CHARLESWORTH'S

COMPANY LAW

CHARLESWORTH'S
COMPANY LAW

EIGHTEENTH EDITION

By

Stephen D. Girvin, BA, LLB, LLM (Natal),
PhD (Aberdeen)
Advocate of the High Court of South Africa,
Professor of Law, Faculty of Law,
National University of Singapore

and

Sandra Frisby, LLB, PhD (Nottingham)
Baker & McKenzie Associate Professor and
Reader in Company and Commercial Law,
School of Law, University of Nottingham

Alastair Hudson, LLB, LLM,
PhD (London) FRSA, FHEA
Barrister, Professor of Equity and Law,
School of Law, Queen Mary,
University of London

SWEET & MAXWELL

 THOMSON REUTERS

First Edition 1932 by His Honour Judge Charlesworth
Second Edition 1938 by His Honour Judge Charlesworth
Third Edition 1940 by His Honour Judge Charlesworth
Fourth Edition 1961 by O.R. Marshall
Second Impression 1947 by His Honour Judge Charlesworth
Third Impression 1948 by His Honour Judge Charlesworth
Fifth edition 1949 by His Honour Judge Charlesworth
Second impression revised 1950 by His Honour Judge Charlesworth
Sixth edition 1954 by His Honour Judge Charlesworth
Second impression revised 1956 by His Honour Judge Charlesworth
Seventh edition 1960 by T.E. Cain
Second impression 1962 by T.E. Cain
Eighth edition 1965 by T.E. Cain
Ninth edition 1968 by T.E. Cain
Tenth edition 1972 by T.E. Cain
Eleventh edition 1977 by T.E. Cain
Second impression 1980 by T.E. Cain
Twelfth edition 1983 by Geoffrey Morse
Thirteenth edition 1987 by Geoffrey Morse
Fourteenth edition 1991 by Geoffrey Morse
Fifteenth edition 1995 by Geoffrey Morse
Second impression 1997 by Geoffrey Morse
Sixteenth edition 1999 by Geoffrey Morse
Seventeenth edition 2005 by Geoffrey Morse
Eighteenth edition 2010 by Stephen D. Girvin, Sandra Frisby and Alastair Hudson

Published in 2010 by Thomson Reuters (Legal) Limited (Registered in Engalnd &
Wales, Company No 1679046. Registered Office and address for service:
100 Avenue Road, London NW3 3PF) trading as Sweet & Maxwell

*For further information on our products and services,
visit www.sweetandmaxwell.co.uk*

Typeset by LBJ Typesetting of Kingsclere
Printed in the UK by CPI William Clowes, Beccles, NR34 7TL

*No natural forests were destroyed to make this product;
only farmed timber was used and re-planted.*

A CIP catalogue record for this book is available from the British Library.

ISBN-13 978-1-84703-919-4

Thomson Reuters and the Thomson Reuters logo are trademarks of Thomson Reuters.
Sweet & Maxwell® is a registered trademark of Thompson Reuters (Legal) Limited

FOREWORD

For most students, coming to company law for the first time is a daunting experience. It is not that company law is any more intrinsically difficult than any other branch of the law but that the factual matrix upon which it operates seems to be more difficult to comprehend. Company law, of necessity, deals with all aspects of corporate activity but the subject cannot be taught in that way. It has to be divided into topics. Each topic may be understandable on its own but the relationship and overlap between them is not really comprehensible until the end of the course. Company law is like the proverbial elephant, difficult to comprehend unless the whole animal is in view. This can lead to misunderstandings. I once asked a particularly bright student why she had answered question 8 on the exam paper on issues of minority protection whereas the question was aimed at directors' duties. The answer was that tutorial 8 had been on minority protection and so . . .

Against that background how does one set out to write a student textbook? In 1932 His Honour Judge Charlesworth, who sat in the North Riding of Yorkshire, produced the first edition of his book on company law. Those were very different times (one edition was produced in war time). The volume of the law was far less, but there was still a substantial amount of detail and procedure which had to be sifted through to produce a coherent text. The result was an excellent balance between giving sufficient information so as to produce a coherent whole and not simply providing endless lists so as to drown the reader. So successful was his book that Judge Charlesworth wrote five further editions, ending in 1956. The mantle was then taken over by Tom Cain who wrote five more editions between 1960 and 1977. I took over in 1982, having been lunched at the Savoy by the publishers to discuss this—how times have changed. The combined effect of the 1980 and 1981 Companies Acts required a significant rewrite but I always bore in mind the need to retain the balance achieved in the previous editions. In all I have been responsible for a total of six editions (the same number as the Judge), although pressure of work and the increasing specialisation involved allowed me to bring in the editors of this edition. I also had the great benefit of both Richard Morris as accounting editor and Enid Marshall as Scottish editor (and a fearsome critic of my grammar in the proofs!).

Charlesworth's Company Law has now been in existence for nearly 70 years. During that time company law teaching has become more sophisticated and the subject more open to scholarly (in RAE terms) analysis. This can be legal, social or economic and there have undoubtedly been more scholarly books on company law and more academically comprehensive ones. Jim Gower's, and latterly Paul Davies', *Modern Company Law* and Brenda Hannigan's *Company Law* are outstanding examples, respectively, of each of those. There have also been many other "basic" textbooks on company law. *Charlesworth* remains unique, however. It manages to carry a substantial amount of information but in an understandable way which does not frighten the reader. For some students and courses it will be sufficient; for others it will be a useful (for some indispensible) safety net below the more erudite texts. Any scholarly analysis depends first upon mastering the often quite complex fundamentals of the subject and no book does that better than *Charlesworth*.

Having now reached a stage in life when grandchildren seem at least as important as academic work, and given the need to reshape *Charlesworth* again (as I did in 1982) following the 2006 Companies Act, I decided that it was time to hand over the baton. That decision was made much easier by the knowledge that Stephen, Sandra and Alastair were already involved in, and had absorbed the unique ethos of, the book. The book is in excellent hands—it must continue to evolve to meet the dictates of the subject but not so as to destroy its qualities. That is not an easy task (deciding what not to include is often the hardest part) but as the reader will see from this edition, that constructive evolutionary process is still evident. Long may it continue to be so.

Geoffrey Morse
Worcestershire, May 2010.

PREFACE

It is customary, when writing book prefaces for new editions of textbooks, to refer to the many changes in the subject since the last edition. This is no less the case with this new edition of *Charlesworth*. The five years since the publication of the previous edition have been marked by continuing change in the field of company law. The previous edition focused at many points on the work of the Company Law Review (CLR) undertaken by what was known then as the DTI (the Department of Trade and Industry) but which has during the years since the last edition changed its name twice, first as BERR (the Department for Business Enterprise and Regulatory Reform) and currently as BIS (the Department for Business, Innovation and Skills). At the time of writing that previous edition in 2005, a Draft Companies Bill had just been published.

The Companies Act 2006, which has the dubious distinction of being the largest statute on the statute book, was passed by Parliament and achieved Royal Assent later that year. Following a complicated implementation timetable, during which parts of the Act were brought into force with over ten commencement orders, the Act came fully into force on October 1, 2009. Few areas of company law have been left untouched in the new Act which, though also consisting of many provisions imported verbatim from the Companies Act 1985, nevertheless contains much that is new or re-ordered. Two well-known instances of new law in the Act are the codifying provisions on directors duties in Part 10 (discussed in Chapter 17 of this book) and the new provisions on statutory derivative actions in Part 11 (discussed in Chapter 22). However, statutory development did not end with the 2006 Act and, indeed, even before the Act was finally brought fully into force in October last year, further changes, mostly at European level, but also consequential changes, had to be made to the Act. In addition to the Act itself there are, at last count, well over sixty statutory instruments concerned with the further development and elaboration of its substantive provisions. Many of these have, of necessity, had to be dealt with in this new edition. There have also been substantial changes to securities, takeover and merger regulation in the United Kingdom to implement successive EU directives, and to the UK's financial regulations (in the *FSA Handbook*): all of these changes are explored here in detail. Other new statutes with some impact on company law include the Fraud Act 2006 and the controversial Corporate Manslaughter and Corporate Homicide Act 2007, both of which are also considered in this new edition.

The law relating to corporate insolvency continues to evolve at a bewildering rate. The decision of the House of Lords in *Buchler v Talbot* has, since the previous edition of this work, been reversed by statute and the Insolvency Rules have been subject to a raft of amendments, many in anticipation of their eventual consolidation, planned for April 2011.

It is not only in the area of statute law that much has changed. The courts continue with their vital role of interpreting the statute and throughout this new edition will be found illustrations and examples of cases which do just that and, in some instances, set down new and important principles. And while no new case is likely to have the impact of *O'Neill v Phillips*, the Privy Council, the House of Lords, the Court of Appeal, as well as the Companies Court have added to the store of that which requires account to be taken in this new edition. In corporate insolvency, the major case law developments have been in relation to the administration procedure, streamlined by the Enterprise Act 2002, and the rise of the "pre-pack" administration has received some judicial attention. Moreover, the decision of the House of Lords in *Re Spectrum Plus* on the fixed/floating charge dichotomy has gone some way to resolving this troubled area.

The new Companies Act and this new 18th edition has brought with it the opportunity to freshen up *Charlesworth*. While the essential character of the book remains unchanged, namely the provision of a comprehensive analytical overview of the subject as a whole, we have taken the opportunity to reorder some of the chapters and the substantive content and also to expand the treatment of some topics. Some areas of the law have inevitably required more detailed treatment. An important change for some will be the fact that this new edition no longer attempts to cover developments in Scots law. Although the Companies Act 2006 applies throughout the United Kingdom and the courts in Scotland continue to play a vital role in the development of company law jurisprudence, none of us can claim contemporary and informed expertise in Scots law. We therefore thought it better to leave coverage of those developments to our colleagues north of the border.

This new edition also marks a change in authorial responsibility. After his involvement in the last seven editions of the book, starting with the 12th edition in 1983, Professor Geoffrey Morse, presently Professor of Corporate and Tax Law at the University of Birmingham, decided that the new Act was the time to hand over the reins to us, his three colleagues who had assisted him in the writing of the 17th edition. Each of us have had a connection with Geoffrey over many years. Stephen and Sandra were his colleagues at the School of Law, University of Nottingham and Stephen also for a short time at the University of Birmingham. Sandra was a student of both Geoffrey and Stephen at Nottingham. All of us share the unique privilege, with Geoffrey, of being members of the Editorial Board of *Palmer's Company Law*, the leading practitioner work on company law from the publishers of this book. As General Editor for many years, Geoffrey brought each of us onto the *Palmer* team. It is therefore right to record our gratitude and appreciation to him for entrusting us with that important task. We hope that he feels that the new *Charlesworth*, very much his baby for the last 22 years, has been left in capable hands. Also retiring from *Charlesworth* after many years involvement in the chapters on accounts and auditors, is Professor Richard Morris, Professor Emeritus of Accounting at the University of Liverpool. We pay tribute to them and indeed to all those who have gone before us. The influence of their work will be apparent to all who use this book.

The division of the labour in this new edition has been as follows: Stephen Girvin, Chapters 1–6, 16, 18–24; Alastair Hudson, Chapters 7–15, 17, 32–34; and

Sandra Frisby, Chapters 25–31. Stephen has (loosely) held the reins together for the new edition.

We should like to thank those who have had to put up with us during the writing of this new edition. They know who they are! Final responsibility for this new edition of course remains with each one of us individually and collectively. It is entirely right and proper to record here our appreciation to our publishers and Nicola Thurlow, in particular, for patiently steering us through the new edition and putting up with several requests for extensions to the deadline for submission of the manuscript.

We have all worked to the law as we understood it to be as on December 1, 2009, but have also included later developments, wherever possible.

Stephen Girvin
Alastair Hudson
Sandra Frisby

Singapore, London and Nottingham
March 31, 2010

CONTENTS

THE NATURE OF COMPANIES AND COMPANY LAW

THE COMPANY AS A CORPORATE ENTITY

CORPORATE CAPACITY

CORPORATE FINANCE

CORPORATE SECURITIES

CORPORATE GOVERNANCE

CORPORATE LIABILITY

CORPORATE INSOLVENCY

CORPORATE REORGANISATION

TABLE OF CASES

TABLE OF STATUTES

TABLE OF STATUTORY INSTRUMENTS

TABLE OF RULES OF THE SUPREME COURT

REFERENCES TO CITY CODE ON TAKEOVERS
AND MERGERS

THE NATURE OF COMPANIES AND COMPANY LAW

Chapter 1

THE NATURE AND FORMATION OF
REGISTERED COMPANIES

INTRODUCTION

This book is concerned with the law relating to registered companies, which may **1–001** be public or private, limited by shares or guarantee, or unlimited and are the most important type of business organisation in the United Kingdom.[1] The term "registered company" now means a company incorporated pursuant to the registration requirements laid down in the Companies Act 2006,[2] the principal Act.[3] Before that the Companies Act 1985[4] consolidated a series of Acts passed between 1948 and 1983, invariably in response to the United Kingdom's obligations as a member of the European Union.[5] Many companies currently on the companies register would have been registered under the provisions of that Act. The 1985 Act was amended on several occasions,[6] starting with the Companies Act 1989[7] and ending with The Companies (Audit, Investigations and Community Enterprise) Act 2004.[8] A significant characteristic of company law, therefore, is that it is overwhelmingly and increasingly statute-based.[9]

WHAT IS A REGISTERED COMPANY?

A registered company, namely an entity incorporated by registration under the **1–002** Companies Act, is regarded in law as a person, just as a human being is a person.

---

[1] For discussion of other types of business organisation, see Ch.2.

[2] c.46 s.1(1). This Act was fully in force as from October 1, 2009. In this book, unless otherwise stated, references to sections and schedules are to those of the Companies Act 2006 and references to "the Act" are to the Companies Act 2006. See now Geoffrey Morse (ed), *Palmer's Company Law: Annotated Guide to the Companies Act 2006* 2nd edn (London: Sweet & Maxwell, 2009).

[3] A company may exist only by being registered in accordance with the provisions of this Act: s.2(1). See *Ooregum Gold Mining Co of India Ltd v Roper* [1892] A.C. 125 at 133, per Lord Halsbury L.C. Thus, an industrial and provident society registered under the Industrial and Provident Societies Act 1965, c.12, would not qualify as a company for the purposes of the Act: see *Re Dairy Farmers of Britain Ltd* [2009] EWHC 1389 (Ch); [2010] Ch. 63.

[4] c.6. Some parts of the Act, such as those relating to companies investigations, remain in force.

[5] The UK became a full member of what was then known as the EC on January 1, 1973.

[6] For the details of some of these changes, see para.1–009, below.

[7] c.40. See para.1–011, below.

[8] c.27. Parts of this Act, namely those relating to community interest companies (see para.2–15, below), remain in force: see s.2(1).

[9] The Companies Act 2006 now codifies provisions on directors fiduciary and common law duties which were previously solely articulated in case law: see Pt 10 of the Act and the discussion in Ch.17.

This artificial or juristic person[10] can own land and other property,[11] enter into contracts,[12] sue and be sued,[13] have a bank account in its own name, owe money to others and be a creditor of other people and other companies, and employ people to work for it. The company's money and property belong to the company and not to the members or shareholders, although the members or shareholders may be said to own the company. Similarly, the company's debts are the debts of the company and the shareholders cannot be compelled to pay them, although if, for example, the company is being wound up and its assets do not realise a sum sufficient to pay its debts, a shareholder whose liability is limited by shares is liable to contribute to the assets up to the amount, if any, which remains unpaid on his shares. A company, of course, can only act through human agents, and those who manage its business are called directors. The directors[14] are agents of the company and transact business, etc., on behalf of the company. They may authorise other agents to act on the company's behalf, e.g. the company secretary.[15] The company will be bound by any transaction entered into on its behalf if the agent is acting within his authority. The company is also liable for torts and crimes committed by its servants and agents within the scope of their employment or authority. This concept of the company as a corporation, i.e. a person separate and distinct from the other persons who are its members and directors,[16] is the fundamental principle of company law.

A company must have members,[17] otherwise it would not exist, and in the case of a company with a share capital these members are known as shareholders. A shareholder's position with regard to the company itself and to other shareholders is regulated by the Act, by the articles of association,[18] by resolutions of the company, and by any agreement between the shareholders,[19] and also by the principle that controlling shareholders, i.e. those with sufficient votes to pass a resolution in general meeting, must act bona fide for the benefit of the company as a whole.[20] The articles[21] vary considerably among different companies, but in every

---

[10] In *Continental Tyre & Rubber Co (Great Britain Ltd) v Daimler Co Ltd* [1915] 1 K.B. 813, CA, at 916, Buckley L.J. stated that

"[t]he artificial legal person called the corporation has no physical existence. It exists only in contemplation of law. It has neither body, parts, nor passions. It cannot wear weapons nor serve in the wars. It can be neither loyal nor disloyal. It cannot compass treason. It can be neither friend nor enemy. Apart from its corporators it can have neither thoughts, wishes, nor intentions, for it has no mind other than the minds of the corporators."

[11] See, e.g. *Bowman v Secular Society Ltd* [1917] A.C. 406 at 441; *Macaura v Northern Assurance Co Ltd* [1925] A.C. 619 at 630.

[12] *Ferguson v Wilson* (1866) L.R. 2 Ch. App. 77 at 89.

[13] *Foss v Harbottle* (1843) 2 Hare 461 at 490–491; 67 E.R.189 at 202.

[14] See Ch.17.

[15] See Ch.18.

[16] As developed in the leading case, *Salomon v Salomon & Co Ltd* [1897] A.C. 22, para.1–037, below.

[17] i.e. at least one member: s.7(1).

[18] Formerly, the memorandum would also be so regarded, but the status of the memorandum is now much diminished in importance: see s.8 and the discussion at para.3–019.

[19] These collectively constitute the company's constitution: s.17.

[20] The traditional formulation of this duty is to be found in *Allen v Gold Reefs of West Africa* [1900] 1 Ch. 656 at 671, para.4–005, below. See now, however, s.172(1) and para.17–020, below.

[21] As already pointed out, the memorandum now plays a minor role in companies (at least those companies formed under the 2006 Act).

case the shareholder's position is that he is the owner of one or more shares in the company, which shares usually carry a right to vote at general meetings, and, if profits are made, a right to receive dividends, if declared, on his shares. His shares are something which he has bought—perhaps from the company, or perhaps from somebody else—and something which he can sell or give away, either in his lifetime or by his will.

The general rule is that a shareholder cannot get his money back from the company so long as the company is in existence, because his position is not that of a person who has lent money to the company or has deposited his money as with a bank or a building society—it is that of the owner of property, namely, the shares, which can only be turned into money if a buyer can be found to pay for them. Shares may be fully paid or partly paid. When the shares are only partly paid, the shareholder can be compelled to pay them up fully if called upon by the company or, if the company is being wound up and its debts exceed its assets, by the liquidator. In any event, it is the general policy of the Act to see that the issued share capital is maintained intact, except for losses in the way of business, so that it may be available to satisfy the company's debts. Accordingly, while the company is a going concern, the general rule is that no part of the paid-up capital may be returned to the shareholders without the consent of the court, or by following procedures intended to protect creditors.[22]

A company may be formed to acquire and carry on an existing business,[23] which **1–003** may or may not belong to the promoters,[24] or to start some new business. However, a company is commonly formed as a private company to acquire the promoters' business. In this case, a price is put on the business and paid by the issue to the promoters of shares credited as fully or partly paid in the company. Most of the price will be left owing to the promoters so that if the company is later wound up they will rank for repayment of it as unsecured creditors; otherwise if they take the whole price in the form of shares credited as fully paid they will rank for repayment of capital after the unsecured creditors. If a company is formed to acquire a business which does not belong to the promoters they may provide the necessary funds for the company by taking shares in the company for cash.

Many companies also raise money by borrowing.[25] Persons who lend money to a company may be issued with debentures[26] to show that they have lent money and are entitled to interest on their loans. Unlike shareholders, they are not members of the company and they have no right to vote at general meetings. Creditors may take a charge over the company's property by way of security for repayment of their debt. Such charges must be registered with the Registrar of Companies.[27]

Shares in, and debentures of, public companies are extensively bought as investments by persons who wish to derive an income from their capital and/or achieve

---

[22] At least in the case of public companies. The rules for private companies have been relaxed. For fuller discussion, see Ch.9.

[23] As in the leading case, *Salomon v Salomon & Co Ltd* [1897] A.C. 22, para.1–037, below.

[24] See Ch.5.

[25] Money borrowed by a company is sometimes called "loan capital". It should not be confused with "share capital".

[26] See Ch.25.

[27] See s.860.

capital growth. In order to facilitate transactions in such securities, the companies involved will be quoted on the London Stock Exchange[28] and are known as quoted companies.[29] To protect investors from dishonest or incompetent people who form companies in which the investors are likely to lose their money, disclosure of such things as the company's past financial record and the benefits of being a director, is required in the document on the strength of which the public is invited to subscribe for shares or debentures of the company. Provision is also made for a company's accounts to be audited every year by auditors appointed by the shareholders and for the balance sheet and the profit and loss account and certain other documents to be circulated to every shareholder and debenture holder. With the exception of unlimited companies,[30] a copy of the balance sheet and the other documents must also be lodged with the Registrar of Companies.[31] The London Stock Exchange itself also provides detailed rules[32] regulating the affairs of quoted companies.

1-004   The directors of a company, who are usually appointed by the members at general meetings,[33] have wide powers to manage the company's business conferred upon them by the articles. The members cannot control the exercise of these powers,[34] although they can, e.g. alter the articles.[35] The directors, in turn, owe certain duties of good faith[36] and care to the company.[37] The Acts have increasingly required disclosure by companies, their directors and substantial shareholders of many financial and other particulars. Usually this will be to the Registrar who will keep the information on the company's file. Such information is then available to anyone who makes a search of that file and is seen as one of the prices of incorporation. There is no constructive notice of such information, however.

A registered company is capable of perpetual succession[38] but it may become insolvent or it may decide to retire from business. In such a case it is wound up, i.e. it is put, or it goes, into liquidation, and a person, known as a liquidator, is appointed to wind up its affairs.[39] He sells the company's property and pays as much of its debts as he can do out of the proceeds of sale. If there is a surplus, he distributes it among the shareholders. When the liquidation is completed the company is dissolved and ceases to exist.[40]

THE DEVELOPMENT OF MODERN COMPANY LAW

1-005 The modern commercial company, incorporated by registration under the Act, is the result of the fusion of two different legal principles. A registered company,

---

[28] See *http://www.londonstockexchange.com* [accessed May 20, 2010].
[29] See s.385.
[30] See now para.20–055, below.
[31] See para.20–048, below.
[32] These Rules are known as "The Listing Rules" and are controlled by the UK Listing Authority (the UKLA): see *http://www.fsa.gov.uk/Pages/Doing/UKLA/* [accessed May 20, 2010]. See Ch.13, below.
[33] Only public companies are now required to hold annual general meetings: see s.336. See para.19–002, below.
[34] See, e.g., *Automatic Self-cleansing Filter Syndicate Co Ltd v Cuninghame* [1906] 2 Ch. 34, CA.
[35] See s.21.
[36] See now s.172(1) and para.17–020, below.
[37] See s.174 and para.17–029, below.
[38] *Stepney Corporation v Osofsky* [1937] 3 All E.R. 289, CA.
[39] See Ch.26.
[40] See s.1001.

like a statutory company or a chartered company, is a "corporation", i.e. in the eyes of the law it is a person, capable of perpetual succession as we have seen, and quite distinct from the natural persons who are its members at any given moment.[41] However, the expression "company" is not confined to a corporation but can include a partnership, which is not a corporation but is merely the relationship between the individual partners.[42] The present-day registered company represents the fusion of the principle of incorporation with that of partnership.

At common law, the Crown has always had the right of granting charters of incorporation.[43] Non-trading companies, such as the Law Society and the Institute of Chartered Accountants, are the kind of company now incorporated by charter but trading companies have in the past been formed in this way. The right was first used for creating commercial corporations at the end of the sixteenth and the beginning of the seventeenth centuries, when such companies as the Levant Company, the East India Company, the Hudson's Bay Company and the notorious South Sea Company (afterwards incorporated by special Act of Parliament) were incorporated. As these corporations were legal entities quite distinct from their members, it followed that at common law the members were not liable for the debts of the corporation, and, indeed, the Crown had no power to incorporate persons so as to make them liable for the debts of the corporation.[44] In a partnership, on the other hand, the partners were always liable for all the debts of the firm and their liability was unlimited.[45]

In England, trading companies were originally regulated companies, that is, companies in which each member traded with his own stock subject to the rules of the company, but towards the end of the seventeenth century the joint-stock company emerged.[46] This is the form of the company in common use today. In a joint-stock company, the company traded as a single person with a stock which was jointly contributed by its members. Such companies could only be formed by special Act of Parliament or by charter but, as the advantages of the joint-stock form of trading became better known, these methods proved too expensive and dilatory to meet the growing commercial needs of the nation. Accordingly, there grew up a new type of company based upon contract. This contract took the form of an elaborate deed of settlement containing provisions regulating the relations of the members among themselves and providing for the transfer of shares. A body formed in this way was only a partnership in the eyes of the law and the liability of the members was unlimited. This type of unincorporated company fell into disfavour with the legislature, largely owing to the activities of fraudulent promoters and unscrupulous share dealers,[47] and in 1720 the Bubble Act[48] was passed to deal with it. Unfortunately, that Act had the effect of suppressing unincorporated companies without satisfying the want which had given rise to their existence, so that "joint-stock" enterprises had to wait till the

---

[41] *Salomon v Salomon & Co Ltd* [1897] A.C. 22, below, para.1–037.
[42] See Partnership Act 1890 s.1(1).
[43] A chartered company is sometimes referred to as "a common law corporation".
[44] See *Elve v Boyton* [1891] 1 Ch. 501, CA at 507.
[45] See, e.g. Partnership Act 1890 s.9.
[46] W.S. Holdsworth, *History of English Law*, Vol.8, pp.206–222.
[47] See particularly, Richard Dale, *The First Crash: Lessons from the South Sea Bubble* (2004).
[48] 6 Geo I, c.18.

middle of the nineteenth century before incorporation "for any lawful purpose" could be obtained by the simple process of registration, and personal liability be limited by "one magic word".[49]

1–006   In 1825, by the Bubble Companies, etc., Act, the 1720 Bubble Act was repealed and the Crown was empowered in grants of future charters to provide that the members of the corporation should be personally liable for the debts of the corporation to such extent as the Crown should think proper. This was the beginning of "limited liability". By the Chartered Companies Act 1837,[50] the Crown was empowered to grant letters patent, i.e. to grant the advantages of incorporation without granting a charter, to a body of persons associated together for trading purposes. The persons in question had to register a deed of partnership dividing the capital into shares and providing for transfers, and satisfy the other requirements of the Act; limited liability was then granted to them. The association to which the letters patent were granted did not become a body corporate and the grant of limited liability was an advantage to which they would otherwise not have been entitled.

By the Joint Stock Companies Registration Act 1844,[51] provision was made in England for the incorporation of companies by registration without the necessity of obtaining a Royal Charter or a special Act of Parliament. The peculiarity of this statute, however, was that, instead of allowing the usual common law consequences of incorporation to follow, it proceeded on the lines of the Chartered Companies Act 1837 and merely gave a corporate existence to a body which it still evidently regarded as a partnership, because it imposed much the same liability on the members for the debts of the company as they would have had for the debts of a partnership. This Act also made it compulsory to register as companies all partnerships with more than 25 members.[52] Liability limited by shares, i.e. where a member's liability is limited to the amount, if any, unpaid on his shares, was introduced in the case of registered companies by the Limited Liability Act 1855,[53] and the Joint Stock Companies Act 1856[54] substituted two documents, the memorandum of association and articles of association, for the deed of settlement.

The Companies Act 1862[55] repealed and consolidated the previous Acts. It also established liability limited by guarantee and, in general, prohibited any alteration in the objects clause[56] of the memorandum of association. This prohibition remained until the Companies (Memorandum of Association) Act 1890[57] enabled the objects to be altered for some purposes with the leave of the court, after a special resolution[58] had been passed by the members in general meeting. The

---

[49] Cecil T. Carr, *Select Charters of Trading Companies 1530–1707* (Selden Society, 1913) Vol.28 p.xx.

[50] 7 Will. 4 & 1 Vict., c.73.

[51] 7 & 8 Vict., c.110.

[52] The maximum number of members for a partnership used to be 20, with exceptions for most professional firms, but that provision of the Companies Act 1985 was repealed by the Regulatory Reform (Removal of 20 Member Limit in Partnerships, etc.) Order 2002 (SI 2002/3203).

[53] 18 & 19 Vict., c.133.

[54] 19 & 20 Vict., c.47.

[55] 25 & 26 Vict., c.89.

[56] Dealt with below, para.4–026.

[57] 53 & 54 Vict., c.62.

[58] 53 & 54 Vict., c.62.

Companies Act 1867[59] contained a power to reduce share capital. The Directors' Liability Act 1890[60] introduced the principle of the liability of the directors to pay compensation to persons who have been induced to take shares on the strength of false statements in a prospectus. The Companies Act 1900[61] contained the first provisions relating to the contents of prospectuses, the compulsory audit of the company's accounts and the registration of charges with the Registrar. The Companies Act 1907[62] made provision for the private (as opposed to the public) company, i.e. a company which is prohibited from inviting the public to subscribe for its shares or debentures.[63] Modern company law was taking shape.

The 1948 Act and its successors

The 1948 Companies Act[64] made far-reaching changes in the law relating to **1–007** company accounts. As the Cohen Report[65] (on which the 1948 Act was based) said,

> "[t]he history of company legislation shows the increasing importance attached to publicity in connection with accounts. The Act of 1862 contained no compulsory provisions with regard to audit or accounts, though Table A[66] to that Act did include certain clauses dealing with both matters. In 1879, provision was made for the audit of the accounts of banking companies, but it was not until 1900 that any such provision was made generally applicable. It was only on July 1, 1908, when the Companies Act 1907 came into force, that provision was made for including a statement in the form of a balance sheet in the annual return to the Registrar of Companies, and that provision exempted private companies from this requirement."

The Companies Act 1929[67] required a balance sheet and a profit and loss account to be laid before the company every year, while the present Acts set out in great detail the contents of those accounts, with stringent provisions for their audit. The 1948 Act also for the first time required the auditor of a public or a private company to have a professional qualification.[68]

A number of the recommendations contained in the Jenkins Report[69] were given effect in the 1967 Act[70] which amended the 1948 Act in a number of respects, including new provisions in connection with a company's accounts.

---

[59] 30 & 31 Vict., c.131.
[60] 53 & 54 Vict., c.64.
[61] 63 & 64 Vict., c.48.
[62] 7 Edw.7, c.50.
[63] Below, para.3–007.
[64] 11 & 12 Geo.6, c.38.
[65] Report of the Committee on Company Law Amendment (1945), Cmd.6659, para.96.
[66] A model set of articles of association. See now para.4–004.
[67] 19 & 20 Geo.5, c.23.
[68] For a fuller treatment of the history of company law, see L.C.B. Gower, *Modern Company Law*, 6th edn (1997), Chs 2 and 3.
[69] Report of the Company Law Committee (1962), Cmnd.1749. This Report has never been implemented in full or dealt with in any consistent manner although certain of its recommendations were implemented by the 1989 Act after a gap of 27 years.
[70] c.81.

1972 saw the European Communities Act,[71] s.9 of which related solely to company law since the UK was obliged on accession to comply with an existing EC Directive of 1968 on the harmonisation of company law.[72] This section's principal change was to modify the law relating to ultra vires and the problems of agency in relation to companies.[73]

The Companies Act 1976[74] enacted, among other things, some but not all of the clauses and Schedules of the abortive Companies Bill 1973. The 1976 Act amended the law relating to the filing of company accounts and the keeping of accounting records. It provided, amongst other things, for the disqualification of persons taking part in the management of companies if they were persistently in default in complying with the requirements to deliver documents to the Registrar.

1–008   The Companies Act 1980[75] was inspired by an EC Directive of 1976 regulating the control of public companies. It provided for the first time a major distinction between public and private companies, including minimum financial requirements for the former. It also contained new provisions relating to the issuing of shares and the payment for them. Payment of dividends became the subject of statutory rules. Tighter restrictions on directors were imposed following the many "unacceptable faces of capitalism" which manifested themselves in the 1970s. Insider dealing,[76] one of the most obvious of those, became a criminal offence.

The 1981 Companies Act[77] was likewise prompted by an EC Directive, this time on company accounts. It provided a new format for accounts and for the public disclosure of them. In addition, however, new rules for company names, the purchase and redemption by a company of its own shares and for more stringent disclosure of shareholders were included. Various other reforms were also appended. The technical nature of much of this legislation was so complex that mistakes were made. One particularly embarrassing one, the accidental prohibition of many employee share and pension trusts had to be corrected, in haste, by the Companies (Beneficial Interests) Act 1983.[78]

The 1985 consolidation and after

1–009   In 1981 proposals were made for a consolidation of the various Acts from 1948 onwards. There were two joint Reports of the Law Commission and the Scottish Law Commission[79] which recommended many technical amendments to the existing law in order to assist consolidation. These amendments were effected by the Companies Acts (Pre-Consolidation Amendments) Order 1984[80] and the

---

[71] c.68.
[72] EC Directives have had a significant impact on UK company law: see para.1–024, below.
[73] This worked along the lines of the Jenkins Committee recommendations in para.42 of the Report. It proved to be defective in many ways, however, and was rewritten by the 1989 Act. See para.4–027, below.
[74] c.69.
[75] c.21.
[76] See Ch.24.
[77] c.62.
[78] c.50
[79] Amendment of the Companies Acts: Consolidation Report (1983) Cmnd.9114; Further Amendments to the Companies Acts (1984) Cmnd.9272.
[80] SI 1984/134.

Companies Acts (Pre-Consolidation Amendments) (No.2) Order 1984[81] which, by virtue of s.116 of the Companies Act 1981, only took effect on the consolidation itself coming into force. After consultation it was decided to produce a single main Act, the Companies Act 1985,[82] with 747 sections and 25 Schedules (up to seven separate Acts had been canvassed) with three small satellite Acts. The 1981 Act provisions relating to the use of business names by all traders, including companies, were separated into the Business Names Act 1985,[83] and those of the 1980 Act relating to insider dealing were also hived off into a separate Act, the Company Securities (Insider Dealing) Act 1985,[84] since those rules applied to securities other than those belonging to companies. The fourth Act, the Companies Consolidation (Consequential Provisions) Act 1985,[85] dealt with transitional matters, savings provisions, repeals and consequential amendments to other Acts.

While the consolidation was proceeding through Parliament, the Companies (Accounts and Audit) Regulations 1984 and the Companies (Share Premium Account) Regulations 1984 were passed and had to be taken into account. The resulting consolidation, taking into account the various amendments referred to above and the need to harmonise legislative styles and phrases over a 30-year period, was by no means a "scissors and paste" consolidation. In the main, it used short subsections and many of the pre-existing sections were divided. It was a triumph of draftsmanship in what was then the largest consolidation ever undertaken. By way of departure from previous practice, Tables A to F, the model forms of memorandum and articles, were now contained in separate regulations, the Companies (Tables A to F) Regulations 1985,[86] rather than in a Schedule to the Act. Table A itself was redrafted for this purpose. The whole consolidation came into effect on July 1, 1985.

Unfortunately the 1985 Act proved to be short-lived as a unified source of company legislation. Two more EC Directives, the third (on mergers)[87] and the sixth (on divisions),[88] were implemented by the Companies (Mergers and Divisions) Regulations 1987,[89] which added a new section and Schedule to the 1985 Act in the area of schemes of arrangement.[90] More importantly, the Insolvency Act 1985, implementing some of the recommendations of the Cork Committee[91] repealed many of the sections of the 1985 Act relating to liquidation and other aspects of corporate insolvency and replaced them with several new concepts, e.g. administration orders, as well as making several amendments to the rules governing insolvent liquidations. The Act was based on a White Paper,[92] itself based on the Cork Report. The resulting legislation on corporate liquidation and insolvency was itself consolidated into the Insolvency Act 1986,[93] apart from

---

[81] SI 1984/1169.
[82] c.6.
[83] c.7.
[84] c.8.
[85] c.9.
[86] SI 1985/805.
[87] Directive 78/855/EC [1978] OJ L295/36.
[88] Directive 82/891/EC [1982] OJ L378/47.
[89] SI 1987/1991.
[90] See Ch.32, below.
[91] Insolvency Law and Practice: Report of the Review Committee (1982) Cmnd.8558.
[92] A Revised Framework for Insolvency Law (1984) Cmnd.9175.
[93] c.45.

the provisions relating to directors' disqualification which were consolidated into the Company Directors Disqualification Act 1986.[94] The result is that some of the 1948 Act winding up provisions were consolidated in 1985, amended in that year and re-consolidated in 1986.

1–010   In addition the reform of the law governing the investment industry, prompted by a report by Professor L.C.B. Gower commissioned by the Department of Trade and Industry, was suggested by a White Paper,[95] and implemented by the Financial Services Act 1986.[96] Whilst this Act was largely concerned with regulating the City and the investment industry generally, it had a double impact on company law. The first was indirect in that company securities were investments for this purpose and those who deal in them were, therefore, subject to the Act's new regulatory system. The second was direct. The Financial Services Act provided new rules for the public issue of shares whether listed on the London Stock Exchange or otherwise. It also recast the provisions in the Companies Act 1985 relating to the compulsory acquisition of shares on a takeover and amended the rules relating to insider dealing in the Company Securities (Insider Dealing) Act 1985.[97] The Financial Services Act thus repealed many of the 1985 Act sections relating to the public issue of shares and the Stock Exchange (Listing) Regulations 1984.[98] The latter were passed to implement yet another set of EC directives, on listing particulars, the admission of securities to listing and the continuing disclosure of information by listed companies.[99]

Companies Act 1989

1–011 More substantial changes were made by the Companies Act 1989[100] which was occasioned by the need to implement two further EC Directives, the seventh on group accounts[101] and the eighth on the qualification of auditors.[102] The opportunity was also taken to amend and extend the 1985 Act provisions relating to investigations (together with investigations under the Insolvency Act 1986 and the Financial Services Act 1986), the doctrine of ultra vires and application of the agency law to corporate transactions and in several other areas, some of which had been recommended by the Jenkins Committee back in 1962. Finally, several amendments to other Acts were made, most importantly to the Financial Services Act 1986. Most of the 1989 Act changes were effected by adding, substituting or amending sections in the earlier Acts.

Parts of the 1989 Act never came into force. One important example of this[103] was Pt IV of the 1989 Act, on the registration of company charges. Although

---

[94] c.46.
[95] Financial Services in the United Kingdom: A New Framework for Investor Protection (1985) Cmnd.9432.
[96] c.60.
[97] c.8.
[98] SI 1984/716.
[99] Directive 80/390/EC [1980] OJ L100/1, Directive 79/279/EC [1979] OJ L66/21, and Directive 82/121/EC [1982] OJ L48/26.
[100] c.40.
[101] Directive 83/349/EC [1983] OJ L193/1.
[102] Directive 84/253/EC [1984] OJ L126/20.
[103] A further example of non-implementation was in relation to the abolition of the doctrine of constructive notice, provided for in s.142 of the 1989 Act, which would have added s.711A to the 1985 Act.

certain of the interim recommendations of the Diamond Committee on Security Interests over Personal Property[104] were implemented in the 1989 Act, a more radical proposal which would have involved a US-style notice filing system, was not acted upon then. Indeed, the Department of Trade and Industry (the DTI) in 1996 advised that it was not intending to implement Pt IV. In more recent times, the Law Commission published two consultation papers on this.[105]

Post-1989 developments

A number of important company law developments have occurred after 1989 **1–012** necessitating still further changes and additions to the 1985 Act. One of the principal sources of these changes was new EC Directives on company law, with the changes implemented by statutory instrument.[106] These included the directive amending the fourth and seventh directives on company accounts;[107] the eleventh directive on disclosure requirements for branches of overseas companies;[108] and the major shareholdings directive relating to disclosure of such interests in listed companies.[109] The most fundamental of the changes[110] was the introduction of the single member company, i.e. whereby one person may form a private company, as the result of the implementation of the twelfth directive on single member private limited companies[111] by the Companies (Single Member Private Limited Companies) Regulations 1992.[112] Implementation of the directive co-ordinating regulations on insider dealing[113] led to the repeal of the Company Securities (Insider Dealing) Act 1985, part of the 1985 consolidation, and its replacement by Pt V of the Criminal Justice Act 1993.[114]

The Companies (Audit, Investigations and Community Enterprise) Act 2004

This Act was passed in 2004 and was brought into force in stages during the **1–013** course of 2005.[115] The Act made changes to both the Companies Act 1985 and the Companies Act of 1989 and was part of the Government's strategy to restore

---

[104] *A Review of Security Interests in Personal Property* (DTI, November 1988). See Michael Bridge, "Form, substance and innovation in personal property security law" [1992] J.B.L. 1.

[105] Registration of Security Interests: Company Charges and Property other than Land, L.C.C.P. No.164 (2002); Company Security Interests: A Consultative Report, L.C.C.P. No.176 (2004). See below.

[106] Under powers to amend legislation in this way given by s.2(2) of the European Communities Act.

[107] Directive 90/604 [1990] OJ L317/57.

[108] Directive 89/666 [1989] OJ L395/36.

[109] Directive 88/627/EC.

[110] Other changes to the 1985 Act came from other sources, such as the Welsh Language Act 1993, c.38.

[111] Directive 89/667 [1989] OJ L395/40.

[112] SI 1992/1699.

[113] Directive 89/592 [1989] OJ L334/30.

[114] c.36.

[115] See The Companies (Audit, Investigations and Community Enterprise) Act 2004 (Commencement) and Companies Act 1989 (Commencement No.18) Order 2004 (SI 2004/3322). The Act came into force on October 1, 2005.

investor confidence in the wake of major corporate scandals such as those involving Enron and WorldCom. Thus, a key objective was to strengthen audit practice and corporate governance. Part I of the Act contained provisions which strengthened the independence of the system of supervising auditors (ss.1–7),[116] and enforced accounting and reporting requirements (ss.8–18). Other important provisions in Pt I were those amending the company investigations regime (ss.21–24),[117] and those relaxing the prohibition on provisions made by companies to indemnify directors against liability to third parties (ss.19–20).[118]

Much of the Act was concerned with making provision for the establishment of a new corporate vehicle, the Community Interest Company (CIC),[119] which is intended to make it simpler and more convenient to establish a business whose profits and assets are to be used for the benefit of the community.[120] Companies wishing to become a CIC are required to pass a community interest test and to produce an annual report showing that they have contributed to community interest aims.[121] There is a statutory "lock" on the profits and financial assets of CICs and, where a CIC is limited by shares, there is a power to impose a "cap" on any dividend.[122] An independent regulator[123] is responsible for approving the registration of CICs and ensuring they comply with their legal requirements,[124] as well as having a whole range of other powers, such as suspending or removing CIC directors.[125] During the course of 2009 there was a consultation exercise[126] by the regulator on whether to vary the share dividend cap, aggregated dividend cap, or performance related interest cap and, following that consultation, a response was published by the regulator in January 2010.[127]

REFORM OF COMPANY LAW

The Law Commission

1–014 The mandate of the Law Commission of England and Wales,[128] which was set up in 1965,[129] is to keep the law of England and Wales under review and to recom-

---

[116] Section 7 has since been repealed: see Companies Act 2006 Sch.16.

[117] See para.22–053, below.

[118] These sections have since been repealed: see Companies Act 2006 Sch.16.

[119] See *http://www.cicregulator.gov.uk* [accessed May 20, 2010].

[120] There are currently 3,323 such companies registered.

[121] See ss.37–38.

[122] See s.30.

[123] The powers of the regulator are specified in the Community Interest Companies Regulations 2005 (SI 2005/1788). See too *http://www.cicregulator.gov.uk/* [accessed May 20, 2010].

[124] s.27.

[125] s.46.

[126] *Community Interest Companies: Consultation on the dividend and interest caps* (March 30, 2009). See *http://www.cicregulator.gov.uk/consultation.shtml* [accessed May 20, 2010].

[127] *Response to the Consultation on the dividend and interest caps* (January 2010). Available at *http://www.cicregulator.gov.uk/consultation.shtml* [accessed on May 20, 2010].

[128] See *http://www.lawcom.gov.uk* [accessed on May 20, 2010].

[129] See Mr Justice Scarman, "The Work of the Law Commission for England and Wales", (1969) 33 Western Ontario L.R. 33.

mend reform, when needed.[130] There have been a number of instances when the Commission has undertaken work in the company law area.[131] Most notably, this included a report on *Shareholder Remedies*[132] and a report on *Company Directors: Regulating Conflicts of Interests and Formulating a Statement of Duties*,[133] both of which, to some extent, fed into the work of the Company Law Review (CLR).[134] The Commission has also worked on registration of company charges.[135] In the related area of partnership law, the Law Commission also produced a report on *Partnership Law*.[136]

The Company Law Review (CLR) and the Government response

On March 4, 1998, the then Department of Trade and Industry (DTI)[137] published **1–015** a consultative document entitled *Modern Company Law for a Competitive Economy*.[138] This heralded a fundamental review of modern company law with terms of reference to make recommendations having:

(1) considered how core company law could be modernised in order to provide a simple, efficient and cost-effective framework for carrying out business activity which provided the maximum freedom and flexibility while protecting those involved in the enterprise and was drafted in clear, concise and unambiguous language that can be readily understood by those involved in business;

(2) considered whether company law, partnership law and other legislation together provided an adequate choice of legal vehicle for business at all levels;

(3) considered the proper relationship between company law and non-statutory standards of corporate behaviour;[139]

(4) reviewed the extent to which foreign companies operated in Great Britain should be regulated under British company law.

In the ensuing years, virtually no aspect of company law was left unscrutinised by those responsible for conducting the review. In all, the review produced a significant

---

[130] See Law Commissions Act 1965 (c.22) s.3.
[131] Often in conjunction with the Scottish Law Commission.
[132] Law Com. Rep. No.246 (1997).
[133] Law Com. Rep. No.261 (1999).
[134] Below, para.1–015.
[135] See now para.25–023, below.
[136] Law Com. Report No.283 (2003). This has not lead, however, to a revision of the Partnership Act 1890. See Geoffrey Morse, *Partnership Law* 6th edn (2006), para.1.08; Elspeth Deards, "Partnership law in the twenty-first century" [2001] J.B.L. 357; "The Partnership Bill: Under starter's orders" (2004) 25 *Company Lawyer* 41.
[137] Now the Department for Business, Innovation and Skills (BIS). See *http://www.bis.gov.uk* [accessed May 20, 2010].
[138] Available at *www.bis.gov.uk/policies/business-law/company-and-partnership-law/company-law/publications-archive* [accessed July 23, 2010].
[139] Para.5.3.

amount of work in consultation and other documents,[140] culminating in *Modern Company Law for a Competitive Economy—Final Report*, in two volumes.[141] The government published a response to the review in a White Paper, *Modernising Company Law*,[142] published in July 2002, also in two volumes.[143] This White Paper set out the government's policy on modernizing company law including draft clauses.

1–016   There was little further progress until 2004, when the DTI published a further consultation document, *Company Law: Flexibility and Accessibility*.[144] Patricia Hewitt, the then Secretary of State, stated that:

> "[the Government] will be following the route-map that the Company Law Review (CLR) provided except where there are compelling reasons to depart from it. We will legislate as soon as parliamentary time allows and will publish beforehand a draft Bill for consultation."[145]

The document clearly recognised that parliamentary time was at a premium and outlined a hugely controversial new system of legislating for company law via a special form of secondary legislation[146] "making it easier to keep the legislation updated over time",[147] and was later withdrawn.[148]

A further White Paper was published in March 2005[149] and responses to it in August 2005.[150] Although generally favourable to the CLR's proposals, there were a number of areas in which the Government rejected specific proposals.[151]

---

[140] *Company Law Review: The Strategic Framework* URN 99/654; *Company General Meetings and Shareholder Communication* URN 99/1144; *Company Formation and Capital maintenance* URN 99/1145; *Reforming the Law Concerning Overseas Companies* URN 99/1146; *Company Law Review—Developing the Framework* URN 00/656; *Company Law Review—Capital Maintenance: Other Issues* URN 00/880; *Company Law Review—Registration of Company Charges* URN 00/1213; *Company Law Review—Completing the Structure* URN 00/1335; *Company Law Review—Trading Disclosures, a Consultation Paper* URN 01/542. These are all available at *www.bis.gov.uk/policies/business-law/company-and-partnership-law/company-law/publications-archive*.

[141] Presented to the Secretary of State on July 26, 2001.

[142] Cm.5553.

[143] See Robert Goddard, " 'Modernising Company Law': The Government's White Paper" (2003) 66 Modern L.R. 402.

[144] May 2004.

[145] At p.4

[146] The Regulatory Reform Order procedure, as established by the Regulatory Reform Act 2001.

[147] And see the response of the House of Commons Trade and Industry Committee's Ninth Report, Updating Company Law: the Government's consultation document on "Company Law: Flexibility and Accessibility" (September 21, 2004). For a critical reaction to this consultation paper, see Len Sealy, "The reform of company law: selling British business short" (2004) *Sweet & Maxwell's Company Law Newsletter* 1.

[148] When the Companies Bill was in Grand Committee of the House of Lords in early 2006. See below.

[149] *Company Law Reform*, Cmnd.6456.

[150] URN 05/928.

[151] See Claire Howell, "The Company Law Whitepaper: A descriptive overview" (2005) 26 *Company Lawyer* 203.

From Bill to Royal Assent

In an admirable attempt at forward momentum, a Company Law Reform Bill[152] **1–017** was introduced in the House of Lords[153] on November 1, 2005 and published on November 3, 2005.[154] It received its Second Reading in the House of Lords on January 11, 2006 and Lord Sainsbury of Turville, then Under-Secretary of State for the DTI, emphasised the "need constantly to update our company law in response to changes in the way that companies do business and how that is often best done, as in this Bill, based on a previous review by independent experts".[155] He too emphasised the clear focus of the Bill on "simplification, on the needs of small businesses, which are so important to our economy, and on deregulation" which he believed represented a "break with the past".[156] The Bill entered a Grand Committee of the House of Lords on January 30, 2006 and at this stage a substantial number of changes were made and, in particular, the very controversial power to reform future company law by means of delegated legislation already referred to.[157] The removal of this power meant that it was necessary to include many sections of the earlier Acts which had not been amended and the net result was that the Bill became considerably longer than intended. After considering 1,144 amendments in all, the Grand Committee completed its work on April 25, 2006.[158] The Report Stage followed on May 9, 2006 and the Bill completed its passage through the House of Lords on May 16, 2006.[159] Thereupon the Bill went to the House of Commons, with the First Reading on May 24, 2006 and the Second Reading on June 6, 2006. Alistair Darling, the then Secretary of State, confirmed that it was hoped to

> "restate without substantive change those parts of the Companies Act 1985 that have not until now been incorporated in the legislation during the passage of the Bill through this House. We do so simply because it has been put to us that it would be convenient for practitioners to have as much of our corporate law in one place as possible."[160]

After consideration by a House of Commons Committee, the Bill was reprinted and, following the summer break, progressed swiftly through the remaining parliamentary stages before finally achieving Royal Assent on November 8, 2006.

---

[152] Subsequently renamed, during the House of Commons stage, as the Companies Bill.
[153] For detailed consideration of the progress of the Bill through Parliament, see Geoffrey Morse (ed.), *Palmer's Company Law: Annotated Guide to the Companies Act 2006* 2nd edn (London: Sweet & Maxwell, 2009), 50.
[154] Bill 218.
[155] *Hansard*, HL, col.181 (January 11, 2006).
[156] *Hansard*, HL, col.181 (January 11, 2006).
[157] Para.1–016 above.
[158] *Hansard*, HL, col.GC100 (April 25, 2006).
[159] *Hansard*, HL, col.190 (May 16, 2006).
[160] *Hansard*, HC Vol.447, Col.123.

The Companies Act 2006 and company law

1–018 The 2006 Act is by any standards a major piece of legislation and has the rather dubious distinction of being the longest Act of Parliament ever passed. There are 1,300 sections in all, sub-divided within 47 Parts, and supplemented by 16 Schedules. Although much earlier legislation has largely been displaced by the new Act and there are also many new provisions, the Act is substantially a restatement of the existing law.

Even after the passage of the new Act it proved necessary to make amendments to the Act, in some cases where the implementation of new EU Directives was required.[161] However, even more important than these changes to the Act has been the significant number of statutory instruments which have had to be passed. While some of these have been concerned with implementation and amendment of the Act, many others have been passed to expand on the treatment of discrete areas in the Act.[162]

The 2006 Act was brought into force in stages. There were a relatively small number of matters which came into force on Royal Assent on November 8, 2006. Other matters were to come into force "on such day as may be appointed by order of the Secretary of State or the Treasury".[163] Between Royal Assent and final implementation on October 1, 2009, eight commencement orders brought the provisions of the Act into force.[164]

Other legislative changes

1–019 There have in the past few years been other changes which have had an impact in ancillary areas of company law. One of the most important among these, which predates the 2006 Act, is the Financial Services and Markets Act 2000,[165] which creates the Financial Services Authority (FSA),[166] a "super-" or "mega-" regulator which covers a wide regulatory scope and embraces not only investment business but also banking and insurance. Under this Act, the Treasury and the FSA are given extensive delegated powers. One important impact of this is that the FSA is now the "competent authority" for the purposes of listed securities.[167]

The Fraud Act 2006,[168] which achieved Royal Assent on the same day as the Companies Act,[169] while not specific to company law, nevertheless has important

---

[161] Such as the Shareholders Rights Directive 2007/36 EC [2007] OJ L 184/17 and the Company Reporting Directive 2006/46 EC [2006] OJ L224/1.

[162] There are well over 60 such statutory instruments. These are all available at *http://www.bis.gov.uk./policies/business-law/company-and-partnership-law/company-law/regulations-statutory-instruments* [accessed July 23, 2010].

[163] s.1300(2).

[164] All are available at *http://www.bis.gov.uk./policies/business-law/company-and-partnership-law/company-law/regulations-statutory-instruments* [accessed July 23, 2010]

[165] The Financial Services Act 1986 was repealed. See the Financial Services and Markets Act 2000 (Consequential Amendments and Repeals) Order 2001 (SI 2001/3649), reg.3(1)(c).

[166] See *http://www.fsa.gov.uk* [accessed May 20, 2010].

[167] The Stock Exchange, which has been demutualised, plays a less prominent regulatory function.

[168] c.35. The Act is largely based on the Law Commission Report on *Fraud* (Law Com No.276, Cm 5560, 2002).

[169] In force from January 15, 2007: see the Fraud Act 2006 (Commencement) Order 2006 (SI 2006/3200).

consequences for company law in a number of respects. One of these is the offence of "fraud or abuse of position" in s.4. This section makes it an offence to commit a fraud by dishonestly abusing one's position and will apply where a defendant has been put in a privileged position, and by virtue of this position is expected to safeguard another's financial interests or not act against those interests. This privileged position can include the relationship between a director and his company, but other relationships can also be caught by it.[170] A further implication for company law lies in the extension of the offence of fraudulent trading[171] to sole traders in s.9.

The Corporate Manslaughter and Corporate Homicide Act,[172] which received Royal Assent on July 26, 2007[173] is the culmination of more than ten years of campaigning by a variety of interest groups inter alia to introduce a greater degree of corporate accountability following a number of high profile disasters, such as the rail crashes at Southall, Paddington, Hatfield and Potter's Bar, the sinking of the passenger ferry, *Herald of Free Enterprise*, off Zeebrugge, the sinking of the pleasure cruiser, *Marchioness*, following a collision with the *Bowbelle* on the Thames,[174] and the Piper Alpha and King's Cross fires. The central feature of the Act is the introduction of a statutory offence of corporate manslaughter in terms of which a company[175] will be guilty of an offence if the way in which its activities are managed or organised cause the death of another person and where this amounts to a gross breach of a relevant duty of care which is owed by the company to the deceased.[176]

In the field of insolvency law, there have been a number of important changes. The Insolvency Act 2000 made a number of changes to the law on company voluntary arrangements (CVAs)[177] and also introduced a new deregulated procedure for the disqualification of unfit directors.[178] These changes were integrated into the Insolvency Act 1986 and the Company Directors Disqualification Act 1986, respectively. The Enterprise Act 2002 has made further changes to personal and corporate insolvency law, competition law and consumer protection law. In relation to corporate insolvency, the objective has been to introduce measures which encourage the use of collective insolvency procedures, increase the prospects of recovery for unsecured creditors, and promote a culture of rescuing ailing companies.[179]

---

[170] See Law Commission Report on *Fraud* (Law Com No.276), para.7.38:

> "The necessary relationship will be present between trustee and beneficiary, director and company, professional person and client, agent and principal, employee and employer, or between partners. It may arise otherwise, for example within a family, or in the context of voluntary work, or in any context where the parties are not at arm's length. In nearly all cases where it arises, it will be recognised by the civil law as importing fiduciary duties, and any relationship that is so recognised will suffice."

[171] Now dealt with in s.993.

[172] c.19. For fuller discussion, see para.23–004.

[173] Most of the Act came into force from April 6, 2008. See the Corporate Manslaughter and Corporate Homicide Act 2007 (Commencement No.1) Order 2008 (SI 2008/401).

[174] For a case arising out of the incident, see *The Bowbelle* [1990] 1 Lloyd's Rep. 532.

[175] See s.1(2)(a).

[176] s.1(1).

[177] ss.1–4.

[178] ss.5–8. As to disqualification, see below, para.17–086.

[179] See Sandra Frisby, "In search of a rescue regime: the Enterprise Act 2002" (2004) 67 Modern L.R. 247.

CURRENT UNITED KINGDOM COMPANY LAW

1–020 To sum up, current UK company law is to be found mainly in the 2006 Act and partly in the Companies Act 1985 and the Companies (Audit, Investigations and Community Enterprise) Act 2004. Also relevant are six major Acts of Parliament: the Insolvency Act 1986, the Company Directors Disqualification Act 1986, the Criminal Justice Act 1993 and the Financial Services and Markets Act 2000, the Insolvency Act 2000, and the Enterprise Act 2002. No thorough attempt has been made to fully codify company law,[180] i.e. to reduce to a code all the statute law and common law on the topic, although it is increasingly the case that more and more matters have been codified.[181] Nevertheless, a significant part of company law is based on decided cases[182] and this aspect of company law jurisprudence has shown no signs of diminishing in either volume or importance.[183]

IMPACT OF THE EUROPEAN UNION

In general

1–021 From the preceding discussion it will have become clear that it is not enough for the UK company lawyer merely to absorb legislative changes emanating from Parliament sitting at Westminster. Since joining what was then the European Economic Community (EEC) in 1972, it has become necessary for every company lawyer to take cognisance of the harmonisation programme of the company laws of the Member States. The source for this programme is what is now art.44 of the Consolidated Treaty of the European Union and of the Treaty Establishing the European Community, which enjoins the Council of Ministers to "act by means of directives"[184] and then goes on to specify that the Council and the Commission are to coordinate safeguards for "companies and firms".[185] National legislatures are required to give effect to these and to amend their law, if necessary, to comply with them.[186] The 1980s in particular was an era of marked influence on UK company law but that influence waned in the 1990s.

Developments in the last decade

1–022 In September 2001, the European Commission set up a Group of High Level Company Law Experts with the objective of initiating a discussion on the need

---

[180] i.e. unlike Acts such as the Partnership Act 1890, the Sale of Goods Act 1893 (now 1979, as amended), and the Marine Insurance Act 1906.

[181] Such as directors fiduciary duties and duty of care: see 2006 Act Part 10. See Ch.17, below.

[182] As the volumes in Butterworths Company Law Cases (B.C.L.C.) and British Company Cases (B.C.C.) provide more than ample testimony.

[183] See David Milman, "The Courts and the Companies Acts: The Judicial Contribution to Company Law" [1990] L.M.C.L.Q. 401.

[184] Art.249.

[185] Art.44(2)(g).

[186] Whether or not other Member States have done so: see *Ministère Public v Blanguernon* (C-38/89) [1991] B.C.L.C. 635, ECJ; [1990] E.C.R. I-83.

for the modernisation of company law in Europe. The Group was given a dual mandate, which included providing the Commission with recommendations for a modern regulatory European company law framework. The Group duly presented its *Final Report of the High Level Group of Company Law Experts* on November 4, 2002[187] and this focused on corporate governance in the EU and the modernisation of European Company Law. The European Commission responded with *Modernising Company Law and Enhancing Corporate Governance in the European Union—A Plan to Move Forward* on May 21, 2003. This set out a comprehensive plan of action for company law reform throughout the EU. During 2004, the Commission consulted on (1) directors' remuneration; (2) cross border transfer of companies' registered offices; (3) board responsibilities and improving financial and corporate governance information; (4) shareholder rights; (5) independent directors and board committees; (6) corporate governance; and (7) companies' capital.

In relation to these consultations, the Commission invited Member States to reinforce the presence and role of independent non-executive directors on listed companies' boards.[188] Simultaneously, the Commission adopted a Recommendation on directors' remuneration.[189]

Two other developments should be highlighted. The first of these was the establishment in October 2004 of a European Corporate Governance Forum to examine best practices in Member States with a view to enhancing the convergence of national corporate governance codes and providing advice to the Commission.[190] More importantly, in January 2005, the Commission announced that it intended to set up a consultative committee, the Advisory Group on Corporate Governance and Company Law, in order to enable it to obtain technical advice on the implementation of the 2003 Plan. The Advisory Group has, at the time of writing, met on eleven occasions.[191]

Implementation of directives

Within the United Kingdom steps have, in the past, been taken to implement a **1–023** whole range of directives. Implementation of these directives by primary legislation does not present any real difficulty in domestic law, but the trend of implementing such changes by means of delegated legislation can lead to problems connected with whether the changes go further than was needed. Further, the difficulty of adapting the changes to existing law may apply to a wider spectrum of companies than those covered by the directive, in effect creating a two-tier system of law. Problems arise when either the directive has not been implemented by the due date or the implementing legislation does not properly comply with the terms of the directive. In such a case, the European Court of Justice has held that

---

[187] Available at *http://ec.europa.eu/internal_market/company/modern/index_en.htm* [accessed May 20, 2010].
[188] Press release IP/04/1182, October 6, 2004.
[189] Press release IP/04/1183, October 6, 2004.
[190] Press release IP/04/1241, October 18, 2004. This forum held its first meeting on January 20, 2005.
[191] See now *http://ec.europa.eu/internal_market/company/advisory/index_en.htm* [accessed May 20, 2010].

directives have vertical direct effect, meaning that as between the Member State and an individual or company, the provisions of the directive must be given precedence over the national law.[192] Although this is said not to apply as between two companies and/or individuals (so-called horizontal direct effect), the European Court has stated that, in applying national law, whether passed before or after the date for implementing the directive, the national court must interpret its law so far as possible in the light of the wording and purpose of the directive in order to achieve the result required by the directive.[193] In another area of law, the same court has allowed a claim for damages against a Member State for non-implementation of a directive.[194]

Of importance too, perhaps more so than directives on company law, have been arguments which arise under art.43 of the Treaty, as to rights of establishment. This provides that restrictions on the freedom of establishment of nationals in the territory of another Member State "shall be prohibited" and goes on to say that such rights of freedom of establishment "shall include . . . companies or firms". This right of corporate mobility was accepted by the court in *Centros Ltd v Erhverus-og Selkabsstyrelsen*,[195] and has been followed subsequently.[196]

Directives implemented in UK law

1–024 A full consideration of the fast moving and changing face of European company law is well beyond the scope of this book.[197] For ease of reference, the following are the main directives which have been implemented in UK law:

(1) The First Company Law Directive 68/151/EEC, which inter alia provided for relief against the doctrine of ultra vires and limits on directors' authority, was implemented in s. 9 of the European Community Act 1972.[198]

(2) The Second Company Law Directive 77/91/EEC provided minimum requirements on the formation of companies, and the maintenance, increase and reduction of capital and this was implemented in the Companies Act 1980 and amended in the Companies Act 1981.[199]

(3) The Third Company Law Directive 78/855/EEC was directed at the co-ordination of mergers within a Member State and was implemented in

---

[192] See *Karella v Greek Ministry for Industry, Energy and Technology* (joined cases C-19/90 and C-20/90) [1994] 1 B.C.L.C. 774, ECJ; [1991] E.C.R. I-2691.

[193] See *Marleasing SA v La Comercial Internacional de Alimentacion SA* (C-106/89) [1993] B.C.C. 421, ECJ; [1990] E.C.R. I-4135.

[194] *Andrea Francovich v The Republic (Italy)* (joined cases C-6/90 and C-9/90) [1993] 2 C.M.L.R. 66; [1990] E.C.R. I-5357.

[195] (C-212/97) [2000] Ch. 446, ECJ; [1999] E.C.R. I-1459.

[196] *Überseering BV v Nordic Construction Company Baumanagement GmbH* (C-208/00) [2005] 1 C.M.L.R. 1, ECJ; [2002] E.C.R. I-9919. See also *Kamer van Koophandel en Fabrieken voor Amsterdam v Inspire Art Ltd* (C-167/01), ECJ; [2003] E.C.R. I-10155.

[197] For detailed analysis, see *Palmer's Company Law* (London: Sweet & Maxwell), Pt 16.

[198] See the discussion of these provisions, which are now to be found in ss.39–40 of the Companies Act 2006.

[199] See now Companies Act 2006 Pt 17.

the UK via the Companies (Mergers and Divisions) Regulations 1987[200] and by inserting s.427A and Sch.15A into the Companies Act 1985.[201]

(4) The Fourth Company Law Directive 78/660/EEC (the "Fourth Directive"), on the disclosure of financial information and the contents of the company's annual accounts, was implemented in the Companies Act 1981.[202]

(5) The Sixth Company Law Directive 82/991/EEC, on the division of public companies, was implemented in the UK in the Companies (Mergers and Divisions) Regulations 1987.[203]

(6) The Seventh Company Law Directive 83/349/EEC (the "Seventh Directive") on consolidated accounts, supplementing the Fourth Directive, was implemented in the Companies Act 1989.

(7) The Eighth Company Law Directive 84/253/EEC on the qualification and independence of auditors in both private and public companies was implemented in the Companies Act 1989.[204]

(8) The Eleventh Company Law Directive 89/666/EEC, on disclosure requirements for branches opened in a Member State, was implemented by the Overseas Companies and Credit and Financial Institutions (Branch) Disclosure Regulations 1992.[205]

(9) The Twelfth Company Law Directive 89/556/EEC, on the formation of private companies with one member, was implemented by the Companies (Single Member Private Limited Companies) Regulations 1992.[206]

(10) The Major Shareholdings Directive 88/629/EEC, relating to the disclosure of such interests in listed companies was implemented by the Disclosure of Interests in Shares (Amendment) Regulations 1993.[207]

(11) The Directive Co-ordinating Regulations on Insider Dealing 89/592/EEC was implemented in the Criminal Justice Act 1993.[208]

(12) The Directive amending the Fourth and Seventh Directives on Company Accounts 90/604/EEC was implemented in the Companies Act 1985 (Accounts of Small and Medium-Sized Enterprises and Publication of Accounts in ECUS) Regulations.[209]

---

[200] (SI 1987/1991).
[201] See now, however, Companies Act 2006 Pt 27.
[202] See now, Companies Act 2006 Pt 24.
[203] (SI 1987/1991).
[204] See now Companies Act 2006 Pt 16.
[205] (SI 1992/3179). See now, on overseas companies, Companies Act 2006 Pt 34.
[206] (SI 1992/1699). See now Companies Act 2006 s.7(1).
[207] SI 1993/1819. See now Companies Act 2006 Pt 22.
[208] See Ch.24, below.
[209] (SI 1992/2452).

(13) Directive 2005/56/EC on cross-border mergers of limited liability companies[210] was implemented in the Companies (Cross-Border Mergers) Regulations 2007.[211]

(14) Directive 2007/36/EC on shareholder's rights[212] was implemented in the United Kingdom by the Companies (Shareholders Rights) Regulations 2009[213] and necessitated a number of changes to the 2006 Act.

Other measures

1–025   The Council Regulation 2001/2157/EC,[214] on the statute for a European company (SE), and Council Directive 2001/86/EC supplementing the statute for a European Company (SE) with regard to the involvement of employees,[215] were implemented in The European Public Limited Liability Company Regulations 2004.[216] Also implemented were a number of Regulations and Directives in relation to accountancy standards, which were implemented in the Companies Act 1985 (International Accounting Standards and Other Accounting Amendments) Regulations 2004, and Directive 2003/6/EC of the European Parliament and Council on insider dealing and market manipulation[217] in the Financial Services and Markets Act 2000 (Market Abuse) Regulations 2005.[218] Attention should also be drawn to Directive 2004/25/EC on takeover bids[219] and the proposal of the European Commission for a directive on cross-border mergers,[220] both of which have been implemented in the United Kingdom.

OTHER DEVELOPMENTS

The Human Rights Act

1–026   In 1998, the Human Rights Act was passed by Parliament and came into force on October 2, 2000.[221] The main effect of the Act has been to implement into UK law the provisions of the European Convention on Human Rights. Although it may not seem that this Act would have an impact on company law decisions, certain decisions have indicated that it could have potential. One area is in relation to art.6.1 of the Convention, which provides that in the determination of any civil rights and obligations or any criminal charge, everyone is entitled to a fair

---

[210] [2005] OJ L310/1.
[211] (SI 2007/2974).
[212] [2007] OJ L184/17.
[213] (SI 2009/1632).
[214] [2001] OJ L294/1.
[215] [2001] OJ L294/22. See para.34–009, below.
[216] (SI 2004/2326).
[217] [2003] OJ L96/16.
[218] (SI 2005/381).
[219] [2004] O.J. L142/12. This was implemented in the Takeovers Directive (Interim Implementation) Regulations 2006 (SI 2006/1183), but ceased to have effect from April 6, 2007, when Pt 28 of the 2006 Act came into force. See para.33–002, below.
[220] Press release IP/03/1564, November 18, 2003.
[221] The Human Rights Act 1998 (Commencement No.2) Order 1998 (SI 2000/1851).

hearing by an independent and impartial tribunal. The impact of this Article has been felt in relation to DTI investigations,[222] but was dismissed in relation to the Company Directors Disqualification Act.[223] Similarly, the Provisions of Protocol I, art.1,[224] which were raised by a petitioner in relation to a scheme of arrangement under s.895,[225] were rejected by the Court on the basis that it was established that a scheme which was purely financial did not infringe Protocol I.[226] However, yet other cases have shown that the Convention is capable of protecting corporate rights, for example in relation to art.8 of the Convention, which lays down the basic principle that everyone has the right to respect for his private and family life, his home and his correspondence.[227]

PROCEDURE FOR OBTAINING REGISTRATION OF A COMPANY

Introduction

To obtain the registration of a company certain documents must be delivered to **1–027** Companies House[228] and certain fees must be paid.[229] If the registered office[230] is situated in England or in Wales, the appropriate registrar is the Registrar of Companies for England and Wales,[231] and the address is Companies Registration Office, Crown Way, Maindy, Cardiff CF14 3UZ.[232] If the registered office is situated in Scotland the appropriate registrar is the Registrar of Companies for Scotland[233] and the address is Companies House, 4th Floor, Edinburgh Quay 2, 139 Fountainbridge, Edinburgh EH3 9FF. If the registered office is situated in Northern Ireland,[234] the registrar is the Registrar of Companies for Northern Ireland and the address is Companies House, Waterfront Plaza, 8 Laganbank Road, Belfast BT1 3BS.

---

[222] See *Saunders v United Kingdom* [1998] 1 B.C.L.C. 362, ECHR; *I.J.L., G.M.R., and A.K.P. v United Kingdom* [2002] B.C.C. 380, ECHR.

[223] See *Secretary of State for Trade and Industry v Eastaway* [2001] 1 B.C.L.C. 653. See now also *Eastaway v Secretary of State for Trade and Industry* [2007] EWCA Civ 425; [2007] B.C.C. 550; [2008] 1 B.C.L.C. 153.

[224] This inter alia provides that every natural or legal person is entitled to the peaceful enjoyment of his possessions and that no one shall be deprived of his possessions except in the public interest and subject to the conditions provided for by law and by the general principles of international law.

[225] i.e. of the 2006 Act. See para.32–016, below.

[226] *Re Waste Recycling Group Plc* [2003] EWHC 2065; [2004] 1 B.C.L.C. 352.

[227] See *R. v Broadcasting Standards Commission Ex p British Broadcasting Corporation* [2001] Q.B. 885, CA.

[228] See *http://www.companieshouse.gov.uk* [accessed May 20, 2010]. Companies house is an Executive Agency of the Department for Business, Innovation and Skills (BIS).

[229] The standard registration fee is £20, but Companies House also offers a Same Day Incorporation Service, for which the registration fee is £50.00: see s.1063 and the Registrar of Companies (Fees)(Companies and Limited Liability Partnerships) Regulations 2009 (SI 2009/2010) Sch.1.

[230] See s.9(2)(b).

[231] s.1060(1)(a). The current Registrar of Companies for England and Wales and Chief Executive of Companies House is Gareth Jones, a civil servant.

[232] There is also an Information Centre in London at Companies House Executive Agency, 21 Bloomsbury Street, London WCIB 3XD.

[233] s.1060(1)(b).

[234] s.1060(1)(c).

Documents which must be delivered to the Registrar

1–028 The documents which must be delivered to the Registrar of Companies[235] under the Act are a memorandum of association in the prescribed form[236] stating that the subscribers wish to form a company under this Act, and agree to become members of the company and, in the case of a company that is to have a share capital, to take at least one share each.[237] Also required is an application for registration of the company[238] stating the company's proposed name, the situation of the company's registered office, whether the liability of the company's members is limited and, if so, whether the company is limited by shares or by guarantee, and whether the company is a private or public company,[239] and a statement of compliance.

The application for registration must contain a statement of the company's share capital[240] and initial shareholdings[241] but only where the company is to have a share capital. Where the company is limited by guarantee, a statement of guarantee[242] is required.[243] Also required is a statement of the company's proposed officers,[244] namely the required particulars of the intended first director or directors and first secretary or joint secretaries, together with an expression of their consent.[245] The application for registration must also contain a statement of the intended address of the company's registered office[246] together with a copy of the company's articles of association,[247] to the extent the model articles do not apply by default.[248] Typically, the articles[249] will provide for such matters as the transfer of shares in the company, the holding of general meetings, i.e. meetings of the members or shareholders, the directors' powers of management and the extent to which they can delegate their powers to a managing director, and the payment of dividends. Finally, it should be noted that where the application is delivered for registration by an agent for the subscribers to the memorandum, the application must state the name and address of that person.[250]

Once complete, the memorandum, together with the application for registration must be delivered to the relevant Registrar of Companies[251] together with a statement of compliance,[252] to the effect that the requirements of the Act as to

---

[235] See s.9.
[236] See s.8(2). This is laid down by the Companies (Registration) Regulations 2008 (SI 2008/3014) Sch.1.
[237] s.8(1).
[238] See s.9(2).
[239] s.9(2).
[240] s.9(4)(a).
[241] See s.10.
[242] s.9(4)(b).
[243] s.11.
[244] s.9(4)(c).
[245] s.12.
[246] s.9(5)(a).
[247] It is now mandatory for a company to have articles: see s.18(1). The articles are dealt with in greater detail in para.4–003, below.
[248] See s.20.
[249] See now the Companies (Model Articles) Regulations 2008 (SI 2008/3229).
[250] s.9(3). See para.1–027.
[251] s.9(6).
[252] s.9(1).

registration have been complied with.[253] The Registrar may accept such a statement as sufficient evidence of compliance.[254]

Registrar's requirements: form, etc. of documents

The Registrar is empowered to impose requirements as to the form, authentica- **1–029** tion and manner of delivery of the documents which are required to be delivered to him.[255] As to form, he can require the contents of the document to be in a standard form and impose requirements for the purpose of enabling the document to be scanned or copied.[256] He has further powers with respect to the authentication of documents and their manner of delivery.[257]

Delivery of documents by electronic means

The Secretary of State may make regulations requiring documents that are autho- **1–030** rised or required to be delivered to the registrar to be delivered by electronic means.[258] He may, likewise, agree with a company that documents relating to that company can be delivered by electronic means.[259] Companies House permits registration electronically and this is often effected by incorporation agents and professional intermediaries[260] who typically can offer their customers a web-based electronic service. Electronic incorporation is cheaper [261] and speedier than making a paper application.

Duty of the Registrar

The duty of the Registrar on receiving the future company's registration docu- **1–031** ments is to satisfy himself that the statutory requirements have been complied with.[262] If he is so satisfied, then he must register the documents that have been delivered to him.[263] He must ensure, of course, that the memorandum contains the relevant statements by the first members of the company, that it is in the required form and has been authenticated by the subscribers.[264] He must satisfy himself that the documents listed in s.9 have been correctly provided and, in relation to the company's name, that it does not fall foul of Part 5 of the 2006 Act or the

---

[253] s.13(1).
[254] s.13(2).
[255] s.1068(1).
[256] s.1068(2).
[257] s.1068(3)(4).
[258] s.1069(1).
[259] s.1070(1).
[260] In 2003–2004, for example, this accounted for some 67 per cent of the new companies incorporated. See *Companies in 2003–2004* (DTI, 2004), p.26.
[261] For electronic incorporations the fee is £15 (£30 for same day): see s.1063 and the Registrar of Companies (Fees)(Companies and Limited Liability Partnerships) Regulations 2009 (SI 2009/2010) Sch.1.
[262] s.14.
[263] s.14.
[264] See s.8.

requirements of the Company and Business Names (Miscellaneous Provisions) Regulations 2009.[265] Apart from these statutory requirements, the Registrar must satisfy himself that the company is not being formed for an unlawful purpose.[266] If the company is being formed for a purpose prohibited by law,[267] the Registrar will decline to register it. If the Registrar does register a company with illegal objects the court will cancel the registration on an application by the Attorney General.[268]

Certificate of incorporation

1–032 On the registration of a company the Registrar issues a certificate that the company is incorporated.[269] At this time he will also allocate the company a registered number.[270] The certificate must state the name and registered number of the company; the date of its incorporation; whether it is a limited or unlimited company, and if it is limited whether it is limited by shares or limited by guarantee; whether it is a private or a public company; whether the company's registered office is situated in England and Wales (or in Wales), in Scotland or in Northern Ireland.[271] The certificate must be signed by the registrar or authenticated by the registrar's official seal[272] and, once issued, is conclusive evidence that the requirements of this Act as to registration have been complied with and that the company is duly registered.[273] The certificate of incorporation has also been held to be conclusive as to the date of incorporation.[274] It cannot be argued that a company is not validly incorporated except where a statutory provision as to substance invalidates the registration.[275] The reason for this section is that once a company is registered and has begun business and entered into contracts, it would be disastrous if any person could allege that the company was not duly registered.[276] The certificate will not, however, be conclusive if a trade union should be registered as a company[277] as the registration of a trade union under the Companies Acts is void by statute.[278] Again, the certificate is not conclusive as to the legality of a company's objects[279] and proceedings may be brought to have the

---

[265] SI 2009/1085.

[266] s.7(2).

[267] *R. v Registrar of Companies, Ex p. More* [1931] 2 K.B. 197, CA.

[268] *R. v Registrar of Companies, Ex p. Attorney General* [1991] B.C.L.C. 476.

[269] s.15(1).

[270] As to this, see s.1066. The registered number must be displayed on the company's business letters, order forms, and its websites: see the Companies (Trading Disclosures) Regulations 2008 (SI 2008/495) reg.7(1)(2).

[271] s.15(2).

[272] s.15(3). As to the registrar's official seal, see s.1062.

[273] s.15(4).

[274] *Jubilee Cotton Mills Ltd v Lewis* [1924] A.C. 958.

[275] *Gaiman v National Association for Mental Health* [1971] Ch. 317 at 329. See also the speech of Lord Wrenbury in *Cotman v Brougham* [1918] A.C. 514 at 523.

[276] *Peel's Case* (1867) L.R. 2 Ch. App at 682, per Lord Cairns.

[277] *British Association of Glass Bottle Manufacturers Ltd v Nettlefold* (1911) 27 T.L.R. 527.

[278] Trade Union and Labour Relations (Consolidation) Act 1992 (c.52) s.10(3)(a).

[279] As to which, see now s.31 and the discussion at para.4–030, below.

registration cancelled where objects are illegal.[280] The Registrar publishes, in the appropriate Gazette[271] or by some alternative means,[272] notice of the issue of a certificate of incorporation and this must specify the name and registered number of the company and the date of issue of the certificate.[273]

Form of the certificate

The certificate of incorporation, which may be described as the company's birth **1–033** certificate, is in the following form for private companies[284]:

CERTIFICATE OF INCORPORATION OF A PRIVATE LIMITED COMPANY
Company No.
The Registrar of Companies for England and Wales hereby certifies that [Name of the Company] is this day incorporated under the Companies Act 2006 as a private company and that the company is limited.
Given at Companies House, Cardiff, the [date].

Off-the-shelf companies

Those business individuals who choose to form a registered company may not **1–034** have any special requirements regarding the company's constitution or name. Indeed, they may wish to have the company incorporated as quickly as possible without incurring the trouble of starting from scratch. Thus the commercial practice has developed of buying a dormant company off the shelf, from one of the several agencies who offer this particular service, instead of registering a new company. Such companies have no trading history and, upon purchase, can begin trading immediately. The great advantage is the speed of the process; all the incorporators have to do is pay the agency[285] and to take transfers of the original subscriber's shares and take custody of the company's registers. They would be obliged to send to the Registrar notices of changes in the directors and company secretary as required under the Act. Any changes to the memorandum[286] or to the articles could be effected at their leisure. The disadvantage of this process is that until any changes are made—including the name of the company—there is likely to be little resemblance between the business of the new company and its predecessor.

---

[280] *R. v Registrar of Companies, Ex p. Attorney General* [1991] B.C.L.C. 476, adopting the words of Lord Parker of Waddington in *Bowman v Secular Society Ltd* [1917] A.C. 406, at 439.

[281] s.1064(1)(a). The appropriate Gazette is either the London or the Edinburgh Gazette depending upon the company's domicile. See *http://www.gazettes-online.co.uk* [accesed May 20, 2010].

[282] See s.1116.

[283] s.1064(2).

[284] Public companies would have a different name and the additional declaration that it is a public limited company (see s.4(2)(a)).

[285] The costs are usually greater than registering a new company, simply because of the agency's costs, such as paying a holding fee to Companies House and the annual costs of making annual returns.

[286] Particularly in the case of a company formed under the Companies Act 1985.

Inspection of registration (and other) documents

1–035 Any person may, on payment of a fee,[287] inspect the originals of documents which have been delivered to the Registrar.[288] On payment of a fee, any person is also entitled to a copy[289] of any material on the register.[290] Such copies may be furnished in an electronic form.[291] Certain material specified in the Act is not, however, available for public inspection.[292]

EFFECT OF REGISTRATION OF A COMPANY

Statutory effect

1–036 From the date of incorporation mentioned in the certificate of incorporation,[293] the subscribers of the memorandum, together with such other persons as may from time to time become members of the company, form a body corporate by the name stated in the certificate of incorporation,[294] capable forthwith of exercising all the functions of an incorporated company.[295] Where the company has a share capital, the subscribers to the memorandum become holders of the shares specified in the statement of capital and initial shareholdings.[296] The persons who are named as directors or secretary (or joint secretary) are from that date deemed to have been appointed to that office.[297]

The company as a body corporate with a separate legal personality

1–037 Once registered, the company exists as a body corporate, i.e. a legal person separate and distinct from its members.[298] In the case of *Continental Tyre & Rubber Co (Great Britain Ltd) v Daimler Co Ltd*, the leading company law judge of the day stated that:

> "The artificial legal person called the corporation has no physical existence. It exists only in contemplation of law. It has neither body, parts, nor passions. It cannot wear weapons nor serve in the wars. It can be neither loyal nor disloyal.

---

[287] The Companies (Fees for Inspection and Copying of Company Records) Regulations 2007 (SI 2007/2612) specifies that the fee is £3.50 for each hour or part thereof: reg.2. A similar fee is payable for inspection of the register of directors and of secretaries: see the Companies (Fees for Inspection of Company Records) Regulations 2008 (SI 2008/3007) reg.2.

[288] s.1085(1)(2).

[289] s.1086.

[290] The Companies (Fees for Inspection and Copying of Company Records) Regulations 2007 (SI 2007/2612) regs 3, 4.

[291] s.1086(2); s.1090.

[292] See s.1087.

[293] s.16(1). In *Jubilee Cotton Mills Ltd v Lewis* [1924] A.C. 958 it was held that "from the date of incorporation" in s.[16(1)] included any portion of the day on which the company was incorporated.

[294] s.16(2).

[295] s.16(3).

[296] s.16(5).

[297] s.16(6).

[298] See Murray Pickering, "The company as a separate legal entity" (1968) 31 M.L.R. 481.

It cannot compass treason. It can be neither friend nor enemy. Apart from its corporators it can have neither thoughts, wishes, nor intentions, for it has no mind other than the minds of the corporators."[299]

This independent corporate existence of a registered company is a principle of the first importance in company law and was confirmed by the House of Lords in the leading case, *Salomon v Salomon & Co Ltd*.[300] S had for many years carried on business as a boot manufacturer. His business was solvent when it was converted into a company, i.e. a company limited by shares was formed, the subscribers to the memorandum of which were S and his wife, daughter and four sons (for one share each), and the business was sold to the company at a price of £39,000. The terms of sale were approved by all the shareholders. £9,000 was paid in cash. £20,000 fully paid shares of £1 each were allotted to S so that S's wife and children held one share each and S held 20,001 shares. S left the rest of the price on loan to the company and for this sum of £10,000 he was given debentures secured by a charge on the company's assets. It seems that the directors were S and his sons and that S was appointed managing director. After a depression the company went into liquidation. The assets were sufficient to satisfy the debentures, but the unsecured creditors, with debts amounting to £7,000, received nothing. The House of Lords held that the proceedings were not contrary to the true intent and meaning of the Companies Act; that the company was duly registered and was not a mere "alias" or agent of or trustee for the vendor; that S was not liable to indemnify the company against creditors' claims; that there was no fraud upon creditors (or shareholders); that the company (or the liquidator) was not entitled to rescission of the contract of purchase. In a famous dictum, Lord Macnaghten stated that

"The company is at law a different person altogether from the subscribers to the memorandum; and, though it may be that after incorporation the business is precisely the same as it was before, and the same persons are managers, and the same hands receive the profits, the company is not in law the agent of the subscribers or trustee for them. Nor are the subscribers as members liable, in any shape or form, except to the extent and in the manner provided by the Act."[301]

Effect of separate legal personality

In a registered company the assets and liabilities are those of the corporation and **1–038** not of the members.[302] It is the company that can hold land and other property and can sue and be sued.[303] This separation of the corporation and its members, which is sometimes referred to by the phrase "the veil of incorporation" means that the members are not liable for the company's debts. Members of a company limited by

---

[299] [1915] 1 KB 813, CA, at p. 916, per Buckley L.J.
[300] [1897] A.C. 22.
[301] At 51. cf. *Broderip v Salomon* [1895] 2 Ch. 323, CA.
[302] See *Ferguson v Wilson* (1866) L.R. 2 Ch. App. 77, at 89.
[303] See *Foss v Harbottle* (1843) 2 Hare 461 at 490–491; 67 E.R.189 at 202. See the discussion, below at para.22–005.

shares are liable to contribute to the company's assets to the extent, if any,[304] unpaid on their shares.[305] Thus if a member has taken one thousand shares of £1 each in the company and the shares are fully paid up he will be under no further liability to contribute to the assets. This was reaffirmed by the House of Lords in *J. H. Rayner (Mincing Lane) Ltd v Department of Trade and Industry*.[306] That case arose out of the collapse of the International Tin Council in 1985 which left it owing millions of pounds to a number of metal traders and banks. The Council had been formed by several states and the Council's creditors sought to recover its debts from those member states. The House of Lords first decided that the Council was a body corporate with its own separate legal personality distinct from its members and it followed therefore that only the Council and not its members could be liable for the debts. Under English law only the party to a contract can be liable on that contract and the only contracting party here was the Council. It would be for Parliament to provide otherwise in any given case. Lord Oliver expressed the decision thus:

> "Once given the existence of the I.T.C. as a separate legal person and given that it was the contracting party in the transactions upon which the appellants claim . . . there is no room for any further inquiry as to what type of legal person the contracting party is. The person who can enforce contracts and the persons against whom they can be enforced in English law and the parties to the contract and in identifying the parties to the contract there are no gradations of legal personality."[307]

A further consequence of the separate personality of the company is that the property of the company belongs to the company itself and not to the individual members.[308] Thus, even the largest shareholder has no insurable interest in the property of the company.[309] The managing director, even if he owns all the shares except one, cannot lawfully pay cheques to the company into his own banking account or draw cheques for his own purposes upon the company's banking account,[310] and two sole shareholder/directors can be convicted of theft from "their" company.[311]

Piercing the veil of incorporation: the courts

1–039 In general, the law will not go behind the separate personality of the company to the members,[312] so that, e.g. in *Macaura v Northern Assurance Co Ltd*,[313] it was

---

[304] Many companies require shares to be paid for in full at the time of subscription.
[305] s.1(2).
[306] [1990] 2 A.C. 418.
[307] [1990] 2 A.C. 418 at 508.
[308] See *Bowman v Secular Society Ltd* [1917] A.C. 406.
[309] *Macaura v Northern Assurance Co Ltd* [1925] A.C. 619.
[310] *A.L. Underwood Ltd v Bank of Liverpool & Marine Ltd* [1924] 1 K.B. 775, CA.
[311] *Attorney-General's Reference (No.2 of 1982)* [1984] Q.B. 624; *R. v Phillipou* (1989) 5 B.C.C. 33.
[312] There is a significant body of academic writing on this subject. See particularly, Marc Moore, " 'A temple built on faulty foundations': Piercing the corporate veil and the legacy of *Salomon v Salomon*" [2006] J.B.L. 180; Tan Cheng Han, "Piercing the Separate Personality of the Company: A Matter of Policy" [1999] Singapore J. of Legal Studies 531; S. Ottolenghi, "From peeping behind the corporate veil to ignoring it completely" (1990) 53 M.L.R. 338.
[313] [1925] A.C. 619.

held that the largest shareholder had no insurable interest in the property of the company. However, there are cases when the courts permit the corporate veil to be lifted, or pierced, and the law disregards the corporate entity and pays regard instead to the economic realities behind the legal façade, i.e. where the facts supersede form. These exceptions may be classified into those under judicial interpretation and those expressly provided by statute.

The grounds upon which the courts will lift the corporate veil are difficult to categorise. Initially there were a number of fairly random examples. Thus, a company registered in England was held to be an alien enemy if its agents or the persons in de facto control of its affairs were alien enemies, and in determining whether alien enemies have such control, the number of alien enemy shareholders and the value of their holdings were material.[314] A further example was *Express Engineering Works Ltd, Re*,[315] where the decision of all the shareholders was held to be the decision of the company, e.g. something less formal than a resolution, even a special resolution, duly passed at a general meeting was regarded as the act of the company. Further, it was held in *Bugle Press Ltd, Re*[316] that if A Ltd makes an offer for the shares in B Ltd and in substance A Ltd is the same as the majority shareholding in B Ltd, A Ltd will not be able to invoke s.979[317] and compel the minority shareholders in B Ltd to sell their shares to A Ltd. In these circumstances the law goes behind the corporate personality of A Ltd to the individual members. The court will not allow that section to be invoked for an improper purpose. The case of *Gilford Motor Co Ltd v Horne*[318] shows that the courts will not allow a company to be used as a device to mask the carrying on of a business by a former employee of another person and to enable the former employee to break a valid covenant in restraint of trade contained in the contract under which he was formerly employed. In that case the employee convenanted that after the termination of the employment he would not solicit his employer's customers. Soon after the termination of his employment he formed a company of which the two directors and shareholders were his wife and one other person and which sent out circulars to customers of his former employer. An injunction was granted against the ex-employee and the company.[319]

Some judges in the past adopted a more general approach based on the interests of justice as being the guiding light. Thus, Lord Denning M.R. was prepared to lift the veil in *Wallersteiner v Moir*[320]—he said that in that case the plaintiff was also in breach of what is now s.197 (which in general prohibits a company making a loan to a director) because the company of which he was a director made a loan to another company which was his puppet, so that the loan should be treated as made to him. In 1985, the Court of Appeal lifted the veil when a

---

[314] *Daimler Co Ltd v Continental Tyre etc. Ltd* [1916] 2 A.C. 307.
[315] [1920] 1 Ch. 466, CA.
[316] [1961] Ch. 270, CA.
[317] See para.33–021, below.
[318] [1933] Ch. 935, CA.
[319] See also *Jones v Lipman* [1962] 1 W.L.R. 832. These cases are said to be examples of the veil being pierced where the situation is a "sham". They are equally explicable on the basis that extending the injunction to the companies was simply necessary for its enforcement.
[320] [1974] 1 W.L.R. 991, CA.

defendant in a company fraud case took elaborate steps to conceal his assets by a complex network of companies and trusts. The court allowed the veil to be lifted in order to establish exactly what he owned and where it was located. They stated that this could be done in the interests of justice irrespective of the legal efficacy of the corporate structure provided he either substantially or effectively controlled the company concerned. The network of companies had been set up in an attempt to confuse and conceal.[321] This interests of justice approach was also applied in *Creasey v Breachwood Motors Ltd*[322] where an employee who had a claim for unfair dismissal against a company found that, after the claim had arisen, all the assets of the company had been transferred to another company owned by the same individuals and the first company had been dissolved. The second company was added as a defendant to the action. In doing so the judge had to distinguish the decision of the Court of Appeal in *Adams v Cape Industries Plc*.[323] He did so on the basis that the cause of action had not accrued at the time in that case whereas it had done so at the time of the actions of the defendants in the present case.

1–040   In the *Adams* case the court had to consider whether the veil of incorporation should be pierced with respect to an action brought against one company in a group[324] in the United Kingdom where liability (for asbestos claims) arose against another company in that group in the United States. The court refused to pierce the veil of incorporation and Scott J. expressly stated that

> "save in cases which turn on the wording of particular statutes or contracts, the court is not free to disregard the principle of *Salomon v Salomon & Co Ltd* merely because it considers that justice so requires."[325]

The Court of Appeal in *Adams* instead applied the test as stated by Lord Keith in the Scottish case of *Woolfson v Strathclyde Regional Council*[326] that the veil would only be pierced where special circumstances exist indicating that it is a mere façade concealing the true facts.[327] That case, like *Adams*, concerned the question as to whether a group of companies could be regarded as a single entity for legal purposes. In *Woolfson*, the issue was whether a subsidiary and parent company could be regarded as a single entity in order to enable them to claim compensation for disturbance on a compulsory purchase. The issue had previously arisen in *D.H.N. Food Distributors Ltd v Tower Hamlets LBC*[328] where the

---

[321] *A Company, Re* [1985] B.C.L.C. 333, CA.

[322] [1993] B.C.L.C. 480.

[323] [1990] Ch. 433, CA.

[324] *The Albazero* [1977] A.C. 774:

> "Each company in a group of companies (a relatively modern concept) is a separate legal entity possessed of separate legal rights and liabilities so that the rights of one company in a group cannot be exercised by another company in that group . . ."

  per Roskill J. at 807.

[325] [1990] Ch. 433, CA, at 536.

[326] 1978 S.C., HL, 90.

[327] At 96.

[328] [1976] 1 W.L.R. 852, CA.

Court of Appeal in England allowed the claim on the basis that D.H.N. was in a position to control its subsidiaries in every respect. The House of Lords in *Woolfson* distinguished the D.H.N. case on its facts but also doubted whether it was a correct application of the general principle, stated above, that the veil should only be pierced where special circumstances exist indicating that it is a mere façade concealing the true facts.

The approach taken by the House of Lords in the *Woolfson* case was also applied in *National Dock Labour Board v Pinn & Wheeler Ltd.*[329] The judge refused to regard three related companies as being a single entity for the purposes of a demarcation dispute. Only where there was a mere façade concealing the true facts would the corporate veil be pierced. In this case the companies had been retained for good commercial reasons. The test was also applied by Lightman J. in *Acatos & Hutcheson Plc v Watson*[330] in relation to the purchase by a company of another company whose principal asset was shares in the purchaser. Since this was neither a façade nor a sham[331] he regarded the purchaser as having acquired shares in the second company and not its own shares.

The position is therefore becoming clearer. There must be some evidence of impropriety or fraud[332] before the corporate veil can be pierced. Thus the Court of Appeal in *H, Re*,[333] upheld an order made against the assets of two companies controlled by two individuals accused of excise fraud, rejecting the argument that the assets of the companies and those of the individuals were separate. Basing their judgment on *Adams v Cape Industries*, the Court of Appeal held that this was an "appropriate case" in which to lift the veil:

"As to the evidence, it provides a prima facie case that the defendants control these companies; that the companies have been used for fraud, in particular the evasion of excise duties on a large scale; that the defendants regard the companies as carrying on a family business, and that company cash has benefitted the defendants in substantial amounts."[334]

In *Trustor AB v Smallbone (No.3)*,[335] the Chancery Division confirmed this general approach, holding that where the defendant, a managing director, had transferred substantial sums to another company, the court was entitled to pierce the veil and recognise the receipt of that company as that of the individual in control, because it was used as a device or façade to conceal the true facts.[336]

---

[329] (1989) 5 B.C.C. 75.
[330] [1995] 1 B.C.L.C. 218.
[331] As to the meaning of "sham", see e.g. *Snook v London and West Riding Investments Ltd* [1967] 2 Q.B. 786, CA, 802.
[332] See, e.g., *R. v Omar (Bassam)* [2004] EWCA Civ 2320; [2005] 1 Cr.App.R. 86 at [18].
[333] [1996] 2 B.C.L.C. 500.
[334] [1996] 2 B.C.L.C. 500 at 511. See also *Gencor ACP Ltd v Dalby* [2002] 2 B.C.L.C. 734 at 744.
[335] [2001] 1 W.L.R. 1177. Applied in *Buckinghamshire County Council v Briar* [2002] EWHC 2821; [2003] Envir. L.R. 25.
[336] At 1185. See too *Kensington International Ltd v Congo* [2005] EWHC 2684 (Comm); [2006] 2 B.C.L.C. 296.

1–041   On the other hand, in the absence of such impropriety or fraud, the courts will not pierce the corporate veil.[337] This approach was taken by Toulson J. in *Yukong Line Ltd v Rendsburg Investments Corporation*.[338] An individual signed a charter-party on behalf of one company. That company was in breach of the agreement and the other party obtained an injunction against that company's assets. It then discovered that that company had closed its account and transferred it to another company. The individual controlled both companies. The judge refused either to regard the individual as therefore being a party to the agreement or to make the second company liable in damages for the breach.

A similar approach was also taken by the Court of Appeal in *Ord v Belhaven Pubs Ltd*.[339] On facts similar to *Creasey v Beachwood Motors Ltd*,[340] the Court of Appeal refused to pierce the corporate veil. They rejected any idea that a group of companies could be regarded as a single entity except in very limited circumstances where there was some impropriety or the company was a façade concealing the true facts.[341] Even in that situation it was suggested that the situation was best dealt with by applying insolvency law. The Court also expressly stated that the decision in the *Creasey* case should no longer be regarded as authoritative.[342]

Piercing the veil of incorporation: statute

1–042   There are some instances where the effect of the statute[343] is to lift the veil. This is not, however, the focus of the 2006 Act where the emphasis is rather on making directors and others liable for corporate wrongs in specified circumstances.[344] Nevertheless, there are several statutory examples of lifting the veil under the Insolvency Act 1986[345] and these include:

1.   liability for fraudulent trading under s.213[346];

2.   liability for wrongful trading under s.214[347];

---

[337] See *Ringway Road Marking v Adbruf Ltd* [1998] 2 B.C.L.C. 625; *Kensington International Ltd v Congo* [2005] EWHC 2684 (Comm); [2006] 2 B.C.L.C. 296; *Print Factory (London) 1991 Ltd v Millam* [2007] EWCA Civ 322; [2008] B.C.C. 169; *Coles v Samuel Smith Old Brewery (Tadcaster)* [2007] EWCA Civ 1461; [2008] 2 E.G.L.R. 159; *Ben Hashem v Ali Shayif* [2008] EWHC 2380 (Fam); [2009] 1 F.L.R. 115; *R. v Seager (Mornington Stafford)* [2009] EWCA Crim 1303; [2010] 1 W.L.R. 815.

[338] [1998] 1 W.L.R. 294. See also *R. v K* [2005] EWCA Crim 619; [2006] B.C.C. 362.

[339] [1998] 2 B.C.L.C. 447, CA.

[340] Above at para.1–039.

[341] See also *Skjevesland v Geveran Trading Co Ltd* [2000] B.P.I.R. 523.

[342] The Court of Appeal also doubted the decision in *D.H.N. Food Distributors Ltd v Tower Hamlets LBC* [1976] 1 W.L.R. 852, CA, 1–040, above.

[343] But see *R. v Warrington Crown Court* [2002] UKHL 24; [2002] 1 W.L.R. 1954, HL, where the House of Lords held that withholding information as to the identity of the members of the company was not indicative of the lack of fitness or bona fides of the members for the purpose of the Licensing Act 1964, c.26.

[344] See para.17–065, below.

[345] c.45.

[346] See para.23–019, below.

[347] See para.23–021, below.

    3.   liability for improper use of an insolvent company's name under ss.216 and 217.[348]

A further statutory example is s.15 of the Company Directors Disqualification Act 1986[349] which penalises a person who acts in breach of a disqualification order by making him personally responsible for all the relevant debts of a company.

---

[348] See para.23–023, below.
[349] c.46. See the discussion at para.17–102.

Chapter 2

OTHER BUSINESS ORGANISATIONS

INTRODUCTION

2–001 Business entrepreneurs contemplating setting up a business have a wide choice of business vehicles available to them. At one level this could consist of a sole tradership or, with the collaboration of others, an ordinary partnership or limited partnership, or closest to the registered company, a limited liability partnership (LLP).

SOLE TRADERS

2–002 This is the simplest form of business structure available to anyone who wishes to carry on business. A sole tradership simply amounts to the carrying on of business on one's own, without anyone else. The type of business which is carried on could be a commercial activity, such as a newsagent, or the provision of a specialist service, such as an electrician or a plumber. The major advantage of this type of business is that sole traders only require start-up capital to commence business and are not dependent upon the investment of capital by others. From a legal perspective there are few controls on the setting up of sole traderships and UK law has not adopted a system of regulation of sole traderships. One area in which controls are maintained is in relation to the professions. Thus, it would be an offence for someone to purport to carry on business as a solicitor without being duly qualified as such.[1] Another area in which controls are exercised is where someone purports to carry on a consumer credit business, which would be subject to the control of the Office of Fair Trading.[2]

A major disadvantage, however, is that the owner of a sole tradership will be personally liable for the firm's debts; sole traders have unlimited liability. One area, however, in which control may be exercised is in relation to the choice of name of the business. Sole traderships are subject to statutory controls on the choice of name for the business, previously found in the Business Names Act 1985.[3] These controls are now to be found in the Company and Business Names (Miscellaneous Provisions) Regulations 2009[4] and the Company, Limited

---

[1] See the Solicitors Act 1974 (c.47) ss.20–21.
[2] See *http://www.oft.gov.uk* [accessed May 20, 2010].
[3] c.7. This Act is repealed by the Companies Act 2006 Sch.16.
[4] SI 2009/1085 as amended by the Company and Business Names (Miscellaneous Provisions) (Amendment) Regulations 2009 (SI 2009/2404).

Liability Partnership and Business names (Sensitive Words and Expressions) Regulations 2009.[5]

PARTNERSHIPS

The law of partnership[6] evolved during the course of the eighteenth and nine- **2–003** teenth centuries. The principles of law developed by the courts were eventually codified in the Partnership Act of 1890,[7] drafted by Sir Frederick Pollock,[8] although not intended to supersede the rules of common law and equity which prevail unless they are inconsistent with the Act.[9] In its simplest terms, a partnership is the relation which subsists between persons carrying on a business in common with a view of profit.[10] A partnership firm is not, however, a body corporate and so does not have a separate legal personality[11]: it is only a description of the relationship between the partners.[12] The property of the firm belongs to the partners and the firm's debts are the debts of the partners, i.e. the partners are personally liable for the firm's debts.[13] On the death or bankruptcy of a partner, subject to any agreement between the partners the partnership is dissolved as regards all the partners.[14] In practice the share of a partner who dies or retires has to be found out of the business or provided for by the other partners, and this may cause serious financial embarrassment to the firm.

Partnerships have certain advantages over a registered company. In particular, there are fewer formalities to be observed, and therefore there is less publicity and less expense involved in forming a partnership. There is no need to be registered, or to file articles of association with the registrar. There are therefore no registration fees, and legal costs are less. A partnership agreement may be oral or even inferred from conduct. The internal management structure is also fluid—there are no requirements for directors or meetings.[15] A further advantage of a partnership is that information about the partnership, including the accounts will, since there is no registration, never be open to public scrutiny. A partnership is also not subject to the rules in connection with raising and maintenance of share capital, to which a registered company which is not an unlimited company is subject.[16]

---

[5] SI 2009/2615.

[6] s.1. See generally on partnerships, Geoffrey Morse, *Partnership Law*, 7th edn (2010).

[7] 53 & 54 Vict., c.39.

[8] Sir Frederick was also the writer of *A Digest of the Law of Partnership* (1877). See now Neil Duxbury, *Frederick Pollock and the English Juristic Tradition* (2004).

[9] See s.46 of the Partnership Act 1890.

[10] Partnership Act 1890 s.1(1).

[11] See s.4(1) of the Partnership Act 1890. In Scots law, however, the partnership is treated as having legal personality: Partnership Act 1890, s.4(2).

[12] Although the Law Commission recommended in 2003 that partnerships should have a separate personality, this has not (and is not likely to be) implemented: see *Partnership Law: A Joint Report* (2003) Law Com No.283, para.5.1 et seq.

[13] Partnership Act 1890 s.9.

[14] Partnership Act 1890 s.33(1). As to dissolution by the court in the event of the mental disorder of a partner, see Partnership Act 1890 s.35, and Mental Health Act 1959, c.72, s.103. As to dissolution by notice by a retiring partner, see Partnership Act 1890 s.32.

[15] Although in relation to the latter, this requirement has now been removed also for private companies under the 2006 Act.

[16] Below, Ch.9.

Each partner is normally an agent for the firm for the purpose of the business of the partnership[17] and, subject to any agreement to the contrary between the parties, may take part in the management of the partnership business.[18]

SOLE TRADERSHIPS AND PARTNERSHIPS COMPARED WITH REGISTERED COMPANIES

2–004 A registered company has many advantages over a partnership, A registered company has the same advantages over an individual trader. These include the following:

1. as we have seen, a registered company is a corporation,[19] i.e. a separate legal person distinct from the members, whereas a partnership is merely the aggregate of the partners.[20] Consequently:

    (a) the debts and contracts of a registered company are those of the company and not those of the members, whereas in the case of a partnership firm every partner is jointly and severally liable with the other partners for all the firm's debts and obligations incurred while he is a partner[21];

    (b) unless it is dissolved, a registered company continues in existence so that it is not affected by the death, bankruptcy, mental disorder or retirement of any of its members. In the case of a partnership, on the other hand, on the death or bankruptcy of a partner, subject to any agreement between the partners the partnership is dissolved as regards all the partners.[22] In practice the share of a partner who dies or retires has to be found out of the business or provided for by the other partners, and this may cause serious financial embarrassment to the firm;

    (c) the property of a registered company belongs to and is vested in the company, so that there is no change in the ownership of, or in the formal title to, the property on a change in the ownership of shares in the company. In a partnership, the property belongs to the partners and is vested in them. Consequently there are changes in the ownership of, and in the formal title to, the firm's property from time to time on the death or retirement of a partner or trustee;

    (d) a registered company can contract with its members and can sue and be sued on such contracts. In England, a partner probably cannot contract with the firm;

---

[17] Partnership Act 1890 s.5.

[18] Partnership Act 1890 s.24(5).

[19] Companies Act 2006 s.16(2); *Salomon v Salomon & Co Ltd* [1897] A.C. 22; para.1–037, above.

[20] Although a partnership in Scotland has one of the attributes of a corporation in that it is "a legal person distinct from the partners of whom it is composed": Partnership Act 1890 s.4(2).

[21] Partnership Act 1890 s.9.

[22] Partnership Act 1890 s.33(1). As to dissolution by the court in the event of the mental disorder of a partner, see Partnership Act 1890 s.35, and Mental Health Act 1959 s.103 (the latter is not applicable to Scotland). As to dissolution by notice by a retiring partner, see Partnership Act 1890 s.32.

(e) each partner is normally an agent for the firm for the purpose of the business of the partnership[23] and, subject to any agreement to the contrary between the parties, may take part in the management of the partnership business.[24] The members of a registered company as such are not its agents and have no power to manage its affairs—the directors are agents and managers, i.e. they have the powers given to them by the articles;

(f) subject to any restrictions in the articles, which there may be in the articles of a private company,[25] shares in a registered company can be transferred or mortgaged without the consent of the other shareholders. Subject to any agreement to the contrary, a person cannot be introduced as a partner without the consent of all the existing partners[26] and if in England a partner charges his share of the partnership for his separate debt the other partners normally have the option to dissolve the partnership[27];

2. the liability of a member of a registered company to contribute to its assets may be, and usually is, limited, e.g. in the case of a company limited by shares, to the amount unpaid on his shares[28] (although the person controlling a private company may have to give a personal guarantee of the company's bank overdraft) but the members of a partnership are jointly and severally liable for all the debts of the firm[29];

3. a registered company has greater facilities for borrowing than a partnership, e.g. the company may borrow on debentures[30];

4. floating charges can be created by a registered company but not by a partnership.[31]

LIMITED PARTNERSHIPS

Limited partnerships were established in 1907 by the Limited Partnerships Act of **2–005** that year.[32] The concept is an importation from abroad; it is an adaptation of the type of business organisation known in French law as a *société en commandite*. The Partnership Act 1890 and the rules of common law and equity apply "subject to the provisions of this Act".[33] The number of partners under the Act is limited, where the business is that of banking to ten, and in the case of any other business

---

[23] Partnership Act 1890 s.5.
[24] Partnership Act 1890 s.24(5).
[25] These have not been compulsory for private companies since 1980.
[26] Partnership Act 1890 s.24(7).
[27] Partnership Act 1890 s.33(2).
[28] s.3(2).
[29] Partnership Act 1890 s.9.
[30] Below, Ch.25.
[31] Below, Ch.25.
[32] 7 Edw. 7, c.24.
[33] s.7.

to twenty.[34] There must in every case be at least one general partner and one limited partner.[35] A general partner is any partner who is not a limited partner and is liable for all the debts and obligations of the firm.[36] Under the Act a limited partner is someone who contributes to the partnership a stated amount of capital in cash or in property valued at a stated amount and whose liability for the debts and obligations of the firm is limited to that amount.[37] If a limited partner withdraws any part of the capital contributed by him he is liable for the firm's debts and obligations up to the amount he has withdrawn.[38]

Limited partnerships, unlike general partnerships, are required to be registered with the Registrar of Companies.[39] Registration is effected by sending to the Registrar a statement signed by the partners containing the following information[40]:

1. the firm name;

2. the general nature of the business;

3. the principal place of business;

4. the full name of each of the partners;

5. the term, if any, for which the partnership is entered into and the date of its commencement;

6. a statement that the partnership is limited and the description of every limited partner as such;

7. the sum contributed by each partner and whether paid in cash or how otherwise.

Any changes in these particulars must be notified to the Registrar within seven days).[41] Because of this requirement of registration (and much like registered companies in this respect), the particulars relating to each registered partnership are open to public inspection.[42]

While the powers and liabilities of a general partner as regards person dealing with the firm are the same as those of a member of an ordinary partnership, a limited partner is precluded from taking part in the management of the partnership business. If he does so, he will be liable for all the debts and obligations of the firm incurred while he so takes part in the management, as though he were a general partner.[43] The Act does not define what amounts to taking part in

[34] s.4(1).
[35] s.4(2).
[36] s.4(3).
[37] s.4(4).
[38] s.4(5).
[39] See s.5 of the Limited Partnerships Act 1907. In 2008–2009 there were 16,487 limited partnerships on the register: see *Statistical Tables on Companies Registration Activities 2008–2009* (BIS), Table E2.
[40] s.8.
[41] s.9.
[42] s.16.
[43] s.6.

management—other than saying, in the proviso to s.6(1) that a limited partner may by himself of his agent at any time inspect the books of the firm and examine the state and prospects of the partnership business. Other modifications of the general law of partnership are set out in the remaining provisions of s.6. Thus, although in certain respects allowing an investor the protection of limited liability—rather like the shareholder of a company—an investor will suffer from the major drawback that his investment and management of the partnership are incompatible activities.

Limited partnerships have proved to be a successful business form for venture capital and private equity investment funds and are widely used for other types of fund, including real estate and film finance. Nevertheless, this was one of the areas considered by the Law Commission[44] and, as a result, the government eventually responded and brought forward proposals for comment which resulted in a Legislative Reform Order[45] being brought before Parliament in June 2009.[46] This came into effect on October 1, 2009 and has effected a number of changes to the principal Act, relating to the duty to register,[47] the application for registration,[48] the name of the limited partnership,[49] and the certificate of registration.[50] These provisions inter alia specify that a limited partnership is formed on the date of registration,[51] and that the certificate issued by the registrar is conclusive evidence of its formation.[52] All new limited partnerships are required to include at the end of their names an indication of their status (i.e. "limited partnership", "lp" or a Welsh equivalent).[53]

LIMITED LIABILITY PARTNERSHIPS (LLPs)

Establishment

On May 22, 1997 the Government announced that it intended to consult on draft **2–006** legislation to introduce a new form of corporate business association in the United Kingdom, the LLP. The impetus for such a new business format arose from pressure exerted by the large accountancy firms which are prevented, by their professional rules, from becoming incorporated as companies. These firms were unhappy with the general partnership rule of joint and several liability for all partnership debts.[54] This arose particularly in connection with such firms' potential liability for negligence damages (awarded on a few occasions against audit firms).

---

[44] See *Partnership Law: A Joint Report* (2003) Law Com No.283, Pts XV–XIX.
[45] i.e. exercising powers conferred by s.1 of the Legislative and Regulatory Reform Act 2006, c.51.
[46] The Legislative Reform (Limited Partnerships) Order 2009 (SI 2009/1940).
[47] New s.8A.
[48] New s.8B.
[49] New s.8C.
[50] New s.8D.
[51] See Legislative and Regulatory Reform Act 2006 s.8C(4).
[52] Legislative and Regulatory Reform Act 2006 s.8C(4).
[53] See Legislative and Regulatory Reform Act s.8B(2)(3).
[54] Partnership Act 1890 s.9.

Legislation

2–007 After a remarkably swift gestation[55] LLPs came into being with effect from April 6, 2001, following the passing of the Limited Liability Partnership Act 2000.[56] Of great importance, besides the relatively short provisions of the Act, was the delegated legislation which was passed to extend provisions of the then Companies Act 1985 to LLPs.[57] This created difficulties of nightmare proportions for those seeking to interpret the legislation.[58] Notwithstanding this and comments that the LLP is premised on an "ungainly mixture of company law and partnership law", the LLP appears to have achieved a significant success in the first decade of its existence.[59]

Following the introduction of the Companies Act 2006 the then Department for Business Enterprise and Regulatory Reform (BERR) in November 2007 issued a consultation document on the application of the new Act to LLPs.[60] The government published a response in May 2008 and three statutory instruments followed the same year, all of them concerned with accounts and, in one case, also with audit.[61] The declared aim, in considering the application of the remaining provisions of the Act to LLPs, is

> "to ensure that LLPs are able to take advantage of the benefits to business of modernising and simplifying company law; remain an attractive corporate vehicle for businesses and retain their distinctive characteristics from companies".[62]

The Draft Limited Liability Partnerships (Application of Companies Act 2006) Regulations[63] and the Limited Liability Partnerships (Amendment) Regulations[64] affect trading disclosures, members' names and addresses, the requirement to have at least two members, e-communications, and many other matters.

Main features of LLPs

2–008 The principal features, compared with companies and ordinary partnerships, are as follows:

---

[55] Following two DTI consultation papers: Limited Liability Partnership—A New Form of Business Association for Professionals (Consultation Paper, URN 97/597, 1997); Limitation Liability Partnerships—Draft Bill (Consultation Paper, URN 98/874, 1998).

[56] For detailed treatment, see Geoffrey Morse (ed.), *Palmer's Limited Liability Partnership Law* (2002). See too Judith Freedman and Vanessa Finch, "The limited liability partnership: pick and mix or mix-up?" [2002] J.B.L. 475.

[57] See Limited Liability Partnerships Regulations 2001 (SI 2001/1090); Limited Liability Partnerships (No.2) Regulations 2002 (SI 2002/913).

[58] See, e.g. Geoffrey Morse, "Partnerships for the 21st century—Limited Liability Partnerships and Partnership Law Reform in the United Kingdom" [2002] *Singapore Journal of Legal Studies* 455, 464.

[59] In 2008–2009 there were 36,763 registered LLPs in the UK. See *Statistical Tables on Companies Registration Activities 2008–2009* (BIS), Table E4.

[60] Available at *http://webarchive.nationalarchives.gov.uk/20102160924443/http://www.berr.gov.uk/consultations/page42363.htm/* [accessed July 23, 2010].

[61] The Limited Liability Partnerships (Accounts and Audit) (Application of Companies Act 2006) Regulations 2008 (SI 2008/1911); The Small Limited Liability Partnerships (Accounts) Regulations 2008 (SI 2008/1912); The Large and Medium-sized Limited Liability Partnerships (Accounts) Regulations 2008 (SI 2008/1913).

[62] See *http://*.

[63] SI 2009/1804.

[64] SI 2009/1833.

1. unlike an ordinary partnership, but like companies, the LLP is a body corporate with a legal personality which is separate to that of its members[65];

2. unlike companies, which may be formed by one person,[66] LLPs, rather like partnerships, can only be formed by two or more persons[67];

3. rather like companies, LLPs must go through a process of registration with the Registrar of Companies[68] and must lodge an "incorporation document"[69] before the granting of a certificate of registration which, once issued, is conclusive evidence that the requirements for registration have been satisfied[70];

4. again, rather like companies, the members of the LLP are agents for the LLP and not for one another,[71] and so there will be no liability for members for one another's wrongdoing;

5. unlike an ordinary partnership, but like (most) companies, the members of an LLP have limited liability, viz. they have such liability to contribute to its assets in the event of its being wound up[72];

6. internally, LLPs reflect a compromise between the principles of ordinary partnership law and companies, with some provisions, e.g. equality of participation in capital, profits, and management, being derived from ordinary partnership law, while others, e.g. the availability of the remedy for unfair prejudice, are derived from company law;

7. LLPs, like companies, but unlike ordinary partnerships, are obliged to file with the Registrar information regarding members, designated members and registered office.[73] Furthermore, LLPs must publish annual accounts and, in general are subject to the regime for accounting and audit of the Companies Act 2006[74];

8. for tax purposes, LLPs are like partnerships, not corporate entities[75];

9. for the purposes of insolvency, LLPs are treated in the much the same way as corporate insolvencies.[76]

---

[65] s.1(2).
[66] See para.1–012, above.
[67] s.2(1)(a).
[68] s.3(1).
[69] See s.2(1)(b) and s.2(2).
[70] s.3(4).
[71] s.6(1); cf. Partnership Act 1890 s.5.
[72] s.1(4).
[73] s.9.
[74] As to this, see the Limited Liability Partnership (Application of Companies Act 2006) Regulations 2009 (SI 2009/1804).
[75] s.10.
[76] s.14.

SPECIALIST TYPES OF COMPANIES

Community interest companies

2–009 One of the purposes behind the passing of the Companies (Audit, Investigations and Community Enterprise) Act 2004[77] was the introduction of a new type of company, the community interest company (CIC).[78] CICs are designed specifically for those wishing to operate for the benefit of the community rather than for the benefit of the owners of the company and may not be formed or used solely for the personal gain of a particular person, or group of people. As they are companies, CICs have to follow the procedure for incorporation under the Companies Act 2006,[79] and the requirements for a CIC, which are detailed in the 2004 Act.[80] Existing companies may convert to being CICs.[81] Once established, a CIC has a statutory "asset lock" which prevents the assets and profits being distributed, except as permitted by legislation.[82] This ensures the assets and profits are retained within the CIC for community purposes, or transferred to another asset-locked organisation, such as another CIC or charity. CICs are subject to the supervision of the Regulator of Community Interest Companies.[83] During the course of 2009 the Regulator consulted on "Dividend Caps and the Performance Related Interest Cap under the Community Interest Company Regulations 2005" and published her findings in January 2010[84] and the result is that there will be a 10 per cent increase in the differential between the Bank of England base rate and the interest and dividend per share cap.[85]

The European Economic Interest Grouping (EEIG)

2–010 The EEIG was created by an EC regulation,[86] Council Regulation 2173/85,[87] as supplemented by the European Economic Grouping Regulations 1989.[88] The intention behind this Regulation was to allow the creation of a separate legal entity for cross-border co-operation between businesses in different Member States. These may or may not be companies. Formation is by contract, registered

---

[77] c.27. In force from July 1, 2005: The Companies (Audit, Investigations and Community Enterprise) Act 2004 (Commencement) and Companies Act 1989 (Commencement No.18) Order 2004 (SI 2004/3322) Sch.3. See also the Community Interest Company Regulations 2005 (SI 2005/1788).

[78] See *http://www.cicregulator.gov.uk/* [accessed May 20, 2010]. There are currently 3,373 CICs.

[79] Both the Act and the Regulations have had to be amended in the light of the 2006 Act. See the Companies Act 2006 (Commencement No.2, Consequential Amendments, Transitional Provisions and Savings) Order 2007 (SI 2007/1093) Sch.4.

[80] See s.36. Note that the provisions of the 2004 Act on CICs remain in force.

[81] See ss.37–38.

[82] See ss.30–31.

[83] See s.27.

[84] The changes came into effect on April 6, 2010.

[85] See *Response to the Consultation on the Dividend and Share Caps*, January 2010, para.75. This is available at *http://www.cicregulator.gov.uk/consultationresponse.shtml* [accessed May 20, 2010].

[86] i.e. a document which has direct legislative effect in the UK unlike a directive which must in general terms be implemented by the UK Parliament to be effective.

[87] [1985] OJ L199/1.

[88] (SI 1989/638).

with the registrar of companies. This contract must include the objects of the EEIG—since making profits in its own right is not allowed, these must require the EEIG to enhance the activities of its members, e.g. by joint research or development. The members of the EEIG will have unlimited liability for its debts, no public investment is allowed and the maximum number of employees is limited to 500. An EEIG can be formed in any Member State[89] and is subject to some aspects of the national law in which it is registered, e.g. as to the use of name, certain winding-up rules, etc. UK law must equally recognise an EEIG registered in another Member State.[90]

The European company (SE)

The idea of a cross-border European company (or Societas Europaea—SE),[91] to   **2–011** facilitate mergers of companies, after a long parturition, finally became a reality in mid-2004. Although first mooted in 1970, interest in the idea revived in 2001, with a Council Regulation on the Statute for a European Company,[92] supplemented by a directive on the involvement of employees.[93] Now in force in the EU,[94] the initiative is aimed at large multinational companies and is organised on the basis of supranational law, rather than the law of just one Member State. Nevertheless, much of the applicable law will be the public company law of the Member State. The SE was brought into force in the UK by the European Public Limited-Liability Company Regulations 2004.[95]

Open-ended investment companies

In 1996, a new type of company, the open-ended investment company (or "oeic"),   **2–012** by now rather well known in the EU, became possible also under UK company law.[96] Initially, oeics were subject to the scrutiny of the Securities and Investment Board (SIB), but with the enactment of the Financial Services and Markets Act in 2000,[97] oeics became subject to the Financial Services Authority (FSA) and new regulations were passed to reflect this change.[98] Oeics are specialised investment companies which, in effect, allow for an incorporated form of unit trust. The investors in such a company purchase and sell shares—rather like units in a unit trust—in the company, reflecting the underlying value of the investments held by

---

[89] In 2008–2009 there were 205 EEIGs with their principal establishment in the UK: see *Statistical Tables on Companies Registration Activities 2008–2009* (BIS), Table E3.

[90] See too the European Economic Interest Grouping Regulations 1989 (SI 1989/638) and the European Economic Interest Grouping (Amendment) Regulations 2009 (SI 2009/2399).

[91] For detailed consideration see below, para.34–009.

[92] Regulation 2157/2001, [2001] OJ L294/1.

[93] Directive 2001/86, [2001] OJ L254/64.

[94] Press release IP/04/1195, October 8, 2004.

[95] As from October 8, 2004: SI 2004/2326. In 2008–2009 there were 14 SEs on the companies register: see *Statistical Tables on Companies Registration Activities 2008–2009* (BIS), Table E3.

[96] See the Open-Ended Investment Companies (Companies with Variable Capital) Regulations 1996 (SI 1996/2827).

[97] See s.236.

[98] The Open-Ended Investment Companies Regulations 2001 (SI 2001/1228), revoking SI 1996/2827, above. See also the Open-Ended Investment Companies (Amendment) Regulations 2009 (SI 2009/553).

the company, but do not acquire any proprietary rights in the company's property. Participants in an oeic are able to redeem any part of their shareholding and, because this means that such companies must buy back their own shares, oeics are permitted to buy back their own shares in a way not currently permitted for other types of company. Shareholders in an oeic are not liable for the debts of the company. The detailed rules applicable to these companies are, however, beyond the scope of this book.[99]

---

[99] But see, for a detailed account, *Palmer's Company Law*, Pt 5A.

THE COMPANY AS A CORPORATE ENTITY

Chapter 3

CLASSIFICATION AND FORMATION OF REGISTERED COMPANIES

COMPANIES LIMITED BY SHARES, COMPANIES LIMITED BY GUARANTEE AND UNLIMITED COMPANIES

Introduction

A registered company may be: (1) a company limited by shares, if the liability of **3–001** its members is limited by its constitution and if the liability of a member to contribute to the company's assets is limited to the amount, if any, unpaid on his shares[1]; or (2) a company limited by guarantee, in which case the liability of a member is limited to the amount which he has undertaken to contribute in the event of its being wound up[2]; or (3) an unlimited company, in which case the liability of a member is unlimited.[3] We shall now look in greater detail at each of these basic types.

Companies limited by shares

The vast majority of registered companies on the register of companies[4] are **3–002** companies limited by shares.[5] Such companies must have a share capital, whereas unlimited companies may or may not have a share capital.

Companies limited by guarantee

The majority of companies limited by guarantee are formed to incorporate **3–003** professional, trade and research associations, or clubs supported by annual subscriptions and they are invariably private companies, rather than public

---

[1] s.3(1)(2).

[2] s.3(1)(3).

[3] s.3(4). This section provides the statutory rules for the liability of the members of a company for its debts. The common law position is that there is otherwise no liability at all: see *J.H. Rayner (Mincing Lane) v DTI* [1990] 2 A.C. 418, HL, para.1–038, above.

[4] The Registrar is obliged to maintain this register: see s.1080.

[5] In 2008–2009 there were 2,270,000 companies incorporated and on the register: see *Statistical Tables on Companies Registration Activities* 2008–2009 (BIS), Table A2. As at January 3, 2010 this figure had increased slightly to 2,607,522 companies on the register: see *Companies House Monthly Statistics* (December, 2009), available at *http://www.companieshouse.gov.uk/about/business RegisterStat.shtml* [accessed May 20, 2010].

companies.[6] A company limited by guarantee is a registered company in which the liability of members is limited to such amount as they respectively undertake to contribute to the assets of the company in the event of its being wound up.[7] The members are not required to contribute to the assets whilst the company is a going concern. The statement of guarantee which has to be delivered to the Registrar for registration must contain such information as may be prescribed for the purpose of identifying the subscribers to the memorandum of association[8] and must state that each member undertakes to contribute to the assets of the company in the event of its being wound up while he is a member such amount as may be required for (a) payment of the debts and liabilities of the company contracted before he ceases to be a member, (b) payment of the costs, charges and expenses of winding up, and (c) adjustment of the rights of the contributories among themselves, not exceeding a specified amount.[9] Whatever the amount of the guarantee specified in the memorandum, it cannot be increased or reduced and the amounts which the members have agreed to contribute in a winding up cannot be mortgaged or charged by the company whilst it is a going concern. They are not assets of the company whilst it is a going concern.

Prior to the 1980 Act,[10] a company limited by guarantee could be formed either with or without a share capital, but was usually formed without a share capital, in which event money to acquire such things as premises may be raised by loans from the members. Since the 1980 Act, no such company can be formed with, or acquire, a share capital.[11] Private companies limited by guarantee formed before October 1, 2009 are exempt from including the word "Limited" from their names so long as two conditions are fulfilled.[12] The first is that the objects of the company are the promotion of commerce, art, science, education, religion, charity or any profession, and anything incidental or conducive to any of those objects.[13] The second condition is that the company's articles: (a) require its income to be applied in promoting its objects; (b) prohibit the payment of dividends to its members; and (c) require all the assets that would otherwise be available to its members generally to be transferred on its winding up either (i) to another body with objects similar to its own, or (ii) to another body the objects of which are the promotion of charity and anything incidental or conducive thereto (whether or not the body is a member of the company).[14]

Companies limited by guarantee are obliged to register articles of association.[15] If articles are not registered or if articles are registered, in so far as they do not

---

[6] For this distinction, see para.3–005, below.
[7] s.3(3).
[8] s.11(2). The name and address of each subscriber must be provided: see the Companies (Registration) Regulations 2008 (SI 2008/3014) reg.4.
[9] s.11(3).
[10] Companies Act 1980, c.21. See para.1–008, above.
[11] s.11(3).
[12] s.62(1).
[13] s.62(2).
[14] s.62(3).
[15] s.18(2).

exclude or modify the relevant model articles, the relevant model articles[16] so far as applicable form part of the company's articles in the same manner and to the same extent as if articles in the form of those articles had been duly registered.[17] Provided that the articles are contained in a single document and are divided into paragraphs numbered consecutively[18] the draftsman of the articles is free to add, subtract or vary as the needs of the case suggest.[19]

Every provision in the articles of a company limited by guarantee and not having a share capital, or in any resolution of the company, purporting to give any person a right to participate in the divisible profits of the company otherwise than as a member is void,[20] and every provision in the constitution of a company purporting to divide the undertaking of the company into shares or interests is treated as a provision for share capital and this applies whether or not the nominal value or number of the shares or interests is specified by the provision.[21]

Unlimited companies

A company may be registered as an unlimited company, in which case there is no **3–004** limit on the members' liability to contribute to the assets.[22] In the years immediately preceding 1967, comparatively few such companies were formed, although they are the oldest class of registered company,[23] but the exemption from publication of accounts[24] given by the 1967 Act, made them more popular.

The memorandum of an unlimited company must be in the prescribed form.[25] Although unlimited companies must also have articles of association[26] the form is not laid down in the Companies (Model Articles) Regulations 2008.[27] Since 1980 unlimited companies cannot be public companies.[28] An unlimited company is exceptional in that its members may be associated on the terms that they may withdraw in the mode pointed out by the articles, so as to be free from liability in the event of a winding up,[29] and it seems that such a company may validly provide for a return of capital to its members without the consent of the court. Similarly an unlimited company may purchase its own shares if its constituent documents authorise it to do so.

---

[16] See now the Companies (Model Articles) Regulations 2008 (SI 2008/3229) reg.3 and Sch.2 (Model Articles for Private Companies Limited by Guarantee).

[17] s.20(1).

[18] s.18(3).

[19] *Gaiman v National Association for Mental Health* [1971] Ch.317.

[20] s.37.

[21] s.5(3).

[22] s.3(4).

[23] Limited liability only became possible following the passage of the Limited Liability Act 1855, 18 & 19 Vict., c.133. See para.1–006, above.

[24] See now para.20–004 below.

[25] See s.8(2). The prescribed form is to be found in the Companies (Registration) Regulations 2008 (SI 2008/3014) reg.2(b) and Sch.2.

[26] In accordance with s.18(1).

[27] SI 2008/3229.

[28] See now s.4(2).

[29] *Re Borough Commercial and Building Society* [1893] 2 Ch.242.

PUBLIC AND PRIVATE COMPANIES

Introduction

3–005 A registered company may be a public company[30] or a private company.[31] A public company limited by shares or guarantee is a company which has a share capital and whose certificate of incorporation states that it is a public company and in relation to which the requirements of the Act as to registration or re-registration as a public company have been complied with on or after the relevant date.[32] A company which is not a public company is, by default, a private company. Thus the private company is the residual class of companies, without any special requirements.[33] This is a complete reversal of the position prior to 1980, whereby all companies were public companies unless their articles contained certain restrictions, e.g. as to the transferability of shares. The vast majority of registered companies are private companies.[34]

Public companies

3–006 Public companies are no longer required to state in the memorandum of association[35] that the company is a public company.[36] Nor may public companies now only be formed by two or more persons[37]; the Act provides that "one or more persons" may form any type of company.[38] Whether a company is a public company or a private company will need to be stated in the company's application for registration[39] and will also be reflected in the certificate of incorporation issued by the Registrar.[40] However, the name of a public company must end with the words "public limited company", (frequently abbreviated to "Plc").[41] A private company, unless otherwise exempted,[42] uses the traditional "Limited" or "Ltd" at the end of its name.[43] Public companies must have an authorised capital figure (the amount of shares it may issue to the public) of at least the authorised minimum,

---

[30] Public companies can only be limited by shares or by guarantee: s.4(2).

[31] Any company may be a private company: s.4(1).

[32] s. 4(2). The "relevant date" is December 22, 1980 for companies in Great Britain: s.4(3).

[33] s.4(1).

[34] In 2008–2009, the 9,600 registered public companies constituted just 0.4% of the register. There were 2,260,400 private companies: see *Statistical Tables on Companies Registration Activities 2008–2009* (BIS), Table A2. By January 3, 2010 this had changed to 10,704 public companies and 2,607,522 private companies: *Companies House Monthly Statistics* (December, 2009), available at *www.companieshouse.gov.uk/about/businessRegisterStat.shtml* [accessed May 20, 2010].

[35] This is because of the diminished role of the memorandum of association. See para. 3–019, below.

[36] See Companies Act 1985 s.1(3)(a).

[37] See Companies Act 1985 s.1(1)).

[38] s.7(1).

[39] See s.9(2)(d).

[40] s.15(2)(d).

[41] s.58(1).

[42] See s.60.

[43] s.59(1).

currently[44] £50,000 or the prescribed Euro equivalent.[45] Public companies must have at least two directors[46] whereas a private company need only have one.[47]

There are substantial differences in the capital requirements as applied to public and private companies. In particular a public company cannot commence business or exercise any borrowing powers until the Registrar issues a so-called "trading certificate".[48] Once issued, a trading certificate has effect from the date on which it is issued and is conclusive evidence that the company is entitled to do business and exercise any borrowing powers.[49] In making application for a trading certificate the application must state that the nominal value of the company's allotted share capital is not less than the authorised minimum, specify the amount, or estimated amount, of the company's preliminary expenses, specify any amount or benefit paid or given, or intended to be paid or given, to any promoter of the company, and the consideration for the payment or benefit, and be accompanied by a statement of compliance.[50] The Registrar will only issue a trading certificate if he is satisfied that the nominal value of the company's allotted share capital is not less than the authorised minimum.[51] A share allotted in pursuance of an employees' share scheme will not be taken into account unless paid up as to at least one-quarter of the nominal value of the share and the whole of any premium on the share.[52]

One of the most important potential advantages of forming a public company, as opposed to a private company, is the possibility of access to capital to grow the business. This arises because only public companies may apply under Pt VI of the Financial Services and Markets Act 2000 to be quoted[53] on the London Stock Exchange.[54]

Private companies

As we have just noted, the overwhelming majority of companies on the register **3–007** are private companies.[55] A private company, unlike a public company,[56] needs no minimum capital either for registration or the commencement of business. Since 1980, private companies have not been required either to restrict the transferability of their shares or to limit the number of members involved, although most private companies do have such restrictions and are small in size. Private companies would not be able to apply to be quoted on the London Stock Exchange and it is specified in the Companies Act 2006 that a private company may not make

---

[44] The Secretary of State may alter the authorised minimum: s.764.
[45] s.763(1).
[46] s.154(2).
[47] s.282(3).
[48] s.761(1).
[49] s.761(4).
[50] s.762(1).
[51] s.761(2).
[52] s.761(3).
[53] i.e. "listed", to use the terminology of the 2000 Act.
[54] See *www.londonstockexchange.com* [accessed May 21, 2010] and Ch.15, below.
[55] Above, para.3–005.
[56] Above, para.3–006.

an offer to the public[57] of its securities.[58] This may be regarded as the only real disadvantage of registration as a private company. The advantages, however, are potentially much greater and include the following:

1. private companies are no longer required to have a company secretary[59];

2. private companies need have only one director[60];

3. as we have seen, private companies may make use of written resolutions[61] and are no longer required to hold an annual general meeting[62];

4. a private company need not convene a general meeting in the event of a serious loss of capital[63];

5. private companies follow a simplified procedure for the allotment of shares, particularly where that company has just one class of shares[64];

6. private companies may, in their articles, exclude all or any of the requirements in the Act relating to existing shareholders' rights of pre-emption or the communication of pre-emption offers to shareholders[65];

7. in relation to the payment for shares, private companies are subject to less onerous restrictions than public companies[66];

8. similarly, in relation to reductions of capital, private companies are subject to the less onerous requirement of only requiring a special resolution supported by a solvency statement[67];

9. a private company may give itself wider charges on its own shares to recover debts owed to it by its members whereas public companies are restricted in this respect[68];

10. private companies are not subject to the ban on giving financial assistance for the acquisition of shares in a company, while public companies are[69];

11. private companies may redeem redeemable shares out of capital[70] whereas public companies may only do so out of distributable profits or out of the proceeds of a fresh issue of shares[71];

---

[57] See s.756.
[58] See s.755(1).
[59] s.270. See also Ch.18, below.
[60] s.154(2).
[61] s.288.
[62] cf. s.336 (for public companies).
[63] s.656.
[64] See s.550.
[65] s.567.
[66] e.g. public companies may not accept in payment for shares an undertaking given by any person that he or someone else should do work or perform services for the company or any other person: see s.585. For further restrictions, see ss.586–587.
[67] See s.641(1)(a).
[68] See s.670.
[69] See now ss.678–679.
[70] See ss.708 et seq.
[71] See s.687(1)(2).

12. private companies may purchase their own shares out of capital, whereas public companies may only do so out of distributable profits or out of the proceeds of a fresh issue of shares[72];

13. private companies need not make provision for unrealised capital losses when distributing dividends[73];

14. many private companies will be subject to the "small companies regime"[74] concerning company accounts and reports, whereas public companies are not eligible for this[75];

15. there is no obligation to disclose information about interests in a private company's shares, however substantial the holding, whereas public companies do have such an obligation[76];

16. private companies though subject to the regulation of compromises and arrangements between creditors or members[77] are subject to a less onerous regime than public companies.[78]

Re-registration

Generally

The Act makes provision for altering the status of a company by a process of re- **3–008** registration. The following possibilities are available: (1) re-registration from a private company to a public company; (2) re-registration from a public company to a private company; (3) re-registration from a private limited company to an unlimited company; (4) re-registration from an unlimited private company to a limited company; (5) re-registration from a public company to an unlimited private company.[79]

Re-registration of a private company to a public company

A private company, whether limited or unlimited, may re-register as a public **3–009** company limited by shares if it complies with the following conditions:

1. it must pass a special resolution that it be so re-registered[80];

2. it must satisfy certain conditions[81] (that the company has a share capital, that certain share capital requirements are met,[82] that requirements

---

[72] See s.692(1)(2).
[73] See s.831.
[74] See particularly s.382.
[75] s.384(1)(a).
[76] See s.791.
[77] See s.895.
[78] For public companies, see Pt 27 of the Act.
[79] s.89.
[80] s.90(1)(a).
[81] s.90(1)(b).
[82] s.91.

regarding net assets are met,[83] that certain requirements concerning non-cash consideration are met,[84] and that the company has not previously been re-registered as unlimited[85];

3.   it must make an application for re-registration to the Registrar in accordance with s.94, together with the documents required by that section and a statement of compliance.[86]

The company must also make such changes to its name and to its articles as are necessary for becoming a public company.[87] If the company is also unlimited, then it must make such changes to its articles consistent with it becoming a company limited by shares.[88] If the company does not have a secretary, as is permitted for private companies,[89] then the application for re-registration needs to contain a statement of the company's proposed secretary.[90]

If the Registrar is satisfied that the company is so entitled to be re-registered, he must re-register the company[91] and issue a certificate of incorporation altered to meet the circumstances of the case.[92] The certificate must state that it is issued on re-registration and the date on which it is so issued.[93] On issue of the certificate the company becomes a public company and the changes in the company's name and articles take effect.[94] Where the application also contained a statement about the proposed secretary or joint secretary, they are deemed to have been appointed to that office.[95] This is conclusive evidence that the company is a public company and that all the procedures as to re-registration have been complied with.[96]

Re-registration of a public company as a private company

3–010 A public company may be re-registered as a private company limited by shares (or guarantee) if it complies with the following conditions:

1.   it must pass a special resolution that it be so re-registered[97];

2.   it must satisfy certain conditions,[98] namely (i) that no application has been made for the cancellation of the resolution because no application could be made because of insufficient votes against the resolution[99] or

---

[83] These are elaborated in s.92.
[84] See s.93.
[85] s.90(2).
[86] s.90(1)(c).
[87] s.90(3).
[88] s.90(4).
[89] See s.270.
[90] s.94(1)(b).
[91] s.96(1).
[92] s.96(2).
[93] s.96(3).
[94] s.96(4)(a)(b).
[95] s.96(4)(c).
[96] s.96(5).
[97] s.97(1)(a).
[98] s.97(1)(b).
[99] s.97(2)(a).

(ii) where such an application has been made the application has been withdrawn or a court order has been made confirming the resolution[100];

3. it must make an application for re-registration to the Registrar in accordance with s.100, together with the documents required by that section and a statement of compliance.[101]

The company must also make such changes to its name and to its articles as are necessary for becoming a private company limited by shares or guarantee.[102]

If the Registrar is satisfied that the company is so entitled to be re-registered, he must re-register the company[103] and issue a certificate of incorporation altered to meet the circumstances of the case.[104] The certificate must state that it is issued on re-registration and the date on which it is so issued.[105] On issue of the certificate the company becomes a private limited company and the changes in the company's name and articles take effect.[106] This is conclusive evidence that the company is a private limited company and that all the procedures as to re-registration have been complied with.[107]

Where a resolution has been passed, as required, an application may be made to the court for the cancellation of the resolution:[108]

1. by the holders of not less in the aggregate than 5 per cent in nominal value of the company's issued share capital or any class of the company's issued share capital (disregarding any shares held by the company as treasury shares);

2. if the company is not limited by shares, by not less than 5 per cent of its members; or

3. by not less than 50 of the company's members; but not by a person who has consented to or voted in favour of the resolution.[109]

The application must be made within 28 days after the passing of the resolution and may be made on behalf of the persons entitled to make it by such one or more of their number as they may appoint for the purpose.[110] On the hearing of the application the court shall make an order either cancelling or confirming the resolution.[111] The court's extensive powers also include adjourning the proceedings for an arrangement to be made,[112] altering the articles,[113] and, if necessary,

---

[100] s.97(2)(b).
[101] s.97(1)(c).
[102] s.97(3).
[103] s.101(1).
[104] s.101(2).
[105] s.101(3).
[106] s.101(4).
[107] s.101(5).
[108] Notice of such an application also needs to be made to the Registrar: s.99.
[109] s.98(1).
[110] s.98(2).
[111] s.98(3).
[112] s.98(4)(b).
[113] s.98(5)(b).

providing for the purchase by the company of the shares of the dissentient members.[114]

Re-registration of public companies by law

3–011 If a public company reduces its capital[115] and the court makes an order which has the effect that the nominal value of its allotted share capital is less than the authorised minimum[116] the Registrar must not register the order unless either the court so directs[117] or the company is first re-registered as a private company.[118] In such a case, there is an expedited procedure for re-registration[119] which also does not require a special resolution[120] which would ordinarily be required for re-registration as a private company.[121]

Re-registration of private limited company as an unlimited company

3–012 A limited private company (not previously re-registered as limited)[122] may be re-registered as unlimited provided that the unanimous consent of its members is obtained.[123] An application for re-registration must be made to the Registrar in accordance with s.103, together with the documents required by that section and a statement of compliance.[124] The company must also make such changes to its name and to its articles as are necessary for its becoming an unlimited company and, if it is to have a share capital, such changes as are necessary for it to become an unlimited company having a share capital.[125]

If the Registrar is satisfied that the company is so entitled to be re-registered, he must re-register the company[126] and issue a certificate of incorporation altered to meet the circumstances of the case.[127] The certificate must state that it is issued on re-registration and the date on which it is so issued.[128] On issue of the certificate the company becomes an unlimited company and the changes in the company's name and articles take effect.[129] This is conclusive evidence that the company is an unlimited company and that all the procedures as to re-registration have been complied with.[130]

---

[114] s.98(5)(a).
[115] s.641.
[116] s.650(1). See also para.3–006, above.
[117] s.650(2)(a).
[118] s.650(2)(b).
[119] This is detailed in s.651.
[120] s.651(1).
[121] See s.97.
[122] s.102(2).
[123] s.102(1)(a). A community interest company is, however, excluded from doing so: Companies (Audit, Investigations and Community Enterprise) Act 2004 s.52(1).
[124] s.102(1)(c).
[125] s.102(3).
[126] s.104(1).
[127] s.104(2).
[128] s.104(3).
[129] s.104(4).
[130] s.104(5).

Re-registration of unlimited private company as a limited company

An unlimited company (not previously re-registered as unlimited)[131] may make **3–013** an application to be re-registered as a private company limited either by shares or by guarantee[132] if a special resolution to that effect has been passed.[133] An application for re-registration must be made to the Registrar in accordance with s.106, together with the documents required by that section and a statement of compliance.[134] The company must also make such changes to its name and to its articles as are necessary for its becoming a company limited by shares or guarantee.[135]

If the Registrar is satisfied that the company is so entitled to be re-registered, he must re-register the company[136] and issue a certificate of incorporation altered to meet the circumstances of the case.[137] The certificate must state that it is issued on re-registration and the date on which it is so issued.[138] On issue of the certificate the company becomes a limited private company and the changes in the company's name and articles take effect.[139] This is conclusive evidence that the company is a limited private company and that all the procedures as to re-registration have been complied with.[140]

A company which on re-registration already has an allotted share capital must, within 15 days after re-registration, deliver a statement of capital[141] to the Registrar[142] unless such information has already been sent to the Registrar.[143] Failure to provide this information is an offence.[144]

Re-registration of a public company as private and unlimited

A public company limited by shares may be re-registered as an unlimited private **3–014** company with a share capital provided that the unanimous consent of its members is obtained.[145] The company must not, however, previously been re-registered as limited or as unlimited.[146] An application for re-registration must be made to the Registrar in accordance with s.110, together with the documents required by that section and a statement of compliance.[147] The company must also make such changes to its name and to its articles as are necessary for its becoming an unlimited private company.[148]

---

[131] s.105(2).
[132] s.105(3).
[133] s.105(1)(a).
[134] s.105(1)(c).
[135] s.105(4).
[136] s.107(1).
[137] s.107(2).
[138] s.107(3).
[139] s.107(4).
[140] s.107(5).
[141] The specific requirements as to what has to be stated are listed in s.108(3).
[142] s.108(1).
[143] s.108(2).
[144] s.108(4)(5).
[145] s.109(1)(a).
[146] s.109(2).
[147] s.109(1)(c).
[148] s.109(3).

If the Registrar is satisfied that the company is so entitled to be re-registered, he must re-register the company[149] and issue a certificate of incorporation altered to meet the circumstances of the case.[150] The certificate must state that it is issued on re-registration and the date on which it is so issued.[151] On issue of the certificate the company becomes an unlimited private company and the changes in the company's name and articles take effect.[152] This is conclusive evidence that the company is an unlimited private company and that all the procedures as to re-registration have been complied with.[153]

UK-REGISTERED COMPANIES, HOLDING AND SUBSIDIARY COMPANIES

Introduction

3–015 It is sometimes important to know whether a registered company is a subsidiary or a holding company. This can be for a number of reasons. One of these is that the Act generally prevents a subsidiary from being a member of its holding company.[154] A further reason is that the financial assistance prohibition applies when a public company[155] acquires shares in its private holding company.[156]

UK-registered companies

3–016 The Act introduces a new definition, of a "UK-registered company", and this means a company registered under the Act.[157]

Holding and subsidiary companies

3–017 There are three ways of establishing that a company (B) is a subsidiary of another company (A):

1. where A holds a majority of the voting rights in B (this may be called voting control)[158];

2. where A is a member of B and can appoint or dismiss a majority of its directors (this may be called director control)[159];

3. where A is a member of B and controls alone or under an agreement with others a majority of the voting rights in B (this may be called contract control).[160]

---

[149] s.111(1).
[150] s.111(2).
[151] s.111(3).
[152] s.111(4).
[153] s.111(5).
[154] See s.136.
[155] The prohibition for private companies has now been removed. See now Ch.11, below.
[156] See s.679.
[157] s.1158.
[158] s.1159(1)(a). See now *Enviroco Ltd v Farstad Supply A/S* [2009] EWCA Civ 1399; [2010] Bus L.R. 1008.
[159] s.1159(1)(b).
[160] s.1159(1)(c).

If C is a subsidiary of B and B is a subsidiary of A, then C is also regarded as being a subsidiary of A.[161] A wholly-owned subsidiary is one whose shares are all owned by one company, its wholly-owned subsidiaries and their and its nominees.[162]

Schedule 6 of the Act expands upon this basic framework. Thus, when calculating the voting rights (for voting control or contract control) it is the rights attached to the shares which count.[163] For the purposes of calculating a majority of the board (for director control) it is the majority of the voting rights on the board on all, or substantially all, matters which must be taken into account and not a numerical majority.[164] A company will be treated as being able to control the appointment or dismissal of the director of another company if either that director's appointment follows necessarily from his appointment as a director of the first company or the directorship is held by the first company itself.[165] Rights to appoint or dismiss a director which require another's consent or concurrence do not count unless there is no one else who has those rights of appointment or removal.[166]

The final aspect of the definition is to discover which rights, either as to voting or as to the appointment or dismissal of directors, should be attributed to whom for the purpose of establishing any of the three methods of control. The following rules will apply:

1. rights which are applicable at all times will count. Restricted rights, i.e. ones which only apply in certain circumstances, will only count if they are in fact exercisable at the relevant time or when the circumstances are within the control of the person having the rights.[167] On the other hand a general right which is in a temporary abeyance will still count[168];

2. rights held by a person in a fiduciary capacity will be treated as not held by him[169];

3. nominee rights (i.e. those exercisable only on instructions or with consent)[170] are to be attributed to the beneficial owner[171];

4. where shares are mortgaged, the rights attached to those shares count as those of the lender and not the borrower only if, apart from normal creditor protection rights, they are exercisable only by or with the lender's, or the lender's subsidiaries', instructions[172];

---

[161] s.1159(1).
[162] s.1159(2).
[163] Sch.6 reg.2
[164] Sch.6 reg.3.
[165] Sch.6 reg.3(2).
[166] Sch.6 reg.3(3).
[167] Sch.6 reg.4(1).
[168] Sch.6 reg.4(2).
[169] Sch.6 reg.5. Further, where the shares are held in a fiduciary capacity only because the transferor retains them under a contract to transfer them at a future date, the voting rights remain with the transferor: *Michaels v Harley House (Marylebone) Ltd* [2000] Ch.104, CA.
[170] Sch.6 reg.6(2).
[171] Sch.6 reg.6(1).
[172] Sch.6 reg.7.

5. the rights of a subsidiary count as those of its holding company and rules 3. and 4. above must not be read as applying to the contrary[173];

6. any voting rights held by a company in itself must be discounted when making the calculation[174]; and

7. rights held under 2.–6. are cumulative if necessary.[175]

The above, complex, definition may be amended by regulations made by the Secretary of State.[176]

FORMATION OF REGISTERED COMPANIES

Introduction

3–018 As we saw previously, the requirements for forming a registered company have been simplified, with much less reliance on information which previously had to be contained in the company's memorandum of association. This information has now to be submitted as one of a bundle of documents when an application for registration is made. We now look in greater detail at these requirements.

The memorandum

3–019 Under previous Companies Acts, every registered company was required to have a memorandum of association, which was usually described as being the registered company's charter.[177] Its purpose was to enable persons who invest in or deal with the company, to ascertain, whether it was a public company or private company, whether it was an English (or a Scottish) company, what its objects were, whether the liability of its members was limited and what share capital it was authorised to issue. However, the CLR recommended that both the memorandum and articles be replaced with a single document constitution[178] and this was accepted by the government.[179] The result is that the memorandum now plays a minor role in company formation in that it is merely a memorandum which states that the subscribers wish to form a company under the Act and agree to become members of the company and, in the case of a company that is to have a share capital, to take at least one share.[180] The memorandum is required to be in the prescribed form and must be authenticated by each subscriber.[181] The Companies (Registration) Regulations 2008[182] specify that the memorandum of

---

[173] Sch.6 reg.8.
[174] Sch.6 reg.9.
[175] Sch.6 reg.10.
[176] See s.1160.
[177] *Ashbury Railway Carriage Co Ltd v Riche* (1875) L.R. 7 H.L. 653 at 667 and 668, per Lord Cairns, L.C.
[178] *Final Report* Vol.1 (2002), para.9.4.
[179] See *Modernising Company Law* (Cm 5553-II, 2002).
[180] s.8(1).
[181] s.8(2).
[182] SI 2008/3014.

association of a company having a share capital must take the form specified in Sch.1, as follows:

Memorandum of association of [*insert name of company*]

Each subscriber to this memorandum of association wishes to form a company under the Companies Act 2006 and agrees to become a member of the company and to take at least one share.

Name of each subscriber   *Authentication by each subscriber*

Dated

For a company not having a share capital, the form specified in Sch.2 is as follows:

Memorandum of association of [*insert name of company*]

Each subscriber to this memorandum of association wishes to form a company under the Companies Act 2006 and agrees to become a member of the company.

Name of each subscriber   *Authentication by each subscriber*

Dated

The company name—general provisions

The application for registration must state the company's proposed name.[183] The general rule is that any name may be selected but this is now dealt with in Pt 5 of the Act. Thus, a company cannot be registered by a name if, in the opinion of the Secretary of State, its use would constitute an offence, or because it is offensive.[184] Further, the last word of the name of a private limited company must be the word "limited" or "ltd",[185] unless the company is able to comply with the criteria for exemption in the Act[186] and dispenses with the word. The last words of a limited company which is a public company must be "public limited company" or "Plc".[187] Where the company has its registered office in Wales, the last word of the name of the company may be "cyfyngedig" or "cyf" if the company is a private company,[188] or "cwmni cyfyngedig cyhoeddus" or "ccc" if it is a public company.[189] In selecting a name, it is not necessary to use the word "Company", and the modern tendency is to omit it. A short name is an obvious practical convenience.

3–020

---

[183] s.9(2)(a). Previously required to be stated in the memorandum: see Companies Act 1985 s.2(1)(a).
[184] s.53.
[185] s.59(1).
[186] s.59(3). See particularly s.60.
[187] s.58(1).
[188] s.59(2).
[189] s.58(2).

The important thing about the name is that it should show to others that the company is a body corporate, and not a mere unincorporated partnership. The Secretary of State can make provision by regulations prohibiting a person from carrying on business under a name consisting of specified words, expressions or other indications associated with a particular type of company.[190] A person must also not carry on business under a name that gives so misleading an indication of the nature of the business as to be likely to cause harm to the public.[191]

The company name—sensitive words and expressions

3–021 Where a company is to be registered with a name that would be likely to give the impression that the company is connected with the government, a local authority,[192] or any public authority specified in regulations, the approval of the Secretary of State is required.[193] His approval is also required for a company to be registered under a name that includes a word or expression specified in regulations made by him.[194] The regulations in point, the Company, Limited Liability Partnership and Business Names (Sensitive Words and Expressions) Regulations 2009,[195] specify the relevant words in Sch.1 and these include such words as "assurer", "banking", "Britain", "charter", "England", "King", "Parliament" and "Royal". The Regulations[196] also specify words which require approval of the Secretary of State or of a specified Government department.[197] The applicant is required to request the specified department or other body in writing to indicate whether (and if so why) it has any objections to the proposed name.[198] The Secretary of State may also make regulations as to the letters or other characters, signs or symbols (including accents and other diacritical marks) and punctuation that may be used in the name of a company and specifying a standard style or format for the name of a company for the purposes of registration.[199] The regulations may prohibit the use of specified characters, signs or symbols when appearing in a specified position (such as at the beginning of a name).[200] The relevant regulations are the Company and Business Names (Miscellaneous Provisions) Regulations 2009.[201]

The company name—similarity to other names

3–022 A company must not be registered under this Act by a name that is the same as another name appearing in the Registrar's index of company names.[202] The Act

---

[190] See s.1197(1) and para.3–021.
[191] s.1198(1).
[192] See s.54(2).
[193] s.54(1).
[194] s.55(1).
[195] SI 2009/2615.
[196] See Sch.2.
[197] See s.56.
[198] s.56(2).
[199] s.57(1).
[200] s.57(2).
[201] SI 2009/1085. See also the Company and Business Names (Miscellaneous Provisions) (Amendment) Regulations 2009 (SI 2009/2404) and the Company, Limited Liability Partnership and Business names (Sensitive Words and Expressions) Regulations 2009 (SI 2009/2615).
[202] s.66(1).

provides that regulations may supplement this provision as to matters which are to be disregarded and as to words, expressions, signs or symbols that are, or are not, to be regarded as the same.[203] The onus of checking the index is on those who wish to register the name. There is no pre-registration control on registration of names similar or "too like" those already on the index but applicants intent on forming a company would be well-advised to make use of the index of company names operated by Companies House[204] and also to check the Trade Marks Register of the UK Intellectual Property Office[205] to ensure that the proposed name does not infringe an existing trade mark. Thus, giving an example, Companies House advises its customers that if, for example, "Hands Limited" was already registered, they would reject the following applications: "Hand-S Limited or Ltd"; "H and S Public Limited Company (or PLC)"; "H & S Services Limited (or Ltd)"; "@H & S Limited (or Ltd)"; "Hands: Limited (or Ltd)"; "# H & S Limited (or Ltd)".[206]

The Secretary of State has the authority to direct a company to change its name if it has been registered in a name that is the same as or too like a name appearing at the time of the registration or a name that should have appeared at the time of registration in the index of company names—so called "post registration control".[207] If a direction to change a name is given it must be given within 12 months of the company's registration by the name in question and must specify the period within which the company is to change its name.[208] The Secretary of State may by a further direction extend that period and this must be given before the end of the period for the time being specified.[209] It is an offence for failing to comply.[210]

Since similar names can be registered, there is a possibility of passing-off actions being brought against registered companies. Under the general law, the court has jurisdiction to grant an injunction to restrain a company from using a trade name colourably resembling that of the claimant if the defendant's trade name, though innocently adopted, is calculated, i.e. likely to deceive,[211] either by diverting customers from the claimant to the defendant or by occasioning confusion between the two businesses, by suggesting that the defendant's business is in some way connected with that of the claimant. Thus, in *Ewing v Buttercup Margarine Co Ltd*,[212] the claimant, who carried on business under the trade name of the Buttercup Dairy Company, was held entitled to restrain a newly registered company from carrying on business under the name of the Buttercup Margarine Company Ltd on the ground that the public might reasonably think that the

---

[203] s.66(2). See the Company and Business Names (Miscellaneous Provisions) Regulations 2009, (SI 2009/1085) Sch.3.
[204] The Companies House WebCheck service is readily available 24 hours a day, 7 days a week: see *http://www.companieshouse.gov.uk* [accessed May 21, 2010].
[205] See *http://www.ipo.gov.uk* [accessed May 21, 2010].
[206] See *Companies House: Incorporation and names* (GP1), 18.
[207] s.67(1).
[208] s.68(2).
[209] s.68(3).
[210] s.68(5)(6).
[211] *The North Cheshire and Manchester Brewery Co Ltd v The Manchester Brewery Co Ltd* [1899] A.C. 83 at 84, per Earl of Halsbury L.C.
[212] [1917] 2 Ch. 1, CA.

registered company was connected with his business. However, if the company's business is or will be different from that of the complaining party, confusion is not likely to arise, and an injunction will not be granted.[213] A company having a word in ordinary use as part of its name cannot prevent another company from using the same word. Thus, a company called Aerators Ltd were unable to prevent the registration of Automatic Aerators Patents, Ltd because the word "aerator" was a word in common use in the English language and Aerators Ltd had no monopoly on it.[214]

The position under the general law has now been extended by the Act[215] which provides that a person may object to a company's registered name on the ground that it is the same as a name associated with the applicant in which he has goodwill, or that it is sufficiently similar to such a name that its use in the United Kingdom would be likely to mislead by suggesting a connection between the company and the applicant.[216] The objection has to be made to an adjudicator,[217] the company names adjudicator.[218] If the ground is established it is then for the respondent to show—

1.   that the name was registered before the commencement of the activities on which the applicant relies to show goodwill;[219]

2.   that the company is operating under the name, or is proposing to do so and has incurred substantial start-up costs in preparation, or was formerly operating under the name and is now dormant;

3.   that the name was registered in the ordinary course of a company formation business and the company is available for sale to the applicant on the standard terms of that business;

4.   that the name was adopted in good faith; or

5.   that the interests of the applicant are not adversely affected to any significant extent. If none of these is shown, the objection will be upheld.[220]

---

[213] *Dunlop Pneumatic Tyre Co Ltd v Dunlop Motor Co Ltd* [1907] A.C. 430, where the respondents carried on a motor repairing company.

[214] *Aerators Ltd v Tollitt* [1902] 2 Ch. 319.

[215] But it has been held that an application to the company names adjudicator is neither an alternative nor an equivalent to an action for passing off: see the arbitration reported as *Barloworld Handling Ltd v Unilift South Wales Ltd* [2009] F.S.R. 21.

[216] s.69(1).

[217] s.69(2).

[218] See s.70. The Secretary of State may also make rules about proceedings before a company names adjudicator: s.71. See the Company Names Adjudicator Rules 2008 (SI 2008/1738).

[219] "Goodwill" is defined in s.69(7) as "including reputation of any description". In *Knight v Beyond Properties Pty Ltd* [2007] EWHC 1251 (Ch); [2007] F.S.R. 34, at [66], it was held that a claim in passing off could not be sustained to protect goodwill that any reasonable person would consider to be trivial. Thus, while the claimant had shown that by the end of 1993 he had established a reputation in connection with the use of the word "Mythbusters" to describe the investigation of myths for a children's audience of primary school age, on a very minor scale but sufficient to attract protection under the law of passing off, that reputation had significantly diminished by 1996, and by November 2003 the applicant had had no more than a trivial, if any, reputation in the "Mythbusters" name.

[220] s.69(4).

If the facts in 1, 2, or 3, above, are established, the objection will nevertheless be upheld if the applicant shows that the main purpose of the respondents (or any of them) in registering the name was to obtain money (or other consideration) from the applicant or prevent him from registering the name.[221] If the objection is not upheld, it will be dismissed.[222] If upheld, the adjudicator will make an appropriate order specifying the date by which the company's name is to be changed.[223] The decision of the adjudicator must be made public within 90 days of the decision, together with reasons.[224] There is a right of appeal to a court against the order.[225]

The company name—exemption from using the word "limited"

A private company is exempt from the requirement to have a name ending in "limited" or "ltd" if it is a charity, exempted from the requirements by regulations, or it meets certain conditions[226] relating to the continuation of an existing exemption for companies limited by shares[227] or for companies limited by guarantee.[228] The Registrar may refuse to register a private limited company by a name that does not include the word "limited" (or "ltd") unless a statement has been delivered to him that the company meets the conditions for exemption.[229] The Registrar may accept the statement as sufficient evidence of the matters stated in it.[230] A private company which is exempt from the requirement of using "limited" in its name may not amend its articles so that it ceases to comply with the conditions for exemption under the relevant section of the Act.[231] The right to the exemption may be revoked and the Secretary of State can direct the company to change its name so that it ends with "limited".[232] Associations taking advantage of this exemption are typically chambers of commerce, schools and colleges, research associations, learned societies, professional qualifying bodies and charitable bodies doing social work.

3–023

Company names—minor variations

In considering a company's name, the Act provides that no account[233] is to be taken of whether upper or lower case characters (or a combination of the two) are used, whether diacritical marks or punctuation are present or absent, and whether the name is in the same format or style as is specified[234] for the purposes of

3–024

---

[221] s.69(5).
[222] s.69(6).
[223] s.73.
[224] See s.72(1).
[225] See s.74.
[226] s.60(1).
[227] See s.61.
[228] See s.62.
[229] s.60(2).
[230] s.60(3).
[231] s.63.
[232] See s.64.
[233] s.85(1).
[234] i.e. under s.57(1)(b).

registration, provided there is no real likelihood of names differing only in those respects being taken to be different names. This does not affect the operation of regulations[235] which permit only specified characters, diacritical marks or punctuation.[236]

Company names—misleading information

3–025 If the Secretary of State considers that misleading information has been given for the purposes of a company's registration by a particular name or that an undertaking or assurance has been given for that purpose and has not been fulfilled, the Secretary of State may direct the company to change its name.[237] Any such direction must be given within five years of the company's registration by that name, and must specify the period within which the company is to change its name.[238] The Secretary of State may by a further direction extend the period within which the company is to change its name and such direction must be given before the end of the period for the time being specified.[239] A direction under this section must be in writing.[240] Failure to comply is an offence.[241] Furthermore, if in the opinion of the Secretary of State the name by which a company is registered gives so misleading an indication of the nature of its activities as to be likely to cause harm to the public, the Secretary of State may, in writing, direct the company to change its name.[242] The direction must be complied with within a period of six weeks from the date of the direction or such longer period as the Secretary of State may think fit to allow.[243] The company may apply to the court to set the direction aside within the period of three weeks from the date of the direction.[244] In *Association of Certified Public Accountants of Britain v Secretary of State for Trade and Industry*,[245] the court held that on such an application the burden of proof was on the Secretary of State to show that the company's name is so misleading that it is likely to cause harm to the public. The court may set the direction aside or confirm it and if the direction is confirmed, the court shall specify the period within which the direction is to be complied with.[246] Failure to comply is an offence.[247]

---

[235] i.e. under s.57(1)(a). See the Company and Business Names (Miscellaneous Provisions) Regulations 2009 (SI 2009/1085) Sch.1.
[236] s.85(2).
[237] s.75(1).
[238] s.75(2).
[239] s.75(3).
[240] s.75(4).
[241] s.75(5)(6).
[242] s.76(1)(2).
[243] s.76(3).
[244] s.76(4).
[245] [1997] 2 B.C.L.C. 307.
[246] s.76(5).
[247] s.76(6)(7).

Company names—right to change name

Companies may change their registered names voluntarily by special resolution or **3–026** by other means provided for by the company's articles.[248] Additionally,[249] a company's name may be changed by resolution of the directors acting to change a company's name so as to comply with direction of Secretary of State[250]; on the determination of a new name by a company names adjudicator[251]; on the determination of a new name by the court[252]; and where a company is restored to the register.[253] Where the change of name is agreed by special resolution the company is obliged to give notice of this to the Registrar and forward a copy of the resolution to him.[254] In the event that the change of name is conditional on some event, then the notice must specify that the change is conditional and state whether the event has occurred.[255] If the notice states that the event has not occurred the Registrar is not required to act[256] until further notice and when the event occurs, the company must give notice to the Registrar stating that it has occurred.[257] The Registrar may rely on the statement as sufficient evidence of the matters stated in it.[258] Where a change of a company's name has been made by other means provided for by its articles the company must give notice to the Registrar, and the notice must be accompanied by a statement that the change of name has been made by means provided for by the company's articles.[259] The Registrar may rely on the statement as sufficient evidence of the matters stated in it.[260]

When the Registrar receives notification of a name change and he is satisfied that the new name complies with the requirements of the Act and any relevant requirements of the company's articles, with respect to a change of name are complied with, the Registrar must enter the new name on the register in place of the former name.[261] On the registration of the new name, the Registrar must issue a certificate of incorporation altered to meet the circumstances of the case.[262] The new name takes effect from the date of issue of the new certificate of incorporation[263] but the change does not affect any rights or obligations of the company or render defective any legal proceedings by or against it[264] and any legal proceedings

---

[248] s.77(1). This requirement cannot be circumvented by the court: see *Halifax Plc v Halifax Repossessions Ltd* [2004] EWCA Civ. 331; [2004] 2 B.C.L.C. 455, CA, at 461.
[249] See s.77(2).
[250] i.e. under s.64. See particularly s.64(3).
[251] i.e. under s.73.
[252] i.e. under s.74.
[253] Under s.1033.
[254] s.78(1).
[255] s.78(2).
[256] i.e. registering the new name and issuing a new certificate of incorporation (see s.80).
[257] s.78(3)(a)(b).
[258] s.78(3)(c).
[259] s.79(1).
[260] s.79(2).
[261] s.80(2).
[262] s.80(3).
[263] s.81(1). The old name continues until then: see *Shackleford, Ford & Co Ltd v Dangerfield* (1868) L.R. 3 C.P. 407.
[264] s.81(2).

that might have been continued or commenced against it by its former name may be continued or commenced against it by its new name.[265]

Company names—trading disclosures

3–027 The Act provides that the Secretary of State may make regulations as to the display of information as to its name and other matters.[266] This has been done in the Companies (Trading Disclosures) Regulations 2008[267] and in the Companies (Trading Disclosures) (Amendment) Regulations 2009.[268] These are to the following effect:

1. The company is obliged to display its registered name at its registered office and at any inspection place,[269] save where the company has at all times since incorporation been dormant[270] or where a liquidator, administrator or administrative receiver has been appointed and the registered office or inspection place is also a place of business of that liquidator, administrator or administrative receiver.[271]

2. The company is obliged to display its name at any location at which it carries on business.[272] The exceptions are where the location is primarily used for living accommodation,[273] where a liquidator, administrator or administrative receiver has been appointed and the location is also a place of business of that liquidator, administrator or administrative receiver,[274] and to any location at which business is carried on by a company of which every director who is an individual is a relevant director.[275]

3. The registered name is required to be so positioned that it may be easily seen by any visitor to that office, place or location.[276]

4. The registered name is also required to be displayed continuously but where any such office, place or location is shared by six or more companies, each such company is only required to display its registered name for at least fifteen continuous seconds at least once in every three minutes.[277]

---

[265] s.81(3).
[266] s.82.
[267] SI 2008/495.
[268] SI 2009/218.
[269] Companies (Trading Disclosures) Regulations 2008 (SI 2008/495) reg.3(1).
[270] reg.3(2).
[271] reg.3(3), inserted by the Companies (Trading Disclosures) (Amendment) Regulations 2009 (SI 2009/218) reg.2.
[272] reg.4(2).
[273] reg.4(3).
[274] reg.4(4), inserted by Companies (Trading Disclosures) (Amendment) Regulations 2009 (SI 2009/218) reg.3(2).
[275] *Ibid.*
[276] reg.5(2).
[277] reg.5(3).

5.   Every company must disclose its registered name on (a) its business letters, notices and other official publications; (b) its bills of exchange, promissory notes, endorsements and order forms; (c) cheques purporting to be signed by or on behalf of the company; (d) orders for money, goods or services purporting to be signed by or on behalf of the company; (e) its bills of parcels, invoices and other demands for payment, receipts and letters of credit; (f) its applications for licences to carry on a trade or activity; and (g) all other forms of its business correspondence and documentation.[278]

6.   Every company is also obliged to disclose its registered name on its websites.[279]

7.   A company which has a common seal must engrave its name in legible characters on its seal.[280]

Fines may be imposed on the company and its officers for non-compliance with the above requirements.[281]

Company names—civil consequences of making disclosure

Previously, under the Companies Act 1985, there was a provision to the effect that **3–028** if an officer of the company or any person on its behalf, signed or authorised to be signed on behalf of the company any bill of exchange, cheque or order for money or goods in which the company's name is not correctly mentioned, he was liable to a fine and was personally liable to the holder of the bill of exchange, cheque or order, for its amount, unless it is paid by the company.[282] This was strictly interpreted by the courts[283] and the Company Law Review thought that it could operate unduly harshly and should be narrowed.[284] Thus the new Act now provides that if the company brings legal proceedings to enforce a right arising out of a contract made in the course of a business in respect of which the company was, at the time the contract was made, in breach of the disclosure regulations,[285] those proceedings will be dismissed if the defendant to the proceedings shows: (a) that he has a claim against the claimant arising out of the contract that he has been unable to pursue by reason of the latter's breach of the regulations, or (b) that he has suffered some financial loss in connection with the contract by reason of the claimant's (pursuer's) breach of the regulations, unless the court before which the proceedings are brought is satisfied that it is just and equitable to

---

[278] reg.6(1).

[279] reg.6(2).

[280] s.45(2). Where a company entered into a bond by way of deed and used a seal engraved with its trading name rather than its registered name, it was held that this did not render the bond a nullity or enforceable by a third party beneficiary against a surety: *OTV Birwelco Ltd v Technical and General Guarantee Co Ltd* [2002] EWHC 2240, TCC; [2002] 2 B.C.L.C. 723.

[281] See the Companies (Trading Disclosures) Regulations 2008 (SI 2008/495) reg.10; s.45(3)(4)(5).

[282] s.394(4).

[283] See the discussion in the previous edition of this book at pp.56–57.

[284] CLR, *Final Report*, para.11.57.

[285] s.83(1).

permit the proceedings to continue.[286] The section does not affect the right of any person to enforce such rights as he may have against another person in any proceedings brought by that person.[287]

The registered office

3–029   A company must at all times have a registered office to which communications and notices may be addressed.[288] The application for registration must state whether the registered office is to be in England and Wales, Scotland, or Northern Ireland[289] and its intended address.[290] This statement of the registered office is important because it fixes the company's nationality and domicile, e.g. if the statement is to the effect that the registered office is to be in England and Wales, the company is an English company with British nationality and an English domicile. A corporation is domiciled where it is incorporated and cannot change this domicile,[291] except by Act of Parliament, and the law of a corporation's domicile governs all questions of its status. The nationality of a corporation, seldom relevant in private international law, also depends on the place of incorporation.[292] The reason for requiring a company to have a specific registered office is that, since the company has a legal existence but does not have a physical existence, it is necessary to know where the company can be found, where the communications and notices may be addressed and where documents can be served on it. A company need not, and very frequently does not, carry on its business at its registered office. There is nothing, for example, to prevent a company with a registered office in England from carrying on its business abroad.

A document can be served on a company by leaving it at, or sending it by post to, the registered office of the company.[293] It is not, however, necessary to send it by registered post.[294] If a company registered in Scotland or Northern Ireland carries on business in England and Wales, the process of any court in England and Wales can be served on the company by leaving it at, or sending it by post to, the company's principal place of business in England and Wales, addressed to the manager or other head officer in England and Wales of the company.[295] Where process is served on a company, the person issuing process must send a copy of it by post to the company's registered office.[296]

---

[286] s.83(2).

[287] s.83(3).

[288] s.86(1). This is so even where the company ceases trading. In *Oakwood Storage Services Ltd, Re* [2003] EWHC 2807, Ch; [2004] 2 B.C.L.C. 404 a company ceased trading when Customs and Excise took over its bonded premises, which was also its registered office. The Court held that, in such circumstances, the directors must put in place arrangements to ensure that documents served on the company at its registered office came to their notice.

[289] s.9(2)(b).

[290] s.9(5)(a).

[291] *Gasque v I.R.C.* [1940] 2 K.B. 80.

[292] See *Konamaneni v Rolls Royce Industrial Power (India) Ltd* [2002] 1 W.L.R. 1269 at 1284; *Reeves v Sprecher* [2007] EWHC 117, Ch; [2008] B.C.C. 49 at 54.

[293] s.1139(1).

[294] See *T.O. Supplies (London) Ltd v Jerry Creighton Ltd* [1952] 1 K.B. 42.

[295] s.1139(4).

[296] s.1139(4).

As we have already seen, the Act provides that the Secretary of State may make regulations as to the display of information as to its name and other matters.[297] These "other matters" include the place of registration. Thus the Companies (Trading Disclosures) Regulations 2008[298] provide that particulars of the address of the company's registered office[299] are to be disclosed on its business letters, its order forms, and its websites.[300] The company must also disclose, within five working days, the address of its registered office to any person it deals with in the course of business who makes a written request to the company for that information.[301] Failure to do so is an offence.[302]

Change of address of the registered office

A company may change the address of its registered office on giving notice to the **3–030** Registrar.[303] The new address takes effect on the entry of that address on the register by the Registrar but until the end of the period of 14 days beginning with the date on which it is registered a person may validly serve any document on the company at the address previously registered.[304] For the purposes of any duty of a company to keep available for inspection at its registered office any register, index or other document, or to mention the address of its registered office in any document, a company that has given notice to the Registrar of a change in the address of its registered office may act on the change as from such date, not more than 14 days after the notice is given, as it may determine.[305] If a company is unavoidably unable to keep its registers, etc., at its registered office in circumstances in which it was impracticable to give the Registrar prior notice, the company and its officers will not be liable if it can show that it resumed performance of that duty at other premises as soon as practicable and notified the Registrar of that new address within 14 days of doing so.[306] The Registrar must publish in the Gazette notice of the receipt by him of notice of a change in the situation of a company's registered office;[307] i.e. he must officially notify it.[308]

Items which must be kept at the registered office

The following must be kept at the registered office of a company although these **3–031** may also be kept at a single alternative location[309] provided that it is a place that is situated in the part of the United Kingdom in which the company is registered,

---

[297] s.82.
[298] SI 2008/495.
[299] reg.7(2)(c).
[300] reg.7(1).
[301] reg.9.
[302] reg.10.
[303] s.87(1).
[304] s.87(2).
[305] s.87(3).
[306] s.87(4).
[307] s.1077(1); s.1078(1).
[308] On the other hand official notification does not constitute notice of such a change to anyone: *Official Custodian of Charities v Parway Estates* [1985] Ch. 151, CA.
[309] See s.1136.

must be the same place for all the relevant provisions, and must have been notified to the Registrar as being the company's alternative inspection location:[310]

1. the register of members[311] and, if the company has one, the index of members[312];

2. the register of directors[313];

3. where there is a resolution of a meeting concerning directors, long-term service contracts this must be kept at the registered office for not less than 15 days ending with the date of the meeting[314];

4. a resolution approving a loan to a director must be kept at the registered office for not less than 15 days ending with the date of the meeting[315];

5. a resolution approving a quasi-loan to a director must be kept at the registered office for not less than 15 days ending with the date of the meeting[316];

6. a resolution approving a loan or quasi-loan to persons connected with the directors must be kept at the registered office for not less than 15 days ending with the date of the meeting[317];

7. a resolution approving the entering into a credit transaction as creditor for the benefit of a director of the company or of its holding company, or a person connected with such a director, or approving of a guarantee or the provision of security in connection with a credit transaction entered into by any person for the benefit of such a director or a person connected with such a director must be kept at the registered office for not less than 15 days ending with the date of the meeting[318];

8. in the case of related arrangements approved by resolution at a meeting this must be kept at the registered office for not less than 15 days ending with the date of the meeting[319];

9. A resolution approving a payment for loss of office to a director of the company must be kept at the registered office for not less than 15 days ending with the date of the meeting[320];

10. a resolution approving a payment in connection with the transfer of an undertaking must be kept at the registered office for not less than 15 days ending with the date of the meeting[321];

[310] See the Companies (Company Records) Regulation 2008 (SI 2008/3006) reg.3.
[311] s.114.
[312] s.115(4).
[313] s.162(3).
[314] s.188(5).
[315] s.197(3).
[316] s.198(4).
[317] s.200(4).
[318] s.201(4).
[319] s.203(3).
[320] s.217(3).
[321] s.218(3).

11. a resolution approving a payment in connection with a share transfer must be kept at the registered office for not less than 15 days ending with the date of the meeting[322];

12. a copy of each director's contract of service or memorandum of terms[323];

13. a copy or memorandum of a qualifying indemnity to a director[324];

14. the register of secretaries[325];

15. all records of resolutions and meetings of the company[326];

16. a company's accounting records[327];

17. any proposed contract or option for an off-market purchase by a company of its own shares, for 15 days prior to the resolution to approve it or, in the case of a written resolution, by being sent or submitted to every eligible member at or before the time at which the proposed resolution is sent or submitted to him[328];

18. any proposed release by a company of its rights under an off-market purchase contract or option to purchase its own shares and any contract for the purchase by a company of its own shares approved by the company must be kept at the registered office for 10 years from the purchase of the shares or the determination of the contract[329];

19. the requisite statutory declaration of solvency and auditors' report where a private company intends to purchase or redeem its own shares out of capital[330];

20. if the company has one, the register of debenture holders[331];

21. reports made by a company following an investigation instigated at the behest of the members must be retained by the company for at least six years from the date on which they are first made available for inspection[332];

22. a public company may, by giving notice to any person, require information about that person's interest in its shares and the information once received must be kept in a register[333] and this, together with the mandatory index,[334] must be kept at the registered office;

---

[322] s.219(3).
[323] s.228(2).
[324] s.237(3).
[325] s.275(3).
[326] s.358(1).
[327] s.388(1).
[328] s.696(2).
[329] s.702(4).
[330] s.720(2).
[331] s.743(1).
[332] s.805(4).
[333] s.808(1).
[334] See s.810(1).

23. a copy of every instrument creating or evidencing any charge requiring registration and the company's register of charges affecting property of the company.[335]

Inspection and copying of records held at the company's registered office

3–032　The Secretary of State is empowered to make provision by regulations as to the obligations of a company which is required by any provision of the Act to keep available for inspection and copying the documents kept at the company's registered office.[336] The Companies (Company Records) Regulations 2008[337] make separate provision for private and public companies. Private companies are required to make their company records available for inspection by a person on a day which has been specified by that person, provided that this is a working day and the company has been given the required notice of the specified day.[338] The required notice is at least 2 working days' notice of the specified day if the notice is given during the period of notice for a general meeting or a class meeting or where the company circulates a written resolution, during the period provided for in s.297(1) of the Act, provided that the notice given both begins and ends during the periods referred to.[339] In all other cases the required notice is at least 10 working days' notice of the specified day.[340] A person giving notice of the specified day is also required to give notice of the time on that day at which he wishes to start the inspection (any time between 9 am and 3 pm) and the company is required make its company records available for inspection by that person for a period of at least two hours beginning with that time.[341] Public companies are required to make their company records available for inspection for at least two hours between 9 am and 5 pm on each working day.[342] A company is not required for the purposes of inspection of a company record to present information in that record in a different order, structure or form from that set out in that record.[343]

A company is required to permit a person to make a copy of the whole or any part of a company record in the course of inspection at the location at which the record is made available for inspection and any time during which the record is made available for inspection, but it is not required to assist that person in making his copy of that record.[344] Where a company is requested to provide a copy of a company record in hard copy form, the company is required to provide that copy in hard copy form.[345] Where, however, a person requests a company to provide a copy of a company record in electronic form, the company is required to provide

---

[335] s.877(2).
[336] s.1137.
[337] SI 2008/3006.
[338] reg.4(1).
[339] reg.4(2).
[340] reg.4(3).
[341] reg.4(4).
[342] reg.5.
[343] reg.6(1).
[344] reg.6(2).
[345] reg.7.

that copy in such electronic form as it (the company) decides.[346] But where a company keeps a company record in hard copy form only, it is not required to provide a copy of that record in electronic form.[347] Finally, where a company provides a copy of a company record in electronic form to a member of the company or to a holder of the company's debentures, the company is not required to provide a hard copy of that record in accordance with s.1145 of the Act.[348] A company is not required to present information in a copy of a company record that it provides in a different order, structure or form from that set out in the record.[349]

The fees for inspection and copying of records are specified in a series of statutory instruments. The Companies (Fees for Inspection of Company Records) Regulations 2007[350] specifies that the fee for inspection of all documents is £3.50 per hour.[351] The fee for copying of certain registers[352] is £1 for each of the first 5 entries, £30 for the next 95 entries or part thereof, £30 for the next 900 entries or part thereof, £30 for the next 99,000 entries or part thereof, and £30 for the remainder of the entries in the register or part thereof.[353] The fee for the copy of certain records is 10 pence per 500 words or part thereof copied and the reasonable costs incurred by the company in delivering the copy of the company record to the person entitled to be provided with that copy.[354]

Limitation of liability

Whether the liability of the members is limited by shares or by guarantee must be **3–033** stated in the company's application for registration.[355]

Share capital

In the case of a company that is to have a share capital, the registration docu- **3–034** ment[356] is no longer required to state the company's authorised share capital.[357] Instead, it must state the total number of shares of the company to be taken on formation by the subscribers to the memorandum of association, the aggregate nominal value of those shares and, for each class of shares (a) prescribed

---

[346] reg.8(1).

[347] reg.8(2).

[348] reg.8(3).

[349] reg.9.

[350] SI 2007/2612.

[351] reg.2. The fee is similar for the inspection of the register of debenture holders: Companies (Fees for Inspection of Company Records) (No.2) Regulations 2007 (SI 2007/3535) reg.2. See too the Companies (Fees for Inspection of Company Records) Regulations 2008 (SI 2008/3007) reg.2.

[352] i.e. those specified in reg.3(1).

[353] reg.3(2). The fee structure is similar for a copy of the register of debenture holders: Companies (Fees for Inspection of Company Records) (No.2) Regulations 2007 (SI 2007/3535) reg.3.

[354] reg.4.

[355] See s.9(2)(c).

[356] s.9(4)(a).

[357] See the Companies Act 1985, s.2(5). The CLR recommended that the requirement as to authorised share capital fall away, to be replaced by a statement as to the share capital to be allotted to members on formation. See CLR, *Final Report*, para.9.4. This was accepted by the Government: see *Modernising Company Law*, above, cl.6.

particulars of the rights attached to the shares, (b) the total number of shares of that class, and (c) the aggregate nominal value of shares of that class, and the amount to be paid up and the amount (if any) to be unpaid on each share (whether on account of the nominal value of the share or by way of premium).[358] It must contain such information as may be prescribed for the purpose of identifying the subscribers to the memorandum of association.[359] It must state, with respect to each subscriber to the memorandum the number, nominal value (of each share) and class of shares to be taken by him on formation and the amount to be paid up and the amount (if any) to be unpaid on each share (whether on account of the nominal value of the share or by way of premium).[360] Where a subscriber to the memorandum is to take shares of more than one class, the information required is required for each class.[361]

A public company will not be issued a trading certificate[362] unless the Registrar is satisfied that the nominal value of the company's allotted share capital is not less than the authorised minimum.[363] This is currently £50,000 or the equivalent euro equivalent,[364] a low figure in practical terms. The Secretary of State has the power to alter this authorised minimum.[365]

In the case of a company limited by guarantee, the registration document must include a statement of guarantee[366] which must contain such information as may be prescribed for the purpose of identifying the subscribers to the memorandum of association.[367] Thus, it must state that each member undertakes that, if the company is wound up while he is a member, or within one year after he ceases to be a member, he will contribute to the assets of the company such amount as may be required for (a) payment of the debts and liabilities of the company contracted before he ceases to be a member, (b) payment of the costs, charges and expenses of winding up, and (c) adjustment of the rights of the contributories among themselves, not exceeding a specified amount.[368]

Statement of proposed officers

3–035 The application for registration must provide a statement of the company's first officers.[369] This statement must contain the required particulars of the person who is, or persons who are, to be the first director or directors of the company.[370] If the company is to be a private company, the statement must contain the details of any person who is (or any persons who are) to be the first secretary (or joint

---

[358] s.10(2).
[359] s.10(3).
[360] s.10(4).
[361] s.10(5).
[362] There are also penal consequences of doing business as a public company without a trading certificate: see s.767.
[363] s.761(2).
[364] s.763(1).
[365] s.764.
[366] This replaces s.2(4) of the Companies Act 1985.
[367] s.11(1)(2).
[368] s.11(3).
[369] s.9(4)(c).
[370] s.12(1)(a).

secretaries) of the company.[371] For a public company, the person who is (or the persons who are) to be the first secretary (or joint secretaries) of the company must be stated.[372] The relevant required particulars for a director[373] are those that will have to be stated in the register of directors and the register of directors' residential addresses.[374] In the case of the secretary[375] these will be the particulars required for the company's register of secretaries.[376] The statement must also contain a consent by each of the persons named as a director, as secretary or as one of the joint secretaries, to act in the relevant capacity.[377] If all the partners in a firm are to be joint secretaries, consent may be given by one partner on behalf of all of them.[378]

Other clauses

The application for registration is also required to include a copy of the proposed **3–036** articles of association of the company[379] to the extent that the model articles do not apply by default.[380]

The statement of compliance

The documents for registration are, as we have now seen, the memorandum **3–037** of association, the various documents specified in the Act, and a statement of compliance.[381] This statement is a statement to the effect that the requirements of the Act as to registration have been complied with.[382] The Registrar is entitled to accept this statement as sufficient evidence of compliance.[383]

---

[371] s.12(1)(b).
[372] s.12(1)(c).
[373] See ss.162–165.
[374] s.12(2)(a).
[375] ss.277–278.
[376] s.12(2)(b).
[377] s.12(3).
[378] s.12(3).
[379] See para.4–003, below.
[380] s.12(5)(b).
[381] s.9(1).
[382] s.13(1).
[383] s.13(2).

Chapter 4

THE CORPORATE CONSTITUTION

INTRODUCTION

4-001 Hitherto, company law has depended upon two constitutional documents of importance for registration: the memorandum of association and the articles of association. The implementation of the 2006 Act has, however, seen a major change in the importance of these two documents with the recognition of a much-reduced role for the memorandum[1] and a correspondingly more important one for the articles of association. In the context of the corporate constitution, however, the Act goes further and recognises more than the company's articles as forming the constitution.

THE COMPANY'S CONSTITUTION

4-002 For the purposes of the Act, the constitution of the company includes the following two matters: the company's articles and also any resolutions and agreements affecting a company's constitution.[2]

THE ARTICLES OF ASSOCIATION

General provisions

4-003 It is mandatory for a company to have articles of association.[3] In general terms, the articles are the regulations for the internal arrangements and the management of the company. They are intended to help ensure that a company's business runs as smoothly and efficiently as possible. Typically, they deal with the issue of shares, transfer of shares, alteration of share capital, general meetings, voting rights, directors (including their appointment and powers), managing director, secretary, dividends, accounts, audit of accounts, winding up and various other matters which will be referred to later. However, under the Companies Act 2006, the articles have come to assume greater importance because of the corresponding diminution in importance of the memorandum of association. The articles of

---

[1] The CLR recommended that both the memorandum and articles be replaced with a single document constitution: see *Final Report*, vol.1 (2002), para.9.4. This was accepted by the government in its then draft Bill: see *Modernising Company Law* (Cm.5553-II, 2002), cl.5. See now s.8 of the Act.
[2] s.17.
[3] See s.18(1).

association must be contained in a single document and be divided into paragraphs which are numbered consecutively.[4] If a company does not register its own articles, model articles will apply by default.[5]

Model articles

The Secretary of State is empowered to make regulations which prescribe model **4–004** articles of association for companies.[6] He may make different model articles for different descriptions of company.[7] He has done so in the Companies (Model Articles) Regulations 2008[8] and made provision for model articles for private companies limited by shares,[9] for private companies limited by guarantee[10] and for public companies.[11] A company may adopt all or any of the provisions of the model articles.[12] The model articles will apply on formation of a limited company if articles are not registered.[13] If articles are registered, in so far as they do not exclude or modify the relevant model articles, the relevant model articles (so far as applicable) form part of the company's articles in the same manner and to the same extent as if articles in the form of those articles had been duly registered.[14]

Alteration of articles

A company may by special resolution alter or add to its articles,[15] subject to **4–005** special provision being made for entrenched provisions in articles.[16] An alteration or addition so made is as valid except in so far as the alteration requires a member of a company to take or subscribe for more shares than the number held by him at the date on which the alteration is made, or in any way increases his liability as at that date to contribute to the company's share capital or otherwise to pay money to the company.[17] This will not apply in a case where the member agrees in writing, either before or after the alteration is made, to be bound by the alteration.[18] A provision in the articles which purports to deprive the company of its power to alter them is void,[19] e.g. a provision that no alteration of the articles shall be effective without the consent of X, or that on a proposed alteration only the shares of those opposed shall have a vote.[20] The power to alter articles is subject, in the case of companies which are charities, to the provisions of the relevant

---

[4] s.18(3).
[5] s.18(2).
[6] s.19(1).
[7] s.19(2).
[8] SI 2008/3229.
[9] See Sch.1.
[10] Sch.2.
[11] Sch.3.
[12] s.19(3).
[13] s.20(1)(a).
[14] s.20(1)(b).
[15] s.21(1).
[16] s.22, discussed below, para.4–007.
[17] s.25(1).
[18] s.25(2).
[19] *Malleson v National Insurance Corp* [1894] 1 Ch. 200.
[20] *Bushell v Faith* [1969] 2 Ch. 438, CA, at 448, per Russell L.J.

legislation.[21] Whenever a company amends its articles there is a statutory requirement that the company must send to the Registrar a copy of the articles, as amended, not later than 15 days after the amendment takes effect.[22] Failure to do so amounts to an offence.[23] In the event of a failure to send the Registrar the amended articles, he may give notice to the company requiring compliance within 28 days of the date of issue.[24] There are civil and criminal penalties for failure to comply.[25]

Alterations and rights attached to shares

4–006 If special rights are attached to a class of shares[26] by the articles, as opposed to the terms of issue of the shares, then a so-called "modification of rights clause" which provides for alteration of the class rights only with the consent of a specified proportion or the sanction of a specified resolution of the shareholders of the class, ensures that those class rights can only be altered with such consent or sanction.[27] This special position with respect to class rights is protected also by the Act which provides that where rights attaching to a class of shares are varied, consent is required from the holders of at least three-quarters in nominal value of the issued shares of that class, excluding treasury shares.[28] Dissentient holders of not less in the aggregate than 15 per cent of the issued shares of the class may, within 21 days after the consent was given, apply to the court to have the variation cancelled.[29] This restriction on the alteration of the articles has been held in one case to apply not only to rights actually attached to a specific class of shares, e.g. preference shares, but also to rights given by the articles to certain members in their capacity as members. This means that a group of shareholders can enjoy the protection of the variation of a class rights procedure if they qua shareholders enjoy different rights, e.g. of pre-emption of other shares, even though the shares they own are in no way distinguished from other shares; i.e. if their class rights attach to them as shareholders and not specifically to the shares themselves.[30]

Alterations and entrenched provisions of the articles

4–007 The CLR recommended in its *Final Report* that provision should be made for the possibility of having entrenched provisions in a company's articles.[31] Under the Act it is now provided that the articles may contain so-called "provisions for entrenchment". Although the Act provides that such provisions for entrenchment

[21] See s.21(2)(3).
[22] s.26(1).
[23] s.26(3)(4).
[24] s.27(1)(2).
[25] s.27(4). If the company does comply, no criminal proceedings may be brought: s.27(3).
[26] Under the Act shares are of one class if the rights attached to them are in all respects uniform: s.629(1).
[27] Below, para.7–008.
[28] s.630(4) (for companies having a share capital); s.631(4) (for companies without a share capital).
[29] s.633(2); s.634(2).
[30] *Cumbrian Newspapers Group Ltd v Cumberland and Westmorland Herald Newspaper & Printing Co Ltd* [1987] Ch. 1. See also *Harman v BML Group Ltd* [1994] 2 B.C.L.C. 674.
[31] para.9.8.

can be made on formation[32] or by an amendment of the company's articles which is agreed to by all the members of the company,[33] this subsection has been prevented from coming into force.[34] This is because it is thought that the provision might catch rules governing class rights that appear in articles, even though those rights are covered elsewhere in the Act[35] and that this could have the unintended consequence of making it difficult to create or modify rules for classes of shares.[36] The BIS has decided that it will consider and consult further on this.[37] Provision for entrenchment will not prevent amendment of the company's articles by agreement of all the members of the company[38] or by an order of the court or other authority having power to alter the company's articles.[39] Further, nothing will affect any power of a court or other authority to alter a company's articles.[40] Two further consequences follow the provision on entrenched provisions. The first is that there has to be notice to the Registrar of the existence of such a provision, whether in the articles from formation, or whether included or subsequently removed either by the members or by a court.[41] Furthermore, the company is required to deliver to the Registrar a statement of compliance, certifying that the amendment has been made in accordance with the company's articles and, where relevant, any applicable order of a court or other authority.[42] The Registrar is entitled to rely on the statement as sufficient evidence of the matters stated in it.[43]

Alterations and the general law

The courts have always considered the statutory power of alteration as being **4–008** subject to implied limitations,[44] although the principles of natural justice are not applicable.[45] In particular, the power to alter the articles must be exercised bona fide for the benefit of the company as a whole.

In *Allen v Gold Reefs of West Africa Ltd*,[46] articles gave the company a lien on partly paid shares for all debts and liabilities of a member to the company. Z, on his death, owed money to the company (arrears of calls on partly paid shares), and was the only holder of fully paid shares. The articles were altered so as to give the company a lien on fully paid shares. The court held that the alteration was valid and, as from the date of the alteration, gave the company a lien on Z's fully paid shares in respect of the debts contracted before the date of the alteration.

---

[32] s.22(2)(a).
[33] s.22(2)(b).
[34] See the Companies Act 2006 and Limited Liability Partnerships (Transitional Provisions and Savings) (Amendment) Regulations 2009 (SI 2009/2476) reg.2(2).
[35] See ss.629 et seq.
[36] See the Explanatory Memorandum to SI 2009/2476, para.7.6.
[37] See the Explanatory Memorandum to SI 2009/2476, para.7.6.
[38] s.22(3)(a).
[39] s.22(3)(b).
[40] s.22(4).
[41] See s.23.
[42] s.24(2)(3).
[43] s.24(4).
[44] See *Citco Banking Corp NV v Pusser's Ltd* [2007] UKPC 13; [2007] B.C.C. 205 at 209.
[45] *Gaiman v National Association of Mental Health* [1971] 1 Ch. 317 at 335, per Megarry J.
[46] [1900] 1 Ch. 656, CA. cf. *Liquidator of W. & A. M'Arthur Ltd v Gulf Line Ltd* 1909 S.C. 732.

Lord Lindley M.R. stated that the power conferred on companies to alter articles

"must, like all other powers, be exercised subject to those general principles of law and equity which are applicable to all powers conferred on majorities and enabling them to bind minorities. It must be exercised, not only in the manner required by law, but also bona fide for the benefit of the company as a whole, and it must not be exceeded. These conditions are always implied, and are seldom, if ever expressed".[47]

He also stated that

"The fact that Zuccani's executors were the only persons practically affected at the time by the alterations made in the articles excites suspicion as to the bona fides of the company. But, although the executors were the only person who were actually affected at the time, that was because Zuccani was the only holder of paid-up shares who at the time was in arrear of calls. The altered articles applied to all holders of fully paid shares, and made no distinction between them. The directors cannot be charged with bad faith".[48]

The burden of proof is upon the person who challenges the validity of the amendment.[49]

4–009   However, it is for the shareholders, and not for the court to say whether an alteration of articles is for the benefit of the company, unless no reasonable man could so regard it.

In *Shuttleworth v Cox Bros & Co (Maidenhead) Ltd*[50] the articles provided that S and four others should be permanent directors of the company unless they should become disqualified by any one of six specified events. None of the six events had occurred. S on 22 occasions within 12 months failed to account for the company's money he had received, and the articles were accordingly altered by adding a seventh event disqualifying a director, namely, a request in writing signed by all the other directors that he should resign. Such a request was made to S who was also a shareholder. It was held that the contract, if any, between the plaintiff and the company contained in the original articles was subject to the statutory power of alteration, and the alteration was bona fide for the benefit of the company as a whole and valid. Bankes L.J. stated that

"Then the first thing to be considered is whether, in formulating the test I have mentioned, Lindley M.R. [in *Allen's* case] had in mind two separate and distinct matters; first, bona fides, the state of mind of the persons whose act is complained of, and secondly, whether the alteration is for the benefit of the company, apart altogether from the state of mind of those who procured it. In my opinion this view of the test has been negatived by this Court in *Sidebotham's* case.[51] So the test is whether the alteration of the articles was in the opinion of the shareholders for the

---

[47] At 671. But cf. the view of the High Court of Australia in *Gambotto v WCP Ltd* (1995) 182 C.L.R. 432.
[48] At 675, per Lord Lindley M.R. On this point see also *Mutual Life Insurance Co of New York v The Rank Organisation* [1985] B.C.L.C. 11.
[49] *Peters' American Delicacy Co v Heath* (1939) 61 C.L.R. 457, at p. 482, per Latham C.J.
[50] [1927] 2 K.B. 9, CA.
[51] Below, para.4–010.

benefit of the company.[52] By what criterion is the Court to ascertain the opinion of the shareholders upon this question? The alteration may be so oppressive as to cast suspicion on the honesty of the persons responsible for it, or so extravagant that no reasonable man could really consider it for the benefit of the company".[53]

Scrntton L.J. stated that:

"Now when persons, honestly endeavouring to decide what will be for the benefit of the company and to act accordingly, decide upon a particular course, then, provided there are grounds on which reasonable men could come to the same decision, it does not matter whether the Court would or would not come to the same decision or a different decision. It is not the business of the Court to manage the affairs of the company. That is for the shareholders and directors. The absence of any reasonable ground for deciding that a certain course of action is conducive to the benefit of the company may be a ground for finding lack of good faith or for finding that the shareholders, with the best motives, have not considered the matters which they ought to have considered. On either of these findings their decision might be set aside. But I should be sorry to see the Court go beyond this and take upon itself the management of concerns which others may understand far better than the Court does".[54]

In particular, an alteration of articles is liable to be impeached if its effect is to **4–010** discriminate between the majority shareholders and the minority so as to give the former an advantage of which the latter are deprived. It is not necessary that persons voting for an alteration of articles should dissociate themselves altogether from their own prospects.[55] If an alteration of articles is bona fide for the benefit of the company, it is immaterial that it prejudices a minority of the members.

In *Sidebottom v Kershaw, Leese & Co*[56] a private company, in which the directors held a majority of the shares, altered its articles so as to give the directors power to require any shareholder who competed with the company's business to transfer his shares, at their fair value to nominees of the directors. S who had a minority of the shares and was in competition with the company, brought an action for a declaration that the special resolution was invalid. The court held that as a power to expel a shareholder by buying him out was valid in the case of original articles, it could be introduced in altered articles, provided that the alteration was made bona fide for the benefit of the company as a whole. In this case the alteration was so made and was valid. Lord Sterndale M.R. stated that

"I think . . . that it is for the benefit of the company that they should not be obliged to have amongst them as members persons who are competing with

---

[52] This has been said to include both present and future members of the company: *Gaiman v National Association of Mental Health* [1971] 1 Ch. 317 at p. 338, per Megarry J.

[53] [1927] 2 K.B. 9, CA, at 18. Thus, the alternative view, as propounded in *Dafen Tinplate Co Ltd v Llanelly Steel Co (1907) Ltd* [1920] 2 Ch. 124, that the alteration must in fact genuinely be for the benefit of the company was rejected.

[54] At 23.

[55] *Greenhalgh v Arderne Cinemas* [1951] Ch. 286, CA at p. 291, per Lord Evershed M.R. See too *Citco Banking Corp NV v Pusser's Ltd* [2007] UKPC 13; [2007] B.C.C. 205.

[56] [1920] 1 Ch. 154, CA.

them in business and who may get knowledge from their membership which would enable them to compete better".[57]

4–011 It has been held that the members of a company, acting in accordance with the Act and the constitution of the company, and subject to any necessary consent on the part of the class affected, can alter the relative voting powers attached by the articles to various classes of shares, provided that the special resolution is passed in good faith for the benefit of the company as a whole.

In *Rights and Issues Investment Trust Ltd v Stylo Shoes Ltd*[58] the issued capital of S Ltd comprised 400,000 management shares, which under the articles carried eight votes each, and 3,600,000 ordinary shares. On the acquisition by S Ltd of the shares in B Ltd in consideration of the issue of 8,400,000 ordinary shares in S Ltd, the articles were altered so as to double the votes carried by management shares in order to ensure continuity of management. The special resolution was passed by a large majority at an extraordinary general meeting of the company. The holders of management shares, directors of S Ltd, did not vote in respect of these shares or their ordinary shares. Nor did they vote at a separate class meeting of the ordinary shareholders which sanctioned the special resolution. It was held that the alteration was valid.

A company cannot agree not to alter its articles.[59] The members can, however, as between themselves agree not to vote in favour of an alteration unless they all consent, provided that this does not bind future members.[60] In *Russell v Northern Bank Development Corp Ltd*,[61] the House of Lords upheld an agreement between the four shareholders of a company not to vote in favour of an increase in the company's share capital unless they and the company agreed in writing. In doing so they emphasised that the company could not be bound by this agreement and only allowed the agreement to stand because it was valid as between the shareholders without the company's involvement. An agreement involving the company would have been void if it had been included in the company's articles and an extraneous agreement such as this would involve the company effectively fettering its statutory power. The agreement between the shareholders was personal to them and did not bind their successors.

4–012   If a company alters its articles in breach of a contract to which it is a party, such an alteration is valid but it may give rise to an action for damages against the company for breach of contract. Although there were earlier decisions which suggested that a third party could obtain an injunction to prevent a company altering its articles in breach of a contract,[62] the above statement was made by Lord Porter in *Southern Foundries (1926) Ltd v Shirlaw*[63] and approved by Scott J. in *Cumbrian Newspaper Group Ltd v Cumberland and Westmorland Herald Newspaper and Printing Co Ltd*.[64] It is perfectly possible for a contract to incor-

---

[57] At 166.
[58] [1965] Ch. 250.
[59] *Southern Foundries (1926) Ltd v Shirlaw* [1940] A.C. 701, at 739, per Lord Porter; *Allen v Gold Reefs of West Africa Ltd* [1900] 1 Ch. 656, at 671, per Lindley M.R.
[60] *Welton v Saffery* [1987] A.C. 299, at 331, per Lord Davey.
[61] [1992] B.C.L.C. 1016, HL.
[62] *Bailey v British Equitable Assurance Co* [1904] 1 Ch. 374; *British Murac Syndicate v Alperton Rubber Co* [1915] 2 Ch.186.
[63] [1940] A.C. 701 at 740.
[64] [1987] Ch. 1.

porate the articles as a term in the contract but any such clause is subject to alteration in the normal way.

It is clear that any alteration of the articles may, in an appropriate case, be used as the basis for bringing a petition under what is now s.994 of the Act.[65] An example of this is in *Smiths of Smithfield Ltd, Re*,[66] which arose in connection with an alteration of the articles which was alleged to exclude the petitioner from his pre-emption rights and constituted a variation of his class rights.[67] One of the issues was whether the alteration could be challenged as constituting unfairly prejudicial conduct under s.994. The judge agreed that it could[68] but confirmed that such allegation had to be specifically pleaded, which they had not been on the facts of the case.

Inspection of articles

A company is required to furnish an up-to-date copy of its articles to its members **4–013** on request,[69] as well as the following documents:

1. a copy of any resolution or agreement relating to the company to which the Act applies and that is for the time being in force;

2. a copy of any document required to be sent to the Registrar under s.34(2) or s.35(2)(a);

3. a copy of any court order sanctioning a compromise or arrangement[70] or an order facilitating reconstruction or amalgamation[71];

4. a copy of any court order altering the company's constitution[72];

5. a copy of the company's current certificate of incorporation, and of any past certificates of incorporation;

6. in the case of a company with a share capital, a current statement of capital[73];

7. in the case of a company limited by guarantee, a copy of the statement of guarantee.[74]

Failure to comply with a request from a member is an offence.[75]

Interpretation of the articles

As a general proposition, the articles will be construed in accordance with the **4–014** established rules for the interpretation of contracts. The court has no power to

---

[65] Previously CA 1985 s.459. See below, para.22–026.
[66] [2003] EWHC 568 (Ch); [2003] B.C.C. 769.
[67] It was argued that the variation was therefore in breach of s.630. See above, para.4–006.
[68] [2003] B.C.C. 769 at 782.
[69] s.32(1).
[70] s.899.
[71] s.900.
[72] s.996.
[73] As elaborated in s.32(2).
[74] Ibid.
[75] s.32(3)(4).

improve upon them and nor can it introduce terms to make them fairer or more reasonable. Its task is to discover what they mean.[76] In other words, the court must give the words used their ordinary meaning derived from the context in which they appear.[77] Nevertheless, the interpretation of the contract is not carried out in vacuum and has to be conducted against the background knowledge which would reasonably have been available to the contracting parties at the time of the contract.[78] Accordingly, as part of the relevant background, it has been held to be legitimate to have regard to the original form of the articles of association of a Plc.[79] However, the court will exclude from the admissible background the previous negotiations of the parties and their declarations of subjective intent.[80]

The court will not imply any terms into the articles other then those which are needed to give effect to the language of the articles, for questions of business efficacy or otherwise.[81] The question for the court is whether such implied wording would spell out in express words what the articles, read against the relevant background, would reasonably be understood to mean:

In *Attorney General of Belize v Belize Telecom Ltd*,[82] articles of a company provided that there would be two classes of ordinary shares, B and C, and one special share. Articles provided that, if the holder of the special share also owned 37.5 per cent of the issued share capital in C shares, the special shareholder became entitled to appoint two of the four directors allocated to the C shareholders, regardless of the wishes of the majority of C shareholders, and that those directors could only be removed by the special shareholder holding the additional 37.5 per cent in C shares. BT purchased the special share and, inter alia, 37.5 per cent in C shares from the Government. It then appointed two directors in its capacity as special shareholder holding 37.5 per cent in C shares. Within a year BT found itself in financial difficulties and, although retaining the special share, it ceased to hold 37.5 per cent in C shares. The articles of association made no provision for the removal of directors appointed by a party acting in its capacity as special shareholder holding 37.5 per cent in C shares in circumstances where such a party no longer existed. The Attorney General sought a declaration that the articles should be construed as having an implied term that, in such circumstances, the directors concerned would vacate once. The judge made the declaration but the Court of Appeal found that there was no scope for reading words into the articles of association and set aside the order. The Privy Council held that it appeared that the overriding purpose of the machinery of appointment

---

[76] *Attorney General of Belize v Belize Telecom Ltd* [2009] UKPC 10; [2009] 1 W.L.R. 1988 at 1993, per Lord Hoffmann.

[77] See *Towcester Racecourse Co Ltd v The Racecourse Association Ltd* [2002] EWHC 2141 (Ch); [2003] 1 B.C.L.C. 260 at 268.

[78] *Investors Compensation Scheme Ltd v West Bromwich Building Society* [1998] 1 W.L.R. 896 at 912; *Folkes Group Plc v Alexander* [2002] EWHC 51 (Ch); [2002] 2 B.C.L.C. 254 at 257; *Attorney General of Belize v Belize Telecom Ltd* [2009] UKPC 10; [2009] 1 W.L.R. 1988 at 1993.

[79] *Folkes Group Plc v Alexander* [2002] EWHC 51 (Ch); [2002] 2 B.C.L.C. 254.

[80] See *Investors Compensation Scheme Ltd v West Bromwich Building Society* [1998] 1 W.L.R. 896 at 913; *Folkes Group Plc v Alexander* [2002] EWHC 51 (Ch); [2002] 2 B.C.L.C. 254 at 257.

[81] See *Bratton Seymour Service Co Ltd v Oxborough* [1992] B.C.L.C. 693; *Towcester Racecourse Co Ltd v The Racecourse Association Ltd* [2002] EWHC 2141 (Ch); [2003] 1 B.C.L.C. 260; *Equitable Life Assurance Society v Hyman* [2002] 1 A.C. 408 at 459, per Lord Steyn.

[82] [2009] UKPC 10; [2009] 1 W.L.R. 1988.

and removal of directors was to ensure that the board rejected the appropriate shareholder interest in accordance with the scheme laid down in the articles; and that, accordingly, there was an implied term that directors would vacate once when there was no longer any shareholder with a shareholding appropriate to authorise their appointment. Lord Hoffman stated that:

> "There is only one question: is that what the instrument, read as a whole against the relevant background, would reasonably be understood to mean?
>
> There are dangers in treating these alternative formulations of the question as if they had a life of their own. Take, for example, the question of whether the implied term is 'necessary to give business efficacy' to the contract. That formulation serves to underline two important points. The first, conveyed by the use of the word 'business', is that in considering what the instrument would have meant to a reasonable person who had knowledge of the relevant background, one assumes the notional reader will take into account the practical consequences of deciding that it means one thing or the other. In the case of an instrument such as a commercial contract, he will consider whether a different construction would frustrate the apparent business purpose of the parties . . . The second, conveyed by the use of the word 'necessary', is that it is not enough for a court to consider that the implied term expresses what it would have been reasonable for the parties to agree to. It must be satisfied that it is what the contract actually means.
>
> The danger lies, however, in detaching the phrase 'necessary to give business efficacy' from the basic process of construction of the instrument. It is frequently the case that a contract may work perfectly well in the sense that both parties can perform their express obligations, but the consequences would contradict what a reasonable person would understand the contract to mean."[83]

Rectification of articles

The court has no inherent jurisdiction to rectify the articles, even if it is proved **4–015** that they were not in accordance with the intention of the original signatories.[84]

RESOLUTIONS AND AGREEMENTS

Introduction

Under the Companies Act 2006, the articles and any resolutions and agreements **4–016** as specified in the Act constitute the company's constitutional documents.[85]

Resolutions and agreements included

The resolutions and agreements which will form part of the company's constitu- **4–017** tional documents are specified in the Act and include: (a) any special resolution;

---

[83] At 1994.
[84] *Scott v Frank F Scott (London) Ltd* [1940] Ch. 794, CA.
[85] See s.17(b).

(b) any resolution or agreement agreed to by all the members of a company that, if not so agreed to, would not have been effective for its purpose unless passed as a special resolution; (c) any resolution or agreement agreed to by all the members of a class of shareholders that, if not so agreed to, would not have been effective for its purpose unless passed by some particular majority or otherwise in some particular manner; (d) any resolution or agreement that effectively binds all members of a class of shareholders though not agreed to by all those members; (e) any other resolution or agreement brought in by virtue of any enactment.[86]

Resolutions and agreements to be sent to the Registrar

4–018　The Act goes on to say that a copy of every resolution or agreement to which the Act applies, or (in the case of a resolution or agreement that is not in writing) a written memorandum setting out its terms, must be forwarded to the Registrar within 15 days after it is passed or made.[87] Failure to do so constitutes an offence.[88]

EFFECT OF THE COMPANY'S CONSTITUTION

Special contract

4–019　The provisions of the company's constitution bind the company and its members to the same extent as if there were covenants on the part of the company and each member to observe those provisions.[89]

The members and the company

4–020　The articles (and the memorandum) form a contract binding the members to the company. A shareholder may therefore bring an action to enforce any personal rights contained in the articles but may also bring a statutory derivative action or a petition for unfairly prejudicial conduct.[90]

In *Hickman v Kent or Romney Marsh Sheep-Breeders' Association*[91] the articles provided for the reference of differences between the company and any of the members to arbitration. H, a shareholder, brought an action against the company in connection with a dispute as to his expulsion from the company, i.e. a dispute between the company and him in his capacity, as a member. The court held that the company was entitled to have the action stayed, as the articles constituted a contract between the company and its members in respect of their ordinary rights as members. Astbury J. stated that

---

[86] s.29.
[87] s.30(1).
[88] See s.30(2)(3).
[89] s.33(1). As to the special nature of what was previously CA 1985 s.14, see *Bratton Seymour Service Company Ltd v Oxburgh* [1992] B.C.L.C. 693, CA, at 698. See too R.R. Drury, "The Relative Nature of a Shareholder's Right to Enforce the Company Contract" [1986] C.L.J. 219.
[90] Ch.22, below.
[91] [1915] 1 Ch. 881.

". . . articles regulating the rights and obligations of the members generally as such do create rights and obligations between them and the company respectively".[92]

In *Beattie v E & F Beattie*[93] a dispute as to a director's right to inspect the company's books, and accounts, including minutes of board meetings, i.e. a dispute between the company and the director in his capacity as director, is not within the terms of articles like those in *Hickman's* case, even though the director is also a member. The plaintiff sued for, inter alia, a declaration in a representative capacity as a shareholder. It was then claimed that a director had received remuneration to which he was not entitled. He asked for a stay but was refused it.

The company and the members

The Act also stipulates that the company is contractually bound by the constitution. **4–021**

Thus, in *Wood v Odessa Waterworks Co*[94] a company declared a dividend and passed a resolution to pay it by giving to the shareholders debenture bonds bearing interest and redeemable at par, by an annual drawing, over 30 years. The articles empowered the company to declare a dividend "to be paid" to the shareholders. It was held that the words "to be paid" meant paid in cash, and a shareholder could restrain the company from acting on the resolution on the ground that it contravened the articles.

The courts will imply two terms into this contract insofar as it relates to the powers of the directors: (a) they must be exercised in good faith and in the interests of the company; and (b) they must be exercised fairly as between shareholders (which does not mean identically).[95]

Contract binding qua member

Members are only bound by and entitled on the above-mentioned contract qua **4–022** members, i.e. in their capacity as members.[96]

Contract binding each member

The articles (and the memorandum) constitute a contract between each individual **4–023** member and every other member but in most cases the court will not enforce the contract as between individual members,[97] it is enforceable only through the company or, if the company is being wound up, the liquidator. In *Welton v Saffery*, Lord Herschell stated that:

---

[92] At 900, per Astbury J.

[93] [1938] Ch. 708, CA.

[94] (1889) 42 Ch.D. 636. On the other hand the fact that the articles are not so executed by the company limits the time for enforcing such a contract against the company to 6 years and not the 12 years allowed for contracts under seal: *Compania de Electricidad de la Provincia de Buenos Aires Ltd, Re* [1978] 3 All E.R. 668.

[95] *Mutual Life Insurance Co of New York v The Rank Organisation Ltd* [1985] B.C.L.C. 11.

[96] *Beattie v E. & F. Beattie Ltd* [1938] Ch. 708, CA; *Eley v Positive Life Assurance Co Ltd* (1876) 1 Ex. D. 88, CA.

[97] *Salmon v Quin and Axtens Ltd* [1909] 1 Ch. 311, CA, per Farwell L.J.

"It is quite true that . . . there is no contract in terms between the individual members of the company; but the articles . . . regulate their rights inter se. Such rights can only be enforced by or against a member through the company, or through the liquidator representing the company; but . . . no member has, as between himself and another member, any right beyond that which the contract with the company gives".[98]

It seems that it is the rule in *Foss v Harbottle*[99] which prevents an individual member enforcing the contract. However, the rule is irrelevant where the articles give a member a personal right. In such a case the contract is directly enforceable by one member against another without the aid of the company.

In *Rayfield v Hands*,[100] articles of a private company provided that if a member intending to transfer his shares should inform the directors, the directors "will take the said shares equally between them at a fair value". It was held that the articles bound the defendant directors to buy the plaintiff's shares and related to the relationship between the plaintiff as a member and the defendant, not as directors, but as members of the company,[101] and it was not necessary for the company to be a party to the action.

Outsiders not bound

4–024 The provisions of the articles and the memorandum do not constitute a contract binding the company or any member to an outsider,[102] i.e. a person who is not a member of the company, or to a member in a capacity other than that of member, e.g. that of solicitor, promoter or director of the company.[103] This is on the general principle that a person who is not a party to a contract has neither rights nor liabilities under it.

In *Eley v Positive Life Assurance Co Ltd*,[104] the articles provided that E should be the solicitor to the company. He was employed as such for a time but subsequently the company ceased to employ him. The court held that E was not entitled to damages for breach of contract against the company. The articles did not create a contract between E and the company.

4–025   However, if a director takes office on the footing of an article providing for remuneration for the director, although the article is not in itself a contract between the company and the director, its terms may be implied into the contract between the company and the director.

In *New British Iron Co, Re*,[105] an article provided that the remuneration of the directors should be the annual sum of £1,000. The directors were employed and accepted office on the footing of the article. For some time the directors, who

---

[98] [1897] A.C. 299 at 315, per Lord Herschell.

[99] Below, para.

[100] [1960] Ch. 1.

[101] As is usual, the directors had shares in the company and so were members.

[102] See *Hickman v Kent or Romney Marsh Sheepbreeders Association* [1915] 1 Ch 881, at p. 900, *per* Astbury J.

[103] *Globalink Telecommunications Ltd v Wilmbury Ltd* [2002] EWHC 1988; [2003] 1 B.C.L.C. 145.

[104] (1876) 1 Ex.D. 88, CA.

[105] [1898] 1 Ch. 324. In *Globalink Telecommunications Ltd*, above, there was insufficient evidence to support an incorporation of article provisions into an external contract.

were also members, acted as directors but were not paid. The company went into liquidation. The court held that the article was embodied in the contract between the company and the directors and they were entitled to recover the arrears of remuneration.

THE OBJECTS OF THE COMPANY

Background and ultra vires

In the past,[106] it was mandatory for the memorandum of association to state the **4–026** objects of the company.[107] As Lord Parker of Waddington said in *Cotman v Brougham*,[108] the statement of the objects in the memorandum was originally intended to serve the dual purpose of protecting the subscribers (who learn from it the purposes to which their money can be applied) and of protecting persons dealing with the company (who can discover from it the extent of the company's powers).

The courts developed the ultra vires doctrine to ensure that companies only exercised powers to carry out the objects together with anything incidental thereto. Anything done which was outside the scope of the objects clause was ultra vires and void. The result of this doctrine was that objects clauses became very lengthy because companies stated all the objects they could conceivably require. Nevertheless the ultra vires doctrine continually caused unnecessary hardship for innocent third parties and introduced extreme complexity into the law. An additional "protection" for shareholders and third parties was provided by the original rule that the objects clause could not be altered except by a special Act of Parliament or a reconstruction of the company. Later, the objects could be altered but only for specified purposes, initially with the court's consent.

Statutory reform

The first EC directive[109] required a change in the law of ultra vires and this was **4–027** implemented by s.9(1) of the European Communities Act 1972[110] which later became s.35 of the Companies Act 1985. As drafted, that section proved to have serious defects and in 1985 Dan Prentice of Oxford University[111] was commissioned by the DTI[112] to write a report on the ultra vires rule.[113] This report led to major reforms in the 1989 Act and effectively abolished the ultra vires rule so far as third parties were concerned. The reforms allowed for a catch-all short-form objects clause, gave companies a general power of alteration of all such clauses,

---

[106] The CLR recommended that this requirement be abolished: see *Final Report*, para.9.10.

[107] CA 1985 s.2(1)(c).

[108] [1918] A.C. 514 at 520. See also per Lord Wrenbury at 522 and 523.

[109] Directive 68/151/EEC on Co-ordination of safeguards which are required of companies [1968] OJ L65/8.

[110] c.68.

[111] Allen & Overy Professor of Corporate Law at Oxford, 1990–2008. See John Armour & Jennifer Payne (eds), *Rationality in Company Law: Essays in Honour of DD Prentice* (2009).

[112] i.e. the predecessor of BIS.

[113] "Reform of the ultra vires doctrine". For discussion, see Brenda Hannigan, "The reform of the ultra vires rule" [1987] J.B.L. 173.

and limited even their internal effects. Most of the old law was swept away. This
has continued under the 2006 Act, which contains similar provisions, although
with further modifications, as detailed in the discussion below.

Form of the objects clause

4–028   Under the Companies Act 1985, companies were required to have an objects
clause.[114] As the result of the legacy of the ultra vires doctrine objects clauses
were often very long and contained general clauses specifying that every object
is a separate main object[115] or that the company may do, in addition to the objects
listed, anything which the directors consider can be carried on in conjunction with
its other objects.[116] Such clauses, developed in response to the courts attempts to
limit long objects clauses by discovering main objects and winding up a company
for failure of that main object, were perfectly valid.

Objects clauses under the 1989 Act

4–029   The 1989 Act provided that where the memorandum stated that the object of the
company was to carry on business as a general commercial company, that
company was deemed to be able to carry on any trade or business whatsoever and
have the power to do anything which is incidental or conducive to the conduct of
any trade or business by it.[117] The 1989 Act also substantially changed the power
of a company to alter its objects by permitting a company to alter its objects
clause by a special resolution.[118] The 1985 Act provided a mechanism whereby
dissentients[119] might, within 21 days of the passing of the special resolution,
apply to the court for the alteration of the objects to be cancelled, and then the
alteration is of no effect unless it is confirmed by the court.[120]

Objects clauses under the 2006 Act

4–030   As we have previously noted, the memorandum of association is now of minor
importance in the formation of a company.[121] This has also had an impact on the
former mandatory requirement to have an objects clause.[122] As the memorandum
now has a different function, the requirement to have an objects clause no longer
exists. Companies,[123] instead, may elect to have an objects clause which will be
contained in the articles of association. In such an event, the Act provides that

---

[114] s.2(1)(c).
[115] See, e.g. *Cotman v Brougham* [1918] A.C. 514.
[116] See, e.g. *Bell Houses Ltd v City Wall Properties Ltd* [1966] 2 Q.B. 656.
[117] s.110 (s.3A of the 1985 Act).
[118] *Ibid.* See s.4 of the 1985 Act.
[119] The application for cancellation could only be made by the holders of not less than 15 per cent in
     nominal value of the company's issued share capital or any class thereof or, if the company is not
     limited by shares, not less than 15 per cent of the members: s.5(2).
[120] See s.5(1).
[121] See para.3–019, above.
[122] CA 1985 s.2(1)(c).
[123] i.e. companies registered under the 2006 Act.

unless the articles restrict the objects of the company, its objects are unrestricted.[124] Further, where a company amends its articles so as to add, remove, or alter a statement of the company's objects it is obliged to give notice to the Registrar who is required to register it.[125] Such an amendment does not affect any rights or obligations of the company or render defective any legal proceedings by or against it.[126]

In the case of those companies formed under earlier Companies Acts, including the 1985 Act (as amended), the 2006 Act now provides that provisions (such as objects clauses) which, immediately prior to the commencement of Pt 3 of the Act,[127] were contained in the company's memorandum will henceforth be treated as provisions of the company's articles[128]—and hence subject to the provisions of this Act as to the articles, e.g. alteration.[129]

Effect of the objects clause on corporate capacity

As we have seen, the doctrine of ultra vires severely restricted the capacity of a **4–031** company in the sense that any act by the company (and its agents) outside the objects clause was ultra vires and void. Above all an ultra vires act could not be ratified—even by all the members.[130] A company could not be sued on any such act[131] and probably could not enforce it.[132] A company was, however, allowed to do things which were reasonably incidental to its stated objects.[133] Third parties were deemed to have constructive notice of the contents of the objects clause. An example of the potential injustice caused by a combination of these restrictions is *Jon Beauforte Ltd, Re.*[134] In this case, a company, authorised by its memorandum to carry on business as costumiers and gown makers, started the business of making veneered panels. This was ultra vires. They ordered and received coke for this business from coke merchants. Correspondence showed that the coke suppliers had actual notice that the coke was required for the business of veneered panel manufacturers, and since they had constructive notice of the objects clause that this was an ultra vires activity.[135] It was held that they could not prove for their debts in the company's liquidation. Nor in practice could they recover the coke, which legally remained theirs, since it had been consumed.

The ultra vires doctrine therefore proved to be both unduly restrictive on shareholders and a trap for unwary third parties. In 1986, however, its operation was

---

[124] See s.31(1).
[125] s.31(2).
[126] s.31(3).
[127] i.e. October 1, 2009.
[128] s.28(1).
[129] See para.4–005, above.
[130] *Ashbury Railway Carriage & Iron Co Ltd v Riche* (1875) L.R. 7 H.L. 653.
[131] *Ashbury Railway Carriage & Iron Co Ltd v Riche* (1875) L.R. 7 H.L. 653.
[132] *Bell Houses Ltd v City Wall Properties Ltd* [1966] 2 Q.B. 656; *Cabaret Holdings Ltd v Meeance Sports & Radio Club Inc* [1982] N.Z.L.R. 673.
[133] *Attorney General v Great Eastern Railway Co* (1880) 5 App. Cas. 473.
[134] [1953] Ch. 131.
[135] It would have been different if the coke merchant had not known that the coke was to be used for an ultra vires purpose because he could have assumed that it was for an intra vires business.

restricted by the Court of Appeal in *Rolled Steel Products Ltd v British Steel Corp*,[136] so that it only applied to the capacity of the company strictly construed. Earlier cases had decided that a company had no capacity to exercise any of its powers, e.g. to borrow or lend money, otherwise than for the authorised objects of the company. This approach was rejected in the *Rolled Steel* case[137] which held that if a company had a power in its objects clause, e.g. to give guarantees, then it had the capacity to give a guarantee for any purpose. Thus, the common law doctrine of ultra vires was finally refined so that a transaction or act would only be void for lack of corporate capacity if it was not capable of falling within the terms of the objects clause either as an object or as a power.[138]

Statutory amendments to corporate capacity

4–032 The original provision of the 1985 Act provided that in favour of a person dealing with a company in good faith any transaction decided upon by the directors was deemed to be within the capacity of the company.[139] Good faith was presumed in the absence of evidence to the contrary and the third party was not bound to enquire as to the company's capacity, reversing the doctrine of constructive notice. This section was defective in several areas: it did not protect the company, it was limited to dealings and so arguably not to gratuitous transactions,[140] it required a transaction decided on by the directors and gave no definition of good faith. In *International Sales & Agencies Ltd v Marcus*[141] it was suggested that good faith would be destroyed if the third party had actual knowledge that the transaction was ultra vires or could not in all the circumstances have been unaware of the ultra vires nature of the transaction. It was also suggested that a decision by a sole director or managing director would suffice if the full board had properly delegated the appropriate powers to him.[142]

As a result of the general dissatisfaction with the ultra vires concept and the perceived inadequacies of s.35, the 1989 Act substituted a new s.35 into the 1985 Act. This provided that "the validity of an act done by a company shall not be called into question on the ground of lack of capacity by reason of anything in the company's memorandum".[143] This subsection effectively abolished the ultra vires doctrine insofar as it affected the capacity of the company. The section went on to say that a member of a company might bring proceedings to restrain the doing of an act which but for Act would be beyond the company's capacity; but that no such proceedings would lie in respect of an act to be done in fulfilment of a legal obligation arising from a previous act of the company.[144] Further, any action by

---

[136] [1986] Ch. 246, CA.
[137] [1984] Ch. 246, CA.
[138] For a modern example of this approach see *Halifax Building Society v Meridian Housing Association Ltd* [1994] 2 B.C.L.C. 540.
[139] s.35.
[140] See, e.g. *Halt Garage, Re (1964) Ltd* [1982] 3 All E.R. 1016 at 1024, per Oliver J.
[141] [1982] 3 All E.R. 551, approved in *International Factors (N.I.) Ltd v Streeve Construction Ltd* [1984] 12 N.I.J.B.
[142] Agreement by all the directors individually would also suffice: *T.C.B. Ltd v Gray* [1987] Ch. 458.
[143] s.35(1).
[144] s.35(2).

the directors which but for the Act would be beyond the company's capacity may only be ratified by the company by special resolution.[145]

The general approach of s.35 has been retained in the 2006 Act which retains the same wording,[146] though with the substitution of "constitution" for the word "memorandum". In effect, the two provisions are substantially similar. Thus, if there is any limitation on the company's corporate capacity, whether in an objects clause in the articles (assuming the company has an objects clause), or some other kind of limitation as to the kind of transactions that the company can enter into, then any act which is carried out in contravention of such a limitation will not be invalid. There are, however, two further important differences with the 1985 Act. The first is that the provision of the 1985 Act as to members bringing proceedings to restrain an act outside the company's constitution has not been retained. This was considered unnecessary for two reasons, namely that the statement of the objects was no longer a legal requirement for the formation of a company, although a company might elect to have such a statement in the articles. The second reason is that directors under the 2006 Act are subject to a statutory duty to act in accordance with the company's constitution.[147] A further reason is that it is, relatively speaking, rather easier for members of a company to bring a statutory derivative claim in respect of any "proposed act or omission involving negligence, default, breach of duty or breach of trust by a director of the company".[148] A final point to note is that while s.35 of the 1985 Act referred to the possibility of ratification of an ultra vires act by special resolution, this possibility has not been retained in the 2006 Act.

These provisions of the Act only apply to an act done by a company. They do not deal with the question whether those acting on the company's behalf have the authority to act on the company's behalf so that it was an act of the company. The fact of the company having the necessary capacity is therefore only the first element in deciding whether the company is bound by an act. The second element, whether there is authority to act, is dealt with separately.[149]

Effect of the objects clause on shareholders' rights and directors' duties

As suggested above, a company's objects clause in addition to its effects on **4–033** corporate transactions vis-à-vis third parties, always fulfilled a role in the internal aspects of company law. As a consequence of the contractual nature of the company's constitutional documents,[150] any member would have a personal right[151] to seek an injunction to prevent the commission of any act which is outside the objects clause,[152] i.e. the investor was entitled to see that the objects

---

[145] s.35(3).

[146] See s.39(1).

[147] s.171(a). The consequences of a breach are laid down in s.178. Generally, see para.17–065.

[148] See s.260(3) and the discussion at para.22–013.

[149] See para.6–011, below.

[150] Formerly CA 1985 s.14(1). See now s. 33(1) of the 2006 Act and the discussion at paras.4–019, above.

[151] See para.22–010 below.

[152] *Colman v Eastern Counties Railway Co* (1846) 10 Beav. 1; 50 E.R. 481.

for which he invested are adhered to. The 1989 Act reforms expressly preserved this right to seek an injunction by permitting a member of a company to bring proceedings to restrain the doing of an act which but for the Act would be beyond the company's capacity.[153] However, in an important restriction, no such proceedings would lie in respect of an act to be done in fulfilment of a legal obligation arising from a previous act of the company.[154] Further, the directors, acting in the exercise of their powers, were under a duty to act both within the limits of the objects clause and bona fide for the benefit of the company.[155] These duties were owed to the company and not to individual members per se and in this connection the Act provided that, notwithstanding the new rules as to corporate capacity, "it remains the duty of the directors to observe any limitations on their powers flowing from the company's memorandum".[156]

Under the 2006 Act, it is likely that members could still avail themselves of their personal right under the articles to ensure that the company's agents comply with any restrictions as to corporate capacity in the articles. Although there is no statutory right to seek an injunction, at least in s.39 of the Act, members' rights against the directors are in a sense enhanced in a number of ways in the Act, notably by the statutory duty to act only in accordance with the company's constitution already referred to.[157] Such statutory duties are owed only to the company,[158] as was the position also at common law,[159] which would mean that such duties would only be enforceable at the behest of the company.[160] Although common law derivative actions were beset by egregious difficulties for those pursuing them,[161] the availability of a statutory derivative action under the Act[162] ought to remedy this.

---

[153] s.35(2).
[154] s.35(2).
[155] See generally, Ch.17, below.
[156] s.35(3).
[157] i.e. in s.171(a). See para.17–016, below.
[158] s.170(1).
[159] *Percival v Wright* [1902] 2 Ch. 421.
[160] Because of the rule in *Foss v Harbottle* (1843) 2 Hare 461 at 493–494; 67 E.R. 189 at 203, per Wigram V-C.
[161] See para.22–007 below.
[162] See s.260 and discussion at para.22–012, below.

CORPORATE CAPACITY

Chapter 5

PROMOTERS

Introduction

Before a company is formed and registered, there must be some persons who have **5–001** an intention to form a company, and who take the necessary steps to carry that intention into operation. Such persons are called "promoters". Promoters stand in a fiduciary position towards the company and, as a result, they owe the company certain fundamental duties.

Meaning of Term "Promoter"

The term promoter was originally defined by reference to the preparation of a **5–002** prospectus to accompany a public offer of shares only for the purposes of liability for a misstatement in a prospectus. This was repealed by the Financial Services Act 1986,[1] which used the term "promoter" but did not define it.[2] However, a promoter has been described judicially, as "one who undertakes to form a company with reference to a given project and to set it going, and who takes the necessary steps to accomplish that purpose".[3]

A company may have several promoters and, as is shown by cases such as the *Leeds Theatres* case,[4] one existing company may promote another new company. Persons who give instructions for the preparation and registration of the articles of association are promoters. So, too, are persons who obtain the directors (very often a promoter is himself a prospective director), issue a prospectus, negotiate underwriting contracts or a contract for the purchase of property by the company, or procure capital. A person may become a promoter after the company is incorporated, e.g. by issuing a prospectus or preparing listing particulars, or by procuring capital to enable the company to carry out a preliminary agreement. Whether a person is actually a promoter and, if so, the date when he became one and whether he is still one, are questions of fact.

A person who has taken no active part in the formation of a company and the raising of the necessary share capital but has left it to others to set up the company

---

[1] Itself now repealed: see the Financial Services and Markets Act 2000 (Consequential Amendments and Repeals) Order 2001 (SI 2001/3649) art.3(1)(c).
[2] Financial Services and Markets Act 2000 s.90(8). The former definition was in s.67(2)(c) of the 1985 Act, repealed by s.150(6) of the Financial Services Act 1986.
[3] *Twycross v Grant* (1877) 2 C.P.D. 469, CA, at 541, per Cockburn C.J.
[4] *Leeds and Hanley Theatres of Varieties Ltd, Re* [1902] 2 Ch. 809.

on the understanding that he will profit from the operation is a promoter.[5] However, anyone who acts merely as the employee or agent of a promoter is not himself a promoter. Thus a solicitor who merely does the legal work necessary to the formation of a company is not as such a promoter.[6]

At one time, the business of a company promoter was almost a separate business in itself, but this is not so today. Further, the increasingly strict provisions of successive Companies Acts, culminating in the Financial Services and Markets Act 2000, in relation to the issue and contents of listing particulars or a prospectus have almost eliminated the fraudulent company promoter.

POSITION AND DUTIES OF PROMOTERS

5–003 A promoter is not an agent for the company which he is forming because a company cannot have an agent before it comes into existence.[7] Furthermore, he is usually not treated as a trustee for the future company.[8] However, from the moment he acts with the company in mind, a promoter stands in a fiduciary position towards the company and therefore he must not make any secret profit out of the promotion, e.g. a profit on a sale of property to the company. These liabilities are independent of any liability for misstatements, etc. in listing particulars or a prospectus. A promoter must disclose a profit which he is making out of the promotion to either an independent board of directors,[9] or the existing and intended shareholders, e.g. by making disclosure in a prospectus.[10]

The requirement of an independent board of directors is one which, in most cases, cannot be complied with, as the promoters, or some of them, are usually the first directors of the company. In the formation of a private company, the promoter usually sells his business to a company, of which he is managing director, and in which he is the largest shareholder, but, nevertheless, the transaction cannot be impeached on the ground that there is no independent board of directors.[11]

> "After *Salomon's* case I think it is impossible to hold that it is the duty of the promoters of a company to provide it with an independent board of directors, if the real truth is disclosed to those who are induced by the promoters to join the company."[12]

Remedies for breach of duty

5–004 If a promoter fails to make full disclosure of a profit made by him out of the promotion the following remedies may be open to the company. Since the

---

[5] See *Emma Silver Mining Co Ltd v Lewis* (1879) 4 C.P.D. 396 at 408, per Lindley J., and *Tracy v Mandalay Pty Ltd* (1952–53) 88 C.L.R. 215.
[6] *Re Great Wheal Polgooth Ltd* (1883) 53 L.J. Ch.42.
[7] *Kelner v Baxter* (1866) L.R. 2 C.P. 174, para.6–001 below.
[8] *Omnium Electric Palaces Ltd v Baines* [1914] 1 Ch. 332.
[9] *Erlanger v New Sombrero Phosphate Co* (1878) 3 App.Cas. 1218, PC; *Tracy v Mandalay Pty Ltd* (1952–53) 88 C.L.R. 215.
[10] *Lagunas Nitrate Co v Lagunas Syndicate* [1899] 2 Ch. 392, CA.
[11] *Salomon v Salomon Co Ltd* [1897] A.C. 22 at 17. See above, para.1–037.
[12] *Lagunas Nitrate Co v Lagunas Syndicate* [1899] 2 Ch. 392, CA, at 426, per Lindley M.R.

promoter's duties are owed to the company the rule in *Foss v Harbottle*[13] is relevant to their enforcement.

Where the promoter has, e.g. sold his own property to the company, the company may rescind the contract and recover the purchase-money paid.

A syndicate, of which E was the head, purchased an island in the West Indies said to contain valuable mines of phosphates for £55,000. E formed a company to buy this island, and a contract was made between X., a nominee of the syndicate, and the company for its purchase at £110,000. Held, as there had been no disclosure by the promoters of the profit they were making, the company was entitled to rescind the contract and recover the purchase-money from E and the other members of the syndicate.[14]

The right of rescission may be lost in a number of ways. For example, it will be lost if the parties cannot be restored to their original positions, as where the property has been worked so that its character has been altered.[15] However, even if restitution is strictly not possible, rescission may be allowed if restitution is substantially possible. The right to rescind will also be lost if third parties have acquired rights for value, by mortgage or otherwise, under the contract.[16]

The company may compel the promoter to account for any profit he has made.   **5–005**

Intending to buy property and to form a company and resell the property to the company or another purchaser, a syndicate of four persons bought charges on the property at a discount. They afterwards bought the property for £140,000, formed a company of which they were the first directors and resold the property to the company for £180,000. As a result of this, they made a profit of £40,000 on the property and one of £20,000 on the charges which were paid off in full with the £140,000 received for the property. A prospectus was issued, disclosing the profit of £40,000 but not that of £20,000. It appears that rescission had become impossible. Held, the £20,000 was a secret profit made by a syndicate as promoters of the company and they were bound to pay it to the company.[17]

The company may sue the promoter for damages for breach of his fiduciary duty.

The F Co contracted to purchase two music halls for £24,000 and had the property conveyed to its nominee, R, intending to sell it to the T Co when formed. The F Co then promoted the T Co and agreed to sell the music halls to it for £75,000 and directed R to convey them. The board of directors of T Co was not an independent board. A prospectus was issued to the public by the T Co, giving R as the vendor, and not disclosing the interest of F Co or the profit it was making. *Held*, the prospectus should have disclosed that F Co was the real vendor and the amount of profit it was making. For breach of their fiduciary duty to those invited to take shares the promoters were liable in damages to the company and the measure of damages was the promoters' profit.[18]

---

[13] Below, Ch.17.
[14] *Erlanger v New Sombrero Phosphate Co* (1878) 3 App. Cas. 1218, PC.
[15] As in *Lagunas Nitrate Co v Lagunas Syndicate* [1899] 2 Ch. 392, CA.
[16] As in *Re Leeds and Hanley Theatres of Varieties Ltd* [1902] 2 Ch. 809, below, where the mortgagee of the property had sold it.
[17] *Gluckstein v Barnes* [1900] A.C. 240.
[18] *Leeds and Hanley Theatres of Varieties Ltd, Re* [1902] 2 Ch. 809, CA.

Where promoters sell their own property to the company, the company cannot affirm the contract and at the same time ask for an account of profits or for damages as this would be, in effect, asking the court to vary the contract of sale and order the defendants to sell their assets at a lower price.[19]

PAYMENT FOR PROMOTION SERVICES

5–006 A promoter has no right against the company to payment for his promotion services in the absence of an express contract with the company. In England such a contract will normally have to be under seal since the company cannot make a valid contract before incorporation and when the contract can be made the consideration by the promoter will normally be past.[20] In the absence of such a contract he cannot even recover from the company payments he has made in connection with the formation of the company.

Any amount or benefit paid or given within the two preceding years, or intended to be paid or given, to a promoter must normally be disclosed in a prospectus or listing particulars.[21]

SUSPENSION OF PROMOTERS

5–007 A person who has been convicted on indictment of any offence in connection with the promotion or formation of a company may have an order made against him by the court that he shall not, without leave of the court, be a director, liquidator, receiver or take part in the management of a company for a period of up to 15 years.[22]

---

[19] *Cape Breton Co, Re* (1885) 29 Ch.D. 795, CA; *Jacobus Marler Estates Ltd v Evatt* [1971] A.C. 793, PC.

[20] *Clinton's Claim* [1908] 2 Ch. 515, CA.

[21] See Ch.7, below.

[22] Company Directors Disqualification Act 1986, s.2, para.17–00, below.

Chapter 6

CORPORATE TRANSACTIONS

CONTRACTS MADE BEFORE INCORPORATION OF COMPANY

Effect on company

If, before the formation of a company, some person purports to make a contract on **6–001** its behalf, or as trustee for it, e.g. a contract for the sale of property to the company, the contract, or "preliminary agreement" as it is sometimes called, is not binding on the company when it is formed, even if the company takes the benefit of the contract. Before incorporation the company lacks capacity to make the contract[1] and an agent cannot contract on behalf of a principal who is not in existence.[2]

In *English & Colonial Produce Co Ltd, Re*[3] solicitors, on the instructions of persons who afterwards became directors of the company, prepared the memorandum and articles of association of the company, and paid the registration fees. The court held that the company was not liable to pay their costs.

Similarly, a company cannot, after incorporation, enforce a contract made in its name before incorporation, or sue for damages for breach of such a contract since it was not a party to that contract. Thus, in *Natal Land & Colonization Co Ltd v Pauline Colliery & Development Syndicate Ltd*[4] N Co agreed with a person acting on behalf of a future company, P Co, that N Co would grant a mining lease to P Co. P Co discovered coal whereupon N Co refused to grant the lease. It was held that P Co could not compel N Co to grant the lease.

Further, such a contract cannot be ratified by the company after it is incorporated—the company was not a principal with contractual capacity at the time when the contract was made—although, as is explained later, the contract may be novated.[5]

In *Kelner v Baxter*[6] the Gravesend Royal Alexandra Hotel Company Ltd was being formed to buy a hotel from K. At a time when all concerned knew that the company had not been formed, a written contract was made "on behalf of" the proposed company by A, B and C for the purchase of £900 worth of wine from

---

[1] "If somebody does not exist they cannot contract", per Harman J. in *Rover International Ltd v Cannon Film Sales Ltd* [1987] 1 W.L.R. 1597 at 1599.

[2] This does not apply to a company which contracts in a new name prior to the change of name becoming operative. Such a company is at all times in existence: *Oshkosh B'Gosh Incorporated Ltd v Dan Marbel Inc Ltd* [1989] B.C.L.C. 507.

[3] [1906] 2 Ch. 435, CA.

[4] [1904] A.C. 120, PC.

[5] See para.6–004, below.

[6] (1866) L.R. 2 C.P. 174.

K The company was formed, and the wine handed over to it and consumed, but before payment was made the company went into liquidation. It was held that A, B and C were personally liable on the contract, and no ratification could release them from their liability.

> "Where a contract is signed by one who professes to be signing 'as agent', but who has no principal existing at the time, and the contract would be altogether inoperative unless binding on the person who signed it, he is bound thereby; and a stranger cannot by a subsequent ratification relieve him from that responsibility".[7]

This situation cannot be remedied either by the operation of the doctrine of estoppel by convention. That requires an assumption of fact, i.e. that the company would be bound, by both parties to a contract prior to the "agreement". Since the company was not then in existence it could make no such assumptions.[8]

Effect on individuals

6–002 At common law, if an individual contracts as "agent"[9] for a future company, whether there is a contract between him and the other person involved depends upon whether the agent was intended to be a party to the contract.[10] That is a question of construing the terms of the written contract and does not depend simply upon the way that the individual signed the contract.[11] In *Kelner v Baxter*,[12] it was intended that A, B and C should contract personally. In *Newborne v Sensolid (Great Britain) Ltd*[13], the intention was that only the future company should contract. Tinned ham was sold to S. Ltd. The contract was "We have this day sold to you ... (Signed) Leopold Newborne (London) Ltd". The signature was typed and underneath was written "Leopold Newborne". The market price of ham fell and S. Ltd. refused to take delivery. When an action was brought it was found that Leopold Newborne (London) Ltd had not been incorporated at the time of the contract and Leopold Newborne tried to enforce the contract in his own name. It was held that neither Leopold Newborne (London) Ltd nor Leopold Newborne could enforce the contract. It was not a case of an agent undertaking to do certain things himself as agent for somebody else. It was a contract in which a company purported to sell. Leopold Newborne did not purport to contract as principal or agent—the contract purported to be made by Leopold Newborne (London) Ltd, on whose behalf it was signed by a future director. Morris L.J. stated that "This company was not in existence and ... the signature on that document, and indeed, the document itself ... is a complete nullity".[14]

---

[7] At 183, per Erle C.J.

[8] *Rover International Ltd v Cannon Film Sales Ltd* [1987] 1 W.L.R. 1597.

[9] Strictly, one cannot be agent for a principal not yet in existence.

[10] *Phonogram Ltd v Lane* [1982] Q.B. 938 at 945, per Oliver L.J. Approved in *Cotronic (UK) Ltd v Dezonie* [1991] B.C.L.C. 721, CA and *Badgerhill Properties Ltd v Cottrell* [1991] B.C.L.C. 805, CA.

[11] e.g. whether he signs "per pro" the company or "for and on behalf of the company".

[12] (1866) L.R. 2 C.P. 174, see above para.6–001.

[13] [1954] 1 Q.B.45. See also *Cotronic (UK) Ltd v Denozie* [1991] B.C.L.C. 721, CA and *Badgerhill Properties Ltd v Cottrell* [1991] B.C.L.C. 805, CA.

[14] At 52.

The position of the individual was, however, changed substantially by s.9(2) of the European Communities Act 1972, which became s.36(4) of the 1985 Act.[15] That section was repealed by the 1989 Act and replaced by s.36C of the 1985 Act[16] and is unchanged in the 2006 Act:

"A contract that purports to be made by or on behalf of a company at a time when the company has not been formed has effect, subject to any agreement to the contrary, as one made with the person purporting to act for the company or as agent for it, and he is personally liable on the contract accordingly."[17]

This means that in circumstances like those in *Newborne's* case, above, today, unless there is an agreement to the contrary, there will be a contract between the individual who purports to act for the company and the other person involved. The words "subject to any agreement to the contrary" allow for the case where there is a novation.

In *Phonogram Ltd v Lane*,[18] the Court of Appeal considered the effect of the **6–003** old s.36(4) which was identical in all relevant respects to s.51(1). They held that it rendered the individual "agent" liable even though the company was not at the time in the course of formation.[19] Further, a contract can be "purported" to be made by a company even though both parties to the contract knew that the company had not then been formed. They also considered that signing the contract as an agent, or as in the *Newborne* case, above, would not amount to an agreement to the contrary so as to avoid personal liability. Lord Denning M.R. considered that only a clear exclusion of personal liability would suffice.[20]

It used to be thought that individuals contracting on behalf of an unformed company might not be entitled to sue on the contact,[21] but this has now been resolved in *Braymist Ltd v The Wise Finance Co Ltd*.[22] W entered into an agreement with an unformed company for the purchase of a piece of land and this was signed on behalf of the company by its solicitors. Subsequently, when W refused to complete the purchase, the solicitors rescinded the agreement and brought an action for breach of contract. At first instance,[23] the judge held that the solicitors, as agents, could enforce the contract under s.36C(1). This was confirmed by the

---

[15] See the discussion in *Braymist Ltd v The Wise Finance Co Ltd* [2002] EWCA Civ 127; [2002] Ch. 273 at 283–285.

[16] Introduced by CA 1989 s.130(4).

[17] s.51(1). Section 51(2) extends this liability to deeds in England and Wales or Northern Ireland. The section applies equally to companies incorporated overseas: see the Overseas Companies (Execution of Documents and Registration of Charges) Regulations 2009 (SI 2009/1917).

[18] [1982] Q.B. 938.

[19] A contrary argument based on the French text of the Directive implemented by the 1972 Act was rejected.

[20] But signing the contract in the *Newborne* manner prevents the individual enforcing the contract: *Cotronic (UK) Ltd v Denozie* [1991] B.C.L.C. 721.

[21] See *Cotronic (UK) Ltd v Denozie* [1991] B.C.L.C. 721; *Badgerhill Properties Ltd v Cottrell* [1991] B.C.L.C. 805.

[22] [2002] EWCA Civ 127; [2002] Ch. 273, CA.

[23] *The Times*, March 27, 2001.

Court of Appeal, the majority[24] of whom were of the view that s.36C(1) not only made a party who entered into a contract as agent for an unformed company personally liable on the contract, it also entitled the agent to enforce the contract himself.[25] In so far as there were any further difficulties arising from this, such as the identity of the contracting party,[26] this could be dealt with on ordinary common law principles.[27] On the facts, as it was clear that the identity of the seller of the land had been of no importance to W, the solicitors could enforce the agreement.[28]

Section 51(1) only applies, however, to a contract made on behalf of a company which has not been formed. Thus it has been held not to apply to a contract made on behalf of a company which no longer existed[29] or on behalf of a company which had been formed but was not properly named in the contract.[30]

New contract after incorporation—novation

6–004   Of course, a company may, after incorporation enter into a new contract with the other party to the same effect as a contract made on its behalf before incorporation, in which event there is a novation, i.e. the old contract is discharged and replaced by the new. Such a new contract may be inferred from the acts of the parties after incorporation.

In *Howard v Patent Ivory Manufacturing Co*[31] J had agreed with W, acting on behalf of a company about to be formed, to sell certain property to the company. After the company's incorporation, the directors resolved to adopt the agreement, and to accept J's offer to take part of the purchase-money in debentures instead of cash. The court held that a contract was entered into by the company with J to the effect of the previous agreement as subsequently modified.

However, such a new contract will not be inferred if the acts of the company after incorporation are due to the mistaken belief that it is bound by the contract made before incorporation. Thus, in *Northumberland Avenue Hotel Co, Re*[32] a contract was made between W and D, who was acting on behalf of an intended company, for the grant of a lease to the company. The company, on its formation, entered on the land the subject of the lease and began to erect buildings on it but did not make any fresh agreement with respect to the lease. The court held that the agreement, being made before the formation of the company, was not binding on the company, and was incapable of ratification; and the acts of the company were done in the erroneous belief that the agreement was binding on the company and not evidence of a fresh agreement between W and the company.

---

[24] Arden L.J. considered that parliament had not intended s. 51(1) to determine the rules which should apply where an agent made a contract as agent on behalf of a principal then claimed to enforce the contract: [2002] Ch. 273, CA, at p.289.

[25] At p.291.

[26] See, e.g. at p.293.

[27] The case law is referred to in the judgment of Arden L.J.: at pp.286–288.

[28] Judge L.J. confirmed that the normal incidents appropriate to any contract applied equally to deemed or statutory contracts, such as that created by s.51(1): at p.293.

[29] *Cotronic (UK) Ltd v Denozie* [1991] B.C.L.C. 721.

[30] *Badgerhill Properties Ltd v Cottrell* [1991] B.C.L.C. 805.

[31] (1888) 38 Ch.D. 156.

[32] [1886] 33 Ch.D. 16, CA.

Modern practice

Agreements to sell property to a company about to be formed are not now, as a **6–005** rule, made with a person expressed to be acting on behalf of the company, because of the liability incurred by such person, and the absence of liability incurred by the company unless there is a novation. Although the other party will not be bound before the company is formed, the modern practice is for the promoters[33] to have prepared, before the company is incorporated, a draft agreement to which the company is expressed to be a party, and for the agreement to be executed by the other party and on behalf of the company after incorporation, pursuant to a clause in the company's memorandum to that effect. If, as is common, a company is being formed to acquire the promoters' business, it does not matter that the promoters are not bound.

Contracts made prior to commencement of business

Any contract made by a public company after it is incorporated but before it is **6–006** entitled to commence business[34] is nevertheless valid, but in such cases if the company fails to comply with its obligations within 21 days of being asked to do so the directors are liable to compensate the other party for any loss or damage consequent on its inability to commence business.[35]

FORM OF CONTRACTS

Introduction

A company in England and Wales or Northern Ireland may make contracts either **6–007** in writing under its common seal or by an agent acting within his authority, express or implied, on the company's behalf.[36] The rules as to the form of contracts for companies are the same as those for individuals, e.g. as to whether the contract needs to be in writing or under seal or can be made orally.

Execution of documents—England and Wales and Northern Ireland

A company may execute any document by affixing its common seal.[37] However, a **6–008** company is not required to have a common seal[38] and so, alternatively, a document

---

[33] Above, Ch.5.

[34] See s.761, para.3–006, above.

[35] s.767(3).

[36] s.43(1). This section together with s.44, applies with modifications to overseas companies: the Overseas Companies (Execution of Documents and Registration of Charges) Regulations 2009 (SI 2009/1917).

[37] s.44(1)(a). It has been held, however, that there is nothing in s.44 which requires a company to use its registered name rather then its trading name in the body of a deed or bond. Accordingly, on the facts, a contractor was held entitled to enforce the bond against a surety: *OTV Birwelco Ltd v Technical and General Guarantee Co Ltd* [2002] EWHC 2240 (TTC); [2002] 2 B.C.L.C. 723.

[38] s.45(1).

may be executed by signature.[39] A document will be validly executed by a company if it is signed on behalf of the company by two authorised signatories, or by a director of the company in the presence of a witness who attests the signature.[40] The authorised signatories for this purpose are every director of the company and in the case of a private company with a secretary or a public company, the secretary (or any joint secretary) of the company.[41]

A document which is signed in this way expressed, in whatever words, to be executed by the company has the same effect as if executed under the common seal of the company.[42]

To protect third parties purchasers acting in good faith for valuable consideration,[43] a document so signed will be deemed to have been duly executed by a company.[44] Thus third parties need not investigate the validity of the appointment of those signing the document.[45]

Use of the seal

6–009   Art. 49 of the Model Articles for Private Companies Limited by Shares provides as follows:[46]

1. any common seal may only be used by the authority of the directors;

2. the directors may decide by what means and in what form any common seal is to be used;

3. unless otherwise decided by the directors, if the company has a common seal and it is affixed to a document, the document must also be signed by at least one authorised person in the presence of a witness who attests the signature;

4. for the purposes of this article, an authorised person is—

   (a) any director of the company;
   (b) the company secretary (if any); or
   (c) any person authorised by the directors for the purpose of signing documents to which the common seal is applied.

A company which continues to have a common seal may have an official seal for use outside the UK.[47] The official seal must be a facsimile of the company's common seal, with the addition on its face of the name of the place or places where it is to be used.[48] The official seal has the same effect as the company's

---

[39] s.44(1)(b).
[40] s.44(2).
[41] s.44(3).
[42] s.44(4).
[43] Including lessees and mortgagees: s.44(5).
[44] s.44(5).
[45] This is similar to the general protection given to conveyancers generally in the Law of Property Act 1925 s.74.
[46] See too art.81 of the Model Articles for Public Companies.
[47] s.49(1).
[48] s.49(2).

common seal.[49] A company which continues to have a common seal may have an official seal for use in sealing securities issued by the company and for sealing documents creating or evidencing securities issued by the company.[50] This official seal must be a facsimile of the common seal of the company with the addition on its face of the word "Securities".[51]

Bills of exchange

Bills of exchange and promissory notes can be drawn, accepted or indorsed on behalf of a company by any person acting under the company's authority.[52] When a director signs the modern form of company cheque with the company name and account number printed on it, he has been held to be signing only as an agent and is not personally liable on the cheque, even though he has not expressly signed on behalf of the company or as its agent.[53] **6–010**

TRANSACTIONS BY AGENCY

Introduction

Unless a company contracts in writing using its common seal, or the equivalent procedures discussed in the previous section, it can only enter into a transaction through the medium of its human agents, including its directors[54] and company secretary,[55] or others to whom authority is delegated. The transaction made by an agent acting on behalf of the company must be those of an agent who either has authority to bind the company to that transaction at the time or whose actions are subsequently validly ratified by the company. In general, therefore, the central question is whether the agent has the requisite authority to bind the company (his principal). In this respect companies are no different from individuals as the ordinary rules of agency apply as to establishing authority. But companies are artificial persons with a corporate constitution. We have already seen that the objects clause in the memorandum used to restrict the capacity of the company itself to enter into transactions which were outside that clause and a company could not authorise an agent to do what it itself had no capacity to effect.[56] The Act removes any such constitutional restrictions based solely on corporate capacity[57] but the articles may equally restrict the authority of a company's agents to act on its behalf. In such a case any person dealing with the company would not be able to rely on an agent having authority if the transaction was contrary to the company's constitution, e.g. if it was contrary to a restriction in the articles. **6–011**

---

[49] s.49(3).
[50] s.50(1).
[51] s.50(2).
[52] s.52.
[53] *Bondina Ltd v Rollaway Shower Blinds* [1986] 1 W.L.R. 517, CA.
[54] See Ch.17, below.
[55] See Ch.18, below.
[56] See para.4–031 above.
[57] s.39(1)—as did s.35 of the 1985 Act. See the discussion at para.4–032, above.

Limitations under the company's constitution—background

6–012   The effect of company law on the general law of agency therefore has been that even if an agent is otherwise acting within his authority to bind the company, a third party will not be able to enforce the transaction if the agent was acting contrary to the company's constitution. Since a third party was deemed to have constructive notice of all the company's registered documents, including the articles, he could not rely on the agent having authority where the act was contrary to such documents.[58] This doctrine was, however, subject to an exception, known as the rule in *Royal British Bank v Turquand*,[59] whereby if an agent was acting apparently consistently with the company's constitution, the third party was not affected by any internal irregularity, e.g. the lack of disclosure of a director's interest in a contract to the board as required by the articles, since he could not have discovered whether such disclosure had or had not been made.[60] Third parties did not have constructive notice of matters not on the register.[61] Only actual notice of such an irregularity would affect the transaction.[62]

This situation was substantially changed, however, in 1972 by s.9(1) of the European Communities Act 1972, which became s.35 of the 1985 Act. That section, which attempted to remove the limits on corporate capacity, also restricted the effect of limitations on the authority of the company's agents arising from the company's constitution. It suffered from serious defects, however, and was repealed by the 1989 Act. The 1989 Act substituted a new s.35 and added new s.35A and s.35B into the 1985 Act. These new sections applied as to the effects of the company's constitution on the authority of a company's agents as from 1991 onwards. The 2006 Act has now replaced these provisions, though retaining much of the substance.

Limitations under the company's constitution—the current law

6–013   We have already seen that nothing in a company's constitution can affect the capacity of a company to enter into a transaction.[63] However the Act also removes any constitutional limitations on the powers of the board of directors and those authorised by them to act on behalf of the company so far as bona fide third parties are concerned, whilst preserving the existing internal rights of members to control the directors if they do act contrary to the company's constitution. The

---

[58] "If [third parties] do not choose to acquaint themselves with the powers of the directors, it is their own fault, and if they give credit to any unauthorised persons they must be contented to look to them only, and not to the company at large":

per Lord Wensleydale in *Ernest v Nicholls* (1857) 6 HL Cas. 401 at 491; 10 E.R. 1358.

[59] (1856) 6 El. & Bl. 327; 119 E.R. 886.

[60] per Jervis C.J. at 332; 119. E.R. 888. See too *Cowan de Groot Properties Ltd v Eagle Trust Plc* [1991] B.C.L.C. 1045.

[61] Thus whether or not an ordinary resolution had been passed would not matter since there is no requirement to register an ordinary resolution, whereas the lack of a required special resolution authorising the deal would destroy the agent's authority—special resolutions must be registered.

[62] But see para.6–025, below.

[63] See s.39(1) and the discussion in para.4–032.

position is different, however, if the third party is himself a director (or an associate of the director) of the company concerned.[64]

Section 41(1) provides that:

"In favour of a person dealing with a company in good faith, the power of the directors[65] to bind the company, or authorise others to do so, shall be deemed to be free of any limitation under the company's constitution."

The policy of the section was described as follows by Carnwath L.J.:

"The general policy seems to be that, if a document is put forward as a decision of the board by someone appearing to act on behalf of the company, in circumstances where there is no reason to doubt its authenticity, a person dealing with the company in good faith should be able to take it at face value".[66]

Putting this another way, the section removes any restrictions imposed upon the authority of the directors, either to act themselves or to empower others to act, by the company's constitution if the third party is dealing in good faith. If the section applies the sole question is whether the agent was acting within his authority irrespective of the company's constitution.

The section only applies in favour of a third party—"a person"—who deals with a company. While this does not include the company and its members,[67] it seems that a third party could include a director of a company.[68] Of course, the company, like any other principal, may always ratify any agent's acts, unless they are illegal, and then enforce the transaction. Such ratification will need to be by special resolution only if the transaction is contrary to a provision in the articles since a special resolution would be required to alter such a provision.[69]

The third party must be "dealing with a company" and the Act provides that **6–014** anyone who is a party to any transaction[70] or other act to which the company is a party is dealing with that company.[71] The use of the words "transaction" and "act" seem to indicate that gratuitous acts will be included. It has been established that a third-party non-member will not "deal with" a company for the purposes of the

---

[64] See s.41, para.6–016 below.
[65] Note that s.35A(1) of the 1985 Act contained the wording "board of directors"; below, para.6–014.
[66] *Smith v Henniker-Major & Co* [2002] EWHC Civ 762; [2003] Ch. 182, CA, at 213, citing *Friedrich Haagga GmbH* [1974] E.C.R. 1201 at 1210 (per Advocate General Mayras).
[67] It has been held, overruling the court below (see [2003] EWHC 1507; [2003] 1 W.L.R. 2360), that a member receiving a bonus share issue is not a "person": *EIC Services Ltd v Phipps* [2004] EWCA Civ 1069, [2004] 2 B.C.L.C. 589, CA.
[68] See *Smith v Henniker-Major & Co* [2002] EWCA Civ 762; [2003] Ch. 132, CA, at 213. But cf. Schiemann L.J. at 215.
[69] i.e. under s.21(1).
[70] See *T.C.B. Ltd v Gray* [1986] Ch. 621 for the court's views as to what constitutes a transaction in this context.
[71] s.40(2)(a). See, e.g. *International Sales and Agencies Ltd v Marcus* [1982] 3 All E.R. 551; *Halt Garage (1964) Ltd, Re* [1982] 3 All E.R. 1016; *International Factors (N.I.) Ltd v Streeve Construction Ltd* [1984] 12 N.I.J.B.

section merely because the company receives and registers a transfer of shares.[72] On the other hand, the grant of a debenture and of an option agreed by the board of directors[73] will be a "transaction" for the purpose of the section.[74]

The third party dealing with a company must be acting in good faith.[75] This requirement is strengthened by a presumption of good faith in his favour unless the contrary is proved,[76] and the provision which states that the third party is not bound to enquire whether a transaction[77] is subject to any limitation on the powers of the directors to bind the company or authorise others to do so.[78] The Act further states that bad faith is not to be assumed simply because the third party knew that the act was contrary to the directors' powers under the constitution.[79] This was intended to reverse the judicial interpretation of the phrase in the original version of s.35 of the 1985 Act that good faith would be defeated if the third party actually knew or could not in all the circumstances have been unaware of the defect.[80] Something more than mere awareness is now required, presumably understanding, although it is unclear whether this is to be subjectively or objectively tested. What was intended no doubt was a distinction between notice and knowledge, with only the latter counting, as it would for liability for receipt of trust property under constructive trust.[81] The wording of the section is such, however, that a third party may on the one hand be able to plead the validity of the transaction against the company on the basis that, although he has objective but not subjective knowledge of the defect, that is not enough to defeat a presumption of good faith, whilst on the other hand he may be liable to the company as a constructive trustee under the doctrine of knowing receipt because he has such objective knowledge of the defect. If the third party is not acting in good faith, the company may always ratify the transaction either by an ordinary resolution, or by special resolution if the defect relates to the articles.

The Act states that in favour of a third party, the power of the directors to bind the company or authorise others to do so are to be free of any limitations under the company's constitution.[82] A company's constitution would include its

---

[72] In such a case, it was doubted whether the company was in any "meaningful sense" a party to the transaction or act, which had taken place between a notional transferor and the claimant: *Cottrell v King* [2004] EWHC 397 (Ch); [2004] 2 B.C.L.C. 413 at 421.

[73] Albeit that there was, inter alia, an alleged failure to give notice to all of the special directors of these meetings.

[74] *Ford v Polymer Vision Ltd* [2009] EWHC 945 (Ch); [2009] 2 B.C.L.C 160.

[75] s.40(1).

[76] s.40(2)(b)(ii).

[77] But not in this case an act.

[78] s.40(2)(b)(i).

[79] s.40(2)(b)(iii).

[80] *International Sales and Agencies Ltd v Marcus* [1982] 3 All E.R. 551, approved in *International Factors (N.I.) Ltd v Streeve Construction Ltd* [1984] 12 N.I.J.B.

[81] *El Ajou v Dollar Land Holdings Plc* [1994] 1 B.C.L.C. 464, CA; *Brown v Bennett* [1999] 1 B.C.L.C. 649, CA; *Crown Dilmun v Sutton* [2004] EWHC 52; [2004] 1 B.C.L.C. 468. It may be that the criteria for liability as a constructive trustee for "knowing receipt" will be whether dishonesty can be shown. That test has been applied to the related liability for "knowing assistance": *Royal Brunei Airlines v Tan* [1995] 2 A.C. 378, PC; *Twinsectra Ltd v Yardley* [2002] UKHL 12; [2002] 2 A.C. 164. For fuller discussion, see para.17–070, below.

[82] A failure properly to call two meetings has been held to be within the scope of the expression "limitation under the company's constitution" in s.40(1): see *Ford v Polymer Vision Ltd* [2009] EWHC 945 (Ch); [2009] 2 B.C.L.C 160 at [78] per Blackburne J.

articles,[83] any resolution of the company or of any class of its shareholders,[84] and any shareholder agreement.[85]

As previously noted,[86] there is a potentially important change in the wording of s.40(1) when compared with the wording of s.35A(1) of the 1985 Act. The 1985 Act provision referred to the "power of the board of directors", whereas the new provision merely refers to the "power of the directors". On one view, this changed wording is intended to widen the application of the provision such as to effectively permit individual directors to commit the company to obligations with third parties acting in good faith. However, as this was not covered in any way in the parliamentary debates, in the explanatory notes, or indeed by the CLR, it is submitted that "power of the directors" should, in the absence of judicial guidance, be taken to be a reference to the board acting as such. Thus, it is submitted that the freedom given by s.40(1) should apply to any acts of the directors as a whole or of any agent to whom they have delegated the transaction expressly or impliedly. It should not apply to the powers of a single director without authorisation from the board.[87] The section is not intended to extend the authority of an agent, simply to remove fetters if he would otherwise have authority to bind the company.

Internal consequences

Any limitations on the powers of the directors contained in the company's consti- **6–015** tution remain binding on the directors as a statutory limitation on their powers[88] and a contractual right for the members. The liberalisation of the effects of such limitations on third parties under s.40 does not affect any right of the members to petition for an injunction preventing any breach of their powers by the directors or the liability of the directors and others for such breaches.[89] No injunction can be granted, however, if the company is already legally obliged to carry out the transactions.[90]

Directors and their associates as third parties

The general rule, discussed above, that if the third party dealing with the company **6–016** is in good faith no restrictions imposed upon the company's directors by the company's constitution will affect him, is modified where that third party is himself a director or a person connected with that director of the company or of its holding company.[91] This is emphasised by s.40(6) which, inter alia, provides

---

[83] See s.17(a).

[84] See s.40(3)(a).

[85] s.40(3)(b). All but special resolutions were covered by the rule in *Turquand's* case which is still valid, in any event.

[86] Para.6–013, above.

[87] By analogy with the decision in *Mitchell & Hobbs (UK) Ltd v Mill* [1996] 2 B.C.L.C. 102 on directors' powers under the articles.

[88] See s.171(a).

[89] s.40(4). Unlike, however, the position with respect to the company's capacity: see para.4–032, above.

[90] *ibid.*

[91] For persons connected with a director, see s.252 (s.41(7)(b)).

that that section "has effect subject to" s.41. There are two issues to be considered. The first is whether, so far as s.40 is concerned, a director can be person "dealing with a company". The second is the scope of s.41.

The first issue arose on the special facts of the case of *Smith v Henniker-Major & Co.*[92] The issue here was whether the chairman of the board of a company, S, who purported to act as an inquorate board[93] meeting to assign the company's rights of action to himself, could rely on the protection afforded by s.40(1). Although the transaction was one in which S clearly had a self-interest, he was seeking to combat the misconduct of two of his fellow directors from making off with a corporate opportunity. At first instance,[94] the judge concluded that s.40 only applied to a properly constituted board, which was a pre-condition to the exercise of board power, and so the section was not available to S. Although agreeing with the outcome and dismissing the appeal, the Court of Appeal was nevertheless divided. All the judges concluded that the phrase "person dealing with a company" was wide enough to include a director,[95] but differed as to the impact of this on S.[96] The majority thought that, because S was not simply a director dealing with the company, but the chairman of the board, he was under a duty to ensure that the company's constitution was properly applied. He could not seek to turn a decision which had no validity under the company's constitution into one of the board of directors properly convened.

The second issue concerns the scope of the section which applies to a transaction with a company if or to the extent that its validity depends on s.40.[97] Thus, where a director or a person connected with him is a third party and the directors exceed any limitation on their powers under the company's constitution, then the transaction[98] is voidable at the instance of the company.[99] The transaction remains valid, however, until it is avoided by the company, unless it is void for some reason (e.g. if it is illegal under some Act or because it infringes the equitable rules imposing liability for knowing assistance in a breach of fiduciary duty or for knowing receipt of trust property).[100] The purpose of s. 41 was interpreted as follows by one judge:

". . . it seems to me that the purpose of Section [41] is to protect a company in circumstances where its directors exceed their powers in connection with transactions entered into by the Company with one or more of their number (or their associates) to the disadvantage of the Company and to the advantage of one or more of the directors (or associates). It is true that the effect of the section is wider than that, and that it may well have been intended to ensure that directors are penalized if they fail to behave with particular propriety in connection

---

[92] [2002] EWCA Civ 762; [2003] Ch. 182, CA. Carnwath L.J. described the facts as "quite exceptional" (at 214).

[93] The board meeting was attended by S only.

[94] [2002] B.C.C. 544.

[95] [2002] EWCA Civ 762; [2003] Ch. 182, CA, at 213 and 216 per Carnwath L.J. and Schiemann L.J. respectively).

[96] Robert Walker L.J. dissenting. See especially at 198.

[97] s.41(1).

[98] Defined so as to include any "act": see s.41(7)(a).

[99] s.41(2).

[100] s.41(1).

with transactions between the company and themselves. However, I do not think that detracts from the main mischief at which the Section is directed."[101]

The company will lose the right to rescind (avoid) the transaction in any of the **6–017** following circumstances:[102] (i) restitution of property supplied is no longer possible; (ii) the company is indemnified against any loss or damage arising from the transaction; (iii) bona fide purchasers without actual notice of the defect have acquired rights which would be affected by the avoidance, e.g. if the subject matter has been deposited as security with a bank; or (iv) the transaction is affirmed by the company. It is important to remember that to be valid the transaction does not need to be ratified in this way, it is valid unless avoided by the company. The right to rescind or avoid a transaction may be limited under the general law, e.g. by undue delay.

Where there are two (or more) persons dealing with a company, one of whom is a director and the other is neither a director nor connected with one, and where that second person is dealing in good faith then he may continue to rely on the protection given by s.40, above, although the director will be subject to s.41. To avoid the difficult situation of a transaction which is valid for one person under s.40 but voidable against another (the director) under s.41, either the third party or the company may apply to the court to settle the matter. The court may then affirm the transaction as a whole, set it aside on just terms or sever it.[103]

Whether or not the transaction is avoided, any party to the transaction and any director who authorised the transaction must account to the company for any gain arising from the transaction and indemnify the company against any loss.[104] The company may, however, waive this right by the appropriate resolution.

Agency—persons acting in good faith

If the outsider is dealing with the company in good faith,[105] as defined in s.40, he **6–018** will be able to enforce any contract made by an agent on the company's behalf if that agent was acting within his authority, irrespective of any limitations on his powers under the company's constitution. If the outsider is not acting in good faith, the position is different.[106] An agent may bind his principal (in this case the company) if he has acted within his actual, implied or apparent authority.

Agency—actual authority

An individual director or committee of the board may be specifically authorised by **6–019** the board of directors to make a particular contract on behalf of the company.[107]

---

[101] *Torvale Group Ltd, Re* [1999] 2 B.C.L.C. 605 at 622, per Neuberger J. See too *Smith v Henniker-Major & Co* [2002] EWCA Civ 762; [2003] Ch. 182, CA, at 216, per Schiemann L.J.

[102] s.41(4).

[103] s.41(6). See *Re Torvale Group Ltd* [1999] 2 B.C.L.C. 605, where the court validated certain scheme debentures.

[104] s.41(3).

[105] Good faith has been described as the "touchstone" for the third party's reliance: see *Ford v Polymer Vision Ltd* [2009] EWHC 945 (Ch); [2009] 2 B.C.L.C 160, at [73] per Blackburne J.

[106] Below, para.6–025.

[107] Or a board of directors may pass a resolution authorising two of their number to sign cheques: per Lord Denning M.R. in *Hely-Hutchinson v Brayhead Ltd* [1968] 1 Q.B. 549, CA, at 583.

Alternatively, this may be defined in the individual director's contract of employment.[108] As a matter of general agency law, a grant of actual authority would be implied as being subject to a condition that it is to be exercised honestly and on behalf of the principal.[109] In *Rolled Steel Products (Holdings) Ltd v British Steel Corp*[110] Slade L.J. stated that the directors had no actual authority to exercise any express or implied power of the company other than for the purposes of the company as set out in the memorandum; although if the shareholders unanimously consented this might not be so. Browne-Wilkinson L.J. expressed no opinion on this point and it would seem that on agency principles a simple majority will suffice to give the directors such actual authority. Whether the directors are then acting in breach of their fiduciary duties is a separate question which does not per se affect the outsider.[111]

Agency—implied authority

6–020   A director may, under a power in the articles, be appointed to an office, e.g. that of managing director,[112] which carries with it authority to make certain contracts on behalf of the company.[113] However, the question of implication does not stop there and authority may be implied from the conduct of the parties and the circumstances of the case.[114] A person with actual authority to obtain quotations of prices has no implied authority to communicate acceptance of such quotes where no decision to purchase has been made by his principal—at most such a person may have apparent authority.[115] On the other hand, a director will have implied authority to enter into transactions where these are ordinarily incidental to his duties. Thus, where the terms of a director's contract of employment were potentially ambiguous, a director was nevertheless still held to have implied authority to enter into commission agreements generally, such that his company was held liable on profits on sales to another company.[116]

Agency—apparent authority

6–021   A company is also bound by the acts of an agent acting within his apparent authority[117] where he lacks actual authority (although actual authority and apparent

---

[108] As in *SMC Electronics Ltd v Akhter Computers Ltd* [2001] 1 B.C.L.C. 433, CA.

[109] See *Lysaght Bros & Co Ltd v Falk* (1905) 2 C.L.R. 421; *Hopkins v TL Dallas Group Ltd* [2004] EWHC 1379 (Ch); [2005] 1 B.C.L.C. 543 573.

[110] [1986] Ch. 246, CA.

[111] Below, Ch.17.

[112] A managing director's functions are not fixed by law but depend on the terms of his appointment: see *Harold Holdsworth & Co (Wakefield) Ltd v Caddies* [1955] 1 W.L.R. 352, HL.

[113] per Willmer L.J. in *Freeman & Lockyer v Buckhurst Park Properties (Mangal) Ltd* [1964] 2 Q.B. 480, CA, at 488, 489. Diplock L.J. agreed.

[114] As in *Hely-Hutchinson v Brayhead Ltd* [1968] 1 Q.B. 549, CA. See too *Fusion Interactive Communication Solutions Ltd v Venture Investment Placement Ltd* [2005] EWHC 224 (Ch); [2005] 2 B.C.L.C. 250.

[115] *Crabtree-Vickers Pty Ltd v Australia Direct Mail Advertising Co Pty Ltd* (1976) 50 A.L.J.R. 203, following *Freeman & Lockyer v Buckhurst Park Properties (Mangal) Ltd* [1964] 2 Q.B. 480, CA, and *Turquand's* case.

[116] *SMC Electronics Ltd v Akhter Computers Ltd* [2001] B.C.L.C. 433, CA.

[117] *Panorama Developments (Guildford) Ltd v Fidelis Furnishing Fabrics Ltd* [1971] 2 Q.B. 711, CA, where the secretary had apparent authority to hire cars on behalf of the company.

authority are not mutually exclusive and may often co-exist). It has been said that apparent authority is a form of estoppel by implied representation.[118] Thus an outsider may be protected where an individual director acts on behalf of the company without actual authority but with apparent authority, which apparent authority may arise from a representation that he has authority made by the board of directors or such a representation contained in the company's public documents.[119] In *Rolled Steel Products (Holdings) Ltd v British Steel Corp.*,[120] Slade L.J. thought that the directors would have such authority in relation to any transaction which falls within the company's express or implied powers. In such a case the company will be bound if the other party can prove:

1. that he was induced to make the contract by the agent being held out as occupying a certain position in the company;

2. that the representation, which is usually by conduct, was made by the person with actual authority to manage the company, generally or in respect of the matters to which the contract relates, who are usually the board of directors;[121] and

3. that the contract was either one which a person in the position which the agent was held out as occupying would usually have actual authority to make or one which the company had by its conduct as a whole represented that he had authority to make.[122]

Condition 2. is due to the fact that the principal, the company, is not a natural person.

In *Hely-Hutchinson v Brayhead Ltd*[123] R, the chairman of the directors of the defendant company, B Ltd, acted as its de facto managing director. The board knew of and acquiesced in that and the articles of B Ltd empowered the board to appoint a managing director. H was the chairman and managing director of a public company, P Ltd, which needed financial assistance. B Ltd was prepared to help and accordingly in January, 1965 B Ltd bought shares in P Ltd from H for £100,000 and proposed to inject £150,000 into P Ltd. H became a director of B Ltd but never saw its memorandum and articles and did not attend board meetings until May 19, 1965. After that meeting, R and H agreed that H would put more money into P Ltd if B Ltd would secure his position. R, on behalf of B Ltd, signed letters to H in which B Ltd purported to indemnify H against loss on his guarantee of a bank loan of £50,000 to P Ltd and to guarantee a loan by H to P Ltd. H then advanced £45,000 to P Ltd. When P Ltd went into liquidation, H had to honour his guarantee and he claimed the £50,000 and the £45,000 from B Ltd. B Ltd denied liability and said that R had no authority to sign the letters (and that

---

[118] *Freeman & Lockyer v Buckhurst Park Properties (Mangal) Ltd* [1964] 2 Q.B. 480, CA, at 498, 503 (per Pearson L.J. and Diplock L.J., respectively). See now also *ING Re (UK) Ltd v R & V Versicherung AG* [2006] EWHC 1544 (Comm); [2007] 1 B.C.L.C. 108.

[119] See *Lovett v Carson Country Homes Ltd* [2009] EWHC 1143 (Ch); [2009] 2 B.C.L.C. 196.

[120] [1986] Ch. 246.

[121] But occasionally the shareholders: *Mahony v East Holyford Mining Co* (1875) L.R. 7 H.L. 869.

[122] *Ebeed v Soplex Wholesale Supplies Ltd* [1985] B.C.L.C. 404, CA. Usually these will be the same.

[123] [1968] 1 Q.B. 549, CA, applying *Freeman & Lockyer v Buckhurst Park Properties (Mangal) Ltd* [1964] 2 Q.B. 480, CA.

the contracts were unenforceable for non-disclosure of H's interest in accordance with s. 182). It was held that that on the facts R had actual authority implied from the conduct of the parties and the circumstances of the case to enter into the contracts with H (and that it was too late to avoid them for non-disclosure of H's interest as required by the articles).

In *Freeman & Lockyer v Buckhurst Park Properties (Mangal) Ltd*[124] K, a director, was never appointed managing director but, to the knowledge of the board, he acted as such. On behalf of the company he instructed architects to do certain work in connection with the estate. The court held that the company was bound by the contract and liable for the architects' fees. K had apparent authority because he had been held out by the board as managing director and, therefore, as having authority to do what a managing director would usually be authorised to do on behalf of the company, and this act was within the usual authority of a managing director. Accordingly, the plaintiffs could assume that he had been properly appointed.

In *Mahony v East Holyford Mining Co*[125] the persons who signed the articles of a company, and who under the articles were entitled to appoint directors, treated some of themselves as directors although there was no proper appointment. The articles provided that cheques should be signed as directed by the board. The person acting as secretary informed the company's bank that the "board" had resolved that cheques should be signed by two of three named directors and countersigned by the secretary. The bank acted on the communication and honoured cheques so signed. The court held that the bank was entitled to honour the cheques and was not liable to refund the money paid. The rule in *Turquand's* case applied.

6–022 The outsider cannot, as a rule,[126] rely on the agent's own representation that he has authority.[127] Also, any representation must be made by a person with "actual" authority to manage the business. Thus if the representation is made by someone with no such authority the outsider cannot rely on it.

In *British Bank of the Middle East v Sun Life Assurance of Canada (UK) Ltd*[128] sales representative, with the title of "unit manager", purported to bind his company to repay sums advanced by the bank to another company. He had no actual or apparent authority to do so. The bank sought confirmation from the company's "general manager" of its City branch. He confirmed the "unit manager's" authority, but he himself had no authority to make loans. It was held that the bank could not rely on the general manager's statements as to the unit manager's authority.

6–023 Where the outsider relies on a representation by the board of directors it is of course not necessary that he should actually have inspected the company's public

[124] [1964] 2 Q.B. 480, CA. Applying *Biggerstaff v Rowatt's Wharf Ltd* [1896] 2 Ch. 93, CA, and *British Thomson-Houston Co v Federated European Bank Ltd* [1932] 2 K.B. 176, CA. See also *Clay Hill Brick Co Ltd v Rawlings* [1938] 4 All E.R. 100; *Rhodian River Shipping Co S.A. v Halla Maritime Corp* [1984] B.C.L.C. 139.

[125] (1875) L.R. 7 H.L. 869.

[126] See *Crabree-Vickers Pty Ltd v Australia Direct Mail Advertising Co Pty Ltd* (1976) 50 A.L.J.R. 203.

[127] Per Diplock L.J. in *Freeman & Lockyer v Buckhurst Park Properties (Mangal) Ltd* [1964] 2 Q.B. 480, CA, at 505 and Lord Pearson in the *Hely-Hutchinson v Brayhead Ltd* [1968] 1 Q.B. 549, CA, at 593.

[128] [1983] B.C.L.C. 78, HL. Quaere the effect of the wording of s.40 on this situation? Now the power of the director to authorise others to act on behalf of the company is free of any limitation under the company's constitution. Does this allow any representation to bind the company in such situations?

documents but where he is seeking to rely on a representation in the public documents it is essential that he inspected them. A party seeking to set up an estoppel must show that he relied on the representation which he alleges, be it a representation in words or a representation by conduct. Reliance on the part of the third party may continue until a withdrawal of authority is communicated.[129]

In *Houghton & Co v Nothard, Lowe and Wills Ltd* [130] a director purported to make, on behalf of the company, an agreement whereby an outsider was to sell on commission goods imported by the company and to retain the proceeds as security for a debt due from another company. The outsider had not inspected the company's public documents and did not know of the power of delegation contained in the articles. Further, the agreement was so unusual as to put the outsider upon inquiry to ascertain whether the director had authority in fact. It was held that the company was not bound.

In *Rama Corp v Proved Tin & General Investments Ltd*[131] R. Co, by their principal director, A, purported to enter into an oral contract with B, who was a director of and purported to act for P. Co but had no actual authority. The alleged contract was that the two companies should finance the sale of a telephone directory holder produced by a third company. R. Co claimed repayment of money paid by them to B as agent for P. Co in pursuance of the contract. R. Co alleged that P. Co were estopped from denying B's authority because the P. Co's articles provided that the directors could delegate their powers to a committee of one or more directors. However, A had not inspected the articles until after the action began (and even if A had inspected the articles a single director would not normally have authority to act for the company). It was held that because A had not inspected the articles when the contract was made, they could not be relied on as conferring ostensible or apparent authority on B, and the action failed.

Ratification

There is another issue, which has already been mentioned in the context of s.40,[132] **6–024** and that is, as a matter of general agency law, that a company may adopt, expressly or impliedly, a transaction purportedly entered into in its name, but not, in fact, authorised at the time. The form that the ratification takes, in the company context, will be special resolution only where the transaction is contrary to a provision of the articles.[133] The doctrine of ratification, which is "equivalent to an antecedent authority",[134] has retrospective effect and the transaction in question must be adopted in its entirety.[135] Ratification will not be permitted where, to do so, would prejudice a third party. In particular, an act which has to be done within

---

[129] See *SEB Trygg Holding AG v Manches* [2005] EWCA Civ 1237; [2006] 1 W.L.R. 2276 at 2291.
[130] [1927] 1 K.B. 246, CA; affirmed on other grounds [1928] A.C. 1.
[131] [1952] 2 Q.B. 147.
[132] Above, para.6–014.
[133] Pursuant to s.491) and s.9(1).
[134] See *Koenigsblatt v Sweet* [1923] 2 Ch. 314 at 325, per Lord Sterndale M.R.
[135] See *Smith v Henniker-Major & Co* [2002] EWCA Civ 762; [2003] Ch. 182, CA, at 203. There is authority which suggests that the adoption of part of a transaction may amount to a ratification of the whole: see *Re Mawcon Ltd* [1969] 1 W.L.R. 78.

a certain time cannot be ratified after the expiration of that time[136] and the ratification must be reasonable in all circumstances.[137] A party wishing to rely on retrospective ratification would not succeed in such a bid where they were serious allegations involved and where there was clear prejudice to them caused by delay in bringing proceedings.[138] Silence and inaction would not amount to ratificatory conduct.[139]

Agency—persons acting otherwise than in good faith

6–025 If the third party is not acting in good faith, he cannot rely on s.40 and will by definition have subjective knowledge of the express limitation in the company's constitution. Unless the transaction is ratified therefore the company will not be bound. In addition, the rule in *Turquand's* case has never applied in four situations, which in effect provide that an outsider acting in bad faith will be bound by internal irregularities as well. In such cases even if the agent is otherwise acting within his implied or apparent authority the outsider will be bound by the irregularity and the company will not be liable.

The rule in *Turquand's* case does not apply, i.e. the company is not bound and the outsider is not protected, where the outsider knows of the irregularity or lack of actual authority.[140]

In *Howard v Patent Ivory Manufacturing Co*[141] the directors had power under the articles to borrow up to £1,000 on behalf of the company without the consent of a general meeting and to borrow further money with such consent. The directors themselves lent £3,500 to the company without such consent, and took debentures. The court held that the company was liable, and the debentures were valid, only to the extent of £1,000.

The rule in *Turquand's* case will also not apply where the outsider purported to act as a director in the transaction, i.e. to act for and on behalf of the company in the transaction. On the other hand, if a director, acting in his private capacity, contracts with his company, acting by another director, the former director is not automatically to be treated as having constructive knowledge of any defect in the latter's authority, so as to exclude the rule.[142]

6–026 The rule in *Turquand's* case will also not apply where there are suspicious circumstances putting the outsider on inquiry.[143] Thus, in *A.L. Underwood Ltd v Bank of Liverpool & Martins*,[144] the sole director of and main shareholder in a company paid cheques, drawn in favour of the company, into his own account.

---

[136] See *Presentaciones Musicales SA v Secunda* [1994] Ch. 271, CA.

[137] As to this point, see *Re Portuguese Consolidated Copper Mines Ltd* (1890) 45 Ch.D. 16, CA.

[138] See *Smith v Henniker-Major & Co* [2002] EWCA Civ 762; [2003] Ch. 182, CA, at 207.

[139] See *ING Re (UK) Ltd v R & V Versicherung AG* [2006] EWHC 1544 (Comm); [2007] 1 B.C.L.C. 108.

[140] See *Criterion Properties Plc v Stratford UK Properties LLC* [2004] UKHL 28; [2004] 1 W.L.R. 1846 at 1856.

[141] (1888) 83 Ch.D. 156.

[142] *Morris v Kanssen* [1946] A.C. 459; *Hely-Hutchinson v Brayhead Ltd* [1968] 1 Q.B. 549.

[143] See, e.g., *Wrexham Association Football Club v Crucialmove Ltd* [2006] EWCA Civ 1237; [2007] B.C.C. 139.

[144] [1924] 1 K.B. 775, CA. Followed in *Rolled Steel Products (Holdings) Ltd v British Steel Corp* [1986] Ch. 246, CA.

The court held that the bank was put upon inquiry and not entitled to rely on his ostensible authority, and could not rely on the rule.

In *Kreditback Cassel GmbH v Schenkers Ltd*,[145] the articles of a company carrying on business as forwarding agents empowered the directors to determine who should have authority to draw bills of exchange on the company's behalf. C, the company's Manchester manager, drew bills on the company's behalf in favour of K, who took them, believing C to be authorised to draw them. C had no such authority, and it was unusual for a branch manager to have such authority. The court held that the company was not liable to the holders on the bills because (1) K did not know of the power of delegation in the articles and therefore could not rely on its supposed exercise; (2) the bills were forgeries; (3) even if K had known of the power of delegation, he was not entitled to assume that a branch manager had ostensible authority to draw bills on behalf of his company.

Finally, the rule in *Turquand's* case will not apply where a document is forged **6–027** so as to purport to be the company's document, unless, perhaps, it is held out as genuine by an officer of the company acting within the scope of his authority.[146]

Validity of acts of directors—procedural defects in appointment

Where there is a defect in the appointment of a director who has acted for the company, the outsider may be protected by the provision of the Act which states that the acts of a director or manager are valid notwithstanding any defect that may afterwards be discovered in his appointment or qualification.[147] The effect of this provision is to validate the acts of a director who has not been validly appointed because there was some procedural slip or irregularity in his appointment. Thus, an outsider dealing with the company, or a member, is entitled to assume that a person who appears to be a duly appointed and qualified director is so in fact.

In *Dawson v African Consolidated Land & Trading Co*,[148] the articles included an article like Table A, art.92. T, N and S, de facto directors, made a call, payment of which was resisted by some shareholders on the ground that T, N and S were not de jure directors. For example, unknown to his co-directors, N had vacated office by parting with his qualification shares, although he later acquired a share qualification and continued to act as a director. The court held that the article operated not only as between the company and outsiders but also as between the company and its members, and covered the irregularities alleged, so that the call was valid.

It is immaterial that it is clear from the company's public documents that a director is not duly qualified to act.[149]

The Act will not validate acts where there has been no appointment at all.[150] Thus they have no effect on substantive rather than procedural defects. So they

---

[145] [1927] 1 K.B. 826, CA.
[146] *Ruben v Great Fingall Consolidated* [1906] A.C. 439, particularly per Lord Loreburn L.C. at 443.
[147] s.161(1). cf. also art.92 of Table A.
[148] [1898] 1 Ch. 6, CA.
[149] *British Asbestos Co Ltd v Boyd* [1903] 2 Ch. 439 at 444, per Farwell J. In this case a director vacated office on becoming secretary.
[150] *Morris v Kanssen* [1946] A.C. 459, applied in *Grant v John Grant & Sons Pty Ltd* (1950) 82 C.L.R. 1.

cannot validate acts which could not have been done even by a properly qualified director. In *Craven-Ellis v Canons Ltd*,[151] for example, what is now s.161 did not empower improperly qualified directors to do what properly qualified directors could not do, namely, appoint an improperly qualified director as managing director.

---

[151] [1936] 2 K.B. 403, CA.

CORPORATE FINANCE

Chapter 7

SHARES

INTRODUCTION

The commercial aspects of a share

A share can be thought of in many different ways. From the shareholder's **7–001** perspective, an ordinary share in a public company entitles the shareholder to receive a dividend if there are sufficient distributable profits in any given financial year, it entitles the shareholder to sell the share on the stock exchange for a profit if the share price has risen on that market between the time of acquisition and disposal, and it entitles the shareholder to vote at company meetings. Each share carries a right to the same dividend of any other share of the same class. The shareholder has no legal entitlement to receive a dividend, however, unless and until the company's directors declare a dividend over those shares. There may well be different classes of shares in a company. Ordinary shares differ from preference shares, for example, in that preference shares entitle their "preferred shareholders" to a fixed dividend, although a preference share may not carry any voting rights: this makes preference shares equivalent to a bond which pays a fixed rate of interest. There may be other securities in a company which are "convertible": that is, they may begin life as a bond (constituting a loan by a large number of investors to the company, in return for which the company must pay interest to the investors and repay the capital amount of the loan at the expiry of the bond), but the bondholder may elect to convert some or all of the bonds into shares in the company at identified times or in identified contexts. It is possible to structure many different sub-species of shares and other securities building on these basic blocks. In a public company, the single vote which is carried by each share is often of little practical use to a private shareholder because no single shareholder has sufficient voting power to exercise control as an individual, and so it is a club of so-called "institutional investors" in relation to public companies which tend to exercise control and who are consulted closely by management. In the Takeover Code, for example, a shareholding of 30 per cent of the shares in a public company is generally taken to constitute control of such a company.

For the investor in a public company, therefore, the dividend may be a source of income in the long-term. Alternatively, the investor may have an eye to a short-term speculative profit by means of buying shares when they seem likely to increase in value: buying them, in a perfect world, at the bottom of the market, and then selling them at the top. In a private company, by comparison, there is no public market for the shares (because private companies may not offer their shares to the public as provided by s.755 of the Companies Act 2006 ("CA 2006")). Therefore, the shareholder in a private company is likely to have a different relationship with his shareholding. For an entrepreneur like Aron Salomon,[1] for example, his shareholding is simply an expression of the means by which he has transferred his sole trading business[2] to a company which he had created so as to attract the protection of limited liability under the companies' legislation. The entrepreneur may extract money from the company either by means of a dividend or by means of a salary, often depending on which approach is more tax efficient. Alternatively, the company may be the vehicle used by a family business to organise and allocate the profits from that business among family members. In this situation, company law lends those family members a model through which they can organise the management of their business: including the management of meetings, the various rights of the participants, and so forth. The purpose of a private company is to attract all of the benefits of limited liability and corporate personality without seeking the concomitant benefits of access to a public securities market to raise financing. Private companies need to raise their capital through ordinary bank debt or through admitting identified people to the company with limited issues of shares or subscription to the company on its formation. Some very large businesses are organised as private companies where the participants in the business want to keep matters among a defined group of investors and managers.

Even though the company law model of the limited liability company was derived historically from the trust, unlike beneficiaries under a trust who have proprietary rights in the trust fund, it is only if the company is wound up that the shareholder will acquire rights to the company's property directly. Therefore, the shareholder's property rights are expressed solely by ownership of the share as a form of "chose in action" (that is, a bundle of rights which can be transferred or turned to account). Shareholding is not a proprietary concept, in that sense, unless and until the company is wound up. That is, a shareholder does not own any of the company's property until the company is wound up and property is allocated to the shareholder in that winding up. Before a winding up, all that the shareholder owns is the share itself. Nor do the shareholders own any of the company's profits until a dividend is declared out of distributable profits. The expectation of a dividend distributed from the company's profits is nothing more than a mere expectation unless and until a dividend is declared by the directors.

The legal conception of a share

7–002   A share was defined by Farwell J. in *Borland's Trustee v Steel Bros & Co Ltd* as being:

> "the interest of a shareholder in the company measured by a sum of money, for the purpose of liability in the first place, and of interest in the second, but also

---

[1] The principal protagonist in *Salomon v A Salomon & Co Ltd* [1897] A.C. 22.
[2] There is a pun in there. A "sole trader" is someone who trades on their own account and who owns their own business. Aron Salomon, of course, was also a "sole trader" in the sense that he manufactured and sold boots.

consisting of a series of mutual covenants entered into by all the shareholders inter se in accordance with [the Companies Act, s.33]. The contract contained in the articles of association is one of the original incidents of the share."[3]

The articles of association constitute a contract between the shareholders: therefore, one of the important aspects of shareholding is the mix of rights and obligations which are bestowed on the shareholder by the company's constitution. Therefore, beyond the commercial aspects of a share considered above, the share also embodies a web of contractual terms. More prosaically, s.541(1) of the CA 2006 defines a share as being a "share in the company's share capital". A share in a company is in itself a form of personal property.[4] All shares must have a fixed nominal value.[5] The share is measured by a sum of money, namely, the nominal amount of the share, and also by the rights and obligations belonging to it as defined by the Companies Acts and by the memorandum and articles of the company. The undivided profits form an integral part of the shares to which they appertain.[6] A share certificate, which specifies the shares held by the member and which is prima facie evidence[7] of his title to the shares,[8] is usually issued to a shareholder except where the share is held in a de-materialised form. Shares are transferable in the manner provided by the articles of the company or under the provisions of the Stock Transfer Act 1963, except for uncertificated shares which are transferable in accordance with the Uncertificated Securities Regulations (as considered below). Shares are intangibles (that is, they are choses in action[9]) and are located in the country in which the register of members is kept.[10] A shareholder may borrow money on the security of his shares: so, by way of example, in England a shareholder may give the lender a mortgage over the shares to secure the payment of interest and repayment of the principal sum.

CLASSES OF SHARES

Introduction

There may be a number of commercial or marketing advantages in providing **7–003** different types of rights to different classes of shareholders or other investors in a company. Some investors may prefer to know with certainty that they will receive a fixed dividend, others may prefer to speculate on the company generating higher profits than a fixed dividend might require, and yet others may not require voting rights in relation to the company because they prefer a higher fixed dividend or loan

---

[3] Per Farwell J. in *Borland's Trustee v Steel Bros & Co Ltd* [1901] 1 Ch. 279 at 288. See also *Whittome v Whittome (No.1)* 1994 S.L.T. 114 (OH).

[4] Companies Act 2006 s.541.

[5] Companies Act 2006 s.542(1).

[6] *Carron Co v Hunter* (1868) 6 M.H.L. 106.

[7] Or in Scotland, sufficient evidence unless the contrary is shown.

[8] Companies Act 2006 s.768.

[9] In Scotland shares are incorporeal moveable property. See *Whittome v Whittome (No.1)*, 1994 S.L.T. 114 (OH).

[10] *International Credit and Investment Co (Overseas) Ltd v Adham* [1994] 1 B.C.L.C. 66. If, unusually, the shares are negotiable instruments it is the place where the paper constituting the negotiable instrument is kept: *Harvard Securities Ltd, Re* [1997] 2 B.C.L.C. 369.

interest instead. Consequently, a company is not bound to issue all its shares with the same rights but may confer different rights on different classes of shares, thus giving different rights to different shareholders.[11] Such classes may be described as ordinary shares and preference shares but the name which a class of shares is given provides us with only an indication of the rights attaching to it in any particular company; so instead, to ascertain the precise nature of those rights reference must be made to the articles or the terms of issue of the shares.

Preference shares

The rights of preferred shareholders in the abstract

7–004   Preference shares are shares which are entitled to some priority over the other shares in the company. They usually carry a "right to preference" in payment of dividend (if a dividend is declared) at a fixed rate, and a "right to preference" in the repayment of capital in a winding up. There may be several classes of preference shares, first, second and third, ranking one after the other. The rights attached to preference shares are always a question of construction of the memorandum, the articles or the terms of issue of the shares. However, unless the company's constitution otherwise provides, the rights which attach to preference shares are as described below. These prima facie rights differ according to whether the company is a going concern or in liquidation.

Preferred shareholder rights while the company is a going concern

When the company is a going concern, the rights of a holder of preference shares are as follows:

1. When a right to a preferential dividend is given without more, the right of a preferred shareholder is a right to a cumulative dividend, i.e. if no preference dividend is declared in any year the arrears of dividend are carried forward and must be paid before a dividend is paid on the other shares.[12] If, however, the shares are declared to be non-cumulative preference shares, or the preferential dividend is to be paid out of the yearly profits,[13] or out of the net profits of each year,[14] the dividend will not be cumulative.

2. Preference shares are non-participating, which means that they do not confer any right to a participation in the surplus profits of the company, after payment of a specified rate of dividend on the ordinary shares, in the absence of anything to that effect in the articles. Where a special resolution

---

[11] The CLR recommended continuation of such variable rights, e.g. voting: *Final Report*, Vol.1, para.7.29.

[12] *Webb v Earle* (1875) L.R. 20 Eq. 556; *Ferguson & Forrester Ltd v Buchanan*, 1920 S.C. 154. Interest is not payable on the arrears: *Partick, etc. Gas Co Ltd v Taylor* (1888) 15 R. 711.

[13] *Adair v Old Bushmills Distillery* [1908] W.N. 24.

[14] *Staples v Eastman Photographic Materials Co* [1896] 2 Ch. 303, CA; contrast *Miln v Arizona Copper Co Ltd* (1899) 1 F. 935.

that the holders of preference shares were entitled to a cumulative prefer-ence dividend at the rate of 10 per cent per annum and that such shares should rank, both as regards capital and dividend in priority to the other shares, the holders were only entitled to a 10 per cent dividend in the distri-bution of profits—the provision defined the whole terms of the bargain between the shareholders and the company.[15] Sometimes, however, cumu-lative and participating preference shares are created, conferring a right to participate in surplus profits up to a fixed percentage, for example a right to a preferential dividend of 7 per cent may be given, together with a further right, after 7 per cent has been paid on the ordinary shares, to participate in the surplus profits equally with the ordinary shares until an additional 7 per cent has been paid, but no more. In effect, the shareholder is striking an ordinary contract with the company as to the terms on which the shareholder will invest in that company.

3.   Unless the company's constitution otherwise provides, preference shares carry the same voting rights at general meetings as the other shares. However if, as is common, the preference shareholders are expressly given a right to vote in certain specified circumstances, e.g. when their preference dividend is in arrears[16] or the rights attached to the preference shares are being varied, prima facie they have no right to vote in other circumstances. There are also circumstances in which preference shares do not carry any voting rights at all. In essence, the precise nature of any given class of preference shares depends on the rights attached to those shares by any given company's articles of association, although for the most part they express some compilation of the characteristics considered in this section.

Preference shareholder rights during a winding up

When the company is being wound up, the rights of a holder of preference shares **7–005** are as follows:

1.   In the absence of a provision in the company's constitution, arrears of cumulative preference dividend are not payable out of the assets in a liquidation, unless the dividend has been declared.[17] If, however, as is usual, the articles provide for the payment of arrears, such arrears are payable out of the surplus assets after payment of the company's debts, whether or not any undistributed profits are included in the assets.[18] If

---

[15] *Will v United Plantations Co Ltd* [1914] A.C. 11.

[16] Preference dividend is in arrears if it has not been paid even though that is because there are no available profits: *Bradford Investments Plc, Re* [1991] B.C.L.C. 224.

[17] *Crichton's Oil Co* [1902] 2 Ch. 86, CA; *Catalinas Warehouses & Mole Co Ltd, Re* [1947] 1 All E.R. 51; *Robertson-Durham v Inches*, 1917, 1 S.L.T. 267 (OH).

[18] *Springbok Agricultural Estates Ltd, Re* [1920] 1 Ch. 563; *Wharfedale Brewery Co Ltd, Re* [1952] Ch. 913. The rules as to the payment of dividends (below, Ch.22) have no application to the surplus assets in a winding up.

the articles provide only for payment of all arrears "due" at the date of winding up, no arrears will be payable unless dividends have been declared, because a dividend is not due until it has been declared.[19]

2.   Prima facie, preference shares have no priority in the repayment of capital in a winding up. However, such a right may be, and usually is, given by the articles, and its effect is that after the company's debts and liabilities, and any arrears of preference dividend which are payable, have been paid, the preference shareholders are entitled to repayment of their capital in full before the ordinary shareholders are repaid their capital.[20]

3.   Where there are surplus assets available after the discharge of all the company's liabilities and the repayment of the capital to the share-holders, such surplus assets are divisible rateably among all classes of shareholders in the absence of any provision in the articles to the contrary.[21] However, if, as is common, the articles set out the rights attached to a class of shares to participate in profits while the company is a going concern or to share in the property of the company in liqui-dation, prima facie those rights are exhaustive. Thus, articles giving preference shareholders priority in the repayment of capital in a liquida-tion but containing no reference to any further rights in the capital do not entitle the preference shareholders to participate in such surplus assets.[22]

7-006   By way of illustration, in *Wilsons and Clyde Coal Co Ltd v Scottish Insurance Corp Ltd*,[23] the colliery assets of a coal mining company had been transferred to the National Coal Board under the Coal Industry Nationalisation Act 1946 and the company was to go into voluntary liquidation. Meanwhile the company proposed to reduce its capital by returning capital to the holders of the preference stock. The articles provided that in the event of a winding up the preference stock ranked before the ordinary stock to the extent of repayment of the amounts, called up and paid thereon. It was held that the proposed reduction was not unfair nor inequitable. Even without it, the preference shareholders would not be entitled in a winding up to share in the surplus assets nor to receive more than a return of their paid up capital. Accordingly, they could not object to being paid, by means of the reduction, the amount which they would receive in the proposed liquidation.

It follows from this decision that where the preference shareholders have priority as to repayment of capital on a winding up they should also be paid off first on a reduction of capital due to over-capitalisation, and have no right to complain about any variation of their class rights,[24] since it is in accord with their

---

[19] *Roberts and Cooper Ltd, Re* [1992] 2 Ch. 383.

[20] See, e.g. *Walter Symons Ltd, Re* [1934] Ch. 308; *E. W. Savory Ltd, Re* [1951] 2 All E.R. 1036.

[21] *Monkland Iron, etc. Co Ltd v Henderson* (1883) 10 R. 494; *Liquidators of Williamson-Buchanan Steamers Ltd, Petitioners*, 1936 S.L.T. 106 (OH); *Town and Gown Ass Ltd, Liquidator, Petitioner*, 1948 S.L.T. (Notes) 71 (OH).

[22] *Wilsons and Clyde Coal Co Ltd v Scottish Insurance Corp Ltd*, 1949 S.C. HL 90; 1948 S.C. 360; *The Isle of Thanet Electricity Supply Co Ltd, Re* [1950] Ch. 161, CA.

[23] 1949 S.C. HL 90; [1949] A.C. 462.

[24] *Prudential Assurance Co Ltd v Chatterley-Whitfield Collieries Ltd* [1949] A.C. 512, HC.

rights[25] unless the articles expressly make such a reduction as such a class right, in which case the variation of class rights procedure must be used.[26]

If a company's articles expressly give preference shareholders a right to share in surplus assets after the repayment of capital, then they are entitled to share in accumulated profits in a liquidation even if the articles give the ordinary shareholders a right to exclusive enjoyment of accumulated profits not required for the preference dividend—the right of the ordinary shareholders depends on the appropriate resolutions being passed before a winding up.[27]

The variation of class rights

Variation of class rights in general terms

If the rights of any given class of shareholders are varied, this will clearly affect **7–007** the power which those shareholders have in relation to the company (whether positively or negatively) and it may also affect the value of their investment. The variation of class rights of shareholders is generally conducted in accordance with the following principles.

1. Where a company's shares are divided into classes, "class rights" are special rights of a class of shares, such as a preferential right to a dividend attached to preference shares where a company's shares are divided between preference shares and ordinary shares. Section 630 of the CA 2006 applies to alterations governing the rights attaching to any class of shares in a company whose share capital is divided into shares of different classes. Section 630 requires that an alteration is carried on in such a context in accordance with any provision in the articles dealing with variation of rights of shareholders, or if there is no such provision then the shareholders of the class in question must "consent" to the variation in writing with a three-quarters majority. It has, however, been held that it is not necessary for those rights to be attached to particular types of shares as long as they are given to a class of members in their capacity as members or shareholders, for example a right of pre-emption over other shares. For the purposes of s.630 therefore the share capital of a company is to be regarded as being divided into different classes, if shareholders, qua shareholders, enjoy different rights. It follows that the shares could come into or go out of a particular class on their acquisition or disposal by a particular individual.[28] Where a quorum right has been held to be a class right, it cannot be overridden by an order under s.306 of the CA 2006 to hold a general meeting with a reduced quorum.[29]

---

[25] *Saltdean Estate Co Ltd, Re* [1968] 1 W.L.R. 1844; *House of Fraser Plc v A.C.G.E. Investments Ltd* [1987] A.C. 387, HL, 1987 S.C. HL 125.

[26] *Northern Engineering Industries Plc, Re* [1994] 2 B.C.L.C. 704, CA.

[27] *Dimbula Valley (Ceylon) Tea Co Ltd v Laurie* [1961] Ch. 353.

[28] *Cumbrian Newspaper Group Ltd v Cumberland and Westmorland Newspaper and Printing Co Ltd* [1987] Ch. 1; *Harman v BML Group Ltd* [1994] 2 B.C.L.C. 674, CA.

[29] *Harman v BML Group Ltd* [1994] 2 B.C.L.C. 674, CA.

Class rights are usually given to preference shareholders and if the articles give the ordinary shareholders a right to the distributable profits after payment of a dividend on the preference shares, and a right to surplus assets on a liquidation, these are not class rights—they are no more than would be implied if the articles did not refer to them.[30] However, by way of example, it seems that the original ordinary shares in *Greenhalgh v Arderne Cinemas*[31] formed a class of shares within the meaning of an article providing for variation of the rights attached to a class of shares. Again, in *Lord St David's v Union-Castle Mail Steamship Co Ltd*,[32] where under the articles the large number of preference shares carried a right to vote when the preference dividend was in arrears and, such dividend being in arrears, the preference shareholders proposed to alter the articles so as to give themselves a right to vote on all resolutions, it was held that the proposed resolution would not affect the rights of the small number of ordinary shares unless the ordinary shareholders approved it in accordance with an article providing for variation of class rights, that is the class rights were attached to the ordinary shares.[33]

7–008   2.   If the articles attach class rights to a class of shares and contain a "modification of rights clause" the class rights may in general be varied, with the consent of the specified proportion or resolution of the holders of shares of the class, by a valid alteration of the articles by a special resolution of the company in general meeting. In essence, the rights can be varied in accordance with the articles or if the articles are silent then by a three-quarters majority of the shareholders.[34] By way of example, in *Holders Investment Trust Ltd, Re*[35] a reduction of capital was to have been effected by cancelling the five per cent £1 cumulative preference shares and allotting the holders an equivalent amount of "six per cent unsecured loan stock repayable 1985/90". The majority of the preference shareholders, who supported the reduction, were also holders of 52 per cent of the company's ordinary stock and non-voting ordinary shares. Minority preference shareholders opposed the reduction. The court refused to confirm it. The majority preference shareholders had considered what was best in their own general interests, based on their large holdings of ordinary shares, without considering what was best specifically for preference shareholders as a class. Furthermore, the court considered that the reduction was unfair and that the advantages of the exchange into unsecured stock did not compensate for the disadvantages.

3.   Where there is in the articles (or the memorandum) an express or implied power to vary class rights, the exercise of that power is subject

---

[30] *Hodge v James Howel & Co, The Times*, December 13, 1958, CA.
[31] [1946] 1 All E.R. 512, CA.
[32] *The Times*, November 24, 1934.
[33] See too, *Rights and Issues Investment Trust Ltd v Stylo Shoes Ltd* [1965] Ch. 250.
[34] Companies Act 2006 s.630.
[35] [1971] 1 W.L.R. 582.

to s.633 of the CA 2006. This section provides that if, in the case of a company with a share capital divided into different classes of shares, provision is made by the articles (or memorandum) for the variation or abrogation of the rights attached to any class of shares, subject to the consent of a specified proportion of the holders of the shares of the class or the sanction of a resolution passed at a separate meeting of the holders of such shares, and in pursuance of such provision the rights attached to any such class of shares are varied, an application can be made to the court to have the variation cancelled, whereupon it has no effect unless and until it is confirmed by the court. The section also applies to variations under the procedure required by s.630.[36]

Various detailed requirements apply. Those who can apply are the holders of not less than 15 per cent of the issued shares of the class, discounting treasury shares, and who did not consent to or vote for the variation. The application must be made within 21 days after the giving of the consent or the passing of the resolution. The court may disallow the variation if, after hearing the various parties interested, it is satisfied that the variation would unfairly prejudice the shareholders of the class in question. If the court is not so satisfied it must confirm the variation. The company must, within 15 days, send a copy of the order made by the court to the Registrar of Companies.[37] The object of this provision is to protect shareholders from being prejudiced by the voting of other shareholders who hold shares of another class in addition to those of the class affected by the variation. For example, if a variation reduces the dividend on preference shares from seven per cent to six per cent per annum, and 80 per cent of the preference shareholders are also ordinary shareholders, the requisite consent of the preference shareholders is likely to be obtained, since the variation will leave more profits for a dividend on the ordinary shares. This would be unfair to the 20 per cent of the preference shareholders who are not ordinary shareholders.

4.   A variation of class rights, includes an abrogation of those rights.[38] **7–009** However, it has been held that class rights are not "varied" by the subdivision of other shares, under a power in the articles, which results in the holders of the shares with the class rights being outvoted by the holders of the other shares. In *Greenhalgh v Arderne Cinemas Ltd*[39] there were two categories of ordinary shares with equal voting rights, such that the 2s. ordinary shares ranked pari passu with the 10s. ordinary shares. Each 10s. share was sub-divided into five 2s. ordinary shares. It was held that the voting rights of the original 2s. shares had not been varied.

---

[36] Companies Act 2006 s.633.
[37] Companies Act 2006 s.635(1)–(3).
[38] Companies Act 2006 s.630(6). Preference shareholders' rights are not abrogated by being repaid first on a reduction of capital: *House of Fraser Plc v A.C.G.E. Investments Plc* [1987] A.C. 387; 1987 S.C. HL 125, unless such a reduction is made a specific class right: *Northern Engineering Industries Plc, Re* [1994] 2 B.C.L.C. 704, CA.
[39] [1946] 1 All E.R. 512, CA.

The only voting right attached to that class was one vote per share, and that right remained.

Class rights are not "affected" by the creation or issue of new shares of the class ranking equally with the old. So, in *White v Bristol Aeroplane Co Ltd*[40] capital was being increased by the issue of 600,000 £1 preference shares ranking pari passu with the existing 600,000 £1 preference stock, and 2,640,000 ordinary shares of 10s. each ranking pari passu with the existing £3,300,00 ordinary stock. The new shares were to be issued to the ordinary stockholders and paid for out of the reserve fund. It was held that the proposed issue of new capital did not "affect" the rights of the existing preference shareholders. Only the enjoyment of the rights was affected, the rights themselves were not. It should be noted that a modification of rights clause in the articles cannot be altered by special resolution without the appropriate consent of shareholders of the class under that procedure.[41]

Deferred shares

7–010   Deferred shares, which are sometimes called founders' or management shares, are usually of small nominal amount with a right to take the whole or a proportion of the profits after a fixed dividend has been paid on the ordinary shares. The rights of the holders of deferred shares depend on the articles or the terms of issue. Deferred shares are rarely issued today. The modern tendency is to convert existing deferred shares into ordinary shares.

Employees' shares

7–011   Some companies issue special shares to their employees. Modern tax legislation, however, in general only provides tax incentives for companies who provide their employees with ordinary shares, i.e. those not specifically available only to employees.

TRANSFER OF SHARES

7–012   There is a distinction between a transfer of shares and a transmission of shares. A transfer is carried out by the act of the member, while a transmission occurs by operation of law on the death or the bankruptcy of a member. The procedure on transfer is set out below, but it requires at least a valid contractual agreement or gift to be effective.[42] In *Harvela Investments Ltd v Royal Trust Company of Canada (C.I.) Ltd*[43] the House of Lords held that the holder of shares in a private company could not validly invite other parties to submit sealed bids for those shares and then accept a bid which is referential, i.e. one which is given as an

---

[40] [1953] Ch. 65, CA. See also *John Smith's Tadcaster Brewery Co Ltd, Re* [1953] Ch. 308, CA.
[41] Companies Act 2006 s.334(7), s.630(5).
[42] If the full transfer formalities are not complied with, there will still be an equitable transfer or assignment under the contract or gift.
[43] [1986] A.C. 207, HL.

amount above that submitted by the other bidder. If such bids were allowed one party could not lose and the other party could not win.

The following account as to the form and procedure of transfers of shares does not apply to transfers of shares held in electronic or uncertified form under the CREST system which operates in respect of some listed companies. A note on that system is included at the end of this section.

Form of transfer

Section 770(1) of the CA 2006, which effects a policy of ensuring that there is an **7–013** instrument which can be stamped so as to be subject to stamp duty, provides that it is unlawful for a company to register a transfer of shares unless a "proper instrument of transfer" has been delivered to the company. Consequently it is unlawful to have an article that upon the death of a shareholder his shares shall be deemed to have passed to his widow, without any transfer.[44] While the precise form of the transfer may be prescribed by the articles, nevertheless for an instrument to be a "proper instrument" that instrument must be the sort of instrument which attracts stamp duty, as was held in *Re Paradise Motor Co Ltd*, and it does not necessarily mean an instrument which complies with the formalities prescribed by the articles.[45] Therefore, a transfer document which failed to state the consideration for the transfer was held to be valid since it was still appropriate for stamping purposes because the Revenue could look behind the information provided on the form to ascertain that amount.[46] Where the shares are only partly paid it is essential that the transferee signs the transfer document to accept the liability on the shares.[47] In the case of a company limited by shares, if shares are fully paid they may be transferred by a simplified form of transfer, namely a stock transfer under hand in the form set out in Sch.1 to the Stock Transfer Act 1963.[48]

Procedure on transfer

If a shareholder has sold or given all his shares comprised in one share certificate[49] **7–014** to one person,[50] the transfer is effected as follows. First, the transferor sends the transferee the "proper instrument of transfer" required by s.770(1) of the CA 2006 and executed by the transferor,[51] together with the share certificate relating to the shares comprised in the transfer. Then, the transferee executes the transfer[52] if it is

---

[44] *Greene, Re* [1949] Ch. 333.
[45] *Paradise Motor Co Ltd, Re* [1968] 1 W.L.R. 1125, CA; *Dempsey v Celtic Football and Athletic Co Ltd* [1993] B.C.C. 514; *Nisbet v Shepherd* [1994] 1 B.C.L.C. 300.
[46] *Nisbet v Shepherd* [1994] 1 B.C.L.C. 300.
[47] *Dempsey v Celtic Football and Athletic Co Ltd* [1993] B.C.C. 514.
[48] As amended by the Stock Transfer (Amendment of Forms) Order 1974 (SI 1974/1214). Such a transfer need be executed only by the transferor and need not be attested: 1963 Act s.1.
[49] As to shares comprised in a share warrant.
[50] As to the procedure when, e.g. part only of the holding is being sold, see para.7–015, below.
[51] Where there is a dispute as to whether the transferor signed the transfer form the burden of proof is on the transferee to show that it was so signed: *Elliott v The Hollies Ltd* [1998] 1 B.C.L.C. 627.
[52] If he is required to do so under the articles and see *Dempsey v Celtic Football and Athletic Co Ltd* [1998] B.C.C. 514.

in accordance with the articles, and forwards it, with the share certificate and the registration fee, to the company for registration. A transfer may also be registered, at the request of the transferor, in the same manner and subject to the same conditions as if registration were applied for by the transferee.[53]

Certification of transfer

7–015 The company is then required to register the transfer under s.771(1) of the CA 2006 or to give the transferee notice of refusal to accept the transfer. A refusal to accept the transfer requires that the company give reasons for that refusal.[54] When the transfer is accepted, the company must enter the name of the transferee in the register of shareholders.[55]

Rights as between transferor and transferee

7–016 On a sale of shares ordinarily the terms of the contract between the parties is that the vendor shall give the purchaser a valid transfer and do all that is required to enable the purchaser to be registered as a member in respect of the shares, the purchaser's duty being to get himself registered.[56] The vendor's duty is not only to give a valid transfer but also, where the vendor is not the transferor, one which is signed by a transferor willing that the transfer shall be registered. In *Hichens, Harrison, Woolston & Co v Jackson & Sons*,[57] solicitors instructed stockbrokers to sell stock and enclosed the certificate and a blank transfer form signed by the stockholder but on which the transferee's name still had to be inserted. The stockbrokers sold the stock but the stockholder repudiated the contract and the company, on her instructions, refused to register the transfer. The stockbrokers replaced the stock by a purchase on the Stock Exchange and sued the solicitors for an indemnity. It was held that the solicitors were principals of the stockbrokers as regards the sale; that it was the solicitor's duty to deliver a transfer executed by a transferor willing that it should be registered; and that the solicitors were liable accordingly.

If the directors, in pursuance of a power in the articles, decline to register the transfer, the purchaser, unless he bought "with registration guaranteed", will be unable to sue the vendor for damages or rescind and recover the price from the vendor—there is no implied condition subsequent to the contrary effect.[58] In such a case the vendor will be a trustee of the shares for the purchaser.[59] The vendor is, of course, under a duty to the purchaser not to prevent or delay the registration of the transfer.[60]

---

[53] Companies Act 2006 s.772.
[54] Companies Act 2006 s.771(2).
[55] Companies Act 2006 s.773.
[56] *Skinner v City of London Marine Ins Corp* (1885) 14 Q.B.D. 882, CA.
[57] [1943] A.C. 266.
[58] *London Founders Assn Ltd v Clarke* (1888) 20 Q.B.D. 576, CA.
[59] *Stevenson v Wilson*, 1907 S.C. 445; this quasi-trust would not, however, defeat a subsequent arrestment of the shares by a creditor of the transferor: per Lord Moncrieff (Ordinary) in *National Bank of Scotland Glasgow Nominees Ltd v Adamson*, 1932 S.L.T. 492 (OH) at 495.
[60] *Hooper v Herts* [1906] 1 Ch. 549, CA.

As from the time of the contract of sale the equitable or beneficial interest in the shares passes to the purchaser, and the vendor holds the shares on trust for the purchaser.[61] No transferee can obtain absolute title until his name is entered on the register of members.[62] In the case of a gift, delivery of the share transfer form is usually required to effect on equitable assignment of the shares.[63] That may not always be required if, in the circumstances, it would be unconscionable for the donor to recall the gift.[64] The issue which arises in relation to these cases, however, is that in relation to a private company in relation to which the directors have a right to refuse a transfer of shares, an assignment of the shares may be effected even though at common law the directors may latterly decide to refuse the transfer.[65]

Until the transfer is registered, the vendor will receive any dividends or other **7–017** benefits declared on the shares and, in the case of partly paid shares, calls may be made on him. As between the vendor and the purchaser the rights and liabilities depend on the terms of the contract. The shares may be bought "cum" or "ex" dividends or rights, or with a specified sum paid. In the absence of any such agreement, the purchaser is entitled to dividends or other benefits declared after the date of the contract.[66] In *Wimbush Re*,[67] R sold shares privately to W in September 1935. In April 1936, the company declared a dividend for the year ending December 31, 1935. It was held that because the sale was conducted by means of private bargain rather than under Stock Exchange rules, W was entitled to the whole dividend and therefore it was not apportionable between W and R.

Subject to contrary agreement, the purchaser must indemnify the vendor against calls made after the date of the contract.[68] Again, until the transfer is registered, the vendor is entitled to exercise any vote conferred by the shares but he must vote as directed by the purchaser.[69] An unpaid vendor of shares who remains on the register of members after the contract of sale retains vis-à-vis the purchaser the right to vote in respect of those shares. Where the contract expressly provides for delay in payment and makes alternative arrangements as to voting then the unpaid vendor will lose his right to vote,[70] but not where the purchaser defaults in payment even though the voting rights have passed to the purchaser under the contract.[71]

---

[61] *Hawks v McArthur* [1951] 1 All E.R. 22.
[62] See per Lord Gifford in *Morrison v Harrison* (1876) 3 R. 406 at 411; see also *Tennant's Trustees v Tennant*, 1946 S.C. 420.
[63] Since equity will not assist a volunteer, the donor must have done everything required of him to effect the gift: *Rose, Re* [1952] Ch. 499, CA.
[64] *Pennington v Waine* [2002] 2 B.C.L.C. 448, CA.
[65] See Alastair Hudson, *Equity & Trusts*, 6th edn (Routledge Cavendish, 2009), p.230.
[66] *Black v Homersham* (1878) 4 Ex.D. 24; *Kidner, Re* [1929] 2 Ch. 121.
[67] [1940] Ch. 92.
[68] *Spencer v Ashworth, Partington & Co* [1925] 1 K.B. 589, CA.
[69] *Dempsey v Celtic Football and Athletic Co Ltd* [1993] B.C.C. 514.
[70] *Musselwhite v C.H. Musselwhite & Son Ltd* [1962] Ch. 964, where a contract for the sale of shares provided that the transfer and share certificate should be held by a third party until the price was paid by instalments over a period of years.
[71] *JRRT (Investments) Ltd v Haycroft* [1993] B.C.L.C. 401.

Shares held in electronic form

The market process

7–018 Where shares are listed on the London Stock Exchange transfers are effected through members of the Exchange who may also act as principal traders and market makers and there is no direct link between a buyer and seller. They will sell and buy shares to their clients' instructions but there still has to be payment by the buyer and transfer of the legal title to the buyer. This process is known as "settlement". In order to speed up this process an optional new form of electronic transfer was introduced in 1996, known as CREST. Under this system, where the company, the operator of the system and the shareholder all agree, transfers are effected without the need for either a written instrument of transfer or a share certificate. In that sense, they are "uncertificated".

Uncertificated securities

7–019 It used to be the case that ownership of shares was demonstrated by the issue and possession of a share certificate. In the modern world, share ownership has become "dematerialised" in many circumstances: that means, ownership of shares is demonstrated by the entry of a person's ownership of shares on an electronic register.

The Uncertificated Securities Regulations 2001[72] govern dealings with securities which exist in dematerialised form. It is a requirement of the admission of securities to listing that those securities are eligible for electronic settlement: therefore the shares of all major public companies are in uncertificated form.[73] The regulations provide for a mechanism for the approval of an operator of the uncertificated securities system.[74] The purpose of the regulations is to "enable title to units of a security to be evidenced otherwise than by a certificate and transferred otherwise than by a written instrument".[75] The regulations require that the company's articles of association permit an uncertificated form for that company's securities, in that a special procedure is required if the articles do not permit such a form. If the articles do not permit uncertificated securities, then the directors may resolve to issue securities and to transfer securities by means of an uncertificated system,[76] at which point the regulations provide that the articles cease to have effect.[77] Notice of that directors' resolution, if not given to the members in advance, must be given within 60 days of the resolution.[78] The members of the company may by ordinary resolution decide that the directors' resolution shall have no effect or shall cease to have effect, as appropriate.[79] The members may change the articles of association in the ordinary way.

[72] SI 2001/3755.
[73] Listing Rules, 6.1.23R.
[74] In Pt 2 of the Uncertificated Securities Regulations 2001 reg.2.
[75] Uncertificated Securities Regulations 2001 reg.2.
[76] Uncertificated Securities Regulations 2001 reg.15(2).
[77] Uncertificated Securities Regulations 2001 reg.15(3).
[78] Uncertificated Securities Regulations 2001 reg.15(4).
[79] Uncertificated Securities Regulations 2001 reg.15(6).

Registers of holders of securities must be maintained by the operator of the system and by the issuer.[80] There is also a separate register of public sector securities.[81] In general terms, entry of ownership on an appropriate register is prima facie evidence of the ownership of the person recorded as the owner.[82] Once a transfer has taken place, the operator is required to register that change in ownership on its register[83]; unless the transfer has been prohibited by a court order, or is void under some legislation, or would constitute a transfer to a deceased person.[84] The operator is only entitled to register uncertificated securities other than under the procedure in the regulations if there has been a court order requiring the recognition of the ownership of some other person.[85] The operator must notify the participating issuer of the transfer of securities. Rectification of the issuer's register may not take effect without rectification of the operator's register.[86] If a person suffers loss as a result of a forged dematerialisation instruction, then that person may apply to the court for an order that the operator compensate him for his loss.[87]

Dealings on CREST

Dealings in uncertificated securities take place mainly on CREST.[88] CREST is an **7–020** electronic system for the holding and transfer of securities, which also enables payment to be made simultaneously with transfer. The CREST system is governed by the "CREST Rules", which were effected in July 2007, the CREST Manual and the Security Application Form.[89] CREST is not the only possible system but it is the system which is used most commonly in the United Kingdom. Admission to CREST is dependent on the securities qualifying under the Uncertificated Securities Regulations 2001. The shares must be fungible, they must be freely transferable and their issue must not be subject to any condition. Admission to CREST is made formally by completion of a Security Application Form.

PRIORITIES

English law

The question arises as to which of a variety of owners of shares takes priority. **7–021** There are two general principles in this area. First, the party who is entered on the

---

[80] Uncertificated Securities Regulations 2001 reg.20.
[81] Uncertificated Securities Regulations 2001 reg.21.
[82] Uncertificated Securities Regulations 2001 reg.24.
[83] Uncertificated Securities Regulations 2001 reg.27(1).
[84] Uncertificated Securities Regulations 2001 reg.27(2).
[85] Uncertificated Securities Regulations 2001 reg.27(5).
[86] Uncertificated Securities Regulations 2001 reg.25.
[87] Uncertificated Securities Regulations 2001 reg.36.
[88] See Tuckley, "Settlement Arrangements—CREST", in Maule (ed.) *A Practitioner's Guide to the AIM Rules* (City & Financial Publishing, 2006), p.225, which sets out an excellent summary of the appropriate regulations.
[89] Available at *http://www.euroclear.com* [accessed May 27, 2010]. See also the *CPSS-IOSCO Disclosure Framework*, 2005.

register of members, and who therefore has the legal title, has priority. Second, if neither party is entered on the register, then the party whose equitable interest was created first in time has priority.

So, for example, if X, the registered owner, is trustee of the shares for Y and, in breach of trust sells the shares to Z, who buys without notice of the trust and becomes registered as owner before the company knows of the trust, then Z will have priority over Y. Nor can Y bring an action for conversion against Z. Y only has an equitable interest in the shares whereas Z is a bona fide purchaser of the shares without notice of Y's interest.[90] Y's interest has therefore effectively been extinguished.[91] A company, however, is entitled to a reasonable time for the consideration of every transfer before it registers the transfer, and therefore if Y, in the example just given, had given notice of his claim to the company before Z was actually registered as owner, he would have been entitled to priority over Z, as his equitable interest would have been first in time. So, in *Peat v Clayton*,[92] C assigned all his property to P as trustee for C's creditors. The property included some shares. P asked for the share certificates but was unable to obtain them from C; he then gave notice of the assignment to the company. C, after the date of the assignment to P, sold the shares to X, who applied for registration. It was held that because P had acquired his equitable interest first in time that he was therefore entitled to be registered as the owner of those shares because he had priority.

Entry on the register after notice of a prior equitable claim will not give priority. So, in *Coleman v London County and Westminster Bank Ltd*,[93] in 1893 X transferred debentures of a private company to Y on trust for X for life with remainder to X's sons. The transfer was not registered. In 1894 one son sold his share of the debentures to Z. In 1911 X deposited the debentures with the bank as security for the company's overdraft. In 1914 the bank, on learning of the settlement and transfer to Y, took a transfer of the debentures from X, and were registered as owners. In line with the general principle it was held that Z was entitled to priority over the bank because Z's rights came into existence first. As mentioned, where there is notice of the prior rights then simply having registered your rights will not give you priority over someone whose rights arose earlier in time.

It was held by Romer J.[94] that in relation to a person whose legal title has not been perfected, then provided that that person has a present, absolute, and unconditional right to registration of his rights before the company learns of a better title, he has the same priority as if he were actually registered. It is doubtful, however, whether anything short of registration will give priority, except perhaps in very special circumstances. Directors should refuse to register a transfer after receiving notice of an adverse equitable claim to the shares, unless the transfer has already been passed for registration.[95]

Delay in obtaining registration is dangerous to a transferee for two reasons: a later transferee may gain priority by obtaining registration first, or an earlier

---

[90] See e.g. *Westdeutsche Landesbank v Islington* [1996] A.C. 669.
[91] *M.C.C. Proceeds Inc v Lehman Bros Int (Europe)* [1998] 2 B.C.L.C. 659.
[92] [1906] 1 Ch. 659.
[93] [1916] 2 Ch. 353.
[94] Per Romer J. in *Moore v North Western Bank* [1891] 2 Ch. 599 at 602 and 603.
[95] Per Joyce J. in *Ireland v Hart* [1902] 1 Ch. 522 at 529.

equity may come to light. So, in *Ireland v Hart*[96] a husband mortgaged shares of which he was trustee for his wife. Before the mortgagee was registered the wife successfully claimed that her equitable interest prevailed over that of the mortgagee because the equitable interest had been in existence first in time. To protect himself such a transferee should issue a stop notice.

SHARE CERTIFICATES

Every company issuing certificates must complete the share certificates and have **7–022** them ready for delivery within two months[97] after the allotment of any of its shares or after the date on which a transfer of its shares is lodged for registration, unless the conditions of issue otherwise provide, under a penalty of a default fine.[98] The form of the certificate is governed by the articles. Ordinarily, the articles of association will give the right to a certificate without payment and provides that it shall be under the seal of the company, and shall specify the shares to which it relates and the amount which has been paid up on those shares.

The certificate is a formal statement by the company that the person named on the certificate is the holder of the number of shares in the company specified in the certificate at the date of issue. It is prima facie evidence of the title of that person to the shares.[99] It is not, however, a document of title (as the register of members is), but wrongful interference with the right to possession of it can be the subject of a claim in the tort of conversion for which damages can be recovered for the whole of the value which is lost (as opposed to damages merely for the loss of the value of a mere piece of paper).[100] The object of the certificate is to facilitate dealings with the shares, whether by way of sale or security, and so make them more valuable to their owner. On the other hand, a share certificate is not a negotiable instrument, so that its accidental loss or destruction is not a matter of great moment. The articles usually make provision for the granting of a new certificate in such a case.

Estoppel[101] as to statements in a certificate

The principle in general terms: the company will be estopped from denying the trust of the certificate

The issue of a share certificate may give rise to an estoppel against the company **7–023** on the basis that the company may not deny the truth of the certificate against a person who has relied on the certificate and in consequence has changed his position. So, in *Bahia and San Francisco Railway Co, Re*[102] T was a registered holder

---

[96] [1902] 1 Ch. 522.

[97] Except for shares held in electronic form.

[98] Companies Act 2006 s.765.

[99] Companies Act 2006 s.768. See *Baku Consolidated Oilfields Ltd, Re* [1994] 1 B.C.L.C. 173.

[100] *M.C.C. Proceeds Inc v Lehman Brothers International (Europe)* [1998] 2 B.C.L.C. 659, CA; see also *International Credit and Investment (Overseas) Co Ltd v Adham* [1994] 1 B.C.L.C. 66.

[101] Personal bar is the Scottish equivalent of "estoppel". See Lord Kyllachy (Ordinary) in *Clavering, Son & Co v Goodwins, Jardine & Co Ltd* (1891) 18 R. 652 at 657.

[102] (1868) L.R. 3 Q.B. 584.

of shares who left her share certificate with her broker. T's signature was forged to a transfer in favour of S. T did not reply to notice of the transfer sent to her by the company and a new certificate in the name of S was issued by the company. A bought from S and paid for the shares on delivery of the share certificate and a new share certificate was issued to A. The fraud was subsequently discovered and T's name was restored to the register. It was held that the company was liable to indemnify A because the giving of the certificate to S amounted to a statement by the company, intended to be acted upon by purchasers of shares in the market; that S was entitled to the shares; and that because A had acted on the statement, the company was estopped from denying it. It was therefore held that A was entitled to recover damages from the company equal to the value of the shares at the time when the company first refused to recognise him as a shareholder, together with interest.

No estoppel in favour of a person who procures the certificate on the basis of a forged transfer

7–024 There will be no estoppel in favour of a person, such as S in *Bahia, Re*, who procures the granting of a certificate on a forged transfer[103] or forged power of attorney,[104] even if he has acted in good faith. In fact the company may be able to claim an indemnity from such a person. Nor will there be any estoppel in favour of a person who relies on the certificate either to establish that the person named is still the owner or that the person in possession is in fact the owner. It applies only to someone relying on the fact that the person named was the owner at the date of issue.[105]

In *Cadbury Schweppes Plc v Halifax Share Dealing Ltd*[106] fraudsters procured duplicate share certificates from a company by claiming that the proper shareholders had not received their certificates, and then the fraudsters purported to sell the shares relating to those certificates in the open market. The company was required to buy up the fraudulently issued, duplicate shares and to pay dividends on those shares to the genuine shareholders. The company then sought to recover its losses from the stockbrokers through whom the transactions had been conducted and against the company's Registrar. The stockbrokers sought an estoppel on the basis that the company ought not to be able to deny the truth of the duplicate share certificates which appeared to be genuine on their face. The company contended that the stockbrokers had suffered no detriment. Lindsay J. held, in essence, that the detriment was bound up with the stockbrokers' reliance on the ostensible validity of the certificates. Therefore, the stockbrokers were entitled to rely on the estoppel. It is a disappointment that the precise source of the detriment is not made clear because there is little evidence of detriment on the facts, except that the stockbrokers would suffer detriment if they were in the

---

[103] *Sheffield Corporation v Barclay* [1905] A.C. 392.

[104] *Starkey v Bank of England* [1903] A.C. 114.

[105] *Longman v Bath Electric Tramways Ltd* [1905] 1 Ch. 646; *International Credit and Investment Co (Overseas) Ltd v Adham* [1994] 1 B.C.L.C. 66; *Royal Bank of Scotland Plc v Sandstone Properties Ltd* [1998] 2 B.C.L.C. 429.

[106] [2007] 1 B.C.L.C. 497.

future required to compensate the company for the loss which it suffered in recovering the duplicate shares and compensating the genuine shareholders.[107]

Company estopped from denying title to people who have a share certificate

The company may be estopped from denying the title to shares of the person to **7-025** whom it has issued a share certificate.[108] So, in *Dixon v Kennaway & Co*[109] D bought 30 shares through a broker, L, who was also secretary of the company, and paid L. She received and returned to L a transfer of shares executed to L's direction by his clerk, P, who was never a man of substance and who did not hold any shares. The transfer, which did not specify the numbers of the shares, was put before the board by L and passed without production of P's certificate being required, and a new certificate prepared by L was issued to the effect that D held 30 shares, numbers 115–144 inclusive. The chairman, who did not sign the certificate, did not notice that the shares were part of his holding (numbers 1–133). The board properly relied on the secretary to check transfers and certificates with the register. Two years later the board notified D that P's transfer was invalid and declined to recognise her as a shareholder. L was bankrupt by then and the company could not prove that he could not have reimbursed D if, when the certificate was issued, the company had refused to issue it. It was held that D was entitled to damages.

The company may also be estopped from denying the amount stated to be paid up on shares. So, in *Bloomenthal v Ford*,[110] B lent money to a company on the security of fully paid shares in the company and was handed by the company share certificates for 10,000 shares of £1 each which the certificates stated to be fully paid up. No money had been paid on the shares, which had been issued direct by the company to B, but B did not know this. On the company's going into liquidation, B was placed on the list of contributories in respect of these shares. It was held that the company was estopped by the certificate from denying that the shares were fully paid up and B was entitled to have his name removed from the list of contributories.

The company may be made liable in damages to the person who has relied on the statement in the share certificate.[111] So, if B in the *Bloomenthal* had known that the shares were not fully paid up, there would have been no estoppel—there is no estoppel in favour of a person who knows the untruth of statements in a share certificate.[112] An original allottee, therefore, will seldom be in a position to benefit from the principle.[113]

---

[107] cf. *Gillett v Holt* [2001] Ch. 210.

[108] *Balkis Consolidated Co Ltd v Tomkinson* [1893] A.C. 396.

[109] [1900] 1 Ch. 833.

[110] [1897] A.C. 156. cf. *Waterhouse v Jamieson* (1870) 8 M. H.L. 88, in which it was held that statements in the memorandum and articles, which also appeared in share certificates, as to the amount paid up on shares could not be contradicted by the liquidator.

[111] *Clavering, Son & Co v Goodwins, Jardine & Co Ltd* (1891) 18 R. 652.

[112] See *Crickmer's Case* (1875) L.R. 10. Ch. App. 614. In England, if the shares had been transferred to a purchaser without notice that they were not fully paid up he could give a good title to a purchaser from him without notice: *Barrow's Case* (1880) 14 Ch.D. 432, CA.

[113] *Liquidator of Scottish Heritages Co Ltd* (1898) 5 S.L.T. 336 (OH): contrast *Penang Foundry Co Ltd v Gardiner*, 1913 S.C. 1203 (OH).

Company not estopped where certificate is a forgery

7-026 The company is not estopped where a certificate is a forgery. So, in *Ruben v Great Fingall Consolidated*,[114] R lent money to the secretary of a company for his own purposes on the security of a share certificate issued to R by the secretary and certifying that R was registered as transferee of the shares. The secretary issued the share certificate without authority, affixed the common seal and forged the signatures of two directors, so that the certificate apparently complied with the articles. R sued the company for damages for refusal to register him as a shareholder. It was held that, in the absence of evidence that the company had held out the secretary as having authority to do more than the mere ministerial act of delivering share certificates when duly made to the people who were entitled to them, that the company was not estopped from disputing the claim or responsible for the secretary's act.

Forged transfers

7-027 A forged transfer of shares is a nullity and cannot affect the title of the shareholder whose signature has been forged. Therefore, if a company has registered the forged transfer and removed the true owner of the shares from the register, then it can be compelled to replace him.[115] The company can then claim an indemnity from the person who sent the forged transfer for registration if it has sustained a loss through acting on it. The person who sent the form is usually either the transferor or his broker.

Ordinarily, no estoppel will arise in favour of such a person in relation to a share certificate which is issued to him even though he knows nothing of the forgery on the basis that he has not relied on the act of the company in issuing the certificate. By way of illustration, in *Sheffield Corporation v Barclay*,[116] B sent to the corporation for registration a transfer of stock which stood in the names of T and H. The transfer was a forgery, T having forged H's signature to the transfer, but B was ignorant of this. The corporation registered the transfer. B transferred the stock to third parties to whom certificates were issued. The corporation was estopped from denying that those registered were the stockholders entitled. H subsequently discovered the forgery and compelled the corporation to buy him an equivalent amount of stock and to pay him the missing dividends with interest. It was held that B was bound to indemnify the corporation upon an implied contract that the transfer was genuine.

It has been suggested that the company may not, however, be able to claim a complete indemnity if it is guilty of negligence in failing to spot the forgery, by virtue of s.2(1) of the Civil Liability (Contribution) Act 1978.[117] This view was

---

[114] [1906] A.C. 439.

[115] *Barton v N. Staffordshire Railway Co* (1888) 38 Ch.D. 458.

[116] [1905] A.C. 392. In *Royal Bank of Scotland Plc v Sandstone Properties Ltd* [1998] 2 B.C.L.C. 429, this principle was applied even where the company had issued the fraudster with a duplicate share certificate which was then used in the forged transfer. The duplicate certificate was not the proximate cause of the loss. That was the request for the transfer; cf. Lord Kyllachy (Ordinary) in *Clavering, Son & Co v Goodwins, Jardine & Co Ltd* (1891) 18 R. 652 at 657.

[117] *Yeung v Honk Kong and Shanghai Bank Ltd* [1980] 2 All E.R. 599, PC. In Scotland see Law Reform (Miscellaneous Provisions) (Scotland) Act 1940 s.3.

doubted, however, in *Royal Bank of Scotland Plc v Sandstone Properties Ltd*,[118] on the basis that the whole principle of the right to an indemnity would be affected by such a claim for contribution.

In an effort to prevent the registration of a forged transfer, companies usually, on a transfer being lodged for registration, write to the shareholder informing him of the transfer and of their intention to register it unless by return of post they hear that he objects. The neglect of the shareholder to reply to this communication does not estop him from proving that the transfer is a forgery.[119]

RESTRICTIONS ON TRANSFER

Every shareholder has a right to transfer his shares to whom he likes, unless the **7–028** articles provide to the contrary.[120] As Buckley LJ explained the principle in *Lindlar's Case*[121]:

"[By the Companies Acts] it is provided that the shares in a company under these Acts shall be capable of being transferred in manner provided by the regulations of the company. The regulations of the company may impose fetters upon the right of transfer. In the absence of restrictions in the articles the shareholder has by virtue of the statute the right to transfer his shares without the consent of anybody to any transferee, even though he be a man of straw, provided it is a bona fide transaction in the sense that it is an out-and-out disposal of the property without retaining any interest in the shares—that the transferor bona fide divests himself of all benefit. . . . In the absence of restrictions it is competent to a transferor, notwithstanding that the company is in extremis to compel registration of a transfer to a transferee notwithstanding that the latter is a person not competent to meet the unpaid liability upon the shares. Even if the transfer be executed for the express purpose of relieving the transferor from liability, the directors cannot upon that ground refuse to register it unless there is in the articles some provision so enabling them."

In the case of a private company, the articles may, and usually do, restrict the right of the company to transfer its shares.[122] In the case of a public company, shares must normally be free from restrictions on the right of transfer if a stock exchange quotation is to be obtained: that is, those shares must be freely transferable, in the manner discussed in Chs 14 and 15 below.[123]

---

[118] [1998] 2 B.C.L.C. 429. That case equally suggests there is no joint liability as joint tortfeasors.

[119] *Bahia and San Francisco Railway Co, Re* (1868) L.R. 3 QB 584, above, 220, *Barton v L. & N.W. Railway Co* (1890) 24 Q.B.D. 77, CA.

[120] *Weston's Case* (1868) L.R. 4 Ch. App. 20; *O'Meara v The El Palmar Rubber Estates Ltd*, 1913; 1 S.L.T. 383 (OH). It is otherwise, e.g. where the company is being wound up and a transfer is prevented by IA 1986 s.127.

[121] [1910] 1 Ch. 312, CA at 316. See also *Borland's Trustee v Steel Bros & Co Ltd* [1901] 1 Ch. 279. For Scottish authority to the same effect, see, e.g. Lord Kincairney (Ordinary) in *Stewart v James Keiller & Sons Ltd* (1902) 4 F. 657 at 667.

[122] Until the 1980 Act such restrictions were obligatory for private companies.

[123] Admission of securities to listing. The main advantage of a stock exchange quotation is that it makes the securities more marketable.

In traditional company law theory, any restrictions on the transfer of shares are a derogation from the common law right of free transfer. It follows that: any rights conferred by the articles will not be extended to situations not covered by them,[124] the procedure laid down in the articles for the exercise of the rights must be strictly followed,[125] and if the rights are not actively exercised the right of free transfer will revive.[126] If there has been a registered transfer in breach of the articles the only remedy available to an aggrieved shareholder is rectification of the register. This is a discretionary remedy, however, and will not be granted to third parties for extraneous purposes.[127]

Such restrictions usually fall within one of two categories: pre-emption clauses and refusal clauses. Each is considered in the sections to follow.

Pre-emption clauses

7–029   The articles of a private company usually contain a pre-emption clause: that is a clause which provides that if rights are to be sold then they must be offered to identified people first. In company law, this is a clause which requires that if new shares are to be issued, then they must be offered to existing shareholders first. For example, a pre-emption provision may provide that no shares shall be transferred to any person not being an existing member of the company so long as a member can be found to purchase them at a fair price to be determined in accordance with the articles.[128] Such a pre-emption clause does not entitle the company to refuse to register a transfer of shares from one member to another member of the company.[129] Where the value of shares for the purpose of such a clause falls to be fixed by the directors, the court will not review the directors' valuation provided that they have acted fairly and honestly.[130] Furthermore, a member whose shares have been offered to other members under a pre-emption clause has been held entitled to withdraw his offer at any time before its acceptance.[131]

Sometimes the pre-emption clause provides that a member who wants to sell any of his shares must inform the directors of the number of shares, the price and the name of the proposed transferee, and the directors must first offer the shares at that price to the other shareholders. In such a case, any member to whom the shares are offered cannot buy part only of the shares, and if none of the members is willing to buy all the shares the proposed transfer can be carried out.[132] Many pre-emption clauses also provide the machinery whereby the shares may be offered to the existing members, for example by making the company secretary

---

[124] *Furness & Co v Liquidators of "Cynthiana" Steamship Co Ltd* (1893) 21 R. 239.

[125] *Neilson v Ayr Race Meetings Syndicate Ltd*, 1918 1 S.L.T. 63 (O.H.).

[126] *Shepherd's Trustees v Shepherd*, 1950 S.C. HL 60 (application for registration granted, the two directors having failed to agree to refuse registration); *New Cedos Engineering Co Ltd, Re* [1994] 1 B.C.L.C. 797.

[127] *Piccadilly Radio Plc, Re* [1988] B.C.L.C. 683.

[128] Valued as at the date of the transfer under the clause, unless the contrary is expressed: *Pennington v Crampton* [2004] B.C.C. 611.

[129] *Delavenne v Broadhurst* [1931] Ch. 234.

[130] *Stewart v James Keiller & Sons Ltd* (1902) 4 F. 657.

[131] *J. M. Smith Ltd v Colquhoun's Trustees* (1901) 3 F. 981.

[132] *The Ocean Coal Co Ltd v The Powell Duffryn Steam Coal Co Ltd* [1932] 1 Ch. 654.

as agent for their sale. In *Tett v Phoenix Property and Investment Co*[133] the articles simply provided that there should be no transfer if any member indicated that he was willing to purchase the shares. The Court of Appeal, reversing Vinelott J., read a term into the articles which required a transferor to take reasonable steps to give the other members a reasonable opportunity to offer to purchase the shares at a fair value. (Strictly speaking such a clause is not a pre-emption clause since it simply forbids a transfer to outsiders where a member has indicated his willingness to buy.)

Application to transfers of beneficial interests

Most disputes centre around the question as to whether transfers of beneficial **7–030** interests in shares will be caught by a pre-emption clause or whether it will only operate on transfers of the legal title. The issue was brought into focus by the decision of the Court of Appeal in *Safeguard Industrial Investments Ltd v National Westminster Bank Plc.*[134] In that case, an executor was registered as a member in that capacity and so held the testator's shares on trust for the beneficiaries under the terms of the will. The beneficiaries gave instructions to the executor that they did not wish to have the shares transferred into their own names. It was held that this did not invoke the pre-emption clause.[135] That clause only operated against a proposed transfer of, what a property lawyer would understand as being, the absolute title in the shares,[136] but that was not proposed in those circumstances.[137] The Court distinguished the earlier case of *Lyle & Scott Ltd v Scott's Trustees*,[138] in which case the shareholders had given an outside purchaser, who was making a bid to take over the company, general voting proxies and had also agreed to execute transfers and to deliver up their share certificates when asked to do so. They were held to be desirous of transferring their shares and so invoked the pre-emption clause. The difference was said to be that in *Lyle* the shareholders had done everything they had to do to transfer the shares and were bound to transfer them on request; whereas in *Safeguard*, although the beneficiaries could ask for transfer of the legal title in the shares, they had no intention of doing so.

---

[133] [1986] B.C.L.C. 149, CA.

[134] [1982] 1 W.L.R. 62.

[135] The beneficiaries were not existing members so that a transfer of the legal title to them would have invoked the clause.

[136] That is, the beneficiaries would require transfer of the legal title to them (or rather, properly, the termination of the trust so that the legal title owned by the trustees can be transferred to the beneficiaries), with the result that the beneficiaries would then be in a position to take absolute ownership of the shares in the proportions which would be agreed between them: in accordance with the principle in *Saunders v Vautier* (1841) 4 Beav. 115, as discussed in Alastair Hudson, *Equity & Trusts*, 6th edn (Routledge Cavendish, 2009), p.152.

[137] It would have been different if the company had adopted regs 31 and 32 of Table A which applies the pre-emption provisions to the registration of the executors as shareholders in the first place. The reasoning in *Safeguard* was followed in similar circumstances in *Pennington v Crampton* [2004] B.C.C. 611, where the main issue was whether the company's articles had impliedly overruled regs 31 and 32 which were supposedly incorporated into them. That case also decided that the particular clause would not operate on a change of executor.

[138] [1959] A.C. 763.

A different aspect of the distinction between legal and equitable interests in this context arose in *Theakston v London Trust Plc*.[139] One member agreed to sell his shares to another member but in fact the purchase price was paid by a non-member, in whose name the shares were charged and according to whose instructions the "purchaser" was to vote. Harman J. held that this was a transfer from one member to another and so outside the pre-emption clause. The fact that the transferee had equitable obligations to an outsider did not affect the position.

Nevertheless, in general the position is that if the transferor, as in *Lyle*, has put himself into a position whereby he must transfer the legal title to his shares on request, then he will be caught by the pre-emption clause.[140] The trick is to somehow give the intending purchaser the benefits and security of a transfer without becoming bound to transfer the shares on request. An ingenious solution was found in *Sedgefield Steeplechase (1927) Ltd, Re*.[141] The company had a pre-emption clause applying to those intending to transfer their shares to an outsider. An outside buyer for the company had entered into agreements with about 80 per cent of the members to the effect that they were bound to vote and otherwise comply with any instructions given to them by the bidder and to use their best endeavours to alter the articles to remove the pre-emption clause. However, these agreements were specifically subject to an obligation on the part of the members not to do anything contrary to the pre-emption clause. When the other member sought to invoke the pre-emption clause her application was rejected, first by Lord Hoffmann (sitting at first instance)[142] and then by the Court of Appeal. Lord Hoffmann held that since the members were not under an obligation to transfer the shares in violation of the clause the clause could not apply. As Lord Hoffmann held:

> "The general principle which I would derive from the cases is that a shareholder who has done nothing inconsistent with an intention to comply, at the appropriate moment, with the subsisting provisions of the articles, cannot be required to serve a transfer notice at an earlier stage. The obligation attaches only when the shareholder has entered into arrangements . . . which place him under a contractual obligation to execute and deliver a transfer in violation of the rights of pre-emption."[143]

7–031 The Court of Appeal were dismissive of any such principle but upheld the decision as a matter of construction in the circumstances of that particular clause.

It is true that each clause has to be interpreted on its own merits and the principles on which such interpretation have been conducted have become more complex as a result of the weight of case law. Many now seek to cover transfers of beneficial interests as well as the legal title. That difficulties of construction remain can be seen from the pre-action case of *Rose v Lynx Express Ltd*.[144] In that

---

[139] [1984] B.C.L.C. 390.
[140] *Macro (Ipswich) Ltd, Re* [1994] 2 B.C.L.C. 354; *Hurst v Crampton Bros (Coopers) Ltd* [2003] B.C.L.C. 304.
[141] [2003] B.C.C. 889.
[142] Sitting as a judge at first instance and not for a short time in the House of Lords.
[143] [2003] B.C.C. 889 at 996E.
[144] [2004] 1 B.C.L.C. 455.

case, the pre-emption clause in question applied to the transfer of the legal or beneficial ownership of the shares, and also to any sale or disposition of any legal or equitable interest in a share whether or not by the registered owner. The registered owner was the nominee for two limited partnerships. The question was whether the pre-emption clause applied where there was a change in the membership of those limited partnerships. On one construction whereby the clause would not apply, any member could easily circumvent the clause by transferring his shares to a nominee and then assigning his beneficial interest. The other construction, however, whereby the clause would apply, would arguably require the nominee to give a transfer notice in respect of the entire holding even where there was no proposed purchaser of that holding. In the circumstances the Court of Appeal felt unable to resolve the point without a full trial.

Transfers in breach of the clause

If the provision in the articles relating to the offer of the shares to the existing **7–032** shareholders before a transfer is made is disregarded, then the directors cannot validly register the transfer since it is a transfer in breach of the articles.[145] Under English law the same is true in the case of a sale, made in disregard of the articles, by a mortgagee under his power of sale.[146] However, a transfer by a shareholder, in breach of the pre-emptive rights given by the articles, to a person who has paid for the shares operates as a transfer of the beneficial interest in the shares, so that the transferee takes priority over a judgment creditor who subsequently obtains a charging order on the shares.[147] Yet, if the transferee is not a purchaser for value, then he takes subject to the equitable interests arising under the option given by the pre-emption clause to the other shareholders.[148] There must be substantial and substantive compliance with the pre-emption procedure before a transfer outside its terms can be effective. If there is no such compliance the court can award an injunction to prevent such transfer.[149] It has also been held that a company enforcing a power of sale under a lien on its own shares must itself comply with the pre-emption clause in its articles in effecting that sale.[150] One should bear in mind what is said below as to the duty of care owed by an auditor who values shares in the knowledge that his valuation will determine the price to be paid under a contract.

---

[145] *Tett v Phoenix Property and Investment Co Ltd* [1986] B.C.L.C. 149, CA.

[146] *Hunter v Hunter* [1936] A.C. 222.

[147] *Hawks v McArthur* [1951] 1 All E.R. 22. In *Tett v Phoenix Investment and Property Co Ltd*, above, Vinelott J. upheld *Hawks v McArthur* and rejected any general argument to the contrary based on *Hunter v Hunter*, above. This part of his judgment was not challenged in the Court of Appeal. Similarly, in Scotland, in a competition between a transferee and an arrester, the arrester was held not to be entitled to found on an alleged failure on the part of the company to observe the proper procedure relating to pre-emption and registration of transfers, with the result that the court declared that the shares had vested in the transferee: *National Bank of Scotland Glasgow Nominees Ltd v Adamson*, 1932 S.L.T. 492 (OH).

[148] *Cuttrell v King* [2004] 2 B.C.L.C. 814.

[149] *Curtis v J.J. Curtis & Co Ltd* [1986] B.C.L.C. 86 NZ.

[150] *Champagne Perrier-Jouet SA v H. H. Finch Ltd* [1982] 1 W.L.R. 1359.

Directors' powers to refuse transfers ("refusal clauses")

7–033 The question arises as to the circumstances in which a transfer of shares may be refused. In addition to containing a pre-emption clause, the articles of a private company often contain an article that the directors may, in their absolute discretion and without giving any reason for any exercise of that discretion, refuse to register any transfer of any share. For example, directors may choose to refuse to accept a transfer of shares in relation to a private company if that company operates a family business if the transfer would have the effect of taking control of the company out of the hands of family members. By contrast, it is a requirement of the law on the offer of shares to the public that shares in relation to public companies are freely transferable, as considered in Chs 14 and 15, below. If the shares in public companies were not freely transferable, then stock exchanges could not operate properly because the buyers and sellers of shares could not know if their transactions would be enforced.

In relation to private companies, where the directors have a discretionary power of refusal then they must both act within the terms of that power, and also act bona fide in what they consider to be the interests of the company and not for any collateral purpose. This is true of any fiduciary power of course. Where the power is unrestricted (the normal case) the courts, in considering whether the directors have so acted bona fide for the benefit of the company use the presumption that the directors have been acting in good faith and the onus of proving the contrary is therefore on those challenging the decision.[151] Thus the courts will not impugn the decision simply because the directors disliked the transferor or transferee. Personal relationships are a fact of life in small companies. The problem which is created is that directors' personal, private views may interfere with what might otherwise have been thought was in the best interest of the company. The private views of the directors would only affect the issue if they displaced their dispassionate views as to what was in the best interests of the company.[152] So, in *Smith and Fawcett Ltd, Re*[153] the articles of association gave the directors "an absolute and uncontrolled discretion" to refuse to register any transfer of shares. The two directors each held 4,001 of the 8,002 ordinary shares. F died and his son, as the executor, applied for the shares to be registered in his name. S refused, but offered to register 2,001 shares if 2,000 were sold to him at a fixed price. F's son applied for rectification of the register but failed. It was held that there was nothing on the facts to show that the director's power had not been exercised bona fide in the company's interest, and therefore that exercise of the director's power was permitted to stand. This approach was applied in *Mactra Properties Ltd v Morshead Mansions Ltd*[154] to the effect that refusal to register a transfer of shares could only be based on a power in the articles if that power was being exercised in the best interests of the company. The central principle, as expressed by Lord Greene M.R. in *Smith and Fawcett* was that the directors

---

[151] *Village Cay Marina Ltd v Acland* [1998] 2 B.C.L.C. 327, PC; *Charles Forte Investments Ltd v Amanda* [1964] Ch. 240, CA, per Willmer L.J. at 252–254 and per Danckwerts L.J. at 260–261.
[152] *Popely v Planarrive Ltd* [1997] 1 B.C.L.C. 8.
[153] [1942] Ch. 304 CA.
[154] [2009] 1 B.C.L.C. 179.

"must exercise their discretion bona fide in what they consider—not what a court may consider—is in the interests of the company, and not for any collateral purpose . . . The question therefore, simply is whether on the true construction of the particular article the directors are limited by anything except their bona fide view as to the interests of the company".

(This concept is considered in detail in Ch.17 in relation to the directors' duty to prosecute the best interests of the company.)

If the articles empower the directors to decline to register transfers on certain grounds, for example on the grounds that the transferor is indebted to the company or that the transferee is a person of whom they do not approve, then they can be interrogated as to the ground on which they have refused registration. The directors may be interrogated as to the reasons for their refusal, unless the articles provide that they shall not be bound to specify the grounds for their refusal, in which case they cannot be interrogated at all.[155] If the directors give reasons for their refusal, the court can decide whether they are sufficient to justify the refusal. An illustration of these principles arose in *Bede S.S. Co Ltd, Re*.[156] In that case the articles of association empowered the directors to refuse to register a transfer if they certified that "in their opinion it is contrary to the interests of the company that the proposed transferee should be a member thereof." The directors declined to register transfers of single shares, stating that it was contrary to the interests of the company that shares should be transferred singly or in small amounts to outside persons with no interest in, or knowledge of, shipping. It was held that this was a bad reason for refusing—on the basis that refusal should have been on grounds personal to the transferee—and so the transfers were directed to be registered.

The directors are not, however, confined to the reasons they have given, at least **7–034** in the normal case where they are not bound by the articles to make a certification as to their opinion. Rather, it is for the court to decide whether the directors were acting bona fide in the interests of the company, and the reasons given are merely evidence of that.[157] (A different approach is taken, however, in relation to the directors' duties to act in the best interests of the company (on which see Ch.17).)

A formal active exercise of the right of refusal to register is required before the company is authorised to refuse to register shares in the names of the transferees. Where directors are equally divided and so come to no decision to decline to register, the transfer must be registered.[158] As considered above, a refusal to register a person as a shareholder may be the result of conflict within the company. So, in circumstances in which the articles of the association provided that no share could be transferred to a person who was not already a member of the company without the consent of the directors, one of the directors sought to prevent a particular transfer from being registered by deliberately abstaining from attending board meetings so that a quorum could not be obtained to approve that

---

[155] *Berry and Stewart v Tottenham Hotspur Football Club Co Ltd* [1935] Ch. 718.
[156] [1917] 1 Ch. 123 CA.
[157] *Village Cay Marina Ltd v Acland* [1998] 2 B.C.L.C. 327, PC.
[158] *Shepherd's Trustees v Shepherd*, 1950 S.C. HL 60, per Lord Porter at 66; *Hackney Pavilion Ltd, Re* [1924] 1 Ch. 276.

transfer. In that case it was held that the transferee was entitled to an order directing the company to register the transfer.[159] Another stratagem for refusing a transfer, in relation to companies whose articles give the directors the power to refuse transfers, is simply to delay voting to approve it. In one decided case the board of directors lost their right to veto a transfer because they were guilty of an unreasonable delay of four months in deciding whether or not to exercise the veto, whereas the legislation at the time provided for a period of two months to give an intended transferee notice of a refusal to register a transfer. It was considered that four months constituted an unnecessary delay in this context, unless in an exceptional case it is impossible to constitute a board.[160] Where there are no properly appointed directors to constitute a quorum to decide whether to exercise the right of refusal any refusal to register is a nullity,[161] but the transferee has no right to registration until the end of the period within which a properly constituted board could have exercised the power. It follows that any purported registration during that period is invalid.[162]

In a rare case, the remedy of the transferee, or of the transferor, on a refusal to register a transfer is to apply to the court to rectify the register of members by substituting his name for that of the transferor. Unnecessary delay in registering a transfer does not in itself constitute a ground for rectification, and a transferor applying for rectification must be able to show that he has been prejudiced by the delay.[163] A winding up petition is not the proper remedy for the transferor where registration of a transfer is refused.[164]

Transmission of Shares

7-035 Section 770(2) of the CA 2006 provides that s.770(1), does not prejudice any power of a company to register as a shareholder any person to whom the right to any shares in the company has been transmitted by operation of law. Transmission of shares occurs on the death or the bankruptcy of a member, or, if the member is a company, on its going into liquidation.

On the death of a sole shareholder the shares vest in his personal representative.[165] The company is bound to accept production of the probate of the will or, in the case of an intestacy, letters of administration of the estate, or, in Scotland, the confirmation as executor, as sufficient evidence of the grant.[166] Subject to any restrictions in the articles, the personal representative may be registered as a member or transfer the shares without himself becoming a member.[167]

---

[159] *Copal Varnish Co Ltd, Re* [1917] 2 Ch. 349.
[160] *Swaledale Cleaners Ltd, Re* [1968] 1 W.L.R. 1710, CA; *Inverdeck Ltd, Re* [1998] 2 B.C.L.C. 242.
[161] *New Cedos Engineering Co Ltd, Re* [1994] 1 B.C.L.C. 797.
[162] *Zinotty Properties Ltd, Re* [1984] 1 W.L.R. 1249.
[163] *Property Investment Co of Scotland Ltd v Duncan* (1887) 14 R. 299.
[164] *Charles Forte Investments Ltd v Amanda* [1964] Ch. 240, CA.
[165] *Greene, Re* [1949] Ch. 333.
[166] See, e.g. *Baku Consolidated Oilfields Ltd, Re* [1994] 1 B.C.L.C. 173.
[167] Companies Act 2006 s.773. If any pre-emption or refusal powers in the articles to the executor or administrator becoming the registered member are disapplied then the executor is not subject to them unless or until he transfers the legal title: *Safeguard Industrial Investments Ltd v National Westminsters Bank Ltd* [1982] 1 W.L.R. 589, CA.

MORTGAGE OF SHARES (ENGLISH LAW)

Under English law, a shareholder who borrows money on the security of his shares **7–036** may give the lender either a legal mortgage or an equitable mortgage over the shares.[168] Like any other form of property, a share can be used as security for a loan.

Legal mortgage

A legal mortgage of shares is effected by transfer of the shares to the lender (the **7–037** mortgagee) followed by registration of the transfer by the company. There should also be a document setting out the terms of the loan and containing an agreement to retransfer the shares on repayment of the amount borrowed with interest. The document will empower the lender to sell the shares in the event of default by the borrower (the mortgagor). When exercising a power of sale the lender is under a duty to take reasonable care to obtain a proper price for the shares. He does not have to wait for a higher price but he must obtain the true market value of the shares. Any clause in the deed which purports to exclude this liability for negligence must be expressly worded to that effect.[169]

This form of mortgage gives the lender with security up to the value of the shares. He will be entitled to dividends and to exercise any voting rights in respect of the shares, unless it is agreed that the dividends shall be paid to the borrower and that he shall exercise the voting rights as the borrower directs.[170] However, restrictions on the transfer of shares contained in the articles may prevent this kind of mortgage being made. Further, it might not be advisable where the shares are not fully paid because the lender on the register would be personally liable for calls.

Equitable mortgage

Mortgages can arise in equity in various situations in which the formalities for the **7–038** creation of a valid, legal mortgage have not been observed. So, an equitable mortgage of shares may be made by depositing the share certificate with the lender as security for such a loan. In such a case the lender can enforce his security by applying to the court for a sale of the shares or for an order for transfer and foreclosure.[171] Alternatively, a method which is more commonly adopted is for the borrower to deposit the share certificate with the lender together with a blank transfer form.[172] In such a case the lender has an implied power to sell the shares if default is made by the borrower in making repayment at the agreed time or, if no time for repayment is agreed, within a reasonable time after notice.[173] The implied power of sale includes power to insert the name of the buyer in the blank transfer if, as is usual, the articles provide for transfers to be in writing. The

---

[168] The general law on mortgages and charges is set out in Alastair Hudson, *The Law of Finance* (London: Sweet & Maxwell, 2009), para.23–30 et seq.

[169] *Bishop v Bonham* [1988] B.C.L.C. 656, CA.

[170] *Siemens Brothers & Co Ltd v Burns* [1918] 2 Ch. 324.

[171] *Harrold v Plenty* [1901] 2 Ch. 314.

[172] i.e. a transfer signed by the borrower with the transferee's name left blank.

[173] *Hooper v Herts* [1906] 1 Ch. 549.

borrower is under an implied obligation not to delay registration of the transfer so filled up.[174]

No equitable mortgage is in itself absolutely secure because the borrower remains on the register and may sell the shares and procure the registration of the purchaser with priority over the lender, who would have no remedy against the company. So, in *Rainford v James Keith & Blackman Co Ltd*,[175] C deposited his share certificate and a blank transfer with R as a security for a loan. The following wording was printed on the certificate: "Without the production of this certificate no transfer of the shares mentioned therein can be registered." C sold the shares to Y and induced the company to register Y as owner of the shares without the production of the share certificate. R sued the company for wrongfully registering the shares in Y's name. It was held that the company was not liable as it owed no duty of care to R, and the statement on the certificate was only a warning to the owner of the shares to take care of the certificate and not a statement of fact giving rise to an estoppel.[176] However, as a general principle, the mortgagor must exercise any voting rights as directed by the mortgagee.[177]

Stop notice

7–039 To obtain complete protection, an equitable mortgagee of shares should serve a stop notice. This is done by filing an affidavit setting out the facts, and a notice in the prescribed form, in the Central Office of the Supreme Court or in a District Registry and serving an office copy of the affidavit and a duplicate notice on the company. The effect of the notice is that, whilst it continues in force, if the company receives any request to register a transfer of the shares in question it must give notice in writing to the person who has served the notice. Within eight days, such person must apply for an injunction restraining the transfer or the company will be at liberty to register the transfer.[178]

Charging order

7–040 A judgment creditor of the registered owner of shares may obtain an order charging the shares with payment of the judgment debt,[179] after which, until the order is discharged, the company cannot permit a transfer except with the authority of the court. A charging order will not have priority over a mortgage created by deposit of the share certificate and a blank transfer before the date of the charging order, as the judgment creditor can be in no better position than the judgment debtor at the time when the order was made.

---

[174] *Powell v London and Provincial Bank* [1893] 2 Ch. 555, CA.

[175] [1905] 1 Ch. 296.

[176] Reversed on the facts [1905] 2 Ch. 147, CA. On the facts the company was affected with notice of R's charge and he was able to recover the price of the shares which had been paid to the company in repayment of a loan made by the company to C.

[177] *Wise v Lansell* [1921] 1 Ch. 420.

[178] RSC, Ord.50, rr.11–15. See also the Charging Orders Act 1979.

[179] RSC, Ord.50, rr.2–7.

ASSIGNATION OF SHARES IN SECURITY (SCOTS LAW)

The only effective way of assigning shares in security is by the execution and **7–041** registration of a transfer in favour of the lender. See para.7–037, above.

No form of the equitable mortgage recognised by English law gives the lender any real security in competition with the general creditors of the borrower.[180] Accordingly, where a borrower delivers the share certificate to the lender and undertakes to transfer the shares to the lender when requested to do so, a transfer executed within six months before the borrower's sequestration or his granting of a protected trust deed is reducible as an unfair preference under s.36 of the Bankruptcy (Scotland) Act 1985.[181] For the purposes of that section the day on which a preference was created is the day on which the preference became "completely effectual",[182] and that would only be so when the transfer had been registered. It may be, however, that where a completed transfer has been delivered to the lender along with the share certificate so that the lender is in a position to have himself registered as a member without further interposition of the borrower, registration of the transfer on the eve of the borrower's sequestration is not open to challenge as an unfair preference provided the delivery of the documents to the lender was made more than six months before the borrower's sequestration.[183]

Stop notices and charging orders are not part of Scots law. When a company called on to register a transfer receives intimation from some person other than the transferee that that other person has an interest in the shares, the company is entitled to proceed to register the transfer unless the intimation is followed up by an application for interdict or other legal measure.[184]

Shares are subject to arrestment at the instance of the creditors of the shareholder, whether the arrestment is in execution,[185] or merely to found jurisdiction.[186] Where competition arises between a transferee and an arrester the transferee has the preferable right to the shares as soon as his transfer has been lodged, even although it is not registered before the lodging of the arrestment.

The principle was illustrated in *Harvey's Yoker Distillery Ltd v Singleton*.[187] In **7–042** that case, in January, S transferred 200 shares to M and 1,000 shares to F, and the transfers were received by the secretary of the company on January 19, and February 2, respectively. Because of an arrestment lodged the previous November against S at the instance of a bank, the transfers were not registered. On March 30, arrestments

---

[180] *Gourlay v Mackie* (1887) 14 R. 403; per Lord Gifford in *Morrison v Harrison* (1876) 3 R. 406 at 411; cf. *Guild v Young* (1884) 22 S.L.R. 520 (OH).

[181] This provision is the successor to the repealed Bankruptcy Act 1696 (Scots Act 1696, c.5) which made fraudulent preferences reducible on the ground of notour bankruptcy.

[182] Bankruptcy (Scotland) Act 1985 s.36(3).

[183] *Guild v Young* (1884) 22 S.L.R. 520 (OH), decided under the 1696 Act, can give at best slender support to the proposition. Whereas the 1696 Act affected only voluntary preferences conferred by the bankrupt on favoured creditors, s.36 of the 1985 Act applies to any transaction entered into by the debtor. Although s.36 is not restricted to the challenge of voluntary preferences, it is submitted that the registration by the creditor of an already executed transfer in circumstances such as arose in *Guild v Young* would not be classed as a transaction entered into by the debtor.

[184] Per Lord M'Laren in *Shaw v Caledonian Railway Co* (1890) 17 R. 466 at 482.

[185] *Sinclair v Staples* (1860) 22 D. 600.

[186] *American Mortgage Co of Scotland Ltd v Sidway*, 1908 S.C. 500.

[187] (1901) 8 S.L.T. 369 (OH)

were executed at the instance of D against S. It was held, the transfers to M and F were preferable to D's arrestments. Lord Stornmonth Darling held that[188]:

> "An arrestment can only attach property belonging truly and in substance to the common debtor. Now these shares did not belong in substance to Singleton at the time of the arrestment, because he had by that time done all in his power to dispose of them by executing the transfers".

An arrester is not entitled to found on any irregularity in the registration procedure to the effect of defeating the transferee's title.[189] Intimation to the company of a transfer, even without registration, has the effect, in a question between the transferee and a subsequent arrester of cutting out the arrestment.[190]

CALLS ON SHARES

7-043 A call on shares is a demand by the directors that a member pay to the company money which is unpaid on his shares, whether on account of the nominal value of the shares or by way of premium.[191] If, when shares are issued, the full amount of each share is not payable at once, the terms of issue will provide that part is payable on application, part on allotment and the remainder by instalments at fixed dates: in such a case, the instalments are not calls because the obligation of the shareholder to pay is not dependent on a call from the company. However, in a rare case, the company may not require all the nominal amount of a share, or the full amount of a premium on a share, to be paid at or soon after allotment but may leave part to be called up in accordance with the provisions of the articles as and when required by the company or, in the event of a winding up, by the liquidator. If so, a shareholder is bound to pay the whole or part of the balance unpaid on his shares "as and when called on", in accordance with the provisions of the articles. Calls, including communication of the call notice, must be made in the manner laid down in the articles.[192]

LIEN ON SHARES (ENGLISH LAW)

7-044 The articles of a private company may give the company a lien on the shares held by a member for his unpaid call or instalment, or for some other debt due from him to the company. Public companies however may only have a lien on such shares for an unpaid call or instalment on those shares.[193] A lien is expressed by

---

[188] (1901) 8 S.L.T. 369 (OH) per Lord Stormonth Darling (Ordinary) at 370.

[189] *National Bank of Scotland Glasgow Nominees Ltd v Adamson*, 1932 S.L.T. 492 (OH); for an arrestment made effective by the granting by the court of a warrant to sell the shares, see *Valentine v Grangemouth Coal Co Ltd* (1897) 35 S.L.R. 12 (OH).

[190] *Jackson v Elphick* (1902) 10 S.L.T. 146 (OH).

[191] For Scots dicta on the nature of a call see Lord President M'Neill in *Wryght v Lindsay* (1856) 19 D. 55 at p.63; affirmed (1860) 22 D. HL 5.

[192] See, e.g. *Hunter v Senate Support Services Ltd* [2004] EWHC Ch. 1085.

[193] Companies Act 2006 s.670. The articles may grant a lien on shares which are fully paid but that would interfere with the principle in the Listing Rules that the shares must be freely transferable. If the lien given by the articles extends only to shares not fully paid, the company can alter its articles so as to give a lien on all shares, even if only one member will be affected by the alteration. See *Allen v Gold Reefs of West Africa Ltd* [1900] 1 Ch. 656, CA.

s.670 of the CA 2006 as being a form of equitable charge upon the shares, and has been understood by the case law as giving rise to the same rights as if the shares had been expressly charged by the member in favour of the company.[194]

Commonly, a public company's articles of association will provide that the company shall have a first and paramount lien on every share which is not a fully paid share for all moneys which are payable in respect of that share. The articles of a private company may extend this concept to cover any debt owed by a member to the company. In *Champagne Perrier-Jouet SA v H.H. Finch Ltd*[195] where a director had incurred a debt by virtue of the company paying bills on his behalf, the company was held to have a lien on his shares even though it was also, by virtue of another article, prohibited from making a loan to that director on security of its shares. It was held that the company had not made a loan to the director but rather that he had simply become indebted to the company. A shareholder against whom a lien is to be enforced can compel the company to assign its lien to his nominee who is willing to pay off the amount of the lien.

How a lien is enforced

A lien is enforced, like any other equitable charge, by a sale. However, the sale of **7–045** the shares is subject to any restrictions on the transferability of those shares contained in the articles of a private company, for example a pre-emption clause requiring them to be offered to existing shareholders.[196] It has been held that a lien cannot be enforced by forfeiture even if power to forfeit is contained in the articles. In *Hopkinson v Mortimer*[197] the articles of association provided that the company should have a lien on shares for the debts of the shareholder, and also provided that the lien could be enforced by forfeiture. It was held that forfeiture for debts generally, as distinct from debts due from the shareholder as a contributory, amounted to an illegal reduction of capital; and furthermore that the power to forfeit on failure to redeem after notice amounted to a clog on the shareholder's equity of redemption, and was invalid and was ultra vires the company.

Priority of lien

When a third party advances money on the security of shares, a question may arise **7–046** as to whether the third party has priority over the company's lien. In such a case, if the third party gives notice of his security to the company before the company's lien arises, the third party will have priority, but otherwise not. So, in *Bradford Banking Co v Briggs & Co*[198] the articles of association gave "a first and paramount lien and charge" on shares for debts due from the shareholder. A shareholder created an equitable mortgage of his shares by depositing the share certificate with a bank

---

[194] *Everitt v Automatic Weighing Machine Co* [1892] 3 Ch. 506. However, in ordinary property law theory, there is a distinction drawn between a lien and a charge in that the former ordinarily gives rise to a right of possession and then to taking property rights with a court order.

[195] *Champagne Perrier-Jouet SA v H.H. Finch Ltd* [1982] 1 W.L.R. 1359.

[196] *Champagne Perrier-Jouet SA v H.H. Finch Ltd* [1982] 1 W.L.R. 1359.

[197] *Hopkinson v Mortimer, Harley & Co Ltd* [1917] 1 Ch. 646.

[198] *Bradford Banking Co v Briggs & Co* (1886) 12 App. Cas. 29.

as security for an overdraft and the bank gave notice of the deposit to the company. The shareholder subsequently became indebted to the company whereupon a lien arose in favour of the company. It was held that the bank had priority as the company's lien arose after notice of their equitable mortgage. The notice was not notice of a trust but rather a notice affecting the company, in its personality as a trading entity, with knowledge of the bank's interest.[199]

Where the shareholder is a trustee, the company's lien will prevail over the claims of the beneficial owners unless the company is given notice, before the lien arises, that the shareholder is a trustee. In *New London and Brazilian Bank v Brocklebank*[200] a trustee held shares in a company, the articles of which gave the company a lien on shares standing either in a single name or in joint names for any debt due from any of the holders, either separately or jointly with any other person. Long after the registration of the shares in the trustee's names, one of the trustees incurred a liability to the company. It was not alleged that the company had notice of the trust before the lien arose. It was held that the company's lien prevailed over the trust. However, the title of the beneficiaries under a trust will have priority if the company has notice, before the lien arises, that the shareholder is a trustee of the shares.[201] The company has no lien on the shares registered in the name of a trustee for debts due to it from the beneficial owner.[202]

More generally, if a lien in favour of the company has arisen and the shareholder sells part only of his shares, the purchaser can require the company to discharge the lien primarily out of the shares not sold.[203] A lien does not cease on the shareholder's death, but may be enforced against his executors.[204]

Lien on Shares (Scots Law)

7–047   A company has at common law and independently of any provision in its articles a lien on shares held by a member for debts due by the member to the company.[205] Articles, however, usually make express provision to the same effect. The lien enables the company to refuse to register any transfer of the shares until the transferor's debt to the company has been satisfied. A company whose articles expressly limit the lien to partly paid shares may alter the articles so as to extend the lien to all shares, but if such an alteration is not made until after a transfer of fully paid shares has been presented for registration the transferee's right to be registered is not affected by that alteration.[206]

A lien can be enforced by a sale in Scots Law only if the power of sale has been conferred by the articles, or a warrant is obtained from the court. A lien in respect of debts other than calls or instalments could not be enforced by forfeiture, since

---

[199] See *Hopkinson v Mortimer, Harley & Co Ltd* [1917] 1 Ch. 646.
[200] (1882) 21 Ch.D. 302, CA.
[201] *Mackereth v Wigan Coal Co Ltd* [1916] 2 Ch. 293.
[202] *Perkins, Re* (1890) 24 Q.B.D. 613, CA.
[203] *Gray v Stone* (1893) 69 L.T. 282.
[204] *Allen v Gold Reefs of West Africa Ltd* [1900] 1 Ch. 656, CA.
[205] *Hotchkis v Royal Bank* (1797) 3 Paton 618; (1797) M. 2673; *Burns v Lawrie's Trustees* (1840) 2 D. 1348; *Bell's Trustee v Coatbridge Tinplate Co Ltd* (1886) 14 R. 246.
[206] *Liquidator of W & A M'Arthur Ltd v Gulf Line Ltd*, 1909 S.C. 732.

that would be an illegal reduction of capital. Where X, a shareholder, has assigned his shares in security to Y who has completed his title to the shares by being registered as the holder of them, the company is no longer entitled to a lien on the shares in respect of debts due to it by X, since X is not the registered holder.[207]

FORFEITURE OF SHARES

Although a forfeiture of a member's shares by the company is recognised by the **7–048** Act, the directors may forfeit shares only if expressly authorised to do so by the articles and only for non-payment of a call or an instalment.[208] Forfeiture, being in the nature of a penal proceeding, is valid only if the provisions of the articles are followed strictly, for example those requirements relating to notice. Any irregularity will avoid the forfeiture.[209] The forfeiture will also be voidable if the directors fail to take into consideration a material fact, such as the alternative possibilities.[210] To protect purchasers of the forfeited shares against possible irregularities in the forfeiture, the articles usually provide that the title of the purchaser shall not be affected by any invalidity in the proceedings in reference to the forfeiture. However, where the purchaser took the shares with full knowledge of the material facts giving rise to the irregularity it was held to be bound by the irregularity.[211]

Forfeited shares may be sold or reissued by a private company according to the provisions of the articles. A public company however must cancel the forfeited shares unless they are disposed of within three years. In the interim period the company may not vote with the shares. If this cancellation takes the public company below the authorised minimum capital it must re-register as a private company.[212]

Forfeited shares can be reissued at less than the amount which has been paid on them. In *Morrison v Trustees, etc., Corp Ltd* [213] a company had forfeited a number of shares of £5.25 each, £2.25 paid, and proposed to reissue them at the price of £1.50 per share. It was held that the company could do so, as it was not bound to treat the forfeited shares as if nothing had been paid upon them.

The purchaser of the reissued shares is liable for the payment of all future calls duly made, including one for the amount of the call which occasioned the forfeiture.[214] Consequently, there is no issue of shares at a discount, as the company has already received the amount paid up. The purchaser should be credited with any subsequent payments made by the ex-owner.[215]

---

[207] *Paul's Trustee v Thomas Justice & Sons Ltd*, 1912 S.C. 1303.
[208] Companies Act 2006 s.659(2)(c).
[209] *Johnson v Lyttle's Iron Agency* (1877) 5 Ch.D. 687, CA.
[210] *Hunter v Senate Support Services Ltd* [2004] EWHC Ch. 1085.
[211] *Hunter v Senate Support Services Ltd* [2004] EWHC Ch. 1085.
[212] Companies Act 2006 s.662.
[213] (1898) 68 L.J. Ch. 11 CA.
[214] *New Balkis Eersteling Ltd v Randt Gold Mining Co* [1904] A.C. 165, where the purchaser was to hold the shares "discharging from all calls due prior to such purchase".
[215] *Randt Gold Mining Co, Re* [1904] 2 Ch. 468. *Bolton, Re*, below, shows that the converse is true.

7–049   The effect of the forfeiture on the former owner of the shares is to discharge him from his liability on the shares.[216] To prevent this position from arising, the articles usually preserve the liability of the former owner.

The company cannot recover more than the difference between the calls due and the amount received on reissue. In *Bolton, Re*[217] B underwrote two blocks of shares in a company. The issue to the public was a failure and B was consequently allotted (inter alia) 8,200 £1 shares in the company. He was unable to pay the calls on these shares, which were forfeited. They were then reissued so that the company received the balance of the calls in full, but to obtain the new allottees the company had to pay £1,018 by way of commission. B became bankrupt. The articles provided that the holder of forfeited shares should remain liable for calls notwithstanding the forfeiture and the company attempted to prove for the balance of calls due from B. It was held that the company could not receive payment of the calls twice over and could only prove for the actual loss sustained, that is the £1,018 commission.

SURRENDER OF SHARES

7–050 The Act does not give a company any express power to accept a surrender of his shares by a member. A company's articles, however, frequently give power to the directors to accept a surrender of shares where they are in a position to forfeit such shares, i.e. for non-payment of calls or instalments on those shares.[218] Surrender in these circumstances has been described as an "apparent exception" only to the principle of maintenance of capital, since "the extinction of the obligation of a bankrupt shareholder can injure nobody."[219]

A surrender of partly paid shares, not liable to forfeiture, is unlawful, because it releases the shareholder from further liability in respect of the shares, because it amounts to a purchase by the company of its own shares, and because it is a reduction of capital without the sanction of the court. So, in *Bellerby v Rowland & Marwood, Steamship Co Ltd*[220] a company sustained a loss of £4,000 and the directors agreed to share the loss between themselves. They therefore surrendered shares to the amount of £4,000. The shares were £11 each, £10 paid, and the intention was that the directors should be released from the remaining £1 a share unpaid. The company subsequently became more prosperous and the directors took proceedings to have the surrender declared invalid. It was held that the surrender was invalid as amounting to a purchase by the company of its own shares. Furthermore, shares which have been validly surrendered can be reissued in the same way as forfeited shares, if the articles authorise their reissue.

---

[216] *Stocken's Case* (1868) L.R. 3 Ch. App. 412; in *Goldsmith v Colonial Finance, etc. Corp Ltd* [1909] 8 C.L.R. 241, Griffith C.J. at 249, and Barton J. at 253, thought that what Lord Cairns L.J. said in *Stocken* was founded on the particular article there in question.

[217] [1930] 2 Ch. 48.

[218] Companies Act 2006 s.659(1), (2).

[219] Per Lord M'Laren in *Gill v Arizona Copper Co Ltd* (1900) 2 F. 843 at 860.

[220] [1902] 2 Ch. 14 CA.

SHARE WARRANTS

A share warrant, as set out in s.779 of the CA 2006, is a document issued by a **7–051** company stating that the bearer of the warrant is entitled to the shares specified in it. This is an alternative means of establishing ownership of shares to allotting those shares to a shareholder. Such a share warrant may be issued either under the company's common seal under s.779(2) or otherwise in accordance with s.44. The share warrant may enable the company, if the articles so provide, to pay the dividends which accrue in relation to the shares in respect of the warrant.[221] In essence, further to s.779, before share warrants can be issued the following conditions must be satisfied: the company must be a company limited by shares; there must be authority in the articles to issue share warrants in this manner; and the shares must be fully paid up. When the issue of share warrants is authorised, the articles usually provide for such matters as the deposit of the share warrant with the company a certain number of days before any right is exercised, and for the giving of notices of meetings by advertisement.

On issuing a share warrant, the company must comply with s.122 of the CA 2006, which include making the following entries in the register: the fact of the issue of a warrant; a statement of shares included in the warrant, distinguishing each share by its number, so long as the share has a number; and the date of issue of the warrant. The holder of a warrant may be deemed to be a member of the company if the articles so provide[222]; alternatively, a share warrant can, subject to the articles, be surrendered for cancellation, whereupon the holder is entitled to be entered in the register of members.[223]

Share warrants are not very common. This is because until 1979, they could only be issued with Treasury consent and had to be deposited with an authorised depository, because of the serious consequences of loss or theft, and also because of the heavy stamp duty. Another reason is that the company has to advertise in newspapers to get in touch with the shareholders. With the abolition of exchange controls in 1979 there are fewer restrictions on their use.

CHALLENGING THE VALUATION OF SHARES

Articles of private companies often provide that a member who wants to sell his **7–052** shares must first offer them to the existing members at a price to be fixed by the auditors. Similar provisions are often applicable in the case of a member's death. When the auditor or other expert makes a valuation the question may arise as to whether either side may validly challenge that valuation. Originally it was held that the valuation could be set aside on the grounds of mistake by the valuer,[224] but later that it could only be so set aside if the valuer had given reasons (a "speaking certificate") but not if no reasons were given ("a non-speaking certificate").[225]

---

[221] Companies Act 2006 s.779(3).
[222] Companies Act 2006 s.122(3).
[223] Companies Act 2006 s.122(4).
[224] *Dean v Prince* [1954] Ch. 409, CA.
[225] *Burgess v Purchase and Son (Farms) Ltd* [1983] Ch. 216; analysing *Campbell v Edwards* [1976] 1 W.L.R. 403, CA and *Baber v Kenwood Manufacturing Co Ltd* [1978] 1 Lloyd's Rep. 175, CA.

Such a distinction has now been rejected by the Court of Appeal in *Jones v Sherwood Computer Services Plc*.[226] On principle they decided that any valuation could only be set aside if the valuer had departed from his instructions in a material respect, for example if he valued the wrong number of shares or failed to employ an expert valuer for a specific item which he was required to do,[227] or valued shares by reference to assets otherwise than those specified in his instructions[228] and not on the basis of a mistake as to matters such as the identity of the assets. The reason for this change in the courts' approach has been the possibility of the aggrieved party suing the valuer in negligence, which did not exist at the time of the original decisions. In *McKinlay v Nexia Smith*[229] it was found on the facts that "no reasonable valuer, acting properly, could have certified" the valuation which had been arrived at, and consequently the claimant was entitled to receive the difference between the valuation which was arrived at and the proper valuation.[230] However, Mann J. has held that the deliberations of the valuer should be kept behind a curtain, including whether or not the valuer had valued the business on the basis that not all of the shareholders would continue to support the business[231]—this attitude of English law to secrecy strikes this writer as somewhat unnecessary. Its effect is to make it very difficult for shareholders and others to know what has been done in their name and more importantly why.

A valuer may now therefore be liable in negligence to either party even though the valuation may not be liable to be set aside. To be liable in this way a valuer must be acting as a valuer and not as an arbitrator, i.e. settling a dispute between at least two parties which was sent to him to resolve in such a way that he had to exercise a judicial discretion.[232] An auditor of a private company who, on request, values its shares in the knowledge that this valuation will determine the price to be paid under a contract owes a duty of care to both the vendor and the purchaser. An agreement for valuation is not generally one for an arbitration. The function of a valuer is usually to settle a price so that no differences arise between the parties. His function is not to make an award after a difference has arisen. Only in the latter case will no duty of care arise.[233] Even if a duty of care does arise, the standard of care expected of an ordinary auditor is not that of a specialist valuer. This "auditor standard" will only be displaced by express contrary intention.[234]

---

[226] [1992] 1 W.L.R. 277.
[227] *Jones (M.) v Jones (R.R.)* [1971] 1 W.L.R. 840.
[228] *Macro v Thompson (No.2)* [1997] 1 B.C.L.C. 626.
[229] [2009] 1 B.C.L.C. 43.
[230] See also *Dashfield v Davidson* [2009] 1 B.C.L.C. 220.
[231] *Doughty Hanson & Co Ltd v Roe* [2008] 1 B.C.L.C. 404.
[232] *Sutcliffe v Thackrah* [1974] A.C. 727.
[233] See *Leigh v English Property Corporation* [1976] 2 Lloyd's Rep. 298.
[234] *Whiteoak v Walker* (1988) 4 B.C.C. 122.

Chapter 8

ALLOTMENT AND COMMENCEMENT OF BUSINESS

INTRODUCTION

Shares must be allotted to shareholders before they formally acquire rights against **8–001** the company as shareholders. It may be that there are more subscribers for shares than there are shares to satisfy their orders, and consequently a shareholder cannot be the owner of shares until an identified number of shares are actually allotted to that shareholder.[1] Traditionally, company law scholarship traces the principles of company law from the creation of a company by an entrepreneur, via the operation of that company through to the winding up of that company. If we think of the history of a company from birth through life and into death in this way, the allotment of shares is an essential part of the company's weaning process, as is the moment when a trading company commences business. The allotment of shares is the moment at which shareholders and the company itself acquire rights in relation to one another; and the commencement of business is the moment at which a trading company comes to life. If a company issues further shares after it has commenced business, as discussed in Chs 13 through 15, below then those shares will also have to be allotted to the shareholders.

The concept of "allotment" for these purposes includes the grant of rights to subscribe for ordinary shares or the grant of a right to convert securities into ordinary shares.[2] The power to allot shares and the principles surrounding the commencement of business are therefore important phenomena in the legal treatment of companies. This chapter deals first with the powers of the directors and the company to allot shares, then with the contract of allotment under which shares are allotted by a company to a person who has applied for them, certain statutory restrictions on allotment by a public company, and the return which the company usually must deliver to the Registrar after it has allotted shares. Finally, the chapter deals with certain statutory restrictions on the commencement of business by a public company.

---

[1] For a more detailed discussion of the principles governing the allotment of shares, see Alastair Hudson, *Securities Law* (London: Sweet & Maxwell, 2008), Ch.28.

[2] Companies Act 2006 s.560(2). It also includes the sale of shares as ordinary shares which had previously been held as treasury shares.

THE STATUTORY ALLOTMENT CODE

A summary of the key provisions of the allotment code

8–002 A new code on the allotment of shares was introduced by the Companies Act 2006 by means of Chs 2 through 6 of Pt 17 of the Companies Act 2006 (referred to here collectively as "the Allotment code"). Controls were placed on the ability of directors to allot shares originally so as to prevent the inappropriate issue of shares so as to block takeovers of companies[3]: directors had been able to issue shares to whomever they chose, in accordance with the articles of association, and so had been able to block takeovers simply by issuing shares to people who would agree to frustrate the takeover bid. Statute therefore limited the powers of directors to issue shares.[4] However, the 2006 Allotment code has liberalised the authority of directors to allot shares, provided they are permitted to do so by the articles of association.[5] The heart of the directors' authority to allot shares is encapsulated in the general principle in s.549 of the CA 2006 to the effect that directors of a company may not issue shares unless the situation falls within one of the broad exemptions from that principle in the statute. The CA 2006 then provides for a number of exemptions from that provision. Directors of a company may only allot shares in that company, grant rights to subscribe for shares in that company, or convert any security into a share in that company if they have complied either with s.550 of the CA 2006 (in relation to private companies with only one class of shares) or s.551 of the CA 2006 (in relation to other forms of company).[6] Each of these provisions is considered in turn below.

Significantly, the allotment code retains existing shareholders' rights of pre-emption, which means that the voting power and the proportion of each shareholder's holding of the company's equity cannot be diluted without first offering new shares to existing shareholders. This prevents directors from being able to ride roughshod over the wishes of the majority of shareholders by issuing enough new shares so as to overwhelm their voting power. Instead, the agreement of those shareholders must be acquired in the way considered below. There are also statutory controls on the way in which payment can be made for shares, with the aim being to prevent shares being issued at a reduced consideration in a way which would alter the composition of the shareholdings in the issuing company without increasing the size of its equity capital to the same extent.

The directors' power to allot shares

8–003 The powers of directors to allot shares are governed by s.549 of the CA 2006 and the sections following that section. Section 549(1) of the CA 2006 provides:

---

[3] See, e.g. *Hogg v Cramphorn* [1967] Ch. 254; *Bamford v Bamford* [1970] Ch. 212.
[4] Whereas s.80 of the Companies Act 1985 placed a limit on the number of shares which directors were entitled to allot by means of a maximum authorised capital, s.549 of the 2006 Act removes the need to provide such a maximum authorised capital in the company's constitution for private companies with only one class of shares. The approach taken in the 2006 Act is to permit an authorisation for a period of up to five years stating the maximum amount of shares which may be allotted by the directors.
[5] Companies Act 2006 s.549.
[6] Companies Act 2006 s.549(1).

"The directors of a company must not exercise any power of the company—

(a) to allot shares in the company, or

(b) to grant rights to subscribe for, or to convert any security into, shares in the company,

except in accordance with section 550 (private company with single class of shares) or section 551 (authorisation by company)."

A director who knowingly and wilfully contravenes, or permits or authorises, a contravention of s.549 of the CA 2006, commits a criminal offence and is therefore liable to a fine under s.549(4) of the CA 2006.[7] The board of directors cannot in any event issue shares beyond the amount fixed as the authorised capital of the company. Furthermore, the directors may issue shares only for a proper purpose: that is, they may only issue shares in the best interests of the company. Directors are required to act in the way which they consider, in good faith, "would be most likely to promote the success of the company for the benefit of its members as a whole".[8] An issue for an ulterior motive, such as altering the voting power in the company[9] or for serving only the self-interest of the directors,[10] would be void.

Exemptions from the prohibition on allotting shares

Allotment in relation to private companies with only one class of shares

Section 549(1) of the CA 2006 divides between private companies with one class **8–004** of shares on the one hand, and then both private companies with more than one class of shares and public companies on the other hand. In effect, the powers of directors to allot shares in relation to private companies with one class of shares have been greatly simplified.[11] Section 550 of the CA 2006 provides that the directors of a private company with only one class of shares may "exercise any power of the company" to do any of the three activities related to allotment: namely, allot shares in that company, grant rights to subscribe for shares in that company, or convert any security into a share in that company.[12] However, the directors may not exercise this power if they are "prohibited from doing so by the company's articles".[13]

---

[7] Companies Act 2006 s.549(4) and (5).

[8] Companies Act 2006 s.172(1).

[9] *Fraser v Whalley* (1864) 2 Hem. & M. 10; *Punt v Symons & Co Ltd* [1903] 2 Ch. 506; *Piercy v S. Mills & Co Ltd* [1920] 1 Ch. 77; *Hogg v Cramphorn Ltd* [1967] Ch. 254; *Howard Smith Ltd v Ampol Ltd* [1974] A.C. 821.

[10] See the cases referred to in the previous footnote and *Ngutli Ltd v McCann* (1953) 90 C.L.R. 425.

[11] Companies Act 2006 s.549.

[12] Companies Act 2006 s.550. This provision repeals the requirement in s.80 of the 1985 Act that the directors have a prior authorisation from the company's members for an allotment of shares, provided that the company is a private company with only one class of shares. This refinement was recommended by para.4.5 of the Company Law Review.

[13] Companies Act 2006 s.550.

Allotment authorised by the articles of association

8–005 In general terms the directors of a company are permitted to allot shares if they are expressly authorised to do so by the company's articles or by a resolution of the company.[14] More precisely, s.551 of the CA 2006 provides that the directors of a company (which by inference from s.550) is not a private company with only one class of shares may "exercise any power of the company" to do any of the three activities related to allotment: namely, allot shares in that company, grant rights to subscribe for shares in that company, or convert any security into a share in that company.[15] Significantly, however, the directors are only permitted to exercise such a power if they are "authorised to do so by the company's articles or by resolution of the company".[16] Therefore, it is suggested, that one of two things must be the case. Either, the articles of association must expressly grant a power to the directors to allot shares, whether by reference to some conditions precedent[17] or not; or, alternatively, the company must have passed a resolution to authorise such an allotment if there is no such power in the company's articles of association, or have passed a resolution to waive a condition precedent to such an allotment. Even though a resolution of the company may be used to amend the company's articles for the purposes of this provision, there is no requirement that that resolution be anything other than a general resolution.[18] Except in the case of a private company, the authority of the directors to issue relevant securities is limited to five years and must not exceed that time limit.[19]

Further exemptions

8–006 There are two further exemptions. The first further exemption from s.549(1) relates to an employees' share scheme. The second further exemption relates to shares allotted pursuant to an employee share scheme, and rights to convert any security into an allotted share are also exempt.

The enforceability of allotments of shares without authorisation

8–007 The question arises as to the enforceability of an allotment of shares made by directors beyond the scope of their authority. It is provided in s.40 of the CA 2006 "the power of the directors to bind the company . . . is deemed to be free of any limitation under the company's constitution". Therefore, from the perspective of the allottee, there may be a valid allotment which cannot be doubted on the basis that the directors did not have the power to make such an allotment under the company's constitution, provided that the allottee was acting in good faith.

---

[14] Companies Act 2006 s.551(1).
[15] Companies Act 2006 s.551.
[16] Companies Act 2006 s.551.
[17] Companies Act 2006 s.551(2).
[18] Companies Act 2006 s.551(8).
[19] Companies Act 2006 s.551.

The time at which allotment takes place

Section 558 of the CA 2006 provides that shares in a company are deemed to have **8–008** been allotted at the time at which "a person acquired the unconditional right to be included in the company's register of members in respect of the shares".[20] A company is required to *register* any allotment of shares "as soon as practicable and in any event two months after the date of allotment".[21] It is an offence to fail to comply with this requirement: that offence is committed by the company and every officer of the company who is in default.[22] Furthermore, a company must make a *return* of any allotment of shares.[23] This provision applies to two forms of company: a company limited by shares and a company limited by guarantee which also has a share capital.[24] The company is required to make delivery of that return of the allotment to the Registrar within one month of the date of the allotment.[25]

The pre-emption rights of existing shareholders

Directors are prevented from issuing shares to new shareholders or otherwise allot- **8–009** ting shares in a way which dilutes the rights of existing shareholders by giving existing shareholders the right to object to a new issue of shares. This is referred to as a right of pre-emption. It is provided in s.561(1) of the CA 2006 that:

"A company must not allot equity securities to a person on any terms unless—

(a) it has made an offer to each person who holds ordinary shares in the company to allot to him on the same or more favourable terms a proportion of those securities that is as nearly as practicable equal to the proportion in nominal value held by him of the ordinary share capital of the company, and

(b) the period during which any such offer may be accepted has expired or the company has received notice of the acceptance or refusal of every offer so made."

Therefore, offers of equity securities can only be made once an offer of an appropriate proportion of those shares has been made to existing shareholders. Section 562 of the CA 2006 sets out the means by which this offer must be made to existing shareholders. Breach of these provisions provides a right to compensation under s.563 of the CA 2006.

Allotment of shares in public companies to be subscribed for in full

Further to the policy expressed by art.28 of the Second Council Directive,[26] **8–010** people who apply for shares are to be protected to the extent that the capital base

[20] Companies Act 2006 s.558.
[21] Companies Act 2006 s.554.
[22] Companies Act 2006 s.554(3).
[23] Companies Act 2006 s.555(1).
[24] Companies Act 2006 s.555(1).
[25] Companies Act 2006 s.555(2).
[26] Directive 77/91/EEC on co-ordination of safeguards which are required of companies [1977] OJ L26/1.

of the company will not be increased if the issue is not fully subscribed, or that the company's capital base will only be increased if the terms of the issue envisaged an increase even if the issue was not fully subscribed. Section 578 of the CA 2006 provides that:

> "(1) No allotment shall be made of shares of a public company offered for subscription unless—
>
> (a) the issue is subscribed for in full, or
> (b) the offer is made on terms that the shares subscribed for may be allotted—
>
> (i) in any event, or
> (ii) if specified conditions are met (and those conditions are met)."

Thus, much turns on the precise terms of the proposed issue: it is only if the issue is to be made on terms that it may be carried out even if the issue has not been fully subscribed, or on some other terms contained in the issue, that that issue can indeed be so made. If an allotment is made in breach of s.578 then s.579 of the CA 2006 provides that that allotment is not automatically void. Rather, the allotment is "voidable at the instance of the applicant within one month after the date of the allotment".[27] This principle applies even if the company is in the course of being wound up.[28] Any director of a company who "knowingly contravenes, or permits or authorises the contravention" of s.578 in respect of an allotment of shares is "liable to compensate the company and the allottee respectively for any loss, damages, costs or expenses that the company and the allottee respectively may have sustained or incurred by the contravention".[29]

THE CREATION OF A CONTRACT FOR THE ALLOTMENT OF SHARES

Ordinary principles of contract law apply

8–011 Contracts for the allotment of shares are subject to the ordinary principles of contract law. The ordinary law of contract requires an offer and an acceptance if there is to be an agreement.[30] This requirement for an offer and acceptance applies to agreements to take shares in a company. An offer is made by the applicant in sending a form of application for shares to the company or issuing house and it is accepted by the allotment of shares to the applicant.

Common law principles on the acceptance of an offer of shares

8–012 This section considers the common law principles which govern the making of an offer and an acceptance of that in relation to an allotment of shares. Shares will be allotted when the board passes the appropriate resolution, in compliance (it is

---

[27] Companies Act 2006 s.579(1).
[28] Companies Act 2006 s.579(2).
[29] Companies Act 2006 s.579(3).
[30] For a more detailed analysis of the applicable common law principles, see Alastair Hudson, *Securities Law* (London: Sweet & Maxwell, 2008), paras 28–57 et seq.

suggested) with the statutory principles considered in this chapter. Those shares will not actually be issued, however, until they are entered into the register of members.[31]

An acceptance of an offer of shares must be unconditional[32] and must correspond to the terms of the offer. As was suggested at the beginning of the chapter, it is possible that a share issue will be over-subscribed such that investors may not be able to acquire as many shares as they may have agreed to buy. Therefore, the company's offer of shares may have caused an investor to apply for 100 shares but due to the demand for those shares only 25 shares may have been allotted to that investor. Consequently, because the number of shares allotted was different from the 100 shares for which the investor applied, the allotment would be deemed to be a counter-offer of 25 shares and the applicant could refuse to take any shares. In practice, in order to circumvent these difficulties, it is common for the application to provide: "I [the investor] agree to accept such shares or any smaller number that may be allotted to me."

To constitute a binding contract, an acceptance must be communicated to the offeror.[33] If the parties contemplated that the post might be used to communicate acceptance, then the posting of a letter of allotment is sufficient communication to the applicant. So, in one decided case, where an investor applied for shares in a company, a letter of allotment was posted by the company but never reached the investor. It was held that the investor was a shareholder in the company because the mere posting of the letter was sufficient to constitute communication of the company's acceptance of the investor's offer to buy shares.[34] Communication, however, may be made in any way which shows the applicant that the company has accepted his offer:[35] for example, by means of a letter demanding payment of an instalment on the shares,[36] or by receipt of a notice calling a general meeting and notification given orally by the secretary that shares have been allotted.[37] The applicant must, however, have agreed to take shares and not merely expressed a "willingness" to take them.[38] Sending notices of meetings and letters making calls on the shares to a person who has not so agreed does not of itself make the recipient a shareholder.[39]

Significantly, an offer can be revoked at any time before acceptance is communicated. The question therefore arises as to what will constitute revocation. To be effective, revocation of an offer must be communicated to the offeree. Thus notice of the revocation of an application must reach the company before the letter of allotment is posted.[40] If the revocation is communicated by post, it is not effective

8–013

---

[31] *National Westminster Bank Plc v IRC* [1994] 2 B.C.L.C. 239, HL.
[32] *Liquidator of the Consolidated Copper Co, etc. Ltd v Peddie* (1877) 5 R. 393.
[33] See *Entores Ltd v Miles Far East Corporation* [1955] 2 Q.B. 327, CA.
[34] *Household Fire Insurance Co v Grant* (1879) 4 Ex.D. 216, CA. This principle has been doubted in Scotland: *Mason v Benhar Coal Co Ltd* (1882) 9 R. 883, per Lord Shand at 890.
[35] *Chapman v Sulphite Pulp Co Ltd* (1892) 19 R. 837.
[36] *Forget v Cement Products Co of Canada* [1916] W.N. 259, PC.
[37] *Chapman v Sulphite Pulp Co Ltd* (1892) 19 R. 837; see also *Curror's Trustee v Caledonian Heritable Security Co Ltd* (1880) 7 R. 479 and *Nelson v Fraser* (1906) 14 S.L.T. 513 (OH).
[38] *Mason v Benhar Coal Co Ltd* (1882) 9 R. 883.
[39] *Goldie v Torrance* (1882) 10 R. 174; and see *Liquidator of the Florida, etc. Co Ltd v Bayley* (1890) 17 R. 525.
[40] *Byrne v Van Tienhoven* (1880) 5 C.P.D. 344; *Thomson v James* (1855) 18 D. 1.

until the letter is received by the company. Similarly, in *National Savings Bank Association, Re*[41] an investor applied for shares in a company. Shares were allotted to him, and the letter of allotment sent to the company's agent to deliver by hand to the investor. However, before the letter was delivered, the investor withdrew his application. It was held that the investor was not a shareholder in the company.

Otherwise, an offer lapses if it is not accepted within the time prescribed or, if none is prescribed, within a reasonable time. Thus an allotment must be made within a reasonable time after the application, otherwise the application will lapse and the applicant will be entitled to refuse to take the shares. So in *Ramsgate Victoria Hotel Co Ltd v Montefiore*[42] an investor offered to take shares in a company on 8 June, but he heard nothing from the company until 23 November, when he received a letter of acceptance. The investor refused to take the shares, and so the question arose whether or not he was obliged to take the shares. It was held that the investor was entitled to refuse because the offer was deemed to have lapsed due to effluxion of time.

Further issues arise in relation to offers which are made subject to a condition. The principle is that an offer will be terminated by the failure of a condition subject to which it was made. So, if an application for shares is made subject to a condition—for example, that the applicant is granted a contract to supply goods to the company,[43] that all capital in the company must be subscribed for[44]—then if the condition is not fulfilled when shares are allotted to him, the applicant is under no obligation to take those shares. Nevertheless, a conditional application must be distinguished from an application for shares which is coupled with a collateral agreement. An example of such an arrangement would be the situation in which £10 shares are to be paid up to the extent of £1.50 in cash on allotment and that the balance is to be set-off against goods to be supplied to the company by the allottee. In the latter case, when shares are actually allotted, the investor will become a shareholder with the right merely of suing the company on the collateral agreement.[45]

---

[41] *National Savings Bank Association, Re* (1867) L.R. 4 Eq. 9.
[42] *Ramsgate Victoria Hotel Co Ltd v Montefiore* (1866) L.R. 1 Ex. 109.
[43] *Shackelford's Case* (1866) L.R. 1 Ch. App. 567.
[44] *Swedish Match Co Ltd v Seivwright* (1889) 16 R. 989.
[45] *Elkington's Case* (1867) L.R. 2 Ch. App. 511; cf. *Liquidator of the Pelican, etc. Insurance Co Ltd v Bruce* (1904) 11 S.L.T. 658 (OH), and see opinions in *National House, etc. Investment Co Ltd v Watson*, 1908 S.C. 88.

Chapter 9

SHARE CAPITAL

Introduction

The central principles

This chapter considers the law governing the maintenance of a company's share **9–001** capital. There are two central principles. First, that a company's share capital must be raised and, once raised, must be maintained for the benefit of creditors. Secondly, the law then controls the circumstances in which there can be a reduction of a company's share capital. These long-established rules were rehearsed in the Second Council Directive 77/91/EEC on Co-ordination of Safeguards which are required of companies.

Thinking about the company's capital position in the abstract

The current trend, however, is to regard the two central principles as being anti- **9–002** quated, and that they should be replaced by solvency and liquidity criteria. In essence, the issue is this. In the nineteenth century in particular, there was a large amount of fraud conducted in relation to companies. For example, in Charles Dickens's novel *Martin Chuzzlewit* the possibilities for fraud using companies were clearly illustrated in the business of the (fictional) Anglo-Bengali Disinterested Life Assurance and Loan Company whose leading light, Montague Tigg, used false statements of the company's capital and lies about its profitability to induce investors to plough their wealth into the company because it appeared that the company both had a large amount of capital and was very profitable. Therefore, the focus of the early case law was on ensuring that the statement of the company's capital reflected the company's actual capital base, in part by preventing the company from reducing its capital and in part by ensuring that the company's capital was appropriately paid up. If a company has a large amount of capital this will lead potential investors and the company's creditors to believe that the company is dependable because there is a large amount of capital to which they can have recourse even if something should happen to the company. The purpose of the company law rules considered in this chapter is to prevent this sort of fraud by ensuring the maintenance of the company's capital.

There is another current in the thinking that focuses on the solvency of the company. Previously, one used to think solely about the "net worth" of the company on its balance sheet: that means, creditors used to look to the excess of the company's capital assets over its liabilities. However, the weakness of net worth as a means of measuring a company's credit worth is that the balance sheet only presents a snapshot of the company's capital position on a single day in the financial year and therefore can be manipulated.[1] By contrast, finance theory has changed its attention to measurements of a company's solvency by looking at the amount of cash it holds and uses during its financial year. If the concern is to ensure that the company has sufficient worth to meet its obligations to its creditors, then the concern ought to be to assess the ability of that company to generate enough cash to meet those obligations. Therefore, the suggestion for the future is that what should be measured is both the solvency of the company (that is, the extent to which it is able to meet its obligations) and its cash flow position. While it is possible to manipulate profit and loss accounts and balance sheet accounts, it is not possible to manipulate a company's cash position in the same way without straightforward fraud.

The meaning of "capital"

9–003 The nature of the "capital" of a company should be understood in the first place in contradistinction to its "income". An example of a trading company's income would be the profits which it makes from its ordinary trading activities in any financial year. The central portion of a company's capital when that company is first created is the share capital which the original subscribing members of the company (that is, its very first shareholders) contribute to the company at the outset. Over time, the company's borrowings and profits which are held in reserve will also be added to the capital base of the company (the equivalent of moving money from your current account to your deposit account), and also any capital assets like buildings, business premises and plant and machinery which are acquired over time.

However, there are other, more complex accounting concepts which affect the capital and income position of the company: for example, the need to account for the reduction in the value of capital assets over time ("depreciation") and the way in which cash or other assets are moved into reserves held for different purposes. In these accounting senses, the word "capital" used in connection with a company has several different meanings, thus it may mean the nominal or authorised share capital, the issued or allotted share capital, the paid-up share capital or the reserve share capital of the company. Each of these terms relates to different aspects of the company's capital. We shall consider the meaning of each in turn.

The "nominal" or "authorised" capital is merely the amount of share capital which the company is authorised to issue, but that is not necessarily the same as what it has actually issued. So, a company may choose to grant the directors the power to issue 100,000 shares with a nominal value of £10 each, but may decide only actually to issue 50,000 shares at the outset because that is all the capital that is needed at that time or because only a limited number of investors can be

---

[1] See Alastair Hudson, *The Law of Finance* (London: Sweet & Maxwell, 2009), para.33-27; and see in particular Terry Smith, *Accounting for Growth* (1992) on the possibilities for manipulating corporate accounts.

found. In the case of a limited company the amount of potential share capital with which it proposes to be registered, and the division of that capital into individual shares of a fixed value (the nominal amount), must be set out in the company's constitution, but this amount may be increased or reduced as explained later. Companies may fix on any figure which is large enough for its potential requirements.[2] It must be remembered that public companies must have at least £50,000 in authorised capital.[3]

By contrast with the nominal share capital, the "issued" or "allotted" capital **9–004** refers to that part of the company's nominal capital which has actually been issued or allotted to the shareholders. A private company is not bound to allot all its capital at once; whereas a public company must allot at least £50,000 by way of the nominal value of shares before it may commence business.[4] The law concerning the allotment of shares is considered in Ch.8. Allotments of capital are made as they are needed by the directors, provided that the directors have been properly authorised to do so under the Act, up to the amount identified in the company's constitution as that company's authorised capital. There is a subtle difference between a share being allotted, which is when the company and the shareholder have agreed contractually to issue and acquire those shares, and it being "issued", which is when the shareholder's ownership of that share is registered by the company. There are circumstances in which that distinction may be important. For example, the restrictions and controls imposed by the CA 2006 relate in general to the allotted shares. In the context of taxation the distinction may also be significant, as in *National Westminster Bank Plc v IRC*[5] in which a majority of the House of Lords held that a share is allotted when the company and shareholder are contractually bound and it is only issued when the shareholder is registered as such on the register of members.

The "paid-up" capital is that part of the issued capital which has actually been paid up by the shareholders. There may clearly be a time between a shareholder agreeing to acquire shares and the payment for those shares being made. There are controls on the company seeking to issue shares at a discount or issuing shares with payment only needing to be made later: otherwise, clearly, the company could claim to have a much larger share capital than it had actually received in cash. As a company grows, it may seek to issue tranches of shares as it needs to draw in more capital. Having the power to issue shares in advance makes it easier for the directors to issue shares as and when they need to do so. Suppose a company has a nominal capital of £500,000 which would be divided into 500,000 shares of a nominal amount of £1 each. The directors may decide that the company only needs £400,000 and therefore only 400,000 shares would be issued, with 100,000 shares which the directors have the power to issue in the future being held back. Alternatively, if the director only required £100,000 immediately, or if their shareholders agreed with the company that they would

---

[2] In earlier times, stamp duty was payable on this figure which had the effect of keeping it as low as possible, but that no longer applies.
[3] Companies Act 2006 s.761(2) (to acquire trading certificate) and s.763 (the authorised minimum).
[4] Companies Act 2006 s.761.
[5] [1994] 2 B.C.L.C. 239, HL.

only pay for their shares in bits, then 400,000 shares may be issued, but only £100,000 actually paid up in that the company has so far required only 25p. to be paid up on each share. Therefore, the issued share capital would be £400,000 but the actual, paid-up share capital at that time would only be £100,000. The uncalled (i.e. not paid-up) capital is the remainder of the issued capital and can be called up at any time by the company from the shareholders in accordance with the provisions of the company's articles. Section 586 of the CA 2006 requires public companies to call up at least one quarter of the nominal value of a share and all the premium on allotment.

9–005   Uncalled capital is rare today.[6] Indeed, it might be thought that other than in exceptional circumstances, for example where investors will only agree to pay for their shares a bit at a time, that it would be undesirable for a company to have an issued share capital which is so far in excess of its actual paid-up capital because a creditor who focused on the issued share capital might then get a misleading impression as to the company's capital position. Consequently, any references in correspondence to the amount of the share capital must be to paid-up share capital.

It is possible that shares will be sold for an excess over the nominal value of the shares. The paid-up share capital includes the nominal value of the shares paid-up and any premium on such shares. For example, if 10,000 £1 shares are sold for £2 each, then the paid up capital will be £20,000. The excess £1 paid for each share is then paid into a "share premium account" distinct from the nominal share capital. So, this will be expressed as £10,000 share capital and £10,000 share premium account in the balance sheet. It has even been held that where the shareholders agree to increase a company's capital without any formal allocation of shares—so that each shareholder contributes more money to the company's share capital without receiving more shares in return—then that increase will be treated like a share premium and so subject to the capital maintenance rules.[7]

Raising Share Capital, Capital Maintenance and the Protection of Creditors

9–006   The issued share capital of a company is considered by company law theory to be the fund to which creditors of the company can look for payment of their debts, and so, to protect the creditors, it has been held that the issued share capital must actually be raised. This means that shares can be treated as paid up only to the extent of the amount actually received by the company in cash or in kind, and must not be issued at a discount, which means that they must not be issued as fully paid for a consideration less than payment or the promise of payment of the nominal amount of each share,[8] although the company may not necessarily require payment in full of the nominal amount on allotment. This needs some explanation: it means, a share with a nominal value of £2 may not be sold for £1, although it is possible for the company to agree that the shareholder will only pay £1 at the date

---

[6] So too is the part of that uncalled capital designated a reserve capital under s.120. That was a fund only to be called up on a winding up.

[7] *Kellar v Williams* [2002] 2 B.C.L.C. 390, PC.

[8] *Ooregum Gold Mining Co v Roper* [1892] A.C. 125.

of allotment and then pay the remaining £1 at a later date. In effect, the full amount must be paid eventually but it is permissible for that payment to be made over time. There must be payment made in full eventually, however.[9] There is no objection to shares being issued at a premium, that is being issued at more than the nominal value with the excess being paid into a separate share premium account.

In one particular case, no additional funds will be received by the company on an issue of shares. This is where a company makes an issue of "bonus shares". This involves the capitalisation of distributable profits.[10] That means some profits being held back instead of being paid out in dividends to the shareholders or ploughed back into investment in the business; instead those profits which are held back are added to the company's capital. The issue of bonus shares is therefore the allotment to each existing shareholder of new shares which are effectively paid for out of the profits which are to be capitalised.[11] The effect for the shareholders is that the shareholders acquire more shares with the result that they have more shares which can be sold in the future or which can receive a dividend; the effect for the company is that the company has retained an amount of its profits in that financial year instead of paying them out to the shareholders by way of dividend. However, while the shareholders acquire new shares, that does not necessarily mean that their future dividends will lead to them receiving a larger aggregate amount of cash unless the company increases its total profits by means of investing the retained, capitalised profits back into the business; and of course the existence of more shares simply means that the distributable profits in the company are simply being divided up among a larger number of shares such that the profits-per-share falls. Thus the shareholders receive additional shares but the overall value of the company is unchanged. The issuing process has been described as being analogous to a contract.[12] The draft articles of association require an ordinary resolution authorising the directors to issue bonus shares and there must be sufficient distributable profits.[13]

THE ISSUE OF SHARES AT A DISCOUNT

The general rule has always been that shares must not be issued at a discount, **9–007** which means that a share may not be issued as "fully paid" if in fact the consideration paid for that share is less than the nominal amount set out in the company's constitution.[14] The general principle was first established in England

---

[9] What is more difficult perhaps, is the circumstance in which the company and the shareholder may agree that the remaining portion of the payment will be delayed in practice indefinitely: there would be a seemingly lawful agreement for the allotment of shares but the share capital would never actually be paid up. It is suggested that such a scheme would be outwith the mischief of the legislation.

[10] Which are not subject to the capital maintenance rules. Bonus share can also be used to convert other capital funds, such as the share premium account, into issued shares. That will simply increase the number of shares but leave the overall amount of share capital unaffected.

[11] If this has not been done then the shareholders have no rights to the shares: *Topham v Charles Topham Group Ltd* [2003] 1 B.C.L.C. 123.

[12] *Cleveland Trust Plc, Re* [1991] B.C.L.C. 424.

[13] For the consequences of a defect in the procedure see *EIC Services Ltd v Phipps* [2004] B.C.C. 814, CA.

[14] The Company Law Review ultimately recommended that the nominal value of shares be retained, although the requirement, enshrined in the Second EC Directive, is under review by the EC Commission. CLR *Final Report*, Vol.1, para.10.7.

by the House of Lords in 1892 in *Ooregum Gold Mining Co of India Ltd v Roper*.[15] In that case the market value of the £1 ordinary shares of a company was "2s 6d".[16] The company thereupon issued preference shares of £1 each with 15s credited as having been paid, leaving a liability of only 5s per share to be paid to make up the £1. A contract to this effect was registered under the companies, legislation. It was held that the issue was beyond the powers of the company and consequently that the allottees were liable to pay for the shares in full. As Lord Macnaghten held[17]:

> "The dominant and cardinal principle of [the Companies] Acts is that the investor shall purchase immunity from liability beyond a certain limit on the terms that there shall be and remain a liability up to that limit . . . It is plain that this [principle] is one which cannot be dispensed with by anything in the articles of association, or by any resolution of the company, or by any contract between the company and outsiders who have been invited to become members of the company and who do come in on the faith of such a contract."

This principle is now expressly set out in s.580 of the CA 2006. The shareholder must pay the full nominal value of his shares, whether he pays in cash or in kind. If the share is not paid for in full at the outset then the shareholder owes the balance plus interest to the company and any subsequent holder of the shares may also be held liable for any amount which remains outstanding unless he is a bona fide purchaser for value without actual notice of the discount issue or a subsequent transferee of the shares from such a person. The court may grant relief in appropriate circumstances under s.589 of the CA 2006 if it considers it "just and equitable" to do so.[18] Contravention of s.580 of the CA 2006 is a criminal offence by the company and any officer in default under s.590.[19] The general rule is subject to the following exceptions: first, there is in effect a discount when shares are issued by a private company for an overvalued non-monetary consideration, as in *Wragg Ltd, Re*, considered below. Secondly, where, under s.553, commission is paid to a person who agrees to subscribe, or to procure subscriptions, for shares in a company.

There is nothing to prevent debentures or bonds (which are debt securities, as opposed to shares) being issued at a discount because such debt securities merely represent a loan to the company and do not constitute part of the company's equity capital. However, in the case of convertible bonds (that is, bonds which can be

---

[15] [1892] A.C. 125. See also earlier Scottish case to the same effect, *Klenck v East India Co, etc. Ltd* (1888) 16 R. 271, where the memorandum contained a power to issue shares at a discount.

[16] This is an old measurement of money in England, where "s" refers to shillings and "d" refers to pence. This form of money measurement was removed with the decimalisation of sterling in 1971. In "old money" there were twenty shillings in a pound: so 20s made up £1. Therefore, in the case discussed in the text, when 15s is paid up, there are still 5s owing to make up the nominal value of each share of £1.

[17] [1892] A.C. 125 at 145.

[18] Companies Act 2006 s.589(2).

[19] There is no issue at a discount if the shares are issued at par (e.g. after the exercise of an option to take them up at par), even though they could otherwise be issued at a premium (*Hilder v Dexter* [1902] A.C. 474), or where shares are issued at a lesser premium than that at which they might have been paid (*Cameron v Glenmorangie Distillery Co Ltd* (1896) 23 R. 1092.

converted into shares) may not be issued at a discount, because otherwise the right to exchange those bonds for shares as if those shares were fully paid-up would effectively circumvent the prohibition on issuing shares at a discount.[20] The right will be valid if it is a right to fully paid shares equal in nominal amount to the issue price of the debentures—the shares will not then be issued at a discount.

CONSIDERATION FOR ALLOTMENT

Section 578 of the CA 2006 provides that an allottee must pay for his shares in full, as is discussed in Ch.8.[21] In essence, the principles are as follows. Shares are only treated as paid up to the extent that the company has received money or money's worth (including goodwill and know-how) in return for them. Public companies may not accept an undertaking by any person to do work or perform services in return for shares.   **9–008**

Payment of non-cash consideration—public companies

Section 587 of the CA 2006 prohibits a public company[22] from accepting as consideration for shares any undertaking, for example to transfer property, which is to be or may be performed more than five years after the date of the allotment. Any variation of a valid undertaking (i.e. within five years) taking it outside the five-year period is void. Any allotment in contravention of this requirement, or a failure by the purchaser to fulfil a valid undertaking within the contract period, renders the allottee liable to pay the company the amount owed on the shares, together with interest. Any subsequent holder of the shares is also liable, subject to the bona fide purchaser exemption noted above.[23]   **9–009**

Sections 593 and 594 of the CA 2006 provide that a public company, and not just a listed company, may not allot shares for any non-cash consideration unless a report on the value of the consideration had been made by an independent person qualified to be an auditor of the company. His report must be sent to the company within six months prior to the allotment and to the proposed allottee. He may accept another's valuation if it is reasonable to do so, provided that that person is also independent and appears to be qualified and provided that such facts are disclosed in the report. The company's auditor may be so used.[24] The report must state the amount payable on the shares, a description of the consideration and the valuation methods used, the date of valuation and the extent to which the shares are to be treated as paid up by the consideration and in cash. It must be filed with the Registrar.[25] In making his report, the expert may require from the officers of the company such information and explanation as he thinks necessary to enable him to carry out the valuation or to make the report. False,

---

[20] *Mosely v Koffyfontien Mines Ltd* [1904] 2 Ch. 108, CA.
[21] See generally Alastair Hudson, *Securities Law* (London: Sweet & Maxwell, 2008), para.28–81 et seq.
[22] The Second EC Directive which instigated these sections does not apply to private companies.
[23] Companies Act 2006 ss.588 and 605.
[24] Companies Act 2006 s.596.
[25] Companies Act 2006 s.597.

misleading or deceptive statements made in this context constitute criminal offences under s.1153 of the CA 2006.

There is a general exemption for shares issued generally to shareholders in another company on a take-over or merger with the other company.[26] Such issues are, however, subject to the extra-statutory rules on takeovers discussed in Ch.33. There is also an exemption for shares issued in return for the transfer of shares in another company under an arrangement which is open to all the shareholders at that company.[27]

In default of such a report, the allottee will be liable to pay any amount owed on the shares in cash if either he did not receive a copy of the report or he knew or ought to have known of the breach.[28] Subsequent holders may also be liable subject to the bona fide purchaser exemption. Relief may again be given by the court if it is just and equitable to do so, taking into account the actual amount received for the shares and other liabilities of the allottee under the contract.[29] It is for the allottee to show that the company has actually received assets to the value of the nominal value and premium of the shares in order to obtain this relief.[30]

These provisions only apply if the shares are issued "otherwise than for cash." Issues for cash are defined in s.583(2) of the CA 2006 so as to include payment by a cheque received by the company in good faith, or the release of liability of the company for a defined sum (i.e. a set-off)[31] or an undertaking to pay cash at a future date. This may be thought to cover a multitude of sins although it does not include the assignment of a debt. It is convenient to note here that similar provisions apply, by virtue of ss.598 and 600 of the CA 2006, to the acquisitions by public companies of non-cash assets from any subscriber of the memorandum, within two years of the issue of the certificate entitling it to commence business, if the consideration to be given by the company is not less than 10 per cent of the nominal value of the company's issued shares at that time.

Payment of non-cash consideration—private companies

9–010 Sections 587 et seq. of the CA 2006 as just considered do not apply to private companies, but where shares are allotted as fully or partly paid up otherwise than in cash, a contract constituting the title of the allottee to the allotment together with any contract of sale, or for services or other consideration for the allotment, or, if such a contract is not in writing, particulars of the contract, must, with the return as to allotments, be delivered to the Registrar, usually within a month after the allotment.[32] Default renders the officers of the company liable to penalties but does not make the allotment void.

---

[26] Companies Act 2006 s.595.
[27] Companies Act 2006 s.593(2) and s.594(1)(2), excluding treasury shares.
[28] Companies Act 2006 s.593(3).
[29] Companies Act 2006 s.593. See, e.g. *Ossory Estates Plc, Re* (1988) 4 B.C.C. 460. In *Bradford Investments Plc, Re* [1991] B.C.L.C. 224 the failure to obtain a report led to the shareholders losing their right to vote under the articles.
[30] *Bradford Investments Plc, Re (No.2)* [1991] B.C.L.C. 688.
[31] Thus preserving the decision in *Spargo's Case* (1873) L.R. 8 Ch. App. 407.
[32] Companies Act 2006 s.555.

Any such contract must be supported by consideration. Consideration must be real but it need not be adequate: which means that the courts will not inquire into the adequacy of that consideration, unless it is manifestly inadequate, provided there is some consideration. Thus provided property is transferred to the company in return for shares the court will not examine whether that property is actually worth the value of the shares.[33] These issues arose in *Wragg Ltd, Re*[34] where the goodwill, stock-in-trade and property of a business was sold to a company for £46,000, of which £20,000 was to be paid in fully-paid shares. The stock-in-trade was shown in the company's books at a figure of £11,000 less than the sum allocated to it in the agreement. On the company's going into liquidation, a misfeasance summons was taken out to obtain payment for the shares. It was held that, because the agreement could not be impeached, the adequacy of the consideration could not be gone into.

Past consideration is, however, no consideration under English law.[35] In *Eddystone Marine Insurance Co, Re*[36] a private company decided to turn itself into a public company. Before doing so it resolved to allot £6,000 of fully paid shares to the existing directors and shareholders, and a contract was made agreeing to allot the shares in consideration of their past services and expenses in forming the company and establishing the business. The contract was registered and the shares were allotted. The company afterwards went into liquidation. It was held that the director and shareholders were liable to pay for the shares, as there was no consideration in money or money's worth for the allotment, past services being no consideration.

An agreement by a private company to allot shares in consideration of services **9–011** to be performed in the future also renders the allottee liable to pay for the shares.[37] It has been held that "[i]t is not open to a company to agree with the holder or proposed holder of its shares to replace the statutory liability by a special contract sounding in damages only".[38] However, a private company may agree to pay a fixed sum immediately for services to be performed in the future (for example, for the construction of a building) and to satisfy that debt by the allotment of shares.[39]

Where the contract is fraudulent or shows on the face of it that the consideration is illusory, the allottee is liable to pay for the shares. So, in *Hong Kong and China Gas Co Ltd v Glen*[40] G agreed to sell a concession to a company which agreed to allot him as fully paid 400 shares forthwith and also one-fifth of any future increase of capital. It was held that the agreement was good so far as it obliged the company to allot one-fifth of any future increase of capital but void so far as it relieved G from paying for the shares. It was apparent that the value of the concession bore no relation to the amount of the shares. Sargant J. held that:

---

[33] *Wragg Ltd, Re* [1897] Ch. 796; *Park Business Interiors Ltd v Park* [1992] B.C.L.C. 1034.
[34] [1897] 1 Ch. 796, CA.
[35] In Scotland past consideration is valid consideration so that, e.g. shares can be issued in return for the past services of the company's promoters: *Park Business Interiors Ltd v Park* [1992] B.C.L.C. 1034.
[36] [1893] 3 Ch. 9, CA.
[37] *National House, etc. Investment Co Ltd v Watson*, 1908 S.C. 888.
[38] Per Parker J. in *Gardner v Iredale* [1912] 1 Ch. 700 at 716.
[39] [1912] 1 Ch. 700 at 716.
[40] [1914] 1 Ch. 527.

"If the agreement were that the property to be purchased should be valued, and that against this property shares should be issued as fully paid to an extent exceeding the amount of the valuation by one-third, the arrangement would . . . be bad as to this excess of one-third. It would to this extent be apparent on the face of the contract that the attempted discharge of a part of the liability was illusory".[41]

ISSUE OF SHARES AT A PREMIUM

The general principle

9–012 As was discussed above, the company's articles will permit a company to issue shares at a "nominal value". However, where a company's issued shares have a market value greater than the amount paid up on them, then, when further shares are being issued, the company may require applicants to agree to pay more than the nominal amount of the new shares. Paying an amount above the nominal amount is known as paying a "premium". So, if the company's value in the open market increases above its given value at the time that the company's constitution was created, then the company may decide to seek to raise more cash than the nominal value would suggest for a share issue of a given size. It has been held that a company may issue its shares at a premium without any special power in its articles. There is no requirement for a company to issue its shares above par simply because they could be sold at a premium in the market if the company does not wish to do so.[42] However, by s.610 of the CA 2006, if shares are issued at a premium then a sum equal to the premium amounts received on each share must be transferred to the "share premium account". Although share premiums are regarded as capital, it is not capital belonging to any individual shareholder. The shareholder paying the premium has no dividend rights in respect of it and has no automatic right to repayment of it in a winding up.

Section 610 of the CA 2006 extends the general principle that the share capital of a company must be maintained[43] so as to apply it to the share premium account, because the section provides that the rules relating to the reduction of capital also apply to the share premium account. This principle has the effect that the share premium account cannot be reduced without the leave of the court. The exceptions to this principle apply where the share premium account is applied in one of the following ways: paying up unissued shares of the company to be issued to members as fully paid bonus shares; or writing off either the preliminary expenses or the expenses of, or the commission paid or discount allowed on, an issue of shares or debentures of the company; or providing for the premium payable by the company on the redemption of shares or debentures.

The issue of shares at a premium accentuates the unreality of the nominal or par value of a share. The capital in the share premium account is an anomalous

---

[41] [1914] 1 Ch. 527 at 539.
[42] Per Lord Davey in *Hilder v Dexter* [1902] A.C. 474 at 480.
[43] *Moorgate Mercantile Holdings Ltd, Re* [1980] 1 All E.R. 149.

form of capital because it is capital on which no dividend is paid, which is not attributable to the ownership of any class of shares, which is not part of the company's nominal capital, and which the ordinary investor may not realise is part of the company's actual capital.

Share premium account and issues other than for cash

Shares can be issued at a premium not only for cash but also for consideration **9–013** other than cash. Shares might be issued, for example, in exchange for land or in exchange for shares in another company. In each instance, there will be a question of valuing the assets which are given as consideration in exchange for the shares. If the value of the consideration received exceeds the nominal value of the shares issued then there is an issue of shares at a premium and s.610 applies. So, in *Head (Henry) & Co Ltd v Ropner Holdings Ltd*[44] a company acquired a majority of the shares in another company by virtue of an exchange of shares, and the value of the shares acquired exceeded the value of the shares issued. The excess had to be transferred to the share premium account, with the result that the pre-acquisition profits of the acquired company, reflected in the value of its shares, were frozen and could not be distributed as dividends by the acquiring company. This decision was regarded as wrong in principle by many lawyers and accountants, with the result that few such transfers to share premium accounts were made. The principle was, however, confirmed in *Shearer v Bercain*,[45] and, following that decision, the Act provides two forms of relief from the obligations of s.610 in certain defined circumstances, as considered in the next section.

Acquisition of shares at a premium in relation to corporate reorganisations

Merger relief

There is an exception from the ordinary s.610 requirements in relation to mergers **9–014** of companies. Where the issuing company acquires a 90 per cent holding in another company[46] by way of a share-for-share exchange no transfer to the share premium account need be made.[47] This is because the regulation of mergers (as considered in Ch.32) deals with the procedure for dealing with mergers and so the metamorphosis of shares in one company into shares in another company in relation to mergers is dealt with differently. In fact this is a wide relief as it applies whether or not the issuing company owned any shares in the other company, e.g. it applies to a company owning 60 per cent of the shares of a subsidiary acquiring another 30 per cent. There is no obligation in such cases to disclose any premiums in the balance sheet. It also applies if the consideration provided by the acquired company is a cancellation of its issued shares rather than an issue, which is a frequent practice in schemes of reconstruction.

---

[44] [1952] Ch.124.
[45] [1980] 3 All E.R. 295.
[46] This is 90 per cent of the nominal value of the equity share capital excluding any shares held as treasury shares.
[47] Companies Act 2006 s.612.

Group reconstruction relief

9–015 As with mergers, there is a separate procedure for group reconstructions which deal with reconstructions differently from ordinary acquisitions of shares with non-cash consideration. Where a wholly-owned subsidiary acquires a shareholding (not necessarily 100 per cent) in a fellow subsidiary (not necessarily wholly-owned) in return for an allotment of its own shares or other non-cash assets to its holding company or another of its wholly-owned subsidiaries, relief from s.610 is available.[48] Only the lower of the cost or book value to the issuing company of the acquired shares need be taken into account.

ALTERATION OF SHARE CAPITAL

Alterations of share capital: the general principle

The power to effect alterations under s.617 CA 2006

9–016 Section 617 provides for the only ways in which a company may alter its share capital. They are as follows in the following provisions of s.617:

"(2) The company may—

(a) increase its share capital by allotting new shares in accordance with this Part, or

(b) reduce its share capital in accordance with Chapter 10.

(3) The company may—

(a) sub-divide or consolidate all or any of its share capital in accordance with section 618, or

(b) reconvert stock into shares in accordance with section 620.

(4) The company may redenominate all or any of its shares in accordance with section 622, and may reduce its share capital in accordance with section 626 in connection with such a redenomination."

There are a number of exceptions to these requirements whereby the s.617 regime does apply, as delineated in s.617(5) as follows:

(5) Nothing in this section affects—

(a) the power of a company to purchase its own shares, or to redeem shares, in accordance with Part 18[49];

(b) the power of a company to purchase its own shares in pursuance of an order of the court under—

(i) section 98 (application to court to cancel resolution for re-registration as a private company),

---

[48] Companies Act 2006 s.611.
[49] As discussed in Ch.10.

    (ii) section 721(6) (powers of court on objection to redemption or purchase of shares out of capital),

    (iii) section 759 (remedial order in case of breach of prohibition of public offers by private company), or

    (iv) Part 30 (protection of members against unfair prejudice);

(c) the forfeiture of shares, or the acceptance of shares surrendered in lieu, in pursuance of the company's articles, for failure to pay any sum payable in respect of the shares;

(d) the cancellation of shares under section 662 (duty to cancel shares held by or for a public company);

(e) the power of a company—

    (i) to enter into a compromise or arrangement in accordance with Part 26 (arrangements and reconstructions), or

    (ii) to do anything required to comply with an order of the court on an application under that Part."

These forms of capital alteration in s.617 are considered in turn.

Subdivision and consolidation of shares

A subdivision or a consolidation of shares may take place further to s.617(3)(a) **9–017** and s.618 of the CA 2006, although a resolution of the company's members is required under s.618(3). A consolidation occurs when several shares are consolidated into one share: for example, when twenty shares with a nominal value of 5p each are consolidated into a single £1 share. Consolidation is effected by the passage of a resolution which is to be specified in the articles. If the articles are silent, a special resolution to give authority and to effect the consolidation is necessary. Notice must be given to the Registrar within a month of the consolidation.

Increase in share capital

A company can increase its share capital further to s.617(2)(a) of the CA **9–018** 2006 provided that the procedure in Pt 17 of the CA 2006 is followed. The law and regulation dealing with the raising of capital are considered in Chs 13 through 15 of this book. The principles governing the allotment of shares are considered in Ch.8. Every increase of the nominal or authorised capital figure in the memorandum must be effected by the company in general meeting. If the articles authorise the increase of capital, whether an ordinary or a special resolution is required depends on the articles. If the articles do not give authority to increase capital, the articles must be altered by special resolution so that they do give authority but the one special resolution can both authorise and effect an increase.[50] The notice convening the meeting must specify the amount of the

---

[50] *Campbell's Case* (1873) I.R. 9 Ch. App. 1. Remember that the Company Law Review recommended the abolition of this figure.

proposed increase.[51] Within 15 days after the passing of the resolution effecting the increase, a notice in the prescribed form of the amount of the increase must be filed with the Registrar. A printed copy of the resolution effecting the increase, or a copy in some other form approved by him, must also be filed with the Registrar.

Conversion of shares into stock

9–019 It was once the practice to convert shares in companies into "stock" in particular because stock allows shares effectively to be sold in smaller units. Section 540(2) of the CA 2006 provides that "a company's shares may no longer be converted into stock". Therefore, this practice has been stopped for the future. The difference between stock and shares was described by Lord Hatherley as follows:

> "Shares in a company, as shares, cannot be bought in small fractions of any amount, fractions of less than [the nominal value] but the consolidated stock of a company can be bought just in the same way as the stock of the public debt can be bought, split up in as many portions as you like, and subdivided into as small fractions as you please."

His lordship referred to stock as "simply a set of shares put together in a bundle".[52] A company could not issue stock directly but could only convert shares into stock. The prohibition under s.540(2) now effectively precludes the practice for the future, although companies may still seek to reconvert stock back into shares in the future further to the procedure in s.617 of the CA 2006. A subdivision of shares is the division of shares into shares of smaller amount. Effectively it is the inverse of a consolidation of shares: for example, the division of a single £1 share into twenty shares with a nominal value of 5p each. This process is often used to improve the marketability of expensive shares by breaking them up into a greater number of less expensive shares. Subdivision is effected under s.617 of the CA 2006.

REDUCTION OF CAPITAL

Introduction

9–020 The share capital of the company must be subscribed in money or money's worth. This capital may be lost or diminished according to the fluctuations of the business, but otherwise, subject to the Act, it cannot be reduced without the sanction of the court.[53] Yet, if a company has more than enough capital, it may reduce the nominal amount of shares by repaying paid-up capital. The concern is that a company might seek to reduce its capital by bleeding it out and distributing it

---

[51] *MacConnell v E. Prill & Co Ltd* [1916] 2 Ch. 57.

[52] In *Morrice v Aylmer* (1875) L.R. 7 HL 717 at 724, 725. Although it is suggested that more commonly stock are units bundled together into a share.

[53] This is generally known as the rule in *Trevor v Whitworth* (1887) 12 App. Cas. 409, HL.

among its shareholders to the detriment of unsecured creditors and others. Thus any agreement which has the effect of returning capital to a shareholder is void, however indirect that effect might be.[54] The object of requiring the court's sanction is threefold: first, to protect persons dealing with the company, so that the fund available for satisfying their claims shall not be diminished except by ordinary business risks; secondly, to ensure that the reduction is equitable as between the various classes of shareholders in the company; and, thirdly, to protect the interests of the public.[55] The limited means by which there may be a reduction of capital are delineated by s.641 of the CA 2006, considered next.

Reduction procedure

The two possible methods

Section 641 of the CA 2006 provides that: **9–021**

"(1) A limited company having a share capital may reduce its share capital—

(a) in the case of a private company limited by shares, by special resolution supported by a solvency statement (see sections 642 to 644);

(b) in any case, by special resolution confirmed by the court (see sections 645 to 651)."

Therefore, a reduction of capital may take place in one of two ways. Under the first method, if the company is a private company, then the company may pass a special resolution together with a "solvency statement", which does not need to be confirmed by the court. If the company is a public company, then it may not rely on that first method.[56]

So, if the company is a public company it is obliged to use the second method; or alternatively, if it is a private company it may elect to use the second method. The second method is to pass a special resolution and to have it confirmed by the court. It was held under the predecessor legislation (and may now apply only to the second method), the court cannot condone a reduction which has been carried out without its prior approval.[57] The special resolution must be in the correct form and comply with the requirements of s.378 as to the exact notice required.[58] The reference to "the court" is a reference to the court with jurisdiction to wind up the company. The courts with jurisdiction to wind up a company are set out in ss.117 and 120 of the Insolvency Act 1986.

---

[54] For a complex agreement which had this effect see *Barclays Bank Plc v British & Commonwealth Holdings Plc* [1996] 1 B.C.L.C. 1.
[55] Per Lord Watson in *Trevor v Whitworth* (1887) 12 App. Cas. 409 at 423; per Lord MacNaghten in *British and American Finance Corporation Ltd v Couper* [1894] A.C. 399 at 411.
[56] The first method was suggested by the Company Law Review.
[57] *Alexander Henderson Ltd, Petitioners*, (Notes) 1967 S.L.T. 17.
[58] *Moorgate Mercantile Holdings Ltd, Re* [1980] 1 All E.R. 40. However, if there is an error in the actual resolution as passed which is so insignificant that no one would be prejudiced by its correction the court will allow the reduction to proceed: *Willaire Systems Plc, Re* [1987] B.C.L.C. 67. See also *European Homes Products Plc, Re* (1988) 4 B.C.C. 779.

Importantly, this provision (as with the whole of Ch.10 which contains the provisions on reduction of capital) is "subject to any provisions of the company's articles restricting or prohibiting the reduction of the company's share capital".[59] If the articles do not authorise the reduction of capital, two special resolutions— one to alter the articles so as to give authority and the other to effect the reduction—will be necessary, in addition to the consent of the court.[60] Moreover, no reduction of capital is permissible if it would leave no shareholders.[61] For this purpose, it is not enough that there is only a shareholder with redeemable shares.[62]

The first method: reduction of capital supported by a solvency statement

9–022 The first method is supported by a statutory procedure set out in ss.642 through 644 of the CA 2006. The nature of the solvency statement is set out in s.643 of the CA 2006 in the following terms:

"(1) A solvency statement is a statement that each of the directors—

(a) has formed the opinion, as regards the company's situation at the date of the statement, that there is no ground on which the company could then be found to be unable to pay (or otherwise discharge) its debts; and

(b) has also formed the opinion—

(i) if it is intended to commence the winding up of the company within twelve months of that date, that the company will be able to pay (or otherwise discharge) its debts in full within twelve months of the commencement of the winding up; or

(ii) in any other case, that the company will be able to pay (or otherwise discharge) its debts as they fall due during the year immediately following that date."

The statement is therefore a statement as to the continued financial viability of the company. The statement must be made by all of the directors, and therefore if just one director wished to refuse to agree to that statement then that director would need to resign.[63] This is the stringency bound up in a new procedure which otherwise enables the company to avoid the need to acquire the approval of the court.

---

[59] Companies Act 2006 s.641(6).

[60] *Patent Invert Sugar Co, Re* (1885) 31 Ch.D. 166, CA; *Oregon Mortgage Co Ltd, Petitioners*, 1910 S.C. 964.

[61] Companies Act 2006 s.641(2).

[62] Companies Act 2006 s.641(2).

[63] See, perhaps, *In A Flap Envelope Co Ltd* [2004] 1 B.C.L.C. 64 where a director was held to have remained as a de facto director of the company even though he had purported to resign as a director so that such a statement could be made purportedly unanimously by the other directors. It is suggested that such a sham resignation is no more objectionable than a genuine resignation (perhaps in disgust) by a director who genuinely disagreed with the solvency statement and whose dissent was lost as a result of his resignation as opposed to being shared with the outside world in pursuance of the general policy that unsecured creditors should have their position protected by the unanimity of the directors.

In essence, it is a requirement that there cannot be a reduction of capital unless the company is able to meet its debts. The ability to meet one's debts as they become due is the essence of being a solvent person. The directors are therefore required to certify that the company is solvent in this sense, before the company then passes a special resolution. This supports the underlying policy requirement that the company must maintain its capital so that the company's obligations to its creditors will be met. When preparing their statement, "the directors must take into account all of the company's liabilities" which includes any contingent or prospective liabilities.[64] The ramifications for the directors personally of making a solvency statement under s.643 "without having reasonable grounds for the opinions expressed in it" is the commission of a criminal offence.[65]

A reduction of capital supported by a solvency statement must comply with the requirements in s.642 of the CA 2006 that a notice containing the proposed reduction to be voted on by special resolution and the solvency statement is circulated "to very eligible member".[66] A copy of the special resolution and of the solvency statement must be lodged with the Registrar within 15 days of the resolution having been passed.[67]

Examples of reductions of capital

Reductions of capital take effect in many different ways. Some illustrations from **9–023** the decided cases may serve to demonstrate this. In *Saltdean Estate Co Ltd, Re*,[68] the reduction of capital involved repaying the capital paid-up on each of the company's preference shares of 50p each plus a premium of 25p per share: the court confirmed the reduction. A reduction may involve the company paying off part of its share capital not with money but by transferring to its shareholders shares of another company.[69] Alternatively it can be used to create a reserve out of the share premium account arising on an acquisition which will then be available to set off against that "surplus" on consolidated account.[70] Moneys withdrawn from the capital and set free by the reduction can be employed in the purchase of the company's own shares which it is intended to extinguish. The procedure can also be used to convert ordinary shares into redeemable shares, at least where there is a specific date for the redemption.[71]

The reduction procedure cannot be used as a device to raise new capital to replace capital which has disappeared, for example by the conversion of £1 fully paid shares into £1 shares with only 75p paid, thus imposing an additional liability on shareholders.[72] On the other hand it can be used as a method of

---

[64] Companies Act 2006 s.643(2). See *MacPherson v European Strategic Bureau Ltd* [2000] 2 B.C.L.C. 683 at [39] in relation to contingent liabilities being liabilities which will have to be met even though they have not accrued at the date of the statement.

[65] Companies Act 2006 s.643(4).

[66] Companies Act 2006 s.642(2).

[67] Companies Act 2006 s.644(1).

[68] [1968] 1 W.L.R. 1844.

[69] *Westburn Sugar Refineries Ltd, Petitioners*, 1951 S.C. HL 57; [1951] A.C. 625.

[70] Per Lord Macnaghten in *British and American Finance Corporation v Couper* [1894] A.C. 399 at 414.

[71] *Forth Wines Ltd, Petitioners*, 1993 S.L.T. 170.

[72] See s.16 and also *W. Morrison & Co Ltd, Petitioners* (1892) 19 R. 1049.

varying the type or denomination of capital. In such cases the reduction resolution will be contingent on the corresponding increase of capital taking place. This practice was approved in *TIP-Europe Ltd, Re*[73] provided the increase has taken place prior to the court's approval being given. In this way shares may be converted into a different currency, for example from sterling into dollars, by cancelling the sterling shares and immediately issuing dollar shares.[74]

Questions for the court on reduction

9–024   The statute does not prescribe the precise manner in which any reduction must take place. Instead, a scheme for the reduction is to be identified by the company and it is that scheme which is to be the subject of the special resolution. If the question is referred to the court, because the company is a public company or because a private company has chosen to do so, the question whether there should be a reduction of capital and how it should be effected is a domestic question for the prescribed majority of the shareholders to decide.[75] Ordinarily, the court should sanction a reduction unless what is proposed to be done is unfair or inequitable in the several interests of the creditors, the shareholders or any section of the public who may have dealings with the company or may invest in its securities.[76] The court has to decide, on the evidence as a whole, whether to approve the reduction. Since many applications are unopened there is a duty on the company of full and frank disclosure to the court.[77] The introduction of the new procedure relating to solvency statements, however, means that in relation to private companies many fewer applications will come before the court in any event.

Reductions due to over-capitalisation

9–025   Reductions in capital may be sought in circumstances in which the company simply has more capital than it requires. In such circumstances it is suggested that the interests of creditors are not at issue because the reduction does not involve the diminution of any liability in respect of unpaid capital or the payment to any shareholder of any paid-up capital. It is suggested that in this context the questions to be considered by the court are whether reduction should not be granted permission because the court is concerned about those members of the public who may be induced to take shares in the company, and furthermore whether the reduction is fair and equitable as between the different classes of shareholders.[78] When capital is being returned as surplus to the company's requirements, it

---

[73] (1987) 3 B.C.C. 647. See also *M.B. Group Plc, Re* (1989) 5 B.C.C. 684 and *B.A.T. Industries Plc, Re*, September 3, 1998.

[74] *Anglo-American Insurance Co Ltd, Re* [1991] B.C.L.C. 564.

[75] *British and American Finance Corp v Couper* [1894] A.C. 399. See Lord President Inglis in *Hoggan v Tharsis Sulpher, etc. Co Ltd* (1882) 9 R. 1191 at 1212.

[76] *Westburn Sugar Refineries Ltd, Petitioners*, 1951 S.C. HL 57; [1951] A.C. 625. *Ratners Group Plc, Re* [1988] B.C.L.C. 685.

[77] *Ransomes Plc, Re* [1999] 2 B.C.L.C. 591.

[78] *Poole v National Bank of China Ltd* [1907] A.C. 229. See Lord Parker of Waddington in *Caldwell & Co Ltd v Caldwell*, 1916 S.C. HL 120 at 121. *Ratner Group, Re*, above, *Ransomes Plc, Re*, above.

should normally[79] be returned first to the class of shareholders with priority as to capital in a winding up,[80] at any rate where preference shares are not entitled to participate in surplus assets.[81]

An illustration of a case involving such a reduction in capital is *Prudential Assurance Co Ltd v Chatterley-Whitfield Collieries Ltd*[82] in which a coal company had a capital of £400,000, half of which was in ordinary shares and half in 6 per cent preference shares. The company had a surplus of capital as a result of nationalisation. A special resolution was passed reducing the capital by paying off the preference shares. Under the company's articles of association, in the event of a winding up the preference shareholders had a right to priority of repayment of capital but no further right to participate in the surplus assets. It was held that the reduction should be confirmed as being fair and equitable. It was found that the preference shareholders had no right to a continuance of their rate of dividend during the life of the company if the company desired and had the means to pay them off. The preference shareholders were being treated in accordance with their rights and it was immaterial that the elimination of their shares extinguished any hopes which they had of obtaining some additional advantage as a result of regulations to be made under s.25 of the Coal Industry Nationalisation Act 1946.

It is not necessary for the company to show by how much its capital is surplus to its requirements. It is suggested that "public policy" is not a ground for the court refusing to confirm a reduction which is otherwise unobjectionable. For example, a reduction may be confirmed although the motive for it may have been avoidance of the consequences of possible future nationalisation, or the minimisation of tax liability.[83]

A modification of rights clause in the articles has no application to a cancellation **9–026** of shares on a reduction of capital which is in accord with the rights attached to the shares under the articles.[84] It follows, therefore, that if the reduction of capital of a class of share is itself made a class right by the articles, then any reduction will be subject to the modification procedure, usually approved by three quarters of that class, before it can be confirmed by the court.[85] If the necessary approval has been obtained, the reduction will be approved unless it is unfair or has been sanctioned by the influence of some improper or extraneous consideration.[86] There is a duty on the company to explain the reduction to its shareholders. The court will also consider the financial risk to the remaining shareholders.[87]

---

[79] But not always: see *William Dixon Ltd, Petitioners*, 1948 S.C. 511.

[80] *Wilsons and Clyde Coal Co Ltd v Scottish Insurance Corporation Ltd*, 1949 S.C. HL 90; 1948 S.C. 360; *Prudential Assurance Co Ltd v Chatterley-Whitfield Collieries Ltd* [1949] A.C. 512.

[81] Per Lord Greene M.R. in the *Prudential* case, above, in the Court of Appeal [1948] 2 All E.R. 593 at 596, 600.

[82] [1949] A.C. 512.

[83] *David Bell Ltd, Petitioners*, 1954 S.C. 33.

[84] *Saltdean Estate Co Ltd, Re* [1968] 1 W.L.R. 1844; *House of Fraser v A.C.G.E. Investments Ltd* [1987] A.C. 387; 1987 S.C. HL 125; cf. *Old Silkstone Collieries Ltd, Re* [1954] Ch. 169, CA.

[85] *Northern Engineering Industries Plc, Re* [1994] 2 B.C.L.C. 704, CA.

[86] *Welsbach Incandescent Gas Light Co Ltd, Re* [1904] Ch. 87, CA. A scheme of arrangement is not necessary: *Oban and Aultmore-Glenlivet Distilleries Ltd, Petitioners* (1903) 5 F. 1140, and *Marshall, Fleming & Co Ltd, Petitioners*, 1938 S.C. 873 (OH).

[87] See *Ransomes Plc, Re* [1999] 2 B.C.L.C. 591.

In one decided case, where there were special circumstances, a reduction involving a variation of class rights was confirmed.[88] There had not been a meeting of the class of shareholders at issue, in that case it was the preference shareholders. Nevertheless no one objected to the lack of a meeting. On the facts, there was no prospect of a liquidation which would have given the preference shareholders the right to participate in surplus assets after repayment of capital. In consequence the preference shareholders received more than they would have received by selling. When one part of a class of equity shareholders is treated differently from another, the usual practice is to proceed by a scheme of arrangement under s.895 of the CA 2006, under which the interests of the minority are better protected.[89]

Reductions due to loss of capital

9–027   Under English law, when a reduction is sought on the ground that capital has been lost or is not represented by available assets, evidence must be given about the loss or evidence must be provided to the effect that the available assets do not represent the capital.[90] A reduction may be confirmed where capital has been lost but it is still represented by available assets. In *Re Hoare & Co Ltd*[91] a company had built up a reserve fund. It had incurred a loss arising from the depreciation in the value of its public-houses below the amount stated in the balance sheet, and it proposed to reduce its capital by apportioning the loss between its capital account and the reserve. It was held that the loss ought to be rateably apportioned between the capital account and the reserve, and the company was not bound to apply the whole of its reserve to wipe out the loss.

Capital is not lost unless it is permanently lost.[92] If the evidence is therefore that the loss might not be permanent, the courts will not allow a reduction unless the company gives an undertaking to protect the creditors in the event of the loss being made good. In one case[93] the judge required an undertaking to place any sums recovered in respect of the loss (by way of compensation) into capital reserve so that it could not be distributed as dividend. However, in a subsequent case[94] Nourse J. refused to accept that such an undertaking must always require a reserve to be set aside indefinitely to safeguard the interests of future creditors and shareholders. The undertaking in most cases need only safeguard the interests of creditors at the time of the reduction. This approach was followed in *Quayle Munro Ltd, Petitioners*,[95] where the court confirmed a petition to cancel

[88] *William Jones & Sons Ltd, Re* [1969] 1 W.L.R. 146.
[89] *Robert Stephen Holdings Ltd, Re* [1968] 1 W.L.R. 522.
[90] Per Lord Parker of Waddington in *Caldwell & Co Ltd v Caldwell*, 1916 S.C. HL 120 at 121. Scottish courts dispense with such evidence where there is no reason to suspect the bona fides of the parties: *Caldwell's* case.
[91] [1904] 2 Ch. 208, CA.
[92] *Haematite Steel Co, Re* [1901] 2 Ch. 746 at 749, per Romer L. J.; *Walsbach Incandescent Gas Light Co Ltd, Re* [1904] 1 Ch. 87.
[93] *Jupiter House Investments (Cambridge) Ltd, Re* [1985] 1 W.L.R. 975.
[94] *Grosvenor Press Plc, Re* [1985] 1 W.L.R. 980.
[95] 1992 S.C. 24; [1994] 1 B.C.L.C. 410.

the share premium account to allow for past losses leaving a credit balance as a special reserve fund. Undertakings were only needed for present creditors with respect to that reserve, and could allow for the writing off of future losses irrespective of any creditors.

Creditors' rights to object to reduction

Creditors are entitled to object to the reduction if they would have been able to prove **9–028** against the company if it was being wound up, provided that the circumstances surrounding the proposed reduction of share capital involves one of the following: either a diminution of liability in respect of unpaid share capital; or a payment to any shareholder of any paid-up capital[96]; or any other case where the court so directs. For this purpose the court must settle a list of creditors, with the nature and amount of their claims, and may publish notices fixing a day by which creditors not entered on the list are to claim to be entered. Any creditors who do not consent to the reduction must be paid off or the company must secure payment of their claims by appropriating such amount as the court directs.[97] In special circumstances, however, the court may dispense with these requirements.[98] However, before dispensing with a list of creditors, the court must be satisfied that no creditor who might be entitled to object to the reduction would be prejudiced by it.[99]

If there is no overall diminution in the company's issued and paid up share capital, for example where the cancelled shares are to be replaced by equivalent shares, then the creditors cannot in practice object to the proposed reduction of capital because no asset could satisfy their claims is being given up or returned to the shareholder.[100] So, in *Meux's Brewery Co Ltd, Re*[101] a company had a paid-up share capital of £1,000,000, and had also issued £1,000,000 debentures secured by a trust deed constituting a floating charge. In 1904, losses to the extent of £800,000 were incurred and no dividends had since been paid, any profits being applied in reduction of the deficiency. By 1917 the deficiency had been reduced to £640,000, and the company proposed to reduce its capital to £360,000 by writing off the lost capital. The latest balance sheet showed assets worth £1,500,000. The debenture holders objected to the reduction of capital. It was held that, as the reduction involved no diminution of unpaid capital or repayment to shareholders of paid-up capital, that the creditors were not entitled to object unless a strong case was made out, and the debenture holders had not made out any such case. It is not clear whether creditors may object to such a reduction of capital which is intended to be followed by a distribution of assets. In *B.A.T. Industries Plc, Re*[102] Neuberger J. was of the opinion that they could not.

---

[96] Replacement of preference shares with loan stock, which became a common practice for the purposes of reducing liability to corporation tax, counts as such payment, although the loan stock does not fall to be repaid by the company until a future date: *Lawrie & Symington Ltd, Petitioners*, 1969 S.L.T. 221.

[97] Companies Act 2006 ss.645 and 646.

[98] Companies Act 2006 s.645(2),(3).

[99] *Lucania Temperance Billiard Halls (London) Ltd, Re* [1966] Ch. 98.

[100] *B.A.T. Industries Plc, Re*, September 3, 1998.

[101] [1919] Ch. 28.

[102] *B.A.T. Industries Plc, Re*, September 3, 1998.

The object of reducing capital, where capital has been lost or is not represented by available assets, is to enable the accounts to present a realistic picture of the company's financial position, which may permit the company to pay dividends. To safeguard the creditors in the case of an application by a company to write off capital not lost or unrepresented by available assets, thereby setting free capital which might be distributed among the shareholders, the court is empowered by s.645 of the CA 2006 to give effect to a creditor's objection "in any other case".

Procedural requirements of the second method requiring court sanction

Order for reduction; minute of reduction

9–029   The court may "make an order confirming the reduction of capital on such terms and conditions as it thinks fit".[103] Confirmation by the court must precede the actual reduction of capital.[104] On making an order confirming the reduction, the court may direct that the company add the words "and reduced" to its name for a specified time,[105] and furthermore that the reasons for reduction and the causes leading to the reduction be published so that proper information is given to the public.[106]

A copy of the order for reduction and a minute approved by the court showing the amount of the share capital, the number of shares into which it is divided, the amount of each share and the amount, if any, deemed to be paid up on each share, must be registered with the Registrar.[107] The Registrar then grants a certificate of registration, which is conclusive evidence of the reduction and that all the requirements of the Act with respect to reduction have been complied with, even if it is later discovered that the special resolution for a reduction was not properly passed,[108] or that there was no power in the articles to reduce capital.[109] The reduction takes effect as from the date of registration.

Reduction below authorised minimum capital

9–030   A question arises when the proposed reduction of capital would reduce the company's capital below the statutory authorised minimum. When the court confirms a reduction of capital of a public company which has the effect of bringing the nominal value of the company's allotted share capital below the authorised minimum capital (as considered above, £50,000) this will only be registered (and so will only be effective) if the company is first re-registered as a private company.[110] To ease this process the court may authorise the company to

---

[103] Companies Act 2006 s.648(1).
[104] *Alexander Henderson Ltd, Petitioners*, (Notes) 1967 S.L.T. 17.
[105] Companies Act 2006 s.648(4).
[106] Companies Act 2006 s.648(3).
[107] Companies Act 2006 s.649. Where the reduction takes the share capital to nil for a split second and new shares are then issued, this fact can be included in the minute of reduction: *Anglo-American Insurance Co Ltd, Re* [1991] B.C.L.C. 564.
[108] *Ladies' Dress Association v Pullbrook* [1900] 2 Q.B. 376, CA.
[109] *Walker and Smith Ltd, Re* [1903] W.N. 82.
[110] Companies Act 2006 s.650.

re-register as a private company without passing a special resolution and will also specify the necessary alterations to the company's memorandum and articles. In practice many public companies prohibit any reduction of capital below the authorised minimum in their articles.[111]

SERIOUS LOSS OF CAPITAL

Following the Second EC Directive,[112] under s.656 the directors of a public **9–031** company are obliged to call an extraordinary meeting of the company within 28 days from the earliest date on which any director knew that the company had suffered a serious loss of capital. A serious loss of capital occurs where the net assets of the company are half or less of the amount of the company's called up share capital. In other words if it has lost half or more of its called up share capital. The meeting must be fixed for a date not later than 56 days from when the obligation arose. It is to consider whether any, and if so what, measures should be taken to deal with the situation. Directors who knowingly and wilfully authorise or permit a failure to convene such a meeting are liable on conviction to a fine. There is some ambiguity as to what may actually be discussed. Section 656(6) of the CA 2006 provides that the meeting may not be used to discuss anything "which could not have been considered at that meeting apart from this section."

---

[111] But see *M.B. Group Plc, Re* (1989) 5 B.C.C. 684; *Anglo-American Insurance Co Ltd, Re* [1991] B.C.L.C. 564.
[112] Art.17.

Chapter 10

ACQUISITION OF OWN SHARES

INTRODUCTION

The scope of this chapter

10–001 The principle that a company cannot reduce its capital except in accordance with the CA 2006 means that it is unlawful for a company to buy its own shares or to redeem its own shares without statutory authorisation, irrespective of the extent to which such a purchase is in the interests of the company or its shareholders as a whole.[1] If a company was allowed to purchase its own shares back from its shareholders with impunity, this would mean that the company's capital could be depleted and its assets distributed to its shareholders with the effect that the company's creditors would have fewer assets left to satisfy obligations owed to them. Similarly, if shares could be redeemed, that is repurchased by the company and cancelled, then that would also reduce the company's capital. Clearly, if some shareholders could withdraw the company's capital on a whim then it would be possible to raise money for a company and to trade through a company on the basis that the company had capital of £x, when the withdrawal of capital would leave the company worth only £y once those shareholders stripped their investment out of the company in cash by having their shares purchased back from them by the company. Therefore, the circumstances in which these activities may be conducted are tightly controlled. There is of course no hindrance on shareholders selling their shares to third parties in the ordinary way.

However, this general principle against the purchase and redemption of shares does not prevent a company from buying the shares of another company even if that second company's assets consist entirely of a holding of shares in the purchaser. After all, the court will not pierce the corporate veil in such a circumstance. The purchasing company would be treated as buying shares in the second company and not as buying its own shares.[2] Companies were, however, able to issue preference shares which were expressly redeemable at a future date under s.58 of the 1948 Act. The 1981 Act replaced that narrow power with a general power to issue redeemable shares of any type and gave companies the additional power for the first time to purchase their own shares. Changes introduced in 2003

---

[1] See *Trevor v Whitworth* (1887) 12 A.C. 409.

[2] *Acatos & Hutcheson Plc v Watson* [1995] 1 B.C.L.C. 218. The judge suggested that it might be different if the second company was formed expressly for the purpose of avoiding the rule.

allowed public companies to retain and re-issue such shares: these are known as "treasury shares".

This chapter is concerned with these powers of purchase and redemption. Within Part 18 of the CA 2006, there are three separate activities covered: a company purchasing its own shares (considered below); a company redeeming its own shares (considered below); and the prohibition of financial assistance from the company to acquire shares in that company (which is considered separately in Ch.11). This chapter therefore considers a company's ability to purchase its own shares and to redeem its own shares, the methodology required for each activity, the funding of these activities, and the effects on the company's capital of each activity. These powers were originally part of a "package" designed to assist small companies in finding outside investors who might wish to be able to withdraw such investment at will. To this end it will be seen that there are different rules still within Ch.5 of Pt 18 of the CA 2006 so that private companies can, in some cases, fund the acquisition or redemption of shares out of capital. The effect is that subject to certain procedures and authority all shares are now potentially redeemable either by the terms of their issue or by subsequent agreement.

The policy reasons against acquisition of own shares

One of the underpinning policies of company law is the protection of creditors **10–002** and of shareholders against abuse. One of the principal, potential forms of abuse in relation to companies would be for a company's capital to be stripped away so that only a shell is left for creditors and others to recover what is owed to them. Consequently, in general terms, companies are precluded from acquiring their own shares because if a company was able to buy back its own shares from shareholders with impunity then that would allow the company's capital to be diverted to those shareholders and away from others. As discussed above, if third parties dealt with a company on the understanding that its paid-up share capital was £x, before the company used £y to buy back shares from some of its shareholders, then the company's paid-up share capital would be much less than the amount on which those third parties were relying. Therefore, the restriction on buying back shares promotes fair dealing, transparency in the affairs of companies, the accuracy of published corporate accounts, and prevents one particular avenue of fraud. After all, as the *Salomon* litigation demonstrated, one of the principal uses of companies is to conceal from the outside world both the true worth of a business and the true ownership of a business, unless the information which is required to be published about that business through the companies legislation is entirely transparent.

There are, however, limited circumstances in which shares may be bought back or redeemed. Those exceptions are considered in detail below. They fall into two broad categories. First, there are investment companies which were created specifically so that investors would be able to redeem their shares and so realise their share of the company's investment profits. Second, there is the corporate practice of convincing the investing public that they return sufficient profits for each share held, known as "earnings-per-share". This measurement is important for professional investors who want to generate investment income by means of the dividends paid on shares, and the amount of profit earned relative to the number of shares which have been issued. To soak up excess profits in the good times, a company's management may decide to pay a dividend and then to use excess profits to buy up some of the company's shares so that there are fewer shares in issue. If there are fewer shares in issue, then the ratio of profits per share must increase. As a result, the earnings-per-share ratio would appear to be impressive and the market value of the company would remain strong. Consequently, the need to allow share buy-backs in particular circumstances passed into the statute book, as considered below.

This policy underpins the law on the repurchase and redemption of shares in this chapter. It also informs the material in the next chapter relating to *Financial Assistance* by reference to which the management of companies are prevented from using the company's money to help other people to acquire shares in that company. The reasoning is, in large part, to prevent the company's capital from being reduced to assist share purchases and to prevent a fraudulently active market in the company's shares from being created. Furthermore, the discussion of dividends in Ch.12 centres on the requirement that dividends may not be paid out in any way that management sees fit, but rather dividends and other distributions may only be paid out of "available profits" so that the company's capital is not allowed to leak out to shareholders so that there is no capital left to meet the company's obligations.

THE RESTRICTION ON A COMPANY BUYING ITS OWN SHARES

Introduction

10–003   As was set out above, there has long been a restriction on a company buying its own shares. The purpose behind this rule is the need to preserve the company's capital. In some circumstances it might also make it appear that a company's shares were more valuable than their "true" value if the company itself were to generate speculation in those shares. This would tend to distort the market in those shares.

Restrictions on a company buying its own shares

10–004   Further to s.658 of the CA 2006, a limited company may not acquire its own shares, "whether by purchase, subscription or otherwise", unless that is done in accordance with the provisions of Pt 18 of the CA 2006.[3] Breach of that prohibition is a criminal offence[4] and any purported acquisition of shares in that manner is void.[5] Void acquisitions cannot be effected retrospectively once they have taken place.[6]

---

[3] Companies Act 2006 s.658(1). Thus continuing to enact the common law principle in *Trevor v Whitworth* (1887) 12 A.C. 409.
[4] Companies Act 2006 s.658(2)(a).
[5] Companies Act 2006 s.658(2)(b). See also *RW Peak (King's Lynn) Ltd, Re* [1998] 1 B.C.L.C. 193.
[6] *R. W. Peak (Kings Lynn) Ltd, Re* [1998] 1 B.C.L.C. 193. This does not apply where the irregularity relates only to the number of treasury shares exceeding the maximum allowed under statute.

The exceptions to the general rule are contained in s.659 of the CA 2006. The first exception is that a limited company may acquire any of its own fully paid shares "otherwise than for valuable consideration".[7] So, for example, the company may acquire its own shares by way of gift. The second exception relates to acquisitions on a reduction of capital under s.135 of the CA 2006.[8] The third exception relates to purchases authorised by the court under ss.98, 721 or 759 of the CA 2006.[9] These forms of purchases relate to the cancellation of a re-registration as a private company; in relation to the powers of the court connected to an objection to the redemption of purchase of shares out of capital; in relation to remedial orders relating to public offers of shares by a private company; or to protect minority shareholders against unfair prejudice.[10] The fourth exception relates to the forfeiture of shares or acceptance of any shares surrendered in lieu for failure to pay for them.[11] It has also been held that the acquisition of a company which owns shares in the acquiring company falls outside the central principle.[12]

Where shares are subscribed for by a nominee and held for the company by that nominee, then those shares are to be treated as belonging beneficially to the nominee.[13] Otherwise, if the company gives financial assistance to the nominee to acquire those shares otherwise than by subscription then those shares will be treated as being owned beneficially by the company.[14] The provisions relating to the cancellation of shares by public companies are governed by ss.662 et seq. of the CA 2006.

REDEMPTION AND PURCHASE OF SHARES

The power to issue redeemable shares

Section 684 of the CA 2006 allows companies to issue redeemable shares in the **10–005** following contexts:

> "(1) A limited company having a share capital may issue shares that are to be redeemed or are liable to be redeemed at the option of the company or the shareholder ("redeemable shares"), subject to the following provisions.
>
> (2) The articles of a private limited company may exclude or restrict the issue of redeemable shares.
>
> (3) A public limited company may only issue redeemable shares if it is authorised to do so by its articles.
>
> (4) No redeemable shares may be issued at a time when there are no issued shares of the company that are not redeemable."

---

[7] Companies Act 2006 s.659(1).
[8] Companies Act 2006 s.659(2)(a).
[9] Companies Act 2006 s.659(2)(b).
[10] Companies Act 2006 s.659(2).
[11] Companies Act 2006 s.659(2)(c).
[12] *Acatos & Hutcheson Plc v Watson* [1995] 1 B.C.L.C. 218.
[13] Companies Act 2006 s.660(1) and (2).
[14] Companies Act 2006 s.660(3).

Therefore, in the first place, any company with a share capital (thus excluding companies which do not have share capital, like companies limited by guarantee) may issue redeemable shares. Those shares may be redeemed at the option of the company or at the option of the shareholder who holds those redeemable shares. This general power exists for private companies unless the articles of association of a private company exclude that power. The reverse is true for public companies: that is, a public company may only issue redeemable shares if its articles of association expressly permit it to issue redeemable shares. It is a requirement that the company has shares which are not redeemable making up its share capital, hence the prohibition on the issue of redeemable shares when there are no shares in issue which are not redeemable. So, no company may issue only redeemable shares[15] but one non-redeemable share will technically be enough.

The mechanics of redeeming shares

10–006   The redemption of shares can work in a number of different ways. Redeemable shares may be issued on one of two bases. First, redeemable shares may be issued on the basis that they are redeemable at a fixed date or on the happening of an identified event. For example, a venture capitalist investing money in the company may specify that its shares are to be redeemed by the company after five years, or if the company's profits falls below an identified level. Secondly, redeemable shares may be redeemable at the option of the company or the shareholder. That means that the company or the shareholder itself may have the right to elect that the shares are redeemable whenever it chooses.

The directors may, however, set the "terms, condition and manner of redemption" provided that they have authorisation to do so in the company's articles of association or by a resolution of the company,[16] and provided that they identify those terms, conditions and manner of redemption before the shares are allotted.[17] If the directors do not have such an authorisation, then the method of redemption must be identified in the company's articles of association.[18] Any shares which are redeemed may not be redeemed unless they are fully paid.[19] However, the company and the shareholder may agree that the amount payable on redemption may be paid later than the redemption date.[20] Otherwise, the redemption amount must be paid for on redemption.[21] It is a key part of the policy in this area, following the decision in *Trevor v Whitworth*,[22] that there must be no incidental reduction in the company's capital. Furthermore, the terms of redemption must provide for payment at the time of redemption. This requirement has been interpreted as meaning payment in full and not by instalments.[23] In one case, the court

---

[15] Nor can a company purchase its own shares if that would leave only redeemable shares in existence.
[16] Companies Act 2006 s.685(1). The resolution may be an ordinary resolution: Companies Act 2006 s.685(2).
[17] Companies Act 2006 s.685(3).
[18] Companies Act 2006 s.685(4).
[19] Companies Act 2006 s.686(1).
[20] Companies Act 2006 s.686(2). This was a new addition to company law in the 2006 Act.
[21] Companies Act 2006 s.686(3).
[22] (1887) 12 A.C. 409.
[23] *Petna v Dale* [2004] 2 B.C.L.C. 508.

allowed a company to issue redeemable shares on a reduction of capital as a replacement for ordinary shares which were cancelled under the scheme.[24] Apart from those basic requirements, the terms and conditions of redemption are to be as specified in the company's articles.

When redeemable shares are redeemed, those shares are "treated as cancelled" and the company's issued share capital is "diminished accordingly by the nominal value of the shares redeemed".[25] In consequence, because those shares are treated as being cancelled automatically, there is no option for treating those redeemed shares as being held as treasury shares. The company must give notice of the redemption of those shares to the Registrar within one month of redemption.[26]

Private limited companies benefit from a different regime from other types of company. A private limited company may pay for the redemption of shares out of its capital in accordance with ss.705 et seq. of the CA 2006 relating to the power of private companies to purchase or redeem their own shares.[27] In essence, the redemption of shares by private limited companies may only be redeemed out of the distributable profits of the company (a concept which is discussed in relation to *Dividends and Distributions* in Ch.12) or out of "the proceeds of a fresh issue of shares" made so as to fund the redemption.[28] By requiring that redemption is paid for out of distributable profits or by means of an issue of fresh shares the effect that the company's remaining capital is not reduced to pay for the redemption because the redemption is paid for either out of income or by means of a new capital issue.

Purchase by a company of its own shares

The general principle

Companies are permitted to purchase their own shares in accordance with Ch.4 **10–007** of Pt 18 of the CA 2006, provided that there is no restriction on the company doing so contained in its articles of association.[29] This central principle is contained in s.690 of the CA 2006. While s.690 appears to be permissive, the remainder of Ch.4 provides the limits to the company's power. The first limit on the power of a limited company is that the company may not purchase its own shares if the effect of that purchase would be that there "would no longer be any issued shares of the company other than redeemable shares or shares held as treasury shares".[30] The second limit on the power is that a limited company "may not purchase its own shares unless they are fully paid".[31] Thirdly, the purchase

---

[24] *Forth Wines Ltd, Petitioners*, 1993 S.L.T. 170.
[25] Companies Act 2006 s.688.
[26] Companies Act 2006 s.689(1).
[27] Companies Act 2006 s.687(1).
[28] Companies Act 2006 s.687(2). Shares can only be redeemed at a premium in the circumstances identified in s.687(4).
[29] Companies Act 2006 s.690(1). It is doubtful whether a majority of the shareholders can be given a general power to do this because of the doctrine of a fraud on the minority: *Brown v British Abrasive Wheel Co* [1919] 2 Ch. 290; *Dafen Tinplate Co Ltd v Llanelly Steel Co* [1920] 2 Ch. 124; cf. *Sidebotham v Kershaw, Leese and Co* [1920] 1 Ch. 154.
[30] Companies Act 2006 s.690(2).
[31] Companies Act 2006 s.691(1).

price for the shares must be "paid for on purchase" and not at some later date.[32] The other terms on which a purchase takes place (that is, except for the date of payment) can be arranged between the parties,[33] except that the remainder of Ch.4 sets out further limits on the company's powers.

Private limited companies benefit from a different regime from other types of company. A private limited company may pay for the purchase of its own shares out of its capital in accordance with ss.705 et seq. of the CA 2006 relating to the power of private companies to purchase or redeem their own shares (considered below).[34] In essence, the purchase of shares by a private limited company may only be paid for out of the distributable profits of the company[35] (a concept which is discussed in relation to *Dividends and Distributions* in Ch.12) or out of "the proceeds of a fresh issue of shares" made so as to fund the redemption.[36] Any premium paid must similarly be funded out of the company's distributable profits.[37] The premium on any such shares may, however, only be paid for out of distributable profits; unless the shares themselves were originally issued at a premium, in which case the proceeds of a fresh issue may be used up to the amount of the company's share premium account at the time. In effect the share premium account may be used to fund the purchase or redemption and then be replaced by a fresh issue of shares. That payment can only be made in the first place out of distributable profits means that the company's remaining capital is not used in the acquisition; and that payment can only be made in the second place by way of an issue of fresh shares means that the company's remaining capital is similarly not reduced.[38]

Authority for purchase of own shares

10–008   A limited company may purchase shares under s.693 of the CA 2006 if it complies with one of two procedures: the "off market purchase" procedure or the "market purchase" procedure.[39] In essence, the two procedures govern a purchase by the company either by means of a private purchase conducted outside a recognised investment exchange (and in that sense "off market") or by means of a purchase which is conducted on a recognised investment exchange (in that sense a "market

---

[32] Companies Act 2006 s.691(2).

[33] *Pena v Dale* [2004] 2 B.C.L.C. 508.

[34] Companies Act 2006 s.692(1).

[35] These include a non-capital reserve created on a reduction of capital: *Quayle Munro Ltd, Petitioners*, 1992 S.C. 24; [1994] 1 B.C.L.C. 410. Payment in kind rather than in cash is allowed: *BDG Roof-Bond Ltd v Douglas* [2000] 1 B.C.L.C. 401. In so far as the company uses distributable profits for such payments the funds available for dividends are thereby reduced. Further, in such a case an amount equal to the amount of profits used must be transferred on the company's balance sheet to a fund known as the capital redemption reserve. This is a capital fund to which the rules relating to reduction of capital apply. The object of this section is to prevent the balance sheet showing a paper profit which might be distributed by way of dividend. That profit would otherwise arise through the current assets being reduced once by the amount necessary to redeem or purchase the shares, whereas both the share capital and the revenue reserve would be reduced by that amount.

[36] Companies Act 2006 s.692(2)(a).

[37] Companies Act 2006 s.692(3). Shares can only be redeemed at a premium in the circumstances identified in s.692(3) and (4).

[38] Companies Act 2006 s.692(2)(b).

[39] Companies Act 2006 s.693(1).

purchase"). In either event, a copy of the contract must be kept available for inspection[40] (or a memorandum setting out its main terms if the contract was not made in writing) for a period of ten years after its creation.[41] A market is a "recognised investment exchange" if it is identified as such by the Financial Services Authority further to Pt 18 of the Financial Services and Markets Act 2000.

An "off-market purchase" must be in the form of a contract which complies with s.694 of the CA 2006. The definition of an "off-market purchase" is set out in s.693(2) in the following terms:

"(2) A purchase is "off-market" if the shares either—

(a) are purchased otherwise than on a recognised investment exchange, or

(b) are purchased on a recognised investment exchange but are not subject to a marketing arrangement on the exchange."

So, such a purchase is "off-market" if it is conducted outside the market, primarily where the shares in question are shares in a private company which by definition is not quoted on an exchange, or if the purchase is not conducted on the basis of the standard rules of that exchange in the form of its "marketing arrangement". A transaction is conducted on the basis of an exchange's "marketing arrangement", and so does not fall within the off-market regime, if the shares are listed under the listing rules (considered in Ch.15) or if the company has been afforded specific facilities for dealing in those shares under different terms from the exchange's marketing arrangement.[42] The contract of purchase can only be performed if there is a special resolution of the company approving the purchase and if it is a term of the contract that a special resolution is required before the contract is performed.[43] In *R. W. Peak (Kings Lynn) Ltd, Re*[44] it was said that since such approval must take place prior to the contract, authorisation cannot therefore be given informally by the terms of the contract itself. The authorisation granted by the company's special resolution may be varied or revoked without the authorisation being ineffective at all times.[45] In relation to public companies, the authorisation must contain an expiry date when it will no longer be effective.[46]

A "market purchase" must comply with s.701 of the CA 2006. A transaction **10–009** is a "market purchase" if it is conducted on a recognised investment exchange otherwise than through special facilities made available to the company by that

---

[40] Companies Act 2006 s.703.

[41] Companies Act 2006 s.702. This right may not be assigned: Companies Act 2006 s.704.

[42] Companies Act 2006 s.693(3).

[43] Companies Act 2006 s.694(2). Any variation of the terms of that contract must be approved by a special resolution of the company: Companies Act 2006 s.697; as must a release of rights under such a contract: Companies Act 2006 s.700. No shareholder who holds shares affected by the resolution is an eligible member for voting purposes in relation to the resolution, except on a poll: Companies Act 2006 s.695; the same principle applies to votes to approve a variation of the contract by special resolution: Companies Act 2006 s.698. Furthermore, the terms of the contract must be disclosed to the company's members: Companies Act 2006 s.696; the same principle applies to votes to approve a variation of the contract by special resolution: Companies Act 2006 s.699.

[44] [1998] 1 B.C.L.C. 193.

[45] Companies Act 2006 s.694(4).

[46] Companies Act 2006 s.694(5).

exchange.[47] A company may only make a market purchase of its own shares if the purchase has first been approved by a resolution of the company.[48] The authorisation may be unconditional or it may be subject to conditions.[49] Furthermore, the "authority must specify the maximum number of shares authorised to be acquired", and "determine both the maximum and minimum prices that may be paid for the shares".[50] Given that this is a market purchase, the parameters within which the company may acquire the shares on a volatile market will need to be identified.

It is not clear whether a breach of the various procedural requirements will make the purchase void. It has been said that failure to pass the required resolution prior to the contract being made and a breach of the voting restrictions will have that effect.[51] On the other hand, a breach of the former statutory rule requiring a memorandum of the contract to be available for 15 days prior to the meeting was said not to invalidate the purchase, at least where all the shareholders were aware of the terms of the contract.[52] The answer may well be that if the requirement can be seen as protecting only the shareholders and they all in effect waive that protection then the purchase will be valid.

Validation of otherwise unenforceable purchases at common law

10–010 It has been held in Scotland that a contract to purchase shares which has not complied with the statutory requirements for approval cannot be enforced.[53] In *Vision Express (UK) Ltd v Wilson (No.2)*,[54] however, it was held that an agreement by the company to acquire its own shares as part of an agreed settlement of litigation and which was as such illegal under statute could be effected by the introduction of an implied term that the acquisition should be carried out so as to comply with the statutory provisions, in that case the off-market procedure.[55] Thus, since the company had in fact passed the necessary resolution, specific performance of the agreement would be ordered. However, in the ordinary case where the transaction has already been completed the transaction cannot be validated in this way.[56]

Disclosure of purchases

10–011 The company must deliver a return to the Registrar within 28 days of a purchase of its own shares under the foregoing provisions which either cannot or do not

---

[47] Companies Act 2006 s.693(4).
[48] Companies Act 2006 s.701(1).
[49] Companies Act 2006 s.701(2).
[50] Companies Act 2006 s.701(3).
[51] *R.W. Peak (Kings Lynn) Ltd, Re* [1998] 1 B.C.L.C. 193 at 198–205; *Wright v Atlas Wright (Europe) Ltd* [1999] 2 B.C.L.C. 301 at 310–315.
[52] *BDG Roof-Bond v Douglas* [2000] 1 B.C.L.C. 401.
[53] *Western v Rigblast Holdings Ltd*, 1989 G.W.D. 23–950 (Sh.Ct.).
[54] [1998] B.C.C. 173.
[55] On the basis that where an agreement can be performed in a lawful or unlawful manner there was a presumption that the parties intended to carry it out in the lawful manner. See, e.g. *Brady v Brady* [1989] A.C. 755.
[56] *R.W. Peak (Kings Lynn) Ltd, Re* [1998] 1 B.C.L.C. 193.

lead to the company exercising the treasury share option.[57] The return must distinguish between treasury shares, cancelled shares and so forth, and it must identify the number, the nominal value of the shares and the date on which they were delivered to the company. Notice of cancellation of shares must also be given within 28 days to the Registrar.[58] Where the company is able, and intends to, retain some or all of the shares as treasury shares, their acquisition and subsequent disposal must be notified to the Registrar within 28 days of the relevant event.

Funds available for redemption or purchase

The process of funding

The funding of purchase of own shares and the redemption of shares by private **10–012** companies is dealt with by ss.709 et seq. of the CA 2006. The core principle is as follows:[59]

"A private limited company may in accordance with this Chapter, but subject to any restriction or prohibition in the company's articles, make a payment in respect of the redemption or purchase of its own shares otherwise than out of distributable profits or the proceeds of a fresh issue of shares."

These provisions were reinstated to the CA 2006 at the last minute because there may be situations in which, for example, a company wished to purchase its own shares but where there were insufficient reserves in the company's accounts. The means of making such a payment out of capital is as follows. "Capital" in this context is any fund other than distributable profits and the proceeds of a fresh issue, whether or not it is technically capital for the rules relating to reduction of capital and so forth. Thus undistributable profits[60] may be used. Private companies must first utilise distributable profits before resorting to "capital". To use the power a private company must have authority to do so in its articles. Moreover, there must be a shortfall in the funds available to all companies (distributable profits and issue proceeds). To ascertain whether there is a genuine shortfall the company must calculate its available distributable profits by reference to accounts drawn up at any date within the three months immediately preceding the date on which the directors make the required declaration of solvency, which initiates the procedure. The accounts must enable a reasonable judgment to be made.

The shortfall between available profits and the amount needed for purchase or redemption is known as the "permissible capital payment" ("PCP"). If the PCP and the proceeds of any issue used for the redemption or purchase are together less than the nominal value of the shares redeemed or purchased, the remainder must have come from distributable profits. In that case s.734(2) of the CA 2006

---

[57] Companies Act 2006 s.707.
[58] Companies Act 2006 s.708.
[59] Companies Act 2006 s.709(1).
[60] e.g. the revaluation reserve.

provides that an equivalent amount to those profits must be transferred to the capital redemption reserve as in the general funding power and for the same reasons. However, if the PCP and the proceeds of any issue used for the redemption or purchase amount to more than the nominal value of the shares redeemed or purchased, part of those capital funds must have been used to cover the redemption or purchase of the premium on those shares. In such a case s.734(3) provides that the excess must be deducted either from the capital redemption reserve, share premium account, share capital figure or unrealised profits of the company. If such profits are subsequently realised they cannot then be used for dividends.

Exercise of the power

10–013 Section 713 of the CA 2006 makes it unlawful for a company to use its PCP unless the procedure laid down in that section is followed. This procedure is in addition to that required for the approval of the purchase; it is to approve the redemption or purchase out of capital. Just as a specific off-market purchase requires the prior authority of a special resolution, so does the use of capital. However in this case it must be preceded not by details of the contract but by a statutory declaration of solvency by the directors. This declaration must relate both to the company's immediate ability to pay its debts after using its PCP and its ability to do so for the following year, taking into account the company's resources and the directors' management intentions. It must be accompanied by an auditors' report that the PCP has been properly ascertained and that the declaration of solvency itself is not unreasonable. That declaration must be followed on the same day or within one week by the necessary special resolution. After it has been passed no payment can be made for five weeks. (This is to enable any objection to the payment to be made to the court, as considered below.) The resolution must then be implemented within two further weeks. The proposed vendor will invalidate the resolution if he votes with the shares in question in such a way as to affect the result.

The requirement of a special resolution will put the shareholders on notice as to what is intended. However, since this involves "capital," the company's creditors need to know. It may affect their guarantee fund. Accordingly s.175 requires the company to place a notice both in either the London or the Edinburgh *Gazette*, as appropriate,[61] and in a national newspaper.[62] The latter can, theoretically, be avoided by giving a notice to each creditor of the company. The notice must state that the resolution has been passed and what its effect is. It must also specify the PCP and the date of the resolution and state first that the statutory declaration of solvency and auditors' report are available for inspection at the company's registered office and second that a creditor may apply to the court, within five weeks of the date of the resolution, to have the resolution set aside. The proposed vendor will invalidate the resolution if he votes with the shares in question in such a way as to affect the result. The declaration of solvency and the auditors' report must

---

[61] Depending on the location of the company's registered office.
[62] In England and Wales, or Scotland, as appropriate.

be available both for shareholders at the meeting, and subsequently, for either shareholders and creditors at the registered office during the five-week holding period. Further, they must be registered with the Registrar by the first notice date—i.e. the date of publication in the *Gazette* or the newspaper, whichever is earlier.

Objections by members and creditors

Under s.721 and 722 of the CA 2006, any member who did not vote for the special **10–014** resolution authorising the use of capital, or any creditor may petition the court to have the resolution set aside within five weeks of the date of the resolution. For a creditor the effective time limit may be four weeks since the advertisements putting him on notice can be put in up to a week after the resolution. On such a petition the court has all the powers available to it as on a petition to prevent a public company re-registering as a private company. Thus it may order a compulsory purchase of the shareholder's shares by the company, alter the company's constitution, cancel, amend or confirm the resolution or impose new time scales for its implementation.[63] If either there are no objections, or the court overrides them, the PCP may be used by the company for the purchase or redemption as appropriate.

Liability of shareholders and directors

Where a private company which has made a payment out of capital for the **10–015** purchase or redemption of its own shares is wound up as being unable to pay its debts within one year of the payments being made, then s.76 of the Insolvency Act 1986 applies. In such a case the recipient of the payment, known as the relevant payment, and any director who signed the statutory declaration of solvency without having reasonable grounds for doing so, are liable to repay the amount of the relevant payment up to the amount needed to cover the company's insolvency.

This liability is linked to the amount of the relevant payments needed to cover the company's outstanding debts. Liability is joint and several so that any of the recipients or directors may be sued for the whole amount leaving him to recover a contribution from the others. By way of protection anyone who might be liable to make payment under this section may petition to wind up the company on the grounds of its insolvency or on the just and equitable ground under s.122(1)(f) or (g) of the Insolvency Act 1986.

Failure by a company to redeem or purchase its own shares

If a company has issued redeemable shares and fails to redeem them, or agrees to **10–016** purchase its own shares and fails to honour that agreement, the shareholder has a right of action for breach of contract under s.735 of the CA 2006. Section 735(2), however, provides that the company shall not be "liable in damages for any failure

---

[63] Companies Act 2006 s.721(3)–(7).

on its part to redeem or purchase the shares".[64] In *Barclays Bank Plc v British and Commonwealth Holdings Plc*,[65] the Court of Appeal held that this restriction was limited to a claim for damages in respect of the company's breach of its actual agreement to purchase or redeem its shares. It did not apply to an action by a party other than the shareholder for breach of a covenant by the company, even though the breach of that covenant, failure to maintain its assets value, caused the failure to redeem and the damages for breach of covenant were measurable by the failure to redeem. The Court of Appeal also indicated that in any event the prohibition was probably restricted to actions by shareholders. A shareholder may apply for an order of specific performance,[66] but this will only be made if the company is able to fulfil its obligations out of distributable profits.

If the company goes into liquidation after the obligation to redeem or purchase has arisen the shares are regarded as being cancelled on the liquidation but the vendor/shareholder may seek to recover (or, "apply for") any loss suffered as a creditor in the liquidation unless the company could not have fulfilled its obligations out of distributable profits at any time between the date of redemption or purchase and the date of liquidation. Such a vendor/shareholder is a deferred creditor and, as such, will be paid after all the other creditors but before the shareholders.

Treatment of purchased shares—treasury shares

The general principles dealing with treasury shares

10–017   Changes made in 2003 by two regulations[67] allowed some companies the option to retain and, if desired, reissue the shares which they have purchased.[68] These regulations were re-enacted without substantive change in ss.724 et seq. of the CA 2006. These shares are known as "treasury shares". Treasury shares are shares which are held by the company in treasury, a sort of abeyance, pending disposal or cancellation. The ability to diminish or increase the number of its shares owned by shareholders is seen as an advantage to companies in managing their capital structures, in particular their debt/equity ratios which are usually significant in their corporate finance covenants. Briefly put, it gives the company greater flexibility in managing its capital.

The treasury share option is in fact a very limited one. It only applies if three requirements are met. First, the shares (referred to as "qualifying shares" in the statute) must either be listed, or else traded on the Alternative Investment Market or on a regulated market.[69] That excludes all private companies at a stroke

---

[64] Such a claim if made by a shareholder would gain priority over other shareholders' rights against the company in the event of a liquidation since it would in effect turn the right for a repayment of capital into a creditor's claim for damages.

[65] [1996] 1 B.C.L.C. 1, CA.

[66] See *Vision Express (UK) Ltd v Wilson (No.2)* [1998] B.C.C. 419.

[67] Companies (Acquisition of Own Shares) (Treasury Shares) Regulations 2003 (SI 2993/1116); Companies (Acquisition of Own Shares) (Treasury Shares) (No.2) Regulations (SI 2003/3031). See now Ch.6 of Pt 18 of the Companies Act 2006.

[68] These are allowed under the terms of the EU's Second Company Law Directive 77/91/EEC.

[69] Companies Act 2006 s.724(2).

because private companies may not offer their shares to the public in general terms, which in turn prohibits all of these markets.[70] Second, the shares must have been purchased out of distributable profits,[71] and third, they cannot exceed in total more than ten per cent of the nominal value of the shares or of the shares of the class concerned.[72] Shares above that limit are known as excess shares and must be either disposed of or cancelled within 12 months.[73]

If those three conditions are met then the company may hold some or all of them, or it may deal with all or any of them[74] either by sales for cash[75] or pursuant to an employee share scheme,[76] or it may do both things. It may of course cancel them at any time. If the shares are resold for cash, then insofar as the proceeds are equal to or less than the price paid by the company to acquire them, they are to be regarded as distributable profits.[77] Any excess of receipts over the purchase price is, however, regarded as capital and an equivalent amount must be transferred to the share premium account.

The company is to be registered as the owner of treasury shares in the Register of members, but this is a purely nominal ownership as no rights such as voting or attending meetings can be exercised by the company in respect of such shares. The exceptions to this are as follows: the company may keep any bonus shares issued in respect of the treasury shares, but such bonus shares will themselves become treasury shares; and since the company may acquire redeemable shares as treasury shares, it may redeem them and make any payment due on them.

ONE EXCEPTION TO THE GENERAL RULE: OPEN-ENDED INVESTMENT COMPANIES

The principal exception to the notion that a company may not buy its own shares **10–018** is the open-ended investment company.[78] Open-ended investment companies ("oeics") were introduced to English company law so that collective investment scheme structures akin to unit trusts could be marketed in jurisdictions where there are no trusts. Unit trusts are "collective investment schemes" governed by the UCITS Directive[79] which permit investors to acquire units in a mutual fund

---

[70] If the shares cease to be qualifying shares they must be cancelled immediately: Companies Act 2006 s.729(2).

[71] Companies Act 2006 s.725.

[72] Companies Act 2006 s.725. This is the maximum currently permitted by the Second EC Directive but there is a proposal from the EC Commission to amend that directive to allow purchases in total up to the level of a company's distributable reserves: COM 04, October 2004.

[73] Here are penalties in default under Companies Act 2006 s.732(1) and (2).

[74] Under Companies Act 2006 s.727.

[75] This does not apply where there has been a takeover offer and the offeror has achieved a 90 per cent acceptance rate and wishes to invoke ss.979 et seq. of the Companies Act 2006 to acquire the rest. In such a case the company cannot dispose of its shares to anyone else.

[76] In practice, assenting shares to such a scheme may be one of the most useful aspects of treasury shares.

[77] Thus they are available for distribution on the basis that they are replacing the profits used to acquire the shares.

[78] Alastair Hudson, *The Law on Investment Entities* (London: Sweet & Maxwell, 2000) 215 et seq.; Alastair Hudson, *The Law of Finance* (London: Sweet & Maxwell, 2009), para.52–28 et seq.

[79] Directive 85/611/EEC on the coordination of laws relating to undertakings for collective investment in transferable securities [1985] OJ L375/3.

and to terminate their investments by selling their units back to the fund for their then market price expressed as a proportionate share at the value of the fund at the time of redemption.[80] In much of the rest of the EU the only way in which these funds are replicated is by means of company structures because trusts did not form a natural part of those jurisdictions' jurisprudence. Therefore, oeics were created in the UK to form a corporate form of unit trust to compete with the rest of the EU for the mutual fund market. For an oeic to function it is important that an investor is able to terminate his investment by selling his units back to the company. Only in this instance the units which are being sold are not equitable interests in a unit trust but rather shares in a company. Thus, an oeic must be able to buy back its own shares whenever an investor requires it too. Consequently, oeics are exceptions to the rule against companies buying back their own shares.[81]

---

[80] See Alastair Hudson, *The Law of Finance* (London: Sweet & Maxwell, 2009), Ch.52; and on unit trusts specifically: Thomas and Hudson, *Law of Trusts*, 2 edn (Oxford University Press, 2010) Ch.53.

[81] See Alastair Hudson, "Open-ended investment companies", Pt 5A, *Palmer's Company Law* (London: Sweet & Maxwell).

Chapter 11

FINANCIAL ASSISTANCE

INTRODUCTION

Financial assistance is the process by which a company makes a gift of money or **11–001** a loan or otherwise enables another person to buy that company's shares. It is a practice with a long pedigree. The giving of financial assistance by a company to purchase that company's shares is prohibited by s.678 of the CA 2006 in perpetuation of a policy which has long formed part of company law. The motives for the prohibition were originally to preserve the company's share capital, but later to prevent the misuse of assets by those in control of a company[1] and to prevent the creation of a false market in that company's shares, such as by artificially stimulating demand for the shares at a time when the share price may be particularly important, for example in a takeover situation.[2] This policy motivation was considered in Ch.10, above. (The approach taken in this chapter is to set out the provisions of the Companies Act 2006 applying to financial assistance, and then to analyse the case law which was decided on the basis of various provisions in predecessor companies legislation as they would apply to the 2006 Act.)

To understand modern company law, it is often important to understand its history. When the South Sea Company collapsed in 1720, it planted the seed of a policy which remains deep-rooted in modern company and securities law. The promoters of the South Sea Company—principally a man called John Blunt—had sought to transform the national debt by offering to exchange loans made to the Government for shares in the South Sea Company. To encourage people to give up their rights against the Government for shares in the South Sea Company, Blunt needed to make those shares seem attractive, and to do that he needed to encourage some select individuals to buy those shares. To assist those individuals to buy shares, Blunt organised for the company to lend money covertly to them. In effect, therefore, investors were being loaned money by the South Sea Company to acquire shares in the South Sea Company. What this meant was that investors were paying a comparatively small amount to acquire what purported to be valuable shares, and having the difference made up by the company itself. This had the effect of making the value of the shares in the Company seem artificially

---

[1] By using corporate funds to assist a takeover bidder in the acquisition of the controlling interest by way of a loan, see, e.g. *Selangor United Rubber Estates Ltd v Cradock (No.3)* [1968] 1 W.L.R. 1555. It is suggested that this above is better covered by controls on directors' activities: see Ch.16 below.

[2] Other provisions are now aimed at controlling this—see Ch.33—which might be said to render this part of the rationale redundant.

high because there was such an ostensibly high demand for them among people who were respected in society. The attraction of the shares became the fact that the price of the shares kept rising and yet the company's loans made the shares seem so cheap. When the company crashed—because in truth it had never had any trading activities of any sort in the South Seas or anywhere else, other than the fraudulent issue of shares to a credulous public—the shareholders were still obliged to pay for their shares and they lost their paper profits too. Blunt had created an entirely artificial market in shares by making people believe that the shares were much sought after, when in truth the original subscribers for the shares were often having those shares bought for them or were receiving them at a reduced price. In consequence, there are strict controls to this day on the circumstances in which assistance can be given to acquire shares in a company when that assistance comes from the company itself.

The lessons of the South Sea bubble, as it became known, were learned by company law long ago. Similar scandals in France in 1719 bound suspicion of companies giving assistance to shareholders to buy shares into the warp and weft of much European company law. As will emerge later in this chapter, the prohibition on companies giving financial assistance is inconvenient in many circumstances in which it becomes necessary to reorganise a company or group of companies but not all of the participants have sufficient funds for the purpose. The principal reason historically for preventing financial assistance is to prevent a false market being created in a company's securities. The modern reasons for preventing financial assistance are generally explained as being the need to preserve the company's share capital or alternatively to prevent the company's assets being misused. The preservation of the company's share capital would only be relevant if the company were seeking to acquire its own shares (as considered in the previous chapter), which is not necessarily the case at all in relation to financial assistance. The company's assets may be being misused if, for example, a person seeking to take over a company sought to use the target company's own assets to fund the takeover. This has become a problem in relation to transactions, such as leveraged buy-outs, in which the use of the company's assets is a prerequisite of the success of the transaction. As considered below, it will be a complex question on the cases whether or not there has been financial assistance, whereas the Companies Act 2006 has altered the statutory principles dealing with financial assistance. Before turning to the difficulties of the case law, however, we shall consider the statutory prohibition itself.

THE PROHIBITION ON FINANCIAL ASSISTANCE IN THE COMPANIES ACT 2006

The extent of the prohibitions on financial assistance

11–002 There are three prohibitions on financial assistance in the CA 2006. The first prohibition in s.678(1) of the CA 2006 provides that:

> "Where a person is acquiring or proposing to acquire shares in a public company, it is not lawful for that company, or a company that is a subsidiary of

that company, to give financial assistance directly or indirectly for the purpose of the acquisition before or at the same time as the acquisition takes place."

Thus financial assistance is unlawful. As will emerge below, there is a conditional exception in relation to assistance provided by private companies.[3] It is significant that the company involved must be a public company. The most significant change to this area of law since the repeal of the Companies Act 1985 is that the ban on the giving of financial assistance no longer applies to private companies.

The term "financial assistance" is defined for this purpose so as to include assistance by way of gift,[4] or by way of guarantee or indemnity,[5] or by way of a loan,[6] or by way of any other arrangement such that the company's net assets are reduced[7] (thus implying that value has shifted from the company to some other person so as to acquire shares). This terminology is considered in the next section of this chapter.

The second prohibition on financial assistance will arise under s.678(3) of the **11–003** CA 2006 if the purchaser of those shares takes on a liability in so doing and if the company then undertakes to reduce or expunge that liability: thus, indirectly passing value to the purchaser and so giving financial assistance.[8]

The third prohibition under s.679 of the CA 2006 on financial assistance will arise if a person is acquiring shares in a private company, it is not lawful for a public company which is a subsidiary of that private company to give direct or indirect financial assistance for that acquisition.[9] There is also a prohibition, which is akin to s.678(3), to the effect that it is not lawful to reduce a liability so as to facilitate the acquisition.[10] The prohibition under s.679 is considered in detail below.

The potential width of the prohibitions means that they may well strike down transactions which in no way threaten any of the original reasons for their existence. It is essential, however, to realise that the prohibitions will only apply if there is assistance given by the company for the purpose of the acquisition of its shares[11] and if that assistance is financial. It is not enough to show either that there is a financial transaction involving a company and a person acquiring its shares if there was no assistance, or that there was the necessary assistance if it is not also financial. These concepts are explored in greater detail below in relation to the decided cases on financial assistance.

A breach of any of the prohibitions is a criminal offence

A contravention of any of the prohibitions on the giving of financial assistance in **11–004** s.678(1) or (3), or s.679(1) or (3) CA 2006 constitutes a criminal offence.[12]

---

[3] Companies Act 2006 s.682(1)(a).
[4] Companies Act 2006 s.677(1).
[5] Companies Act 2006 s.677(2).
[6] Companies Act 2006 s.677(3).
[7] Companies Act 2006 s.677(4).
[8] Companies Act 2006 s.678(3).
[9] Companies Act 2006 s.679(1).
[10] Companies Act 2006 s.679(3).
[11] Or for reducing the liability in the case of post-acquisition assistance.
[12] Companies Act 2006 s.680(1).

THE MEANING OF FINANCIAL ASSISTANCE AS DEVELOPED IN THE CASE LAW

The pattern in the cases

11–005 The law on financial assistance has undergone frequent changes with re-drafting of the principles in successive Companies Acts. The current exceptions are the result of successive dilutions of the original principle, inter alia, to permit assistance in relation to private companies and with the larger objective of permitting otherwise unobjectionable transactions. This section presents a short survey of the types of transaction which have been found to constitute financial assistance, observing that the judiciary has tended to tighten the effective meaning of financial assistance, culminating in the decision of the House of Lords in *Brady v Brady*.[13] What emerges from the case law is that the financial assistance must be financial in nature[14] and that it must be given for the purpose of acquiring the shares.[15] We shall deal first with the categories of activity which have been treated as constituting financial assistance and then with the purpose for which the assistance was given within the scope of a larger transaction. All of these cases were decided on the basis of subtly but significantly different statutory provisions predating the Companies Act 2006.

The types of activity which constitute financial assistance

11–006 Financial assistance may be given directly or indirectly. The clearest example of direct financial assistance would be an outright transfer of money to an individual who stands at arm's length from the company so that that individual becomes able to acquire a parcel of the company's shares. Another example of direct financial assistance would be a company lending money to the third party so that the third party could acquire shares, even if the party's intention was that latterly the loan would be repaid: the company would nevertheless have assisted the acquisition of the shares by making their acquisition possible. The simplest means of taking over a company remains procuring the agreement of that company to agree to pay for its own shares by lending the money to do so to the person who intends to take the company over. Private equity typically operates on a subtly different basis by borrowing money at arm's length and then undertaking to repay those loans once the company has been acquired out of the company's own assets. If the private equity purchaser had acquired the loan from the company then that would constitute financial assistance, as would a guarantee over the loan from the company, or some other means of making the loan available. It is not necessary for the company to have had its assets reduced so as to facilitate the acquisition: all that seems to be required is that the company assisted the financing.[16]

---

[13] [1989] A.C. 755, [1988] 2 All E.R. 617.
[14] *Barclays Bank v British and Commonwealth Holdings Plc* [1996] 1 W.L.R. 1.
[15] See generally the cases considered below: e.g. *Brady v Brady* [1989] A.C. 755, [1988] 2 All E.R. 617.
[16] *Belmont Finance Corporation v Williams Furniture Ltd (No.2)* [1980] 1 All E.R. 393.

The examples of cases involving loans have begun to veer into indirect financial assistance. In *Belmont Finance Corporation v Williams Furniture Ltd (No.2)*[17] Buckley L.J. considered a company buying goods from a supplier and the supplier then using that money to buy shares in the company. His Lordship considered that there would not be financial assistance if the company had needed the goods which it had acquired, so that the payment of money only constituted a part of a larger transaction and was not intended solely to assist the purchase of shares. By contrast, if the company had not required the goods and had acquired them merely as a means of paying money to the supplier so that the supplier would be able to acquire the company's shares, then there would have been financial assistance. What is more difficult is to decide on cases in which there was a mixture of objectives: partly to fund the acquisition and partly to acquire goods. These "mixed motives" cases are considered in the next section.

In *Charterhouse Investment Trust Ltd v Tempest Diesels Ltd*,[18] a company, as part of a management buy-out, had sold all of the shares in a subsidiary company to one of its directors and thus sold a part of its business to that director. The issue was whether a transfer of tax losses between the two companies when the subsidiary was hived off would constitute financial assistance. Hoffmann J. held that the transfer of the tax losses constituted a part of a much larger transaction and therefore could not be viewed as financial assistance in isolation. Hoffmann J. suggested that the acid test for financial assistance should be whether or not the company's net assets were reduced by the transaction.[19] Hoffmann J. held that the question, in essence, was whether there had been a net transfer of value by the company to the acquirer. Since, in that case, that could not be shown, there was no financial assistance. The test should be applied by looking at the commercial realities of the transaction as a whole and not be strained to cover transactions not fairly within it. So, it has been held that if there was a genuine commercial reason for a payment to a shareholder, such as a payment being made as part of a security agreement in relation to a company's indebtedness, then that would not be financial assistance under the *Charterhouse* approach.[20]

Other examples of transactions which have been held to constitute financial **11–007** assistance are as follows. An agreement between two active shareholders and the only other active shareholder that those two shareholders would sell their shares to the remaining shareholder for their nominal value plus a share of future profits would constitute financial assistance from the company by way of a share in those future profits.[21] When a loan is procured from a company by one shareholder to enable another person to acquire shares in that company, even though there was no compulsion to use the loan moneys for that purpose, then there will be financial assistance, especially if the parties' true intention was that that would be the

---

[17] [1980] 1 All E.R. 393.
[18] [1986] 1 B.C.L.C. 1.
[19] *Charterhouse Investment Trust Ltd v Tempest Diesels Ltd* [1986] 1 B.C.L.C. 1. However, this was considered to constitute a lacuna outside the scope of the *Belmont* decision because in *Belmont* cash was made available to the purchaser, whereas it was not in the *Charterhouse* case.
[20] *Anglo Petroleum Ltd v TFB (Mortgages) Ltd* [2008] 1 B.C.L.C. 185.
[21] *MacPherson v European Strategic Bureau Ltd* [2000] 2 B.C.L.C. 683.

purpose for which the loan moneys would in fact be used.[22] Where a company provides security for a loan, whether by way of a guarantee or by way of a debenture, then that will constitute financial assistance.[23]

The following are examples of transactions which have not been held to constitute financial assistance. Where a company agreed to pay a shareholder a salary and a bonus if he transferred his shareholding to another person, it was held that there had not been financial assistance because the net assets of the company had not been reduced by the salary and bonus being paid out of distributable profits.[24] Where a company gave financial incentives to acquire shares, it was held that that was not the same as granting financial assistance to acquire those shares.[25] However, this decision of Laddie J. has been criticised[26] and does seem out of step with the other cases. As part of the reconstruction of a group of private companies run by a family, there was no financial assistance ultimately where the shares in the group companies were divided between two brothers to settle ongoing disputes even though one group company was worth more than the other and so a transfer of assets from one company had to be made to the other.[27] Care should be exercised with this particular approach: in this circumstance the House of Lords was prepared to hold that there had not been an infringement of the financial assistance prohibition because the companies were private companies and the parties gave an undertaking to keep the transaction within the parameters of the private companies exemption, as considered below.

To consider the term "financial assistance" more generally it should be observed that it is inclusively defined in s.678 of the CA 2006, as set out above. If the transaction does not fall within this definition then the sections cannot apply. It includes gifts,[28] the giving of a guarantee,[29] security[30] or indemnity,[31] loans and other forms of credit agreements, and releases and waivers. It also includes any "other financial assistance" which reduces the net assets of the company "to a material extent"[32] or in relation to a company which has no net assets.[33] Only in the last of

---

[22] *Harlow v Loveday* [2004] B.C.C. 732.

[23] *Selangor United Rubber Estates Ltd v Cradock (No.3)* [1968] 1 W.L.R. 497 (providing security for a loan will render that debenture security void); *Heald v O'Connor* [1971] 1 W.L.R. 497 (providing a guarantee will render that guarantee void).

[24] *Parlett v Guppys (Bridport) Ltd* [1996] 2 B.C.L.C. 34.

[25] *MT Realisations Ltd v Digital Equipment Co Ltd* [2002] 2 B.C.L.C. 688, Laddie J.

[26] *Chaston v SWP Group Ltd* [2003] 1 B.C.L.C. 675. See also Charlesworth and Morse, *Company Law*, p.176.

[27] *Brady v Brady* [1989] A.C. 755, [1988] 2 All E.R. 617.

[28] Which may well include overpayments made by a company: see *Plat v Steiner* (1989) 5 B.C.C. 352.

[29] This has been defined in *Yeoman Credit Ltd v Latter* [1961] 1 W.L.R. 828 at 831 as: "a contract to answer for the debt, default or miscarriage of another who is to be primarily liable to the promisee."

[30] For the definition of a security see *Singer v Williams* [1921] 1 A.C. 41, HL.

[31] This has been given its strict legal meaning, i.e. "a contract by one party to keep the other harmless against loss": *Barclays Bank Plc v British and Commonwealth Holdings Plc* [1996] 1 B.C.L.C. 1, CA. Thus it was held in that case not to apply to a contract whereby the damages recoverable for its breach were the same as would have been recovered under an indemnity.

[32] Net assets for this purpose are defined by reference to the company's assets and liabilities.

[33] In *MT Realisations Ltd v Digital Equipment Co Ltd* [2002] 2 B.C.L.C. 688, Laddie J. said that this meant that if a company had net assets there must be a material reduction but that if it did not, any reduction would suffice—the concept was otherwise the same. But this was doubted by the Court of Appeal in *Chaston v SWP Group Plc* [2003] 1 B.C.L.C. 675 where the two were said to be alternatives—either a material reduction in net assets, or no assets.

these is there any requirement that the company has actually lost assets. The others need no such element and so can hardly be said to be part of the maintenance of capital regime. In *Parlett v Guppys (Bridport) Ltd*,[34] the Court of Appeal held that where a number of independent companies had agreed to pay the plaintiff a salary and bonus if he transferred his shares in one of them, the net assets of that company had not been reduced since there were sufficient distributable profits to pay the sums due. They did not therefore have to decide as to whether they were reduced by "a material extent" but rejected the idea, put to them by both counsel, that 5 per cent would be the relevant criteria. It would be a question of degree.

Whether the purpose of acquiring shares is incidental to a larger transaction

As outlined above, the financial assistance must be financial in nature and that it **11–008** must be given for the purpose of acquiring the shares. Much of the difficulty relates to the question whether the assistance was given solely for the purpose of acquiring shares, or whether the assistance was only part of a larger transaction addressed at other commercial goals but which incidentally involved the acquisition of the shares: the real problem here is identifying how incidental or collateral the acquisition of shares must be to the main purpose for there not to have been financial assistance. In practice this raises great difficulty. If a transaction will involve a company granting some benefit to a third party—whether directly in the form of transferring money or indirectly by granting some benefit which will facilitate the acquisition of shares in some way—then the risk is that that would be held to constitute financial assistance.

The leading case in this context is the decision of the House of Lords in *Brady v Brady*[35] which caused a great deal of consternation because of its restrictive interpretation of the financial assistance prohibition, even though (it is suggested) that interpretation was entirely feasible on an ordinary reading of the statute at the time. In that case two brothers fell into a dispute with one another. To resolve the dispute it was agreed that the two private companies which ran the family businesses would be divided between them. However, one business was considerably more valuable than the other and therefore it was agreed that one company would transfer assets to the other company to pay off loan stock which had been issued as part of the purchase price for shares. The question arose whether or not this transfer of assets to pay off the loan stock constituted financial assistance in the acquisition of shares. It was contended that there had not been financial assistance because that transfer of assets was part of a much larger transaction concerned with the reconstruction of the group of companies. It was argued before the court (and accepted by the Court of Appeal) that the purpose of this transfer had been to resolve the deadlock between the brothers and therefore that the financial assistance was entirely incidental to the parties' principal objectives. Nevertheless, the House of Lords held that there was clearly financial assistance on these facts and that the broader context of the transaction did not affect that analysis. Lord Oliver held that even though the *reason* for the transaction was to reorganise the group

---

[34] [1996] 2 B.C.L.C. 34, CA.
[35] [1989] A.C. 755, [1988] 2 All E.R. 617.

of companies, nevertheless the *purpose* of the redemption of the loan stock was simply to acquire shares, and therefore it constituted financial assistance.[36]

The concern to which this decision gave rise was that perfectly unobjectionable transactions would be held to be financial assistance as a result of this distinction between the reason for a transaction and the purpose of the individual activity which was said to constitute the financial assistance. Here, for example, the deadlock in the group of companies was resolved by a reorganisation of the group and the concomitant preservation of the two separate businesses intact in two different companies. As a result the two businesses were faring very well indeed. It therefore seemed a very technical matter to find that these transactions could be unenforceable because they fell within a literal reading of the legislation. On the facts, as was mentioned in an earlier section, the parties' affairs fell within the private companies' exemptions under the old statute and therefore the parties were entitled to attract the protection of those exemptions on the giving of an undertaking to conduct their affairs in accordance with those exemptions.

Latterly, adopting the so-called "commercial reality" test suggested by Hoffmann J. in *Charterhouse Investment Trust Ltd v Tempest Diesels Ltd*,[37] subsequent cases have excused ostensible financial assistance in circumstances in which the commercial reality was that the financial assistance was an incidental part of a larger transaction. So, in *Dyment v Boyden*[38] the two shareholders in a company which ran a nursing home agreed, when one of them had been disqualified from operating a nursing home, that the disqualified shareholder would transfer his shares to the other party but that the company would rent property from him above a market rate. It was held by Hart J. that in these circumstances the parties were simply identifying how they could best run the nursing home business for the future and were not intending to provide one shareholder with financial assistance after the acquisition of the shares. By contrast, but applying the same approach in effect, in *Harlow v Loveday*[39] it was held that when the parties to a loan knew that the money was intended to be used to buy shares in the company, then an argument that there was no compulsion to use the loan moneys for that purpose would not blind the court to the fact that the loan was intended to be a form of financial assistance.

Assistance for the purpose

11–009 The financial assistance must be also be given for the purpose of the acquisition of the shares. When the sections were redrafted into their present form an attempt

---

[36] The Court of Appeal was prepared to allow that the division of the group was a larger purpose of which the giving of the financial assistance was but an incidental part, but refused to apply the exception on the grounds that it was not given in good faith in the interests of the company, apparently on the basis that in the context of financial assistance the company includes the creditors as well as the shareholders, and the former had never been taken into consideration. The House of Lords reversed the Court of Appeal on that point. Without deciding whether the interests of the creditors had to be considered, since at all times the group was solvent so that the creditors were not at risk and, in other respects, since the division of the group had prevented deadlock and expensive winding up petitions, it was in the interests of the company.

[37] [1986] 1 B.C.L.C. 1.

[38] [2004] 2 B.C.L.C. 427; affirmed [2005] B.C.C. 79, CA.

[39] [2004] B.C.C. 732.

was made to solve the Belmont problem by reference to the principal purpose or main purpose of the company. Before turning to these ill-fated and largely irrelevant "purpose exceptions", however, it is necessary to consider the interpretation of the reworded s.678. The initial consideration was given by the Court of Appeal in *Barclays Bank Plc v British and Commonwealth Holdings Plc*[40] as to the approach to be adopted in deciding whether, assuming there was financial assistance, there has been a breach of either of the prohibitions in s.678. Aldous L.J., with whose judgment the other members of the Court of Appeal agreed, adopted the following approach of Mahoney J. in *Burton v Palmer*[41] to the equivalent provision in the New South Wales legislation:

"There may, of course, be circumstances in which the obligations entered into by a company are entered into for a collateral purpose: in such circumstances it may be that the company will, in the particular case, be giving financial assistance. But, collateral purpose aside, if [s.678] is to be relevant, there must be more than the incurring, in connection with the transfer of shares, of an obligation which may involve the company in the payment of money. The obligation must be such that it is properly to be categorised as financial assistance . . . I do not mean by this that the relevance of [the provision] is to be determined by a schematic analysis of the obligation undertaken. The words 'financial assistance' are words of a commercial rather than a conveyancing kind and the form of the obligation or transaction will not be conclusive."

On that basis, assuming always that the assistance is financial within the meaning of the section, the primary test to establish whether there has been a breach of s.678 is whether the obligation on the company can properly be categorised as financial assistance in a commercial sense.[42] That clearly mirrors the "commercial reality" approach to the equivalent provision in former legislation applied by Hoffmann J. in *Charterhouse v Tempest Diesels*. If, in reality, that obligation involves the collateral purpose of giving such assistance, then the section will apply. An example of that concept, given by Mahoney J. in *Burton v Palmer*, is where a company gives a warranty with the intention that it will have to pay damages in order to provide the funds for an acquisition of its shares. If there is no such obvious collateral purpose, however, then applying the commercial reality test has proved to be more difficult.[43]

An example is the Court of Appeal's view in *MacPherson v European Strategic Bureau Ltd.*[44] That case concerned an agreement whereby, as part of an exit package, two of the three active shareholders agreed to sell their shares to the

---

[40] [1986] 1 B.C.L.C. 1, CA.

[41] [1980] 2 N.S.W.L.R. 878 at 889–890.

[42] If so, then it seems that the section will apply if the assistance is given to the vendor rather than to the purchaser of the shares: *Armour Hick Northern Ltd v Whitehouse* [1980] 3 All E.R. 833; *Partlett v Guppy's (Bridport) Ltd [1996]* 2 B.C.L.C. 34, CA.

[43] The absence of any such collateral purpose meant that the Court of Appeal in the *Barclays Bank* case were able to validate a covenant entered into by a company as part of a complex deal to persuade another to take shares in the company even though breach of that covenant gave rise to an action for damages against the company.

[44] [2000] 2 B.C.L.C. 683, disagreeing with the judge below, [1999] 2 B.C.L.C. 203.

other for a nominal value and a share of the future profits accruing to the company from a contract they had helped to set up. The Court indicated that in their provisional view this was in breach of s.678. Without referring to any previous decisions, the Court held that the agreement provided a strong incentive for the sale of the shares and that it was inconceivable that the vendors would have transferred their shares for a nominal value unless they had also had the benefit of the future profits share agreement. That obligation was therefore the financial assistance involved.[45]

11–010   In *MT Realisations Ltd v Digital Equipment Co Ltd*,[46] Laddie J., in a clear attempt to limit the scope of the section, said that in the absence of a collateral purpose there was a distinction between a company giving financial incentives for another to enter into an agreement or concurrent benefits (outside the section) and financial assistance for the actual acquisition of the shares. There was a difference between assistance given in connection with a transfer and assistance given for the actual transfer.[47] This approach was, however, roundly criticised by the Court of Appeal in *Chaston v SWP Group Ltd*.[48] The company had paid the fees for the drawing up of a report on its parent company for the benefit of a prospective purchaser of the parent company's shares. Rejecting Laddie J.'s approach,[49] the Court of Appeal said that this payment had assisted the purchaser, helped smooth the course of the acquisition and was to further it. It must therefore have been for the purpose of the acquisition. Arden L.J. also made the following points: first, there was no need for the company to suffer a detriment (except for a loss to the net assets if required to establish that the assistance was financial);[50] second, it was sufficient if the assistance was an inducement; third, there was no need to establish any impact on the company's share price; and, fourth, the assistance need only be one of the purposes of the obligation.[51]

However, the Court of Appeal also stressed the commercial reality test first stated by Hoffman J. in *Charterhouse* and this has been applied in the cases since *Chaston*. In *Dyment v Boyden*,[52] for example, two shareholders jointly owned a nursing home and the company which ran it. One of them, Mr Boyden, was disqualified from running a nursing home and agreed to transfer his shares to Mrs Dyment in return for the other shareholder surrendering her interest in the

---

[45] It could be argued that they were therefore in fact finding that here was a collateral purpose. The judge took a different view, that the profit share agreement was in reality compensation for unpaid work the shareholders had performed for the company and not for the shares. The case was actually decided on different issues.

[46] [2002] 2 B.C.L.C. 688.

[47] The Court of Appeal upheld this actual decision but on other grounds based on a complex analysis of the facts which in their view did not establish that there had been any financial assistance by the company concerned. They did also stress the commercial reality test; [2003] 2 B.C.L.C. 117.

[48] [2003] 1 B.C.L.C. 675. The Court of Appeal in *MT Realisations* refused to be drawn into this dispute.

[49] And explaining the *Barclays Bank* case on the curious basis that there was no intention that the covenant would ever be used (but it was).

[50] Under s.152(1)(iv), above.

[51] Given the very narrow interpretation applied to the purpose exceptions, below, which might have been expected to have come into play in this situation, this is not surprising. And, in fact, Arden L.J. used s.153 to come to this conclusion. It is hard to see, however, the mischief in the facts of *Chaston* which would have made it a criminal offence.

[52] [2004] 2 B.C.L.C. 427; affirmed [2005] B.C.C. 79, CA.

property. He then negotiated a rental from the company in excess of the market rate. Hart J. and the Court of Appeal held that the excess rental agreement was not post-acquisition unlawful financial assistance for the transfer because although it was connected with the sale of the shares it was not for the purpose of that sale in a commercial sense. The clear purpose of the company (as inferred from Mrs Dyment's acts) was to enter into an agreement which would allow its business to continue. Mr Boyden's objective may well have been to make up for his loss of income from the company, but that was not the company's objective.

Similarly in *Harlow v Loveday*,[53] commercial reality dictated that a charge given by the company to A as security for a loan made by A to B, which was used by B to purchase shares in the company, was given for the purpose of the acquisition. Although B was not bound to use the loan monies to purchase the shares, each of the parties knew what the loan and security were for.

Subsidiaries

The prohibitions apply equally to a subsidiary providing financial assistance for **11–011** the acquisition of shares in its holding company. In *Arab Bank Plc v Mercantile Holdings Ltd*[54] it was held that the mere fact that a subsidiary provides such assistance does not mean that the assistance has been provided by the holding company, although there may be circumstances, for example where the holding company transfers an asset to the subsidiary which the latter then uses to provide the assistance, where the holding company may do so indirectly. That case also decided that the prohibitions do not apply to foreign subsidiaries providing assistance in relation to the shares of a UK holding company. This approach was applied in *AMG Global Nominees (Private) Ltd v Africa Resources Ltd*[55] where it was held that there could not be alleged to have been financial assistance by a subsidiary company within a group simply because the value of the assets of the holding company in that group were diminished as a result of the transaction.

STATUTORY EXCLUSIONS FROM FINANCIAL ASSISTANCE

Circumstances in which there will not be financial assistance under section 678(1), CA 2006

There will not be financial assistance, however, either if the principal purpose for **11–012** giving the assistance was not to give it for so as to make such an acquisition of the company's own shares or if the giving of the assistance was only an incidental part of some larger purpose of the company.[56] It is also required that the assistance was given in good faith.[57] This exemption from a finding of financial assistance also applies, mutatis mutandis, to what would otherwise be financial

[53] [2004] B.C.C. 732.
[54] [1994] 1 B.C.L.C. 330.
[55] [2009] 1 B.C.L.C. 281.
[56] Companies Act 2006 s.678(2).
[57] Companies Act 2006 s.678(2).

assistance given by way of reduction of a liability. Section 678(2) of the CA 2006 provides that the prohibition in s.678(1) of the CA 2006:

> "does not prohibit a company from giving financial assistance for the acquisition of shares in it or its holding company if
>
> (a) the company's principal purpose in giving the assistance is not to give it for the purpose of any such acquisition, or
> (b) the giving of the assistance for that purpose is only an incidental part of some larger purpose of the company,
>
> and the assistance is given in good faith in the interests of the company."

Therefore transactions without a corporate group which are bona fide in the interests of the company do not constitute financial assistance.

Unconditional, authorised transaction exceptions under section 681, CA 2006

11–013 Section 681(2) of the CA 2006 sets out eight specific transactions permitted under company law which are not to be subject to the prohibition on financial assistance. These are as follows:

1. the distribution of lawful dividends.[58] The rules relating to the funds available for dividends are considered strong enough to protect companies. One of the old abuses was to extract unusually large dividends from a company to repay a loan used by the borrower to gain control of the company;

2. distributions made in the course of a winding up[59];

3. the allotment of bonus shares[60];

4. any reduction of capital confirmed by the court[61];

5. a redemption of shares or a purchase of its own shares by a company[62];

6. anything done under a court order under Pt 26 of the CA 2006[63];

7. anything done under an arrangement between a company and its creditors under s.1 of the Insolvency Act 1986[64];

8. anything done under an arrangement made in pursuance of s.110 of the Insolvency Act 1986.[65]

---

[58] Companies Act 2006 s.681(2)(a)(i). Below, Ch.12.
[59] Companies Act 2006 s.681(2)(a)(ii).
[60] Companies Act 2006 s.681(2)(b). Discussed in Ch.8.
[61] Companies Act 2006 s.681(2)(c).
[62] Companies Act 2006 s.681(2)(d). Above, Ch.10.
[63] Companies Act 2006 s.681(2)(e).
[64] Companies Act 2006 s.681(2)(f).
[65] Companies Act 2006 s.681(2)(g).

Conditional exceptions under statute

A series of conditional exceptions to the prohibition on financial assistance[66] is **11–014** provided in s.682 of the CA 2006. There are two species of exception under s.682: first, if the company is a private company;[67] second, in relation to assistance given by public companies where their net assets are not reduced or where any reduction in those assets is paid out of distributable profits.[68] Both exceptions are then conditional on there being one of the following types of transactions. The listed transactions under s.682 are as follows: lending money where the company's business is lending money; the good faith provision of financial assistance in the interests of the company's employees' share scheme; in relation to the company's bona fide employees or former employees or their designated relatives acquiring shares in the company; or the making of loans by the company to enable the borrower to acquire fully paid shares in the company "to be held by them by way of beneficial ownership."[69]

In relation to the exception where the principal purpose of giving the financial assistance was not for the purpose of the acquisition and was given in good faith in the interests of the company, this exception was designed to protect groups of companies with relevance to the post-acquisition assistance prohibition. For example, where, following the acquisition of a new subsidiary company, the acquiring company has to charge the assets of that subsidiary to comply with a prior debenture which requires all the assets of the group to be charged on security. In such a case, the security would not be given for the principal purpose of reducing a liability incurred for the purpose of acquiring the subsidiary.

In relation to the exception relating to transactions in which, even if the principal purpose of giving the financial assistance was for the acquisition of shares, it was an incidental part of some larger purpose and was given in good faith in the interests of the company. This exception was also defined with reference to post-acquisition financial assistance within a group of companies. For example, when a subsidiary company provides funds to its parent company some years after it has been acquired to effect a more efficient deployment of assets within the group, the proviso may relieve the parent company of indebtedness incurred for the purpose of acquiring the subsidiary but if the larger purpose can be established it will be exempt.

These two purpose exceptions contain an inherent difficulty. They could be interpreted very widely so that if there is any overall scheme, e.g. a takeover bid, which involves financial assistance being given for the purpose of the acquisition of shares, the overall scheme will serve as the principal or larger purpose for the exceptions to apply, even though the narrow purpose of giving the assistance was the acquisition (the latter is, as we have seen, necessary for the prohibition to apply in the first place). On the other hand if the purpose of giving the assistance is the acquisition of shares (as above, the starting point) how can the giving of that

---

[66] Companies Act 2006 s.681(1).
[67] Companies Act 2006 s.682(1)(a).
[68] Companies Act 2006 s.682(1)(b).
[69] Companies Act 2006 s.682(2).

assistance (as distinct from the acquisition of the shares) ever be part of a larger or principal purpose? In either extent what is meant by good faith in this context?

11–015 As discussed above, in *Brady v Brady*[70] a group of private companies which ran two businesses was controlled by two brothers who quarrelled and so caused a deadlock within the group. The proposed solution was a division of the businesses between them, but one business was more valuable than the other. To equalise the division, a complex series of transactions followed, one of which involved the transfer of a large proportion of one company's assets to pay off loan stock which had been issued as the purchase price of that company's shares. This was clearly a breach of what is now s.678 since at least part of the purpose was to assist[71] the acquisition of the shares. The question arose as to whether the transaction could be saved under either of the purpose exceptions. It was held that they would not. The House of Lords refused to find (as the Court of Appeal had done) that the financial assistance was merely part of a larger transaction. The House of Lords did not consider whether the interests of the creditors had to be considered, nor the fact that the group was solvent at all times so that the creditors were not at risk, nor the fact that the proposed division of the group would resolve deadlock and remove the need for expensive winding up petitions, and was therefore arguably in the broader interests of the company. Following that decision the purpose exceptions will be of little use where as the result of a transaction a company provides financial assistance to a person acquiring its shares. Whether that is a collateral purpose of an otherwise innocent-looking transaction or whether the transaction itself can properly be categorised as financial assistance in a commercial sense, then any reference to a larger or main purpose will be regarded as one motive or reason. The situation will be best resolved on the issue as to whether the whole transaction can properly be categorised as financial assistance within s.678(1), rather than on the wording of s.678(2) and s.679(2).[72]

There is, however, a suggested alternative application of the purpose exceptions. The test would be whether there was some overall corporate purpose, i.e. one for the benefit of the company itself, which would then remove a transaction otherwise in breach of s.678 (under either the collateral purpose or proper categorisation test). In *Brady v Brady* after all the transaction was for the benefit of solving the shareholders' dispute and not for the company as such.

Assistance by public company for acquisition of shares in its private holding company

11–016 There are specific provisions in relation to assistance given by a public company for acquisition of shares in its private holding company under s.679 of the CA 2006. Section 679(1) provides that:

---

[70] [1989] A.C. 755, HL; [1988] B.C.L.C. 20, CA.

[71] cf. *Dyment v Boyden*, where on not dissimilar facts there was held to be no financial assistance in a commercial sense. Section 153 was not in issue in that case.

[72] This seems to have happened in the not dissimilar case of *Dyment v Boyden* [2005] B.C.C. 79, CA, above.

"Where a person is acquiring or proposing to acquire shares in a private company, it is not lawful for a public company that is a subsidiary of that company to give financial assistance directly or indirectly for the purpose of the acquisition before or at the same time as the acquisition takes place."

There is, however, an exception to this provision in s.679(2) in the following terms:

"Subsection (1) does not prohibit a company from giving financial assistance for the acquisition of shares in its holding company if—

(a) the company's principal purpose in giving the assistance is not to give it for the purpose of any such acquisition, or
(b) the giving of the assistance for that purpose is only an incidental part of some larger purpose of the company,

and the assistance is given in good faith in the interests of the company."

This exception is similar to s.678(2), as considered above.

THE EFFECT OF TRANSACTIONS BEING TAINTED WITH FINANCIAL ASSISTANCE UNDER PRIVATE LAW

The question

There is a question under private law as to the effect of a transaction being found **11–017** to have fallen foul of the prohibition on financial assistance. The breach of the prohibition in s.678(1) CA 2006, and the other prohibitions, is a criminal offence.[73] In private law, a transaction which is held to constitute financial assistance is void.[74] That much is plain from the decision of the House of Lords *Brady v Brady*.[75] On the one hand it is argued that the financial assistance regime is intended to protect the company and therefore there ought to be no conceptual problem with allowing third parties to enforce financial assistance agreements between them. To achieve this objective on the authorities one would have to sever that portion of an agreement which is intended to be saved from the element which constitutes the financial assistance.[76] The question would then arise whether the financial assistance was merely collateral to a larger transaction such that it could be severed, or whether the financial assistance is so integral to the

---

[73] Companies Act 2006 s.680(1).
[74] *Selangor United Rubber Estates Ltd v Cradock (No.3)* [1968] 1 W.L.R. 497 (providing security for a loan will render that debenture security void); *Heald v O'Connor* [1971] 1 W.L.R. 497 (providing a guarantee will render that guarantee void); *Carney v Herbert* [1985] A.C. 301; *Harlow v Loveday* [2004] B.C.C. 723.
[75] [1989] A.C. 755, [1988] 2 All E.R. 617. And consequently an action for specific performance of an agreement for a transaction which constitutes financial assistance will not stand. See also *Plaut v Steiner* (1989) 5 B.C.C. 352, where it was held that it could never be in the interests of the company if it became insolvent as a result of giving the assistance. See also Dyment v Boyden [2005] B.C.C. 79, CA.
[76] *South Western Mineral Water Co v Ashmore* [1967] 1 W.L.R. 1110; *Carney v Herbert* [1985] A.C. 301.

remainder of the transaction that a substantively different agreement would be left if severance were attempted.[77] If the company loses money or other assets due to the financial assistance then it will have to seek to recover its loss by means of the imposition of a constructive trust on the person who has committed or induced any breach of the fiduciary duties of any director,[78] or by means of imposing personal liability to account as a constructive trustee on any person who has knowingly received property in breach of fiduciary duty.[79]

Authorities avoiding the transaction

11–018 After some initial hesitation,[80] the courts have held that the actual financial assistance provided by the company, such as security for a loan[81] or guaranteeing an illegal security,[82] is void. It is clear that no such unlawful financial assistance may be enforced against the company. There is still some doubt, however, as to whether the company may enforce a loan against the borrower even if it constitutes financial assistance on the basis that the prohibitions are designed to protect the company.[83] In any event, the further question then arises as to whether the whole transaction for the acquisition of shares is also void. This question arises in two different situations, where the financial assistance has actually been given and where it might potentially be given.

Validity of the transaction—actual financial assistance

11–019 In *South Western Mineral Water Co v Ashmore*[84] Cross J. suggested that the agreement might be saved if the parties proceeded with the acquisition of the shares in a manner dissociating the purchase from the invalid security, for example by means of the seller/lender waiving his rights in the security or by the buyer paying the price at once. In the absence of this, however, the whole agreement to acquire the shares was in his opinion void.

In *Carney v Herbert*,[85] however, the Privy Council decided that if the unlawful elements in the transaction could be severed from the overall transaction and their elimination would leave the basic contract of sale of the shares unchanged, then the remainder of the agreement could be enforced. Only the unlawful elements would be void. The fact that the vendor might have refused to enter into the transaction unless the unlawful elements had been included was not a relevant factor

---

[77] Alastair Hudson, *The Law on Financial Derivatives*, 4th edn (Sweet & Maxwell, 2006) para.3–126.
[78] *Selangor United Rubber Estates Ltd v Cradock (No.3)* [1968] 1 W.L.R. 497. See Ch. 24.
[79] *Agip (Africa) Ltd v Jackson* [1991] Ch. 547.
[80] *Victor Battery Co Ltd v Curry's Ltd* [1946] Ch. 242.
[81] *Selangor United Rubber Estates Ltd v Cradock* (No.3) [1968] 1 W.L.R. 497; *Carney v Herbert* [1985] A.C. 301, PC; *Harlow v Loveday* [2004] B.C.C. 723.
[82] *Heald v O'Connor* [1971] 1 W.L.R. 497.
[83] See the statements of Lord Denning M.R. and Scarman L.J. in *Wallersteiner v Moir* [1974] 1 W.L.R. 991 at 1014, 1033, and of Buckley L.J. and Goff L.J. in *Belmont Finance Corp Ltd v Williams Furniture Ltd* [1979] Ch. 250 at 261, 271.
[84] [1967] 1 W.L.R. 1110.
[85] [1985] A.C. 301, PC. This decision was approved in *Neilson v Stewart*, 1991 S.C. HL 22. See also *Motor & General Insurance Co Ltd v Gobin* (1987) 3 B.C.C. 61.

in determining their severability. The effect of this is to allow a contract of sale to be enforced where there is no damage to the company. H, A and J were directors of A Ltd and of its subsidiary N Ltd C was the fourth director of these companies and he decided to buy the shares of the other directors. They agreed to sell their shares to I Ltd, a company controlled by C, the purchase price to be payable in three instalments by I Ltd. C guaranteed I Ltd's payments, which were also secured by mortgages executed over N Ltd's property. I Ltd failed to pay for the shares and H, A and J sued C on his guarantee. C alleged that the whole transaction was void for unlawful financial assistance. The Privy Council held that the only unlawful financial assistance was the mortgage over N Ltd's property and that this could be severed so as to leave the sale and guarantee intact and enforceable.[86]

Validity of the transaction—potential financial assistance

In *Carney v Herbert*[87] two further allegations of financial assistance were made. **11–020** First, it was said that payment for the shares had been made by means of a cheque drawn on the company's account. The Privy Council held that since there were a number of ways that such payment could have been effected without breaching the section it would not be assumed that it was in breach. Second, it was shown that the vendor/directors had been released from liability on their loan accounts with the company as part of the agreement with a consequent reduction in the purchase price of the shares. That was again held not to be necessarily financial assistance since it was more than offset by a credit balance in the purchaser/director's loan account. Since that could be reduced to the extent of the release it would leave the company in an identical position as before.

That part of the decision illustrates the courts' desire to preserve the validity of a transaction if there is only potential financial assistance. Thus where there is a contract for the acquisition of shares which could be performed in a number of ways, only one of which would contravene s.678, the courts will assume that it was intended to perform the contract in a lawful manner, consistent with the benefit of the company, and order specific performance accordingly. In *Parlett v Guppys (Bridport) Ltd*,[88] therefore the Court of Appeal held that even assuming that the agreement to pay the vendor's salary would have amounted to financial assistance if it had been paid by the company whose shares were being acquired, it was reasonable to assume that in reality it would be paid by the other companies involved in the agreement. Such a solution would be beneficial to the companies as a whole.[89]

---

[86] *Carney v Herbert* [1985] A.C. 301, PC. However, where the guarantee is of an illegal security it cannot be severed from the illegality and cannot therefore be enforced: *Heald v O'Connor* [1971] 1 W.L.R. 497.

[87] [1985] A.C. 301, PC.

[88] [1996] 2 B.C.L.C. 34, CA.

[89] See also *Lawlor v Gray* [1984] 3 All E.R. 345; *Grant v Cigman* [1996] 2 B.C.L.C. 24. Such a solution cannot apply, however, if the transaction has been completed and no order for specific performance is sought: see *R.W. Peak (Kings Lynn) Ltd, Re* [1998] 1 B.C.L.C. 198.

Liability of those participating in the breach

11–021 It was held that s.54 of the 1948 Act was passed to protect the company from having its assets misused and not merely to protect its creditors[90] and this will also apply to s.678. Thus any director who is knowingly a party to a breach of this section will be in breach of duty as a trustee of company funds to the company and liable to repay the loss.[91] In addition anyone who receives the funds of the company so misapplied is liable to it as a constructive trustee if his knowledge makes it unconscionable for him to retain the benefit. Dishonesty is not essential.[92] Anyone who assists in the breach is also liable as an accessory but only if he acted dishonestly.[93] It appears from the *Belmont* case that the company may also recover in the tort of conspiracy[94] if it can prove: first, that the conspirators combined to participate in a common agreement with a common purpose; second, that the combination was to carry out an unlawful purpose; i.e. the provision of financial assistance contrary to s.678; and, third, that the company suffered damages as a consequence. Damage must be proved.

---

[90] *Wallersteiner v Moir* [1974] 1 W.L.R. 991, 1014, per Lord Denning M.R.

[91] *Belmont Finance Corp v Williams Furniture Ltd (No.2)* [1980] 1 All E.R. 393; *Wallersteiner v Moir*, above; *Karak Rubber Co v Burden* (No.2) [1972] 1 W.L.R. 602.

[92] See *Bank of Credit and Commerce International (overseas) Ltd v Akindele* [2000] 4 All E.R. 221, CA.

[93] *Royal Brunei Airlines v Tan* [1995] 2 A.C. 378. In *Twinsectra Ltd v Yardley* [2002] A.C. 164, it was held that the dishonesty required was both objective (dishonest by reasonable standards) and subjective (he was aware of his dishonesty).

[94] Or in Scots law under the general law of delict.

Chapter 12

DIVIDENDS AND DISTRIBUTIONS

INTRODUCTION

The commercial context of dividends

Investors in a company have two means of profiting from their investment. The **12–001** first method is to sell their shares at a profit: this is more easily achieved in relation to public companies whose shares are quoted on public markets and so are easier to buy and sell. The second method is to receive a stream of dividend payments over time. Banks make profits from loan transactions by charging interest; whereas shareholders receive income from their shareholding by means of dividend payments. The focus of this chapter is on the payment of dividends and on all other sorts of "distributions" made by companies to their shareholders. Any payment made by a company to its shareholders—whether in the form of a dividend or otherwise—is referred to as a "distribution".

The question as to when dividends may be paid to shareholders is a matter partly of accounting practice and partly of law.[1] There is a difficult calculation for company directors: how much profit should be ploughed back into the business to generate future profit, to expand the brand and to reward employees, and how much profit should be distributed to the shareholders by way of dividend? A public company which pays too little by way of dividend will have difficulty in raising equity capital from shareholders and other investors in the future because for institutional investors the receipt of dividend income over time is a key part of their investment strategy. The desirability of shares in public companies as an investment is measured typically by reference to the "earnings per share". This encapsulates two things: first, the size of the dividend which is paid per share in each financial year and, secondly, the profits which the company has made when theoretically divided equally among the shareholders. A company which has too many shareholders will generate a comparatively small amount of profit per shareholder. Similarly, a company with profits which are too low or which do not grow will seem unattractive to investors. A key part of encouraging investors to buy shares in a company is to maintain growth in the earnings-per-share ratio year on year. This need to keep the earnings per share growing can have the effect of skewing management policy either towards increasing the dividend or organising

---

[1] These principles were introduced by the Companies Act 1980 for the first time to embody accounting practice in legislative form.

the company's activities so that profits appear to grow (for example, by cutting costs or delaying payments to suppliers).

In private companies, the calculations are different because private companies are not permitted to offer their shares for sale to the public,[2] therefore their shares are not quoted on the stock exchange and therefore there is no ordinary market for those shares. Shareholders in private companies can only generate profit from their shareholdings by effecting private sales of their shares at a profit (provided that the company's articles of association permit those sales) or by receiving dividend income. Consequently, the motivations for management to pay dividends of varying sizes may differ from company to company. In a private family company, for example, where the company was formed to conduct a family business, the management and the shareholders are likely to be the same people and therefore discussions as to the level of dividend which needs to be paid may depend upon a family discussion about the nature of the business. You probably belong to a family, and if so you will know how these sorts of family discussions play out. Otherwise, private companies will tend to involve small groups of people who need concern themselves only with the needs and ambitions of the people who are managers and shareholders, but not with the interests of many other people. A private company will have bankers who have lent it money, possibly a private company will have arm's length investors (known as "venture capitalists") who have acquired shares in return for making a large cash investment in the company,[3] and a private company will ordinarily have a group of people who act as the managers of the business as well as being its principal shareholders. For private companies it may be preferable for tax purposes to distribute profits as directors' fees and salaries. However, for closely held companies (i.e. those whose shares are owned or controlled by a small group of persons), revenue law even deems that a certain amount of profits may be treated as distributed to shareholders, regardless of whether or not such dividend payments have been made.

The core principle in a nutshell

12–002   There are two potential problems with dividends. First, the concern must be that those who control the company might seek to distribute the company's capital among themselves by means of declaring a large dividend payable out of the company's capital as opposed to its income, which is precluded as discussed in Ch.10. This would be prejudicial to the interests of unsecured creditors and others if the company became worth less than it had been previously as a result of the company's profits being bled out of it as dividends. Secondly, the company may wish to pay a large dividend to its shareholders when its profits for the financial

---

[2] Companies Act 2006 s.755.

[3] Venture capitalism is discussed (along with its cousin, private equity) in Alastair Hudson, *The Law of Finance* (Sweet & Maxwell, 2009). In essence, the venture capitalist may simply be contributing money to the business without participating in its management. In that sense, the venture capitalist will be concerned either to earn large dividend income, or alternatively a deal will have been struck whereby the venture capitalist is entitled to take dividend income as a shareholder or to convert its shares to debt so that it can seek repayment of the capital amount of its investment after an identified period of time.

year have been insufficiently large. To do this, a company may seek to declare a dividend which includes an amount of profits which it expects to earn, for example, from sales which have been agreed but for which the purchase price has not yet been paid. Profit and loss accounts frequently include sales which have been made even if the money has not been received; whereas cash flow statements exclude amounts which have not actually been paid yet.

Consequently, the central rule on dividends in s.830 of the CA 2006 requires that any company "may only make a distribution [to its members] out of profits available for the purpose". This has the effect of limiting all distributions from the company to income amounts (that is, the profits) which can be paid out at that time. There is a further requirement in relation only to public companies, under s.831 of the CA 2006, that the company's net assets will still exceed its share capital and its reserves after the distribution. Even though the core policy here is predicated on the protection of unsecured creditors by preventing money from being bled out of the company, in fact it is not possible to provide fully effective protection to creditors in this way. Nevertheless, the general philosophy of capital maintenance has nevertheless been behind the development of the law relating to the distribution of dividends as it has evolved over the past 150 years. However, in many of the cases at the start of the twentieth century judges went out of their way not to impose unreasonable restrictions which might potentially lead to a misallocation of resources within the economy.[4] Paid-up capital must not be paid to the shareholders except by leave of the court or under strictly defined circumstances. It must be spent only on the objects defined in the company's constitution. Any other expenditure is beyond the company's powers as it reduces the fund available for the company's creditors. The rules on capital were considered in Ch.10.

PROVISIONS DEALING WITH DISTRIBUTIONS

Restrictions on when distributions may be made

The definition of "distribution"

The term "distribution" is defined in s.829(1) of the CA 2006 as encompassing **12–003** "every description of distribution of a company's assets to its members, whether in cash or otherwise". The exceptions to this broad definition are issues of bonus shares and reductions in share capital (both of which are considered in Ch.9), and distributions to the members on the winding up of a company.

The central principle: distributions may only be made out of available profits

Section 830(1) of the CA 2006 provides the central principle against unfettered **12–004** distributions being made to shareholders in the following terms:

---

[4] See French, "The Evolution of the Dividend Law of England," in Baxter and Davidson (eds) *Studies in Accounting*, 3rd edn (London: Institute of Chartered Accountants in England and Wales 1977), pp.306–331.

"A company may only make a distribution out of profits available for the purpose."

The purpose of the provision is clear. Distributions of all kinds are covered by this provision. Those distributions may only be made out of "profits". In this sense, a profit may be an income profit (for example, the profit earned from selling goods to the public in a given financial year) and a profit may also be a capital profit (for example, a profit made in a financial year by selling a capital asset for more than its purchase price). However, profits cannot be made out of the assets set out in s.831 (considered below).

Furthermore, and very importantly, those profits must be "available for the purpose". This element is in the province of accounting theory. A "profit" in accountancy terms is the amount of income which is left after the "cost of sales" have been deducted, or the profit shown on the disposal of an asset for more than was paid for it. To focus on the income profits for the moment, there are numerous expenses which appear on the profit and loss account below the ordinary calculation of profit: for example, taxation, interest, depreciation and amortisation.[5] Therefore, under s.830(1) it is necessary to show that the profits are free to be distributed and are not required to be allocated to meet, for example, the company's tax bill, the company's interest payments on its debt and similar expenses on the company's profit and loss account. The company may not, therefore, seek to pay dividends out of "profits" which are needed to pay the corporate tax bill because they are not "available".

Section 830(2) defines the concept of "available profits" in the following terms:

"A company's profits available for distribution are its accumulated, realised profits, so far as not previously utilised by distribution or capitalisation, less its accumulated, realised losses, so far as not previously written off in a reduction or reorganisation of capital duly made."

12–005 Two concepts of particular importance in the definition of "available profits" emerge. First, the profits must be "accumulated" and "realised" profits, which means that they must be profits which have actually been received in cash and not simply paper profits which are recorded in the company's books for sales made for which payment has not been received. The same principle applies to the company's losses. Secondly, if the company has lawfully reduced or reorganised its capital base (as considered in Ch.9) then any such changes in the company's capital do not count in the calculation of its available profits.

Section 831(1) of the CA 2006 provides a further restriction on the ability of companies to make distributions:

"(1)   A public company may only make a distribution—

(a)   if the amount of its net assets is not less than the aggregate of its called-up share capital and undistributable reserves, and

---

[5] Where these last two items reflect the fall in value of the company's assets, such as plant and machinery, from year to year as they get older.

(b) if, and to the extent that, the distribution does not reduce the amount of those assets to less than that aggregate."

In essence, this subsection prohibits a public company from making a distribution of such a size that its assets would become less than its liabilities and its capital. This is made clearer by s.831(2), which provides that "a company's 'net assets' means the aggregate of the company's assets less the aggregate of its liabilities". Again, the purpose of this provision is to preserve the company's net worth (a key measure, for example of a company's credit worth in most loan contracts[6]) so that that value is available to the company's unsecured creditors.[7] Matters in s.831(1) are, of course slightly more complicated than this. The "capital" in this sense includes its "undistributable reserves" (that is, its share premium account, its capital redemption reserve and any other part of its reserves which the articles of association prohibit it from distributing).[8] Capital also includes the company's called-up share capital: that means, in effect, shares which have actually been allotted and paid for, as opposed to shares which have not actually been called-up even though the directors have a power to allot them. Shares which have not been called-up are not to be included in the company's accounts for these purposes.[9]

Accounting approaches to realised profits

Given that the notion of what is and is not a realised profit is a subtle one, which **12–006** has caused some controversy among accountants, the professional accountancy bodies issued guidance on the matter in March 2003.[10] Essentially this endorses guidance given previously in September 1982. In general terms the accounts must present a "true and fair view" of the company's financial position. The guidance reaches three conclusions. First, accounting standards[11] would constitute evidence of generally accepted accounting principles and the profits calculated

---

[6] See Alastair Hudson, *The Law of Finance* (London: Sweet & Maxwell, 2009), para.33–23 et seq.

[7] It was suggested in earlier editions of this work that, in view of the underlying rationale behind the law in this area, the realised profits test introduced for the first time by the Companies Act 1980 can be viewed as a retrograde step. However, in practice it is unlikely to prove an effective constraint. In the rare cases in which companies might wish to distribute more than their accumulated realised profits, they could always convert unrealised gains into realised income by selling off assets (and, if necessary, buying or leasing them back); purchase their own shares; or apply to the court for a reduction of capital: these provisions were considered in Chs 9 and 10.

[8] Companies Act 2006 s.831(4).

[9] If such uncalled shares could be included in the company's accounts then it would be possible to skew the company's accounts by holding large numbers of uncalled shares in abeyance so as to make it appear that the company had much more capital than in fact it did, so that larger dividends could be paid out to shareholders.

[10] "Guidance on the determination of realised profits and losses in the context of distributions under the Companies Act 1985". The March 2003 statement gives specific guidance with respect to a number of issues: e.g. the translation of foreign currencies, valuing securities at their current market values ("marking to market"), payments in kind ("top slicing"), and the treatment of positive and negative goodwill.

[11] The status of accounting standards has been examined in terms of clarifying the meaning of the phrase "a true and fair view" in the case of *Lloyd Cheyham and Co Ltd v Littlejohn and Co* [1986] P.C.C. 389.

applying such standards should in general be regarded as "realised profits", even where the usual criteria for establishing "realisation" (such as receipt of cash, or the creation of a contractual obligation to pay a specific sum of money) are not met. This would mean, for instance, that the procedures for gradually recognising profits on long-term contracts and the inclusion in the profit and loss account of foreign currency translation gains and losses on net monetary items would both give rise to "realised profits". Secondly, where no accounting standard is applicable a profit can be regarded as "realised" where the policy followed is consistent with the accounting accruals concept and prudence doctrine. Thirdly, where necessary a company must, in order for its accounts to show a "true and fair view" of its financial performance and position, depart from accepted accounting principles and include an unrealised profit in its income statement, provided that the accounts contain a note indicating the nature of the departure, the reasons for it, and the effect of this accounting treatment.[12]

The relevant accounts

12–007 Section 836 of the CA 2006 identifies the accounting documentation which can be referred to in deciding the level of the company's distributable profits. The relevant accounts are: profits, losses and liabilities; "provisions"[13] (including provisions for depreciation); and share capital and reserves (including undistributable reserves).[14] The documents to be used to identify these accounting materials are ordinarily the company's last annual accounts[15]; unless other, interim accounts are necessary to enable a reasonable judgment to be made to determine distributable profits, or unless the distribution is proposed to be made during the company's first year before any annual accounts are prepared.[16] Those accounts must have been prepared in accordance with the Companies Act provisions in relation to company accounts in ss.237 through 239 of the CA 2006.[17]

The consequences of an unlawful distribution

12–008 The question then arises as to the consequences of a distribution in breach of the provisions in the CA 2006 relating to the preparation of accounts. The accounts may not be relied upon unless they comply with those provisions.[18] Consequently, a breach of the statutory requirements relating to the relevant accounts for

---

[12] Apart from these general considerations, realised profits and losses are, under s.830, all profits and losses, whether income or capital, which are deemed to have been realised. It follows that when a company sells an undepreciated fixed asset (such as freehold land) which has been revalued in the accounts for consideration above its original cost, and the revaluation has been credited direct to reserves, the relevant part of the revaluation reserve has to be regarded as realised profit, even though it has never been credited to the profit and loss account. Similar considerations relate to wasting fixed assets, although the provisions are more complex.

[13] That is, amounts set aside.

[14] Companies Act 2006 s.836(1).

[15] Companies Act 2006 s.836(2) and also s.837.

[16] Companies Act 2006 s.836(2). The requirements governing interim accounts are set out in s.838 of the Companies Act 2006, and s.839 where initial accounts are used.

[17] Companies Act 2006 s.836(3).

[18] Companies Act 2006 s.836(4).

determining whether or not profits were available constitutes a breach of the test as to whether or not those profits may be distributed. Section 847 of the CA 2006 provides that any shareholder who receives a distribution which he knows, or has reasonable grounds to believe, has been paid in breach of the 2006 Act rules as to the preparation of accounts, must repay that amount to the company. This is expressly made an addition to the shareholders' existing liabilities set out below, but it does not apply in relation either to financial assistance given by a company to a person to help him purchase its shares, nor to any payment made by a company in respect of the redemption or purchase by the company of shares in itself.

With regard to payments of dividends out of capital, it was established prior to the 1980 Act that directors who are knowingly parties to such payments are jointly and severally liable to the company to replace the amounts of dividends so paid, with interest, and ratification is impossible so as to bind the company.[19] In such a case they are entitled to be indemnified by each shareholder who received dividends, knowing them to be paid out of capital, to the extent of the dividends received.[20] A shareholder who has knowingly received a dividend paid out of capital cannot individually, nor on behalf of the company, maintain an action against the directors to replace the dividends so paid, at any rate until he has repaid the money he has received.[21]

Distributions by investment companies

There are different principles in play in relation to investment companies. An **12–009** investment company is a company which seeks investors who want to speculate on financial and other markets, and who do so by means of buying shares in an investment company before that investment company makes speculative investments on their behalf. Investment companies are public companies which explicitly carry on the business of "investment companies", as described in s.833 of the CA 2006. Such companies can only make distributions out of "accumulated, realised revenue profits" in accordance with s.832 of the CA 2006. This creates an alternative to the s.830 principle. The alternative test is a realised profits test which only applies to revenue and not to capital profits or losses. Accumulated, realised revenue profits are calculated as constituting realised revenue profits minus realised and unrealised revenue losses. The corresponding net assets test requires that the value of the assets must be at least 1.5 times the aggregate of the company's liabilities (including provisions) both before and after the proposed distribution. However, where a distribution by an investment company reduces

---

[19] For example, where debts known to be bad were entered as assets in reports and balance sheets, so that an apparent profit was shown, and the shareholders, relying on these documents, declared dividends: *Flitcroft's Case* (1882) 21 Ch.D. 519 (C.A.). See also *Liquidators of City of Glasgow Bank v Mackinnon* (1881) 9 R. 535. Directors who authorise dividend payments other than out of distributable profits may be personally liable to reimburse the company: *Bairstow v Queens Moat Houses Plc* [2000] 1 B.C.L.C. 549, QBD.

[20] *Moxham v Grant* [1900] 1 Q.B. 88 (C.A.).

[21] *Towers v African Tug Co* (1904) 1 Ch. 558 (C.A.); *Liquidators of City of Glasgow Bank v Mackinnon* (1881) 9. R. 535.

the amount of its net assets below the aggregate of its called-up share capital and undistributable reserves, this fact must be disclosed in the notes to its financial statements.

PAYMENT OF DIVIDENDS

12–010   As was considered at the beginning of this chapter, from a commercial perspective dividends are payable in accordance with management decisions as to the profitability of the company and the need to invest for the future. From a general, legal perspective, management must observe the rules about *paying out* dividends out of distributable, available profits. More specifically, the decision whether or not to pay dividends from a legal perspective is governed by the procedure laid down in the company's articles of association. Ordinarily, the company may declare a final dividend by ordinary resolution at the annual general meeting but so that no dividend shall exceed the amount recommended by the directors. It is possible to declare an interim dividend: that is, a dividend paid on some date between two annual general meetings of the company.[22] The articles of association typically provide that the directors may pay such a dividend if it appears to be justified by the profits available for distribution.

Before recommending a dividend, directors should have a complete and detailed list of the company's assets and investments prepared for their information, and they should not rely for their value merely on the opinion of the chairman or the auditors.[23] In the absence of anything to the contrary in the articles,[24] a company cannot be compelled to declare a dividend and no action can be brought for its recovery until it has been declared.[25] In England the declaration of a dividend creates a simple contract debt due from the company to the shareholder which will be barred in six years from the date of declaration.[26]

There are different types of shareholding in a company. Ordinarily, preference shares entitle the holder to receive a fixed dividend out of the profits of the company for each year. In that circumstance, the "profits of the company" are the profits available for paying a dividend after setting aside such reserves as the directors think fit. If the whole of the profits are transferred to a reserve, then the preference shareholders are not entitled to any dividend.[27] More generally, the rights of holders of preference and other special shares must be observed, since infringement of such rights will give aggrieved members the right to apply for an injunction or other relief. Moreover, if dividends are paid infringing such rights, any class of members which suffers will be able to take legal action against the

---

[22] *Jowitt, Re* [1922] 2 Ch. 442 at 447, per Lawrence J.

[23] *City Equitable Fire Insurance Co Ltd, Re* (1925) Ch. 407 at 471, 474, per Romer J.

[24] For articles which were interpreted as requiring whole profits to be divided, see *Paterson v R. Paterson & Sons Ltd*, 1917 S.C. HL 13; 1916 S.C. 452.

[25] *Bond v Barrow Haematite Steel Co* [1902] 1 Ch. 353.

[26] *Compania de Electricidad de la Provincia de Buenos Aires Ltd, Re* [1978] 3 All E.R. 668.

[27] *Buenos Ayres Great Southern Railway Co Ltd, Re* [1947] Ch. 384; cf. the Scottish case *Wemyss Collieries Trust Ltd v Melville* (1905) 8 F. 143, in which transfer of a sum to reserve was, on an interpretation of the articles, held to be valid, although preference shareholders were thereby deprived of an additional non-cumulative dividend.

company, while the directors who wrongly paid the dividends will be liable to replace the sum involved.

In English law, unless the articles otherwise provide, dividends are payable to the shareholders in proportion to the nominal amounts of their shares, irrespective of the amounts paid up.[28] Where there is no provision in the articles as to how dividends are to be paid, the common law principle applicable is that they are payable in proportion to the amounts paid up on the shares.[29] The articles usually provide that dividends payable in cash may be paid by a cheque sent through the post to the registered address of the shareholder, or to such persons and to such address as the shareholder may in writing direct. In the absence of such a provision in the articles, the company will have to issue a fresh dividend cheque to the shareholder should the cheque first sent be lost in the post.[30] However, unless power is given in the articles, dividends declared must be paid in cash, and a shareholder can restrain the company from paying them in any other way.[31] When the articles give the directors power to pay interim dividends, a resolution by the company in general meeting requiring the directors to declare an interim dividend is inoperative.[32]

CAPITALISATION AND DIVIDENDS

Creation of a reserve

Sections 415 et seq. of the CA 2006 require, inter alia, that the directors should **12–011** state in their report the amount, if any, which they recommend should be paid as a dividend. It used to be the case that the directors were also required to state the amount, if any, which they proposed to carry to reserves. Consequently companies' articles often contain provisions dealing with the creation of a reserve. Yet even where no power to create a reserve is included in its articles, a company may nevertheless create one as this is a business matter to be decided by the company itself.[33] "The general practice of companies certainly is not to divide the total available profits, but to carry forward a part to make provision for meeting current liabilities."[34] Moreover, a reserve may at any time be distributed as dividend or be employed in any other way authorised by the articles.[35] The fact that it has been used in the business does not show that it has been capitalised so as not to be available for dividend.[36]

---

[28] *Birch v Cropper* (1889) 14 App. Cas. 525.
[29] *Hoggan v Tharsis Sulphur etc. Co Ltd* (1882) 9 R. 1191.
[30] *Thairlwall v Great Northern Railway* [1910] 2 KB 509.
[31] *Wood v Odessa Waterworks Co* (1889) 42 Ch.D. 636.
[32] *Scott v Scott* [1943] 1 All E.R. 582.
[33] *Burland v Earle* [1902] A.C. 83, PC. Scottish cases decided on the interpretation of articles were *Cadell v Scottish Investment Trust Co Ltd* (1901) 9 S.L.T. 299, affirming (1901) 8 S.L.T. 480 (OH) (power to carry forward profits to the next year instead of paying a larger dividend on deferred shares); and *Wemyss Collieries Trust Ltd v Melville* (1905) 8 F. 143 (transfer of profits to reserve fund instead of paying additional dividend on preference shares).
[34] Per Lord M'Laren in *Cadell v Scottish Investment Trust Co Ltd* (1901) 9 S.L.T. 299 at 300.
[35] e.g. *Blyth's Trustees v Milne* (1905) 7 F. 799.
[36] *Hoare & Co Ltd, Re* [1904] 2 Ch. 208, CA.

Capitalisation of reserves

12–012 A company may decide to retain profits within the company by adding those profits to the company's capital (the equivalent, perhaps, of paying a part of one's salary into a deposit account). This is referred to as "capitalisation". Capitalisation of a company's profits is defined in s.853 as relating either to the creation of bonus shares, or to the transfer of profits to the company's capital redemption reserve. However, a company must have a power in its articles to be able to issue "bonus" shares. Scrip dividends (where rights to receive bonus shares are issued instead of a cash dividend being paid) have become increasingly popular amongst listed companies: originally, this was because many companies had unrelieved Advance Corporation Tax as a result of substantial overseas earnings and were able to use scrip dividends to soak up this liability to tax. These tax advantages were effectively removed by the Finance Act 1993, but the practice continued because offering scrip dividends still enables companies to retain cash which would otherwise have been paid out in dividends, with the result that it added to its capital without the costs of raising capital through new share issues. Consequently, listed companies now frequently offer shareholders the option of taking dividends in cash or as scrip.[37] If bonus shares are to be issued, then five things must be the case: there must be authority in the company's articles[38]; the company's nominal share capital must be sufficient; the members must resolve by ordinary resolution to capitalise profits or to apply the share premium account or the capital redemption reserve fund, and to issue bonus shares; the shares must be allotted by the board in the proportions specified in the articles, usually the same proportions as those in which the members would have received a cash dividend; and a return of allotments and a contract between the members and the company (which may be signed on the members' behalf by the person authorised by the articles) must be delivered to the Registrar within one month after the allotment.

---

[37] When a company capitalises its distributable reserves, it reduces at a stroke its accumulated realised profits available for dividend and issues in their place to existing ordinary shareholders in proportion to their holdings. Those shares are then credited as being fully paid up. From an accounting viewpoint, the distributable reserves figure in the balance sheet is reduced and the share or loan capital accounts increased by an equivalent offsetting amount. As a result, other things being equal, the net effect on the value of an individual's holding in the company remains unchanged. The term "bonus" used to describe such issues is therefore misleading, and more appropriate descriptions are "capitalisation-", "scrip-" or "script-issues".

[38] *Wood v Odessa Waterworks Co* (1889) 42 Ch.D. 636. Also see the current Table A, art.110.

CORPORATE SECURITIES

Chapter 13

SECURITIES REGULATION, PROSPECTUSES AND TRANSPARENCY

INTRODUCTION

The issue of securities, for example in the form of shares or bonds, is one of the **13–001** principal means by which companies raise capital, especially on the Anglo-American model of finance. In the European Union in the late twentieth and early twenty-first centuries, the policy was to augment the securities markets available to businesses in Europe by facilitating their growth and by creating a single market for securities. This meant moving the focus away from ordinary borrowing in many continental European jurisdictions towards the "deep, liquid pools of capital" which were thought to reside in securities markets as in the USA and the United Kingdom. The policy was intended to facilitate growth for companies in the EU. Consequently, much of the law governing the raising of capital through securities markets and the regulatory architecture in the United Kingdom is predicated on EC directives. While the regulatory rulebooks are complex and large, there are a few key themes which can be identified at the outset. The regulation of securities is concerned principally with two things: first, the regulation of the information which must be disclosed to the marketplace by the issuer of securities and, second, the preservation of the integrity of those markets.

This chapter performs three different functions. First, it provides a general map to the whole of securities regulation. This book cannot consider the whole of securities regulation, but there is an important overlap between company law and the formal regulation which governs the means by which companies raise capital on securities markets by means of issuing shares, bonds and other securities.[1] Therefore, this chapter will present an overview of that regulation. Second, it considers the requirement that a prospectus in prescribed form must be authorised by the Financial Services Authority ("FSA") and published before securities may be offered to the public. This requirement is at the heart of modern securities regulation. This discussion analyses the regulations which are contained in the FSA Prospectus Rules, which in turn implement the provisions of the EC Prospectus Directive. Third, it considers the "transparency obligations" imposed on companies with securities in issue to inform the market as to the identity of those people who control voting rights in those companies. This includes a

---

[1] See Alastair Hudson, *Securities Law* (Sweet & Maxwell, 2008) generally for a detailed analysis of securities regulation.

discussion of the FSA Disclosure and Transparency Rules, which in turn implement the EC Transparency Obligations Directive 2004/109/EC. The next chapter considers the various heads of liability which arise (and on which persons those obligations are imposed) when loss is suffered as a result of some defect in a prospectus or some failure to comply with transparency obligations. The chapter following that considers the regulations governing shares which are to be listed on the Official List maintained by the FSA, and the FSA Listing Rules which govern such issues.

THE SOURCES OF THE LAW ON THE PUBLIC ISSUE OF SHARES

The fundamentals relating to the public issue of shares

13–002 There are two principal means by which companies can acquire capital: either by borrowing it or by issuing shares. Borrowing can take the form of ordinary loans or it can take the form of debt securities, such as bonds. In market parlance, shares provide the investor with "equity" in the company in the form of a share, entitling the shareholder to the rights considered in Chs 7 though 9. Both debt securities and shares are forms of security. That is, when investing in a public company, the investor acquires an item of property (the security) which can be traded on the open market. An investor in shares also acquires a potential entitlement to receive a dividend if a dividend is declared over those shares (as discussed in Ch.12) and also acquires the right to vote in general meeting (if the shares are voting shares, as discussed in Ch.7); whereas an investor in bonds acquires no right to vote in general meeting but rather acquires a right to receive a payment of interest (known as "coupon") on each bond that is held. Securities can be listed on any "regulated market" if the issuer sees a commercial advantage in such a listing, or they need not be listed. The decision whether or not to list is a commercial one depending on the perceived marketing advantage in having complied with the listing rules and thus reassuring investors as to the bona fides of the securities issue. This chapter will focus on securities which are issued by public companies which are to be marketed to the public. There are restrictions on the ability of private companies issuing shares to the public as considered below in s.755 of the CA 2006.

EC Directives concerning the public offers of securities

13–003 The underpinnings of law and the regulation of public offers of securities are to be found in the following directives: the Consolidated Admission and Reporting Directive of 2001,[2] the Prospectus Directive of 2003,[3] and the Transparency Obligations Directive of 2004.[4] The first goal of the EC securities directives in this

---

[2] Directive 2001/34/EC on the admission of securities to official stock exchange listing [2001] OJ L184/1.
[3] Directive 2003/71/EC on the prospectus to be published when securities are offered [2003] OJ L345/64.
[4] Directive 2004/109/EC on the harmonisation of transparency requirements [2004] OJ L390/38.

area is to harmonise the treatment of the public issue of securities across the European Union. Consequently those directives have sought to establish minimum requirements for the publication of prospectuses and minimum requirements for domestic regulation dealing with the marketing and issue of securities to the public. However, those directives do permit the regulations in the United Kingdom to be more stringent than the minimum requirements in those directives. In consequence the directives are in truth aimed at the "co-ordination" or "approximation" of national laws rather than their complete harmonisation. The second goal of the securities directives is to create a single market for securities in the EU. This is intended to be achieved by enabling a regulatory approval of a securities issue in one Member State automatically to acquire a "passport" so as to be valid in all Member States in the EU. For reasons of space, rather than consider the terms of these directives in detail, we shall instead consider the manner in which the general principles established in the directives have been implemented in the United Kingdom in principal legislation and by FSA regulation.[5]

The role of the Financial Services and Markets Act 2000

There has been a transformation in the regulation of public offers of securities **13–004** from a system of self-regulation and regulation by the London Stock Exchange under its own Listing Rules to a new system after the enactment of the Financial Services and Markets Act 2000 ("FSMA 2000") in relation to financial services generally. Rather than relying on the development of regulations by the Stock Exchange itself, the FSA now functions as a external regulator of most of the financial services industry in the United Kingdom, acting on the basis of the statutory principles set out in Pt 6 of FSMA 2000, the statutory instruments created thereunder, and the relevant provisions of the *FSA Handbook* (in the specific regulations contained in the sub-divisions of that *Handbook* known as the Listing Rules, the Prospectus Rules and the Disclosure and Transparency Rules).

The FSMA 2000 established the FSA as the principal regulator for financial services activity in the UK in place of the previous system containing a series of different self-regulatory organisations which regulated different market sectors.[6] The FSA was granted a range of powers and sanctions by the FSMA 2000 which should have given it a more formidable standing in the regulation of financial markets. The effect of the global financial crisis of 2007–09 was that the FSA appeared to have been very ineffectual in the regulation of banks and in particular of the complex derivatives markets which contributed to a systemic collapse of the financial markets in 2008.[7] The Coalition Government in the UK has announced that it will replace the FSA in 2012. However, all of the principles discussed in this part of the book will remain in effect because they are based on EC directives. The FSMA 2000 set out general objectives for the FSA when carrying out its functions: these objectives were focused not only on the

---

[5] See more generally Alastair Hudson, *Securities Law* (London: Sweet & Maxwell, 2008).
[6] The regulation of financial markets in the UK is considered in detail in Pt 2 of Alastair Hudson, *The Law of Finance*, (London: Sweet & Maxwell, 2009).
[7] See Alastair Hudson, *The Law of Finance*, Ch.32.

preservation of the integrity of financial markets but also on the enhancement of the UK economy and the education of the investing public.

Market abuse

13–005　Securities law also contains a range of regulation to do with "market abuse". In this regard there are criminal offences connected to insider dealing and market abuse, as is discussed in Ch.24.[8] In this regard, the FSA also has powers to impose "penalties" in relation to market abuse connected to dealing with "inside information". The Listing Rules also contain a code on market conduct which prohibits dealing with inside information. The common objectives of these regulations are to maintain the integrity of the market in the eyes of the investing public and to ensure that transactions between buyers and sellers of securities are conducted on an equal footing. The regulation of market abuse is set out in the Code on Market Conduct contained in the FSA Market Abuse rulebook ("MAR1") which was created further to s.119 of FSMA 2000. Section 118 of the FSMA 2000 sets out the categories of behaviour which constitute market abuse, and then MAR1 provides detail as to the FSA's approach to those various categories. The three categories of market abuse which arise under MAR1 are as follows: first, when a person is "dealing on the basis of inside information which is not trading information"[9]; second, when an insider discloses inside information to another person; and, third, when a person fails to observe proper market conduct when dealing with price sensitive information which is not in the public domain.

Private companies may not offer shares to the public

13–006　A private company—that is, a company which is not a public company[10]—which is limited by shares or limited by guarantee may not "offer to the public any securities of the company" nor "allot or agree to allot any securities of the company with a view to their being offered to the public".[11] It is a cornerstone of securities law that offers of securities to the public may only be made by public companies which are expressly subject to the FSA securities regulations.

THE PRINCIPLES OF PROSPECTUS REGULATION

13–007　In essence, when an offer of transferable securities is made to the public or when a request is made to admit securities to trading on a regulated market, it is criminal offence not to have had a prospectus in the prescribed form authorised by the FSA and then published.[12] The definition of "the public" for these purposes is very broad indeed, encompassing an offer to any person,[13] with the statute then identifying a range of exempt categories of offer. The legislative purpose was to capture a large

---

[8] See also Alastair Hudson, *The Law of Finance*, Ch.14.
[9] MAR, 1.3.2(1)E.
[10] Companies Act 2006 s.4(1).
[11] Companies Act 2006 s.755(1).
[12] Financial Services and Markets Act 2000 s.85.
[13] Financial Services and Markets Act 2000 s.102B.

number of offers so as to expand the scope of securities regulation with only a few, narrowly-defined carve-outs. The statute creates a right to compensation for any loss suffered as a result of an incorrect or misleading statement in a prospectus.[14] The purpose of prospectus regulation is to ensure that the investing public has access to the all "necessary information" to make an informed decision about whether or not to invest in those securities.[15] Once the securities have been issued, the issuer and others bear transparency obligations,[16] which ensure that the investing public has information about the ownership and control of voting rights in the company.

In 2005, the UK Prospectus Regulations[17] ("the Prospectus Regulations 2005") implemented the EC Prospectus Directive by means of amending existing sections of Pt 6 of FSMA 2000 and also by introducing new sections to that Pt 6. The Prospectus Regulations 2005 repealed the Public Offers of Securities Regulations 1995[18] (which had previously dealt with unlisted securities) and also repealed the Financial Services and Markets Act 2000 (Official Listing of Securities) Order 2001[19] (which had dealt with offers of listed securities before 2005).

The Prospectus Regulations 2005 completely changed the manner in which prospectus material is to be prepared and the legal principles governing prospectuses, as was required by the EC Prospectus Directive. Before the Prospectus Regulations 2005 were introduced, it had been important to know whether securities were to be listed on the Official List or were to be unlisted so that one could identify which regulatory code would deal with those securities. For the purposes of prospectus regulation today, as a result of the Prospectus Regulations 2005, it is now important to know whether securities are to be offered to the public, or whether they are to be the subject of a request for admission to trading on a regulated market; or alternatively whether the offer falls outside either of these categories, or is an exempt offer under the prospectus regulations. These categories of offers of securities will be considered below. After 2005, it is only important to know whether securities are listed or unlisted so that one can know whether or not the FSA Listing Rules—as considered in Ch.15—will apply to those securities. In the wake of the Prospectus Regulations 2005, the FSA was empowered to create further securities regulations in the form of the "Prospectus Rules", which are considered next.

THE REQUIREMENT FOR A PROSPECTUS

The nature of a prospectus

A prospectus is a document which makes prescribed forms of information about **13–008** securities and about their issuer available to the investing public. That prospectus will therefore constitute a series of representations on which purchasers of those securities will rely when making the decision whether or not to acquire them. The

---

[14] Financial Services and Markets Act 2000 s.90.
[15] Financial Services and Markets Act 2000 s.87A.
[16] Companies Act 2006 Pt 43 generally.
[17] SI 2005/1433.
[18] SI 1995/1537
[19] SI 2001/2958. Also revoked are the Financial Services and Markets Act 2000 (Official Listing of Securities) Regulations 2001 (SI 2001/2956).

prospectus is therefore the root of any contract for the acquisition of securities, and consequently the approach of securities regulation in this context has been to prescribe the minimum contents of a prospectus for certain types of issuer and for certain types of security, and to demand the continued accuracy of that prospectus during its lifetime so that the investing public is provided with sufficient, appropriate material with which to make informed investment decisions. This chapter, then, considers both the requirements for a prospectus, the circumstances in which a prospectus will not be required, the continuing obligations associated with prospectuses, and the required contents of such a prospectus.

The criminal offence for failure to prepare a prospectus

13–009 It is a criminal offence[20] under s.85 the FSMA 2000 either to offer transferable securities for sale to the public in the United Kingdom[21] or to request the admission of securities to trading on a regulated market[22] without a prospectus in relation to that issue having first been approved by the competent authority (which is the FSA) and then having been published.[23] Consequently, a prospectus is required in relation to an issue of securities when those securities are to be offered to the public in the United Kingdom, that prospectus must be approved by the FSA, provided that the offer is not of a type which is exempted from this requirement by the terms of the statute.[24] The concept of an "offer to the public" is very broad indeed in that it encompasses an offer to only one person and does not require that the offer is made to a number of people.[25] There will have been an "offer of transferable securities to the public" if there is "a communication to any person which presents sufficient information" to enable the recipient of that communication to decide whether or not to buy those securities.[26] In criminal law terms, a failure to comply with either of these requirements constitutes a criminal offence[27]; in private law terms, a failure to comply with either of these requirements is "actionable" on behalf of any person who suffers loss as a result that contravention either under s.90 of the FSMA 2000 or under the general law. Each of these provisions within s.85 is considered in turn in the paragraphs to follow.

Offers of transferable securities require the publication of an approved prospectus: section 85(1) FSMA 2000

13–010 It is a criminal offence to fail to have a prospectus approved and to publish it in the following circumstances, under s.85(1) of FSMA 2000:

---

[20] Financial Services and Markets Act 2000 s.85(3).
[21] Financial Services and Markets Act 2000 s.85(1).
[22] Financial Services and Markets Act 2000 s.85(2).
[23] Financial Services and Markets Act 2000 s.85, as amended by the Prospectus Regulations 2005 (SI 2005/1433) in the manner discussed in the text.
[24] This is the effect of Financial Services and Markets Act 2000 s.85(1).
[25] Financial Services and Markets Act 2000 s.102B.
[26] Financial Services and Markets Act 2000 s.102B.
[27] Financial Services and Markets Act 2000 s.85(3).

"It is unlawful for transferable securities to which this subsection applies to be offered to the public in the United Kingdom unless an approved prospectus has been made available to the public before the offer is made."

Thus, a prospectus must be approved and "made available" to the public before transferable securities are offered to that public. The breadth of an offer to the public is set out in s.102B of the FSMA 2000, as is considered below. However, Sch.11A of the FSMA 2000 provides for a variety of categories of exempt instruments which would otherwise be transferable securities but which are excluded from the ambit of "transferable securities" for the purposes of s.85(1) FSMA 2000. The definition of these various terms is considered in detail below.

Requests for admission to trading on a regulated market require a prospectus

Section 85(2) of FSMA 2000 sets out a second criminal offence, which may also **13–011** give rise to a civil liability to compensate for loss, in the following terms:

"It is unlawful to request the admission of transferable securities to which this subsection applies to trading on a regulated market situated or operating in the United Kingdom unless an approved prospectus has been made available to the public before the request is made."

This second offence, then, relates to the admission to trading on any regulated market, not necessarily the Official List (considered in Ch.15) and not necessarily in conjunction with an offer falling under s.85(1). Notably, it is not a requirement that securities have already been admitted to trading on that regulated market: rather, it is sufficient that a mere "request" for their admission to trading has been made. The term "transferable securities" in this context refers to all transferable securities except for units in an open-ended investment scheme, non-equity transferable securities issued by a public body in an EEA state, shares in the capital bank of an EEA state, securities guaranteed by a public body in an EEA state, non-equity transferable securities issued in a repeated manner by a credit institution,[28] and non-fungible shares of capital intended to provide a right in immoveable property which cannot be sold without giving up that right.[29] These exemptions are considered in greater detail below.

The meaning of an "offer to the public"

The requirement that an offer must have been made to the public does not require **13–012** that the offer is made to an appreciable section of the public at large nor that it is made to more than a fluctuating class of private individuals. Section 102B of the FSMA 2000 draws the concept of an "offer of transferable securities to the public" very broadly indeed. Section 102B(1) provides:

---

[28] Which are not subordinate, convertible or exchangeable.
[29] Financial Services and Markets Act 2000 Sch.11A.

"For the purposes of [Part 6 of FSMA 2000] there is an offer of transferable securities to the public if there is a communication to any person which presents sufficient information on—

(a) the transferable securities to be offered, and
(b) the terms on which they are offered,

to enable an investor to decide to buy or subscribe for the securities in question."

The communication need be received by only "any person". Therefore, the concept of an "offer" is very broad indeed in that it encompasses an offer to only one person and does not require that the offer is made to a number of people. The communication will be an "offer" if there is sufficient information about the securities and the terms of the offer to enable the offeree to make up her mind whether or not to buy them. So, the mere suggestion: "are you interested in some shares?" would not be an "offer" in this sense; whereas, the statement: "are you interested in subscribing for ordinary shares in A Plc carrying ordinary voting rights at a price of 100p each" would constitute an "offer", because it is more specific as to the identity of the securities and the terms on which they are offered, if it is made to "any person" whatsoever.

The offeror must intend to make an offer which, if accepted, would bind her to the agreement.[30] The Irish Prospectus Regulations 2005 make it plain that an "offer" includes "an invitation to treat"; and it is suggested that that interpretation should be placed on s.102B of the FSMA 2000 in the United Kingdom. In relation to the offer of securities to the public, no offer can be made which breaches the terms of the financial promotion code. Section 21 of the FSMA 2000 provides that there may not be any "promotion" or advertisement of financial services without authorisation to do so from the FSA.

13–013   Furthermore, it is required that a "communication" was made and that that communication "presented sufficient information" as to the securities themselves and the terms on which those securities are offered. The communication can be made, it would seem, in any form and by any means. There is no formality required to constitute a communication for these purposes.[31] The communication can be made directly by the offeror or it can be made through an intermediary.[32] However, a communication for the purposes of this section will not have been effected if it is connected with trading on a regulated market, or a multilateral trading facility,[33] or on a market which has been prescribed as a regulated market under FSMA 2000.[34] Therefore, there need not be a binding contract in place for there to have been a communication made. Instead, it is sufficient that an offer has been made which was intended to effect legal relations. If such an offer is made

---

[30] *Storer v Manchester CC* [1974] 1 W.L.R. 1403.
[31] Financial Services and Markets Act 2000 s.102B(3).
[32] Financial Services and Markets Act 2000 s.102B(4).
[33] Financial Services and Markets Act 2000 s.102B(6).
[34] Financial Services and Markets Act 2000 s.102B(5).

to a person in the United Kingdom then it is taken to be an offer of transferable securities in the United Kingdom.[35]

Therefore, the liability to comply with prospectus regulation is very broadly drawn. Indeed, that was the policy underpinning the Prospectus Directive. The aim was to bring all offers to the public, even very small offers, theoretically within the scope of prospectus regulation. However, having thrown the net very widely indeed, the Directive then excluded a number of different types of offer, as discussed below.

The definition of "securities" and "transferable securities"

For the purposes of the Prospectus Directive 2003, the term "securities" is defined so as to constitute[36]: **13–014**

"–   shares in companies and other securities equivalent to shares in companies,
  –   bonds and other forms of securitised debt which are negotiable on the capital market [sic] and
  –   any other securities normally dealt in giving the right to acquire any such transferable securities by subscription or exchange or giving rise to a cash settlement excluding instruments of payment."

However, the Prospectus Directive provides that national legislation may supplement this definition.[37] The definition of "transferable security" in the Glossary to the *FSA Handbook* is "anything which is a transferable security for the purposes of MiFID, other than money—market instruments for the purposes of that directive which have a maturity of less than 12 months". The definition[38] of "transferable security" in MiFID is[39]:

" 'Transferable securities' means those classes of securities which are negotiable on the capital market, with the exception of instruments of payment, such as:

(a)   shares in companies and other securities equivalent to shares in companies, partnership or other entities, and depositary receipts in respect of shares;
(b)   bonds or other forms of securitised debt, including depositary receipts in respect of such securities;
(c)   any other securities giving the right to acquire or sell any such transferable securities or giving rise to a cash settlement determined by reference to transferable securities, currencies, interest rates or yields, commodities or other indices or measures".

---

[35] Financial Services and Markets Act 2000 s.102B(2).
[36] Prospectus Directive art.2(1)(a), as supplemented by the definition in art. 1(4) of Directive 93/22/EEC on investment services [1993] OJ L141/27.
[37] Prospectus Directive art.2(1)(a).
[38] "Indicative" in the sense that we are told only what is included with the concept "transferable securities" rather than being given a comprehensive definition of the term.
[39] MiFID, art.4(18).

This definition is self-evidently very wide indeed. The aim of the regulation is to capture as many forms of securities issue as possible. Issues must fall within one of the statutory exemptions to elude regulatory coverage, as considered below.

Private law liability further to section 85 FSMA 2000

13–015   Breach of the duties created by s.85 of the FSMA 2000 leads to a right to recover compensation for any loss suffered as a result of that breach. The nature of the private law liability which might arise further to s.85 of the FSMA 2000 is expressed in s.85(4) FSMA 2000 in the following terms:

> "A contravention of subsection (1) or (2) is actionable, at the suit of a person who suffers loss as a result of the contravention, subject to the defences and other incidents applying to actions for breach of statutory duty."

A person who commits a breach of statutory duty which causes another person loss will be liable in tort for damages.[40] The tort of "breach of statutory duty simpliciter"[41] will render the defendant liable for damages.[42] The source of the claim is the loss suffered "as a result of" the contravention of s.85: that is, a loss which is caused by the breach of s.85.

Exemptions and exclusions from the prospectus regulations

13–016   Schedule 11A to the FSMA 2000 provides for three categories of securities which are excluded from the ambit of the term "transferable securities" for the purposes of the offence committed under s.85(1) of FSMA 2000. The first category deals primarily with government and similar securities. The second category relates to securities in not-for-profit organisations. The third category then divides between two further types of security: non-equity transferable securities which are "issued in a continuous or repeated manner by a credit institution" if the total consideration for the offer is less than €50 million, and an offer in which the total consideration for the offer is less than €2.5 million.

   The exemptions from liability for failure to make available an approved prospectus in relation to the offences in s.85 are provided in s.86 of the FSMA 2000.[43] There is no contravention of s.85 in any of these circumstances. The first exemption relates[44] to an offer which is only made to or directed at people (whether financial institutions, public bodies or recognised individuals) who are registered by the FSA as being qualified investors. The second exemption relates to offers made to fewer than one hundred people, because such a small group

---

[40] *Groves v Lord Wimborne* [1898] 2 Q.B. 402; *X (minors) v Bedfordshire County Council* [1995] 2 A.C. 633; *O'Rourke v Camden LBC* [1998].

[41] *X (minors) v Bedfordshire County Council* [1995] 2 A.C. 633. See generally *Clerk & Lindsell on Torts*, 19th edn Sweet & Maxwell, (2006), para.9–06 et seq.

[42] *Cutler v Wandsworth Stadium Ltd* [1949] A.C. 398.

[43] These provisions are expanded on in broadly similar terms in Prospectus Rules, para.1.2.2R "exempt securities—offers of securities to the public" and Prospectus Rules, para.1.2.3R "exempt securities—admission to trading on a regulated market".

[44] Financial Services and Markets Act 2000 s.86(1).

would not be "the public".[45] The third exemption relates to large issues beyond the reach of ordinary, retail investors in which the minimum consideration is at least €50,000. The fourth exemption relates to large denomination issues where the securities being offered are denominated in amounts of at least €50,000. The fifth exemption relates to small issues where the total consideration for the transferable securities being offered cannot exceed €100,000. The sixth possible exemption relates to situations in which a non-qualified investor engages a qualified investor to act as his agent and where that agent has discretion as to his investment decisions,[46] because the expertise of the qualified investor will shield the issuer from liability to comply with the prospectus requirement in s.85 of the FSMA 2000.

The FSA is given a power, further to s.85(5)(b) of the FSMA 2000, to create regulations under the Prospectus Rules to exempt further categories of offers of securities. In relation to offers of securities to the public, they include shares issued in substitution for shares of the same class[47]; transferable securities offered in connection with a takeover[48] or with a merger[49]; shares which are to be offered or allotted free of charge to existing shareholders and dividends which are to be paid in the form of shares[50]; or transferable securities offered or allotted to existing or former directors or employees by their employer where those transferable securities have already been admitted to listing.[51] Securities which are to be admitted to trading on a regulated market may be exempt under this head where they are shares representing less than 10 per cent of the shares of the same class already admitted to trading on the same regulated market over a period of twelve months[52]; or securities of the type mentioned above in relation to offers of securities to the public.

The "persons responsible" for the contents of a prospectus

There is an issue, first, as to the people who are responsible for the contents **13–017** of the prospectus under the securities regulations. The definition of the persons responsible for the contents of a prospectus or of a supplementary prospectus are set out in Ch.5 of the FSA Prospectus Rules.[53] In relation to equity securities, the persons responsible for the prospectus are[54]; the issuer; directors and those authorising themselves to be named as responsible for the prospectus; any other person who accepts responsibility for the prospectus; in relation to an offer, each person who is a director of a body corporate making an offer of securities; in relation to applications for admission to trading, each person who is a director of a body corporate making an offer of securities; and other persons who have authorised the contents of the prospectus. In relation to securities which are not equity

---

[45] Financial Services and Markets Act 2000 s.86(3).
[46] Financial Services and Markets Act 2000 s.86(2).
[47] Prospectus Rules, para.1.2.2(1)R.
[48] Prospectus Rules, para.1.2.2(2)R.
[49] Prospectus Rules, para.1.2.2(3)R.
[50] Prospectus Rules, para.1.2.2(4)R.
[51] Prospectus Rules, para.1.2.2(5)R.
[52] Prospectus Rules, para.1.2.3(1)R.
[53] Prospectus Rules, Ch.5.
[54] Prospectus Rules, para.5.5.3R.

securities, the persons responsible for the prospectus are[55]: the issuer; anyone who accepts and is stated in the prospectus as accepting responsibility for the prospectus; any other person who is the offeror of the securities; any person who requests an admission to trading of transferable securities; any guarantor for the issue in relation to information about that guarantee; and any other person who has authorised the contents of the prospectus. That someone has given advice in a professional capacity about the contents of a prospectus does not make that person responsible for the contents of the prospectus in itself[56]; unless they consent to being so named or they authorise those contents of the prospectus which are the subject of the action, and even then they are liable only to the extent that they have agreed to be so liable.[57]

The duty of disclosure in section 87A FSMA 2000

The section 87A duty in essence

13–018   There is a general duty of disclosure of information in a prospectus set out in s.87A of the FSMA 2000. The effect of this duty of disclosure is that prospectuses must contain all of the information which investors would require to make an informed assessment of the securities. The duty of disclosure is rooted in the requirement that the prospectus must contain the "necessary information" before it can be approved by the FSA. Section 87A(1) of the FSMA 2000 provides as follows:

> "The competent authority may not approve a prospectus unless it is satis-fied that—
>
> (a) the United Kingdom is the home State in relation to the issuer of the transferable securities to which it relates,
> (b) the prospectus contains the necessary information, and
> (c) all of the other requirements imposed by or in accordance with this Part or the prospectus directive have been complied with (so far as those require-ments apply to a prospectus for the transferable securities in question)."

Therefore it is s.87A(1)(b) which contains the requirement that the "necessary information" be contained in the prospectus. The term "necessary information" is defined in s.87A(2) of FSMA 2000 in the following terms:

> "The necessary information is the information necessary to enable investors to make an informed assessment of—
>
> (a) the assets and liabilities, financial position, profits and losses, and prospects of the issuer of the transferable securities and of any guarantor; and
> (b) the rights attaching to the transferable securities."

---

[55] Prospectus Rules, para.5.5.4R.
[56] Prospectus Rules, para.5.5.9R.
[57] Prospectus Rules, para.5.5.8R.

There are therefore four significant elements to this general duty of disclosure, which are considered in the sections to follow.

The "informed assessment" criterion

The principle which governs the type of information which should be contained **13–019** in the prospectus is an "informed assessment" test. This is not a requirement of "reasonableness", nor is it a test based on the information which a professional advisor would require. In this regard, s.87A(4) of the FSMA 2000 provides that:

> "The necessary information must be prepared having regard to the particular nature of the transferable securities and their issuer."

Thus, the information must be relative to the nature of the securities in question and to the nature of the issuer. It also requires the prospectus to present information about the securities themselves, as opposed to generic information, and about the issuer particularly such that an unusual issue would require more information, or a little known start-up company issuing securities would require more information, and so forth, than would a well-known company in a well-known market. Well-known companies in well-known markets (such as high street retailers or clearing banks) making issues of plain vanilla securities (such as ordinary shares of the same class as those already in issue) would not require a large amount of specialist information beyond that normally found in prospectuses. Thus, the provision of information can start at a level relative to the issuer's particular market and particular corporate structure and financial condition. However, a technology company developing new products in new markets and which is little known in the markets in which a general offer to the public is being made would require a much larger amount of background information as to the company's organisation, products, markets and so forth to be made available to investors. It is when there are matters which may not be obvious to all investors—as to the issuer's market, or as to the manner in which the issuer's accounts were prepared, or as to the issuer's group structure, or some such—that the issuer is required to begin to provide information which goes further than might ordinarily be required.

The relevant information to be provided

The information which must be provided is not *all* information which may **13–020** possibly relate to the issuer. Rather, the information which is required is that information which enables an investor to make an informed assessment of four things: the assets and liabilities of the issuer, the financial position of the issuer, the profits and losses of the issuer, and the prospects of the issuer. The prospectus is likely to range across other issues which are likely to be of significance to an investor, but the types of information which are identified in s.87A of the FSMA 2000 are limited to these four. A discussion of the issuer's prospects, for example, will require a greater range of types of information than simply accounting information. As is considered below, the nature of the information which is required may also be dependent on the likely pool of investors, where more expert investors may require less information (for example) as to the basic risk profile of ordinary securities than retail investors.

Information as to the rights attaching to the securities

13–021   The prospectus must provide information as to the rights which will attach to the securities which are to be issued. In relation to debt securities or convertible securities, this may be more complex than in relation to the voting and other rights attaching to ordinary shares.

The requirement for comprehensible and easy-to-analyse presentation of the necessary information

13–022   The manner in which the necessary information is to be set out is described in s.87A(3) of the FSMA 2000 in the following way:

> "The necessary information must be presented in a form which is comprehensible and easy to analyse."

The obligation to make the information comprehensible and easy to analyse is a result of requiring disclosure of information which will satisfy ordinary investors. The dictionary definition of "comprehensible" in the *Oxford English Dictionary* is that the matter "may be understood". If something may be understood by someone, then it might be comprehensible even if it cannot be understood by everyone. What is important, it is suggested, in relation to prospectuses is that an ordinary investor would be able to understand what assertion is being made by the statement in the prospectus on a reasonable basis. That is, no ambiguity must be permitted which would conceal the true meaning of a statement in a prospectus which is otherwise encouraging investors to acquire securities; and there must also be sufficient disclosure of the basic information.

The requirement for a supplementary prospectus: section 87G FSMA 2000

13–023   Even after the preparation of a prospectus is complete there may be events which take place which affect the prospects or condition of the issuer significantly, and therefore a supplementary prospectus may be required to be published which deals with those intervening events. Section 87G of the FSMA 2000 provides that a supplementary prospectus is required to be published in the following circumstances:[58]

> "if, during the relevant period, there arises or is noted a significant new factor, material mistake or inaccuracy relating to the information included in a prospectus [or in a supplementary prospectus][59] approved by the competent authority."

[58] Financial Services and Markets Act 2000 s.87G(2).
[59] Financial Services and Markets Act 2000 s.87G(7).

The "relevant period" is the time between the regulatory approval of the prospectus and the start of trading in the securities. This obligation arises in relation to prospectuses which have already been approved. If the prospectus had not been approved when such a matter came to the parties' attention then, it is suggested, the obligation under s.87A of the FSMA 2000 to provide all necessary information would require that the prospectus was amended and that this information was added to it before approval could take place. The requirement of "significance" is defined by s.87G(4) to be something which is significant in relation to the categories of "necessary information" in s.87A(2).

Criteria for the approval of a prospectus by the FSA

An application for approval of the prospectus by the FSA must be made on the **13–024** appropriate form (Form A) together with a copy of the prospectus.[60] The FSA may impose conditions before it will approve a prospectus. Such conditions must be given to the issuer by notice in writing.[61] Section 87C of the FSMA 2000 provides the timetable by reference to which the FSA must give its decision in relation to an application for the approval of a prospectus. Approval or disapproval of a prospectus must be given in writing to the issuer.[62] In either event, the notice of the decision must give the FSA's reasons for that decision[63] and inform the applicant of its right of appeal to the FSA Markets Tribunal under the 2000 Act.[64]

The required contents of a prospectus

The central principle as to the contents of a prospectus

As was considered above, a prospectus must comply with the general obligation to **13–025** make disclosure under s.87A of the FSMA 2000 to the effect that the prospectus must provide all of the "necessary information" to enable an investor to be able to make "an informed assessment" as to those securities. The Prospectus Rules then provide more detailed requirements. The building blocks in the Commission's PD Regulation and the detailed provisions of the Prospectus Rules take the following approach.[65] A base prospectus is required: that is, a vanilla form of prospectus which contains basic information which is required of all prospectuses. Then, the regulations divide between the different types of prospectus requirements for the different types of security. It is a little like a pizza: there is a generic base to the pizza just like the generic form of the base prospectus; and then depending on the type of pizza that is required there are different toppings placed on the pizza, just as different types of security issue require different types of information to be provided to supplement the base prospectus.

---

[60] Prospectus Rules, para.3.1.1R.
[61] Financial Services and Markets Act 2000 s.87J.
[62] Financial Services and Markets Act 2000 s.87D(1), and (2) and (4) respectively.
[63] Financial Services and Markets Act 2000 s.87D(3).
[64] Financial Services and Markets Act 2000 s.87D(5).
[65] Prospectus Rules, para.2.2.10: PD Regulation, art.25.2.

Appendix 3 to the FSA Prospectus Rules then contains a large amount of material divided between schedules of required minimum information, and building blocks containing additional information required for different types of issue. The lists of information which must be provided are far too long to be reproduced here, but can be viewed on the FSA's web site.[66] In essence, those preparing the prospectus are given a large number of "headings" under which they must provide information which must comply with the general duty of disclosure in s.87A, as discussed above.

The general obligation to obey the Prospectus Rules

13–026 There is a general obligation imposed on all persons to whom any individual rule is specified as being applicable to obey that rule.[67] Further to s.91(1A) of FSMA 2000, any contravention of the listing rules opens an issuer or any persons offering securities for sale to the public or seeking their admission to a regulated market up to a penalty from the FSA if there has been either a contravention of Pt 6 of FSMA 2000 generally, or a contravention of the prospectus rules, or a contravention of the transparency rules. Penalties may also be imposed on directors of the perpetrator if the FSA considers it to be appropriate.[68] In place of financial penalties, the FSA may instead issue a statement of censure.[69]

TRANSPARENCY OBLIGATIONS

Introduction

13–027 The purpose of transparency regulation is to ensure that the investing public has information about the control of voting rights in a company and consequently that the investing public is aware of any hidden ownership or control of that company. Consequently, the ownership and control of the company is said to become transparent. This species of regulation was created by the Transparency Obligations Directive,[70] which was implemented in the UK by means of Pt 43 of the CA 2006 and by means of the "Disclosure and Transparency Rules" ("DTR", which forms part of the *FSA Handbook*). In essence, transparency obligations impose continuing obligations on the issuers of securities traded on regulated markets to provide certain types of information to investors about those securities once those securities have been issued. Obligations are also imposed on the professional advisors and directors of those issuers, and on shareholders. Breach of these provisions which causes loss creates a liability to compensate that loss further to s.90A of the FSMA 2000.

---

[66] *http://www.fsa.gov.uk* [accessed May 30, 2010].
[67] Prospectus Rules, para.1.1.3R.
[68] Financial Services and Markets Act 2000 s.91(2).
[69] Financial Services and Markets Act 2000 s.91(3).
[70] Directive 2004/109/EC. This directive has been referred to as the "Transparency Directive" for some time in the literature but the Companies Act 2006 refers to this directive as the "Transparency Obligations Directive".

The scope of the transparency regulations

The Disclosure and Transparency Rules relate to dealings on "regulated markets" **13–028**
generally, rather than simply admission to listing on the Official List.[71] The term
"regulated market" is defined as being:[72]

">... a multilateral system operated and/or managed by a market operator,
which brings together or facilitates the bringing together of multiple third party
buying and selling interests in financial instruments—in the system and in
accordance with non discretionary rules—in a way that results in a contract in
accordance with the provisions of Title II [of the Directive]."

The transparency rules extend to cover not only people who hold shares but also
"persons who hold comparable instruments".[73] The term "comparable instruments" is qualified by s.89F(1)(c) of FSMA 2000 which refers to an "article 13
instrument". The term "article 13 instrument" refers to article 13 of the
Transparency Obligations Directive. There is a code in the Directive relating to
people who hold financial instruments which, although not vote-carrying shares,
grant rights equivalent to such shares which is set out principally in new ss.89B
through 89E of the FSMA 2000. Article 13(1) of the Transparency Obligations
Directive defines such an instrument to be one which provides a person with:

"an entitlement to acquire, on such holder's own initiative alone, under a
formal agreement, shares to which voting rights are attached, already issued, of
an issuer whose shares are admitted to trading on a regulated market".

These instruments are further defined by Commission technical regulation in
similar terms. This category of instrument seems to cover bonds which are convertible into voting shares and physically-settled options to acquire shares.[74] It is not
clear whether an option to buy a share which is automatically exercisable, however,
would be an option exercisable on "such holder's own initiative", unless that
initiative includes the creation of such a contract in the first place.

The information required by the transparency regulations

The purpose of transparency regulation is to specify the types of information which **13–029**
must be provided to the marketplace. An issuer of securities must provide the
following types of information to the FSA: "voteholder information" at the date of
the Directive coming into effect, and subsequent changes in that information;

---

[71] Disclosure and Transparency Rules, 1.1.1R (as to the disclosure rules)
[72] Transparency Obligations Directive, art.4(14), as implemented by Companies Act 2006 Sch.15
   para.11.
[73] Financial Services and Markets Act 2000 s.89A(3)(b).
[74] On the legal treatment of derivatives like options, see Alastair Hudson, *The Law of Finance*
   (London: Sweet & Maxwell, 2009) Ch.43, and Alastair Hudson, *The Law on Financial Derivatives*,
   (4th edn London: Sweet & Maxwell, 2006), para.2–30 et seq. in particular.

annual and half-yearly accounts, and interim management statements as described in the Directive; information relating to the rights attaching to any and all securities; information relating to any new loans or related security interests connected to them; information as to voting rights held by the issuer in the issuer itself; information as to any proposed amendments to the issuer's constitution. Secondly, investors must provide "voteholder information" to the issuer. Thirdly, the FSA may demand information from the following types of person: the issuer; a voteholder, or a person who controls or is controlled by a voteholder; an auditor of an issuer or a voteholder; or a director of an issuer or a voteholder.

Chapter 14

LIABILITY FOR ISSUES OF SECURITIES

INTRODUCTION

This chapter considers the potential liability of various people for loss caused to **14–001** third persons by issues of securities, whether in the form of misleading statements in a prospectus or breaches of transparency obligations. The regulation governing the contents of prospectuses and the requirements of transparency regulation were considered in the previous chapter. Here we shall divide our attention between liabilities relating to prospectuses and then liabilities relating to transparency obligations. The first focus of this chapter is on the categories of people who are responsible for a prospectus, then we shall consider liability for loss caused by the contents of a prospectus at common law and then liability under s.90 of the FSMA 2000. In essence, liability for an incorrect or misleading statement in a prospectus has long given rise at common law to liability for damages under the tort of negligence. However, the introduction of s.90 of the FSMA 2000 created a further head of liability. Liability for losses caused by failure to observe transparency obligations is the sole preserve of s.90A of the FSMA 2000. Each head of liability is considered in turn.

LIABILITY FOR LOSS CAUSED BY THE CONTENTS OF A PROSPECTUS

Introduction

This section is concerned with the various heads of liability which may be **14–002** occasioned by an investor acquiring securities on the basis of a misstatement in a prospectus. First, we consider liability under the general law for the torts of negligent misrepresentation and deceit. Second, we consider liability to pay compensation under s.90 of the FSMA 2000 for incorrect or misleading statements.

Negligent misrepresentation

The traditional approach at common law to prospectuses

The case law has always taken the approach that those preparing a prospectus **14–003** relating to the issue of securities must do so with complete honesty. The nineteenth-century approach to the preparation of prospectuses was set out by Kindersley V.C. in *New Brunswick, etc., Co v Muggeridge*[1] in the following way:

> "Those who issue a prospectus, holding out to the public the great advantages which will accrue to persons who will take shares in a proposed undertaking, and inviting them to take shares on the faith of the representations therein contained, are bound to state everything with strict and scrupulous accuracy, and not only to abstain from stating as fact that which is not so, but to omit no one fact within their knowledge, the existence of which might in any degree affect the nature, or extent, or quality, of the privileges and advantages which the prospectus holds out as inducements to take shares."

This approach—that a prospectus must be prepared with "strict and scrupulous accuracy"—in the case law was approved in many subsequent cases. So, in *Central Railway of Venezuela v Kisch*,[2] Lord Chelmsford held that no misstatement nor concealment of any material facts or circumstances ought to be permitted. In his Lordship's opinion the public, who were invited by a prospectus to join in any new venture, ought to be given the same opportunity as the promoters themselves to judge everything which had a material bearing on the true character of the company's proposed undertakings. Consequently, it was held that the utmost candour ought to characterise the promoters' public statements.

It is interesting to note that the FSA Prospectus Rules take a broadly similar approach to the obligations of those preparing the prospectus to include all necessary information. It is mandatory to produce a prospectus when making an offer of securities to the public or when seeking admission of securities to listing on a regulated market, in that it is an offence not to make such a prospectus available beforehand.[3] Consequently, securities regulation now imposes positive, continuing obligations on companies as to the full disclosure of relevant information and are not limited to "strict and scrupulous accuracy" as to the things which the issuer chooses to mention in the preparation of the initial prospectus.

Negligent misstatement at common law

14–004 The principle underpinning liability in tort for negligent misrepresentation is contained in the decision in *Hedley Byrne v Heller & Partners Ltd*.[4] That principle was summarised for the purposes of negligent misrepresentations made in prospectuses by Lightman J. in *Possfund v Diamond*[5] in the following terms:

> "In 1963 the House of Lords in *Hedley Byrne v Heller & Partners Ltd*[6] established that at common law a cause of action exists enabling the recovery of

---

[1] (1860) 1 Dr. & Sm. 363 at 383.
[2] (1867) L.R. 5 H.L. 99 at 123.
[3] Financial Services and Markets Act 2000 s.85.
[4] [1963] 2 All E.R. 575, [1964] A.C. 465.
[5] *Possfund Custodian Trustee Ltd v Diamond* [1996] 2 All E.R. 774, [1996] 1 W.L.R. 1351, [1996] 2 B.C.L.C. 665, per Lightman J.
[6] [1963] 2 All E.R. 575, [1964] A.C. 465.

damages in respect of a negligent misrepresentation occasioning damage and loss where the necessary proximity exists between the representor and representee. It is clearly established (and indeed common ground on these applications) that in a case such as the present, where the defendants have put a document into more or less general circulation and there is no special relationship alleged between the plaintiffs and the defendants, foreseeability by the defendants that the plaintiffs would rely on the prospectus for the purposes of deciding whether to make after-market purchases is not sufficient to impose upon the defendant a duty of care in such a situation requires a closer relationship between representor and representee, and its imposition must be fair, just and reasonable."

There are three criteria for the imposition of a duty of care in any given situation: foreseeability of damage, proximity of relationship and reasonableness.[7]

The position was expressed in the following terms by Lord Oliver in *Caparo Industries Plc v Dickman*[8]:

"What can be deduced from the *Hedley Byrne*[9] case, therefore, is that the necessary relationship between the maker of a statement or giver of advice (the adviser) and the recipient who acts in reliance on it (the advisee) may typically be held to exist where (1) the advice is required for a purpose, whether particularly specified or generally described, which is made known, either actually or inferentially, to the adviser at the time when the advice is given, (2) the adviser knows, either actually or inferentially, that his advice will be communicated to the advisee, either specifically or as a member of an ascertainable class, in order that it should be used by the advisee for that purpose, (3) it is known, either actually or inferentially, that the advice so communicated is likely to be acted upon by the advisee for that purpose without independent inquiry and (4) it is so acted on by the advisee to his detriment. That is not, of course, to suggest that these conditions are either conclusive or exclusive, but merely that the actual decision in the case does not warrant any broader propositions."[10]

What this formulation does not take into account is a regulatory requirement under the Prospectus Rules that the statement in question was included in the prospectus and that there would be continuing obligations under those same regulations to ensure the continued accuracy of that statement. In such a circumstance, it is suggested, that the issuer must have known that the statement would be relied upon by investors in the after-market as well as initial subscribers for the securities.

Absent the provisions of financial regulation, the principle in *Hedley Byrne v Heller & Partners Ltd*[11] imposes liability under a duty of care in the following circumstances. First, one party must seek information or advice from another party

---

[7] See *Smith v Bush* [1990] 1 A.C. 861, HL at 865 per Lord Griffiths, and also *Caparo Industries Plc v Dickman* [1990] 2 A.C. 605.

[8] [1990] 2 A.C. 605.

[9] [1964] A.C. 465.

[10] [1991] 2 A.C. 605 at 638. See also Lord Bridge at 620–621 and Lord Jauncey at 659–660 (esp. at 660E "the fundamental question of the purpose").

[11] [1964] A.C. 465.

in circumstances in which the party seeking advice relies on that other party to exercise due care. It must be reasonable for the party seeking advice to rely on the other party to exercise such care and it must also be the case that the party giving the advice knows or ought to know that reliance is being placed on his skill, judgment or ability to make careful inquiry. Furthermore, the party giving the advice must not expressly disclaim responsibility for his representation.[12]

The narrow model of liability set out in Caparo v Dickman

14–005 The restrictive nature of this form of liability was affirmed by the House of Lords in *Caparo Industries Plc v Dickman*[13] in which case their Lordships stressed that the defendant's liability was limited to those whom he knew would receive the statement and would rely upon it for the purposes of a particular transaction. For that reason it was held that there was no liability in tort to purchasers of shares in the after market[14] because the prospectus had been issued in respect of the original purchase only.[15]

Caparo Industries Plc v Dickman related to a claim brought by a claimant which had acquired shares in a target company, Fidelity Plc, as part of a takeover. The claimant contended that it had relied on Fidelity's accounts for the accounting year 1983–84, which had been audited by the accountants Touche Ross and which showed a pre-tax profit of £1.3 million. After acquiring a controlling shareholding in the target company, the claimant discovered that the company's true financial position demonstrated a loss of £0.4 million. Consequently, the claimant sought to establish a breach of a duty of care in negligence on the part of the accountants when acting as the auditors of the company. The claimant argued that, as a person intending to acquire a controlling shareholding in the company, the accountants owed it a duty of care when auditing the company's accounts. Lord Bridge held that

> "[i]f a duty of care were owed so widely, it is difficult to see any reason why it should not equally extend to all who rely on the accounts in relating to other dealings with a company as lenders or merchants extending credit to the company".[16]

Therefore, it was held that on policy grounds a general duty of care ought not to be imposed on auditors in such situations.[17]

---

[12] See now *Caparo v Dickman* [1990] 2 A.C. 605 at 638, per Lord Oliver reiterating this principle. See also Lord Bridge at 620–621 and Lord Jauncey at 659–660 (esp. at 660E "the fundamental question of the purpose"). Also see *James McNaughton Papers Group Ltd v Hicks Anderson & Co (a firm)* [1991] 1 All E.R. 135, but cf. *Morgan Crucible Co Plc v Hill Samuel Bank Ltd* [1991] 1 All E.R. 148.

[13] [1990] 1 A.C. 605, HL.

[14] That is, purchasers of the securities who were not original subscribers for the shares but who acquired them subsequently in the open market.

[15] *Al-Nakib Investments (Jersey) Ltd v Longcroft* [1991] B.C.L.C. 7. See also *Morgan Crucible Co v Hill Samuel Bank Ltd* [1991] B.C.L.C. 178.

[16] [1990] 2 A.C. 605.

[17] Approving *Al Saudi Banque v Clark Pixley* [1990] Ch. 313.

As to the circumstances in which there may be liability for misstatements when making offers to the public, Lord Bridge suggested that general statements as to the condition of company would generally be unlikely to attract liability in tort on the basis that:

"The situation is entirely different where a statement is put into more or less general circulation and may foreseeably be relied on by strangers to the maker of the statement for any one of a variety of different purposes which the maker of the statement has no specific reason to anticipate."[18]

Therefore, his lordship's view was that statements put into general circulation **14–006** would be less likely to attract liability in tort because the maker of that statement could not ordinarily know the purposes to which his statement would be put to use by the claimant. On the facts of *Caparo Industries Plc v Dickman* it was recognised that an auditor's role is primarily to verify for the benefit of shareholders that the accounts constitute a true and fair view of the financial position of the company. It was therefore held that an auditor cannot also be said to be liable for the reliance which a person, even if a current shareholder, might choose to put on that auditor's report in deciding whether or not to acquire a controlling stake in the company.

Similarly, in *Al-Nakib Investments (Jersey) Ltd v Longcroft*[19] the claimants, who had acquired shares in the after-market, alleged that the prospectus and two interim reports issued by M Ltd contained misrepresentations as to the identity of the person who would be manufacturing the company's products. The defendants successfully applied to have these claims struck out, in so far as they related to purchases of the company's securities in the after-market, on the basis that they disclosed no reasonable cause of action. As to the prospectus, it was held by Mervyn Davies J. that it had been issued for a particular purpose, namely to encourage subscription for shares by a limited class of subscribers and that any duty of care in relation to its issue was directed to that specific purpose only. It had not been directed at purchases in the after-market and therefore any misrepresentation therein could not found a claim based on the tort of negligence.[20]

Different approaches to negligent misrepresentations

There are two cases which have taken a different approach on the facts in front of **14–007** them from the cases considered above. First, in *Morgan Crucible Co Plc v Hill Samuel Bank Ltd*,[21] the directors and financial advisors of the target company had

---

[18] [1990] 2 A.C. 605, [1990] 1 All E.R. 568 at 576. Approving *Scott Group v Macfarlane* [1978] 1 N.Z.L.R. 553 at 566, per Richmond P.
[19] [1990] 3 All E.R. 321.
[20] Reliance was placed on *Peek v Gurney* (1873) L.R. 6 HL 377 in which similar conclusion was reached. In this regard, Mervyn Davies J. relied, inter alia, on dicta of Lord Jauncey in *Caparo Industries Plc v Dickman* [1990] 2 A.C. 605; [1990] 1 All E.R. 568 at 607. His lordship also placed reliance on dicta of Lord Griffiths in *Smith v Eric S. Bush* [1989] 2 All E.R. 514 at 536, to similar effect.
[21] [1991] 1 All E.R. 148.

made express representations in the course of a contested takeover forecasting a 38 per cent increase in pre-tax profits at a time when an identified bidder for the company had emerged. The purpose behind these and other representations had been to induce the bidder to make a higher bid because the bidder had relied on those statements. The Court of Appeal held that there was therefore a relationship of sufficient proximity between the bidder and those who had been responsible for the statements to found a duty of care in negligence.

Second, in *Possfund Custodian Trustee Ltd v Diamond*[22] there had been a placement of shares on the Unlisted Securities Market[23] and subsequent purchases of those shares after the placement in the after-market. The prospectus prepared in relation to the initial placement greatly understated the issuer's liabilities to pay extra premiums to syndicates at the Lloyds of London insurance market. The company subsequently went into receivership due, in no small measure, to the burden of paying those extra premiums. Purchasers of those shares in the after-market contended that they had relied on those statements made in the prospectus, that it had been reasonable for them to rely on the prospectus in that way in making their purchases, and that those responsible for the prospectus had breached a duty of care owed to purchasers of the shares. Lightman J. held that the purpose of a prospectus at common law and under statute in English law had always been:[24]

"... to provide the necessary information to enable an investor to make an informed decision whether to accept the offer thereby made to take share on the proposed allotment, but not a decision whether to make after-market purchases."

Further, his Lordship held that:

"What is significant is that the courts have since 1873 (before any legislation) recognised a duty of care in case of prospectuses when there is a sufficient direct connection between those responsible for the prospectuses and the party acting in reliance (see *Peek v Gurney*), and the plaintiffs' claim may be recognised as merely an application of this established principle in a new fact situation . . . I can find nothing in the authorities or textbooks which precludes the finding of such a duty and at least some potential support in them."

14–008 Therefore, Lightman J. refused to strike out this claim on the basis that in these circumstances the investors had been justified in relying on the statements made in the prospectus when making their investment decisions. It was held that such a duty of care would exist if the subsequent purchaser could show the following things: that he relied reasonably on the prospectus; that he reasonably believed that the defendant intended him to act on them; and that there was a sufficiently direct connection between the parties to make such a duty fair, just and reasonable. This in effect reverses the burden in *Caparo* in that all that needs to be

---

[22] [1996] 2 All E.R. 774.
[23] The forerunner of the Alternative Investment Market.
[24] [1996] 2 All E.R. 774 at 787.

shown is that it was reasonable for the buyer to rely on the statement and not that the representor must have realised that the claimant was within the class of people who would be relying on it.

It is suggested that the effect of the FSA Prospectus Rules, considered in the previous chapter, is that the entire investing public is necessarily within the cognisance of any person involved in the preparation of a prospectus for an offer of securities to the public. Consequently, any loss caused by a negligent misstatement in such a prospectus must now be actionable in tort. Consequently, the precise ratio decidendi of the decision of the House of Lords in *Caparo v Dickman* has now been superseded in relation to issues of securities falling within s.85 of the FSMA 2000 because the makers of representations in prospectuses may not necessarily be able to hide behind a claim that their statements were intended to be made only to a limited class of buyers (so as to avoid liability to the marketplace at large).

Negligent misrepresentation under statute

Damages in lieu of rescission may be recovered in England and Wales under **14–009** section 2(2) of the Misrepresentation Act 1967. That provision states that where a person has entered into a contract after a misrepresentation made to him otherwise than fraudulently, and provided he would be entitled to rescind that contract, then the court may award damages in lieu of rescission if it appears to the court that it would be equitable to do so. Damages for negligent misrepresentation may be recovered from the company under s.2(1) of the Misrepresentation Act 1967, which provides that where a person has entered into a contract after a misrepresentation made to him by another party thereto and as a result has suffered loss, then the representor is liable in damages unless he proves that on reasonable grounds he believed up to the time when the contract was made that the representation was true.[25]

Fraudulent misrepresentation

The basis of the liability for fraudulent misrepresentation in relation to a prospectus

Promoters, directors, experts or the persons making an offer for sale, are liable for **14–010** fraud if it can be shown that they signed, or authorised the issue of, a prospectus containing a false statement which they did not honestly believe to be true (or if they were reckless as to its truth or falsity)[26] with the intention that another person should act upon it, and that he acted on it to his detriment. The test is subjective, which means that the court must ask: did he honestly believe the statement to be true according to its meaning as understood *by him*, albeit erroneously, when it was made.[27]

---

[25] A similar provision to s.2(1) applies in Scotland under s.10(1) of the Law Reform (Miscellaneous Provisions)(Scotland) Act 1985.
[26] *Derry v Peek* (1889) 14 App. Cas. 337 at 374, per Lord Herschell.
[27] *Akerhielm v De Mare* [1959] A.C. 789, PC.

The measure of damages for fraudulent misrepresentation

14-011 The measure of damages for fraud is prima facie the difference between the actual value of the shares at the time of allotment and the sum paid for them.[28] The plaintiff is entitled to recover all the actual damage directly flowing from the fraudulent misrepresentation.[29] This principle means that in some cases the value as at the date of allotment will not be applied, for example where the plaintiff is locked into the shares by reason of the fraud.[30] It is not an action for breach of contract, however, and therefore no damages in respect of prospective gains can be recovered, merely the out-of-pocket loss.

The House of Lords in *Smith New Court Securities Ltd v Scrimgeour Vickers (Asset Management) Ltd*[31] was required to consider the measure of damages available for fraudulent misrepresentation, and particularly the extent to which the size of the loss suffered by the claimant had been foreseeable. In that case there had been two entirely unrelated frauds. The first fraud related to deliberately misleading information given to the claimant by the defendant concerning the number of bids already acquired for those shares. The second fraud was unrelated to the first although the discovery of the second fraud brought the first fraud to light. The value of the shares had fallen sharply on the discovery of the second fraud. The question arose whether the quantum of damages should reflect the value after the discovery of the second fraud or irrespective of that fraud. Lord Browne-Wilkinson set out seven principles which are to inform decisions in this area:[32]

> "(1) The defendant is bound to make reparation for all the damage directly flowing from the transaction.
>
> (2) Although such damage need not have been foreseeable, it must have been directly caused by the transaction.
>
> (3) In assessing such damage, the plaintiff is entitled to recover by way of damages the full price paid by him, but he must give credit for any benefits which he has received as a result of the transaction.
>
> (4) As a general rule, the benefits received by him include the market value of the property acquired as at the date of acquisition; but such general rule is not to be inflexibly applied where to do so would prevent him obtaining full compensation for the wrong suffered.
>
> (5) Although the circumstances in which the general rule should not apply cannot be comprehensively stated, it will normally not apply where either (a) the misrepresentation has continued to operate after the date of the acquisition of the asset so as to induce the plaintiff to retain the asset or (b) the circumstances of the case are such that the plaintiff is, by reason of the fraud, locked into the property.

---

[28] *McConnel v Wright* (1903) 1 Ch. 546, CA; *Davidson v Tulloch* (1860) 3 Macq. 783; 22 D. HL 7.

[29] *Doyle v Olby (Ironmongers) Ltd* [1969] 2 Q.B. 158, CA.

[30] *Smith New Court Securities Ltd v Scrimgeour Vickers (Asset Management) Ltd* [1997] 1 B.C.L.C. 350, HL.

[31] [1996] 4 All E.R. 769.

[32] [1996] 4 All E.R. 769 at 778–779, per Lord Browne-Wilkinson.

(6) In addition, the plaintiff is entitled to recover consequential losses caused by the transaction.

(7) The plaintiff must take all reasonable steps to mitigate his loss once he has discovered the fraud."

It was held that, while there was a duty on the claimant to mitigate his loss, where the investments had been acquired in this case as part of a long-term investment strategy there was no obligation on the claimant to sell the shares immediately where that would not have been a sensible strategy because of the low price which could have been acquired for those shares after the second fraud had been discovered. In any event, the claimant is entitled to recover the difference between the price at which the shares were acquired and the real value of those shares. Therefore, the claimant was entitled to recover the loss suffered even though the added loss caused by the discovery of the second fraud had not been foreseeable.

Rescission on grounds of misrepresentation

In order to obtain rescission of a contract of allotment of shares on the ground that **14–012** it was induced by misrepresentation, the allottee must prove, first, a material false statement of fact which, second, induced him to subscribe.

Material false statement of fact

It is not sufficient to claim rescission of a contract of allotment to demonstrate **14–013** that there was some mistake made in the prospectus or in some other statement. First, then, the statement must have been an assertion of a fact and not merely a statement of opinion.[33] Therefore, a statement that the property of the company is worth a certain sum of money, or that the profits are expected to reach a certain figure, is only opinion and gives no right to rescission, except where it can be proved that the maker of the statement did not hold the opinion. Statements, on the other hand, such as "the surplus assets, as appear by the last balance sheet, amount to upwards of £10,000"[34] and that certain persons have agreed to be directors,[35] are all assertions of fact and, if false, will give rise to a right to rescission. The second requirement is that the statement be material to the investor's decision to invest and not a statement as to a peripheral matter. On the authorities it has been held that a representation in a prospectus to the effect that the members of the company were comprised of "a large number of gentlemen in the trade and others", when only a dozen out of a total membership of 55 were in fact in the trade, was not a material misrepresentation.[36] Statements as to the company's assets or the condition of its accounts would be material representations.[37]

---

[33] *Liverpool Palace of Varieties Ltd v Miller* (1896) 4 S.L.T. 153 (OH).
[34] *London and Staffordshire Fire Insurance Co, Re* (1883) 25 Ch.D. 149.
[35] *Scottish Petroleum Co, Re* (1883) 23 Ch.D. 413, CA; *Blakiston v London and Scottish Banking, etc. Corp Ltd* (1894) 21 R. 417; contract *Chambers v Edinburgh, etc. Aerated Bread Co Ltd* (1891) 18 R. 1039.
[36] *City of Edinburgh Brewery Co Ltd v Gibson's Trustee* (1869) 7 M. 886.
[37] *London and Staffordshire Fire Insurance Co, Re* (1883) 25 Ch.D. 149.

Where the facts are not equally well known to both side a statement of opinion by one who should know the facts often implies a statement of fact, i.e. that there are reasonable grounds for his opinion, and there is misrepresentation of fact if it can be proved that he could not as a reasonable man honestly have had the opinion.[38] Again, a statement of intention does not amount to a representation of fact unless it can be proved that the alleged intention never existed.[39]

If a prospectus refers to a report which contains inaccurate statements of fact, then the contract can be rescinded if the company has vouched for the accuracy of the report, but otherwise it cannot. Thus, if the company employs an accountant to go through the books and make a report, and then sets out the report in a prospectus, it will not be liable for an inaccuracy in the report.[40] But if the company makes statements of its own, although they are expressed to be based upon a report, it will be liable for an inaccuracy unless in clear and unambiguous terms it has warned intending applicants that it does not vouch for the accuracy of the report, or of any statement based on it. So, in *Pacaya Rubber and Produce Co Ltd, Re*[41] the prospectus contained extracts from a report of a Peruvian expert as to the condition of a rubber estate which the company sought to acquire. It was held that these extracts from the report contained in the prospectus formed the basis of the contract. On the basis that the company had not distanced itself from the report nor suggested that it did not vouch for the accuracy of the report, the company was taken to have contracted on the basis of the contents of the report. Therefore, the contracts of allotment could be rescinded.

Non-disclosure of a material fact amounts to misrepresentation if the omission renders that which is stated misleading. It has been held[42] that "[i]t is not that the omission of material facts is an independent ground for rescission, but the omission must be of such a nature as to make the statement actually made misleading."[43]

The allottee must have been induced to subscribe by the false statement

14–014 Whether or not an allottee was induced to subscribe by reason of the misrepresentation is a question of fact depending on the circumstances of each case. It is not sufficient that the prospectus has been widely advertised in the locality if there is proof that the applicant relied, not on the prospectus, but on independent advice.[44] He is entitled to rely upon the prospectus, however, and is not bound to verify the statements it contains. Where, therefore, a prospectus simply gave information as to the dates of and parties to contracts, and stated where they could be inspected, without indicating that they were material contracts, the omission of the applicant to inspect them did not fix him with notice of their contents.[45] The false statement need not

[38] *Smith v Land, etc. Corp* (1884) 28 Ch.D. 7 at 15, per Bowen L.J.
[39] *Edgington v Fitzmaurice* (1885) 29 Ch.D. 459, CA.
[40] *Bentley & Co v Black* (1893) 9 T.L.R. 580, CA.
[41] [1914] 1 Ch. 542. See also *Mair v Rio Grande Rubber Estates Ltd* (1913) S.C. HL 74.
[42] *McKeown v Boudard Peveril Gear Co Ltd* (1896) 74 L.T. 712 at 713, per Rigby L.J.
[43] *Coles v White City (Manchester) Greyhound Assn Ltd* (1929) 48 T.L.R. 230, CA.
[44] *M'Morland's Trustees v Fraser* (1896) 24 R. 65.
[45] *Aaron's Reefs Ltd v Twiss* [1896] A.C. 273.

have been the decisive factor inducing the claimant to enter into the contract. It is enough that it was one of the contributory causes.[46] Rescission enables the allottee to recover what he paid for the shares or debentures, plus interest.

Loss of the right to rescind

The right to rescind is lost in four circumstances. First, if, after discovering the **14–015** misrepresentation, the allottee performs an act which shows that he elects to retain the shares and so affirms the contract (for example, if he attends and votes at general meetings).[47] Second, if he fails to act within a reasonable time of discovering the true facts. The right to rescind must be exercised promptly if the company is a going concern, and even a delay of a fortnight has been held to be too long.[48] Third, if restitution is impossible,[49] for example because he has sold the shares. Fourth, if the company goes into liquidation.[50]

Compensation under section 90 of the FSMA 2000

The basis of the right to compensation under section 90 FSMA 2000

Section 90 of the FSMA 2000 creates a means of acquiring compensation for **14–016** defects in a prospectus which is not stated as being subject to all of the requirements of proximity, causation and foreseeability which arise in the common law, particularly on the case law decided before the creation of the Prospectus Rules. Section 90(1) of the FSMA 2000 provides that:

"Any person responsible for [a prospectus] is liable to pay compensation to a person who has

(a) acquired securities to which the [prospectus] apply; and
(b) suffered loss in respect of them as a result of

(i) any untrue or misleading statement in the [prospectus];
(ii) or the omission from the [prospectus] of any matter required to be included by [the duties of disclosure in] section [*87A or 87B*]".[51]

There are three heads of liability resulting from this provision. The first head of liability relates to untrue statements. It is not a requirement of the statutory language that there must have been fraud or any other intention to deceive; rather, the statement made must have been untrue. The second head of liability relates to

---

[46] *Edgington v Fitzmaurice* (1885) 29 Ch.D. 459, CA.
[47] *Sharpley v South and East Coast Ry. Co* (1876) 2 Ch.D. 663, CA.
[48] See *Scottish Petroleum Co, Re* (1883) 23 Ch.D. 413, CA.
[49] *Western Bank v Addie* (1867) 5 M. HL 80.
[50] *Oakes v Turquand* (1867) L.R. 2 HL 325; *Western Bank v Addie* (1867) 5 M. HL 80; *Houldsworth v City of Glasgow Bank* (1880) 7 R. HL 53; (1880) 5 App. Cas. 317.
[51] Financial Services and Markets Act 2000 s.90(1). Words in square brackets added by the author to reflect Financial Services and Markets Act 2000 s.90(11)(a) and the fact that this discussion focuses on prospectuses, and not the limited regime relating to listing particulars for offers only to expert investors.

misleading statements made in a prospectus. The element of causation in the statute is satisfied if the loss is "a result of" the misleading statement. It is not a requirement of the statutory language that there has been fraud or any other intention to deceive; rather, the statement made must have misled the claimant. As above, it is duty of the person responsible for the prospectus to ensure that all statements made in the prospectus or any omissions made from the prospectus are not likely to be misleading. The effect of this provision is therefore to place an implied obligation on those responsible for the contents of a prospectus not to make any misleading statements in that prospectus, whether advertently or inadvertently. The third head of liability relates to the omission of material which would otherwise be required by the duty of disclosure in s.87A of the FSMA 2000, as was discussed above. The duty of disclosure is rooted in the requirement that the prospectus must contain the "necessary information" before it can be approved by the FSA.

Persons responsible for the contents of a prospectus

14-017 There is an issue, first, as to the people who are responsible for the contents of the prospectus under the securities regulations. The definition of the persons responsible for the contents of a prospectus or of a supplementary prospectus are set out in Ch.5 of the FSA Prospectus Rules. In relation to shares (encompassed within the term "equity securities" in the regulations), the persons responsible for the prospectus are[52]: the issuer; directors and those authorising themselves to be named as responsible for the prospectus; any other person who accepts responsibility for the prospectus; in relation to an offer, each person who is a director of a body corporate making an offer of securities; in relation to applications for admission to trading, each person who is a director of a body corporate making an offer of securities; and other persons who have authorised the contents of the prospectus. In relation to securities which are not equity securities (principally bonds and securitised derivatives), the persons responsible for the prospectus are[53]: the issuer; anyone who accepts and is stated in the prospectus as accepting responsibility for the prospectus; any other person who is the offeror of the securities; any person who requests an admission to trading of transferable securities; any guarantor for the issue in relation to information about that guarantee; and any other person who has authorised the contents of the prospectus. That someone has given advice in a professional capacity about the contents of a prospectus does not make that person responsible for the contents of the prospectus in itself[54]; unless they consent to being so named or they authorise those contents of the prospectus which are the subject of the action, and even then they are liable only to the extent that they have agreed to be so liable.[55]

Defences to liability under section 90

14-018 In Sch.10 to the FSMA 2000 there are five possible defences to a claim under s.90. The first defence applies when the defendant believed in the truth of the statement

[52] Prospectus Rules, 5.5.3R.
[53] Prospectus Rules, 5.5.4R.
[54] Prospectus Rules, 5.5.9R.
[55] Prospectus Rules, 5.5.8R.

that was made in the prospectus.[56] The second defence applies when the statement was made by an expert, when the statement is included in a prospectus or a supplementary prospectus with that expert's consent, and when it is stated in that document that the statement was included as such.[57] The third defence requires the publication, or the taking of reasonable steps to secure publication, of a correction.[58] The fourth defence requires the taking of all reasonable steps to secure the publication of a correction of a statement made by an expert.[59] The fifth defence applies when the statement was made by an official person or contained in a public, official document, provided that the statement was accurately and fairly reproduced.[60] The sixth defence applies if the court is satisfied that the investor acquired the securities with knowledge that the statement was incorrect, and therefore that the investor was not misled by it.[61]

The persons who can bring a claim under section 90 FSMA 2000

The category of potential claimants under s.90 includes any person who has **14–019** acquired or who has contracted to acquire securities or any interest in some of the securities to which the defective prospectus relates.[62] Further that person must have suffered a loss in respect of the securities; and the loss must have been suffered as a result of the relevant untrue or misleading statement or omission.

The interpretation of section 90 of FSMA 2000 in the light of the decided cases

The current policy underpinning the regulation of the preparation of prospectuses **14–020** is predicated on the need to provide as much information in an accurate fashion as investors could reasonably require in making their investment decisions. This was effectively the approach of the cases which comprised the so-called "golden legacy" in the case law,[63] although without the giant architecture of positive obligations created by FSA regulation in the form of continuing obligations, conduct of business rules and so forth. The golden legacy itself, in relation to the obligations of those who issued prospectuses, was described by Kindersley V.C. in *New Brunswick, etc. Co v Muggeridge*[64] as requiring that those responsible for the prospectus

"are bound to state everything with strict and scrupulous accuracy, and not only to abstain from stating as fact that which is not so, but to omit no one fact

---

[56] Financial Services and Markets Act 2000 Sch.10, para.1.
[57] Financial Services and Markets Act 2000 Sch.10, para.2(1).
[58] Financial Services and Markets Act 2000 Sch.10, para.3.
[59] Financial Services and Markets Act 2000 Sch.10 para.2(3), and para.4.
[60] Financial Services and Markets Act 2000 Sch.10, para.5.
[61] Financial Services and Markets Act 2000 Sch.10, para.6.
[62] Financial Services and Markets Act 2000 s.90(7).
[63] When giving judgment in *Henderson v Lacon* (1867) L.R. 5 Eq. 249 at 262, Page-Wood V.C. described these common law principles as being a "golden legacy".
[64] (1860) 1 Dr. & Sm. 363 at 383.

within their knowledge, the existence of which might in any degree affect the nature, or extent, or quality, of the privileges and advantages which the prospectus holds out as inducements to take shares."

In the light of the Prospectus Directive and of the Prospectus Rules of 2005[65] this conceptualisation of the golden legacy seems unremarkable. The key focus of securities regulation at the time of writing is in the public availability of information. As a result, where securities regulations—principally the prospectus rules—apply, then the issuers and people responsible for that prospectus know that that prospectus will be published. Indeed, its publication is a requirement of s.85 FSMA 2000 whether securities are to be offered to the public or admitted to trading on a regulated market. Therefore, those "people responsible" for the prospectus know that any potential investor—whether a subscriber, or a placee, or a purchaser in the after-market—will consult and rely on the statements made in that prospectus. Consequently, all potential investors must be within the issuer's contemplation when the prospectus is prepared. This issue is considered in detail in Alastair Hudson, *Securities Law*.[66]

MISLEADING STATEMENTS IN THE DISCHARGE OF TRANSPARENCY OBLIGATIONS

14–021 Section 90A of the FSMA 2000 provides for compensation to be paid in relation to untrue or misleading statements contained in, or in relation to omissions from, the annual financial reports, the half-yearly financial reports, or interim management statements which are required to be published by arts 4, 5 and 6 of the Transparency Obligations Directive, as discussed in Ch.40. Thus s.90A in effect extends the effect of s.90 to the new dimension which is added to securities regulation by the Transparency Obligations Directive. Section 90A(2), introduced to the bill in its final stages, makes clear that the Act relates only to securities traded on regulated markets. Section 90A of FSMA 2000 provides that the issuer of securities will be liable to "pay compensation" to any person who has both

> "(a) acquired such[67] securities issued by it, and
> (b) suffered loss in respect of them as a result of—
>
>> (i) any untrue or misleading statement in a publication to which this section applies, or
>> (ii) the omission from any such publication of any matter required to be included in it."[68]

There is one important caveat to the issuer's liability, however. As provided in s.90A(4):

[65] SI 2005/1433.
[66] Alastair Hudson, *Securities Law* (London: Sweet & Maxwell, 2008), Ch.23.
[67] The reference to "such securities" seems to be a reference to the particular securities which have been issued and in relation to which the loss must have been suffered.
[68] Financial Services and Markets Act 2000 s.90A(3).

"The issuer is so liable only if a person discharging managerial responsibilities within the issuer in relation to the publication—

(a) knew the statement to be untrue or misleading or was reckless as to whether it was untrue or misleading, or
(b) knew the omission to be dishonest concealment of a material fact."[69]

Therefore, the basis of liability is predicated, first, on the making of an untrue or misleading statement and, secondly, also the requisite knowledge of someone discharging managerial responsibilities within the issuer. It is provided in s.90A(6) of FSMA 2000 that the defendant issuer is not to be liable for "any other liability than that provided for" by the preceding provisions of s.90A of FSMA 2000.[70]

---

[69] Financial Services and Markets Act 2000 s.90A(4).
[70] Financial Services and Markets Act 2000 s.90A(6).

Chapter 15

LISTED SECURITIES

INTRODUCTION

The regulation of listed securities

15–001 The Official List of securities is the principal market for the securities of public limited companies which are offered for sale to the public.[1] In essence, the largest public companies will seek admission to listing on the Official List, and so make themselves subject to the demanding requirements of the FSA Listing Rules (referred to here as "the Listing Rules") as a result, because there is perceived to be a marketing advantage for companies of that type to have their shares admitted to the Official List. The types of securities on this list include shares, bonds, convertible bonds, warrants, securitised derivatives, and other securities as discussed in this chapter, all of which are required to be transferable so that they can be bought and sold. These securities are also admitted to trading on a market such as the London Stock Exchange's "Main Market" in the United Kingdom because it is a requirement of listing that those securities be available on such a regulated market. This chapter considers three elements of the Listing Rules in particular: the interpretative principles which underpin the regulation of the Official List maintained by the FSA; the regulations governing admission to listing; and the regulations governing the maintenance of listing. This chapter therefore focuses specifically on so-called "listed securities", which are securities which have been admitted to the Official List.

The statutory regime governing the official listing of securities is contained in Pt 6 of the FSMA 2000, comprising ss.72–103 (as amended and added to over time). In this context it is the EC Consolidated Admission and Reporting Directive which is being implemented by Pt 6 of the FSMA 2000 and by the Listing Rules. The Official List in the United Kingdom is the list maintained by the "competent authority" under the EC securities directives for the purposes of Pt 6. The FSA is acting specifically in its role as the UK Listing Authority ("UKLA") which is the competent authority in this context. The FSA therefore has two capacities in this

---

[1] There are other markets, such as the London Stock Exchange's Alternative Investment Market ("AIM") but that market deals in the securities of smaller public companies: as discussed in Alastair Hudson, *Securities Law* (London: Sweet & Maxwell, 2008), Ch.19. There are also on-line markets. However, the market in securities which have been admitted to the Official List ("listed securities") remains the market for the most significant corporate securities admitted to trading in the UK.

context: first as the general financial services regulator in the United Kingdom and secondly, more specifically, as the authority responsible for the maintenance of the Official List in the UK. It is also responsible for the creation of Listing Rules. The Official List is regulated by means of the Listing Rules.

Importantly, if securities are offered to the public or if securities are to be admitted to trading on a regulated market, then the issuing company must comply with the prospectus rules and the disclosure and transparency rules considered in Ch.13; whereas the Listing Rules constitute a further tier of regulations with which a company must comply only if it chooses to seek the admission of its securities to the Official List, as considered in this chapter. The principal advantage of admission of securities to the Official List is the confidence which this process inculcates in investors that the issuing company has complied with the stringent demands of the Listing Rules. Therefore, admission to the Official List is thought to have a marketing advantage even though the cost of compliance with the Listing Rules is generally considered to be high in comparison with compliance only with the general prospectus rules and the disclosure and transparency rules which were considered in Ch.13. Admission to the Official List has important consequences for the issuer in that the issuer will be subject to the continuing obligations contained in the listing rules which are imposed on issuers whose securities are listed. The procedure for admission to listing is considered below.

Statutory obligations on the FSA's performance of its duties

Section 73 of the FSMA 2000 provides that the FSA must itself observe six regu- **15–002** latory principles when acting as the UKLA and when "determining the general policy and principles by reference to which it performs particular functions" under Pt 6 of the FSMA 2000.[2] First, the FSA bears a duty of economic efficiency in relation to the use of its own resources.[3] Secondly, the FSA must ensure that a burden or restriction which is imposed on a person should be proportionate to the benefits which are expected to accrue from it.[4] Thirdly, when exercising its powers in relation to the admission of securities to listing, the FSA must consider "the desirability of facilitating innovation".[5] Fourthly, the FSA must have regard to "the international character of capital markets and the desirability of maintaining the competitive position of the United Kingdom".[6] Fifthly, the FSA must consider "the need to minimise the adverse effects on competition of anything done in the discharge of those functions".[7] Sixthly, the FSA must have regard to "the desirability of facilitating competition in relation to listed securities and in relation to financial instruments which have otherwise been admitted to trading on a regulated market or for which a request for admission to trading on such a market has been made."[8]

---

[2] Financial Services and Markets Act 2000 s.73(2).
[3] Financial Services and Markets Act 2000 s.73(1)(a).
[4] Financial Services and Markets Act 2000 s.73(1)(b).
[5] Financial Services and Markets Act 2000 s.73(1)(c); as supplied by Financial Services and Markets Act 2000 (Market Abuse) Regulations 2005 (SI 2005/381), reg.4, Sch.1, para.1(1), (2).
[6] Financial Services and Markets Act 2000 s.73(1)(d).
[7] Financial Services and Markets Act 2000 s.73(1)(e).
[8] Financial Services and Markets Act 2000 s.73(1)(f); as supplied by Financial Services and Markets Act 2000 (Market Abuse) Regulations 2005 (SI 2005/381), reg.4, Sch.1, para.1(1), (3).

The Listing Principles

15–003 The Listing Rules are governed by a set of over-arching principles known as the "Listing Principles". These are principles which govern the manner in which issuers and their professional advisors are required to act when complying with the Listing Rules and when dealing with the competent authority. The listing rules provide that[9]:

> "The purpose of the Listing Principles is to ensure that listed companies pay due regard to the fundamental role they play in maintaining market confidence and ensuring fair and orderly markets."

Further, the listing rules provide that[10]:

> "The Listing Principles are designed to assist listed companies in identifying their obligations and responsibilities under the listing rules and the disclosure rules and transparency rules."

The obligations imposed on issuers by the Listing Principles require: that the company's directors understand their obligations; that the issuer maintains adequate procedures, systems and controls; that the issuer conduct its activities in relation to the Listing Rules with integrity; that information is communicated in a way that avoids the creation or continuation of a false market in listed equity securities; that the issuer ensures the equal treatment of all shareholders; and that the issuer conducts its dealings with the FSA in an open and co-operative manner. The Listing Rules are therefore to be interpreted in the accordance with these general principles.

The Model Code

15–004 A key part of securities regulation is the prevention of market abuse: principally the prevention of the abuse of inside information relating to securities. The Model Code is concerned with corporate governance within listed companies as it relates to the misuse of inside information. As such it is that part of the Listing Rules which seeks to prevent market abuse. Briefly put, during prohibited periods in relation to a company's securities, any insider (such as a person discharging management responsibilities or an employee in an applicable role) who wishes to deal in that company's securities must seek clearance under the procedure identified in the rules. The aim is not only to prevent actual abuse but also to prevent the suspicion of abuse, so as to preserve confidence in the market for those securities.

Corporate governance

15–005 The Listing Rules provide that the annual financial report of a listed company must include a statement as to the extent of that company's compliance with the

---

[9] Listing Rules, 7.1.2G. The Listing Rules are subject to periodic amendment. This discussion refers to that version of the Listing Rules introduced after the last comprehensive revision in 2007.
[10] Listing Rules, 7.1.3G.

Combined Code on Corporate Governance.[11] Also to be included with this statement is a further statement as to whether or not the listed company has complied with the Combined Code throughout the accounting period or whether there are any provisions in relation to which there has not been compliance.

The power of UKLA to modify or dispense with its rules

The FSA, acting as the UKLA, has the power[12] to modify or dispense with individual **15–006** listing rules where it considers it to be appropriate to do so on an application from a company. The FSA may dispense with any of its rules on application by a company.[13] This power to waive rules is subject to the FSMA 2000 and to the EC Securities Directives.[14] The precise form of the waiver which the FSA may grant is either a "modification" or a "dispensation" such that an issuer may have particular obligations merely modified or alternatively may have particular modifications dispensed with altogether.[15] There is nothing in the listing rules which stipulates precisely who must make the application, although it is envisaged in the rules that either the issuer or a sponsor may make an application.[16] Where it is the issuer or a sponsor who has made an application or been granted a waiver, there is a continuing obligation imposed on that person to inform the FSA "immediately" of any "matter which is material to the relevance or appropriateness of the dispensation or modification".[17]

One of the common reasons for seeking a modification or dispensation is that the issuing company is in "severe financial difficulty". In the event that that is the reason for seeking the modification or dispensation, the issuing company is expected to comply with section 10.8 of the Listing Rules[18] which deals, inter alia, with dispensations generally for companies in severe financial difficulty from requirements of providing information to the public, or from the need to seek shareholder approval for its actions in an extraordinary general meeting, in either event due to pressures of time which make such actions impossible in the circumstances.

ADMISSION TO LISTING

Sources of law on admission to listing

This section considers the process of seeking admission of securities to listing. **15–007** There are three principal sources of regulation in this area: the EC Consolidated Admission and Reporting Directive 2001 ("CARD"), which is the core EC directive relating to the admission of securities to listing; the FSMA 2000; and the FSA Listing Rules, part of the *FSA Handbook*.[19]

---

[11] Listing Rules, para.9.8.6(5)R.
[12] Listing Rules, para.1.2.2R.
[13] Listing Rules, para.1.2.2R.
[14] Listing Rules, para.1.2.1R.
[15] Listing Rules, para.1.2.1R.
[16] Listing Rules, para.1.2.1(3)R.
[17] Listing Rules, para.1.2.1(3)R.
[18] Listing Rules, para.1.2.4G.
[19] These sources are considered in detail in Alastair Hudson, *The Law of Finance* (London: Sweet & Maxwell, 2009), Ch.37.

The Consolidated Admission and Reporting Directive 2001

15–008 The CARD[20] consolidated four earlier "listing directives" and has been amended by the Prospectus Directive and the Transparency Obligations Directive. CARD is limited to "admission to official listing on a stock exchange",[21] as opposed to private offerings or issues of securities in general terms outside the official list. CARD takes account of "present differences in the structures of securities markets in Member States"[22] of the EU so as to enable member states to take into account "any specific situations with which they may be confronted".[23] Furthermore, "co-ordination should first be limited to the establishment of minimum conditions"[24] with the result that the regulations of each Member State may differ beyond those minimum conditions. The purpose is to enable approvals to be passported in time between Member States. The directive is concerned to achieve "closer alignment" of national regulatory rules,[25] through a "first step" which in time led to the Prospectus Directive and the Transparency Directive. One of the principal misalignments between different national systems of securities regulations are the "safeguards" for investor protection in those different codes. CARD is intended to eliminate them by "coordinating the [various national] rules and regulations without necessarily making them completely uniform".[26]

There are two underlying policies in CARD beyond the coordination of laws. First, mutual recognition in all Member States of any authorised listing of securities in the issuer's home Member State.[27] This is the "passport" granted to such securities which enables a security admitted to listing in one Member State to be admitted to listing as a result in any other Member State. The second objective is "to ensure that sufficient information is provided for investors".[28] The provision of information is to be achieved by making accounts available, principally by means of making annual reports and other information available to investors, with some exceptions in relation to debentures.

There were three results which were expected to flow from the implementation of CARD. First, the improvement of investor protection. This was intended principally to arise from issuers being required to make information available to investors. Secondly, an increase in investor confidence, principally by virtue of requiring issuers of listed securities to bear continuing obligations to provide identified classes of information to the investing public and so reassuring investors about the efficacy of the information available to them. Thirdly, ensuring that securities markets function correctly. As for the more general viability of the mooted pan-European market in securities, CARD provides that its expectation "by making [investor] protection more equivalent" is that "coordination of that policy at community level is likely to make for greater inter-penetration" of securities

[20] 2001/34/EC.
[21] CARD, art.1(a) and art.2.
[22] CARD, recital 5.
[23] CARD, recital 5.
[24] CARD, recital 6.
[25] CARD, recital 7.
[26] CARD, recitals 9 to 11.
[27] CARD, recital 13.
[28] CARD, recital 21.

markets.[29] That is, by generating a greater equivalence between national securities regulations it is hoped that issuers and investors will be prepared to act across borders within the EU.

Applications for admission to listing

An application for listing must be made in accordance with s.75 of the FSMA **15–009** 2000. That means, the application must be made to the competent authority in the manner required by the Listing Rules.[30] Over and above those regulations, however, the FSA is empowered to make admission to listing subject to any special condition which it considers appropriate. The general conditions in the Listing Rules divide between conditions relating to the applicant itself, conditions relating to the nature of the securities which are to be issued, and conditions as to the documentation which is to be provided. There are requirements that the applicant issuer must be duly authorised, have appropriate accounts prepared, have published the prescribed financial information, have appropriate management, have appropriate working capital, and so forth. There are also requirements as to the nature of the securities themselves, which relate severally to the admission of the securities to trading on a recognised investment exchange, the need for the securities to be validly issued and freely transferable, the market capitalisation of the securities, that a sufficient number of securities are to be issued, and the preparation of an appropriate prospectus, as considered below. Applicants must also have a sponsor who is, in effect, an expert in matters such as admission to listing, who will be required to ensure that the application and its supporting materials are appropriate and suitably prepared.

Provision of information

It is important that the issuer is compelled to make full and frank disclosure of all **15–010** material facts in such a way that they will be publicly available. Under the listing rules, the issuer is under a duty in general terms to "take reasonable care to ensure that any information it notifies to a [regulatory information service][31] or makes available through the FSA is not misleading, false or deceptive".[32] Furthermore the issuer must not only ensure that all information is not misleading and so forth, but also to ensure that it does not "omit anything likely to affect the import of the information".[33]

In relation to an application for admission to listing the FSA may request any information which the FSA may "reasonably require to decide whether to grant an application for admission".[34] The FSA may also require that the issuer provide

---

[29] CARD, recital 32.
[30] Financial Services and Markets Act 2000 s.75(1).
[31] If information cannot be made through a recognised information service then it must be made in not less than two national newspapers, two newswire services in the United Kingdom and a recognised information service as soon as one opens: Listing Rules, Chap.1, para.1.3.4R.
[32] Listing Rules, Chap.1, para.1.3.3R.
[33] Listing Rules, Chap.1, para.1.3.3R.
[34] Listing Rules, Chap.1, para.1.3.1(1)R.

any information which the FSA considers "appropriate to protect investors or ensure the smooth operation of the market".[35] Finally, the FSA may request any further information which it requires to verify whether or not the listing rules are being complied with or whether the listing rules have been complied with at some point in the past.[36]

The preconditions for making an application for listing

15–011　There are numerous conditions to be fulfilled by the applicant before the applicant's securities will be admitted to listing. It is in Chs 2 and 6 of the Listing Rules that the principles dealing with the pre-requisites for admission to listing are set out. Briefly put, the company is required to be duly incorporated,[37] and the securities must have been duly authorised for listing under the company's constitution,[38] the shares must be freely transferable,[39] the shares must be admitted to trading on an RIE's market for listed securities,[40] and the issuer's securities must have a minimum capitalisation.[41] Significantly, an approved prospectus must have been published in respect of those securities, as was considered in Ch.13.[42]

The second tranche of information relates to the company's financial condition. The company must have published and filed audited accounts for at least three previous years,[43] the company must have an independent business and the company's business activities must have been continuous for the previous three years,[44] and it must have a minimum working capital identified in the rules.[45] The securities themselves must be 25 per cent in public hands after the issue within the EU and EEA,[46] and they must be capable of electronic settlement.[47]

Special conditions on a particular listing application

15–012　The Listing Rules empower the FSA to impose special conditions on any application for listing. CARD provides that any special conditions should be used "solely in the interests of protecting investors" and so may relate, for example, to the provision of particular information necessary to keep the investing public informed about the issuer's business activities.[48] Admission to listing may not be permitted unless and until those general conditions and any special conditions have been complied with.[49] The admission procedure is set out in the Listing

---

[35] Listing Rules, Chap.1, para.1.3.1(2)R. See also CARD, art.16.1.
[36] Listing Rules, Chap.1, para.1.3.1(3)R.
[37] Listing Rules, para.2.2.1R.
[38] Listing Rules, para.2.2.2R.
[39] Listing Rules, para.2.2.4R.
[40] Listing Rules, para.2.2.3R.
[41] Listing Rules, para.2.2.7R.
[42] Listing Rules, para.2.2.10R.
[43] Listing Rules, para.6.1.3R.
[44] Listing Rules, para.6.1.4R.
[45] Listing Rules, para.6.1.16R.
[46] Listing Rules, para.6.1.19R.
[47] Listing Rules, para.6.1.23R.
[48] CARD, art.12.
[49] Financial Services and Markets Act 2000 s.75(4); and Listing Rules, Ch.2, para.2.1.2G.

Rules, with the provisions as to the need for a prospectus being set out primarily in the Prospectus Rules. The requirements of the Listing Rules, especially as to the form of any prospectus, vary according to the nature and circumstances of the listing application. Those requirements will also differ depending on the method by which the securities are brought to listing.

Requirements as to working capital

The final significant requirement in relation to issues of equity securities to primary listing in Ch.6 of the Listing Rules is that the issuer must have "sufficient working capital"[50] and must make a statement to that effect. The issuer is required to satisfy itself after "due and careful enquiry" that it (and its subsidiaries, where appropriate) have sufficient working capital for the group's requirements for a 12-month period after the publication of the prospectus.[51] There are two stated exceptions to this requirement. The first applies where the applicant already has securities listed and instead provides proposals as to how working capital will be obtained in the future to make good any shortfall in working capital at the time.[52] The second applies where the applicant's business is that of banking or insurance.[53] **15–013**

The application procedure for admission to the Official List

The Listing Rules contain a detailed application procedure for companies to gain admission to listing in Ch.3, setting out all of the documents which must be lodged with the FSA before, in accordance with its guidance notes, the FSA will consider the application. There are different, detailed rules for different types of security.[54] The FSA guidance notes provide that it will consider applications only once all the documentation has been delivered, and that the FSA will consider any and all information which it considers appropriate, possibly going beyond the documentation which has been lodged with it in accordance with Ch.3 of the Listing Rules.[55] This may result in the FSA conducting enquiries, verifying the accuracy of the documentation, and requesting any further information which it requires, as mentioned above. The FSA may then impose any further conditions on the application which it considers appropriate.[56] In the ordinary case of events, the specified documents must be lodged by the issuer at least two business days prior to the FSA hearing the listing application (hence them being known as "the 48-hour documents"),[57] including the application for listing in prescribed form, any declaration required from a sponsor, and a copy of the prospectus, and any **15–014**

---

[50] Listing Rules, Chap.6, para.6.1.16R. Note the exceptions in favour of banking, insurance or other companies providing financial services, in Listing Rules, Chap.6, para.6.1.18G.
[51] Listing Rules, Chap.6, para.6.1.16R. It is also required that the sponsor accede to this statement and the information contained in it.
[52] Listing Rules, Ch.6, para.6.1.17G.
[53] Listing Rules, Ch.6, para.6.1.18(1)G.
[54] See Alastair Hudson, *Securities Law* (London: Sweet & Maxwell, 2008), Pt 4 generally.
[55] All of the material considered in this paragraph is set out at Listing Rules, Ch.3, para.3.2.6G.
[56] Listing Rules, Ch.3, para.3.2.6(5)G.
[57] Listing Rules, Ch.3, para.3.3.2R.

other document required by the regulations in that context.[58] Other documentation may include a copy of any circular which has been published in connection with the application[59]; any approved supplementary prospectus[60]; a copy of the board resolution of the issuer allotting the securities[61]; any accounts or interim financial statement; and so on. The application processes for block listing[62] relate to applicants who issue securities "on a regular basis" and "in circumstances which do not require the production of a prospectus".[63]

The role of sponsors in listing applications

The requirement for a sponsor

15–015 To bring securities to listing, the issuer must engage a sponsor.[64] The sponsor's primary role is to assist the issuer to bring an issue of securities to market; and the other role of the sponsor is to supply information to the FSA and in effect to certify to the FSA that the application is properly made and that the issuer is in compliance with the Listing Rules. The sponsor is required to have sufficient professional expertise in securities issues to be authorised to act as such by the FSA. The FSA maintains a list of approved sponsors on its website.[65] To be included on the list of approved sponsors, the sponsor must be authorised under the FSMA 2000[66] or must be a person regulated by a professional body recognised by that Act.[67] To be appointed as a sponsor, a person must be competent to perform designated services, including being able to assure the FSA that the listed company's obligations have been fulfilled,[68] and being able to guide the applicant as to its responsibilities under the Listing Rules and other regulations.[69] A sponsor must have a "sufficient number of suitably experienced employees" to discharge its responsibilities[70]; and thus experience of a suitable range of types of issue. While the sponsor may appear at first blush to be the applicant's agent in seeking admission to listing, it is the FSA which must be satisfied as to the sponsor's abilities and competence.[71]

Principles governing the activity of sponsors

15–016 There are four principles governing the activities of sponsors. First, the sponsor must exercise due care and skill in advising the listed company as to its obligations

---

[58] Listing Rules, Ch.3, para.3.3.2R.
[59] Listing Rules, Ch.3, para.3.3.2(3).
[60] Listing Rules, Ch.3, para.3.3.2(4).
[61] Listing Rules, Ch.3, para.3.3.2(5).
[62] Listing Rules, Ch.3, para.3.5.1R.
[63] Listing Rules, Ch.3, para.3.5.2G.
[64] Listing Rules, Ch.8, para.8.2.1R.
[65] Listing Rules, Ch.8, para.8.6.1G.
[66] Listing Rules, Ch.8, para.8.6.2R.
[67] Listing Rules, Ch.8, para.8.6.5R.
[68] Listing Rules, Ch.8, para.8.3.1(1)R.
[69] Listing Rules, Ch.8, para.8.3.1(2)R.
[70] Listing Rules, Ch.8, para.8.3.10R.
[71] Listing Rules, Ch.8, para.8.3.2G.

under the securities regulations.[72] Second, the sponsor must take reasonable steps to ensure that the directors of the listed company understand the nature and extent of their obligations under the listing rules.[73] Third, the sponsor must deal with the FSA in an open and co-operative manner, dealing promptly with all of the FSA's enquiries and disclosing any "material information" of which it has knowledge to the FSA in a "timely manner".[74] Broadly, this mirrors the obligation placed on listed companies by the Listing Principles in Ch.7 of the Listing Rules. Fourth, the sponsor is required to be independent of the listed company[75] and to complete a form attesting to its independence in relation to each admission for listing in which it participates.[76] The definition of independence here requires that the sponsor not own more than 30 per cent of the equity of the listed company nor have a "significant interest" in the listed company's debt securities.[77]

The obligations imposed on sponsors as to the suitability of the issue

The sponsor is required to form the "reasonable opinion", after making due and **15–017** careful inquiry, that the applicant has satisfied all of the requirements of the Listing Rules and Prospectus Rules, that the directors of the applicant have put in place adequate procedures to enable the applicant to comply with the Listing Rules, and that the directors of the applicant have also put in place procedures on the basis of which they are able to make "proper judgments on an ongoing basis" as to the applicant's financial position and prospects.[78] A sponsor must also ensure that no shares are placed with connected clients of the sponsor or with any financial intermediary involved in the issue except for the purposes of market-making for on-sale to clients[79]; that the results of any marketing or any allotment are notified to a recognised information service[80]; and that a recognised information service is notified if any of the listed company's advisors or intermediaries acquires more than 3 per cent of a class of equity shares.[81]

A sponsor is also required in two further situations: in relation to further issues of equity securities which are already listed[82]; and when a listed company is seeking to refinance its own shares up to 25 per cent of the issued share capital[83] such that it is required to produce a Class 1 Circular. In each of these circumstances, the sponsor must have formed the reasonable opinion after a due and careful enquiry that the applicant satisfies all of the requirements of the Listing Rules and the Prospectus

---

[72] Listing Rules, Ch.8, para.8.3.3R.
[73] Listing Rules, Ch.8, para.8.3.4R.
[74] Listing Rules, Ch.8, para.8.3.5R.
[75] Listing Rules, Ch.8, para.8.3.6R.
[76] Listing Rules, Ch.8, para.8.7.12R.
[77] Listing Rules, Ch.8, para.8.3.6R.
[78] Listing Rules, Ch.8, para.8.4.2R.
[79] Listing Rules, Ch.8, para.8.4.5(1)R.
[80] Listing Rules, Ch.8, para.8.4.5(2)R.
[81] Listing Rules, Ch.8, para.8.4.5(3)R.
[82] Listing Rules, Ch.8, para.8.4.7R.
[83] See Listing Rules, Ch.10.

Rules and that the directors can attest to the working capital requirements for listing, before the application may be presented to the FSA.[84]

Deciding on a listing application

15–018 The FSA must reach a decision on an application for listing within six months of the application or a longer period if further information is required.[85] In the event that such a decision to admit the securities to listing is not reached within that time period, the application is deemed to have been refused.[86] In the event of a decision to refuse admission to listing, the competent authority is required to give the applicant a warning notice[87] and a decision notice.[88] A decision to admit securities to listing is to be accompanied by a written notice from the competent authority.[89] The FSA may refuse an application if it does not comply with the Listing Rules,[90] or if any special condition imposed on the issue has not been complied with[91]; alternatively, if the FSA considers "that granting it would be detrimental to the interests of investors"[92]; or third, if the securities are already in issue and "if the issuer has failed to comply with any obligations to which he is subject as a result of that listing".[93]

MAINTENANCE OF LISTING

General continuing obligations in the Listing Rules

15–019 The Listing Rules create a number of rules which can be understood as continuing obligations. The securities which are listed must continue to be admitted to trading on a regulated market.[94] The securities must also remain in public hands as to 25 per cent of their number.[95] There are a number of mini-codes of obligations within the Listing Rules dealing with a listed company's dealings with its shares, requiring, in effect, notification of certain information to the FSA and compliance with the Listing Rules.[96]

Among the most important form of information required by securities regulations is accounting information. Listed companies must publish a preliminary statement of their annual results as soon as such a statement has been approved, in any event within 120 days of the end of the period to which it relates.[97] This information must be published through a recognised information service once

---

[84] Listing Rules, Ch.8, para.8.4.12R.
[85] Financial Services and Markets Act 2000 s.76(1).
[86] Financial Services and Markets Act 2000 s.76(2).
[87] Financial Services and Markets Act 2000 s.76(4).
[88] Financial Services and Markets Act 2000 s.76(5).
[89] Financial Services and Markets Act 2000 s.76(3).
[90] Listing Rules, Ch.2, para.2.1.2(1)G.
[91] Listing Rules, Ch.2, para.2.1.2(2)G.
[92] Financial Services and Markets Act 2000 s.75(5). Also Listing Rules, Ch.2, para.2.1.3(1)G.
[93] Financial Services and Markets Act 2000 s.75(6).
[94] Listing Rules, para.2.2.3R.
[95] Listing Rules, para.6.1.19R
[96] See Alastair Hudson, *Securities Law* (London: Sweet & Maxwell, 2009), generally.
[97] Listing Rules, Ch.9, para.9.7.1R.

those matters have been agreed with the company's auditors, together with any decision as to the payment of a dividend.[98] As to its annual report and accounts, a listed company must publish these documents as soon as possible after they have been approved,[99] and in any event with six months after the end of the accounting period.[100] However, the FSA may authorise the omission of any of this information if its disclosure would be either "contrary to the public interest or seriously detrimental to the listed company".[101] This power to condone omission of information is nevertheless subject to a proviso that the omission would not be "likely to mislead the public with regard to facts and circumstances, knowledge of which is essential for the assessment of the shares".[102]

Continuing obligations in relation to market abuse and inside information

One of the most significant continuing obligations in relation to the Listing Rules **15–020** relates to the obligation to disclose inside information. This principle derives from the Market Abuse Directive, as implemented by the Disclosure and Transparency Rules. In general terms, the FSA Disclosure and Transparency Rules oblige an issuer to notify a recognised information service "as soon as possible"[103] of any inside information which "directly concerns the issuer",[104] unless the issuer (on its own initiative) considers the prevention of disclosure to be necessary to protect its own "legitimate interests".[105] Section 119 of FSMA 2000 requires the FSA to create a code to specify what sorts of behaviour may constitute market abuse.[106] This code is known as the Code on Market Conduct: or more commonly by the acronym "MAR 1". It is contained in Ch.1 of the FSA Market Abuse Rulebook.[107]

The obligation on listed companies to make prescribed communications

This section considers the legal principles which govern the content of commu- **15–021** nications by listed companies, the need for corporate communications in certain situations under the Listing Rules, and the requirement to distribute circulars under the Listing Rules. The fourth of the Listing Principles provides that:

> "A listed company must communicate information to holders and potential holders of its listed equity securities in such a way as to avoid the creation or continuation of a false market in such listed equity securities."

---

[98] Listing Rules, Ch.9, para.9.7.2R.
[99] Listing Rules, Chap.9, para.9.8.1(1)R.
[100] Listing Rules, Chap.9, para.9.8.1(2)R.
[101] Listing Rules, Chap.9, para.9.7.3R.
[102] Listing Rules, Chap.9, para.9.7.3R.
[103] This will be satisfied if the issuer acted as soon as was possible in the circumstance of factors which were only gradually coming to light: Disclosure and Transparency Rules, Ch.2, para.2.2.2R. A short delay in publication of the information will be acceptable if it is "necessary to clarify the situation": Disclosure and Transparency Rules, Ch.2, para.2.2.9G.
[104] Disclosure and Transparency Rules. Ch.2, para.2.2.1R.
[105] Disclosure and Transparency Rules, Chap.2, para.2.5.1R. See Market Abuse Directive ("MAD"), art.6(1).
[106] Financial Services and Markets Act 2000 s.119.
[107] Published under the Financial Services Authority, *Market Conduct Sourcebook Instrument 2001* (MAR 1).

There are a number of matters about which a listed company must make disclosure either at the time of making an issue of securities or on a continuing basis thereafter. The keynote here is the avoidance of the creation of a "false market" in the equity securities at issue.

Circulars are required in a number of circumstances, many of which are those set out in s.13.8 of the Listing Rules. Circulars are required in relation to votes connected with the authority to allot shares, disapplying pre-emption rights in relation to the allotment of shares, increasing authorised share capital, reducing the company's capital, in relation to a capitalisation or bonus issue, in relation to a scrip dividend, giving notice of meetings, making amendments to the company's constitution, in relation to an employees' share scheme, in relation to discounted option arrangements and in relation to reminders of conversion rights over convertible securities. Other circumstances in which circulars of particular sorts are required include Class 1 transactions relating to corporate acquisitions or disposals or to takeovers generally.

Penalties for breach of the Listing Rules

15–022 There are two potential penalties for breach of the listing rules as provided in s.91 of FSMA 2000. The first arises when there has been any contravention of the listing rules such that the issuer, or any of its managers or any person connected to a manager, is subject to such penalty as the FSA thinks fit. Liability for a second form of penalty arises under s.91(1A) of the FSMA 2000 when there has been a contravention of Pt 6 of the FSMA 2000 or of the Prospectus Rules: the penalty is such as the FSA considers appropriate.

FSA powers of punishment: discontinuance and suspension of listing

15–023 The FSA has four separate powers under FSMA 2000 to prohibit or suspend or otherwise control securities transactions: first, a power to discontinue or to suspend listing further to s.77 of the FSMA 2000; second, a power to suspend or prohibit an offer of transferable securities to the public under s.87K of the FSMA 2000; third, a power to suspend or prohibit admission to trading on a regulated market under s.87L of the FSMA 2000; and, fourth, a power to suspend trading in a financial instrument on grounds of breach of the disclosure rules under s.96C of the FSMA 2000. Further to s.87M of FSMA 2000, UKLA may publish a statement of censure if an issuer of transferable securities, or a person offering transferable securities to the public, or a person requesting the admission of transferable securities to trading on a regulated market, has in either case failed to comply with its obligations under any provision of the securities regulations stemming from Pt 6 of FSMA 2000.[108]

---

[108] Financial Services and Markets Act 2000 s.87M(1).

CORPORATE GOVERNANCE

Chapter 16

MEMBERSHIP

MEMBERSHIP OF A COMPANY

Introduction

The members of a company consist of two categories of person. The first category **16–001**
are the subscribers of a company's memorandum who are deemed to have agreed
to become members, and on the registration of the company they become members
and must be entered as such in its register of members.[1] The second category is
every other person who has agreed to become a member of the company and
whose name is entered in the register of members.[2]

Members—subscribers to the memorandum

A subscriber to the company's memorandum becomes a member on registration **16–002**
of the company, and an entry in the register of members is not necessary to make
him a member of the company. It is the duty of the directors to enter his name in
the register, but their failure to do this will not enable him to escape liability for
calls on the shares for which he has signed the memorandum.[3] A subscriber's
obligation to take the shares for which he has subscribed is not satisfied by the
(later) allotment of shares credited as fully paid and to which someone else is
entitled.

M signed the memorandum for five shares. The company had agreed to allot
paid up shares to C, as the purchase price of property sold to the company, and C
directed the company to allot five of these shares to M. This was done and the
company was afterwards wound up. *Held*, M was liable to pay for the five shares
for which he had signed the memorandum.[4]

If, however, the entire share capital has been allotted to others, the subscriber is
under no liability to take shares.[5] A subscriber to the memorandum cannot rescind

---

[1] s.112(1).

[2] s.112(2). The section is not conclusive as to membership for voting purposes if the entry on the
register is wrongly made, e.g. if those who have agreed to become members and who have been put
on the register have failed to comply with other requirements for membership under the articles:
POW Services Ltd v Clare [1995] 2 B.C.L.C. 435.

[3] *London, Hamburgh, & Continental Exchange Bank, Re (Evans's Case)* (1867) L.R. 2 Ch. App. 427.

[4] *South Blackpool Hotel Co, Re (Migotti's Case)* (1867) L.R. 4 Eq. 238.

[5] *Tal v Drws Slate Co, Re (Mackley's Case)* (1875) L.R. 1 Ch.D. 247.

the contract to take shares on the ground of a misrepresentation made by a promoter, because (a) the company could not appoint an agent before it came into existence and it is therefore not liable for the promoter's acts, and (b) by signing the memorandum the subscriber became bound, on the registration of the company, not only as between himself and the company, but also as between himself and the other persons who should become members on the footing that the contract existed.[6]

Members—every other person

16–003 A person, other than a subscriber, who has agreed to become a member of the company does not actually become one until his name is entered in the register of members. The Act makes the placing of the name of a shareholder on the register a condition precedent to membership.[7] Registration is essential for membership[8] but it does not necessarily make the person a member[9] so far as the company is concerned. A member agrees to become a member, however, if he consents to do so even though there is no contract between him and the company that he should be entered on the register.[10] Such a person may take an allotment of his shares direct from the company,[11] or may purchase shares from an existing member,[12] or he may succeed to shares on the death or bankruptcy of a member.[13]

Minors as members

16–004 In English law a minor, i.e. a person under the age of 18,[14] may be a member unless this is forbidden by the articles. However, a minor's contract to take shares is voidable by him before or within a reasonable time after he attains the age of 18. If he avoids he cannot recover the money paid for the shares unless there has been a total failure of the consideration for which the money was paid.

S, an infant,[15] agreed to take 500 £1 shares from a company, and paid 10s. on each share. She received no dividend on the shares. While still an infant she repudiated the shares, and brought an action (a) for a declaration that she was entitled to avoid the contract, and (b) to recover the money she had paid. *Held*, (a) S was entitled to rescind and so was not liable for future calls, but (b) there was no total failure of consideration and S could not recover money already paid because she had got the thing for which the money was paid, a thing of value.[16]

If the company is wound up the minor member loses his right to avoid unless the liquidator agrees.[17] A person of 18 years of age or over has full legal capacity.

---

[6] *Metal Constituents Ltd, Re (Lord Lurgan's Case)* [1902] 1 Ch. 707.
[7] *Florence Land & Public Works Co, Re (Nicol's Case)* (1885) L.R. 29 Ch.D. 421, CA, at 447, per Fry L.J.
[8] See *Baku Consolidated Oilfields Ltd, Re* [1994] 1 B.C.L.C. 173.
[9] *POW Services Ltd v Clare* [1995] 2 B.C.L.C. 435.
[10] *Re Nuneaton Borough A.F.C. Ltd* [1989] B.C.L.C. 454.
[11] Above, Ch.8.
[12] Above, Ch.7.
[13] Above, Ch.7.
[14] Family Law Reform Act 1969, c.46, s.1(1).
[15] The age of majority was formerly 21 and persons under that age were called "infants".
[16] *Steinberg v Scala (Leeds) Ltd* [1923] 2 Ch. 452, CA.
[17] *Asiatic Banking Corp, Re (Symons' Case)* (1870) L.R. 5 Ch. App. 298.

Personal representatives

Ownership of the shares of a deceased member is transmitted to his executors or **16–005** administrators. They must produce to the company the grant of probate of the will, or of letters of administration of the estate and such a document must be accepted by the company as sufficient evidence of the grant.[18] Production to the company does not, however, make the representatives members of the company. The deceased member's estate is the member for some purposes, such as an article providing that on an increase of capital the new shares are to be divided among the existing members in proportion to their existing shareholdings.[19]

The personal representatives are liable for calls[20] on partly paid shares only to the extent of the deceased's assets in their hands, and if in England the personal representatives default on a winding up in paying sums due from the deceased, the company can obtain an order for administration of the estate of the deceased member.[21]

The personal representatives are entitled to transfer the shares without being registered as members,[22] and to receive all dividends, bonuses or other benefits from the shares, but the articles usually prevent them from voting at general meetings. Article 27(3) of the Model Articles for Private Companies Limited by Shares provides that

"transmittees do not have the right to attend or vote at a general meeting, or agree to a proposed written resolution, in respect of shares to which they are entitled, by reason of the holder's death or bankruptcy or otherwise, unless they become the holders of those shares."[23]

If personal representatives are registered as members, they become personally liable for calls, although they have a right of indemnity against the deceased's estate.[24]

Trustees in bankruptcy

A bankrupt may be a member of a company, although the beneficial interest in his **16–006** shares will be vested in his trustee in bankruptcy as from the time when he is adjudged bankrupt.[25] Unless the articles provide to the contrary, a shareholder does not cease to be a member of the company on becoming bankrupt. Accordingly, as long as he is on the register he is entitled to exercise any vote conferred by his shares at the meetings of the company, even though the articles provide[26] that notice

---

[18] s.774(a). For foreign personal representatives, see *Baku Consolidated Oilfields Ltd, Re* [1994] 1 B.C.L.C. 173.

[19] *James v Buena Ventura Nitrate Grounds Syndicate Ltd* [1896] 1 Ch. 456, CA, at 464, per Lord Herschell.

[20] See para.7–001, above.

[21] Insolvency Act 1986, s.81(3).

[22] s.773. See *Safeguard Industrial Investments Ltd v National Westminster Bank Ltd* [1982] 1 W.L.R. 589, CA.

[23] See too art.66(2) of the Model Articles for Public Companies. cf. also Table A, art.31.

[24] *Cheshire Banking Co, Re (Duff's Executors' Case)* (1886) 32 Ch.D. 301, CA, at 309, per Cotton L.J.

[25] Insolvency Act 1986 s.306(1).

[26] cf. art.38 of Table A.

of meetings is to be sent to the trustee in bankruptcy and not to the bankrupt.[27] The bankrupt must vote in accordance with the directions of the trustee.

Other companies

16–007 A company may, if authorised by its memorandum, take shares in and be a member of another company. It attends meetings of the other by a representative authorised by resolution of its directors.[28]

In general a company cannot be a member of itself, either directly or through a nominee[29] but, as we have already seen, companies may, in certain circumstances purchase or acquire their own shares.

The Act provides that, for similar reasons and subject to certain exceptions, a subsidiary company cannot be a member of its holding company and any allotment or transfer of shares in a holding company to its subsidiary is void.[30] This prohibition cannot be evaded by having a nominee for the subsidiary. There are exceptions, namely where the subsidiary is concerned as a personal representative or trustee (unless in the latter case the holding company or a subsidiary of it is beneficially interested under the trust[31]) or where the subsidiary is acting as an authorised dealer in securities.[32]

Examples

Y, who holds shares in X Bank Ltd, appoints its subsidiary, X Bank (Executor & Trustee) Ltd, as his executor and on Y's death the subsidiary is registered in respect of the shares.

Y transfers his shares to the subsidiary on trust for a beneficiary, Z, who borrows money from X Bank Ltd and secures repayment by mortgaging his interest in the shares to X Bank Ltd.

THE REGISTER OF MEMBERS

Mandatory obligation

16–008 Every company must keep a register of its members[33] containing the following information: (1) the names and addresses[34] of the members, and, if the company has a share capital, a statement of the shares held by each member, distinguishing each share by its number[35] so long as it has one and by its class if there is more

---

[27] *Morgan v Gray* [1953] Ch. 83.
[28] s.323.
[29] s.658(1).
[30] s.136(1).
[31] s.138.
[32] See s.141.
[33] s.113(1).
[34] s.113(2)(a). This means the address given by the member and not an address substituted by someone else: *POW Services Ltd v Clare* [1995] 2 B.C.L.C. 435.
[35] s.113(3)(a)(i).

than one class of shares,[36] and the amount paid or agreed to be considered as paid on the shares of each member.[37] If the company has converted shares into stock, the register must show the amount and class of stock held by each member.[38] In the case of companies which do not have a share capital and have more than one class of members the register must show the class to which each member belongs as well as their names and addresses.[39] (2) The date on which each person was entered in the register as a member[40]; and (3) the date at which any person ceased to be a member.[41] Default in the keeping the relevant information in the register gives rise to penalties for the company and every officer in default.[42]

In the case of a limited company formed under the Act with just one member, the register must, in addition to the name and address of that member, contain a statement that the company has only one member.[43] In addition, where a limited company's number of members falls to one then, in addition to the name and address of the sole member, the register must state: (a) that the company only has one member; and (b) the date on which the company became a single member company.[44] If the number of members subsequently increases to two or more the register must state both the fact that the company has ceased to have only one member and the date of the change.[45] Default renders the company and every officer in default liable to a fine.[46]

The register may be kept in hard copy or electronic form and may be arranged in such manner as the directors of the company think fit, provided the information is adequately recorded.[47] If the register is kept in electronic form, it must be capable of being reproduced in hard copy form.[48] Any entry relating to a former member may be removed from the register after 10 years from the date on which he ceased to be a member.[49]

Index of members

A company with more than 50 members must, unless the register of members consti- **16–009** tutes in itself as an index, keep an index of the names of its members,[50] and must alter the index within 14 days after any alteration in the register.[51] The index must contain sufficient indication to enable the account of each member to be readily

---

[36] s.113(3)(a)(ii).
[37] s.113(3)(b).
[38] s.113(4).
[39] s.113(6).
[40] s.113(2)(b).
[41] s.113(2)(c).
[42] s.113(7)(8).
[43] s.123(1).
[44] s.123(2).
[45] s.123(3).
[46] s.123(4)(5).
[47] s.1135(1).
[48] s.1135(2).
[49] s.121.
[50] s.115(1).
[51] s.115(2).

found.[52] The index must be kept at the same place as the register.[53] Default renders the company and every officer in default liable to a fine.[54]

Effect of the register

16–010 The register of members is prima facie evidence of any matters directed by the Act to be inserted in it.[55] This does not mean, however, that a person so included is a member for the purpose of attending meetings, etc.[56]

Location of the register

16–011 The register must be kept available for inspection at the company's registered office or at some other place specified in regulations.[57] The relevant regulations[58] specify that the alternative place must be a place situated in the part of the United Kingdom in which the company is registered, must be the same place for all the relevant provisions, and must have been notified to the Registrar as being the company's alternative inspection location.[59] A company must give notice to the Registrar of the place where its register of members is kept available for inspection and of any change in that place.[60] No such notice is required, however, if the register has, at all times since it came into existence been kept available for inspection at the company's registered office.[61]

Rights to inspect and require copies of the register

16–012 The register and index are to be open to the inspection of any member without charge, and of any other person on payment of the appropriate fee.[62] Any person may also require a copy of, or any part of, the register on payment of the appropriate charge.[63] A person requiring to inspect the register or who requires a copy of some part of it, is obliged to make a request to the company to this effect,[64] together with the following information[65]: the name and address of an individual responsible for making a request, where that request is from an organisation; an indication of the purpose for which the information will be used.[66] The request

---

[52] s.115(3).
[53] s.115(4).
[54] s.115(5)(6).
[55] s.127.
[56] *POW Services Ltd v Clare* [1995] 2 B.C.L.C. 438.
[57] s.114(1).
[58] The Companies (Company Records) Regulations 2008 (SI 2008/3006).
[59] Reg.3.
[60] s.114(2). Default renders the company and every officer in default liable to a fine: s.114(5)(6).
[61] s.114(3).
[62] s.116(1). The Companies (Fees for Inspection and Copying of Company Records) Regulations 2007 (SI 2007/2612) specifies that the fee is £3.50 for each hour or part thereof: reg.2.
[63] s.116(2). See the Companies (Fees for Inspection and Copying of Company Records) Regulations 2007 (SI 2007/2612) regs 3, 4.
[64] s.116(3).
[65] It is an offence to make any statement that is misleading, false, or deceptive in a material particular: s.119(1).
[66] s.116(4)(a)(b)(c).

must also indicate whether the information will be disclosed to others and, if so, the purpose for which the information will be used by those people.[67] Private companies are required to make their company records available for inspection by a person on a day which has been specified by that person provided that this is on a working day and the person gives the company the required notice of the specified day.[68] The required notice is at least two working days notice of the specified day if the notice is given during the period of notice for a general meeting or a class meeting or where the company circulates a written resolution during the period specified in s.297 of the Act.[69] In all other cases the required notice is at least 10 working days notice of the specified day.[70] A person giving notice of the specified day also has to given notice of the time on that day at which he wishes to start the inspection (to be between 9am and 3pm) and the company is required to make its company records available for inspection by that person for a period of at least two hours beginning at that time.[71]

Company's response to a request for inspection or copies

Where a request to inspect the register is made, the company must, within five working days either comply with the request or apply to the court.[72] In the case of an application to court, the company must notify the person who made the request of this fact.[73] The court has a discretion either to accede or refuse the request.[74] If the court is satisfied that the request has not been sought for a proper purpose then it may direct the company not to comply with the request and it may order that the costs associated with the application be paid in whole or in part by the person who made the request, even if he is not a party to the application.[75] The court can also direct that the company need not comply with other requests made for a similar purpose, whether by the same person, or different persons.[76] If, on the other hand, the court does not direct the company not to comply with the request, then the company is required to comply with the request immediately upon the court giving its decision.[77]

16–013

Information as to the state of the register

The company must, when providing an individual with a copy of the register (or any part of it), inform him of the most recent date on which any alterations were

16–014

[67] s.116(4)(d).
[68] The Companies (Company Records) Regulations 2008 (SI 2008/3006) reg.4(1).
[69] Reg.4(2).
[70] Reg.4(3).
[71] Reg.4(4). Public companies are required to make their company records available for inspection for at least two hours between 9am and 5pm on each working day: reg.5.
[72] s.117(1).
[73] s.117(2).
[74] For cases arising under CA 1985 s.356(6), see *Pelling v Families Need Father Ltd* [2001] EWCA Civ 1280; [2002] 1 B.C.L.C. 645; *O'Brien v Sporting Shooters Association of Australia* [1999] 3 V.R. 251.
[75] s.117(3).
[76] s.117(4).
[77] s.117(5).

made to the register.[78] Likewise, when a person inspects the index, there is again a requirement that the company must inform the individual whether there is any alteration which is not reflected in the index.[79] If the company fails to provide this information, an offence is committed by the company and every officer of the company who is in default.[80]

Consequences of the company's refusal or default in providing a copy

16–015 The Act specifies certain consequences where there has been a refusal to allow for inspection of the register or where default is made in providing a copy, an offence is committed by the company and also every officer of the company who is in default.[81] In addition, the court may by order compel an immediate inspection or direct that the copy required be sent to the person who has requested it.[82]

Importance of register

16–016 The importance of the register as a public representation of who the members are and what their liability is has often been emphasised, and a company has no power to create a right of pledge or lien over the register, since that would deprive the public of their statutory right of access and inspection. The register and not the share certificate is the document of title to shares, the share certificate being merely an acknowledgement on the part of the company that, at the time of its issue, the name of the person mentioned in it is duly recorded in the register.[83] There is a distinction, however, between the liability of the company and the individuals on the register to third parties as a result of that representation on the one hand, and the internal question as to whether the individual is actually a member for voting purposes, etc., on the other.[84]

16–017 Any liability incurred by a company as the result of making or deleting an entry in its register, or failing to do either, cannot be enforced against it more than 10 years after the date of first default.[85]

Power of court to rectify register

16–018 If there is some error in the contents of the register, it has long been a principle of company law that this cannot be rectified by the company, but must be made on application to the court. The Act therefore provides that the register may be rectified in two categories of case: (1) where the name of any person is, without sufficient cause, entered in or omitted from the company's register; (2) where default is made or unnecessary delay takes place in entering on the register of the

---

[78] s.120(1).
[79] s.120(2).
[80] s.120(3)(4).
[81] s.118(1)(2).
[82] s.118(3).
[83] *Re Baku Consolidated Oilfields Ltd* [1994] 1 B.C.L.C. 173.
[84] *POW Services Ltd v Clare* [1995] 2 B.C.L.C. 438.
[85] s.128.

fact of any person having ceased to be a member.[86] In such a case, the person aggrieved,[87] or any member of the company, or the company itself, may apply to the court for the register to be rectified.

A court hearing an application may either refuse the application or it may order rectification of the register[88] and payment by the company of any damages sustained by an aggrieved party.[89] The Act also provides that where a company is required to send a list of its members to the Registrar, the court in making an order for rectification shall direct notice of the rectification to be given to the Registrar.[90]

The court may also decide any question relating to the title of a person who is a party to the application, whether this arises between members and alleged members, or between members or alleged members on the one hand and the company on the other. Indeed, the court may generally decide any question necessary or expedient to be decided for rectification of the register.[91] There is older authority to the effect that rectification of the register is the only method of resolving disputes as to legal title to shares.[92] Some doubt was cast on this at first instance in *Hoicrest Ltd, Re*,[93] when the court was asked to rectify the register in relation to a number of shares alleged to be held by K. The judge decided that the court had no jurisdiction to entertain K's application because he could not produce a legal transfer of the shares alleged to be held by him[94] and, until he could do so, there was sufficient cause for omitting his name from the register. The Court of Appeal[95] reversed this decision and emphasised that the court a general discretionary power to resolve a dispute on title, although it would not follow that the power of determination should always be exercised.[96] While true that the court would not make an order which required the company or its board to act in contravention of the Act or the articles, this did not prevent the court from resolving, prior to deciding whether or not to make an order for rectification, relevant disputes about entitlement to shares.[97]

The courts have always regarded the jurisdiction as discretionary.[98] Thus, the **16–019** general approach of the courts has been to emphasise that a remedy should not be given other than in a straight-forward, uncomplicated case. The main criterion is that there must be a legitimate interest[99] and if rectification of the register would

---

[86] s.125(1).

[87] This includes a person who is alleging that the shares ought to have been allotted to him and that another has been registered in respect of those shares, even though he does not yet have a right to be registered: *Thundercrust Ltd, Re* [1995] 1 B.C.L.C. 177.

[88] The mere fact of a potential order for rectification of the register would not lead to the court striking out an application under what was s.459 of the 1985 Act (now s.994, below para.): *Starlight Developers Ltd, Re* [2007] EWHC 1660 (Ch).

[89] s.125(2). See *BTR Plc, Re* (1988) 4 B.C.C. 45.

[90] s.125(4).

[91] s.125(3).

[92] Based on *Shaw, Ex p. Re Diamond Rock Boring Co Ltd* (1877) 2 Q.B.D. 463.

[93] [1998] 2 B.C.L.C. 175.

[94] In reliance on s.183(1) of the 1985 Act.

[95] [2001] W.L.R. 414, CA.

[96] At p.419. Mummery L.J. made directions for the trial of a preliminary issue on whether the parties had agreed that the shares should be transferred to K: at p.420.

[97] [2001] W.L.R. 414, CA, at p.419.

[98] See, e.g, *Re Sussex Brick Co* [1904] 1 Ch. 598, CA, at p. 606–607, per Vaughan Williams L.J.; *Re Piccadilly Radio Plc* [1989] B.C.L.C. 683.

[99] See *New Millennium Experience Co Ltd, Re* [2003] EWHC 1823 (Ch); [2004] 1 B.C.L.C. 19, where no legitimate interest was shown.

directly affect the legal rights of another person, then the court may not order recti-fication without hearing that other person.[100] It has been confirmed that the court's discretion is the same as its discretion to grant or refuse specific performance and, as such, would be affected by delay and prejudice.[101]

Orders have been made in the following situations:

1. where the directors have power under the articles to refuse to register a transfer of shares and they have failed to act[102];

2. where new shares were wrongfully allotted by the directors to themselves and a provisional allotment letter had not been delivered to an existing shareholder who wishes to take the shares[103];

3. where the share transfer documentation had been lodged with a company but the directors failed to notify the transferee of their refusal to register the transfer within two months[104];

4. where, due to an administrative oversight, a member's name had not been entered on the register[105];

5. where an accountant's letter did not have the effect of constituting a transfer notice triggering rights of pre-emption under a company's articles[106];

6. where a share transfer was torn up, but later stuck together and registered, but where there had been no intention to effect a transfer.[107]

On the other hand, orders have not been made in the following situations:

1. where a member who had no interest in shares and was not aggrieved by an error in the register applied for relief as a tactical step in a takeover battle[108];

2. where directors bona fide exercised an absolute discretion to refuse to register a transfer of shares[109];

3. where an application would prejudice persons who had not had the opportunity to be before the court and who might wish to challenge any change being sought[110];

---

[100] *Joint Stock Discount Co, Re (Sichell's Case)* (1867) 3 L.R. Ch. App. 119.

[101] See *Dulai v Isis Factors Plc* [2003] EWHC 1653 (Ch); [2003] 2 B.C.L.C. 411.

[102] *Swaledale Cleaners Ltd, Re* [1968] 1 W.L.R. 1710, CA.

[103] *Thundercrust Ltd, Re* [1995] 1 B.C.L.C. 117.

[104] *Inverdeck Ltd, Re* [1998] 2 B.C.L.C. 242.

[105] *New Millennium Experience Co Ltd, Re* [2003] EWHC 1823 (Ch); [2004] 1 B.C.L.C. 19.

[106] *Romer-Ormiston v Claygreen Ltd* [2005] EWHC 2032; [2006] B.C.L.C. 175.

[107] *Smith v Charles Building Services Ltd* [2006] EWCA Civ 14; [2006] B.C.C. 334, upholding [2005] EWHC 654; [2005] B.C.C. 513.

[108] *Piccadilly Radio Plc, Re* [1989] B.C.L.C. 683.

[109] *Popely v Planarrive Ltd* [1997] 1 B.C.L.C. 8.

[110] *R.W. Peak (King's Lynn) Ltd, Re* [1998] 1 B.C.L.C. 193.

4. where it could not be shown that the former member of a pop band had signed a stock transfer form[111];

5. where defendants had been held liable in damages for injurious falsehood[112];

6. where there was no legal foundation for the claim and where the applicant has delayed unduly.[113]

The court may order rectification of the register by deleting a reference to only **16–020** some of the registered shareholder's shares. It need not delete his name entirely. Thus when an existing shareholder was registered as the holder of an additional number of shares issued in breach of the then Exchange Control Regulations the court deleted the reference to those shares only.[114]

An order for rectification may be made even if the company is being wound up.

B, a transferee of shares in a company, sent in his transfer for registration but, by mistake, registration of the transfer was omitted. The company then went into liquidation with a view to reconstruction and B, thinking that he was on the register of members, served the liquidator with notice of dissent to the scheme. The liquidator disregarded the notice on the ground that B was not a member. *Held*, there was such "default or unnecessary delay" in registration as entitled B to rectification of the register.[115]

Where the person on the register has been wrongly included, the court will examine, for the purposes of voting, etc., whether that person is properly a member without rectification of the register.[116] The court has exclusive jurisdiction as to the rectification of the registers of British registered companies, irrespective of the nationality of the parties.[117]

Trusts not to be entered on register in England

The Act provides that no notice of any trust shall be entered on the register, or be **16–021** received by the Registrar, in the case of companies registered in England, Wales, or Northern Ireland.[118] This means that, subject as below, the company is entitled to treat every person on the register of members as the beneficial owner of shares, even if in fact he holds them on trust for another, i.e. the company need not take notice of equitable interests in shares. Nominee shareholdings are common[119] and potential abuses (such as tax evasion) are legion but the only current anti-avoidance provisions concern substantial shareholding disclosure rules.[120] Under current law,

---

[111] *Elliott v The Hollies Ltd* [1998] 1 B.C.L.C. 627.
[112] *Lloyd v Popely* [2000] 1 B.C.L.C. 19.
[113] *Dulai v Isis Factors Plc* [2003] EWHC 1653 (Ch); [2003] 2 B.C.L.C. 411.
[114] *Transatlantic Life Assurance Co Ltd, Re* [1979] 3 All E.R. 357.
[115] *Sussex Brick Co, Re* [1904] 1 Ch. 598, CA.
[116] *POW Services Ltd v Clare* [1995] 2 B.C.L.C. 438.
[117] *Fagin's Bookshop Plc, Re* [1992] B.C.L.C. 118; *International Credit and Investment Co (Overseas) Ltd v Adham* [1994] 1 B.C.L.C. 66.
[118] s.126.
[119] See para.16–022, below.
[120] See para.16–023, below.

therefore, if the company registers a transfer of the shares held by a person as trustee, it is under no liability to the beneficiaries even if the sale was a breach of trust and in fraud of the beneficiaries.

X's shares were, on his death, registered in the name of his executors. They subsequently transferred the shares to Y in breach of the terms of X's will, and the transfer was registered by the company. The company had a copy of the will in its possession, and its president was one of X's executors. *Held*, the company did not act wrongfully, as it was only bound to satisfy itself from the will that the executors were executors, and was not concerned with the disposition by X of his property.[121]

A further result is that the company is not a trustee for persons claiming the shares under an equitable interest. For example, if A, the owner of shares, makes an equitable mortgage of his shares by depositing his share certificate and a blank transfer with B as security for a debt and afterwards makes another equitable mortgage of the same shares by depositing another blank transfer of them with C as security for another debt, saying that he has lost his share certificate, C cannot by giving notice to the company affect the company with notice of his interest in the shares or gain any priority of B.[122] The proper way to protect the interest of a beneficiary in shares is to serve a stop notice. As a rule, if a company receives notice of an equitable claim it should allow the person giving the notice to apply for a restraining order, if he makes a request to that effect, before registering a transfer to his prejudice.[123]

The articles frequently deal with notice of trusts. Thus the Model Articles for Private Companies Limited by Shares states that

"Except as required by law, no person is to be recognised by the company as holding any share upon any trust, and except as otherwise required by law or the articles, the company is not in any way to be bound by or recognise any interest in a share other than the holder's absolute ownership of it and all the rights attaching to it."[124]

16–022   A trustee of shares who is entered on the register is entitled to exercise any vote conferred by the shares although he may be bound to vote in accordance with the directions of the beneficiary. The trustee is personally liable to the company for any calls or other obligations attaching to the shares but is entitled to an indemnity from the beneficiary, not only out of the trust property but to the full extent of his indebtedness in respect of the shares.[125] The company cannot put the beneficiary on the list of contributories but it can, through the trustee, enforce the trustee's right to an indemnity.[126]

A purchase of shares in the name of a nominee, even if a minor or a man of straw, is legal. In such a case the company cannot go behind the nominee to the beneficial owner.

---

[121] *Simpson v Molson's Bank* [1895] A.C. 270.
[122] *Société Générale de Paris v Walker* [1885] 11 App. Cas. 20.
[123] *Société Générale de Paris v Tramways Union Co* (1884) 14 Q.B.D. 424, CA, at 453, per Lindley L.J.
[124] See also the Model Articles for Public Companies, art.45. cf. also Table A, art.5.
[125] *Hardoon v Belilios* [1901] A.C. 118, PC.
[126] *European Society Arbitration Acts, Re* (1878) 8 Ch.D. 679, CA, at 708, per James L.J.

M and G, a firm of stockbrokers, bought shares which were registered in the name of L, their clerk. L was an infant. On the company's going into liquidation, the liquidator applied that M and G's names might be substituted for that of L in the register of members and the list of contributories. *Held*, the application failed, as there was no contractual relation between the company and M and G.[127]

If a person applies for shares in a fictitious name, or in the name of a person who has never agreed to accept the shares, rectification of the register can be obtained so as to place the name of the real owner upon the register.[128]

DISCLOSURE OF SUBSTANTIAL SHAREHOLDINGS

Part 22 of the Act contains provisions for securing the disclosure and registration **16–023** of substantial individual interests in share capital carrying unrestricted voting rights. The aim is to ensure that despite the nominee-friendly rules relating to the register of members, directors, shareholders and employees of a public company[129] may ascertain the identity of, for instance, any person who may be in the process of buying shares in the company through nominees whose name will only appear on the register, to gain control of it or of any person who is in a position to veto a special resolution of the company not only at the date of the request but also in respect of the previous three years.[130] In addition they allow companies to carry out their own investigations into such matters without necessitating intervention by the Secretary of State under ss.442–444 of the 1985 Act.[131]

For the purpose of the Act, a reference to an interest in shares[132] includes an interest of any kind whatsoever in the shares.[133] Any restraints or restrictions to which the exercise of any right attached to the interest is or may be subject are to be disregarded.[134]

Interests to be notified: interest of a person

A person will be regarded as having an interest in shares[135] if he either enters **16–024** into a contract to acquire them,[136] or not being the registered holder, is entitled to exercise any right conferred by the holding of the shares, or to control the exercise of any such right.[137] A person is treated as having an interest in shares[138] if he has a right to call for delivery of the shares to himself or to his order,[139] or

---

[127] *National Bank of Wales Ltd, Re* [1907] 1 Ch. 582.
[128] *Hercules Insurance Co, Re (Pugh and Sharman's Case)* (1872) L.R. 13 Eq. 566; *Imperial Mercantile Credit Association, Re (Richardson's Case)* (1875) L.R. 19 Eq. 588.
[129] Not private companies: see s.791.
[130] *Geers Gross, Re* [1987] 1 W.L.R. 837.
[131] Below, para.???.
[132] The reference to shares is to the company's issued share of a class carrying rights to vote in all circumstances at general meetings of the company (and including treasury shares): s.792(1).
[133] s.820(2)(a).
[134] s.820(2)(b).
[135] It is immaterial that shares in which a person has an interest are unidentifiable: s.820(8).
[136] s.820(4)(a).
[137] s.820(4)(b).
[138] Persons having a joint interest are treated as each having that interest: s.820(7).
[139] s.820(6)(a).

he has a right to acquire an interest in shares or is under an obligation to take an interest in shares.[140] A person is entitled to exercise or control the exercise of a right conferred by the holding of shares if he has a right (whether subject to conditions or not) the exercise of which would make him so entitled,[141] or is under an obligation the fulfilment of which would make him so entitled.[142]

Interests to be notified: family interests

16–025 A person will be taken to be interested in shares in which his spouse, civil partner, infant child, or step-child, is interested.[143]

Interests to be notified: corporate interests

16–026 The Act provides that a person will also be taken to be interested in shares if a body corporate is interested in them and the body or its directors are accustomed to act in accordance with his directors or instructions or he is entitled to exercise or control the exercise of one-third or more of the voting power at general meetings.[144] Likewise, a person will be treated as entitled to exercise or control the exercise of voting power if another body corporate is entitled to exercise or control the exercise of that voting power and is entitled to exercise or control the exercise of one-third or more of the voting power at general meetings.[145]

Agreements to acquire interests in a particular company

16–027 An interest in shares may arise from an agreement[146] between two or more persons which includes provision for the acquisition by any one or more them of interests in shares of a particular public company (the target).[147] The Act will apply to such an agreement if the agreement includes provisions[148] imposing obligations or restrictions on any one or more of the parties to it with respect to their use, retention or disposal of their interests in the shares of the target company[149] acquired in pursuance of the agreement and an interest in the target company's shares is in fact acquired by any of the parties in pursuance of the agreement.[150] Once an interest

---

[140] s.820(6)(b). This applies whether the right or obligation is conditional or absolute.

[141] s.820(5)(a).

[142] s.820(5)(b).

[143] s.822(1).

[144] s.823(1). A person is to be treated as entitled to exercise or control the exercise of voting power if he has a right the exercise of which would make him so entitled, or he is under an obligation, the fulfilment of which would make him so entitled: s.823(3).

[145] s.823(1).

[146] An agreement includes any agreement or arrangement: s.824(5)(a). Not all agreements are, however, included: s.824(6).

[147] s.824(1).

[148] Provisions of an agreement include undertakings, expectations or understandings operative under an arrangement, and any provision whether express or implied and whether absolute or not: s.824(5)(b).

[149] A reference to the use of interests in shares in the target company is to the exercise of any rights or of any control or influence arising from those interests, including the right to enter into an agreement for the exercise, or for control of the exercise, of any of those rights by another person: s.824(3).

[150] s.824(2).

in shares in the target company has been acquired in pursuance of the agreement, the section will continue to apply to it so long as it continues to include provisions of any description mentioned in the section.[151] This is stated to apply irrespective of whether or not any further acquisitions of interests in the company's shares take place in pursuance of the agreement; any change in the persons who are for the time being parties to it, or any variation of the agreement.[152]

Extent of the obligation in the case of a share acquisition agreement

For the purposes of the provisions in Pt 22 of the Act, each party to an agreement **16–028** will be treated as interested in all shares in the target company in which any other party to the agreement is interested apart from the agreement, whether or not the interest of the other party was acquired, or includes any interest that was acquired, in pursuance of the agreement.[153] This is then further elaborated, to the effect that an interest of a party to such an agreement in shares in the target company is an interest apart from the agreement if he is interested in those shares otherwise than by virtue of the application of s.824.[154] Any such interest of that person will include, for these purposes, any interest treated as his under s.822 or s.823 or by the application of s.824 and s.825 in relation to any other agreement with respect to shares in the target company to which he is a party.[155] Finally, the form that the notification to the company must take must state that the person making the notification is a party to such an agreement, include the names and (so far as known to him) the addresses of the other parties to the agreement, identifying them as such, and state whether or not any of the shares to which the notification relates are shares in which he is interested by virtue of s.824 (and this section) and, if so, the number of those shares.[156]

Notices from the company requiring information about interests in shares

A company can give notice to any person who it knows or has reasonable cause **16–029** to believe who is interested in the company's shares or to have been interested in them during the three years preceding the date on which the notice is issued.[157] The notice can require that person to confirm that fact or state whether or not it is the case and to give any further information as may be required[158] and the notice may require the person to whom it is addressed to give particulars[159] of his own present or past interest in the company's shares.[160] The notice may require the person to whom it is addressed to give such particulars as may be required

---

[151] s.824(4).
[152] s.824(4).
[153] s.825(1).
[154] s.825(2).
[155] s.825(3).
[156] s.825(4).
[157] s.793(1).
[158] s.793(2).
[159] The particulars referred to can include the identity of the person interested in the shares in question and whether persons interested in the same shares are or were parties to certain agreements (such as those under s.824) or an agreement or arrangement relating to the exercise of any rights conferred by the holding of the shares: s.793(5).
[160] s.793(3).

where his interest is a present interest and another interest in the shares subsists or another interest subsisted during that three-year period at a time when his interest subsisted.[161] The information required by the notice must be given "within such reasonable time as may be specified in the notice".[162]

A person is under no obligation to comply with a notice from the company if he has been exempted from doing so by the Secretary of State.[163] In such a case the Secretary of State must have consulted the Governor of the Bank of England and be satisfied that there are special reasons why that person should not be subject to the obligations imposed by s.793.[164]

Non-compliance: application for an order imposing restrictions on shares

16–030 Where a notice has been given by the company and the relevant person fails to give the company the information required by the notice the company can apply to the court for an order directing that the shares be subject to restrictions.[165] Pursuant to this, the court may, if it is satisfied that this may unfairly affect the rights of third parties in respect of the shares, direct that such acts by such persons shall not constitute a breach of the restrictions.[166] The court may make an interim order, either unconditionally, or on such terms as the court thinks fit.[167]

Consequences of an order imposing restrictions

16–031 The Act spells out the effect of an order made pursuant to s.794.[168] This is as follows: any transfer of the shares is void[169]; no voting rights are exercisable in respect of the shares; no further shares may be issued in right of the shares or in pursuance of an offer made to their holder[170]; except in a liquidation, no payment may be made of sums due from the company on the shares, whether in respect of capital or otherwise.[171]

Relaxation of restrictions

16–032 The restrictions imposed may be relaxed where these unfairly affect the rights of third parties in respect of the shares.[172] Application can be made by the company

---

[161] s.793(4).
[162] s.793(7).
[163] s.796(1).
[164] s.796(2).
[165] s.794(1).
[166] s.794(2).
[167] s.794(3).
[168] All the provisions of the section are expressed to be subject to s.792(2), s.799(3), and s.794(3): s.797(4).
[169] Where any transfer of shares is made void, any agreement to transfer the shares is void (although this would not, however, apply to an agreement under s.800(3)(b)): s.797(2).
[170] An agreement to transfer any right to be issued with other shares in right of those shares, or to receive any payment on them (otherwise than in a liquidation), is void, except that this does not apply to an agreement under s.800(3)(b): s.797(3).
[171] s.797(1).
[172] s.799(1).

or any aggrieved person[173] and, if the court is satisfied that the application is well-founded, it may, subject to such terms as it thinks fit, order that certain acts by such persons do not constitute a breach of the restrictions.[174]

Removal of restrictions

It is possible for an application to be made to court for an order directing that the **16–033** shares cease to be subject to any restrictions.[175] As was the case under s.799, an application under this section may be made by the company or by any aggrieved person.[176] The court must not, however, make an order, unless two criteria are fulfilled.[177] The first is that the court must not make an order unless it is satisfied that the relevant facts about the shares have been disclosed to the company and no unfair advantage has accrued to any person as a result of the earlier failure to make the disclosure. The second is that the court must not make an order unless the shares are to be transferred for valuable consideration and the court approves the transfer. Where an order is made in relation to the latter, subs.(4) specifies that an order may continue, in whole or part, the restrictions listed in s.797(1)(c) and (d) so far as they relate to a right acquired or offer made before the transfer. Where these restrictions continue in force an application may be made for an order directing that the shares are to cease to be subject to those restrictions and subs.(3) will not apply (subs.(5)).

Penalties for evasion of restrictions

Where there is an attempted evasion of the restrictions imposed under s.794, an **16–034** offence is committed by the company and also every officer of the company who is in default.[178] Such an offence will be committed where a person:

1. exercises or purports to exercise any right to dispose of shares that to his knowledge, are for the time being subject to restrictions, or to dispose of any right to be issued with any such shares;

2. votes in respect of any such shares (whether as holder or proxy), or appoints a proxy to vote in respect of them;

3. being the holder of any such shares, fails to notify of their being subject to those restrictions a person whom he does not know to be aware of that fact but does know to be entitled (apart from the restrictions) to vote in respect of those shares whether as holder or as proxy; or

4. being the holder of any such shares, or being entitled to a right to be issued with other shares in right of them, or to receive any payment on

---

[173] s.799(2).
[174] s.799(3).
[175] s.800(1).
[176] s.800(2).
[177] s.800(3).
[178] s.798(3). A person found guilty is liable on conviction on indictment to a fine and, on summary conviction, to a fine not exceeding the statutory maximum: s.798(4).

them (otherwise than in a liquidation), enters into an agreement which is void under s.797(2) or (3).[179]

Order for sale of shares

16–035 On application being made by the company[180] the court has the power to order the shares which are subject to restrictions are sold, subject to the court's approval as to the sale.[181] Where the court does make an order, it is empowered to make such further order relating to the sale or transfer of the shares as it thinks fit.[182] In relation to this further order, the application may be made by the company, by the person appointed to effect the sale, or by any person interested in the shares.[183] The court may also order that the costs be paid out of the proceeds of the sale.[184]

Application of the proceeds of the sale

16–036 Where shares are sold by court order under s.801, the proceeds, less the costs, are required to be paid into court for the benefit of those who are beneficially interested in the shares.[185] A person beneficially interested may apply to the court for the whole or part of the proceeds to be paid to him.[186] The court is then enjoined to order the payment to the applicant of the whole of the proceeds of sale together with any interest on them or, if some other person had a beneficial interest in them at the time of sale, such proportion of the proceeds and interest as the value of the applicant's interest in the shares bears to the total value of the shares.[187] Where, however, the court orders the costs to be paid out of the proceeds, the applicant is entitled to payment of his costs out of those proceeds before any person interested in the shares receives any part of them.[188]

Members requests to the company to act

16–037 The members of the company are empowered to require that the company should exercise its powers under s.793.[189] The company can be required to do so where it has received requests[190] from members holding at least 10 per cent of the paid-up

---

[179] s.798(2).
[180] s.801(2).
[181] s.801(1).
[182] s.801(3).
[183] s.801(4).
[184] s.801(5).
[185] s.802(1).
[186] s.802(2).
[187] s.801(3).
[188] s.801(4).
[189] s.803(1).
[190] Section 803(3) provides that the request must be made in hard copy form or in electronic form and state that the company is requested to exercise its s.793 powers, specifying the manner in which the company is requested to act and giving reasonable grounds for the request. It must be authenticated by those making it.

capital of the company which carries the right to vote at general meetings of the company, excluding voting rights attached to treasury shares.[191]

Register of substantial shareholders

Requirement to keep a register

A company is obliged to keep a register of the information which it has received **16–038** under a s.793 notice.[192] However, the company will not, by virtue of anything done for the purpose of the section, be affected with notice or put on enquiry as to the rights of any person in relation to any shares.[193]

Information on the register

The company must, within three days of receipt of the information, enter in the **16–039** register the fact that the information was imposed, the date on which it was imposed, and the information received in pursuance of the requirement.[194] The record of this information must be entered against the name of the present holder of the shares in question or if there is no present holder (or he or she is unknown) against the name of the person holding the interest.[195] The register must be made up so that the entries against the names appear in chronological order.[196] An offence is committed by the company and every officer of the company who is in default.[197]

Index to the register

The Act provides that the company must keep an index of the names entered **16–040** on the register, unless the register is itself in such a form as to constitute an index.[198] The index must be kept available for inspection at the same place as the register.[199] The company is required to make any necessary entry or alteration in the index within 10 days after the date on which any entry or alteration is made in the register.[200] The index must also contain a sufficient indication to enable the information entered to be readily found.[201] There are penalties for default.[202]

Availability of the register for inspection

There are similar requirements as for the register of members. The register has to **16–041** be kept available for inspection at the company's registered office or at the place

---

[191] s.803(2).
[192] s.808(1).
[193] s.808(7).
[194] s.808(2).
[195] s.808(3).
[196] s.808(4).
[197] s.808(5)(6).
[198] s.810(1).
[199] s.810(4).
[200] s.810(2).
[201] s.810(3).
[202] s.810(5)(6).

where the company's register of members is kept.[203] A company must give notice to the Registrar of companies of the place where the register is kept available for inspection and also of any change in that place.[204] However, no notice will be required if the register has, at all times, been kept available for inspection at the company's registered office.[205] There are penalties for default.[206]

Rights of inspection and copies of entries

16–042 There are similar statutory requirements as for the register of members. Thus, the register and its associated index must be kept open to inspection by any person without charge.[207] On payment of the prescribed fee, any person may request to be provided with a copy of any entry in the register.[208]

Company's response to the request for inspection and copies

16–043 Where a request is made, the company must comply if it is satisfied that the request is made for a proper purpose.[209] If it decides to refuse the request, the company must inform the person who has made the request, stating the reasons why it is not satisfied.[210] That person, in turn, may apply to court[211] and, if so, the person must notify the company. The company must then use its best endeavours to notify any person whose details would be disclosed if the company were required to comply with the request.[212] If the court is not satisfied that the inspection or copy is sought for a proper purpose it may direct that the company need not comply with the request.[213] If the court makes such a direction and it appears to it that the company may be subject to further requests, it may direct that the company need not comply.[214] If the court orders the company to comply, it must do so immediately on the court giving the decision or on the proceedings being discontinued.[215]

Consequences of refusal or default

16–044 The Act provides for the imposition of penalties for default in the case of an inspection required under s.811 and where this is refused or default is made in providing a copy.[216] The court may by order compel an immediate inspection or direct that the copy required be sent to the person requesting it.[217]

---

[203] s.809(1).
[204] s.809(2).
[205] s.809(3).
[206] s.809(4)(5).
[207] s.811(1).
[208] s.811(2).
[209] s.812(1).
[210] s.812(2).
[211] s.812(3).
[212] s.812(4).
[213] s.812(5).
[214] s.812(6).
[215] s.812(7).
[216] s.813(1)(2).
[217] s.813(3).

Removal of entries

A company is permitted to remove an entry if more than six years have elapsed **16–045** since the entry was made.[218] Subject to that, entries must not be deleted except where there has been an incorrect entry relating to a third party.[219] If an entry is wrongly deleted, the company is obliged to restore it as soon as is reasonably practicable.[220]

Adjustment of entries

Where a person is identified in the register as party to an agreement to which s.824 **16–046** applies and then ceases to be a part to the agreement, the Act provides that he may apply to the company for the inclusion of that information in the register.[221] Where the company is satisfied that he has ceased to be a party to that agreement, it must record that information (if not already recorded) in every place where his name appears in the register as a party.[222] Where the application is refused, the applicant may apply to the court for an order directing the company to include that information in the register and the court may make such an order as it thinks fit.[223]

Company ceasing to be a public company

Where the company ceases to be public company, the Act provides that it must **16–047** continue to keep any register as required under s.808 as well as any associated index, for a period of six years after it ceased to be such a company.[224] Failure to do so is an offence and the extent of the default and its consequences is spelt out by the Act.[225]

ANNUAL RETURN

Further details as to shareholders must also be disclosed in the company's annual **16–048** return. Every company must make such a return to the Registrar each year made up to a date not later than the company's "return date".[226] That date is fixed initially at one year from the date of the company's incorporation, and subsequently it is one year from the date when the last return was made up.[227] Each return must contain the information required and be delivered to the Registrar within 28 days after the date to which it is made up.[228] It is an offence for the

---

[218] s.816.
[219] s.815(1). For the requirements for removal of an incorrect entry, see s.817.
[220] s.815(2). There are penalties for default: s.815(3)(4).
[221] s.818(1).
[222] s.818(2).
[223] s.818(3).
[224] s.819(1).
[225] s.819(2)(3).
[226] s.854(1).
[227] s.854(2).
[228] s.854(3).

company, any director of the company, the company secretary, or officer of the company to fail to comply with these obligations.[229]

Contents of the annual return

16–049 The contents of the annual return for all companies are specified by the Act. The following information is required:

1. the date to which it is made up[230];

2. the address of the company's registered office[231];

3. the type of company it is and its principal business activities[232];

4. the required particulars of the directors of the company,[233] and in the case of a private company with a secretary or a public company, the secretary or joint secretaries[234];

5. if any company records are kept at a place other than the company's registered office, the address of that place and the records that are kept there[235];

6. whether the company was a traded company at any time during the return period.[236]

In addition, if the company has a share capital, the Act requires the annual return to contain details as to the company's capital at the date to which the return is made up.[237] Information is also required specifically about the shareholders in non-traded[238] and traded[239] companies.

The required contents of an annual return can be amended by regulations made by the Secretary of State.[240]

[229] s.858.
[230] s.855(1).
[231] s.855(1)(a).
[232] s.855(1)(b).
[233] See s.855A. This section was inserted by the Companies Act 2006 (Annual Return and Service Addresses) Regulations 2008 (SI 2008/3000).
[234] s.855(1)(c).
[235] s.855(1)(d).
[236] s.855(1)(f).
[237] s.856.
[238] s.856A. This section was inserted by the Companies Act 2006 (Annual Return and Service Addresses) Regulations 2008 (SI 2008/3000).
[239] s.856B. This section was also inserted by the Companies Act 2006 (Annual Return and Service Addresses) Regulations 2008 (SI 2008/3000).
[240] s.857.

Chapter 17

DIRECTORS

DIRECTORS AND COMPANY LAW

Introduction

While companies are treated by English law as being distinct legal persons, all of **17–001** the activities of a company must necessarily be conducted through the medium of human beings. After all, a company cannot pick up a telephone, or post a letter or type an email, even though company law theory treats companies as having sufficient legal personality to create contracts, to own property and so forth. In general terms, the most significant human beings in the conduct of the activities of a company are its directors. The management of a company's affairs are ordinarily entrusted ultimately to its directors.[1] The legal responsibilities and powers of directors are the concerns of this chapter. Company law has requirements as to the requisite number of directors and as to those directors' ordinary duties and powers. Among other things, this chapter deals with the appointment, remuneration and removal of directors. It also shows that the directors of a company act as a board, that articles of association ordinarily give the directors extensive powers to manage the company's business, that usually the company in general meeting cannot overrule the directors provided that they act within their powers, and that the articles of association can empower the directors to appoint a managing director and to delegate any of their powers to him. The most important topics dealt with in this chapter are the general fiduciary duties and duties of care which a director owes to his company in exercising these powers: the analysis of those duties comprises the bulk of this chapter.

The structure of this chapter

This chapter is divided up as follows. The first section defines what a "director" **17–002** is. The second section continues with a brief summary of the previous case law principles (to provide a map through the remaining discussion) and an introduction to the over-arching provisions of the statutory code.[2] The bulk of this chapter is made up of the discussion in the second section which considers the statutory code for directors' general duties in Pt 10 of the Companies Act 2006 and of the

---

[1] However, in larger companies middle and junior management may well conduct important functions.
[2] At p.321.

old case law dealing with those same principles. The discussion of the statutory
code considers each statutory principle in turn, and then, because those statutory
principles are explicitly predicated on the old case law, that discussion considers
the case law applicable to each statutory principle. The third section of the
chapter considers other aspects of fiduciary law which are significant in the liabilities of directors beyond the statutory code.[3] The fourth section of the chapter
considers miscellaneous other aspects of the law relating to directors.[4] The fifth
section of this chapter considers the disqualification of directors from their
office.[5] The sixth section of this chapter considers the non-legal requirements of
corporate governance regulation which have been introduced in recent years in an
effort to impose practical controls on the behaviour and remuneration of directors
particularly in large public companies.

The legal nature of directorship

What is a director?

17–003   The nature of directorship is central to company law. Directors are fiduciaries, as
considered below, but they may also have other capacities: not least their personal
capacities. For example, in a private company the directors are usually substantial shareholders as well as being the company's managers. Therefore, there is a
possibility for conflicts between such a person's fiduciary and personal capacities. In a public company, the directors normally have few shares as a proportion
of the total shareholding in the company, and so their fees and other emoluments,
rather than their dividends from their shareholding, are their main source of
profit from the company. Consequently, in the context of public companies, the
management and the ownership of the company are more likely to be separated.
     Importantly, there are also different types of directors. In practice, companies
will have different grades of director. There will usually be full-time, executive
directors, and part-time, non-executive directors. In large public companies, good
corporate practice generally requires that executive directors may not control all
aspects of management (as considered below), especially decisions relating to
their own remunerations. Consequently, non-executive directors (generally drawn
from backgrounds which give them useful perspectives on the company's business) are used to decide issues which executive directors ought not to decide alone,
and are used to advise the executive directors on the most appropriate way for the
company to act in a number of circumstances. The more complex the company or
group of companies, the more likely it is that different directors will have very
different responsibilities within the organisation: whether managing a particular
trading unit, or supervising the organisation's financial affairs, or personnel, or
whatever. Consequently, there can be differences in the levels of power, influence
and remuneration of directors. A number of different types of people may be
treated as being a director, as considered next.

---

[3] At p.371.
[4] At p.380.
[5] At p.387.

Who is a director?

The exact name or title which is given to a person who occupies the position of **17–004**
director is immaterial because under s.250 of the CA 2006 the term "director" is
defined so as to include "any person occupying the position of director, by whatever name called". Although there is some dispute, the current view is that this
provision only applies to persons properly appointed as "directors" but who operate
under a different title, e.g. as a "governor".[6] A person who has been lawfully
appointed as a director is known as a "de jure" director; as opposed to people who
may appear to discharge the functions of a director in practice but without having
been appointed as a director. However, on a normal interpretation, the definition in
s.250 allows for others who are not properly appointed as directors to be regarded
as directors. There are two such categories of director beyond those people who
have been officially appointed as directors: "de facto" directors and "shadow"
directors. Each category is considered in turn in the sections to follow.

De facto directors

The courts have long accepted that a person who has never been properly **17–005**
appointed as a director may nevertheless be regarded as being a director for the
purposes of imposing some liability or restriction on him, usually in the context
of imposing a disqualification order (as considered below). Such persons are those
who have acted as if they were directors although they have never been appointed
as such. They are known as "de facto" directors. The essential element is that
they are openly acting as directors and, as such, should be contrasted with the
statutory category of "shadow" directors, dealt with below, who exert control from
behind the scenes. In most cases, these categories are mutually exclusive since
one claims to be a director whilst the other claims not to be one.[7] Nevertheless in
both cases they will have exercised an influence over the governance of the
company.

More precisely, the question is what does a person have to do to become a de
facto director? There have been a number of judicial attempts to provide an answer
to this question. In *Hydrodan (Corby) Ltd, Re*, Millett J. held that[8]:

> "A de facto director is a person who assumes to act as a director. He is held out
> as a director by the company, and claims and purports to be a director, although
> never actually or validly appointed as such. To establish that a person was a de
> facto director of a company, it is necessary to plead and prove that he undertook
> functions in relation to the company which could properly be discharged only
> by a director. It is not sufficient to show that he was concerned in the manage-
> ment of a company's affairs or undertook tasks in relation to his business which
> cannot properly be performed by a manager below board level."

---

[6] *Lo-Line Electric Motors Ltd, Re* [1988] B.C.L.C. 698 at 706, per Browne-Wilkinson V.C.;
cf. *Eurostem Maritime Ltd, Re* [1987] P.C.C. 190, per Mervyn Davies J.
[7] See *Kaytech International Plc, Re* [1999] 2 B.C.L.C. 351 at 422, per Robert Walker L.J.
[8] [1994] 2 B.C.L.C. 180 at 183.

Although that definition was applied in *Secretary of State for Trade and Industry v Morrell*,[9] it was criticised by Lloyd J. in *Richborough Furniture Ltd, Re*[10] principally on the basis that there ought not to be a requirement that such a person should be holding himself out as being a director nor that he be held out by the company as being a director. Instead Lloyd J. substituted a revised version of the principle in the following terms:

"It seems to me that for someone to be made liable . . . as a de facto director, the court would have to have clear evidence that he had either been the sole person directing the affairs of the company . . . or, if there were others who were true directors, that he was acting on an equal footing with the others in directing the affairs of the company. It also seems to me that, if it is unclear whether the acts of the person in question are referable to an assumed directorship, or to some other capacity such as a shareholder or, as here, a consultant, the person in question must be entitled to the benefit of the doubt."[11]

17–006 This test was approved and applied in *Secretary of State for Trade and Industry v Laing*[12] with the additional element that even if one particular act could be regarded as amounting to a de facto directorship, that does not mean that the person is still acting as such. Instead it was held that one can cease to be a de facto director simply by ceasing to act as such. The idea that if the acts could be attributable to acting in a capacity other than a director, the person should be given the benefit of the doubt, was also approved in *Secretary of State for Trade and Industry v Hickling*[13] and *Sykes (Butchers) Ltd, Re.*[14]

In *Secretary of State for Trade and Industry v Tjolle*,[15] Jacob J. considered both the tests set out above. He held that it may be difficult to formulate a single test, and that it would not be sufficient to make a person a de facto director simply on the basis that he was held out as being a director, or even used the title. That would, however, be a factor to be taken into account and may require the person to rebut a presumption of directorship. What was required was evidence of activities which could only be discharged by a director and/or either that the person was the sole person directing the affairs of the company, in the sense of taking major decisions on proper financial information, or was acting on an equal footing with others in directing the affairs of the company. With regard to the idea of an equal footing, Jacob J. pointed out that this meant the right to participate in management decisions and not necessarily equal power in coming to those decisions. After all, that is the reality in most boardrooms in larger companies.

It seems, therefore, that there is no single decisive factor and that those mentioned above are not exhaustive. In *Kaytech International Plc, Re*, the Court of Appeal[16]

---

[9] [1996] B.C.C. 229.
[10] [1996] 1 B.C.L.C. 507.
[11] [1996] 1 B.C.L.C. 507 at 524.
[12] [1996] 2 B.C.L.C. 324.
[13] [1996] B.C.C. 678.
[14] [1998] 1 B.C.L.C. 110.
[15] [1998] 1 B.C.L.C. 333.
[16] [1999] 2 B.C.L.C. 351.

said that overall the court must be satisfied that the individual had assumed the status and functions of a director, so as to have openly exercised real influence in the corporate governance of the company. In that case, the individual had been the moving spirit in setting up the company, had pretended to raise the capital and variously described himself as a director and as chief executive. Even though he apparently did not consider himself to be one, the court had little difficulty in finding that he was a de facto director. Likewise in *Secretary of State for Trade and Industry v Jones*,[17] a similar finding was made against a substantial shareholder in a small company who had taken an active part in running the company in order to protect his investment and had signed a letter as "joint managing director". When the company, with the connivance of the defendant, holds the defendant out as being a director, then the defendant will be deemed to be a de facto director.[18]

On the other hand no such finding was made against the defendant in *Red Label Fashions Ltd, Re*.[19] There was no clear indication that she had acted as a director rather than as a manager or "a compliant and dutiful wife willing to perform any role which [her husband] wanted her to perform in the hope that this might lead to the saving of their marriage and further their jointly owned company". Again, in *Secretary of State v Becker*,[20] there was found to be no evidence of the defendant undertaking functions in relation to the company which could properly be discharged only by a director. Similarly in *Gemma Ltd v Davies*[21] even though a wife had been held out by her husband as being a director of a company, she had never done so herself and it could not be proved that she had participated in the company's decision-making processes nor that she had influence over them: in consequence it was held that she was neither a de facto director nor a shadow director.

Shadow directors

Several of the statutory provisions in both the Companies Act and the Insolvency **17–007** Act relating to directors also apply to "shadow directors".[22] Section 251 of the 2006 Act[23] provides that these are persons in accordance with whose instructions the directors are accustomed to act, excluding purely professional advice. These types of directors are different from "de facto directors" because they do not purport to act as directors. On the contrary, they claim not to be directors and so seek to hide behind those who are. In that sense, they "lurk in the shadows". In *Hydrodam (Corby) Ltd, Re*,[24] the question arose as to whether two directors of a parent company could be regarded as shadow directors of a subsidiary company. It was

---

[17] [1999] B.C.C. 336.
[18] *Shepherds Investments Ltd v Walters* [2007] 2 B.C.L.C. 202.
[19] [1999] B.C.C. 308. This was so even though the defendant had consistently lied about her role and functions.
[20] [2003] 1 B.C.L.C. 555.
[21] [2008] 2 B.C.L.C. 281.
[22] Fiduciary duties could also apply to such persons: see *Yukong Line Ltd v Rendsburg Investments Corporation of Liberia (No.2)* [1978] 1 W.L.R. 294 at 311.
[23] See also IA 1986 s.251.
[24] [1994] 2 B.C.L.C. 180.

held that for a person to be a shadow director, four things must be shown: first, the identity of the formally-appointed directors and the de facto directors of the company; second, that the person in question directed those formally-appointed and de facto directors as to how to act in relation to the company[25]; third, that those directors acted in accordance with that person's directions[26]; and, fourth, that the directors were accustomed to act in that manner. The judge was prepared to accept that the parent company may have been a shadow director of its subsidiary[27] but the two directors of the parent company could not be liable as shadow directors of the subsidiary simply because they took part in board meetings of the parent company. Further, if they acted in implementing board decisions with respect to the subsidiary, they were only acting as agents of the parent company. It would have been different if they had acted individually with respect to the subsidiary company.

The definition was expanded on by Morritt L.J. in *Secretary of State for Trade and Industry v Deverell*.[28] His lordship set out the following propositions, noting as he did so that "lurking in the shadows" was not an essential part of the definition of what constituted a shadow director. First, the definition should be construed in the normal way to give effect to Parliament's intention, especially the protection of the public, even though the provision may be quasi-penal.[29] Secondly, the purpose of the definition is to identify those who are not professional advisers but who have a real influence on corporate affairs; but it is not necessary that the influence should be exercised over the whole field of its corporate activities. So, it would be enough to make a person a shadow director that that person took day-to-day control of the logistical aspects of ordering a company's raw materials and the manner in which the board of directors approached raw materials issues, but did not supervise the production of the finished goods: it is not necessary that the entire business is under his control. Thirdly, whether a communication is a direction or instruction must be construed in the light of the evidence and not simply by reference to the label used, but it is not necessary to prove the understanding of either party. Communication and its consequences will suffice in most cases. So, for example, calling a memorandum an "Information Sheet, for information only" which in practice was treated by all of the members of the board of directors as instructions as to their duties from the person who in practice controlled the company from outside the board of directors, would render that person a shadow director. Fourthly, advice given in a non-professional capacity may well come within the category of direction or instruction. So, for example, if a solicitor gave an instruction to the directors so as to comply with contract law then that would not render the solicitor a shadow director because a solicitor would commonly give such instructions simply in a legal capacity. By contrast, if a person who was not a solicitor gave instructions as to the contents of

---

[25] Directing, only one or two out of several directors will not be enough: *Kuwait Asia Bank E.C. v National Mutual Life Nominees Ltd* [1990] B.C.L.C. 868, *Unisoft Group Ltd, Re (No.2)* [1994] B.C.C. 766.

[26] But not if it is rescue plan initiated by a creditor in return for extending credit. The directors had a choice to "take it or leave it". *PFTZM Ltd, Re* [1995] 2 B.C.L.C. 354.

[27] This depends upon the wording of the particular statutory provision, many of which negate this possibility.

[28] [2000] 2 B.C.L.C. 133.

[29] Such as wrongful trading or disqualification proceedings.

contracts as part of his control of the board of directors at arm's length, then that would indicate that that person was a shadow director. Fifthly, although it would be sufficient to indicate a shadow director, there is no need to show in all cases that the properly appointed directors cast themselves in a subservient role or surrendered their respective discretions to the shadow director because that would be to put a gloss on the phrase "accustomed to act".[30]

Directors as fiduciaries

Directors as fiduciaries and agents

A director owes fiduciary duties to the company and will act as an agent of the **17–008** company.[31] The director's fiduciary duties and duties of care to the company will be considered in detail below. As Lord Cranworth L.C. held[32]:

> "The Directors are a body to whom is delegated the duty of managing the general affairs of the Company. A corporate body can only act by agents, and it is of course the duty of those agents so to act as best to promote the interests of the corporation whose affairs they are conducting. Such agents have duties to discharge of a fiduciary nature towards their principal. And it is a rule of universal application that no one, having such duties to discharge, shall be allowed to enter into engagements in which he has, or can have, a personal interest conflicting, or which possibly may conflict, with the interests of those whom he is bound to protect".

Even though the company is clearly the legal owner, directors have long been regarded as the equivalent of trustees of the company's property and money under their control,[33] and as being in a fiduciary position in relation to the exercise of their powers of management of the company. Thus in their dealings with the company's assets and so forth, the directors will be liable for breach of trust if they misapply them, giving rise to a constructive trust in many circumstances[34] or to an action against them for damages or equitable compensation for any loss caused to the company or, even if there is no loss, to account for any gain they may have made as a result of the breach.[35] Similarly, such liability to compensate

---

[30] Millet J. in *Hydrodam* suggested otherwise. But those words do require some pattern and a single instruction, however significant, will not suffice: *Secretary of State v Becker* [2003] 1 B.C.L.C. 555.

[31] "Directors of a company are fiduciary agents, and a power conferred upon them cannot be exercised in order to obtain some private advantage or for any purpose foreign to the power": per Dixon J. in *Mills v Mills* (1938) 60 C.L.R. 150 at 186.

[32] *Aberdeen Rlwy Co v Blaikie Bros* (1854) 1 Macq. 461 at 471.

[33] See e.g. per Lord Selborne L.C. in Great Eastern Rlwy Co *v Turner* (1872) L.R. 8 Ch. 149 at 152. Sometimes they are referred to as constructive trustees but more properly they are treated as being equivalent to a trustee: *JJ Harrison (Properties) Ltd v Harrison* [2002] 1 B.C.L.C. 174.

[34] *Regal v Gulliver* [1942] 1 All ER 378; *Boardman v Phipps* [1967] 2 A.C. 47; *CMS Dolphin Ltd v Simonet* [2001] 2 B.C.L.C. 704, Lawrence Collins J.; *Sinclair Investment Holdings SA v Versailles Trade Finance Ltd (No.3)* [2007] EWHC 915, 10 ITELR 58, Rimer J.

[35] *Selangor United Rubber Estates Ltd v Cradock (No.3)* [1968] 1 W.L.R. 1555; *Bishopsgate Investment Management v Maxwell (No.1)* [1993] B.C.L.C. 1282; *Gwembe Valley Development Co Ltd v Koshy (No.3)* [2004] 1 B.C.L.C. 131.

or to account will attach to the directors if they act in breach of any of their fiduciary duties in the exercise of their powers of management. In certain cases the company may also recover its property (or its loss) from third parties who have either received the property or assisted in the breach. The obligations of directors are considered in greater detail below.[36]

On the basis that directors are regarded as being trustees, or as having trustee-like responsibilities, it has now been accepted that actions against them for breach of fiduciary duty are subject to s.21 of the Limitation Act 1980. That requires any action by a beneficiary to recover trust property or in respect of any trust to be brought within six years, after which it is said to be time barred. There is no such limitation, however, if either the action is in respect of fraud or for a fraudulent breach of trust,[37] or to recover trust property or its proceeds from the trustee or property previously received by the trustee and converted to his own use.[38]

Directors as agents

17–009 Directors are agents through whom a company acts,[39] and it is largely because they are agents that they were originally regarded as owing fiduciary duties and certain duties of care to the company. Like other agents, directors incur no personal liability on contracts made by them on behalf of the company, within the scope of their authority.[40] If, however, directors exceed the powers given to them by the memorandum and articles they will be liable for breach of warranty of authority.[41] Their actions may be ratified by the company in general meeting even if they have acted contrary to the company's constitution. Directors may be specifically appointed agents for the shareholders to negotiate a sale of the company's shares; and if so, the shareholders are liable for their fraud.[42] Further, directors may hold themselves out to the shareholders as agents for the shareholders, in which case the directors must disclose any profit made by them to the shareholders.[43]

DIRECTORS' GENERAL DUTIES

Directors' duties at the heart of company law

17–010 The nature of directors' duties is one of the most interesting aspects of company law. Given that the activities of companies are in fact conducted by human beings, albeit under the disguise of corporate personality, and given that a company's

---

[36] Where a person has improperly profited from his fiduciary position the court has equitable jurisdiction to award interest on the judgment for damages for misfeasance or breach of duty as a director: *Wallersteiner v Moir (No.2)* [1975] Q.B. 373, CA, where the interest awarded was compound interest at one per cent per annum above the official bank rate or minimum lending rate in operation at the time.

[37] See *Gwembe Valley Development Co Ltd (No.3) v Koshy* [2004] 1 B.C.L.C. 131, CA.

[38] See *JJ Harrison Properties Ltd v Harrison* [2002] 1 B.C.L.C. 162.

[39] See, e.g. per Lord Selborne L.C. in *Great Eastern Rlwy Co v Turner* (1872) L.R. 8 Ch. 149 at 152. See Ch.6.

[40] *Elkington & Co v Hürter* [1892] 2 Ch 452.

[41] *Firbank's Exors v Humphreys* (1886) 18 Q.B.D. 54, CA.

[42] *Briess v Woolley* [1954] A.C. 333.

[43] *Allen v Hyatt* (1914) 30 T.L.R. 444; *Munro v Bogie* [1994] 1 B.C.L.C. 415 CS (OH)

directors are its principal human actors, then the duties of those directors to the company, and the effect of those duties on third persons such as the shareholders, employees, creditors and others, are central to the legal control of companies. The Companies Act 2006 introduced a statutory code of directors' general duties for the first time. Interestingly, this statutory code expressly preserves the effect of the previous case law and allows the precise nature of those duties to develop with any later case law. The case law relates specifically to the common law on directors' duties and significantly applies the equitable principles which govern the liabilities of all fiduciaries, including directors. The purpose of the statutory code was to formalise directors' duties so that non-lawyers could understand their duties as directors more clearly.

THE STATUTORY SCHEME IN OUTLINE

The extent of the statutory scheme on directors' general duties in Pt 10 of the CA 2006

The ambit of the statutory scheme

The statutory scheme on directors' duties is contained in Ch.2, Pt 10 of the CA **17–011** 2006 titled "General Duties of Duties". That Chapter covers the principles in s.170 through to s.177, and attendant legislation. The ambit of the statutory scheme is set out in s.170 of the CA 2006 in the following terms:

"(1) The general duties specified in sections 171 to 177 are owed by a director of a company to the company."

Significantly, then the director owes the duties considered below to the company itself and not, for example, to the shareholders of the company. Therefore, the company is confirmed as being the proper plaintiff in relation to claims for any breach of such a duty by a director.

The term "director" in this context is expanded by s.170(5) of the CA 2006 so that "[t]he general duties apply to shadow directors where, and to the extent that, the corresponding common law rules or equitable principles so apply". Therefore, as considered at the beginning of this chapter, shadow directors are treated as being directors. As a result, a person who controls a company or who performs the duties of a director without being formally appointed as such, may not avoid liability for breach of duty simply by virtue of not being appointed formally as a director if he is in truth a shadow director, as discussed immediately above.

The interaction of the statutory scheme with the case law

It is very important to understand the unusual interaction between the statute **17–012** and the case law. The statutory scheme is best understood as a statement of a director's general obligations qua director, and as such as an attempt to reduce the case law principles to a short, comprehensible code. To this effect, s.170(3) of the CA 2006 provides as follows:

"The general duties are based on certain common law rules and equitable principles as they apply in relation to directors and have effect in place of those rules and principles as regards the duties owed to a company by a director."

Therefore, the statutory scheme can be interpreted in accordance with the pre-existing case law in that the general duties are based on those common law and equitable principles. Significantly, the statutory principles have effect "in place of" the case law. Therefore we might assume that, in the ordinary course of events, the statute has displaced all of the pre-existing case law, except to the extent that the pre-existing case law might be referred to in the event that the statutory principles are unclear or their genesis is obscure. However, s.170(4) of the CA 2006 provides as follows:

"The general duties shall be interpreted and applied in the same way as common law rules or equitable principles, and regard shall be had to the corresponding common law rules and equitable principles in interpreting and applying the general duties."

Therefore, while the statutory rules act "in place of" the pre-existing case law, the statutory rules are nevertheless to be interpreted as though they were themselves case law principles. That means that the high-level principles set out on ss.171 through 177 of the CA 2006 are capable of being developed by subsequent case law. What is unclear is how we can understand these principles as being a sort of case law principle given that presumably the courts are not permitted to overrule nor materially alter the sense of the statutory rules. Furthermore, as s.170(4) provides, "regard shall be had" to the case law principles in the development of the statutory principles. In effect, then, it is suggested that the effect of this statutory scheme is that the previous case law principles have been distilled down to the statutory code (and therefore that any earlier cases which conflict with this statutory scheme are deemed to be of no further effect) but that in the future the courts may develop those principles as with any case law principle which is (presumably) binding upon it.

The purpose and effect of the statutory scheme

17–013 The purpose behind creating a statutory code for directors' duties for the first time was to enable non-lawyers to understand their duties as directors more easily. The Companies Act 2006, as with its predecessor legislation, is drafted in as accessible a way as possible. Therefore, having all of a directors' general duties reduced from reams of complex case law down to a brief code of statutory principles means that all directors should be able to understand what their obligations are. The continued importance of the old case law and the natural development of the case law principles mean that those general principles are still illustrated by centuries of jurisprudence. On a more cynical note, one might think that the principal effect of the statutory code (which contains clear expression of the limitations on each principle) is to provide directors with clear instructions as to how they can avoid their duties. For example, in relation to the principles on conflicts of interest it is made clear in s.175 how directors can give one another authorisation to take profits from their fiduciary duties, as well as setting out a conceptualisation of the core principle. Therefore, the effect is likely to be that the legislation enables directors to avoid their obligations and consequently has the practical effect of reducing the strictness of fiduciary and similar duties in the corporate context.

The statutory scheme provisions in outline

Those duties on each director in outline are: a duty to act within the terms of his **17–014** powers under the company's constitution[44]; a duty to promote the success of the company as the director sees it in good faith[45]; a duty to exercise independent judgment[46]; a duty to exercise reasonable care, skill and diligence[47]; a duty to avoid conflicts of interest[48]; a duty not to accept benefits, such as bribes and secret commissions[49]; and a duty to declare interests in transactions.[50] It should be noted that under s.179 of the CA 2006 that more than one of the general duties may apply at the same time. Each is considered in turn below.

The methodology of this chapter in discussing the statutory code

In the discussion to follow, each of the statutory general duties is taken in turn. **17–015** This chapter takes the approach that, if the statutory provisions now act "in place of" the case law, then the discussion must begin with an analysis of the statutory principles. Then, after the discussion of each statutory principle, our focus turns to an analysis of the case law applicable to that principle. By knitting the discussion of the case law together with the statutory provisions in this way it is possible to see more clearly how the statutory provisions relate to the case law principles and how they may be interpreted in the future.

DUTY TO ACT WITHIN POWERS

The statutory principle

A company is a person which must act not only in compliance with the **17–016** general law but also in accordance with the terms of its own constitution. Its directors are therefore similarly constrained. Consequently, s.171 of the CA 2006 provides that:

"A director of a company must—

(a) act in accordance with the company's constitution, and
(b) only exercise powers for the purposes for which they are conferred."

[44] Companies Act 2006 s.171.
[45] Companies Act 2006 s.172.
[46] Companies Act 2006 s.173.
[47] Companies Act 2006 s.174.
[48] Companies Act 2006 s.175.
[49] Companies Act 2006 s.176.
[50] Companies Act 2006 s.177.

Under s.171(a) each director is obliged to act in accordance with the company's constitution. This means both that the director must use his own powers within the terms specified in the company's constitution and that the director must not seek to make the company act outwith the terms of its own constitution. Furthermore, under s.171(b), in relation to the director's powers, the director must only exercise those powers for the purposes for which they were granted. Under the case law there have been a number of situations in which, for example, directors have used a power to issue new shares, which was intended to enable the company to raise capital, so as to frustrate a takeover attempt without asking the shareholders whether or not they wanted that takeover to go ahead. Consequently, a power intended for one purpose was being used for a different, inappropriate purpose. In *Smith and Fawcett Ltd, Re* it was held that the directors were required to act "bona fide in what they consider—not what a court may consider—is in the interests of the company, and not for any collateral purpose".[51] If a director breaches any of the obligations under s.171, then that director will be liable to compensate the company for any loss suffered by the company as a result.

The principle in the case law

17–017   As was set out above, in *Smith and Fawcett Ltd, Re* it was held that the directors were required to act "bona fide in what they consider—not what a court may consider—is in the interests of the company, and not for any collateral purpose".[52] This principle has given birth to two statutory principles: the principle that directors must act in accordance with the company's constitution and their powers, and the principle that directors must promote the success of the company (under s.172, considered next). As considered above, one of the ways in which directors have abused their powers has been to obstruct takeovers. In *Punt v Symons*[53] it was found by Byrne J that the power to issue shares had been given to the directors

> "for the purpose of enabling them to raise capital when required for the purposes of the company . . . but when I find a limited issue of shares to persons who are obviously meant and intended to secure the necessary statutory majority in a particular interest [to prevent a vote in favour of a takeover], I do not think that is a fair and bona fide exercise of the power."[54]

Similarly, in *Hogg v Cramphorn*[55] the controlling director, Colonel Cramphorn, wanted to stop Baxter from taking the company over and so convinced his compliant fellow directors to issue shares to people who would vote against the takeover. It was held that the power to issue share capital was a fiduciary power which could be set aside if it was exercised for an improper motive even if the issue was made in good faith in the belief that it was in the interests of the company. Consequently, the use of the power was held to be ultra vires. It was,

[51] [1942] Ch. 304 at 306, per Lord Greene MR.
[52] [1942] Ch. 304 at 306, per Lord Greene MR.
[53] [1903] 2 Ch. 506.
[54] [1903] 2 Ch. 506 at 515.
[55] [1967] Ch. 254.

however, ratifiable (and eventually ratified) by the shareholders in that case, and so that ratification made the exercise of the power enforceable as a result.[56]

An alternative approach to *Hogg v Cramphorn* was taken in Canada in the case of *Teck Corporation Ltd v Millar*[57] on the basis that, when new shares were issued to prevent a takeover, directors were entitled to consider the reputation, experience and policies of anyone seeking to take over the company. If they decided on reasonable grounds that the takeover would cause substantial damage to the company's interests then they were entitled to use their powers to protect the company. Consequently, it was held that it was not correct to say that issuing shares otherwise than to raise capital was always a breach of duty.

What may be significant about the drafting of s.171(b) is that it imposes a posi- **17–018** tive obligation on directors to act in accordance with the company's constitution and to operate their powers properly. This differs from the *Smith and Fawcett* formulation which requires that directors refrain from committing a breach of their duties.[58]

The question is then how the court is to identify an improper exercise of a power. The case law approach to the obligations of directors to the exercise of their powers was set out by Parker J. in *Regentcrest Ltd v Cohen*[59]:

"The duty imposed on directors to act bona fide in the interests of the company is a subjective one . . . The question is not whether, viewed objectively by the court, the particular act or omission which is challenged was in fact in the interests of the company; still less is the question whether the court, had it been in the position of the director at the relevant time, might have acted differently. Rather, the question is whether the director honestly believed that his act or omission was in the interests of the company. The issue is as to the director's state of mind. No doubt, where it is clear that the act or omission under challenge resulted in substantial detriment to the company, the director will have a harder task persuading the court that he honestly believed it to be in the company's interest; but that does not detract from the subjective nature of the test."

Therefore the court will not substitute its own view of what a director should have done for the director's own decision.[60] Instead, the court is concerned to identify whether or not the director acted honestly in the exercise of his power. The appropriateness of the director's actions will be thrown into relief, in his lordship's opinion, by whether or not it causes detriment to the company. However, it is suggested that a director may act in good faith in the exercise of a power but nevertheless cause loss. The better approach, it is suggested, would be whether or not, on a proper interpretation of the purpose of the power, the directors were

---

[56] That a breach may be ratified was approved in *Howard Smith Ltd v Ampol Petroleum Ltd* [1974] A.C. 821.

[57] (1972) 33 D.L.R. (3d) 288.

[58] See *Hunter v Senate Support Services Ltd* [2004] EWHC 1085, [2005] 1 B.C.L.C. 175; *Edge v Pensions Ombudsman* [2000] Ch. 602 at 627, CA.

[59] [2001] 1 B.C.L.C. 80 at 105b. See also *Smith and Fawcett Ltd, Re* [1942] Ch. 304.

[60] The final sentence of that quote allows the court in effect to import some basic reasonableness test in the sense that the alleged honest belief must be credible. Sometimes the word is actually used: see, e.g. *Pantone 485 Ltd, Re* [2002] 1 B.C.L.C. 266.

genuinely pursuing that purpose or whether they were pursuing some alternative goal. Therefore, it is not enough that a director have been honest, but rather they must also be exercising their powers for the purpose for which they were granted. So, as considered above, a power to allot new shares may not be used to prevent a takeover bid.[61] In this vein, in *Colin Gwyer & Associates v London Wharf (Limehouse) Ltd*,[62] it was said that where the directors had failed to separate their own interests from those of the company, their assertion that they had acted in the best interests of the company should be examined with particular care. In essence, would an intelligent and honest man in the directors' position have reasonably believed that a particular course of action was for the benefit of the company?

17–019 The duty to consider the best interests of the company is also considered below in relation to the duty in s.172 of the CA 2006. An issue clearly arises not only as to whether or not the director is acting honestly but also as to whether or not the action which the directors propose to take is in the company's interests. In that sense, the directors may choose to be conservative as well as progressive in choosing to protect the company's position instead of moving into new territory. The Privy Council in *Howard Smith Ltd v Ampol Petroleum Ltd*[63] considered similar facts to *Hogg v Cramphorn* where shares were allotted so as to frustrate an attempted takeover by one company so as to improve the chances of another bidder. In essence, the directors allotted enough shares to convert a majority shareholding into a minority shareholding because the majority shareholding was considered likely to vote for what they considered to be the "wrong" takeover bid. It was established on the facts that the primary purpose of the allotment was not to raise money but was intended instead to destroy the existing majority shareholding; although it was also found that the directors were not motivated by the advancement of their own self-interest, but their rather their view of the interests of the company. The Privy Council rejected both the argument that allotments of shares can only be carried out to raise capital and also the argument that any finding of self-interest in the exercise of the power necessarily invalidates it. Instead it was held that no limitation can be placed in advance on the exercise of the directors' powers. Rather, the court must examine the purpose for which the power was exercised and consider whether that purpose was proper or not. This requires a close interpretation of the precise power in the articles of association on which the directors were relying. It was held on those facts that the power to allot shares had been exercised improperly because it had been used solely to frustrate a takeover offer.

It was held further in *Howard Smith v Ampol* that the court must respect the directors' opinion on questions of management; although that is a question to be considered on the circumstances of each case. In the abstract there could be two ways in which the law could operate: either the law could take an objective view of what the court thinks the director ought to have done, or the law could leave the decision subjectively to the director and consider whether or not the directors were acting in the best interests of the company. The law takes the latter

---

[61] *Piercy v S. Mills & Co Ltd* [1920] 1 Ch. 77; *Hogg v Cramphorn Ltd* [1967] Ch. 254; *Bamford v Bamford* [1970] Ch. 212, CA.
[62] [2003] 2 B.C.L.C. 153.
[63] [1974] A.C. 821, PC.

approach. In *Mutual Life Insurance v The Rank Organisation*,[64] Goulding J. applied this distinction between questions relating solely to management of the company and other questions in upholding a rights issue which was not made available to certain US shareholders. Unlike the *Howard Smith* case it was held that this particular arrangement did not upset the status quo within the company but rather maintained the investment policy of the company. As considered above, in *Howard Smith v Ampol* it was held that it was unconstitutional for the directors to exercise their powers purely for the purpose of destroying an existing majority or creating a new majority which had not previously existed, and consequently it was not a question relating solely to the management of the company over which the directors had exclusive competence.

The company's constitution is separate and distinct from the powers themselves. Thus it would be a breach of duty for the directors to operate contrary to the memorandum or articles of the company or to enter into a contract on behalf of the company whereby they remained in post as directors so that the shareholders could not exercise their constitutional rights to appoint new directors.[65] Similarly, using company funds other than for the commercial purposes of the company is contrary to the purpose for which management is delegated to the board.[66] In other cases which are regarded as being management areas, however, the courts will simply apply the principles considered above to decide whether the directors have acted in breach of their duty in exercising a power under the articles, for example to vary the terms of the managing director's service contract.[67]

If the directors act in breach of their duty, then they will be liable to account for any profits made and to compensate the company for any loss incurred. If the director actually obtains corporate assets for himself, he becomes a constructive trustee of those assets and the company will be able to recover the property or its proceeds from him. These various remedies, together with any defences, are discussed later in this section. But there is one further issue. If the directors, in abuse of their powers, have entered into a contract with a third party, clearly the members can ratify it, but in what circumstances can that third party enforce the contract against the company anyway? This issue arose in *Criterion Properties Ltd v Stratford UK Properties LLC*.[68] The alleged abuse of power was an agreement entered into by the then managing director of a company which allowed for the sale of certain assets to S if another party obtained control of Criterion. This is an example of what is known as a "poison pill" in the world of takeovers, since it makes the company less attractive to outside predators because valuable assets could be sold off before a takeover is completed. Since there was evidence that this contract would damage the company more than an outsider gaining control of the company, the Court of Appeal held that it was an abuse of power. The question, however, was whether the contract could be enforced by S. The

---

[64] [1985] B.C.L.C. 11.
[65] *Lee Panavision Ltd v Lee Lighting Ltd* [1992] B.C.L.C. 22, CA.
[66] *Extrasur Travel Insurances Ltd v Scattergood* [2003] 1 B.C.L.C. 598.
[67] *Runciman v Walter Runciman Plc* [1992] B.C.L.C. 1084. See also *CAS (Nominees) Ltd v Nottingham Forest FC Plc* [2002] B.C.L.C. 613, where a statutory provision was not regarded as being mandatory.
[68] [2004] 1 W.L.R. 1846, HL, cf. [2003] 2 B.C.L.C. 129, CA.

Court of Appeal held that it was a question of whether it would be unconscionable for S to retain the benefit of the contractual right. The House of Lords disagreed on that issue. In their view the situation was purely one of agency: that is, did the managing director have authority to make that contract? If he did, then it was enforceable; whereas if he did not, then it was not.

DUTY TO PROMOTE THE SUCCESS OF THE COMPANY

The statutory principle

The genesis of the principle; and the significance of the six factors

17–020 One of the most interesting innovations in the CA 2006 is the creation of a statutory duty for directors "to promote the success of the company". The policy behind this development was set out in the Company Law Review in the following terms:

> "We believe there is value in inserting a reference to the success of the company, since what is in view is not the individual interests of members, but their interests as members of an association with the purposes and the mutual arrangements embodied in the constitution; the objective is to be achieved by the directors successfully managing the complex relationships and resources which comprise the company's undertaking."[69]

The breadth of this duty is potentially enormous and, significantly, is not focused exclusively on the profitability of the company alone, but rather takes a much more "three-dimensional"[70] approach to the company's place in the community and in its interactions with third parties other than the shareholders. It is important, however, to note that the statutory principle requires the promotion of the success of the company "for the benefit of its members", which does focus attention on the members' needs as opposed to success in a more general sense. If this concept is read in accordance with the paragraph quoted from the Company Law Review above, then it could be interpreted as requiring that it is the *collective* interests of the members as a body which must be considered by the directors and not the individual interest of any one member. The statutory principle does also require that other factors are to be borne in mind at the same time, even though those other factors may be of lesser importance within s.172. Section 172 of the CA 2006 provides that:

> "(1) A director of a company must act in the way he considers, in good faith, would be most likely to promote the success of the company for the benefit of its members as a whole, and in doing so have regard (amongst other matters) to—
>
> (a) the likely consequences of any decision in the long term,
> (b) the interests of the company's employees,

---

[69] Company Law Review, *Modern Company Law for a Competitive Economy: Developing the Framework* (URN 00/656), para.3.51.

[70] Apologies: the term is my own. It suggests that instead of looking solely at profit, or solely at the interests of shareholders, the directors should also properly consider the broader role of a company within society.

(c) the need to foster the company's business relationships with suppliers, customers and others,

(d) the impact of the company's operations on the community and the environment,

(e) the desirability of the company maintaining a reputation for high standards of business conduct, and

(f) the need to act fairly as between members of the company."

It is suggested that while the statutory principle requires the promotion of the success of the company "for the benefit of its members", this does suggest that even though other factors should be borne in mind (or, more importantly, may be borne in mind by the directors without them having breached their duties) nevertheless pursuing the interests of the members does remain first among equals: that is, pursuing the interests and promoting benefits of members is the primary objective of the directors in promoting the success of the company, although other factors may be borne in mind so as to deviate from a course of action which might otherwise advance the naked financial interests of the shareholders in high dividends and a buoyant share price. Historically, Anglo-American company law was focused on the best financial health of the company. There were celebrated cases in the USA where, for example, directors were precluded from using the company's money for any purpose other than developing the business or distributing profits to shareholders.[71] Consequently, on this limited model of company law, charitable contributions or non-salary benefits for employees were prohibited. However, company law thinking has developed since. From the perspective of business theory, investment in good public relations and in a happy workforce is considered to be more important now than used to be the case.[72] So, the inclusion of this list of factors which directors may take into account in considering the success of the company, we see company law moving beyond the longstanding debates in the cases and the journals about what constituted the "best interests of the company"—a concept which was mentioned briefly in the previous section relating to directors under the case law being required to exercise their powers in the best interests of the company. In essence, it might be said that some of these principles derive from the old case law and from s.391 of the now-repealed Companies Act 1985, but the discussion of this provision was one of the most controversial in the passage of the 2006 Act and marks a departure in many senses from the old law because of the inclusion of the six further factors in statutory form, as considered next.

Interpreting the six factors

In relation to the six factors listed in s.172(1), three things should be observed. First, **17–021** a natural reading of the prefatory words of s.172(1) *requires* the director to consider the six factors. The subsection opens with the verb "must" and ends by saying that

---

[71] *Dodge v Ford* 204 Mich. 459, 170 N.W. 668, Michigan Supreme Court.
[72] See, for example, in England: *Hutton v West Cork Railway* (1883) 23 Ch.D. 654 where it was held that there may be "cakes and ale" on a limited scale. For a more modern discussion of the role of public relations in company management, see Reich, *Supercapitalism* (2008).

"in doing so" regard is to be had to the six factors. Therefore, it is suggested that the verb "must" qualifies the entire provision and so requires that the six factors are considered, even if the directors decide that they are not of overriding importance in any given context. This is important because, if the directors are required to consider these factors, then those factors become (arguably for the first time) issues which directors are compelled to consider as part of their duties as directors. Second, the prefatory words in s.172(1) make it clear that these factors should be considered "amongst other" factors not included on the list. Consequently, the directors may establish what in their professional judgment is most likely to promote the success of the company. In that sense, the legislation encapsulates the principle set out by Parker J. in *Regentcrest Ltd v Cohen*[73] to the effect that the court will not substitute its view of what the directors ought to have done for what the directors actually did do, because the power and the responsibility rests with professional directors to make their own decisions. What the directors must be able to do, it is suggested, is to justify the actions they have taken or not taken as being sufficiently likely to promote the success of the company at the time. This idea is mirrored in the opening words of s.172(1) to the effect that "a director of a company must act in a way which *he* considers . . . would be most likely to promote the success of the company": therefore, each director individually bears a responsibility as well as holding a power. (It is suggested that this chimes in with the requirement that each director exercise independent judgment (considered below) in that each director has this power and responsibility.) Third, each director must be acting in good faith in supposing that a given course of action will promote the success of the company. Each provision is considered in turn. It should be recalled that s.172(1) places the "benefit of the members" as a principal aspect of the success of the company, as discussed above.

The six factors

17–022   First, it has long been a complaint among radical economists that capitalist markets are orientated too closely around short-term considerations. In stock markets the key determinant for much investment activity is the return that is generated on each share by way of dividend in each financial year. Therefore, to ensure easy access to capital, there is pressure on management to maximise short-term earnings per share at the expense, it is said, of the long-term health of the company and of the economy more broadly. Therefore, the first factor is "the likely consequences of any decision in the long term". This chimes in with the concerns of the Blair-Brown administrations, being social democratic, mildly left-of-centre governments, to ensure investment for the longer term and the operation of companies for the longer term benefit of the economy and all involved.

Second, the traditional matrix of English company law focuses on the rights of the company, the rights of the shareholders and the duties of the directors. No one else had a *right* to be considered. In practice, management would consider the need for good industrial relations (up to a point) and the need to keep creditors and others content so that the company could continue to function. However, there was no legal

---

[73] [2001] 1 B.C.L.C. 80 at 105b. See also *Smith and Fawcett Ltd, Re* [1942] Ch. 304.

right for those people to be considered by the company's directors when managing a company. The inclusion of the second factor that "the interests of the company's employees" must be considered has the effect of empowering the directors to consider the interests of employees. This is not the same as giving the employees rights to act against the management or the company itself, but it does free the directors from liability for breach of duty for considering employees instead of shareholders, and the directors are required to "have regard" to the interests of employees inter alia when making decisions.

Third, a successful economy requires that all participants in the economic chain—whether suppliers, customers, service providers, or whoever—are entitled to rely on one another. Particularly in difficult economic times, it is important that companies do not decide arbitrarily not to pay moneys owed to other people nor to treat customers badly. Therefore, requiring directors to consider the position of such people is hoped to have a beneficial effect on the economy: thus, "the need to foster the company's business relationships with suppliers, customers and others" is included in s.172.

Fourth, and following on from the discussion of the social role of companies in **17–023** the previous paragraph, the directors are to have regard to "the impact of the company's operations on the community and the environment". As opposed, for example, to pursuing solely profitable but potentially polluting activities, the directors may now consider the effect of the company's operations on both the community more broadly and also on the environment without being held liable for breaching a common law obligation to act in the best interests of the company. It is an important development in the scope of company law that directors are to have regard to the impact of the company's operations. In an age where more responsible business practices are required by policymakers and by consumers, this is an important maturing in the law.[74]

Fifth, the movement away from a single-minded focus on profit is also part of an ethical project to raise standards of behaviour among commercial people. Therefore, paragraph 172(1)(e) of the CA 2006 provides that directors must have regard to "the desirability of the company maintaining a reputation for high standards of business conduct". Whereas a quick profit might be earned by unscrupulous conduct, this provision empowers directors to consider the need to maintain high standards in their business ethics. The concomitant benefit in the broader economy is then a higher mean level of ethical business behaviour in the economy. Importantly, directors cannot be held liable for breach of duty on the basis that they acted reasonably in putting business ethics before profit.

Sixth, the ensuring of equal treatment of shareholders and members of a company is an important part of company law. The provisions ensuring minority protection from abusive behaviour in ss.994 et seq. of the CA 2006 are one aspect of this process. Relieving the directors from a claim for breach of duty where they act so as to ensure equal and fair treatment of the company's members is another aspect of that process. Hence, s.172(1)(f) requires that directors have regard to "the need to act fairly as between members of the company."

---

[74] See Alastair Hudson, *Understanding Company Law* (Routledge-Cavendish, 2011), Ch.14 "Corporate Social Responsibility".

The nature of the success of the company: consequent provisions

17–024 The success of any given company must be decided on its own merits, specifically by reference to the objectives of that company on its formation as expressed in its constitutional documents. Subsections (2) and (3) of s.172 are new. Section 172(2) of the CA 2006 provides that:

> "Where or to the extent that the purposes of the company consist of or include purposes other than the benefit of its members, subsection (1) has effect as if the reference to promoting the success of the company for the benefit of its members were to achieving those purposes."

Therefore, if the company is created with constitutional purposes which are beyond the mere benefit to members (much as a co-operative industrial and provident society is organised around a common bond between members such that the altruistic goals of the organisation outweigh the individual rights of individual members[75]), then those alternative purposes may be taken to constitute a part of the evaluation of the success of that company.[76]

Section 172(3) of the CA 2006 provides that:

> "The duty imposed by this section has effect subject to any enactment or rule of law requiring directors, in certain circumstances, to consider or act in the interests of creditors of the company."

Section 214 of the Insolvency Act 1986, for example, requires the directors to contribute to the company's assets in the event of wrongful trading. More generally, it is a contested idea in company law whether or not the company and its directors should owe more than contractual duties to its creditors.[77] On one view, the common law held that the directors owed their duties in this sense to the company and not to third parties.[78] In any event, the directors' duties were to ensure that the creditors were not placed in a worse position by the insolvency proceedings, as opposed to advancing their interests actively.[79]

The principle in the case law

The "best interests" approach

17–025 The case law did not have a principle relating to the promotion of the success of the company directly. Instead, the case law was concerned that the directors

---

[75] See Alastair Hudson, *The Law of Finance* (London: Sweet & Maxwell, 2009) p.1310 et seq.

[76] *CAS (Nominees) Ltd v Nottingham Forest FC Plc* [2002] 1 B.C.L.C. 613.

[77] See, for example, *West Mercia Safetywear Ltd v Dodd* [1988] B.C.L.C. 250.

[78] *Kuwait Asia Bank v National Mutual Life* [1991] 1 A.C. 187, 217; *Yukong Line Ltd v Rendsburg Investments (No.2)* [1998] 1 W.L.R. 294.

[79] *Weldfab Engineers Ltd, Re* [1990] B.C.L.C. 833, Hoffmann J. However, identifying where reasonable continuation of activities has been carried on by the directors, as opposed to looking after creditors, is difficult to establish: *Facia Footwear Ltd v Hinchcliffe* [1998] 1 B.C.L.C. 218 at 228.

should act in the best interests of the company. As considered in the previous section, there were cases such as *Punt v Symons*,[80] *Hogg v Cramphorn*[81] and *Howard Smith v Ampol*[82] in which the directors had sought to obstruct potential takeovers of their companies by using their powers to allot new shares (so that there would not be a majority of shareholders able to vote in favour of the takeover). In those instances it was held that the directors must use their powers for the purposes for which they were intended and also that they must act in the best interests of the company, and not for some collateral purpose. So, in *Punt v Symons*, Byrne J. held that issuing shares so as to frustrate the takeover was not "bona fide for the general advantage of the company". In relation to the use of director's powers, this also involved identifying the proper purpose behind that power in the company's constitution.

Interpreting the "success of the company" where there are different interests

It is possible that the ongoing interests of the company are at odds with the short-term goals of shareholders: for example, the company may need to invest in its plant and machinery so as to make profits in the future, whereas some of the shareholders may prefer to receive a large dividend pay-out immediately. It is suggested that it would be a breach of duty if the directors chose in the abstract to prefer the interests of one group of shareholders over another group of shareholders.[83] Alternatively, a shareholder may be in competition with the company and so may wish to have the directors protect his own personal interests as opposed to advancing the company's business. That the directors owe their duties to the company under s.170 is important because it means that the directors must look to the company's interests as an abstract entity; and when taken with the prefatory words to s.172(1), it would suggest that the directors must consider the interests of the shareholders as a collective group (and thus as a "company" or association of people) instead of looking at the separate interests of individual shareholders.[84] It has been held in *Neath Rugby Club Ltd, Re*[85] that where a director has been appointed by a nominator, then it is acceptable for that director to consider the interests of his nominator when exercising his powers provided that he also considers the best interests of the company. This last principle merely shows how directors may be required to considered many contrary factors in exercising their duties.

The court's response

On the decided cases, it is not always a straightforward matter to know how to **17–026** deal with a contention that a director was not promoting the success of the

---

[80] [1903] 2 Ch. 506.
[81] [1967] Ch. 254.
[82] [1974] A.C. 821.
[83] *Mills v Mills* (1938) 60 C.L.R. 150, HCA.
[84] See, perhaps, *Mutual Life Assurance Co of New York v Rank Organisation* [1985] B.C.L.C. 11, 21, Goulding J.; *BSB Holdings Ltd (No.2)* [1996] 1 B.C.L.C. 155 at 251, Arden J.
[85] [2009] 2 B.C.L.C. 427.

company in good faith. On the basis, as discussed above, that the court will not substitute its own decision for the director's decision, then it will be necessary to show that the director could not have believed either reasonably[86] or in good faith that his decision was likely to promote the success of the company. So, it is likely that it is only in cases of egregious default that the court will be confident in upholding a breach of duty, and furthermore it is only in such cases that a claimant will be confident in commencing an action.[87] For example, in *Item Software (UK) Ltd v Fassihi*[88] a director of IS encouraged a distributor company dealing with IS to make its terms more stringent and to consider dealing with him directly. In the event negotiations between IS and the distributor company collapsed, as a result of the director's intervention. In such circumstances the director was clearly not acting in the best interests of the company (nor promoting its success, in modern parlance), and was operating on the basis of a conflict of interest. Similarly, if a director invoices a company fraudulently so as to divert money to himself, then that director would not be promoting the success of the company (and would also be involved in a conflict of interest).[89] However, the cases are unlikely always to be so clear cut.

DUTY TO EXERCISE INDEPENDENT JUDGMENT

17–027 It is an essential part of the duties of any fiduciary that that fiduciary is responsible for acts which he performs and also that he is responsible for acts which he ought to have performed: otherwise a fiduciary would be able to avoid liability for breach of duty in circumstances in which he simply failed to act. This would be an opiate on the conscience of fiduciaries.[90] Therefore, company directors are required to perform their duties under Pt 10 of the CA 2006 and, under s.173 specifically, they are required to act independently of control by any other person. Therefore, from the perspective of fiduciary law at the very least, company directors are required to exercise their own judgment as to the discharge of their duties and as to the issues which confront the board of directors. Company directors may not simply act as the proxies or nominees of other people. It will certainly not be a good defence to an action for breach of a fiduciary duty that a director was simply taking instructions from another person. Section 173(1) of the CA 2006 provides that:

"A director of a company must exercise independent judgment."

However, it is not only direction from a third person which is considered (such as the person who ultimately controls a shareholding in the company, or who employs or retains the director in question), but rather it also encompasses senior executives or shadow directors in the company who exercise a de facto power over the directors. In *City Equitable Fire Insurance, Re* there was a senior executive,

---

[86] It is suggested that, given that this was originally a common law test, a notion of reasonableness is appropriate.
[87] *Item Software (UK) Ltd v Fassihi* [2004] EWCA Civ. 1244 at [44].
[88] [2004] EWCA Civ. 1244.
[89] *Tesco Stores Ltd v Pook* [2003] EWHC 823. See also *Fulham FC v Tigana* [2004] EWHC 2585.
[90] To borrow from *Bahin v Hughes* (1886) 31 Ch.D. 390.

Bevan, who controlled the other directors so that Bevan was able to commit numerous frauds with the company's property. The collapse of the Mirror group of companies revealed that Robert Maxwell had the same control over the directors in those companies. The Enron and WorldCom collapses revealed similar patterns of control by a small group of senior executives. It is a feature of many human organisations that one or two people may exercise de facto control far in excess of their legal powers. These sorts of control are also phenomena against which directors are expected to be strong enough to exercise independent judgment. It has been held in *Neath Rugby Club Ltd, Re*[91] that if a director has been appointed by a nominator, then it is acceptable for that director to consider the interests of his nominator when exercising his powers provided that he also considers the best interests of the company, and also provided that this involves no oppression of minority shareholders.

There are then two exclusions from that duty in s.173(2) in the following terms:

"(2)   This duty is not infringed by his acting—

(a)   in accordance with an agreement duly entered into by the company that restricts the future exercise of discretion by its directors, or

(b)   in a way authorised by the company's constitution."

First, if the company has properly entered into an agreement that the company will act in a particular way, then it is permissible for its directors to fetter their judgment and act in accordance with that agreement. Secondly, the company's articles of association and other constitutional documents may authorise the directors to fetter their discretion by acting in a way required by the company's constitution. The case law provided that a director could not fetter his own discretion.[92] Similarly it was held that a director may not excuse himself from liability in general terms simply by arguing that another person has instructed him how to act.

DUTY TO EXERCISE REASONABLE CARE, SKILL AND DILIGENCE

The statutory principle

Section 174 of the CA 2006 creates a statutory duty to exercise reasonable care, **17–028** skill and diligence. This encapsulates one trend in the case law before 2006 as to the duties of directors. Section 174(1) provides as follows:

"A director of a company must exercise reasonable care, skill and diligence."

This is an obligation, as indicated by the word "must". There is a question as to whether or not there is a need to exercise reasonable care or alternatively skill or alternatively diligence, or whether there is one, single duty which is a duty to

---

[91] [2009] 2 B.C.L.C. 427.
[92] See variously: *Kregor v Hollins* (1913) 109 LT 225; *Fulham FC Ltd v Cobra Estates Plc* [1994] 1 B.C.L.C. 363; *Scottish Co-operative Wholesale Society Ltd v Meyer* [1959] A.C. 324; *Kuwait Asia Bank EC v National Mutual Life Nominees Ltd* [1990] 1 A.C. 187.

exercise reasonable care, skill and diligence as one composite expression. The statute does not make this clear. The cases have not differentiated between these three terms and therefore it is supposed that there is one composite obligation imposed on directors.

An important question which has arisen on the case law is whether the director must be measured subjectively against his own level of competence or whether the director must be measured against an objective concept of what constitutes reasonable care, skill and diligence for any director. Section 174(2) provides in this context as follows:

> "This means the care, skill and diligence that would be exercised by a reasonably diligent person with—
>
> (a) the general knowledge, skill and experience that may reasonably be expected of a person carrying out the functions carried out by the director in relation to the company, and
> (b) the general knowledge, skill and experience that the director has."

Therefore, the statute requires us to consider both the objective knowledge of anyone acting as a director and also the individual director when deciding whether or not that individual director has breached this duty. What is measured is the general knowledge (as opposed specifically to technical knowledge, it appears) and the skill and also the experience associated with an ordinary director, even if the defendant in a particular case does not have, for example, that level of experience. Therefore, all directors are required to live up to standards expected of an objective director. The alternative would be an opiate on the conscience of directors everywhere because directors could rely on being ill-informed, lacking skill and having little or no experience so as to avoid any effective liability as a director. In effect, then, an individual director should not be able to rely on his subjective level of experience and so forth unless that subjective level of experience is higher than would be expected from an objective director. In the case law, as will emerge below, the approach drifted from a subjective to an objective test in the late twentieth century. It is suggested that the effect of this drift has been embodied in the statute.

The principle in the case law

The roots of the principle in City Equitable Fire Insurance Co Ltd, Re

17–029   In essence, the modern case law history of this principle begins with the decision of Romer J. in of *City Equitable Fire Insurance Co Ltd, Re*[93] and then is traced by more recent decisions resiling from that judgment on the basis, in effect, that the uses of companies in the modern context have made the approach of Romer J. appear to be a little antiquated. Principally, Romer J. took the approach that directors bore little personal responsibility to turn up for anything more than board meetings and that

---

[93] [1925] Ch. 407 at 428.

they could delegate the day-to-day administration of the company's business to subordinate managers and employees. This gloriously Edwardian approach to the idea of the gentleman director attending at meetings, lending his good name to the company, but taking only light responsibility for the day-to-day machinations of the corporation, seems very old-fashioned. If one were to read some of the great Victorian novels which consider companies then this attitude to directors seems less unusual. In Anthony Trollope's novel *The Way We Live Now*, for example, the powerful financier Melmotte created a company to build a railroad in America and filled the board of directors with aristocratic idiots who would do his bidding and whose family names lent allure to the company's reputation. Meetings of the board took place at speed and it was clear that no one except Melmotte really understood the business which was being conducted nor the decisions which were being made. Board meetings were in effect an excuse to have lunch together. This is not how directors of companies are expected to behave today. It is expected that executive control will be exercised by professional directors who are well-paid for their hard work and expertise. While non-executive directors may be permitted to behave differently, executive directors generally may not. The modern understanding of the responsibilities of directors necessitates a more hands-on approach and direct responsibility for the failings of the company. However, duties of care, as is the case with fiduciary duties, can always be ratified by the company.[94] The case law has, it is suggested, recognised this drift in the understanding of the role of directors.

The facts of *City Equitable Fire Insurance Co Ltd, Re* are interesting. They are typical of those corporate frauds where one senior executive tends to dominate the organisation with the result that the other directors follow his orders and either wittingly or unwittingly assist him to commit fraud. So, in *City Equitable Fire, Re*, the leading light of the company, Bevan, committed widespread fraud in a notorious corporate collapse in the 1920s. The issue was whether or not some of his fellow directors and the company's auditors were liable to the company for allowing Bevan to do what he did: in particular, those directors who had signed blank cheques for Bevan and the auditors who were alleged to have overlooked fraud with "wilful default". Romer J. acknowledged that the "position of a director of a company carrying on a small retail business is very different from that of a director of a railway company", in that large businesses had different challenges for a director from smaller businesses. As Romer J. held, "in discharging the duties of his position thus ascertained a director must, of course, act honestly; but he must also exercise some degree of both skill and diligence".[95] It was held that the directors who had signed blank cheques in favour of third parties had not done so in circumstances in which there was anything to have caused them to be suspicious and so they were not liable.

So, to begin at the beginning, directors' duties of care towards the company were, for many years, defined in the propositions laid down by Romer J. in *City Equitable Fire Insurance Co Ltd, Re*.[96] These principles, which have been doubted in more recent cases and by s.174 of the CA 2006, were set out as being

---

[94] *Pavlides v Jensen* [1956] Ch. 565.
[95] *Pavlides v Jensen* [1956] Ch. 565.
[96] [1925] Ch. 407 at 428.

three in number in his lordship's judgment. Each is considered separately in the sections to follow, including subsequent case law dealing with them.

17–030 **(1) The subjective level of skill.** First, Romer J. held that, on the basis of earlier authority, "[a] director need not exhibit in the performance of his duties a greater degree of skill than may reasonably be expected from a person of his knowledge and experience".[97] As Lindley M.R. held elsewhere:

> "[i]f directors act within their powers, if they act with such care as is reasonably to be expected from them, having regard to their knowledge and experience, and if they act honestly for the benefit of the company they represent, they discharge both their equitable as well as their legal duty to the company".[98]

This means that a director was to have been held to his own, subjective standard of ability, knowledge and experience, and not that of the reasonable man. Such a director was required, however, to take the same level of care in the performance of his duties as an ordinary man might be expected to take when acting on his own behalf.

This understanding of a director's standard of care in relation to the company was first modified in respect of an executive director: that is, by someone who has a service contract with the company. There is an implied term in such a contract that the director will use reasonable skill in the performance of the duties of the office based on what might reasonably be expected from a person in his position.[99] However, more significantly, the general standard of care for all directors has been restated by Hoffmann L.J. in two cases, with virtually no discussion as to the rationale for the change, as being the same as the test for establishing wrongful trading under s.214(4) of the Insolvency Act 1986. In *Norman v Theodore Goddard*,[100] the standard of care expected of directors was held to be that of a reasonably diligent person having the knowledge, skill and experience both of a person carrying out that director's functions and of that person himself. Thus the test was expressed as being both objective and subjective.

This test was also applied by Hoffmann L.J. in *Re D'Jan of London Ltd*[101] to establish the negligence of a director in signing an inaccurate fire insurance proposal form to insure the company's property. The facts of that case are interesting. The director signed an insurance form without having read it. As a result, the company failed to disclose the information required by the insurance company so as to make the insurance contract valid. Consequently, when the company's warehouse caught fire and destroyed a large amount of stock worth £174,000, the company was uninsured. It was found by his lordship that the director "did not strike [his lordship] as a man who would fill in his own forms".[102] Hoffmann L.J.

---

[97] [1925] Ch. 407 at 428.
[98] *Lagunas Nitrate Co v Lagunas Syndicate* [1899] 2 Ch. 392 at 435.
[99] *Lister v Romford Ice and Cold Storage Co Ltd* [1957] A.C. 555.
[100] [1991] B.C.L.C. 1028. The director was excused liability on the basis of reasonable reliance on another under the third of Romer J.'s propositions.
[101] [1994] 1 B.C.L.C. 561, CA, see also *Cohen v Selby* [2001] 1 B.C.L.C. 176, CA.
[102] [1994] 1 B.C.L.C. 561 at 562.

considered that the amount of work and the amount of diligence required of a director would differ from circumstance-to-circumstance:

> "I do not say that a director must always read the whole of every document **17–031** which he signs. If he signs an agreement running to 60 pages of turgid legal prose on the assurance of his solicitor that it accurately reflects the board's instructions, he may well be excused from reading it all himself. But this was an extremely simple document asking a few questions which Mr D'Jan was the best person to answer."

Therefore, the director was personally liable to compensate the company on these facts because this was a simple form which the director should personally have read and dealt with, even though there might be circumstances in which a director might be absolved from liability. In essence, it is suggested that a director is well-advised to seek advice in more complex circumstances so that he cannot be held to have negligently failed to attend to this sort of duty. On either test, whether subjective or objective, it was held that the director in *D'Jan* had failed to act with reasonable diligence. The remedy was expressed to be an obligation to "compensate" the company.[103]

Since it is now accepted that the wrongful trading standard is the standard of care for negligence,[104] the cases on wrongful trading (and disqualification) on what is expected of a director, set out later in this chapter, will be of great significance in any negligence action.

(2) The quality of attention which a director must give to the affairs of the 17–032 company. Second, and somewhat at odds with the modern understanding of the duties of a director, Romer J. held that:

> "A director is not bound to give continuous attention to the affairs of his company. His duties are of an intermittent nature to be performed at periodical board meetings, and at meetings of any committee of the board upon which he happens to be placed. He is not, however, bound to attend all such meetings, though he ought to attend whenever, in the circumstances, he is reasonably able to do so."[105]

A more modern and appropriate approach, it is suggested, is that set out in *Dorchester Finance Co Ltd v Stebbing*,[106] in which two non-executive directors were held to be negligent in not attending board meetings of a subsidiary company even though it was shown that it was not the usual business practice in that company to do so. Directors also signed blank cheques for a director who rarely attended the company's offices, with the result that that director embezzled

---

[103] [1994] 1 B.C.L.C. 561 at 564.
[104] See e.g. the Government's position as set out in *Modernising Company Law*, Cmn. 5553–1, paras 3.2–3.7, accepting the suggestions of the Company Law Review.
[105] [1925] Ch. 407 at 428.
[106] [1989] B.C.L.C. 498.

money from the company. Foster J. approved the test set out by Romer J.,[107] although he came to conclusions on the facts in front of him which seemed different from those which Romer J. would have reached. It was held that it was important to recognise that the directors were accountants and people with long experience of acting in the financial affairs of various bodies, and consequently that they could not assert that non-executive directors had no duties to perform. Foster J. expressed himself as being "alarmed" at the very suggestion. The signing of blank cheques was held to have been negligent. As for the director who misused the blank cheques, such that he took £400,000 from the company, it was held that he had "knowingly and recklessly misapplied the assets" of the company with the effect that he had committed gross negligence and so was liable for "damages".[108]

17–033   **(3) The extent to which a director may delegate responsibilities to another person.** Third, it was held by Romer J. that a director is entitled to trust a manager or other official to perform any duties which are delegated to him honestly, provided that this is in compliance with the exigencies of business and the articles of association, and provided that there were no grounds for suspicion when delegating tasks to that official.[109] This proposition is of particular relevance to the supervisory role of the non-executive directors in larger companies.[110] In *Equitable Life Assurance Society v Bowley*,[111] it was said, without a detailed examination of the issue since it was a summary application, that the law in this area is developing and that the third proposition in *City Equitable Fire* no longer represents the modern law. It was plainly arguable that a company may look to its non-executive directors for independence of judgement and supervision of the executive management.

An alternative formulation of the third proposition is that set out by Parker J. and approved by the Court of Appeal in the disqualification case of *Barings Plc, Re (No.5)*[112]:

"(i) Directors have, both collectively and individually, a continuing duty to acquire and maintain a sufficient knowledge and understanding of the company's business to enable them properly to discharge their duties as directors. (ii) Whilst directors are entitled (subject to the articles of association of the company) to delegate particular functions to those below them in the management chain, and to trust their competence and integrity to a reasonable extent, the exercise of the

---

[107] [1989] B.C.L.C. 498 at 501.
[108] [1989] B.C.L.C. 498 at 505.
[109] As Romer J. put the same idea, somewhat inelegantly:

"In respect of all duties that, having regard to the exigencies of business, and the articles of association, may properly be left to some other official, a director is, in the absence of grounds for suspicion, justified in trusting that official to perform such duties honestly".
[1925] Ch. 407 at 428.

[110] For the situation of a non-active director of a small company see the sections on wrongful trading and disqualification, below.
[111] [2004] 1 B.C.L.C. 180.
[112] [1999] 1 B.C.L.C. 433 at 489, approved [2000] 1 B.C.L.C. 523 at 535–536, CA.

power of delegation does not absolve a director from the duty to supervise the discharge of the delegated functions. (iii) No rule of universal application can be formulated as to the duty referred to in (ii) above. The extent of the duty, and the question whether it has been discharged, must depend on the facts of each particular case, including the director's role in the management of the company."

That formula was concerned with delegation by all directors down the chain of management but it could equally well apply to supervision of those above the non-executive directors in that chain. It is suggested that this approach is more successful in understanding the modern expectation of directors, particularly in public companies. Securities regulation expects that management and in particular the board of directors will understand the company's obligations under those regulations.[113] Investors will expect that the directors and the company's management structure maintains a firm hand on the tiller in relation to all business issues and also in relation to its understanding of any changing market in which it operates. The corporate world has changed radically from the world of Trollope's characters in *The Way We Live Now* or the non-existent board of the Anglo-Bengali Disinterested Life Assurance Company in Dickens's *Martin Chuzzelwit*, into an age of professional directors taking responsibility for the success or failure of a business. The *Barings* litigation dealt with a cadre of management in a long-standing bank which had failed to supervise or to put in place systems which would supervise the activities of one employee in particular in Singapore who was able as a result to manufacture large numbers of false transactions which bankrupted the entire institution when they unwound. In an era of gentleman directors it might have been appropriate to excuse them from liability for the fraudulent acts of a single employee many thousands of miles away, but in the modern era it is not.[114] Particularly in relation to investment business and banking, there are regulatory requirements in the FSA Handbook's "SYSC" rulebook on financial institutions to maintain adequate systems and management processes. In this new world, the company director bears positive obligations to ensure the well-being of the company which were not understood to be the norm in 1925 when *City Equitable Fire Insurance Co, Re* was decided.

DUTY TO AVOID CONFLICTS OF INTEREST

Introduction

One of the core tenets of the law on fiduciary duties is the obligation to avoid **17–034** conflicts of interest. This is a core principle of equity.[115] The conflict of interest which is referred to here is a conflict between a director's fiduciary's duties and

---

[113] See Alastair Hudson, *Securities Law* (London: Sweet & Maxwell, 2008), para.6–07.
[114] In *Lexi Holdings Plc v Luqman* [2009] 2 B.C.L.C. 1 it was found that it was in breach of directors' duties and dishonest for directors to fail to disclose the existence of false accounts and the embezzlement of money by other directors. See also *Green v Walkling* [2008] 2 B.C.L.C. 332 where it was held that a director had discharged his duties in this context by acting on the advice of his solicitor throughout. cf. *Kappler v Secretary of State DTI* [2008] 1 B.C.L.C. 120.
[115] See Alastair Hudson, *Equity & Trusts* 6th edn (Routledge-Cavendish, 2009), section 12.5.

his personal interests. For example, there would be a conflict of interest in a situation in which a director of a company was also carrying on business as a sole trader in competition with the company and so voted at a meeting of the board of directors against exploiting a specific business opportunity so that he could exploit it on his own account. That the fiduciary must avoid conflicts of interest has two consequences in equity. First, the fiduciary will be required to account for any unauthorised profit acquired as a result of a conflict of interest.[116] This account takes the form of holding any profit on constructive trust for the beneficiaries of that fiduciary duty, or of holding any property acquired with that profit on constructive trust for the beneficiaries of that fiduciary duty, or (if the property or its traceable proceeds cannot be identified) of accounting personally to the beneficiaries of that fiduciary duty for the amount of the profit.[117] Second, the fiduciary must not only avoid actually taking profits from such a conflict but must also prevent any possibility that there has been a conflict of interest.[118] In consequence the general equitable principles have been applied very strictly indeed, as Lord Chancellor King intended in the early case of *Keech v Sandford*.[119] Recent decisions of the Court of Appeal in the company law context have suggested a distaste for the rigour of these fiduciary obligations.[120] It will be suggested that this drift in the cases does not, however, show sufficient appreciation for the significance of the fiduciary principles and that its effect can be doubted in yet more recent decisions. We shall begin with the statutory expression of the principle.

The statutory expression of the principle

The core duty

17–035 The duty to avoid conflicts of interest[121] is contained in s.175 of the CA 2006 in the following terms:

> "(1) A director of a company must avoid a situation in which he has, or can have, a direct or indirect interest that conflicts, or possibly may conflict, with the interests of the company."

The obligation is incumbent on each individual director separately. The duty specifically is a duty to avoid situations where there may possibly be conflicts of

---

[116] *Regal v Gulliver* [1942] 1 All E.R. 378; *Boardman v Phipps* [1967] 2 A.C. 47.

[117] *Boardman v Phipps* [1967] 2 A.C. 47; *CMS Dolphin Ltd v Simonet* [2001] 2 B.C.L.C. 704, Collins J.; *Sinclair Investment Holdings SA v Versailles Trade Finance Ltd (No.3)* [2007] EWHC 915, 10 ITELR 58, Rimer J.

[118] Companies Act 2006 s.175. See also the decisions of variously constituted Houses of Lords asserting the need to avoid potential conflicts of interest as part of the equitable principle in *Aberdeen Railway Co v Blaikie Bros* (1854) 1 Macq 461 at 471, [1843–60] All E.R. 249 at 252, per Lord Cranworth; *Bray v Ford* [1896] A.C. 44, at 51; [1895–99] All E.R. 1009 at 1011, per Lord Herschell; *Regal v Gulliver* [1942] 1 All E.R. 378; *Boardman v Phipps* [1967] 2 A.C. 47 relating to the need under the general equitable principle to avoid conflicts of interest.

[119] (1726) 2 Eq. Cas. Abr. 741.

[120] *Murad v Al-Saraj* [2005] EWCA Civ 959; *Foster v Bryant* [2007] Bus LR 1565, considered below.

[121] It is provided in CA 2006 s.175(7) that "Any reference in this section to a conflict of interest includes a conflict of interest and duty and a conflict of duties."

interest, and not simply a duty to refrain from benefiting from a conflict of interest. The duty is therefore much broader than, for example, a duty simply to avoid taking profits from conflicts of interest or of causing loss to the company or to its shareholders by means of exploiting a conflict of interest. Therefore, the duty is breached (subject to the defences considered below) simply by failing to avoid a situation where there may be a conflict of interest. The precise conflict of interest which is at issue here is a conflict between the director's personal interests and the interests of the company. The director's interest may be direct, for example where he stands to take a fee for providing a personal service to the company; or it may be indirect, for example where the director owned shares in a company which would have taken a profit from a transaction.

It is important that it is the interests of the company which are at issue and not, for example, the personal interests of some of the shareholders nor of any particular shareholder.[122] Thus, to take two hypothetical examples: there may be a distinction between the interests of the company in developing a successful business in the long-term in relation to which a director may benefit personally from supplying that company with raw materials, which would be a conflict of interest falling under s.175 because it impacts on the interests of the company; and a situation in which one of the minority shareholders wished to have the company earn large short-term profits so as to realise a large dividend for him personally in the short-term (as opposed to contracting with the director to acquire raw materials at a fair price in the long-term) where that would concern an interest of the shareholder personally and not necessarily an interest of the company. Something which is solely in the interests of a shareholder personally is not within s.175(1), whereas it is only if it also conflicts with the interests of the company that it would fall within s.175(1). The question as to whether or not the duty had been breached would centre on the interests of the company and not on the interests of the shareholder. Therefore, if the dealing between the director and the company was considered to be appropriate (on the basis of s.175(3) of the CA 2006 considered below) then it would not matter if it conflicted with the wishes of one of the minority shareholders to earn a short-term dividend profit. The remaining provisions of s.175 qualify this general duty, as considered next.

The application of section 175 to former directors

At first blush, there would seem to be a very simple way of avoiding this **17–036** duty if a director were to resign his directorship either immediately before or immediately after taking a profit from a conflict of interest and so claim an entitlement to keep it. With this sort of problem in mind, s.170(2) of the CA 2006 provides that:

"A person who ceases to be a director continues to be subject—

---

[122] This is the key difference between companies and trusts because it would be the equitable interests of the beneficiaries which would be important because a trust has no distinct legal personality, whereas because companies have distinct legal personalities and because CA 2006 s.170 requires that it is company which is owed these duties then the particular, personal interests of the shareholders are not significant.

(a) to the duty in section 175 (duty to avoid conflicts of interest) as regards the exploitation of any property, information or opportunity of which he became aware at a time when he was a director . . .

To that extent those duties apply to a former director as to a director, subject to any necessary adaptations."

Section 175 therefore applies both to current directors and also to former directors. The issue is therefore whether the conflict of interest related to "the exploitation of any property, information or opportunity" and furthermore whether or not the director "became aware at a time when he was a director" of that "exploitation".[123]

Application of the general duty

17–037 The scope of the duty is illustrated by s.175(2) in the following terms:

"(2) This applies in particular to the exploitation of any property, information or opportunity (and it is immaterial whether the company could take advantage of the property, information or opportunity)."

This provision gives one clear example of circumstances in which the general duty applies. That relates to an "exploitation", which is a term which could be interpreted either narrowly as a pejorative abuse of property or equally as simply any use of property with a view to a personal profit for a director. It is suggested that the broader interpretation of exploitation as any use of property with a view to profit fits better with the general statement of the principle in s.175(1). Where that exploitation relates to the company's property then that would be straightforwardly to misapply property belonging to another person (i.e. the company) for personal gain. In relation to the company's commercial activities, it will also be important to cover "information" or an "opportunity" because information which is of commercial value (whether because it is confidential information in the form of intellectual property, or simply information which has general commercial worth), or an opportunity which could have been exploited profitably by the company itself are akin to property in that they may generate profit for a trading company.[124]

Limitations on the general duty in relation to transactions

17–038 The entire statutory scheme of directors' duties is hemmed in by exceptions, and (if you will pardon the expression) s.175 is no exception to that. The scope of the duty is further qualified by s.175(3) in the following terms:

---

[123] The syntax of the subsection requires that it is the "exploitation" which must have been within the director's contemplation, and not the presence of a conflict of interest. This is a rather odd limitation given that it focuses the director only on avoiding exploitation of property, etc., and not straightforwardly on avoiding all forms of conflict of interest (whether or not they relate to exploitation of property, etc.).

[124] See for example *Don King v Warren* [1998] 2 All E.R. 609 where it was held that the benefit which would flow from a non-transferable contract could itself form the subject matter of a trust and was therefore property.

"(3) This duty does not apply to a conflict of interest arising in relation to a transaction or arrangement with the company."

The provisions relating to dealings with the company are dealt with by s.177 of the CA 2006, as considered below.

Limitation on the duty where there has been authorisation

The central principle that fiduciaries may not permit conflicts of interest is clear, **17–039** and the case law has always upheld that general principle strictly. Consequently, the heart of the case law on fiduciaries being involved in conflicts of interest has always been deciding whether or not any given defendant has had authorisation to profit from a conflict of interest so that no liability to account attaches to him. This concept of authorisation is therefore effectively a defence to the general duty. In s.175, the ambit of this defence and the procedure which must be followed so as to benefit from it are set out in the following four subsections of s.175. To begin with, s.175(4) provides that:

"(4) This duty is not infringed—

(a) if the situation cannot reasonably be regarded as likely to give rise to a conflict of interest; or
(b) if the matter has been authorised by the directors."

There are effectively two defences to a claim based on a conflict of interest. Thus paragraph (a) permits the introduction of a modicum of common sense to be used to decide whether or not a conflict of interest is likely. Alternatively, paragraph (b) provides for a defence where the directors (which, in the plural, is taken to constitute a majority of the board of directors, as considered below) have "authorised" the particular matter at issue. The definition of what constitutes authorisation is considered in s.175(5) in the following terms:

"(5) Authorisation may be given by the directors—

(a) where the company is a private company and nothing in the company's constitution invalidates such authorisation, by the matter being proposed to and authorised by the directors; or
(b) where the company is a public company and its constitution includes provision enabling the directors to authorise the matter, by the matter being proposed to and authorised by them in accordance with the constitution."

The concept of authorisation therefore applies differently to private companies and **17–040** public companies. In relation to a private company, the articles of association may prevent an authorisation being granted by the directors. If there is no such prevention of authorisation being granted in the private company's constitution, then the directors may authorise something which might otherwise be a conflict of interest. By contrast, in relation to public companies the company's constitution must contain a power for directors to authorise what would otherwise be a conflict of interest. What is less clear is whether the constitution may empower the directors to authorise such conflicts of interest in general terms, or whether only one particular transaction may be authorised at a time. It is suggested that the subsection would be satisfied if the constitution permitted the directors in general terms to approve what would otherwise be conflicts of interest.

The statute appears to anticipate simply that a majority of the directors is permitted to authorise a conflict of interest. An alternative reading would be that the use of the term "the directors" means *all* of the directors agreeing to the authorisation. However, the manner in which authorisation must take place is qualified by s.175(6) of the CA 2006 in the following terms, which appears to suggest that any quorum permitted in the company's constitution is sufficient:

"The authorisation is effective only if—

(a) any requirement as to the quorum at the meeting at which the matter is considered is met without counting the director in question or any other interested director, and

(b) the matter was agreed to without their voting or would have been agreed to if their votes had not been counted."

Thus the statute provides a mechanism for directors avoiding liability stemming from conflicts of interest. In essence, s.175 provides that a director bears an obligation to avoid even potential conflicts of interest, although that duty does not exist if the directors have authorised the conflict of interest, or if there is not likely to be any reasonable conflict of interest.

The principle in the case law

The principle in essence

17–041 As considered above, the principle in s.175 is predicated on the case law which has come before it. The earliest decision of the House of Lords in this context is that in *Keech v Sandford*[125] which held that a fiduciary may not take unauthorised profits from his office.[126] The basis for this principle is said to be that the fiduciary may not permit conflicts between his personal capacity and his fiduciary capacity.[127] The proper approach to the nature of the company's rights when a fiduciary acquires an unauthorised profit is set out by Rimer J. in *Sinclair Investment Holdings SA v Versailles Trade Finance Ltd (No.3)*[128] and by Collins J. in *CMS Dolphin Ltd v Simonet*.[129] The company's rights have always been generally described by the courts on the basis that the

---

[125] (1726) 2 Eq. Cas. Abr. 741.
[126] This principle is discussed in detail in Alastair Hudson, *Equity & Trusts*, 6th edn (Routledge-Cavendish, 2009), section 12.5, p.535–564.
[127] *Boardman v Phipps* [1967] 2 A.C. 47.
[128] [2007] EWHC 915, 10 ITELR 58.
[129] [2001] 2 B.C.L.C. 704.

fiduciary is "liable to account" for the unauthorised profit. The question then is: what is meant by this obligation to account? The answer is that the principal right of the company (or beneficiary under a trust or principal in an agency arrangement) is to have the fiduciary's personal profit held on constructive trust (and in turn any property acquired with that profit[130]). If there is no property which can be separately identified as being held on trust (for example, because the profits have all been dissipated), then the director owes a personal obligation to the company to account in money or money's worth for the amount of the profits. Rimer J. has explained this doctrine accurately in *Sinclair Investment Holdings SA v Versailles Trade Finance Ltd (No.3)*[131] in the following terms:

". . . any identifiable assets acquired by fiduciaries in breach of their fiduciary duty are, and can be declared to be, held upon constructive trust for the principal[132] (*Boardman v Phipps*,[133] *AG Hong Kong v Reid*,[134] *Daraydan Holdings Ltd v Solland*)[135] . . . There will in practice often be no identifiable property which can be declared by the court to be held upon such a constructive trust, in which case no declaration will be made and the principal may at most be entitled to a personal remedy in the nature of an account of profits. In Boardman's case the court made a declaration that the shares that had been acquired by the fiduciaries were held on constructive trust (a proprietary remedy), and directed an account of the profits that had come into their hands from those shares (a personal remedy). Boardman's case can be said to have been a hard case as regards the fiduciaries, whose integrity and honesty was not in doubt; and it well illustrates the rigours of the applicable equitable principle. The recovery by the trust of the shares was obviously a valuable benefit to it; and equity's softer side was reflected in the making of an allowance to the fiduciaries for their work and skill in obtaining the shares and profits. On the very different facts of *Reid's* case, there was no question of any such allowance being made."

Therefore, the position is clear: the company's primary right is for a proprietary constructive trust over the director's profits; the secondary right (if there is no property over which the constructive trust can take effect) entitles the company to a personal remedy in the form of an account of profits from the director; and thirdly the court may make some equitable accounting to reduce the amount of any such account if the court considers the circumstances to be appropriate for the equitable relief of such a defendant (as considered below).[136]

---

[130] As is suggested by *Attorney General for Hong Kong v Reid* [1994] A.C. 324 and *Westdeutsche Landesbank v Islington* [1996] A.C. 669.

[131] [2007] EWHC 915, 10 ITELR 58.

[132] In the context of company law, the "principal" is the company further to Companies Act 2006 s.170.

[133] [1967] 2 A.C. 47.

[134] [1994] A.C. 324.

[135] [2005] Ch. 1.

[136] See also *Markel International Insurance Co Ltd v Surety Guarantee Consultants Ltd* [2008] EWHC 1135 (Comm.) illustrating the principle that secret profits made by a fiduciary must be subject to an account.

17–042   The primary form which the liability to account takes is in the form of a constructive trust, whereby a proprietary right is imposed over those profits such that the fiduciary becomes a constructive trustee over those profits. Because the company acquires a proprietary right over the profits, that beneficiary also has a proprietary right over any property that is acquired with those profits. This constructive trust right also means that even if those profits are mixed with other money, then the beneficiary acquires a right to trace into that mixture or into any substitute property and to impose a proprietary right over it.[137] The secondary form which the liability to account takes is predicated on the idea either that the profits cannot be traced or that the property substituted for the profits can be traced but has become worthless. In such a situation, the proprietary right would be worthless. In this second context, the fiduciary's liability is instead to account for the amount of the unauthorised profits personally by paying money or money's worth to the company equal to the amount of the profits. Therefore, equity provides the company with a remedy in one way or the other.

So, in the leading case of *Boardman v Phipps*[138] the beneficiaries suffered no loss when Boardman, a solicitor who advised their trustees, acquired shares in a private company on his own account while advising the trustees as to the trust's shareholding in that same company, but the beneficiaries were nevertheless entitled to force Boardman to account for the unauthorised profits which he made through his fiduciary office on those shares.[139] The basis of this liability is predicated on an actual or even a potential conflict between the fiduciary's personal interests and his fiduciary office.[140]

The roots of the principle are in equity and in the need to prevent fiduciaries from acting unconscionably in the sense of permitting conflicts of interest.[141] As this principle was expressed by Lord Herschell in *Bray v Ford*[142]:

> "It is an inflexible rule of the court of equity that a person in a fiduciary position . . . is not, unless otherwise expressly provided [in the terms of that person's fiduciary duties], entitled to make a profit; he is not allowed to put himself in a position where his interest and duty conflict. It does not appear to me that this rule is, as had been said, founded upon principles of morality.[143] I regard it rather as based on the consideration that, human nature being what it is, there is danger, in such circumstances, of the person holding a fiduciary

---

[137] *Westdeutsche Landesbank v Islington* [1996] A.C. 669. See Alastair Hudson, *Equity & Trusts*, 6th edn (Routledge-Cavendish, 2009), Ch.19.

[138] [1967] 2 A.C. 46.

[139] Consequently this is not a restitutionary remedy because the fiduciary need not have earned her profits at the beneficiaries' expense, as the theory of restitution of unjust enrichment requires. Instead, it is enough that the equitable wrong of earning unauthorised profits from a fiduciary office has been committed.

[140] e.g. *Boardman v Phipps* [1967] 2 A.C. 46.

[141] See *Yugraneft v Abramovich* [2008] EWHC 2613 (Comm.), [2008] All E.R. (Comm.) 299 at para [373], per Clarke J. where this explanation of the principle in *Attorney General for Hong Kong v Reid* [1994] 1 A.C. 324 is advanced, further to the speech of Lord Browne-Wilkinson in *Westdeutsche Landesbank v Islington* [1996] A.C. 669 asserting that unconscionability is the central, organising principle in cases of constructive trust, and indeed all trusts.

[142] [1896] A.C. 44 at 51; [1895–99] All E.R. 1009 at 1011.

[143] Although see, e.g. Parker L.J. in *Bhullar v Bhullar* [2003] 2 B.C.L.C. 241 at para [17] referring to the "ethic" in these cases.

position being swayed by interest rather than by duty, and thus prejudicing those whom he was bound to protect. It has, therefore, been deemed expedient to lay down this positive rule."

So, the rule is considered to be a strict rule, as was accepted by separately **17–043** constituted Houses of Lords in *Regal v Gulliver*[144] and in *Boardman v Phipps*,[145] considered in detail below. As Lord King held in *Keech v Sandford*[146]:

"This may seem hard, that the trustee is the only person of all mankind who might not have [the property]: but it is very proper that rule should be strictly pursued, and not in the least relaxed; for it is very obvious what would be the consequence of letting trustees have the [property] . . ."

That same principle applies mutatis mutandis to company directors, instead of trustees. Its base is the need to avoid conflicts of interest between a fiduciary's personal and fiduciary capacities, and is not dependent on proof of bad faith. As Lord Cranworth expressed this principle[147]:

". . . it is a rule of universal application that no one having such duties to discharge shall be allowed to enter into engagements in which he has or can have a personal interest conflicting or which possibly may conflict with the interests of those whom he is bound to protect."

Nevertheless, it is important that the defendant be shown to have been acting in a fiduciary capacity for this principle to take effect. As emerges from Lord Cranworth's dicta, it is necessary that the defendant had appropriate duties before the principle would apply.[148]

The application of this principle in Boardman v Phipps and in Regal v Gulliver

The most recent decision of the House of Lords considering this equitable prin- **17–044** ciple in general terms was that in *Boardman v Phipps*,[149] a case which relates to

---

[144] [1942] 1 All E.R. 378.
[145] [1967] 2 A.C. 47.
[146] *Keech v Sandford* (1726) Sel. Cas. Ch. 61.
[147] *Aberdeen Railway Co v Blaikie Bros* (1854) 1 Macq 461 at 471; [1843–60] All E.R. 249 at 252.
[148] So, in *Biss, Re* [1903] 2 Ch 40, a son was entitled to take possession of a renewed lease where, acting in good faith, he had sought a renewal in his own name of a lease which had formerly been held by his father's business, after his father had died intestate. It was held that the son did not occupy a fiduciary position in respect of his father's business, unlike the trustee in *Keech v Sandford* (1726) 2 Eq. Cas. Abr. 741, who clearly occupied the fiduciary position of trustee in relation to the infant's settlement. Therefore, the son in *Biss, Re* would not be subject to a constructive trust over the renewed lease in his own name. So, if those profits were not earned in a fiduciary capacity, then an account for the profits earned will not be ordered: see e.g. *Experience Hendrix LLC v PPX Enterprises Inc* [2003] EWCA Civ 323; [2003] 1 All E.R. (Comm.) 830; [2003] EMLR 515, where royalties had not been paid to a musician further to a contract, but in circumstances in which the defendant was not in a fiduciary relationship to the claimant, there was a right to contractual recovery of money but no equitable accounting.
[149] [1967] 2 A.C. 46 at 67. See also *Blair v Vallely* [2000] WTLR 615; *Ward v Brunt* [2000] WTLR 731.

trusts. This case followed and applied the decision of the House of Lords in *Regal v Gulliver*,[150] relating to companies. The respondent, Boardman, was solicitor to a trust who was consequently taken to be acting in a fiduciary capacity. The trust fund included a minority shareholding in a private company. While making inquiries as to the performance of the company on behalf of the trust, Boardman and the one active trustee learned of the potential for profit in controlling the company through information which they obtained as a result of being permitted to attend a general meeting of this private company on behalf of the trust. Boardman and the trustee decided to acquire enough shares personally so that they would hold a majority shareholding in the company together with the trust's shareholding. Boardman informed the active trustee that he intended to do this. However, it was held that Boardman had not provided all of the trustees with enough information to be able to rely on the defence of their authorisation for his plans. Boardman was able to assume control of the company and to generate a large profit for all concerned. The question arose whether or not he was liable to account for the personal profits which he had earned from the transaction. The majority of the House of Lords held that Boardman should hold the profits on constructive trust for the beneficiaries of the existing trust. The minority, Viscount Dilhorne and Lord Upjohn, dissented on the basis that Boardman had not acted in bad faith and therefore that he ought not to be subjected to a constructive trust. Boardman was entitled to some compensation (known as "equitable accounting") for his efforts in spite of the imposition of the constructive trust. All of their lordships agreed on the core equitable principle, however; they disagreed only as to their application to the particular facts of this case. As Lord Upjohn held:

> "Rules of equity have to be applied to such a great diversity of circumstances that they can be stated only in the most general terms and applied with particular attention to the exact circumstances of each case. The relevant rule for the decision of this case is the fundamental rule of equity that a person in a fiduciary capacity must not make a profit out of his trust which is part of the wider rule that a trustee must not place himself in a position where his duty and his interest may conflict."

These dicta contained the central statement of principle to the effect that the constructive trust in this species of case is predicated on the need to prevent conflicts of interest.

The House of Lords in *Regal v Gulliver*[151] considered a situation in which four directors of a company which operated a cinema sought to divert a business opportunity to acquire two further cinemas to a separate company which they controlled. The first company could not afford to acquire the rights to all of the cinemas out of its own resources and its directors were reluctant to give personal guarantees for the extra sums needed. Therefore, the four directors of the plaintiff company and a solicitor subscribed for shares in the second company which

---

[150] [1942] 1 All E.R. 378.
[151] [1942] 1 All E.R. 378.

took up the opportunity. Control of the original company passed into new hands and so that company (prompted by its new owners) brought proceedings against the four directors to account for the profits which they had realised from these transactions. It was held that the directors' profits on these shares were profits made from their fiduciary offices as directors. Therefore, they were required to account for those profits to the company. Lord Russell was clear that the obligation to account for profits was in no way predicated on proof of fraud or mala fides on the part of the directors. "The liability arises from the mere fact of a profit having, in the stated circumstances, been made", in the words of Lord Russell, by a fiduciary. Because the four directors were acting as directors of the plaintiff company at the time they entered into this transaction and made their profits, they were liable to account for them to the plaintiff company. Lord Russell relied on the principle in *Keech v Sandford* and the other cases referred to above in finding that this was intended to be a strict rule. All of their lordships delivered concurring speeches affirming the importance of the strict principle that fiduciaries may not earn unauthorised profits from their fiduciary offices. The four directors were not able to rely on their purported grant of authorisation to themselves to pursue this opportunity on their own account. Equally, if a director seeking authorisation from the other directors fails to make sufficiently full disclosure of all the relevant facts, then that director will not be taken to have acquired authorisation to earn personal profits.[152] It was held by Lord Russell that the directors could have acquired authorisation by seeking a vote of the general meeting of the company's shareholders to agree to the transaction. Under s.175(4) and (5) of the CA 2006, that would no longer be required, as discussed above.

The general principle that the profit must relate to a conflict of interest

The general principle is predicated on the need for any person acting in a fiduciary capacity to avoid conflicts of interest, and will therefore not be excluded where the fiduciary suggests that the profit was earned outwith the scope of his precise duties or that it was not predicated directly on misuse of the company's property. So, in the Court of Appeal in *Bhullar v Bhullar*,[153] the principle has been reasserted that the constructive trust in this context is not dependent on any interference with the company's property, but rather is based on the avoidance of conflicts of interest. In that case, the directors of a family company learned of an opportunity to acquire land neighbouring the company's land but acquired it on behalf of a second company which was under their exclusive control. The background circumstances were that the various family members who owned shares in the family company had fallen out and consequently it was difficult to forge a consensus among the shareholders as to how the company should proceed. It was held by Parker L.J. that the principle is a simple one, even if it may occasionally

17–045

---

[152] *IDC v Cooley* [1972] 1 W.L.R. 443; *Gwembe Valley Development Co Ltd v Koshy (No.3)* [2004] 1 B.C.L.C. 131, where the managing director of a company formed to farm in Zambia failed to disclose his personal interest in activities in which the company was engaged and therefore was held to be liable to account to the company for the profits which he had made.

[153] [2003] 2 B.C.L.C. 241 at para.[27], per Parker L.J.

be difficult or seemingly harsh to apply. The directors were bound by their fiduciary duties to the family company, the acquisition of the neighbouring land was an opportunity which would have been attractive to the family company, but the directors had not made that opportunity known to the family company. Therefore, the directors had not acquired authorisation to proceed on their own account. Consequently, it was held that there was a "sensible possibility of conflict" on these facts and therefore the equitable principle in *Regal v Gulliver* applied. Another decision has similarly held that this form of constructive trust is based on the fiduciary's obligation to permit no conflict between his personal benefit and his duties to others.[154]

Furthermore, it has been held that there is no need to demonstrate that the profit was earned directly "from the fiduciary office" as opposed to being made in general terms in a manner which involved a conflict between the fiduciary's personal interest and her fiduciary duties.[155] So, as Morritt V.C. has held[156]:

> "If there is a fiduciary duty of loyalty and if the conduct complained of falls within the scope of that fiduciary duty as indicated by Lord Wilberforce in *NZ Netherlands Society v Kuys*[157] then I see no justification for any further requirement that the profit shall have been obtained by the fiduciary 'by virtue of his position'. Such a condition suggests an element of causation which neither principle nor the authorities require. Likewise it is not in doubt that the object of the equitable remedies of an account or the imposition of a constructive trust is to ensure that the defaulting fiduciary does not retain the profit; it is not to compensate the beneficiary for any loss."

Therefore, if, for example, a director took some advice from the stockbrokers advising a company which was in the business of investing in shares that there was only one remaining parcel of shares which were expected to realise a massive profit, and if the director acquired those shares for herself rather than for the company, it would not be open to the director to argue that she acquired the shares on her own account and not while working for the company. Otherwise it would be too simple for fiduciaries to argue that they were acting in a different capacity when taking direct or indirect advantage of their office. Instead, the strict principle in *Keech v Sandford* and *Bray v Ford* is to be enforced so that no possible conflict of interest can be allowed to generate an unauthorised profit for a fiduciary. This, it is suggested, is the reason for supporting the decision of the majority of the House of Lords in *Boardman v Phipps*: if Boardman had been permitted to retain his profits, then the purity of the principle derived from *Keech v Sandford* and from *Bray v Ford* would have been fatally compromised.

---

[154] Deane J. in *Chan v Zacharia* (1984) 154 C.L.R. 178.
[155] *United Pan-Europe Communications NV v Deutsche Bank* [2000] 2 B.C.L.C. 461; *Button v Phelps* [2006] EWHC 53.
[156] *United Pan-Europe Communications NV v Deutsche Bank* [2000] 2 B.C.L.C. 461 at para.[47]; approved in *Button v Phelps* [2006] EWHC 53 at para.[66].
[157] [1973] 1 W.L.R. 1126.

The defence of authorisation in the case law

There is, effectively, a defence to an action for constructive trust on grounds of **17–046**
making personal profits that the fiduciary had authorisation so to do. The effect of
s.175(5) of the CA 2006 is that it formalises the way in which fiduciaries can
acquire the necessary authorisation, whereas on the authorities there were few
circumstances in which authorisation was found to have been granted. It was
suggested by the House of Lords in *Boardman v Phipps* that the solicitor could have
avoided liability had he made a disclosure of his intention to make share purchases
on his own account, whereas on the facts no such disclosure was made and moreover one of the trustees had been too ill to have received such a disclosure.
Similarly, in *Regal v Gulliver* there was no disclosure and therefore no authorisation, except in the form of a purported authorisation by the directors themselves for
the action which they proposed to take. It was held, in essence, that the fiduciaries
could not authorise themselves. As s.170 of the CA 2006 provides, while the directors owe their duties to the company they may nevertheless acquire authorisation
from the other directors in accordance with s.175(5).[158] The cases on authorisation
may nevertheless retain some significance if s.175(5) cannot be complied with.

In the Privy Council decision in *Queensland Mines v Hudson*,[159] the defendant
had been managing director of the plaintiff mining company and had therefore
been in a fiduciary relationship with that company. The defendant had learned of
some potentially profitable mining contracts. The board of directors of the
company decided not to pursue these opportunities after they had had all of the
relevant facts explained to them. The board of directors decided not to pursue
the opportunity in the knowledge that the managing director intended to do so on
his own account. Importantly, then, one director received the informed consent of
the remainder of the board that this opportunity would not be pursued by the
company, thus impliedly giving that individual director the authorisation to
pursue the opportunity on his own account. The managing director resigned and
pursued the business possibilities offered by the contracts on his own account,
taking great personal risk in so doing. When that individual director made profits
from the opportunity, the company sought to recover the profits generated by the
contract from the director. The court held that the repudiation of the contracts by
the company meant that the director was entitled to pursue them on his own
account without a conflict with his fiduciary responsibility to the company, even
though the opportunity had come to the managing director's attention originally
by means of his fiduciary office. This decision was, however, a rare case in which
authorisation was found.

The mainstream English law was illustrated in *Industrial Development
Consultants Ltd v Cooley*,[160] where a managing director was offered a contract by
a third party. The offer was made expressly on the basis that the third party would
deal only with the managing director, not with his employer company. Without
disclosing this fact to the company and claiming to be in ill-health, the managing

---

[158] Companies Act 2006 s.174.
[159] (1977) 18 ALR 1. See also *Framlington Group Plc v Anderson* [1995] B.C.C. 611.
[160] [1972] 2 All E.R. 162.

director left his employment and entered into a contract with the third party within a week of his resignation. It was held that the managing director occupied a fiduciary position in relation to his employer company throughout. He was therefore required to disclose all information to the company and to account for the profits he made under the contract. It was significant, in the judgment of Roskill J., that the director had misled his employer on these facts.

Similarly, in *Crown Dilmun v Sutton*,[161] a director learned of an opportunity to develop a football ground which he exploited on his own account once his contract of employment had been terminated. It was found that he had not made full disclosure to the claimant company of the extent of the opportunity. Consequently, he was liable to account to the claimant for the personal profits realised from the transaction. Equally, if a director sought to tempt a client away from her employers, that would constitute a breach of fiduciary duty with the effect that any profits so earned would have to be accounted for by way of constructive trust to the employer company.[162]

What remains unclear is whether the case law principles will continue to apply over-and-above the means of acquiring authorisation under s.175, for example relying on the dicta of Lord Russell in *Regal v Gulliver* to the effect that a vote by the shareholders in general meeting would constitute authorisation (even if, for example, the directors had voted against the transaction, or if all of the directors stood to take a benefit from the transaction and so there were no directors without a conflict of interest who could vote). It is suggested that this general equitable principle, that the company (by means of a shareholder vote) can ratify the directors' actions,[163] ought to continue to apply in such circumstances even after the passage of the 2006 Act.

The corporate opportunity doctrine and acquiring authorisation on the case law

17–047 Company law has developed a concept whereby the directors will be liable for breach of duty only if an opportunity is taken from the company by the director, or if the company's property is misused. (The way in which this ties in with the equitable principle is considered below.) There are, it is suggested, three circumstances in which a company director may earn personal profits: first, if he has authorisation to do so, in line with s.175 of the CA 2006; second, if he has resigned from his employment before commencing the activities which led to the profit; and, third, if the director had no powers at all to act as a director in practice before then making those personal profits. Each of these approaches is taken in turn.

First, the complex question of the acquisition of authorisation in relation to companies. Before considering this question in detail, it is important to understand the subtle differences between companies and trusts. A number of cases

---

[161] [2004] 1 B.C.L.C. 468.

[162] *Item Software (UK) Ltd v Fassihi* [2003] EWHC 3116; [2003] 2 B.C.L.C. 1.

[163] It is suggested that it is important to ratify the directors' decision and not simply to agree not to sue because the company may in time be taken over by other shareholders who may not agree with the policy of agreeing not to sue.

dealing with companies have been considered already. More recent cases in company law have suggested that this corporate opportunity doctrine will be pursued so that a director may be absolved from liability for secret profits if the company is not intending to pursue the opportunity from which the director earned his profits. So, in *Island Export Finance Ltd v Umunna*,[164] the company had a contract with the government of Cameroon to supply the government with post boxes. Mr Umunna resigned from the company once the contract was completed, having worked on that contract and acquired a great deal of expertise in that particular activity. The company ceased pursuing this line of business and after his resignation Mr Umunna entered into a similar contract on his own behalf. The company sued him for the personal profits which he made for himself under this second contract. The court held that Mr Umunna's fiduciary obligations towards the company did not cease once he resigned from its employment. This makes sense: if it were not the case, then no fiduciary could ever be bound by their fiduciary office if they had the good sense to resign immediately before breaching their duties. However, in this instance, the court found that the company had not been seeking to develop this sort of business opportunity at the time Mr Umunna had done so and therefore he had not interfered with a corporate opportunity. Consequently, he bore no liability to the company.

Second, we should consider the position of directors who have resigned from their employment and who then seek to exploit an opportunity on their own account. In *Balston v Headline Filters Ltd*,[165] a director had resigned from a company and leased premises with a view to starting up in business on his own account before a client of the company approached him and asked him to work for the company. Falconer J. held that there was no breach of duty in these circumstances because there was nothing wrong with a director leaving his employment and setting up in business on his own account and, furthermore, there had not been any maturing business opportunity in this case which the director had diverted to himself. Therefore, in company law, it has been held that company directors may, assuming nothing in their contracts to the contrary prohibiting such an action under contract law, resign from their posts and on the next day begin activities which would previously have been in breach of their fiduciary duties, provided that they have not taken a maturing business opportunity away from the company in so doing.[166] Although, a director may not, even after resigning from her post, use either the company's property or information which she had acquired while still a director of the company to generate personal profits.[167] Clearly, if such behaviour were possible then it would constitute all too easy a method for eluding the principle against fiduciaries earning unauthorised profits: one could learn commercially useful information at work on Monday, resign on Tuesday, and make a huge personal profit on Wednesday from that information. Instead, the law of contract permits a person to leave one

---

[164] [1986] B.C.C. 460.
[165] [1990] F.S.R. 385.
[166] *CMS Dolphin v Simonet* [2001] 2 B.C.L.C. 704 (Lawrence Collins J.); *Quarter Master UK Ltd v Pyke* [2005] 1 B.C.L.C. 245 at 264 (Mr Paul Morgan QC) and *British Midland Tool Ltd v Midland International Tooling Ltd* [2003] 2 B.C.L.C. 523 (Hart J).
[167] *Ultraframe UK Ltd v Fielding* [2005] EWHC 1638 (Ch), [2005] All E.R. (D) 397, per Lewison J.

employment and begin work elsewhere, but the law on constructive trust prevents that person also taking advantage of a conflict between her personal interests and her fiduciary office for that previous employer.

17–048   Third, we must consider the position of directors who have no effective powers to act as a director. In the case of *In Plus Group Ltd v Pyke*[168] Mr Pyke was a director of a company, In Plus Ltd, but he had "fallen out with his co-director" and in consequence he had been "effectively excluded from the management of the company". Mr Pyke decided to set up a company on his own while he was still a director of In Plus Ltd. So, he set up his own company and that company entered into contracts on its own behalf with a major customer of In Plus Ltd. Remarkably, the Court of Appeal held that Mr Pyke was not in breach of his fiduciary duties to In Plus Ltd because he had not used any property belonging to In Plus Ltd and also because he had not made any use of any confidential information which he had acquired while he was a director of In Plus Ltd. As Sedley L.J. held:

> "Quite exceptionally, the defendant's duty to the claimants had been reduced to vanishing point by the acts (explicable and even justifiable though they may have been) of his sole fellow director and fellow shareholder Mr Plank. Accepting as I do that the claimants' relationship with Constructive was consistent with successful poaching on Mr Pyke's part, the critical fact is that it was done in a situation in which the dual role which is the necessary predicate of [the claimants'] case is absent. The defendant's role as a director of the claimants was throughout the relevant period entirely nominal, not in the sense in which a non-executive director's position might (probably wrongly) be called nominal but in the concrete sense that he was entirely excluded from all decision-making and all participation in the claimant company's affairs. For all the influence he had, he might as well have resigned."

It is suggested that this is an exceptional decision and it is difficult to square with the strictness of the approach in cases such as *Regal v Gulliver*. Had Mr Pyke been a non-executive director of In Plus it would still have been difficult to see how he could have used information acquired while on company business for his personal gain without there being some suggestion that there was at the very least a conflict between his personal interests and the fiduciary duties which he owed to the company.

17–049   This case does raise a more general point which is of importance in relation to company law—and one which is little discussed in the cases: how should equity deal with people who are directors of more than one company? In practice such matters would be dealt with by a well-drafted contract of employment for that director or by the company's constitutional documents (in the form of its articles of association) and so may not be a question for equity to resolve necessarily. The question is still likely to arise in practice, especially in relation to directors of subsidiary companies within a group where each company is strictly a separate

---

[168] [2002] 2 B.C.L.C. 201; considered in *Ultraframe UK Ltd v Fielding* [2005] EWHC 1638 (Ch), [2005] All E.R. (D) 397.

entity with its own interests.[169] In part it is resolved by the principle whereby a fiduciary is bound by duties of confidentiality and therefore ought to respect the confidence of the company on whose business that confidential information was learned. The effect of s.175(7) of the CA 2006 is that the duty applies to conflicts between various duties between, it is suggested, different directorships.[170]

The way in which Collins J. conceived of this company law form of the doctrine was explicitly by way of analogy with the law of trusts. So, in *CMS Dolphin Ltd v Simonet*[171] Simonet left a company, an advertising agency, after a falling-out with his co-founder of that agency, Ball. Both men had been directors of that company. Simonet established a rival agency and attracted clients from his former employer. The first advertising agency claimed that Simonet was in breach of his fiduciary duties as a director in diverting business opportunities from the first advertising agency to his new agency. Collins J. upheld Simonet's liability for diverting a corporate opportunity and so made him liable to account as a constructive trustee for the profits that had been earned from this activity. What is particularly important for present purposes is that manner in which Collins J. concluded his judgment by explaining the operation of this doctrine, as his lordship saw it:

"In my judgment the underlying basis of the liability of a director who exploits after his resignation a maturing business opportunity of the company is that the opportunity is to be treated as if it were property of the company in relation to which the director had fiduciary duties. By seeking to exploit the opportunity after resignation he is appropriating for himself that property. He is just as accountable as a trustee who retires without properly accounting for trust property. In the case of the director he becomes a constructive trustee of the fruits of his abuse of the company's property, which he has acquired in circumstances where he knowingly had a conflict of interest, and exploited it by resigning from the company."

Therefore, in summary, if a director diverts a maturing business opportunity away from the company to himself personally or to some entity under his control, then he will be required to account for any profits made by way of constructive trust and to account to the company for any loss suffered by the company as a result. It is suggested that this approach must be correct in principle and that *In Plus* should not be applied beyond its own particular facts.

Cases suggesting a dilution of the principle

In two recent cases there have been signals that the Court of Appeal is reluctant **17–050** to persist with the strict approach of the principle against secret profits being made by fiduciaries. The principal concern among these judges has been the

---

[169] It may be, of course, that one subsidiary is sold off such that "the company" after the sell off may seek to enforce its rights differently from "the company" before the sell-off.

[170] cf. *London Mashonaland Exploration Co Ltd v New Mashonaland Exploration Co Ltd* [1891] WN 165.

[171] [2001] 2 B.C.L.C. 704.

perceived strictness of the test. So, in *Murad v Al-Saraj*[172] the Murad sisters entered into a joint venture with Al Saraj to buy a hotel but Al-Saraj did not disclose that he stood to earn personal profits in the form of a commission from the vendor for setting up the transaction. It was found that he had committed fraudulent misrepresentations in relation to the Murad sisters and furthermore that he had owed fiduciary duties to them. The profits had been earned from his fiduciary office without authorisation. Accordingly, he was held liable to account to the Murad sisters for his profits. Arden L.J. chose to cast doubt on the suitability of the doctrine in the leading cases to the extent that that doctrine imposed liability to hold property on constructive trust on people who had not been demonstrated to have acted wrongly. She expressed a preference for liability being based on some fault by the defendant. However, speaking in the Court of Appeal she acknowledged that it was not open to her to overrule *Regal v Gulliver* and *Boardman v Phipps*.[173] It should be noted that the majority in *Boardman v Phipps* were all too aware that they were imposing a constructive trust on a person who had acted in good faith. Rix L.J. in *Foster v Bryant*[174] was as equivocal as Arden L.J. about the inflexibility of the test in *Boardman v Phipps*. His lordship, with respect, became overly concerned in his survey of the cases with the notion that the defendant must be misusing trust (or company) property in some way so as to be liable to hold his profits on constructive trust, and thus overlooked the central point of the principle reiterated by Lord Upjohn in *Boardman v Phipps* and Lord Cranworth in *Aberdeen Railway v Blaikie* that its purpose was to prevent both actual conflicts of interest and even the possibility that there was a conflict of interest. The purpose of that principle is to provide that once one acts in a fiduciary capacity it is simply impossible to take personal profits from a transaction in which the trust (or company) has or may have a direct or an indirect interest.

In *Foster v Bryant*[175] the defendant director of a company was effectively forced to resign by his co-director (who was also the majority shareholder of the company). The defendant resigned from the company after his co-director "truculently" made the defendant's wife redundant. The defendant was found to have been excluded from the operation of the business, just like the defendant in *In Plus* above. One of the company's principal clients wanted to retain the services of both directors. Before the defendant's resignation came into effect (i.e. while he was still technically a director but after he had tendered his resignation) the client began to talk to the defendant about the way in which the defendant could work with this client. Importantly, the defendant had resigned at this stage. When the defendant's resignation took effect, he began to work for the client. The company sued the defendant on the basis that he had been a director of the company when the business opportunity came to light and therefore it was argued that any profits earned from that opportunity should be subject to an account in favour of the company. While it was the company which brought the action, in

---

[172] [2005] EWCA Civ. 959.
[173] In that case, on the facts, the principle was not one which was at all harsh in the final analysis.
[174] [2007] Bus. L.R. 1565.
[175] [2007] Bus. L.R. 1565.

practice it was the majority shareholder (who was also the defendant's co-director) who was driving the litigation. It was the same person who had driven the defendant to resign his directorship. Consequently, the sympathy of Rix L.J. was evidently with the defendant.

Rix L.J. sought to distinguish the decided cases considered in previous sections on the basis severally that they concerned a misuse of the company's property, that many of them concerned "faithless fiduciaries" who took wrongful or deceitful advantage of their employers (as in *IDC v Cooley*), or that they were diversions of maturing business opportunities by the fiduciary. Rix L.J. did not doubt that a director needed to deal in good faith with the company nor that a fiduciary could not earn profits in secret from her office from an opportunity which belonged to the company or for which the company was negotiating. However, Rix L.J. held that those principles must be applied in a "fact-sensitive" way—considering the ripeness of the business opportunity, the specificity of the opportunity, and thus whether the director had diverted the specific opportunity open to the company. It was held that the position changed in this company after the defendant's resignation such that he was excluded from the business and thus had only to act honestly in his role as director, and therefore that he was not required to account for his subsequent profits. Importantly, while agreeing with Rix L.J., Buxton L.J. pointed out that just because a fiduciary had not sought to create a conflict of interest, that did not necessarily mean that there was no conflict of interest. Furthermore, the fiduciary is required to account for profits in general terms even if no loss is suffered by the company.

It is suggested that the developments mooted in these three cases are unfortunate and should be resisted. Three points emerge. First, when one is a fiduciary then one may not take an unauthorised profit from one's fiduciary capacity: end of story. We live in a world where we expect to be able to take whatever we want, to earn quick profits, and to please ourselves. The concept of a fiduciary derives from the idea that in some contexts people should be required to act selflessly for others, especially where they have voluntarily accepted that office and are being paid for it (like directors of trading companies). As Moses L.J. put it in *Foster v Bryant*,[176] the need to take a "fact-sensitive" approach to each case might almost "make one nostalgic for the days in when there were inflexible rules, inexorably enforced by judges who would have shuddered at the reiteration of the noun-adjective [fact-sensitive]". One such inflexible rule is the rule that a fiduciary may not take an unauthorised profit in circumstances in which there may possibly be a conflict between her personal interests and her fiduciary duties. Second, this rule is not as strict as all that. Equity does have an ability to relieve a worthy defendant (as in *Boardman v Phipps*) by requiring some account to be given to him for the work that he had done in the transaction, in that case, so as to generate large profits for the beneficiaries of a trust. Third, for those who argue that equity is too uncertain for commercial use, it is not open to them to criticise the ancient doctrine which was put to work in *Boardman v Phipps* which unquestionably has the virtue of predictability about it. More recent cases which have re-affirmed the traditional principle are considered in the next section.

---

[176] [2007] Bus. L.R. 1565, 1598.

Reaffirming the traditional principle

17–051 None of the three cases considered in the preceding section were referred to by the Court of Appeal in *Allied Business and Financial Consultants Ltd, Re*[177] which instead reinforced the significance of the "no conflict" principle even in circumstances in which the other directors may have been reluctant to pursue a business opportunity because of the risk to the company. In that case, directors learned of an opportunity, as part of the company's business of arranging financial services, involving the development of a large building in central London. One of the directors diverted this opportunity to another undertaking when one of the company's clients could not be interested in investing in this building's development. The company later went into insolvency. It was held that the principles in *Aberdeen Railway* and *Regal v Gulliver* continued to apply so that the directors owed an undivided loyalty to the company which was akin to the obligations of a trustee. The Court of Appeal thus reversed the decision at first instance[178] which had found no breach of duty on the basis that it was the practice within the company to allow individual directors to pursue some commercial opportunities on their own account. The overriding duty of loyalty incumbent on fiduciaries was prioritised over other considerations. This reaffirmation of the traditional principle, it is suggested, should be applauded.

In *Berryland Books Ltd v BK Books Ltd*[179] a publishing company was operated de facto by the second defendant who was the only director resident in the UK where the company carried on its business. In essence, the second defendant set up a new company, the first defendant, and resigned from the publishing company to go and work for the new company. Briefly put, the new company took over the business and the maturing business opportunities which had previously belonged to the publishing company, as well as soliciting its staff. The publishing company (through its remaining shareholders and directors) sued the defendants on the basis that they had been involved in a conspiracy to divert the publishing company's business to the new company. It was held by Judge Hodge QC (sitting as a High Court judge) that the second defendant was bound by a "fundamental duty of loyalty" as a fiduciary (in the form of being a director of the publishing company) and that this duty had been breached when the new company was created to carry on the publishing company's business and also when the defendants set up web domains and marketing stands at industry conferences while working for the publishing company (often using the publishing company's name falsely to enable permission to do so). The various actions which constituted a breach of this duty were: undermining the publishing company by competing with it; acting contrary to the best interests of the publishing company; seeking to make personal profits by establishing the new company to conduct what was in effect the business of the publishing company; and soliciting and procuring the publishing company's staff to work for the new company. It was only acceptable for a director to prepare to set up a new business if he did not cross the line

---

[177] [2009] 2 B.C.L.C. 666.
[178] [2009] 1 B.C.L.C. 328.
[179] [2009] 2 B.C.L.C. 709.

between legitimate preparation for a new business and taking illegitimate acts which were in competition with his existing employer's business.

There will even be a conflict between a person's fiduciary duties and his personal interests if he exercises a right to vote at board meetings so as to obtain a personal benefit. So, in *PNC Telecom Plc v Thomas (No.2)*[180] it was held that there would be a conflict of interest when the defendant director had voted in relation to the change of control of a company which was bound up with his own removal from his directorship, even though there was no evidence of fraud. This took place in relation to the ousting of the founder of a telecoms company and generally speaking the sort of boardroom shenanigans which so upset Rix L.J. in *Foster v Bryant*: and yet Thomas Ivory QC (sitting as a High Court judge) did not seek to dilute the "no conflict" principle out of sympathy for the director.

DUTY NOT TO ACCEPT BENEFITS FROM THIRD PARTIES

The statutory principle

Section 176 of the CA 2006 provides that a director bears a duty not to accept **17–052** benefits from third parties in the following terms:

"(1) A director of a company must not accept a benefit from a third party conferred by reason of—

(a) his being a director, or
(b) his doing (or not doing) anything as director."

In this context, s.176(2) provides that the term "third party" means "a person other than the company, an associated body corporate or a person acting on behalf of the company or an associated body corporate". However, a director does not take a benefit if that benefit is paid "from a person by whom his services (as a director or otherwise) are provided to the company are not regarded as conferred by a third party".[181] The kernel of the directors' liability is based on conflicts of interest under s.176. Consequently, s.176(4) of the CA 2006 provides that "[t]his duty is not infringed if the acceptance of the benefit cannot reasonably be regarded as likely to give rise to a conflict of interest."[182]

The application of section 176 to former directors

Section 170(2) provides that: **17–053**

"A person who ceases to be a director continues to be subject—

. . .

---

[180] [2008] 2 B.C.L.C. 95.
[181] Companies Act 2006 s.176(3).
[182] Further to s.176(5), "Any reference in this section to a conflict of interest includes a conflict of interest and duty and a conflict of duties".

(b) to the duty in section 176 (duty not to accept benefits from third parties)
as regards things done or omitted by him before he ceased to be a
director.

To that extent those duties apply to a former director as to a director, subject
to any necessary adaptations."

Therefore s.176 applies to former directors as well as to current directors.

The principle as developed in the case law

Bribes

17–054   As considered above, the principle in s.176 is predicated on the case law which has
come before it. The Privy Council in *Attorney General for Hong Kong v Reid*[183]
established the modern principle that a bribe received by a fiduciary must be held
on constructive trust from the moment of its receipt and consequently that any
property acquired with that bribe is also held on constructive trust. The former
Director of Public Prosecutions for Hong Kong had accepted bribes not to prosecute certain individuals accused of having committed crimes within his jurisdiction. The bribes which he had received had been profitably invested. The question
arose whether or not the property bought with the bribes and the increase in value
of those investments should be held on constructive trust. Lord Templeman, giving
the leading opinion of the Privy Council, held that a proprietary constructive trust
is imposed as soon as the bribe is accepted by its recipient, with the effect that the
employer is entitled in equity to any profit generated by the cash bribe received
from the moment of its receipt. Similarly, Lord Templeman held that the constructive trustee is liable to account to the beneficiary for any *decrease* in value in the
investments acquired with the bribe, as well as for any increase in value in such
investments. There are therefore two forms of liability: first, to hold the bribes and
any property acquired with the bribes on constructive trust; and, secondly, if the
value of any property held on such a constructive trust should decrease in value,
the defendant is required to account personally for that diminution in value as well
as holding the property on constructive trust. As Lord Templeman has expressed
the basis for this principle[184]:

"A bribe is a gift accepted by a fiduciary as an inducement to him to betray his
trust. A secret benefit, which may or may not constitute a bribe is a benefit which
the fiduciary derives from trust property or obtains from knowledge which he
acquires in the course of acting as a fiduciary. A fiduciary is not always accountable for a secret benefit but he is undoubtedly accountable for a secret benefit
which consists of a bribe. In addition a person who provides the bribe and the
fiduciary who accepts the bribe may each be guilty of a criminal offence. In the
present case the first respondent was clearly guilty of a criminal offence."

---

[183] [1994] 1 A.C. 324, [1994] 1 All E.R. 1.
[184] [1994] 1 A.C. 324 at 330–31; [1994] 1 All E.R. 1 at 4–5.

The fiduciary is thus liable to account to the beneficiaries for the receipt of a bribe. Lord Templeman considered bribery to be an "evil practice which threatens the foundations of any civilised society". As such, the imposition of a proprietary constructive trust was the only way in which the wrongdoer could be fully deprived of the fruits of his wrongdoing.

It has been held latterly that the reason for the constructive trust in *Reid* was that it would have been "as a fiduciary unconscionable for him to retain the benefit of it"[185]; even though that was not the precise rationale used by Lord Templeman. The manner in which Lord Templeman constructed his proprietary remedy started from the premise that equity acts *in personam*. The defendant had acted unconscionably in accepting the bribe in breach of his fiduciary duty. In consequence of that breach of duty, it was held that the bribe should have been deemed to pass to the beneficiary of the fiduciary power at the instant when it was received by the wrongdoer. Given that equity considers as done that which ought to have been done, it was held that the bribe should have been considered to have been the property of the beneficiary from the moment of its receipt. The means by which title passes to the beneficiary in equity in such circumstances is a proprietary constructive trust. As such, the bribe, any property acquired with the bribe and any profit derived from such property fell to be considered as the property of the person wronged in equity.[186]

The approach of the Privy Council in *Attorney General for Hong Kong v Reid* **17–055** has been applied in subsequent High Court cases.[187] So, in *Tesco Stores v Pook*,[188] Mr Pook had tendered invoices in the aggregate of about £500,000 for services which had not in fact been rendered. Out of these amounts, the case concerned a total sum of £323,749 which had allegedly been paid as a bribe indirectly to Pook, who had been appointed as a manager in Tesco's e-commerce business in South Korea, by third parties. Pook claimed that the money had been paid to him as a loan to help him start up in business. It was held by Peter Smith J. that these payments should be taken to have been a bribe because they were documented by the payer by means of false invoices and a fraudulent VAT claim, rather than as an ordinary loan. His Lordship applied the decision in *Attorney General for Hong Kong v Reid* to the effect that this bribe should be held on constructive trust.[189] He approved the idea both that the bribe is held on constructive trust and also that when there is any decrease in the value of any property acquired with the bribe then the fiduciary "is required to make up the difference". On these facts, because

---

[185] *Yugraneft v Abramovich* [2008] EWHC 2613 (Comm.), [2008] All E.R. (Comm.) 299 at [373], per Clarke J.

[186] Applied in *Corporacion Nacional Del Cobre De Chile v Interglobal Inc* (2003) 5 ITELR 744; and *Sumitomo Bank v Thahir* [1993] 1 S.L.R. 735.

[187] *Ocular Sciences Ltd v Aspect Vision Care Ltd* [1997] RPC 289; *Fyffes Group Ltd v Templeman* [2000] 2 Lloyd's Rep 643 (where this case was obiter); *Dubai Aluminium Company Ltd v Alawi* [2002] EWHC 2051; *Tesco Stores Ltd v Pook* [2003] EWHC 823; *Daraydan Holdings Ltd v Solland International Ltd* [2004] EWHC 622. In relation to interlocutory relief, such as Mareva injunctions, the *Lister v Stubbs* approach has also been displaced in favour of the approach in *Attorney General v Reid: Mercedes Benz AG v Leiduck* [1996] A.C. 284 at 300. This approach has not been followed in *Attorney General v Blake* [1997] Ch 84 at 96, per Sir Richard Scott V.C.; *Halifax Building Society v Thomas* [1996] Ch. 217, 229, preferring the approach in *Lister v Stubbs*.

[188] [2003] EWHC 823.

[189] [2003] EWHC 823 at [45] and [69].

the bribe had been made by means of a false invoice together with a fraudulent claim for recovery of VAT (that is, a claim for recovery of VAT which had purportedly been paid under this false invoice for a service rendered), it was held that the value of the bribe which should be accounted for was the amount of the invoice falsely rendered together with the VAT amount. Thus, any value received as part of the transaction comprising the bribe will be deemed to be held on constructive trust.

Similarly, in *Daraydan Holdings Ltd v Solland International Ltd*,[190] a married couple, who were directors of a company which was involved in the refurbishment of property in London, connived in the appropriation of a secret commission which was procured by arbitrarily increasing the budget for a refurbishment project by 10 per cent and then diverting that extra 10 per cent so as to pay "kickbacks"[191] to K. It was found as a fact that K was employed by the person who ultimately controlled a group of organisations which included the company, and thus was acting as a fiduciary. The secret commission, or "kickback", of 10 per cent was held to have been equivalent to a bribe in this case. Collins J. began his judgment by quoting that sentence from Lord Templeman in *Reid* to the effect that. "[b]ribery is an evil practice which threatens the foundations of any civilised society". It was held that an agent ought not to put herself into a situation in which her duty and her personal interest conflict. Thus, the constructive trust here was based on avoidance of conflict of interest as well as the need to deal with the "evil practice" of bribery. It was explained that the constructive trust in this case was further justified because the bribes were drawn from the claimant's property (being the payments for the refurbishment) and also on the basis that the bribes were paid as part of a fraudulent misrepresentation exercised by S. It was held further that where, as on these facts, a bribe has been paid here by an employee (S) to a third party (K), and when that third party is acting in a fiduciary capacity, then both parties are required to account jointly and severally for the receipt of that bribe. Consequently, the bribe was deemed to have been held on constructive trust, just as in *Reid*.

Secret commissions

17–056 There are occasions on which the principles relating to "bribes" are treated together with "secret commissions". A secret commission is in many cases synonymous with a bribe, in that a person is in receipt of money covertly. Usually the purpose of such a transaction would be to induce the recipient to act in a corrupt manner. An example of patterns of secret commissions are set out in *Pakistan v Zadari*,[192] a case which—at a purely interlocutory stage—relates to allegations that payments were made at the behest of the husband of a former Prime Minister of Pakistan through a series of companies to acquire a 350-acre estate in Surrey and in connection with a variety of other transactions. While it was not necessary to dispose of the facts at this interlocutory stage in the proceedings, in the event that it could be proved that the estate was acquired with secret

---

[190] [2004] EWHC 622, [2004] 3 W.L.R. 1106; [2005] Ch. 1.
[191] [2004] EWHC 622; [2004] 3 W.L.R. 1106 at para.[63].
[192] [2006] EWHC 2411 (Comm.), [2006] All E.R. (D) 79 (Oct).

commissions or bribes then Collins J. indicated that that estate would be held on constructive trust for the state of Pakistan. Similarly, in *Imageview Management Ltd v Jack*[193] it was held that an agent was required to commit himself completely to the interests of his principal in the conduct of his fiduciary duties. Therefore, when a footballer's agent took secret commissions as part of the negotiations connected with the transfer of a footballer from one football club to another then that was found to constitute a direct conflict of interest between his fiduciary duties and his personal interests.[194] That profit meant that the agent lost the right to further remuneration on the facts, applying *Boston Deep Sea Fishing v Ansell*.[195]

DUTY TO DECLARE INTEREST IN PROPOSED TRANSACTION

The statutory principle

The core principle

It is a key facet of fiduciary law that a fiduciary may not permit conflicts of **17-057** interest so that he deals, for example, with a company for which he acts as a director in circumstances in which he has some interest of his own bound up in the transaction (the "self-dealing" rule). This principle is clearly covered by s.175 of the CA 2006, as considered above. However, there is a duty which can be thought of as being connected with it, and that is the duty in s.177 of the CA 2006 which requires that a company director must disclose any personal interest in a proposed transaction. Section 177 provides as follows:

"(1) If a director of a company is in any way, directly or indirectly, interested in a proposed transaction or arrangement with the company, he must declare the nature and extent of that interest to the other directors."

That a director has an interest in a transaction may arise in a number of circumstances. The term is not defined in the legislation. It would clearly encompass a situation in which the director was acting as a sole trader and was the other party to a contract with the company. The interest in the transaction may be indirect as well as direct. Consequently, it is suggested, the principle would cover transactions with a subsidiary company in which the director owns shares or in which the director also acts as a director; or even a transaction in which the director's spouse has a direct interest so as to grant the director an indirect interest in that transaction.[196] The former example would mean that the director's indirect interest was constituted through his share-holding in the company entering into the transaction, whereas the latter example

---

[193] [2009] 1 B.C.L.C. 724.
[194] For those who are interested by these things (a class which includes me), the footballer was Kelvin Jack and the club was Dundee United.
[195] (1888) 39 Ch.D. 339; and *Andrews v Ramsay & Co* [1903] 2 K.B. 635.
[196] This last proposition depends on meeting the argument that a husband does not own his wife's property and therefore an "indirect" benefit in this context would have to encompass the context of taking a practical benefit in that more money would come into the marriage even if the husband-director himself did not have any personal rights under the contract.

requires that the concept of an indirect interest includes a tangible benefit (in the form of more money in the marriage) without any personal legal rights under the contract.

The methodology for making a declaration

17–058 The statute identifies a manner in which the director may make this declaration. Section 177(2) of the CA 2006 provides that:

> "(2) The declaration may (but need not) be made—
>
> (a) at a meeting of the directors, or
> (b) by notice to the directors in accordance with—
>
> (i) section 184 (notice in writing), or
> (ii) section 185 (general notice)."

Therefore, the director may either make a declaration at a meeting of the board of directors[197] or by means of a notice under s.184 or s.185. The declaration may be made in other ways which are not defined in the section. It is suggested that for a director to acquire authorisation for continuing to have that interest in the transaction, a majority of the directors who have no interest in the transaction must agree to the company continuing with the transaction in which one of their number has an interest. It may be that, if there was only a subset of the directors who were authorised by the company's constitution or management structure to effect the particular transaction at issue (for example, because it relates to business conducted with a particular business unit) then there may be situations in which authorisation on behalf of the company could be given by the relevant director or directors. However, it is suggested that this would be a worse mechanism than enabling all of the directors to know of the circumstances and to activate a broader corporate policy as to the treatment of such transactions.

It is important that the director involved must keep the other directors informed of any changes in circumstance. Section 177(3) provides that:

> "If a declaration of interest under this section proves to be, or becomes, inaccurate or incomplete, a further declaration must be made."

Significantly, all such declarations must be made *before* the company enters into the transaction. Section 177(4) provides that:

> "Any declaration required by this section must be made before the company enters into the transaction or arrangement."

It makes complete sense the declaration must be made before the transaction is completed so that the other directors are able to enter into that transaction with informed consent as to the interests of any of their fellow directors.

---

[197] This is suggested by the term "*the* directors" which suggests all of them.

Exclusions of liability and exclusions from the need to make a declaration

Section 177 provides for situations in which there will not be an obligation to **17–059** comply with the duty in s.177. So, s.177(5) provides:

> "(5) This section does not require a declaration of an interest of which the director is not aware or where the director is not aware of the transaction or arrangement in question.
>
> For this purpose a director is treated as being aware of matters of which he ought reasonably to be aware."

Consequently, the s.177 duty does not apply to a person who is not aware of the transaction. It is not enough that one is not aware or does not remember that one has an indirect interest in the transaction. Rather, for example in a complex corporate group, it is anticipated that a director may not know of all of the transactions created by that company and so may not know that he has some interest in the transaction.

There are three situations in which the director is not obliged to declare an interest:

> "(6) A director need not declare an interest—
>
> (a) if it cannot reasonably be regarded as likely to give rise to a conflict of interest;
> (b) if, or to the extent that, the other directors are already aware of it (and for this purpose the other directors are treated as aware of anything of which they ought reasonably to be aware); or
> (c) if, or to the extent that, it concerns terms of his service contract that have been or are to be considered—
>
> (i) by a meeting of the directors, or
> (ii) by a committee of the directors appointed for the purpose under the company's constitution."

In essence the common root of these principles is that there is no genuine conflict of interest.

The principle in the case law

The self-dealing principle in equity

The basis of the original equitable principle was expressed in the following dicta **17–060** of Lord Cranworth in *Aberdeen Railway Co v Blaikie Bros*[198]:

> "... it is a rule of universal application, that no one, having such [fiduciary] duties to discharge, shall be allowed to enter into engagements in which he has,

---

[198] (1854) 2 Eq. Rep. 1281.

or can have, a personal interest conflicting, or which possibly may conflict, with the interests of those whom he is bound to protect."

The effect of s.177 of the CA 2006 is that a director may be involved in such a transaction provided that a declaration of that interest has been made in the manner considered above before the transaction was created. In equity, the self-dealing principle entitles the beneficiary to avoid any such transaction on the basis, set out in *Keech v Sandford*,[199] that even the possibility of fraud or bad faith being exercised by a fiduciary is to be resisted.[200] Megarry V.C. in *Tito v Waddell (No.2)*[201] enunciated the self-dealing principle in the following terms:

"If a trustee purchases trust property from himself, any beneficiary may have the sale set aside ex debito justitiae, however fair the transaction."

The right of the beneficiary under the case law is therefore to set aside the transaction. The effect of s.177, however, is to preserve the effect of the transaction provided that the director in question has complied with the s.177 procedures considered above. There is no defence to the exercise of such a right that the transaction was entered into as though it was created between parties acting at arm's length. The same principle applies to purchases by directors from their companies,[202] although most articles of association in English companies expressly permit such transactions, as is considered below.[203] Where the beneficiary acquiesces in the transaction, that beneficiary is precluded from seeking to have that transaction set aside.[204] A fiduciary will not be able to avoid this principle simply by selling to an associate or a connected company or similar person—although the authorities on this point relate primarily to sales to relatives,[205] to trustee's children[206] and to trustee's spouses.[207]

Disclosure of directors' interests in corporate transactions under the self-dealing rule

17–061 Before the 2006 Act was passed, the application of fiduciary principles to directors allowed a company automatically to avoid any contract which the board entered into on its behalf in which one or more of the directors had an interest, unless that interest had been disclosed to the company and approved by the

[199] (1726) 2 Eq. Cas. Abr. 741.
[200] *Ex p. Lacey* (1802) 6 Ves. 625.
[201] [1977] Ch. 106. cf. *Prince Jefri Bolkiah v KPMG* [1999] 1 All E.R. 517—with reference to "Chinese walls".
[202] *Aberdeen Railway Co v Blaikie Brothers* (1854) 1 Macq 461.
[203] As in *Ireland Alloys Ltd v Dingwall* 1999 S.L.T. 267, OH, where the disclosure requirements in the articles were not followed and this invalidated decisions taken at a meeting of the directors of the company.
[204] *Holder v Holder* [1968] Ch. 353.
[205] *Coles v Trecothick* (1804) 9 Ves. 234—which may be permitted where the transaction appears to be conducted as though at arm's length.
[206] *Gregory v Gregory* (1821) Jac. 631.
[207] *Ferraby v Hobson* (1847) 2 Ph. 255; *Burrell v Burrell's Trustee* 1915 S.C. 333.

general meeting.[208] This was so, whether or not the director was acting bona fide for the benefit of the company. Any benefit derived by the director from such a contract could also be recovered.[209] This is, broadly speaking, the effect of s.177 as discussed above. This need to disclose an interest was extended to include not only contracts made directly with a director (such as a director's service contract) but also those in which he had an interest (for example as a shareholder[210] or as a partner[211] of the other contracting party). It does not apply to interests of a director's spouse or other personal contacts. In such a case only the usual fiduciary duty will apply but it has been suggested that the burden of proving good faith and so forth should be placed on the directors.[212]

What constitutes an interest which must be disclosed

Another difficult issue in the case law related to the sorts of material which would **17–062** amount to an interest which must be disclosed. In *Cowan de Groot Properties Ltd v Eagle Trust*,[213] the question arose as to whether in a contract of sale between A Ltd and B Ltd a director of A who was either a creditor of B, or of shareholders of B, had a disclosable interest. The judge was of the opinion that in most cases that would not amount to a disclosable interest but that circumstances could exist where the director would have an interest in B making that contract. He did, however, state that a director who was a bare trustee for another would not have a disclosable interest. In *Runciman v Walter Runciman Plc*,[214] this was expressly decided despite the "apparent absurdity" of requiring such a disclosure where it is patently obvious that the director has an interest.

Whether disclosure can be implied in the circumstances

Situations in which a director has an interest in a transaction but in which it is **17–063** contended that the other directors ought to have known that fact raise the further question of whether there can ever be implied disclosure to the board. This issue arose in *Lee Panavision v Lee Lighting*[215] where the directors all knew of each others' interest in the agreement being discussed by the board. The Court of Appeal, unlike Harman J. at first instance, were reluctant to regard this as a breach of duty. However, it could be argued that that approach might seem to miss the point that a formal declaration would not only require the other directors to expressly consider the conflict of interest position, it would also be recorded in the minutes of the directors and there could be no suspicion of secret dealings. For

---

[208] *Aberdeen Railway Co v Blaikie Bros* (1854) 1 Macq. 461. The right to avoid a contract for non-disclosure is not affected by the provisions of the first EU Directive: *Coöperative Rabobank "Vecht en Plassengerbeid" BA v Minderhoud* [1998] 2 B.C.L.C. 507, ECJ.

[209] *Parker v McKenna* (1874) L.R. 10 Ch. App. 96 at 118, per Lord Cairns L.C.

[210] *Transvaal Lands Co v New Belgium (Transvaal) Land, Co* [1914] 2 Ch. 488, CA.

[211] *Costa Rica Ry v Forwood* [1901] 1 Ch. 746, CA.

[212] *Newgate Stud Company v Penfold* [2004] EWHC 2993 (Ch).

[213] [1991] B.C.L.C. 1045.

[214] [1992] B.C.L.C. 1084. See also *Neptune (Vehicle Washing Equipment) Ltd, Re (No.1)* [1995] 1 B.C.L.C. 352.

[215] [1991] B.C.L.C. 575; affirmed [1992] B.C.L.C. 22, CA.

those reasons, and the possible abuses concerning shadow directors, Lightman J. in *Neptune (Vehicle Washing Equipment) Ltd, Re*[216] held that a single director was obliged to disclose a redundancy payment he authorised for himself to a 'meeting' of the board and record that fact in the minutes. It remains, however, to be decided what the penalty might be for such a technical non-disclosure.[217]

That issue was left open by Lightman J. in the *Neptune* case. In the *Runciman* case, Simon Brown J. also declined to give any definitive view but he did refuse to allow the company to rescind the contract. Rescission is a discretionary remedy which the courts may refuse to allow even where it has not been lost by acquiescence or delay. In *Dominion International Group Plc, Re,*[218] Knox J. held that where there was genuine informed consent by all the directors, a failure to make a declaration would be a technical and not a substantive default, although he did not say what, if any, consequences would follow. Other cases have also stressed the need for a formal rather than an informal disclosure; "piecemeal and informal" information gathered by the directors would not suffice.[219] However, in one case the lack of a formal minute as to disclosure was held not to be decisive of the matter.[220]

Whether rescission is available in cases of non-disclosure

17–064 A more complex situation arose under the case law where there was no disclosure of an interest by a director: does non-disclosure allow the company to rescind the contract? All three members of the Court of Appeal in *Hely-Hutchinson v Brayhead Ltd*[221] held that the fact of non-disclosure under the section simply brought the normal principles of equity into play. The emphasis of each judge was, however, different. It is arguable that Lord Denning M.R. thought that the contract would be voidable since the articles could not allow the directors to contract out of their statutory duty to disclose. This was also the opinion of Lord Templeman in *Guinness v Saunders.*[222]

CONSEQUENCES OF BREACH OF DUTY

17–065 It is provided in s.178(1) of the CA 2006 that the consequences of any breach or threatened breach of a director's general duties under ss.171 to 177 of the CA 2006 "are the same as would apply if the corresponding common law rule or equitable principle applied". Except for the duty in s.174 to exercise reasonable care,

---

[216] [1995] 1 B.C.L.C. 352.

[217] At a subsequent full trial the non-disclosure in that case was held to be substantive and not technical and further that the director had no authority anyway to authorise the payment: *Neptune (Vehicle Washing Equipment) Ltd (No.2), Re* [1995] B.C.C. 1000. The Company Law Review recommended that there should be no need to disclose interests, the material provisions of which were known to the board: *Completing the Structure* (2000) paras 4.11–4.16

[218] [1996] 1 B.C.L.C. 572.

[219] *Gwembe Valley Development Co Ltd v Koshy (No.3)* [2004] 1 B.C.L.C. 131, CA; *MDA Investment Management Ltd, Re* [2004] 1 B.C.L.C. 217.

[220] *Marini Ltd, Re* [2004] B.C.C. 172.

[221] [1968] 1 Q.B. 549.

[222] [1990] 2 A.C. 663 at 695.

skill and diligence, which takes effect as a common law principle, the directors' general duties are "enforceable in the same way as any other fiduciary duty owed to a company by its directors".[223] Therefore there is no codification of the appropriate remedies relevant to each duty, and instead one is thrown back on the case law remedies which were considered in relation to each section in the discussion above.

Section 180 of the CA 2006 deals with consent, approval or authorisation by the company's members. In cases where the duty to avoid conflicts of interest or the duty to declare an interest in a proposed transaction or arrangement) is complied with, then "the transaction or arrangement is not liable to be set aside by virtue of any common law rule or equitable principle requiring the consent or approval of the members of the company".[224]

FIDUCIARY DUTIES OUTWITH PART 10 OF THE COMPANIES ACT 2006

Introduction

Beyond the reach of Pt 10 of the Companies Act 2006, a company or any person **17–066** (whether employee, agent or otherwise) advising or acting of behalf of a company (or in relation to any other fiduciary office) may be held liable for dishonest assistance in a breach of fiduciary duty or for unconscionable receipt of property further to a breach of fiduciary duty.[225] The defendant's liability is a personal liability to account as a constructive trustee to the company or any other beneficiary of a fiduciary duty for the whole of loss occasioned by the breach of fiduciary duty. Each head of liability is considered in turn.[226]

Dishonest assistance

The principle in outline

A person, even if otherwise unconnected with the fiduciary duty, who dishonestly **17–067** assists in a breach of fiduciary duty will be personally liable to account to the company for any loss caused by that breach.[227] The dishonest assistant himself will not need to be a fiduciary; it is enough that he assists the breach of some other person's fiduciary duty.[228] It is a pre-requisite that there was a breach of fiduciary duty.[229] There is very little authority as to what will constitute "assistance" in a breach of fiduciary duty—it seems that any act which facilitates the breach of fiduciary duty will suffice. The bulk of the discussion in the case law has revolved around the question of what constitutes "dishonesty".

---

[223] Companies Act 2006 s.178(2).
[224] Companies Act 2006 s.180(1).
[225] Alastair Hudson, *Equity & Trusts*, 5th edn (Routledge Cavendish, 2009) Ch.20.
[226] See *Primlake Ltd v Matthews* [2007] 1 B.C.L.C. 666, Lawrence Collins J., for an overview of the general principles, although neither claim is made out definitively on the facts.
[227] *Royal Brunei Airlines v Tan* [1995] 2 A.C. 378.
[228] [1995] 2 A.C. 378.
[229] [1995] 2 A.C. 378.

The test for dishonesty

17–068 The source of the current law on the meaning of "dishonesty" in relation to
dishonest assistance is the decision of the Privy Council in *Royal Brunei Airlines
v Tan*[230] in the judgment of Lord Nicholls. In that case a company carried on business as a travel agency and entered into a contract to sell the claimant airline's
tickets on the basis that all receipts for ticket sales were to be held on trust by the
company prior to being paid to the airline periodically. The defendant was the
managing director of the company who organised for trust money to be used to
pay the company's debts. The issue arose whether or not the defendant was liable
for dishonest assistance in the breach of trust committed by the company. It
was held that the managing director had dishonestly assisted in that breach of
trust: there was no requirement that the company as trustee had to be shown to
have acted dishonestly. The principal issue was as to the nature of the test for
"dishonesty".[231] In this regard, Lord Nicholls held the following:

> "Before considering this issue further it will be helpful to define the terms
> being used by looking more closely at what dishonesty means in this context.
> Whatever may be the position in some criminal or other contexts (see, for
> instance, *Reg. v Ghosh*[232]), in the context of the accessory liability principle
> acting dishonestly, or with a lack of probity, which is synonymous, means
> simply not acting as an honest person would in the circumstances. This is an
> objective standard. At first sight this may seem surprising. Honesty has a
> connotation of subjectivity, as distinct from the objectivity of negligence.
> Honesty, indeed, does have a strong subjective element in that it is a descrip-
> tion of a type of conduct assessed in the light of what a person actually knew
> at the time, as distinct from what a reasonable person would have known
> or appreciated. Further, honesty and its counterpart dishonesty are mostly
> concerned with advertent conduct, not inadvertent conduct. Carelessness is not
> dishonesty. Thus for the most part dishonesty is to be equated with conscious
> impropriety. However, these subjective characteristics of honesty do not mean
> that individuals are free to set their own standards of honesty in particular
> circumstances. The standard of what constitutes honest conduct is not subjec-
> tive. Honesty is not an optional scale, with higher or lower values according to
> the moral standards of each individual. If a person knowingly appropriates
> another's property, he will not escape a finding of dishonesty simply because
> he sees nothing wrong in such behaviour."

What is important to take from this passage, it is suggested, is that Lord Nicholls
stressed the objective nature of the test for dishonesty. It may be argued that
within this objectivity is a need to consider the circumstances in which the

---

[230] [1995] 2 A.C. 378; *Twinsectra v Yardley* [2002] UKHL 12.
[231] In *Lexi Holdings Plc (in administration) v Luqman* [2009] 2 B.C.L.C. 1 it was held by Morritt C.
that it was dishonest for directors to fail to disclose their knowledge of the embezzlement of funds
in relation to a company which provided bridging finance by way of business.
[232] [1982] Q.B. 1053.

defendant was acting, and by considering those circumstances to admit some subjectivity. However, this should not be overstated and in any event subjectivity is not what Lord Nicholls intended. By taking into account the circumstances, one is simply asking what would an objectively honest person have done in this context and not asking what the defendant personally considered appropriate in that context. Lord Nicholls is clear that the test is a strictly objective one. His lordship was even careful to dismiss any instinct to suppose that dishonesty is connected to a subjective state of mind. The most significant section of this passage, it is suggested, is the following:

". . . acting dishonestly, or with a lack of probity, which is synonymous, means simply not acting as an honest person would in the circumstance. This is an objective standard."[233]

The test of "dishonesty" in this context is actually a test asking whether or not the defendant did or did not do what an honest person would have done in the same circumstances. Thus, the court will ask what an objectively honest person would have done. That this test is clearly stated by Lord Nicholls to be an objective test means that it does not matter that the defendant may have thought that what she was doing was honest: instead the question is what an objectively honest person would have done in those circumstances. Interestingly, this test does not require that there is any active *lying* on the defendant's part.[234] Rather, it is sufficient that the defendant fails to live up to an objective standard of probity.[235] It is also not required that the assistant be proved to have been acting fraudulently, as indeed it could not be shown that the defendant in *Royal Brunei Airlines v Tan* was because he had aimed to return the money to the trust fund: it is enough that an honest and reasonable person would not have behaved in the way that the defendant behaved.

The development of the test for dishonesty

The precise nature of the test for dishonesty has seemed to change and then to change back in subsequent cases. In *Twinsectra v Yardley*[236] Lord Hutton suggested that the test for dishonesty should be a hybrid test combining elements of objectivity and subjectivity. This meant that the test for dishonesty required *both* that objectively an honest person would not have behaved as the defendant behaved (being the test in *Royal Brunei Airlines v Tan*) and also that the defendant appreciated that his actions would be considered to be dishonest by honest and reasonable people. The effect of this change to the test would have been that a defendant would have been able to resist a finding of dishonesty if his personal

17–069

---

[233] [1995] 2 A.C. 378 at 386.

[234] cf. *Eagle Trust Plc v SBC Securities Ltd* [1992] 4 All E.R. 488 at 499, per Vinelott J.; *Polly Peck International v Nadir (No.2)* [1992] 4 All E.R. 769 at 777, per Scott L.J.

[235] This is to be contrasted with the action for knowing receipt which, in the judgement of Scott L.J. in *Polly Peck v Nadir (No.2)* [1992] 3 All E.R. 769, sets out a form of subjective test of whether or not the recipient "ought to have been suspicious" and thereby have constructive notice of the breach of trust in those particular circumstances.

[236] *Twinsectra v Yardley* [2002] UKHL 12; approving *Abbey National Plc v Solicitors Indemnity Fund Ltd* [1997] P.N.L.R. 306.

morality would not have considered the behaviour to have been dishonest or would not have recognised that other people would have thought it dishonest. In this way, a person with questionable morals would be able to rely on moral relativism to escape liability for dishonesty. In *Twinsectra v Yardley* itself, a solicitor escaped liability for dishonest assistance when he passed moneys in breach of trust to his client on the basis that he had not appreciated the trust obligations on him and importantly on the basis that he had not appreciated that honest people would have considered his behaviour to have been dishonest.[237]

This interpretation of the correctness of Lord Hutton's test was doubted in the decision of the Privy Council in *Barlow Clowes v Eurotrust*[238] when the defendant argued, in spite of assisting the unlawful transmission of large amounts of money out of investment funds in breach of fiduciary duty for a client, in a manner which the judge at first instance decided was dishonest, that his personal morality meant that he would never ask questions of a client and that he did not appreciate that such behaviour would be considered to be dishonest by honest people. The defendant relied explicitly on Lord Hutton's test in *Twinsectra v Yardley*. The unanimous Privy Council found that the test for dishonesty in this context should be an objective test in the manner argued for by Lord Nicholls in *Royal Brunei Airlines v Tan*.[239] The defendant was held to have been dishonest, relying principally on the finding of the judge at first instance (having heard lengthy evidence from the defendant) that he was simply dishonest and must have known that the money came from a tainted source.

Importantly, an intervening decision of the House of Lords in *Dubai Aluminium v Salaam*[240] found that the test for dishonesty should be that set out by Lord Nicholls in *Royal Brunei Airlines v Tan*[241] but without making reference to the decision in *Twinsectra v Yardley*. The leading speech was delivered by Lord Nicholls, not surprisingly approving his own judgment in *Royal Brunei Airlines v Tan*. In *Dubai Aluminium v Salaam* a partner in an accountancy firm had assisted a client to commit a breach of fiduciary duty, and the question arose, inter alia, whether or not he should have been held liable as a dishonest assistant in the breach of fiduciary duty.[242] It was found that the appropriate test was an objective one. The objective test approach in *Royal Brunei Airlines v Tan* has been supported latterly by a majority of the Court of Appeal in *Abou-Rahmah v Abacha*,[243] albeit that the phrasing used by Arden L.J. suggested that the defendant must not only be objectively dishonest but also must subjectively appreciate

---

[237] While the extent to which each member of the House of Lords intended to agree with Lord Hutton's re-expression of the test has been doubted, the analysis that Lord Hutton intended to introduce subjectivity to the test was accepted by Lewison J. in *Ultraframe (UK) Ltd v Fielding* [2005] EWHC 1638 (Ch.), [2005] All E.R. (D) 397, although it was contested by Lord Hoffmann in *Barlow Clowes v Eurotrust* [2006] 1 All E.R. 333.

[238] [2006] 1 W.L.R. 1476; [2006] 1 All E.R. 333.

[239] See Alastair Hudson, *Equity & Trusts*, 6th edn (Routledge-Cavendish, 2009) p.855 et seq.

[240] [2002] 3 W.L.R. 1913; [2003] 1 All E.R. 97.

[241] [1995] 2 A.C. 378.

[242] The case relates primarily to the transmission of liability to the partnership as a whole from the individual partner. This, it is suggested, is why so few commentators have noticed it in spite of the extensive discussion of the test of dishonesty.

[243] *Abou-Rahmah v Abacha* [2006] EWCA Civ. 1492, [2007] Bus. L.R. 220.

this interpretation of her behaviour. It is suggested that this is a straightforward misreading of the judgment of Lord Nicholls in *Royal Brunei Airlines v Tan*.[244]

Unconscionable receipt of property further to a breach of fiduciary duty

The concept in outline

The doctrine of personal liability to account on grounds of unconscionable receipt   **17–070**
of property held subject to a fiduciary duty concerns people who are neither directors nor the company itself who receive some such property when that property has been transferred away from the company in breach of some fiduciary duty. This doctrine used to be referred to in the cases as "knowing receipt" because liability was predicated on both the receipt of company property and on the defendant having "knowledge" that there had been a breach of fiduciary duty.[245] Latterly, a number of Court of Appeal decisions have taken the view that liability should be based on receipt of company property and on the defendant having acted both with knowledge and "unconscionably", as opposed simply to having had one of the identified forms of "knowledge" of the breach of fiduciary duty.[246] While there are some cases which have resisted this development,[247] it is suggested that the weight of authority is now that the test has developed into one of unconscionability[248]: as considered below. It is suggested that this concept of "unconscionability" should be understood as encompassing "knowledge" of the breach of fiduciary duty as traditionally understood, "dishonesty" of the sort considered above in relation to dishonest assistance,[249] and then more general forms of unconscionability such as breach of extant regulatory rules prescribing commercially acceptable and unacceptable behaviour[250] for a person in the defendant's circumstances (such as being an investment firm governed by financial services regulation).

That there must have been a breach of fiduciary duty

There must have been a breach of some fiduciary duty, before the stranger will   **17–071**
bear liability for unconscionable receipt of property passed out of the fund held subject to the fiduciary duty.[251] If the property had been passed from the company

[244] See Alastair Hudson, *Equity & Trusts*, 6th edn (Routledge-Cavendish, 2009) p.868.
[245] *Baden v Société General pour Favoriser le Developpement du Commerce et de l'Industrie en France SA* [1993] 1 W.L.R. 509; *Montagu's Settlements, Re* [1987] Ch. 264.
[246] *BCCI v Akindele* [2000] 4 All E.R. 221; *Criterion Properties Ltd v Stratford UK Properties* [2003] 1 W.L.R. 218, CA; *Charter Plc v City Index Ltd* [2008] 2 W.L.R. 950, CA.
[247] *Twinsectra v Yardley* [1999] Lloyd's Rep. Bank 438, CA.
[248] *BCCI v Akindele* [2000] 4 All E.R. 221; *Niru Battery v Milestone Trading* [2004] 2 W.L.R. 1415; *Criterion Properties Ltd v Stratford UK Properties* [2003] 1 W.L.R. 218, CA; *Charter Plc v City Index Ltd* [2008] 2 W.L.R. 950, CA.
[249] See the discussion of *Charter Plc v City Index Ltd* [2008] 2 W.L.R. 950 at [31], per Carnwath L.J.
[250] See for example the discussion of the judgment of Knox J. in *Cowan de Groot Properties Ltd v Eagle Fiduciary Duty Plc* [1992] 4 All E.R. 700 at 761 below.
[251] *Eagle Fiduciary Duty Plc v SBC Securities Ltd* [1992] 4 All E.R. 488; *El Ajou v Dollar Land Holdings* [1994] 1 B.C.L.C. 464 at 478, per Hoffmann J.; *Brown v Bennett* [1998] EWCA Civ. 1881.

to the stranger within the terms of the fiduciary duty then no liability could lie. As Morritt V.C. put it:

> "[a] claim for 'knowing receipt' is parasitic on a claim for breach of fiduciary duty in the sense that it cannot exist in the absence of the breach of fiduciary duty from which the receipt originated."[252]

Once a breach of fiduciary duty has been proved, it is incumbent on the claimant to demonstrate that the defendant had acted unconscionably or that he had the requisite knowledge.

The nature of "receipt"

17–072 The first question is what actions will constitute "receipt" in this context.[253] There are, in essence, two competing views. On the one hand, it could be said that there has been receipt when the defendant takes company property into his possession or has it under his control; whereas on the other hand, it could be said that there has been receipt only when the defendant has purportedly acquired sufficient rights in that property to have satisfied an equitable tracing claim: which would have the effect, it is suggested, of potentially narrowing the claim. An example of the former approach appears in the decision of Millett J. in *Agip v Jackson*,[254] his lordship held that "there is receipt of fiduciary duty property when a company's funds are misapplied by any person whose fiduciary position gave him control of them or enabled him to misapply them". An example of the second, narrower approach to what constitutes "receipt", which has been cited in numerous cases in this context,[255] was set out by Hoffmann L.J. in *El Ajou v Dollar Land Holdings* to the effect that[256] "the plaintiff must show, first, a disposal of his assets in breach of fiduciary duty; secondly, the beneficial receipt by the defendant of assets which are traceable as representing the assets of the plaintiff; and thirdly, knowledge on the part of the defendant that the assets he received are traceable to a breach of fiduciary duty."

The concept of "knowledge" of a breach of fiduciary duty

17–073 Knowledge was held by Lord Browne-Wilkinson in *Westdeutsche Landesbank v Islington* to be a central aspect of liability for knowing receipt:

> "If X has the necessary degree of knowledge, X may himself become a constructive trustee for B on the basis of knowing receipt.[257] But unless he has

---

[252] *Charter Plc and another v City Index Ltd* [2006] EWHC 2508 (Ch), [2007] 1 W.L.R. 26.

[253] Lack of proof of receipt will prevent a claim for knowing receipt being commenced, such a claim will be struck out: *Fraser v Oystertec* [2004] EWHC 2225; see also *Compagnie Noga D'Importation et D'Exportation v Abacha* [2004] EWHC 2601.

[254] *Agip v Jackson* [1990] Ch. 265 at 286, per Millett J., CA [1991] Ch. 547.

[255] e.g. *Charter Plc v City Index Ltd* [2007] 1 W.L.R. 26 at 31, per Morritt C.

[256] [1994] 2 All E.R. 685 at 700.

[257] [1996] A.C. 669.

the requisite degree of knowledge he is not personally liable to account as trustee.[258] Therefore, innocent receipt of property by X subject to an existing equitable interest does not by itself make X a trustee despite the severance of the legal and equitable titles."[259]

The key to liability for knowing receipt is that the defendant has acted wrongfully by receiving property with the requisite knowledge as to the breach of fiduciary duty which led to his possession of the property. Given this acceptance by his lordship in the House of Lords that knowledge is the foundation of knowing receipt, it remains arguable that the development of a concept of unconscionability by variously constituted Courts of Appeal can only be effective so long as they are interpreted in accordance with this need for knowledge in relation to knowing receipt.

The question is as to what a person can be taken to "know". The most significant judicial exposition of the various categories of knowledge was set out by Gibson J. in *Baden v Sociéte Générale pour Favoriser le Développement du Commerce et de l'Industrie en France SA*[260] and then whittled down to the following three categories for the purposes of liability for knowing receipt by Megarry V.C. in *Montagu, Re*[261]: first, actual knowledge[262]; second, wilfully shutting one's eyes to the obvious[263]; third, wilfully and recklessly failing to make inquiries which an honest person would have made. In *Montagu, Re* Megarry V.C. wished to exonerate a defendant from liability who had knowledge of circumstances which would have put an honest person on inquiry, but had forgotten what he had been told and so was considered by his lordship not to have acted wilfully. As Scott L.J. held in *Polly Peck*, these categories are not to be taken as rigid rules and "one category may merge imperceptibly into another".[264]

The concept of "unconscionability"

The evolution of the doctrine of "knowing receipt" into a doctrine predicated **17–074** more generally on 'unconscionability' emerged from the decision of the Court of Appeal in *Bank of Credit and Commerce International v Akindele*[265] where Nourse L.J. held[266]:

"What then, in the context of knowing receipt, is the purpose to be served by a categorisation of knowledge? It can only be to enable the court to determine whether, in the words of Buckley LJ in *Belmont Finance Corpn Ltd v Williams*

---

[258] *Diplock, Re* [1948] Ch. 465 and *Montagu's Settlement Trusts, Re* [1987] Ch. 264.
[259] [1996] 2 All E.R. 961 at 990.
[260] [1993] 1 W.L.R. 509.
[261] [1987] Ch. 264.
[262] Where there is proof that a defendant actually knew, then that will be sufficient to make out the claim: *Bank of Tokyo-Mitsubishi Ltd v Baskan Gida* [2004] EWHC 945, [2004] 2 Lloyd's Rep. 395.
[263] See *Manifest Shipping Co Ltd v Uni-Polaris Shipping Co Ltd* [2003] 1 A.C. 469.
[264] *Polly Peck International v Nadir (No.2)* [1992] 4 All E.R. 769.
[265] [2000] 4 All E.R. 221.
[266] [2001] Ch. 437, 455.

Furniture Ltd (No 2),[267] the recipient can 'conscientiously retain [the] funds against the company' or, in the words of Sir Robert Megarry V-C in *In re Montagu's Settlement*,[268] '[the recipient's] conscience is sufficiently affected for it to be right to bind him by the obligations of a constructive fiduciary duty'. But, if that is the purpose, there is no need for categorisation. All that is necessary is that the recipient's state of knowledge should be such as to make it unconscionable for him to retain the benefit of the receipt.

For these reasons I have come to the view that, just as there is now a single test of dishonesty for knowing assistance, so ought there to be a single test of knowledge for knowing receipt. The recipient's state of knowledge must be such as to make it unconscionable for him to retain the benefit of the receipt. A test in that form, though it cannot, any more than any other, avoid difficulties of application, ought to avoid those of definition and allocation to which the previous categorisations have led. Moreover, it should better enable the courts to give commonsense decisions in the commercial context in which claims in knowing receipt are now frequently made . . .".

Therefore, the defendant is taken to have acted unconscionably if his knowledge was such that (to borrow from Nourse L.J.) it would be unconscionable for him to retain any benefit taken from the receipt of the property, or (preferably, it is suggested) it would cause the beneficiaries uncompensated loss without the defendant having a good defence or an absence of knowledge. The significance of this model is the approximation of "unconscionability" to the pre-existing test of "knowledge". What remains unclear, however, is the range of other factors which may be considered "unconscionable" beyond the requirement of knowledge.

17–075   In *Bank of Credit and Commerce International v Akindele*[269] itself Chief Akindele, the defendant, was a client of the bank, which later collapsed amid endemic and systematic fraud among many of that bank's officers.[270] The defendant had effectively been promised a very high return on his investments by the bank's officers and those bank officers sought in breach of their fiduciary duties to the bank to procure the defendant that return on his investments even though his investments had not performed nearly so well. The question at issue was whether in relation to a series of payments to the defendant he had at any time had knowledge of the breaches of fiduciary duty involved. It was found on the facts that the defendant had heard rumours about skulduggery inside the bank. Under the test for knowledge set out in *Baden v Societe Generale*, it might have been enough to demonstrate knowledge to show that the defendant had had knowledge of factors which would have put an honest and reasonable man on inquiry as to the propriety of the actions of the bank's officers. However, Nourse L.J. held that in general terms there was nothing on the facts to demonstrate that the defendant had acted unconscionably in general terms and therefore

---

[267] [1980] 1 All E.R. 393 at 405.
[268] [1987] Ch. 264 at 273.
[269] [2000] 4 All E.R. 221.
[270] See, for example, J. Adams and D. Frantz, *A Full Service Bank* (Simon & Schuster, 1991).

it was held that the defendant would not be liable for knowing receipt. The effect of the notion of unconscionability was to permit the court to absolve the defendant of liability when the stricter test of "knowledge" would have made him liable to account to the bank because he had had knowledge of factors which might have put a reasonable person on inquiry.

Carnwath L.J. took a similar approach to Nourse L.J. in the Court of Appeal in *Charter Plc v City Index Ltd*.[271] Carnwath L.J. (with whom Mummery L.J. agreed) took the view that the test of unconscionability in *BCCI v Akindele* is now to form part of the appropriate test in cases of receipt of property in breach of fiduciary duty.[272] As his lordship put it:

". . . liability for 'knowing receipt' depends on the defendant having sufficient knowledge of the circumstances of the payment to make it 'unconscionable' for him to retain the benefit or pay it away for his own purposes".

The notion of unconscionability is therefore linked to the requirement of knowledge. On this model of the test, it is not that the defendant has acted unconscionably in general terms which imposes liability, but rather it is a question as to whether or not the defendant had such knowledge of the circumstances so as to make his retention or dealing with the property unconscionable.

Attributing knowledge to companies

A company will be taken to have knowledge of something if the controlling mind **17–076** or the directing will of the company had that knowledge. So in *El-Ajou v Dollar Land Holdings*[273] the plaintiff had been defrauded of his money in Geneva by an investment manager who diverted that money into companies controlled by two men who had bribed him to do so. The plaintiff's money was moved around the world in an attempt to disguise its source before the traceable proceeds of that money were ultimately invested in a London property company called "DLH". The investment had come to DLH through its non-executive chairman, a man who ordinarily took no part in the day-to-day management of the company. It was found that only the chairman had sufficient knowledge of the manner in which the money had come to be invested in DLH, but not any of the other directors of DLH. It was held at first instance by Millett J. that while it was possible to trace the moneys into the hands of DLH, it was nevertheless not possible to prove that DLH had knowledge of the fraud because only the chairman, who did not participate in the ordinary management of the company, had had the requisite knowledge. The matter was then appealed to the Court of Appeal.

It was confirmed by the Court of Appeal that the test for demonstrating that a company has knowledge of something is that "the controlling mind" or "the directing mind and will" of the company had knowledge of whatever has been alleged. On these facts, there were different people within DLH who acted as the

---

[271] *Charter Plc v City Index Ltd* [2008] 2 W.L.R. 950.
[272] *Charter Plc v City Index Ltd* [2008] 2 W.L.R. 950 at [31].
[273] [1994] 2 All E.R. 685; [1994] 1 B.C.L.C. 464; [1994] B.C.C. 143.

directing mind and will of DLH in different contexts. In that case, it was necessary to identify the person who was the directing mind and will in the particular
context in relation to the act or omission which was the basis of the complaint.
On these facts, even though the non-executive chairman of the company ordinarily played no part in the day-to-day management of the company, he had been
the person who had organised the investment by the Canadians in DLH and he
had acted without any of the requisite resolutions of the board of directors in so
doing: these factors suggested that the chairman was the directing mind and will
in this particular context for this particular transaction because he had assumed
managerial control of this transaction. Therefore, any knowledge which the
chairman had about these transactions could be attributed to DLH. Consequently,
on the facts it was held that the chairman and consequently DLH had had the
requisite knowledge of the circumstances which had led to the Canadians making
the investment in DLH. By contrast, a person who had been merely the chairman
of a company, but who never carried out the day-to-day management of that
company nor took control of *any* given transaction, would not be the controlling
mind of that company. Therefore, sometimes one must look for the person or
people who actually control the company, and not simply look at the people who
are installed as figureheads. The issue, therefore, is as to the seniority or influence
of the person who has the requisite knowledge of the breach of fiduciary duty so
as to fix the company with that same knowledge and make it liable to account to
the beneficiaries of that fiduciary duty relationship. If the person with the knowledge is a junior employee acting outside the limits of his authority, then the
company might not be fixed with his knowledge as suggested by *Stone & Rolls
Ltd (In Liquidation) v Moore Stephens (A Firm)*.[274]

SPECIFIC ASPECTS OF DIRECTORSHIP

General rules relating to the need for, appointment and removal of directors

17-077   Every public company must have at least two directors.[275] If it has only one director,
then that one director may not act[276] except to appoint another director.[277] Whereas
every private company need have only one director.[278] While a company may itself
act as a director, at least one director of every company must be a natural person.[279]

The first directors of a newly formed company must be identified in the application for the company's registration.[280] Those directors then become the first
directors of the company when it is formed.[281] There is no specific statutory
provision about who can appoint subsequent directors; instead that is a matter for

---

[274] [2009] UKHL 39; [2009] Bus, L.R. 1356.
[275] Companies Act 2006 s.154(2).
[276] See generally on the inability of a non-quorate number of directors to act: *Alma Spinning Co, Re
Bottomley's Case* (1880) 16 Ch.D. 681. Specifically on a single director: *Jalmoon Pty Ltd v Bow*
[1996] QCA 516.
[277] *Channel Colleries Trust Ltd v Dover St Margarets Railway Co* [1914] 2 Ch. 506.
[278] Companies Act 2006 s.154(1).
[279] Companies Act 2006 s.155(1).
[280] Companies Act 2006 s.9(4)(c), s.12(1)(a).
[281] Companies Act 2006 s.16(6).

the articles of association to set out. Ordinarily, under the draft articles of association for example, a director can be appointed by an ordinary resolution of the shareholders. The articles may, however, typically permit the directors themselves to appoint new directors. The power to appoint directors is to used only for the benefit of the company as a whole.[282]

An undischarged bankrupt must not act as director of, or be concerned in the promotion, formation or management of, a company without the leave of the court by which he was adjudged bankrupt,[283] under penalty of imprisonment or a fine or both.[284] Such a person may be personally liable if he acts while disqualified. No director may be under the age of 16.[285]

Directors may be removed in the following circumstances. First, where the articles deem that the office of director has been vacated. Second, where the articles require that the directors retire in rotation at the annual general meeting, and where appropriate seek reappointment by a resolution at the annual general meeting. Third, where the director is dismissed from office under s.168 of the Companies Act 2006 by means of an ordinary resolution at the annual general meeting, following service of an appropriate notice of the resolution.[286] The director is then entitled to communicate with the shareholders and to speak at the meeting under s.169 of the 2006 Act. Fourth, where there is some other power, for example in the company's articles of association, to dismiss a director for some specific reason. Dismissal of a director for insufficient cause may give rise to claims in employment law for unfair dismissal[287] or may in itself constitute a breach of contract if the director had been appointed for example for a fixed term.[288] The company cannot validly contract not to remove a director although the shareholders may do so as between themselves.[289] Fifth, by resignation of his office by the director.[290]

Register of directors

Section 162 of the Companies Act 2006 requires that a company must keep a **17–078** register of its directors and secretaries. In the case of an individual director, ss.162 and 165 provide that the register must contain his name[291] and any former names,[292] address, nationality and business occupation, together with particulars of any other present or past directorships held by him (except directorships of

---

[282] *HR Harmer Ltd, Re* [1959] 1 W.L.R. 62.
[283] For Scotland, substitute "sequestration of his estates was awarded" for "he was adjudged bankrupt."
[284] Company Directors Disqualification Act 1986 s.11.
[285] Companies Act 2006 s.157(1).
[286] This procedure has been upheld even where a private company had weighted voting rights: *Bushell v Faith* [1970] A.C. 1099.
[287] *Cobley v Forward Technology Industries Plc* [2003] EWCA Civ. 646, [2003] ICR 1050.
[288] *Southern Foundries Ltd v Shirlaw* [1940] A.C. 701; *Shindler v Northern Raincoat Ltd* [1960] 1 W.L.R. 1038.
[289] *Russell v Northern Bank Development Corp Ltd* [1992] B.C.L.C. 1016.
[290] See, for example, *CMS Dolphin Ltd v Simonet* [2001] 2 B.C.L.C. 704.
[291] A corporate director will use its corporate name. An LLP and a Scottish partnership can use its firm name.
[292] This does not include the maiden name of a married woman, the previous name of a peer or a name changed before the director was 18 or more than 20 years ago.

companies of which the company is the wholly-owned subsidiary, or which are wholly-owned subsidiaries either of the company or of another company of which the company is the wholly-owned subsidiary) and the date of his birth.

The board of directors

17–079 The ordinary understanding of the powers of directors is that the directors are required to act collectively as a board, and as such the members of that board should have no separate powers to bind the company.[293] However, the articles of association of any particular company may empower the directors to act differently and in particular may empower the directors to delegate their responsibilities to other people, as suggested by the draft articles of association for public companies. Decisions of the board of directors were expected by the case law to be unanimous and to be made at a formal meeting of the board of directors.[294] It is suggested that this approach would make it difficult to operate many companies because the refusal of a single director could effectively bring the business of a company to a halt. Therefore, well-drafted articles of association would provide for a looser management and decision-making system. The more modern case law by the late twentieth century accepted the enforceability of decisions which were not made at a formal meeting with all directors present, provided that all the directors agreed with or acquiesced in the decision.[295] Article 7 of the draft articles for public companies provides that directors' decisions must either be taken at a meeting of the board or must be in the form of a written resolution. The manner in which directors will conduct themselves in practice in public companies is considered in greater detail below in relation to corporate governance requirements for the proper discharge of directors' duties. More generally, the ordinary principles governing meetings must be complied with: that is, a notice of the meeting must be circulated, a quorum must be present, and votes must be taken in a proper manner. A decision taken at a board meeting which has been inappropriately convened or improperly conducted will not ordinarily be binding on the company,[296] although the company may not use that as a defence to a claim by a third party seeking to rely on a contract or some other right formed as a result of such a decision.[297]

The directors' report

17–080 The directors of a company are required to prepare a directors' report for each financial year.[298] This is an important part of a director's duties and also an important part of providing information to the company's members (and where appropriate to third parties). At the general level, the directors' report must give

---

[293] *Marseilles Extension Railway Co, Re* (1871) LR 7 Ch. App. 161, CA; *HR Harmer Ltd, Re* [1959] 1 W.L.R. 62.

[294] *D'Arcy v Tamar* (1867) LR 2 Ex. 158.

[295] *Charterhouse Investment Trust Ltd v Tempest Diesels Ltd* [1986] B.C.L.C. 1; *Hunter v Senate Support Services Ltd* [2004] EWHC 1085 (Ch.).

[296] *Greymouth Point Elizabeth Railway, Re* [1904] 1 Ch. 32.

[297] *Bonelli's Telegraph Co, Re Collie's Claim* (1871) LR 12 Eq. 246.

[298] Companies Act 2006 s.415.

the names of the people who were directors and also set out the principal activities of the company during the course of that financial year. More specifically, and importantly, further to s.417 the directors are required to set out a business review from that company in that financial year. There is an exemption from this requirement in relation to small companies: in effect this protects directors of small companies from this additional administrative burden. The purpose of the business review is to give information to the company's members so that they can assess how the directors perform in that financial year.[299] Importantly, this is not intended to be a report for the investing public generally; instead it is intended for the use of the company's members.

The business review is required to contain two things: first, "a fair review of the company's business" and, second, "a description of the principal risks and uncertainties facing the company".[300] That the review must present a "fair review" of the company's performance, and thereby the directors' performance also, means that the report cannot be biased. In that sense, the review is required to present "a balanced and comprehensive analysis" of three things: the development of the business, the performance of the business, and ultimately the position of the business at the end of the financial year.[301] In relation to a quoted company (that is, one whose securities traded on a regulated market), the business review must consider the main trends and factors affecting the future success of the business and also information about the impact of the company's business on the environment, the company's employees, and social and community issues. The review must also consider key performance indicators relevant to the measurement of the success of the particular business in question.

The directors report is also required, further to s.418(2), to contain a statement that as far as each director is aware there is no relevant information which is not being provided to the company's auditors and that each director has also taken all of the steps which he ought to have taken to make himself aware of any such information. The directors' report is then required to be approved by the board of directors and signed on behalf of the board.[302]

The directors of a quoted company must also prepare a report into their remuneration.[303] It is an important part of corporate governance in the United Kingdom in relation to public companies in particular, that directors' remuneration is not left entirely to the directors themselves but rather is passed on to a specific remuneration committee made up primarily of non-executive directors. The annual accounts and the directors' report must be circulated to every member of the company, to every holder of the company's debentures, and to every person entitled to receive notice of general meetings.[304] The directors of public companies are required to lay a copy of the company's annual accounts of the directors

---

[299] Companies Act 2006 s.417(2).
[300] Companies Act 2006 s.417(3).
[301] Companies Act 2006 s.417(4).
[302] Companies Act 2006 s.419(1).
[303] Companies Act 2006 s.420.
[304] Companies Act 2006 s.423. Moreover, a quoted company must ensure that its annual accounts and reports are made available on the website (s.430). In the modern age the Internet has the effect that information can be more easily and efficiently published online, and company law has consequently seized on the opportunity which it presents.

report before the company's general meeting.[305] A corporate governance statement is also required under the FSA disclosure and transparency rules in relation to public companies governed by them.[306]

Significantly, in s.463(2), a director will be liable to compensate the company for any loss that the company suffers as a result of any untrue or misleading statement in a directors' report or as a result of any omission from such report of anything required to be included in it. Again, this approach is necessitated by the importance of the provision of accurate information by company law.

Remuneration of directors

Where the director does not have a service contract

17–081   Directors acting as directors are not employees of the company, but are instead managers or controllers of the company's affairs and, in that capacity, are regarded as fiduciaries. Accordingly, as with any fiduciary, they have no claim to payment for their services (due to the no profits rule) unless, as is usual, there is a provision for the payment of directors in the company's articles of association.[307] If there is no authorisation for payment of directors in the articles or elsewhere then a director cannot make a claim for payment by way of quantum meruit or in equity for special work performed. Thus in *Guinness Plc v Saunders*,[308] above, the House of Lords refused such a claim by a director who had successfully negotiated a takeover bid for the company but whose remuneration was not properly authorised either by the directors or the company.[309]

Directors' service contracts—executive pay

17–082   The ordinary understanding among non-lawyers as to the status of directors of companies is that they are retained by the company and paid large salaries by those companies. So, as considered above, the articles of association will usually provide that the directors have a right to be paid. In addition to being a director, a person may also be appointed to a post within the company, such as the managing or finance director, in which case he will be given a service contract as an employee of the company. Such persons are often referred to as the "executive directors" of the company, as opposed to its "non-executive directors". It is usual for the articles to provide that the terms of such contracts be fixed by the board or a committee of the board, and they must act bona fide in the interests of the company in exercising this power.[310] Similar rules apply to the variation or renewal of such contracts.[311]

---

[305] Companies Act 2006 s.437.

[306] Companies Act 2006 s.472A.

[307] *Hutton v West Cork Railway Co* (1883) 23 Ch. D. 654 at 672, per Bowen L.J.; *Moriarty v Regent's Garage Co Ltd* [1921] 1 K.B. 423 at 446, per McCardie J. cf. Lord President Inglis in *M'Naughtan v Brunton* (1882) 10 R. 111 at 113.

[308] [1990] 2 A.C. 663.

[309] See also *Zemco Ltd v Jerrom-Pugh* [1993] B.C.C. 275.

[310] The contract will not be binding on the company if it has been issued otherwise than as required by the articles: *UK Safety Group Ltd v Heane* [1998] 2 B.C.L.C. 208.

[311] *Runciman v Walter Runciman Plc* [1992] B.C.L.C. 1084.

Where a director has been paid fees out of the company without proper authorisation he cannot claim a set-off against money owed to him under a service contract. He must repay the money improperly paid, since he is a constructive trustee of it, and sue under his contract for damages.[312]

The Companies Act 2006 imposes some controls on directors' service contracts. Section 228 provides that every company must keep a copy of each director's contract of service[313] (or a record of its terms if it is not in writing) in one place. This obligation extends to the directors of any subsidiary companies. The place where the service contracts are lodged may be: the company's registered office; or the other place where the register of members is kept; or its principal place of business in England, if the company is registered in England, or in Scotland if the company is registered in Scotland. Notice of such place and of any changes in it must be given to the Registrar except where the documents have always been kept at the registered office.[314] There are default fines for contravention of s.228 and the court is empowered to order an inspection.

To prevent possible abuse by directors granting themselves long-term service contracts in order to obtain large compensation payments in the event of a dismissal, s.188 of the 2006 Act seeks to limit the length of such contracts without the approval of a general meeting at which a copy of the proposed contract is available. Any term in such a contract which entitles a director to employment with the company for longer than two years must be approved by the company in general meeting.

Compensation for loss of office

It is unlawful for a company to make to a director any payment by way of compensation for loss of office, or as consideration for or in connection with retirement, unless particulars of the proposed payment, including the amount, are disclosed to the members and the proposal is approved by the company.[315] It was held in *Duomatic Ltd, Re*[316] that disclosure must be made to all members, even those with no right to attend and vote at general meetings, whilst the payment is still a proposed payment. However, in *Wallersteiner v Moir*[317] Lord Denning M.R. held that he imagined that payment could be later approved by the company in general meeting. This principle does not apply, however, to compensation for breach of a service contract or other payments which the company is contractually bound to make.[318] As a result the section has little effect. It was also said that the section does not apply, even to gratuity payments, in relation to a position other than as a director.

17–083

---

[312] *Zemco Ltd v Jerrom-Pugh* [1993] B.C.C. 275.

[313] This applies also to shadow directors.

[314] Contracts requiring a director to work wholly or mainly outside the United Kingdom are excluded although a memorandum of the duration of the contract, and, if appropriate, the name and place of the subsidiary company, must be kept. Also excluded are those where the unexpired term of the contract is less then 12 months or the contract can be terminated by the company without payment of compensation within 12 months.

[315] Companies Act 2006 s.215.

[316] [1969] 2 Ch. 365.

[317] [1974] 1 W.L.R. 991, CA, at 1016.

[318] *Taupo Totara Timber Co Ltd v Rowe* [1978] A.C. 537, PC; *Lander v Premier Pict Petroleum Ltd*, 1997 S.L.T 1361, OH [1998] B.C.C. 248; *Mercer v Heart of Midlothian Plc* 2002 S.L.T. 945, OH.

Substantial property transactions involving directors

17–084 Section 190 of the Companies Act 2006 provides a check on dealings between a company and its directors. It provides that no arrangement may be made without the approval of the general meeting between a director and his company involving the transfer, either way,[319] of a substantial non-cash asset.[320] The purpose of this principle has been said to be:

> "The thinking . . . is that if the directors enter into a substantial commercial transaction with one of their number, there is a danger that their judgment may be distorted by conflicts of interest and loyalties, even in cases where there is no actual dishonesty. The section is designed to protect a company against such distortions. It enables members to provide a check. Of course that does not necessarily mean that the members will exercise a better commercial judgment; but it does make it likely that the matter will be more widely ventilated and a more objective decision reached."[321]

The mischief aimed at by the section is the acquisition of an asset by the company at an inflated price or a disposal at an undervalue. Thus it has been held[322] that the necessary approval of the arrangement, although not requiring approval of every last detail, must cover the central aspects of the arrangement, such as the price involved, or at least a minimum price or a yardstick by reference to which the price is to be fixed. Moreover, what has been approved must actually be what happens in practice.

If the company avoids the transaction such loss is limited to the expenses of the transaction plus interest and any expenses of maintaining the asset. In other cases, however, the loss would include not only the difference between the market value of the asset at the date of the transaction and the price paid or received by the company, but also any subsequent loss of value after the date of the transaction, for example due to a subsequent reduction in the value of the asset, together with maintenance expenses and interest on the total amount. This is because the liability of those in breach of the section is regarded as a liability for breach of a fiduciary obligation and not for damages for breach of contract.[323]

---

[319] Thus applying both to sales to the company by a director, e.g. *Pavlides v Jensen* [1956] Ch. 565; and sales to a director by the company, e.g. *Daniels v Daniels* [1978] Ch. 406. But a disposal to a corporate body, as opposed to one which is to a person connected only with the directors, would not be caught by s.320: see *Clydebank Football Club v Steadman* 2002 S.L.T. 109, OH

[320] Under the predecessor legislation it was held that this can include the benefit of a contract or a beneficial interest in property: *Duckwari Plc (No.1), Re* [1997] 2 B.C.L.C. 713, CA. It does not, however, include the right of a director to compensation in cash for termination of his service contract. That was not an asset since it could not be assigned and in any event it was a right to cash: *Lander v Premier Pict Petroleum Ltd* [1998] B.C.C. 248. The burden of proof is on those alleging that the monetary limits have been exceeded: *Receivers of Niltan Carlton Ltd v Hawthorne* [1998] 2 B.C.L.C. 298. The time for valuing the asset is the time of the agreement: *Lander v Premier Pict Petroleum Ltd* [1998] B.C.C. 248.

[321] Per Carnwath J. in *British Racing Drivers' Club Ltd v Hextall Erskine & Co* [1997] 1 B.C.L.C. 182 at 198. For those reasons failure by a firm of solicitors to advise the directors of the need to comply with the section with consequent loss to the company was held to be negligence giving rise to liability for such losses.

[322] *Demite Ltd v Protec Health Ltd* [1998] B.C.C. 638 at 649 per Park J.

[323] *Duckwari Plc, Re (No.2)* [1998] 2 B.C.L.C. 315, CA.

A good illustration of this principle arose from the *Duckwari* litigation.[324] **17–085**
O Ltd agreed to purchase some land for £495,000 and paid a deposit of £49,500
to stakeholders. O Ltd then made an agreement with D Ltd whereby the property
was actually conveyed to D Ltd, D Ltd paying £49,500 to O Ltd. C was a director
of D Ltd and a 20 per cent shareholder in O Ltd. D Ltd completed the purchase,
partly by raising a loan at a substantial rate of interest. Subsequently the value of
the land fell. D Ltd spent £24,000 on obtaining planning permission but even then
only sold the land for £178,000. D Ltd claimed that the transaction was in breach
of s.190 and that O Ltd was liable to indemnify D Ltd against the loss arising on
the sale, the costs of obtaining the planning permission, the costs of financing the
bank loan, the costs of maintaining the land and interest on the whole amount. It
was held that s.320 applied because: (i) this was the transfer of a non-cash asset
(the right under the contract of purchase or the beneficial ownership of the land);
(ii) it was between a company, D Ltd, and a person connected with one of its
directors, O Ltd, (C owned 20 per cent of O Ltd); and (iii) the value of the asset,
£49,500, was more than 10 per cent of the net assets of D Ltd. Having sold the
land, D Ltd could not, however, avoid the transaction. Although there was no
evidence that the price paid by D Ltd was more than the market value at the time,
it was held to be entitled to recover the loss caused by the subsequent fall in value
of the property, the costs of the planning permission and the maintenance costs,
together with interest on the whole amount. All those liabilities flowed from the
transaction itself. The planning permission costs had in fact increased the resale
price and so reduced the overall loss on the sale. But D Ltd could not recover the
costs of the bank loan because those did not flow from the transaction itself.
There was no liability for the means by which the requisition was made.

The section does not apply if the director concerned received the assets solely
by virtue of being a member (e.g. on a general reduction of capital), or the transaction was entered into by the liquidator during the course of the compulsory
winding up of an insolvent company. However, in *Demite Ltd v Protec Health
Ltd*,[325] it was held, somewhat unrealistically, that there was no implied exception
for a sale by a receiver acting as the company's agent,[326] so that the prior approval
of the transaction by the general meeting was required. Most transactions within
a group of companies are also excluded.

DISQUALIFICATION OF DIRECTORS

The law relating to the disqualification of directors

The law surrounding disqualification of directors is one of the most litigated areas **17–086**
of company law. In essence, this area of law concerns the prohibition of people
from acting as company directors. The fact that companies operate through
the agency of human beings means that inappropriate people must be prevented

---

[324] *Duckwari Plc, Re (No.1)* [1997] 2 B.C.L.C. 713, CA; *Duckwari Plc, Re (No.2)* [1998] 2 B.C.L.C.
315, CA; *Duckwari Plc, Re (No.3)* [1999] 1 B.C.L.C. 168, CA.
[325] [1998] B.C.C. 638.
[326] For alternative ways around this see [1998] B.C.C. 638 at 647.

from acting as directors to prevent the inappropriate use of companies. Consequently, s.1 of the Company Directors Disqualification Act 1986 ("CDDA 1986") empowers the court to make a disqualification order against a person relating to him being a director of that company or a receiver of the company's property.[327] The maximum length of a disqualification order in any given set of circumstances is set out in s.6 of the CDDA 1986, as considered below. Alternatively, the court may accept an undertaking from a person not to act as a director or a receiver of a company's property for up to fifteen years.[328]

Grounds for disqualification

The effect of a disqualification order under all grounds

17–087 The CDDA 1986 provides for a number of different grounds on which disqualification may be ordered from sections 2 through 8 of that Act, as it has been amended by subsequent legislation. The effect of the disqualification order is that the person in question may not, without the leave of the court, be a director of a company, he may not act as the receiver of a company's property, he shall not "in any way, whether directly or indirectly, be concerned or take part in the promotion, formation or management of a company", and he shall not act as an insolvency practitioner.[329] Each head of disqualification is considered in turn.

Disqualification on conviction for an indictable offence

17–088 The court may make a disqualification order in relation to a person, further to s.2 of the CDDA 1986, if he has been convicted of an indictable offence in connection with the promotion, formation, management, liquidation or striking off of a company, or with the receivership of a company's property, or with his being the administrative receiver of a company.[330] The maximum period of disqualification is fifteen years, unless it is made by a court with only summary jurisdiction in which case the period is five years.[331]

Disqualification for persistent breaches of companies legislation

17–089 Section 3 of the 1986 Act provides that a person may alternatively be disqualified from being a director of, or being concerned in the management of, a company if he has been "persistently in default in relation to any provision of the companies legislation requiring any return, account or other document to be filed with, delivered, or sent to the Registrar of companies".[332] The fact that a person has been persistently in default in relation to any provision of the Companies Acts may be

---

[327] The law relating to disqualification orders was consolidated from the Companies Act 1985 and the Insolvency Act 1985 into the Company Directors Disqualification Act 1986, as amended by the Insolvency Act 2000.

[328] Company Directors Disqualification Act 1986 s.1A. See *Morija Plc, Re* [2008] 2 B.C.L.C. 313.

[329] Company Directors Disqualification Act 1986 s.1(1).

[330] Company Directors Disqualification Act 1986 s.2(1). See *R v Creggy* [2008] 1 B.C.L.C. 625.

[331] Company Directors Disqualification Act 1986 s.2(3).

[332] Company Directors Disqualification Act 1986 s.3(1).

conclusively proved by showing that in the five years ending with the date of the application he has been adjudged guilty (whether or not on the same occasion) of three or more defaults.[333] In that context, a person is to be treated as being adjudged guilty of a default in the following circumstances: if he is convicted of any offence by virtue of any contravention of or failure to comply with any provision of the Companies Acts (whether on his own part or on the part of the company); or if a default order is made against him under ss.242 and 713 or ss.41 and 170 of the Insolvency Act 1986.[334] However, it is not necessary to show three such convictions. In *Arctic Engineering Ltd, Re*[335] failure to send 35 required returns to the Registrar was held to be sufficient evidence for the making of an order. An order made on this basis may only last for a maximum of five years.[336]

Disqualification for fraud in a winding up

A disqualification order may be made under s.4 of the CDDA 1986 if in a **17–090** winding up it "appears" that a person has been guilty of fraudulent trading[337] or that he has been guilty of fraud or breach of duty in relation to the company while an officer of that company. The word "appears" is not defined in s.4. An offence is committed in connection with the management of a company if it has some factual connection with the management of a company; it does not have to be committed in the actual management of the company. Thus it includes insider dealing in the relevant company's shares[338] and carrying on an unlawful business through the medium of a company.[339]

The maximum length of the disqualification order in this context is 15 years.[340] The period of disqualification must date from conviction; and not, for example, from the convicted person's release from prison.[341] The restriction on taking part in the management of the company is very wide. In particular the words "be concerned in" the management do not mean "take part in," and so include acting as a management consultant.[342]

Successive convictions or default orders

A disqualification order may be made under s.5 of the CDDA 1986 if a person is **17–091** convicted of any offence by virtue of or failure to comply with any provision of

---

[333] Company Directors Disqualification Act 1986 s.3(2).
[334] Company Directors Disqualification Act 1986 s.3(3).
[335] [1986] 1 W.L.R. 686.
[336] Company Directors Disqualification Act 1986 s.3(5).
[337] This applies whether or not he is actually convicted of the offence.
[338] *R. v Goodman* [1994] 1 B.C.L.C. 349.
[339] *R. v Georgiou* (1988) 4 B.C.C., CA. See also *R. v Austen* (1985) 1 B.C.C. 99.
[340] Disqualification orders may run concurrently.
[341] *R. v Bradley* [1961] 1 W.L.R. 398, CA.
[342] *R. v Campbell* [1984] B.C.L.C. 83, CA. See also *Drew v H.M. Advocate*, 1996 S.L.T. 1062. In *R. v Young* [1990] B.C.C. 549 the director had had a three and a half year record of successful business after committing the offence before the matter came to court. On the offence he was given a conditional discharge but disqualified for two years. This was quashed by the Court of Appeal (Criminal Division) on the basis of the intolerable delay and his recent record. Disqualification was a punishment which should be linked to the conditional discharge.

the Act and in the five-year period up to that conviction he has been convicted of other such offences or received three default orders. The court making the conviction can impose a disqualification order which may last for five years. In *Civica Investments Ltd, Re*[343] the judge held that deciding the length of the disqualification was similar to the passing of a sentence in a criminal case and consequently that elaborate reasoning was unnecessary because it would be undesirable for the judge to be taken through the facts of previous cases as more of the cases arose. It was held further that the five-year period was a maximum and should be reserved for serious cases. In the case before him, since most of the defaults had been remedied the judge imposed a one-year disqualification only.

Disqualification orders following corporate insolvency

17–092 Section 6 of the CDDA 1986 deals with disqualification of directors of insolvent companies on grounds of unfitness.[344] The core question which the court has to consider is whether a defendant director's conduct, viewed cumulatively (i.e. taking all behaviour into account) and taking into account any extenuating factors, fell below the standards of probity and competence appropriate for directors of companies.[345] For example, in *Kappler v Secretary of State*[346] the court was required to consider the mixed question of law and fact as to whether or not there was sufficient evidence that the director had been dishonest, and it was found that there was sufficient evidence that the director had known that false invoices had been raised by the company. If, for example, directors leave all the company's financial matters to other people, that will not absolve them from the charge that they have acted without sufficient probity when those other people act dishonestly in relation to the company's finances.[347] It was held that the director's high degree of incompetence, even if he had not himself been dishonest, justified a period of disqualification as a director. A director will not be found to have acted inappropriately or dishonestly if he acted throughout on the advice of his solicitor.[348]

If the court is satisfied that a person is or has been a director of a company which has become insolvent within the past two years, and that his conduct as such makes him unfit to be concerned in the management of a company, it must make a disqualification order against him for at least two years.[349] The

---

[343] [1983] B.C.L.C. 458.
[344] See *Official Receiver v Key* [2009] 1 B.C.L.C. 22 and *Secretary of State for BERR v Aaron* [2009] 1 B.C.L.C. 55 for recent reviews of the principles considered in the text.
[345] In *Lexi Holdings Plc v Luqman* [2009] 2 B.C.L.C. 1 it was found that it was in breach of directors' duties and dishonest for directors to fail to disclose the existence of false accounts and the embezzlement of money by other directors.
[346] *Kappler v Secretary of State for Trade and Industry* [2008] 1 B.C.L.C. 120.
[347] *Secretary of State for Trade and Industry v Thornbury* [2008] 1 B.C.L.C. 139.
[348] *Green v Walkling* [2008] 2 B.C.L.C. 332 where it was held that a director had discharged his duties in this context by acting on the advice of his solicitor throughout.
[349] Company Directors Disqualification Act s.6. This section applies equally to non-residents and to conduct which occurred outside the United Kingdom: *Seagull Manufacturing Co Ltd, Re (No.2)* [1994] 1 B.C.L.C. 273.

order may be stayed pending an appeal.[350] The conduct may relate to one or more companies as specified, provided it tends to show unfitness. There may be evidence relating to a "lead" company (or companies)[351] and collateral companies: where a lead company is the company through which the principal acts of unfitness were performed, and where collateral companies are different companies but companies which are connected in some way. However, there is no requirement that the conduct in relation to a collateral company should be the same as, similar to, or explanatory or confirmatory of the conduct relied on in relation to the lead company. The only connection required is that the defendant was a director of both companies and the conduct shows unfitness.[352]

The application for such an order must be made by the Secretary of State. In practice, this is an order made by the Disqualification Unit of the appropriate government department acting on behalf of the Secretary of State. The application will be made if it appears to the Secretary of State to be in the public interest as a result of information received from a liquidator, administrator, or administrative receiver. Those officials are under a duty to report information about a director's conduct in such matters to the Secretary of State.[353] Although the proceedings are civil, involving the civil standard of proof,[354] and not criminal, they do nevertheless involve penal consequences for the director. However, the European Court of Human Rights has held that only art.6(1) of the European Convention on Human Rights applies (that is, the right to a fair trial within reasonable time) and not arts 6(2) and (3) (that is, the presumption of innocence and the specific right of defence in criminal trials).[355] It has therefore been held that natural justice requires that the director should know the substance of the charges he has to meet.[356] Consequently, a different charge cannot be introduced during the trial.[357] However, the defendant's conduct during the proceedings may be used as an additional ground of unfitness.[358] The proceedings will not be automatically stayed if criminal charges are also being brought,[359] or because they are taking place after other proceedings.[360] Further to s.6(2) of the CDDA 1986, a company becomes insolvent for the purpose of such orders, broadly, in the three following circumstances: when it goes into liquidation at a time when its assets are insufficient to pay its debts, and so forth[361]; or when an administration

---

[350] *Secretary of State v Bannister* [1995] 2 B.C.L.C. 271.

[351] *Surrey Leisure Ltd, Re* [1999] 2 B.C.L.C. 457, CA.

[352] *Secretary of State v Ivens* [1997] B.C.C. 801, CA.

[353] Company Directors Disqualification Act 1986 s.7. See also Insolvent Companies (Reports on Conduct of Directors) Rules 1996 (SI 1996/1909).

[354] *Living Images Ltd, Re* [1996] 1 B.C.L.C. 348.

[355] *DC v United Kingdom* [2000] B.C.C. 710, ECHR.

[356] See e.g. *Sutton Glassworks Ltd, Re* [1997] 1 B.C.L.C. 26; and also *Blackspur Group Plc, Re* [2008] 1 B.C.L.C. 153.

[357] *Secretary of State for Trade and Industry v Crane* [2001] 2 B.C.L.C. 222.

[358] *Secretary of State for Trade and Industry v Ragna* [2001] 2 B.C.L.C. 48.

[359] *Cubelock Ltd, Re* [2001] B.C.C. 523.

[360] *Secretary of State for Trade and Industry v Reynard* [2002] 2 B.C.L.C. 625, CA.

[361] The effective date here is the making of the winding up order: *Walter L. Jacob & Co Ltd, Re* [1993] B.C.C. 512. "Debts" in this context includes the liquidator's remuneration: *Gower Enterprises Ltd, Re* [1995] 2 B.C.L.C. 107.

order is made in respect of the company[362]; or when an administrative receiver is appointed[363].

Disqualification following a departmental investigation

17–093 The Secretary of State may apply for a disqualification order against a person if it appears to him to be expedient in the public interest following a report by inspectors, or from the production of books and papers or the entry and search of premises. The decision of the Secretary of State not to apply may be challenged by way of judicial review by a person with sufficient interest but only if the decision was perverse or that the only lawful and proper decision would have been to make an application.[364] The court may make an order if it is satisfied that the person's conduct makes him unfit to be concerned in the management of a company.[365] This is the same test as is applied in relation to orders made following a corporate insolvency and the courts apply similar criteria both as to unfitness and as to the length of the period imposed,[366] although there is no mandatory minimum period. Evidence which the defendant has been compelled to give to the inspectors may be used in the disqualification proceedings,[367] but not the inspectors' own notes or drafts.[368]

Time limit for applications

17–094 The director must be given ten days clear notice before the institution of proceedings. Failure to do so may make the proceedings invalid under s.16(1) of the CDDA 1986. However, failure to give such notice will not invalidate proceedings commenced without it unless there has been substantial prejudice caused to the defendant.[369] More importantly, s.7(2) of the CDDA 1986 provides that no application for a disqualification may be made after the end of the period of two years beginning with the day when the relevant company first became insolvent unless the court gives leave or the defendant consents to the delay.[370] This means the earliest of the insolvent acts set out above.[371] In deciding whether to give

---

[362] However, not an interim order: *Secretary of State for Trade and Industry v Palmer* [1993] B.C.C. 650; 1994 S.C. 707.

[363] Whether or not that appointment was valid: *Secretary of State for Trade and Industry v Jabble* [1998] 1 B.C.L.C., CA.

[364] *R. v Secretary of State, Ex p. Lonrho Plc* [1992] B.C.C. 325.

[365] Company Directors Disqualification Act 1986 s.8. See *Secretary of State for BERR v Sullman* [2009] 1 BCLC 397; *TransTec Plc, Re (No.2)* [2007] 2 B.C.L.C. 495.

[366] *Samuel Sherman Plc, Re* [1991] 1 W.L.R. 1070; *Looe Fish Ltd, Re* [1993] B.C.L.C. 1160 (improper allotment of shares to maintain control).

[367] *R. v Secretary of State, Ex p. McCormick* [1998] B.C.C. 379, CA.

[368] *Astra Holdings Plc, Re* [1998] 2 B.C.L.C. 44. But in that case a side letter to the report expressing the view that the directors should not be disqualified had to be produced by the Secretary of State.

[369] *Secretary of State for Trade and Industry v Langridge* [1991] B.C.L.C. 543; followed in *Secretary of State for Trade and Industry v Lovat*, 1996 S.C. 32.

[370] *New Technology Systems Ltd, Re* [1997] B.C.C. 810.

[371] *Tasbian Ltd, Re* [1990] B.C.C. 318; *Secretary of State for Trade and Industry v Normand*, 1994 S.L.T. 1249 OH; *Secretary of State for Trade and Industry v Campleman* 1999 S.L.T. 787, OH.

leave for an application out of time the court must take into account all the circumstances of the case, including the purpose for which the discretion was given and the public interest.[372] Among the factors to be considered are[373]: the length of the delay; the reasons for the delay[374]; the strength of the case against the director; and the degree of prejudice caused to the director by the delay. In assessing the third of those factors the courts have allowed hearsay evidence to be used.[375] In general they will not go into the merits of the case in the same way as in a full trial. If there is a conflict of evidence then the courts must decide on the supporting evidence but if there is no conflict but an explanation by the defendant, these can be taken together.[376]

Striking out the application

As in all civil litigation an application to disqualify a director may be struck out **17–095** by the courts for want of prosecution once the original application has been made. The Court of Appeal in *Manlon Trading Ltd, Re*[377] held that the fact that the proceedings were brought in the public interest had to be balanced against the prejudice caused to the defendant by an inordinate or inexcusable delay. That could include consideration of delay in bringing the proceedings, i.e. at the end of the two-year time limit as well as delay after such commencement. Prejudice which might be caused by such delay would include the fact that the defendant would not be able to obtain other directorships during the delay. The European Court of Human Rights has held that such prejudice together with the impact on the defendant's reputation requires special diligence and expedition so that a delay of four and a half years after proceedings had been started was found to be a breach of art.6(1) of the European Convention on Human Rights which requires all civil proceedings to be heard within a reasonable time.[378] An action may also be struck out for reasons other than delay such as the loss of documents by the applicant. In such a case the question is whether or not that loss can be compensated for at the substantive hearing.[379] Other reasons for striking out include a situation where it is plain and obvious that the case will fail,[380] or where the defendant has already been subject to proceedings on the same facts.[381] However, it is not the courts' role to decide whether the Secretary of State has been over zealous in bringing the action.[382]

---

[372] *Secretary of State for Trade and Industry v Davies* [1997] 2 B.C.L.C. 317, CA.
[373] *Probe Data Systems Ltd, Re (No.3)* [1992] B.C.L.C. 405, CA; *Polly Peck International Plc, Re (No.2)* [1994] 1 B.C.L.C. 574; *Packaging Direct Ltd, Re* [1994] B.C.C. 213; *Secretary of State for Trade and Industry v Cleland* [1997] 1 B.C.L.C. 437.
[374] See e.g. *Noble Trees Ltd, Re* [1993] B.C.L.C. 1185; *Copecrest Ltd, Re* [1994] 2 B.C.L.C. 284, CA; *Cedar Developments Ltd, Re* [1994] 2 B.C.L.C. 714.
[375] *Polly Peck International Plc, Re (No.2)* [1994] 1 B.C.L.C. 574.
[376] *Packaging Direct Ltd, Re* [1994] B.C.C. 213.
[377] [1995] 1 B.C.L.C. 578, CA.
[378] *EDC v United Kingdom* [1998] B.C.C. 370, ECHR.
[379] *Dexmaster Ltd, Re* [1995] 2 B.C.L.C. 430.
[380] *Barings Plc, Re (No.3)* [1998] 1 B.C.L.C. 590, C.A.
[381] *Secretary of State for Trade and Industry v Baker (No.4)* [1999] 1 B.C.L.C. 226, CA.
[382] [1999] 1 B.C.L.C. 226, CA.

Disqualification undertakings

17–096 The sheer volume of proceedings for disqualification orders following an insolvency put great pressure on the system. Therefore, a means was sought to speed up the process of disqualifying directors, and to enable directors to be effectively disqualified without the need for lengthy court proceedings.[383] Consequently, amendments made to the CDDA 1986 by the Insolvency Act 2000 granted the Secretary of State the power to accept a disqualification undertaking from the defendant that he will not act as a director, receiver, promoter or manager of a company or as an insolvency practitioner for a stated period of between two and 15 years.[384] The legal effect of such an undertaking is the same as a disqualification order made by the court. The Secretary of State must be satisfied both that the disqualification is justified and that it is expedient in the public interest to accept an undertaking. In *Blackspur Group Plc, Re (No.3)*,[385] the Court of Appeal held that in delegating this matter to the Secretary of State, Parliament had intended the Secretary of State to have a better appreciation of what was expedient in the public interest than the courts, so that the Secretary of State was quite entitled to refuse to accept an undertaking which did not have a schedule of the grounds of unfitness attached. Whilst the use of such undertakings will save much unnecessary expense, there is a danger that it may be seen as a way of avoiding the possibility of having to pay the substantial costs involved in defending any formal proceedings.

Unfitness to be concerned in the management

17–097 In deciding whether a person's conduct makes him unfit to be concerned in the management of a company, s.9 of the CDDA 1986 requires the court to have regard to the matters specified in Sch.1 to that Act. These are: first, any misfeasance, breach of duty or misapplication of assets[386]; secondly, failure to comply with the requirements under the companies legislation relating to books and records, returns and accounts[387]; and, where the company has become insolvent, thirdly, responsibility for the cause of insolvency or for losses of customers who furnished advance payments and involvement in any transaction (or preference) which can be set aside[388]; and, fourthly, failure to comply with the statutory requirements relating to insolvency.

---

[383] To help alleviate this, a summary procedure, known as the *Carecraft* procedure, first used in *Carecraft Construction Co Ltd, Re* [1993] B.C.L.C. 1259, was adopted by the common law for non-contentious cases. In essence this involved an agreed statement by the parties of the facts and the appropriate period of disqualification. However, this procedure still involved going to court and the court was not bound by the agreement.

[384] Company Directors Disqualification Act 1986 s.1(1A) and 7(2A).

[385] [2002] 2 B.C.L.C. 263, CA.

[386] See e.g *Keypak Homecare Ltd, Re (No.2)* [1990] B.C.C. 117; *T. & D. Services Ltd, Re* [1990] B.C.C. 592; *Tansoft Ltd, Re* [1991] B.C.L.C. 339; *Dominion International Group Plc, Re (No.2)* [1996] 1 B.C.L.C. 572; *Ward Sherrard Ltd, Re* [1996] B.C.C. 418.

[387] See, e.g. *Rolus Properties Ltd, Re* (1988) 4 B.C.C. 446; *T. & D. Services Ltd, Re*, above; *New Generation Engineers Ltd, Re* [1993] B.C.L.C. 435 and *Firedart Ltd, Re* [1994] 2 B.C.L.C. 340.

[388] See *Secretary of State for Trade and Industry v Gray* [1995] 1 B.C.L.C. 276, CA; *Living Images Ltd, Re* [1996] 1 B.C.L.C. 348; *Secretary of State for Trade and Industry v Creegan* [2002] 1 B.C.L.C. 99, CA and Ch.29, below.

In addition to such specific criteria the judges have laid down various tests to determine whether a director's conduct is deserving of disqualification. *In Dawson Print Group Ltd, Re*[389] Hoffmann J. held as follows:

"There must, I think, be something about the case, some conduct which if not dishonest is at any rate in breach of standards of commercial morality, or some really gross incompetence which persuades the court that it would be a danger to the public if he were allowed to continue to be involved in the management of companies, before a disqualification order is made."

In *Churchill Hotel (Plymouth) Ltd, Re*[390] Gibson J. construed this to mean that gross incompetence without a breach of commercial morality would suffice for a disqualification, whilst the statement was approved by Browne-Wilkinson V.C. in *McNulty's Interchange Ltd, Re*[391] together with his own test in *Lo-Line Electric Motors Ltd, Re*[392] to the effect that:

"Ordinary commercial misjudgment is in itself not sufficient to justify disqualification. In the normal case, the conduct complained of must display a lack of commercial probity although I have no doubt that in an extreme case of gross negligence or total incompetence disqualification could be appropriate."

However, the Court of Appeal in *Sevenoaks Stationers (Retail) Ltd, Re*[393] warned **17–098** against treating them as paraphrases of the wording of the section, even though it acknowledged that such statements would be helpful in identifying particular circumstances in which a person would clearly be unfit to act as a director. The central question was held to be whether particular conduct makes a director unfit to be concerned in the management of a company. The Court of Appeal held in addition that incompetence to a marked degree would be sufficient for disqualification: that incompetence did not need to be total incompetence. It must, however, amount to more than a simple commercial misjudgement, involving some form of lack of probity or abuse of the system.

In *Secretary of State v Goldberg*,[394] Lewison J. held that the question of unfitness required a broad-brush approach and rejected an argument that it was based on three criteria of competence, discipline and honesty.[395] However, his lordship did hold that it would require a high standard before the court would disqualify someone who had acted honestly and had not broken any duty to anyone. Lewison J. held that:

---

[389] (1987) 3 B.C.C. 322 at 324.
[390] (1988) 4 B.C.C. 112 at 117.
[391] (1988) 4 B.C.C. 533 at 536.
[392] [1988] Ch. 477 at 479. See also *Chartmore Ltd, Re* [1990] B.C.L.C. 673; *Tansoft Ltd, Re* [1991] B.C.L.C. 339; *Austinsuite Furniture Ltd, Re* [1992] B.C.L.C. 1047.
[393] [1991] B.C.L.C. 325.
[394] [2004] 1 B.C.L.C. 597.
[395] See to *Secretary of State for Trade and Industry v Mitchell* 2002 S.L.T. 658, OH, where Lord Carloway confirmed that unfitness had to be looked at in the context of the circumstances at the time, including the director's mental state, but disregarding improvement in conduct and expressions of remorse afterwards.

"In considering whether a director is unfit, it is important to consider the cumulative effect of such of the allegations as are proved against him."

The clearest case where the courts regard the conduct as amounting to unfitness is where successive companies are formed which each become insolvent in turn, often transferring the business from one to the other.[396]

The general intention is to protect the public from abuse of the limited liability given by a company. However, the Court of Appeal, including Hoffmann L.J., in *Secretary of State for Trade and Industry v Gray*[397] made it quite clear that no such requirement is needed for an order to be made. It was irrelevant that the judge had decided that the director was no longer such a danger. The intention is also to raise standards of those who act as directors. The same idea is sometimes phrased by reference to the test being whether the director has forfeited the right to enjoy the privileges of limited liability by failing to perform the attendant duties.[398] A similar view was taken by Lord Woolf M.R., giving the judgment of the Court of Appeal in *Secretary of State for Trade and Industry v Griffiths*.[399] The fact that between the time of the acts complained of and the date of the hearing the defendant has shown that he has mended his ways and is no longer a danger to the public does not mean that no order should be made. There is a deterrent element involved in the procedure. Lord Woolf M.R. also said that the question for the court as to unfitness should be answered by the use of common sense and by adopting a practical and flexible approach so as to confine the evidence to that which is probative. Detailed or repetitive evidence should not be allowed. Over-elaboration in the preparing and hearing of cases and a technical approach to evidence simply leads to delay.

Disqualification orders have been refused where the director's conduct was only imprudent and improper[400] and where there was a reasonable reliance on advice which indicated that the director had none of the badges of a man who had exploited limited liability in a cynical way, with disregard for proper responsibility, or by incompetence.[401] Allegations of incompetence alone have been said to require a high standard. The order should not be made out of sympathy for the creditors nor to appease them.[402]

17–099 On the other hand, it has been held that there are minimum standards which can be expected of all directors. In small companies, directors have been disqualified even where they have taken no active part in the management of the company.

---

[396] *Travel Mondial Ltd, Re* [1991] B.C.C. 224; *Linvale Ltd, Re* [1993] B.C.L.C. 654; *Swift 736 Ltd, Re* [1995] 1 B.C.L.C. 896, CA.

[397] [1995] 1 B.C.L.C. 276, CA.

[398] This test was used by Vinelott J. in *Stanford Services Ltd, Re* (1987) 3 B.C.C. 326, Peter Gibson J. in *Bath Glass Ltd, Re*, above, Mervyn Davies J. in *Majestic Recording Studios Ltd, Re* (1988) 4 B.C.C. 519, and Hoffmann J. in *Ipcon Fashions Ltd, Re* (1989) 5 B.C.C. 773 and Nicholls V.C. in *Swift 736 Ltd, Re* [1993] B.C.L.C. 896.

[399] [1998] 2 B.C.L.C. 646, CA.

[400] *Bath Glass Ltd, Re, ibid.* See also *ECM (Europe) Electronics Ltd, Re* [1991] B.C.C. 268 and *Wimbledon Village Restaurant Ltd, Re* [1994] B.C.C. 753; *Secretary of State for Trade and Industry v Blackwood* 2003 S.L.T. 12, IH

[401] *Douglas Construction Services Ltd, Re* (1988) 4 B.C.C. 553.

[402] *Cubelock Ltd, Re* [2001] B.C.C. 523.

A director cannot simply abrogate his responsibilities as a director to others[403]; he has to keep himself informed and will be unfit otherwise.[404] Even reliance on professional advice may be insufficient where the director has asked no questions and done exactly as he was told to do.[405] As applied to larger companies, this has been stated in the context of responsibility to supervise others, whether as executive directors supervising senior employees or non-executive directors supervising the executives. The leading case is *Barings Plc, Re (No.5)*,[406] following the spectacular collapse of Barings Bank as a result of the activities of a single trader in Singapore. Failure by the directors to control that trader's activities, in particular failure to implement internal audit requirements, rendered the directors unfit. The existing controls were described as crass and an absolute failure. It was held that there had been incompetence to a high degree in a management role and that was enough. It was held further that errors of judgment could amount to unfitness.

Failure to resign as a director is not fatal, however. If the director protests against further trading and stays on to use his influence,[407] he will not be unfit unless he has also been directly involved in the breaches of statutory duty, for example as to the production of accounts.[408]

One area of dispute has been the relevance of a director allowing his company to run up arrears of money which it ought to have paid over to the tax authorities. The significant point is that these debts are not trading debts in the ordinary sense since they arise out of the use for other purposes of money which the company actually receives on behalf of the Crown, e.g. VAT collected from suppliers, income tax deducted at source from employees' wages under the Pay As You Earn system and national insurance contributions similarly deducted and not handed over to the correct authorities. In *Dawson Print Group Ltd, Re*[409] Hoffmann J. rejected the idea that in some way these sums amounted to quasi-trust moneys so that misappropriation was a serious matter. Failure to pay such debts was not a sufficient breach of commercial morality as to justify a disqualification. In *Stanford Services Ltd, Re*,[410] Vinelott J., whilst deciding that failure to set aside sums to cover those debts was not in itself a breach of commercial morality, stated that the Crown was nevertheless an involuntary creditor and if a company went into liquidation with such sums owing and irrecoverable the directors would be regarded as either being improperly informed as to the company's financial position or as acting improperly in using the money to finance the company's current trade.

---

[403] *Official Receiver v Vass* [1999] B.C.C. 516 (the defendant was named as a director of a large number of companies registered in Sark in the Channel Islands—this is known as the "Sark Lark").

[404] Even if he has an honest but unreasonable belief that he is not a director: *Kaytech International Ltd, Re* [1999] 2 B.C.L.C. 351, CA.

[405] *Bradcrown Ltd, Re* [2001] 1 B.C.L.C. 547.

[406] [2000] 1 B.C.L.C. 521, CA, upholding [1999] 1 B.C.L.C. 433.

[407] Unless he has no realistic chance of doing so and is staying on for his fees: *Secretary of State for Trade and Industry v Gash* [1997] 1 B.C.L.C. 341.

[408] *C S Holdings Ltd, Re* [1997] B.C.C. 172; *Secretary of State v Arif* [1997] 1 B.C.L.C. 34.

[409] (1987) 3 B.C.C. 322. See also *CV Fittings Ltd, Re* (1989) 5 B.C.C. 210; *Keypak Homecare Ltd, Re (No.2)* [1990] B.C.C. 117.

[410] (1987) 3 B.C.C. 326. This approach was followed in other cases, e.g. in *Lo-Line Motors Ltd, Re* [1988] Ch. 477.

In *Sevenoaks Stationers (Retail) Ltd, Re*[411] the Court of Appeal, agreeing with Hoffmann J.'s statement, regarded non-payment of Crown debts as important, not because of the fact that they were such debts, but because their non-payment indicated that the director was only paying those creditors who were pressing for their debts at the time to the detriment of other creditors, including the Crown. Viewed in that light such non-payment was a factor to be taken into account when deciding whether a director was unfit to be concerned in the management of a company. This approach has since been adopted in other cases.[412]

Period of disqualification

17–100 If the court finds that a director is unfit to be concerned in the management of a company under s.6 of the Company Directors Disqualification Act 1986, it has no choice but to impose a period of disqualification of between two and 15 years.[413] This is the only area where a disqualification order must be imposed; the court has no discretion except as to the length of the order. This approach was criticised by Vinelott J. in *Re Pamstock Ltd*[414] as being unduly rigid, especially as no minimum period is required in other areas such as fraudulent trading. There is no equivalent in this context of a conditional discharge in mainstream criminal law.

The Court of Appeal in *Sevenoaks Stationers (Retail) Ltd, Re*[415] laid down what, in effect, amounts to sentencing guidelines, which have been adopted in all the cases decided thereafter. The 15-year ambit should be divided into three bands. The band over 10 years should be used only for very serious cases such as a second disqualification[416]; that between six and 10 years for serious cases involving some form of breach of duty such as misappropriation of assets or deliberate misuse of the corporate form to prejudice creditors, and that from two to five years for less serious cases such as gross negligence or incompetence.[417] The length of the period is a matter for the court and not for agreement between the parties.[418]

In *Secretary of State for Trade and Industry v Griffiths*,[419] the Court of Appeal approved its earlier decision in *Secretary of State for Trade and Industry v McTigue*,[420] that fixing the appropriate period was a matter for the judge in accordance with the *Sevenoaks* principles. The Court of Appeal also said that although imposing a disqualification period is not technically a "punishment", in reality it is a sentencing exercise and must contain a deterrent element. "Plea bargaining"

---

[411] [1991] B.C.L.C. 325.
[412] See e.g. *City Investment Centres Ltd, Re* [1992] B.C.L.C. 956; *New Generation Engineers Ltd, Re* [1993] B.C.L.C. 435; *Park House Properties Ltd, Re* [1997] 2 B.C.L.C. 530; *Verby Print for Advertising Ltd, Re* [1998] 2 B.C.L.C. 23; *Amaron Ltd, Re* [2001] 1 B.C.L.C. 562 (where an attempt to negotiate with the Inland Revenue failed).
[413] Company Directors Disqualification Act 1986 s.6(4).
[414] [1994] 1 B.C.L.C. 716.
[415] [1991] B.C.L.C. 325, CA.
[416] For examples of such a serious case see *Secretary of State for Trade and Industry v McTigue* [1996] 2 B.C.L.C. 477, CA. *Sever Ltd, Re* [1999] B.C.C. 221; *Official Receiver v Vass* (1999) B.C.C. 316.
[417] See also *Vintage Hallmark Plc, Re* [2007] 1 B.C.L.C. 788.
[418] *Barings Plc, Re* [1998] B.C.C. 583.
[419] [1998] 2 B.C.L.C. 646, CA.
[420] [1996] 2 B.CLC. 477, CA.

as such is not allowed but credit may be given for admission of facts which would otherwise have taken a great deal of time and expense to prove. There should be no need to be over-elaborate in deciding this question and the citation of previous cases as to the period of disqualification will usually be unnecessary and inappropriate. The best approach would be to fix the period on the basis of the gravity of the offence and then take into account any mitigating factors such as the age and health of the defendant, delay in proceedings and admission, and so forth.

There are many reported examples of this system operating in practice, two **17–101** may suffice by way of illustration. In *A & C Group Services Ltd, Re*[421] the allegations against three directors included not only responsibility for the company's failure by ineffective stewardship of its affairs such as defective accounting procedures, failure to take into account excessive trading losses and non-payment of Crown debts, but also more serious allegations of improper use of company funds, making misleading statements, taking excessive remuneration and illegal use of directors' loan accounts. One of the directors was identified as being responsible for all of these and was disqualified within the middle band, for six years. That ruling took into account the delay in bringing the proceedings and the fact that he had admitted the charges. The other two directors were held not to be primarily responsible for the more serious allegations and to have been influenced by the other at a time of ill health. Nevertheless it was held that they were responsible for the poor management and should be disqualified for the minimum period of two years. In *Official Receiver v Stern*,[422] a 12-year penalty was imposed where the defendant had taken money out of the company and allowed it to trade at a time when he knew it was insolvent, had financed the business out of monies owed to the Crown and been party to the Phoenix syndrome. This was a particularly serious case.

Both parties can appeal against the length of the disqualification period and it is possible for the period to be increased on appeal if the judge is found to have erred in principle rather than simply as to the exercise of his discretion. In *Swift 736 Ltd, Re*[423] the defendant had been a director of sixteen insolvent companies. In respect of six of these, which had carried on the same business in succession as the previous one failed, he had not been the principal director. The other directors had already been disqualified for five years in separate proceedings. With regard to the other ten companies the complaints were of failure to keep proper accounts and to file returns, etc. The judge disqualified him for three years. The Court of Appeal decided that the judge had been over-concerned with the periods given to the other directors and had failed to take into account the other ten companies. Taken together this was serious misconduct and justified a six-year period.

The court has the power under s.17 of the CDDA 1986 when making a disqualification order to make an exception for a particular company. It may also hear applications for exceptions to a disqualification undertaking. The Court of Appeal in *Secretary of State for Trade and Industry v Griffiths*[424] held that whether such

---

[421] [1993] B.C.L.C. 1297.
[422] [2002] 1 B.C.L.C. 119, CA.
[423] [1993] B.C.L.C. 312, CA.
[424] [1998] 2 B.C.L.C. 646, CA.

a discretion is likely to be exercised is not a relevant factor in determining the period of disqualification. The principles for exercising this discretion were set out in *Secretary of State for Trade and Industry v Collins*.[425] The company must be shown to need the defendant's services; there must be no risk to the public; and there must be no subversion of the order, even if only of its deterrent effect. The burden of proof is on the defendant.

The court may impose conditions on the granting of leave.[426] Failure to observe these conditions may lead to such leave being withdrawn. It could also mean acting as a director contrary to the order, which could involve criminal penalties and personal liability.[427]

Costs

17–102 The normal rule is that costs are awarded against the losing party but the court has a discretion. There has been some dispute as to the basis upon which costs are to be awarded against a disqualified director. Some judges have awarded costs on an indemnity basis, (that is, full costs unless the defendant can prove that they are unreasonable) rather than the normal standard basis (where costs have to be justified) on the grounds that these are public interest proceedings.[428] Others have used the standard basis unless the defendant has acted unreasonably.[429] The matter appears to have been resolved by the Court of Appeal in *Dicetrade Ltd, Re*,[430] in favour of the latter approach. These are civil proceedings and the Secretary of State must take his chance. Cases where the indemnity basis would be appropriate include where the defendant makes extravagant claims or a wholly false and futile defence, or defends claims with no conceivable defence. With regard to orders for costs made against the Secretary of State the court again has a complete discretion as to the basis used.[431] An indemnity basis was used where the allegations were misconceived and no explanation had ever been sought from the defendants.[432]

Personal liability of persons acting while disqualified through bankruptcy or by a disqualification order or undertaking

17–103 Any person disqualified by reason of his personal bankruptcy under s.11 of the CDDA 1986 or by a disqualification order or undertaking and who becomes involved in the management of the company,[433] or acts in breach of a condition attached to leave to act as a director of a specific company under s.17 is personally

---

[425] [2000] B.C.L.C. 233.
[426] *Chartmore Ltd, Re* [1990] B.C.L.C. 673; *Secretary of State for Trade and Industry v Palfreman*, 1995 S.L.T. 156, OH; [1995] 2 B.C.L.C. 301.
[427] *Brian Sheridan Cars Ltd, Re* [1996] 1 B.C.L.C. 327.
[428] See e.g. *Brooks Transport (Purfleet) Ltd, Re* [1993] B.C.C. 766.
[429] See e.g. *Synthetic Technology Ltd, Re* [1993] B.C.C. 549.
[430] [1994] 2 B.C.L.C. 113, CA. See also *Godwin Warren Ltd, Re* [1993] B.C.L.C. 80, CA.
[431] *Southbourne Sheet Metal Co Ltd, Re (No.2)* [1993] B.C.L.C. 135.
[432] *Secretary of State for Trade and Industry v Blake* [1997] 1 B.C.L.C. 728.
[433] This includes acting as a director or directly or indirectly taking part in the management of the company: CDDA 1986 s.15(4). See *R. v Campbell*, above.

liable for all debts incurred while he was so involved. This liability extends to those who although not disqualified themselves act or are willing to act on the orders of someone who is so disqualified and whom he knows is so disqualified. Anyone who has so acted is presumed to be willing to act in the future. The liability extends to debts incurred while they were so acting or willing to act.[434] Liability under this head can also lead to a criminal offence under s.13 of the Act. The offence is one of strict liability so that it is no defence that the defendant thought that he was no longer bankrupt.[435]

Register of disqualification orders and undertakings

Section 18 of the CDDA 1986 provides that the prescribed officer of any court **17–104** which makes an order that a person shall not, without the leave of the court, be a director of or be concerned in the management of a company for a specified period or grants leave in relation to such an order, must furnish the Secretary of State with particulars of the order or the grant of leave where the order is made under that Act. The Secretary of State must maintain a register of such orders, undertakings accepted by her, and grants of leave, which register is open to inspection on payment of such fee as may be specified by the Secretary of State in regulations made by statutory instrument.[436]

CORPORATE GOVERNANCE

The development of corporate governance codes in the United Kingdom

Beyond the strict statutory and case law principles which govern directors' offices **17–105** and duties, there are also very significant non-legal principles which inform the way in which companies should be operated in practice. In the wake of a number of scandals involving large public companies, and amidst growing concern about the audit of such companies and about directors awarding themselves excessive remuneration, a number of reports have been generated which deal with "corporate governance" in recent years, leading to the current Combined Code on Corporate Governance. There was a renewed interest in corporate governance after the Enron and WorldCom scandals in the USA where small cabals of directors procured the falsification of corporate accounts and caused enormous losses. This led to the much-criticised Sarbanes-Oxley Act. In the United Kingdom, however, there had already been much debate about corporate governance in the wake of scandals involving, among others, the Mirror newspaper group, the Polly Peck group and Barings Bank in which case each group of companies were made insolvent as a result of the actions of their chief executives or, in the case of Barings Bank, the actions of one improperly supervised junior employee in Singapore. Therefore, in the USA and the United Kingdom the public policy agenda embraced the need to control the power of directors which was frequently

---

[434] Company Directors Disqualification Act 1986 s.15.
[435] *R. v Brockley* [1994] 1 B.C.L.C. 606.
[436] See the Companies (Disqualification Orders) Regulations 2001 (SI 2001/967).

unfettered in practice. It was clear that while company law may provide for rights for various actors relating to a company, the reality of the day-to-day operation of public companies is that directors hold the real power and therefore those directors may require controlling.

In particular, the corporate governance of listed companies was the subject of three specific reports prepared for the London Stock Exchange, initially those of the Cadbury Committee[437] and the Greenbury Committee,[438] and then later the Hempel Committee which produced a final report,[439] leading in turn to the Combined Code on Corporate Governance. A further report, the Higgs Report,[440] commissioned by the Chancellor of the Exchequer, was published in January 2003. In September 2002, Sir Robert Smith was charged by the Financial Reporting Council (FRC),[441] the guardians of the Combined Code on Corporate Governance, to undertake a review of audit committees. His report[442] was also published in January 2003.[443] The Revised Combined Code ("the Code") was approved by the FRC in July 2003 and came into effect on November 1, 2003. This new code has been described, perhaps a little over-excitedly, as being "the biggest shake-up of boardroom culture in more than a decade".[444]

The Revised Combined Code on Corporate Governance

The Code's methodology

17–106 The Code contains 17 principles of good corporate governance. The Code creates general principles with which public companies are expected to comply in a way that is appropriate in their own circumstances, as opposed to having a Code which creates rigid rules covering all circumstances. The Preamble to the Code states that:

> "While it is expected that listed companies will comply with the Code's provisions most of the time, it is recognised that departure from the provisions of the Code may be justified in particular circumstances. Every company must review each provision carefully and give a considered explanation if it departs from the Code provisions."[445]

The reference to "listed companies" is to companies which are listed on regulated markets like the London Stock Exchange, which was discussed in Ch.15. The overlap with the Listing Rules is considered in the next section. More generally,

---

[437] *Report of the Committee on the Financial Aspects of Corporate Governance*, 1992.
[438] *Directors' Remuneration: Report of a Study Group*, 1995.
[439] *Committee on Corporate Governance: Final Report*, January 1998.
[440] Review of the role and effectiveness of non-executive directors.
[441] See *http://www.frc.org.uk* [accessed July 1, 2010].
[442] *Audit Committees—Combined Code Guidance*.
[443] See the joint DTI and Treasury News Release P/2003/31, which followed the publication of these two reports.
[444] Tony Tassel, "Investors urged to adopt Higgs Standards", *Financial Times*, July 24, 2003.
[445] Preamble, para.5. See generally Alastair Hudson, *Securities Law* (London: Sweet & Maxwell, 2008) on the listing rules.

the Code deals in five parts with: the activities of the board of directors; directors' remuneration; audit committees to oversee the corporate audit process; institutional shareholders; and relations with shareholders. Each is considered in turn below. The Code divides between core principles, as considered below, and supporting principles and code provisions which expand on the core principles.

The overlap between the Listing Rules and the Code

The Code has been incorporated tangentially into the Listing Rules in that listed **17–107** companies are required to make a declaration as to whether or not they comply with the Code in their corporate governance procedures.[446] The Listing Rules provide that the annual financial report must include:

> "a statement of how the listed company has applied the principles set out in Section 1 of the Combined Code, in a manner that would enable shareholders to evaluate how the principles have been applied".[447]

Also to be included with this statement is a further statement as to whether or not the listed company has complied with the Code throughout the accounting period or whether there are any provisions in relation to which there has not been compliance.[448] It is a requirement that an auditor review the accuracy of this disclosure statement.[449] Overseas companies are required to explain their corporate governance arrangements but not strictly to comply with the Code.[450]

Directors

One of the principal arenas for corporate governance is in relation to the manage- **17–108** ment of the company by its directors. If the directors' means of conducting business are inadequate, or if their personal qualifications or knowledge as individuals are inadequate, then that will evidently have a negative effect on the company's business. Contrariwise, effective management will be to the benefit of a company and its shareholders. To this end, Principle A.1 of the Code, relating to "The Board", provides that the company must be headed by an effective board which is collectively responsible for the success of the company. The Supporting Principles provide that the board's role is to provide entrepreneurial leadership, although that is to be done within a framework of prudent and effective controls which enables risk to be assessed and managed while the directors take risks in pursuing the company's business. Therefore, the board should set strategic aims, it should ensure that the company has the necessary financial and human resources, and it should review the performance of management. In particular,

---

[446] This overlap is recognised in Combined Code 2006, recital 2.
[447] Listing Rules, 9.8.6(5)R.
[448] Listing Rules, 9.8.6(6)R.
[449] Listing Rules, 9.8.6(10)R
[450] Listing Rules, 9.8.7R

non-executive directors ("NEDs")[451] should challenge the executive directors' decisions constructively and should help the board to develop proposals on strategy, they should scrutinise the performance of management, they should satisfy themselves on the integrity of the company's financial information, they should determine the level of directors' remuneration and they should have a prime role in succession planning so that the success of the company's activities can be rolled out into the future.

The Code suggests that the board should meet sufficiently regularly to discharge its duties, including the creation of a formal schedule of matters reserved for its decision. To ensure that all of the shareholders are fully informed, the company's annual report should include a statement of how the board of directors operates and should identify the chairman and other company officials, such as the chairman and the members of the nomination, audit and remuneration committees. Further, the chairman should hold meetings with NEDs, without the executives present, and the NEDs should meet, without the chairman, at least once a year. If the directors have concerns about the running of the company or any proposed action which cannot be resolved, then they should ensure that these concerns are recorded in the board minutes. On resignation, an NED should provide a written statement to the chairman, for circulation to the board, if they have any such concerns. Finally, the company should arrange appropriate insurance cover in respect of legal action against its directors.

Principle A.2 of the Code, "Chairman and chief executive", provides that there should be a clear division of responsibilities at the head of the company between the running of the board and the executive responsibility for the running of the company's business. Many of the corporate scandals in the United Kingdom and in the USA leading up to the creation of the Code were caused by the unfettered power within companies of one individual who had complete effective control over the management of the company, or by a small cabal of senior executives who had similar control. Consequently, the approach of corporate governance codes on both sides of the Atlantic has been to require that there are two senior executives—a Chief Executive who controls the day-to-day business of the company, and a Chairman whose role is to observe the Chief Executive—so that each balances out the other. No single individual should have unfettered powers of decision. The Supporting Principles provide that the chairman is responsible for leadership of the board and for ensuring that all directors receive accurate, timely and clear information. He is also responsible for ensuring effective communication with shareholders and for facilitating the contribution of NEDs. Thus, he should ensure that executive directors and NEDs maintain a good relationship. The Code Provisions then provide that the roles of chairman and chief executive should not be exercised by the same person and the exact division of responsibilities should be set out in writing and agreed to by the board. The chairman should, on appointment, meet the independence criteria set out in principle A.3, below. In particular, a chief executive should not go on to be chairman so that a particular culture of management does not take hold; but exceptionally,

---

[451] See too Sch.B of the Code, which is headed, "Guidance on liability of non-executive directors: care, skill and diligence".

if this does happen, the board should consult major shareholders and set out the reasons in their next annual report.

Principle A.3 of the Code, "Board balance and independence", provides that **17–109** the board should include a balance of executive and NEDs (and in particular independent NEDs), such that no individual or small group of individuals can dominate the board's decision taking. The Supporting Principles are to the effect that the board should not be unwieldy. It should have a balance of skills and experience, should ensure power and information are not concentrated, be regularly refreshed, not place undue reliance on individuals, and ensure that only members should attend audit, nomination and remuneration committee meetings. The Code Provisions are that the board should identify each NED which it considers to be independent. A list of indicative independence criteria are then set out. Except for smaller companies,[452] at least half the board, excluding the chairman, should be independent NEDs. The board should appoint a senior independent NED, who should be available to shareholders if they have concerns which contact through the normal channels has failed to resolve or for which such contact is inappropriate.

Principle A.4 of the Code, "Appointments to the Board", provides that there should be a formal, rigorous and transparent procedure for the appointment of new directors to the board. The Supporting Principles state that appointments should be on merit and against objective criteria, that appointees should have enough time available to devote to the job, and that the board should satisfy itself that plans are in place for an orderly succession. The Code Provisions then state that there should be a nomination committee consisting of a majority of members who are independent NEDs and that the chairman or an NED should chair the committee except when choosing a new chairman. The committee should make available its terms of reference and should prepare a description of the role and capabilities required. For the appointment of a chairman, a job specification should be prepared, which includes an assessment of the time commitment expected. The terms and conditions of the appointment of NEDs should also be made available for inspection.[453] A chairman's other significant commitments should be disclosed to the board before appointment and included in the annual report. Changes to external commitments should be reported as they arise and included in the annual report. No individual should chair more than one FTSE 100 company, to ensure that the chairman's attention is focused on one company and to ensure that FTSE 100 companies do not fall under the control of a small clique of chairmen. Further, other significant appointments of NEDs should be disclosed and the board informed of subsequent changes. An executive director should not be allowed to become an NED of more than one FTSE 100 company nor the chair of such a company. A separate section of the annual report should set out the work of the nomination committee and an explanation given if neither an external search consultancy nor open advertising has been used in the appointment of a chairman of NED.

---

[452] This is defined as one that is below the FTSE 350 throughout the year immediately prior to the reporting year.

[453] cf. *Oxford Legal Group Ltd v Sibbasbridge Services Plc* [2008] 2 B.C.L.C. 381.

Principle A.5 of the Code, "Information and professional development", provides that the board should be supplied in a timely manner with information in a form and of a quality appropriate to enable it to discharge its duties. Further, all directors should receive an induction on joining the board and should regularly update and refresh their skills and knowledge. The Supporting Principles are that the chairman is responsible for ensuring that directors receive accurate, timely and clear information. He should ensure that directors continually update their skills and knowledge and the company should provide the necessary resources for them to do so. Under the direction of the chairman, the company secretary's responsibilities include facilitating information flows to and from the board and advising the board on governance matters. The Code Provisions provide that the chairman should ensure that new directors receive a full formal induction, including an offer to major shareholders to meet a new NED. There should also be access to independent professional advice at the company's expense. Finally, it is stated that all directors should have access to the advice and services of the company secretary, who is responsible for ensuring that board procedures are complied with. Both the appointment and removal of the company secretary should be a matter for the board as a whole.

Principle A.6 of the Code, "Performance evaluation", provides that the board should undertake a formal and rigorous annual evaluation of its own performance and that of its committees and individual directors. The Support Principle states that evaluation should ensure that each director contributes effectively and demonstrates commitment to the role. In particular, the chairman should seek appointments and resignations on the basis of strengths and weaknesses of the board. The Code Provisions provide that the board should state in the annual report how performance evaluation of the board, its committees and its individual directors has been conducted. The NEDs, led by the senior independent director, should be responsible for a performance evaluation of the chairman, taking into account the views of the executive directors.

Principle A.7 of the Code, "Re-election", provides that all directors should be submitted for re-election at regular intervals, subject to continued satisfactory performance and that the board should ensure planned and progressive refreshing of the board. The Code Provisions state that all directors should be subject to election confirmed at the first annual general meeting and then re-elected at intervals of no more than three years. NEDs should be appointed for specified terms and the board should set out why they believe that such an individual should be elected. Any term over six years should be subject to rigorous review and should take into account the need for progressive refreshing of the board and serving more than nine years could be relevant to the determination of a NED's independence.[454]

Remuneration[455]

17–110 At the time of writing, in the wake of the global financial crisis of 2007 through 2009, the levels of pay of bankers is at the forefront of public debate. Similar

---

[454] As set out in Code Provision A.3.1, above.
[455] As to this, see too The Directors' Remuneration Report Regulations 2002 (SI 2002/1986).

concerns have been a part of the corporate governance debate for some time. The concern is that directors are able to pay themselves overly high salaries and other "remuneration packages" unless corporate governance procedures within companies provide that the executive directors' salaries are set by an independent committee staffed by NEDs. The approach of the Code is to balance the need to attract talent to public companies with a need to ensure that pay levels do not escalate unduly. Consequently, Principle B.1 of the Code, "The Level and Make-up of Remuneration", provides that levels of remuneration should be sufficient to attract, retain and motivate quality directors, but that the company should avoid paying more than is necessary for this purpose. A significant portion of executive director's remuneration should be structured so as to link rewards to corporate and individual performance. In practice this often means that executive directors are paid in part in shares and in share options[456] in the company so that the directors have a personal commitment to ensure the profitability of the company. The Supporting Principle states that the remuneration committee should judge the position of the company relative to other companies, albeit using such comparisons with caution. They should also be sensitive to pay and employment conditions elsewhere in the group, especially when determining annual salary increases.

The Code Provisions are then broken down between remuneration policy on the one hand, and service contracts and compensation on the other. In relation to remuneration policy, it is provided that performance related elements should form a significant portion of the total package and should be designed to align the interests of executive directors with those of the shareholders and to give the directors keen incentives to perform at the highest levels. In designing such schemes, the remuneration committee should, in this respect, follow the provisions attached to Sch.A of the Code.[457] Executive share options should not be offered at a discount, save as permitted under the Listing Rules. On the other hand, levels of remuneration for NEDs should reflect the time commitment and responsibilities of the role, but should not include share options. Where, exceptionally, these are granted, shareholder approval should be sought in advance. Where external NED posts are held by executive directors, the remuneration report should state whether the earnings are retained as well as the amount. As to service contracts and compensation, the remuneration committee should aim to avoid rewarding poor performance and should take a robust line on reducing compensation to reflect departing director's obligations to mitigate loss. Notice or contract periods should be set at one year or less.

Principle B.2 of the Code, "Procedure", provides that there should be a formal and transparent procedure for developing policy on executive remuneration and for fixing the remuneration packages of individual directors. No director should be involved in deciding his or her own remuneration. The Support Principles provide that the remuneration committee should consult the chairman and or chief executive about their proposals relating to the remuneration of the other

---

[456] By using share options, the directors are not able to sell their shares immediately but rather have a long-term involvement with the company, at least until their options can be exercised.

[457] "Provisions on the design of performance related remuneration".

executive directors and should be responsible for appointing external consultants in respect of executive director remuneration. Potential conflicts of interest should be recognised and avoided and the chairman should ensure communication with shareholders with regards to remuneration. The Code Provisions are to the effect that the board should establish a remuneration committee, who should all be independent NEDs and that the remuneration committee should make available its terms of reference. Where remuneration consultants are used, there should be a statement as to whether they have any connection with the company. The committee should have delegated responsibility for all remuneration for all executive directors and the chairman, including pension and compensation payments. It should also monitor remuneration for senior management (the first layer of management below board level). The board itself (or the shareholders, if required by the articles) should set the NEDs remuneration and shareholders should be invited to approve all long-term incentive schemes, as defined in the Listing Rules.

Audit committee and auditors

17–111 The integrity of the company's accounting information is particularly important in providing investors and other businesses dealing with the company with the information which they need to make assessments of the risks associated with that company. If the company's audited accounts cannot be relied upon, then a central plank of company law and of securities regulation falls away. The requirements of posting accounts and of making other financial information available to securities markets are at the heart of the logic of how the integrity of the economy and the financial markets function. The Enron collapse was fuelled in large part by auditors being in cahoots with the senior executives who were falsifying the company's accounts.[458] Therefore, there is a need to ensure the company's processes for generating audited accounts are appropriate and robust. Principle C.1 of the Code, "Financial Reporting", provides that the board should present a balanced and understandable assessment of the company's position and prospects. The Supporting Principle states that responsibility extends to interim and other price-sensitive public reports and reports to regulators as well as to information required to be presented by statutory requirements. The Code Provisions then go on to state that the directors should explain in the annual report their responsibility for preparing the accounts and there should be a statement by the auditors about their accounting responsibilities. The directors should report that the business is a going concern statement, with supporting assumptions or qualifications as necessary.

Principle C.2 of the Code, "Internal Control", provides that the board should maintain a sound system of internal control to safeguard shareholders' investments and the company's assets. There are no Supporting Principles, but the Code Provisions are that there should be an annual review by the board of the system of internal controls which should be reported to the shareholders. This

---

[458] See, for example, McLean and Elkind, *The Smartest Guys in the Room* updated edition, (Penguin, 2004) and Fox, *Enron: the rise and fall* (John Wiley & Sons, 2003).

should cover all material controls, including financial, operational and compliance controls and risk management systems.

Principle C.3 of the Code, "Audit Committee and Auditors", provides that the board should establish formal and transparent arrangements for considering how they should apply the financial reporting and internal control principles and for maintaining an appropriate relationship with the company's auditors. There are no Supporting Principles, but the Code Provisions are that the board should establish an audit committee consisting of independent NEDs with at least one member with recent and relevant financial experience. The main role and responsibilities of the audit committee should be set out and should include monitoring, review, recommendations, and the development and implementation of an external auditor to supply non-audit services. The terms of reference of the audit committee should be made available and a separate section in the annual report should describe work done in discharging their responsibilities. The audit committee should review arrangements in place for staff concerns to be raised in confidence and should also review internal audit activities and the reasons for an absence of an internal audit function, if applicable. It should have primary responsibility for making a recommendation on the appointment, reappointment and removal of external auditors. The annual report should explain to shareholders how, if the auditor provides non-audit services, auditor objectivity and independence is safeguarded.

Relations with shareholders

Principle D.1 of the Code, "Dialogue with Institutional Shareholders", provides **17–112** that there should be a dialogue with shareholders based on mutual understanding of objectives. The board as a whole has responsibility for ensuring that a satisfactory dialogue with shareholders takes place. The Supporting Principles provide that the chairman should ensure that sufficient contact is maintained, whilst recognising that most contact will be through the chief executive and finance director. The board is encouraged to keep in touch with shareholder opinion in whatever ways are most practical and efficient. The Code Provisions are to the effect that the chairman should ensure that the views of shareholders are communicated to the board and that he should discuss governance and strategy with major shareholders. Further, NEDs should be offered the opportunity to meet major shareholders and the senior independent director should attend sufficient meetings with a range of major shareholders for a balanced view. There should be a statement in the annual report by the board as to the steps taken to develop an understanding of the views of major shareholders, for example through face-to-face contact, analyst's or broker's briefings, and surveys of shareholder opinion.

Principle D.2 of the Code, "Constructive Use of the AGM", provides that the board should use the annual general meeting to communicate with investors and to encourage their participation. There is no Supporting Principle, but the Code Provisions elaborate that the company should count all proxy votes and ensure that votes cast are properly recorded. In particular, there should be a separate resolution for each substantially separate issue and there should be a resolution relating to the report and accounts. The chairman should arrange for the chairmen of the audit, remuneration and nomination committees to be available to answer questions and for all directors to attend. Finally, the company should arrange for the notice and working papers for AGM to be sent to shareholders at least 20 working days before the meeting.

Institutional shareholders

17–113 Principle E.1 of the Code, "Dialogue with companies", provides that institutional shareholders should enter into a dialogue with companies based on the mutual understanding of objectives. The Supporting Principle states that institutional shareholders should apply the principles set out in the Institutional Shareholders' Committee's "The Responsibilities of Institutional Shareholders and Agents— Statement of Principles". The provisions of this part contain no Code Provisions.

Principle E.2 of the Code, "Evaluation of Governance Disclosures" provides that when evaluating companies' governance arrangements, particularly those relating to board structure and composition, due weight should be given to all relevant factors drawn to their attention. The Support Principle states that institutional shareholders should carefully consider explanations given for departure from the Code and communicate in writing where appropriate. They should avoid a box-ticking exercise in assessing the company's corporate governance and should bear in mind the size and complexity of the organisation and the nature of the risks and challenges it faces.

Principle E.3 of the Code, "Shareholder Voting", provides that institutional shareholders have a responsibility to make considered use of their votes. The Supporting Principles are to the effect that institutional shareholders should take steps to ensure voting intentions are being translated into practice. They should, on request, make available to their clients information on the proportion of resolutions on which votes were cast and non-discretionary proxies lodged. Finally, major shareholders should attend annual general meetings where appropriate and practicable and this should be facilitated by companies and registrars.

The future for corporate governance

17–114 Corporate governance is an area in which the European Commission has begun to take an interest, as was heralded in *Modernising Company Law and Enhancing Corporate Governance in the European Union—A Plan to Move Forward*. Following a consultation on the matter, the Commission formally invited Member States, through a Commission Recommendation, to reinforce the presence and role of independent non-executive directors on listed companies' boards. The protection of shareholders, employees and the public against potential conflicts of interest, by an independent check on management decisions, was seen to be particularly important to restore confidence in financial markets after recent scandals.[459] Commissioner McCreevy has stated, in relation to corporate governance, that:

---

[459] See Press Release IP/04/1182, October 6, 2004.

"Europe has a role to play. That role is to co-ordinate where possible Member States' efforts to improve corporate governance practices, through changes in their national company law, securities law or in corporate governance codes. There are different traditions in different Member States and those should be respected, but we must avoid unnecessary divergences which distort the single market and make life difficult for investors. Member States want and need to learn from each other's experience. The Corporate Governance Forum brings together a vast amount of high-level experience and expertise. It has a key strategic role to play".[460]

It remains, of course, to be seen what impact these developments are likely to have on the future development of UK company law in this area. In that respect the Cadbury Code was considered by Jonathan Parker J. in *Astec (BSR) Plc, Re*[461] in the following terms:

"So far as corporate governance is concerned, members of the public buying shares in listed companies may well expect that all relevant rules and codes of best practice will be complied with in relation to the company. But that expectation cannot, in my judgment, give rise to an equitable constraint on the exercise of legal rights conferred by the company's constitution (of which . . . the Cadbury Code form[s] no part) so as to found a petition [to protect the rights of minority shareholders]. It is in essence little more than an expectation that the company's affairs will not be conducted in a manner which is unfairly prejudicial to the interests of the members generally, or of some part of its members, an expectation which one would expect to be present in every case."[462]

Two points emerge from these dicta, it is suggested. First, simply put, a corporate **17–115** governance code will not found a claim under s.994 of the CA 2006 on the basis of unfair prejudice to the interest of a minority shareholder. Secondly, investors who rely on a company's statement as to its corporate governance will not be able to recover damages for loss in the way in which they will be able to recover damages for loss if those same matters had been the subject of a representation in a prospectus or listing particulars.

Corporate governance is now an important part of the management of large public companies which are listed on regulated stock markets. While they do not create legally-enforceable rights in the abstract (as discussed in the earlier sections of this chapter), institutional investors in particular will require that companies are well-managed and in part that will be measured by whether or not the company's management complies with the Combined Code on Corporate Governance.

---

[460] See Press Release IP/05/78, January 20, 2005.
[461] [1998] 2 B.C.L.C. 556.
[462] [1998] 2 B.C.L.C. 556 at 590.

Chapter 18

THE COMPANY SECRETARY

STATUTORY REQUIREMENT TO HAVE A COMPANY SECRETARY

Introduction

18–001 The requirement to have a company secretary was the subject of consideration at a number of points by the Company Law Review (CLR).[1] Under the previous companies legislation, the requirement to have a company secretary was common to all companies, including private companies. In practice such functions are contracted out to external advisors and for this reason the CLR stated that:

> "while properly qualified secretaries can provide a very valuable service to many private companies, the statutory *requirement* to appoint a secretary imposes a burden to very little effect. The decision whether to use the services of a secretary should be made by the market rather than by law. We recommend, therefore, that the requirement for private companies to appoint a secretary should be abolished. This would not, of course, remove the obligation on the company to carry out the functions that a secretary normally carries out. However, the proposal would give greater flexibility to companies in their internal administrative arrangements."[2]

Private companies

18–002 The Act accordingly now provides that a private company is not required to have a secretary.[3] In such a case anything authorised or required to be given or sent to, or served on, the company by being sent to its secretary may be given or sent to, or served on, the company itself, and if addressed to the secretary shall be treated as addressed to the company.[4] Further, anything else required or authorised to be done by or to the secretary of the company may be done by or to a director, or a person authorised generally or specifically in that behalf by the directors.[5]

---

[1] Generally on the work of the CLR, see para.1–015, above.
[2] *Final Report*, para.4.7.
[3] s.270(1).
[4] s.270(3)(a).
[5] s.270(3)(b).

Public companies

Public companies are required to have a secretary.[6] If it appears to the Secretary **18–003** of State that a company is in breach of this requirement, the Act now provides a mechanism whereby he can give such a company a direction[7] which specifies what the company must do to comply and the period within which it must do so.[8]

The Act requires the directors of a public company to take all reasonable steps to secure that the secretary (or each joint secretary) is a person who appears to them to have the requisite knowledge and experience to discharge the functions of secretary of the company.[9] In addition, a public company secretary must have either been a public company secretary for three out of the five years before his present appointment,[10] or be a barrister, advocate or solicitor,[11] or a member of one of the professional accountancy bodies[12] or of the Institute of Chartered Secretaries and Administrators,[13] or be someone who because of his position or qualifications appears to the directors to be capable of discharging the duties of a public company secretary.[14]

REQUIREMENTS APPLICABLE TO PUBLIC COMPANIES AND THOSE PRIVATE COMPANIES WITH A SECRETARY

Vacancies

The Act recognises that there may be situations where the office of secretary is **18–004** vacant. Accordingly, it is provided that his functions may be done by an assistant or deputy (if any) or, if there is no such person, by any person authorised generally or specifically by the directors.[15]

Duty to keep a register of secretaries

The Act requires a company to keep a register of its secretaries[16] which must **18–005** contain the particulars specified in the Act for individuals[17] who are secretaries and corporate secretaries and firms.[18] The register is required to be kept available for inspection at the company's registered office, or at a place specified in

---

[6] s.271.
[7] s.272(1).
[8] s.272(2).
[9] s.273(1).
[10] s.273(2)(a).
[11] s.273(2)(c).
[12] s.273(2)(b); s. 273(3).
[13] s.273(3)(e).
[14] s.273(2)(d).
[15] s.274.
[16] s.275(1).
[17] s.277. The Secretary of State is empowered to make regulations amending these requirements: s.279(1).
[18] s.278. The Secretary of State is also empowered to make regulations amending these requirements: s.279(1).

regulations.[19] The company must give notice to the Registrar of the place at which the register is kept available for inspection, and of any change in that place, unless it has at all times been kept at the company's registered office.[20] The register must be open to the inspection of any member of the company without charge, and of any other person on payment of such fee as may be prescribed.[21] Every company and every officer in default commits an offence if there is a failure to comply with these requirements.[22]

Duty to notify the Registrar of changes

18–006 A company is obliged to ensure that the Registrar is informed of changes to the register. Thus, within the period of 14 days from a person becoming or ceasing to be its secretary or one of its joint secretaries, or the occurrence of any change in the particulars contained in its register of secretaries, the company must give notice to the Registrar of the change and of the date on which it occurred.[23] Notice of a person having become secretary, or one of joint secretaries, of the company must be accompanied by a consent by that person to act in the relevant capacity.[24] Every company and every officer in default commits an offence if there is a failure to comply with these requirements.[25]

POSITION OF COMPANY SECRETARY

Appointment

18–007 The secretary is usually appointed by the directors, but sometimes he is named in the articles.[26] Table A, art.99, provides that:

> "Subject to the provisions of the Act, the secretary shall be appointed by the directors for such term, at such remuneration and upon such conditions as they may think fit; and any secretary so appointed may be removed by them."[27]

Status of the company secretary: older cases

18–008 The position of a company secretary has changed a great deal in the last 100 years. In 1887 it was said that

> "a secretary is a mere servant; his position is that he is to do what he is told, and no person can assume that he has any authority to represent anything at all; nor

---

[19] s.275(3).
[20] s.275(4).
[21] s.275(5).
[22] s.275(6)(7).
[23] s.276(1).
[24] s.276(2).
[25] s.276(3)(4).
[26] See e.g. *Eley v Positive Life Assurance Co Ltd* (1876) 1 Ex.D. 88, CA.
[27] There is no equivalent provision in the Model Articles for Public Companies or the Model Articles for Private Companies Limited by Shares.

can anyone assume that statements made by him are necessarily to be accepted as trustworthy without further inquiry".[28]

Accordingly, it has in the past been held that a company is not liable for the acts of its secretary in fraudulently making representations to induce persons to take shares in the company,[29] or in issuing a forged share certificate.[30] It has also been held that the secretary has no implied authority to bind the company by contract[31] and no implied authority to borrow money on behalf of the company[32] or issue a writ in the company's name.[33] Thus, it could justifiably be said that the secretary of a company is not "an official who *virtute officii* can manage all its affairs with or without the help of servants, in the absence of a regular directorate".[34]

Status of the company secretary: modern law

The modern status of the company secretary was explored in the leading case of **18–009** *Panorama Developments (Guildford) Ltd v Fidelis Furnishing Fabrics Ltd.*[35]

The secretary, purportedly on behalf of the company, fraudulently hired cars, ostensibly for the purpose of meeting customers, and used the cars for his own private purposes. It was held that the secretary had implied authority to enter into contracts for the hire of cars on behalf of the company and the company was liable to pay the hire charges.[36]

> "Times have changed. A company secretary is a much more important person now than he was in the past. He is the chief administrative officer of the company with extensive duties and responsibilities. This appears not only in the modern Companies Acts but in the role which he plays in the day-to-day business of the company. He is no longer a mere clerk. He regularly makes representations on behalf of the company and enters into contracts on its behalf which come within the day-to-day running of its business. So much so that he may be regarded as held out as having authority to do such things on behalf of the company. He is certainly entitled to sign contracts connected with the administrative side of a company's affairs, such as employing staff and ordering cars. All such matters come within the implied or apparent authority of a company's secretary."[37]

Although it would appear from this case that company secretaries may undertake a wide range of functions within the company, it has been held that they have no implied authority to make representations about the company in relation to a

---

[28] *Barnett, Hoares & Co v South London Tramways Co* (1887) 18 Q.B.D. 815, CA, at 817, per Lord Esher M.R.

[29] (1887) 18 Q.B.D. 815, CA, at 817.

[30] *Ruben v Great Fingall Consolidated* [1906] A.C. 439.

[31] *Houghton & Co v Nothard, Lowe & Wills Ltd* [1928] A.C. 1. He may of course be given actual authority to do anything: see *UBAF Ltd v European Banking Corp* [1984] Q.B. 713.

[32] *Cleadon Trust Ltd, Re* [1939] Ch. 286, CA.

[33] *Daimler Co Ltd v Continental Tyre & Rubber Co (Great Britain) Ltd* [1916] 2 A.C. 307.

[34] At 377, per Lord Parker.

[35] [1971] 2 Q.B. 711, CA.

[36] *Panorama Developments (Guildford) Ltd v Fidelis Furnishing Fabrics Ltd* [1971] 2 Q.B. 711, CA.

[37] [1971] 2 Q.B. 711, CA, per Lord Denning M.R. at 716–717. See too at 717–718, per Salmon L.J.

commercial transaction, e.g. a syndicated loan.[38] The company secretary's duties will ultimately depend very much on the size and nature of the company, and on the arrangement made with him. In any case he will be present at all meetings of the company,[39] and of the directors,[40] and will make proper minutes of the proceedings.[41] He will issue, under the direction of the board, all notices to members and others.[42] In practice he will usually countersign every instrument to which the seal of the company is affixed.[43] He is one of those whose signature will validate a document as executed by the company.[44] He or his department will conduct all correspondence with shareholders in regard to transfers and otherwise, will certify transfers, and will keep the books of the company, or such of them as relate to the internal business of the company, e.g. the register of members,[45] the register of charges,[46] etc. He will also make all necessary returns to the Registrar, e.g. the annual return,[47] notices, etc. If a provision requires or authorises a thing to be done by or to a director and the secretary it is not satisfied by the thing being done by or to the same person acting both as director and as secretary.[48]

If a person is secretary of two companies, a fact which comes to his knowledge as secretary of one company is not notice to him as secretary of another company, unless it was his duty to the first company to communicate his knowledge to the second company.

H was secretary to two companies, A Co and B Co. B Co drew a bill on a third company, C Co, and indorsed it in favour of A Co. The bill was dishonoured by C Co and no notice of dishonour was given to B Co. It was claimed that as H, in his capacity of secretary, knew of the dishonour, no notice was necessary. It was held notice to H, as secretary of A Co, was not notice to B Co.[49]

In England, a full-time secretary has been held to be an employee so as to be entitled to preferential payment of his salary on a winding up but a part-time secretary is not.[50] The Act regards the secretary as an officer of the company.[51] Thus, it is perfectly possible for the secretary to be liable[52] following a breach of

---

[38] *UBAF Ltd v European American Banking Corp* [1984] Q.B. 713.

[39] As to meetings generally, see s.302, and Ch.19, below.

[40] Thus, he may be authorised to call a meeting of the directors: Model Articles for Private Companies Limited by Shares, art.9(1) (also Model Articles for Public Companies, art.8(2)).

[41] Thus, a company has a statutory obligation to cause minutes of the proceedings of meetings of its directors to be recorded and kept for ten years from the date of the meeting: see s.248(1)(2).

[42] Thus, the Model Articles for Public Companies provides that he must propose a directors written resolution if so directed (art.17.2) and must keep a written record of such resolutions for ten years (art.18(4)). He can be instructed to call a meeting to appoint directors (art.28) and notices of amendment to ordinary resolutions are made by notice to him (art.40(1)).

[43] See Model Articles for Private Companies Limited by Shares, art.49(4) and Model Articles for Public Companies, art.81(4).

[44] See s.44(2)(3). See para.6–008 above.

[45] i.e. as required by s.113. See para.16–008, above.

[46] i.e. pursuant to s.876. See para.25–024, below.

[47] i.e. under s.854. See para.16–048, above.

[48] s.280.

[49] *Fenwick, Stobart & Co, Re* [1902] 1 Ch.507.

[50] *Cairney v Back* [1906] 2 K.B. 746.

[51] See now s.1173(1).

[52] See too s.1121(2).

trust or fiduciary duty by the directors under the "knowing assistance" head of liability, or under the tort of conspiracy, provided, in either case that the requisite criteria are satisfied.[53] It will also be possible, in an appropriate case, for a company secretary to be held liable as a director if, on the facts, the secretary is a de facto director.[54] The court can relieve a company secretary from liability for negligence, default, breach of duty or breach of trust, in certain cases.[55]

[53] See, e.g. *Brown v Bennett* [1998] 2 B.C.L.C. 97.
[54] cf. *Re Gemma Ltd* [2008] EWHC 546 (Ch); [2008] B.C.C. 812, where the court found that the company secretary was not a de facto director. Generally on de facto directors, see para.17–005, above.
[55] See s.1157, discussed at para.23–017, below.

Chapter 19

MEETINGS

INTRODUCTION

19–001 The law relating to meetings and resolutions has been the subject of extensive consideration, both by the CLR, and subsequently.[1] Reflecting the emphasis on deregulation for private companies, such companies are no longer required to hold any formal meetings (including an AGM) but may instead use written resolutions. The elective resolution regime, an important feature of the 1985 Act, has been discontinued.[2] Quoted companies will be subject to the right to demand an independent audit of any poll conducted by the company while traded companies will have additional obligations, including the need to make provision for electronic voting, allow voting in advance and answer questions at a meeting.

KINDS OF MEETING: THE ANNUAL GENERAL MEETING

Requirement to hold an annual general meeting

19–002 The regime in earlier companies acts made it mandatory for all companies to hold an annual general meeting (AGM). This is no longer the case. It is now only public companies, traded companies (which can also be private companies),[3] and those private companies whose articles require it that must hold an AGM. Every public company must hold a general meeting as its annual general meeting in each period of six months beginning with the day following its accounting reference date[4] (in addition to any other meetings held during that period).[5] Every private company that is a traded company must hold a general meeting as its annual general meeting in each period of nine months beginning with the day following its accounting reference date (in addition to any other meetings held during that period).[6] Failure to comply with these requirements is an

---

[1] See, e.g. Company General Meetings and Shareholder Communication (URN 99/1144); *Final Report*, Ch.2.

[2] Extraordinary resolutions are now no longer possible.

[3] A traded company is a company which carries rights to vote at general meetings and are admitted to trading on a regulated market in an EEA State by or with the consent of the company: s.360C. This section was added by the Companies (Shareholders Rights) Regulations 2009 (SI 2009/1632).

[4] See s.391.

[5] s.336(1).

[6] s.336(1A).

offence and every officer of the company in default will be liable on conviction to a fine.[7]

The directors may call the AGM as they may call a general meeting.[8] The original object of requiring the company to hold an AGM was to ensure that those members who wished to do so could meet together and confront the directors at least once a year. The usual business at an annual general meeting can include: the declaration of a dividend, the consideration of the accounts, balance sheets and the reports of the directors and auditors, the election of directors in place of those retiring, and the appointment of, and the fixing of the remuneration of, the auditors.[9]

Notice of the AGM

At least 21 days notice must be given of the calling of an AGM of a public **19–003** company,[10] although the company's articles may specify a longer period of notice.[11] An AGM of a public company that is not a traded company may, however, be called by shorter notice if all the members entitled to attend and vote at the meeting agree to the shorter notice.[12]

A notice calling an AGM of a public company or a private company that is a traded company must state that the meeting is an AGM.[13] Where a notice calling an AGM of a traded company is given more than six weeks before the meeting, the notice must include—if the company is a public company—a statement of the right under the Act to require the company to give notice of a resolution to be moved at the meeting, and whether or not the company is a public company, a statement of the right under the Act to require the company to include a matter in the business to be dealt with at the meeting.[14]

Members' powers to require circulation of resolutions

Members of a public company[15] may require the company to give, to members of **19–004** the company entitled to receive notice of the next AGM, notice of a resolution which may properly be moved and is intended to be moved at that meeting.[16] Such a resolution may properly be moved at an AGM unless it would, if passed, be ineffective, is defamatory of any person, or is frivolous or vexatious.[17] A company is required to give notice of a resolution once it has received requests that it do so from members representing at least 5 per cent of the total voting

---

[7] s.336(3)(4).
[8] s.302.
[9] Although in modern practice some of these will be considered at other general meetings.
[10] s.307(2).
[11] s.307(3).
[12] s.337(2).
[13] s.337(1).
[14] s.337(3).
[15] There is a similar provision for traded companies whose members wish to include other matters in business dealt with at the AGM: see s.338A, inserted by the Companies (Shareholders Rights) Regulations 2009 (SI 2009/1632).
[16] s.338(1).
[17] s.338(2).

rights of all the members who have a right to vote on the resolution at the AGM to which the requests relate[18] or at least 100 members who have a right to vote on the resolution at the annual general meeting to which the requests relate and hold shares in the company on which there has been paid up an average sum, per member, of at least £100.[19] A request may be in hard copy form or in electronic form, must identify the resolution of which notice is to be given, must be authenticated by the person or persons making it, and must be received by the company not later than six weeks before the AGM to which the requests relate or, if later, the time at which notice is given of that meeting.[20]

Public companies[21] are obliged to circulate members' resolutions for the AGM[22] and failure to do so is an offence to which every officer in default is liable to a fine.[23] The expenses[24] of the company in complying need not be paid by the members who requested the circulation of the resolution if requests sufficient to require the company to circulate it are received before the end of the financial year preceding the meeting.[25] Otherwise the expenses of the company in complying with that section must be paid by the members who requested the circulation of the resolution unless the company resolves otherwise and unless the company has previously so resolved, it is not bound to comply with that section unless there is deposited with or tendered to it, not later than six weeks before the annual general meeting to which the requests relate or, if later, the time at which notice is given of that meeting, a sum reasonably sufficient to meet its expenses in complying with that section.[26]

KINDS OF MEETING: GENERAL MEETINGS

19–005 All company meetings, whether for public or private companies and other than AGMs, are now known as general meetings. The directors have the power to call a general meeting of the company.[27]

Members power to require the calling of a general meeting

19–006 The Act provides that the members of a company can require the directors to call a general meeting of the company.[28] The directors are required to do so once the company has received requests to do so from members representing at least

---

[18] This excludes any voting rights attached to any shares in the company held as treasury shares. See para.10–017, below.

[19] s.338(3).

[20] s.338(4).

[21] There is a similar duty on traded companies in respect of a request by members (under s.338A) to include other matters in the AGM: see s.340A, inserted by the Companies (Shareholders Rights) Regulations 2009 (SI 2009/1632).

[22] s.339.

[23] s.339(4)(5).

[24] There is a similar provision for traded companies in respect of a request by members (under s.338A) to include other matters in the AGM: see s.340B, inserted by the Companies (Shareholders Rights) Regulations 2009 (SI 2009/1632).

[25] s.340(1).

[26] s.340(2).

[27] s.302.

[28] s.303(1).

5 per cent[29] of such of the paid-up capital of the company as carries the right of voting at general meetings of the company (excluding any paid-up capital held as treasury shares).[30] In the case of a company not having a share capital, the members must represent at least 5 per cent of the total voting rights of all the members having a right to vote at general meetings.[31] A request is required to state the general nature of the business to be dealt with at the meeting and may also include the text of a resolution that may properly be moved and is intended to be moved at the meeting.[32] A resolution may properly be moved at a meeting unless it would, if passed, be ineffective, is defamatory of any person, or is frivolous or vexatious.[33] A request from such members may be in hard copy form or in electronic form, and must be authenticated by the person or persons making it.[34]

The directors are required by the Act to call a meeting within 21 days of the date on which they became subject to the requirement with the meeting to be held not more than 28 days after the date of the notice convening the meeting.[35] If the request includes a proposed resolution, the notice of the meeting is required also to include notice of the resolution.[36] If the resolution is proposed as a special resolution,[37] the directors will be treated as not having duly called the meeting if they do not give the required notice.[38] The business of the meeting will include the resolution of which notice has been given under this part of the Act.[39]

If the directors do not act in calling the meeting, the members themselves (representing more than one half of the total voting rights of all of them) may do so.[40]

Members power to require the circulation of statements

The members of a company may require the company to circulate a statement of **19–007** not more than 1,000 words with respect to a matter referred to in a proposed resolution to be dealt with at that meeting or other business to be dealt with at that meeting.[41] The company is obliged to comply once it has received requests to do so from members representing at least 5 per cent of the total voting rights of all the members who have a relevant right to vote[42] (excluding any voting rights attached to any shares in the company held as treasury shares)[43] or at least 100 members who have a relevant right to vote and hold shares in the company on

---

[29] This requirement was introduced by the Companies (Shareholders' Rights) Regulations 2009 (SI 2009/1632), reg.4.
[30] s.303(2)(a).
[31] s.303(2)(b).
[32] s.303(4).
[33] s.303(5).
[34] s.303(6).
[35] s.304(1).
[36] s.304(2).
[37] See s.283.
[38] s.304(4).
[39] s.304(3).
[40] s.305.
[41] s.314(1).
[42] Defined in s.314(3).
[43] s.314(2)(a).

which there has been paid up an average sum, per member, of at least £100.[44] A request may be in hard copy form or in electronic form, must identify the statement to be circulated, must be authenticated by the person or persons making it, and must be received by the company at least one week before the meeting to which it relates.[45]

A company that is required to circulate a statement must send a copy of it to each member of the company entitled to receive notice of the meeting in the same manner as the notice of the meeting and at the same time as, or as soon as reasonably practicable after, it gives notice of the meeting.[46] Failure to comply is an offence on the part of every officer of the company who is in default and a person guilty of an offence is liable to a fine.[47] The company will not, however, be required to comply if an application is made by the company or another person who claims to be aggrieved and the court is satisfied that the section is being abused.[48]

The expenses of the company in complying need not be paid by the members who requested the circulation of the statement if the meeting is an AGM of a public company and requests sufficient to require the company to circulate it are received before the end of the financial year preceding the meeting.[49] Otherwise the expenses of the company in complying with that section must be paid by the members who requested the circulation of the statement unless the company resolves otherwise and unless the company has previously so resolved, it is not bound to comply with that section unless there is deposited with or tendered to it, not later than one week before the meeting, a sum reasonably sufficient to meet its expenses in doing so.[50]

Meetings convened by the court

19–008 If for any reason it is impracticable to call a meeting in any manner in which meetings may be called, or to conduct a meeting in the manner prescribed by the company's articles or the Act,[51] the court may, either of its own motion or on application by any director or any member entitled to vote at the meeting, order a meeting to be called, held and conducted in such manner as the court thinks fit.[52] The court may give such ancillary directions as it thinks expedient,[53] including a direction that one member present in person or by proxy shall be deemed to constitute a quorum.[54] A meeting so held is deemed for all purposes to be a meeting duly called, held and conducted.[55]

---

[44] s.314(2)(b).
[45] s.314(4).
[46] s.315(1).
[47] s.315(3)(4).
[48] s.317(2). The court can make an order for costs against the members who requested the circulation of the statement: s.317(2).
[49] s.316(1).
[50] s.316(2).
[51] s.306(1). Formerly s.371 of the 1985 Act.
[52] s.306(2).
[53] s.306(3).
[54] s.306(4).
[55] s.306(5).

Where a meeting has been requisitioned under these provisions, it may competently deal with business proposed by the board additional to that specified in the requisition.[56]

The question for the court is whether it is impracticable to call a meeting not whether it is impossible.[57] Thus, the courts have used this power to prevent a minority shareholder using the quorum provisions as a weapon in a dispute, i.e. by refusing to attend meetings so that no quorum under the articles or shareholders agreement can be obtained.[58] The section is designed to enable companies to conduct their business. The company must be able to manage its affairs and a majority shareholder to exercise his rights without being subject to a veto. But since it is a procedural section this will not apply, if the right of a member to be present for a quorum to be obtained is a class right of that member.[59]

E Ltd had three members, A, B and C. A and B were directors and held five per cent of the shares each. C, who was not a director, held 90 per cent of the shares. No general meetings were held. The articles provided that a quorum at a meeting should be two members. A and B frustrated C's efforts to call a meeting under s.306 by refusing to attend. C gave special notice of his intention to move ordinary resolutions to remove the directors at the next extraordinary general meeting, and asked the court to call a meeting under s.306 and to direct that one member should be a quorum. C's application was opposed by the directors. It was held the application should be granted because (1) otherwise C would be deprived of his right to remove the directors under s.168, (2) the directors were in breach of their statutory duty by not holding an annual general meeting.[60]

"The word 'impracticable' is not synonymous with the word 'impossible'; and it appears to me that the question necessarily raised by the introduction of that word 'impracticable' is merely this: examine the circumstances of the particular case and answer the question whether, as a practical matter, the desired meeting of the company can be conducted, there being no doubt, of course, that it can be convened and held. Upon the face of the section there is no express limitation which would operate to give those words 'is impracticable' any less meaning than that which I have stated, and I can find no good reason in the arguments which have been addressed to me on behalf of the respondents for qualifying in any way the force of that word 'impracticable' or the interpretation which I have placed upon it, and therefore upon that point I am in favour of the applicant".[61]

O Ltd had two members, A and B, who were the sole directors. A owned 51 per cent of the votes and B the remainder. They fell out and A called a meeting to dismiss B as a director. B refused to attend so that the quorum provisions for

---

[56] *Rose v McGivern* [1998] 2 B.C.L.C. 593.

[57] See *El Sombrero Ltd, Re* [1958] Ch. 900.

[58] *Opera Photographic Ltd, Re* [1989] W.L.R. 684; *Woven Rugs Ltd, Re* [2002] 1 B.C.L.C. 324; *Vectone Entertainment Holding Ltd v South Entertainment Ltd* [2004] 2 B.C.L.C. 224.

[59] *Harman v BML Group Ltd* [1994] 2 B.C.L.C. 704, CA.

[60] *El Sombrero Ltd* [1958] Ch. 900.

[61] [1958] Ch. 900 at 904, per Perry J.

meetings (two) could not be complied with. On A's application under s. 306, the court ordered a meeting with a quorum of one, otherwise there would be a deadlock situation. The quorum provisions did not give B a veto. A's conduct in dismissing B was a matter for other proceedings.[62]

The jurisdiction of the court under the section is very wide and will apply whenever "as a practical matter the desired meeting of the company cannot be conducted". Thus it has been used to order a meeting restricted to a few members to be followed by a postal ballot of all the members, where it was feared that a normal meeting would lead to a riot, even though there was no problem with obtaining a quorum or otherwise complying with the articles.[63]

19–009   Where there is a dispute between the shareholders which is the subject of other proceedings[64] and one of the parties seeks an order under the Act because the other party refuses to attend meetings, the court has a discretion whether to make an order under the section. If the application under s.306 is made prior to the other proceedings it is more likely to be granted then if the application is made after the other proceedings have commenced.[65] A s.306 application is not the appropriate forum to discuss allegations relevant to s.994.[66] But it is a procedural section and so, where the company is "deadlocked", e.g. where there are two shareholders, each with equal voting rights, so that either can prevent a resolution being passed, the Court of Appeal held that s.306 could not be used by one of them to break the deadlock by ordering a meeting of the applicant alone. The section was not designed to shift the balance of power in a case where the shareholders have specifically agreed that it be shared equally.[67]

Section 306 is concerned with ensuring that the company's business can be carried on—it is not as such a minority protection section. In *Union Music Ltd v Watson*[68] the company was the singer, Russell Watson's, manager. It owned 51 per cent of the shares in Arias Ltd. Watson owned the other 49 per cent. They were also the only directors. Under the articles, a quorum for any meeting was two and under a shareholders' agreement the consent of both shareholders was needed for a meeting to be held. The two parties fell out on a grand scale and the company became deadlocked at both board and meeting level. Union wanted to call a meeting with a quorum of one solely to appoint another director so as to enable the company to function. The judge refused to do so on the basis that it would be wrong to interfere with the situation as agreed by the parties. The Court of Appeal reversed this decision. Subject to not interfering with class rights or the case where there are two equal shareholders, the court could make the order if the majority shareholder was being improperly prevented from exercising its rights and the company was not able to manage its affairs properly. The quorum agreement in

---

[62] *Opera Photographic Ltd, Re* [1989] 1 W.L.R. 634.

[63] *British Union for the Abolition of Vivisection, Re* [1995] 2 B.C.L.C. 1. The court may impose conditions on any order it makes: *Woven Rugs Ltd, Re* [2002] 1 B.C.L.C. 324.

[64] Usually a petition under s.994. See para.22–026 below.

[65] *Sticky Fingers Restaurant Ltd, Re* [1992] B.C.L.C. 84; *Whitchurch Insurance Consultants Ltd, Re* [1993] B.C.L.C. 1359; *Opera Photographic Group Ltd, Re* [1989] 1 W.L.R. 634.

[66] *Woven Rugs Ltd, Re* [2002] 1 B.C.L.C. 324; *Vectone Entertainment Holding Ltd v South Entertainment Ltd* [2004] 2 B.C.L.C. 224.

[67] *Ross v Telford* [1998] 1 B.C.L.C. 82, CA. In such cases it is unlikely that s.994 will assist, so that deadlocked companies really are so.

[68] [2003] 1 B.C.L.C. 453.

this case was not a class right and Union, as majority shareholder, could properly appoint another director under normal circumstances. By way of contrast, in *Might SA v Redbus Interhouse Plc*,[69] the court refused to make an order under the section to restrain any of the directors of the company from chairing the meeting. It had been argued that each of them would have a conflict of interest in doing so. That did not make it impractical to call the meeting. There were other remedies available to the minority shareholders if the chairman actually abused his position.

Persons entitled to receive notice of General Meetings

To be validly held, notice of a general meeting must be called in accordance with **19–010** the Act and the company's articles. Thus all members[70] of the company and every director must be given notice.[71] In one case, where a number of persons attending a meeting were subsequently found not to be members of the company because of an irregularity in their membership the meeting was declared to be invalid.[72] The judge in that case also said that the meeting was invalid because the addresses of the members were not correctly entered on the register of members. That omission prevented free communication between members, without which "a meeting cannot be valid".[73] If notice of a meeting is not given to every person entitled to notice, any resolution passed at the meeting will be of no effect.

In *Young v Ladies' Imperial Club Ltd*,[74] a committee of a club met and passed a resolution expelling Y from the club. X, a member of the committee, was not summoned to the meeting, as she had previously informed the chairman that she would be unable to attend meetings. It was held that the omission to summon X invalidated the proceedings of the committee.

To obviate this result the Act provides that where a company gives notice of a general meeting any accidental omission[75] to give notice to one or more persons shall be disregarded for the purpose of determining whether notice of the meeting is duly given.[76] The onus of proof is on those claiming that the meeting was valid to show that the omission was accidental and not deliberate.[77]

Manner of giving notice

Notice of a general meeting of a company may be given in hard copy form, in **19–011** electronic form, or by means of a website, or partly by one such means and partly

---

[69] [2004] 2 B.C.L.C. 449.
[70] See s.310(2)(3).
[71] s.310(1).
[72] *POW Services Ltd v Clare* [1995] 2 B.C.L.C. 435.
[73] At 451, per Jacob J.
[74] [1920] 2 K.B. 523, CA.
[75] See *West Canadian Collieries Ltd, Re* [1962] Ch. 370. But cf. *Musselwhite v C. H. Musselwhite & Sons Ltd* [1962] Ch. 964 where the omission to give notice of a general meeting to the unpaid vendors of shares who remained on the register of members because the directors erroneously believed the vendors were no longer members, was due to an error of law and was not an accidental omission within such an article.
[76] s.313(1)(a). This section has effect subject to any provision of the articles save for s.304, s.305, and s.339: s.313(2).
[77] *POW Services Ltd v Clare* [1995] 2 B.C.L.C. 435 at 450, per Jacob J.

by another.[78] Where website notification is used, the notification must state that it concerns a notice of a company meeting, specify the place, date and time of the meeting and, in the case of a public company, state whether the meeting will be an AGM.[79] The notice must be available on the website throughout the period beginning with the date of that notification and ending with the conclusion of the meeting.[80]

Contents of notices of meetings

19–012   A notice of a general meeting of a company must state the time and date of the meeting and the place of the meeting.[81]

Notice of an annual general meeting was in common form and included in the business was "to elect directors". C, the retiring director, offered himself for re-election, but was not elected. A motion was proposed for the election of three new directors to fill up the places of the retiring director and two vacancies, but the chairman refused to accept it. It was held that the refusal was wrong, as the notice sufficiently specified the general nature of the business to bring it within the competence of the meeting to elect directors up to the number permitted by the articles.[82]

Subject to any provision of the company's articles,[83] the notice must also state the general nature of the business to be dealt with at the meeting.[84]

Directors of a holding company had from 1907 to 1914 been receiving remuneration as directors of a subsidiary company without the knowledge of the shareholders of the holding company. Special resolutions, authorising the directors to retain the remuneration and altering the articles to allow the directors to receive remuneration as directors of subsidiary companies, were proposed and an extraordinary general meeting summoned to pass them. The notice did not specify the amount of the remuneration, which was £44,876. The resolution was passed. A shareholder brought an action on behalf of himself and all other shareholders of the company against the company and its directors claiming, inter alia, a declaration that the resolution was not binding upon the company. It was held that the resolution was not binding as the notice was insufficient.[85]

For traded companies, the notice must include a statement giving the address of the website on which the information required by Act[86] is published and various other matters.[87]

---

[78] s.308.
[79] s.309(2).
[80] s.309(3).
[81] s.311(1).
[82] *Choppington Collieries Ltd v Johnson* [1944] 1 All E.R. 762, CA.
[83] Except traded companies: s.311(1).
[84] s.311(2).
[85] *Baillie v Oriental Telephone, etc. Co Ltd* [1915] 1 Ch. 503, CA. Benefits to directors particularly must be disclosed. See e.g. *Kaye v Croydon Tramways Co* [1898] 1 Ch. 358, CA.
[86] s.311A. This section was inserted by the Companies (Shareholders' Rights) Regulations 2009 (SI 2009/1632).
[87] s.311(3).

Length of notice for calling meetings

The notice period for general meetings of both public and private companies[88] is **19–013** 14 days[89] although the Act recognises that the articles may specify a longer period of notice.[90] The Act also makes provision for the calling of a meeting by shorter notice,[91] but to be effective this must be agreed to by a majority in number of the members having a right to attend and vote at the meeting, being a majority who together hold not less than the requisite percentage[92] in nominal value of the shares giving a right to attend and vote at the meeting (excluding any shares in the company held as treasury shares) or, in the case of a company not having a share capital, together represent not less than the requisite percentage of the total voting rights at that meeting of all the members.[93] If a resolution is to be passed on short notice, it must be appreciated that the resolution is being so passed.[94] Prior to the enactment of statutory rules as to shorter period, various cases established that it is competent for the shareholders to waive formalities for notice periods of meetings.

Five persons formed a private company in which they were the sole shareholders. They sold to the company for £15,000 a property which they had just bought for £7,000. The price was to be paid by the issue of debentures for £15,000 by the company. The transaction was carried out at a "board" meeting of the five individuals who appointed themselves the directors. The articles forbade a director to vote in respect of a contract in which he was interested. It was held that there was no fraud and the company was bound in the matter by the unanimous agreement of the members. Consequently the debentures were valid.[95]

It is no longer necessary for special notice to be given of special resolutions.[96] Nevertheless, some provisions of the Act do require special notice of a resolution to be given: the sections concern proposals to remove a director,[97] the removal of an auditor,[98] and the failure to appoint an auditor.[99] The Act provides that where such a resolution is required, the resolution will not be effective unless notice of intention to move it has been given to the company at least 28 days before the meeting at which it is moved.[100] Where practicable, the company must give its members notice of any such resolution in the same manner and at the same time

---

[88] The notice period for traded companies is governed by s.307A (inserted by the Companies (Shareholders' Rights) Regulations 2009 (SI 2009/1632)).

[89] s.307(1)(2).

[90] s.307(3).

[91] s.307(4).

[92] The requisite percentage is, for private companies, 90 per cent or such higher percentage (not exceeding 95 per cent) as may be specified in the company's articles; for public companies, the requisite percentage is 95 per cent: s.307(6).

[93] s.307(5).

[94] *Pearce Duff & Co Ltd, Re* [1960] 1 W.L.R. 1014.

[95] Applied in *Bailey, Hay & Co Ltd, Re* [1971] 1 W.L.R. 1357. See too *Oxted Motor Co Ltd, Re* [1921] 3 K.B. 32 where both members of a company waived the normal length of notice of a meeting at which an extraordinary resolution for voluntary winding up was validly passed.

[96] i.e. as required previously under the 1985 Act, s.378. See now s.283, para.19–026, below.

[97] Pursuant to s.168(2).

[98] See s.510(2); s.511.

[99] See s.514.

[100] s.312(1).

as it gives notice of the meeting.[101] Where that is not practicable, the company must give its members notice at least 14 days before the meeting by advertisement in a newspaper having an appropriate circulation, or in any other manner allowed by the company's articles.[102] If, after notice of the intention to move such a resolution has been given to the company, a meeting is called for a date 28 days or less after the notice has been given, the notice will be deemed to have been properly given, though not given within the time required.[103] There must be complete identity between the substance of the resolution as passed and the substance of the resolution set out in the notice. Thus in a resolution for a reduction of capital a change of £321 in the amount proposed to be reduced out of a total of £1,356,900 as shown in the notice was held to invalidate the notice. Changes because of grammatical or clerical errors or the use of more formal language might however be allowed.[104]

PROCEEDINGS AT GENERAL MEETINGS

Quorum

19–014 Under art.38 of the Model Articles for Private Companies Limited by Shares,[105] no business other than the appointment of the chairman of the meeting is to be transacted at a general meeting if the persons attending it do not constitute a quorum. The quorum must be an effective quorum, i.e. it must consist of members qualified to take part in and decide upon questions before the meeting.[106] The Act provides that in the case of a company limited by shares or guarantee and having only one member, one qualifying person present at the meeting constitutes a quorum.[107] Subject to that and the articles, in every other case two qualifying persons[108] present are a quorum,[109] unless each is a qualifying person only because he is authorised to act as the representative of a corporation in relation to the meeting,[110] and they are representatives of the same corporation; or each is a qualifying person only because he is appointed as proxy of a member in relation to the meeting, and they are proxies of the same member.[111]

Chairman

19–015 The Act provides that, unless the articles otherwise provide, the members present at a general meeting may elect any member as a chairman.[112] However, the articles

[101] s.312(2).
[102] s.312(3).
[103] s.312(4).
[104] *Moorgate Mercantile Holdings Ltd, Re* [1980] 1 W.L.R. 227.
[105] See also art.40 of the Model Articles for Public Companies. cf. Table A, art.40.
[106] *POW Services Ltd v Clare* [1995] 2 B.C.L.C. 435.
[107] s.318(1).
[108] As defined in s.318(3).
[109] In *East v Bennett Bros Ltd* [1911] 1 Ch. 163 it was held that one member, who held all the shares of a class, constituted a class meeting.
[110] See s.323.
[111] s.318(2).
[112] s.319.

usually provide who is to be chairman. The Model Articles[113] provide that the chairman of the board of directors shall preside at generals meetings of the company if present and willing to do so. If there is no such chairman, or if he is not present within 10 minutes after the time appointed for the meeting or is unwilling to act, the directors present or if no directors are present), the meeting, must appoint a director or shareholder to chair the meeting, and the appointment of the chairman of the meeting must be the first business of the meeting.[114] It is the duty of the chairman:

1. to preserve order;

2. to see that the proceedings are regularly conducted[115];

3. to take care that the sense of the meeting is properly ascertained with regard to any question properly before it[116];

4. to decide incidental questions arising for decision during the meeting, e.g. whether proxies are valid.[117]

The Chairman must allow the minority of the shareholders to have a reasonable time to put forward their arguments, but at the expiration of that time he is entitled, if he thinks fit, to put a motion to the meeting that the discussion be terminated.[118] The chairman has no casting vote unless expressly given one by the articles.[119]

Conduct of a meeting

In *Byng v London Life Association Ltd*,[120] it was held that a meeting could be **19–016** properly held in more than one room provided that all the rooms are properly provided with audio-visual links so that those in all the rooms can see and hear what is going on in the other rooms and that all due steps are taken to direct to the overflow rooms those unable to get into the main meeting. Where there are insufficient audio-visual links, as in that case, the main meeting may still constitute a meeting although it will be incapable of proceeding to business. The chairman may therefore validly adjourn this "meeting". There is no rule of law that a meeting at which members are validly excluded is a nullity for that purpose.[121]

---

[113] Model Articles for Companies Limited by Shares art.39; Model Articles for Public Companies art.31. See too Table A, arts 42–43.
[114] In *Bradford Investments Plc, Re* [1991] B.C.L.C. 224 it was held that where no directors are present and there is a dispute as to who may vote then any member may appoint a chairman. This could later be challenged only if the voting rights were themselves subject to challenge.
[115] *Byng v London Life Association Ltd* [1990] Ch. 170, CA.
[116] *National Dwellings Society v Sykes* [1894] 3 Ch. 159.
[117] Below, para.19–021, below.
[118] *Wall v London and Northern Assets Corporation* [1898] 2 Ch. 469, CA.
[119] *Nell v Longbottom* [1894] 1 Q.B. 767. There is no casting vote for the Chairman in the Model Articles. cf. however Table A, art.50.
[120] [1990] Ch. 170, CA.
[121] Mustill L.J. dissented on this point.

Subject to provisions of the Companies Act and the articles, the way in which the business at a meeting is to be conducted is decided by the meeting itself.

"There are many matters relating to the conduct of a meeting which lie entirely in the hands of those persons who are present and constitute the meeting. Thus it rests with the meeting to decide whether notices, resolutions, minutes, accounts, and such like shall be read to the meeting or be taken as read; whether representatives of the Press, or any other persons not qualified to be summoned to the meeting, shall be permitted to be present, or if present shall be permitted to remain; whether and when discussion shall be terminated and a vote taken; whether the meeting shall be adjourned. In all these matters, and they are only instances, the meeting decides, and if necessary a vote must be taken to ascertain the wishes of the majority. If no objection is taken by any constituent of the meeting, the meeting must be taken to be assenting to the course adopted".[122]

Adjournment

19–017 A chairman must adjourn a meeting if the persons attending a general meeting within half an hour of the time at which the meeting was due to start do not constitute a quorum, or if during a meeting a quorum ceases to be present.[123] He must also adjourn a general meeting if directed to do so by the meeting.[124] He may adjourn a meeting if the meeting consents to an adjournment, or it appears to him that an adjournment is necessary to protect the safety of any person attending the meeting or ensure that the business of the meeting is conducted in an orderly manner.[125]

When adjourning a general meeting, the chairman of the meeting must either specify the time and place to which it is adjourned or state that it is to continue at a time and place to be fixed by the directors and have regard to any directions as to the time and place of any adjournment which have been given by the meeting.[126] If the chairman exercises this power of adjournment he must act not only in good faith but also reasonably in deciding when to reconvene the meeting, so that adjourning to another location for the afternoon of a morning meeting was held not to be reasonable since it did not give all members a reasonable opportunity for attending.[127] If the meeting is adjourned it may elect another chairman and proceed with the business.[128]

---

[122] per Lord Russell of Killowen in *Carruth v ICI Ltd* [1937] A.C. 707 at 761.
[123] Model Articles for Private Companies Limited by Shares art.41(1) (art.33(1) of the Model Articles for Public Companies).
[124] Model Articles for Private Companies Limited by Shares art.41(3) (art.33(3) of the Model Articles for Public Companies). He is not otherwise bound to do so: see *Salisbury Gold Mining Co Ltd v Hathorn* [1897] A.C. 268.
[125] Model Articles for Private Companies Limited by Shares art.41(2) (art.33(2) of the Model Articles for Public Companies).
[126] Model Articles for Private Companies Limited by Shares art.41(4) (art.33(4) of the Model Articles for Public Companies).
[127] *Byng v London Life Association Ltd* [1990] Ch. 170, CA.
[128] *East v Bennett Bros Ltd* [1911] 1 Ch. 163.

If the continuation of an adjourned meeting is to take place more than 14 days after it was adjourned, the company must give at least 7 clear days' notice of it (excluding the day of the adjourned meeting and the day on which the notice is given) to the same persons to whom notice of the company's general meetings is required to be given, and containing the same information which such notice is required to contain.[129] No business may be transacted at an adjourned general meeting which could not properly have been transacted at the meeting if the adjournment had not taken place.[130] It is thought that a single member can constitute a quorum at an adjourned meeting.[131] Where a resolution is passed at an adjourned meeting of a company, the resolution is for all purposes to be treated as having been passed on the date on which it was in fact passed, and is not to be deemed passed on any earlier date.[132]

Voting on a show of hands

It has been held that a "shareholder's vote is a right of property, and prima facie **19–018** may be exercised by a shareholder[133] as he thinks fit in his own interest".[134] Indeed, shareholders are also under no duty to vote at all.[135] The common law rule is that, unless the articles otherwise provide, a resolution put to a meeting is normally decided in the first instance by a show of hands.[136] Each member present has one vote.[137] The Model Articles[138] provide that voting must be decided on a show of hands unless a poll is duly demanded in accordance with the articles. The Model Articles also provide that:

"(1) No objection may be raised to the qualification of any person voting at a general meeting except at the meeting or adjourned meeting at which the vote objected to is tendered, and every vote not disallowed at the meeting is valid. (2) Any such objection must be referred to the chairman of the meeting, whose decision is final."[139]

In *Marx v Estates & General Investments Ltd*,[140] Brightman J. suggested that there was much to be said for such an article. In that case a proxy form, which was liable to stamp duty because it authorised a proxy to vote at more than one

---

[129] Model Articles for Private Companies Limited by Shares art.41(5) (art.33(5) of the Model Articles for Public Companies). See too Table A, art.45.

[130] Model Articles for Private Companies Limited by Shares art.41(6) (art.33(6) of the Model Articles for Public Companies). See too Table A, art.45.

[131] See *Jarvis Motors (Harrow) Ltd v Carabott* [1964] 1 W.L.R. 1101.

[132] s.332.

[133] A bankrupt shareholder may vote if he is still on the register: see *Morgan v Gray* [1953] Ch. 83.

[134] *Carruth v ICI Ltd* [1937] A.C. 707 at 765, per Lord Maugham. See too *Northern Counties Securities Ltd v Jackson & Steeple Ltd* [1974] 1 W.L.R. 1133 at 1145.

[135] See *Kuwait Asia Bank EC v National Mutual Life Nominees Ltd* [1991] 1 A.C. 187, PC, at 221, per Lord Lowry.

[136] *Horbury Bridge Coal Co, Re* (1879) 11 Ch.D. 109, CA.

[137] s.284(2).

[138] art.42 (art.34 for Public Companies).

[139] art.43 (art.35 for Public Companies).

[140] [1976] 1 W.L.R. 380.

meeting but which was unstamped, was not void but a valid authority capable of being stamped, and since the company had accepted it without objection at the meeting the votes cast by the proxy were valid. Further, the objection taken several days after the meeting was made too late.

On a vote on a resolution at a meeting on a show of hands, a declaration by the chairman that the resolution has or has not been passed or passed with a particular majority, is conclusive evidence of that fact without proof of the number or proportion of the votes recorded in favour of or against the resolution.[141] Likewise, an entry in respect of such a declaration in minutes of the meeting is also conclusive evidence of that fact without such proof.[142] If, however, the declaration of the chairman is fraudulent, or shows on the face of it that the proper majority has not been obtained, it is not conclusive.

A special resolution was put to the meeting. The chairman then said: "Those in favour 6; those against 23; but there are 200 voting by proxy,[143] and I declare the resolution carried". It was held that the declaration was not conclusive, and the resolution was not passed.[144]

Voting on a poll

19–019 Although a show of hands can be taken quickly, it is not an accurate method of ascertaining the wishes of the members of a company because the votes of those voting by proxy are not counted. Further, it does not pay due regard to the wishes of a member holding a large number of shares since he has only one vote on a show of hands. Consequently, although the right to demand a poll exists at common law, this is also protected by statute. Thus, the Act provides that any provision of the articles will be void in so far as it excludes the right to demand a poll at a general meeting, on any question other than the election of the chairman of the meeting or the adjournment of the meeting.[145] The Act also provides that a provision of a company's articles is void in so far as it would have the effect of making ineffective a demand for a poll on any such question which is made: (a) by not less than five members having the right to vote on the resolution or (b) by a member or members representing not less than 10 per cent of the total voting rights of all the members having the right to vote on the resolution (excluding any voting rights attached to any shares in the company held as treasury shares), or (c) by a member or members holding shares in the company conferring a right to vote on the resolution, being shares on which an aggregate sum has been paid up equal to not less than 10 per cent of the total sum paid up on all the shares conferring that right.[146]

---

[141] s.320(1). This does not have effect if a poll is demanded in respect of the resolution (and the demand is not subsequently withdrawn): s.320(3).

[142] s.320(2).

[143] Those voting by proxy could not vote on a show of hands (though this has now changed: see s.324(1)).

[144] *Caratal (New) Mines Ltd, Re* [1902] 2 Ch. 498.

[145] s.321(1).

[146] s.321(2). Shares in the company conferring a right to vote on the resolution which are held as treasury shares are excluded.

The Model Articles[147] provide that a poll may be demanded[148] by the chairman of the meeting, the directors, two or more persons having the right to vote on the resolution; or a person or persons representing not less than one tenth of the total voting rights of all the shareholders having the right to vote on the resolution. A proper demand for a poll does away with the need for, or the result of, a show of hands. A poll on a resolution may be demanded in advance of the general meeting where it is to be put to the vote or at a general meeting, either before a show of hands on that resolution or immediately after the result of a show of hands on that resolution is declared.[149]

No procedure is specified for private companies[150] other than that the Model Articles provide that the poll must be taken immediately and in such manner as the chairman of the meeting directs.[151] Where, under articles similar to Table A, a poll was demanded on a question of adjournment and taken, but the scrutineers informed the chairman that the result could not be announced within the time during which the meeting hall was available, it was held that the meeting subsequently convened to hear the result was a continuation of the original meeting, with the result that no proxies deposited between the date of the original meeting and the date of the continuation meeting were valid, as the articles required proxies to be deposited 48 hours before the meeting.[152]

The number of votes which a member has on a poll depends upon the articles. **19–020** However the Act states that, unless the articles otherwise provide, a member shall have one vote in respect of each share and, in the case of a company having a share capital, every member has one vote in respect of each £10 of stock held by him.[153] Further, a member entitled to more than one vote need not, if he votes, use all his votes or cast all the votes he used in the same way.[154] This provision was introduced to meet the difficulties of a large trust corporation which might hold shares in a company on behalf of two or more different trusts, whose respective interests might well require different exercises of its votes.[155]

The Act provides that a company's articles may contain provision to the effect that on a vote on a resolution on a poll taken at a meeting, the votes may include votes cast in advance.[156] In the case of a traded company any such provision in relation to voting at a general meeting may be made subject only to such requirements and restrictions as are necessary to ensure the identification of the person voting and proportionate to the achievement of that objective.[157] Any provision of

---

[147] art.44(2) (art.36(2) for public companies).

[148] A poll may also be withdrawn: art.44(3) (art.36(3) for public companies).

[149] art.44(1) (art.36(1) for public companies). This confirms the dicta of Jenkins L.J. in *Holmes v Keyes* [1959] Ch. 199, CA, at 212.

[150] But cf. art.37 of the Model Articles for Public Companies.

[151] art.44(4).

[152] *Jackson v Hamlyn* [1953] Ch. 577, applying *Shaw v Tati Concessions Ltd* [1913] 1 Ch. 292.

[153] s.284(3).

[154] s.322.

[155] *Northern Counties Securities Ltd v Jackson & Steeple Ltd* [1974] 1 W.L.R. 1133 at 1147, per Walton J.

[156] s.322A(1). This section was added by reg.5 of the Companies (Shareholders Rights) Regulations 2009 (SI 2009/1632).

[157] s.322A(2). This does not affect any power of a company to require reasonable evidence of the entitlement of any person who is not a member to vote.

a company's articles is void in so far as it would have the effect of requiring any document casting a vote in advance to be received by the company or another person earlier than the following time in the case of a poll taken more than 48 hours after it was demanded, 24 hours[158] before the time appointed for the taking of the poll and, in the case of any other poll, 48 hours before the time for holding the meeting or adjourned meeting.[159]

A poll is complete when the result is ascertained, not on an earlier day when the votes are cast.[160] Further, a proxy has the same right to demand a poll as the member he represents. If the articles could require a considerable number of members to demand a poll the right would be worthless.

Public companies are additionally subject to a number of additional requirements for polls. Thus, in the case of a quoted company which is not a traded company,[161] the company has to ensure that certain information is made available on its website.[162] Although there are penal consequences for failure to comply, this does not affect the validity of the poll or the resolution or other business (if passed or agreed to) to which the poll relates.[163] Members of a quoted company also have the power to require the directors to obtain an independent report on any poll taken, or to be taken, at a general meeting.[164] Such a request may be in hard copy or electronic form, must identify the poll or polls to which it relates, must be authenticated by the person or persons making it, and must be received by the company not later than one week after the date on which the poll is taken.[165] The directors are obliged to comply by appointing an "independent assessor"[166] to prepare a report and he must state his opinion as to whether the poll or polls were adequate[167] as well as a range of other matters.[168] He is entitled to attend the meeting at which the poll may be taken and any subsequent proceedings in connection with the poll[169] and is also entitled to access to the company's records relating to any poll on which he is to report and as to the meeting at which the poll or polls may be, or were, taken.[170] He is also entitled to require a director or secretary of the company and others to provide him with information or explanations for the purpose of preparing his report.[171] It is an offence to fail to comply.[172]

---

[158] No account is to be taken of any part of a day that is not a working day: s.322A(4).

[159] s.322A(3).

[160] *Holmes v Keyes* [1959] Ch. 199, CA.

[161] See s.341(1A)(1B), inserted by reg.19 of the Companies (Shareholders' Rights) Regulations 2009 (SI 2009/1632).

[162] s.341(1).

[163] See s.341(5).

[164] See s.342.

[165] s.342(4).

[166] See s.343. As to the independence requirement, see s.344 and s.345.

[167] s.347(1)(a).

[168] i.e. those specified in s.347(1)(b)–(e).

[169] s.348.

[170] s.349.

[171] s.349(2).

[172] s.350.

Proxies

Although there is no common law right to vote by proxy,[173] the Act gives such a   **19–021**
right and provides that a member of a company is entitled to appoint another
person as his proxy to exercise all or any of his rights to attend and to speak and
vote at a meeting of the company.[174] In the case of a company having a share
capital, a member may appoint more than one proxy in relation to a meeting,
provided that each proxy is appointed to exercise the rights attached to a different
share or shares held by him, or to a different £10, or multiple of £10, of stock held
by him.[175] The proxy must vote in accordance with any instructions given by the
member who has appointed him.[176]

Every notice calling a meeting must state this right of a member to appoint a
proxy and any more extensive rights conferred by the articles to appoint more
than one proxy.[177] Although there were formerly a number of important differences between the rights of members and proxies (such as that a proxy could only
vote on a poll) these differences have now fallen away under the 2006 Act. Thus,
as we have seen, the Act provides that a proxy can attend, speak and vote at a
meeting.[178] Similarly, he may demand or join in demanding a poll[179] and, subject
to the articles, he may be elected to be the chairman of a general meeting by
resolution of the company passed at the meeting.[180]

The Act provides that articles cannot require the instrument appointing a proxy to
be deposited with the company more than 48 hours before a meeting or an adjourned
meeting.[181] In the case of a poll taken more than 48 hours after it was demanded, the
articles cannot require notice earlier than 24 hours before the time appointed for the
taking of the poll.[182] If articles could require the instrument to be deposited a considerable time before a meeting the right to appoint a proxy would be worthless.

In the case of a traded company, the Act states that the appointment of a proxy
must be notified in writing.[183] In such circumstances, the company may require
reasonable evidence of the identity of the member and of the proxy, the member's
instructions (if any) as to how the proxy is to vote and, where the proxy is
appointed by a person acting on behalf of the member, authority of that person to
make the appointment.[184] The Model Articles provide that proxies may only
validly be appointed by a "proxy notice" in writing which:

---

[173] *Cousins International Brick Co Ltd* [1931] 2 Ch. 90, CA, at 100, per Lord Hanworth M.R.
[174] s.324(1).
[175] s.324(2).
[176] s.325. The Model Articles provide that proxy notices may specify how the proxy appointed under
them is to vote (or that the proxy is to abstain from voting) on one or more resolutions: see art.45(3)
of the Model Articles for Private Companies Limited by Shares (art.38(3) for public companies).
[177] s.325(1). Failure to comply does not affect the validity of the meeting but is an offence on the part
of every officer in default giving rise to a fine: s.325(2)–(4).
[178] See s.324(1).
[179] See s.329.
[180] See s.328.
[181] s.327(2)(a).
[182] s.327(2)(b).
[183] s.327(A1)(a).
[184] s.327(A1)(b). This was inserted by reg.13 of the Companies (Shareholders Rights) Regulations
2009 (SI 2009/1632).

1. states the name and address of the shareholder appointing the proxy;

2. identifies the person appointed to be that shareholder's proxy and the general meeting in relation to which that person is appointed;

3. is signed by or on behalf of the shareholder appointing the proxy, or is authenticated in such manner as the directors may determine; and

4. is delivered to the company in accordance with the articles and any instructions contained in the notice of the general meeting to which they relate.[185]

Unless a proxy notice indicates otherwise, it must be treated as allowing the person appointed under it as a proxy discretion as to how to vote on any ancillary or procedural resolutions put to the meeting, and appointing that person as a proxy in relation to any adjournment of the general meeting to which it relates as well as the meeting itself.[186]

19–022   There are two forms of proxy in use[187]—a general proxy appointing a person to vote as he thinks fit, having regard to what is said at the meeting, and a special proxy appointing a person to vote for or against a particular resolution. A special proxy is often called "a two-way proxy".

The Act provides that if invitations to appoint a proxy by a person or one of a number of persons specified in the invitations are issued at the company's expense to only some of the members entitled to vote at a meeting, the invitation must be issued to all members entitled to vote at the meeting.[188] Every officer of the company who knowingly and wilfully authorises or permits their issue is liable to a fine,[189] although an officer is not liable by reason only of the issue to a member, at his written request, of a form of appointment naming the proxy or of a list of persons willing to act as proxy, if the form or list is available to every member entitled to vote.[190] If this were not so the directors might send the proxy papers to friendly shareholders only.

It is the duty of the chairman to decide on the validity of proxies. If the articles provide that votes tendered at a meeting and not disallowed shall be deemed to be valid,[191] the court will not review the chairman's decision, even if it is wrong, in the absence of fraud or bad faith on his part.[192] A mere misprint or some quite palpable mistake on the face of a proxy form does not entitle the company to refuse to accept the proxy.[193]

---

[185] Model Articles for Private Companies Limited by Shares art.45(1) (art.38(1) for public companies).

[186] art.45(4) (art.38(4) for public companies).

[187] Note that the company may require proxy notices to be delivered in a particular form, and may specify different forms for different purposes: art.45(2) (art.38(2) for public companies).

[188] s.326(1).

[189] s.326(3)(4).

[190] s.326(2).

[191] See Table A, art.58. There is no equivalent provision in the Model Articles.

[192] *Wall v Exchange Investment Corporation* [1926] Ch. 143, CA. See also *Marx v Estates & General Investments Ltd* [1976] 1 W.L.R. 380.

[193] *Oliver v Dalgleish* [1963] 1 W.L.R. 1274, where the proxies referred to the "annual general meeting" instead of the "extraordinary general meeting" and there was no other meeting which could be confused with the date which was stated in the proxies.

A shareholder who has given a proxy is free to attend the meeting and vote in **19–023** person,[194] in which case the vote tendered by the proxy may properly be rejected.[195] He does not thereby revoke the proxy, however, and the proxy may, e.g. vote on a second resolution on which the shareholder does not vote.[196] The Act provides a mechanism for the notice required to terminate a proxy's authority.[197] The Model Articles provide that an appointment under a proxy notice may be revoked by delivering to the company a notice in writing given by or on behalf of the person by whom or on whose behalf the proxy notice was given.[198] However, a notice revoking a proxy appointment only takes effect if it is delivered before the start of the meeting or adjourned meeting to which it relates.[199]

A corporation, whether a company within the meaning of the Act or not, may, if it is a member of another corporation which is such a company, by resolution of its directors or other governing body[200] authorise such person as it thinks fit to act as its representative at any meeting of the company or any class of members of the company.[201] The representative is entitled to exercise on behalf of the corporation the powers which the corporation could exercise if it were an individual shareholder of the company.[202]

RESOLUTIONS

Kinds of resolution

Private companies considering resolutions may act under the written resolution **19–024** procedure specified in the Act[203] or may do so at a meeting of the members.[204] Resolutions of the members (or of a class of members) of a public company may only be passed at a meeting of the members.[205] In the absence of a contrary provision in the Act or the articles specifying a particular type of majority (or unanimity) the company in general meeting acts by ordinary resolution.[206]

---

[194] The Model Articles also confirm that a person who is entitled to attend, speak or vote (either on a show of hands or on a poll) at a general meeting remains so entitled in respect of that meeting or any adjournment of it, even though a valid proxy notice has been delivered to the company by or on behalf of that person: art.46(1) (art.39(2) for public companies).

[195] See *Cousins v International Brick Co Ltd* [1931] 2 Ch. 90, CA, where the proxy had not been revoked.

[196] *Ansett v Butler Air Transport Ltd (No.2)* (1958) 75 W.N. NSW 306.

[197] See s.330.

[198] art.46(2) (art.39(6) for public companies). If a proxy notice is not executed by the person appointing the proxy, it must be accompanied by written evidence of the authority of the person who executed it to execute it on the appointor's behalf: art.46(4) (art.39(8) for public companies).

[199] art.46(3) (art.39(7) for public companies).

[200] See, e.g. *Hillman v Crystal Bowl Amusements Ltd* [1973] 1 W.L.R. 162, CA.

[201] s.323(1).

[202] s.323(2). The Act also makes provision for the scenario where more than one person is so authorised: see s.323(2)(4).

[203] s.288. See para.19–028, below.

[204] s.281(1).

[205] s.281(2).

[206] s.281(3).

Ordinary resolutions

19–025 An ordinary resolution of the members (or of a class of members) means a resolution passed by a simple majority.[207] In the case of a written resolution, this will be passed by a simple majority if it is passed by members representing a simple majority of the total voting rights of the eligible members.[208] Where there is a show of hands,[209] then the resolution is passed by a simple majority of the votes cast by those entitled to vote.[210] Finally, a resolution passed on a poll taken at a meeting is passed by a simple majority if it is passed by members representing a simple majority of the total voting rights of members who vote in person, by proxy or in advance on the resolution.[211] The Act provides that anything that may be done by ordinary resolution may also be done by special resolution.[212]

Special resolutions

19–026 A special resolution is defined as a resolution of the members (or of a class of members) passed by a majority of not less than 75 per cent.[213] Where a resolution is passed at a meeting, the resolution is not a special resolution unless the notice of the meeting included the text of the resolution and specified the intention to propose the resolution as a special resolution and, if the notice of the meeting so specified, the resolution may only be passed as a special resolution.[214] In the case of a written resolution of a private company,[215] this is passed by a majority of not less than 75 per cent if it is passed by members representing not less than 75 per cent of the total voting rights of eligible members.[216] A resolution passed at a meeting on a show of hands is passed by a majority of not less than 75 per cent of the votes cast by those entitled to vote.[217] A resolution passed on a poll taken at a meeting is passed by a majority of not less than 75 per cent if it is passed by members representing not less than 75 per cent of the total voting rights of the members who vote in person, by proxy or in advance on the resolution.[218]

---

[207] s.282(1).
[208] s.282(2). See also *Bushell v Faith* [1970] A.C. 1099. A shareholders' agreement may, however, prevent a member voting in a particular way on a particular resolution: *Russell v Northern Bank Development Corp Ltd* [1992] B.C.L.C. 1016.
[209] Above, para.19–018.
[210] s.282(3).
[211] s.282(4).
[212] s.282(5).
[213] s.283(1).
[214] s.283(6).
[215] Where a resolution of a private company is passed as a written resolution the resolution is not a special resolution unless it stated that it was proposed as a special resolution and if the resolution so stated, it may only be passed as a special resolution: s.283(3).
[216] s.283(2).
[217] s.283(4).
[218] s.283(5).

Amendments to resolutions

If a positive amendment, pertinent to the subject-matter of the resolution, is **19–027** proposed, it must be voted upon first. If the chairman refuses to put a proper amendment to the meeting, the resolution, if passed, is not binding.[219]

The Model Articles provide that an ordinary resolution to be proposed at a general meeting may be amended by ordinary resolution if notice of the proposed amendment is given to the company secretary in writing by a person entitled to vote at the general meeting at which it is to be proposed not less than hours before the meeting is to take place (or such later time as the chairman of the meeting may determine) and the proposed amendment does not, in the reasonable opinion of the chairman of the meeting, materially alter the scope of the resolution.[220] Thus where a notice of a meeting stated that it was to pass, with such amendments as should be determined, a resolution that three named persons be appointed directors, an amendment to elect two other directors as well was held valid.[221]

The Model Articles provide that a special resolution to be proposed at a general meeting may be amended by ordinary resolution if the chairman of the meeting proposes the amendment at the general meeting at which the resolution is to be proposed and the amendment does not go beyond what is necessary to correct a grammatical or other non-substantive error in the resolution.[222] Thus, there is little scope for amendment of special resolutions since, the notice of such resolutions must set out the exact wording of the resolution.[223] However, where a notice of a meeting stated that it was to pass special resolutions to wind up voluntarily and to appoint X as liquidator, and the second resolution was dropped and a new one to appoint Y as liquidator was passed, it was held that Y's appointment was valid because as soon as the resolution to wind up was passed a liquidator could be appointed, without notice, under the Act.[224]

Written resolutions

The 1989 Companies Act[225] introduced a new statutory procedure to allow private **19–028** companies to pass any resolution without holding a meeting, a so-called "written resolution",[226] provided all those who could have attended the meeting and voted sign the resolution instead. That procedure has been retained under the 2006 Act but with further modification of the requirements. Written resolutions may not be used in two instances: where the company proposes to remove a director before the expiration of his period of office[227] and where an auditor is to be removed

---

[219] *Henderson v Bank of Australasia* (1890) 45 Ch.D. 330, CA.

[220] art.47(1) (art.40(1) for public companies).

[221] *Betts & Co Ltd v Macnaghten* [1910] 1 Ch. 430.

[222] art.47(2) (art.40(2) for public companies).

[223] *Swindon Town Football Co Ltd, Re* [1990] B.C.L.C. 467 at 468, per Harman J.

[224] *Trench Tubeless Tyre Co, Re* [1990] 1 Ch. 408, CA.

[225] That Act introduced four new sections: 381A, 381B, 381C and 382A, and one new Schedule: 15A, into the 1985 Act.

[226] See s.288(1).

[227] See s.168.

before the expiration of his term[228] of office.[229] When passed, a written resolution has effect as if passed by the company in general meeting or by a meeting of a class of members of the company.[230] It should be noted that the Act also provides that a provision of the articles of a private company will be void in so far as it would have the effect that a resolution is required by or otherwise provided for in an enactment could not be proposed and passed as a written resolution.[231] This ensures that the company's articles cannot remove the ability of a private company and its members to propose and pass a statutory resolution using the statutory written resolutions procedure.

If the directors propose a written resolution, they must send or submit a copy of the resolution to every eligible member[232]: (a) by sending copies at the same time (so far as reasonably practicable) in hard copy form, in electronic form[233] or by means of a website,[234] or (b) if it is possible to do so without undue delay, by submitting the same copy to each eligible member in turn (or different copies to each of a number of eligible members in turn), or by sending copies to some members in accordance with para.(a) and submitting a copy or copies to other members in accordance with para.(b).[235] The copy of the resolution must be accompanied by a statement informing the member how to signify agreement to the resolution and as to the date by which the resolution must be passed if it is not to lapse.[236] Default in compliance with these requirements is an offence, which is committed by every officer of the company in default.[237]

An alternative is for the members of the company to require the company to circulate a resolution as a written resolution.[238] The request may be in hard copy or electronic form,[239] must identify the resolution and any accompanying statement, and must be authenticated by the person or persons making it.[240] Any resolution may properly be moved as a written resolution unless it would, if passed, be ineffective, is defamatory of any person or is frivolous or vexatious.[241] Where the members require a company to circulate a resolution they may require the company to circulate with it a statement of not more than 1,000 words on the subject matter of the resolution.[242] A company is required to circulate the resolution and any accompanying statement once it has received requests that it do so from members representing not less than the requisite percentage[243] of the total voting rights of all members entitled to vote on the resolution.[244]

---

[228] See s.510.
[229] s.288(3).
[230] s.288(5).
[231] s.300.
[232] See as to this s.289.
[233] See s.298.
[234] s.291(3)(a). See s.299.
[235] s.291(3)(b).
[236] s.291(4).
[237] s.291(5)(6).
[238] s.292(1).
[239] See s.298.
[240] s.292(6).
[241] s.292(2).
[242] s.292(3).
[243] 5 per cent or such lower percentage specified in the articles: s.292(5).
[244] s 292(4).

A company that is required to circulate a resolution[245] must send or submit to **19–029** every eligible member a copy of the resolution and a copy of any accompanying statement.[246] The company must do so: (a) by sending copies at the same time (so far as reasonably practicable) to all eligible members in hard copy form, in electronic form[247] or by means of a website[248] or, (b) if it is possible to do so without undue delay, by submitting the same copy to each eligible member in turn (or different copies to each of a number of eligible members in turn), or by sending copies to some members in accordance with para.(a) and submitting a copy or copies to other members in accordance with para.(b).[249] The company must send or submit the copies (or, if copies are sent or submitted to members on different days, the first of those copies) not more than 21 days after the members require it.[250] The copy of the resolution must be accompanied by guidance as to how to signify agreement to the resolution and the date by which the resolution must be passed if it is not to lapse.[251] Default in compliance with these requirements is an offence, which is committed by every officer of the company in default.[252] The expenses of the company in complying must be paid by the members who requested the circulation of the resolution unless the company resolves otherwise.[253] Unless the company resolves otherwise, it is not obliged to comply unless there is deposited with or tendered to it a sum reasonably sufficient to meet its expenses in doing so.[254]

A member signifies his agreement to a proposed written resolution when the company receives from him (or from someone acting on his behalf) an authenticated document identifying the resolution to which it relates, and indicating his agreement to the resolution.[255] The document must be sent to the company in hard copy form or in electronic form.[256] Once signified, it may not be revoked.[257] A written resolution is passed when the required majority of eligible members have signified their agreement to it.[258]

A written resolution lapses if it is not passed before the end of the period specified for this purpose in the company's articles or, if none is specified, the period of 28 days beginning with the circulation date.[259] Agreement will be ineffective if signified after the expiry period.[260]

---

[245] See s.295 as to those circumstances in which the company is not required to circulate a members' statement.
[246] s.293(1).
[247] See s.298.
[248] See s.299.
[249] s.293(2).
[250] s.293(3).
[251] s.293(4).
[252] s.293(5)(6).
[253] s.294(1).
[254] s.294(2).
[255] s.296(1).
[256] s.296(2).
[257] s.296(3).
[258] s.296(4).
[259] s.297(1).
[260] s.297(2).

Informal resolutions: the Duomatic principle

19–030 The courts have evolved a principle known as the *Duomatic* principle,[261] that if
all the members who have the right to attend and vote at a general meeting
assent[262] to a transaction which the meeting could carry into effect, that assent is
as binding as a resolution of the meeting would be. Mummery L.J. has stated that

> "[The *Duomatic* principle] is a sound and sensible principle of company law
> allowing the members of the company to reach an agreement without the need for
> strict compliance with formal procedures, where they exist only for the benefit of
> those who have agreed not to comply with them. What matters is the unanimous
> assent of those who ultimately exercise power over the affairs of the company
> through their right to attend and vote at a general meeting. It does not matter
> whether the formal procedures in question are stipulated for in the articles of asso-
> ciation, in the Companies Acts or in a separate contract between the members of
> the company concerned. What matters is that all the members have reached an
> agreement. If they have, they cannot be heard to say that they are not bound by it
> because the formal procedure was not followed".[263]

It is not necessary that they should hold a meeting in one room or one place to
express that assent simultaneously.[264] In the words of Neuberger J.:

> "The essence of the *Duomatic* principle, as I see it, is that, where the articles
> of a company require a course to be approved by a group of shareholders at a
> general meeting, that requirement can be avoided if all members of the group,
> being aware of the relevant facts, either give their approval to that course, or so
> conduct themselves as to make it inequitable for them to deny that they have
> given their approval. Whether the approval is given in advance or after the
> event, whether it is characterised as agreement, ratification, waiver, or estoppel,
> and whether members of the group give their consent in different ways at
> different times, does not matter".[265]

This principle has been applied to an assent to vary the articles of a company
even though no formal special resolution to that effect had been passed.[266] It has
also been applied to override shareholders' agreements,[267] and to meetings of a

---

[261] Formulated by Buckley J. in *Duomatic Ltd, Re* [1969] 2 Ch. 365 from earlier cases (such as
Express Engineering Works Ltd, Re [1920] 1 Ch. 466).

[262] See *Tulsesense Ltd, Re* [2010] EWHC 244 (Ch.) where the relevant members, the ultimate beneficial owners of the shares, were held not to have assented.

[263] *Euro Brokers Holdings Ltd v Monecor (London) Ltd* [2003] EWCA Civ. 105; [2003] 1 B.C.L.C.
506 at [62].

[264] *Parker & Cooper Ltd v Reading* [1926] Ch. 975. In *Petna v Dale, Re* [2004] 2 B.C.C. 508 it was
held that this principle could apply where the four apparent shareholders assented, even though,
unknown to everyone involved, there was another shareholder.

[265] *EIC Services Ltd v Phipps* [2003] EWHC 1507 (Ch); [2003] 1 W.L.R. 2360 at [122].

[266] *Cane v Jones* [1980] 1 W.L.R. 1451. See also *Bailey, Hay & Co Ltd, Re* [1971] 1 W.L.R. 1357.

[267] *Euro Brokers Holdings Ltd v Monecor (London) Ltd* [2003] 1 B.C.L.C. 506, CA.

class of shareholders,[268] on the basis that those who have agreed to procedural restrictions can agree to waive them. It has also been applied where shareholders assented to a transaction such that a director was not in breach of fiduciary duty.[269] The principle cannot apply where the assentors could not validly have passed the resolution at a formal meeting,[270] or where, although the members have been informed, their assent has not been sought.[271] It is not clear whether the assent must be given by the registered owner or whether it can be given by the beneficial owner.[272] But if it must be given by all the members, a majority will not suffice.[273]

A more complex question is whether the principle can override a statutory **19–031** requirement for a resolution. In *R. W. Peak (Kings Lynn) Ltd, Re*,[274] the judge left open the question whether it could be used in cases where the Act required a specific procedure to be followed, e.g. the requirements for a company validly to purchase its own shares, on the basis that the matter involved more than protection of the shareholders. The earlier cases suggested that all lack of formalities could be cured by the relevant assents but they were not faced with such procedures. Although in *Demite Ltd v Protec Health Ltd*[275] a judge expressed doubts as to whether the principle could apply to the necessary approval of a transaction between a director and his or her company under what was s.320 of the 1985 Act,[276] the judge in the case of *N.B.H. Ltd v Hoare* held that there was no reason why the *Duomatic* principle should not apply to that section.[277] Similarly it has been held that unanimous assent would suffice to satisfy the requirements for an off-market purchase of shares[278] because the resolution authorising the terms of the agreement, whilst headed ordinary resolution, was in substance a special resolution which had been passed by the requisite majority of members entitled to vote and the sole shareholder had validly waived the usual notice requirement for a special resolution.[279] On the other hand, the principle would have to give way to a mandatory statutory provision to the contrary.[280]

This issue was considered by the Court of Appeal in *Atlas Wright (Europe) Ltd v Wright*.[281] The Court applied the *Duomatic* principle in the context of the approval of a director's service contract which requires an ordinary resolution.[282]

---

[268] *Torvale Group Ltd, Re* [1999] 2 B.C.L.C. 605.

[269] See *Progress Property Co Ltd v Moore* [2008] EWHC 2577 (Ch.).

[270] *New Cedos Engineering Co Ltd, Re* [1994] 1 B.C.L.C. 797.

[271] *EIC Services Ltd v Phipps* [2003] B.C.C. 931 (note that the Court of Appeal was not concerned with this point).

[272] *Domoney v Godinho* [2004] 2 B.C.L.C. 15; *Shahar v Tsitsekkos* [2004] EWHC 2659 (Ch.).

[273] *Extrasure Travel Insurance Ltd v Scattergood* [2003] 1 B.C.L.C. 598.

[274] [1998] B.C.C. 596.

[275] [1998] B.C.C. 637 at 648.

[276] See now s.190 of the 2006 Act.

[277] [2006] EWHC 73 (Ch.); [2006] 2 B.C.L.C. 649, at [43], per Park J.

[278] i.e. under s.164 of the 1985 Act. See now s.694 of the 2006 Act.

[279] *Kinlan v Crimmin* [2006] EWHC 779 (Ch.); [2007] B.C.C. 106. See too *Dashfield v Davidson* [2008] B.C.C. 222.

[280] Such as art.13 of the Companies (Cross-Border Mergers) Regulation 2007 (SI 2007/2974): see *Oceanrose Investments Ltd, Re* [2008] EWHC 3475 (Ch.); [2009] Bus. L.R. 947.

[281] [1999] 2 B.C.L.C. 301, CA.

[282] s.319 of the 1985 Act. See now s.188 of the 2006 Act.

The answer is to be found by looking at the purpose of the statutory requirement in question which was passed purely for the protection of the shareholders. Accordingly, they could properly waive its formalities, assuming that they were properly informed. The purpose of some aspects of the share purchase legislation[283] and the substantial transactions legislation[284] was to protect a wider constituency, e.g. the creditors, and so the shareholders alone could not waive the formalities. That dichotomy has since been applied to prevent the principle applying to the rules for financial assistance and distributable profits, again on the basis of creditor protection.[285]

Table A, art.53,[286] provides that a written resolution signed by all the members entitled to attend and vote at general meetings shall be as effectual as if passed at a general meeting of the company duly convened and held. However, Nourse J. in *Barry Artist Ltd, Re*,[287] whilst approving the use of such an informal resolution as a special resolution for a reduction of capital, stated that he would not do so again since the reduction of capital procedure requires confirmation by the court.[288] This decision cast doubt on the exact parameters of Art.53 similar to those concerning the *Duomatic* principle.

Records of resolutions

19–032 A company is required under the Act to keep records comprising all resolutions of members passed otherwise than at general meetings and also the minutes of all proceedings of general meetings.[289] Such records must be kept for at least ten years from the date of the resolution.[290] Default in compliance with these requirements is an offence, which is committed by every officer of the company in default.[291] The record of a resolution passed otherwise than at a general meeting is evidence of the passing of the resolution.[292] Unless the articles otherwise provide, the record is not conclusive evidence and so, if a resolution has been passed, but is not entered in the minutes, other evidence to prove it will be admitted.[293] In the case of a private company, the record of a written resolution will be deemed to comply with the requirements of the Act.[294]

Such records of the resolutions of the company must be kept available for inspection at the company's registered office or at some other place specified in

---

[283] *R.W. Peak, Re (Kings Lynn) Ltd* [1998] B.C.C. 596. Other aspects of the share purchase procedures have been said to be for the protection of the shareholders only and so susceptible to the principle: *BDG Roof-Bond Ltd v Douglas* [2000] 1 B.C.L.C. 401.

[284] As in *Demite Ltd v Protect Health Ltd* [1998] B.C.C. 637.

[285] *Bairstow v Queens Moat Houses Plc* [2001] 2 B.C.L.C. 531. This flexibility persuaded the Government not to adopt the Company Law Review's proposal to codify the *Duomatic* principle: see *Modernising Company Law*, Cmn 5553-1, paras 2.31–2.35.

[286] This provision has not been reproduced in the Model Articles.

[287] [1985] B.C.L.C. 283.

[288] Although this is now mandatory only for public companies: see s.641.

[289] See s.355(1)(a).

[290] s.355(2).

[291] s.355(3)(4).

[292] s.356(2).

[293] *Re Fireproof Doors* [1916] 2 Ch. 142.

[294] s.356(3).

regulations.[295] The relevant regulations[296] specify that the alternative place must be a place situated in the part of the United Kingdom in which the company is registered, must be the same place for all the relevant provisions, and must have been notified to the Registrar as being the company's alternative inspection location.[297] The company must give notice to the Registrar as to where the records are kept and of any change in that place unless they have at all times been kept at the company's registered office.[298] The records must be open for inspection of any member, without charge,[299] and any member may require a copy of the relevant records on payment of the prescribed fee.[300] If there is default in complying with the notice requirement for 14 days or an inspection is refused or a copy is not sent, then an offence is committed by every officer of the company in default.[301] In any event, a court may compel an immediate inspection of the records or direct that copies be sent to those who have requested them.[302]

Minutes of meetings

Mandatory requirement

Every company must also keep minutes of all proceedings of general meetings.[303] **19–033** Such records must be kept for at least ten years from the date of the resolution.[304] Default in compliance with these requirements is an offence, which is committed by every officer of the company in default.[305] The minutes of proceedings of a general meeting, if purporting to be signed by the chairman of that meeting or by the chairman of the next general meeting, are evidence of the proceedings at the meeting.[306] However, when the articles provide that the minutes, signed by the chairman, shall be "conclusive evidence without any further proof of the facts therein stated," as between those bound by the articles, namely the company and the members qua members,[307] evidence cannot be called to contradict the minutes unless they have been fraudulently written up.[308] Where there is a record of proceedings of a general meeting of a company, then, until the contrary is proved the meeting isdeemed duly held and convened, all proceedings at the meeting are deemed to have duly taken place, and all appointments at the meeting are deemed valid.[309]

---

[295] s.358(1).
[296] The Companies (Company Records) Regulations 2008, SI 2008/3006.
[297] reg.3.
[298] s.358(2).
[299] s.358(3).
[300] s.358(4). See the Companies (Fees for Inspection and Copying of Company Records) Regulations 2007 (SI 2007/2612).
[301] s.358(5)(6).
[302] See s.358(7).
[303] s.355(1)(b).
[304] s.355(2).
[305] s.355(3)(4).
[306] s.356(4).
[307] See s.33(1) and the discussion at para.4–019, above.
[308] *Kerr v Mottram* [1940] Ch. 657.
[309] s.356(5).

Where a sole member takes a decision which may be taken by the company in general meeting and this has effect as if agreed by the company in general meeting, he must (unless the decision is taken by way of a written resolution)[310] provide the company with details of that decision.[311] He commits an offence if he fails to comply[312] but this does not affect the validity of any decision that he has made.[313]

Such records of the minutes of all proceedings of general meetings of the company must be kept available for inspection at the company's registered office or at some other place specified in regulations.[314] The relevant regulations[315] specify that the alternative place must be a place situated in the part of the United Kingdom in which the company is registered, must be the same place for all the relevant provisions, and must have been notified to the Registrar as being the company's alternative inspection location.[316] The company must give notice to the Registrar as to where the records are kept and of any change in that place unless they have at all times been kept at the company's registered office.[317] The records must be open for inspection of any member, without charge,[318] and any member may require a copy of the relevant records on payment of the prescribed fee.[319] If there is default in complying with the notice requirement for 14 days or an inspection is refused or a copy is not sent, then an offence is committed by every officer of the company in default.[320] In any event, a court may compel an immediate inspection of the records or direct that copies be sent to those who have requested them.[321]

---

[310] See above, para.19–028.
[311] s.357(2).
[312] s.357(3)(4).
[313] s.357(5).
[314] s.358(1).
[315] The Companies (Company Records) Regulations 2008 (SI 2008/3006).
[316] reg.3.
[317] s.358(2).
[318] s.358(3).
[319] s.358(4). See the Companies (Fees for Inspection and Copying of Company Records) Regulations 2007 (SI 2007/2612).
[320] s.358(5)(6).
[321] See s.358(7).

Chapter 20

ACCOUNTS

INTRODUCTION

For 50 years after legislation was enacted permitting limited liability companies **20–001** to be set up by registration, there was little regulation of financial disclosures and the preparation of annual accounts. Such matters were perceived as being domestic matters to be determined by a company's shareholders,[1] the assumption being that they would decide how much information (independently attested or not) the business should publish in order to help lower its financing costs. This non-interventionist philosophy was also reflected in a number of decisions concerning the payment of dividends, the view being that the courts should not in general interfere in the business decision-making process, unless there were good grounds for believing that the rights of creditors and shareholders were being prejudiced.

Towards the end of the nineteenth century, attitudes began to change as the effects of inequalities of information between parties and of manipulation of data became apparent. Moreover, with a third of new companies failing shortly after incorporation, there was increasing support for the view that unsecured creditors had insufficient information on which to base their decisions. The result was that the statutory audit was introduced in 1900, and in 1908 the 10,000 businesses in the newly created "public" class of company were required to file their balance sheets.[2] However, the 30,000 or so "private" concerns were still exempt from this provision.

By 1925, the numbers of companies registered had risen to around 95,000 (of which some 85,000 were private), but the 1929 Companies Act[3] nevertheless did not extend the duty to file accounts to private companies, nor did it substantially expand the disclosure requirements for company financial statements. It was only following the Report of the Cohen Committee in 1945[4] that the central role of the modern corporation in the economy and in society was recognised. As a result, the 1948 Companies Act[5] outlawed reserve accounting, which had made it extremely easy to manipulate reported earnings, and required the preparation of

---

[1] See, for example, *Spanish Prospecting Co Ltd, Re* [1911] 1 Ch. 92.
[2] See the Company Law Amendment Act 1907, Edw.7, c.50.
[3] 19 & 20 Geo.5, c.23.
[4] Report of the Committee on Company Law Amendment (1945), Cmd.6659.
[5] 11 & 12 Geo.6, c.38.

group accounts and slightly more elaborate profit and loss accounts. By that time, there were some 200,000 registered companies, of which over 90 per cent enjoyed private status, and the Act required some of these (a small proportion, described as "non-exempt") to file their annual accounts for the first time.

20–002 The Jenkins Committee, reporting in 1962,[6] favoured further compulsory disclosure, and it proposed that exempt private companies, which comprised some 75 per cent of the 400,000 or so companies then registered, should also be made to file their financial statements, the purpose being to benefit unsecured creditors. A requirement to this effect was included in the 1967 Companies Act,[7] and this led to a rapid increase in the annual number of company searches, which rose from 600,000 in 1960 to 3.1 million in 1985 and to over 4 million by the 1990s.[8] The 1967 Companies Act also greatly extended the disclosures which had to be made in the income statement, in notes to the accounts, and in the directors' report (e.g. turnover, hire charges, movements in fixed assets and segmental analyses of activities).

Companies and unincorporated businesses had effectively been required to prepare annual accounts for income tax purposes since the latter half of the nineteenth century. But the 1960s and the 1970s witnessed an upsurge in activity aimed at regulating the ways in which companies publicly reported their financial affairs, most of it of a quasi-legal nature (e.g. in order to control inflation between 1965 and 1979; for monitoring monopolies; and from 1973 for assessing VAT). But by the 1960s and 1970s the business community was becoming ever more concerned about the "signalling properties" of accounting numbers. On the one hand, this related to the 2,000 or so UK listed companies, for which it was important to try to indicate to investment analysts the trend in permanently sustainable earnings; and on the other, for credit suppliers and bank lenders dealing with the much larger number of unlisted public and private companies.[9]

With conflicts of interest becoming more prevalent in relation to financial disclosures, the leading accountancy bodies set up the Accounting Standards Committee (ASC) in 1969, and over the next 20 years it issued a number of mandatory statements concerning the preparation and publication of companies' annual accounts. The ASC's efforts were reinforced by statements of the International Accounting Standards Committee (IASC), set up in 1973, and the London Stock Exchange's Listing Agreement, published in 1972.[10] In the meantime, attempts to harmonise accounting regulations within the Common Market countries led to the introduction of new rules in the Companies Acts of 1980, 1981 and 1989,[11] the avowed aim being to encourage the efficient allocation of capital within the EU.

---

[6] Report of the Company Law Committee (1962), Cmnd.1749.

[7] c.81.

[8] Annual searches in the year to March 31, 2004, totalled nearly 40 million, of which well over 90 per cent were by computer.

[9] For a discussion of the economic case for mandatory financial disclosures, see Bromwich, *Financial Reporting, Information and Capital Markets* (1992).

[10] From 1993 these became the Listing Rules. Since 2000 these rules have been published by the Financial Services Authority (FSA) rather than by the London Stock Exchange. See para.13–004, below.

[11] The 1980 and 1981 Acts were consolidated in the Companies Act 1985, some of whose sections and Schedules have been substituted by the 1989 Act and various SIs.

The opportunity was also taken when framing the 1989 Act to reform the insti- **20–003**
tutional framework for setting accounting standards. The process is now supervised
by a broadly based Financial Reporting Council (FRC),[12] which guides the work of
six operating bodies, including the Accounting Standards Board (ASB).[13] The ASB
is recognised[14] as the delegated authority empowered to establish accounting standards under s. 464 of the Act. It publishes Financial Reporting Standards (FRSs),[15]
which have to be applied by companies when preparing their statutory accounts.[16]

Since the early 1970s, there have been various initiatives to introduce global
accounting and auditing standards, but in recent years added impetus has come
from the European Commission. This culminated in 2002 with the Commission
requiring that from 2005 onwards, listed companies within the EU would have to
prepare their consolidated accounts in accordance with International Financial
Reporting Standards (IFRSs)[17] and have them audited in accordance with international auditing standards. IFRSs are published by the International Accounting
Standards Board (IASB), which has endorsed many of the International
Accounting Standards (IASs) published by its predecessor body, the International
Accounting Standards Committee (IASC). IFRSs and endorsed IASs are now
collectively referred to as "international accounting standards" (IASs). Individual
EU states are permitted to extend the application of these standards to unlisted
companies and individual company accounts.

The 2006 Act has reordered and redrafted the provisions which were formally
to be found in Pt 7 of the 1985 Act.[18] A major innovation has been to remove the
detailed schedules which were in place under the 1985 Act and to replace this by
giving the Secretary of State the power to make regulations. This was highlighted
by the government in its White Paper in March 2005 who noted that

> "A number of consultees, particularly smaller firms and their advisors, have said
> that it is hard for them to find and understand the requirements which relate to
> them because in the interests of brevity the approach has been to express some
> provisions as modifications of those which apply to larger companies."[19]

The government's response was to "set out sequentially a separate, comprehensive 'code' for each of the different sizes of company, starting with small, private
companies, which can be read independently". Thus, the result of this policy is
two major parts of the 2006 Act are concerned with accounting[20] and auditing

---

[12] See *http://www.frc.org.uk/* [accessed on June 2, 2010].

[13] See *http://www.frc.org.uk/asb/* [accessed on June 2, 2010]. For the background, see especially Peter Holgate, *Accounting Principles for Lawyers* (2006), Ch.2.

[14] See the Accounting Standards (Prescribed Body) Regulations 2008 (SI 2008/651).

[15] Available at *http://www.frc.org.uk/asb/technical/standards/accounting.cfm* [accessed on June 2, 2010].

[16] The ASB has adopted the standards established by its predecessor body, the ASC, until such time as it issues new standards to supersede them.

[17] reg.1606/2002 of the European Parliament and of the Council of July 19, 2002 ("The International Accounting Standards (IAS) Regulation") [2002] OJ L243.

[18] Those parts of Pt 7 relating to audit are now to be found in Pt 16. See Ch.21, below.

[19] At para.410.

[20] i.e. Pt 15. A detailed consideration of the law relating to accounts is, however, beyond the scope of this book. See, however, *Palmer's Company Law Annotated Guide to the Companies Act 2006*, 2nd edn (London: Sweet & Maxwell, 2009), at pp.345–453.

regulations,[21] supplemented by 12 statutory instruments on accounts and reports[22] and six on audits.

THE STATUTORY ACCOUNTS FRAMEWORK FOR DIFFERENT KINDS OF COMPANIES

The basic distinction

20–004 Although the directors of private companies have always had to prepare statutory accounts to lay before their shareholders in general meeting, prior to 1967 most were exempted from the need to file these financial statements with the Registrar of Companies. From then until 1981, however, the only concessions were that companies below a certain size did not have to disclose details of turnover and directors' remuneration, nor in their directors' reports the value of exports, the average number of employees and their aggregate remuneration, and turnover and pretax profit or loss by each class of business. It was the view of the Bolton committee of enquiry on small firms that these concessions did not seriously prejudice the work of credit assessment agencies and the interests of unsecured creditors.[23]

The provisions of the 2006 Act apply to different types of company[24] and the first distinction is between companies which are subject to the small companies regime and those which are not.[25] The second distinction is between quoted companies and companies that are not quoted.[26] A third distinction is introduced later in Pt 15 of the Act, namely a company which is medium-sized.[27]

Companies subject to the small companies regime

20–005 The small companies regime applies to a company for a financial year in relation to which the company qualifies as small and is not excluded from the regime.[28] A company qualifies as small in relation to its *first financial year* if the qualifying condition is met in that year.[29] It qualifies as small in relation to a *subsequent* financial year

1. if the qualifying conditions are met in that year and the preceding financial year;

2. if the qualifying conditions are met in that year and the company qualified as small in relation to the preceding financial year;

---

[21] i.e. Pt 16. See below, Ch.21.

[22] See now *http://www.bis.gov.uk/policies/business-law/company-and-partnership-law/company-law/regulations-statutory-instruments* [accessed June 2, 2010].

[23] (1972) Cmnd. 4811, Ch.17.

[24] s.380(2).

[25] s.380(3)(a).

[26] s.380(3)(b).

[27] ss.465–467.

[28] s.381.

[29] s.382(1).

3. if the qualifying conditions were met in the preceding financial year and the company qualified as small in relation to that year.[30]

The qualifying conditions are that it should meet two or more of three requirements, as follows:

1. a turnover of not more than £6.5 million;

2. balance sheet total[31] of not more than £3.26 million;

3. number of employees[32] of not more than 50.[33]

A parent company may also qualify as small if certain conditions are met. The principal criterion is that it will qualify only if the group[34] headed by it qualifies as a small group.[35] A group qualifies as small in relation to the parent company's first financial year if the qualifying conditions are met in that year.[36] It qualifies as small in relation to a subsequent financial year of the parent company:

1. if the qualifying conditions are met in that year and the preceding financial year;

2. if the qualifying conditions are met in that year and the group qualified as small in relation to the preceding financial year;

3. if the qualifying conditions were met in the preceding financial year and the group qualified as small in relation to that year.[37]

The qualifying conditions are that it should meet two or more of three requirements, as follows:

1. aggregate[38] turnover of not more than £6.5 million net[39] (or £7.8 million gross[40]);

2. aggregate balance sheet total[41] of not more than £3.26 million (or £3.9 million gross);

3. aggregate number of employees[42] of not more than 50.[43]

---

[30] s.382(2). The maximum figures have to be adjusted where the company's financial year is not a year: s.382(4).
[31] i.e. the aggregate of the amounts shown as assets in the company's balance sheet: s.382(5).
[32] See s.382(6).
[33] s.382(3).
[34] i.e. a parent undertaking and its subsidiary undertakings: see s.474(1).
[35] s.383(1).
[36] s.383(2).
[37] s.383(3).
[38] The aggregate figures are ascertained by aggregating the relevant figures determined in accordance with s.382 for each member of the group: s.383(5).
[39] See s.383(6).
[40] See s.383(6).
[41] i.e. the aggregate of the amounts shown as assets in the company's balance sheet: s.382(5).
[42] See s.382(6).
[43] s.383(4).

The figures for each subsidiary undertaking shall be those included in its individual accounts for the relevant financial year, that is if its financial year ends with that of the parent company, that financial year and, if not, its financial year ending last before the end of the financial year of the parent company.[44] If those figures cannot be obtained without disproportionate expense or undue delay, the latest available figures shall be taken.[45]

Companies excluded from the small companies regime

20–006 The small companies regime will *not* apply to a company which was, at any time within the financial year to which the accounts relate,

1. a public company;

2. a company that

    (a) is an authorised insurance company, a banking company, an e-money issuer,[46] a MiFID investment firm[47] or a UCITS management company[48]; or

    (b) carries on insurance market activity, or

3. a member of an ineligible group.[49]

A group is ineligible if any of its members is:

1. a public company;

2. a body corporate other than a company whose shares are admitted to trading on a regulated market in an EEA State;

3. a person (other than a small company) who has permission under Pt 4 of the Financial Services and Markets Act 2000[50] to carry on a regulated activity;

4. a small company[51] that is an authorised insurance company, a banking company, an e-money issuer, a MiFID investment firm or a UCITS management company; or

5. a person who carries on insurance market activity.[52]

[44] s.383(7).
[45] s.383(7).
[46] See s.474(1).
[47] See s.474(1).
[48] See s.474(1).
[49] s.384(1).
[50] c.8.
[51] See s.384(3).
[52] s.384(2).

Quoted and unquoted companies

Quoted[53] and unquoted companies are subject to a separate accounts regime. A **20–007** quoted company means a company whose equity share capital has been included in the official list in accordance with the provisions of Pt 6 of the Financial Services and Markets Act 2000[54] or is officially listed in an EEA State or is admitted to dealing on either the New York Stock Exchange or Nasdaq.[55] An unquoted company, on the other hand, is simply one which is not a quoted company.[56]

Medium-sized companies

A company qualifies as medium-sized[57] in relation to its first financial year if the **20–008** qualifying conditions are met in that year.[58] It qualifies as medium-sized in relation to a subsequent financial year:

1. if the qualifying conditions are met in that year and the preceding financial year;

2. if the qualifying conditions are met in that year and the company qualified as medium-sized in relation to the preceding financial year;

3. if the qualifying conditions were met in the preceding financial year and the company qualified as medium-sized in relation to that year.[59]

The qualifying conditions are that it should meet two or more of three requirements, as follows:

1. turnover of not more than £25.9 million;

2. balance sheet total[60] of not more than £12.9 million;

3. number of employees[61] of not more than 250.[62]

A parent company may also qualify as medium-sized if certain conditions are met. The principal criterion is that it will qualify only if the group headed by it qualifies as a medium-sized group.[63] A group qualifies as medium-sized in relation to the parent company's first financial year if the qualifying conditions are

---

[53] See s.385(1).
[54] See Financial Services and Markets Act 2000 s.103(1).
[55] s.385(2).
[56] See s.385(3).
[57] Note the exclusions in s.467.
[58] s.465(1).
[59] s.465(2). The maximum figures have to be proportionately adjusted where the company's financial year is not a year: s.465(4).
[60] i.e. the aggregate of the amounts shown as assets in the company's balance sheet: s.465(5).
[61] See s.465(6).
[62] s.465(3).
[63] s.466(1).

met in that year.[64] It qualifies as medium-sized in relation to a subsequent financial year of the parent company:

1. if the qualifying conditions are met in that year and the preceding financial year;

2. if the qualifying conditions are met in that year and the group qualified as small in relation to the preceding financial year;

3. if the qualifying conditions were met in the preceding financial year and the group qualified as small in relation to that year.[65]

The qualifying conditions are that it should meet two or more of three requirements, as follows:

1. aggregate[66] turnover of not more than £25.9 million net[67] (or £31.1 million gross[68]);

2. aggregate balance sheet total of not more than £12.9 million (or £15.5 million gross);

3. aggregate number of employees of not more than 250.[69]

The figures for each subsidiary undertaking must be those included in its individual accounts for the relevant financial year, that is if its financial year ends with that of the parent company, that financial year and, if not, its financial year ending last before the end of the financial year of the parent company.[70] If those figures cannot be obtained without disproportionate expense or undue delay, the latest available figures shall be taken.[71]

THE COMPANY FINANCIAL YEAR AND ACCOUNTING REFERENCE PERIODS

The financial year

20–009   The financial year of a company[72] is determined in accordance with the criteria laid down by the Act. A company's first financial year begins with the first day of its first accounting reference period[73] and ends with the last day of that period or such other date, not more than seven days before or after the end of that period,

---

[64] s.466(2).

[65] s.466(3).

[66] The aggregate figures are ascertained by aggregating the relevant figures determined in accordance with s.465 for each member of the group: s.466(5).

[67] See s.466(6).

[68] s.466(6).

[69] s.466(4).

[70] s.466(7).

[71] s.466(7).

[72] This may or may not be the same as a fiscal year for taxation purposes.

[73] See above, para.20–008, and s.391.

as the directors may determine.[74] Subsequent financial years begin with the day immediately following the end of the company's previous financial year and end with the last day of its next accounting reference period or such other date, not more than seven days before or after the end of that period, as the directors may determine.[75] Directors of a parent company are required to secure that, except where in their opinion there are good reasons against it, the financial year of each of its subsidiary undertakings coincides with the company's own financial year.[76]

Accounting reference periods and accounting reference date

A company's accounting reference periods are determined according to its **20–010** accounting reference date in each calendar year.[77] If the company[78] is incorporated *before* April 1, 1996, this will be the date specified by notice to the Registrar in accordance with s.224(2) of the 1985 Act or, failing such notice, for a company incorporated before April 1, 1990, this will be March 31 and in the case of a company incorporated on or after April 1, 1990, this will be the last day of the month in which the anniversary of its incorporation falls.[79] If the company was incorporated *on or after* April 1, 1996 and before the commencement of this Act, or after the commencement of this Act, the accounting reference date is the last day of the month in which the anniversary of its incorporation falls.[80] A company's first accounting reference period is the period of more than six months, but not more than 18 months, beginning with the date of its incorporation and ending with its accounting reference date.[81] Subsequent accounting reference periods are successive periods of 12 months beginning immediately after the end of the previous accounting reference period and ending with its accounting reference date.[82]

A company may alter it accounting reference date if notice is given to the Registrar specifying a new accounting reference date.[83]

ACCOUNTING RECORDS

Keeping records

The Act requires every company to ensure that adequate accounting records are **20–011** kept,[84] sufficient to show and explain its transactions.[85] Moreover, they must be such as to disclose with reasonable accuracy, at any time, the financial position of

---

[74] s.390(2).
[75] s.390(3).
[76] s.390(5).
[77] s.391(1).
[78] For Northern Ireland companies, see s.391(3).
[79] s.391(2).
[80] s.391(4).
[81] s.391(5).
[82] s.391(6).
[83] See s.392.
[84] s.386(1).
[85] s.386(2)(a).

the company,[86] and also enable the directors ensure that any accounts required are prepared to comply with the requirements of the Act.[87] Parent companies are equally required in relation to subsidiaries to which the provisions of the Act do not apply to take reasonable steps to ensure such undertakings keeps sufficient accounting records as to enable the directors of the parent to ensure that any accounts prepared pursuant to the Act comply with the Act.[88] In particular, the accounting records must contain entries from day to day of all monies received and expended, with details of transactions, and a record of assets and liabilities.[89] In addition, a company dealing in goods must keep statements of stock held at the end of each financial year and of stocktakings from which the year-end statements are made up, as well as records of all goods sold and purchased (other than in ordinary retail trade transactions), showing goods, buyers and sellers so as to allow identification.[90] Failure to comply with these requirements is an offence, which is committed by every officer of the company in default and such a person is liable, on conviction on indictment, to imprisonment for up to two years, or a fine (or both) and, on summary conviction, to imprisonment for up to twelve months or to a fine (or both).[91] It would be a defence for such a person to show that he acted honestly and that in the circumstances in which the company's business was carried on the default was excusable.[92]

Duration and place

20–012   The Act requires that the accounting records must be kept at the registered office or such other place as the directors think fit and must, at all times, be open for inspection by the officers of the company.[93] There is, however, no express statutory provision authorising the court to compel inspection. If accounting records are kept at a place outside the United Kingdom, accounts and returns with respect to the business dealt with in the accounting records so kept must be sent to, and kept at, a place in the United Kingdom, and must at all times be open to such inspection.[94] The accounts and returns to be sent to the United Kingdom must be such as to (a) disclose with reasonable accuracy the financial position of the business in question at intervals of not more than six months and (b) enable the directors to ensure that the accounts required to be prepared comply with the requirements of this Act.[95]

Accounting records that a company is required by s.386 to keep must be preserved by it (a) in the case of a private company, for three years from the date

---

[86] s.386(2)(b).
[87] s.386(2)(c).
[88] s.386(5).
[89] s.386(3).
[90] s.386(4).
[91] s.387(1)(3).
[92] See s.387(2).
[93] s.388(1).
[94] s.388(2).
[95] s.388(3).

on which they are made; (b) in the case of a public company, for six years from the date on which they are made.[96] However, the Taxes Management Act 1970[97] effectively requires a six-year retention period, and in order to cover against possible actions for negligence under the Limitation Act 1980 (as amended)[98] the retention period would have to be as long as 15 years. Failure to keep accounting records as required is an offence for which officers of the company are liable, the penalty being imprisonment and/or a fine.[99]

ANNUAL ACCOUNTS

Introduction

The traditional view is that annual accounts[100] represent an historical stewardship **20–013** record of a company's financial affairs. Unfortunately, however, the only objective historical record of this type is afforded by a company's cash flow.[101] On the other hand, any attempt to measure profit, an artificial construct, inevitably involves valuation, either of the business itself as a going concern, or of the individual net assets it owns. Yet what potential users want above all seems to be a measure of profit, even though this must inevitably involve an element of subjectivity in its calculation. The traditional accounting approach has been to value the net assets according to a reasonably flexible set of conservatively biased rules, the overall effect of which is to delay the recognition of profit through time. However, inflation can defeat the accountants' aim to exercise prudence in determining income.

In practice, most users of financial statements are well aware of the shortcomings of conventional accounts and refer to other information to help them assess a business's current position and likely future prospects. Where accounting figures are used not as one of a number of signals of likely future performance, but rather as the basis of a particular calculation (such as a share of profits, the liability to corporation tax, or a restriction under a debt covenant), the interested parties must specify more carefully the exact accounting conventions that are to be adopted in preparing the company's relevant annual financial statements. A framework justifying the use of particular accounting conventions is provided by the Statement of Principles published by the ASB.

It is against this background that the statutory disclosure requirements contained in the Act should be seen. They establish a basic minimum of information which must be disclosed and be subjected to audit, thus increasing its credibility in the eyes of the reader and so hopefully reducing his uncertainty about future likely outcomes. Many companies will disclose more, either in the

---

[96] s.388(4).
[97] c.9.
[98] s.58.
[99] See s.389.
[100] See s.471 for the meaning of the phrase "annual accounts".
[101] For a usual explanation of basic accounting terms, see Peter Holgate, *Accounting Principles for Lawyers* (2002), pp.6–8.

statutory accounts themselves and in supplementary statements demanded by the
ASB and by other regulatory authorities; or by other means (e.g. for quoted
companies through the chairman's report, press releases, or news leaked onto the
market via stockbrokers' reports; and for unquoted companies by disclosing relevant information directly to bank managers, other major creditors and employee
representatives).

Basic principles

20–014 The Act requires that the directors of every company must prepare accounts for
the company for each of its financial years—the company's "individual
accounts".[102] The applicable accounting framework for these accounts is laid
down by s.395. The individual accounts must comprise a balance sheet as at the
last day of the financial year and a profit and loss account.[103] In the case of the
balance sheet, the accounts must give a true and fair view of the state of affairs of
the company as at the end of the financial year and, in the case of the profit and
loss account, give a true and fair view of the profit or loss of the company for the
financial year.[104] The accounts must comply with provision made by the
Secretary of State by regulations as to the form and content of the balance sheet
and profit and loss account and additional information to be provided by way of
notes to the accounts.[105]

The directors of a company must not approve accounts unless they are satisfied
that they give a true and fair view of the assets, liabilities, financial position and
profit or loss in the case of the company's individual accounts, of the company.[106]
The auditor of a company in carrying out his functions under this Act in relation
to the company's annual accounts must have regard to the directors' duty.[107]

Group accounts and small companies

20–015 Where a company is subject to the small companies regime and it is a parent
company, the directors, as well as preparing individual accounts may prepare
group accounts.[108]

Group accounts: other companies

20–016 A number of sections of the Act are devoted to the duty to prepare group
accounts. Thus, if at the end of a financial year the company is a parent company
the directors, as well as preparing individual accounts for the year, must
prepare group accounts for the year unless the company is exempt from that
requirement.[109] There are exemptions for companies included in EEA accounts of

---

[102] s.394.
[103] s.396(1).
[104] s.396(2).
[105] s.396(3).
[106] s.393(1)(a).
[107] s.393(2).
[108] s.398.
[109] s.399(2).

larger groups,[110] for companies included in non-EEA accounts of larger groups,[111] and for companies where none of whose subsidiary undertakings need to be included in the consolidation.[112]

Where group accounts are required, companies must comply with the applicable accounting framework.[113] The accounts must comprise a consolidated balance sheet dealing with the state of affairs of the parent company and its subsidiary undertakings and a consolidated profit and loss account dealing with the profit or loss of the parent company and its subsidiary undertakings.[114] The accounts must also give a true and fair view of the state of affairs as at the end of the financial year, and the profit or loss for the financial year, of the undertakings included in the consolidation as a whole, so far as concerns members of the company.[115] The accounts must comply with provision made by the Secretary of State by regulations as to the form and content of the consolidated balance sheet and consolidated profit and loss account and additional information to be provided by way of notes to the accounts.[116]

The directors of the parent company[117] must ensure that the individual accounts of the parent and each of its subsidiaries[118] are all prepared using the same financial reporting framework, except to the extent, in their opinion, there are good reasons for not doing so.[119]

The directors of a company must not approve group accounts, unless they are **20–017** satisfied that they give a true and fair view of the assets, liabilities, financial position and profit and loss of the undertakings included in the consolidation as a whole, so far as concerns members of the company.[120]

The exact meaning of the phrase "a true and fair view" is unfortunately far from clear. However, it seems that adherence to normal accounting practice would be prima facie evidence of giving such a view. Thus the claim that accounts were misleading because they included property at original cost rather than at current market value was rejected by the courts because normal practice had been followed.[121] The status of accounting standards in helping to clarify the meaning of the phrase has been examined in the case of *Lloyd Cheyham & Co Ltd v Littlejohn & Co*[122] where Woolf J. held that

"While they are not conclusive, so that a departure from their terms necessarily involves a breach of the duty of care, and they are not . . . rigid rules, they are

---

[110] See s.400.
[111] s.401.
[112] s.402.
[113] s.403. See also s.405.
[114] s.404(1).
[115] See s.404(2).
[116] s.404(3).
[117] This does not apply if the directors do not prepare group accounts for the parent company: s.404(2).
[118] This only applies to accounts of subsidiary undertakings that are required to be prepared: s.404(3).
[119] s.407(1).
[120] s.393(1)(b).
[121] *Press Caps Ltd, Re* [1949] Ch. 434.
[122] [1987] B.C.L.C. 303.

very strong evidence as to what is the proper standard which should be adopted and unless there is some justification, a departure from this will be regarded as constituting a breach of duty."[123]

Nevertheless, it is clear that the "true and fair view override" cannot be used without proper justification, as was demonstrated in the *Argyll Foods* case.[124] There the company wished, with the agreement of its auditor, to record "economic substance" at the expense of legal form. The magistrates who heard the case decided that the accounts did not show a true and fair view, and subsequently the DTI (which had brought the prosecution)[125] issued a statement interpreting the decision as confirming its view that the "true and fair view override" is confined to the disclosure requirements of the Companies Acts and that it does not enable companies to depart from the other provisions (e.g. definitions) in the Acts. In such circumstances it would seem appropriate where necessary to indicate the underlying economic substance in notes to the accounts or in supplementary pro forma statements.

Notes to the accounts

Information about related undertakings

20–018 The Act provides that the Secretary of State may make provision by regulations[126] requiring information about related undertakings to be given in notes[127] to a company's annual accounts.[128] The regulations may make different provision according to whether or not the company prepares group accounts and may specify the descriptions of undertaking in relation to which they apply, and make different provision in relation to different descriptions of related undertaking.[129] The regulations may provide that information need not be disclosed with respect to an undertaking that is established under the law of a country outside the United Kingdom or carries on business outside the United Kingdom if certain conditions are met.[130] These are: (a) that in the opinion of the directors of the company the disclosure would be seriously prejudicial to the business of that undertaking, the company, any of the company's subsidiary undertakings or any other undertaking which is included in the consolidation, and (b) that the Secretary of State agrees that the information need not be disclosed.[131] Where advantage is taken of any such exemption, that fact must be stated in a note to the company's annual accounts.[132]

---

[123] At 313.
[124] Unreported, but see R.K. Ashton, "The Argyll Foods Case: A Legal Analysis" (1986) 17 *Accounting and Business Research*, No.65, pp.3–12.
[125] Now BIS.
[126] See now the Small Companies and Groups (Accounts and Directors' Report) Regulations 2008 (SI 2008/409) and the Large and Medium-sized Companies and Groups (Accounts and Reports) Regulations 2008 (SI 2008/410).
[127] See too s.472.
[128] s.409(1).
[129] s.409(2).
[130] s.409(3).
[131] s.409(4).
[132] See s.409(5).

A mechanism for alternative compliance is provided for in s.410. This section applies where the directors of the company are of the opinion that disclosing the information required under s.409 would result in information of excessive length being given in the notes to the company's annual accounts.[133]

Information about off-balance sheet arrangements

In the case of a company that is not subject to the small companies regime, if in **20–019** any financial year the company is or has been party to arrangements that are not reflected in its balance sheet and at the balance sheet date the risks or benefits arising from those arrangements are material, required information has to be given in notes to the company's annual accounts.[134] This relates to the nature and business purpose of the arrangements and the financial impact of the arrangements on the company.[135] The information need only be given to the extent necessary for enabling the financial position of the company to be assessed.[136]

Information about employee numbers and costs

The Act makes provision for information about employee numbers and costs, **20–020** although this does not apply to small companies.[137] The following information must otherwise be given in the notes to the company's annual accounts: (a) the average number[138] of persons employed by the company in the financial year[139]; and (b) the average number of persons so employed within each category of persons[140] employed by the company.[141] This applies in relation to group accounts as if the undertakings included in the consolidation were a single company.[142]

Information about directors' remuneration

The Act provides that the Secretary of State can make provision by regulations **20–021** requiring information in the notes about directors' remuneration.[143] The Act provides that the regulations may require information about: gains made by directors on the exercise of share options; benefits received or receivable by directors

---

[133] s.410(1).
[134] s.401A(1). This section was inserted by the Companies Act 2006 (Amendment) (Accounts and Reports) Regulations 2008 (SI 2008/393). Note that a medium-sixed company does not need to comply with s.410A(1)(b): s.410A(4).
[135] s.410A(2).
[136] s.410A(3).
[137] s.411(1).
[138] See s.411(3)(4).
[139] See too s.411(5)(6).
[140] See s.411(2).
[141] s.411(1).
[142] s.411(7). This was inserted by the Companies Act 2006 (Amendment) (Accounts and Reports) Regulations 2008 (SI 2008/393).
[143] s.412(1). See the Small Companies and Groups (Accounts and Directors' Report) Regulations 2008 (SI 2008/409) reg.5 and Sch.3, and the Large and Medium-sized Companies and Groups (Accounts and Reports) Regulations 2008 (SI 2008/410) reg.8 and Sch.5.

under long-term incentive schemes; payments for loss of office[144]; benefits receivable, and contributions for the purpose of providing benefits, in respect of past services of a person as director or in any other capacity while director; consideration paid to or receivable by third parties for making available the services of a person as director or in any other capacity while director.[145] Amounts paid to or receivable by a person connected with a director or a body corporate controlled by[146] a director are treated as paid to or receivable by the director.[147] It is the duty of any director of a company and any person who has at any time in the preceding five years been a director of the company to give notice to the company of such matters relating to himself as may be necessary for the purposes of regulations made under this section.[148] A person who defaults commits an offence and is liable on summary conviction to a fine.[149]

Information about director's benefits

20–022 The Act provides also for information to be placed in the notes to the individual accounts of advances, credit and guarantees. In the case of a company which does not prepare group accounts, details of advances and credits[150] granted to the directors[151] and guarantees[152] of any kind entered into by the company on behalf of its directors must be shown.[153] In the case of a parent company that prepares group accounts, details of advances and credits[154] granted to the directors of the parent company, by that company or by any of its subsidiary undertakings and guarantees[155] of any kind entered into on behalf of the directors of the parent company, by that company or by any of its subsidiary undertakings, must be shown in the notes to the group accounts.[156] The totals of the amounts generated must also be stated.[157] The requirements stated in the Act apply in relation to every advance, credit or guarantee subsisting at any time in the financial year to which the accounts relate whenever it was entered into, whether or not the person concerned was a director of the company in question at the time it was entered into and, in the case of an advance, credit or guarantee involving a subsidiary undertaking of that company, whether or not that undertaking was such a subsidiary undertaking at the time it was entered into.[158]

---

[144] As defined in s.215.
[145] s.412(2).
[146] The expressions "connected with" and "controlled by" have the same meaning as in Pt 10 of the Act: s.412(4).
[147] s.412(4).
[148] s.412(5).
[149] s.412(6).
[150] See s.413(3).
[151] i.e. persons who were a director at any time in the financial year to which the accounts relate: s.413(6).
[152] s.414(4).
[153] s.413(1).
[154] See s.413(3).
[155] s.414(4).
[156] s.413(2).
[157] s.413(5).
[158] s.413(7).

Approval and signing of accounts

The Act requires that the annual accounts are approved by the board of directors and **20–023** signed on behalf of the board by a director of the company.[159] The signature must appear on the company's balance sheet.[160] If the accounts are prepared in accordance with the provisions applicable to companies subject to the small companies regime, the balance sheet must contain a statement to that effect in a prominent position above the signature.[161] If annual accounts are approved that do not comply with the requirements of this Act every director of the company who knew that they did not comply, or was reckless as to whether they complied and failed to take reasonable steps to secure compliance with those requirements or to prevent the accounts from being approved, commits an offence and is liable on conviction to a fine.[162]

The directors' report

Duty to prepare a report

The directors of a company must prepare a directors' report for each financial **20–024** year of the company.[163] For a financial year in which the company is a parent company and the directors of the company prepare group accounts, the directors' report must be a consolidated report[164] relating to the undertakings included in the consolidation.[165] A group directors' report may, where appropriate, give greater emphasis to the matters that are significant to the undertakings included in the consolidation, taken as a whole.[166] In the case of failure to comply with the requirement to prepare a directors' report, an offence is committed by every person who was a director of the company immediately before the end of the period for filing accounts and reports for the financial year in question and failed to take all reasonable steps for securing compliance with that requirement.[167] On conviction, there those liable will have to pay a fine.[168]

Exemption for small companies

A company is entitled to small companies exemption in relation to the directors' **20–025** report for a financial year if it is entitled to prepare accounts for the year in accordance with the small companies regime, or it would be so entitled but for being or having been a member of an ineligible group.[169]

---

[159] s.414(1).
[160] s.414(2).
[161] s.414(3).
[162] s.414(4)(5).
[163] s.415(1).
[164] A "group directors report".
[165] s.415(2).
[166] s.415(3).
[167] s.415(4).
[168] s.415(5).
[169] s.415A(1). This section was inserted by the Companies Act 2006 (Amendment) (Accounts and Reports) Regulations 2008 (SI 2008/393).

Contents of the report in general

20–026 The directors' report for a financial year must state the names of the persons who, at any time during the financial year, were directors of the company and the principal activities of the company in the course of the year.[170] In relation to a group directors' report this has effect as if the reference to the company was to the undertakings included in the consolidation.[171] Except in the case of a company entitled to the small companies exemption, the report must state the amount (if any) that the directors recommend should be paid by way of dividend.[172] The Secretary of State may make provision by regulations as to other matters that must be disclosed in a directors' report.[173]

Business review

20–027 Unless the company is entitled to the small companies exemption, the directors' report must contain a business review[174] which is intended to inform members of the company and help them assess how the directors have performed their duty[175] under s.172.[176] The business review must contain a fair review of the company's business and a description of the principal risks and uncertainties facing the company.[177] The review required is a balanced and comprehensive analysis of the development and performance of the company's business during the financial year and the position of the company's business at the end of that year, consistent with the size and complexity of the business.[178] For quoted companies, the business review must, to the extent necessary for an understanding of the development, performance or position of the company's business, include the main trends and factors likely to affect the future development, performance and position of the company's business.[179] It must also include information about environmental matters (including the impact of the company's business on the environment), the company's employees, and social and community issues, including information about any policies of the company in relation to those matters and the effectiveness of those policies.[180] Finally, it must include information about persons with whom the company has contractual or other arrangements which are essential to the business of the company.[181] If the review does not contain any of the above

---

[170] s.416(1).

[171] s.416(2).

[172] s.416(3).

[173] s.416(4). He has done so in the Small Companies and Groups (Accounts and Directors' Report) Regulations 2008 (SI 2008/409) reg.7 and Sch.5, and the Large and Medium-sized Companies and Groups (Accounts and Reports) Regulations 2008 (SI 2008/410) reg.10 and Sch.7.

[174] s.417(1).

[175] s.417(2).

[176] i.e. the duty to promote the success of the company. See para.17–001.

[177] s.417(3).

[178] s.417(4).

[179] s.417(5)(a).

[180] s.417(5)(b).

[181] s.417(5)(c). Nothing in this subsection requires the disclosure of information about a person if the disclosure would, in the opinion of the directors, be seriously prejudicial to that person and contrary to the public interest.

information it must state which of those kinds of information it does not contain. The review must, to the extent necessary for an understanding of the development, performance or position of the company's business, include analysis using financial key performance indicators[182] and, where appropriate, analysis using other key performance indicators, including information relating to environmental matters and employee matters.[183] Where appropriate, the review must include references to, and additional explanations of amounts included in the company's annual accounts.[184] Nothing requires the disclosure of information about impending developments or matters in the course of negotiation if the disclosure would, in the opinion of the directors, be seriously prejudicial to the interests of the company.[185]

Statement as to disclosure to auditors

The directors' report must contain a statement to the effect that, in the case of **20–028** each of the persons who are directors at the time the report is approved, so far as the director is aware, there is no relevant audit information[186] of which the company's auditor is unaware, and he has taken all the steps that he ought to have taken as a director in order to make himself aware of any relevant audit information and to establish that the company's auditor is aware of that information.[187] This applies to a company unless it is exempt for the financial year in question from the requirements as to audit of accounts and the directors take advantage of that exemption.[188] Where a directors' report containing the statement required by this section is approved but the statement is false, every director of the company who knew that the statement was false, or was reckless as to whether it was false and failed to take reasonable steps to prevent the report from being approved commits an offence.[189] A person guilty of an offence is liable, on conviction on indictment, to imprisonment for a term not exceeding two years or a fine (or both); on summary conviction, to imprisonment for a term not exceeding twelve months or to a fine not exceeding the statutory maximum (or both).[190]

Approval and signature of the report

The directors' report must be approved by the board of directors and signed on **20–029** behalf of the board by a director or the secretary of the company.[191] If in preparing

---

[182] i.e. factors by reference to which the development, performance or position of the company's business can be measured effectively: s.417(6).
[183] s.417(6). Where a company qualifies as medium-sized in relation to a financial year, the directors' report for the year need not comply with these requirements so far as they relate to non-financial information: s.417(7).
[184] s.417(8).
[185] s.417(10).
[186] See s.418(3).
[187] s.418(2). See also s.418(4).
[188] s.418(1).
[189] s.418(5).
[190] s.418(6).
[191] s.419(1).

the report advantage is taken of the small companies exemption, the report must contain a statement to that effect in a prominent position above the signature.[192] If a directors' report is approved that does not comply with the requirements of this Act, every director of the company who (a) knew that it did not comply, or was reckless as to whether it complied, and (b) failed to take reasonable steps to secure compliance with those requirements or, as the case may be, to prevent the report from being approved, commits an offence.[193] A person guilty of an offence under this section is liable to a fine.[194]

Approval and signature of a separate corporate governance statement

20–030 Any separate corporate governance statement must be approved by the board of directors and signed on behalf of the board by a director or the secretary of the company.[195]

Directors' remuneration report for quoted companies

Duty to prepare a report

20–031 The directors of a quoted company must prepare a directors' remuneration report for each financial year of the company.[196] In the case of failure to comply with the requirement to prepare a directors' remuneration report, every person who was a director of the company immediately before the end of the period for filing accounts and reports for the financial year in question and failed to take all reasonable steps for securing compliance with that requirement commits an offence.[197] Such a person is liable to a fine.[198]

Contents of the report

20–032 The Secretary of State may make provision by regulations as to the information that must be contained in a directors' remuneration report, how information is to be set out in the report, and what is to be the auditable part of the report.[199] It is the duty of any director of a company and any person who is or has at any time in the preceding five years been a director of the company, to give notice to the company of such matters relating to himself as may be necessary for the purposes of regulations under this section.[200] A person in default commits an offence and is liable to a fine.[201]

---

[192] s.419(2).
[193] s.419(3).
[194] s.419(4).
[195] s.419A. This section was inserted by the Companies Act 2006 (Accounts, Reports and Audit) Regulations 2009 (SI 2009/1581) reg.2.
[196] s.420(1).
[197] s.420(2).
[198] s.420(3).
[199] s.421(1). See the Large and Medium-sized Companies and Groups (Accounts and Reports) Regulations 2008 (SI 2008/410) reg.11 and Sch.8.
[200] s.421(30).
[201] s.421(4).

Approval and signature of the report

The directors' remuneration report must be approved by the board of directors and **20–033** signed on behalf of the board by a director or the secretary of the company.[202] If a directors' remuneration report is approved which does not comply with the Act, every director of the company who knew that it did not comply, or was reckless as to whether it complied and failed to take reasonable steps to secure compliance with those requirements or, as the case may be, to prevent the report from being approved, commits an offence.[203] A person guilty of an offence is liable to a fine.[204]

Publication of the accounts and reports

Duty to circulate copies of the accounts and reports

Every company must send a copy of its annual accounts and reports for each **20–034** financial year to every member of the company, every holder of the company's debentures, and every person who is entitled to receive notice of general meetings.[205] Copies need not be sent to a person for whom the company does not have a current[206] address.[207] In the case of a company not having a share capital, copies need not be sent to anyone who is not entitled to receive notices of general meetings of the company.[208] Where copies are sent out over a period of days, references in the Act to the day on which copies are sent out are to be read as references to the last day of that period.[209] Every copy must state the name of the person who has signed it on behalf of the board.[210] For unquoted companies this applies to the company's balance sheet and the directors' report[211] and, for quoted companies, this additionally applies to the directors' remuneration report.[212] Failure to do this is an offence which may lead to a fine.[213]

Requirements for publication of the statutory accounts

If a company publishes any of its statutory accounts,[214] they must be accompa- **20–035** nied by the auditor's report on those accounts unless the company is exempt from audit and the directors have taken advantage of that exemption.[215] A company that

---

[202] s.422(1).
[203] s.422(2).
[204] s.422(3).
[205] s.423(1).
[206] See s.423(3).
[207] s.423(2).
[208] s.423(4).
[209] s.423(5).
[210] s.433(1).
[211] s.433(2).
[212] s.433(3).
[213] s.433(4)(5).
[214] A company's "statutory accounts" are its accounts for a financial year as required to be delivered to the Registrar under s.441. See para.20–048, below.
[215] s.434(1). But this does not apply in relation to the provision by a company of a summary financial statement: see s.426. See para.20–041, below.

prepares statutory group accounts for a financial year must not publish its statutory individual accounts for that year without also publishing with them its statutory group accounts.[216] If a company contravenes any provision of this section, an offence is committed by the company and every officer of the company who is in default.[217] A person guilty will be liable to a fine.[218]

Requirements for publication of non-statutory accounts

20–036 If a company publishes non-statutory accounts,[219] it must publish with them a statement indicating:

1. that they are not the company's statutory accounts;

2. whether statutory accounts dealing with any financial year with which the non-statutory accounts purport to deal have been delivered to the Registrar;

3. whether an auditor's report has been made on the company's statutory accounts for any such financial year, and if so, whether the report

   (a) was qualified or unqualified, or included a reference to any matters to which the auditor drew attention by way of emphasis without qualifying the report; or
   (b) contained a statement under s.498(2) or s.498(3).[220]

The company must not publish with non-statutory accounts the auditor's report on the company's statutory accounts.[221] If a company contravenes any provision of this section, an offence is committed by the company and every officer of the company who is in default.[222] A person guilty of an offence is liable to a fine.[223]

Time for compliance with the duty

20–037 The time allowed for sending out copies of the company's annual accounts and reports is specified in the Act. Whether the time allowed is that for a private company or a public company is determined by reference to the company's status immediately before the end of the accounting reference period by reference to which the financial year for the accounts in question was determined.[224] A private company must send out copies of the company's annual accounts and reports not later than the end of the period for filing accounts and reports or, if earlier, the

---

[216] s.434(2).
[217] s.434(4).
[218] s.434(5).
[219] As defined in s.435(3)(4).
[220] s.435(1). This section does not apply in relation to the provision by a company of a summary financial statement (see s.426): s.435(7).
[221] s.435(2).
[222] s.435(5).
[223] s.435(6).
[224] s.424(5).

date on which it actually delivers its accounts and reports to the Registrar.[225] A public company must comply at least 21 days before the date of the relevant accounts meeting.[226] However, if a public company sent out the accounts and report later than is required by this section they will, despite that, be deemed to have been duly sent if it is so agreed by all the members entitled to attend and vote at the relevant accounts meeting.[227] In the event of default under these sections, an offence is committed by the company and every officer and a person guilty is liable to a fine.[228]

Website publication for quoted companies

A quoted company must ensure that its annual accounts and reports are made **20–038** available on a website and remain so available until the annual accounts and reports for the company's next financial year are made available in accordance with this section.[229] The annual accounts and reports must be made available on a website that is maintained by or on behalf of the company and identifies the company in question.[230] Access to the annual accounts and reports on the website, and the ability to obtain a hard copy of the annual accounts and reports from the website, must not be conditional on the payment of a fee or otherwise restricted, except so far as necessary to comply with any enactment or regulatory requirement (in the United Kingdom or elsewhere).[231] The annual accounts and reports must be made available as soon as reasonably practicable and must be kept available throughout the period required by this section.[232] A failure to make the annual accounts and reports available on a website throughout that period is disregarded if the annual accounts and reports are made available on the website for part of that period and the failure is wholly attributable to circumstances that it would not be reasonable to have expected the company to prevent or avoid.[233] In the event of default in complying with this section, an offence is committed by every officer of the company who is in default who, if convicted, will be liable to a fine.[234]

Rights of members or debenture holders to demand copies: unquoted companies

A member of, or holder of debentures of, an unquoted company is entitled to be **20–039** provided, on demand and without charge, with a copy of the company's last annual accounts, the last directors' report and the auditor's report on those

---

[225] s.424(2).
[226] s.424(3).
[227] s.424(4).
[228] See s.425.
[229] s.430(1).
[230] s.430(2).
[231] s.430(3).
[232] s.430(4).
[233] s.430(5).
[234] s.430(6)(7).

accounts (including the statement on that report).[235] The entitlement is to a single copy of those documents, but that is in addition to any copy to which a person may be entitled under s.423.[236] If a demand made under this section is not complied with within seven days of receipt by the company, an offence is committed by the company and every officer of the company who is in default and, if found guilty, such a person will be liable to a fine.[237]

Rights of members or debenture holders to demand copies: quoted companies

20–040 Similar requirements are in place for quoted companies. Thus, in addition to the information which would have to be sent out for an unquoted company, for a quoted company the company must also send to the member or debenture holder a copy of the last directors' remuneration report.[238] The auditors' report must also include the report on the directors' remuneration report.[239]

Summary financial statement

Power to make regulations

20–041 The Secretary of State may make regulations specifying the conditions under which a company may provide a summary financial statement instead of copies of the accounts and reports required to be sent out in accordance with the Act.[240] Copies of those accounts and reports must, however, be sent to any person entitled to be sent them in accordance with that section and who wishes to receive them.[241] The Secretary of State may make provision by regulations as to the manner in which it is to be ascertained, whether before or after a person becomes entitled to be sent a copy of those accounts and reports, whether he wishes to receive them.[242] If default is made in complying with these requirements, an offence is committed by the company and every officer of the company in default and a person found guilty is liable to a fine.[243]

Form and contents for unquoted companies

20–042 A summary financial statement by an unquoted company must be derived from the company's annual accounts and be prepared in accordance with the Act.[244]

---

[235] s.431(1).
[236] s.431(2).
[237] s.431(3)(4).
[238] s.432(1)(b).
[239] s.432(1)(d).
[240] s.426(1). He has done so in the Companies (Summary Financial Statements) Regulations 2008 (SI 2008/374).
[241] s.426(2).
[242] s.426(3).
[243] s.429.
[244] s.427(1).

The summary financial statement must be in such form, and contain such information, as the Secretary of State may specify by regulations.[245] The regulations may require the statement to include information derived from the directors' report.[246] However, nothing prevents a company from including in a summary financial statement additional information derived from the company's annual accounts or the directors' report.[247] The summary financial statement must:

1. state that it is only a summary of information derived from the company's annual accounts;

2. state whether it contains additional information derived from the directors' report and, if so, that it does not contain the full text of that report;

3. state how a person entitled to them can obtain a full copy of the company's annual accounts and the directors' report;

4. contain a statement by the company's auditor of his opinion as to whether the summary financial statement is consistent with the company's annual accounts and, where information derived from the directors' report is included in the statement, with that report, and complies with the requirements of this section and regulations made under it;

5. state whether the auditor's report on the annual accounts was unqualified or qualified and, if it was qualified, set out the report in full together with any further material needed to understand the qualification;

6. state whether, in that report, the auditor's statement under s.496 was qualified or unqualified and, if it was qualified, set out the qualified statement in full together with any further material needed to understand the qualification;

7. state whether that auditor's report contained a statement under s.498(2)(a) or (b) or s.498(3) and, if so, set out the statement in full.[248]

The regulations[249] may provide that any specified material may, instead of being included in the summary financial statement, be sent separately at the same time as the statement.[250] If default is made in complying with these requirements, an offence is committed by the company and every officer of the company in default and a person found guilty is liable to a fine.[251]

---

[245] s.427(2). He has done so in the Companies (Summary Financial Statements) Regulations 2008 (SI 2008/374).
[246] Companies (Summary Financial Statements Regulations 2008 (SI 2008/374).
[247] s.427(3).
[248] s.427(4).
[249] See the Companies (Summary Financial Statements) Regulations 2008 (SI 2008/374).
[250] s.427(5).
[251] s.429.

Form and contents for quoted companies

20–043 The form and contents for quoted companies[252] have a strong similarity with those for unquoted companies, save that additional information has to be provided.[253] If default is made in complying with these requirements, an offence is committed by the company and every officer of the company in default and a person found guilty is liable to a fine.[254]

Public companies' obligations with respect to accounts and reports

General meeting

20–044 The directors of a public company must lay before the company in general meeting copies of its annual accounts and reports.[255] This must be complied with not later than the end of the period for filing the accounts and reports in question.[256] An "accounts meeting" in a public company is a general meeting at which the company's annual accounts and reports are to be laid.[257]

Offences

20–045 If the requirements of s.437 are not complied with before the end of the period allowed, every person who immediately before the end of that period was a director of the company commits an offence.[258] It is, however, a defence for a person charged with such an offence to prove that he took all reasonable steps for securing that those requirements would be complied with before the end of that period.[259] On the other hand, it is not a defence to prove that the documents in question were not in fact prepared as required.[260] A person found liable will be required to pay a fine.[261]

Quoted companies and member approval of the directors' remuneration report

Member approval generally

20–046 A quoted company must, prior to the accounts meeting,[262] give to the members of the company entitled to be sent notice of the meeting notice of the intention to

---

[252] See s.428.
[253] s.428(4).
[254] s.429.
[255] s.437(1).
[256] s.437(2).
[257] s.437(3).
[258] s.438(1).
[259] s.438(2).
[260] s.438(3).
[261] s.438(4).
[262] i.e. the general meeting of the company before which the company's annual accounts for the financial year are to be laid: s.439(6).

move at the meeting, as an ordinary resolution, a resolution approving the directors' remuneration report for the financial year.[263] The notice may be given in any manner permitted for the service on the member of notice of the meeting.[264] The business that may be dealt with at the accounts meeting includes the resolution.[265] The existing directors[266] must ensure that the resolution is put to the vote of the meeting.[267] No entitlement of a person to remuneration is made conditional on the resolution being passed by reason only of the provision made by this section.[268]

Offences

In the event of default in complying, an offence is committed by every officer of **20–047** the company who is in default.[269] If the resolution is not put to the vote of the accounts meeting, an offence is committed by each existing director.[270] It is a defence for a person charged with an offence to prove that he took all reasonable steps for securing that the resolution was put to the vote of the meeting.[271] A person guilty of an offence is liable on summary conviction to a fine.[272]

Filing of accounts and reports

General duty to file

The directors of a company must deliver to the Registrar for each financial year **20–048** the accounts and reports.[273]

Period for filing[274]

The period for a private company is nine months[275] after the end of the relevant **20–049** accounting reference period.[276] For a public company, it is six months after the end of that period.[277] However, if the relevant accounting reference period is the company's first and is a period of more than twelve months, the period is nine months or six months, as the case may be, from the first anniversary of the incorporation of the company or three months after the end of the accounting reference period, whichever last expires.[278] If the relevant accounting reference period is

---

[263] s.439(1).
[264] s.439(2).
[265] s.439(3).
[266] i.e. those persons who are directors of the company immediately before that meeting: s.439(6).
[267] s.439(4).
[268] s.439(5).
[269] s.440(1).
[270] s.440(2).
[271] s.440(3).
[272] s.440(4).
[273] s.441.
[274] See too s.443.
[275] s.442(2)(a).
[276] See s.442(7).
[277] s.442(2)(b).
[278] s.442(3).

treated as shortened by virtue of a notice given by the company under s.392, the period is that applicable in accordance with this section or three months from the date of the notice under that section, whichever last expires.[279] If for any special reason the Secretary of State thinks fit he may, on an application made before the expiry of the period otherwise allowed, by notice in writing to a company extend that period by such further period as may be specified in the notice.[280] Whether the period allowed is that for a private company or a public company is determined by reference to the company's status immediately before the end of the relevant accounting reference period.[281]

Filing: small companies

20–050 The directors of a company subject to the small companies regime must deliver to the Registrar for each financial year a copy of a balance sheet drawn up as at the last day of that year and may also deliver to the Registrar a copy of the company's profit and loss account for that year and a copy of the directors' report for that year.[282] The directors must also deliver a copy of the auditor's report on the accounts (and any directors' report) that it delivers.[283] The copies of accounts and reports delivered to the Registrar must be copies of the company's annual accounts and reports, except that where the company prepares Companies Act accounts[284] the directors may deliver to the Registrar a copy of a balance sheet drawn up in accordance with regulations made by the Secretary of State and there may be omitted from the copy of the profit and loss account delivered to the Registrar such items as may be specified by the regulations.[285] If abbreviated accounts are delivered to the Registrar the obligation to deliver a copy of the auditor's report on the accounts is to deliver a copy of the special auditor's report required by s.449.[286] Where the directors of a company subject to the small companies regime deliver accounts that are not abbreviated accounts and do not deliver to the Registrar a copy of the company's profit and loss account or do not deliver to the Registrar a copy of the directors' report the copy of the balance sheet delivered to the Registrar must contain in a prominent position a statement that the company's annual accounts and reports have been delivered in accordance with the provisions applicable to companies subject to the small companies regime.[287] The copies of the balance sheet and any directors' report delivered to the Registrar under this section must state the name of the person who signed it on behalf of the board.[288] The copy of the auditor's report delivered to the Registrar under this section must state the name of the auditor and (where the

---

[279] s.442(4).
[280] s.442(5).
[281] s.442(6).
[282] s.444(1).
[283] s.444(2). This does not apply if the company is exempt from audit and the directors have taken advantage of that exemption.
[284] So-called "abbreviated accounts": see s.444(3).
[285] s.444(3).
[286] s.444(4).
[287] s.444(5).
[288] s.444(6).

auditor is a firm) the name of the person who signed it as senior statutory auditor or if the conditions in s.506 are met, state that a resolution has been passed and notified to the Secretary of State in accordance with that section.[289]

Filing: small companies exemption for the directors' report

The directors of a company that is entitled to small companies exemption in rela- **20–051** tion to the directors' report for a financial year[290] must deliver to the Registrar a copy of the company's annual accounts for that year and may also deliver to the Registrar a copy of the directors' report.[291] The directors must also deliver to the Registrar a copy of the auditor's report on the accounts (and any directors' report) that it delivers. This does not apply if the company is exempt from audit and the directors have taken advantage of that exception.[292] The copies of the balance sheet and directors' report delivered to the Registrar under this section must state the name of the person who signed it on behalf of the board.[293] The copy of the auditor's report delivered to the Registrar under this section must state the name of the auditor and (where the auditor is a firm) the name of the person who signed it as senior statutory auditor or, if the conditions in s.506 are met, state that a resolution has been passed and notified to the Secretary of State in accordance with that section.[294]

Filing: medium-sized companies

The directors of a company that qualifies as a medium-sized company in relation **20–052** to a financial year must deliver to the Registrar a copy of the company's annual accounts and the directors' report.[295] They must also deliver to the Registrar a copy of the auditor's report on those accounts (and on the directors' report). This does not apply if the company is exempt from audit and the directors have taken advantage of that exemption.[296] Where the company prepares Companies Act accounts, the directors may deliver to the Registrar a copy of the company's annual accounts for the financial year that includes a profit and loss account in which items are combined in accordance with regulations made by the Secretary of State and that does not contain items whose omission is authorised by the regulations.[297] If abbreviated accounts are delivered to the Registrar the obligation to deliver a copy of the auditor's report on the accounts is to deliver a copy of the special auditor's report required by s.449.[298] The copies of the balance sheet and

---

[289] s.444(7).

[290] This does not apply to companies within s.444: s.444A(5).

[291] s.444A(1). This section was inserted by the Companies Act 2006 (Amendment) (Accounts and Reports) Regulations 2008 (SI 2008/393).

[292] s.444A(2).

[293] s.444A(3).

[294] s.444A(4). This was substituted by the Companies Act 2006 (Accounts, Reports and Audit) Regulations 2009 (SI 2009/1581).

[295] s.445(1). This section does not apply to companies within s.444 or s.444A.

[296] s.445(2).

[297] i.e. "abbreviated accounts": s.445(3).

[298] s.445(4).

directors' report delivered to the Registrar must state the name of the person who signed it on behalf of the board.[299] The copy of the auditor's report delivered to the Registrar under this section must state the name of the auditor and (where the auditor is a firm) the name of the person who signed it as senior statutory auditor or, if the conditions in s.506 are met, state that a resolution has been passed and notified to the Secretary of State in accordance with that section.[300]

Filing: unquoted companies

20–053 The directors of an unquoted company must deliver to the Registrar for each financial year of the company a copy of the company's annual accounts, the directors' report and any separate corporate governance statement.[301] The directors must also deliver to the Registrar a copy of the auditor's report on those accounts (and the directors' report and any separate corporate governance statement). This does not apply if the company is exempt from audit and the directors have taken advantage of that exemption.[302] The copies of the balance sheet and directors' report delivered to the Registrar under this section must state the name of the person who signed it on behalf of the board.[303] The copy of the auditor's report delivered to the Registrar must state the name of the auditor and (where the auditor is a firm) the name of the person who signed it as senior statutory auditor, or if the conditions in s.506 are met, state that a resolution has been passed and notified to the Secretary of State in accordance with that section.[304]

Filing: quoted companies

20–054 The directors of a quoted company must deliver to the Registrar for each financial year of the company a copy of the company's annual accounts, the directors' remuneration report, the directors' report and any separate corporate governance statement.[305] They must also deliver a copy of the auditor's report on those accounts (and on the directors' remuneration report, the directors' report and any separate corporate governance statement).[306] The copies of the balance sheet, the directors' remuneration report and the directors' report delivered to the Registrar under this section must state the name of the person who signed it on behalf of the board.[307] The copy of the auditor's report delivered to the Registrar under this section must state the name of the auditor and (where the auditor is a firm) the name of the person who signed it as senior statutory auditor or if the conditions in s.506 are met, state that a resolution has been passed and notified to the Secretary of State in accordance with that section.[308]

---

[299] s.445(5).
[300] s.445(6).
[301] s.446(1). This section does not apply to copies falling within s.444, s.444A and s.445.
[302] s.446(2).
[303] s.446(3).
[304] s.446(4).
[305] s.447(1).
[306] s.447(2).
[307] s.447(3).
[308] s.447(4).

Exemption for unlimited companies

The directors of an unlimited company are not required to deliver accounts and **20–055** reports to the Registrar in respect of a financial year if certain conditions are met.[309] The conditions are that at no time during the relevant accounting reference period: (a) has the company been, to its knowledge, a subsidiary undertaking of an undertaking which was then limited, or (b) have there been, to its knowledge, exercisable by or on behalf of two or more undertakings which were then limited, rights which if exercisable by one of them would have made the company a subsidiary undertaking of it, or (c) has the company been a parent company of an undertaking which was then limited.[310]

Abbreviated accounts

Where the directors of a company deliver abbreviated accounts to the Registrar **20–056** and the company is not exempt from audit (or the directors have not taken advantage of any such exemption)[311] the directors must also deliver to the Registrar a copy of a special report of the company's auditor stating that in his opinion the company is entitled to deliver abbreviated accounts in accordance with the section in question and the abbreviated accounts to be delivered are properly prepared in accordance with regulations under that section.[312] The auditor's report on the company's annual accounts need not be delivered but if that report was qualified, the special report must set out that report in full together with any further material necessary to understand the qualification and if that report contained a statement under s.498(2) or s.498(3) the special report must set out that statement in full.[313] The provisions of ss.503–509 apply to a special report under this section as they apply to an auditor's report on the company's annual accounts prepared under Pt 16 of the Act.[314] If abbreviated accounts are delivered to the Registrar, the references in s.434 or s.435 to the auditor's report on the company's annual accounts are to be read as references to the special auditor's report required by this section.[315]

Approval and signing of the abbreviated accounts

Abbreviated accounts must be approved by the board of directors and signed on **20–057** behalf of the board by a director of the company.[316] The signature must be on the balance sheet.[317] The balance sheet must contain in a prominent position above the signature a statement to the effect that it is prepared in accordance with the

---

[309] s.448(1). The exemption does not apply in certain circumstances: see s.448(3).
[310] s.448(2).
[311] s.449(1).
[312] s.449(2).
[313] s.449(3).
[314] s.449(4).
[315] s.449(5).
[316] s.450(1).
[317] s.450(2).

special provisions of this Act relating to companies subject to the small companies regime or to medium-sized companies.[318] If abbreviated accounts are approved that do not comply with the requirements of regulations under the relevant section, every director of the company who knew that they did not comply, or was reckless as to whether they complied and failed to take reasonable steps to prevent them from being approved commits an offence.[319] A person guilty of an offence is liable to a fine.[320]

Failure to file accounts and reports

20–058 The Act provides for offences in respect of the failure to file accounts and reports.[321] Civil penalties may also follow.[322] Finally, provision is also made for an application to the court for the making of an order under which the directors can be instructed to make good the default.[323]

Revision of defective accounts and reports

Voluntary revision of the accounts and reports

20–059 Where a company's annual accounts, summary financial statement, directors' report and/or directors' remuneration report do not comply with the Act, the directors may voluntarily revise them.[324] Where copies of the previous accounts or report have been sent out to members, delivered to the Registrar or laid before the company in general meeting (in the case of a public company), the revisions must be confined to the correction of those respects in which the previous accounts or report did not comply with the requirements of this Act and the making of any necessary consequential alterations.[325] The Secretary of State may make provision by regulations as to the application of the provisions of the Act in relation to revised annual accounts, a revised directors' remuneration report or directors' report or a revised summary financial statement.[326] The regulations may, in particular,

1. make different provision according to whether the previous accounts, report or statement are replaced or are supplemented by a document indicating the corrections to be made;

2. make provision with respect to the functions of the company's auditor in relation to the revised accounts, report or statement;

3. require the directors to take such steps as may be specified in the regulations where the previous accounts or report have been sent out to

---

[318] s.450(3).
[319] s.450(4).
[320] s.450(5).
[321] See s.451.
[322] s.453.
[323] s.452.
[324] s.454(1).
[325] s.454(2).
[326] s.454(3).

members and others under s.423, laid before the company in general meeting, or delivered to the Registrar, or where a summary financial statement containing information derived from the previous accounts or report has been sent to members under s.426;

4. apply the provisions of the Act subject to such additions, exceptions and modifications as are specified in the regulations.[327]

Secretary of State's notice

The Secretary of State may also give notice to a company's directors indicating **20–060** how he believes the financial statements and/or reports laid before the company or delivered to the Registrar may not comply with the Act's requirements. The directors must within a specified period of up to a month give satisfactory explanations or prepare revised financial statements and/or reports, failing which the Secretary of State may apply to the court.[328]

Application to court

An application[329] may be made to the court by the Secretary of State, after having **20–061** complied with s.455 or by a person authorised by the Secretary of State,[330] for a declaration that the annual accounts of a company do not comply, or a directors' report does not comply, with the requirements of this Act and for an order requiring the directors of the company to prepare revised accounts or a revised report.[331] If the court orders the preparation of revised accounts, it may give directions as to the auditing of the accounts, the revision of any directors' remuneration report, directors' report or summary financial statement, and the taking of steps by the directors to bring the making of the order to the notice of persons likely to rely on the previous accounts, and such other matters as the court thinks fit.[332] If the court orders the preparation of a revised directors' report it may give directions as to the review of the report by the auditors, the revision of any summary financial statement, the taking of steps by the directors to bring the making of the order to the notice of persons likely to rely on the previous report and such other matters as the court thinks fit.[333] If the court finds that the accounts or report did not comply with the requirements of the Act it may order that all or part of the costs of and incidental to the application and any reasonable expenses incurred by the company in connection with or in consequence of the preparation of revised accounts or a revised report, are to be borne by such of the directors as were party to the approval of the defective accounts or report.[334] For this purpose

---

[327] s.454(4).
[328] s.455.
[329] Notice must be given to the Registrar: s.455(2).
[330] See s. 457. As to the powers of the authorised person to require documents, information and explanations, see ss.459–462.
[331] s.456(1).
[332] s.456(3).
[333] s.456(4).
[334] s.456(5). See too s.456(6).

every director of the company at the time of the approval of the accounts or report shall be taken to have been a party to the approval unless he shows that he took all reasonable steps to prevent that approval.[335] On the conclusion of proceedings on an application under this section, the applicant must send to the Registrar for registration a copy of the court order or, as the case may be, give notice to the Registrar that the application has failed or been withdrawn.[336]

---

[335] s.456(5). See too s.456(6).
[336] s.456(7).

Chapter 21

AUTITORS

The Justification for Having a Statutory Audit

Where there is inequality of information between parties, it is desirable, not only **21–001** between the parties concerned, but also from a wider social perspective that the accounts should be attested by an independent third party. A prospective purchaser of a company's shares will require this information before he commits himself to investing in the company. The established convention is to have an independent third party, an auditor, to validate this information.

While it is important for readers of financial statements to have some guarantee that they have been properly prepared under an accepted set of conventions, it is also necessary for them to be able to rely on the word of those persons who certify them as having been so produced. Auditors, who carry out this role, should be recognised as fit and proper persons to carry out the duties of their office. Under the Companies Act 1989 a person could only be appointed as an auditor of a company if he was a member of a professional body recognised by the Secretary of State. Part II of the 1989 Act, concerned with eligibility for company auditors, has introduced the provisions of the EU's Eighth Council Directive on company law harmonisation into UK legislation.[1] This Directive has, however, since been replaced by a new Company Law Directive on Audit in 2006,[2] which has been described as the most comprehensive single piece of legislation to impact on the auditors profession. This was anticipated in the drafting of the 2006 Act and, together with a raft of statutory instruments, the requirements have already been implemented.

Professional Qualifications of Auditors

Supervisory bodies

A Recognised Supervisory Body[3] (RSB) is a body established in the United **21–002** Kingdom which maintains and enforces rules as to the eligibility of persons for

---

[1] Council Directive 84/253 [1984] OJ L126/20.
[2] Directive 2006/43/EC [2006] OJ L157/87.
[3] So far Chartered Accountants Ireland, the Association of Authorised Public Accountants, the Association of Chartered Certified Accountants, the Institute of Chartered Accountants in England & Wales, and the Institute of Chartered Accountants of Scotland have been recognised as RSBs. See *http://www.auditregister.org.uk* [accessed June 4, 2010].

appointment as a statutory auditor[4] and the conduct of statutory audit work which are binding on persons seeking appointment or acting as a statutory auditor.[5] Bodies wishing to become a supervisory body have to apply to the Secretary of State for recognition, and the conditions for granting or revoking recognition are specified in Sch.10 of the Act. Supervisory bodies have to ensure that only individuals with appropriate qualifications and firms controlled by qualified persons are eligible for appointment as statutory auditors.[6] The rules are required to ensure that statutory audit work is conducted by the holders of appropriate qualifications[7]; that auditors are to be fit and proper persons[8]; that statutory audit work is conducted properly and with professional integrity and independence[9]; that certain technical standards are applied[10]; and that procedures exist for ensuring eligible persons maintain an appropriate level of competence.[11] To this end, the Auditing Practices Board (APB),[12] whose aims include establishing high standards of auditing, meeting the developing needs of users of financial information, and ensuring public confidence in the auditing process,[13] has published Auditing Standards (ISAs), Standards for Investment Reporting (SIRs), as well as various Practice Notes and Bulletins. The APB is under the supervision of the Financial Reporting Council (FRC), but from 2005 onwards listed companies have to comply with international auditing standards published by the International Auditing and Assurance Standards Board (IAASB).[14]

The legislation further requires that a supervisory body's rules should deal with monitoring and enforcement of compliance with its rules[15]; membership, eligibility, and discipline[16]; investigation of complaints[17]; independent investigation of public interest cases[18]; and the promotion and maintenance of standards.[19] The APB has published five Ethical Standards (ESs) which take account of the EU requirements and IAASB statements on ethics.[20] The five ESs are: (1) integrity, objectivity and independence; (2) financial, business, employment and personal relations; (3) long association with the audit engagement; (4) fees, remuneration and evaluation policies, litigation, gifts and hospitality; (5) non-audit services provided to audit clients.

---

[4] Defined in s.1210.
[5] s.1217(1).
[6] See particularly Pt 2 of Sch.10.
[7] para.6.
[8] para.8.
[9] para.9.
[10] para.10.
[11] para.11.
[12] *http://www.frc.org.uk/apb* [accessed June 4, 2010].
[13] *Ibid.*
[14] *http://www.ifac.org/iaasb* [accessed June 4, 2010].
[15] Sch.10, para.12.
[16] para.14.
[17] para.15.
[18] para.16.
[19] para.20.
[20] These were revised in April 2008.

Statutory requirements

The Act lays down detailed requirements for individual auditors and firms. The **21–003** fundamental provision is to the effect that an individual or firm is eligible[21] for appointment as a statutory auditor if the individual or firm is a member of a recognised supervisory body and is eligible for appointment under the rules of that body.[22] A person may not be a statutory auditor on the grounds of lack of independence as specified in the Act.[23]

The Secretary of State is empowered to make regulations requiring the keeping of a register of those persons eligible for appointment as a statutory auditor[24] and he has done so.[25] The effect of these regulations is that the Professional Oversight Board (POB)[26] requires the keeping of a register[27] by the by RSPs and has issued its own regulations with respect to the keeping of the register.[28]

Professional qualifications

The Act requires that auditors should hold an appropriate qualification,[29] namely **21–004** a recognised professional qualification obtained in the United Kingdom[30] granted by a recognised qualifying body (RQB) approved by the Secretary of State under s.1220 of the Act. The procedure for recognition is dealt with under Sch.11 to the Act. Basically, the qualification must only be open to persons who have attained university entrance level or have a sufficient period of professional experience.[31]

The Secretary of State's powers and penalties for offences

The Secretary of State has powers under the Act with respect to RSBs and RQBs **21–005** to provide for matters to be notified to him[32]; the payment of fees[33]; to call for information[34]; apply for a compliance order in the event of failure by an RSB or RQB to carry out an obligation which they are otherwise subject to[35]; and to delegate his powers to a separate body.[36] Moreover, penalties are specified in the Act for giving false or misleading information[37] and for offences by bodies corporate, partnerships, and unincorporated associations.[38]

---

[21] The grounds for ineligibility are laid down in s.1213.
[22] s.1212(1). For partnerships which are appointed as auditor, see s.1216.
[23] See s.1214 and s.1215.
[24] s.1239.
[25] See the Statutory Auditors and Third Country Auditors Regulations 2007 (SI 2007/3494).
[26] *http://www.frc.org.uk/pob* [accessed June 4, 2010].
[27] As to what has to be entered in the register, see s.1239(2)(3).
[28] See the Statutory Auditors Registration Instrument 2008, POB 02/2008.
[29] s.1219.
[30] s.1219(1)(a).
[31] See Sch.11 Pt 2.
[32] s.1223.
[33] See s.1251.
[34] s.1224.
[35] s.1225.
[36] ss.1252–1253.
[37] s.1250.
[38] See ss.1255–1257.

Ineligibility to act as an auditor

21–006 The Act defines the circumstances in which a person is ineligible for appointment as a statutory auditor on the grounds of lack of independence—namely, if he is an officer or employee of the audited person, or a partner or employee of such a person; or if there is a connection between him or any associate of his and the audited person.[39] Further guidance on these matters is given in APB's Ethical Standards.

Acting as a statutory auditor when ineligible is an offence, and the guilty party is liable to a fine on conviction.[40] However, it is a defence to show that there was no knowledge and no reason to believe that the person concerned was ineligible. When a person becomes ineligible, he should vacate office and give notice in writing to the company that he has resigned.[41]

Where a company audit has been carried out by an ineligible person, the Secretary of State may direct that an eligible person be appointed, either to undertake a second audit or to review the first audit and report whether a second audit is needed.[42] The company must comply within 21 days or face being fined.[43]

APPOINTMENT OF AUDITORS

Private companies

21–007 Private companies are required to appoint an auditor (or auditors) for each financial year of the company, unless the directors reasonably resolve otherwise on the ground that audited accounts are unlikely to be required.[44] For each financial year for which an auditor or auditors is or are to be appointed (other than the company's first financial year), the appointment must be made before the end of the period of 28 days beginning with the end of the time allowed for sending out copies of the company's annual accounts and reports for the previous financial year or, if earlier, the day on which copies of the company's annual accounts and reports for the previous financial year are sent out.[45] An appointment may be made by the board of directors or the members. In the case of the directors, they may appoint an auditor or auditors of the company at any time before the company's first period for appointing auditors following a period during which the company (being exempt from audit) did not have any auditor, at any time before the company's next period for appointing auditors or to fill a casual vacancy in the office of auditor.[46] The members may appoint an auditor or auditors by ordinary resolution during a period for appointing auditors if the company should have appointed an auditor or auditors during a period for appointing

---

[39] See s.1214.
[40] See s.1213.
[41] s.1215.
[42] s.1248.
[43] s.1248(5).
[44] s.485(1).
[45] s.485(2).
[46] s.485(3).

auditors but failed to do so or where the directors had power to appoint but have failed to make an appointment.[47]

Where no auditors are appointed, a company must within a week of the term of such an appointment elapsing give notice to the Secretary of State so that he can fill the vacancy.[48] Failure to give such notice renders the defaulting company and its officers liable to be fined.[49]

An appointment as auditor of a private company is subject to the terms of the appointment, subject to the requirements that they do not take office until any previous auditor or auditors cease to hold office and they cease to hold office at the end of the next period for appointing auditors unless reappointed.[50] If no auditor has been appointed by the end of the next period for appointing auditors, any auditor in office immediately before that time is deemed to be re-appointed at that time, unless he was appointed by the directors or the company's articles require actual re-appointment or the deemed re-appointment is prevented by the members, or the members have resolved that he should not be re-appointed, or the directors have resolved that no auditor or auditors should be appointed for the financial year in question.[51]

Public companies

In the case of public companies, an auditor (or auditors) must be appointed for **21–008** each financial year of the company, unless the directors reasonably resolve otherwise on the ground that audited accounts are unlikely to be required.[52] For each financial year for which an auditor or auditors is or are to be appointed (other than the company's first financial year), the appointment must be made before the end of the accounts meeting of the company at which the company's annual accounts and reports for the previous financial year are laid.[53] The directors may appoint an auditor or auditors of the company at any time before the company's first accounts meeting; following a period during which the company (being exempt from audit) did not have any auditor, at any time before the company's next accounts meeting; to fill a casual vacancy in the office of auditor.[54] The members may appoint an auditor or auditors by ordinary resolution at an accounts meeting; if the company should have appointed an auditor or auditors at an accounts meeting but failed to do so; where the directors had power to appoint but have failed to make an appointment.[55] As is the case also with private companies, the Secretary of State has a default power to appoint persons to any vacancies.[56] Auditors of public companies hold office with the terms of their appointment, subject to the requirement that they do not take office until the previous auditor

---

[47] s.485(4).
[48] s.486(1)(2).
[49] s.486(3)(4).
[50] s.487(1).
[51] s.487(2).
[52] s.489(1).
[53] s.489(2).
[54] s.489(3).
[55] s.489(4).
[56] s.490.

or auditors have ceased to hold office and they cease to hold office at the conclusion of the accounts meeting next following their appointment, unless re-appointed.[57]

Exemption from audit: small companies

21–009 The reporting-to-shareholder function is effectively redundant for two-thirds or more of the companies on the register where the entire share capital is owned by the directors. As the administrative burden on such small companies was significant legislation was introduced in 1994 to exempt about half of all companies from having to have a statutory audit. Instead, only the largest "small" companies had to have their accounts attested, and then frequently by means of a less demanding examination culminating in a compilation report. This remains the case under the 2006 Act. Thus, a company which meets certain conditions is exempt from the requirements relating to the audit of accounts for that year.[58] The conditions are that the company qualifies as a small company in relation to that year,[59] that its turnover in that year is not more than £6.5 million and that its balance sheet total for that year is not more than £3.26 million.[60]

Notwithstanding this provision, the Act provides that the members of a company that would otherwise be entitled to exemption from audit may by notice require it to obtain an audit of its accounts for a financial year.[61] Such a notice must be given by members representing not less in total than 10 per cent in nominal value of the company's issued share capital, or any class of it or, if the company does not have a share capital, not less than 10 per cent in number of the members of the company.[62] The notice may not be given before the financial year to which it relates and must be given not later than one month before the end of that year.[63]

Exemption from audit: dormant companies

21–010 A company which is dormant is one which has no significant accounting transaction during any period.[64] Such a company is exempt from the requirements of this Act relating to the audit of accounts in respect of a financial year if it has been dormant since its formation or it has been dormant since the end of the previous financial year and provided that certain conditions are met.[65] These are that the company as regards its individual accounts for the financial year in question is entitled to prepare accounts in accordance with the small companies regime[66] or

---

[57] s.491(1).
[58] Certain companies are excluded: see ss.478–479.
[59] See the criteria listed in s.382.
[60] s.477(2).
[61] s.476(1).
[62] s.476(2).
[63] s.476(3).
[64] See s.1169(1)(2).
[65] s.480(1).
[66] i.e. in ss.381–384. See para.20–005, above.

would be so entitled but for having been a public company or a member of an ineligible group and is not required to prepare group accounts for that year.[67] Certain companies are excluded from this dormant companies exception.[68] As was the case with small companies, the Act provides that the members of a company that would otherwise be entitled to exemption from audit may by notice require it to obtain an audit of its accounts for a financial year.[69]

THE LEGAL POSITION OF AUDITORS

Whether an "officer"

The auditor is not a person included in the definition of "officer" in the Act for the purposes of offences under it.[70] However, he is an officer of the company for the purpose of a misfeasance summons under s.212 of the Insolvency Act 1986[71] and for the purpose of offences under ss.206–211 and s.218 of that same Act[72] (which are also concerned with offences by officers of companies in liquidation). An auditor is presumably an officer for the purpose of the Theft Act 1968[73] s.19, which is concerned with false statements by an officer of a body corporate, but an auditor appointed ad hoc for a limited purpose.[74]   **21–011**

Investigations

Under s.434(4) of the 1985 Act, an auditor is specifically identified as an agent of the company for the purpose of an investigation into its affairs,[75] and he may be examined on oath by an inspector. Otherwise the auditor is not (in the absence of a special contract) an agent of the company, and his normal certificate as to whether the accounts represent a true and fair view of the company's affairs under s.495 cannot constitute an acknowledgement by an agent for the purposes of the Limitation Act 1980.[76]   **21–012**

Other provisions

An auditor is treated in the same way as an officer by s.532 (voidness of provisions relieving protecting auditors from liability) and s.1157 (relief of officers and auditors).   **21–013**

---

[67] s.480(2).
[68] See s.481.
[69] See s.476(1).
[70] See s.1121(2); s.1173(1).
[71] c.45. See *London and General Bank, Re* [1895] 2 Ch. 166, CA. See also para.23–024, below.
[72] ss.206–211 and 218 of the Insolvency Act 1986 replace ss.624–629 and s.632 of the 1985 Act.
[73] c.60.
[74] *R. v Shacter* [1960] 2 Q.B. 252, CA.
[75] See para.22–059, below.
[76] c.58. See *Transplanters (Holding Co) Ltd, Re* [1958] 1 W.L.R. 822.

VACATION OF OFFICE BY AUDITORS

Removal of auditors

21–014 A company may, by ordinary resolution, remove an auditor from office at any time.[77] An auditor so removed retains his rights to compensation or damages in respect of the termination of his appointment.[78] Special notice of the resolution is required[79] and a copy must be forwarded to the auditor proposed to be removed.[80] The auditor may make representations in writing to the company (not exceeding a reasonable length) and request their notification to members of the company.[81] The company must (unless the representations are received by it too late for it to do so) in any notice of the resolution given to members of the company, state the fact of the representations having been made and send a copy of the representations to every member of the company to whom notice of the meeting is or has been sent.[82] If a copy of any such representations is not sent out as required because received too late or because of the company's default, the auditor may (without prejudice to his right to be heard orally) require that the representations be read out at the meeting.[83] Copies of the representations need not be sent out and the representations need not be read at the meeting if, on the application either of the company or of any other person claiming to be aggrieved, the court is satisfied that the auditor is using the provisions of this section to secure needless publicity for defamatory matter.[84] The court may order the company's costs on the application to be paid in whole or in part by the auditor, notwithstanding that he is not a party to the application.[85]

Notice of the removal of the auditor, following the passing of the resolution, must be given to the Registrar within 14 days.[86] It is an offence not to do so.[87]

Resignation of auditors

21–015 An auditor may resign by depositing notice in writing at a company's registered office,[88] but it must be accompanied by a statement indicating whether or not there are any circumstances leading to such action.[89] The auditor's period of office ends when such notice is deposited, unless it specifies another date.[90] The company must deliver a copy of the notice to the Registrar within 14 days of its

---

[77] s.510(1)(2).
[78] s.510(3).
[79] See s.511.
[80] s.511(2).
[81] s.511(3).
[82] s.511(4).
[83] s.511(5).
[84] s.511(6).
[85] s.511(6).
[86] s.512(1).
[87] s.512(2)(3).
[88] s.516(1).
[89] s.516(2).
[90] s.516(3).

being deposited at the registered office, failing which the company and its defaulting officers are liable to a fine.[91]

When an auditor's resignation letter is accompanied by a statement of circumstances leading to such action, he may deposit a signed requisition calling on the directors to convene a general meeting to receive such a statement and other explanations he may wish to give.[92] He may also request the company to circulate a written explanation of reasonable length concerning the circumstances before such a meeting is convened, or before a meeting at which his term of office would normally have expired.[93] The company must indicate in the notice of the meeting that such a statement has been made and circulate it to members of the company.[94] The directors must convene a meeting within 21 days of the requisition being lodged, and it must be held within 28 days of the date of the notice of the meeting being given.[95] Failure to do so renders every director who did not take reasonable steps to secure compliance liable to a fine.[96] If the statement is not circulated, the auditor may require it to be read out at the meeting.[97] However, application may be made to the court by the company or other aggrieved party, and if such representations are deemed to be needlessly defamatory they need not be circulated or be read out at the meeting. In such circumstances, the court may require the auditor to pay some or all of the costs involved.[98]

Statement by a person ceasing to hold office as auditor

A person who for any reason has ceased to hold office as auditor is required to **21–016** deposit at the company's registered office within specified periods a statement detailing any circumstances connected with his departure which he considers should be brought to members' or creditors' attention.[99] Where the auditor considers there are no such circumstances, the statement should indicate that fact.[100] The statement required by this section must be deposited, in the case of resignation, along with the notice of resignation; in the case of failure to seek reappointment, not less than 14 days before the end of the time allowed for next appointing an auditor; in any other case, not later than the end of the period of 14 days beginning with the date on which he ceases to hold office.[101] It is an offence for the auditor to fail to comply,[102] although it is a defence for the person charged to show that he took all reasonable steps and exercised all due diligence to avoid the commission of the offence.[103]

---

[91] s.517.
[92] s.518(2).
[93] s.518(3).
[94] s.518(4).
[95] s.518(5).
[96] s.518(6)(7).
[97] s.518(8).
[98] s.518(9).
[99] s.519(1). The auditor of a quoted company is required to deposit such a statement: s.519(3).
[100] s.519(2).
[101] s.519(4).
[102] s.519(5)(7).
[103] s.519(6).

For his part, the auditor must send a copy of his statement to the Registrar within 21 days of depositing it with the company, unless he receives notice that the company has applied to the court.[104] In such a case he has a further seven days to send a copy to the Registrar.[105] If the court is satisfied that the auditor is needlessly using his statement for defamatory purposes, it will direct that copies of it should not be circulated and may order the auditor to pay some or all of the costs involved.[106] Moreover, the company will have to circulate another statement indicating the effect of the court's order within 14 days.[107] If, however, the court is not satisfied that the auditor's statement is vexatious, the company must circulate it within 14 days.[108]

Additionally to the Registrar, there is now also a statutory requirement that the auditor should notify the appropriate audit authority.[109] In certain circumstances the company must notify the audit authority.[110]

REMUNERATION OF AUDITORS

21–017 The remuneration[111] of the auditor of a company appointed by the directors or by the Secretary of State is fixed by the directors[112] or by the Secretary of State,[113] as the case may be. The remuneration of an auditor appointed by the members of a company must be fixed by the members by ordinary resolution or in such manner as they may by ordinary resolution determine.[114]

The Secretary of State may make provision by regulation for disclosure of the terms of appointment, remuneration etc of the audit appointment[115] and disclosure of the services provided by the auditor or associates and related remuneration.[116]

THE AUDITOR'S REPORT

Report addressed to the members

21–018 The auditors must make a report to the company's members[117] on all annual accounts of the company of which copies are, during his tenure of office, in the

---

[104] s.521(1).

[105] s.521(1)(2).

[106] s.520(4). Whether such a statement is defamatory was considered in *Jarvis Plc v PricewaterhouseCoopers* [2001] B.C.C. 670.

[107] ibid.

[108] s.520(5).

[109] See s.522.

[110] s.523.

[111] Remuneration includes sums paid by the company in respect of the auditor's expenses: s.492(4). It also includes benefits in kind as much as to payments of money: s.492(5).

[112] s.492(2).

[113] s.492(3).

[114] s.492(1).

[115] See s.493.

[116] s.494.

[117] The exact terms would normally be established in formal engagement letters, on the form of which professional guidance is available. Following the decision in *Royal Bank of Scotland Plc v Bannerman Johnstone Maclay* [2005] B.C.C. 235 (overruled in part, [2006] B.C.C. 148), auditors have altered the wording of their reports to make it clear that third parties (such as lending bankers) should not rely on the audit opinion.

case of a private company, to be sent out to members under s.423.[118] In the case of a public company, he must do so for copies to be laid before the company in general meeting under s.437.[119]

Content of the report

The auditor's report must include an introduction identifying the annual accounts **21–019** that are the subject of the audit and the financial reporting framework that has been applied in their preparation and a description of the scope of the audit identifying the auditing standards in accordance with which the audit was conducted.[120] The report must state:

1. whether in the auditors' opinion the annual accounts have been properly prepared in accordance with the relevant financial reporting framework[121];

2. whether a true and fair view is given:

    (a) in the case of an individual balance sheet, of the state of affairs of the company at the end of its financial year;

    (b) in the case of an individual profit and loss account, of the profit or loss of the company for the financial year; and

    (c) in the case of group accounts, of the state of affairs at the end of the financial year, and the profit and loss for the financial year, of the undertakings included in the consolidation as a whole, so far as concerns the members of the company[122];

3. whether the accounts have been prepared in accordance with the requirements of the Act.[123]

The auditor's report must be either unqualified or qualified and must include a reference to any matters to which the auditor wishes to draw attention by way of emphasis without qualifying the report.[124]

The auditors are also required to state in their report whether in their opinion the information given in the directors' report is consistent with that given in the accounts.[125] If the company is a quoted company, the auditor, in his report on the company's annual accounts for the financial year, must report to the company's members on the auditable part of the directors' remuneration report and state whether in his opinion that part of the directors' remuneration report has been properly prepared in accordance with this Act.[126] Finally, where the company prepares a separate corporate governance statement in respect of a particular

[118] s.495(1)(a).
[119] s.495(1)(b).
[120] s.495(2).
[121] s.495(3)(b).
[122] s.495(3)(a).
[123] s.495(3)(c).
[124] s.495(4).
[125] s.496.
[126] s.497.

financial year, the auditor must state in his report on the company's annual accounts for that year whether in his opinion the information given in the statement in compliance with rules 7.2.5 and 7.2.6 in the Disclosure Rules and Transparency Rules sourcebook issued by the Financial Services Authority is consistent with those accounts.[127]

Signing of the auditors' report

21–020 The auditors' report must state the name of the auditor and be signed and dated by him.[128] If the auditor is a firm, the report must be signed by the senior statutory auditor[129] in his own name, for and on behalf of the auditor.[130] Similarly, all published copies of the report must state the names of the auditors[131] and the penalty for default of these provisions is a fine.[132]

The duties of auditors in relation to the audit report

21–021 In preparing their report the auditors must carry out certain investigations as will enable them to form an opinion as to:

1. whether proper accounting records have been kept by the company and returns adequate for their audit have been received from branches not visited by them;

2. whether the company's individual accounts are in agreement with the accounting records and returns; and

3. in the case of a quoted company, whether the auditable part of the company's directors' remuneration report is in agreement with the accounting records and returns.[133]

If the auditor is of the opinion that adequate accounting records have not been kept, or that returns adequate for their audit have not been received from branches not visited by him or that the company's individual accounts are not in agreement with the accounting records and returns, or, in the case of a quoted company, that the auditable part of its directors' remuneration report is not in agreement with the accounting records and returns, he must state that fact in his report.[134]

If the auditor fails to obtain all the information and explanations which, to the best of his knowledge and belief, are necessary for the purposes of his audit, he must state that fact in his report.[135]

---

[127] s.497A(1). This section was inserted by the Companies Act 2006 (Accounts, Reports and Audit) Regulations 2009 (SI 2009/1581).
[128] s.503(1)(2).
[129] See s.504.
[130] s.503(3).
[131] Although in certain circumstances the names may be omitted. See s.506.
[132] s.505.
[133] s.498(1).
[134] s.498(2).
[135] s.498(3).

If the requirements of regulations requiring disclosure of directors' benefits, **21–022** remuneration, pensions and compensation for loss of office are not complied with[136] in the annual accounts or, in the case of a quoted company, the requirements of regulations as to information forming the auditable part of the directors' remuneration report[137] are not complied with in that report, the auditor must include in his report, so far as he is reasonably able to do so, a statement giving the required particulars.[138] If the directors of the company have prepared accounts in accordance with the small companies regime or have taken advantage of small companies exemption in preparing the directors' report and, in the auditor's opinion they were not entitled to do so, the auditor must state this fact in his report.[139]

Where the company is required to prepare a corporate governance statement in respect of a financial year and no such statement is included in the directors' report the company's auditor, in preparing his report on the company's annual accounts for that year, must ascertain whether a corporate governance statement has been prepared and if it appears to the auditor that no such statement has been prepared, he must state that fact in his report.[140]

The auditors perform their duty to the members by forwarding their report to the secretary. They are not responsible if the report is not put before the members.[141] However, in an Australian case it was held that they must pay due regard to the possibility of fraud and must warn the appropriate level of management promptly and without waiting for the general meeting to report to the shareholders.[142]

Powers of Auditors

Rights to information

The auditor of a company has a right of access at all times to the books and **21–023** accounts and vouchers of the company (in whatever form), and they are entitled to require from the officers and employees of the company and its subsidiaries[143] such information and explanations as he thinks necessary for the performance of his duties as an auditor.[144] The articles cannot preclude the auditors from availing themselves of all the information to which they are entitled as material for their report.[145]

---

[136] i.e. under s.412.
[137] Under s.421.
[138] s.498(4).
[139] s.498(5).
[140] See s.498A. This section was inserted by the Companies Act 2006 (Accounts, Reports and Audit) Regulations 2009 (SI 2009/1581).
[141] *Allen, Craig & Co (London) Ltd, Re* [1934] Ch. 483.
[142] *Pacific Acceptance Corporation Ltd v Forsyth* (1970) 92 W.N. (N.S.W) 29.
[143] See s.499(2). A statement made by one of these persons cannot be used against them in criminal proceedings, except for an offence under s.501 (s. 499(3)). However, none of these persons is required to breach legal professional privilege in disclosing information (s. 499(4)).
[144] s.499(1).
[145] *Newton v Birmingham Small Arms Co Ltd* [1906] 2 Ch. 378.

A person commits an offence who knowingly or recklessly makes to an auditor of a company a statement (oral or written) that conveys or purports to convey any information or explanations which the auditor requires under s.499, and is misleading, false or deceptive in a material particular.[146] Such a person is liable, on conviction on indictment, to imprisonment for up to two years or a fine or both. On summary conviction such a person may be imprisoned for up to twelve months or to a fine or both.[147]

Rights to information from overseas subsidiaries

21–024 A UK parent company with overseas subsidiaries may be required by the auditor of the parent company to obtain from a range of persons[148] such information or explanations as he may reasonably require for the purposes of his duties as auditor.[149] If so required, the parent company must take all reasonable steps to obtain the information or explanations from the person concerned.[150]

Rights in relation to resolutions and meetings

21–025 Auditors have the right to attend any general meeting of the company and to receive the same notices of general meetings as the members, and to be heard at any general meeting on any part of the business which concerns them as auditors.[151] Where the auditor is a firm, the right of attendance and to be heard is exercisable by an individual authorised by the firm in writing to act as its representative at the meeting.[152] In relation to a written resolution of a private company, the auditor is entitled to receive the same relevant communications relating to the resolution[153] as the members.[154]

Quoted companies: rights of members

21–026 In a series of new provisions, members of quoted companies[155] may require the company to publish on a website[156] a statement setting any matter relating to the audit of the company's accounts (including the auditor's report and the conduct of the audit) that are to be laid before the next accounts meeting or any circumstances connected with an auditor of the company ceasing to hold office since the previous accounts meeting, that the members propose to raise at the next accounts

---

[146] s.501(1).
[147] s.501(2).
[148] Listed in s.500(2).
[149] s.500(1). A statement made by one of these persons cannot be used against them in criminal proceedings, except for an offence under s.501 (s.500(4)). However, none of these persons is required to breach legal professional privilege in disclosing information (s.500(5)).
[150] s.500(3).
[151] s.502(2).
[152] s.502(3).
[153] See para.19–027, above.
[154] s.502(1).
[155] As to this, see s.531.
[156] See s.528 as to website availability.

meeting of the company.[157] A company is required to do so once it has received requests to that effect from members representing at least 5 per cent of the total voting rights of all the members who have a relevant right to vote[158] or at least 100 members who have a relevant right to vote[159] and hold shares in the company on which there has been paid up an average sum, per member, of at least £100.[160] A request may be sent to the company in hard copy or electronic form and must identify the statement to which it relates, be authenticated by the person or persons making it and be received by the company at least one week before the meeting to which it relates.[161] A quoted company is not required to place on a website a statement under this section if, on an application by the company or another person who claims to be aggrieved, the court is satisfied that the rights conferred by this section are being abused.[162] The court may order the members requesting website publication to pay the whole or part of the company's costs on such an application, even if they are not parties to the application.[163]

DUTIES OF AUDITORS

General duties

The duties of auditors depend on the terms of the articles[164] as well as the provisions of the Act. Thus, they must acquaint themselves with their duties under the Act and the articles.[165] They must carry out their duties with respect to the auditors' report as outlined above. They must also ascertain and state the true financial position of the company by an examination of the books. This examination must be not merely to ascertain what the books show, but also to ascertain that the books show the true financial position.[166] This is exemplified in the following judgments: **21–027**

"It was in my opinion the duty of the auditor not to confine himself merely to the task of verifying the arithmetical accuracy of the balance-sheet, but to inquire into its substantial accuracy, and to ascertain that it contained the particulars specified in the articles of association (and consequently a proper income and expenditure account), and was properly drawn up, so as to contain a true and correct representation of the state of the company's affairs".[167]

"An auditor is not to be written off as a professional 'adder-upper and subtractor'. His vital task is to take care to see that errors are not made, be they

[157] s.527(1).
[158] Excluding any voting rights attached to any shares in the company held as treasury shares: s.527(2)(a).
[159] See s.527(3).
[160] s.527(2).
[161] s.527(4).
[162] s.527(5).
[163] s.527(6).
[164] Although there is nothing on auditors in either the Model Articles for Private Companies Limited by Shares or the Model Articles for Public Companies.
[165] *Republic of Bolivia Exploration Syndicate Ltd, Re* [1914] 1 Ch. 139.
[166] *London and General Bank, Re (No.2)* [1895] 2 Ch. 673, CA, at 682, per Lindley L.J.
[167] *Leeds Estate, Building & Investment Co v Shepherd* (1887) 36 Ch.D. 787 at 802, per Stirling J.

errors of computation, or errors of omission or commission, or downright untruths. To perform this task properly he must come to it with an inquiring mind—not suspicious of dishonesty, I agree—but suspecting that someone may have made a mistake somewhere and that a check must be made to ensure that there has been none".[168]

The statutory duty of an auditor (e.g. to state whether in his opinion a true and fair view is given by the company's annual accounts[169]) is a personal one, and if he adopts the opinion of the company's accountant, and he is sued by the company for wrongly stating that a true and fair view is given, it has been held in Australia that he has no cause of action against the accountant.[170]

Skill and care

21–028 Auditors must act honestly, and with reasonable care and skill, as the following observations make clear:

"It is the duty of an auditor to bring to bear on the work he has to perform that skill, care, and caution which a reasonably competent, careful, and cautious auditor would use. What is reasonable skill, care, and caution must depend on the particular circumstances of each case. An auditor is not bound to be a detective, or . . . to approach his work with suspicion or with a foregone conclusion that there is something wrong. He is a watch-dog, but not a blood-hound. He is justified in believing tried servants of the company in whom confidence is placed by the company. He is entitled to assume that they are honest, and to rely upon their representations, provided he takes reasonable care. If there is anything calculated to excite suspicion he should probe it to the bottom; but in the absence of anything of that kind he is only bound to be reasonably cautious and careful".[171]

"An auditor, however, is not bound to do more than exercise reasonable care and skill in making inquiries and investigations. He is not an insurer; he does not guarantee that the books do correctly show the true position of the company's affairs; he does not even guarantee that his balance-sheet is accurate according to the books of the company. If he did, he would be responsible for error on his part, even if he were himself deceived without any want of reasonable care on his part, say, by the fraudulent concealment of a book from him. His obligation is not so onerous as this. Such I take to be the duty of the auditor: he must be honest—i.e., he must not certify what he does not believe to be true, and he must take reasonable care and skill before he believes that what he certifies is true. What is reasonable care in any particular case must depend upon the

---

[168] *Fomento (Sterling Area) Ltd v Selsdon Fountain Pen Co* [1958] 1 W.L.R. 45, HL, at 61, per Lord Denning.

[169] See s.495(3).

[170] *Dominion Freeholders Ltd v Aird* [1966] 2 N.S.W.R. 293, CA, distinguishing *Hedley Byrne & Co Ltd v Heller & Partners Ltd* [1964] A.C. 465.

[171] *Kingston Cotton Mill Co, Re (No.2)* [1896] 2 Ch. 279, CA, at 288–289, per Lopes L.J.

circumstances of that case. Where there is nothing to excite suspicion very little inquiry will be reasonably sufficient, and in practice I believe business men select a few cases at haphazard, see that they are right, and assume that others like them are correct also. Where suspicion is aroused more care is obviously necessary; but, still, an auditor is not bound to exercise more than reasonable care and skill, even in a case of suspicion, and he is perfectly justified in acting on the opinion of an expert where special knowledge is required".[172]

If directors do not allow auditors time to conduct such investigations as are necessary in order to make the statements required to be contained in their report, the auditors must either refuse to make a report or make an appropriately qualified report. They are not justified in making a report containing a statement the truth of which they have not had an opportunity of ascertaining.[173]

Grounds for suspicion

It may be that entries in or omissions from the books ought to make the auditors **21–029** suspicious. In such a case they must make full investigations into the suspicious circumstances, but they are not liable for "not tracking out ingenious and carefully laid schemes of fraud when there is nothing to arouse their suspicion".[174]

Unauthorised borrowing

If payments are made or sums borrowed by the company, the auditors should see **21–030** that they are authorised and made in accordance with the articles and the Act.[175]

Existence of securities

Auditors must satisfy themselves that securities owned by a company in fact exist **21–031** and are in safe custody. This duty is discharged by their making a personal inspection of the securities in question. If, however, the securities are in the possession of a person who in the ordinary course of his business keeps securities for his customers (e.g. a banker) and that person is regarded as trustworthy, the auditors may safely accept his certificate that the securities are in his custody.[176]

Existence of cash balances

Auditors must check the cash in hand and also the balance at the bank, by inspecting **21–032** the pass book (or bank statement) or obtaining a certificate from the bank.[177]

---

[172] *London and General Bank, Re (No.2)* [1895] 2 Ch. 673, CA, at 683, per Lindley L.J.
[173] *Thomas Gerrard & Son Ltd, Re* [1968] Ch. 455 at 477, per Pennycuick J.
[174] *Kingston Cotton Mill Co, Re (No.2)* [1896] 2 Ch. 279, CA, at 290, per Lopes L.J. However, in *City Equitable Fire Insurance Co Ltd, Re* [1925] Ch. 407, CA, it was held that there was no negligence on the part of the auditors because, although the transactions in question, when isolated, should have led them to conclude that fraud had taken place, they only formed one item in a large audit.
[175] *Thomas v The Corporation of Devonport* [1900] 1 Q.B. 16, CA; *Republic of Bolivia Exploration Syndicate Ltd, Re* [1914] 1 Ch. 139 at 171, per Astbury J.
[176] *City Equitable Fire Insurance Co Ltd, Re* [1925] Ch. 407.
[177] *Fox & Son v Morrish, Grant & Co* (1918) 35 T.L.R. 126.

Stocks and work-in-progress

21–033 Auditors are under no duty to take stock,[178] but this is part of the wider question of the auditors' duty as to the value of the assets. However, the auditor must consider the effect of a reservation of title clause, where it exists, particularly where the stocks are unmixed goods. Auditors are entitled to take the values of stocks and work-in-progress from the manager or other responsible official of the company, unless they have any reason to suppose them inaccurate.[179]

Fixed assets

21–034 If the auditors have formed an opinion that the assets are overvalued, they are bound to report it to the shareholders.[180]

Policies of the company

21–035 Auditors are not concerned with the policy of the company or whether the company is well or ill managed.[181] As explained by Laddie J. in *Bank of Credit and Commerce International (Overseas) Ltd v Price Waterhouse*:

> "The skill [the auditor] offers and for which he is paid is the skill in looking at the company's accounts and the underlying information on which they are or should be based and telling the shareholders whether the accounts give a true and fair view of the company's financial position. He is not in possession of facts nor qualified to express a view as to how the business should be run, in the sense of what investments to make, what business to undertake, what prices to charge, what lines of credit to extend and so on. Not only does he not normally have the necessary expertise but those are areas in respect of which his advice is not sought. When the company engages an auditor, it is not seeking his help in steering the management into making better management decisions".[182]

Auditors' liability

Liability generally

21–036 It is clear that most auditors, whether individuals, or professional firms typically have contractual arrangements with their clients. Those clients will have a contractual remedy against the auditor in the event of any breach of contract (and indeed vice versa). However, the auditor also owes a duty of care to the company which can attract damages in the event of breach.

---

[178] *Kingston Cotton Mill Co, Re (No.2)* [1896] Ch. 279, CA.
[179] In *Kingston Cotton Mill Co, Re (No.2)* [1896] Ch. 279, CA, it was held that the auditors were entitled to rely on a certificate; but not in *Thomas Gerrard & Son Ltd, Re* [1968] Ch. 455, where the circumstances were not dissimilar, Pennycuick J. commenting (at 475): "The standards of reasonable care and skill are, upon the expert evidence, more exacting today than those which prevailed in 1896".
[180] *London and General Bank, Re (No.2)* [1895] 2 Ch. 673, CA.
[181] At 682, per Lindley L.J.
[182] [1999] B.C.C. 351 at 369.

A number of cases deal with aspects of this liability. Thus, in *Equitable Life Assurance Society v Ernst & Young*[183] the Court of Appeal had to consider whether the auditors failed to advise Equitable of the need to include provision for liabilities under guaranteed annuity policies in the company's accounts. Equitable also sought damages for loss of sale or loss of the chance of sale of its business and for losses caused by declaring bonuses instead of making provision for guaranteed annuity policies. The Court of Appeal reminded itself that, in a case like this, a court needed to ask itself five questions:

1. Did a legally enforceable duty of care exist?

2. If so, what was the scope of that duty?

3. What was the prospective harm, or kind of harm, from which the person to whom the duty is owed falls to be protected?

4. Had there been a breach of that duty?

5. If so, was the loss complained of caused by that breach, or was it caused by some other event or events unconnected with the breach?[184]

The court found that this was a claim in contract, and like all who rendered professional services for reward, the auditors owed Equitable an implied duty of care in and about the manner in which they performed those services[185] and that they had proved their loss and a breach of the duty by the auditors. The scope of that duty, identified from the letters of engagement and the various documents in which the auditors set out the nature of their services, included preparing a report on the accounts which was free from material error, reporting to Equitable as soon as they found an actual material error, and carrying out risk assessment, paying particular attention to the level of the technical reserves, and giving assurance to Equitable on key risk areas.

Several cases have dealt with aspects of breaches of the auditors, duty of care and skill with share valuations. Thus, in *McKinlay v Nexia Smith & Williamson Audit Ltd*[186] the claimant sought damages against the auditors for losses occasioned by its negligent valuation of the claimant's shareholding in a food distribution company. The court found that, on the facts and having regard to such circumstances that should have been prescient in the mind of a competent auditor, the value of the shares ascribed by the auditors was far below any reasonable sum one might have expected for those shares. The correct value of claimant's interests was £635 per share and the auditors were held liable to make good the deficit between £128 and £635 per share.[187]

---

[183] [2003] EWCA Civ. 1114, [2003] 2 B.C.L.C. 603. See also *Coulthard v Neville Russell* [1998] 1 B.C.L.C. 143; *Sasea Finance Ltd v KPMG* [2000] 1 B.C.L.C. 236.

[184] At [105].

[185] At [108].

[186] [2008] EWHC 1963 (Ch); [2009] 1 B.C.L.C. 43.

[187] See also *Pearce v European Reinsurance Consultants & Run-Off Ltd* [2005] EWHC 1493 (Ch); [2005] 2 B.C.L.C. 366; *Cook v Green* [2009] B.C.C. 204.

The recent case of *Stone & Rolls Ltd v Moore Stephens*[188] has focused attention sharply on the extent to which auditors should be liable for alleged negligence in failing to detect and prevent the dishonest activities of the controlling owner and manager of the company. The company sought damages in the sum of almost US$174 million but the auditors denied negligence. The judge at first instance held[189] that the actions and state of mind of S were to be attributed to the company and that it was artificial to describe the company as the victim of the frauds, but that, since detection of fraud was the very thing the auditors were engaged to undertake, they were not entitled to rely on that fraud as a defence based on the principle of *ex turpi causa non oritur actio*,[190] and he refused the application. The Court of Appeal[191] allowed the auditor's appeal and held that since the company was to be attributed with responsibility for the fraudulent activities against the banks and had relied on that illegality in its claim against the auditors, any failure by the auditors to detect the frauds as "the very thing" they were engaged to undertake could not debar them from relying on the principle of *ex turpi causa non oritur actio*. The House of Lords, by a majority,[192] held that the company was to be imputed with awareness of the fraudulent activities against the banks and was primarily liable for them. Further, that any duty owed by the auditors was to the company as a whole and not to individual shareholders or its creditors; that all whose interests formed the subject of any such duty, namely the company's sole directing mind and will, already knew about and were party to the illegal conduct which formed the basis of the claim; and that, in the circumstances, the auditors could rely on the defence of *ex turpi causa* to debar the company's claim.

Liability to third parties

21–037 Apart from the auditor's contractual duty of care to the company, he owes a duty of care to third persons with whom he is not in contractual or fiduciary relationship if, as a reasonable man, he knows that he is being trusted or that his skill and judgment are being relied on, and he does not make it clear that he accepts no responsibility for information or advice which he gives.[193] For breach of this duty an action for negligence lies if damage results from the negligence.

The scope of this duty was originally defined by Lord Denning in *Candler v Crane, Christmas & Co.*[194] In subsequent cases on professional negligence three

---

[188] [2009] UKHL 39; [2009] 1 A.C. 1391.

[189] [2007] EWHC 1826 (Comm.); [2008] 1 B.C.L.C. 697.

[190] i.e. that no court will lend its aid to a man who founds his cause of action upon an immoral or an illegal act: see *Holman v Johnson* (1775) 1 Cowp. 341 at 343; 98 E.R. 1120 at 1121, per Lord Mansfield. See now especially *Tinsley v Milligan* [1994] 1 A.C. 340.

[191] [2008] EWCA Civ. 644; [2008] 3 W.L.R. 1146.

[192] Lord Philips of Worth Matravers, Lord Walker of Gestingthorpe, Lord Brown of Eaton-under-Heywood; Lord Scott of Foscote and Lord Mance dissenting. See Peter Watts, "Audit contracts and turpitude" (2010) 126 L.Q.R. 14.

[193] *Hedley Byrne & Co Ltd v Heller & Partners Ltd* [1964] A.C. 465, disapproving *Candler v Crane, Christmas & Co* [1951] 2 K.B. 164, CA. See also *Esso Petroleum Co Ltd v Mardon* [1976] Q.B. 801, CA; *Yianni v Edwin Evans & Sons* [1982] Q.B. 438; *Electra Private Equity Partners v KPMG Peat Marwick* [2000] B.C.C. 368, CA.

[194] [1951] 2 K.B. 164, CA, at 180.

principles emerged. Thus in order for a claim by a third party to succeed, the event leading to a loss should be foreseeable; there should be proximity between the two parties (i.e. the third party should not be so remote that his interests would not reasonably have been considered at the time the supposedly negligent statement was made); and the supposedly defective advice had to be given as a normal part of the expert's business.

The question of proximity was left open. Should liability just extend to persons to whom auditors show the accounts and those to whom they knew the company would show them? Or should it also extend to a general class of persons whom the auditors ought reasonably to have foreseen at the time the accounts were prepared might rely on the accounts? In two cases involving takeovers the latter, broader view of proximity was taken[195] and although it was held that the auditors would only be liable if reliance on the accounts caused loss to the other party.

However, this view was rejected in the landmark case of *Caparo Industries Plc* **21–038** *v Dickman*,[196] where the House of Lords preferred the narrow view of proximity as determining liability to third parties.

C brought an action against its auditors, alleging that they were negligent in carrying out their audit and making their report which they were required to do under the 1985 Act. C alleged that it had begun purchasing shares in F some days before the accounts were published to shareholders. In reliance on the accounts they made further purchases of shares so as to takeover F. C argued that the auditors owed both shareholders and potential investors a duty of care in their certification of the accounts; they should have known that F's profits were not as high as projected and that its share price had fallen significantly, making it susceptible to a takeover bid. Reliance on the accuracy of the accounts would be crucial for any potential bidder, such as C. It was held that liability for economic loss due to negligent misstatement would be confined to those cases where the statement or advice was given to a known recipient for a specific purpose of which the maker was aware and upon which the recipient had relied to his detriment. There was no reason in principle or policy why auditors should be deemed to have a special relationship with non-shareholders contemplating investment in the company in reliance on the published accounts, even when the affairs of the company were known to be such as to render it susceptible to an attempted takeover.[197]

"The situation is entirely different where a statement is put into more or less general circulation and may foreseeably be relied on by strangers to the maker of the statement for any one of a variety of different purposes which the maker of the statement has no specific reason to anticipate. To hold the maker of the statement to be under a duty of care in respect of the accuracy of the statement to all and sundry for any purpose for which they may choose to rely on it is not only to subject him, in the classic words of Cardozo C.J. to 'liability in an

---

[195] *JEB Fasteners Ltd v Marks, Bloom, & Co* [1981] 3 All E.R. 289, affirmed [1983] 1 All E.R. 583, CA; *Twomax Ltd v Dickson, McFarlane and Robinson* [1982] S.C. 113.
[196] [1990] 2 A.C. 605. The case also failed on grounds of foreseeability.
[197] *Caparo Industries Plc v Dickman* [1990] 2 A.C. 605.

indeterminate amount for an indeterminate time to an indeterminate class' . . . it is also to confer on the world at large a quite unwarranted entitlement to appropriate for their own purposes the benefit of the expert knowledge or professional expertise attributed to the maker of the statement".[198]

Lord Oliver of Aylmerton stated that:

"It is almost always foreseeable that someone, somewhere and in some circumstances, may choose to alter his position upon the faith of the accuracy of a statement or report which comes to his attention and it is always foreseeable that a report—even a confidential report—may come to be communicated to persons other than the original or intended recipient. To apply as a test of liability only the foreseeability of possible damage without some further control would be to create a liability wholly indefinite in area, duration and amount and would open up a limitless vista of uninsurable risk for the professional man".[199]

The *Caparo*[200] view has prevailed in a number of subsequent cases. However, the courts have also narrowed the potential third party liability of auditors by addressing the issue of causation. Thus in another takeover case, *Galoo Ltd v Bright Grahame Murray*,[201] it was held that negligence was not the dominant cause of the plaintiffs' loss and that consequently their case could not succeed.

What constitutes professional skill and judgment where a reporting accountant or auditor is potentially liable is an interesting point. For instance, it is quite possible that over time as a result of inflation, the conventional historical cost accounts of many companies might show an upward trend in profits, whereas under current cost accounting principles the trend might instead be downwards, which arguably could give a misleading impression to an interested party. However, it would seem likely that adherence to generally accepted principles, as codified by the accountancy profession, would provide a reasonable defence in such circumstances—though in view of the jury's attitude in the *Royal Mail* case in relation to a prospectus, where accounting principles acceptable at that time were properly followed, it is not clear that this would be adequate defence in a criminal prosecution.[202]

More generally, legislation enacted in 1999 has enabled large firms of auditors to become limited liability partnerships (LLPs).[203] The effect has been to reduce drastically the number of negligence lawsuits filed against the Big Five (now the Big Four) multinational accounting firms, widely perceived as having deep pockets.

---

[198] [1990] 2 A.C. 605 at 621.
[199] [1990] 2 A.C. 605 at 643.
[200] [1990] 2 A.C. 605. See also *Rushmer v Mervyn Smith* [2009] EWHC 94 (QB); [2009] Lloyd's Rep. P.N. 41.
[201] [1994] 1 W.L.R. 1360, CA.
[202] *R. v Lord Kylsant* [1932] 1 K.B. 442, CA. Potential criminal liability for auditors arises under ss.17–20 of the Theft Act 1968, c.60.
[203] Above, para.2–006.

Limitation of liability of auditors

Voidness of provisions

The Act provides generally that any provision[204] is void[205] which exempts an   **21–039**
auditor of a company from any liability that would otherwise attach to him in
connection with any negligence, default, breach of duty or breach of trust in relation to the company occurring in the course of the audit of accounts or by which
a company directly or indirectly provides an indemnity (to any extent) for an
auditor of the company, or of an associated company, against any liability
attaching to him in connection with any negligence, default, breach of duty or
breach of trust in relation to the company of which he is auditor occurring in the
course of the audit of accounts.[206]

Exceptions

The Act then goes on to provide a number of exceptions to this provision. Thus, a   **21–040**
company can indemnify an auditor against any liability incurred by him in
defending proceedings (whether civil or criminal) in which judgment is given in his
favour or he is acquitted or in connection with an application under s.1157 in which
relief is granted to him by the court.[207]

The Act also provides that a company can enter into a so-called "liability limitation agreement" with its auditors. This is an agreement that purports to limit the
amount of a liability owed to a company by its auditor in respect of any negligence, default, breach of duty or breach of trust, occurring in the course of the
audit of accounts, of which the auditor may be guilty in relation to the
company.[208] Such an agreement must not apply in respect of acts or omissions
occurring in the course of the audit of accounts for more than one financial year
and must specify the financial year in relation to which it applies.[209] Subject to
that, it is immaterial how a liability limitation agreement is framed. In particular,
the limit on the amount of the auditor's liability need not be a sum of money, or
a formula, specified in the agreement.[210] The Secretary of State may by regulation require liability limitation agreements to contain specified provisions or
provisions of a specified description.[211] He may also by regulation prohibit
liability limitation agreements from containing specified provisions or provisions
of a specified description.[212] His power to regulate may be exercised with a view
to preventing adverse effects on competition.[213]

---

[204] Whether contained in a company's articles or in any contract with the company or otherwise:
   s.532(3).
[205] s.532(2).
[206] s.532(1).
[207] s.533.
[208] s.534(1).
[209] s.535(1).
[210] s.535(4).
[211] s.535(2)(a).
[212] s.535(2)(b).
[213] s.535(3).

A liability limitation agreement between a private company and its auditor may be (a) authorised by the company passing a resolution, before it enters into the agreement, waiving the need for approval, (b) by the company passing a resolution, before it enters into the agreement, approving the agreement's principal terms,[214] or (c) by the company passing a resolution, after it enters into the agreement, approving the agreement.[215]

21–041   A liability limitation agreement between a public company and its auditor may be authorised (a) by the company passing a resolution in general meeting, before it enters into the agreement, approving the agreement's principal terms,[216] or (b) by the company passing a resolution in general meeting, after it enters into the agreement, approving the agreement.[217]

Authorisation may be withdrawn by the company passing an ordinary resolution to that effect at any time before the company enters into the agreement or if the company has already entered into the agreement, before the beginning of the financial year to which the agreement relates.[218]

Though the possibility of such limitation agreements is now clearly supported, such agreements may not limit the auditor's liability to less than such amount as is fair and reasonable in all the circumstances of the case having regard to the auditor's responsibilities, the nature and purpose of the auditor's contractual obligations to the company and the professional standards expected of him.[219] A liability limitation agreement that purports to limit the auditor's liability to less than this will have effect as if it limited his liability to that amount.[220] In determining what is fair and reasonable in all the circumstances of the case no account is to be taken of matters arising after the loss or damage in question has been incurred or matters (whenever arising) affecting the possibility of recovering compensation from other persons liable in respect of the same loss or damage.[221]

A company which has entered into a liability limitation agreement must make such disclosure in connection with the agreement as the Secretary of State may require by regulations.[222] The regulations may provide that any disclosure required by the regulations is required to be made in a note to the company's annual accounts (in the case of its individual accounts), or in such manner as is specified in the regulations (in the case of group accounts), or in the directors' report.[223]

---

[214] i.e. these are terms specifying, or relevant to the determination of the kind (or kinds) of acts or omissions covered, the financial year to which the agreement relates, or the limit to which the auditor's liability is subject. See s.536(4).

[215] s.536(2).

[216] See s.536(4).

[217] s.536(3).

[218] s.536(5).

[219] s.537(1).

[220] s.537(2).

[221] s.537(3).

[222] s.538(1). See now the Companies (Disclosure of Auditor Remuneration and Liability Limitation Agreements) Regulations 2008 (SI 2008/489).

[223] s.538(2).

Chapter 22

MAJORITY RULE AND MINORITY PROTECTION

THE PRINCIPLE OF MAJORITY RULE

Introduction

The members of a company can express their wishes at general meetings by **22–001** voting for or against the resolutions proposed.[1] As such, the will of the majority of the members usually prevails and if the appropriate majority is obtained a resolution binds all the members, including those who voted against it.[2] As we have seen, sometimes the majority is a simple majority, the paradigm case being an ordinary resolution which is passed by a simple majority of the members.[3] A special resolution, on the other hand, is a resolution passed by 75 per cent of the members.[4] This can be said to be the first example of what is called "majority rule". Further, it should be remembered that, subject to a few restrictions,[5] the articles of a company, which constitute a contract binding the company and the members, can be altered by special resolution.[6]

Another example of majority rule, as we shall see, is the rule in *Foss v Harbottle*,[7] by which, subject to certain exceptions, if a wrong to a company is alleged, or if there is an alleged irregularity in its internal management which is capable of confirmation by a simple majority of the members, the court will not interfere at the suit of a minority of the members.

Exercising majority control

It has often been stated that although the directors of a company owe fiduciary **22–002** duties[8] to the company, as such, shareholders do not: "When voting, a shareholder may consult his own interests".[9] Until recently it has thus been accepted that a share is a piece of property which is to be enjoyed and exercised for the owner's

---

[1] See above, Ch.19.
[2] See, e.g., *Attorney General v Davy* (1741) 2 Atk. 212; 26 E.R. 531.
[3] s.282. See para.19–025 above.
[4] s.283. See para.19–026, above.
[5] Articles containing entrenched provisions can only be altered unanimously: see s.22(3) and para.4–007, above.
[6] Above, para.4–005.
[7] (1843) 2 Hare 461; 67 E.R. 189.
[8] See now s.171, para.17–001, above.
[9] *Estmanco (Kilner House) Ltd v GLC* [1982] 1 W.L.R. 2 at 11, per Megarry V.C.

personal advantage.[10] Thus a shareholder may bind himself by contract to vote in a particular way:

"When a director votes as a director for or against any particular resolution in a directors' meeting he is voting as a person under a fiduciary duty to the company for the proposition that the company should take a certain course of action. When a shareholder is voting for or against a particular resolution he is voting as a person owing no fiduciary duty to the company and who is exercising his own right of property, to vote as he thinks fit. The fact that the result of the voting at the meeting (or at a subsequent poll) will bind the company cannot affect the position that, in voting, he is voting simply in exercise of his own property rights . . . a director is an agent, who casts his vote to decide in what manner his principal shall act through the collective agency of the board of directors; a shareholder who casts his vote in general meeting is not casting it as an agent of the company in any shape or form. His act therefore, in voting as he pleases, cannot in any way be regarded as an act of the company".[11]

In *Greenwell v Porter*,[12] where executors and trustees of a will who held shares agreed to sell some to G, who stipulated that he should nominate X as a director and that the executors should, when X retired by rotation, vote for his re-election, it was held that the executors were bound by the agreement. It may be mentioned that there was a voting agreement in *Greenhalgh v Mallard*[13] but it was held that the shareholders who agreed to vote in a certain way were under no obligation to retain their shares and there was no continuing obligation running with the shares.

This right to vote has, however, always been subject to the doctrine of fraud on the minority so that the majority cannot waive a breach of a director's fiduciary duty by approving a misappropriation by him of the company's property which would be a fraud on the minority. That is what the majority tried to do in *Cook v Deeks*.[14] Also, members cannot, by resolution in general meeting, expropriate the company's property.

In *Menier v Hooper's Telegraph Works*,[15] the shareholders in E Co, which was formed with the object of constructing a submarine telegraph, were H Co with 3,000 shares, M with 2,000 and 13 other persons with 325 between them. H Co was to make and lay cables for E Co. The directors of E Co, who were nominees of H Co, and H Co decided not to pursue an action in which E Co was claiming a concession to construct the telegraph, procured the passing of a resolution in general meeting to put E Co into voluntary winding up and concealed the fact that they had agreed to end the agreement between E Co and H Co so that H Co could sell the cable to a third company. M brought an action on behalf of himself and

---

[10] See, e.g. *North West Transportation Co v Beatty* (1887) L.R. 12 App. Cas. 589, PC; *Northern Counties Securities Ltd v Jackson & Steeple Ltd* [1974] 1 W.L.R. 1133 at 1145.

[11] *Northern Countries Securities Ltd v Jackson and Steeple Ltd* [1974] 1 W.L.R. 1133 at 1144, per Walton J.

[12] [1902] 1 Ch. 530. See also *Puddephat v Leith* [1916] 1 Ch. 200.

[13] [1943] 2 All E.R. 234, CA.

[14] [1916] 1 A.C. 554.

[15] (1874) L.R. 9 Ch. App. 350.

the other shareholders, except those who were defendants, in which he joined E Co as a defendant. He claimed, inter alia, a declaration that H Co was a trustee of the resulting profit for M and the other shareholders in E Co. It was held that M succeeded. The majority shareholder had obtained certain advantages by dealing with something which was the property of the whole company.

Controlling majority shareholders of a company do owe a duty to the company, i.e. the corporators as a body, to act bona fide for the benefit of the company as a whole and not to commit a fraud on the minority. It has been held in *Clemens v Clemens Bros Ltd*,[16] however, that the controlling members may in fact be subject to more stringent controls than the accepted doctrine of a fraud on the minority, although not being subject to the full fiduciary duties of a director. Thus, the majority do not have unrestricted voting rights if it is "unjust" in the particular circumstances.

In *Clemens v Clemens Bros Ltd*,[17] the defendant owned 55 per cent of the issued shares of a family company. She was one of five directors and proposed to give the other directors shares and to set up a trust for long-service employees. The plaintiff, who was the defendant's niece, held 40 per cent of the shares and was not a director. The defendant proposed resolutions to increase the capital so that the plaintiff's shares would fall below 25 per cent of the total and her right to veto special resolutions would be lost. It was also clear that she would never now obtain control of the company. It was held that the defendant was not entitled to exercise her majority votes as an ordinary shareholder in any way she pleased. That right was subject to equitable considerations which could make it unjust to exercise them in a particular way. In this case such considerations applied and the resolutions would be set aside.

In *Estmanco (Kilner House) Ltd v Greater London Council*[18] Megarry V.C., **22–003** however, accepted the general proposition that the shareholders do not owe any fiduciary duties but affirmed that in altering the articles they are subject to the doctrine of fraud on the minority, i.e. they must act in what they believe to be in the best interests of the company as a whole. In that case the majority shareholder wished to deprive the company of a right of action under a contract and proposed, and carried, a resolution to that effect. A minority shareholder sought to bring an action on behalf of the company to prevent this. Megarry V.C. considered the situation thus[19]:

> "Plainly there must be some limit to the power of the majority to pass resolutions which they believe to be in the best interests of the company and yet remain immune from interference by the courts. It may be in the best interests of the company to deprive the minority of some of their rights or some of their property, yet I do not think that this gives the majority an unrestricted right to do this, however unjust it may be, and however much it may harm shareholders whose rights as a class differ from those of the majority."

[16] [1976] 2 All E.R. 268.
[17] [1976] 2 All E.R. 268.
[18] [1982] 1 All E.R. 437.
[19] At pp.11–12.

However, in *Re Swindon Town Football Club Ltd*,[20] Harman J. said that the general rule that shareholders are entitled to vote in their own interest remains the law and is the correct proposition, even though it has not been followed on every modern occasion, notably in *Clemens v Clemens Bros Ltd*.[21] The judge also accepted the proposition that "the company is entitled to consider lawful resolutions, however silly, and, if thought fit, to pass them, and it is not for the court to tell the company that it should not be silly".[22]

On the other hand, the courts do retain an inherent power to grant an injunction to prevent a shareholder from voting with his shares if there would otherwise be substantial injury to the company, or to protect secured creditors from destruction of the secured assets.[23]

MINORITY PROTECTION

Introduction

22–004 Both under the general law and under the Companies and other Acts there is now quite considerable scope for protection of minority shareholders. Taking the general law first, the majority of the members must not commit a fraud on the minority but must act bona fide for the benefit of the company as a whole.[24] Also at common law, there were hitherto a number of exceptions to the rule in *Foss v Harbottle*,[25] in which case an individual member could bring what was known as a derivative action on behalf of the company.[26] The strictures for obtaining such actions at common law have now been much ameliorated by the new statutory derivative action in the Act.[27] In addition there is s.122(1)(g) of the Insolvency Act 1986[28] whereby a member can petition the court to wind up the company on the ground that it is just and equitable that the company be wound up. Under s.994[29] of the Companies Act[30] a member can petition the court for other relief where the company's affairs are being conducted in an unfairly prejudicial manner to some or all of the members, including himself. Apart from these provisions, other minority sections enable a number of shareholders to challenge the majority on specific issues. Thus, under s.633(2), where class rights are varied in pursuance of a clause in the articles, dissentient holders of 15 per cent of the issued shares of the class can apply for cancellation of the variation.[31] Further, under s.431(2) and s.442(3) of the 1985 Act,[32] 200 members or the holders of one-tenth of the issued shares can apply for an investigation of the company's affairs or of the ownership of the company.

---

[20] [1990] B.C.L.C. 467.
[21] [1976] 2 All E.R. 268.
[22] [1990] B.C.L.C. 467 at 469.
[23] *Standard Chartered Bank v Walker* [1992] B.C.L.C. 603.
[24] See now s.172 of the 2006 Act.
[25] (1843) 2 Hare 461; 67 E.R. 189.
[26] See para.22–007, below.
[27] i.e. in Pt 11. See below, para.22–011.
[28] Below, para.22–021.
[29] Below, para.22–026.
[30] Previously s.459 of the 1985 Act.
[31] Above, para.7–008.
[32] Note that these provisions are still in force. Below, para.22–053.

Understanding the Rule in Foss v Harbottle

The rule in the case of *Foss v Harbottle*[33] has cast a long shadow over UK and **22–005** commonwealth company law. In that case, two members took proceedings on behalf of themselves and all other members except those who were defendants against the directors of a company to compel them to make good losses sustained by the company owing to the directors buying their own land for the company's use and paying themselves a price greater than its value. It was held that as there was nothing to prevent the company from taking the proceedings, if it thought fit to do so, the action failed.[34]

> ". . . [I]t is only necessary to refer to the clauses of the Act to show that, whilst the supreme governing body, the proprietors at a special general meeting assembled, retain the power of exercising the functions conferred upon them by the Act of Incorporation, it cannot be competent to individual corporators to sue in the manner proposed by the Plaintiffs . . .
>
> The majority of the proprietors . . . as power to bind the whole body, and every individual corporator must be taken to have come into the corporation upon the terms of being liable to be so bound . . . The very fact that the governing body of proprietors assembled at the special general meeting may so bind even a reluctant minority is decisive to show that the frame of this suit cannot be sustained whilst that body retains its functions."[35]

The rule is a combination of two principles: the proper plaintiff principle and the majority rule principle. The first principle, "the proper plaintiff principle", is that in an action to redress an alleged wrong to a company on the part of anyone, whether director, member or outsider, or to recover money or damages alleged to be due to it, is prima facie the company and, where the alleged wrong is any irregularity which might be made binding on the company by a simple majority of members, no individual member can bring an action in respect of it.[36] In other words, the company is normally the proper plaintiff in an action to recover loss or to enforce a duty owed to the company by directors or controlling members. In such a case, the claim is brought by the company with recovery for the company. The process is for the collective benefit of the shareholders and, where there is any issue as to the solvency of the company, the creditors.

The second principle, the "majority rule principle", is that where the alleged wrong is a transaction which might be made binding on the company by a simple majority of the members, no individual member of the company is allowed to bring a claim in respect of it.[37] Thus, Mellish L.J. has stated that

---

[33] (1843) 2 Hare 461; 67 E.R. 189. In *Smith v Croft (No.2)* [1987] B.C.L.C. 206. Knox J. stated that "it is common ground between the parties, and those familiar with the complications of the rule in *Foss v Harbottle* will not find this a matter of surprise, that difficult questions do arise" (at 208).

[34] *Foss v Harbottle* (1843) 2 Hare 461; 67 E.R. 189 Applied in *Hawkesbury Development Co Ltd v Landmark Finance Pty Ltd* [1969] 2 N.S.W.R. 782.

[35] per Wigram V.C. at 493–494; 67 E.R. 203.

[36] See too *Burland v Earle* [1902] A.C. 82, PC, at 93–94, per Lord Davey.

[37] But see now s.239, discussed at para.23–015, below.

"If the thing complained of is a thing which in substance the majority of the company are entitled to do, or if something has been done irregularly which the majority of the company are entitled to do regularly, or if something has been done illegally which the majority of the company are entitled to do legally, there can be no use in having litigation about it, the ultimate end of which is only that a meeting has to be called, and then ultimately the majority gets its wishes"[38]

In *Pavlides v Jensen*,[39] a minority shareholder sought to bring an action on behalf of himself and to all other shareholders, save three who were directors, against those directors and the company for damages, alleging that the directors had been negligent in selling an asset of the company for less than its market value. Most of the shares in the company were held by another company, the directors of which were also directors of the first company. It was held that, since the sale of the mine was intra vires the company, and there was no allegation of fraud by the directors or appropriation of assets of the company by the majority shareholders in fraud of the minority, the action was not maintainable. It was open to the company, on the resolution of a majority of the shareholders, to sell the mine at a price decided by the company in that manner, and it was open to the company by a vote of the majority to decide that, if the directors by their negligence had sold the mine at an undervalue, proceedings should not be taken by the company against the directors. It seems that it is sometimes admissible to go behind the apparent ownership of shares to discover whether a company is in fact controlled by wrongdoers, e.g. where the shares are held by nominees.

22–006   If such a meeting has been held and the breach of duty condoned not only does this prevent a single shareholder from bringing an action it may, depending on the circumstances, also prevent the liquidator from subsequently doing so. It is for this reason also that the employees of a company to whom the directors now owe a duty[40] may find it impossible to enforce such a right. Only the members have the right to enforce it. Thus, the court will not, for example, interfere with irregularities at meetings at the instance of a shareholder.[41]

In *MacDougall v Gardiner*,[42] the articles empowered the chairman, with the consent of the meeting, to adjourn a meeting, and also provided for taking a poll if demanded by five shareholders. The adjournment was moved, and declared by the chairman to be carried; a poll was then demanded and refused by the chairman. A shareholder suing on behalf of himself and all other shareholders except those who were directors brought an action against the directors and the company for a declaration that the chairman's conduct was illegal and an injunction to restrain the directors from carrying out certain arrangements without the

---

[38] *MacDougall v Gardiner* (1875) 1 Ch.D. 13, CA, at 25. See also *Prudential Assurance Co Ltd v Newman Industries Ltd* [1982] Ch. 204, CA, at 210; *Edwards v Halliwell* [1950] 2 All E.R. 1064, CA, at 1066, per Jenkins L.J.

[39] *Pavlides v Jensen* [1956] Ch. 565.

[40] See now s.172(1)(b).

[41] Nor will the court grant a declaration that the accounts are not in the correct form at the instance of a shareholder: *Devlin v Slough Estates Ltd* [1983] B.C.L.C. 497.

[42] (1875) 1 Ch.D. 13, CA.

shareholders' approval. It was held the action could not be brought by a share-holder; if the chairman was wrong, the company alone could sue.

The rule not only avoids multiplicity of suits; it also recognises that litigation at the suit of a minority of the members is futile if the majority do not wish it.[43] Thus the rule prevents the company being subjected to a long and expensive litigation to no ultimate purpose if an independent majority of the company do not wish to pursue the claim. Mallish L.J. has stated that

"I think it is a matter of considerable importance rightly to determine this question, whether a suit ought to be brought in the name of the company or in the name of one of the shareholders on behalf of the others. It is not at all a technical question, but it may make a very serious difference in the management of the affairs of the company. The difference is this: Looking to the nature of these companies, looking at the way in which their articles are formed, and that they are not all lawyers who attend these meetings, nothing can be more likely than that there should be something more or less irregular done at them—some directors may have been irregularly appointed, some directors as irregularly turned out, or something or other may have been done which ought not to have been done according to the proper construction of the articles. Now, if that gives a right to every member of the company to file a bill to have the question decided, then if there happens to be one cantankerous member, or one member who loves litigation, everything of this kind will be litigated; whereas, if the bill must be filed in the name of the company, then, unless there is a majority who really wish for litigation, the litigation will not go on. Therefore, holding that such suits must be brought in the name of the company does certainly greatly tend to stop litigation".[44]

DERIVATIVE ACTIONS

The common law derivative action—a response to the rule in Foss v Harbottle

At common law the rule in *Foss v Harbottle* was subject to an exception that a **22–007** derivative claim[45] could be brought by a minority shareholder[46] on behalf of the company in order to remedy a wrong that would otherwise go without redress. This action was brought instead of an action in the name of the company. The shareholders as such had no such right and if their own personal rights were being infringed they might bring a representative action.[47]

---

[43] As a result the application of the rule is dealt with as a preliminary issue before any full trial is held: see *Prudential Assurance Co Ltd v Newman Industries (No.2) Ltd* [1982] Ch. 204, CA; *Smith v Croft (No.3)* [1987] B.C.L.C. 355.

[44] *MacDougall v Gardiner* (1875) 1 Ch.D. 13, CA, at 22–25.

[45] This type of action is a "derivative action" because the right to sue derives from the company. See *Wallersteiner v Moir (No.2)* [1975] Q.B. 373, CA, per Lord Denning M.R. at p.390 and Scarman L.J. at p.406.

[46] If the company is in liquidation such an action should be taken over by the liquidator if he is willing to do so. See *Fargo Ltd v Godfroy* [1986] B.C.L.C. 370.

[47] See below, para.22–010.

"The form of the action is always A.B. (a minority shareholder) on behalf of himself and all other shareholders of the company against the wrongdoing directors and the company".[48]

Under the CPR, Part 19.9[49] these minority shareholders would sue on behalf of themselves and all other shareholders except those who are defendants and join the company as defendant.[50]

The nature of the common law derivative action was that it was a "procedural device for enabling the court to do justice to a company controlled by miscreant directors or shareholders".[51] It followed that the court would examine the conduct of whoever intended to start such proceedings—the person must be doing so for the benefit of the company and not for some other purpose; i.e. he or she must be a proper person to bring a derivative action. A particular person might not be a proper person because his or her conduct was tainted in some way which under the rules of equity may bar relief; e.g. he or she might not come with "clean hands" (e.g. having participated in the wrong), or have been guilty of delay,[52] or be motivated by purely personal motives which were not bona fide for the benefit of the company.[53]

In *Nurcombe v Nurcombe*[54] a husband was the majority shareholder and his wife the minority shareholder of a company. The husband had appropriated money belonging to the company for his own use, but the wife had previously brought matrimonial proceedings and had been awarded a sum in respect of that money by the court. It was held that that she was not a proper person to bring a derivative action on behalf of the company since she had, with knowledge of the facts, elected to pursue the matrimonial claim, and it would be inequitable to allow a double claim. A defendant to a derivative action can raise any defence which he could have raised had the action been brought by the shareholder personally. Lawton L.J. stated that

"It is pertinent to remember, however, that a minority shareholder's action in form is nothing more than a procedural device for enabling the court to do justice to a company controlled by miscreant directors or shareholders. Since the procedural device has evolved so that justice can be done for the benefit of the company, whoever comes forward to start the proceedings must be doing so for the benefit of the company and not for some other purpose. It follows that the court has to satisfy itself that the person coming forward is a proper person to do so".[55]

---

[48] per Lord Denning M.R. in *Wallersteiner v Moir (No.2)* [1975] Q.B. 373, CA, at 390.

[49] Formerly under RSC, Ord.15, rr.12 and 12A.

[50] CPR, Pt 19.9(2). As such it is separate and distinct from any personal action being brought by the minority shareholder: *Cooke v Cooke* [1997] 2 B.C.L.C. 28.

[51] *Nurcombe v Nurcombe* [1985] 1 W.L.R. 370, per Lawton L.J. at 376. See also *Wallersteiner v Moir (No.2)* [1975] Q.B. 373, per Lord Denning M.R. at 390.

[52] *Towers v African Tug Co* [1904] 1 Ch. 588. See, however, Jennifer Payne, " 'Clean hands' in derivative actions" (2002) 61 C.L.J. 76.

[53] *Barrett v Duckett* [1995] 1 B.C.L.C. 243, CA.

[54] [1985] 1 W.L.R. 370, CA.

[55] At 376. See also per Browne-Wilkinson J.A. at 377–378.

At common law, there was therefore no right to bring a derivative action and the court had a discretion whether to allow an action to be brought. Thus an action was dismissed where there was another viable remedy[56] and where an independent group of shareholders were opposed to the action.[57] It also followed that if the company, either through its directors or majority shareholders had no right to bring an action then no derivative action would be allowed.[58] A minority shareholder[59] cannot have a larger right to relief than the company itself would have if it were the plaintiff. If therefore there was a valid reason why the company, acting through its directors or majority shareholders, should not sue, it would equally prevent a minority shareholder suing on its behalf.[60] For that reason Hart J. refused to allow a derivative action against a director based on the allegation that he had paid one creditor in preference to another. Such matters were to be resolved by the creditors through the medium of liquidation.[61]

At common law, a derivative action could be brought where the wrong complained of was a fraud by the majority of the members on the minority and the wrongdoers were in control of the company in general meeting, i.e. they controlled the majority of the shares in the company, and they would not permit an action to be brought in the name of the company.[62] If the aggrieved minority could not bring a minority shareholders' action in this case their grievance would never reach the courts. Where an action was brought under this exception the wrongdoers were usually both directors and controlling shareholders. Thus in *Cook v Deeks*[63] a shareholder brought a minority shareholders' action to compel the directors to account to the company for the profits made out of the construction contract which they took in their own names.[64]

Later cases widened the exception to the rule in two ways and, possibly, **22–008** narrowed it in others. In *Daniels v Daniels*[65] the minority shareholders of a company were allowed to bring an action where the directors had authorised the sale of company land to one of them at a price alleged to be well below its market value. The directors objected that since fraud had not been alleged the action should not be allowed. Templeman J. laid down a wider definition of "fraud" for this purpose: "If minority shareholders can sue if there is fraud, I see no reason why they cannot sue where the action of the majority and the directors, though without fraud, confers some benefit on those directors and majority shareholders themselves".[66] However, there is no exception where the allegation is simply that the directors were acting with a collateral purpose with no benefit to themselves.[67]

---

[56] ibid.
[57] *Smith v Croft (No.3)* [1987] B.C.L.C. 355.
[58] See *Watts v Midland Bank Plc* [1986] B.C.L.C. 15 at 20, per Peter Gibson J.
[59] This may include a 50 per cent shareholder: *Barrett v Duckett* [1995] 1 B.C.L.C. 243, CA, but cf. *Halle v Trax BW Ltd* [2000] B.C.C. 1020, which seems to contradict this point.
[60] *Smith v Croft (No.3)* [1987] B.C.L.C. 355.
[61] *Knight v Frost* [1999] 1 B.C.L.C. 364.
[62] For other instances, see the seventeenth edition of this book, pp.346–348.
[63] [1916] 1 A.C. 554.
[64] See also *Menier v Hooper's Telegraph Works* (1874) L.R. 9 Ch. App. 350.
[65] [1978] Ch. 406.
[66] [1978] Ch. 406.
[67] *Downs Wine Bar Ltd, Re* [1990] B.C.L.C. 839.

In *Estmanco (Kilner House) Ltd v Greater London Council*[68] the majority shareholder proposed to alter a contract it had with the company in order to deprive the minority shareholders of certain rights. The majority shareholder then proposed a resolution whereby the company should not sue for breach of contract. When a minority shareholder sought to sue on the company's behalf the majority shareholder argued that since it had acted bona fide for the benefit of the company there was no fraud on the minority to allow such an action. Megarry V.C., refused to accept that test of fraud on the minority as applicable for the purposes of bringing an action. It only related to the alteration of the company's articles. In this case the action of the majority shareholder injured one category of shareholder to the benefit of another. Fraud in this sense is abuse of a power.

The second development concerned the requisite element of "control" by the majority. It has always been accepted that this meant actual voting control. But in *Prudential Assurance Co Ltd v Newman Industries Ltd (No.2)*[69] Vinelott J.[70] was prepared to extend the exception when the alleged fraud was committed by directors who did not exercise actual voting control but who exercised control in practice.[71] It was suggested that control could be established by the votes controlled by the defendants together with those voting with them as a result of apathy or influence. Large public companies, such as *Newman*, are in fact controlled by holders of less than 50 per cent of the votes.

22–009 The question whether a minority shareholder should be allowed to bring a derivative action is a preliminary issue tried before the merits of the case, e.g. alleged fraud, are debated. The CPR[72] requires a minority shareholder to apply for leave to continue the action and for the defendant to be served with the claim form.[73] It has been emphasised that the requirement for permission to continue cannot be dismissed as a mere technicality; the provisions of CPR Pt 19.9 underline the need for the court to retain control over all the stages of a derivative action.[74] Where some other remedy is available, such as a statutory remedy for the winding up of the company on the just and equitable ground,[75] or the unfairly prejudicial remedy,[76] then the court will not sanction the continuation of a derivative claim.[77] The test for derivative proceedings is the view of the hypothetical independent board of directors.[78] But it is not for the court to assert its own view of what it would do if it were the board; on the contrary, it merely has to be satisfied that a reasonable board of directors could take the decision that the minority shareholder applying for permission to proceed would like it to take, and it

---

[68] [1982] 1 W.L.R. 2.
[69] [1981] Ch. 257.
[70] The Court of Appeal in that case did not express any opinion on this point.
[71] There was no such control in *Halle v Trax BW Ltd* [2000] B.C.C. 1020.
[72] Formerly 15, r.12A of the RSC.
[73] Pt 19.9(3).
[74] *Portfolios of Distinction Ltd v Laird* [2004] EWHC 2071 (Ch); [2004] 2 B.C.L.C. 741 at 760, citing *Barrett v Duckett* [1995] 1 B.C.L.C. 243, CA.
[75] i.e. under s.122(1)(g) of the Insolvency Act 1986. See para.22–021, below.
[76] Under s.994 of the Act. See para.22–026, below.
[77] *Mumbray v Lapper* [2005] EWHC 1152 (Ch); [2005] B.C.C. 990.
[78] *Airey v Cordell* [2006] EWHC 2728 (Ch); [2007] B.C.C. 785.

would not be right to shut out the minority shareholder on the basis of the court's assessment of what it would do rather than a test which was easier to apply, which was whether any reasonable board could take that decision.[79]

In relation to the jurisdiction of an English court to entertain a derivative claim brought by shareholders on behalf of a foreign company, it has been held that the court would have such a power and that such a claim could be served out of the jurisdiction on the foreign company.[80] On the facts of the case, however,[81] which involved the bringing of a derivative claim by the minority shareholders of a company incorporated in India, the claimants had not shown that England was the appropriate forum for the claim,[82] and so the court set aside an earlier order by the master permitting such service.

The Legal Aid Act 1988 makes no provision for legal aid in a minority shareholders' action since it is regarded as being the company's action and companies are not entitled to legal aid, unless they are acting purely on behalf of an individual.[83] But it is open to the court in such an action to order the company to indemnify the plaintiff against the costs of the action.[84] The minority shareholder should apply for the sanction of the court soon after issuing his claim form. If granted he will be given such indemnity.[85] It has been held that applications for indemnity should be made inter partes and that the court will apply the same criteria as when deciding whether there is a triable case.[86] Further it has been held that costs should not be awarded unless financially necessary. This contradicts an earlier case,[87] where an indemnity order was granted on the basis of whether an honest, independent and impartial board would have authorised the action and the fact that the minority shareholder was not impecunious was held not be a ground for refusing the indemnity order. No order for an indemnity will be made, however, where neither the petitioner nor the defendant is a minority shareholder and the defendant is not in control of a company.[88] Nor would an indemnity be ordered where there was essentially a quasi-partnership break up.[89] It would be unlawful as being contrary to public policy for a solicitor to accept a retainer for the plaintiff(s) to conduct the action on a contingency fee basis (i.e. he is paid the fee if he wins but not if he loses).[90]

---

[79] *Airey v Cordell* [2006] EWHC 2728 (Ch); [2007] B.C.C. 785.
[80] Pursuant to CPR Pt 19.9(3).
[81] *Konamaneni v Rolls Royce Industrial Power (India) Ltd* [2002] 1 W.L.R. 1269.
[82] In accordance with the principles laid down in the case of *Spiliada Maritime Corp v Cansulex Ltd* [1987] A.C. 460.
[83] *R. v Chester and North Wales Legal Aid Area Office, Ex p. Floods of Queenferry* [1998] 2 B.C.L.C. 436, CA.
[84] CPR Pt. 19.9(7). cf. also *Wishart v Castlecroft Securities Ltd* 2010 S.L.T. 371.
[85] However, it has been held that such is not secured by a lien for unrecovered costs on the company's assets, or assets recovered as a result of the action: *Qayoumi v Oakhouse Property Holdings Plc* [2002] EWHC 2547(Ch); [2003] 1 B.C.L.C. 352.
[86] *Smith v Croft* [1986] 1 W.L.R. 580.
[87] *Jaybird Group Ltd v Greenwood* [1986] B.C.L.C. 319.
[88] *Halle v Trax BW Ltd* [2000] B.C.C. 1020.
[89] *Mumbray v Lapper* [2005] EWHC 1152 (Ch); [2005] B.C.C. 990.
[90] *Wallersteiner v Moir (No.2)* [1975] Q.B. 373.

The common law representative action

22–010 In *Hogg v Cramphorn*[91] the plaintiff was held to be justified in suing in a representative capacity in respect of the alleged wrongful disposition of the company's money by the directors which could be condoned by a resolution in general meeting, so that the action should have been dismissed unless it was not a derivative representative action but an individual rights representative action. A member of a company may enjoy a right alone or in common with other members of the company and the rule in *Foss v Harbottle* has no application where individual members sue, not in right of the company, but in their own right to protect their individual rights as members.[92] In such a case a member can bring an action in his own name and may sue on behalf of himself and other members, and the breach of duty owed to an individual shareholder cannot be ratified by a majority of shareholders. Thus in *Pender v Lushington*[93] a shareholder was able to enforce the article giving him a right to vote at meetings and compel the directors to record his vote. Similarly, actions for damages by shareholders in their own right do not come within the rule. Thus where the defendant owes a duty to the shareholder personally, no restrictions apply.[94]

Circumstances in which an individual member can sue in his own name include actions to prevent:

1. the company from acting illegally or contrary to the memorandum[95];

2. proposed acts where a special majority is required and has not been obtained[96];

3. the company from acting contrary to its articles;

4. asserting a statutory right, e.g. to rectify the register of members under s. 125.

Statutory reform

22–011 In 1997, the English Law Commission recommended reform[97] and that the common law derivative action be replaced by a statutory derivative action. In particular, the Commission proposed vesting a discretion in the court whether to allow a derivative action. This proposal involved a reform of the English Civil Procedure Rules and this was effected in what became r.19.9 of the Civil Procedure Rules (CPR) and required a derivative claimant, after a claim form had been issued, to apply to the court for permission to continue the proceedings. At this point the claimant's standing to bring

---

[91] [1967] Ch. 254.

[92] *Pender v Lushington* (1877) 6 Ch.D. 70 at 80, 81, per Sir George Jessel M.R.

[93] (1877) 6 Ch.D. 70.

[94] *Howard & Witchell Ltd v Woodman Matthews & Co* [1983] B.C.L.C. 117.

[95] *Simpson v Westminster Palace Hotel* (1860) 8 H.L.C. 712, 11 E.R. 608 at 610, per Lord Campbell L.C.; *Russell v Wakefield Waterworks Co* (1875) L.R. 20 Eq. 474 at 481. This would no longer be relevant under the regime of the 2006 Act. See para.3–019.

[96] *Edwards v Halliwell* [1950] 2 All E.R. 1064, CA.

[97] *Shareholder Remedies*, Cm.3769 (1997). See particularly Pt 4 of the Report, available at *http://www.lawcom.gov.uk/docs/cp142.pdf* [accessed June 4, 2010].

the claim could be considered, if contested. The Law Commission's proposal was adopted by the Company Law Review[98] and is now Pt 11 of the Act.[99]

Statutory derivative claims and the common law derivative action

The Act explicitly states that a derivative claim may only be brought under this **22–012** Chapter or in pursuance of an order of the court in proceedings under ss.994 (proceedings for protection of members against unfair prejudice).[100] This implements a recommendation by the Law Commission that the new statutory remedy should be the only procedure for bringing a derivative action, taking on board the suggestion that more orderly development of the law would result from one point of access to a derivative action and would allow for a body of experience and precedent to be built up to guide shareholders.[101]

However, the statutory provision is clearly intended only to cover "single" derivative claims, rather than so-called "multiple" derivative actions which arise when a shareholder in a parent company brings a derivative action on behalf of a subsidiary or associated company within a group of companies. The Law Commission in its Report referred to, but did not recommend them.[102] The Company Law Review recommended that multiple derivative actions should be brought within the statutory scheme[103] but this was not implemented and so the Act does not therefore expressly refer to multiple derivative actions.[104] The Hong Kong legislation,[105] which also preserves the common law,[106] came under consideration by the Court of Final Appeal in *Waddington Ltd v Chan Chun*.[107]

In that case W Ltd was a minority shareholder in P Ltd. The claims arose because of alleged wrongdoing by C, the Chairman and Chief Executive of P Ltd, and also the director of a number of subsidiaries and sub-subsidiaries of the company. The alleged wrongs were alleged to be against the sub-subsidiaries of P Ltd. W Ltd suffered loss only indirectly as a shareholder in P Ltd. Could W Ltd bring a derivation action in relation to the alleged wrongdoing? It was held that it could. There were strong policy arguments for multiple derivative actions being maintainable. Lord Millett stated that

---

[98] See *Modern Company Law for a Competitive Economy: Developing the Framework*, paras 4.112 to 4.139; *Final Report*, paras 7.46 to 7.51.

[99] For detailed consideration, see now Reisberg, *Derivative Actions and Corporate Governance* (2007) and by the same author, "Derivative Claims under the Companies Act 2006: Much Ado About Nothing?" in John Armour and Jennifer Payne (eds), *Rationality in Company Law: Essays in Honour of DD Prentice* (2009) p.17.

[100] s. 260(2). See too *Iesini v Westrip Holdings Ltd* [2009] EWHC 2526 (Ch) at [73]; [2010] B.C.C. 420.

[101] *Shareholder Remedies*, Cm.3769 (1997), para.16.13, quoting with approval from Beck, "The Shareholders' Derivative Action" (1974) 52 *Canadian Bar Review* 159, 207.

[102] See para.16.51.

[103] *Developing the Framework* URN 00/656 (2000), para.4.133.

[104] Unlike the legislation in certain other commonwealth countries, including New Zealand, Australia, Singapore and Canada.

[105] s.168BC of the Companies Ordinance, Cap.32. However, that section only came into force two years after the institution of these proceedings and so the matter was governed by the position at common law, which is expressly preserved by s.168BC(4) of the Act.

[106] i.e. unlike the 2006 Act.

[107] [2008] HKEC 1498, CFA. See Reisberg & Prentice, "Multiple derivative actions" (2009) 125 L.Q.R. 200.

"The very same reasons which justify the single derivative action also justify the multiple derivative action. To put the same point another way, if wrong-doers must not be allowed to defraud a parent company with impunity, they must not be allowed to defraud its subsidiary with impunity".[108]

If similar facts arose in the United Kingdom, it is unfortunately the case that a multiple derivative action could not be brought here because the statute does not permit them and common law derivative actions are excluded.

Statutory derivative actions—the framework

22–013 The provisions in the Act apply in favour of a member[109] of a company where the cause of action is vested in the company and where the member[110] seeks relief on behalf of the company.[111] A derivative claim may be brought only in respect of a cause of action arising from an actual or proposed act or omission involving negligence, default, breach of duty or breach of trust by a director[112] of the company.[113] The cause of action may be against the director or another person (or both).[114] As one judge has explained:

"The section contemplates that a cause of action may arise from, say, the default of a director, but nevertheless is a cause of action against a third party. A claim against a person who had dishonestly assisted in a breach of fiduciary duty or who had knowingly received trust property would be paradigm examples. It is also to be noted that it is not a requirement that the delinquent director should have profited or benefited from his misconduct. He may be guilty of no more than negligence in managing the company's affairs. However, since the cause of action must arise from his default (etc.) a derivative claim brought under Part 11 Chapter 1 will not allow a shareholder to pursue the company's claim against a third party where that claim depends on a cause of action that has arisen independently from the director's default (etc.)."[115]

Court permission: first stage

22–014 The central feature of the Act is that a member of a company who pursues a derivative claim must apply to the court for permission.[116] This may be regarded as the *first stage* of the proceedings. Procedurally, the claimant must file a claim form together with an application for permission to continue the claim and the written evidence on which he relies in support of the permission

---

[108] At [75].

[109] A member includes a person who is not a member but to whom shares in the company have been transferred or transmitted by operation of law: s.260(5)(c). cf. also s.994(2).

[110] It is immaterial whether the cause of action arose before or after the person seeking to bring or continue the derivative claim became a member of the company: s.260(4).

[111] s.260(1).

[112] A director includes a former director and also shadow directors: s.260(5)(a)(b).

[113] s.260(3).

[114] s.260(3).

[115] *Iesini v Westrup Holdings Ltd* [2009] EWHC 2526 (Ch), [2010] B.C.C. 420 at [75], per Lewison J.

[116] s.261(1).

application.[117] At this preliminary stage he must not make the company a respondent to the application[118] although he is required to notify the company of the claim by sending it the particulars of his claim.[119] This necessarily entails a decision that there is a prima facie case both that the company has a good cause of action and that the cause of action arises out of a directors' negligence, default, breach of duty, or breach of trust.[120] If it appears to the court that the application and the evidence filed by the applicant in support of it do not disclose a prima facie case for giving permission, the court must dismiss the application and may make any consequential order it considers appropriate.[121] If, on the other hand, the application is not dismissed, the court may give directions as to the evidence to be provided by the company and may adjourn the proceedings to enable the evidence to be obtained.[122] On hearing the application, the court may give permission to continue the claim on such terms as it thinks fit, refuse permission and dismiss the claim, or adjourn the proceedings on the application and give such directions as it thinks fit.[123] Although it has been suggested that this stage of proceedings it would be quite wrong for the court to "embark on anything like a mini-trial of the action"[124] it has also been recognised that the court will have to form a view on the strength of the claim in order properly to consider the requirements of the Act.[125] The court will refuse permission to continue the proceedings where there are other proceedings afoot which might have a material impact on the procedural framework of the derivative claim being sought.[126]

A further provision deals with the case where the company has brought a claim and the cause of action on which the claim is based could be pursued as a derivative claim.[127] As the Law Commission explained:

"We do not want individual shareholders to apply to take over current litigation being pursued by their company just because they are not happy with the progress being made. The provision is intended to deal with those situations where the company's real intention in commencing proceedings is to prevent a successful claim being brought."[128]

In such a situation the Act provides that a member of the company may apply to the court for permission to continue the claim as a derivative claim on the ground

---

[117] CPR Pt 19.9A(2).

[118] CPR Pt 19.9A(3).

[119] CPR Pt 19.9A(4). He may send the notice and documents by any method: CPR Pt 19.9A(5).

[120] See *Iesini v Westrup Holdings Ltd* [2009] EWHC 2526 (Ch), [2010] B.C.C. 420 at [78], per Lewison J. See also *Stainer v Lee* [2010] EWHC 1539 (Ch.).

[121] s.261(2). But if, for example, a director failed to produce corroborative evidence supporting a defence to allegations that he had breached his fiduciary duties, permission to continue would be granted: *Kiani v Cooper* [2010] EWHC 577 (Ch.); [2010] B.C.C. 463.

[122] s.261(3). The court will also notify the claimant and (unless the court orders otherwise) the company of that decision: CPR Pt 19.9A(9).

[123] s.261(4).

[124] *Fanmailuk.com v Cooper* [2008] EWHC 2198 (Ch); [2008] B.C.C. 877 at 879.

[125] See *Iesini v Westrup Holdings Ltd* [2009] EWHC 2526 (Ch), [2010] B.C.C. 420 at [79] per Lewison J.

[126] See *FanmailUK.com Ltd v Cooper* [2008] EWHC 2198 (Ch); [2008] B.C.C. 877. The court will also refuse an application to continue a claim as a derivate claim where the original claim was time-barred under the Limitation Act 1980, c.58: see *Roberts v Gill & Co* [2010] UKSC 22; [2010] 2 W.L.R. 1227.

[127] s.262(1).

[128] *Shareholder Remedies*, Cm.3769 (1997), para.6.63.

that the manner in which the company commenced or continued the claim amounts to an abuse of the process of the court, the company has failed to prosecute the claim diligently and it is appropriate for the member to continue the claim as a derivative claim.[129] As was the case with s.261, if it appears to the court that the application and the evidence filed by the applicant in support of it do not disclose a prima facie case for giving permission (or leave), the court must dismiss the application and may make any consequential order it considers appropriate.[130] Again, similarly to s.261, if the application is not dismissed the court may give directions as to the evidence to be provided by the company and may adjourn the proceedings to enable the evidence to be obtained.[131] On hearing the application, the court has a wide discretion. Thus, it may give permission to continue the claim as a derivative claim on such terms as it thinks fit, refuse permission and dismiss the application, or adjourn the proceedings on the application and give such directions as it thinks fit.[132]

Criteria considered by the court: second stage

22–015 If the hearing is not dismissed at the first stage, the *second stage* of the proceedings, on either of the above bases, involves the court considering a range of criteria. The court is required by the statute to have particular regard to any evidence before it as to the views of members of the company who have no personal interest, direct or indirect, in the matter.[133] Then, in considering whether to give permission, the court must take into account a number of factors.[134] The first of these is whether the member is acting in good faith in seeking to continue the claim,[135] which is an echo of the "clean hands" requirement under the common law derivative action.[136] The second factor[137] is the importance that a director of a company acting in accordance with s.172 would attach to continuing it.[138] That section[139] requires a director to act in the way he considers, in good faith, would be most likely to promote the success of the company for the benefit of the membership as a whole, having regard to a list of factors.[140] One potential

---

[129] s.262(2).

[130] s.262(3).

[131] s.262(4).

[132] s.262(5).

[133] s.263(4). It has been suggested that this sub-section is not easy to understand: see the reasoning of Lewison J. in *Iesini v Westrup Holdings Ltd* [2009] EWHC 2526 (Ch); [2010] B.C.C. 420 at [129].

[134] s.263(3).

[135] s.263(3)(a). The court in *Mission Capital Plc v Sinclair* [2008] EWHC 1339 (Ch); [2008] B.C.C. 866 found that the claimants were acting in good faith but declined to allow the claim to continue for other reasons. See too *Franbar Holdings Ltd v Patel* [2008] EWHC 1534 (Ch); [2008] B.C.C. 885; *Iesini v Westrup Holdings Ltd* [2009] EWHC 2526 (Ch); [2010] B.C.C. 420.

[136] Discussed at para.22–007, above.

[137] s.263(3)(b). Thus, in *Franbar Holdings Ltd v Patel* [2008] EWHC 1534 (Ch); [2008] B.C.C. 885 the court took the view that it was likely that the hypothetical director would be more inclined to regard pursuit of the derivative claim as less important in light of the fact that several of the complaints were more naturally formulated as breaches of the shareholders' agreement.

[138] See too s.263(2), discussed below. See *Mission Capital Plc v Sinclair* [2008] EWHC 1339 (Ch); [2008] B.C.C. 866 where the court felt that a notional director would not attach that much importance to the claim.

[139] See para.17–020, above.

[140] See s.172(1)(a)–(f). See para.17–021, above.

disadvantage of this approach is that the courts will effectively be asked to give weight to the motives of those who are potentially the wrongdoers, although if they are the wrongdoers it could not be then argued that their actions were in "good faith". The third factor[141] is where the cause of action results from an act or omission that is yet to occur, whether the act or omission could be, and in the circumstances would be likely to be authorised by the company before it occurs or ratified by the company after it occurs. The fourth factor[142] is where the cause of action arises from an act or omission that has already occurred, whether the act or omission could be and in the circumstances would be likely to be ratified by the company. The fifth factor[143] is whether the company has decided not to pursue the claim. The sixth and final factor[144] is whether the act or omission in respect of which the claim is brought gives rise to a cause of action that the member could pursue in his own right rather than on behalf of the company.

Refusals by the court

On the other hand, permission to continue the application must be refused if a **22–016** person acting in accordance with s.172 would not seek to continue the claim.[145] This is important because it reflects the status of the derivative action as a vehicle of redress for the company, not the individual members of the company. However this section will apply only where the court is satisfied that *no* director acting in accordance with s.172 would seek to continue the claim. If some directors would, and others would not, seek to continue the claim the case is one for the application of s.263(3)(b).[146] A further ground for refusal is where the cause of action arises from an act or omission that is yet to occur.[147] Finally, permission must be refused where the act or omission has been authorised by the company or where the cause of action arises from an act or omission that has already occurred, that the act or omission was authorised by the company before it occurred or has been ratified by the company since it occurred.[148] Thus, the majority rule principle, which as we have seen is one of the rationales for the rule in *Foss v Harbottle*,[149] is preserved.

The final statutory provision concerns the right of a member to apply for permission to continue a derivative claim which has been brought and continued by another member. The Act provides that, in such a case, another member may apply to the court for permission to continue the claim on the ground that the manner in which the proceedings have been commenced or continued by the claimant amounts to an abuse of the process of the court, the claimant has failed to prosecute the claim diligently and it is appropriate for the applicant to continue the claim as a derivative claim. If it appears to the court that the application and the evidence filed

---

[141] s.263(3)(c).
[142] s.263(3)(d).
[143] s.263(3)(e).
[144] s.263(3)(f).
[145] s.263(2)(a). See *Franbar Holdings Ltd v Patel* [2008] EWHC 1534 (Ch); [2008] B.C.C. 885; *Stimpson v Southern Landlords Association* [2009] EWHC 2072 (Ch); [2010] B.C.C. 387.
[146] *Iesini v Westrup Holdings Ltd* [2009] EWHC 2526 (Ch); [2010] B.C.C. 420 at [86], per Levison J.
[147] s.263(2)(b).
[148] s.263(2)(c).
[149] (1843) 2 Hare 461; 67 E.R. 189.

by the applicant in support of it do not disclose a prima facie case for giving permission, the court must dismiss the application and may make any consequential order it considers appropriate. If the application is not dismissed, the court may give directions as to the evidence to be provided by the company and may adjourn the proceedings to enable the evidence to be obtained. On hearing the application, the court may give permission to continue the claim on such terms as it thinks fit, refuse permission (or leave) and dismiss the application, or adjourn the proceedings on the application and give such directions as it thinks fit.

Reflective losses

22–017   At one time it was thought that where the wrong was a breach of duty to the company and also damaged the rights of individual members, in the sense of lowering the value of their shares, individual members could sue for the damage to themselves as plaintiffs, in their own right.[150] One member could thus sue on behalf of the others by way of a so-called representative action.

In *Prudential Assurance Co Ltd v Newman Industries Ltd (No.2)*,[151] the minority shareholder used this form of action in addition to a derivative action. The basis for the claim was the loss suffered by the shareholders as a result of the directors' alleged fraud on the company and the shareholders argument was that because the company had lost money their own personal profit expectations been diminished. The Court of Appeal inter alia held that, where a company suffered loss caused by a breach of duty owed to it and a shareholder, the latter's loss, in so far as this was measured by the diminution in value of his shareholding, or the loss of dividends, merely reflected the loss[152] suffered by the company in respect of which the company had its own cause of action and the shareholder, in such a case, could not recover damages.[153]

The *Prudential* approach was subsequently followed by the Court of Appeal in *Stein v Blake (No.2)*,[154] where loss was sustained by a shareholder by reason of a misappropriation of the company's assets and primarily involved a diminution in the value of his shares. The Court of Appeal held that such a loss was fully reflected in the loss suffered by the company and fully compensated by restitution to the company.[155] However, this must be distinguished from the situation where the loss is caused directly to the shareholders who, as a result of a breach of duty by the directors to advise them, have parted with their shares at an undervalue.[156]

---

[150] i.e. thereby avoiding the rule in *Foss v Harbottle* (1843) 2 Hare 461; 67 E.R. 189.

[151] [1982] 1 Ch. 204, CA.

[152] See Mitchell, "Shareholders' claims for reflective loss" (2004) 120 L.Q.R. 457.

[153] [1982] 1 Ch. 204, CA, at 222–223. As it was subsequently put, by Arden L.J., "the company's claim, if it exists, will always trump that of the shareholder": *Day v Cook* [2001] EWCA Civ 592; [2002] 1 B.C.L.C. 1, CA, at 15.

[154] [1998] 1 B.C.L.C. 573, CA.

[155] At 579.

[156] See *Heron International Ltd v Lord Grade* [1983] B.C.L.C. 244, CA, where Lawton L.J. explained (at 262) that:

"*Foss v Harbottle* has nothing whatever to do with a shareholder's right of action for a direct loss caused to his own pocket as distinct from a loss caused to the coffers of a company in which he holds shares".

In the last few decades, a clutch of important cases have revisited what has become known as the "*Prudential* principle" and have sought to exploit the personal rights exception in *Foss v Harbottle*.[157] The Court of Appeal has confirmed that the onus will be on the defendant to establish the applicability of the reflective loss principle.[158]

The principle was the subject of comprehensive review by the House of Lords **22–018** in the case of *Johnson v Gore Wood & Co.*[159]

J, a businessman, held shares in W. Ltd and on its behalf instructed a firm of solicitors, G to act for it in connection with a purchase of land. In particular, G was instructed to serve a notice exercising an option to purchase this land, but this was subsequently followed by a dispute as to its validity. In the end, W. Ltd suffered substantial losses and brought proceedings for professional negligence against G. At the same time, solicitors acting for W. Ltd informed G that J also had a personal claim against them. The claim by W. Ltd was eventually settled, but J proceeded with his action, which G sought to strike out as an abuse of process of the court. It was held that J was, in principle, entitled to recover in respect of any loss that he had himself suffered that was not merely a reflection of the loss suffered by W. Ltd. However, he would not be allowed to recover in respect of the diminution in value of his pension and in respect of his majority shareholding in W. Ltd. His other heads of claim in respect of his own quantifiable damage would not be struck out.

The House of Lords affirmed the following essential principles[160]—

1. Where a company suffers loss caused by a breach of duty owed to it, only the company may sue in respect of that loss and no action lies at the suit of a shareholder suing in that capacity to make good a diminution in the value of the shareholder's shareholding where that merely reflects the loss suffered by the company.

2. A claim will not lie by a shareholder to make good a loss which would be made good if the company's assets were replenished through action against the party responsible for the loss, even if the company, acting through its constitutional organs, has declined or failed to make good that loss.

3. Where a company suffers loss but has no cause of action to sue to recover that loss, the shareholder may sue in respect of it if he has a cause of action so to do, even though the loss is a diminution in the value of the shareholding.

4. Where a company suffers loss caused by a breach of duty to it, and a shareholder suffers a loss separate and distinct from that suffered by the company caused by breach of a duty independently owed to the shareholder, each may sue to recover the loss caused to it by breach of the

---

[157] (1843) 2 Hare 461; 67 E.R. 189.
[158] *Shaker v Al-Bedrawi* [2002] EWCA Civ 1452; [2003] Ch. 350, CA, at 378.
[159] [2002] 2 A.C. 1.
[160] At 35–36, per Lord Bingham.

duty owed to it, but neither may recover loss caused to the other by breach of the duty owed to that other.

A number of recent cases have since followed these principles and rejected a number of shareholder claims. Thus, where a claimant sought to recover from his solicitor for the diminution in value of his shares following various disastrous investments made through companies which he owned or set up for the purpose, the Court of Appeal held that he could not so claim as these were reflective losses which were primarily company losses and not personal losses.[161] By a majority, the Court of Appeal held, however,[162] that the claimant did have a claim in relation to a sum invested in an estate agency business as this sum was part of a personal obligation owed to the claimant by his solicitor.

Likewise, in a case where claimant property developers sought to recover against a firm of surveyors for negligent or fraudulent misrepresentation in valuing certain property, the losses suffered by them were held to be reflected losses and not recoverable by them personally.[163] The principle has also been upheld in circumstances where a defendant had a defence to a company's claim[164] and in a case where the court held that the fact that a claim was brought for breach of fiduciary duty did not prevent the claim being barred by the application of the rule against reflective loss.[165] The principle has also been affirmed in a case which involved a loss of chance loss of over £30 million; the Court of Appeal said that the *Prudential* principle extended to heads of loss which the company could have claimed but had chosen not to and, therefore, included the case where the company had settled for less than it might.[166]

22–019   But in two further cases, the *Prudential* principle has been distinguished. In the first case, *Shaker v Al-Bedrawi*,[167] the claimant alleged that he was beneficially entitled to a substantial proportion of the company's shares, held on trust for him by the company's sole director. He brought proceedings on the basis that his case was a claim for the director, as trustee, to account to him, as beneficiary, for a due proportion of a sum deriving from the use of the trust property. The Court of Appeal held that the reflective loss principle would preclude the claim only if the defendant could show that the whole of the claimed profit reflected what the company had lost and which it had a cause of action to recover. Further, it would not be right to bar the action unless the defendants could establish not merely that the company had a claim to recover a loss reflected by the profit, but that such was available on the facts.[168] Peter Gibson L.J. concluded by pointing out that:

---

[161] *Day v Cook* [2001] EWCA Civ 592; [2002] 1 B.C.L.C. 1 at 51.
[162] Arden L.J. dissenting.
[163] *Ellis v Property Leeds (UK) Ltd* [2002] EWCA Civ 32; [2002] 2 B.C.L.C. 175, CA.
[164] See *Barings Plc v Coopers & Lybrand (No.4)* [2002] 2 B.C.L.C. 364.
[165] *Gardner v Parker* [2004] EWHC Civ 781; [2004] 2 B.C.L.C. 554. See too *Gaetano Ltd v Obertor Ltd* [2009] EWHC 2653 (Ch); *Rawnsley v Weatherall Green* [2010] B.C.C. 406.
[166] *Webster v Sandersons Solicitors* [2009] EWCA Civ. 830; [2009] 2 B.C.L.C. 542.
[167] [2002] EWCA Civ. 1452; [2003] Ch. 350, CA.
[168] At 377–378.

"In circumstances where the *Prudential* principle applies to bar a viable claim on the footing of the company's cause of action which it does not assert, the application of the principle can work hardship. Moreover in this case the application of the principle might serve to leave the trustee holding a profit without being accountable for it to his beneficiary, and that may run counter to a basic equitable principle."[169]

The second case, *Giles v Rhind*,[170] involved a claim by one director against another director who, on leaving the company, had diverted his former company's most lucrative contract to another company in which he had an interest. The action by the company against the defendant had had to be discontinued when the latter was unable to put up security for his costs.[171] The claimant now alleged breaches of a shareholders' agreement and claimed damages for the loss of value of his shares in his company and loss of remuneration which he would otherwise have earned. The Court of Appeal confirmed that there were no reasons of principle or policy to prevent a shareholder from recovering damages where the wrong done to the company had made it impossible for it to pursue its own remedy against the wrongdoer by reason of impecuniosity attributable to the wrong which had been done to it.[172]

Derivative actions, reflective losses, and other rights of action

An issue which arises, both in respect of the reflective loss principle and the **22–020** derivative action, is whether such claims may be pursued under the other minority shareholders remedies, particularly s.994. In relation to the derivative action, the issue may be framed as whether the fact of that availability should prohibit the court granting permission for the derivative claim to proceed.

Taking first the reflective loss principle, it has been held that this would not prevent a bar to relief being sought under s.994.[173] Thus, the fact that conduct might give rise to a cause of action at the suit of the company, did not mean that it was incapable of also giving rise to unfair prejudice and preclude the court from awarding financial compensation to the petitioners.[174]

Taking next the statutory derivative action, some cases have suggested that the availability of an alternative statutory remedy might be a bar to proceeding with a derivative action. Thus in *Barrett v Duckett*, Peter Gibson L.J. said that

---

[169] ibid.

[170] [2002] EWCA Civ 1428; [2003] Ch. 618, CA.

[171] The company went into receivership. Chadwick L.J. stated (at 642) that:

"The paradigm case in which, by reason of the wrong done to it, the company is unable, in practice, to pursue its claim against the wrongdoer is one in which the company is obliged to abandon its claim because the wrong has deprived it of the funds needed for that purpose".

[172] In the Hong Kong case of *Waddington Ltd v Chan Chun* [2008] HKEC 1498, CFA, Lord Millett suggested that this case was wrongly decided (at [85]), but this view was rejected by the Court of Appeal who have taken the view that there is no proper basis for declining to follow *Giles v Rhind*: see *Webster v Sandersons Solicitors* [2009] EWCA Civ 830; [2009] 2 B.C.L.C. 542 at [36].

[173] Above, para.22–001.

[174] *Atlasview Ltd v Brightview Ltd* [2004] EWHC 1056 (Ch); [2004] 2 B.C.L.C. 191 at 208.

"The shareholder will be allowed to sue on behalf of the company if he is bringing the action bona fide for the benefit of the company for wrongs to the company for which no other remedy is available. Conversely if the action is brought for an ulterior purpose or if another adequate remedy is available, the court will not allow the derivative action to proceed."[175]

However, in *Konamaneni v Rolls Royce Industrial Power (India) Ltd*[176] it was suggested obiter that the notion that there must be no alternative remedy was not an independent bar to a derivative action, but simply an example of a case where there will be no relevant wrongdoer control.[177] This view has now been followed, in a case concerned with the new statutory provisions.[178]

In *Franbar Holdings Ltd v Patel*[179] the judge considered that the adequacy of the remedy available to the member in his own right was a matter which would go into the balance when assessing the weight of this consideration on the facts of the case.[180] On the facts of that case as most, if not all, of the allegations of breach of duty were likely to be relevant to a complaint of unfair prejudice, these weighed against the grant of permission to continue a derivative action.[181]

WINDING UP BY THE COURT ON THE "JUST AND EQUITABLE" GROUND

Who may bring a petition

22–021   Under the Insolvency Act 1986 a contributory[182] who has held his shares for at least six months[183] may petition the court to wind up a company and where the court is of opinion that it is just and equitable that the company should be wound up, the court may order a winding up.[184] A member of a company is a contributory, and it has been held that a holder of fully paid-up shares is a contributory.[185] Thus in appropriate circumstances even a single member can petition for a winding up.[186]

Criteria for winding up

22–022   In petitioning for a winding up on the just and equitable ground a member is not confined to such circumstances as affect him as a shareholder, i.e. he is not

---

[175] [1995] B.C.C. 362, CA, at 367.
[176] [2002] 1 W.L.R. 1269.
[177] At 1279, per Lawrence Collins J.
[178] *Iesini v Westrup Holdings Ltd* [2009] EWHC 2526 (Ch); [2010] B.C.C.420 at [123], per Levison J. cf. also *Wishart, Petitioner* [2009] CSOH 20; [2010] B.C.C. 161.
[179] [2008] EWHC 1534 (Ch); [2008] B.C.C. 885.
[180] At p.899.
[181] ibid.
[182] Defined in s.79(1) of the Insolvency Act 1986 as "every person liable to contribute to the assets of a company in the event of its being wound up". In certain cases a creditor may also petition for a winding up on this ground. See, e.g. *Morrice v Brae Hotel (Shetland) Ltd* [1997] B.C.C. 670.
[183] Insolvency Act 1986 s.124(2)(b).
[184] s.122(1)(g).
[185] *National Savings Bank Association, Re* (1866) L.R. 1 Ch App. 547.
[186] A petitioner must establish his locus standi to be a contributory, although the court has a discretion in all cases: *A Company, Re* [1996] 2 B.C.L.C. 409.

confined to cases where his position as a shareholder has been worsened by the action of which he complains; he is entitled to rely on any circumstances of justice or equity which affect him in his relations with the company or with the other shareholders,[187] although it may be otherwise on a petition under s.994.[188]

The court will not, as a rule, order a winding up on a contributory's petition unless he alleges in the petition, and proves at the hearing, at least to the extent of a prima facie case, that there will be assets for distribution among the shareholders or that some disadvantage would accrue to him by virtue of his membership which could be avoided or minimised,[189] a purely private advantage will not suffice.[190] The reason is that unless there are such assets the contributory has no interest in a winding up. The courts will not normally strike out a petition before the hearing on that basis, however, unless it has no doubts about the matter. Thus even where the company's only asset was a non-assignable lease with no clear market value the judge let the petition go to trial since it might have been of some value to the company.[191] Similarly, where the petition is based on the fact that there has been a failure to provide accounts and information so that it is impossible for the petitioner to be able to tell whether or not there will be a surplus available to the contributories, the courts will allow the petition to proceed.[192]

Further, a contributory's petition which is opposed by the majority of the contributories will usually not be granted except where the conduct of the majority is something of which the minority have a right to complain,[193] or the main object of the company has failed.[194] The petitioner need not establish that the other members have not acted bona fide in the interests of the company. If the directors who are not contributories wish to bring a petition they must be acting unanimously.[195]

Meaning of just and equitable

An order for winding up on the just and equitable ground may be made in a **22–023** number of different circumstances. One of these is where the main object of the company has failed[196] or the company is engaging in acts which are entirely outside what can fairly be regarded as having been within the general intention or common understanding of the members when they became members.

---

[187] *Ebrahimi v Westbourne Galleries Ltd* [1973] A.C. 360.

[188] The relationship between petitions for winding up and those under s.994 is dealt with at para.22–052, below.

[189] *Rica Gold Washing Co, Re* (1879) 11 Ch.D. 36, CA; *Martin Coulter Enterprises Ltd, Re* [1988] B.C.L.C. 12; *Instrumentation Electrical Services Ltd, Re* (1988) 4 B.C.C. 301.

[190] *Chesterfield Catering Co Ltd, Re* [1976] 3 All E.R. 294. If the petitioner is also a creditor and the company is insolvent the petition may be amended to one seeking a winding up on the grounds of insolvency: *Commercial and Industrial Insulations Ltd, Re* [1986] B.C.L.C. 19.

[191] *Martin Coulter Enterprises Ltd, Re* [1988] B.C.L.C. 12.

[192] *Wessex Computer Stationers Ltd, Re* [1992] B.C.L.C. 366.

[193] *Middlesborough Assembly Rooms Co, Re* (1880) 14 Ch.D. 104, CA; *Tivoli Freeholds Ltd, Re* [1972] V.R. 445.

[194] *German Date Coffee Co, Re* (1882) 20 Ch.D. 169; *Perfectair Holdings Ltd, Re* (1989) 5 B.C.C. 837.

[195] *Instrumentation Electrical Services Ltd, Re* (1988) 4 B.C.C. 301.

[196] However, as we have seen, there is under the 2006 Act no longer a requirement for a company to have an objects clause: see para.4–026 above.

Thus, in *Bleriot Aircraft Co, Re*[197] a company was formed to acquire the English portion of the aircraft business of M. Blériot, a well-known airman. M. Blériot refused to carry out the contract. The court held that the company should be wound up because its substratum had gone.

Another situation is if the company is a "bubble", i.e. there is no bona fide intent on the part of the directors to carry on business in a proper manner.[198] The court will not order a solvent company to be wound up merely because it is making a loss or is deeply indebted if the majority of the shareholders are against a winding up.[199] A company was wound up, however, where it had a contract damages claim against it to which it was defenceless and which the petitioner could have invoked at any time.[200]

The court will also order a winding up where a company was formed to carry out a fraud, or to carry on an illegal business.

In *Thomas Edward Brismead & Sons*[201] T.E.B. and his sons were relatives of, and had been employed by, persons who carried on the business of piano manufacturers under the name of J.B. & Sons. They left J.B. & Sons and formed a company called T.E.B. & Sons Ltd for carrying on a similar business. A prospectus was issued which stated that the price paid for the business was £76,650, when it was really only £1,000 in cash together with £5,000 in shares in the company. Money was subscribed by the public and most of this money found its way into the hands of the persons who were the real, though not the ostensible, promoters. J.B. & Sons obtained an injunction restraining the company from using the name B, and it was found that the company was formed to filch as much trade as possible from J.B. & Sons. Numerous actions were brought against the company for fraud in the prospectus. It was held that the company should be wound up.

Fraudulent misrepresentation in the listing particulars or prospectus[202] or fraud in the course of business with the outside world[203] are not, by themselves, grounds for winding up the company, as the majority of the shareholders may waive the fraud, or there may be a change of management; but fraud in the real, though not the ostensible, object of the company will be such a ground.[204]

The court will order a winding up where the mutual rights of the members are not exhaustively defined in the articles, e.g. where they entered into membership on the basis of a personal relationship involving mutual confidence or an under-standing as to the extent to which each is to participate in the management of the company's business, and that confidence is not maintained or the petitioner is excluded from the management.

In *Ebrahimi v Westbourne Galleries Ltd*[205] E and N were partners in a carpet dealing business with an equal share in the management and profits. In 1958 they

---

[197] (1916) 32 T.L.R. 253. See also *Re Kitson & Co Ltd* [1946] 1 All E.R. 435, CA.
[198] *Re London and County Coal Co* (1866) L.R. 3 Eq. 355; *Loch v John Blackwood Ltd* [1924] A.C. 783, PC.
[199] *Re Suburban Hotel Co* (1867) L.R. 2 Ch.App. 737 (company making a loss).
[200] *Re Dollar Land Holdings Plc* [1994] 1 B.C.L.C. 404.
[201] [1897] 1 Ch. 45, CA.
[202] *Haven Gold Mining Co, Re* (1882) 20 Ch.D. 151, CA.
[203] *Medical Battery Co, Re* [1894] 1 Ch. 444.
[204] See *Millennium Advanced Technology Ltd, Re* [2004] EWHC 711 (Ch); [2004] 1 W.L.R. 2177.
[205] [1973] A.C. 360.

formed a private company to take the business over. E and N were the first directors and each held 500 £1 shares. The articles provided that shares could not be
transferred without the directors' consent. Later, N's son, G, was appointed a
director and E and N each transferred 100 shares to him. The company made
good profits which were all distributed by way of directors' remuneration, i.e. no
dividends were paid. After a disagreement between E and N, with whom G sided,
N and G at a general meeting removed E as director by ordinary resolution under
s.[168], and thereafter excluded him from the conduct of the company's business.
E petitioned for an order under s.[122(1)(g) of the Insolvency Act 1986] that the
company be wound up on the ground that it was just and equitable. It was held
that it was just and equitable that the company be wound up. After a long association in partnership, during which he had had an equal share in the management
and profits, E had joined in the formation of the company; the inference was
indisputable that he and N had done so on the basis that the character of the association would, as a mater of personal faith, remain the same; and E had established that N and G were not entitled, in justice and equity, to make use of their
legal powers of expulsion. Furthermore E was unable to dispose of his interest in
the company without the consent of N and G. In particular, Lord Wilberforce
stated that

". . . there has been a tendency to create categories or headings under which
cases must be brought if the [just and equitable] clause is to apply. This is
wrong. Illustrations may arise but general words should remain general and not
be reduced to the sum of particular instances.[206]

The words [just and equitable] are a recognition of the fact that a limited
company is more than a mere legal entity, with a personality in law of its own:
that there is room in company law for recognition of the fact that behind it, or
amongst it, there are individuals, with rights, expectations and obligations inter
se which are not necessarily submerged in the company structure. That structure is defined by the Companies Act and by the articles of association by
which shareholders agree to be bound. In most companies and in most
contexts, this definition is sufficient and exhaustive, equally so whether the
company is large or small. The 'just and equitable' provision does not . . .
entitle one party to disregard the obligation he assumes by entering a company,
nor the court to dispense him from it. It does, as equity always does, enable the
court to subject the exercise of legal rights to equitable considerations; considerations, that is, of a personal character arising between one individual and
another, which may make it unjust, or inequitable, to insist on legal rights, or
to exercise them in a particular way.

It would be impossible, and wholly undesirable, to define the circumstances
in which these considerations may arise. Certainly the fact that the company is
a small one, or a private company, is not enough. There are very many of these
where the association is a purely commercial one, of which it can safely be said
that the basis of association is adequately and exhaustively laid down in the
articles. The superimposition of equitable considerations requires something

---

more [than the fact that the company is a small one, or a private company], which typically may include one, or probably more, of the following elements: (i) an association formed or continued on the basis of a personal relationship, involving mutual confidence—this element will often be found where a pre-existing partnership has been converted into a limited company; (ii) an agreement, or understanding, that all, or some (for there may be 'sleeping members'), of the shareholders shall participate in the conduct of the business; (iii) restriction on the transfer of the members' interest in the company—so that if confidence is lost, or one member removed from management, he cannot take out his stake and go elsewhere."[207]

22–024 *Ebrahimi v Westbourne Galleries Ltd*[208] was applied in *Re A. & B.C. Chewing Gum Ltd*,[209] where the petitioners held one-third of the company's shares on the basis that they should have equal control with the two individual respondents, who were brothers and directors of the company and owned the other two-thirds of the shares. To achieve equality of control, the articles were altered so as to provide, inter alia, that the petitioners could appoint and remove a director representing them, and that decisions at board meetings should be unanimous. The petitioners, the respondents and the company also signed and sealed a shareholders' agreement setting out the way in which the day-to-day business was to be conducted. The respondents refused to recognise the petitioner's removal of their director and the appointment of another in his place. This was not a case of one side making use of its legal rights to the prejudice of another—the petitioners were excluded from their legal and contractual rights. Their right to management participation was repudiated.

Weinberg and Rothman were the sole shareholders in and directors of a company, with equal rights of management and voting power. After a time they became bitterly hostile to one another and disagreed about the appointment of important servants of the company. All communications between them were made through the secretary. The company made large profits in spite of the disagreement. It was held that mutual confidence had been lost between W and R and the company should be wound up.[210]

Whether it is just and equitable to wind up a company depends on facts which exist at the time of the hearing and a petitioner is confined to heads of complaint set out in his petition.[211]

It is a matter therefore for the petitioner to establish mutual confidence and/or entitlement to management participation. If he can establish neither, then the matter will be left to be dealt with under the company's articles,[212] or possibly by a petition under s. 994.[213] Such confidence or entitlement may be shown either by the very nature of the company and the relationship between the member/directors,

---

[207] At 379.
[208] [1973] A.C. 360.
[209] [1975] 1 W.L.R. 579.
[210] *Yenidje Tobacco, Co Ltd, Re* [1916] 2 Ch. 426, CA. See also *Worldhams Park Golf Course Ltd, Re* [1998] 1 B.C.L.C. 554; *Phoneer Ltd, Re* [2002] 2 B.C.L.C. 241.
[211] *Fildes Bros Ltd, Re* [1970] 1 All E.R. 923.
[212] *A Company, Re* (1988) 4 B.C.C. 80.
[213] *A Company, Ex p. Estate Acquisition and Development Ltd, Re* [1991] B.C.L.C. 154.

as in a quasi-partnership company similar to that in the *Ebrahimi* case,[214] or by representations being made to the petitioner to a similar effect.[215] There is no necessary requirement of establishing equal rights of management. Thus in *Quinlan v Essex Hinge Co Ltd*[216] the remedy was extended to a petitioner who had joined the company as a director and minority shareholder, on the basis that he was akin to a junior partner. The remedy is even available to someone who is part contingent creditor and part contingent shareholder, i.e. a co-venturer with capital at stake who has a right to take shares, and who has been wrongfully excluded from the management he was intended to have, although it will not be available if he is pursuing a separate action for damages based on the same facts.[217] There is no bar to a petition by a shareholder who is guilty of misconduct if that is not the cause of the breakdown in confidence.[218]

If the petitioner can establish that the affairs of the company are not being managed in a proper manner then if the petition is not due to be heard for some time, the court will appoint a receiver[219] to manage the company's affairs to preserve the status quo and avoid any prejudice to either side. That jurisdiction is exercised by analogy with partnership law.[220]

Alternative remedies

If, in the case of a contributories' petition, the court is of opinion that it is just and **22–025** equitable that the company should be wound up and some other remedy, e.g. accepting an offer to purchase his shares, or seeking an order under s.994 is available to the petitioners,[221] the court must nevertheless make a winding up order unless it is of the opinion that the petitioners are acting unreasonably in not pursuing the other remedy: Insolvency Act 1986 s.125(2).

In *A Company, Re*,[222] Warner J. decided that where the petitioner had a potential claim under s.994, that did not make it unreasonable for him to maintain a claim for a winding up order since it was not plain and obvious that the relief that he would get at the hearing would be relief under s.994. The question would be resolved by the judge at the hearing. Even if the winding up petition was damaging to the company it did not follow that a petitioner claiming his rights as a quasi-partner was being unreasonable in preventing a petition. Similarly the Court of Appeal in *Copeland & Craddock Ltd, Re*[223] held that it was not inevitably unreasonable if a petition under s.994 for shares to be bought by the majority has a winding up petition in the alternative. One result of such a winding

---

[214] Such a relationship may be destroyed by agreed changes in the relationship between the parties: *Third v North East Ice & Cold Storage Co Ltd* [1998] B.C.C. 242.

[215] *Tay Bok Choon v Tachansan Sdn. Bhd.* (1987) 3 B.C.C. 132, PC.

[216] [1996] 2 B.C.L.C. 417.

[217] *A Company, Re* (1987) 3 B.C.C. 575.

[218] *Vujnovich v Vujnovich* (1989) 5 B.C.C. 740, PC.

[219] Under s.37 of the Supreme Court Act 1981 c.54.

[220] *A Company, Re* [1987] B.C.L.C. 133.

[221] See *CVC/Opportunity Equity Partners Ltd v Demarco Almedia* [2002] UKPL 16; [2002] 2 B.C.L.C. 108, PC, where no remedy, other than one for winding up was possible, there being no s.994 equivalent in the Cayman Islands.

[222] (1989) 5 B.C.C. 18.

[223] [1997] B.C.C. 294, CA.

up would be to effect a sale of the business as a going concern in the open market and the petitioner could bid for it. The position is even clearer where the court has already refused an application under s.994.[224]

With regard to a bona fide offer being made by the other members under the articles for the petitioner's shares, i.e. at a valuation by an independent valuer, the Court of Appeal in *Virdi v Abbey Leisure Ltd*,[225] overruling the judge below and other earlier decisions, decided that this was not an automatic reason for striking out the winding up petition. There was nothing unreasonable in the petitioner refusing to accept the risk that a valuer's decision might apply a discount for his minority shareholding, since the machinery in a winding up to determine claims against the company was preferable to their worth being estimated by an accountant. Winding up of necessity effects a full assets valuation of the petitioner's shares. If the essence of the decision to allow petitions based on equitable considerations in *Ebrahimi v Westbourne Galleries Ltd*[226] was that the company's constitution, e.g. as to dismissal of a director, might be overridden, then it could be likewise equitable to ignore the share valuation provisions in the articles. Equally, where there are no proper accounts to enable the share valuation provisions to operate, an offer to purchase the petitioner's shares will not be a bar to the petition being brought.[227]

Each case is, however, dependent on its facts. In *A Company, Re*,[228] the judge struck out the winding up petition on the basis that it was a remedy of last resort, there was no realistic possibility of it succeeding, and that an order under s.994 for the purchase of the petitioner's shares would be at a fair price taking into account the allegations of unreasonably low dividend payments.

This case and others have shown a marked degree of reluctance on the part of the courts to grant the "death sentence" involved in a winding up.[229] Thus in *Fuller v Cyracuse Ltd*,[230] the court held that it was an abuse of process for a minority shareholder to persist with a winding up petition under s.122(1)(g) when he had been offered a buyout at a price fixed by an independent valuer.[231] In these circumstances, there was another remedy available to the petitioner within the meaning of s.125(2) and so the petition would be struck out.[232]

REMEDY FOR UNFAIRLY PREJUDICIAL CONDUCT

Background

22–026 Section 210 of the 1948 Act, now repealed, provided that any member who complained that the affairs of the company were being conducted in a manner oppressive to some part of the members, including himself, could petition for

---

[224] *Vujnovich v Vujnovich* (1989) 5 B.C.C. 740.
[225] [1990] B.C.L.C. 342. See also *Copeland & Craddock Ltd, Re* [1997] B.C.C. 294, CA.
[226] [1973] A.C. 360.
[227] *Wessex Computer Stationers Plc, Re* [1992] B.C.L.C. 366.
[228] [1997] 1 B.C.L.C. 479. See now also *McCarthy Surfacing Ltd, Re* [2008] EWHC 464 (Ch.); [2009] B.C.C. 464, where a remedy was granted under s.994 (below, para.22–026) for non-declaration of dividends.
[229] *Shah v Shah* [2010] EWHC 313 (Ch.) at [138], per Roth J.
[230] [2001] 1 B.C.L.C. 187.
[231] See further, para.22–047, below.
[232] See too *Woven Rugs Ltd, Re* [2008] B.C.C. 903; *Shah v Shah* [2010] EWHC 313 (Ch.).

an order under that section. That section suffered from several drawbacks however,[233] and was repealed in 1980 and replaced by ss.459 to 461 of the 1985 Act. The 2006 Act has restated these provisions, with drafting amendments, in Pt 30 of the Act.[234]

The statutory principle

Under the Act a member[235] of the company can petition[236] the court for an order **22–027** on the ground (a)[237] that the affairs of a company are being or have been conducted in a manner which is unfairly prejudicial to the interests of its members generally or of some part of the members (including at least himself)[238] or (b) that any actual or proposed act or omission of the company (including an act or omission on its behalf) is or would be so prejudicial.[239] If the company is a small private company all the members should be joined as respondents since they may well be affected by the petition.[240] This might not be the case in a larger company, however. Unlike a derivative action, the petitioner cannot ask for an indemnity against costs[241] although legal aid is available.[242] The court may in appropriate circumstances either appoint a receiver[243] or grant an interim injunction to protect the petitioner,[244] pending a full hearing of the petition. A majority shareholder can bring a petition if the board and the minority shareholders act together to prejudice him, but not if the board have been dismissed.[245]

---

[233] For details see the 12th edition of this work.

[234] Supplemented by the Companies (Unfair Prejudice Applications) Proceedings Rules 2009 (SI 2009/2469).

[235] This remedy is not available to an employee: *A Company, Re* [1986] B.C.L.C. 391. But it would be available to a 50 per cent shareholder: see *Southern Countries Fresh Foods Ltd, Re* [2008] EWHC 2810 (Ch.).

[236] The petition is required to be in the form set out in the Schedule to the Companies (Unfair Prejudice Applications) Proceedings Rules 2009 (SI 2009/2469) reg.3(1). If proceedings are commenced by a claim form rather than a petition, the proceedings will be struck out: see *Osea Road Camp Sites Ltd, Re* [2004] EWHC 2437 (Ch); [2005] 1 W.L.R. 760,

[237] See also s.994(1A), added by the Statutory Auditors and Third Country Auditors Regulations 2007 (SI 2007/3494).

[238] The reference to all of the members being affected, as distinct from some part of the members, was added by a 1989 Act amendment, to avoid confusion caused by conflicting decisions on whether if all the members were affected a petition would lie. See *A Company, Re* [1988] 1 W.L.R. 1068, cf. *Sam Weller Ltd, Re* (1989) 5 B.C.C. 810.

[239] s.994(1).

[240] *A Company, Re (No.007281 of 1986)* [1987] B.C.L.C. 593. Although cf. *Ravenhart Service (Holdings) Ltd, Re* [2004] EWHC 76 (Ch); [2004] 2 B.C.L.C. 376, which suggests that it is not necessary for all the other culpable shareholders to be joined as respondents (at 396). The Companies (Unfair Prejudice Applications) Proceedings Rules 2009 (SI 2009/2469) reg.4(2) requires that the petition should be served on every respondent named in the petition.

[241] Above, para.22–009. See *A Company, Re* [1987] B.C.L.C. 82.

[242] Thus making it an attractive alternative action: See *Lowe v Fahey* [1996] 1 B.C.L.C. 262.

[243] *A Company, Re* [1987] B.C.L.C. 133; *Wilton-Davies v Kirk* [1998] 1 B.C.L.C. 274. The costs of the receiver are payable out of the assets of the company but the court may direct that they are ultimately born by the respondent: *Worldhams Park Golf Course Ltd, Re* [1998] 1 B.C.L.C. 554.

[244] *Safinia v Comet Enterprises Ltd* [1994] B.C.C. 883; *Rutherford, Petitioner* [1994] B.C.C. 867; cf. *Wright, Petitioners* [1997] B.C.C. 198.

[245] *Baltic Real Estate Ltd, Re* [1993] B.C.L.C. 498.

The conduct must relate to the affairs of the company

22–028   The section only applies if the unfairly prejudicial conduct relates to the affairs of the company.[246] Thus a petition was refused where the allegation was that a major share-holder had paid off the company's bank loan and had taken a transfer of the bank's security over the company's assets. It was held to have been an act by the respondent in her personal capacity and had not affected the company's position as mortgagor.[247] It is a question of fact whether the actions of a parent company can amount to the conduct of the affairs of a subsidiary.[248] This arose in *Gross v Rackind*[249] where the Court of Appeal was asked to consider whether it would have the power to make an order in relation to a holding company where it was the affairs of its wholly-owned subsidiary that were being or had been conducted in an unfairly prejudicial manner. The Court of Appeal held that the expression "the affairs of the company" in s. 994(1) was "one of the widest import" which could include the affairs of a subsidiary of a holding company.[250] More recently, it has been held that this may extend to matters which are capable of coming before the board for its consideration, and are not restricted merely to those that actually come before the board.[251]

In *Re Astec (BSR) Plc*,[252] Jonathan Parker J. held that, whilst the acts of the board of directors as a whole would relate to the affairs of the company, the acts of a minority of the board acting as nominees of a major shareholder in a public company did not amount to such conduct. The judge was also prepared to accept that a resolution passed by the general meeting amounted to conduct relating to the affairs of the company. Shareholder and other agreements may be relevant but it depends upon the context.[253] Where the subject of the dispute is in an agreement (e.g. such as the terms upon which the company was formed) there are divergent authorities, with an earlier case suggesting that the petition will not be allowed to proceed.[254] However this has not been followed in a later case, which has held that the statutory right conferred on members of a company to apply for s.994 relief is inalienable and could not be diminished or removed by contract and that s.9 of the Arbitration Act 1996 did not compel the court to stay the proceedings.[255] Where the petitioners had also obtained a freezing order[256] against the respondent directors, the court held that this would be discharged in view of the

---

[246] As defined by the company's constitution: *Legal Costs Negotiators Ltd, Re* [1998] 2 B.C.L.C. 171, CA.

[247] *A Company, Re* [1987] B.C.L.C. 141.

[248] *Nicholas v Soundcraft Electronics Ltd* [1993] B.C.L.C. 360.

[249] [2004] EWCA Civ 815; [2004] 4 All E.R. 735, CA.

[250] At 741. The Court of Appeal also held that the affairs of the subsidiary could also be the affairs of its holding company, especially where, as on the facts, the directors of the holding company also represented a majority of the directors of the subsidiary.

[251] *Hawkes v Cuddy* [2009] EWCA Civ 291; [2009] 2 B.C.L.C. 427 at [50], per Stanley Burnton J.A., following (in part) *Dernacourt Investments Pty Ltd, Re* (1990) 2 A.C.S.R. 553 at 556, per Powell J.

[252] [1998] 2 B.C.L.C. 556.

[253] *A Company, Re* [1997] 2 B.C.L.C. 1; cf. *Unisoft Group Ltd, Re (No.3)* [1994] 1 B.C.L.C. 609; *Leeds United Holdings Plc, Re* [1996] 2 B.C.L.C. 545.

[254] *Vocam Europe Ltd, Re* [1998] B.C.C. 396.

[255] *Exeter City Association Football Club Ltd v Football Conference Ltd* [2004] EWHC 2304 (Ch); [2004] 1 W.L.R. 2910.

[256] Formerly known as a "Mareva injunction", as developed in England in the case of *Nippon Yusen Kaisha v Karageorgis* [1975] 1 W.L.R. 1093, CA.

s.994 petition, unless the allegations were sufficient to constitute a relevant cause of action against them.[257]

The interests affected must be those of the petitioner as a member

The right to petition is given to "members". The primary reference point for this **22–029** is the definition of "member" in s.112 of the Act.[258] Additionally, the Secretary of State may petition under s.994,[259] and this includes a case where a report has been made to him pursuant to s.437 of the 1985 Act, following an investigation under the relevant provisions of the Act,[260] and also where the Financial Services Authority has exercised its powers under the Financial Services and Markets Act 2000.[261]

It has been held that a "member"[262] includes registered shareholders[263] and those with a perfect transfer of shares to them in equity.[264] It has also been held that a s.994 petition may be founded on conduct which pre-dated a petitioner's registration as shareholder, so long as the petitioner is a member at the time of presentation of the petition.[265] An application for a petition may be stayed in the event of a dispute as to the standing of the petitioner, pending an application for rectification of the register of members.[266] On the other hand, a beneficiary under a trust[267] would not have standing. In *Atlasview Ltd v Brightview Ltd*,[268] the court struck out as petitioners B and his wife, on the basis that neither were members or those to whom shares had been transferred by operation of law.[269] In the same case it was held that a company as a member would not be struck out as a petitioner, although a bare nominee; the interests of such a nominee shareholder were "capable of including the economic and contractual interests of the beneficial owners of the shares".[270]

It has been confirmed in *O'Neill v Phillips*[271] that the requirement of prejudice having been suffered by a member should not be too narrowly or technically construed.[272] The judge at first instance in that case had dismissed the petition because the prejudice suffered was in the petitioner's capacity as an employee rather than as a shareholder.[273] Although this was overturned by the Court of

---

[257] *Premier Electronics (GB) Ltd, Re* [2002] 2 B.C.L.C. 634.

[258] As to which, see para.16–001, above.

[259] Under s.995.

[260] s.995(1)(a). See para.22–064, below.

[261] s.995(1)(c).

[262] Executors of members may bring such a petition: see s.994(2).

[263] So a person who has assented to registration as a shareholder is a member for the purpose of presenting a petition: *Nuneaton Borough Association Football Club Ltd, Re* [1989] B.C.L.C. 454, CA.

[264] See *Quickdome Ltd, Re* [1988] 1 B.C.L.C. 370.

[265] *Lloyd v Casey* [2002] 1 B.C.L.C. 454 at 465.

[266] i.e. under s.125 of the 2006 Act. See *Starlight Developers Ltd, Re* [2007] EWHC 1660 (Ch.); [2007] B.C.C. 929.

[267] *A Company, Re* [1986] B.C.L.C. 39.

[268] [2004] EWHC 1056 (Ch); [2004] 2 B.C.L.C. 191.

[269] There was also no basis under which CPR Pt 19.2(2)(a) could be invoked to support a non-member as a party, since that rule was confined to cases where it was desirable "so that the court can resolve all matters in dispute in the proceedings": at 202.

[270] At 203 (per Jonathan Crow QC).

[271] [1999] 1 W.L.R. 1092, HL, discussed above at para.22–034.

[272] [1999] 1 W.L.R. 1092, HL, at 1105.

[273] Reported as *A Company, Re (No.00709 of 1992)* [1997] 2 B.C.L.C. 739 at 758. See too *A Company, Re* [1986] B.C.L.C. 391.

Appeal,[274] the House of Lords emphasised that it was the terms, agreement, or understanding on which the petitioner became associated as a member which would generate any restraint on a power of expulsion against him.[275]

22–030   Section 994 has no application if the interests of the member which are affected by the unfairly prejudicial conduct are not those which he enjoys qua[276] member. In *A Company, Re*, a petition was rejected where it was brought by petitioners holding shares as executors for two minors, because the conduct affected them *qua* executors and not members.[277] Likewise, in *J.E. Cade & Son Ltd, Re*,[278] a petition was rejected where it related to the petitioner's position as the landlord of a farm, farmed rent-free by his family company on the basis that no tenancy would be created. The petition failed because the petitioner was pursuing his interests as a freeholder and not as a member.

On the other hand, in *R & H Electrical Ltd v Haden*,[279] a petition was allowed even though the petitioner was alleging that his interests as a creditor in relation to a loan he made to the company had been affected by his dismissal as a director. The fact that a creditor is also a member will not normally suffice, but here the petitioner had, in effect, provided all the venture capital for the business and so his right to remain in management of the company while that capital was at risk could amount to an interest as a member. This view was upheld by the Privy Council case of *Gamlestaden Fastigheter AB v Baltic Partners Ltd*,[280] allowing an appeal from the Court of Appeal of Jersey. In that case a 22 per cent shareholder in an insolvent joint-venture company had, in pursuance of the joint-venture agreement, invested not only in subscribing for shares but also in advancing loan capital to it. The Privy Council held that such an investor ought not to be precluded from the grant of relief under the Jersey equivalent of s.994[281] on the ground that the relief would benefit the investor only as loan creditor and not as member of the company.[282]

Meaning of unfairly prejudicial conduct

22–031   The section will be applicable to cases where the petitioner can show that the company's affairs "are being" or "have been" conducted in a manner which is "unfairly prejudicial". There is, however, no statutory definition of what constitutes such unfairly prejudicial conduct. It will be sufficient that a prejudicial act has been proposed[283] or that there has been prejudicial conduct of the company in the past.[284] Thus, the alleged conduct may be past, present or future. The test of unfair prejudice

---

[274] Also reported at [1997] 2 B.C.L.C. 739.
[275] [1999] 1 W.L.R. 1092, HL, at 1105.
[276] i.e. "in the capacity of" member.
[277] [1983] B.C.L.C. 126. See too *Alchemea Ltd, Re* [1998] B.C.C. 964 where, on the unusual facts of the case, it was held that the petitioners were affected as employees only.
[278] [1992] B.C.L.C. 213.
[279] [1995] 2 B.C.L.C. 280. See too *A Company, Re* [1986] B.C.L.C. 382, where the right of the members to sell their shares at the best price was held to be subject to protection under s.994 because it did not relate simply to their interests as vendors.
[280] [2007] UKPC 26; [2007] B.C.C. 272.
[281] art.141 of the Companies (Jersey) Law 1991.
[282] [2007] UKPC 26; [2007] B.C.C. 272 at [37], per Lord Scott of Foscote.
[283] A mere fear of future actions will not suffice, however: see *Astec (BSR) Plc, Re* [1998] 2 B.C.L.C. 556.
[284] See, e.g. *Kenyon Swansea Ltd, Re* [1987] B.C.L.C. 514.

is objective and does not depend on the subjective intention of the respondent[285] and, within certain constraints,[286] the court is given a wide discretion to determine the matter.[287] As the judge put it in the New Zealand case of *Thomas v H W Thomas Ltd*:

"Fairness cannot be assessed in a vacuum or simply from one member's point of view. It will often depend on weighing conflicting interests of different groups within the company. It is a matter of balancing all the interests involved in terms of the policies underlying the companies legislation in general and [s.994] in particular: thus to have regard to the principles governing the duties of a director in the conduct of the affairs of a company and the rights and duties of a majority shareholder in relation to the minority; but to recognise that [s.994] is a remedial provision designed to allow the Court to intervene where there is a visible departure from the standards of fair dealing; and in the light of the history and structure of the particular company and the reasonable expectations of the members to determine whether the detriment occasioned to the complaining member's interests arising from the acts or conduct of the company in that way is justifiable."[288]

As always, a balance has to be struck between the breadth of the discretion given to the court and the principle of legal certainty.[289] For these reasons, therefore, it is also essential for allegations of unfairly prejudicial conduct to be clearly pleaded.[290]

Unfairness—earlier cases

An important group of cases on s.994 has been concerned with whether or not **22–032** particular actions concerning the conduct of the company's business could be regarded as being both unfair and prejudicial. As one judge pointed out, it was not enough for conduct to be unfair without being prejudicial or prejudicial without being unfair.[291] Thus, in *D.R. Chemicals Ltd, Re*,[292] the action of a majority shareholder and director in allotting shares to himself to increase his shareholding from 60 per cent to 96 per cent was held not only to be a breach of the pre-emption rules of the Act but was also a "blatant case" of unfairly prejudicial conduct.[293] On the other hand, the fact that, after that date, the minority shareholder/director was paid no remuneration was not since he had taken no further part in the

---

[285] *Sam Weller & Sons Ltd, Re* [1990] B.C.L.C. 80 at 85; *Anderson v Hogg* [2002] B.C.C. 923 (Ct. Sess.), at 931; *Fisher v Cadman Developments Ltd* [2005] EWHC 377; [2006] 1 BCLC 499 at 527.

[286] Notably those laid down in *O'Neill v Phillips* [1999] 1 W.L.R. 1092, HL.

[287] See, e.g. *J.E. Cade & Son Ltd, Re*, where Warner J. said that "the court . . . has a very wide discretion, but it does not sit under a palm tree": [1992] B.C.L.C. 213 at 227.

[288] [1984] 1 N.Z.L.R. 686 at 694–695, per Richardson J.

[289] *O'Neill v Phillips* [1999] 1 W.L.R. 1092, HL, at 1099, per Lord Hoffmann.

[290] See *Technion Investments Ltd, Re* (1983) 1 B.C.C. 98, 962; *Baker v Potter* [2004] EWHC 1422 (Ch); [2005] B.C.C. 855 at 877.

[291] *A Company, Re (No.005685 of 1988)* [1989] B.C.L.C. 427 at 437, per Peter Gibson J. See too *Legal Costs Negotiators Ltd, Re* [1999] 2 B.C.L.C. 171, CA, at 197.

[292] (1989) 5 B.C.C. 39.

[293] See also *Dalby v Bodilly* [2004] EWHC 3078 (Ch); [2005] B.C.C. 627 where an allotment by a director of the remaining shares in the company's authorised share capital to himself, thereby diluting the petitioner's 50 per cent interest to one of 5 per cent, was held to be unfairly prejudicial conduct.

running of the company. Similarly, in *Ringtower Holdings Plc, Re*,[294] the late presentation of accounts was regarded as non-prejudicial. Where pre-emption provisions in the articles were deleted and the company re-registered as a private company as part of a management buy-out by the majority, this was not unfair to the minority, since the offer was available to them even though it might be prejudicial since they might be locked into the company if they refused the offer.

Further guidance as to the meaning of unfair prejudice was given by the Court of Appeal in *Saul D Harrison & Sons Plc, Re*.[295] Hoffmann L.J. stressed there that fairness was being used "in the context of a commercial relationship".[296] Thus, the starting point should be whether or not the conduct complained of was in accordance with the contractual terms which governed the relationships of the shareholder with the company and each other, i.e. whether or not the conduct complained of was in accordance with the articles.[297] If the board stepped outside their fiduciary duties, e.g. by exercising their powers for an ulterior purpose, they had stepped outside the bargain between the shareholders and the company. In Hoffmann L.J.'s opinion, trivial breaches of the articles would not suffice.[298] However, in cases where the letter of the articles did not reflect fully the understandings on which the shareholders were associated—as, for example in companies such as those in *Ebrahimi v Westbourne Galleries Ltd*[299]—there might be additional equitable rights, arising out of the fundamental understanding between the shareholders, which formed the basis of their association but was not put into contractual form.[300] In the same case, Neill L.J. sought to extract some guidelines from the earlier decisions. In his view the words "unfairly prejudicial" were general words to be applied flexibly to meet the circumstances of the particular case. Thus, in construing the word "unfairly", it would be necessary to take account not only the legal rights of the petitioner, but also any equitable considerations.[301]

Unfairness after Saul D. Harrison

22–033   Following the guidelines laid down in *Re Saul D. Harrison Ltd*,[302] Neuberger J. in *Marchday Group Plc, Re*[303] held that an allegation against the directors which involved no breach of the articles and nothing unlawful or underhand on the part of the directors could not found a petition. It would be different if the allegations had raised the issue of the directors acting ultra vires, e.g. by issuing shares at a

---

[294] (1989) 5 B.C.C. 82. See also *A Company, Re* (1989) 5 B.C.C. 792.

[295] [1995] 1 B.C.L.C. 14, CA.

[296] At 17.

[297] And other collateral agreements between shareholders.

[298] [1995] 1 B.C.L.C. 14, CA, at 18. He took as his starting point for this Lord Cooper's understanding of "oppression" in the Scottish case of *Elder v Elder & Watson* 1952 S.C. 49, viz. "a visible departure from the standards of fair dealing and a violation of the conditions of fair play on which every shareholder who entrusts his money to the company is entitled to rely".

[299] [1973] A.C. 360, above at para.22–023.

[300] [1995] 1 B.C.L.C. 14, CA, at 19.

[301] At 31.

[302] [1995] 1 B.C.L.C. 14, CA.

[303] [1998] B.C.C. 800. See also *Metropolis Motorcycles Ltd, Re* [2006] EWHC 364 (Ch.); [2007] 1 B.C.L.C. 520.

discount. In *Astec (BSR) Plc, Re*,[304] Jonathan Parker J. held that the concept of wider rights outside the articles, etc., had no part to play in a public quoted company. The shareholders had no legitimate expectations based on alleged breaches of the Stock Exchange Listing Rules,[305] the City Code on Take-overs and Mergers[306] or the Combined Code on Corporate Governance.[307] A majority shareholder could exercise its powers under the articles and the board was to be judged by the articles and the Act. To decide otherwise would be a recipe for chaos.

The particular issue in *Saul D. Harrison, Re* was the extent to which mismanagement of the company could amount to unfairly prejudicial conduct. In *Elgindata Ltd, Re*[308] it was said that serious mismanagement causing economic harm to the business could be unfairly prejudicial conduct but that in most cases simply mismanagement would not suffice. The Court of Appeal in *Saul D. Harrison, Re* emphasised that there would have to be a breach of duty involving abuse of power by the directors or ulterior motives, but in *Macro Ipswich Ltd, Re (No.1)*,[309] Arden J. allowed a petition based on serious mismanagement which had caused economic loss to the company and would continue to do so into the foreseeable future. In *BSB Holdings Ltd, Re (No.2)*,[310] the same judge said that what was needed was unfairly prejudicial conduct in a commercial context. She rejected the idea that only an abuse of power or an ulterior motive would suffice and suggested that acting otherwise than for the benefit of the company could suffice.

In *Blackwood Hodge Plc, Re*,[311] Jonathan Parker J. said that not all breaches of fiduciary duty would suffice, finding no evidence of prejudice on the facts of the case.[312] Harman J., however, has held that failure to implement a business plan was not just negligent mismanagement but abandonment of a structure which was the foundation of the petitioner's involvement with the company, so that if it had not been done bona fide in the interests of the company it could amount to unfairly prejudicial conduct.

It is clear that whatever the exact scope of petitions based on mismanagement, there is a real possibility of their being used as an alternative to a derivative action for a breach of fiduciary duty so avoiding the complexities of such actions.[313] If the conduct of the controller is prima facie "above board" it may still, because of surrounding circumstances, be "unfairly prejudicial" for the purposes of s.994.

In *A Company, Re*[314] L owned one-third of the shares of a company and was a director. He was removed from his directorship by the other two shareholders and presented a petition under s.994. An emergency general meeting of the company

---

[304] [1998] 2 B.C.L.C. 556.
[305] Above, para.15–001.
[306] Now the Takeover Code, below, para.33–005.
[307] Now the Revised Combined Code, above, para.17–105.
[308] [1991] B.C.L.C. 959.
[309] [1994] 2 B.C.L.C. 354.
[310] [1996] 1 B.C.L.C. 155.
[311] *Trace v European Healthcare Group Plc*, Unreported, February 4, 1998.
[312] But in *Gerrard v Koby* [2004] EWHC 1763 (Ch.); [2005] B.C.C. 181 where a majority shareholder and director had breached his fiduciary duty by expecting to make a secret profit from a property development, it was held that this destroyed the mutual confidence upon which the company had been founded and entitled the petitioner to relief.
[313] See *Lowe v Fahey* [1996] 1 B.C.L.C. 262.
[314] [1985] B.C.L.C. 80.

was then called to increase the company's capital and to give the directors power to allot the new shares. The majority shareholders only intended to issue the shares pro rata by way of a rights issue. L sued for an injunction to prevent this rights issue. Harman J. granted the injunction. Although the proposed rights issue was prima facie fair since it would not alter the balance, it might in certain circumstances amount to unfairly prejudicial conduct e.g. (i) if it was known that the dissenting shareholder could not afford to take up the offer and this was the reason for making it, or (ii) if the dissenting shareholder was engaged in litigation and the offer was designed to deplete his available funds. The judge also said that when a s.994 petition had been presented the status quo between the parties should be preserved until the hearing except where a change was absolutely essential.

Unfairness: O'Neill v Phillips

22–034   The leading case[315] on s.994 is now *O'Neill v Phillips*,[316] which was the first case to go all the way to the House of Lords on this provision of the Act. Lord Hoffmann stated that

> "In s.[994] Parliament has chosen fairness as the criterion by which the court must decide whether it has jurisdiction to grant relief. It is clear . . . that it chose this concept to free the court from technical considerations of legal right and to confer a wide power to do what appeared just and equitable. But this does not mean that the court can do whatever the individual judge happens to think fair. The concept of fairness must be applied judicially and the content which is given by the courts must be based upon rational principles".[317]

O, a manual worker, was employed by P Ltd, which was owned by P, who held the entire issued share capital of 100 £1 shares. Subsequently, P gave O 25 shares and appointed him as a director of P Ltd, with the declared intention that he should eventually take over the running of the company and be allowed to draw 50 per cent of the profits. This duly occurred, together with an indication that O's shareholding would be increased to 50 per cent once certain targets were reached. This never materialised; during a recession, P resumed personal command of the company, becoming MD. Subsequently, O's entitlement to 50 per cent of the profits was withdrawn, although he continued to receive his salary and any dividends payable on his 25 per cent shareholding. O brought a petition under s.459, founded on P's termination of equal profit-sharing and his repudiation of the alleged agreement for the allotment of more shares. This was dismissed at first instance but an appeal was successful, the Court of Appeal[318] ordering P to purchase O's shares, and holding that O had suffered unfair prejudice. Allowing the appeal, it was held that: (1) unfairness to a member ordinarily required some breach of the terms on which he had agreed that the company's affairs should

---

[315] See, e.g. *Grace v Biagioli* [2005] EWCA Civ. 1222; [2006] B.C.C. 85 at 103.
[316] [1999] 1 W.L.R. 1092, HL.
[317] At 1098.
[318] [1997] 2 B.C.L.C. 739, CA.

be conducted and since P had not agreed unconditionally to give O more shares or to share equally in the profits, he had not acted unfairly in withdrawing this; (2) a member of a company who had not been dismissed or excluded from participation in its management was not entitled to demand the purchase of his shares simply because of a breakdown in trust and confidence between the parties.

The important principles to emerge from this case may be stated as follows. First, confirming a line of reasoning espoused by him in *Saul D. Harrison Ltd, Re,*[319] a member of a company will not ordinarily be entitled to complain of unfairness unless there has been some breach of the terms[320] on which he agreed that the affairs of the company should be conducted.[321] Second, there will be cases in which equitable considerations will make it unfair for those conducting the affairs of the company to rely upon their strict legal powers, and "unfairness" may therefore consist "in a breach of the rules or in using the rules in a manner which equity would regard as contrary to good faith".[322]

This restatement of principle by Lord Hoffmann has not slowed down the **22–035** numbers of cases brought before the courts under s.994. Thus, it has been held that the conduct of a respondent majority shareholder of a company who arranged, without the petitioner's knowledge, for a substantially increased service charge to be paid and for payments to a pension fund, largely for his own benefit, amounted to unfairly prejudicial conduct.[323] In *Brownlow v G H Marshall Ltd,*[324] the petitioner, a member and director of a family company, was removed from office without any reasonable offer having been made for her shares. Her claim for an order that her shares be purchased was upheld on the basis that the company was one in which considerations of a personal character arising out of the relationships between family shareholders, which gave rise to equitable considerations.[325] In *Pettie v Thomson Pettie Tube Products Ltd,*[326] minority shareholders successfully brought a s.994 petition after alleging that a company's actions in allotting shares at par and substantially below their value to other shareholders was unfairly prejudicial to their interests because it reduced the value of prior shareholdings.[327] In *Irvine v Irvine*[328] the petitioners succeeded in establishing that a director was conducting a company's affairs in a manner prejudicial to their interests when it

---

[319] [1995] 1 B.C.L.C. 14, CA.

[320] Such terms are commonly contained in the articles of association and sometimes in collateral agreements (i.e. shareholder agreements) as between the shareholders: [1999] 1 W.L.R. 1092, HL, at 1098.

[321] At 1098–1099. Applied in *Rahman v Malik* [2008] EWHC 959 (Ch.); [2008] 2 B.C.L.C. 403. Lord Hoffmann also said that he did not suggest that such was the only form of conduct which would be regarded as unfair for the purposes of s.994: see 1101.

[322] At 1099, by analogy with *Ebrahimi v Westbourne Galleries Ltd* [1973] A.C. 360, above 356. See too *Guidezone Ltd, Re* [2000] 2 B.C.L.C. 321 at 355–356; *Anderson v Hogg* [2002] B.C.C. 923 (Ct. Sess.) at 931.

[323] *Lloyd v Casey* [2002] 1 B.C.L.C. 454. See too *Anderson v Hogg* [2002] B.C.C. 923 (Ct. Sess.), where a majority of the Court of Session confirmed that it was unfairly prejudicial to the petitioner when the respondent paid himself a sum, described as a redundancy payment, from the company.

[324] [2000] 2 B.C.L.C. 655.

[325] At 674. The court held that the existence of service agreements did not change the position.

[326] 2001 S.L.T. 473, OH

[327] See also *Sunrise Radio Ltd, Re* [2009] EWHC 2893 (Ch.).

[328] [2006] EWHC 406 (Ch.); [2007] 1 B.C.L.C. 349.

was shown that a director had drawn more remuneration than he should have and in consequence this had prevented the petitioners from receiving as much by way of dividends as they should have received.

But s.994 petitions have also failed on many occasions where unfair prejudice could not be shown. Thus, where the petitioner was unable to show, either singly or collectively, that there was unfair conduct for the purposes of s.994, the court declined the petition.[329] In particular, Jonathan Parker J. concluded that "there was nothing . . . which equity would regard as being contrary to good faith".[330] Similarly, where the board of a company had acted in accordance with its powers of general management conferred by the articles in relation to an issue of new shares which altered the control of the company, the court concluded that there was no unfair prejudice to the petitioner.[331]

In a later case, conduct which required a petitioner, who was a director and minority shareholder, to sign certain conditions coupled with a threat to dismiss him if he did not sign did not amount to unfair prejudice.[332] Nor, for that matter, was a minority shareholder successful in alleging that he had suffered unfair prejudice because of the sale of property at an undervalue. The Court of Appeal[333] held that there had been no harm done and no damage or prejudice caused to the appellant as a minority shareholder because the evidence showed that the price obtained was the best price reasonably available.[334] Also unsuccessful was the case involving a forced departure of a director from the board of a company, alleged to be unfair because another director had not been asked to resign and because of the company's refusal to provide relevant financial information to the potential purchaser of his shares.[335]

Exclusion from management and "legitimate expectations"

22–036   A number of earlier cases on s.994 dealt with the position of directors excluded from management in the case of companies formed on the basis of management participation. In *A Company, Re (No.002567 of 1982)*, Vinelott J. said that he thought that it was unlikely that such persons were intended to be excluded from s.994, even though it would not strictly affect his rights as a shareholder.[336] In a leading case of this earlier period, *R.A. Noble & Sons (Clothing) Ltd, Re*,[337] Nourse J. accepted that exclusion from management participation could amount to unfairly prejudicial conduct in cases such as *Ebrahimi v Westbourne Galleries Ltd*,[338] even though the value of the petitioner's shareholding would not have been

---

[329] *Guidezone Ltd, Re* [2000] 2 B.C.L.C. 321.

[330] At 359.

[331] *CAS (Nominees) Ltd v Nottingham Forest FC Plc* [2002] 1 B.C.L.C. 613.

[332] Nor, in the same case, was conduct requiring him to sign a share transfer: *John Reid & Sons (Strucsteel) Ltd, Re* [2003] EWHC 2329 (Ch.); [2003] 2 B.C.L.C. 319.

[333] Affirming the decision at first instance.

[334] *Rock Nominees Ltd v RCO (Holdings) Plc* [2004] EWCA Civ. 118; [2004] 1 B.C.L.C. 439, CA. See also *Wilkinson v West Coast Capital* [2005] EWHC 3009 (Ch.); [2007] B.C.C. 717.

[335] *Mears v R Mears & Co (Holdings) Ltd* [2002] 2 B.C.L.C. 1.

[336] [1983] 1 W.L.R. 927 at 933.

[337] [1983] B.C.L.C. 273.

[338] [1973] A.C. 360.

seriously diminished. A number of subsequent cases accepted that if the company was a quasi-partnership company, dismissal from management would suffice to found an petition under s.994,[339] but in *A Company, Re (No.00709 of 1992)*, it was said that, in such cases, unless another capacity could be attributed, any unfairly prejudicial conduct must affect the petitioner qua member.[340]

However, it was in the case of *A Company, Re*,[341] that Hoffmann J. first considered that exclusion from a legitimate expectation of taking part in a company's long-term management would be unfairly prejudicial. In another case in the same year, he said that in each such case the question was whether the terms on which the relationship came to an end were unfairly prejudicial to any of the participants.[342] Similarly, in *Ringtower Holdings Plc, Re*,[343] Peter Gibson J. accepted that if management participation was a legitimate expectation then its demise could found an petition on the basis of unfair prejudice. Thus, in *Kenyon Swansea Ltd, Re*,[344] attempts by the majority shareholders to alter the articles to regain control was held to be contrary to the legitimate expectations of the petitioner as to control.

In *Regional Airports Ltd, Re*[345] the petitioners complained that, as a quasi-partnership company in which all the shareholders were entitled to participate as directors and to be consulted about all major issues affecting their interests as shareholders, their removal as directors, an excessive claim to remuneration of a 50 per cent shareholder, and a proposed rights issue were unfairly prejudicial to their interests. The court upheld the petition on the basis that, in the context of their legitimate expectations, they were entitled to be dealt with on the basis of mutual trust and confidence. In *Richards v Lundy*[346] the court upheld the petition on the basis that the petitioner had been unfairly excluded from the management of the company and from his position as a director. Additionally, the conduct of the respondents was unfair because there had been a failure to satisfy the petitioner's legitimate expectation that the value of his 10 per cent shareholding should reflect the fact that no dividends were to be declared on the shares and that the shares should be regarded as his pension.

Reliance on arguments as to legitimate expectations have not, however, always **22–037** been successful. Thus, in *Blue Arrow Plc, Re*,[347] Vinelott J., although taking into consideration the wider equitable rights of the petitioner, rejected a petition by the president of a company when the articles were altered to allow her to be removed by a majority of the directors since she had no legitimate expectation that this would not happen on the company becoming a public company. Similarly, in *Posgate & Denby (Agencies) Ltd, Re*,[348] the non-voting shareholders were held to have no legitimate expectation as to a resolution to sell off some of the company's assets and in *Jaber*

---

[339] See, e.g. *Quinlan v Essex Hinge Co Ltd* [1996] 2 B.C.L.C. 417.
[340] [1997] 2 B.C.L.C. 739.
[341] [1986] B.C.L.C. 376.
[342] *A Company, Re* [1986] B.C.L.C. 362.
[343] (1989) 5 B.C.C. 82.
[344] [1987] B.C.L.C. 514.
[345] [1999] 2 B.C.L.C. 30.
[346] [2001] 1 B.C.L.C. 376.
[347] [1987] B.C.L.C. 585.
[348] [1987] B.C.L.C. 28.

v Science and Information Technology Ltd,[349] one shareholder was held to have no such interest in the voting rights of others. A variation on this was applied in *Tottenham Hotspur Plc, Re*,[350] where there was a dispute between a minority shareholder and the controlling shareholder of a quoted public company as to the former's dismissal as chief executive of the company. The dismissed chief executive was held to have no legitimate expectation of remaining in control since there was nothing which indicated to the other shareholders that the company was to be governed by anything other than its constitution, so that the board could dismiss him.

The majority in a quasi-partnership company, having forced the dismissal of a director, cannot complain if that individual refuses to sell his shares in the company to them. A complaint that he is no longer working for the benefit of all does not relate to the affairs of the company.[351] In *a Company, Ex p. Estate Acquisition and Development Ltd, Re*,[352] Mummery J. considered that the dismissal of a director, alteration of the company's constitution and lack of information was sufficient even in a company which was not a quasi-partnership company.

Legitimate expectations after O'Neill v Phillips

22–038   In *Saul D. Harrison & Sons Plc, Re*,[353] Hoffmann L.J. confirmed that he had in the past borrowed from public law the term "legitimate expectation" to describe the personal relationship between a shareholder and those controlling the company which would entitled him to say that it would, in certain circumstances, be unfair for them to exercise a power conferred by the articles upon the board or the company in general meeting.[354] In *O'Neill v Phillips*, Lord Hoffmann (as he now was) recanted from this position and said that such a legitimate expectation could exist only when equitable principles would make it unfair for a party to exercise rights under the articles. He concluded that:

> "the concept of a legitimate expectation should not be allowed to lead a life of its own, capable of giving rise to equitable restraints in circumstances to which the traditional equitable principles have no application".[355]

Thus, applying this approach, the court in the case of *Parkinson v Eurofinance Group Ltd*[356] found that the exclusion of the petitioner from the management of a company was not justified. In particular, the grounds which had been advanced for his immediate exclusion did not justify summary dismissal, and his dismissal without an offer to purchase his interest was unfairly prejudicial to him.[357]

---

[349] [1992] B.C.L.C. 764.
[350] [1994] 1 B.C.L.C. 655. See also *Astec (BSR) Plc* [1998] B.C.L.C. 556 as to the position vis-à-vis public quoted companies generally.
[351] *Legal Costs Negotiators Ltd, Re* [1999] 2 B.C.L.C. 171, CA.
[352] [1991] B.C.L.C. 154. But for public quoted companies, see *Astec (BSR) Plc, Re* [1998] 2 B.C.L.C. 556.
[353] [1995] 1 B.C.L.C. 14, CA.
[354] At 19.
[355] [1999] 1 W.L.R. 1092, HL. See too *Croly v Good* [2010] EWHC 1 (Ch.).
[356] [2001] 1 B.C.L.C. 720.
[357] At 750. See also *Fisher v Cadman* [2005] EWHC 377 (Ch.); [2006] 1 B.C.L.C. 499.

Exit at will or "No-fault divorce"

One of the arguments in *O'Neill v Phillips*, above, was that it was of no conse- **22–039** quence that the respondent had done anything unfair and that because trust and confidence had broken down between the parties the petition ought to be granted. In effect, this would mean that one member of the company ought to be entitled at will to require the others to buy his shares at a fair value.[358] This was flatly rejected by Lord Hoffmann, however, on the basis that there was no support in the authorities for such a right of unilateral withdrawal.[359] Further, he noted the views of the Law Commission's Report on Shareholder Remedies[360] on such a right of exit at will, which was that:

> "In our view there are strong economic arguments against allowing shareholders to exit at will. Also, as a matter of principle, such a right would fundamentally contravene the sanctity of a contract binding the members and the company which we considered should guide our approach to shareholder remedies".[361]

This approach was followed in *Phoenix Office Supplies Ltd, Re*,[362] where the Court of Appeal held that the petitioner had not shown, albeit as a member of a quasi-partnership company, that he had been unfairly prejudiced. A member of a company who wished voluntarily to sever his connection with the company for personal reasons, was not by s.994 given the means of forcing the other members to purchase his shareholding, when he had no contractual right so to do.

Similarly, in *Jayflex Construction Ltd, Re*[363] the court held that it was not sufficient to found a petition for relief to show that trust and confidence between members of a quasi-partnership company had broken down, regardless of whether that breakdown could be said to be the result of the conduct of the respondent. Further, the court said that a refusal by one 50 per cent shareholder to agree to a sealed bids procedure for the compulsory sale of shares did not constitute relevant unfairness.

Conduct of the petitioner

In deciding whether to grant a petition under s.994 the conduct of the petitioner **22–040** is relevant only to the extent either that it might make the conduct of the controllers although prejudicial not unfair, or that it might affect the remedy which the court may make. There is no general rule, as with the old s. 210, that the petitioner must come "with clean hands".[364]

---

[358] As to which see para.22–047, below.
[359] [1999] 1 W.L.R. 1092, HL, at 1104.
[360] Law. Com. No.246 (1997).
[361] [1997] 1 W.L.R. at 1105.
[362] [2002] EWCA Civ. 1740; [2003] 1 B.C.L.C. 76, CA.
[363] [2003] EWHC 2008 (Ch.); [2004] 2 B.C.L.C. 145.
[364] cf. derivative actions, para.22–007 and para.22–015, above.

In *London School of Electronics, Re*[365] X owned 250 and Y Ltd 750 shares in a company which ran degree courses. Y Ltd appropriated the students to its own courses and X was dismissed as a director and teacher. He set up another college and took several intending students with him. It was held that such an act was not a bar to his petition—on the facts there was no justification for Y Ltd's action. Nourse J. held that

> "Even if the conduct on the other side is both prejudicial and unfair, the petitioner's conduct may nevertheless affect the relief which the court thinks fit to grant . . . In my view there is no independent or overriding requirement that . . . the petitioner should come to the court with clean hands".[366]

This was considered further in the case of *Richardson v Blackmore*[367] where Lloyd L.J. stated that:

> "depending on the seriousness of the matter and the degree of its relevance, such conduct would be capable of leading a court to deny the petitioner any relief at all, even though the conditions under s.[994] are made out".[368]

On the facts of that case, however, though the petitioner had at one point forged a letter, the Court of Appeal found that his conduct was neither sufficiently serious nor sufficiently closely related to the respondents' unfairly prejudicial conduct to make it appropriate for the court to exercise its discretion so as to refuse to grant him a remedy.[369]

Further there is no rule that knowledge by the petitioner of any illegality in the company's business will bar a petition. It may, however, be a consideration in deciding the case.[370] On the other hand, a petition based on conduct of the company's affairs in which a petitioner had participated nine years before the presentation of the petition could not succeed.[371] Even though a s.994 petition was not subject to any period of limitation the court should not countenance proceedings such as these where the petition was presented nearly ten years after the events complained of.[372]

Procedural aspects

22–041 It has been held that a petition can be brought against a former controller of a company for unfairly prejudicial conduct whilst he was a member.[373] Nor is it a bar that some of the shares are the subject of disputed ownership.[374] On the other hand a single petition covering a group of companies has been rejected on the basis that a separate petition must be brought for each company.[375]

---

[365] [1986] Ch. 211. See also *Pectel Ltd, Re* [1998] B.C.C. 405.
[366] At 222.
[367] [2005] EWCA Civ. 1356 [2006] B.C.C. 276.
[368] At 289.
[369] At 291.
[370] *Bermuda Cablevision Ltd v Colica Trust Co Ltd* [1998] 1 B.C.L.C. 1, PC.
[371] See *Grandactual Ltd, Re* [2005] EWHC 1415 (Ch.); [2006] B.C.C. 73.
[372] At 79–80, per Sir Donald Rattee.
[373] *A Company* [1986] 1 W.L.R. 281.
[374] *Garage Door Associates Ltd, Re* [1984] 1 W.L.R. 35.
[375] *A Company, Re* [1984] B.C.L.C. 307.

A petitioner is not entitled to an indemnity against costs as in a derivative action[376] and in general costs will follow the result of the petition, although a reduction may be made on a successful petition if some heads prove to have been unsuccessful.[377] In general, no order will be made if the company is under the control of an administrative receiver unless the complaint relates to prevention of the petitioner selling his shares prior to the appointment.[378] A company other than the one directly involved may be joined as a party if it is directly involved in the transactions complained of,[379] but this is a matter for the court's discretion.[380]

Interface with section 306 orders

In general, the courts will act to prevent changes to the company's constitution **22–042** or assets pending the hearing of the petition[381] but the ordinary business of the company must be allowed to proceed. In this context a question can arise whereby during the existence of a s.994 petition the court is asked to order a meeting under s.306 because the necessary quorum for a meeting cannot be obtained, usually due to the dispute.[382] This is particularly difficult if the purpose of the meeting is to appoint new directors of the company. In *Opera Photographic Ltd, Re*,[383] the existence of a s.994 petition was held not to be a bar on the court making a s.306 order and this was followed in *Whitchurch Insurance Consultants Ltd, Re*.[384] In that case the s.994 petition was presented on the eve of the hearing of the s.306 petition and the position may be different if the s.306 petition is presented some time after that under s.994. Thus in *Sticky Fingers Restaurant Ltd, Re*[385] the court in those circumstances made the order under s.306 on the proviso that any director appointed by the meeting should undertake not to interfere with the s.994 petitioner's management rights pending the outcome of that petition. In *Harman v BML Group Plc*,[386] the existence of a s.994(1) petition was regarded as a factor to be taken into account and the Court of Appeal took notice of the fact that the allegations related to misappropriations by those in control who were petitioning under s.306.

Involvement of the company

The courts may also grant an injunction against the company being involved in the **22–043** petition. This is designed to prevent the majority/respondents from dissipating the company's assets in what is essentially a shareholder dispute.[387] This rule may be relaxed to allow the company to be represented at the time when the judgment

---

[376] *A Company, Re* [1987] B.C.L.C. 82. See, however, *Clark v Cutland* [2003] EWCA Civ. 810; [2004] 1 W.L.R. 783, CA, at 794.
[377] *Elgindata Ltd, Re (No.2)* [1993] B.C.L.C. 119.
[378] *Hailey Group Ltd, Re* [1993] B.C.L.C. 459.
[379] *BSB Holdings Ltd, Re* [1993] B.C.L.C. 915.
[380] *Little Olympian Each-Ways Ltd, Re* [1994] 2 B.C.L.C. 420.
[381] See, e.g. *Mountforest Ltd, Re* [1993] B.C.C. 565; *Corbett v Corbett* [1998] B.C.C. 93.
[382] Above, para.19–008.
[383] [1989] 1 W.L.R. 634.
[384] [1993] B.C.L.C. 1359.
[385] [1992] B.C.L.C. 84.
[386] [1994] 2 B.C.L.C. 674.
[387] *Milgate Developments Ltd, Re* [1993] B.C.L.C. 291.

is given so as to have an input into the consequential orders which may be made[388]; but no other costs should be charged to the company and, if they are, an assets valuation will be amended to protect the petitioner.[389] It follows that individual respondents cannot use corporate assets to fund their involvement if the company has not authorised those payments.[390] The company may apply to the court for permission to be involved but in *A Company, Re*[391] the court held that there was a rebuttable presumption that the company should not be involved and it would have to show that it was necessary or expedient in the company's interests to do so. Advance approval would require the most cogent evidence of compelling circumstances although it was not an automatic bar that the majority and the board were the same people.

Available remedies

22–044   If the court is satisfied it may make such order as it thinks fit.[392] No specific request need be made in advance. However, the section also provides five possible orders[393] which the court may make. The first of these is an order regulating the affairs of the company in the future.[394] The second is an order requiring the company to refrain from doing or continuing an act complained of, or to do an act that the petitioner has complained it has omitted to do.[395] The third is an order authorising civil proceedings to be brought in the name and on behalf of the company by such persons and on such terms as the court may direct.[396]

The respondent to a petition argued that the petitioner was too emotionally involved and vindictive to be given control of any litigation. The Court of Appeal still authorised proceedings to be brought but subject to certain conditions: (i) protection of creditors; (ii) the control of the litigation to be solely the affair of the petitioner's solicitor to the entire exclusion of the petitioner; (iii) no other legal proceedings to be commenced without legal opinion in support; and (iv) no direct communication between the petitioner and respondent.[397]

The fourth is an order requiring the company not to make any, or any specified, alterations in its articles without the leave of the court.[398]

The fifth type or order is an order providing for the purchase of the shares of any members of the company by other members or by the company

---

[388] *A Company, Re, Ex p. Johnson* [1992] B.C.L.C. 701.
[389] *Elgindata Ltd, Re* [1991] B.C.L.C. 959.
[390] *Corbett v Corbett* [1998] B.C.C. 93.
[391] [1994] 2 B.C.L.C. 146.
[392] s.996(1). This can include refusing the specific relief sought where that is inappropriate or there is a preferred alternative: *Antoniades v Wong* [1997] 2 B.C.L.C. 419, CA; or where the wrong has already been remedied by other means: *Legal Costs Negotiators Ltd, Re* [1999] 2 B.C.L.C. 171, CA.
[393] For interim orders see para.22–048, below.
[394] s.996(2)(a). This order could be made under the old s.210: see *H.R. Harmer Ltd, Re* [1959] 1 W.L.R. 62, CA. In practice such orders usually now merge with those under the fifth type below to provide a solution: see, e.g. *A Company, Re* (1989) 5 B.C.C. 792.
[395] s.996(2)(b).
[396] s.996(2)(c).
[397] *Cyplon Developments Ltd*, Unreported, March 3, 1982.
[398] s.996(2)(d).

itself[399] and, in the case of a purchase by the company itself, the reduction of the company's capital accordingly.[400] This is invariably the type of order which is made, such that it can be said that there is a general practice of doing so.[401]

In making an order as to the purchase of shares the court has very wide powers. While the court may order that the petitioner buy out the controller's shares,[402] that is relatively unusual and typically the issue is one of the purchase of a minority shareholder's shares.[403] Such an order will usually be made against the controlling shareholders but it can also be made against another company controlled by those shareholders which has been used as a vehicle to deprive the first company of its assets.[404]

Such purchases raise several questions. By what method are those shares to be **22–045** valued and at what date? As to the former it appears that when the shareholding is in a quasi-partnership company,[405] so that the shares were taken up initially and are still held by the shareholder as part of the management agreement, then the sale is in effect one from an unwilling vendor. The shares should therefore be valued pro rata according to the value of the shares as a whole.[406] On the other hand, where the shareholding has simply been acquired as a minority shareholding it should be valued at a discounted value as a minority shareholding.[407] Similarly where the petitioner has chosen to accept the ending of the management participation agreement and to remain as a minority shareholder his shares will be valued at the discounted price.[408] Preference shareholders, particularly those who have brought upon themselves the buy-out of their shares, will be treated the same way.[409] The court will adopt special valuation rules where the company is in a special position, e.g. a football club where the valuation depends upon prestige rather than profits.[410] In general, the shares should be valued taking the most up to date valuation available.[411]

---

[399] As, for example, in *Irvine v Irvine* [2006] EWHC 406 (Ch.); [2007] 1 B.C.L.C. 349. See also *Oak Investment Partners XII Ltd Partnership v Boughtwood* [2010] EWCA Civ. 23 where the buy-out order given by the judge (see [2009] EWHC 2394 (Ch.)) was described as "inevitable and unchallengeable": per Rimer L.J. at [123].

[400] s.996(2)(e).

[401] See *Grace v Biagioli* [2005] EWCA Civ. 1222; [2006] B.C.C. 85 at 108. The Court of Appeal found that the judge had been wrong to decline to order the purchase of the petitioner's shares and instead to order payment by the company of the dividend that was due to him.

[402] *Bovey Hotel Ventures Ltd, Re*, Unreported, June 10, 1982, CA; *Nuneaton Borough AFC Ltd, Re (No.2)* [1991] B.C.C. 44; *Brenfield Squash Racquets Club Ltd, Re* [1996] 2 B.C.L.C. 184.

[403] As in *Dalby v Bodilly* [2004] EWHC 3078 (Ch.); [2005] B.C.C. 627.

[404] *Little Olympian Each-Ways Ltd, Re (No.3)* [1995] 1 B.C.L.C. 636.

[405] i.e. an incorporated partnership such as that in *Ebrahimi v Westbourne Galleries Ltd* [1973] A.C. 360. See *Strahan v Wilcock* [2006] EWCA Civ. 13; [2006] B.C.C. 320.

[406] *Virdi v Abbey Leisure Ltd* [1990] B.C.L.C. 342 at 350; *Brownlow v G.H. Marshall Ltd* [2000] 2 B.C.L.C. 655; *Strahan v Wilcock* [2006] EWCA Civ. 13; [2006] B.C.C. 320.

[407] *Bird Precision Bellows Ltd, Re* [1986] Ch. 658, CA; *London School of Electronics, Re* [1986] Ch. 211; *Ghyll Beck Driving Range Ltd, Re* [1993] B.C.L.C. 1126; *Macro (Ipswich) Ltd, Re* [1994] 2 B.C.L.C. 354; *Irvine v Irvine (No.2)* [2006] EWHC 583 (Ch.); [2007] 1 B.C.L.C. 445; *McCarthy Surfacing Ltd, Re* [2008] EWHC 2279 (Ch.); [2009] B.C.C. 464.

[408] *D.R. Chemicals Ltd, Re* (1989) 5 B.C.C. 39.

[409] *Planet Organic Ltd, Re* [2000] 1 B.C.L.C. 366. In this case, the appropriate discount was assessed to be 30 per cent.

[410] *A Company, Re* (1989) 5 B.C.C. 792.

[411] *Regional Airports Ltd, Re* [1999] 2 B.C.L.C. 30.

Where the court orders that the shares be purchased under the pre-emption rules in the articles, i.e. by a valuer, the court will only subsequently interfere in the valuation if the instructions given to the valuer were wrong or not complied with.[412] If the valuation on that basis subsequently proves to be impossible the court will substitute its own valuation machinery.[413]

In some cases, the court will determine the valuation at trial, especially where the parties are in basic disagreement on the basis of the valuation.[414] Pumfrey J. has provided the following guidance:

"I think that when arriving at a 'fair value' in the absence of a market it is necessary to assume that the notional sale is taking place between the active participants in the transaction, since the whole purpose of the valuation is to be fair as between the parties. There is no market to provide an objective external criterion. The actual parties must be taken to participate in the sale as willing participants."[415]

22–046 Although the date of valuation is prima facie the date of the purchase order[416] this is not a general rule and if the value of the shareholding has been affected by the unfairly prejudicial conduct, the valuation date can be the date when the conduct began,[417] the date of the bringing of the petition,[418] or, in the case of an appeal, the agreed value as at the time of the first instance hearing.[419] The court has no power to make an interim order for payment pending an order for the purchase of the shares except where the only dispute is as to the valuation and the interim order is on the lowest possible contended valuation.[420]

In the case of an order for an interest, it has been held that such is not beyond the powers of the court under s.996.[421] Thus, in *Planet Organic Ltd, Re*,[422] the court found that there was nothing upon which interest should run, Jacob J. concluding that a forced sale was not like a case where damages had been caused and interest ran on the damages and so no interest element would be included in the amount payable to the petitioner.[423] It has been stated that such a power has to be exercised with extreme caution; Robert Walker L.J. has advised that

"If a petitioner seeking an order for the purchase of his shares contends . . . that they should be valued at a relatively early date but then augmented by the equivalent of interest, he must put forward that claim clearly and persuade the

---

[412] *Macro v Thompson (No.2)* [1997] 1 B.C.L.C. 626, CA; *Kranidites v Paschali* [2001] EWCA Civ. 357; [2003] B.C.C. 353, CA.

[413] *Macro v Thompson (No.3)* [1997] 2 B.C.L.C. 36.

[414] See, e.g. *Parkinson v Eurofinance Group Ltd* [2001] 1 B.C.L.C. 720.

[415] At 753. On the facts of the case, he concluded that the company should be valued on a going concern basis, on the usual principles (at 754).

[416] *D.R. Chemicals Ltd, Re* (1989) 5 B.C.C. 39; *Richards v Lundy* [2000] 1 B.C.L.C. 376.

[417] *OC (Transport) Services Ltd, Re* [1984] B.C.L.C. 251.

[418] *London School of Electronics, Re* [1986] Ch. 211; *Cumana Ltd, Re* [1986] B.C.L.C. 430, CA.

[419] *Profinance Trust SA v Gladstone* [2002] EWCA Civ 1031; [2002] 1 W.L.R. 1024, CA, at 1042. See too *Bilkus v King* [2003] EWHC 2516 (Ch.).

[420] *A Company, Re* (1987) 3 B.C.C. 41.

[421] See *Bird Precision Bellows Ltd, Re* [1986] Ch. 658, CA, where the Court of Appeal rejected any claim to interest.

[422] [2000] 1 B.C.L.C. 366.

[423] At 375.

court by evidence that it is the only way, or the best way, to a fair result. It should not be a last-minute afterthought . . . Unless a petitioner is asking for no more than simple interest at a normal rate he should also put before the court evidence on which the court can decide that amount (if any) to allow."[424]

Effect of offer to buy out the petitioner

If there is a breakdown in relations between director/shareholders so that one of **22–047** them brings a petition under s.994 on the basis of unfairly prejudicial conduct, the most likely order that the court will make is that one side, usually the majority shareholders, buy out the other. As we have seen,[425] such an order will provide for the method and date of the valuation of the shares.[426] In several cases, however, the majority will have already made an offer to purchase the petitioner's shares under the terms of the company's articles and the court is then faced with the problem as to whether such an offer, providing usually for valuation by an independent valuer such as the company's auditors, in effect settles the matter and accordingly no court order is necessary.[427]

In *Benfield Greig Group Plc, Re*,[428] the executors of a 30 per cent shareholding brought a petition under s.994 on the basis that they had been unfairly prejudiced, inter alia, by a failure on the part of the auditors to ascertain the true market value of the shares and that their valuation was one which no reasonable valuer could have arrived at, there being prima facie evidence that they had made a mistake. The evidence revealed that, prior to being appointed, the auditors had been engaged by the company to negotiate and agree with the Inland Revenue the value of incentive shares to be issued by the company to its employees. The Court of Appeal reversed the judge at first instance[429] and concluded that it was clearly arguable that the auditors had compromised their ability to be an independent valuer and that the executors had a real prospect of success in establishing a case under s.994.[430]

In *A Company, Re*[431] the articles actually required the dismissed director to offer his shares to the other shareholders. The majority intended to invoke this provision and on that basis Hoffmann J. refused to allow a s.994 petition based on that dismissal to continue. The articles had made provision in advance for what was to happen if there was a breakdown in relations. As in all such cases it was clear that one party had to leave and on the facts that had to be the petitioner

---

[424] *Profinance Trust SA v Gladstone* [2001] EWCA Civ. 1031; [2002] 1 W.L.R. 1024, CA, at 1035. See also *Scitec Group Ltd, Re* [2010] EWHC 1830 (Ch.).
[425] Above, para.22–045.
[426] cf. *Franbar Holdings Ltd v Casualty Plus Ltd* [2010] EWHC 1164 (Ch.) where the court held that a majority shareholder could not rely on a particular year's accounts to calculate the price it would pay for a minority shareholder's shares because it had unilaterally approved the accounts while keeping the minority shareholder in ignorance of them.
[427] No interest is payable on such an agreement unless expressly agreed: *Harrison v Thompson* [1992] B.C.L.C. 833.
[428] [2001] EWCA Civ. 397; [2002] 1 B.C.L.C. 65, CA.
[429] [2000] 2 B.C.L.C. 488.
[430] [2001] EWCA Civ. 397; [2002] 1 B.C.L.C. 65, CA, at 75. See too *Belfield Furnishings Ltd* [2006] EWHC 183 (Ch.); [2006] 2 B.C.L.C. 705.
[431] [1987] 1 W.L.R. 102.

on the terms of the articles. The judge did not, however, confine this principle to cases where the petitioner was obliged to sell his shares, but extended it to all cases where there is a dispute leading to a s.994 petition except where the majority have been guilty of bad faith or plain impropriety or the articles provide an arbitrary or artificial method of valuation. Hoffman J. stated that

> "It is almost always clear from the outset that one party will have to buy the other's shares and it is usually equally clear who that party will be. The only real issue is the price of the shares . . . Not many such petitions go to full hearing. They are usually settled by purchase of the petitioner's shares at a negotiated price. But the presentation of such a petition is a powerful negotiating tactic . . . In these circumstances it seems to me that if the articles provide a method for determining the fair value of a party's shares, a member seeking to sell his shares upon a breakdown of relations with other shareholders should not ordinarily be entitled to complain of unfair conduct if he has made no attempt to use the machinery provided by the articles . . . I therefore do not consider that in the normal case of breakdown of a corporate quasi-partnership there should ordinarily be any 'legitimate expectation' that a member wishing to have his shares purchased should be entitled to have them valued by the court rather than the auditors pursuant to the articles."[432]

22–048   This approach was initially followed in several cases. In *A Company, Re*,[433] such an offer was held to render the s.994 petition inappropriate, and the exact words of Hoffmann J. quoted above were applied by Peter Gibson J. in *A Company, Re*,[434] by Hoffmann J. again, *A Company, Re*[435] and Judge Paul Baker QC in *Castleburn Ltd, Re*.[436] In the latter case it was also said that if the valuers make a mistake the petitioner has a remedy to attack the valuation without resorting to a s.994 petition.

On the other hand, the court ordered a valuation under s.996(2)(e) if the valuer under the articles could not be seen to be wholly independent of the directors and to have no connection with the unfairly prejudicial conduct.[437] Nor did an offer to purchase some shares prevent a petition where the petitioner claimed to be entitled to other shares in the company.[438]

However, the Court of Appeal in *Virdi v Abbey Leisure Ltd*,[439] in rejecting the idea that an offer under the articles would automatically bar a winding up petition on the just and equitable ground[440] and reversing Hoffmann J. on that point, refused either to confirm or reject the idea that it would automatically bar an unfairly prejudicial petition. Following that decision, Harman J. in *A Company Ex*

---

[432] [1987] 1 W.L.R. 102, at 110.
[433] (1987) 3 B.C.C. 624.
[434] (1988) 4 B.C.C. 80.
[435] (1989) 5 B.C.C. 218.
[436] [1991] B.C.L.C. 89.
[437] *Boswell & Co (Steels) Ltd, Re* (1989) 5 B.C.C. 145.
[438] *A Company, Re* (1989) 5 B.C.C. 18.
[439] [1990] B.C.L.C. 342, CA.
[440] Above, para.22–021.

p. Holden, Re[441] decided that an offer to purchase was no bar where the s.994 petition was a management exclusion case, even though the articles included a compulsory share purchase procedure. The petitioner, he said, has no real right to challenge the auditors' valuation or to make representations to him.

In certain circumstances the court makes an interim order under s.994 pending further consideration of an offer made. If this is to be the case, the court must first be satisfied that there is a serious issue to be tried and that damages would not be an adequate remedy.[442] Thus, in *Pringle v Callard*,[443] the Court of Appeal held that it was open to the judge to decide that he could not properly deal with that matter without proper evidence on the offers and therefore to proceed on the basis that there was a serious issue to be tried.[444]

However, in *A Company, Re*[445] a petition was again stayed in a non-exclusion **22–049** case following an offer by the majority shareholder. The respondent was held to have minimised the risk inherent in a valuation under the articles and the petitioner would receive a fair value for his shares. In *West v Blanchet*[446] the petition was stayed when the court found that the respondents, in making an offer, had funds readily available to do so.

Lord Hoffmann has laid down the following guidelines as to what would count as a reasonable offer—

1. The offer must be to purchase the shares at a fair value, ordinarily a value representing an equivalent proportion of the total issued share capital, without a discount for its being a minority holding.

2. The value, if not agreed, should be determined by a competent expert.

3. The offer should be to have the value determined by the expert as an expert, with the objective of economy and expedition.

4. The offer should provide for equality of arms between the parties and both should have the same right of access to information about the company which bears on the value of the shares and both should have the right to make submissions to the expert.

5. As to costs, these need not always be offered. If there is a breakdown between the parties, the majority shareholder should be given a reasonable opportunity to make an offer before he becomes obliged to pay costs. The mere fact that the petitioner has presented his petition before the offer did not mean that the respondent must offer to pay the costs if he was not given a reasonable time.[447]

Furthermore, he has also stated that

---

[441] [1991] B.C.L.C. 597.
[442] See *American Cyanamid Co v Ethicon Ltd* [1975] A.C. 396.
[443] [2007] EWCA Civ. 1075; [2008] 2 B.C.L.C. 505.
[444] At [29].
[445] [1996] 2 B.C.L.C. 192.
[446] [2001] 1 B.C.L.C. 795. In this case the court had to consider the reasonableness of competing offers made by two equal shareholders.
[447] *O'Neill v Phillips* [1999] 1 W.L.R. 1092, HL, at 1107–1108.

". . . parties ought to be encouraged, where at all possible, to avoid the expense of money and spirit inevitably involved in such litigation by making an offer to purchase at an early stage".[448]

Applications to strike-out

22–050 In certain circumstances proceedings under s.994 may be struck out on the basis that the petition fails to disclose a reasonable cause of action.[449] The discretion to do so is now contained in the CPR Pt 3.4.[450]

There has been authority in the past for striking out a petition owing to the lack of standing of the petitioner. Thus, in one case where the petitioner alleged that he was a transferee by operation of law by virtue of an alleged constructive trust of the relevant share in his favour, the court simply disallowed the application which was made.[451] In a case in the Companies Court the same year, the judge held that the petitioner was not a transferee of shares merely because he and his wife had agreed that she should transfer her shares to him in certain circumstances and struck out the petition.[452] But in *Starlight Developers Ltd, Re*[453] the court stayed, rather than struck out, an application where there was a triable claim with reasonable, i.e. not purely fanciful, prospects of success for retrospective rectification from a date ante-dating the presentation of the petition.

In certain cases, the strike out proceedings may be invoked because a reasonable offer has been made to purchase the petitioner's shares. As a matter of principle, in *Re Saul D. Harrison*, Hoffmann L.J. stated that

"I accept that the notoriously burdensome nature of s.[994] proceedings does not lighten the burden on the respondent who applies to have the petition struck out. He must still satisfy the court that the petitioner's case is plainly and obviously unsustainable. But I think that the consequences for the company mean that a court should be willing to scrutinise with care the allegations in a s.[994] petition and, if necessary, the evidence proposed to be adduced in support, in order to see whether the petitioner really does have an arguable case."[454]

Thus, in *Oriental Gas Co Ltd, Re*, the judge accepted that it was appropriate for him, in considering whether to strike out a petition, to ask whether it was "plain

---

[448] At 1106.

[449] As to the arguments for staying an action in Chancery, pending a s.994 petition, see *Jones v Jones* [2002] EWCA Civ. 961; [2003] B.C.C. 226. It was alleged in that case that the Chancery action was being funded out of corporate funds, giving the respondents to the s.994 petition financial support for their defence. The Court of Appeal ordered that the Chancery proceedings be adjourned pending the resolution of the s.994 petition.

[450] Formerly RSC, Ord.18, r.19(1). Generally, see *Lawrance v Lord Norreys* (1890) 15 App. Cas. 210 at 220; *Wenlock v Maloney* [1965] 1 W.L.R. 1239, CA.

[451] See *A Company, Re (No.007828 of 1985)* (1986) 2 B.C.C. 98, 951.

[452] See *A Company, Re (No.003160 of 1986)* (1986) 2 B.C.C. 99, 276. See too *Quickdome Ltd, Re* (1988) 4 B.C.C. 296.

[453] [2007] EWHC 1660 (Ch.); [2007] B.C.C. 929.

[454] [1995] 1 B.C.L.C. 14, CA, at 22. In this case the petition was struck out because the court was satisfied that the claim of unfairness by the minority shareholder was not reasonably arguable. See too *Astec (BSR) Plc, Re* [1998] 2 B.C.L.C. 556, where a petition was struck out where it was being used as a tactical ploy to exert pressure to achieve a collateral purpose (in forcing a takeover bid).

and obvious" that the relief sought would never be granted.[455] In allowing the application to strike out, he warned that litigants should be encouraged to make an application "sooner rather than later".[456] It is clear that the court will strike out the application where there has been an intentional delay, such that it is no longer possible to have a fair trial. Thus, on the unusual facts of *Vitara Foods Ltd, Re* the court found that there had not merely been delay, but the proceedings had become meaningless at law and, in the face of such an inordinate and inexcusable delay, the petition would be struck out.[457]

Subsequent cases have considered striking out in the context of the Woolf **22–051** Reforms to Civil Procedure (the CPR). In *North Holdings Ltd v Southern Tropics Ltd*, the Court of Appeal has emphasised the need, in striking out applications, for active case management, so as to reduce the time and expense involved in ascertaining the fair price to be paid for the petitioner's shares.[458] In *Arrow Nominees Inc v Blackledge*[459] the Court of Appeal found, on the facts, which included forged documents, that there had been a "flagrant and continuing affront to the court" and that striking out was not a disproportionate remedy for such an abuse.[460] A petition to strike out would, however, not follow where, for example, there have been countervailing offers for the purchase of shares by the parties and where "who should buy whose shares had become the battleground of the petition".[461]

In relation to striking out for delay, the authorities establish that any sanction by the court in relation to a particular case of delay has to be proportionate and requires a degree of flexibility by the court. So, in *Hateley v Morris*[462] the court decided not to strike out a petition under s.994 for delay because to do so would not be fair or proportionate. On the facts, both parties were at fault and striking out the petition would not dispose of their dispute.

In declining to strike out an application for abuse of process, Jonathan Crow provided the following succinct summary of the principles in *Atlasview Ltd v Brightview Ltd*[463]—

1. The court had an inherent jurisdiction to prevent its process being abused.

2. The public policy underlying the exercise of the court's discretion was to discourage stale claims and multiple proceedings by encouraging disputes to be brought to a timely conclusion.

3. The question whether or not a particular action was an abuse of process would depend on all the circumstances, taking into account both the public policy issues and the private rights and interests of the particular parties.

---

[455] [1999] B.C.C. 237 at 245.
[456] [1999] B.C.C. 23 at 245.
[457] [1999] B.C.C. 315. But cf. *Guinness Peat Group Plc v British Land Co Plc* [1999] 2 B.C.L.C. 243, CA, which the Court of Appeal decided was not an appropriate case to strike out the petition.
[458] [1999] B.C.C. 746, CA, at 770. See too *Rotadata Ltd, Re* [2000] 1 B.C.L.C. 122 at 127.
[459] [2000] 2 B.C.L.C. 167, CA.
[460] At 202.
[461] *Apcar v Aftab* [2003] B.C.C. 510 at 519.
[462] [2004] EWHC 252 (Ch.); [2004] 1 B.C.L.C. 582.
[463] [2004] EWHC 1056 (Ch.); [2004] 2 B.C.L.C. 191 at 200–201.

4. The circumstances in which proceedings may be held to represent an abuse of process could not be exhaustively defined.

5. It was too dogmatic to suggest that, because an issue could have been raised in earlier proceedings, it should have been so raised.

6. A collateral attack on an earlier decision of a court of competent jurisdiction may be, but was not necessarily, an abuse of process.

7. If an earlier decision was of a court exercising civil jurisdiction, that was binding on the parties and their privies in any later civil proceedings.

8. If the parties bringing the collateral attack were not parties to the earlier decision or their privies, it would only be an abuse if the attack would produce obvious unfairness to another party, or bring the administration of justice into disrepute.[464]

Joint petitions for a just and equitable winding up and the alternative remedy

22–052 In the past, many petitions based on management exclusion cases sought either a just and equitable winding up under s.122 of the Insolvency Act 1986 or relief under s.994, as alternatives. Prior to 1980, it was generally easier to obtain a winding up order. Thus in *R.A. Noble and Sons, Re*,[465] Nourse J. refused to grant a petition under s.994 on the grounds that objectively the management exclusion had not been unfair since it was partly due to the petitioner's disinterest. The judge did, however, make a winding up order since the exclusion had been the substantial cause of the breakdown in mutual confidence. Thus for a winding up the question is whether the management exclusion was a substantial cause of the subjective breakdown of the underlying equitable obligation of mutual trust whereas for an alternative remedy petition the exclusion must amount to unfairly prejudicial conduct affecting the petitioner qua member.[466] Similarly in *Jesner v Jarrad Properties Ltd*,[467] conduct by the controller of two companies in using the assets of one to fund the other was held not to be unfair to the minority shareholders since both companies were owned by the same people, but a winding up order was granted on the basis of breach of underlying management rights.

The Chancery Division warned in a Practice Direction[468] that a petition under s.122(1)g should only be used as an alternative to a s.994 petition if that is either the preferred relief or possibly the only relief available.

The court has a discretion whether to allow one or both of the petitions to proceed. Thus in *Copeland Craddock Ltd, Re*,[469] a joint petition was allowed to

---

[464] On the facts of the case, the judge held that the application should not be struck out because it was not possible to conclude that the petition represented an abuse of process.

[465] [1983] B.C.L.C. 273. See also *Coulson Sanderson & Ward Ltd v Ward, The Financial Times*, October 18, 1985; *A Company, Re* (1989) 5 B.C.C. 18.

[466] *A Company, Re* [1990] B.C.C. 221.

[467] [1993] B.C.L.C. 1032.

[468] Chancery 1/90; [1990] 1 W.L.R. 490.

[469] [1997] B.C.C. 294.

proceed because the relief sought under s.994 was to buy out the respondent and the winding up provided an alternative way of buying back into the company, from which he had been excluded, on a purchase from the liquidator. On the other hand, in *A Company, Re*[470] the judge struck out the winding up petition since the winding up was a remedy of last resort, the company was prosperous, and there was no reasonable chance of such an order being made.

As we have seen, the seminal decision in *O'Neill v Phillips*, has laid down a blueprint for cases involving unfair prejudice, while at the same time accepting that "unfairness" for the purposes of s.994 may consist in a breach of the rules or in using the rules in a manner which equity would regard as contrary to good faith. Lord Hoffmann in that case took pains to point that any parallel drawn between the notion of "just and equitable"[471] and the notion of fairness in s.994 did not mean that conduct will not be unfair unless it would have justified an order to wind up the company. As has recently been pointed out in the case of *Hawkes v Cuddy*:

"In many, if not most, cases the conduct of the respondent may give rise both to the jurisdiction under s.994 and to that under s.122(1)(g); but there may be cases which satisfy the requirements of one jurisdiction but not the other. In addition, it should be borne in mind that a winding up may be ordered on the 'just and equitable' ground where no unfair conduct is alleged, as in the cases in which the so-called substratum has gone. [This] is consistent with the differences in the statutory wording: Parliament would not have used such different wording in s.994 of the Companies Act 2006 and in s.122(1)(g) of the Insolvency Act 1986 if the jurisdictions were intended to be coterminous."[472]

Thus, the mere fact of deadlock and the inability of a company to conduct its business as initially contemplated when the parties trusted and had confidence in each other might be inherent in the breakdown of that trust and confidence, but did not without more satisfy the requirements of s.994.[473]

INVESTIGATIONS AND POWERS TO OBTAIN INFORMATION

Introduction

Notwithstanding the progressive introduction of the 2006 Act, the principal inves-   **22–053**
tigatory provisions relating to companies are contained in Pt XIV of the Companies Act 1985,[474] as amended.[475] The Secretary of State for the Department for Business,

---

[470] [1997] 1 B.C.L.C. 479.
[471] i.e. as explained by Lord Wilberforce in *Ebrahimi v Westbourne Galleries Ltd* [1973] A.C. 360, para.22–023, above.
[472] [2009] EWCA Civ. 291; [2009] 2 B.C.L.C. 427, at [104]–[105], per Stanley Burnton L.J. He expressly overruled the case of *Guidezone Ltd, Re* [2000] 2 B.C.L.C. 321 on this point.
[473] At [108].
[474] See ss.431–453. These provisions are among the very few which remain in the 1985 Act.
[475] By the Companies Act 1989, by the Companies (Audit Investigations and Community Enterprise) Act 2004, and again by the 2006 Act. The latter Act makes some changes to the provisions on investigations (ss.1035–1038), but otherwise leaves the existing provisions intact.

Innovation and Skills (BIS) is given wide powers by the Act to examine the membership, the affairs and the activities of certain personnel of a company.

The work of the Companies Investigation Branch (CIB)

22–054   The work and investigatory powers of the Secretary of State is devolved to the Companies Investigation Branch (CIB),[476] which has since 2006 been located within the Insolvency Service, an Executive Agency of BIS.[477] The principal objective of CIB is to increase confidence in the working of corporate and financial markets through effective enforcement action. In particular, this involves the use of statutory investigative powers to establish the underlying facts in cases of possible commercial wrong-doing, serious misconduct, fraud or sharp practice in the way a company operates. It also involves following up cases investigated and ensuring that cases are referred to other regulatory bodies, such as the Serious Fraud Office (SFO), the FSA[478] and other professional bodies.

Powers in outline

22–055   The powers given to the Secretary of State fall into three main categories:

1.   the power to appoint and give directions to investigative inspectors;

2.   the power to require documents and information; and

3.   the power to enter and remain on premises.

Investigations of a company's affairs

22–056   The Secretary of State is bound to appoint an inspector (or inspectors) where the court having the appropriate jurisdiction declares that the company's affairs ought to be investigated by an inspector appointed by the Department.[479] The Secretary of State will require inspectors appointed to "report the result of their investigations to him".[480]

The Secretary of State *may* appoint inspectors where it appears to him that there are circumstances suggesting that the business of the company is being, or has been

1.   conducted with intent to defraud its own creditors;

2.   with intent to defraud the creditors of any other person, e.g. of any associated company;

---

[476] Companies Investigation Branch, Ground Floor, 21 Bloomsbury Street, London WC1B 3QW, email: *vetting.section@berr.gsi.gov.uk.*

[477] See *www.insolvency.gov.uk/cib/index.htm.*

[478] The Financial Services Authority.

[479] s.432(1). For an example of a case arising out of the appointment of inspectors under s.432, see *Soden v Burns* [1996] 1 W.L.R. 1512.

[480] This wording is substituted for the previous phrase, "report on them in such a manner as he may direct": inserted by Companies Act 2006 s.1035(3).

3. for another fraudulent purpose;

4. for another unlawful purpose;

5. in a manner which is unfairly prejudicial to some part of its members, or that any act or omission of the company is or would be so prejudicial.[481]

The Secretary of State may also act where those concerned with the company's formation or management have been guilty of fraud, misfeasance or other misconduct towards the company or its members[482] and where the company's members have not been given all the information with respect to its affairs which they might reasonably expect.[483]

The Secretary of State is empowered, but not bound, to appoint an inspector (or inspectors) on an application by 200 or more members of a company having a share capital[484] or of members holding not less than one-tenth of the shares issued,[485] excluding any shares held as treasury shares,[486] and, in any case, on application of the company.[487] The application must be supported by such evidence as the Secretary of State may require for the purpose of showing that the applicant or applicants have good reason for requiring the investigation.[488] The Secretary of State, in appointing the inspectors, may require them to "report the result of their investigations to him".[489] Inspectors may be appointed on terms that any report they make will not be for publication and in such cases the usual rules[490] governing the availability and publication of such inspectors' reports do not apply.[491]

Powers of the Secretary of State to give directions to inspectors

The 2006 Act implements a number of new sections in Pt XIV of the Companies Act 1985. Thus, an inspector is required to comply with any direction given to him by the Secretary of State under this section.[492] In relation to appointments under s.431 or s.432(2), the Secretary of State may give the inspector a direction as to the subject matter of his investigation (whether by reference to a specified area of a company's operation, a specified transaction, a period of time or otherwise) or which requires the inspector to take or not to take a specified step in his investigation.[493] The Secretary of the State may order an inspector to take no further steps in his investigation.[494]   **22–057**

---

[481] s.432(2)(a) and (b). For these purposes it would be necessary to show a prima facie case upon the principles relevant to the court's powers under what was s.994 of the 2006 Act.
[482] s.432(2)(c).
[483] s.432(2)(d).
[484] s.431(2)(a).
[485] s.431(2)(b).
[486] Generally as to treasury shares, see para.10–017 above.
[487] s.431(2)(c).
[488] s.431(3).
[489] This wording is substituted for the previous phrase, "report on them in such a manner as he may direct": inserted by Companies Act 2006 s.1035(2).
[490] i.e. those in s.437.
[491] s.432(2A).
[492] s.446A(1).
[493] s.446A(2).
[494] s.446B(1).

Where an inspector resigned or had his appointment revoked,[495] the Secretary of State may direct him to produce documents[496] obtained or generated during the course of his investigation to himself or an inspector appointed by him.[497]

Duties of company and its officers and agents

22–058 In order to enable the inspector to carry out his investigation, a duty is cast upon the officers and agents of the company, and of any other company which is incidentally investigated as a related company under s.433, to produce requested documents within their custody or power,[498] to attend before the inspectors and to give all assistance which they are reasonably[498] able to give.[499]

Powers of inspectors in relation to company's officers and agents

22–059 If inspectors consider that an officer or agent[500] of the company or other body corporate, or any other person, is or may be in possession of information relating to a matter which they believe to be relevant to the investigation, they may require him to produce to them any documents in his custody or power relating to that matter, to attend before them, and otherwise to give them all assistance in connection with the investigation which he is reasonably able to give.[501]

Further powers of the inspector

22–060 Inspectors are given powers to secure the attendance of and production of documents by persons other than directors and agents of the company under investigation.[502] Such other persons can be required to assist the investigations and are placed under a statutory duty so to do. The Secretary of State may obtain a search warrant enabling the police to enter and search premises and take possession of documents.[503]

Giving of evidence and the use of incriminating evidence

22–061 Any person required to give evidence may not attend nor be represented when other persons are giving evidence nor see any transcript of such evidence. As a general principle, the Act provides that there is no privilege against self-incrimination and all evidence given may be used in subsequent proceedings.[504]

---

[495] s.446E(1). This section is inserted into the Companies Act 1985 by s.1037 of the Companies Act 2006.
[496] A "document" includes information recorded in any form: s.446E(8).
[497] s.446E(3).
[498] See as to reasonableness, *An inquiry into Mirror Group Newspapers Plc, Re* [2000] Ch. 194.
[499] s.434(1).
[500] The reference to officers or to agents includes past, as well as present, officers or agents while "agents", in relation to a company or other body corporate, includes its bankers and solicitors and persons employed by it as auditors, whether these persons are or are not officers of the company or other body corporate: s.434(4). A receiver and manager may be the agent of the company: *R. v Board of Trade Ex p. St Martins Preserving Co Ltd* [1965] 1 Q.B. 603, 622.
[501] s.434(2).
[502] s.434(2).
[503] s.448.
[504] s.434(4). See *Bishopsgate Investment Management Ltd (In Provisional Liquidation) v Maxwell* [1993] Ch. 1, CA.

Admissibility of statements in evidence: criminal proceedings

Section 434(5) provides that answers by any person, whether an officer or agent **22–062** of the company or otherwise, are admissible in both civil and criminal proceedings against him.[505] But the only answers admissible in evidence under s.434(5) are those given on oath.[506]

Reports by inspectors: report written or printed

After hearing the evidence, the inspector has to arrive at his conclusions; these **22–063** need not be tentative but may be final.[507] The inspector makes a report to the Secretary of State[508] and he may also, of his own initiative or on direction, make interim[509] reports and may at any time, or shall if directed by the Secretary of State, inform him of any matter of which the inspector is aware as a result of the investigation.[510]

If the inspectors were appointed by order of the court under s.432(1), a copy of their report must be furnished by the Secretary of State to the court.[511] Otherwise, the Secretary of State may, if he thinks fit, supply copies to the company[512] and, on request and on payment of a fee, to any member of the company or any person whose conduct is referred to in the report, the company's auditors, the applicants for the investigation, and any other person whose financial interests appear to be affected by the matters dealt with in the report.[513] The Secretary of State may, moreover, also cause the report to be printed and published.[514] It is the policy of the Secretary of State to publish s.437 reports in the public interest.

An inspector's report is not itself a legal decision, nor are the opinions of the inspector expressed therein binding upon any person in the manner that a judgment of the court is. It is merely an expression of the findings and opinions of the inspector.[515] There is no right of appeal against such findings or opinions nor any way for witnesses to prevent publication of their reports.[516] Since there is no certainty that proceedings will follow, in which a person referred to might defend his name, such investigations are not altogether satisfactory. A copy of all or any reports made by inspectors under Pt XIV of the Act if certified by the Secretary of State to be a true copy is admissible in any legal proceedings as evidence of the opinion of the inspector in relation to any matter contained in the report and

---

[505] On the right of access of a liquidator to evidence produced before the inspector, see *Rolls Razor Ltd, Re (No.1)* [1968] 3 All E.R. 698. On the admissibility of evidence given to inspectors in civil proceedings see *London & County Securities Ltd v Nicholson* [1980] 1 W.L.R. 948.

[506] s.434(3).

[507] *Maxwell v Department of Trade and Industry* [1974] Q.B. 523, CA.

[508] s.437(1).

[509] See Aldous F.C.A. and Kaye QC *Transtec Plc* (HMSO, 2001).

[510] s.437(1A).

[511] s.437(2).

[512] s.437(3)(a).

[513] s.437(3)(b).

[514] s.437(3)(c).

[515] *Grosvenor and West End Railways Terminus Hotel Co* (1897) 76 L.T. 337; *Sba Properties Ltd, Re* [1967] 1 W.L.R. 799 at 806.

[516] *Pergamon Press, Re* [1971] Ch. 388, CA.

in proceedings on an application for a disqualification order under s.8 of the Company Directors Disqualification Act 1986 following a report under s.437 or following the receipt of documents or information obtained under s.447 or s.448, as evidence of any fact stated in the report.[517]

Consequences of an investigation

22–064 Under s.8 of the Company Directors Disqualification Act 1986, the Secretary of State may, if it appears from a report made by inspectors under s.437 to be in the public interest, apply to Court for disqualification of any person who is or who has been a director or shadow director of any company. The court will make such an order where it is satisfied that such a person's conduct in relation to the company makes him unfit to be concerned in the management of a company.[518] The maximum period of disqualification under the section is 15 years.[519]

If the report appears to disclose any offence in relation to the company for which any person should be prosecuted, the Secretary of State may institute criminal proceedings for this purpose. Alternatively, the matter could be placed in the hands of the police or the Serious Fraud Office.

Section 124A[520] of the Insolvency Act 1986 empowers the Secretary of State, after receiving information from various types of investigation,[521] to petition the court that it is expedient and in the public interest that the company investigated be wound up if the court thinks it just and equitable to do so,[522] unless it is already being wound up by the court.[523] The last-mentioned words appear to give the Secretary of State power to petition for a winding up order notwithstanding that the company is already in voluntary liquidation.

If it appears to the Secretary of State (a) that the affairs of a company are being or have been conducted in a manner which is unfairly prejudicial to the interests of its members generally or of some part of its members, or (b) any actual or proposed act or omission of a company, including an act or omission on its behalf, is or would be so prejudicial, he may himself (in addition to or instead of presenting a petition for the winding up of the company) apply to the court by petition for an order.[524]

---

[517] s.441(1). A document which purports to be such a certificate shall be received in evidence and be deemed to be such a certificate, unless the contrary is proved: s.441(2).

[518] s.8(2).

[519] s.8(4).

[520] See *Marann Brooks CSV Ltd, Re* [2003] B.C.C. 239; *Rodencroft Ltd, Re* [2004] EWHC 862 (Ch.); [2004] 1 W.L.R. 1566; *Bell Davies Trading Ltd v Secretary of State for Trade and Industry* [2004] EWCA Civ. 1066; [2005] 1 B.C.L.C. 516; *Secretary of State for Trade and Industry v Atlantic Property Ltd* [2006] EWHC 610 (Ch.).

[521] Including Companies Act investigations, Insider Dealing and other Financial Services investigations, fraud investigations or investigations for overseas regulators.

[522] s.124A(1).

[523] s.124A(2). For the relationship between the Secretary of State's petition for a winding up order and the appointment of a provisional liquidator see *Highfield Commodities Ltd, Re* [1985] 1 W.L.R. 149.

[524] s.460(1).

Investigation of the ownership of a company

The Secretary of State is given powers to investigate and report on the membership **22–065** of a company, and otherwise for the purpose of determining the true persons who are or have been financially interested in the success or failure, or in the apparent success or failure, of the company, or who are able to control or materially to influence the policy of the company.[525] These powers are in very wide terms and, subject to the terms of their appointment, the powers of the inspector extend to the investigation of any circumstances suggesting the existence of an arrangement or understanding which, though not legally binding, is or was observed or likely to be observed in practice and which is relevant to the purposes of the investigation.[526] The Secretary of State is, moreover, empowered but not bound to appoint an inspector (or inspectors) "where it appears to him that there is good reason so to do".[527]

The Secretary of State is bound, subject to certain qualifications, to appoint an inspector (or inspectors) where an application is made by one of the minorities entitled by s.431 to apply for an investigation with respect to particular shares or debentures of the company.[528] The Secretary of State can ask them for security for the costs of an investigation under s.442 to an amount not exceeding £5,000 or such other sum as he may by order specify.[529]

Powers of the inspector

The Secretary of State instructs the inspector as to the scope of his investigation, **22–066** particularly in regard to the period to which it is to extend (for instance, to cover the persons interested in the shares during the past ten years). In the absence of express instructions to the contrary in the terms of reference, the inspector is not restricted in his investigation to the strict facts of his reference. He is empowered to take into account any circumstances suggesting the existence of an arrangement or understanding which, though not legally binding, is or was observed or is or was likely to be observed in practice and which is relevant to the purpose of his investigation,[530] e.g. if employees of one person between them hold a large number of shares in a company sufficient to exercise an influence in its affairs if they were to vote consistently together, such circumstances would be relevant to the inspector's investigation.

The powers of the inspector to investigate are not restricted to the company the membership of which he is instructed to examine. Under the general provisions relating to inspection he may extend his investigation to related companies if he considers this necessary for the purposes of his investigation.[531] In addition, he may extend his investigation to other persons whom he has reasonable cause to

---

[525] See s.442.
[526] s.442(4).
[527] s.442(1).
[528] s.442(3). Such an investigation took place in November 1953 upon the application of 224 members of the Savoy Hotel Ltd. The investigation became known as the *First Savoy Hotel Investigation*. An interim report was published by the inspector HMSO (S.O. Code No.51–9999).
[529] s.442(3B).
[530] s.442(4).
[531] s.433, as referred to in s.443(1).

believe to be or to have been "financially interested in the success or failure or the apparent success or failure of the company . . . or able to control or materially influence its policy . . ." or whom he reasonably believes has information relevant to the investigation.[532]

The report of an inspector

22–067   The Secretary of State is not bound to furnish the company or any other person with a copy of the whole of a report by an inspector appointed under s.442 if he is of opinion that there is good reason for not divulging part of the contents of the report.[533]

Difficulties with shares

22–068   Wherever it appears to the Secretary of State that there is difficulty in finding out the relevant facts about any shares in respect of which it is making an investigation under s.442 or s.444 and the difficulty is due wholly or mainly to the unwillingness of the persons[534] concerned or any of them to assist the investigation, he may direct that the shares shall until further order be subject to any or all of the following restrictions laid down in Pt XV of the Act.[535]

Investigation of option dealings and failure to disclose interests in shares

22–069   Where it appears to the Secretary of State that there may have been a contravention of the provisions of the Act penalising certain option dealings, or requiring disclosure of the interests of directors or their spouses or children in shares or debentures of a company, inspectors may be appointed to carry out such investigations as may be necessary to establish whether such contraventions have occurred and to report their findings.[536] Such an inspector may be appointed to investigate a limited period and his investigation may be confined to a particular class of shares or debentures.[537]

Inspectors appointed under s.446 have the powers conferred upon them under ss.434–436, and the further powers elaborated in that section. No provision is made for the supplying of copies of the report to any person.

Inspection of company's books and papers

22–070   Although, prior to the Companies Act 1967, what was then the Board of Trade had power to call for the production of books and documents by certain special kinds of company for the purposes of inspection, this power was not available in

---

[532] s.443(2).
[533] s.443(3).
[534] As to the position of foreign companies not having a presence in the United Kingdom see *F.H. Lloyd Holdings Plc, Re* [1985] B.C.L.C. 293.
[535] s.445(1).
[536] s.446.
[537] s.446(2).

relation to companies generally. The Act gives the Secretary of State such powers in relation to all companies regulated by the Act (or one of its predecessors) and certain other bodies. The commonest form of investigations are in the form of the production of documents and information under s.447.[538]

The main new power in the new s.447 relates to the provision of information. The Secretary of State, or any authorised person (an investigator), is empowered to give directions to the company requiring it to produce such documents as may be specified in the directions or to provide such information as may be so specified.[539] Alternatively, an investigator may give directions to the company requiring it to produce such documents as he may specify or provide such information as he may specify[540] and, in such a case, the person on whom this requirement is imposed may require the investigator to produce evidence of his authority.[541] A requirement for documents or information must be complied with at such time and place as may be specified in the directions or by the investigator.[552] In general, it would seem that the powers under s.447 are administrative in the sense that they are not encumbered by the rules of natural justice in relation to, for example, advance warning.[543] However, a notice given under the section must not be in excessively wide and unreasonable terms and those giving the notice must have acted fairly.[544]

Legal professional privilege and other exemptions

No document or information need be disclosed where this is protected by legal **22–071** professional privilege[545] and nor is the taking of possession of any such document which is in the person's possession authorised.[546] A person who is a lawyer may, nevertheless, be compelled to disclose the name and address of his client.[547] The Secretary of State must not, under s.447, require or authorise a person to require the production by a person carrying on the business of banking of a document relating to the affairs of a customer of his, or the disclosure by him of information relating to those affairs, unless one of three stated conditions are fulfilled.[548]

Effect of statements made

Any statement which is made by a person who complies with a requirement under **22–072** s.447 may be used in evidence against him[549] but in criminal proceedings in

---

[538] The nature of enquiries under this section were considered by Sir Donald Nicholls V.C. in *Rex Williams Leisure Centre Plc, Re* [1994] Ch. 1 at 12–13 (upheld on appeal: [1994] Ch. 350, CA).
[539] s.447(2). But this power can only be exercised for reasons relating to the company in question: s.447(1).
[540] s.447(3).
[541] s.447(4).
[552] s.447(5). Thus, it could be specified that the documents should be handed over immediately.
[543] *Norwest Holst Ltd v Secretary of State of Trade* [1978] Ch. 201, CA.
[544] *R. v Secretary of State for Trade Ex p. Perestrello* [1981] Q.B. 19.
[545] s.452(2)(a).
[546] s.452(2)(b).
[547] s.452(5).
[548] s.452(3).
[549] s.447A(1).

which that person is charged with a relevant offence,[550] no evidence relating to the statement may be adduced by or on behalf of the prosecution and nor may a question relating to it be asked by or on behalf of the prosecution, unless such is used by or on behalf of the person.[551]

Failure to comply

22–073 If there is a failure so to comply, an inspector, the Secretary of State or an investigator may certify this fact in writing to a court.[542] If, after hearing any witnesses and hearing any statement which may be offered in defence, the court is satisfied that the offender failed without reasonable excuse to comply, it may deal with him as if he had been guilty of a contempt of court.[553]

Provision for security of information

22–074 There is no statutory provision for the publication of reports of investigations made under s.447. Section 449 provides, however, for security of the information so obtained and applies also in relation to s.448A(2) and s.453A.[554] Any person who discloses any information in contravention of the section is guilty of an offence[555] and is liable on conviction to imprisonment or a fine or to both.[556] There is no prohibition on the disclosure of information if the information is or has been available to the public from any other source.[557] The main part of s.449 specifies that information obtained under the relevant sections must not be disclosed unless the disclosure is made to a person specified in Sch.15C,[558] or is of a description specified in Sch.15D.[559]

Protection in relation to disclosures

22–075 The Act sets out detailed requirements protecting parties who make certain types of disclosures and provides that a person who makes a relevant disclosure is not liable by reason only of that disclosure in any proceedings relating to a breach of an obligation of confidence.[560] A "relevant disclosure" is one which must satisfy each of the conditions specified in the Act.[561]

---

[550] See s.447A(3), which provides that a "relevant offence" is any offence other than one under s.451, under s.5 of the Perjury Act 1911.

[551] s.447A(2).

[552] s.453C(2).

[553] s.453C(3).

[554] s.449(1)(b)(c).

[555] s.449(6)

[556] s.449(6A). Sections 732 to 734 also apply to an offence under this subsection: s.449(7).

[557] s.449(9).

[558] Any information which has been disclosed to one of the above persons may be disclosed to any officer or employee of the person: s.449(8).

[559] s.449(2).

[560] s.448A(1).

[561] s.448A(2).

Entry and search of premises

The Act sets out detailed requirements for the entry and search of premises. **22–076** A justice of the peace may issue a warrant[562] if he is satisfied on the basis of information given on oath by or on behalf of the Secretary of State, or by a person appointed or authorised to exercise powers under Pt XVI, that there are reasonable grounds for believing that there are on any premises documents whose production has been required and which have not been produced in compliance with the requirement.[563] He may also issue a warrant if satisfied that there are reasonable grounds for believing that an offence has been committed for which the penalty on conviction on indictment is imprisonment for a term of not less than two years and that there are on any premises documents relating to whether the offence has been committed. He may only do so, however, if satisfied that the Secretary of State, or the person so appointed or authorised, has power to require the production of the documents and if there are reasonable grounds for believing that if production was so required the documents would not be produced but would be removed from the premises, hidden, tampered with or destroyed.[564]

A warrant issued under s.448(3) authorises a constable, together with any other person named in it and any other constable to:

1. enter the premises specified in the information, using such force as is reasonably necessary for the purpose;

2. search the premises and take possession of any documents or to take, in relation to any such documents, any other steps which may appear to be necessary for preserving them or preventing interference with them;

3. take copies of any such documents; and

4. to require any person named in the warrant to provide an explanation of them or to state where they may be found.

Any documents of which possession is taken may be retained for a period of three months or, if within that period proceedings to which the documents are relevant are commenced against any person for any criminal offence, until the conclusion of those proceedings.[565] Any person who intentionally obstructs the exercise of any rights conferred by a warrant issued under this section or fails, without reasonable excuse, to comply with any requirement is guilty of an offence.[566]

---

[562] A warrant issued continues in force until the end of the period of one month beginning with the day on which it is issued: s.448(5).

[563] s.448(1).

[564] s.448(2). The warrant may extend also to "other documents relevant to the investigation": s.448(4).

[565] s.448(6).

[566] s.448(7)(8).

Power to enter and remain on premises

22–077 Under s.453A(2) of the Act an inspector[567] or investigator[568] may at all reasonable times require entry to relevant premises[569] and remain there for such period as he thinks necessary if he is authorised to do so by the Secretary of State, and if he thinks that to do so will materially assist him in the exercise of his functions under this Part in relation to the company.[570] In exercising his powers, an inspector or investigator may be accompanied by such other persons as he thinks appropriate.[571] A person who intentionally obstructs a person acting lawfully under this section is guilty of an offence and is liable on conviction to a fine.[572]

At the time an inspector or investigator seeks to enter relevant premises[573] the inspector or investigator must produce evidence of his identity and evidence of his appointment or authorisation.[574] Likewise, any person accompanying the inspector or investigator must produce evidence of his identity.[575] The inspector or investigator must, as soon as practicable after obtaining entry, give to an appropriate recipient a written statement containing such information as to his powers under s.453A and the rights and obligations of the company, occupier and the persons present on the premises, as may be prescribed by regulations.[576] However, if during the time the inspector or investigator is on the premises there is no person present who appears to him to be an appropriate recipient for the purposes of subs.(8),[577] the inspector or investigator must as soon as reasonably practicable send to the company a notice of the fact and time that the visit took place, and the statement mentioned in subs.(4).[578] As soon as reasonably practicable after exercising his powers, the inspector or investigator must prepare a written record of the visit and, if requested to do so by the company, he must give it a copy of the record.[579] In a case where the company is not the sole occupier of the premises, he must give the occupier a copy of the record, if requested to do so by that occupier.[580]

---

[567] A person appointed under ss.431, 432 or 442: s.453A(7).

[568] A person authorised for the purposes of s.447: s.453A(8).

[569] Relevant premises are premises which the inspector or investigator believes are used (wholly or partly) for the purposes of the company's business: s.453A(3).

[570] s.453A(1))

[571] s.453A(4))

[572] s.453A(5)).

[573] s.453B(2))

[574] s.453B(3)(a).

[575] s.453B(3)(b).

[576] s.453B(4). See the Companies Act 1985 (Power to Enter and Remain on Premises: Procedural) Regulations 2005 (SI 2005/684) reg.2.

[577] If the inspector or investigator thinks that the company is the sole occupier of the premises an appropriate recipient is a person who is present on the premises and who appears to be an officer of the company, or a person otherwise engaged in the business of the company if the inspector or investigator thinks that no officer of the company is present on the premises: s.453B(8). If the inspector or investigator thinks that the company is not the occupier or sole occupier of the premises an appropriate recipient is a person who is an appropriate recipient for the purposes of subs.(8), and (if different) a person who is present on the premises and who appears to the inspector or investigator to be an occupier of the premises or otherwise in charge of them: s.453B(9).

[578] s.453B(5). See the Companies Act 1985 (Power to Enter and Remain on Premises: Procedural) Regulations 2005 (SI 2005/684) reg.2.

[579] s.453B(6)(a).

[580] s.453B(6)(b).

Production of books by court order where offence is suspected

Where it is shown that there is a reasonable cause to believe that any person, while **22–078** an officer of the company, has committed an offence in connection with the management of the company's affairs and that evidence of the commission of the offence may be found in any books or papers of or under the control[581] of the company, the court may order the production of the books or papers.[582] In England and Wales the court is a judge of the High Court.[583] In England the application to the court has to be made by the Director of Public Prosecutions, the Secretary of State or a chief officer of police. The order may authorise any person named in it to inspect the documents[584] in question, or any of them, for the purpose of investigating and obtaining evidence of the offence, or require the secretary of the company, or such other officer of it as may be named in the order, to produce the documents (or any of them) to a person named in the order at a place so named.[585] The decision of the court is not appealable.[586]

Proceedings by Secretary of State in consequence of inspection

The Secretary of State has the same powers to take civil proceedings,[587] or to peti- **22–079** tion for a winding up order or for the relief of an oppressed minority of shareholders, in consequence of any information or document obtained under s.447 and s.448 as they have in consequence of an inspector's report under the Act.

Penalties for destruction or concealment of documents

In addition to the penalties already referred to, it is an offence, punishable by a **22–080** fine or imprisonment, or both, for an officer of a company[588] to destroy, mutilate, falsify, or dispose of any document relating to the property or affairs of the company, or to be a party thereto, with the intention of concealing the company's state of affairs or of defeating the law.[589] A person guilty of an offence under s.450 is liable on conviction on indictment, to imprisonment for a term not exceeding seven years or a fine (or both).[590] On summary conviction such a person is liable, in England and Wales, to imprisonment for a term not exceeding 12 months or to a fine not exceeding the statutory maximum (or both).[591] Similar consequences follow for any person to make a false or reckless statement in purported compliance with an obligation imposed under s.447.[592]

---

[581] *Lonrho Ltd v Shell Petroleum Co Ltd* [1980] Q.B. 358, CA.
[582] s.1132(2).
[583] s.1132(1)(a).
[584] Document includes information recorded in any form: s.1132(6).
[585] s.1132(3))
[586] s.1132(5). See *Racal Communications Ltd, Re* [1981] A.C. 374, HL.
[587] For example, an application under s.8 of the Company Directors Disqualification Act 1986. See *Secretary of State for Trade and Industry v Amiss* [2003] EWHC 532; [2003] 2 B.C.L.C. 206.
[588] This applies to an officer of an authorised insurance company which is not a body corporate, as it applies to an officer of a company: s.450(1A).
[589] s.450(1). See *R. v Chauhan* [2000] 2 Cr. App. R. (S.) 230.
[590] s.450(3)(a).
[581] s.450(3)(b)(i)).
[592] s.451. See *Attorney General's Reference (No.2 of 1998)* [2000] Q.B. 412, CA.

CORPORATE LIABILITY

Chapter 23

CRIMINAL AND CIVIL LIABILITY OF COMPANIES

LIABILITY OF REGISTERED COMPANIES

The alter ego doctrine

One consequence of the concept of a company's separate personality is that it can **23–001** be liable for breaches of contract, torts, crimes, etc. But for obvious reasons, it can only act through human agents or employees, so that, as a general principle, a company can only be liable either where a principal would be liable for the acts of an agent or an employer liable for the acts of an employee. In an earlier chapter the concept of agency, which is central to an understanding of company commercial transactions,[1] was discussed but sometimes the law only imposes obligations or affords benefits to those who actually do the act, or who have a particular state of mind, and since a company cannot physically do anything, or think anything, there can be a problem assimilating companies into the general law. The answer is that in certain circumstances the acts and mind of the governing body of the company are regarded as the acts and mind of the company—thus, for example, if they intend to defraud, so does the company. Sometimes known as the alter ego doctrine, this is the antithesis of the doctrine of separate corporate personality already discussed.[2]

The doctrine was first laid down by the House of Lords in *Lennards Carrying Co v Asiatic Petroleum*[3] where the major shareholder's negligence in navigating the company's ship was held to be the negligence of the company for the purposes of assessing liability. Viscount Haldane L.C. said:

"For if Mr Lennard was the directing mind of the company, then his action must, unless a corporation is not to be liable at all, have been an action which was the action of the company itself."[4]

---

[1] See para.6–011, above.
[2] See para.1–037, above.
[3] [1915] A.C. 705, HL.
[4] At 717. That test was applied in *El Ajou v Dollar Land Holdings Plc* [1994] 1 B.C.L.C. 464, CA. See also *Woodhouse v Walsall MBC* [1994] 1 B.C.L.C. 435.

This doctrine has been applied in various areas of the law[5] but for some years it remained unclear as to exactly whose acts and intentions could be attributed to the company. In *Bolton (Engineering) Co Ltd v Graham & Son*,[6] Lord Denning drew a distinction between the acts of those directors and managers who control what the company actually does and the acts of mere servants who simply carry out the course of action prescribed by those in control.

The doctrine was developed in *Tesco Supermarkets Ltd v Nattrass*,[7] where the supermarket chain was prosecuted under s.11(2) of the Trade Descriptions Act 1968[8] for carrying an incorrect advertisement as to the availability of a brand of washing powder at a reduced price. Their defence was that provided by s.24(1) of the 1968 Act, i.e. that the commission of the offence was due to the act or default of another person and that they had taken all reasonable care, etc., to avoid the commission of the offence. The relevant question was whether the manager of the particular branch, who had failed to check the stock, was "another person" for this purpose, or whether his default was that of the company. The House of Lords held that he was "another person"; a branch manager of his type was not sufficiently senior to be the alter ego of the company. Such an ego would be found among the directors, managers, secretary or other officers of the company, or someone to whom they had delegated control and management, with full discretionary powers, of some sections of the company's business.

23–002   On the other hand, the House of Lords in *Supply of Ready Mixed Concrete, Re*[9] held that the acts of local managers of the company which were in breach of an order made against the company under the Restrictive Trade Practices Act 1976,[10] were to be regarded as the acts of the company. This was so despite the fact that senior managers of the company had issued orders to prevent this. The acts of an employee acting within the course of his employment were the acts of the company for this purpose. Companies should be judged by what they had done rather than by what they have said.[11]

The apparent conflict between these two decisions of the House of Lords was explained by Lord Hoffmann in the subsequent case of *Meridian Global Funds Management Asia Ltd v Securities Commission*.[12] That case, a decision of the Privy Council on appeal from New Zealand, concerned the failure of the company to disclose an interest in shares in another company as required by legislation when that interest was known. The actual failure to disclose was the fault of two senior investment managers of the company who worked without supervision and who were aware of the facts. The question was whether their default was also that of the company.

Lord Hoffmann stated that whether a person's acts or mind could be attributed to the company so as to make it liable in situations where agency or vicarious

---

[5] See, e.g. *Green v Green* [1993] 1 F.L.R. 326 for an example in family law and *Tecnion Investments Ltd, Re* [1985] B.C.L.C. 434, CA on a procedural issue.

[6] [1957] 1 Q.B. 159, CA.

[7] [1972] A.C. 153, HL.

[8] c.29.

[9] [1995] 1 B.C.L.C. 613, HL.

[10] c.32. This Act has since been repealed by the Competition Act 1998, c.41, with effect from March, 2000 (see the Competition Act 1998 (Commencement No.5) Order 2000 (SI 2000/344)).

[11] See also *National Rivers Authority v Alfred McAlpine Homes East Ltd* [1994] 4 All E.R. 286.

[12] [1995] 2 A.C. 500, PC. See also *Crown Dilmun v Sutton* [2004] EWHC 52; [2004] 1 B.C.L.C. 468.

liability would not solve the issue was a matter of construction of the particular provision under which liability was sought. It was a question of construction and not of metaphysics involving alter egos, etc. Thus the *Tesco* and *Ready Concrete* cases could be explained. Applying that approach to the facts in *Meridian*, the Privy Council held that the policy of the Act requiring disclosure was for immediate disclosure by those who knew they had a disclosable interest. For a company that must be by those who had, with the authority of the company, acquired that interest. Any other construction would render the Act inoperative.[13]

On the other hand this attribution doctrine does not apply to misappropriations **23–003** from the company by those in control of its affairs. Such misappropriations are not the act of the company as there is no consensus between the controller and the company.[14] It is also clear that where the company is the victim of fraud it will not be fixed with any knowledge of an employee or officer who is defrauding it. Conversely the application of the doctrine to determine whether a company has been defrauded requires that an employee or officer whose mind is that of the company has been deceived.[15]

The situation where a sole, controlling member of a company perpetrated a fraud on third party banks, brought the attribution doctrine into further focus in the House of Lords in *Stone & Rolls Ltd v Moore Stephens*.[16] The case was concerned with the question whether auditors should be liable for alleged negligence in failing to detect and prevent the dishonest activities of S, the controlling owner and manager of the company. The judge at first instance held[17] that the actions and state of mind of S were to be attributed to the company and that it was artificial to describe the company as the victim of the frauds, but that, since detection of fraud was the very thing the auditors were engaged to undertake, they were not entitled to rely on that fraud as a defence based on the principle of *ex turpi causa non oritur actio*,[18] and he refused the application. The House of Lords, by a majority,[19] held that the company was to be imputed with awareness of the fraudulent activities against the banks and was primarily liable for them. Any duty owed by the auditors was to the company as a whole and not to individual shareholders or its creditors; all whose interests formed the subject of any such duty, namely the company's sole directing mind and will, already knew about and were party to the illegal conduct which formed the basis of the claim. In the circumstances, the auditors could rely on the defence of *ex turpi causa* to debar the company's claim.

---

[13] See now also *Lebon v Aqua Salt Co Ltd* [2009] UKPC 2; [2009] B.C.C. 425 where the knowledge of a company director and shareholder was held by the Privy Council to have been correctly treated as the knowledge of the company. He had used the company to purchase land knowing that there was a prior purchaser whose rights the company had subsequently tried to override.

[14] [1983] S.T.C. 576; *Attorney General's Reference (No.2 of 1982)* [1984] Q.B. 624; *R. v Phillipou* (1989) 5 B.C.C. 33.

[15] *R. v Rozeik* [1996] 1 B.C.L.C. 380, CA.

[16] [2009] UKHL 39; [2009] 1 A.C. 1391. Discussed also at para.21–036, above. See too *Berryland Books Ltd v BK Books Ltd* [2009] EWHC 1877 (Ch.); [2009] 2 B.C.L.C. 709.

[17] [2007] EWHC 1826 (Comm.); [2008] 1 B.C.L.C. 697.

[18] i.e. that no court will lend its aid to a man who founds his cause of action upon an immoral or an illegal act: see *Holman v Johnson* (1775) 1 Cowp. 341 at 343; 98 E.R. 1120 at 1121, per Lord Mansfield. See now especially *Tinsley v Milligan* [1994] 1 A.C. 340.

[19] Lord Philips of Worth Matravers, Lord Walker of Gestingthorpe, Lord Brown of Eaton-under-Heywood; Lord Scott of Foscote and Lord Mance dissenting. See Watts, "Audit contracts and turpitude" (2010) 126 L.Q.R. 14.

Criminal liability of companies: corporate manslaughter

Background

23–004   During the past two decades, a particular focus of the alter ego doctrine has centred around the liability of companies for corporate manslaughter.[20] This followed a number of high-profile transport disasters, namely the rail crashes at Southall,[21] Paddington,[22] Hatfield[23] and Potter's Bar,[24] the sinking of the passenger ferry, *Herald of Free Enterprise*, off Zeebrugge,[25] and the sinking of the pleasure cruiser, *Marchioness*, following a collision with the *Bowbelle* on the Thames.[26] Also in focus were the disastrous fires on board the oil rig *Piper Alpha*[27] and at King's Cross in London.[28]

Common law

23–005   One of the cases to explore the issue was *Attorney General's Reference (No.2 of 1999)*,[29] which arose out of the rail disaster at Southall. At first instance, the court ruled that it was a condition precedent to a conviction for manslaughter by gross negligence for a guilty mind to be proved and, where a human defendant was prosecuted, it might only be convicted via the guilty mind of a human being with whom it might be identified. One of the two questions referred by the Attorney General was whether a non-human defendant could be convicted of the crime of manslaughter by gross negligence in the absence of evidence establishing the guilt of an identified human individual for the same crime. The Court of Appeal answered in the negative; unless an identified individual's conduct, characterisable as gross criminal negligence, could be attributable to the company, the company was not liable for manslaughter.[30] There was no evidence that the courts had started a process of moving from identification to personal liability as a basis for corporate liability; indeed, as the *Meridian* case had showed,[31] the primary "directing mind and will" rule still applied.[32] Thus, as this case served to highlight, at common law it has in the

---

[20] The subject also of work by the Law Commission: see *Legislating the Criminal Code: Involuntary Manslaughter* (Law Commission Rep. No.237, 1996). See to Celia Wells, *Corporations and Criminal Responsibility*, 2nd edn (2001).

[21] This occurred on September 19, 1997 and involved a collision between a Great Western Railway train en route between Swansea and London Paddington station, and a freight train.

[22] This took place on October 5, 1999 at Ladbrooke Grove, two miles outside Paddington station.

[23] This took place on October 17, 2000, when a GNER intercity train derailed just outside Hatfield in Hertfordshire. See *R. v Balfour Beatty Rail Infrastructure Services Ltd* [2006] EWCA Crim. 1586; [2007] 1 Cr. App. R. (S.) 65 which arose out of this incident.

[24] This took place on May 10, 2002 and also involved a train derailing, just outside Potter's Bar railway station.

[25] On March 6, 1987.

[26] On August 20, 1989. For a case arising out of the incident, see *The Bowbelle* [1990] 1 Lloyd's Rep. 532.

[27] The oil platform exploded and caught fire on July 6, 1988, with significant loss of life.

[28] On November 18, 1987.

[29] [2000] Q.B. 796, CA.

[30] At 815.

[31] Above, para.23–002.

[32] [2000] Q.B. 796, CA, at 816. See too *Crown Dilmun v Sutton* [2004] EWHC 52; [2004] 1 B.C.L.C. 468.

past been difficult to achieve a successful prosecution against a company for gross negligence and indeed the number of such prosecutions is low.[33] Such prosecutions for corporate manslaughter may no longer be brought following the coming into force of the Corporate Manslaughter and Corporate Homicide Act.[34]

Statutory background

The issue of corporate manslaughter attracted wider attention when the Law **23–006** Commission of England and Wales published their Report, "Legislating the Criminal Code: Involuntary Manslaughter".[35] This Report included proposals for a new offence of corporate killing that would act as a stand-alone provision for prosecuting companies to complement offences primarily aimed at individuals. This provided the basis for the Government's subsequent consultation paper in 2000, "Reforming the Law on Involuntary Manslaughter: the Government's Proposals". It was not until 2005, however, that a Draft Bill was published. This was eventually enacted in 2007 as the Corporate Manslaughter[36] and Corporate Homicide[37] Act 2007.[38] The Act received the Royal Assent on July 26, 2007 but it was a further year before most of it came into force.[39]

Application of the Act

The organisations to which the Act applies include corporations,[40] certain depart- **23–007** ments or other bodies,[41] a police force,[42] and a partnership,[43] trade union or employers association that is an employer.[44]

The offence

An organisation will be guilty of an offence if the way in which its activities **23–008** are managed or organised causes a person's death and amounts to a gross breach of a relevant duty of care owed by the organisation to the deceased.[45] This will only be the case if the way in which the organisation's activities are managed or

---

[33] As of September 3, 2008, it has been estimated that there have been just eight convictions: see *http://www.corporateaccountability.org/manslaughter/cases/convictions.htm* [accessed June 5, 2010].
[34] See paras 23–005 and 23–011.
[35] Law Com. 237.
[36] i.e. under the law in England and Wales or Northern Ireland: see s.1(5)(a).
[37] In Scotland: s.1(5)(b).
[38] c.19. For fuller discussion, see para.23–003. See also Celia Wells, "Corporate Manslaughter: Why Does Reform Matter?" (2006) 122 South African L.J. 648; David Ormerod & Richard Taylor, "The Corporate Manslaughter and Corporate Homicide Act" (2008) 8 Criminal L.R. 589; Stephen Griffin, "Corporate killing—the Corporate Manslaughter and Corporate Homicide Act 2007" [2009] L.M.C.L.Q. 73.
[39] Most of the Act came into force from April 6, 2008. See the Corporate Manslaughter and Corporate Homicide Act 2007 (Commencement No 1) Order 2008 (SI 2008/401).
[40] s.1(2)(a).
[41] s.1(2)(b). See too Sch.1.
[42] s.1(2)(c). See also s.13.
[43] See s.14.
[44] s.1(2)(d).
[45] s.1(1).

organised by its senior management[46] is a "substantial element" in the breach.[47] Thus, the crucial elements are that the causing of the death amounts to a "gross breach" of "the relevant duty of care". A gross breach is conduct alleged to amount to a breach of duty which falls below what can reasonably be expected of an organisation in the circumstances.[48] The relevant duty of care is elaborated in some detail in the Act as meaning any of the following duties owed to it by the law of negligence[49]:

1. a duty owed to its employees or to other persons working for the organisation or performing services for it;

2. a duty owed as occupier of premises;

3. a duty owed in connection with the supply by the organisation of goods or services (whether for consideration or not), the carrying on by the organisation of any construction or maintenance operations, the carrying on by the organisation of any other activity on a commercial basis, or the use or keeping by the organisation of any plant, vehicle or other thing.[50]

Whether a duty of care is owed to a particular individual is a question of law but the judge may make any findings of fact necessary to decide that question.[51]

Once it is established that an organisation, such as a company, owed a relevant duty of care, it falls to the jury to decide whether there was a "gross breach" of that duty[52] and, in doing so, the jury must consider whether the evidence shows that the organisation failed to comply with any health and safety legislation that relates to the alleged breach and, if so, how serious that failure was and how much of a risk of death it posed.[53]

Exclusions

23–009   In certain situations, the relevant duty of care for the offence is excluded. Thus, a duty of care owed by a public authority in respect of a decision as to matters of public policy, including in particular the allocation of public resources or the weighing of competing public interests is not a "relevant duty of care".[54] Other exclusions include certain types of military activities,[55] policing and law enforcement,[56] emergency circumstances,[57] and child-protection and probation functions.[58]

---

[46] As to the meaning of this, see s.1(4)(c).
[47] s.1(3).
[48] s.1(4)(b).
[49] This includes the Occupiers' Liability Act 1957, c.31, the Defective Premises Act 1972, c.35, and the Occupiers' Liability Act 1984, c.3: s.1(7). See too s.2(4) and s.2(6).
[50] s.2(1).
[51] s.2(5). See as to this, *R. v Evans (Gemma)* [2009] EWCA Crim. 650; [2009] 1 W.L.R. 1999.
[52] s.8(1).
[53] s.8(2).
[54] s.3(1).
[55] s.4.
[56] s.5.
[57] s.6.
[58] s.7.

No individual liability

The Act expressly removes secondary liability from its ambit. Thus, it is stated that **23–010** an individual cannot be guilty of aiding, abetting, counselling, or procuring the commission of an offence of corporate manslaughter.[59]

No common law liability of corporations at common law

The Act abolishes the common law offence of manslaughter by gross negligence **23–011** in its application to corporations and also any application it has to other organisations to which the Act applies.[60]

Civil liability of the company and its officers

Personal liability of directors in tort to third parties

In certain cases a director[61] or other company officer may become personally **23–012** liable for some wrong connected with the company.[62] In *C. Evans & Sons Ltd v Spritebrand Ltd*,[63] the Court of Appeal discussed a director's liability for torts committed by his company. They decided that a director is not automatically liable for such torts even if it is a small company over which he exercised total control. It is necessary to examine the role he played in regard to the commission of the tort. On the other hand it would not always be necessary to prove that the director had acted recklessly or knowing that the company's acts were tortious. If the tort itself required negligence or recklessness then the director's state of mind might well be relevant, but for torts of strict liability different considerations could apply.

But in *Williams v Natural Life Health Foods Ltd*,[64] the House of Lords held that the controller of a small company which had made negligent misstatements to its franchisees, was not personally liable for the tort of negligent misstatement. There was no evidence of personal dealings or conduct which would have led the franchisees to assume that the director was willing to assume personal responsibility to them. Nor was he a joint tortfeasor with the company—the only relationship giving rise to liability was that between the company and the franchisees.

It is clear, however, that the decision in *Williams* was largely based on the peculiarities of the tort of negligent misstatement, which requires a specific finding of the assumption of personal responsibility for the statement by the tortfeasor. The director, acting as an agent, on the facts had not assumed that personal responsibility. As such it had nothing to do with the concept of the company as a separate legal person—the decision would have been the same if the principal had been an individual. That analysis enabled the House of Lords in the subsequent

---

[59] See s.18(1).
[60] See s.20.
[61] Generally as to director's statutory and other duties to the company, see Ch.17, above.
[62] See, generally, Francis Reynolds, "Personal Liability of Company Directors in Tort" (2003) 33 Hong Kong L.J. 51.
[63] [1985] 1 W.L.R. 317, CA.
[64] [1998] 1 W.L.R. 830, HL.

case of *Standard Chartered Bank v Pakistan National Shipping Corporation*,[65] to hold a director personally liable in the tort of deceit and to set aside his defence that he had made the fraudulent misstatement on behalf of the company. Although that may make the company liable, it did not absolve him from liability for his own tort. Deceit does not require any assumption of personal responsibility so it was no defence to say that he made the statement on behalf of another (which happened to be a company).[66]

The principles governing the liability of a director as a joint tortfeasor with the company have been set out in two cases relating to intellectual property. In *MCA Records Inc v Charly Records Ltd*,[67] Chadwick L.J. said that: (i) a director will not be liable as a joint tortfeasor if all he is doing is carrying out his constitutional role as a director, e.g. by voting at board meetings; (ii) but he will be liable if he participates or is involved in committing the tort in ways which go beyond the exercise of constitutional control, even though he could have procured the same acts through the exercise of such control. In the cases, the test was whether the director "intends and procures and shares a common design" that the infringement takes place.

Contribution between directors

23–013   The liability of directors for breaches of duty is joint and several,[68] so that where the directors have misapplied the company's funds, as by paying dividends out of capital or advancing money for an unauthorised purpose, a director who has been sued for the misapplication is entitled to contribution from the other directors who were parties to it.[69] If, however, the money misappropriated has been applied for the sole benefit of one of the directors, that director is not entitled to obtain contribution.[70]

Relief of directors from liability for breach of duty

Ratification by a resolution in general meeting

23–014   Since directors' fiduciary duties are owed to the members as a body,[71] the common law position was that a majority of the members in general meeting might, at least while the company is solvent,[72] after full disclosure of all material circumstances, waive a breach of fiduciary duty by a director.[73] If he was a

---

[65] [2002] UKHL 43; [2003] 1 A.C. 959. These propositions were used by Pumfrey J. in *Koninklijke Philips Electronics NV v Princo Digital Disc GmbH* [2003] EWHC 2588 (Pat); [2004] 2 B.C.L.C. 50.
[66] See too *Invertec Ltd v De Mol Holding BV* [2009] EWHC 2471 (Ch.); *Contex Drouzhba Ltd v Wiseman* [2007] EWCA Civ. 1201; [2008] B.C.C. 301.
[67] [2001] EWCA Civ. 1441; [2002] B.C.C. 650. See also *Partco Group Ltd v Wragg* [2002] EWCA Civ. 594; [2004] B.C.C. 782; *Societa Esplosivi Industriali SpA v Ordnance Technologies (UK) Ltd* [2007] EWHC 2875 (Ch.); [2008] 2 B.C.L.C. 428.
[68] *Bishopsgate Investment Management Ltd v Maxwell (No.2)* [1993] B.C.L.C. 1282.
[69] *Ramskill v Edwards* (1886) 31 Ch.D. 100. See also the Civil Liability (Contribution) Act 1978, c.47.
[70] *Walsh v Bardsley* (1931) 47 T.L.R. 564.
[71] See now s.172(1), above para.17–020.
[72] The position would be different if the company is operating under doubtful solvency since the duties may then be owed to the creditors rather than the members of the company. See *DKG Contractors Ltd, Re* [1990] B.C.C. 903.
[73] *Bamford v Bamford* [1970] Ch. 212, CA; *Gencor ACP Ltd v Dolby* [2000] 2 B.C.L.C. 734. 269.

member, the position at common law was that a director could vote in favour of waiver, provided that there was no fraud on the minority of the members.

In *North-West Transportation Co v Beatty*,[74] the directors of a company contracted to buy a ship from a vendor who was a director. This was a breach of duty by him since the articles contained no clause authorising a director to contract with the company. At a general meeting a resolution affirming the contract was carried, against the wishes of the minority shareholders, by reason of the fact that the vendor held the majority of the shares in the company. It was held that the resolution was valid. As a shareholder, the vendor was merely using his voting power to his own advantage, and there was no question of a fraud on the minority—there was no unfairness or impropriety.

Two directors of a construction company negotiated for a construction contract in the usual way in which the company's business was carried on, and then took the contract in their own names. A meeting of the company was called, and by their votes as holders of three-quarters of the shares a resolution was passed declaring that the company had no interest in the contract. It was held that the benefit of the contract belonged to the company and the directors must account to the company for it, and the purported ratification was a fraud on the minority and ineffective.[75]

Ratification under the Act

The Act now lays down certain minimum standards for effective ratification **23–015** of breaches by the company and applies to the ratification by a company of conduct[76] by a director[77] amounting to negligence, default, breach of duty or breach of trust in relation to the company.[78] As at common law, decisions to ratify such conduct must be made by resolution of the members.[79] This is a minimum requirement, notwithstanding any more lenient alternative provided by the articles of the company or under the general law.

At this point, however, the Act introduces an important change. It provides that where the resolution is proposed as a written resolution[80] neither the director, if he is a member of the company, nor any member connected with him is an eligible member.[81] The Act also provides that where the resolution is proposed at a meeting, it is passed only if the necessary majority is obtained disregarding votes in favour of the resolution by the director, if he is a member of the company, and any member connected with him.[82] However, this does not prevent the director or any such member from attending, being counted towards the quorum and taking part in the proceedings at any meeting at which the decision is considered.[83] This is clearly intended to reverse the effect of *North-West Transportation*

---

[74] (1887) 12 App. Cas. 589, PC.
[75] *Cook v Deeks* [1916] 1 A.C. 554, PC.
[76] Conduct includes acts and omissions: see s.239(5)(a).
[77] This includes a former director and treats a shadow director as a director: s.239(5)(b)(c).
[78] s.239(1).
[79] s.239(2).
[80] See para.19–028, above.
[81] s.239(3).
[82] s.239(4).
[83] s.239(4).

Co Ltd v Beatty[84] and the reasons were articulated by the then Attorney-General, Lord Goldsmith, in the parliamentary debates:

"It seeks to exclude the votes of the wrongdoer and those persons most likely to be biased in favour of the director or under his influence—namely, the persons connected with him—and makes it easier to identify those persons when the votes are counted."[85]

The Act provides that nothing in this section affects the validity of a decision taken by unanimous consent of the members of the company or any power of the directors to agree not to sue, or to settle or release a claim made by them on behalf of the company.[86] Thus, nothing in this provision of the Act changes the law on unanimous consent. The restrictions imposed by this clause as to who may vote on a ratification resolution will not apply when every member votes (informally or otherwise) in favour of the resolution. The subsection also makes clear that nothing in this clause removes any powers of the directors that they may have to manage the affairs of the company.

Finally, it should be noted that the Act provides that this section does not affect any other enactment or rule of law imposing additional requirements for valid ratification or any rule of law as to acts that are incapable of being ratified by the company.[87] Thus, the Act is intended to be clear that the requirements are additional and not an alternative to any other requirements as to ratification which are imposed by statute or under the common law.

Provisions in the articles protecting directors from liability

23–016 Under the general law a director can be exempted from liability for breach of duty by a provision in the articles of the company. However, this is limited by the Act, as was the case also under the 1985 Act as amended.[88] The Act provides that, subject to what is said below, any provision[89] for exempting a director (to any extent) from liability for negligence, default, breach of duty or breach of trust in relation to the company is void.[90] The Act applies a similar rule to any indemnity[91] provided for a director of the company or an associated company against any such liability, whether directly or indirect.[92] However, nothing prevents a company's articles from making such provision as has previously been lawful for dealing with conflicts of interest.[93]

---

[84] (1887) 12 App. Cas. 589, PC. See para.23–014, above.
[85] Hansard HL Report Stage, cols 872–873 (May 9, 2006).
[86] s.239(6).
[87] s.239(7).
[88] The 1985 Act (formerly s.310) was amended on this by the Companies (Audit, Investigations and Community Enterprise) Act 2004: see s.309A.
[89] Defined in all the sections as a provision of any nature whether contained in the company's articles or any contract: s.232(3).
[90] s.232(1).
[91] Subject to s.233, s.234, or s.235: see s.232(2).
[92] s.232(2).
[93] s.232(4).

This ban on indemnities does not prevent the company taking out an indemnity insurance policy as cover against such liability[94] or from providing what is called a qualifying third-party indemnity provision[95] or a qualifying pension scheme indemnity provision.[96] Such an indemnity provision will only be a qualifying one if it does not apply to any liability to the company, or with regard to the payment of any criminal fine or regulatory penalty, or the payment of costs in any proceedings in which he is convicted, or where judgment is given against him on in favour of the company.[97] The existence of such qualifying third-party indemnity provisions must be disclosed in the directors' report[98] and must be available for inspection.[99]

One issue which has still not been resolved by these provisions, is the difficulty of the relationship between these sections and provisions of the articles with which they still appear to be inconsistent. Thus, art.85 of Table A[100] (and similar articles) allow a director to have an interest in a transaction, etc., subject to disclosure to the board. Insofar as this is an attempt to relieve the director from a conflict of interest this would appear to exempt him from a breach of duty or trust and accordingly be void under the Act.[101] In *Movitex Ltd v Bulfield*,[102] Vinelott J. resolved the difficulty by deciding that the conflict of interest rule was a disability imposed by equity and not a duty owed by the director. Thus by modifying the rule the articles are removing a disability and not exempting a breach of duty.[103]

By the court

The Act provides that if, in proceedings for negligence, default, breach of duty or **23–017** breach of trust against an officer or auditor of a company, it appears that he has acted honestly and reasonably, and that, having regard to all the circumstances, including those connected with his appointment, he ought fairly to be excused, the court may relieve him, wholly or partly, from liability on such terms as it thinks fit.[104] A defence under the section can, it seems, be pleaded at trial.[105]

The court has to decide both that the director acted honestly and reasonably and that he ought to be excused. Whilst "honestly" might be subjective, "reasonably" would seem to be objective. In negligence cases this might appear to be difficult to establish.

---

[94] s.233.
[95] s.234.
[96] This is a new provision: see s.235.
[97] See s.234(3).
[98] s.236. See too para.20–024, above.
[99] See s.237 and s.238.
[100] cf. now the Model Articles for Private Companies Limited by Shares art.52 and art.53 (see art.85 and art.86 for the Model Articles for Public Companies).
[100] i.e. under s.232.
[102] [1988] B.C.L.C. 104.
[103] See too the analysis in *Neptune (Vehicle Washing Equipment) Ltd, Re (No.2)* [1995] B.C.C. 1000.
[104] s.1157(1). But a court would not have the power under the section to relieve a former director against liability imposed by ss.216 and 217 of the Insolvency Act 1986: see *First Independent Factors and Finance Ltd v Mountford* [2008] EWHC 835 (Ch.); [2008 B.C.C.598 and the discussion at para.23–023, below.
[105] See *Kirby's Coaches Ltd, Re* [1991] B.C.L.C. 414; *Phillips v McGregor-Paterson* [2009] EWHC 2385 (Ch.) at [36], per Henderson J.

In *City of London Insurance Co, Re*,[106] B and G, two of the directors of a company were present at a finance committee in June at which it was resolved to sell £60,000 War Bonds and to reinvest the proceeds at B's discretion. In September, G inquired about the reinvestment of the proceeds and was told that they had been temporarily invested on the Stock Exchange. B misappropriated the proceeds of sale. The court held that G was negligent in allowing the money to remain in B's hands longer than was reasonable and in not making inquiries as to its permanent investment. Further, that though G had acted honestly, he had not acted reasonably and ought not to be granted relief.

In *Selangor United Rubber Estates Ltd v Cradock (No.3)*[107] directors of a public company who disposed of virtually all its assets without regard for minority shareholders, and without consideration, but blindly at the behest of the majority shareholder who nominated them to the board, did not act reasonably and could not be relieved. In *Duomatic Ltd, Re*[108] a director dealing with payment to another director of compensation for loss of office, who did not seek legal advice but dealt with the matter himself without a proper exploration of what should be done on the company's behalf, did not act reasonably.

23–018 But in *D'Jan of London Ltd, Re*,[109] Hoffmann L.J. held that a director who had acted negligently but "understandably" and who would have suffered a personal loss through his shareholding in the company at the time of the negligence could be excused under the section.

Some of the cases have involved the improper declaration of dividends. In *Bairstow v Queens Moat Houses Plc*,[110] the Court of Appeal emphasised that the burden of proof to establish honesty and reasonableness was on the defendant, and that a finding of dishonesty was total. In *Marini Ltd, Re*,[111] it was doubted whether a director who had received an unlawful dividend to the prejudice of creditors could ever be said to have acted reasonably, however honest he had been.[112]

The Act only applies to proceedings against a director for breach of duty by, on behalf of, or for the benefit of, the company as a whole.[113] It does not apply to claims against a director by a third party to enforce a debt, e.g. arrears of general betting duty.[114] It has no relevance either to a claim by a company for recovery of money paid to a director under an unauthorised and void contract, since that is not founded on a breach of duty,[115] or to a claim for wrongful trading.[116] But in *Duckwari Plc, Re (No.2)*,[117] the Court of Appeal considered that s.1157 could apply to a liability to

---

[106] (1925) 41 T.L.R. 521. See too *PNC Telecom v Thomas* [2007] EWHC 2157 (Ch.); [2008] 2 B.C.L.C. 95; *Ortega Associates Ltd, Re* [2007] EWHC 3251 (Ch.); [2008] B.C.C. 256; *Cook v Green* [2009] B.C.C. 204.

[107] [1968] 1 W.L.R. 1555.

[108] [1969] 2 Ch. 365.

[109] [1994] 1 B.C.L.C. 561; cf. *Brian D. Pierson (Contractors) Ltd, Re* [1997] B.C.C. 26.

[110] [2001] 2 B.C.L.C. 531, CA. See also *Inn Spirit Ltd v Burns* [2002] 2 B.C.L.C. 780.

[111] [2004] B.C.C. 172. Reliance on financial advice might also not be enough.

[112] [2009] EWCA Civ. 625; [2010] B.C.C. 104. See too *Paycheck Services 3 Ltd, Re* [2009] EWCA Civ. 625; [2010] B.C.C. 104, discussed at para.23–025, below.

[113] Whatever remedy is sought: *Colemen Taymor Ltd v Oakes* [2002] 2 B.C.L.C. 749.

[114] *Customs and Excise Commissioners v Hedon Alpha* [1981] 2 All E.R. 697, CA.

[115] *Guinness Plc v Saunders* [1990] 2 A.C. 633, HL.

[116] *Produce Marketing Consortium Ltd, Re* [1989] B.C.L.C. 513.

[117] [1998] 2 B.C.L.C. 315, CA.

indemnify the company under s.195, although it would not avail a director who had a personal interest in the transaction and who has benefited from it.

DIRECTORS LIABILITIES AND INSOLVENCY

Liability for fraudulent trading

The Insolvency Act 1986[118] provides that if in the winding up of a company it appears that business has been carried on with intent to defraud creditors or for any fraudulent purpose, the court, on the application of the liquidator, may declare that any persons who were knowingly parties to the fraudulent trading shall make such contributions to the company's assets as the court thinks proper.[119] It has been held that this provision of the of the 1986 Act imports two essential conditions, quite apart from the need to prove that the business of the company had been carried on with intent to defraud creditors, namely, that the company is in the course of being wound up and that the application is made by the liquidator. For the purposes of the section, commencement of the winding up is the making of the winding up order rather than the presentation of the petition.[120]   **23–019**

In general it may be properly inferred that there is an intent to defraud creditors if a company carries on business and incurs debts when, to the knowledge of the directors, there is no reasonable prospect of the company being able to pay them.[121] It is not necessary to show that there was no prospect of the creditors ever being paid. It is enough that there is no reason for thinking that they will be paid as the debts fall due or shortly thereafter.[122] In general, the courts have used the benchmark of "actual dishonesty" in determining whether the requirements of the section are made out.[123]

The expression "parties to" the fraudulent trading in s.213(2) indicates no more than "take part in" or "concur in" and involves some positive steps. Mere omission by the secretary to give certain advice (that the company is insolvent and should cease to trade) is not being a party to carrying on the business in a fraudulent manner.[124] However, a creditor who, knowing of the circumstances, accepts money fraudulently obtained by the company may be liable to repay it even if he took no part in the fraudulent trading itself.[125]

It is not fraudulent trading for a parent company to give promises of support to a subsidiary which are not implemented. The fraud of the parent company cannot be linked to the subsidiary, since to establish liability the fraudulent trading must be committed by someone carrying on the business, i.e. the subsidiary. In any event such general statements would not be sufficient to prove fraud.[126]   **23–020**

---

[118] s.45.

[119] s.213. Any order is in favour of the liquidator not an individual shareholder: *Esal (Commodities) Ltd, Re* [1997] 1 B.C.L.C. 705, CA.

[120] *Overnight Ltd, Re* [2009] EWHC 601 (Ch.); [2009] Bus. L.R. 1141.

[121] *William C. Leitch Bros Ltd, Re* [1932] 2 Ch. 71.

[122] *R. v Grantham* [1984] Q.B. 675. See also *Bank of India v Morris* [2005] EWCA Civ. 693; [2005] B.C.C. 739; *Carman v Cronos Group SA* [2005] EWHC 2403 (Ch.); [2006] B.C.C. 451.

[123] *Patrick and Lyon Ltd, Re* [1933] Ch. 786; *Bernasconi v Nicholas Bennett & Co* [2000] B.C.C. 921.

[124] *Maidstone Buildings Provisions Ltd, Re* [1971] 1 W.L.R. 1085, *R. v Miles* [1992] Crim. L.R. 657.

[125] *Gerald Cooper Chemicals Ltd, Re* [1978] Ch. 262.

[126] *Augustus Barnett & Son Ltd, Re* [1986] B.C.L.C. 170.

It is also not fraudulent trading to intend to prefer one creditor to another even if all could not be paid in full,[127] nor to sell goods which prove to be defective knowing that liability for such defects might not be met.[128]

The court may charge the liability of a person declared liable under s.213 on any debt due to him from the company, or on any charge on any assets of the company held by him, or any company or person on his behalf, or certain assignees from him or such a company or person.[129]

Fraudulent trading (so defined) is also a criminal offence under s.993 of the 2006 Act and like the Insolvency Act provision there must be an intent to defraud creditors[130] of the company.[131] Thus, there must be a finding of dishonesty for the criminal offence to be committed.[132] The criminal offence, unlike the civil penalties in the Insolvency Act, however, is not linked to a winding up.[133] A person found guilty is liable on conviction on indictment to imprisonment for up to ten years or a fine (or both).[134] On summary conviction, a person is liable to imprisonment for up to 12 months or a fine (or both).[135]

Liability for wrongful trading

23–021 One of the principal aims of the Insolvency Act 1986 was to encourage directors to put their company into liquidation when all reasonable expectation of saving it has gone. Before 1986 the only remedy available to a liquidator against a director who had allowed his company to incur debts after all reasonable hope had gone was to institute proceedings for fraudulent trading. This remedy still exists and, as we have seen,[136] can give rise to both civil and criminal consequences. Under s.214 of the Insolvency Act 1986 there is now an additional liability on directors and shadow directors[137] for those guilty of wrongful trading in such circumstances.[138]

To establish wrongful trading the liquidator of a company must show that the company has gone into an insolvent liquidation,[139] that the director, prior to the liquidation, knew or ought to have concluded that there was no reasonable prospect that the company could avoid going into insolvent liquidation, and that he took insufficient steps in the circumstances to minimise the potential loss to the company's creditors.[140] As Chadwick J. pointed out in *Secretary of State for Trade and Industry v Gash*:

---

[127] *Sarflax Ltd, Re* [1979] Ch. 592.
[128] *Norcross Ltd v Amos* (1981) 131 N.L.J. 1213.
[129] Insolvency Act 1986, s.215.
[130] This includes future creditors: *R. v Smith* [1996] 2 B.C.L.C. 109, CA.
[131] See *R. v Bright* [2008] EWCA Crim. 462; [2008] 2 Cr. App. R. (S.) 102.
[132] *R. v Cox* [1983] B.C.L.C. 169.
[133] s.993(2).
[134] s.993(3)(a).
[135] s.993(3)(b).
[136] Para.23–019 above.
[137] And also for de facto directors. See para. 17–007, above.
[138] No defence under s.1157 is available against a claim for wrongful trading: *Produce Marketing Consortium Ltd, Re* [1989] B.C.L.C. 513.
[139] This is defined as where, at the time of the winding up, its assets are insufficient for the payment of its debts and other liabilities and the expenses of winding up. This is known as balance sheet insolvency.
[140] s.214(2)(3). Any such action must be brought by the liquidator within six years of the insolvent liquidation and the court may strike out the claim if there is inordinate and inexcusable delay by the liquidator in actually commencing the proceedings: *Farmizer (Products) Ltd, Re* [1997] 1 B.C.L.C. 589, CA.

"The companies legislation does not impose on directors a statutory duty to ensure that their company does not trade while insolvent; nor does that legislation impose an obligation to ensure that the company does not trade at a loss. Those propositions need only to be stated to be recognised as self-evident. Directors may properly take the view that it is in the interests of the company and of its creditors that, although insolvent, the company should continue to trade out of its difficulties. They may properly take the view that it is in the interests of the company and its creditors that some loss-making trade should be accepted in anticipation of future profitability. They are not to be criticised if they give effect to such view."[141]

Note that no dishonesty need be involved, simply unreasonable behaviour or negligence.[142] Where, however, the directors have addressed the reality of the situation and have prepared revised business plans and forecasts that may be taken as evidence of a reasonable belief that the company will survive.[143] But a superficial belief that the situation was due to "temporary cash flow shortages", the ignoring of losses in the accounts and an unreasonable failure to realise that many of the company's assets were worth less was held to be clear evidence of wrongful trading.[144] In a case where a company was hopelessly insolvent, it was held that the directors knew or ought to have concluded before making a business sale agreement that there was no reasonable prospect that the company would avoid going into insolvent liquidation.[145] On the other hand, it has been recognised that it

"is easy with hindsight to conclude that mistakes were made. An insolvent liquidation will almost always result from one or more mistakes. But picking over the bones of a dead company in a courtroom is not always fair to those who struggled to keep going in the reasonable (but ultimately misplaced) hope that things would get better."[146]

To decide whether a director ought to have concluded that an insolvent liquidation was unavoidable the court must ask whether that would have been the conclusion of a reasonably diligent person having both the general knowledge, skill and experience that might reasonably be expected of a person carrying out that particular director's duties with regard to the company (including those entrusted to him even if he does not actually carry them out) and the general knowledge, skill and experience which that director actually has.[147] **23–022**

In construing these provisions Knox J. in *Produce Marketing Consortium Ltd, Re (No.2)*,[148] held that each director had to be judged by what might reasonably be expected of a person fulfilling his functions in a reasonably diligent way, always

---

[141] [1997] 1 B.C.L.C. 341.
[142] Becoming aware of pressing creditors will suffice: *DKG Contractors Ltd, Re* [1990] B.C.C. 903.
[143] *Sherborne Associates Ltd, Re* [1995] B.C.C. 40.
[144] *Re Brian D Pierson (Contractors) Ltd* [2001] 1 B.C.L.C. 275; see also *Rubin v Gunner* [2004] EWHC 316 (Ch); [2004] B.C.C. 684.
[145] *Re Bangla Television Ltd* [2009] EWHC 1632 (Ch); [2010] B.C.C. 143.
[146] *Re Hawkes Hill Publishing Co Ltd* [2007] B.C.C. 937, at p. 952, per Lewison J.
[147] s.214(4)(5). See *Singla v Hedman* [2010] EWHC 902 (Ch.). This test has also been applied as to the standard of care of directors generally: see now s.174 of the 2006 Act, para.17–028, above.
[148] [1989] B.C.L.C. 520.

bearing in mind certain minimum standards such as the preparation of annual accounts and a basic awareness of the company's financial position, etc. Further, such a director must be judged not only on the facts as known to him but those which he would have known had the company complied with its obligations under the Act, e.g. as to the publication of accounts, so as to establish when the wrongful trading began. These minimum standards are expected of all directors, even one who takes no part in running the business. There is no such thing as a "sleeping director".[149] Where the liquidator specifies a specific date as to when the wrongful trading began he cannot subsequently ask the court to make such a finding as at a later date instead.[150]

Many companies actually begin life as balance sheet insolvent but in *Cubelock Ltd, Re*[151] it was held that that was not enough to constitute wrongful trading, unless perhaps the company was formed with totally insufficient capital. The liability would only arise if the directors allowed the company to continue to trade when they knew or ought to have known that there was no reasonable prospect of the creditors ever being paid. A reasonable, if mistaken, belief that the company could trade into profit was not enough.

Although all directors must be aware of the company's financial situation, where the non-executive directors questioned that position and actively considered whether to allow the company to continue trading it was held that they had acted reasonably. They had reasonably relied on the accounts and the opinions of the finance director and auditor that the company was insolvent. They were not expected to show "the sort of intricate appreciation of recondite accounting details possessed by a specialist in the field".[152]

If wrongful trading is established the court may require the director to make a contribution to the company's assets.[153] Such an order is to be compensatory, i.e. to provide an amount equal to that by which the company's assets were depleted by the directors' conduct from that date, and not penal.[154] There must be a connection between the wrongful trading and the loss to the company's net assets. A loss caused, e.g. by bad weather would not be included.[155] The absence of fraudulent intent can be taken into account but is not in itself a reason for fixing a low or nominal figure. Any amount is payable with interest from the date of winding up.[156] If the company has failed to keep any records the court can use its discretion in calculating the period of wrongful trading for this purpose.[157] Following such an order the court may also make a disqualification order against the director.[158]

---

[149] *Brian D Pierson Ltd, Re* [2001] 1 B.C.L.C. 275 at 302.
[150] *Sherborne Associates Ltd, Re* [1995] B.C.C. 40.
[151] [2001] B.C.C. 523.
[152] *Continental Assurance of London Plc, Re* [1996] B.C.C. 888.
[153] s.214(1). The liquidator cannot assign that sum to a third party in return for the third party funding the action: *Oasis Merchandising Services Ltd, Re* [1997] 1 B.C.L.C. 689.
[154] For this reason the liability survives the death of the director: *Sherborne Associates Ltd, Re* [1995] B.C.C. 40. That case also suggested that responsibility for the wrongful trading could be reduced by a defence of reasonable reliance on another. If there was no diminution in the company's assets during the wrongful trading, there is no liability: *Marini Ltd, Re* [2003] EWHC 334 (Ch.); [2004] B.C.C. 17.
[155] *Continental Assurance of London Ltd, Re* [1996] B.C.C. 888.
[156] *Produce Marketing Consortium Ltd, Re (No.2)* [1989] B.C.L.C. 520.
[157] *Purpoint Ltd, Re* [1991] B.C.L.C. 491.
[158] Company Directors Disqualification Act 1986, s.10.

Liability for use of insolvent company's name

Another abuse prior to 1986 was the so-called "Phoenix" company operation. The **23–023** liquidator would dispose of the company, its name and assets to the existing directors, who would purchase it with other funds and then continue to trade in exactly the same way as before the insolvent liquidation leaving the creditors of the old company stranded. To prevent this happening, s.216 and s.217 of the Insolvency Act 1986 provide that where a company goes into insolvent liquidation, anyone who was a director (or shadow director) of that company at any time in the previous year and who becomes a director of a company using the name[159] or trading name of the insolvent company within five years commits an offence, unless he either has leave of the court or comes within limited exceptions under the Insolvency Rules 1986.[160] This prohibition extends to being concerned in the promotion, formation, management or taking part in the business of a company using the insolvent company's name. The offence is one of strict liability.[161]

In deciding whether a name is so similar to suggest an association with the first company, the courts will adopt an objective test and a purposive approach. Merely using different stationery etc. will not be enough.[162] The mater will be looked at in the context of all the circumstances in which the two names were actually used or likely to be used. These would include the types of product, location, type of customers and the persons involved in the two companies.[163]

The Insolvency Rules allow, inter alia, the director to act as such in respect of the new company where the business of the old company has been acquired by the new company[164] under arrangements made with an insolvency practitioner provided notice is given to all the creditors of the old company within 28 days of the completion of the acquisition. The court's residual discretion may allow the director to act as such with respect to the new company but may require certain undertakings as to future conduct of the management of that company.[165] In deciding whether to grant such leave, however, the court will only be concerned with the risk to creditors of the old and new companies. In the absence of any evidence to the contrary it is not a question as to the director's fitness to act as such, that is relevant only to the separate question of disqualification. Nor is there any general rule that undertakings must be given as to the new company.[166]

In addition to the criminal offence under s.216, s.217 imposes personal liability on a director who acts either as such or in the management of a company in breach of s.216, for all debts incurred by that company whilst he is in breach. In *Thorne v Silverleaf*,[167] the Court of Appeal upheld a director's liability under this section to an investor in the second company, despite the fact that it was alleged

---

[159] Or any name which is so similar as to suggest an association with the previous company; see below.
[160] s.216.
[161] *R. v Cole* [1998] 2 B.C.L.C. 234, CA.
[162] *Archer Structures Ltd v Griffiths* [2003] EWHC 957 (Ch.); [2004] B.C.C. 156.
[163] *Ricketts v Ad Valorem Factors Ltd* [2004] 1 B.C.L.C. 1, CA.
[164] This does not have to include the old company's liabilities: *Bonus Breaks Ltd, Re* [1991] B.C.C. 546.
[165] *Bonus Breaks Ltd, Re* [1991] B.C.C. 491.
[166] *Penrose v Official Receiver* [1996] 1 B.C.L.C. 389; *Lighting Electrical Contractors Ltd, Re* [1996] 2 B.C.L.C. 302.
[167] [1994] 1 B.C.L.C. 637.

that the latter was fully aware of the breach and had encouraged it. Public policy demanded that the liability under s.217 be strict.[168] A similar view was taken in *Ricketts v Ad Valorem Factors Ltd*,[169] where the liability was imposed, even though the second company was not Phoenix company.

Personal liability of delinquent directors, etc.

23-024   The Insolvency Act 1986 provides that if in a winding up it appears that any person who is or has been an officer[170] of the company, or a promoter, or manager, liquidator, or administrative receiver of a company, has misapplied or retained or became accountable for any money or other property of the company, or has been guilty of any misfeasance or breach of trust or other duty to the company the court may on the application of the Official Receiver, the liquidator or any creditor or contributory,[171] examine his conduct and order him to repay or restore the assets or to contribute to the assets of the company as the court thinks just.[172] A contributory can only bring such an action with the leave of the court. It is for the complainant to prove his case.[173]

This section replaced s.631 of the Companies Act 1985 which had established a similar summary procedure whereby directors and others could be called to account swiftly for any breach of duty or misfeasance prior to the liquidation. In many ways it is identical with s.631 and many of the cases on that section will still apply. The main differences are that s.212 applies to administrative receivers and includes breaches of duty other than breaches of trust, i.e. negligence.[174]

Section 631 was held to be procedural only. It gave a summary remedy, not a new cause of action.[175] It has been said that it "did not create any new liability or any new right, but only provides a summary mode of enforcing rights which must otherwise have been enforced by the ordinary procedure of the Courts".[176] Also, that the applicant "must show something which would have been the ground of an action by the company if it had not been wound up".[177] There seems no reason why this should not apply equally to s.212 of the Insolvency Act 1986.

A summons was taken out by the liquidator against the secretary of a company for sums overdrawn by him on account of his salary on the instructions of the managing director. It was held that as this was a claim for repayment of an

---

[168] But cf. *Ess Production Ltd v Sully* [2005] EWCA Civ. 554; [2005] B.C.C. 435, where the Court of Appeal allowed an appeal from a decision in which a director had been held liable to pay £21,450 to a claimant under s.217 for contravention of s.216 of the 1986 Act by the use of a prohibited company name where an exception under the Insolvency Rules 1986 did not apply.

[169] [2004] 1 B.C.L.C. 1.

[170] This includes a director, manager or secretary (see s.251 of the 1986 Act). Thus while "director" clearly also includes a de facto director, if that fact is not proved then proceedings cannot be brought under s.212: see *Gemma Ltd, Re* [2008] [2008] EWHC 546 (Ch.); [2008] B.C.C. 812.

[171] Defined in s.79(1) of the Insolvency Act 1986 as "every person liable to contribute to the assets of a company in the event of its being wound up".

[172] s.212.

[173] See *Mullarkey v Broad* [2007] EWHC 3400 (Ch.); [2008] 1 B.C.L.C. 638.

[174] Thus overriding the earlier case law on s.631. See *B. Johnson & Co, Re (Builders) Ltd* [1955] Ch. 634.

[175] *Coventry and Dixon's Case* (1880) 14 Ch.D. 660, CA.

[176] At 670 per James L.J.

[177] ibid.

ordinary debt due from the secretary without any wrongful conduct on his part, no order on the summons ought to be made.[178]

Instances of misfeasance under s.631 included the improper receipt by a director **23–025** of his qualification shares from a promoter.[179] No set-off was allowed to a claim for misfeasance under that section.[180] In relation to s.212 it has been held to include transfer of the company's business without requiring payment for goodwill and a non-genuine redundancy payment.[181] Also included is the case where it was established that from the date of a minute of a directors' meeting, a director had had a duty to put a stop to the practice of lending and to recover indebtedness, but had failed to do so.[182] In the recent case of *Paycheck Services 3 Ltd, Re*,[183] the Court of Appeal held that a director of a group[184] of composite companies had failed to show that he acted both honestly and reasonably in causing unlawful dividends to continue to be paid after receiving counsel's advice against doing so. On that basis he would have been liable in principle to make good those misapplications of the companies' assets. The judge at first instance had wrongly granted him relief under s.727 of the 1985 Act[185] but he should not have done so and was in error in limiting his order requiring him to account for the tax that ought to have been paid, rather than the full amount of the dividends unlawfully paid.

The court has a discretion as to the amount to be ordered to be paid on an application under s.212 of the Insolvency Act 1986.

A liquidator negligently admitted a proof, which he should have disallowed, and as a result the company paid £30,000 to a creditor. An attempt to recover this failed, as there was no mistake of fact on the liquidator's part. It was held that the liquidator was liable for misfeasance under s.631, but the court, in the exercise of its discretion, ordered him to pay only such a sum as would enable the creditors to be paid in full with interest at five per cent.[186]

Further, the court's power under s.631 was not merely to specify a sum by way of compensation but to apportion it between co-defendants in such a way and with such priority of liability as the court thought fit.[187] Again there is no reason to suppose that s.212 of the Insolvency Act 1986 has altered this.

---

[178] [1928] Ch. 861.

[179] Which occurred in *Eden v Ridsdales Railway Lamp Co Ltd* (1889) 23 Q.B.D. 368, CA.

[180] *Ex p. Pelly* (1882) 21 Ch.D. 492, CA.

[181] *Brian D. Pierson (Contractors) Ltd, Re* [2001] 1 B.C.L.C. 275. The latter payment was, however, excused under s.1157. See para.23–017, above.

[182] *Neville (Administrator of Unigreg Ltd) v Krikorian* [2006] EWCA Civ. 943; [2006] B.C.C. 937.

[183] [2009] EWCA Civ. 625; [2010] B.C.C. 104.

[184] The question whether he was a de facto director of these companies was also a live issue in the case, although the Court of Appeal overruled the first instance judge on this: at 63, per Rimer L.J.

[185] i.e. s.1157 of the 2006 Act. See para.23–017, above.

[186] *Home & Colonial Insce Co Ltd* [1930] 1 Ch. 102.

[187] *Re Morcambe Bowling Ltd* [1969] 1 W.L.R. 133.

Chapter 24

INSIDER DEALING

NATURE OF INSIDER DEALING

Introduction

24–001 Part V of the Criminal Justice Act 1993[1] deals with certain forms of insider trading and makes them criminal offences.[2] Provisions to regulate dealings in a company's shares came about because of widespread concern prior to 1980 about the misuse of confidential information by officers of the company, in particular, but also by their associates, their families and friends to whom information about the company had been relayed by them, or the misuse by others outside the company such as accountants, auditors and bankers who might equally have access to restricted information about the company which would affect the value of its shares on the market.

Insider dealing occurs where an individual or organisation buys or sells securities while knowingly in possession of some piece of confidential information which is not generally available and which is likely, if made available to the general public, to materially affect the price of these securities. So, for example, there is insider trading where a company director knows that the company is in a bad financial state and sells his shares in it knowing that in a few days' time this news will be made public together with an announcement of a cut in dividend payment. Likewise, the director would be insider dealing if, on being informed, before it was generally known by the public, that the company has discovered oil or gold on its own land, he bought more shares in the company in the not unrealistic expectation of an increase in their market value as a result of the subsequent public announcement. In *R. v McQuoid*[3] Lord Judge C.J. has stated that

> "Those who involve themselves in insider dealing are criminals: no more and no less. The principles of confidentiality and trust, which are essential to the operations of the commercial world, are betrayed by insider dealing and public confidence in the integrity of the system which is essential to its proper function is undermined by market abuse. Takeover arrangements are normally kept

---

[1] c.36.

[2] This Act replaced the provisions first introduced in ss.68–73 of the Companies Act 1980, c.21, and consolidated into the Company Securities (Insider Dealing) Act 1985, c.8.

[3] [2009] EWCA Crim. 1301; [2009] 4 All E.R. 388.

secret. Very few people are permitted to have advance knowledge of them. Those who are entrusted with advance knowledge are entrusted with that knowledge precisely because it is believed that they can be trusted. When they seek to make a profit out of the knowledge and trust reposed in them, or indeed when they do so recklessly, their criminality is not reduced or diminished merely because they are individuals of good character."[4]

Ethical and legal objections

The moral or ethical reasons[5] for prohibiting such activities are that the use of **24–002** insider information is clearly unfair to those who deal with the insider. One of the difficulties, however, is that in many cases it is seen as a victimless crime in that it is difficult to identify those who have lost by the insider dealing where, as the law currently requires, it takes place on a Stock Exchange dealing.

From the point of view of company law, perhaps a more significant reason for attempting to regulate insider trading by law is that the insider with access to confidential information is thereby in a potential conflict-of-interest situation. For example, he may be in such a position within the company as to be able to dictate or at least influence when the public disclosure of price-sensitive information is to be made. In that situation his decision and his own desire to trade advantageously in the company's shares may conflict; in other words the best interests of the company may wrongly take second place to his own self-interest. Directors are duty bound, subject to the considerations contained in Pt 10 of the 2006 Act and s.187 of the Insolvency Act 1986,[6] only to act bona fide in the best interests of the company as a whole.[7]

Furthermore, such unethical conduct is likely to bring not only the reputation of the company concerned but also that of the securities market in this country into disrepute with the possible risk of a consequent adverse investment effect. For this reason in particular, the Financial Services Act 1986[8] extended the scope of the provision aimed at preventing the abuse of information obtained by persons in their official capacity in connection with the new regulation of the securities and investment industry, and provided the innovation of investigations into suspected insider dealing. The Companies Act 1989 allowed for investigations at the request of overseas regulators since insider dealing may well take place on an international scale.

Since then, the Financial Services and Markets Act 2000[9] has been brought into force, effecting very significant changes to financial services regulation in the United Kingdom. Although the Act does not specifically deal with insider dealing, it does

---

[4] At [8].

[5] There are some economic arguments in favour of the practice. See Harry McVea, "What's wrong with insider dealing?" (1995) 15 *Legal Studies* 390; Paul Barnes, *Stock Market Efficiency, Insider Dealing and Market Abuse* (2009).

[6] This permits a company to make provision for the benefit of its employees or ex-employees on the cessation or transfer of the whole or part of its business even if it is not in the best interests of the company and permits a liquidator to make over assets to employees in satisfaction of the amount decided to be provided to them in such circumstances.

[7] *Hutton v W. Cork Railway* (1883) 23 Ch.D. 654, CA; *Lee Behrens & Co, Re* [1932] Ch. 46; *Evans v Brunner Mond & Co* [1921] 1 Ch. 359; *Parke v Daily News* [1962] Ch. 927; *Roith, Re* [1967] 1 W.L.R. 479.

[8] Since repealed.

[9] c.8.

contain a complex provision termed "market abuse" in Pt VIII.[10] Market abuse is defined as behaviour inter alia "which is based on information which is not generally available to those using the market but which, if available to a regular user of the market, would or would be likely to be regarded by him as relevant when deciding the terms on which transactions in investments of the kind in question should be effected".[11] This is very similar to, but not entirely on all fours with, the equivalent definition in the Criminal Justice Act 1993.[12] The Financial Services Authority (FSA)[13] is given a number of sanctions which it may invoke against persons who engage in such market abuse.[14] The FSA has become active in invoking these provisions in respect of insider dealing and since 2009 has secured three prosecutions for insider dealing, the most recent being against a Mr Malcolm Calvert, a former equities market maker at stock broker Cazenove,[15] who was found guilty at Southwark Crown Court on five counts of insider dealing after making approximately £103,883 profit from the trades between June 2003 and October 2004.[16]

Methods of control

24–003 Given that it is recognised as wrong for a director or another to deal in a company's shares knowing of some development which will affect the price of the shares and to which other members or the public generally are not privy, then the question arises how to put an end to such unethical activity. The universal condemnation of this malpractice has produced differing solutions for its eradication. In the USA, which has been in the forefront of the attack on insider trading, the solution adopted is to make the insider disgorge his ill-gotten gains to the company itself or to the individual with whom he dealt.

In the United Kingdom on the other hand the approach has been to progress from a few disparate provisions of the Companies Act and prohibitions contained in various self-regulatory codes to making certain instances of insider dealing a criminal offence. These offences were first created in 1980 partly at the request of the Takeover Panel who acknowledged that their self-regulatory code was inadequate to control the practice. The current provisions are set out in Pt V of the Criminal Justice Act 1993, incorporating changes required by the EU insider dealing directive.[17] These are dealt with in detail below[18] but two general points should be noted at this stage. First, the offences do not apply to private share deals and, second, there

---

[10] See also para.33–024, below.
[11] s.118(2)(a). cf. the amendments introduced by the Financial Services and Markets Act 2000 (Market Abuse) Regulations 2005 (SI 2005/381).
[12] See para.24–005, below.
[13] http://www.fsa.gov.uk [accessed June 4, 2010].
[14] See s.123.
[15] See http://www.cazenove.com [accessed June 4, 2010]. Cazenove is now 100 per cent owned by J.P. Morgan.
[16] See FSA/PN/041/2010, March 10, 2010, available at http://www.fsa.gov.uk [accessed June 4, 2010].
[17] Directive 89/592/EC [1989] OJ L334/30. See Klaus Hopt, "The European Insider Dealing Directive" (1990) 27 C.M.L.R. 51. See too *Comparative Implementation of EU Directives—Insider Dealing and Market Abuse*, City Research Series No.8, (British Institute of International and Comparative Law 2005), available at http://www.cityoflondon.gov.uk/nr/rdonlyres/3950d4a4-5792-412c-ba89-1b30827101c7/0/bc_rs_eudirectives_1205_fr.pdf [accessed June 1, 2010].
[18] See para.24–005.

are no civil consequences of a transaction being a criminal offence. The option for that in the directive was not adopted in the United Kingdom.

Prior to the creation of the criminal offences by the 1980 Companies Act,[19] the only statutory restrictions on insider trading by company officers were the prohibitions on option dealings by directors and the requirement that a register of their share dealings and the dealings of their spouses and children be maintained and available for inspection by an interested person.[20] These 1967 statutory provisions were ineffective because although they purported to create a legal duty or obligation to disclose share dealings, yet they provided no remedy for failure to comply with the Act's requirements.

Also by that time there were sanctions conceived and imposed by the Stock Exchange Authorities and the City Panel under the City Code on Takeovers and Mergers.[21] These, however, were only an extra-statutory form of self-regulation and open to criticism because they had no legal backing.[22] There are strict rules, for example, relating to the disclosure of director's personal interests in shares in relation to certain profitable transactions such as take-over bids; for absolute secrecy before any significant announcement is made, and for regulating dealings by insiders in the shares while negotiations continue.[23] In theory any breach of the rules, at the Panel's direction will be investigated by it or the Financial Services Authority (FSA), and improprieties chastised or corrected by appropriate action.

Civil liability

At common law officers of a company have always been freely permitted to hold **24-004** and deal in the shares of their company. The only sanction which the common law imposed was to make actionable the use of certain confidential information belonging to the company. Such information included industrial or trade secrets and details concerning customers.[24] The misuse of such information by directors, whether it occurred during the course of, or after the termination of, corporate office, was actionable.

The reason why the common law imposed no clear prohibition on the use of insider information in share dealings stems largely from the decision in *Percival v Wright*.[25] In this case where directors had purchased a member's shares in the knowledge that there was a ready buyer for all the shares of the company at a higher price than they paid him, it was held that the transaction could not be set aside for

---

[19] c.21.
[20] See Ch.17, above.
[21] Now the Takeover Panel and the Takeover Code. See paras 33–003 and 33–005.
[22] They rely on private reprimand, public censure or the withdrawal of access to the facilities of the securities market. cf. now para.33–013, below and s.955 of the Act.
[23] The Takeover Code. See *http://www.thetakeoverpanel.org.uk* [accessed on June 4, 2010].
[24] See *British Industrial Plastics v Ferguson* [1938] 4 All E.R. 504, CA (affirmed [1940] 1 All E.R. 479, HL); *Cranleigh Precision Engineering Ltd v Bryant* [1965] 1 W.L.R. 1293; *Measures Bros Ltd v Measures* [1910] 1 Ch. 336 (affirmed [1910] 2 Ch. 248, CA); *Printers & Finishers Ltd v Holloway (No.2)* [1965] 1 W.L.R. 1.
[25] [1902] 2 Ch. 421.

the director's failure to disclose the negotiations which were already taking place at a higher price. There was said to be no duty to disclosure because there was no fiduciary relationship between the directors and individual shareholders. The directors' duty was owed by the company alone.[26] It followed that the ordinary rules of contract applied. Subsequently in the case of *Allen v Hyatt*[27] the courts did recognise special but very limited circumstances in which a duty might be owed by directors to individual shareholders. In that particular case the directors had profited through share purchases from members and were held accountable to them because they had purported to act as agents for the members by inducing the latter to give them purchase options over each member's shares supposedly to facilitate a proposed amalgamation. Unless some special relationship of this type could be shown so as to establish a legal duty to disclose all relevant information, the officer retained his profit without adverse legal consequences.[28]

PART V OF THE CRIMINAL JUSTICE ACT 1993

Introduction

24-005 The criminal offences concerned with insider dealing are contained in Pt V of the Criminal Justice Act 1993. These replace the former offences contained in the Company Securities (Insider Dealing) Act 1985[29] which was repealed by the 1993 Act.[30] The current provisions incorporate the requirement to implement the EU directive on insider dealing,[31] together with other changes in the light of experience with the former provisions.

The three offences

24-006 Section 52 creates three separate offences, each of which may only be committed by an individual and within the United Kingdom.[32] The offences, which must be proved by the prosecution beyond all reasonable doubt, are:

1. where an insider[33] deals in securities to which the inside information relates (the dealing offence)[34];

2. where an insider encourages another person[35] to deal in such securities, knowing or having reasonable cause to believe that the other would do so (the encouraging offence)[36];

---

[26] See now s.172(1).

[27] (1914) 30 T.L.R. 444.

[28] See, e.g. *Munro v Bogie* [1994] 1 B.C.L.C. 415.

[29] See the 14th edition of this work.

[30] See Sch.6, Pt I.

[31] Directive. 89/592/EC [1989] OJ L334/30.

[32] s.62 requires either that the person committing the offence be within the United Kingdom at the relevant time or that the transaction takes place in the United Kingdom. Where the offence is communicating information to another it is sufficient that the recipient be within the United Kingdom at the relevant time.

[33] See para.24–010, below.

[34] s.52(1). See *R. v Butt (Asif Nazir)* [2006] EWCA Crim. 137; [2006] 2 Cr. App. R. (S.) 44.

[35] Not necessarily an individual.

[36] s.52(2)(a)

3. where an insider discloses the inside information to another person, otherwise than in the proper performance of the functions of his employment, office or profession (the disclosure offence).[37]

There is no definition of what is meant by "proper" in this context and as with many other areas this will have to be settled by a judge and jury at the trial.

The dealing and encouraging offences can only be committed if the dealing actually takes place on a regulated market[38] or the person dealing is either a professional intermediary or relying on such a person. A professional intermediary is defined in s.59(1) to mean a person carrying on a business of dealing in securities and who holds himself out to the public as such. The effect of these restrictions is that private off-market transactions are not covered by the Act.

No offence can be committed by a person who is acting on behalf of a public sector body[39] in pursuit of monetary policies or policies with respect to exchange rates or the management of the public debt: s.63(1).

The penalties and civil consequences

On conviction[40] of any of the three offences an individual can be sentenced to a **24–007** maximum of seven years' imprisonment on indictment or six months on a summary conviction, together with a fine.[41] No prosecution can be brought without the consent of either the Secretary of State for Trade and Industry or the Director of Public Prosecutions.[42]

The Court of Appeal has now given the following guidance on sentencing:

"These considerations seem to us to be relevant: (1) the nature of the defendant's employment or retainer, or involvement in the arrangements which enabled him to participate in the insider dealing of which he is guilty; (2) the circumstances in which he came into possession of confidential information and the use he made of it; (3) whether he behaved recklessly or acted deliberately, and almost inevitably therefore, dishonestly; (4) the level of planning and sophistication involved in his activity, as well as the period of trading and the

---

[37] s.52(2)(b).

[38] These are defined in art.9 of the Insider Dealing (Securities and Regulated Markets) Order 1994 (SI 1994/187) as amended by The Insider Dealing (Securities and Regulated Markets) (Amendment) Order 2002 (SI 2002/1874) including all the relevant stock exchanges and investment exchanges in the EU and Austria, Finland, Iceland, Norway, Sweden and Liechtenstein. Those regulated by the United Kingdom, for jurisdictional purposes are set out in art.10 of the Order, principally the London Stock Exchange.

[39] As defined in s.60(3)(b).

[40] In 2002–2004, there were 27 prosecutions under s.52: see *Companies in 2003–2004* (HMSO, 2004), at p.45.

[41] s.61(1). See *R. v Butt (Asif Nazir)* [2006] EWCA Crim. 137; [2006] 2 Cr. App. R. (S.) 44, where a sentence of five years' imprisonment for conspiring to commit insider dealing by the compliance officer of an investment bank engaged over a period of three years, was reduced to four years.

[42] s.61(2). But cf. *R. (Uberoi) v City of Westminster Magistrates' Court* [2008] EWHC 3191 (Admin.); [2009] 1 W.L.R. 1905, where the court held that under s.402(1) of the Financial Services and Markets Act 2000 the FSA could institute proceedings on its own initiative without the need to first obtain consent from the Secretary of State or the Director of Public Prosecutions.

number of individual trades; (5) whether he acted alone or with others and, if so, his relative culpability; (6) the amount of anticipated or intended financial benefit or (as sometimes happens) loss avoided, as well as the actual benefit (or loss avoided); (7) although the absence of any identified victim is not normally a matter giving rise to mitigation, the impact (if any), where proved, on any individual victim; and (8) the impact of the offence on overall public confidence in the integrity of the market; because of its impact on public confidence it is likely that an offence committed jointly by more than one person trusted with confidential information will be more damaging to public confidence than an offence committed in isolation by one person acting on his own. Age and a guilty plea will always be relevant. So, too, will good character. However, it must be borne in mind that it will often be the case that it is the individual of good character who has been trusted with information just because he or she is an individual of good character. By misusing the information, the trust reposed as a result of the good character has been breached."[43]

Section 63(2) provides, however, that no contract shall be void or unenforceable simply because of the fact that an offence was committed. Thus there are to be no civil consequences of an offence of insider dealing. This is intended to protect market transactions and the option to provide a civil remedy allowed for in the directive has not been adopted. The wording of s.63 is different from its predecessor in the 1985 Act which provided that no contract was to be void or voidable as a consequence of an offence. Thus the courts were able to hold that a contract was nevertheless unenforceable by the insider.[44] That is no longer possible so that in theory at least a criminal will be able to enforce a contract which was the subject of his crime.

The three offences each involve consideration of one or more of four concepts: securities, dealing, insider and inside information. It is necessary, therefore, to examine each of these in turn.

Securities

24–008 The dealing or information being communicated must relate to securities which are covered by the Act. These are defined in s.54(1) as those within Sch.2 to the Act subject to any conditions for specific types of security as the Treasury may prescribe.[45] Schedule 2 includes shares and debentures issued by companies. The condition required for these to be securities to which the Act applies is that they must be officially listed within the European Economic Area[46] or to be admitted to, quoted on, or regulated by a regulated market within that area.

---

[43] *R. v McQuoid* [2009] EWCA Crim. 1301; [2009] 4 All E.R. 388 at [14], per Lord Judge C.J.
[44] *Chase Manhattan Equities Ltd v Goodman* [1991] B.C.L.C. 897.
[45] See the Insider Dealing (Securities and Regulated Markets) Order 1994 (SI 1994/187, SI 1996/1561, SI 2000/1923 as amended, and SI 2002/1874).
[46] The EU and certain other European countries, including Norway.

Dealing

The dealing and encouraging offences require a definition of what amounts to **24–009** dealing. Section 55(1) therefore provides that a person deals in securities if he acquires or disposes of them either as principal or agent, or if he procures their acquisition or disposal by another person who may, but does not need to be under his control. Agreements to acquire or dispose of securities, to create securities or ending an agreement which created a security are all caught by the section.

Insiders

All three offences can only be committed by individuals who are insiders. These **24–010** are called by the Act "persons who have information as insiders". Under s.57(1) an individual can only be in that position if the information he has is inside information and he knows both that it is inside information and that he has it from an inside source. The concept of inside information is discussed below. The information will be deemed to have come from an inside source in relation to corporate securities in any of three situations. In other words those within these situations are potential insiders, who may or may not be actual insiders depending upon their knowledge. No one else can be an insider. The situations are specified in s.57(2):

1. information gained by being a director, employee or shareholder[47] of the company (issuer of securities) which has issued the shares or debentures in question;

2. information gained by access to it through the individual's employment, profession or office. Note that there is no requirement, as previously, that the person be connected with the relevant company through his employment, etc. Thus individuals, such as financial journalists, can now be temporary potential insiders;

3. information which an individual has obtained directly or indirectly from a person within 1. or 2. above. These people are known as "tippees" from primary insiders. Because of the word "indirectly", this liability can extend to sub-tippees, i.e. a tippee's tippee, although of course in all cases the requisite degree of knowledge must also be proved. Under the previous law the House of Lords held that a tippee could be regarded as obtaining information even if he did not actively seek the information but was merely a passive recipient of it.[48]

Thus potential insiders are those directly connected with the company in question, those who come across the information professionally and tippees from any of those. To make them actual insiders, and so liable for any of the three offences, it must be shown that the potential insider knows both that it is inside information and came from an inside source.

---

[47] Shareholders as such were not potential insiders under the previous Act.
[48] *Attorney General's Reference (No.1 of 1988)* [1989] A.C. 971.

Inside information

24–011 The concept of inside information is therefore crucial to the definition of an insider and thus to the offences themselves. The definition, which is largely taken from the directive, is in s.56. There are four requirements specified in s.56(1):

1. the information must relate to particular securities or to a particular company or its business but not to securities generally or companies generally;

2. it must be specific or precise;

3. it must not have been made public; and

4. it must be such that if it were made public it would be likely to have a significant effect on the price or value of any securities, which are then known as price affected securities.

Many of these concepts are undefined and will have to be decided on by a jury after judicial guidance in each case. When, for example, does a rumour cease to be rumour and become specific or precise?

The only factor which is defined, non-exhaustively, in the Act is when information is deemed to have been made public and so is no longer insider information. Section 58(2) states that inclusion of the information on records to which the public have access and publication of it in accordance with the rules of a regulated market,[49] such as the information service of the Stock Exchange, will be sufficient. Since the section also makes it clear that such information is to be treated as being made public even if it is communicated to a section of the public for a fee and can only be accessed by observation, it is thought that this will include computer-linked market information systems. If that is correct, the position is different from the previous law where it was agreed that time had to be allowed for the market to digest the information before it could be regarded as being in the public domain.

The defences

24–012 Section 53 provides specific defences to the three offences. With regard to the dealing and encouraging offences there are three defences which must all be proved by the defendant on the balance of probabilities.[50] The specified defences are set out in s.53(1) and s.53(2):

1. that the defendant did not at the time expect the dealing, by himself or another, to result in a profit or the avoidance of a loss. It is not for the prosecution therefore to show a profit motive but for the defence to show that there was none;

---

[49] See above.

[50] Thus it is not for the prosecution to prove that the defence is not applicable if the defendant simply raises the matter. This confirms the decision in *R. v Cross* [1991] B.C.L.C. 125 on the previous, different, wording.

2. that at the time the defendant reasonably believed that the information was widely enough known (although not made public) so as not to prejudice the other parties to the dealing. This is intended to save certain City transactions such as underwriting, etc.;

3. that the defendant would have dealt (or encouraged another to deal) in the securities even if he had not had the inside information. This may protect, e.g. a takeover bidder or possibly a trustee who under his duty as a trustee to do the best he can for the beneficiaries was obliged under trust law to deal. There is no specific defence for such conflict of duty situations,[51] however, as under the previous law.

Section 53(3) provides for two defences, again to be proved on the balance of probabilities by the defendant, for the disclosure offence:

1. that the defendant did not expect that any person (the tippee) would deal as a result of such disclosure; and

2. that, even if the defendant did expect another to deal, he did not expect a profit or avoidance of a loss to arise from such a dealing using inside information.

Schedule 1 to the Act also contains three general defences, available in respect of all three offences: for market makers; those acting reasonably with market information; and those involved in price-stabilisation transactions under s.144(1) of the Financial Services and Markets 2000.[52] These defences are outside the scope of company law.

Investigations into insider dealing

When the offence of insider dealing was first made law by the Companies Act 1980 no provision was made or mechanism included whereby alleged or suspected abuse of insider information might be investigated by a regulatory body other than the police. Despite the fact that this was a serious drawback to any effectiveness that the legislation might have had, no amendment was made to rectify that weakness until the Financial Services Act 1986[53] empowered the Secretary of State to appoint investigators into what appears to him to be a contravention of Pt V of the Criminal Justice Act 1993. In investigating alleged insider dealing the investigators were provided with wide powers[54] similar to those vested in an inspector appointed under the 1985 Act.[55] **24–013**

---

[51] These could include liquidators, executors and administrators among others.
[52] As substituted by the Financial Services and Markets Act 2000 (Consequential Amendments and Repeals) Order 2001 (SI 2001/3649).
[53] Since repealed.
[54] Financial Services Act 1986, c.60, s.177. See *R. (on the application of Clegg) v Secretary of State for Trade and Industry* [2002] EWCA Civ. 519; [2003] B.C.C. 128.
[55] Companies Act 1985, Pt XIV, ss.431–453, above.

Since the repeal of the 1986 Act,[56] however, these powers have been vested in the Financial Services Authority (FSA) which may appoint one or more competent persons to conduct an investigation on its behalf.[57] If an investigator considers that any person is or may be able to give information which is or may be relevant to the investigation, he can require this person to attend before him at a specified time and place and answer questions or otherwise to provide such information as he may require for the purposes of the investigation.[58]

The investigator can also require the person to produce, at a specified time and place, any specified documents or documents of a specified description which appear to the investigator to relate to any matter relevant to the investigation.[59] Finally, the investigator may also otherwise require the person to give him all assistance in connection with the investigation which the person is reasonably able to give.[60] Failure to comply can lead to the investigator certifying that fact in writing to a court.[61] If the court is satisfied that the person in default failed, without reasonable excuse to comply, it may deal with the defaulter as if he were in contempt.[62]

The Secretary of State may vary the terms of the investigation and direct the inspectors to take no further steps. Any person convicted of an offence as a result of an inquiry may be required to contribute towards the costs of the inquiry.

---

[56] See the Financial Services and Markets act 2000 (Consequential Amendments and Repeals) Order 2001 (SI 2001/3649) art.3(1)(c).

[57] s.168(2)(a) and s.168(3) of the Financial Services and Markets Act 2000.

[58] s.173(2).

[59] s.173(3). A journalist would not be exempt from this requirement: see *An Inquiry under the Company Securities (Insider Dealing) Act 1985, Re* [1988] A.C. 660.

[60] s.173(4).

[61] s.177(1).

[62] s.177(2).

CORPORATE INSOLVENCY

Chapter 25

DEBENTURES

This chapter is concerned with the borrowing of money by a company where the **25–001** borrowing is on debentures or on debenture stock, and with fixed and floating charges which a company may create over its property in order to secure the principal sum borrowed and interest thereon until repayment. Thus the chapter deals with the relationship between a company and its creditors, which is also central to the following chapters up to Ch.31.

The most important part of the chapter is that with regard to charges and the registration of charges, particularly registration with the Registrar of Companies under s.860 Companies Act 2006. This system was reviewed by the Law Commission as part of a series of consultations.[1] The Law Commission was in favour of reform of the registration system so as to replicate, at least to some extent, art.9 of the Uniform Commercial Code of the United States, but its recommendations in this regard have not been adopted.

A COMPANY'S POWER TO BORROW MONEY

Prior to the substantial changes to corporate transactions contained in ss.35 and **25–002** 35A and 322A of the Companies Act 1985 Act as substituted by the 1989 Act,[2] it was important to decide whether or not the company had the capacity, i.e. by virtue of an express or implied power, to borrow money, and it was possible for a loan to be ultra vires the company and so void.[3]

Following those changes, however, any borrowing is simply one type of transaction by a company and so its validity is now governed, as with all other corporate transactions, by the new provisions. It follows that unless the lender is either not acting in good faith[4] or is a director of the borrowing company[5] no question of invalidity can arise as a result of the company's constitution. Even if the lender is not

---

[1] See Law Com Consultation Paper 164, *Registration of Security Interests: Company Charges and Property other than Land* (TSO, 2002); Law Com Consultation Paper 176, *Company Security Interests* (TSO, 2004). See also Scot Law Com Rep No.197, *Registration of Rights in Security by Companies* (TSO, 2004).

[2] Ch.6, above. The provisions in question are now substantially replicated by Companies Act 2006 ss.39, 40 and 41.

[3] For the position prior to the 1989 Act changes see the 13th edition of this work at pp.607–611.

[4] So that Companies Act 2006 s.40 cannot apply. See, for example, *Ford v Polymer Vision Ltd* [2009] EWHC 945 (Ch.).

[5] Thus applying s.41.

acting in good faith or is a director, the transaction may still be ratified by the appropriate resolution. Ratification is also possible if the defect arises from a lack of authority on the part of those negotiating the loan on behalf of the company, if it arises under the general law of agency rather than from the company's constitution.[6]

DEBENTURES AND DEBENTURE STOCK

25–003 A debenture is a document which creates or acknowledges a debt due from a company. Such document need not be, although it usually is, under seal,[7] it need not give, although it usually does give, a charge on the assets of the company by way of security, and it may or may not be one of a series.[8] Thus debentures may be either secured or unsecured. As will be seen, debentures may be collaterally secured by a trust deed.[9] Convertible debentures, i.e. debentures which the holder has the right to convert, at stated times, into shares in the company, have already been mentioned.[10]

It may be helpful to mention here that some of the differences between shares and debentures are:

1. the holder of a debenture is a creditor, not a member, of the company; a shareholder is a member[11];

2. debentures may be issued at a discount; shares, in general, may not be[12];

3. a company may purchase its own debentures since that would amount to repaying a debt; it must not purchase its own shares except in accordance with specific procedures[13];

4. interest at the specified rate on debentures may be paid out of capital; dividends on shares must be paid only out of distributable profits.[14]

Section 738 of the Companies Act 2006 defines "debenture" as including debenture stock, bonds, and any other securities[15] of a company whether constituting a charge on the assets of the company or not. A mortgage of land by a company is a debenture.[16] Debentures, including debenture stock, loan stock, bonds and certificates of deposit are investments for the purposes of Pt V of the Criminal Justice Act 1993[17]: see Ch.19, above.

---

[6] i.e. because the agent has no authority to bind the company. See, for example, *Wrexham Associated Football Club Ltd (In Administration) v Crucialmove Ltd* [2006] EWCA Civ. 237.

[7] N.B. the provisions relating to the sealing of documents in Companies Act 2006 s.45, above, p.112.

[8] See *Lemon v Austin Friars Investment Trust Ltd* [1926] Ch. 1, CA.

[9] Below, p.608.

[10] See *Mosely v Koffyfontein Mines* [1904] 2 Ch. 108, above pp.129, 181. See also *Domain Dynamics (Holdings) Ltd v Revenue and Customs Commissioners* [2008] S.T.C. (S.C.D.) 1136.

[11] Above, p.291

[12] Above, p.179

[13] Above, Ch.10.

[14] Above, Ch.14.

[15] "Securities", as used in s.738, does not include shares.

[16] *Knightsbridge Estates Trust Ltd v Byrne* [1940] A.C. 613.

[17] Criminal Justice Act 1993, Sch.2, para.2.

Debenture stock is borrowed money consolidated into one mass for the sake of convenience. This is normally done by a trust deed,[18] which may give the trustees a charge on the company's property. Where there is no charge, debenture stock is commonly called unsecured loan stock. The main advantage of debenture stock is that, unlike a single debenture it is transferable in fractional amounts, although the trust deed may specify the minimum fractional amount which can be transferred. Again, the debenture stockholders will be given simple debenture stock certificates instead of debentures.

ISSUES OF DEBENTURES

Debentures are issued in accordance with the provisions of the articles, usually **25–004** by a resolution of the board of directors. When debentures have been issued, the prospectus[19] cannot be looked at to ascertain the contract, but if the contract was intended to be contained in the prospectus and the debenture together, or if the prospectus contains a collateral contract the consideration for which was the taking up of the debentures, the prospectus can be looked at.[20] Debentures or debentures stock certificates must be completed and ready for delivery within two months after allotment or after the lodging of a transfer, unless the conditions of issue otherwise provide: s.769.

There is no objection to the issue of debentures at a discount but when any commission, allowance or discount has been paid or made to any person in consideration of his subscribing or procuring subscriptions for debentures, particulars of the amount or rate of the commission or discount must be sent to the Registrar within 21 days. The omission to do this does not, however, affect the validity of the debentures. The deposit of debentures as security for a debt of the company does not, for this purpose, amount to the issue of debentures at a discount: ss.863 and 883.

A contract to take up debentures may be enforced by specific performance: s.740. This section provides an exception to the rule, laid down in *South African Territories Ltd v Wallington*,[21] that specific performance will not be granted of a contract to lend money since damages are an adequate remedy for breach of such contract. Apart from the section, an agreement to issue debentures made in consideration of an actual balance of money has the effect in English law of putting the lender in equity in the same position as if the debentures had actually been issued.

A syndicate agreed to sell goods to a company on the terms that, as part payment, £3,000 debentures charged upon all the company's assets were issued. On this agreement the syndicate allowed the company to remove the goods, which were subsequently taken in execution by F. It was held that although no debentures were actually issued, the syndicate was in the same position as if they had been and so F was entitled subject to the charge.[22]

---

[18] See n.9, above.
[19] This presumably also applies to listing particulars.
[20] *Jacobs v Batavia and General Plantations Trust Ltd* [1924] 2 Ch. 329, CA.
[21] [1898] A.C. 309.
[22] *Simultaneous Colour Printing Syndicate v Foweraker* [1901] 1 K.B. 771.

TRUST DEEDS

25–005 Debentures and particularly debenture stock are usually secured by a trust deed. The main terms of a debenture trust deed are:

1. a covenant by the company for payment to the debenture holders of the principal moneys and interest;

2. clauses giving the trustees a legal mortgage (or a charge by way of legal mortgage) by demise of the company's freeholds and leaseholds, which are specified (or fixed), and a floating charge over the rest of the undertaking and property[23];

3. a clause specifying the events on which the security is to become enforceable, e.g. default in the payment of interest or principal moneys, order made or resolution passed for winding up, appointment of a receiver, cessation of business, breach of covenant by the company;

4. a clause giving the trustees power to take possession of the property charged when the security becomes enforceable, to carry on the business and to sell the property charged and to apply the net sale moneys in payment of the principal and interest and to pay the balance to the company;

5. power for the trustees to concur with the company in dealings with the property charged;

6. covenants by the company to keep a register of debenture holders, to insure and to keep in repair the property charged;

7. provision for meetings of debenture holders;

8. power for the trustees to appoint a receiver or an administrator when the security becomes enforceable[24];

9. provision for serving notices on the debenture holders by post.

A debenture stock trust deed, in addition to containing the foregoing terms, constitutes a stock by acknowledging that the company is indebted to the trustees in a specified sum and provides for the issue of debenture stock certificates. A trust deed usually contains a clause providing that the rights of the debenture holders against the company or any property charged by the deed may be modified or compromised by extraordinary resolution of the debenture holders. A debenture holder is entitled to require a copy of the trust deed on payment of the prescribed fee: s.744.

---

[23] It *may* be possible to take fixed equitable charges over other assets, e.g. book debts of a company, but see pp.619 et seq., below.

[24] The power to appoint an *administrative receiver* will only apply to debentures containing a floating charge which pre-dates September 15, 2003: see Ch.27, below.

Liability of trustees

Trustees for debenture holders are in the same position towards their beneficiaries **25–006** as any other trustees, and cannot purchase the debentures, the subject of the deed, without making full disclosure of all the information relating to them which is in their possession.[25] Any provision in a trust deed, or in a contract with the holders of debentures secured by a trust deed, for exempting the trustees from, or indemnifying them against, liability for breach of trust where they fail to show the degree of care and diligence required of them as trustees, is void, except that the trustees may be released from liability by a release given after the liability has arisen; and a provision in a trust deed for the giving of such a release by a majority of not less than three-fourths in value of the debenture holders present and voting in person or by proxy at a meeting summoned for the purpose is not void: ss.750, 751. (Contrast s.532, above,[26] as regards auditors.) Section 1157 (power of court to grant relief), above,[27] does not apply to the trustees although the Trustee Act 1925, s.61 does, and so in an appropriate case the court may relieve the trustees from liability.

REGISTERED DEBENTURES AND CONTENTS OF A REGISTERED DEBENTURE

Debentures or debenture stock may be payable to either (1) the registered holder; **25–007** or (2) the bearer. Where there is a trust deed the usual form of debenture payable to the registered holder is a document issued under the seal of the company and containing two clauses. The clauses are as follows:

1. the company, for valuable consideration received, covenants to pay the registered holder the principal sum on a specified day or on such earlier day as it becomes payable under the indorsed conditions, and in the meantime to pay interest by equal half-yearly payments on specified dates at a specified rate;

2. the debenture is said to be issued subject to and with the benefit of the conditions indorsed thereon.

The indorsed conditions usually include the following:

1. the debenture is said to be one of a series, each for securing a specified sum;

2. the registered holders of all the debentures of the issue are said to be entitled pari passu to the benefit and subject to the provisions of the trust deed, the date of execution of which the parties to which are specified, and the charges conferred by the trust deed are recited. This has the effect of putting all the debentures of the issue on an equal footing; in

---

[25] *Magadi Soda Co, Re* (1925) 41 T.L.R. 297.
[26] p.487.
[27] p.487.

the absence of such a clause the debentures would rank according to the order in which they were executed[28];

3. the company is empowered, at any time after a specified date, by giving not less than a specified number of months' notice, to pay off the principal moneys secured with interest to the date of payment;

4. provision is made for keeping a register of debenture holders at the registered office. We shall see that this will comply with s.743 and that a right of inspection is given by s.744[29];

5. the company is not to be bound to recognise anyone as having any title to the debenture except the registered holder, or his personal representative, and is not to be bound to enter notice of any trust in the register.

Section 126, which provides that trusts are not to be entered on the register of members in England and Wales, does not apply to the register of debenture holders, and consequently such a clause is necessary. If the company does receive notice of a trust, the clause relieves it from the obligation of entering it on the register, but if it deals with the debentures as a trader, e.g. by advancing money on them, after notice of a trust, it will be bound by that trust[30];

6. transfer of the debenture is provided for. Every transfer must be in writing, as will be explained later;

7. equities between the company and any person other than the registered holder are excluded. This will be explained later[31];

8. the principal moneys and interest are made payable at the company's registered office or at its bankers.

If this clause is not inserted it is the company's duty to follow the usual rule and seek out its creditor and pay him.

F held 18 £100 debentures repayable in June, 1913, in the M Corporation. Before the date of redemption F died, and her executors neglected to present the debentures to the company for payment. In June, 1916, the company was sued for principal and interest. It was held that as the debentures contained no clause to the effect set out above, it was the company's duty to seek out the debenture holder and pay her; as this had not been done, the company was liable to pay the principal with interest until the date of actual payment;[32]

9. the company is empowered to purchase any of the debentures of the issue at any time;

[28] *Gartside v Silkstone and Dodworth Coal, etc., Co* (1882) 21 Ch.D. 762.
[29] Below, p.612.
[30] *Bradford Banking Co v Briggs & Co* (1886) 12 App. Cas. 29; *Mackereth v Wigan Coal Co Ltd* [1916] 2 Ch. 293.
[31] Below, p.612.
[32] *Fowler v Midland Electric Corp* [1917] 1 Ch. 656, CA.

10. interest is made payable by warrant on the company's bank payable to the order of the registered holder and sent by post to his registered address;

11. the principal moneys are made immediately payable if the company defaults in the payment of interest for a specified number of months, or if a winding up order is made or resolution passed, or if the security constituted by the trust deed becomes enforceable and the trustees enforce it.

The debenture holder is entitled to repayment of his principal on the company's going into liquidation, whether or not the date fixed for repayment has arrived.[33]

Transfer of registered debentures

The following account does not apply to transfers of debentures held in electronic **25–008** form under the CREST system which operates in respect of some listed companies.[34] Registered debentures are transferred in the manner laid down in the indorsed conditions (which usually require a transfer to be in writing under the hand of the registered holder or of his personal representatives) or by a stock transfer under the Stock Transfer Act 1963. As in the case of a transfer of shares[35] it is unlawful for a company to register a transfer of debentures unless a "proper instrument of transfer" has been delivered to the company: s.770(1).

The company must have the debenture or debenture stock certificate ready for delivery within two months of the lodging of the instrument of transfer unless the conditions of issue otherwise provide: s.776. If registration of a transfer is refused, notice of refusal must be given to the transferee within two months: s.771(1)(b).

Registered debentures are choses in action. They are not negotiable instruments, and consequently a transferee takes them subject to all claims which the company may have against prior holders at the date of the transfer.

After a receiver had been appointed and a winding up petitions had been presented, P, a debenture stockholder, transferred £10,000 debenture stock to X, who was registered as the owner. P, was also a director of the company and a claim was made against him for money had and received by him while a director. It was held that X was not entitled to payment until the amount due from P to the company had been ascertained and deducted.[36]

To avoid this result, the indorsed conditions usually provide that the principal and interest shall be paid to the registered holder without regard to any equities or rights of compensation existing between the company and any prior holder of the debenture. Such a clause amounts to a contract by the company that it will not rely on equities or rights of compensation, and its effect is to make the debentures more marketable.

---

[33] *Hodson v Tea Co* (1880) 14 Ch.D. 859.
[34] See p.143, above.
[35] Above, pp.143 et seq.
[36] *Rhodesta Goldfields Ltd, Re* [1910] 1 Ch. 239.

A company was in liquidation. C, who had been a director of the company, transferred debentures to R as security for a loan. The debentures contained a clause similar to that set out above. It was then discovered that C had been guilty of misfeasance and he was ordered to pay a sum of money to the liquidator in respect thereof. The liquidator refused to register R's transfer. It was held that the right to transfer and to have the transfer registered was not affected by the winding up, and R was entitled to payment without regard to C's debt to the company.[37]

A transferee cannot claim the benefit of such a clause unless either he is registered or the conditions specifically allow the holder to transfer the debenture free of equities.

B held debentures containing a clause similar to that set out above. After a resolution for winding up had been passed he transferred them for value to C, who took without notice of any defect in B's title. Notice of transfer but no request for registration was given to the liquidator. C claimed payment but the court found that B had paid nothing for the debentures and had obtained them by misrepresentation. Held, notwithstanding the clause, C took subject to the company's claim against B. *Goy & Co, Re*, above, was distinguished on the ground that when the transfer in that case was sent for registration the company was not aware of and was not setting up any equities between itself and the transferor.[38] Where the actual agreement specifically allowed the holder to transfer free of all equities it has been held that following such a transfer the issuing company is bound to register the transfer.[39]

Section 775 (certification of transfers) above[40] applies to transfers of debentures as well as to transfers of shares.

Register of debenture holders

25–009   A company is not required to keep a register of debenture holders but there are provisions regulating those companies which do. The register must be kept at the registered office or at any other office of the company where it is made up or, if it is made up by an agent, it may be kept at the agent's office: s.743. Debenture holders and shareholders in the company may, without fee, inspect the register of debenture holders within limits laid down by the Secretary of State. Other persons may inspect the register on payment of a prescribed fee. A copy may be demanded on payment of the prescribed fee: s.744.[41] A computer may be used to keep the register of debenture holders: s.1135.

BEARER DEBENTURES

25–010   Debentures payable to bearer are in the same form as registered debentures except that they are expressed to be made payable to bearer and coupons for the interest

---

[37] *Goy & Co Ltd, Re* [1900] 2 Ch. 149.
[38] *Palmer's Decoration and Furnishing Co, Re* [1904] 2 Ch. 743.
[39] *Hilger Analytical Ltd v Rank Precision Industries Ltd* [1984] B.C.L.C. 301.
[40] p.140.
[41] For the relevant limits and fees see the Companies (Fees for Inspection and Copying of Company Records) (No.2) (SI 2007/3535) reg.2.

are attached. The indorsed conditions are also in the same form with the necessary modifications for bearer, instead of registered, instruments. Bearer debentures are negotiable instruments and consequently a transferee in good faith and for value takes them free from any defects in the title of a prior holder.

The B Company owned some bearer debentures and kept them in a safe. The secretary fraudulently took them from the safe and deposited them with the bank, who took them in good faith and as security for advances to the secretary. It was held that the debentures were negotiable instruments transferable by delivery and the bank was entitled to them as against the B Company.[42]

Bearer debentures are transferable by delivery and no stamp duty is payable on transfer. Interest is payable by means of the coupons which are cut off and presented for payment to the company's bankers when the date of payment arrives.

REDEEMABLE DEBENTURES

25–011 Debentures may be (1) redeemable at the option of the company, or (2) irredeemable or perpetual. Sometimes debentures are issued on the terms that the company is bound to redeem a certain number each year by "drawings" (in which case, in effect, the numbers of the debentures to be redeemable are drawn out of a hat),[43] or that it may purchase, e.g. on the Stock Exchange, or that it is bound to set aside a sinking fund for redemption purposes on a specified date. When debentures have been so redeemed, s.752 empowers the company to reissue them or issue other debentures in their place, unless:

1. the company, in its articles or otherwise, has contracted not to reissue them; or

2. the company has shown an intention to cancel the debentures by passing a resolution to that effect, or by some other act.

On a reissue of redeemed debentures, the person entitled to them has the same priorities as if the debentures had never been redeemed: s.752(2). The date of redemption of the reissued debentures cannot be later than that of the original debentures.[44] Reissued debentures are treated as new debentures for the purpose of stamp duty: s.752(3).

PERPETUAL DEBENTURES

25–012 Debentures are not invalid merely because they are made irredeemable, or redeemable on the happening of a contingency, however remote, e.g. the winding up of the company, or on the expiration of a period, however long, e.g. 100 years after the issue of the debenture, i.e. the legal or contractual date for redemption may be postponed, despite any rule of equity to the contrary: s.739.

---

[42] *Bechuanaland Exploration Co v London Trading Bank* [1898] 2 Q.B. 658.

[43] For difficulties which may arise from the company's inability to trace the holders to whom repayment is due, see *United Collieries Ltd v Lord Advocate*, 1950 S.C. 458.

[44] *Antofagasta (Chile) and Bolivia Ry Co's Trust Deed, Re* [1939] Ch. 732.

CHARGES SECURING DEBENTURES

25–013 A charge on the assets of a company given by a debenture or a trust deed in order to secure money borrowed by the company may be either (1) a specific or fixed charge, or (2) a floating charge. In practice many debentures are secured by both a fixed and a floating charge. Such charges are usually drafted to cover "all moneys" due by the company to the lender including contingent and future liabilities. In *Quest Cae, Ltd, Re*[45] it was held that such wording only covered debts arising as a result of transactions between the company and the lender so that where the lender subsequently acquired loan stock issued by the company to a third party it was not protected by the charge. The debt had not arisen by virtue of a transaction between the company and the lender.

Fixed charges

25–014 A fixed charge is a mortgage of ascertained and definite property, e.g. a legal or an equitable mortgage of a specified factory, and prevents the company from realising that property, i.e. disposing of it free from the charge, without the consent of the holders of the charge. It has been said in one case,[46] however, that a limited licence for the company to deal with the charged property may not be inconsistent with a fixed charge, depending upon the nature of the property charged and the degree of the licence to deal. But in *Cosslett (Contractors) Ltd, Re*[47] the Court of Appeal made it clear that the essence of a fixed charge is that the company cannot deal with the assets without the consent of the chargee. Whether or not a charge is a fixed or floating charge does not depend upon the wording of the charge but upon the extent of the rights and obligations of each party arising under the agreement granting the charge.[48] Only if those rights and obligations are consonant with the charge being a fixed charge, as defined by the courts, will the charge be fixed, notwithstanding the label the parties have chosen to attach to it.[49] Where a charge is on fixed plant and machinery it will only apply to those items physically attached to the company's premises and not to all a company's fixed, i.e. capital, assets.[50] The question of creating a fixed charge over the book debts or other moneys due to the company is considered below.[51]

Floating charges

25–015 In *Yorkshire Woolcombers Association Ltd, Re*[52] Romer L.J. said that if a charge has the three characteristics set out below it is a floating charge:

[45] [1985] B.C.L.C. 266.
[46] *Cimex Tissues Ltd, Re* [1995] 1 B.C.L.C. 409.
[47] [1997] B.C.C. 724, CA.
[48] *G.E. Tunbridge Ltd, Re* [1995] 1 B.C.L.C. 34.; *Agnew v Inland Revenue Commissioner* [2001] 2 A.C. 710.
[49] *Agnew v Inland Revenue Commissioner* [2001] 2 A.C. 710; *Spectrum Plus, Re* [2005] UKHL 41.
[50] *Hi-Fi Equipment (Cabinets) Ltd, Re* (1987) 3 B.C.C. 478, not following *Tudor Heights Ltd v United Dominions Corporation Finance Ltd* [1977] 1 N.Z.L.R. 532.
[51] Below, pp.619 et seq.
[52] [1903] 2 Ch. 284, CA, at 295.

1. it is a charge on a class of assets of a company, present and future;

2. which class is, in the ordinary course of the company's business, changing from time to time;

3. it is contemplated by the charge that, until the holders of the charge take steps to enforce it, the company may carry on business in the ordinary way as far as concerns the class of assets charged.

Thus a floating charge is an equitable charge on some or all of the present and future property of a company, e.g. the company's undertaking, i.e. all its property, present and future.[53] It is effective as to future property only when that property is acquired by the company. It is not necessary for the existence of a floating charge that the company has complete unfettered freedom to deal with the charged assets; the distinction between a fixed and floating charge is whether the chargee is in control of those assets. Under a floating charge the company retains control of the assets and may deal with them so as to withdraw them from the security.[54] A floating charge will be valid even if the assets covered do not yet exist.[55]

However, when the security is enforceable, e.g. there is default with regard to payment of interest or repayment of the principal sum, and the debenture holders or the trustees enforce it, e.g. they appoint an administrative receiver[56] or an administrator over the charged property, the floating charge is said to crystallise; i.e. it becomes a fixed charge on the assets in the class charged at the time of crystallisation or, where the floating charge so provides, assets which come to the company after crystallisation.[57]

Crystallisation also occurs on the commencement of the winding up of the company, even if it is a voluntary winding up for the purpose of reconstruction,[58] or when the company ceases business.[59] The latter, which is a form of "implied automatic crystallisation" in that it needs no act or specific event to bring it about and so may be difficult for other creditors to judge, was disputed until 1986. In coming to his decision on this point, Nourse J. pointed out that cessation of business prevents a company from dealing with its assets and so there is no reason why the charge should not crystallise. Being an implied term it may be excluded by express terms in the agreement but this will only be the case where there is no doubt that that was the intention.[60] Nourse J., however, rejected another such ground for implied crystallisation, i.e. on the crystallisation of a second floating charge which is postponed to the relevant floating charge.[61]

---

[53] *Panama, etc., Royal Mail Co, Re* (1870) L.R. 5 Ch. App. 318.
[54] *Cosslett (Contractors) Ltd, Re* [1997] B.C.C. 724; *Agnew v Inland Revenue Commissioner* [2001] 2 A.C. 710; *Spectrum Plus Ltd, Re* [2005] UKHL 41.
[55] *Croftbell Ltd, Re* [1990] B.C.C. 781.
[56] If the charge in question pre-dates the coming into force of the Pt 10 of the Enterprise Act 2002: see below, pp.659 et seq.
[57] *N. W. Robbie & Co Ltd v Whitney Warehouse Co Ltd* [1963] 1 W.L.R. 1324, CA; *Ferrier v Bottomer* (1972) 126 C.L.R. 597.
[58] *Crompton & Co, Re* [1914] 1 Ch. 954.
[59] *Woodroffes (Musical Instruments) Ltd, Re* [1986] Ch. 366.
[60] *The Real Meat Co Ltd, Re* [1996] B.C.C. 254.
[61] But see as to priority *H & K Medway Ltd, Re* [1997] B.C.C. 853.

It is possible that the charging deed may provide for crystallisation on a certain event, e.g. an attempt by the company to create another charge over the assets in the class charged, or simply by the giving of a notice to that effect. Such "express automatic crystallisation" is valid under English law following the decision of Hoffmann J. in *Brightlife Ltd, Re*.[62] The judge pointed out that floating charges were developed to enable companies to raise money without inhibiting their ability to trade, but this involved potential prejudice to other creditors who could suddenly find assets becoming subject to a charge on crystallisation without anyone else being aware. The appointment of an administrative receiver, administrator or liquidator were public acts, but the giving of a notice or the happening of an event would not be. The judge, however, considered that any restrictions on the contractual freedom of parties to a floating charge were matters for Parliament, and it would be "wholly inappropriate" for the courts to impose restrictions on the ground of public policy. The judge followed a decision of the New Zealand courts to a similar effect,[63] but noted that very clear language would be required to demonstrate the parties' intention to automatically crystallise a floating charge. This was because such crystallisation would, in many cases, be commercially inconvenient, so much so that there existed a strong presumption that the parties did not intend it.[64]

The characteristics of a floating charge are therefore:

1. it is an equitable charge on assets for the time being of the company[65];

2. it attaches to the class of assets charged in the varying condition in which they happen to be from time to time,[66] i.e. it does not fasten on any definite property but is a charge on property which is constantly changing;

3. it remains dormant, subject to any automatic crystallisation until the undertaking charged ceases to be a going concern, or until the person in whose favour it is created intervenes. His right to intervene may be suspended by agreement but if there is no agreement for suspension he may intervene whenever he pleases after default.[67] When this happens the charge is said to "crystallise" and becomes fixed[68];

4. although it is an immediate and continuing charge, until it becomes fixed the company can, without consent,[69] control the assets, including taking

---

[62] [1987] Ch. 200.
[63] *Manurewa Transport Ltd, Re* [1971] N.Z.L.R. 909; cf. *R. v Consolidated Churchill Copper Corp Ltd* [1978] 5 W.W.R. 652. See also the Australian case of *Deputy Commissioner of Taxation v Horsburgh* [1984] V.R. 773.
[64] [1987] Ch. 200, 213.
[65] per Lord MacNaghten in *Governments Stock Investment Co Ltd v Manila Ry Co Ltd* [1897] A.C. 81 at 86. See *G.E. Tunbridge Ltd, Re* [1994] B.C.C. 563.
[66] ibid.
[67] See n.60, above.
[68] *Evans v Rival Granite Quarries Ltd* [1910] 2 K.B. 979, CA.
[69] Limited restrictions on the company's power of disposal do not, however, convert a floating charge into a fixed charge: *G.E. Tunbridge Ltd, Re* [1995] 1 B.C.L.C. 34; see also *Cosslett (Contractors) Ltd, Re*, above n.54, where the company could remove charged plant from a site only with the permission of an architect. The charge was held to be a floating charge.

them outside the scope of the charge, e.g. it has been held that a company can sell all or any of its business or property for shares or debentures of another company if the memorandum gives it power to do so, and the debenture holders cannot prevent such a sale if the company remains a going concern[70]; similarly, a company with three businesses may sell one of the three.[71]

Where, before crystallisation of a floating charge over all the company's assets and undertaking, the company contracted to sell goods to a buyer to whom it owed money under a previous contract, and the goods were delivered after crystallisation, the company's right to sue for the debt due to it was embraced, when it arose, by the floating charge, but the debenture holder could not be in a better position to assert the rights under the previous contract than the company.[72]

A floating charge can be created only by a registered company not by a partnership or a sole trader. One reason is that such a charge created by a firm over chattels would be a bill of sale within the Bills of Sale Acts 1878 and 1882, and would have to be registered and, as a mortgage bill, would have to be in the statutory form and specify the chattels, which is impossible.[73]

Vulnerabilities of the floating charge

The advantage of a floating charge from the company's point of view is that the **25-016** company can give security for a loan to it by charging property which changes in the course of business and over which it is impracticable to create a fixed charge, e.g. the company's stock-in-trade. Further, until crystallisation the company can carry on business in the ordinary way. From the chargee's point of view, an important advantage is that, upon crystallisation of the floating charge, the chargee obtains priority in the payment of debts over the ordinary unsecured creditors and the existence of such a charge entitles the chargee to appoint an administrator or, in certain circumstances, an administrative receiver.[74]

However, there are a number of disadvantages attached to a floating charge from the chargee's point of view. Whilst the charge will confer priority over the general unsecured creditors of the company upon insolvency, it has been rendered, by a series of statutory provisions, vulnerable to certain "preferred" claims in liquidation, administration and, in certain circumstances, administrative receivership. Further, as will be seen below, it may be attacked under the insolvency legislation by a liquidator or an administrator.[75] Claims that are afforded statutory priority in insolvency are as follows:

---

[70] *Borax Co, Re* [1901] 3 Ch. 326.

[71] *H.H. Vivian & Co Ltd, Re* [1900] 2 Ch. 654.

[72] *Rother Iron Works Ltd v Canterbury Precision Engines Ltd* [1974] Q.B. 1, CA, applied in *George Barker (Transport) Ltd v Eynon* [1974] 1 W.L.R. 462, CA.

[73] The Law Commission recommended that the law be changed to allow unincorporated organisations to create such security over personal property under a notice filing system, a recommendation which would require the repeal and replacement of the Bills of Sale Acts: see Law Commission Consultation Paper No.176 (above, n.1), para.1.3.

[74] See Chs 26 and 27, below.

[75] Under s.245 of the Insolvency Act 1986: see below at p.

Preferential debts: Part XII of the Insolvency Act 1986 describes preferential debts as those debts listed in Sch.6 to the Insolvency Act 1986. There are, following the abolition of the first three categories of preferential debts by s.251 Enterprise Act 2002[76], three remaining categories, these being contributions to Occupational Pension Schemes, remuneration of employees[77] and levies on coal and steel production.

Preferential debts rank equally among themselves but in priority to the general creditors of the company and, to the extent that assets available for payment of those creditors are insufficient to discharge the preferential debts, they have priority over the claims of floating charge holders as far as property comprised in the charge is concerned: s.175(2) Insolvency Act 1986. Section 175(2) applies in administration by virtue of para.65 Sch.B1 to the Insolvency Act 1986 and in administrative receivership by virtue of s.40(2) of the Act.

The "Prescribed Part": Section 176A(2) of the Insolvency Act 1986 provides that a liquidator, administrator or receiver of a company must set aside out of the proceeds of property subject to a floating charge (the company's "net property: s.176A(6)) an amount (the "prescribed part") to be distributed to the company's unsecured creditors. Unsecured creditors *do not* include a charge holder whose security, whether fixed or floating, is not sufficient to discharge the full amount of the company's indebtedness to the chargeholder[78]. The level of the prescribed part is 50 per cent of the first £10,000 worth of floating charge realisations and 20 per cent of any amount over that, subject to a ceiling of £600,000[79].

The obligation to set aside the prescribed part does not apply where the company's net property is worth less than £10,000[80], or where the costs of making such a distribution would be disproportionate to the benefits (s.176A(5))[81]. More importantly, however, s.176A does not apply to any floating charge in existence before the provision came into force (s.176A(2)—the relevant date is September 15, 2003).

Expenses of the insolvency procedure: Section 175(2)(a) subordinates the payment of preferential debts to the expenses of the winding up. In *Barleycorn Enterprises Ltd, Re*[82] it was held that such expenses therefore ranked for payment ahead of the claims of floating charge holders out of floating charge assets, but the House of Lords reversed this ruling in *Leyland Daf Ltd, Re.*[83] The former position was restored by s.176ZA of the Insolvency Act[84], so that both liquidation

---

[76] These categories encompassed the "Crown preference" and consisted of debts due to the Inland Revenue, Customs and Excise and Social Security contributions.

[77] See Category 5. A claim for unpaid remuneration is preferential to the extent that it accrues in the period of four months preceding the relevant date (for which see s.387 Insolvency Act 1986) and claims are subject to a ceiling of £800, as prescribed by the Secretary of State (Insolvency Proceedings (Monetary Limits) Order (SI 1986/1996, art.4)).

[78] *In Airbase Services (UK) Ltd, Re* [2008] EWHC 124.

[79] SI 2003/2097.

[80] The "prescribed minimum", as provided for in SI 2003/2097

[81] See *Hydroserve Ltd, Re* [2007] EWHC 3026 and cf. *International Sections Ltd, Re* [2009] EWHC 137.

[82] [1970] Ch. 465.

[83] [2004] UKHL 9.

[84] Inserted by Companies Act 2006 s.1282.

and administration expenses[85] are payable out of the realisations of floating charge assets in priority to the claims of the floating charge holder.

Further, where a company enters administration, the administrator may dispose of or take action in relation to property subject to a floating charge as though it were not subject to the charge[86]. Whilst the holder of the charge retains the same priority in respect of acquired property[87] the administrator's power in this regard to some extent dilutes the control rights of the chargeholder. The disposition of property subject to a *fixed charge* requires the permission of the court on the application of the administrator.[88]

Charges over book debts

Creditors, aware of these drawbacks to a floating charge, yet wishing to give the **25–017** company the maximum flexibility in dealing with its assets, have faced a difficult problem in relation to using the company's book debts as security for a loan. Book debts are moneys owed to the company, which by their nature are constantly being created and paid off and, as an asset group, may often represent a considerable store of value. Creditors have therefore attempted to create fixed charges over the company's book debts and this was accepted as a possibility by Slade J. in *Siebe Gorman & Co Ltd v Barclays Bank Ltd*[89] where the terms of the charge required the chargor to pay the proceeds of book debts (i.e., the cash or cheques collected by the chargor company) into an account with the chargee bank.

The significance of this requirement was taken to be that it restricted the company's freedom to deal with the proceeds of the debts, such freedom being the hallmark of a floating charge and inconsistent with a fixed charge. Thus, where a charge over book debts expressed in the debenture to be fixed nevertheless allowed the company to collect and pay the proceeds into its current account (which was not with the chargee) it was held to be a floating charge.[90] Moreover, in *Keenan Bros Ltd, Re*,[91] the Supreme Court of Ireland placed emphasis on the fact that the charged debts had to be paid into an account with the chargee bank over which significant restrictions on withdrawals existed. These were sufficient to support the parties' denomination of the charge as fixed.

The possibility of creating a genuine fixed charge over book debts which nevertheless allowed the company to use the proceeds in the ordinary course of its business was further tested in *New Bullas Trading Ltd, Re*.[92] In that case, the chargee was granted a fixed charge over the company's uncollected book debts. The charge went on to provide that, in the absence of instructions from the chargee, the company could collect the debts and that the proceeds would be

---

[85] See Sch.B para.99(3). Insolvency Act 1986.
[86] Insolvency Act 1986. Sch.B para.70.
[87] i.e. property which directly or indirectly represents the charged property disposed of: Insolvency Act 1986 para.70(2), (3).
[88] Insolvency Act 1986 para.71.
[89] [1979] 2 Lloyds Rep. 142.
[90] *Brightlife Ltd, Re* [1987] Ch. 200. See also *G.E. Tunbridge Ltd, Re* [1995] 1 B.C.L.C. 34.
[91] [1986] B.C.L.C. 242 (Ir).
[92] [1994] 1 B.C.L.C. 485, CA.

subject to a separate floating charge. No instructions were ever given. At first instance the charge was construed as a floating charge, but the Court of Appeal considered that it was fixed, giving effect to the parties' terms as they stood.

The reasoning of the Court of Appeal was rejected in *Agnew v Inland Revenue Commissioner*,[93] where the Privy Council exhaustively reviewed the authorities on the fixed/floating charge dichotomy. The charge in *Agnew* was in virtually identical terms to that in *New Bullas*, and here it was held to be a floating charge. According to Lord Millett, the critical question in determining the nature of a charge is whether the company "should be free to deal with the charged assets and to withdraw them from the security without the consent of the holder of the charge." If control of the charged assets lies with the chargor the charge is a floating charge, if it lies with the chargee then it is fixed. The Bullas debenture gave the chargor rights of disposal of the debts that were inherently inconsistent with the charge being fixed, and the case was wrongly decided.

The decision in *Agnew* seemed also to have implications for standard form debentures requiring a chargee to pay the proceeds of book debts into a nominated bank account (most often with the chargee). Lord Millett supported the reasoning in *Keenan Bros, Re*[94] and suggested that where the chargor was free to draw on the nominated account the charge would be floating: the requirement of payment into the nominated account would not be an adequate restriction, of itself, on the company's freedom to deal with the charged debts.

This dicta was followed at first instance in *Spectrum Plus Ltd, Re*[95] in relation to a charge, similar to that seen in Siebe Gorman & Co Ltd,[96] requiring the company to pay the proceeds of its book debts into an account with the chargee bank but allowing the company to draw on that account. The judge categorised the charge as floating. However, the Court of Appeal[97] overruled the judge and held the charge to be fixed. This was because, as a matter of banking law, moneys paid into a bank account cease to be the property of the payer and become that of the bank,[98] although the bank may give the account holder a contractual right to make withdrawals from the account. Thus, the chargee bank could be said to have imposed adequate controls on the proceeds of the debt for the charge to be fixed, notwithstanding that the chargee retained a contractual right to draw on the account.

The House of Lords,[99] approving *Agnew v Inland Revenue Commissioner*,[100] overturned the decision of the Court of Appeal and found the charge in question to be a floating charge. In the words of Lord Scott:

". . . the essential characteristic of a floating charge, the characteristic that distinguishes it from a fixed charge, is that the asset subject to the charge is not

---

[93] [2001] 2 A.C. 710.
[94] [1986] B.C.L.C 242 (Ir).
[95] [2004] EWHC 9.
[96] [1979] 2 Lloyd's Rep. 142.
[97] [2004] EWCA 607.
[98] *Foley v Hill* (1848) 2 HLC 28.
[99] *Spectrum Plus Ltd, Re* [2005] UKHL 41.
[100] See n.93, above.

finally appropriated as a security for the payment of the debt until the occurrence of some future event. In the meantime the chargor is left free to use the charged asset and to remove it from the security."[101]

On the facts, the company in question continued to draw on its bank account and such drawings were routinely honoured by the chargee bank. In such circumstances, and whether or not the account in question was in credit or overdrawn, this clearly denoted that the charger company in practice was able to withdraw the charged asset from the security. This freedom was characteristic of a floating rather than a fixed charge, and *Siebe Gorman* had been wrongly decided *on its facts*. The Law Lords were, however, clear that the creation of a fixed charge over book debts remains a legal possibility, and that what is required is that the chargee demonstrates control over both the debts and their proceeds (*New Bullas, Re*[102] is therefore overruled) or, conversely, that the chargor is sufficiently restricted from dealing with the debts or their proceeds.

No guidance was given as to the kind of steps necessary for a chargee to establish the control necessary to render a charge over book debts fixed. In the context of the operation of a typical current account (usually with an overdraft facility), however, it would at first appear difficult for a chargee to adequately "block" the account without at the same time cutting off the source of the cash flow necessary for the company to carry on its day-to-day business. This would seem to be even more clearly the case where the chargee in question is not a clearing bank.[103] However, in *Harmony Care Homes Ltd, Re*[104] a charge was designated by the debenture as a fixed charge over uncollected debts, and, in the absence of directions from the charge holder (the company's landlord), a floating charge on the proceeds of the debts on their receipt.[105] The charge holder in fact required that the collected debts be paid into a designated bank account over which it held a mandate and produced evidence that the company could not draw on that account without the written consent of the charge holder. The charge was held to be fixed.

Retention of title clauses

Sellers, particularly of raw materials, frequently protect themselves by inserting into **25–018** the contract of sale a retention of title or "*Romalpa*" clause whereby they seek to retain title to the materials supplied until the buyer has paid for them. There have been many cases since the original decision in *Aluminium Industrie Vaassen BV v Romalpa Aluminium Ltd*[106] that such a clause could have the effect of retaining the legal title to the goods. Some clauses have failed, e.g. because the raw materials have ceased to exist,[107] or because in purporting to retain *equitable title* to the goods in

---

[101] [2005] UKHL 41, para. 111.
[102] See n.92, above.
[103] As was the case in *Brightlife Ltd, Re* see above at n.90.
[104] [2009] EWHC 1961 (Ch).
[105] i.e. a *New Bullas* type charge.
[106] [1978] 1 W.L.R. 676, CA.
[107] *Borden (UK) Ltd v Scottish Timber Products Ltd* [1981] Ch. 25; *Chaigley Farms Ltd v Crawford Kaye & Grayshire Ltd* [1996] B.C.C. 957; cf. *CKE Engineering Ltd (in administration)* [2007] B.C.C. 975.

question they have created a floating charge which has thus been declared void for non-registration under the Companies Act[108] or because they have created a charge over the book debts of the company, which again is void for non-registration.[109] The distinction is always one of construction of the particular clause–is the buyer conferring a charge on his goods or the proceeds of sale of those goods[110] in favour of the seller,[111] or is the seller retaining title to his goods to provide himself with a security.[112] It may be indicative of the former if the seller attempts to retain title to the goods into which the raw materials have been incorporated.[113]

A seller supplied yarn to some fabric manufacturers. He included a clause whereby the ownership of the yarn was to remain with the seller and if it was incorporated into other goods the ownership of these other goods was to remain with the seller, in either case until payment. The Court of Appeal held that the first part of the clause was a valid retention of title clause whereas the second created a floating charge. Since only the unused yarn was claimed the seller was allowed to succeed: *Clough Mill Ltd v Geoffrey Martin* [1985] 1 W.L.R. 111, CA.

If there is a valid retention of title clause and the purchaser sells on the goods, to a sub-purchaser also subject to such a clause, the original seller can claim title in the goods until the sub-purchaser pays the purchaser.[114] A valid clause can retain the seller's title until all debts due from the buyer have been discharged.[115]

Priority of charges

25–019 While fixed charges over the same assets rank in the order of creation, a company which has created a floating charge cannot later create another floating charge over some of the same assets ranking in priority to or pari passu with the original charge unless the provisions of the original charge allow this.[116]

On the other hand, since a company which has created a floating charge can, without the consent of the holders of the charge, deal with the class of assets in the ordinary course of business, it follows that the company can, in the ordinary course of business, create a later fixed charge, legal or equitable, over specific assets and with priority over the floating charge,[117] unless the floating charge provides that the company is not to create any mortgage or charge ranking pari passu with or in priority to the floating charge, known as a negative pledge clause, in which case any fixed chargee taking with notice of this provision[118] will be postponed to the

---

[108] *Bond Worth Ltd, Re* [1980] Ch. 228; *Stroud Architectural Systems Ltd v John Laing Construction Ltd* [1994] 2 B.C.L.C. 276.

[109] *E. Pfeiffer Weinkellerei-Weineinkauf GmbH & Co v Arbuthnot Factors Ltd* [1988] 1 W.L.R. 150; *Weldtech Equipment Ltd, Re* [1991] B.C.L.C. 393.

[110] *Tatung (UK) Ltd v Galex Telesure Ltd* (1989) 5 B.C.C. 325.

[111] *Peachdart Ltd, Re* [1984] Ch. 131; *Specialist Plant Services Ltd v Braithwaite Ltd* (1987) 3 B.C.C. 119, CA.

[112] *Hendy Lennox (Industrial Engines) Ltd v Grahame Puttick Ltd* [1984] 1 W.L.R. 485; *Andrabell Ltd, Re* [1984] B.C.L.C. 522.

[113] *John Snow & Co Ltd v D.B.G. Woodcroft & Co Ltd* [1985] B.C.L.C. 54.

[114] *Highway Foods International Ltd, Re* [1995] 1 B.C.L.C. 209.

[115] *Armour v Thyssen Edelstahlwerke AG* [1991] 2 A.C. 339.

[116] *Automatic Bottle Makers Ltd, Re* [1926] Ch. 412, CA.

[117] *Wheatley v Silkstone, etc., Coal Co* (1885) 29 Ch.D. 715.

[118] But see n.122, below.

floating charge. In spite of such a provision the holder of a specific charge will obtain priority over a floating charge on all the company's property if:

1. taking a legal charge, he obtains his charge without notice of the provision, even though he has notice of the debentures[119]—the maxim "where the equities are equal the law prevails" will apply; or

2. taking an equitable fixed charge, he obtains the title deeds without notice of the debentures[120]—the maxim "where the equities are otherwise equal the earlier in time has priority" will not apply since the debenture holders left the title deeds with the company so as to enable it to deal with its property as if it was unencumbered so that the equities are not equal.

Further, registration of a floating charge under the Companies Act, below,[121] although amounting to constructive notice under certain circumstances of the charge, is not notice that the charge contains a provision prohibiting the creation of subsequent charges with priority over the floating charge.[122] A floating charge is also postponed to an earlier fixed charge, including an earlier floating charge which has crystallised prior to the creation of the second charge.[123]

The following also have priority over a floating charge:

1. an execution creditor if the goods are sold by the sheriff,[124] or the company pays out the sheriff to avoid a sale,[125] or the creditor obtains a garnishee order absolute[126] (not a garnishee order nisi),[127] before crystallisation of the floating charge;

2. a landlord's distress for rent or a local authority's distress for unpaid business rates levied before crystallisation[128];

3. the rights of persons such as one who has sold goods to the company under a hire-purchase agreement by which the goods are still the property of such person.[129]

---

[119] *English and Scottish Mercantile etc. Co Ltd v Brunton* [1892] 2 Q.B. 700, CA.

[120] *Castell & Brown Ltd, Re* [1898] 1 Ch. 315.

[121] pp.626 et seq.

[122] per Eve J. in *Wilson v Kelland* [1910] 2 Ch. 306 at 313; *Dempsey v Traders' Finance Corp* [1933] N.Z.L.R. 1258, CA; but see *Ian Chisholm Textiles Ltd v Griffiths* [1994] 2 B.C.L.C. 291.

[123] *The Real Meat Co Ltd, Re* [1996] B.C.C. 254, [1997] B.C.C. 537, CA.

[124] *Standard Manufacturing Co, Re* [1891] 1 Ch. 627, CA.

[125] *Heaton and Dugard Ltd v Cutting Bros Ltd* [1925] 1 K.B. 655.

[126] *Evans v Rival Granite Quarries Ltd* [1910] 2 K.B. 979, CA.

[127] *Norton v Yates* [1906] 1 K.B. 112.

[128] *Roundwood Colliery Co, Re* [1897] 1 Ch. 373, CA; *ELS Ltd, Re* [1994] B.C.C. 449. It follows that where distress is levied after crystallisation the floating charge takes priority. However, where a floating charge crystallised before the company's landlord served a distress notice on the company's tenants which assigned their rents to the landlord, the chargee still took priority over the landlord, since the latter had notice of the crystallisation, which was an earlier assignment by the company to the chargee: *Rhodes v Allied Dunbar Pension Services Ltd* [1988] B.C.L.C. 186.

[129] See *Morrison, Jones and Taylor Ltd, Re* [1914] 1 Ch. 50, CA.

On the other hand a floating charge may not be postponed to the holder of a Mareva injunction over the assets. Such an injunction prohibits the company from removing its assets outside the United Kingdom. The holder of the floating charge may apply to have the injunction set aside and will succeed if the holders of the injunction are unsecured creditors.[130]

Avoidance of floating charges

25–020 To prevent those in control of insolvent companies from creating floating charges to secure past debts so as to gain priority over other unsecured creditors, s.245 of the Insolvency Act 1986 provides that floating charges created within 12 months prior to the presentation of a successful petition for a winding up,[131] the making of an administration application or the filing of a notice of intention to appoint an administrator[132] are invalid unless the company was solvent immediately after the charge was created, except insofar as money was paid or goods or services supplied to the company or a debt of the company was reduced or discharged, in consideration of and at the same time as or after the creation of the charge, with interest if appropriate.

The position is different if the floating charge is created in favour of a person who is connected with the company. In such cases the ambit of the section is widened to catch floating charges created within two years prior to the winding up or administration application, or notice of an intention to appoint an administrator, as appropriate, and it is of no consequence that the company was solvent immediately after granting the charge.[133]

The difficulty therefore is to establish whether money was paid, goods or services supplied or a debt reduced or discharged in consideration of the charge and whether that was at the same time as the creation of the charge. The value of any goods or services so supplied are to be valued at the cost which could reasonably be expected to be paid for goods or services supplied at that time in the ordinary course of business and on the same terms (apart from the granting of a floating charge) as those on which they were supplied to the company.[134] Section 245 replaced s.617 of the Companies Act 1985 which invalidated floating charges created within a year of a winding up except to the amount of any cash paid to the company in consideration and at the time of the charge (unless the company was solvent immediately after granting the charge).

Whether cash was paid *at the time when the charge was created* was a question of fact for s.617, and "a payment made on account of the consideration for the security, in anticipation of its creation and in reliance on a promise to execute it, although made some days before its execution, [was] made at the time of its creation within the meaning of the section."[135] Section 245, on the other hand,

---

[130] *Cretanor Maritime Co Ltd v Irish Marine Management Ltd* [1978] 1 W.L.R. 966, CA.
[131] This, and not the date of the winding up order is the relevant date: *Power v Sharp Investments Ltd* [1994] 1 B.C.L.C. 111, CA.
[132] Below, Ch.28.
[133] s.245(3)(a).
[134] s.245(6).
[135] per Neville J. in *Columbian Fireproofing Co Ltd, Re* [1910] 1 Ch. 758 at 765; *F. & E. Stanton Ltd, Re* [1928] 1 Ch. 180.

expressly requires it to be paid at the same time as or after the creation of the charge.

The question arises, therefore, as to whether the relaxed attitude of the courts under the former section has been preserved.

In *Fairway Magazines Ltd, Re*,[136] Mummery J. considered that it had and that the **25–021** advancing of the cash and the creation of the charge should be regarded as a matter of substance rather than form so that a month's gap between the two did not prevent the cash being paid to the company at the same time as the charge. In *Shoe Lace Ltd, Re*,[137] on the other hand, Hoffmann J. considered that the wording between the old and new sections was sufficiently different to justify a new approach which he considered should be whether a reasonable businessman, having knowledge of the statute, would regard the money as having been paid at the same time as the charge.

The reasoning of both judges was, however, rejected by the Court of Appeal in the *Shoe Lace* case.[138] The Court of Appeal decided that the difference in wording was insufficient to justify a distinction from the old cases but that they had been wrongly decided in the first place. It followed that any gap between the advancement of the cash and the creation of the charge would invoke s.245.[139] A mere agreement to create a charge at the time when the money was advanced would not be enough unless that agreement itself created an equitable charge. The words "in consideration for the charge" in s.617 meant "in consideration of the fact that the charge exists".

A company created a floating charge to secure its overdrawn current account with its bank. It was held that (1) Every payment made by the bank to the company. i.e., by way of allowing drawings on the overdrawn account, after the creation of the charge was "cash paid to the company" and was made in consideration of the charge. Consequently the charge was not invalid against the liquidator, and the bank was a secured creditor as to such payments; and (2) the rule in *Clayton's Case*[140] applied. Each payment by the bank after the date of the charge was a provision of "new money" and there was nothing to displace the presumption that payments in by the company after the charge should be set in the first instance against the company's debt to the bank at the date of the charge.[141]

Section 245 of the Insolvency Act uses the phrase "so much of the consideration as consists of". Quaere whether *Yeovil Glove Co Ltd, Re* is still valid?

In *Mace Builders (Glasgow) Ltd v Lunn*[142] it was held that the effect of s.617 was simply to render the charge invalid from the date of the winding up so that where the charge was repaid prior to the winding up the section had no effect.[143] The wording of s.245 is not identical, however, and it may be that the position is now different. Payments made direct to the company's creditors, though made on the company's behalf, have been held not to be within the phrase "Cash paid to the company".[144] The question is one of substance, however.

---

[136] [1992] B.C.C. 924.
[137] [1992] B.C.L.C. 636.
[138] Reported as *Power v Sharp Investments Ltd* [1994] 1 B.C.L.C. 111, CA.
[139] Although they did concede that a short break for coffee might not count!
[140] (1816) 1 Mer. 572.
[141] *Yeovil Glove Co Ltd, Re* [1965] Ch. 148, CA.
[142] (1986) 130 S.J. 839, CA.
[143] See also *Parkes Garage, Re* [1929] 1 Ch. 139.
[144] *Libertas-Kommerz GmbH v Johnston*, 1977 S.C. 191 (O.H.).

D was a director of the company and a partner in the firm of D & Co who supplied goods to the company. The company owed D & Co £1,954 and D & Co refused to supply any more goods until this debt was paid. In March D who wished to save the company, agreed to lend the company £3,000 on the security of a floating charge if the company would, out of this sum, pay £1,954 to D & Co. This was done. The company was insolvent at the time. In July the company went into liquidation. It was held that the floating charge was valid, the whole £3,000 being cash paid to the company.[145]

On the other hand, the cash must have been intended to benefit the company and not certain creditors or the directors.[146]

An insolvent company granted a floating charge to Z to secure £900. The money was provided by D, for whom Z was a nominee, and the same day as it was paid to the company the company paid £350 each to B and S for directors' fees and £200 to D, the amount guaranteed by D in respect of the company's overdraft. Within 12 months, the company went into liquidation. It was held that the charge was invalid, as its object was to benefit B, S and D and not the company—in substance, no cash was paid to the company.[147]

Cash was held not to be paid to the company where the substance of the transaction was the substitution of a better security for the company's debts.[148] It was also said that the section would apply irrespective of the motives of the chargee.[149] These decisions on whether cash has been paid to the company have been applied to s.245.[150]

Preferences and transactions at an undervalue

25–022   Any charge made by a company within six months[151] before the commencement of winding up, or presentation of a successful administration petition is void if it is a preference of any of the company's creditors, or, within a two year period, if it is part of a transaction of an undervalue, or within a three-year period, if it is part of an extortionate credit transaction: Insolvency Act 1986, ss 238–244, Ch.31, below.

REGISTRATION OF CHARGES

25–023   Charges created by a company are required to be registered (1) in the company's own register of charges, and (2) with the Registrar of Companies.

Registration in company's own register of charges

25–024   Section 876 of the Companies Act 2006 provides that every limited company must keep at its registered office a register of all charges specifically affecting the

---

[145] *Orleans Motor Co Ltd, Re* [1911] 2 Ch. 41.
[146] *Matthew Ellis Ltd, Re* [1933] 1 Ch. 458.
[147] *Destone Fabrics Ltd, Re* [1941] Ch. 319, CA.
[148] *G.T. Whyte & Co Ltd, Re* [1983] B.C.L.C. 311.
[149] [1983] B.C.L.C. 311 at 317, per Nourse J.
[150] *Fairway Magazines Ltd, Re* [1992] B.C.C. 924.
[151] Two years for persons connected with the company.

property of the company and all floating charges on the undertaking or any property of the company. The register must give:

1. a short description of the property charged;

2. the amount of the charge;

3. the names of the persons entitled thereto, except in the case of bearer securities.[152]

The omission to comply with s.876 merely results in a fine on every officer who is knowingly a party to the omission. The validity of the charge is not affected.

Every company must keep a copy of every instrument creating a charge required to be registered under s.860(7) (see below) at the registered office of the company. In the case of a series of uniform debentures a copy of one of the series is sufficient: s.875. These copies, and also the company's register of charges, must be kept available for inspection at the company's registered office to[153] any creditor or member of the company without fee: s.877 The documents and the register of charges are similarly open to the general public on payment of a fee of £3.50 per hour of inspection.[154]

Registration with the Registrar of Companies

Section 860 of the Companies Act 2006 provides that prescribed particulars of **25–025** certain specified charges created by companies registered in England, together with the instrument, if any, creating them, must be delivered to the Registrar of Companies. The period allowed for registration of a charge created by the company is 21 days beginning with the day after the day on which the charge is created: s.870(1). The object of registration is to protect the grantee of the charge,[155] although it also allows actual and prospective creditors of the company to ascertain whether, and the extent to which, the company has granted security over its assets.

The charges to which s.860 applies are specified in s.860(7) as follows:

1. a charge on land or any interest in land, other than a charge for any rent or other periodical sum issuing out of land;

The general rule is that a deposit of title deeds by a company to secure a debt, whether owed by the company or a third party creates an equitable charge on the land,[156] and not just a naked lien on the documents themselves, which charge is registerable under s.860 since it is contractual in nature even though created as a result of a presumption of law;[157]

---

[152] Section 876(2).
[153] Or at a place specified by regulations made under Companies Act 2006 s.1136.
[154] Companies (Fees for Inspection of Company Records) Regulations 2008 (SI 2008/3007) s.877.
[155] Per Bankes L.J. in *National Provincial Bank v Charnley* [1924] 1 K.B. 431, CA, at 442.
[156] But see *Alton Corporation, Re* [1985] B.C.L.C. 27.
[157] *Wallis & Simmonds (Builders) Ltd, Re* [1974] 1 W.L.R. 391, distinguishing *London and Cheshire Insce Co Ltd v Laplagrene Property Co Ltd* [1971] Ch. 499 (unpaid vendor's lien created by law not registrable). In *Wallis & Simmonds* there was no lien on the title deeds having a separate existence and the charge was void for non-registration.

2. a charge created or evidenced by an instrument which, if executed by an individual, would require registration as a bill of sale;[158]

3. a charge for the purposes of securing any issue of debentures;

4. a charge on uncalled share capital;

5. a charge on calls made but not paid;

6. a charge on book debts of the company;

If a company which has entered into hire-purchase agreements for the disposal of its products deposits the agreements as security for advances, there is a charge on the company's book debts.[159] Whether a particular agreement amounts to a charge on book debts is a question of construction.[160] In *Morris v Rayners Enterprises Inc*[161] the House of Lords held that it was possible for a creditor to grant a charge-back to the debtor on the debt but left open the question of whether such a charge was registerable as a book debt.

A charge on future book debts is registerable under s.860. However, where the subject-matter of a charge at the date of its creation is the benefit of a contract which does not then comprehend a book debt, e.g. a contract of insurance, the contract cannot be brought within s.860 merely because it might ultimately result in a book debt.[162] The test is whether there is a charge on future book debts as and when they arise or there is simply an assignment of a contingent contractual right;[163]

7. a floating charge on the undertaking or property of the company;

There is no requirement to register a possessory lien over certain assets of a company. The fact that the lien includes a power of sale does not convert it into a floating charge. The distinction is that a lien depends upon possession, whereas a floating charge does not.[164]

8. a charge on a ship or aircraft;

9. a charge on goodwill, or on any intellectual property.

---

[158] See *Stoneleigh Finance Ltd v Phillips* [1965] 2 Q.B. 537, CA. The transfer of goods by way of security is caught by this head: *Welsh Development Agency v Export Finance Co Ltd* [1991] B.C.L.C. 936, reversed on other grounds [1992] B.C.L.C. 148.

[159] *Independent Automatic Sales Ltd v Knowles & Foster* [1962] 1 W.L.R. 974.

[160] *Carreras Rothmans Ltd v Freeman Matthews Treasure Ltd* [1985] 1 All E.R. 155; *Welsh Irish Ferries Ltd, Re* [1985] 3 W.L.R. 610; *Orion Finance Ltd v Crown Financial Management Ltd* [1996] 2 B.C.L.C. 78.

[161] [1998] A.C. 214.

[162] *Paul & Frank Ltd v Discount Bank (Overseas) Ltd* [1967] Ch. 348.

[163] *Brush Aggregates, Re* [1986] B.C.L.C. 320.

[164] *Hamlet International Plc* [1999] 2 B.C.L.C. 506, CA. A lien *may*, however, constitute an equitable charge over a chose in action: see *Welsh Irish Ferries Ltd, Re* [1986] Ch. 471.

Registration: special rules on debentures

In the case of a series of debentures containing, or giving by reference to another **25–026** instrument, a charge to the benefit of which the debenture holders are entitled pari passu, it is sufficient if the following particulars are registered (s.873 Companies Act 2006):

1. the total amount secured by the series;

2. the dates of the resolutions authorising the issue of the series and the date of the covering deed, if any, by which the security is created;

3. a general description of the property charged;

4. the names of the trustees, if any, for the debenture holders.

Particulars entered on the register

The register contains the following particulars: **25–027**

1. in the case of a series of debentures, the particulars set out above: s.869(2);

2. in other cases, by virtue of s.869(4)—

   (a) the date of the creation of the charge;
   (b) the amount secured by the charge;
   (c) short particulars of the property charged;
   (d) the persons entitled to the charge.

It is the duty of the company to register the particulars required by s.860. Registration, however, may be effected by any person interested in the charge and the registration fees may be recovered from the company: s.860(2), (3).

On the registration of a charge the Registrar gives a certificate of registration which is conclusive evidence that the requirements of the Act as to registration have been complied with: s.869(5), (6). The particulars delivered to the Registrar may incorrectly state the property charged, or the amount or date of the charge, but if a certificate is given, the grantee of the charge is protected.[165] The certificate is conclusive evidence that the Registrar has entered the particulars in the register and that the prescribed, i.e. accurate, particulars have been presented to him.[166]

In the course of its business in 1960 a company bought properties. R, a shareholder, advanced money for each purchase and the company undertook to execute formal mortgages on demand. In 1961 the directors and R agreed that the company should implement its undertakings, and memoranda of deposit of title

---

[165] This is equally true where the particulars are delivered late with the consent of the court under s.873, below: *Exeter Trust Ltd v Screenways Ltd* [1991] B.C.L.C. 888.
[166] *C.L. Nye Ltd, Re* [1971] Ch. 442, CA.

deeds purporting to charge some of the properties with payments to R of certain sums on demand were signed but not dated on June 5, 1961. On July 11, the memoranda were registered with the Registrar, the date of execution being given as June 23. On August 4, the company went into voluntary winding up. It was held that the charges were not void since the certificate of registration was conclusive that all the requirements of the Act had been complied with within 21 days of execution, although the particulars submitted for registration incorrectly stated the date of the charges.[167]

The Registrar used to adopt the practice whereby if incorrect particulars of a charge were delivered for registration within the 21-day period he would register the charge after the 21-day period on the delivery of amended particulars. This practice was challenged in the courts and disapproved of by the Court of Appeal, who nevertheless refused to allow the Registrar's certificate to be challenged. No evidence could be adduced to challenge the correctness of his decision—he has jurisdiction finally and conclusively to determine any question of law or fact as to whether the requirements for registration have been complied with. Only the Attorney General can challenge registration by means of judicial review since the Crown is not bound by the section.[168] Following that decision, however, the Registrar has changed his practice so that unless correct forms are submitted within the 21-day period registration will not be allowed without the court's permission under s.873.[169]

25–028 To discover the exact terms of a charge one has to look at the document creating it (which document will have been filed), and not at the register.[170]

In England, a copy of the certificate of registration must be indorsed on every debenture or debenture stock certificate issued by the company and the payment of which is secured by the charge registered. The penalty for non-compliance is a fine: s.865.

When the debt for which any registered charge was given is satisfied, in whole or in part, or part of the property charged is released or ceases to form part of the company's property, the Registrar enters a memorandum of satisfaction or release on the register. The company is entitled to a copy of the memorandum: s.873.[171] The register is open to public inspection: s.869(7).

Effect of non-registration

25–029 If a charge which ought to be registered under s.860 is not so registered:

1. the company and every officer who is knowingly a party to the default, is liable to a default fine (s.860(4);

2. the charge is, so far as any security on the company's property is concerned, void against a liquidator or administrator and any creditor of

---

[167] *Eric Holmes (Property) Ltd, Re* [1965] Ch. 1052, applied in *C.L. Nye Ltd, Re* [1971] Ch. 442, CA.

[168] *R. v Registrar of Companies, Ex p. Central Bank of India* [1986] Q.B. 1114, CA.

[169] Below, p.631.

[170] *Mechanisation (Eaglescliffe) Ltd, Re* [1966] Ch. 20, following *National Provincial Bank v Charnley* [1924] 1 K.B. 431, CA.

[171] See, e.g. *Scottish & Newcastle Plc v Ascot Inns Ltd* (in receivership), 1994 S.L.T. 1140.

the company; but without prejudice to the contract to repay the money secured, which becomes immediately repayable: s.874. The result is that the holder of the charge is reduced to the level of an unsecured creditor.

In March the company gave T, a legal mortgage of specific land to secure £500. The mortgage was not restricted. In December the company issued debentures secured by a floating charge on its undertaking and assets to J to secure another £500. This charge was registered. It was held that although J, when he took his security, had actual notice of T's mortgage, he nevertheless had priority over T.[172]

A council loaned money to a company to purchase plant to be used on the council's land. The loan granted rights to the council which were construed as creating a floating charge over the plant. This charge was not registered. The company defaulted on making the loan repayments and the council sold the plant: it was held that the floating charge was void against the administrator of the company and the council was liable in damages to the company for conversion of the plant.[173]

Rectification of register

Under s.873 of the Companies Act 2006 the court may, on application by the **25–030** company or any person interested, extend the time for registration or rectify the register if:

1. the omission to register a charge within the required time or the omission or misstatement of a particular with respect to a charge is:

    (a) accidental or due to inadvertence[174] or some other sufficient cause; or

    (b) not of a nature to prejudice the creditor or shareholders; or

2. on other grounds it is just and equitable to grant relief.[175]

Section 873 requires the court to be satisfied with respect to certain matters before it orders an extension of time and, therefore, if serious issues of fact are involved it should arm itself with the best information and evidence available.[176] The section does not empower the court to grant interim relief.

If, on an application for late registration, it is shown either that a liquidation of the company is imminent or has actually occurred, the court is unlikely to order

---

[172] *Monolithic Building Co, Re* [1915] 1 Ch. 643, CA.

[173] *Smith (Administrator of Cosslett (Contractors) Ltd v Bridgend CBC* [2002] 1 A.C. 336.

[174] See, e.g. *Chantry House Developments Plc, Re* [1990] B.C.L.C. 813.

[175] See, e.g. *Fablehill Ltd, Re* [1991] B.C.L.C. 830, where the directors registered their own charge during the period of non-registration of the applicant's charge.

[176] *Heathstar Properties Ltd, Re* [1966] 1 W.L.R. 993. In *Heathstar Properties Ltd, Re (No.2)* [1966] 1 W.L.R. 999, it was found that the omission to register was due to inadvertence and the time for registration was extended notwithstanding that an action was proceeding in which the validity of the charge was in issue.

an extension of time. This was held to be a factor against the applicant in *Telomatic Ltd, Re*[177] and in *Barrow Borough Transport Ltd, Re*,[178] where the court refused an application where the company was in administration for the purpose of ensuring the company's survival but that had proved to be incapable of achievement. The company's liquidation was not merely imminent, it was inevitable. The court indicated that the same would apply if the administration had not included the survival of the company as one of its purposes. On the other hand, the imminence of a liquidation is not an absolute bar to a late registration order if there are other circumstances which justify it. Thus in *Braemar Investments Ltd, Re*[179] the court made an order on the basis that the fault was that of the chargee's solicitors and the chargee had acted promptly on discovering the non-registration.

That case also shows that when a chargee discovers that, by mistake, he is unregistered he must apply without delay for an extension of time and not deliberately defer his application in order to see which course would be to his best advantage. Failure to do so will prejudice his application: *Victoria Housing Estates Ltd v Ashpurton Estates Ltd*.[180]

25–031   It has been argued that the court will allow late registration where to do so would prevent one of its officers invoking the non-registration so as to benefit the other creditors unfairly. In *John Bateson, Re*,[181] Harman J. regarded such a rule as strange and that in any event it could only apply if the court officer had acted in an unworthy manner. He also doubted whether a voluntary liquidator was an officer for this purpose.

Relief will usually only be granted "without prejudice to the rights of parties acquired prior to the time when [the charge is] actually registered".[182] This proviso protects rights acquired against the company's property in the extension of time,[183] so that a secured creditor whose charge is created and registered in such time will not lose priority.[184] This is equally true if the later chargee knew of the existence of the unregistered charge at the date of registration of the later charge since the system is based on registration and not upon the actual notice of the chargee.[185] The court always has a discretion in these matters, however, so that in *Fablehill Ltd, Re*[186] the court applied the proviso to give priority to one later registered charge but not another, since the latter had been created by the directors of the company in their own favour with full knowledge that the applicant's charge was unregistered.

The effect of the proviso is different where the second charge is created and registered within the 21-day period allowed by s.874 for registration of the first

---

[177] [1994] 1 B.C.L.C. 90.
[178] [1989] B.C.L.C. 653.
[179] [1989] Ch. 54.
[180] [1983] 3 All E.R. 665, CA. See also *Telomatic Ltd, Re* [1994] 1 B.C.L.C. 90.
[181] [1985] B.C.L.C. 259.
[182] *Joplin Brewery Co Ltd, Re* [1902] 1 Ch. 79.
[183] *Ehrmann Bros Ltd, Re* [1906] 2 Ch. 697, CA.
[184] *Monolithic Building Co, Re* [1915] 1 Ch. 643, CA, above.
[185] *Telomatic Ltd, Re* [1994] 1 B.C.L.C. 90.
[186] [1991] B.C.L.C. 830.

charge, e.g. the second chargee's rights do not gain priority by reason of the proviso—such rights are acquired at the date of execution of the second charge.

On January 22, a company created two floating charges on its undertaking and property by issuing a first debenture to X to secure £10,000 lent by him to the company and a second debenture to Y to secure £5,000. The second debenture was registered on January 28, but, by mistake, the first was returned to X unregistered. On October 20, X applied under s.101 of the 1948 Act for an extension of the time allowed for registration and on October 28, the court ordered an extension to November 11, with a proviso that the order was "without prejudice to the rights of any parties acquired prior to the time when the said debenture is to be registered." Also on October 28, Y appointed a receiver under the second debenture. The first debenture was registered on November 5, and a receiver appointed thereunder on November 8. On November 9, the company went into a creditors' voluntary liquidation.

It was held that (1) Y's rights under the second debenture were acquired at the date of its execution and not at the expiration of the 21 days allowed by s.874 for registration of the first debenture (February 12), when the first debenture being then unregistered became void, nor in the ensuing period, during which it remained void, between the expiration of the 21 days and the date of its actual registration, and accordingly such rights did not gain priority over the first debenture by reason of the proviso to the court order; (2) although the appointment by Y of a receiver crystallised his floating charge, Y did not thereby acquire rights but merely exercised a power acquired when the debenture was executed.[187]

Unsecured creditors with no charge on the company's property do not qualify for the purposes of the proviso. However, if the company has gone into liquidation there will be, as a general rule, no benefit in obtaining an extension of time, as the unsecured creditors will then have acquired rights against the property of the company.[188]

Registration of charges existing on property acquired

If a company acquires any property which is already subject to a charge which, if created by the company, would have required registration under s.860, the company must register particulars of the charge and a copy of the instrument creating or evidencing it within 21 days after the acquisition is completed: s.862. Default renders the company and every officer in default liable to a default fine (s.862(4), (5)) but the validity of the charge is not affected. **25–032**

Registration of charges created in, or over property situated in, other jurisdictions

A company may create charges in jurisdictions outside of the United Kingdom, or charges created within the United Kingdom may apply to property outside the **25–033**

---

[187] *Watson v Duff, Morgan and Vermont (Holdings) Ltd* [1974] 1 W.L.R. 450.
[188] *Re S. Abrahams & Sons* [1902] 1 Ch. 695. The position is likely to be the same where the company subsequently enters administration: see *Salvesen, Petitioner* [2009] CSOH 161.

jurisdiction. If a charge is created outside of the United Kingdom over property similarly outside it, delivery to the Registrar of a verified copy of the instrument creating or evidencing the charge has the same effect, for the purposes of the Chapter, as delivery of the instrument itself: s.866(1). If a charge is created within the United Kingdom but extends to property outside the jurisdiction, the instrument creating the charge may be sent for registration even where further steps may be required to be taken in the jurisdiction in which the property is situated for the charge to be effective: s.866(2).

REMEDIES OF DEBENTURE HOLDERS

25–034 If a debenture confers no charge, a debenture holder is an ordinary unsecured creditor. Thus, if there is default in the payment of principal or interest he may (a) sue for the principal or interest and, after obtaining judgment, levy execution against the company, or (b), as will be explained later,[189] petition either for an administration order or for the winding up of the company by the court on the ground that the company is unable to pay its debts.

When a charge is conferred on the company's assets by way of security, and default is made in the payment of principal or interest, a debenture holder, or the trustees where there is a trust deed, may:

1. sue for the principal or interest;

2. if the charge is a "qualifying floating charge", appoint an administrator of the company[190]; or

3. present a petition for the winding up of the company;

4. if the charge was created prior to September 15, 2003,[191] exercise any powers conferred by the debenture or the trust deed, e.g. of appointing a receiver or administrative receiver of the assets charged, of selling the assets charged or of taking possession of the assets and carrying on the business;

5. if the debenture or the trust deed does not contain powers in that behalf, apply to the court for:

    (a) the appointment of a receiver or a receiver and manager; or
    (b) an order for sale or foreclosure.

A debenture or trust deed will normally contain an express power to appoint a receiver or administrative receiver of, or to sell, the company's assets charged by way of security. If there is no express power there will be an implied power under the Law of Property Act 1925 s.101, if the debenture or trust deed is under seal. Failing an express or an implied power, an application may be made to the court

---

[189] Below, Chs 28 and 29.
[190] Below, Ch.28.
[191] Below, Ch.27.

for the appointment of a receiver or an order for sale. A company's inability to pay its debts for the purpose of appointing a receiver is to be assessed at the date of appointment. Further, where the receiver is to be appointed by a deed, his appointment is not invalidated by an appointment in another manner—that operates as an agreement to perfect the power if necessary.[192]

Where the debenture is an "all moneys" debenture (e.g. one for all sums owed **25–035** to a bank) the demand for payment need not specify the exact sum due and a receiver may be appointed once reasonable time to effect payment has passed.[193] Similarly a demand for an amount less than the full amount due will be sufficient for the appointment of a receiver, although there is no authority if the demand is excessive, i.e. for more than the amount due.[194]

Where there are numerous debentures of the same class, a debenture holders' action is usually brought. This is brought by one debenture holder on behalf of himself and all other debenture holders of the same class as himself. In it a claim may be made for:

1. a declaration that the debenture holders are entitled to a (first) charge on the property of the company;

2. if there is a trust deed, the enforcement of the trust;

3. an account of what is due to the debenture holders;

4. the enforcement of the charge by sale or foreclosure;

5. the appointment of a receiver and manager.

An order for foreclosure will only be made if all the debenture holders of the same class as the plaintiff are before the court. If the assets require immediate protection an application for the appointment of a receiver is made.[195] The various remedies are discussed in detail in Ch.27, below.

---

[192] *Byblos Bank S.A.L. v Al Khudhairy, Financial Times*, November 7, 1986.
[193] *Bank of Baroda v Panessar* [1987] Ch. 335.
[194] *N.R.G. Vision Ltd v Churchfield Leasing Ltd* (1988) 4 B.C.C. 56.
[195] *Continental Oxygen Co, Re* [1897] 1 Ch. 511.

Chapter 26

CORPORATE INSOLVENCY

26–001 The Insolvency Act 1985 enacted major changes to the legal regulation of both corporate and personal insolvencies.[1] It introduced new concepts and controls and also amended (or repealed) several sections of the Companies Act 1985 concerned with corporate insolvency. The interaction of the two Acts led to the consolidation of Parts XIX, XX and XXI of the Companies Act 1985 and the Insolvency Act 1985 into the Insolvency Act 1986. The Insolvency Act 1986 is thus the major Act[2] which applies to this and the next five chapters. The Act itself was significantly modified by the Enterprise Act 2002, and is further supplemented by the Insolvency Rules 1986,[3] which themselves have seen substantial revision since their inception.[4] The Rules are currently undergoing a process of consolidation, which is expected to be complete by April 2011.[5]

The arrangement of the insolvency related Chapters is as follows. Chapter 27 deals with receivers and the concept, introduced by the Insolvency Act 1985, of an administrative receiver, usually appointed by a debenture holder as the most efficient way of protecting his security in the face of possible insolvency. The entitlement to appoint an administrative receiver has been substantially restricted by the Enterprise Act 2002.[6] Such appointments may or may not lead to the ultimate liquidation of the company. Chapter 28 deals with one alternative to the liquidation of an insolvent company—the administration procedure, which was also introduced by the Insolvency Act 1985 and has since been streamlined by the Enterprise Act 2002. Chapters 29 to 31 are, on the other hand, concerned with liquidations, that is to say the effective demise of the company, which may in fact arise otherwise than on an insolvency. The majority of liquidations, however, are caused by such an eventuality. We have already discussed, in Ch.15, one other

---

[1] On the background to these changes, see Final Report of the Insolvency Review Committee (Cork Report) 1982, Cmnd.8558; *A Revised Framework of Insolvency Law*, 1984 Cmnd.9175.

[2] See also the Insolvency Act 1994 and the Insolvency (No.2) Act 1994, above, p.659.

[3] SI 1986/1925.

[4] There are too many amendments to list here. Where provisions contained in the Rules are referred to in the following discourse, the more recent amendments, and the objectives behind them, will be dealt with in the text itself.

[5] The Insolvency Service has published a very useful summary of this project, from which the amending Statutory Instruments can be accessed. See: *http://www.insolvency.gov.uk/insolvencyprofessionandlegislation/consolidation/consolidationhome.htm* [accessed June 4, 2010]

[6] Below, Ch.27.

aspect of insolvency law introduced by the 1985 Insolvency Act, i.e. that in relation to the disqualification of directors of insolvent companies.[7]

The present chapter is concerned with three general matters. The new framework for corporate insolvency, the controls on insolvency practitioners involved in the various aspects of insolvency, e.g. as administrative receivers, liquidators, administrators etc., and a second alternative to the liquidation of an insolvent company—a voluntary arrangement, i.e. a composition with creditors.[8] There remains one further possibility open to an insolvent corporation, and that is to enter into a compromise with its creditors through a scheme of arrangement under Pt 26 of the Companies Act 2006.[9] Whilst this procedure is most commonly used to effect solvent reconstructions or mergers, it has recently re-emerged as a viable choice by which the capital structure of an *insolvent* company can be reorganised so as to accomplish a "rescue" of the entity in question. Because of the expense associated with such schemes, it is likely that they will only be a realistic option for very large companies with complex capital structures, and so will not be considered in detail here.[10]

THE NEW FRAMEWORK FOR INSOLVENCY

One of the two main themes of the Insolvency Act 1986 was to update a system **26–002** which had its origins in the Bankruptcy Act 1914 and was inadequate to deal with unscrupulous liquidators and directors who allowed companies which were hopelessly insolvent to continue to trade. The second aim of the legislation was to provide alternative and less drastic remedies than liquidation for an insolvent company, where such remedies would provide a better opportunity for the creditors to recover their debts and for the companies concerned to remain in existence. Measures designed to assist in the first aim include the regulation of insolvency practitioners,[11] the disqualification of directors' provisions (including the concept of wrongful trading)[12] and the many amendments to the laws relating to receiverships and liquidations, including the new statutory concept of an administrative receiver.[13]

To achieve the second aim the Act introduced the new administration procedure[14] and a simplified procedure, the company voluntary arrangement, for a composition with creditors.[15] The use of these "rescue" procedures was low as compared to the number of insolvencies, and, in an effort to facilitate and increase the incidence of corporate rescue, the Insolvency Act 2002 and the Enterprise Act 2002 introduced provisions intended to make them more attractive to both

---

[7] Above, p.387.
[8] For the other alternative see Ch.28, below.
[9] See, generally, Ch.32, below.
[10] For a recent example of a successful corporate rescue effected through a scheme of arrangement, and the particular issues raised by its use in relation to an insolvent company, see *Bluebrook Ltd, Re* [2009] EWHC 2114 (Ch.).
[11] Below, pp.638 et seq.
[12] Below, Ch.23.
[13] Below, Ch.27.
[14] Below, Ch.28.
[15] Below, p.640.

corporate debtors and their creditors.[16] As noted above, these statutory provisions are supplemented by many rules and regulations,[17] in particular, the Insolvency Rules 1986[18] and the rules relating to Qualified Insolvency Practitioners.[19]

The Insolvency Act 1986 also retained and redefined the role of Official Receivers for England and Wales in all types of corporate proceedings.[20] In effect, although they are civil servants under the control of the Secretary of State, Official Receivers are also officers of the court and are attached to the High Court or to one or more county courts having insolvency jurisdiction. They assume the functions and responsibilities specified in the Act or the Rules in those cases falling within the jurisdiction of the court to which they are attached. Deputy Official Receivers can be appointed and have the same status and functions as an Official Receiver.[21]

By virtue of s.426 of the Insolvency Act 1986, the courts in each part of the United Kingdom are required to recognise and enforce orders made by the courts of all other parts of the United Kingdom in relation to insolvency law. Thus where property exists e.g. in Scotland, but the insolvency proceedings are taking place in London, all such property can be protected and claimed for the benefit of creditors. The United Kingdom courts are also required to assist the courts of other designated jurisdictions.[22] This may be the case notwithstanding that the scheme of distribution under law of the relevant country or territory may differ to that which would apply to the property in question in the United Kingdom.[23] The European Council Regulation on Insolvency Proceedings[24] also provides for the recognition of insolvency proceedings commenced in a Member State on a Europe-wide basis, and for the enforcement of judgments thereunder.

INSOLVENCY PRACTITIONERS

26–003 Part XIII of the Insolvency Act 1986 subjects insolvency practitioners to proper regulation by ensuring that they are "qualified" within the terms of s.390. To act as an insolvency practitioner in relation to a company when not qualified to do so is a criminal offence under s.389. For this purpose "acting as an insolvency practitioner" means acting either as a liquidator,[25] administrator,[26] administrative receiver[27] or as the nominee or supervisor of a company voluntary arrangement,[28]

---

[16] Below, p.642 and Ch.28.
[17] IA 1986 ss.411–413, 419.
[18] SI 1986/1925 as amended.
[19] See Insolvency Practitioners Regulations 2005 (SI 2005/594), revoking and replacing, subject to savings and transitional provisions, the Insolvency Practitioners Regulations 1990 (SI 1990/439).
[20] IA 1986 ss.399–401.
[21] IA 1986 s.401(2).
[22] i.e., courts in "any other part of the United Kingdom or any relevant country or territory": s.426(4), and see *Hughes v Hannover Ruckversicherungs AG* [1997] B.C.C. 921. The Secretary of State may designate by order that a county or territory is a "relevant country or territory": s.426(11).
[23] See *HIH Casualty & General Insurance Ltd, Re* [2008] UKHL 21.
[24] Regulation 1346/2000 on insolvency proceedings [2000] OJ L160.
[25] Below, Ch.30.
[26] Below, Ch.28.
[27] Below, Ch.27.
[28] Below, p.641.

s.388,[29] although such a supervisor is subject to the less stringent authorisation provisions of s.389A. This offence is one of strict liability—the knowledge of the person concerned is irrelevant. It does not, however, apply to the Official Receiver. The Official Receiver does not come within the terms of s.388 and therefore escapes the qualification requirements of s.390 and the criminal penalty in s.389; the control exercised over such public officials within the Department of Trade and Industry is deemed sufficient safeguard.

Section 390 sets out the requirements for qualification. Only an individual can be qualified to act as an insolvency practitioner.[30] He must be currently authorised to act as an insolvency practitioner either by virtue of membership of a professional body recognised under s.391[31] or by a direct authorisation granted by a competent authority under s.393,[32] and must have provided the requisite security for the proper performance of his functions.[33]

Even if a person is so qualified to act he may be disqualified if (a) he is an undischarged bankrupt,[34] or (b) he is subject to a disqualification order under the Company Directors Disqualification Act 1986,[35] or (c) he lacks capacity (within the meaning of Mental Capacity Act 2005) to act as an insolvency practitioner.[36] This is subject to s.389A, Insolvency Act 1986.

Most individuals will qualify by virtue of being members[37] of a recognised **26–004** professional body who are permitted to act as such by the rules of that body. The bodies currently recognised by the Secretary of State include the established accountancy bodies, the Law Society and the Insolvency Practitioners Association. The intention is that the control exercised by such bodies over their members shall be equivalent to that exercised by the competent authority over those directly authorised by that body under ss.392 to 398 of the Insolvency Act 1986. For those who cannot qualify as qualified insolvency practitioners by virtue of membership of a recognised professional body, those sections of the Act allow a direct application to the competent authority appointed to deal with such matters. Currently the Secretary of State is the competent authority for this purpose and he must grant the application if satisfied that the applicant is a fit and proper person to be an insolvency practitioner and satisfies prescribed educational and experience requirements: s.393(2). The previous maximum period of authorisation of three years

---

[29] In relation to insolvent partnerships, see s.388(2A) inserted by the Insolvent Partnerships Order 1994 (SI 1994/2421).

[30] IA 1986 s.390(1).

[31] See Insolvency Practitioners (Recognised Professional Bodies) Order 1986 (SI 1986/1764).

[32] Insolvency Practitioners (Recognised Professional Bodies) Order 1986 (SI 1986/1764) s.390(2)(b). The competent authorities are the Secretary of State or a body designated by him: s.392(2).

[33] s.390(3); by means of a fidelity bond in the amount of £250,000 plus an additional sum varying with the value of the assets in relation to which he is to act in the particular case: Insolvency Practitioners Regulations 2005 Sch.2, para.3 (as amended by the Provision of Services (Insolvency Practitioners) Regulations 2009 (SI 2009/3081)).

[34] See IA 1986, ss.278–282.

[35] See above, p.387.

[36] A person lacks capacity "if, at the material time he is unable to make a decision for himself in relation to the matter because of an impairment of, or a disturbance in the functioning of, the mind or brain": Mental Capacity Act 2005 s.2.

[37] This includes those who, although not members, are subject to the rules of a recognised body in the practice of their profession: IA 1986 s.391(3).

was revoked by the Provision of Services (Insolvency Practitioners) Regulations 2009,[38] but authorisation may be withdrawn on the practitioner's ceasing to comply with the s.393 requirements or where he was authorised by virtue of false, misleading or inaccurate information.[39] There is a right to make representations before a refusal or withdrawal of authorisation and a right to appeal against an adverse decision to the Insolvency Practitioners Tribunal.[40] Withdrawal of authorisation results in automatic vacation of office.

P was acting as liquidator in relation to a number of companies when his authorisation was withdrawn. It was held that, though no longer a liquidator, he was a proper person to apply to the court under s.108 of the Insolvency Act 1986 for a compendious appointment in relation to all the companies with which he had been concerned.[41]

The appointment of an insolvency practitioner as officeholder is a personal appointment not an appointment of his firm. On retirement, meetings of creditors should normally be convened to approve a change of officeholder.[42] An insolvency practitioner's firm can apply to the court for his removal.[43]

VOLUNTARY ARRANGEMENTS—COMPOSITIONS WITH CREDITORS

26–005   Sections 1 to 7 of the Insolvency Act 1986 introduced a new procedure which enabled an insolvent or potentially insolvent company to come to a legally binding arrangement with its creditors. If the procedure is complied with it binds creditors, even those who have not agreed to it[44] (IA 1986, s.5(2)) and so perhaps will avoid a liquidation. There are alternative methods of effecting such a scheme under Pt 26 of the Companies Act 2006[45] or s.110 of the Insolvency Act 1986[46] but these procedures were not designed expressly for the purpose of enabling an insolvent company to rationalise its affairs and proved to be cumbersome in practice for such a purpose. Schemes of arrangement under Pt 26 Companies Act 2006 require the court's involvement at every stage and the court's ultimate consent.[47] Schemes of reconstruction under s.110 do not bind dissentient creditors.[48] The essence of the company voluntary arrangement is to simplify both the procedure and the court's involvement whilst maintaining the ability to bind creditors to the scheme if the requisite procedure is complied with.

[38] SI 2009/3081 Sch.1 para.5.

[39] IA 1986 s.393(4).

[40] IA 1986 ss.395, 396. This Tribunal is governed by IA 1986 Sch.7, and by the Insolvency Practitioners Tribunal (Conduct of Investigations) Rules 1986 (SI 1986/952).

[41] A.J. Adams (Builders) Ltd, Re [1991] B.C.C. 62. In some circumstances the application may be by the recognised professional body: see Stella Metals Ltd, Re [1997] B.C.C. 626.

[42] Sankey Furniture Ltd, Re [1995] B.C.L.C. 594.

[43] A. & C. Supplies Ltd, Re [1998] B.C.C. 708; see also Cork v Rolph (2001) 98(7) L.S.G. 40.

[44] See below, p.644.

[45] See below, Ch.32.

[46] See Ch.32. See also administration orders, below, Ch.28.

[47] See, e.g. Bluebrook Ltd, Re [2009] EWHC 2114 (Ch.).

[48] IA 1986 s.111.

Implementing a voluntary arrangement

Section 1 of the Insolvency Act 1986 allows either a liquidator or administrator of **26–006** a company (if it is in liquidation[49] or administration[50]) or, if there is no liquidator or administrator, the directors, to make a proposal to the company and to its creditors for a composition in satisfaction of its debts or a scheme of arrangement of its affairs, to be known as a voluntary arrangement.[51] This proposal must provide for some person who is qualified to act as an insolvency practitioner in relation to the company[52] to act as the nominee of the scheme, i.e. as trustee or otherwise for the purpose of implementing the scheme. Under s.389A of the IA, a wider range of practitioners may act as nominees and supervisors of voluntary arrangements, and in particular turnaround specialists authorised by the Secretary of State are able to act. It is a criminal offence for an unqualified person to act as a nominee.[53]

If the directors of the company, rather than a liquidator or an administrator, instigate the CVA they must prepare for the intended nominee a proposal explaining why, in their opinion, a voluntary arrangement is desirable and why the company's creditors may be expected to concur in the arrangement: Insolvency Rules 1986, r.1.3(1). The proposal should also contain details of the company's assets and their values, the extent to which they are charged in favour of creditors, those assets to be included in or excluded from the arrangement, the nature and amount of the company's liabilities and a comprehensive raft of further information, ending with "such other matters (if any) as the directors consider appropriate for ensuring that members and creditors are enabled to reach an informed decision on the proposal".[54] This is so as to allow the proposed nominee to consider whether meetings of the company and its creditors should be summoned to consider the proposal.

Where the nominee is not the liquidator or administrator, he must observe the formalities in s.2 of the Insolvency Act 1986, which involve the scrutiny by him of the soundness of the proposed arrangement, with reference to the information provided by the directors under r.1.3(1) of the Insolvency Rules 1986, and the submission of a report to the court stating whether in his opinion meetings of the company and of its creditors should be summoned to consider the proposal, and, if so, the date, time and place he proposes the meetings should be held. In effect he is required to state that the scheme is worth pursuing, in that it has a reasonable prospect of being approved and implemented: s.2(2).

No such report is needed where the nominee is the liquidator or administrator; proper scrutiny by such office holders is assumed. In such a case the liquidator or administrator may proceed directly by virtue of s.3(2) of the Insolvency Act 1986

---

[49] See below, Ch.29.
[50] See below, Ch.28.
[51] For a discussion of the meaning of "scheme of arrangement" see below, Ch.32.
[52] This is someone qualified by virtue of IA 1986 s.390 and not connected with the company so as to be in breach of the professional or regulatory rules.
[53] IA 1986 ss.388, 389.
[54] Insolvency Rules 1986 (hereinafter IR 1986) r.1.3, as amended by the Insolvency (Amendment) Rules 2010 (SI 2010/686).

to summon meetings of the company and its creditors[55] to consider the proposal for such a time, date and place as he shall think fit. The liquidator or administrator should include, in the notice summoning the meetings, a statement of affairs relating to the company, or a summary of it, along with a list of the company's creditors and the amounts of their debts.[56] Following a positive report by a nominee other than a liquidator or administrator, under s.2 of the Insolvency Act, that nominee should call the meetings as stated in that report unless the court orders otherwise: IA 1986 s.3(1). Section 3(3) requires every creditor of the company of whose claim and address the nominee is aware to be given notice of the creditors' meeting. There is no requirement to hold separate meetings for separate classes of creditors[57] which is a feature of schemes of arrangements under Pt 26 of the Companies Act 2006.[58]

Voluntary arrangement with moratorium

26–007 One of the perceived weaknesses of the voluntary arrangement was that it remained possible for creditors to undermine it in its early stages by instituting enforcement actions against the company. This could be avoided by implementing the arrangement under the umbrella of an administration order, during the course of which an automatic moratorium would be in place, but such a step was seen as complex and expensive. Therefore, following a series of consultations,[59] the Insolvency Act 2000 introduced s.1A and Sch.A1 into the Insolvency Act 1986. These provisions came into force on January 1, 2003. Essentially, they are intended to redress the limitation identified above by allowing, in certain circumstances, a moratorium facility to be obtained without the use of administration.

Only the directors of "eligible" companies may take steps to obtain a moratorium during a voluntary arrangement: s.1A(1). The criteria for eligibility are found in Sch.A1 paras 2–5, and are primarily concerned with whether the company satisfies two or more of the requirements for being a "small company" in s.382(3) of the Companies Act 2006. Such small companies are prima facie eligible companies, unless they are subject to some other form of insolvency procedure or are otherwise excluded from eligibility under paras 4A–4J of Sch.A1. These paragraphs exclude from eligibility certain specialised types of company and companies which are parties to certain specialised types of financial arrangements.

The procedure for obtaining a moratorium is contained in paras. 6–11 of Schedule A1. The directors of an eligible company must submit to the nominee[60] a document setting out the terms of the proposed arrangement and a statement of the company's affairs: Sch.A1, para.6(1). The nominee must then submit to the

---

[55] As to the meaning of "creditor" in this context, see *T & N Ltd, Re* [2005] EWHC 2870 (Ch.) and IR 1986 r.13.12, as amended by the Insolvency (Amendment) Rules (SI 2006/1272).

[56] IR 1986 r.1.11, as amended by the Insolvency (Amendment) Rules 2010 (SI 2010/686).

[57] See below, p.643.

[58] See below, Ch.32.

[59] *CVAs and Administration Orders* (DTI, 1993); *Revised Proposals for a New CVA Procedure* (DTI, 1995); *A Review of Company Rescue and Business Reconstruction Mechanisms* (DTI, 2000).

[60] See above as to the nominee.

directors a statement that, in his opinion, the proposed voluntary arrangement has a reasonable prospect of being approved and implemented, that the company is likely to have sufficient funds during the moratorium to enable it to carry on business, and that meetings of the company should be summoned to approve the arrangement: para.6(2). The directors must then file with the court documents setting out the terms of the proposed arrangement, a statement of the company's affairs and the nominee's statement: para.7. The moratorium comes into force at the time the documents are filed with the court and lasts for 28 days or until meetings of the company and its creditors to approve the arrangement are held, whichever is the sooner: para.8. The directors of the company must notify the nominee when the moratorium comes into force[61] and the nominee must then advertise this fact and notify the Registrar of companies, the company itself and any petitioning creditor of the company of whose claim he is aware.[62] Notification is also required of the moratorium coming to an end under r.11 of Sch.A1.

While the moratorium is in force, no petition or resolution for winding up may **26–008** be presented or passed and no administrator or administrative receiver of the company may be appointed and creditors may not take steps to enforce security over the company's property without leave of the court: para.12. The holder of an uncrystallised floating charge[63] may not take steps to cause it to crystallise without leave of the court: para.13. Any company invoices, orders, business letters and order forms issued during the moratorium must state that it is in force and include the nominee's name, as must any website of the company: para.16.

There are restrictions on the amount of credit a company can obtain during the moratorium and on disposals and payments it may make: paras 17–19. Property subject to a charge may only be disposed of with the consent of the chargee or leave of the court, and the chargee has the same priority over the proceeds of disposals as he had over the charged property itself: paras 20, 21. However, transactions entered into in contravention of the provisions of paras 16–23 are not rendered void or unenforceable against the company: para.15. The nominee is required to monitor the company's affairs during the moratorium: para.24, and, notably, is under an obligation to report to the Secretary of State if it appears to him that any past or present officer of the company has been guilty of any offence in connection with the moratorium (or, in the case of a CVA without a moratorium, the voluntary arrangement) for which he is criminally liable: Insolvency Act 1986 s.7A.

Consideration of a voluntary arrangement

It is for the two meetings convened by the nominee to decide whether to approve the **26–009** proposed voluntary arrangement, with or without modifications. Any such modification is allowed, including a change in the nominee, subject to three limitations. First no modification is allowed if the proposal would thereby cease to comply with

---

[61] Insolvency Act 1986 Sch.A1 para.9.
[62] Insolvency Act 1986 para.10: a petitioning creditor is any creditor who has presented a winding up petition before the beginning of the moratorium (para.10(2)).
[63] See Ch.25, above.

the terms of s.1 of the Insolvency Act, i.e. it would no longer be a voluntary arrangement as there defined. Secondly no modification can affect a secured creditor's[64] rights to enforce his security without his consent. Third no modification can interfere with the rights of a preferred creditor, either as against ordinary creditors or other preferred creditors, without his consent.[65] The Insolvency Rules 1986 regulate the conduct of the meetings and it is for the chairman to make a report of the result to the court and other prescribed persons: IA 1986 s.4.

If both the company and creditors' meetings approve the proposal in identical terms, the voluntary arrangement "takes effect as if made by the company at the creditors' meeting" and binds every person who in accordance with the rules had notice of, and was entitled to vote at, that meeting (whether or not he was present or represented at the meeting) as if he were a party to the voluntary arrangement": IA 1986, s.5(1), (2). Where there is disagreement between the meetings of creditors on the one hand, and members on the other, the decision of creditors' meetings prevails by virtue of s.4A(2), although a member of the company may apply to court within 28 days of the creditors' meeting, and the court may order that the decision of the company meeting shall have effect: s.4A(3), (4), (6).

Creditors vote in accordance with the amount of their debt.[66] The Rules provide that a creditor is not entitled to vote in relation to an unliquidated amount except where the chairman agrees to put upon the debt an estimated minimum value.[67] The creditors' consent is not required.

L sought to vote in respect of total future rent arising under a lease. The chairman, bearing in mind the likelihood that L would terminate the lease by forfeiture in the near future, valued L's claim at a minimum of one year's rent. L did not agree and did not vote. L later claimed not to be bound by the arrangement in respect of the future rent. It was held that the chairman had agreed to put a minimum value on the claim and had done so. Therefore L had been entitled to vote and was bound.[68]

26–010 The position is otherwise where a creditor claims a liquidated debt but the company disputes the amount or claims a set off. Here the creditor is entitled to vote in respect of the whole debt subject to his votes subsequently being declared invalid.[69] The chairman's decision on a creditor's entitlement to vote can be challenged by a creditor or member.[70]

---

[64] Defined in s.248. See also *Naeem, Re* [1990] 1 W.L.R. 48; *Peck v Craighead* [1995] B.C.C. 525; and below, p.669 where the term is considered in the context of the administration procedure.

[65] Preferred creditors are defined in the same way as for a liquidation except that they are calculated by reference to the date of the approval of the proposal if there is no liquidation or administration order in force: IA 1986 s.387. For an example of a proposal that did not affect or interfere with such rights, see *Inland Revenue Commissioners v Wimbledon Football Club Ltd* [2004] EWCA Civ. 655.

[66] IR 1986 r.1.17(2).

[67] IR 1986 r.1.17(3). A token value will not do: *Doorbar v Alltime Securities Ltd* [1994] B.C.C. 1007 (Knox J.).

[68] *Doorbar v Alltime Securities Ltd* [1995] B.C.C. 1149, CA. This related to an individual voluntary arrangement but the position was said to be the same for a company voluntary arrangement: at 1155; and see *Sweatfield Ltd, Re* [1997] B.C.C. 744; see also *Newlands (Seaford) Educational Trust (In Administration), Re* [2006] EWHC 1511 (Ch).

[69] IR 1986, r.1.17A(4), and see *Newlands (Seaford) Educational Trust (In Administration), Re* [2006] EWHC 1511 (Ch.).

[70] IR 1986 r.1.17A(3).

While the creditors bound by the arrangement cannot assert claims against the company which are inconsistent with it, they may still be able to sue any co-debtors of the company (unless the arrangement has the additional effect of releasing all co-debtors).[71] However, such an arrangement may be challenged as unfairly prejudicial under s.6.[72]

Payment by a co-debtor may result in an indemnity claim by such co-debtor against the company thus undermining the arrangement. A consequential claim of this sort may perhaps be avoided by ensuring that a co-debtor has notice of the arrangement and is bound by it.[73] Where, under the terms of the arrangement, a particular claim is not brought within it that claim can still be pursued by a creditor bound by the other terms of the arrangement.[74]

Once the arrangement is duly approved a supplier of gas, electricity and other public utilities cannot make it a precondition of any further supply that outstanding charges in respect of earlier supplies are met.[75]

If a proposal is approved while the company is in liquidation or subject to an administration order the court may stay the winding up proceedings or discharge the administration order or give such directions as to their future conduct as will facilitate the arrangement. No such order can be made within 28 days from the date when the court received the reports of the meeting since that is the period allowed for the meetings' approval to be challenged in the court,[76] or at any time when such a challenge is under consideration by the court: IA 1986 s.5(3), (4).

Challenge to a voluntary arrangement

Within 28 days of the report of the meeting having been made to the court, anyone **26–011** who was entitled to vote at either meeting, the nominee or his replacement or the liquidator or administrator (if any) can challenge the approval of the scheme by an application to the court. This challenge can, however, only be made on one of two grounds: either that the scheme will unfairly prejudice[77] the interests of a creditor, member or contributory[78] of the company, or there has been some material irregularity at or in relation to either of the meetings: IA 1986, s.6(1), (2), (3).[79]

Section 6 is not concerned with the conduct of an approved arrangement, but with the process of approval itself. As far as unfair prejudice is concerned, the court will not be concerned with whether an alternative form of arrangement would be

---

[71] By its express or implied terms or the effect of action taken under it: *Johnson v Davies* [1998] 2 All E.R. 649, CA (individual voluntary arrangement); *R.A. Securities Ltd v Mercantile Credit Co Ltd* [1995] 3 All E.R. 581.

[72] See *Prudential Assurance Co Ltd v PRG Powerhouse Ltd* [2007] EWHC 1002 (Ch.).

[73] *Mytre Investments Ltd v Reynolds* [1995] 3 All E.R. 588; *March Estates Plc v Gunmark* [1996] 2 B.C.L.C. 1.

[74] *Alman v Approach Housing Ltd* [2001] B.P.I.R. 203.

[75] IA 1986 s.233 and see below, p.660.

[76] See below.

[77] There is no definition of this but the words are used in s.459 of the Companies Act 1985 (now s.994 Companies Act 2006) in relation to the protection of a minority shareholder generally, see above, p.532. See, generally, *Primlaks (UK) Ltd, Re (No.2)* [1990] B.C.L.C. 234; *Inland Revenue Commissioners v Wimbledon Football Club Ltd* [2004] EWHC 1020.

[78] This is the term used for a member once the company has gone into liquidation.

[79] Irregularities not challenged within 28 days cannot invalidate the approval: IA 1986 s.6(7).

more beneficial to the petitioning creditor or creditors.[80] However, where an approved arrangement compromises the rights of a creditor or creditors without any quid pro quo, this may amount to unfair prejudice for the purposes of the section.

The parent company of a subsidiary subject to a company voluntary arrangement had executed guarantees in favour of the landlords of the subsidiary. The subsidiary company wished to close a number of its retail outlets, and the proposal in question involved the release of the guarantee as far as the closed outlets were concerned. The landlords claimed that the arrangement was unfairly prejudicial to their interests. It was held that the terms of the arrangement gave the guaranteed creditors no more than their unsecured counterparts, and offered no "compensation" for the loss of the benefit of the guarantees, and was therefore unfairly prejudicial.[81]

There may be an irregularity at a meeting of the company or its creditors, but that irregularity must still be shown to be material.

At a meeting of creditors to approve a voluntary arrangement, offers to purchase the company's business were not disclosed by the administrators of the company. Held, whilst the non-disclosure amounted to an irregularity, it was not material as there was no real prospect that disclosure would have affected the approval of the arrangement.[82]

Supervising an approved voluntary arrangement

26–012 An approved scheme which is not subject to a challenge is then put into effect. At this stage the person carrying out the nominee's functions is known as the supervisor: IA 1986 s.7(2). His primary duty is to implement the arrangement according to the law and its terms.[83] The supervisor is under the control of the court and any interested party, including the company,[84] may apply to the court if his conduct is unsatisfactory and the court may make an order to give him directions as it thinks fit: s.7(3). In return the supervisor himself may apply to the court for directions and can petition for a winding up or the making of an administration order: s.7(4), although the fact that directions are sought under this provision does not empower the court to modify the terms of an approved arrangement.[85] In extremis the court can replace the supervisor or appoint an additional one: s.7(5).

Under the Insolvency Rules 1986 the supervisor must keep accounts and records and must report annually upon the progress of the arrangement. A voluntary arrangement is not automatically terminated on a subsequent winding up. It depends on the terms of the arrangement and the nature of the petition. If it is terminated, the liquidator is not automatically entitled to claim funds already held in trust for creditors under the terms of the arrangement.[86]

[80] *Sisu Capital Fund Ltd v Tucker* [2005] EWHC 2170 (Ch.).
[81] *Prudential Assurance Co Ltd v PRG Powerhouse Ltd* [2007] EWHC 1002 (Ch.).
[82] *Trident Fashions Plc, Re* [2004] EWHC 293.
[83] *Appleyard Ltd v Ritecrown Ltd* [2007] EWHC 3515 (Ch).
[84] *County Bookshops Ltd v Grove* [2002] EWHC 1160.
[85] *Re Alpha Lighting Ltd; Re Beloit Walmsley Ltd* [2008] EWHC 1888 (Ch).
[86] *Re Halson Packaging Ltd* [1997] B.C.C. 993; *Re Leisure Study Group Ltd* [1994] 2 B.C.L.C. 65. Cp. *Davis v Martin-Sklan* [1995] B.C.C. 1122 (individual voluntary arrangement) *and Re Arthur Rathbone* [1997] 2 B.C.L.C. 280 and [1998] B.C.C. 450; *Re NT Gallagher & Sons Ltd* [2002] 1 B.C.L.C. 224 (CA).

Reform

As noted earlier,[87] many of the reforming initiatives in the field of insolvency **26–013** law have been designed to achieve more positive results for insolvent companies and their creditors than a straightforward liquidation strategy would achieve. The company voluntary arrangement was itself such an initiative and, when its performance in this regard was considered somewhat disappointing, the Insolvency Act 2000 introduced the CVA with moratorium in an attempt to remedy the perceived deficiencies of the CVA. The most recent reform programme was detailed in a Consultation Document issued by the Insolvency Service in June 2009.[88]

The consultation document sought views as to how to improve further the potential for corporate rescue in the United Kingdom through the mechanism of the CVA procedure. A number of "proposals" were mooted, the first being to extend the CVA with moratorium procedure in Sch.A1 to companies of all sizes.[89] The legislation would be amended so as to allow for an initial 28-day moratorium to come into force where a CVA proposal had been submitted to an insolvency practitioner (the nominee) and that practitioner considered that it had a reasonable prospect of success and would be approved by at least 75 per cent of creditors. If the proposal was then so approved, the proposal would bind all creditors and the nominee would become the supervisor of the arrangement.[90]

The second proposal, aimed at large companies with complex capital structures, was for a court-sanctioned moratorium. The directors of the company would apply to the court for an initial 42-day moratorium, subject to one further extension on further application, which the court could grant if satisfied that (a) the company was unable to pay its debts or likely to become unable to do so, (b) that there was a reasonable prospect of the company's creditors approving the proposal, and (c) that in the circumstances sanctioning the moratorium would be in the interests of the creditors as a whole. The initial application would be required to be supported by a statement from an insolvency practitioner to the effect that the above tests were satisfied. The first and second proposals were viewed as mutually exclusive, i.e. a company could not apply for a moratorium under the first proposal and then again under the second, and vice versa.[91]

The third, and most ambitious proposal was to legislate to provide for super-priority funding in administration, such funding to rank as an expense of the administration and so to take priority over the claims of certain existing secured creditors.[92] This initiative, reminiscent of the "debtor-in-possession" funding (DIP finance) provisions of the Ch.11 of the United States Bankruptcy Code, was intended to address the perceived problem of obtaining "rescue finance" where the company's assets were already subject to one or more security interests, and would apply only in administration. A related proposal was to extend the

---

[87] Above, p.637.
[88] *Encouraging Company Rescue—a consultation*: The Insolvency Service: June 2009.
[89] As noted above, at p.642, it is currently available only to small companies.
[90] See *Encouraging Company Rescue—a consultation*, above, n.88, paras 39–43.
[91] ibid., paras. 45–49.
[92] See Ch.25, above, as to the priority of procedural expenses over floating charges in insolvency and, as to administration expenses generally, see Ch.28, below.

opportunity to create new secured charges in administration and to make provision for CVA rescue finance.[93]

A summary of responses to the consultation was issued by the Insolvency Service in November 2009.[94] At the time of writing, the Insolvency Service is taking forward the proposals involving an extension of the CVA with moratorium and the possibility of a court-sanctioned moratorium, but not those for the provision of rescue finance.[95]

---

[93] See *Encouraging Company Rescue—a consultation*, above, n.88, paras 51–83.
[94] *Encouraging Company Rescue—summary of responses*, The Insolvency Service, November 2009.
[95] See *http://www.insolvency.gov.uk/insolvencyprofessionandlegislation/con_doc_register/responses/Written_Ministerial_Statement.doc* [accessed June 5, 2010].

Chapter 27

RECEIVERS AND ADMINISTRATIVE RECEIVERS

THE LAW OF RECEIVERSHIP

The law relating to receivership is of ancient origin and the position of "receiver" **27–001** encompasses a wide variety of functions going far beyond the realm of corporate insolvency. Receivers may be appointed by the court, under s.109 of the Law of Property Act 1925, or contractually, by virtue of a power afforded to a debenture holder in a contract of loan. As far as receivers of companies are concerned, the practice of appointing a receiver over the property of a company by debenture holders developed during the nineteenth century as a convenient adaptation of the similar practice of mortgagees faced with a defaulting mortgagor. This practice thus amalgamated property and contract law, but was placed on a statutory footing with the coming into force of the Insolvency Act 1986, which recognised, for the first time, the unique position of a receiver and manager of virtually the entirety of a company's property by denominating such a receiver an "administrative receiver".[1]

The Enterprise Act 2002, by inserting s.72A into the Insolvency Act 1986, significantly restricted the right to privately appoint an administrative receiver. However, this provision is only applicable to holders of floating charges granted on or after September 15, 2003. It is therefore likely that the appointment of receivers as administrative receivers will continue for some time into the future and that what follows will remain relevant law whilst ever there remain in existence floating charges pre-dating September 15, 2003. Moreover, there remains the possibility of appointing a receiver over specific corporate property under a charge by way of legal mortgage by virtue of s.109 of the Law of Property Act 1925.

Receivers and other officeholders

A receiver takes possession of the property of the company over which he **27–002** is appointed and realises it for the benefit of the debenture holder(s) appointing him. Where the charged property includes a business, a receiver and manager is usually appointed to preserve the goodwill pending sale or the resumption of control by the company on discharge of the debt[2]. A receiver should not be confused either with a liquidator or an administrator. A liquidator is appointed

---

[1] On administrative receivers generally, see below, pp.658 et seq.
[2] Although this is a highly unlikely outcome.

with the object of winding up the company and terminating its existence. An administrator is appointed with the object of saving a company from a winding up or obtaining a more advantageous realisation of its assets, and acts for the benefit of the company's creditors and shareholders generally,[3] whereas a receiver is usually appointed by a specific debenture holder to protect his security under a fixed or floating charge.[4]

A receiver may take possession of only part of a company's property[5] (e.g. of a specific asset secured by a fixed charge) but if he takes possession of the whole (or substantially the whole) of the company's property and was appointed by the holders of a charge which, as created, was a floating charge, he is known as an administrative receiver, as long as the charge in question was granted before September 15, 2003.[6] Most receivers will in fact be administrative receivers since the major creditors appointing them, e.g. the banks and other institution lenders, usually take extensive fixed and floating charges as a security. Administrative receivers are subject to special rules and given special powers by the Insolvency Act 1986.

As mentioned in Ch.25, a receiver can be appointed: (1) under an express power[7] contained in the debenture or trust deed; or (2) by an order of the court where there is no such power.[8] There is the third possibility, noted above, of appointing a receiver under s.109 of the Law of Property Act 1925.

Receiver appointed by the court

27–003   While the Insolvency Act refers to receivers appointed by the court, and certain of its provisions,[9] applicable to all receiverships, would seem to apply to them, it has little to say about them. It is accepted that the court may appoint a receiver when:

1.   the principal or interest is in arrears[10]; or

2.   the company is being wound up[11]; or

3.   the security is in jeopardy.

A creditor obtained judgment against the company and was in a position to issue execution. There was no default in payment of debenture principal or interest. It was held that the debenture holders with a floating charge on the undertaking and

---

[3] See below, Chs 29 and 30.

[4] Although it is now possible for the debenture holder to appoint an administrator to realise his security: see Ch.28, below.

[5] IA 1986 s.29(1)(a).

[6] IA 1986 s.29(2)(a). So long as his security extends to the whole or substantially the whole of the company's property, the fact that some other person has previously been appointed receiver of the part of the company's property under a charge having priority to the floating charge and that consequently he does not in fact have possession of the whole or substantially the whole of the company's property, does not prevent him from coming within the definition of an administrative receiver: s.29(2)(b).

[7] The court will not imply a term entitling a debenture holder to appoint a receiver on the basis of business efficacy: *Cryne v Barclays Bank Plc* [1987] B.C.L.C. 548.

[8] Where it appears just and convenient to do so: Supreme Court Act 1981 s.37(1).

[9] e.g. IA 1986 ss.31, 39, 40 and 41.

[10] *Bissill v Bradford Tramways* [1891] W.N. 51; *Crompton, Re* [1914] 1 Ch. 594.

[11] *Wallace v Universal Automatic Machines Co* [1894] 2 Ch. 547, CA.

property of the company were entitled to the appointment of a receiver because the security was in jeopardy.[12]

The security is in jeopardy when there is a risk of its being seized and taken to pay claims which are really not prior to the debenture holders' claims. Accordingly a receiver was appointed where the company's works were closed and creditors were threatening actions,[13] where execution was actually levied by a judgment creditor,[14] where a creditor's winding up petition was pending and compulsory liquidation was imminent,[15] where the company proposed to distribute its reserve fund, which was its only asset, among its members[16] and where there was a real risk that assets would be "switched from one shadowy hand to another in breach of a Mareva order".[17] Mere insufficiency of security is not jeopardy where the company is a going concern, is not being pressed by its creditors and there is no risk of its assets being seized by its creditors.[18]

4.   the creditor is unlikely to obtain payment of a judgment debt by the process of legal execution.

The defendant company's assets consisted of payments to become due under a supply contract with a Guernsey company. The ability of the defendant company to manipulate the supply contract and the inability of the plaintiff to ascertain payments due under it made it unlikely that the plaintiff would obtain satisfaction by a garnishee order. It was held that a receiver should be appointed by the court.[19]

Appointments by the court are infrequent[20] and usually occur because there is no **27–004** adequate power of appointment in the instrument of charge or there is some doubt as to the validity of the instrument or the appointment under it.[21] The appointment is made on the application of the debenture holders. It is uncertain whether a receiver appointed by the court can fall within the definition of an administrative receiver, but the better view appears to be that the court does not enjoy the power to appoint an administrative receiver.[22] Where the company is being wound up by the court, the court can appoint the Official Receiver as receiver: IA 1986 s.32. A receiver appointed by the court is an officer of the court, not an agent of the company or of the debenture holders.[23] He is personally liable on contracts he enters into.[24]

[12] *London Pressed Hinge Co Ltd, Re* [1905] 1 Ch. 576.
[13] *McMahon v North Kent Ironworks* [1891] 2 Ch. 148.
[14] *Edwards v Standard Rolling Stock Syndicate* [1893] 1 Ch. 574.
[15] *Victoria Steamboats Ltd, Re* [1897] 1 Ch. 158.
[16] *Tilt Cove Copper Co, Re* [1913] 2 Ch. 588.
[17] per Robert Walker J. in *International Credit and Investment Co (Overseas) Ltd v Adham* [1998] B.C.C. 134 at 137.
[18] *New York Taxicab Co, Re* [1913] 1 Ch. 1.
[19] *Soinco v Novokuznetsk Aluminium Plant* [1998] Q.B. 406. The court accepted that the receiver should be able to execute future, as well as existing, debts. See also *Masri v Consolidated Contractors International Co SAL* [2008] EWHC 2492.
[20] And have disadvantages, see Lightman and Moss, *The Law Relating to Receivers of Companies*, 4th edn (2007) para.29–009.
[21] As in *B.C.C.I. SA v B.R.S. Kumar Bros Ltd* [1994] B.C.L.C. 211 (where a receiver was appointed over the assets of a company to which the chargor company had transferred its assets).
[22] *A & C Supplies Ltd, Re* [1998] B.C.C. 708, per Blackburne J.
[23] See IA 1986, s.29(2).
[24] But not on pre-receivership contracts unless he novates. In some circumstances he may have a duty to perform such contracts: see *Newdigate Colliery Ltd, Re* [1912] 1 Ch. 468.

B was appointed receiver and manager by the court. He gave a signed order for goods, with the words "receiver and manager" appended to his signature. It was held that he was personally liable to pay for the goods.[25]

However, he is entitled to an indemnity out of the assets in respect of which he is appointed[26] for liabilities properly incurred.[27] This may be the case even where the assets in question are beneficially owned by a third party.[28] He "supersedes the company which becomes incapable of making contracts on its own behalf."[29]

His appointment causes floating charges to crystallise and thus prevents the company from dealing with assets without his consent. To enable him to carry on the business of the company or to preserve the property of the company, the court can authorise the receiver to borrow money ranking in priority to the debentures.[30] The company's servants are automatically dismissed[31] (but they may be entitled to damages for breach of contract) although they may be employed by the receiver.[32] As an officer of the court he cannot sue or be sued without leave of the court[33] but such leave may be given to enable an action to be brought against him by a person at whose instance he was appointed.[34] Officers of the court have a duty to act not merely lawfully, but in accordance with the principles of justice and honest dealing.[35] His remuneration is fixed by the court. The criteria relevant to determine the level of remuneration have been set out by Ferris J. in *Mirror Group Newspapers Plc v Maxwell*.[36] The task is to reward value rather than indemnify cost. Remuneration is not a "cost" of the receivership.[37] Notice of his appointment must appear on invoices, business letters, orders for goods, etc. and on all the company's websites.: IA 1986 s.39.

Receivers appointed out of court

27–005 A body corporate is disqualified for appointment as receiver[38]: IA 1986 s.30. Also, an undischarged bankrupt is disqualified from acting as receiver or manager, unless he is appointed by the court: IA 1986 s.31. Persons subject to the

---

[25] *Burt, Boulton and Hayward v Bull* [1895] 1 Q.B. 276, CA.

[26] *Mellor v Mellor* [1992] 4 All E.R. 10.

[27] [1992] 4 All E.R. 10. Where he is appointed manager of the business pending its sale within a limited time, unless the time is extended, expenditure incurred outside that time will be disallowed: *Wood Green Steam Laundry, Re* [1918] 1 Ch. 423.

[28] *Sinclair v Glatt* [2009] EWCA Civ. 176 (receiver appointed under s.77 of the Criminal Justice Act 1988).

[29] *Moss S.S. Co Ltd v Whinney* [1912] A.C. 254, 260.

[30] *Greenwood v Algesiras Rly. Co* [1894] 2 Ch. 205, CA.

[31] The tenure of directors and other officers is unaffected: *South Western of Venezuela Ry, Re* [1902] 1 Ch. 701.

[32] *Reid v Explosives Co Ltd* (1887) 19 Q.B. 264, CA.

[33] *Viola v Anglo American Cold Storage Co* [1912] 2 Ch. 305; *Searle v Choat* [1884] 25 Ch. 723, CA.

[34] *L.P. Arthur Insurance Ltd v Sisson* [1966] 1 W.L.R. 1384.

[35] *Tyler, Re* [1907] 1 K.B. 865. cf. *John Bateson Co Ltd, Re* [1985] B.C.L.C. 259.

[36] [1998] B.C.C. 324. See also the report of Ferris J.'s working party on the remuneration of office holders (July 31, 1998).

[37] *Mirror Group Newspapers Plc v Maxwell (No.2)* [2001] B.C.C. 488.

[38] An attempted appointment of a body corporate is a nullity, and the body corporate does not thereby become an agent for the purpose of the Law of Property Act 1925 s.109, and the Limitation Act 1980: *Portman Building Society v Gallwey* [1955] 1 All E.R. 227.

various disqualification orders under the Company Directors Disqualification Act 1986[39] cannot act as receivers.

Since an administrative receiver, but not an ordinary receiver, is acting as an insolvency practitioner within s.388 of the Insolvency Act 1986, only a qualified insolvency practitioner may be appointed as such[40] and it is a criminal offence for anyone else so to act.[41]

Time of appointment and defects in appointment

A receiver or manager is appointed when the document of appointment is handed **27–006** to him or his agent provided that he accepts such an appointment by the end of the next business day after such receipt[42]; IA 1986 s.33. The person delivering the document to the receiver or his agent must be a person having authority to appoint and the circumstances must be such that it could fairly be said that he was appointing the receiver.[43]

If the appointment of a receiver is discovered to be invalid (e.g. the document of appointment was defective[44] or the charge has been set aside for non-registration) the court can order the person appointing the receiver to indemnify him against any liability which arises solely by reason of that invalidity: IA 1986 s.34. This section will not protect a receiver from liability arising from other causes, e.g. his negligence in managing the company's affairs, simply because his appointment was also invalid. The court has a complete discretion in cases where the section applies and it may well seek to establish where the blame for the invalidity lies.

Effect of appointment of receiver

The following occurs when a receiver is appointed— **27–007**

1. When a receiver is appointed floating charges crystallise and become fixed. This prevents the company from dealing with the assets charged, without the receiver's consent.[45]

2. When a receiver of the undertaking of the company is appointed, the directors' power of controlling the company is suspended[46] but they may have a residual role to play. Thus, where a receiver decides not to get in or realise an asset, which it would be in the interests of the company and its other creditors to get in or realise, the directors have power to act on the company's behalf, so long as the interests of the debenture holders, qua debenture holders, are not threatened.

---

[39] Above, p.387.

[40] Above, p.638.

[41] IA 1986 s.389.

[42] Administrative receivers must confirm in writing within seven days: Insolvency Rules 1986 r.3.1.

[43] *A. Cripps & Sons Ltd v Wickenden* [1973] 1 W.L.R. 944, applying *Windsor Refrigerator Co Ltd v Branch Nominees Ltd* [1961] Ch. 375, CA.

[44] But see *Byblos Bank S.A.L. v Rushingdale SA* [1987] B.C.L.C. 232.

[45] Above, p.615.

[46] *Gomba Holdings UK Ltd v Homan* [1986] 3 All E.R. 94.

The assets in respect of which a receiver was appointed included an action for damages against the debenture holders who had appointed him. It was alleged that they had, in breach of contract, refused further finance causing the company to forfeit its interest in, and profit from, a joint venture. The receivers having refused to sue the debenture holders, the action was initiated by the directors on behalf of the company. It was held that the action could continue.[47]

The directors cannot claim fees from the receiver unless he employs them, but they can still claim from the company any fees to which they are entitled.[48]

3. On the appointment of a receiver by the court the company's employees are dismissed.[49] The company ceases to employ them because it is no longer carrying on business: the receiver may carry on the business but he is not the company's agent. In the case of a receiver appointed by the debenture holders and acting as the company's agent,[50] "the business is still the company's business carried on by the company's agent"[51] and therefore there will generally be no automatic dismissal of company employees. Automatic dismissal will, however, occur if, exceptionally, the receiver is acting as agent for the debenture holders or if the receiver, having transferred the business to a third party, ceases to act as the company's agent in that regard.[52] Further, a particular employee may be subject to automatic dismissal if continuance of his contract of employment is inconsistent with the receiver's role and functions.[53] Where employees are automatically dismissed, the company is liable for breach of contract. Where they are not dismissed, the company remains liable for remuneration, etc., arising. The receiver will not be liable[54] in the absence of novation or adoption.[55]

4. Every invoice, order for goods or business letter which is issued by or on behalf of the company or the receiver and on which the company's name appears must contain a statement that a receiver has been appointed, as must any website of the company: IA 1986 s.39.

5. Within seven days after the appointment, the person who made or obtained the appointment must give notice of the fact to the Registrar who must enter it in his register of charges: Companies Act 2006 s.871(1).

---

[47] *Newhart Developments v Co-operative Commercial Development Bank* [1978] 2 W.L.R. 636; [1978] 2 All E.R. 896. See also *Lascomme Ltd v United Dominion Trusts* [1994] I.L.R.M. 227 (High Court of Ireland); *GE Capital Commercial Finance Ltd v Sutton* [2004] EWCA Civ. 315.; cf. *Tudor Grange Holdings Ltd v Citibank N.A.* [1991] 4 All E.R. 1.

[48] *South Western of Venezuela etc. Rly, Re* [1902] 1 Ch. 701.

[49] Below, n.53.

[50] Most debentures will provide that the receiver is to be the agent of the company and, as to administrative receivers, statute so provides: IA 1986 s.44 (1)(a); See, however, *Silven Properties Ltd v Royal Bank of Scotland Plc* [2003] EWCA Civ. 1409.

[51] Per Dillon L.J. in *Nicoll v Cutts* [1985] B.C.L.C. 322, CA.

[52] *Foster Clark's Indenture Trusts, Re* [1966] 1 W.L.R. 125.

[53] *Griffiths v Secretary of State for Social Security* [1974] Q.B. 468.

[54] *Nicoll v Cutts*, above, n.51.

[55] See below, IA 1986 ss.37, 44.

6.   When a receiver appointed under a power in an instrument ceases to act, he must give notice to the Registrar: Companies Act 2006 s.871(2).

7.   A receiver appointed under a power in a debenture has his remuneration fixed by agreement. The court may, however, on the application of the liquidator, fix the receiver's remuneration. Under this power the remuneration may be fixed retrospectively, and any excess paid before the making of the order must be accounted for: IA 1986 s.36. This power does not entitle the court to interfere with the receiver's right to be indemnified for disbursements which have been properly incurred.[56] A liquidator may use investigatory powers under Insolvency Act 1986 s.236 to require a receiver to furnish him with documents relating to the conduct of the receivership in order to determine whether an application to fix the level of remuneration under s.36 should be made.[57]

Position of receiver other than administrative receiver

In the case of a receiver appointed under a power in a debenture or a trust deed **27–008** the debenture usually provides that he is to be the agent of the company.[58] Consequently the debenture holder(s) or the trustees are not liable for his acts, though the company is. Through this agency the company can claim documents brought into existence in the course of the receivership in discharge of the receiver's duties to the company but not otherwise.[59]

Contracts made by the company and current at the date of his appointment are not binding on the receiver personally, unless they become binding by novation,[60] or, in the case of contracts of employment, adoption: IA 1986, s.37(1), (2).[61] It has been held that the receiver must, however, carry out the company's current contracts if not to do so would injure the company's goodwill,[62] although this proposition must be regarded as doubtful given that the receiver in question was appointed by the court. As far as privately appointed receivers are concerned, it has been held that such a receiver may, as agent of the company, refuse to perform a contract.[63] In *Astor Chemicals Ltd v Synthetic Technology Ltd*[64] it was held that specific performance of a contract could be ordered, or an injunction against repudiation issued, where the consequence of the breach would be to deprive the plaintiff of an equitable interest "ranking ahead of the debenture . . . or, I think, any other proprietary or contractual right binding on the debenture-holder." Clearly, if

---

[56] *Potters Oils, Re* [1986] 1 W.L.R. 201.
[57] *Delberry Ltd, Re* [2008] EWHC 925 (Ch.). As to s.236, see below.
[58] If it does not, he is agent of the debenture holders who are answerable for his faults and omissions: *Vimbos, Re* [1900] 1 Ch. 470.
[59] *Gomba Holdings UK Ltd v Minories Finance Ltd* [1989] B.C.L.C. 115, CA.
[60] *Parsons v Sovereign Bank of Canada* [1913] A.C. 160, PC.
[61] See below.
[62] *Newdigate Colliery Ltd, Re* [1912] 1 Ch. 468, CA; and see also *Astor Chemical v Synthetic Technology Ltd* [1990] B.C.C. 97.
[63] *Lathia v Dronsfield Bros Ltd* [1987] B.C.L.C. 321.
[64] [1990] BCLC 1. See also *Airlines Airspares Ltd v Handley Page Ltd* [1970] Ch. 193, and *Freevale v Metrostore Holdings* [1984] Ch. 199, where it was held that an order for specific performance could be made against a receiver in relation to a pre-appointment contract of the company.

the contracts can only be carried out by borrowing money ranking in priority to the debenture holders and are unprofitable, a receiver need not carry them out.[65]

As agent of the company, he is immune from personal liability for breach of such contracts or for inducing a breach of contract so long as his decision not to carry out the contract is bona fide and within his authority.[66] These cases are, to a considerable extent, dependent on the receiver's status as agent of the company. In a case where the validity of the appointment of the receivers was in some doubt, so that their agency status was also not established, the House of Lords has held that one element of the tort of unlawful interference with contractual relations is the intention to induce a breach of contract, which, on the facts, was not made out.[67]

Under s.37(1), (3) of the Insolvency Act 1986, a receiver appointed under a power in an instrument (other than an administrative receiver) is, to the same extent as if he had been appointed by the court, personally liable on contracts made by him in the performance of his functions except so far as they otherwise provide[68] and on any contract of employment adopted by him in the performance of his functions. Nothing he does or does not do within 14 days of his appointment can be regarded as his adopting such a contract of employment. S.37(1)(a) was in part a response to *Nicoll v Cutts*[69] which decided that a receiver who merely continued a contract of employment on behalf of the company did not incur personal liability. The employee, in relation to post-receivership remuneration, had the status of an unsecured creditor. Now, causing the company to continue the contract of employment amounts to adoption and results in personal liability.[70] The receiver is unable to avoid personal liability unilaterally, as by service of a notice.[71] The liability is restricted to liabilities incurred on the contract while he was receiver.[72] In respect of it he enjoys a right of indemnity against the company's assets under s.37(1)(b). The Insolvency Act 1994, which qualifies the liability of administrative receivers and administrators,[73] is not applicable to ordinary receivers within s.37. It may be that the liability could be excluded or modified by a contract with the employees but such a contract will not readily be implied.[74]

27–009   On the commencement of a winding up of the company the receiver ceases to be the company's agent and his authority to bind the company ceases[75] but his powers with regard to the property charged are unaffected[76] so that he may continue to use the company's name for the purpose of the realisation of its assets.[77] On a

---

[65] *Thames Ironworks Co Ltd, Re* (1912) 106 L.T. 674.

[66] *Lathia v Dronsfield Bros Ltd* [1987] B.C.L.C. 321. See also *Welsh Development Agency v Export Finance Co Ltd* [1992] B.C.L.C. 148.

[67] *OBG Ltd v Allan* [2007] UKHL 21.

[68] Where liability is excluded the receiver may in appropriate circumstances be exposed to a claim under s.213 for fraudulent trading: *Leyland Daf Ltd, Re; Ferranti Ltd, Re* [1994] B.C.C. 658 at 668.

[69] [1985] B.C.L.C. 322, CA.

[70] See *Powdrill v Watson, Leyland Daf Ltd, Re; Ferranti International Plc, Re,* [1995] 2 All E.R. 65, HL (relating to s.19 (administrators) and s.44 (administrative receivers)).

[71] ibid. cf. *Specialised Mouldings Ltd, Re,* Unreported, February 13, 1987 which gave rise to the practice, now known to be ineffective, of sending "Specialised Mouldings" letters opting out of personal liability.

[72] *Powdrill v Watson,* above, n.70.

[73] See below, and see Ch.28.

[74] *Leyland Daf Ltd, Re* [1994] B.C.C. 658.

[75] *Gosling v Gaskell* [1897] A.C. 575; *Thomas v Todd* [1926] 2 K.B. 511.

[76] *Gough's Garages Ltd v Pugsley* [1930] 1 K.B. 615.

[77] *Sowman v David Samuel Trust Ltd* [1978] 1 W.L.R. 22.

liquidation, the receiver may well become the agent of the debenture holder who will then be liable for his acts.[78] Where the appointing debenture holder "intermeddles" with the receiver's performance of his functions (e.g. by giving him instructions) the receiver may also become the agent of the debenture holder rather than that of the company.[79]

A debenture holder or mortgagee must exercise his power to appoint a receiver in good faith for the propose of obtaining repayment.[80] If he complies with this rule, it is irrelevant that the appointment of a receiver is disadvantageous to the company and its other creditors, because, for example, it causes unnecessary expense[81] or frustrates negotiations with a third party for additional funding.[82] Once appointed, a receiver owes a duty of good faith to the company but it is qualified by the recognition that the primary function of the charge is repayment of the debt. Thus, where he is appointed manager of a business, he manages it in order to discharge the debt and not, as would its directors, in order to benefit the company.[83] Where he exercises a power of sale, he can give preference to the interests of the debenture holders regarding the time of sale[84] but he does owe a duty of reasonable care to obtain the true value of the property at the time he chooses to sell it.[85] This may include a duty to pursue a sale of the property and the business as a going concern,[86] but it does not require the receiver to incur expense in improving the secured property in order to obtain a higher price.

Receivers were appointed over mortgaged property and subsequently exercised a power of sale. The mortgagor complained that the sale had been made at an undervalue, because the receivers had failed to pursue planning applications for the property prior to sale and, further, had failed to find tenants for vacant properties. It was held that the receivers were under no duty to incur expense in an attempt to attain a higher price for the property. While they were free to investigate how such a potential could be realised, they were under no obligation to pursue such enquiries and were therefore not liable for any breach of duty.[87]

This duty has been equated with a duty of care in negligence[88] but it is now **27–010** accepted that it is an equitable duty only[89] and it is owed to a limited class,

---

[78] *American Express International Banking Corp v Hurley* [1985] 3 All E.R. 564.

[79] *American Express International Banking Corp v Hurley* [1985] 3 All E.R. 564; *Royal Bank of Scotland Plc v Binnell* [1996] B.P.I.R 352.

[80] cf. *Downsview Nominees Ltd v First City Corp Ltd* [1993] 3 All E.R. 626, PC, where the appointment was made to prevent a subsequent encumbrancer enforcing his security.

[81] *Potter Oils Ltd, Re (No.2)* [1986] 1 All E.R. 890.

[82] *Shamji v Johnson Matthey Bankers Ltd* [1991] B.C.L.C. 36.

[83] *B. Johnson & Co (Builders) Ltd, Re* [1955] 2 All E.R. 775 at 790–91.

[84] *Cuckmere Brick Co Ltd v Mutual Finance Ltd* [1971] 2 All E.R. 633, CA, even if redemption is imminent so long as there has been no valid tender of the redemption price: see *Routestone Ltd v Minories Finance Ltd* [1997] B.C.C. 180, 187. See also *Cohen v TSB Bank Plc* [2002] 2 B.C.L.C. 32, *Silven Properties Ltd v Royal Bank of Scotland Plc* [2003] EWCA Civ. 1409.

[85] ibid. And see *Downsview Nominees Ltd v First City Corp Ltd*, above, n.80.

[86] Unless the business has previously ceased: see *A.I.B. Ltd v Debtors (Alsop & Another)* [1998] B.C.C. 780, CA.

[87] *Silven Properties Ltd v Royal Bank of Scotland Plc* [2003] EWCA Civ. 1409.

[88] e.g. in *Knight v Lawrence* [1991] 01 E.G. 105.

[89] *China & South Sea Bank Ltd v Tan* [1980] 3 All E.R. 839, PC; *Parker-Tweedale v Dunbar Bank, Plc (No.1)* [1990] 2 All E.R. 577, CA; *Downsview*, above, n.80.

namely, the company, subsequent encumbrancers and guarantors.[90] Where a receiver decides to continue the business of the company he owes an equitable duty of care to do so with reasonable competence.

Receivers appointed over a pig-farming business were advised that discounts on orders of feed were available. The receivers failed to request such discounts. It was held that the receivers were liable to compensate the mortgagor in respect of the discounts, as these were lost as a result of their breach of an equitable duty of skill and care.[91]

This duty is owed to the company and to subsequent encumbrancers and guarantors.[92] The duty does not compel the receiver to continue to operate the business where it is not in the interests of the debenture holder to do so,[93] but it will be a breach of duty for a receiver to remain passive where to do so damages the interests of the debenture holder or the company.[94]

A company in receivership cannot interfere with the receiver in the proper exercise of his powers but, in *Watts v Midland Bank Plc*,[95] Peter Gibson J. thought that it could maintain an action against him for the proper performance of his duties and so refused to allow a minority shareholder to bring a derivative action[96] against him.

A receiver appointed out of court, or the person who appointed him, may apply to the court for directions in any matter concerning the performance of his functions: IA 1986 s.35.[97] The court's jurisdiction is not limited to giving guidance and instruction; it may also make an order enforcing a contract of indemnity between the receivers and the debenture holders who appointed them.[98] He must within one month of his first year of appointment, every subsequent period of six months and on ceasing to act, deliver to the Registrar the requisite accounts of his receipts and payments: IA 1986 s.38. Since the receiver is usually the agent of the company he must produce full accounts to the company when required to do so.[99] The court may order the receiver to make any returns or give any notices which he is by law required to give or make: IA 1986 s.41.[100]

Administrative receivers

27–011   The concept of an administrative receiver was introduced, on the recommendation of the Cork Committee, by s.29(2) Insolvency Act 1986. A receiver and manager appointed by or on behalf of debenture holders will be an administrative receiver if he is a receiver and manager of the whole or substantially the whole of

---

[90] *American Express International Banking Corp v Hurley* [1985] 3 All E.R. 564; Parker-Tweedale, above.
[91] *Medforth v Blake* [2000] Ch. 86.
[92] *Medforth v Blake* [2000] Ch. 86.
[93] ibid.
[94] *Silven Properties Ltd v Royal Bank of Scotland Plc* [2003] EWCA Civ. 1409.
[95] [1986] B.C.L.C. 15.
[96] Above, p.511.
[97] This section also applies to administrative receivers. For an example of such an application, see *Cheyne Finance Plc, Re* [2007] EWHC 2402 (Ch).
[98] *Therm-a-Stor Ltd, Re* [1996] 3 All E.R. 228. See also *Munns v Perkins* [2002] B.P.I.R. 120 (guidance on level of receiver's remuneration).
[99] *Smiths Ltd v Middleton* [1979] 3 All E.R. 843.
[100] This section also applies to administrative receivers.

the company's property and the appointment is made or on behalf of debenture holders secured by a charge which as created was a floating charge.[101]

The right to appoint a receiver who qualifies as an administrative receiver has been restricted by s.72A of the Insolvency Act 1986. The legislative purpose behind this provision was to promote the use of the new, streamlined administration procedure,[102] as this regime was seen as fairer, more inclusive for all creditors and, most importantly, as more likely to result in the rescue of the company or its business.[103] Section 72A, however, applies only to the entitlement of the holders of a "qualifying floating charge"[104] to make such an appointment, and is not retrospective in effect: s.72A(4). Therefore, holders of charges granted prior to September 15, 2003 will still be entitled to appoint an administrative receiver and the following exposition of the law will remain of relevance for some time to come.

The prohibition in s.72A is also subject to a number of exceptions found in s.72B–72GA, although these exceptions relate to rather specialist financing transactions. Moreover, it does not prevent a debenture holder from appointing a receiver over the fixed charge element of the secured property, perhaps under s.109 of the Law of Property Act 1925, although such a receiver would not be an administrative receiver.

Section 44 of the Insolvency Act 1986 provides that an administrative receiver is deemed to be the agent of the company unless and until it goes into liquidation[105] so that the company remains liable as principal on all contracts made by him.[106] The section also provides that an administrative receiver is personally liable on all contracts he makes in carrying out his functions and on any contract of employment he adopts (i.e. allows to continue for more than 14 days after his appointment).[107] In respect of contracts of employment adopted on or after March 15, 1994, the administrative receiver's personal liability is limited to liabilities arising under the contract of employment[108] which fall within the definition of a "qualifying liability" (IA 1986 s.44, as amended by IA 1994 s.2) being:

1. a liability to pay a sum by way of wages or salary[109] or contribution to an occupational pension scheme;

---

[101] The charge in question does not have to extend to the whole of the company's property if its holder enjoys the benefit of a package of security which does in fact do so. Moreover, the requisite floating charge need not actually cover any assets for an appointment to be made: see *Croftbell Ltd, Re* [1990] B.C.C. 781.

[102] Below, Ch.28.

[103] See *Productivity and Enterprise: Insolvency—A Second Chance* (DTI: Cm 5234, HMSO, July 2001), para.2.2.

[104] See Insolvency Act 1986 Sch.B1 para.14.

[105] *American Express Banking Corp v Hurley* [1985] 3 All E.R. 564.

[106] A contract within Companies Act 2006 s.190 (see above p.386) is liable to be avoided: *Demite Ltd v Protec Health Ltd* [1998] B.C.C. 638 (Park J.).

[107] In respect of liabilities incurred while he was receiver. See *Powdrill v Watson, Leyland Daf Ltd, Re, Ferranti International Plc, Re* [1995] 2 All E.R. 65, HL. See above, p.656

[108] cf. liabilities arising by virtue of statute in relation to redundancy or unfair dismissal.

[109] s.2(3) of the IA 1994 inserts into IA 1986 s.44 a new subsection, (2C), which includes within the definition of wages or salary amounts payable in periods of absence due to holidays and sickness and also amounts payable in lieu of holidays. Redundancy payments and payments as compensation for unfair dismissal are not "wages or salary" within the meaning of the provision: *Allders Department Stores Ltd, Re* [2005] EWHC 172 (Ch.).

2.   incurred while the administrative receiver is in office; and

3.   in respect of services rendered wholly or partly after adoption of the contract.[110]

27–012   Where the liability arises in respect of services rendered partly before and partly after the adoption, it is provided that only so much of it as relates to the post-adoption period qualifies.[111]

In respect of the s.44 liability, the administrative receiver is entitled to an indemnity out of the assets of the company and this is without prejudice to any indemnity he can claim under any express clause in his appointment or in an order of the court under s.35 of the Act.

An administrative receiver has the powers set out in Schedule 1 to the Insolvency Act 1986, subject to any contrary express terms in the relevant debenture; Insolvency Act 1986 s.42(1). Schedule 1 also applies to administrators and the powers therein are set out in the following chapter of this book. Section 42(2) of the Act adapts those powers to an administrative receiver.[112] Section 42(3) of the Insolvency Act 1986 provides that a person dealing with an administrative receiver in good faith and for value does not need to inquire whether the receiver is acting within his powers.

By virtue of s.43(1) of the Insolvency Act an administrative receiver can sell property[113] which is subject to a security having priority over the security of his appointor[114] free of that security if the court is satisfied that such a sale is likely to promote a more advantageous realisation of the company's assets.[115] The secured creditor whose security is thus overturned is protected by s.43(3) so that the net proceeds of sale must be used to discharge his debt together with, if the court regards such proceeds as less than the open market value of the property, such additional sums as are necessary to make good the deficiency.[116] The receiver must send an office copy of any court order under this section to the Registrar within 14 days, with a fine in default: s.43(5), (6).

Supplies to administrative receivers

27–013   Supplies of gas, electricity, water and telecommunications requested by an administrative receiver are protected: IA 1986 s.233.[117] Supplies of other goods and services are not protected,[118] and the supplier is entitled at common law to stipulate for payment in full of pre-receivership arrears before making further

---

[110] IA 1994 s.2(3) inserting a new subsection, (2A), into IA 1986 s.44.

[111] IA 1994 s.2(3) adding a new section (2B) to IA 1986 s.44.

[112] Note also that IA 1986 ss.233–237 apply to administrative receivers. See below.

[113] Being property in relation to which he is the receiver or would be the receiver but for the appointment of a receiver by a prior chargee: IA 1986 s.43(7).

[114] IA s.43(2).

[115] Following a recommendation of the Cork Report paras 1510–1513; cf. IA below. Sch.B1, para.70, below, p.676.

[116] If there is more than one charge on the property they are to be repaid in order of priority: IA 1986 s.43(4).

[117] See, below p.673.

[118] Whether requested by an administrative receiver or an ordinary receiver.

supplies.[119] Such a demand is not a breach of art.86 of the Treaty of Rome which prohibits abuse of a dominant position.[120]

Where an administrative receiver himself contracts for post-receivership supplies, he will incur personal liability and will be entitled in respect of it to an indemnity out of the company's assets.[121] Where he merely continues the company's contract, he incurs no personal liability.[122] Thus he is not personally liable to pay rent or hire charges under an existing lease or hire-purchase agreement, even where he uses the land or goods. Such amounts are a company liability and "it is to the company that, along with other creditors, the lessor and the owner of the goods must look for payment."[123]

Where goods are hired or leased to the company under a hire purchase or chattel lease agreement, and the appointment of the receiver terminates that agreement that receiver may apply for equitable relief against forfeiture of the subject matter of the agreement.[124] In such circumstances, a receiver should make such an application speedily, rather than pay a premium to the owner of the goods in question and then attempt to avoid that payment on the grounds of economic duress.[125]

Duties of administrative receiver

On appointment, an administrative receiver must forthwith inform the company **27–014** of his appointment and publish that fact in the Gazette and may be advertised in such other manner as the administrative receiver thinks fit: IA 1986 s.46(1), Insolvency Rules 1986, r.3.2(3).[126] The notice must state, as well as the fact of appointment, the date of the appointment and the name of the person making it and a description of the business of the company.[127] Within 28 days of his appointment he must send a notice of his appointment to all the creditors of the company[128] so far as he is aware of their addresses. There are fines in default: IA 1986 s.46(1)(b), (4).

He must also require "forthwith" the provision of a statement of the company's affairs from some or all of the officers of the company (past or present), its promoters (if they acted within the year prior to his appointment), its employees (if they are in

---

[119] *Leyland Daf Ltd v Automotive Products Plc* [1993] B.C.C. 389.

[120] [1993] B.C.C. 389.

[121] IA 1986 s.44. Such indemnity, together with his renumeration and any expenses properly incurred by him is charged on any property of the company in his custody or under his control at the time he vacates office in priority to any security held by the person who appointed him: IA 1986 s.45. Similar provisions apply to ordinary receivers: IA 1986 s.37.

[122] In the absence of novation.

[123] Per Nicholls L.J. in *Atlantic Computer Systems Plc, Re* [1992] 1 All E.R. 476 at 486. Unlike in the case of an administration or liquidation, such amounts are not treated as a prior charge on the assets, but, if not paid, the lessor or owner is free to take legal proceedings. cf. IA 1986 ss.11, 130. As to liability for rates, see *Sobam B.V., Re* [1996] B.C.C. 351; *Beck Foods Ltd, Re* [2001] EWCA Civ. 1934.

[124] *Transag Haulage Ltd v Leyland DAF Finance Plc* [1994] B.C.C. 356, *On Demand Information Plc v Michael Gerson (Finance) Plc* [2000] 4 All E.R. 734.

[125] *Alf Vaughan & Co Ltd v Royscot Trust Plc* [1999] 1 All E.R. (Comm.) 856.

[126] As amended by the Insolvency (Amendment) Rules 2009 (SI 2009/642).

[127] IR 1986, r.3.2(4), as substituted by the Insolvency (Amendment) Rules 2010 (SI 2010/686).

[128] Unless the court otherwise directs, not to the shareholders.

his opinion capable of giving the information required and are either current employees or have been employed within the preceding year) and the officers of any company which is (or has been within the previous year) an officer of the company concerned. The administrative receiver must, under the Insolvency Rules, send a notice to those persons he considers should be responsible for providing the statement of affairs (the "nominated persons").[129] Such a statement must be made within 21 days of being requested, with a fine in default. Nominated persons are entitled to be paid their reasonable expenses by the administrative receiver.[130] The receiver may excuse any person from the obligation or extend the time limits although the court may intervene and exercise the power on his behalf: IA 1986 s.47.

Statements submitted under s.47 must be verified by affidavit and contain particulars of the company's assets, debts and liabilities, the names and addresses of its creditors, any securities held by them and when they were given and such further information as may be prescribed. Similar statements are required to be given to an administrator.[131]

27–015   Within three months of his appointment, unless the court allows an extension, an administrative receiver must report to the Registrar, the trustees for secured creditors and all secured creditors of whose addresses he is aware; IA 1986 s.48(1). This report must include details of the events leading up to his appointment, any dealings of his with company property and his carrying on of the company's business, the amounts of principal and interest payable to those debenture holders who appointed him and the amounts payable to preferential creditors, and the amount (if any) likely to be available for the payment of other creditors. It must also include a summary of the statements of affairs submitted to him under s.47 together his comments: IA 1986 s.48(5). It need not include anything "which would seriously prejudice the carrying out by the administrative receiver of his functions": IA 1986 s.48(6).

In addition, within three months an administrative receiver must also either send a copy of his report to all the company's unsecured creditors (of whose addresses he is aware) or publish an address to which they may write for copies to be sent to them free of charge. In either case he must also summon a meeting of the unsecured creditors on not less than 14 days' notice, before which he must lay a copy of the report. The court may dispense with such a meeting if the report states that the receiver intends to apply for such an order and the other requirements as to publicity are complied with at least 14 days before the application: IA 1986 s.48(2), (3). Such a meeting may appoint a committee, which may summon the receiver to attend before it and to give it such information as is reasonable, provided it gives him seven days' notice: IA 1986 s.49. If the receivership is overtaken by a winding up, the report must be sent to the liquidator within seven days: IA 1986 s.48(4). The administrative receiver must provide annual and final accounts of his receipts and payments to the Registrar of Companies, the company, the person who appointed him and each member of the creditors' committee (where there is one).[132]

---

[129] IR 1986 r.3.3, as amended by the Insolvency (Amendment) Rules 2010 (SI 2010/686).
[130] IR 1986 r.3.7(1).
[131] Below, Ch.28.
[132] *Gomba Holdings UK Ltd v Homan* [1986] 1 W.L.R. 1301; IR 1986, r.3.32(1).

These provisions replaced more limited ones in the Companies Act 1985 and reflect the Cork Committee's intention that creditors should be more aware and receivers more accountable.

Preferential payments

A receiver appointed to enforce a charge which, as created, was a floating charge, **27–016** must pay the preferential debts[133] in priority to any claims for principal and interest in respect of the debentures.[134] This obligation applies even if the charge had crystallised prior to the appointment of a receiver, but it does not apply to a charge which as created was fixed. Creditors relying on a floating charge are thus deferred to the preferential debts but they are entitled to have the consequent depletion of assets made good out of assets available for the payment of general creditors: IA 1986 s.40.[135] A receiver who pays floating charge funds to his debenture holder in the knowledge that preferential creditors have not been paid is liable in the tort of breach of statutory duty, and liable to the preferential creditors.[136]

Share of assets for unsecured creditors

An administrative receiver must make available for the satisfaction of unsecured **27–017** debts a "prescribed part of the company's property": s.176A(2).[137] The company's net property is the amount that would have been available to floating charge holders but for s.176A: s.176A(6). The duty does not apply where the company's net property is less than the "prescribed minimum" and the receiver thinks that the cost of making a distribution to unsecured creditors is disproportionate to the benefits.[138]

The prescribed part is calculated as a percentage of the company's property subject to a floating charge (but not a fixed charge). Where such property does not exceed £10,000 in value, the prescribed part is 50 per cent of that value, where it exceeds £10,000 the prescribed part is 50 per cent of the first £10,000 and 20 per cent of property exceeding £10,000, subject to a maximum of £600,000: SI 2003/2097 para.3. Only floating charges granted on or after September 15, 2003 are affected: s.176A(9).

Vacation of office by receiver

An administrative receiver may only be removed from office by an order of the **27–018** court although he may resign on giving due notice. In addition he must vacate his

---

[133] See s.386 and Sch.6, IA 1986 and below, p.618. In this case the periods mentioned in Sch.6 run from the appointment of the receiver or the taking of possession. The duty does not cease on the claim of the appointor being met: *Re Pearl Maintenance Services Ltd* [1995] B.C.C. 657.

[134] Both the debentures in respect of, and those having priority to, the debentures under which he has been appointed: see *H. & K. (Medway) Ltd* [1997] B.C.C. 853.

[135] See also s.754 Companies Act 2006 and *Re Oval 1472 Ltd* [2007] EWCA Civ. 1262.

[136] *Inland Revenue Commissioners v Goldblatt* [1972] Ch. 498.

[137] As inserted by Enterprise Act 2002 s.252, and see above, Ch.25, p.618.

[138] Section 176A(3)(a). The prescribed minimum is £10,000: The Insolvency Act 1986 (Prescribed Part) Order 2003 (SI 2003/2097) para.2. If the company's net property exceeds the prescribed minimum and the receiver thinks that the cost of making a distribution to unsecured creditors is disproportionate to the benefits, he must apply to court for an order disapplying s.176A(2): s.176A(5).

office if he ceases to be a qualified insolvency practitioner. When he does give up office he must inform the Registrar within 14 days and is subject to a fine in default: IA 1986 s.45. Any administrative receiver must also vacate his office.

When any receiver vacates office any remuneration, expenses or indemnity to which he is entitled at that time take priority over any security held by the person who appointed him: IA 1986. Where the expenses of a receiver appointed by the court exceed the assets in his hands, he is not entitled to recover them from the person who appointed him or the company.[139]

---

[139] *Evans v Clayhope Ltd* [1988] B.C.L.C. 238, CA.

Chapter 28

THE ADMINISTRATION PROCEDURE

The Insolvency Act 1985 introduced an entirely new concept into UK company **28–001**
law—the administration order.[1] It was intended to provide an alternative to liquidation for companies where no administrative receiver could be appointed because
no suitably secured creditor existed to make such an appointment. It was hoped
that the administration regime would prove to be an effective form of "company
rescue". However, the use of administration orders in the years following the
introduction of the procedure was disappointingly low and so, after a series of
Consultations and Reports,[2] the Enterprise Act 2002 made a number of significant
changes to the law, all intended to promote the use of administration and, as a
result, to increase the incidence of rescue amongst financially troubled companies.
These apply to Scotland as well as England and Wales.

One method of achieving this aim was to restrict the power of a floating
charge holder to appoint an administrative receiver,[3] but it was also hoped to
persuade such creditors that the administration procedure would serve their interests equally well. Therefore, Pt 10 of the Enterprise Act 2002 contained provisions designed to "streamline" that procedure. Section 248 of the Enterprise Act
substituted a "new" Sch.B1 to the Insolvency Act 1986 for the "old" Pt II of that
Act. This chapter will focus on the new administration regime, although it should
be noted that for administration orders pre-dating September 15, 2003,[4] the old
Pt II will continue to apply. The reader is referred to the 16th edition of this work
for a full exposition of the old law.

While Sch.B1 makes some significant changes to the administration procedure,
an equally significant number of its provisions mirror those contained
in Pt II of the Insolvency Act. Therefore, authorities decided in relation to
Pt II will remain of relevance to similarly (or identically) worded provisions of
Sch.B1 and will be referred to as appropriate in this chapter. References to paragraphs in the following are to the paragraphs of Sch.B1 unless the contrary is
indicated.

---

[1] See the *Cork Report*, Ch.9.
[2] See *A Review of Company Rescue and Business Reconstruction Mechanisms* (The Insolvency
Service, 1999); *A Review of Company Rescue and Business Reconstruction Mechanisms: Report by
the Review Group* (The Insolvency Service, 2000); *Productivity and Enterprise: Insolvency—A
Second Chance* (Cm 5234 The Insolvency Service, 2001).
[3] Enterprise Act 2002 s.250, inserting s.72A Insolvency Act 1986. See Ch.27, above p.659.
[4] The date on which Enterprise Act 2002 Pt 10 was brought into force: SI 2003/2093.

THE EMPHASIS OF THE ADMINISTRATION REGIME

28–002   "The recognition of administration as an important tool in providing a company in financial difficulties with a breathing space in which to put together a rescue plan or, alternatively, in providing a better return to creditors than would be likely in a liquidation, has increased steadily in recent years. Nonetheless, if administration is to become a fully efficient procedure in all circumstances, it will need to be streamlined."[5]

In order to promote administration as a rescue-orientated regime Sch.B1 provides for a hierarchy of objectives in any administration. The pivotal provision is para.3:

> "3(1) The administrator of a company must perform his functions with the objective of—
>
> (a) rescuing the company as a going concern, or
> (b) achieving a better result for the company's creditors as a whole than would be likely if the company were wound up (without first being in administration), or,
> (c) realising property in order to make a distribution to one or more secured or preferential creditors."

The objective of rescuing the company as a going concern must be pursued unless the administrator thinks that it is not reasonably practicable to achieve that objective or that the company's creditors as a whole would be better served by the pursuit of the objective in para.3(1)(b): para.3(3). The administrator may only realise property in order to make a distribution to secured or preferential creditors if he thinks that it is not reasonably practicable to achieve either of the other objectives and, in any event, he must not unnecessarily harm the interests of the company's creditors as a whole: para.3(4). Subject to this, an administrator must perform his functions in the interests of the company's creditors as a whole,[6] and as quickly and efficiently as is reasonably practicable: para.4. Moreover, where the administrator thinks that the objectives of rescuing the company or achieving a better result for the company's creditors as a whole cannot be achieved he must, in his statement of proposals,[7] explain his reasons for so thinking: para.49(2)(b).

Taken together, these provisions are intended to ensure that, where reasonably practicable, some attempt will be made to devise a rescue strategy in relation to the company, or that the interests of the company's creditors as a whole will be prioritised. The interests of secured creditors, which are seen as the main concern in administrative receivership, are relegated to the lowest rung of this hierarchy.

---

[5] *Productivity and Enterprise* (above n.2), para.2.7.
[6] para.3(2).
[7] Below, p.678.

ENTERING ADMINISTRATION

Prior to the coming into force of Sch.B1 the administration procedure was exclu- **28–003**
sively available through an application to the court. This involved a petition for
an administration order and was seen as unduly cumbersome and expensive.
Sch.B1 now provides three ways for a company to enter administration, thus
streamlining the entry procedure. In all cases an administrator has to be qualified
to act as an insolvency practitioner in relation to a company and so has to satisfy
the requirements of s.390 of the Insolvency Act: para.6.[8] An administrator,
whether appointed by the court or not, is an officer of the court: para.5.

There are certain general restrictions on the appointment (whether or not by the
court) of an administrator. Most obviously, no appointment may be made where
a company is already in administration: para.7.[9] An administrator may not be
appointed if the company is in liquidation,[10] unless an administration application[11] is made by a qualifying floating charge holder[12] (in the case of a court-
ordered winding up) or the company's liquidator[13] (in the case of both a voluntary
and court-ordered winding up), and the court sees fit to make an administration
order. In either case the court shall then discharge the winding up.

Appointment by the court following administration application

Paragraphs 10–13 relate to the appointment of an administrator by the court. It is **28–004**
a pre-condition to any court order appointing an administrator that the court is
satisfied that the company is or is likely to become unable to pay its debts and that
the administration order is reasonably likely to achieve the purpose of the administration: para.11. As to the first requirement, the statutory wording is identical
to that of its predecessor,[14] in relation to which it has been held that the court
must be satisfied that it is more probable than not that the company will become
unable to pay its debts: *Colt Telecom Group Plc, Re* [2002] EWHC 2815.[15] As to
the second, it would appear that the particular purpose out of the para.3 hierarchy
need not be specified in the application.[16]

In a case described as "unusual" an administration order was granted in respect
of a company that had not traded for some time and had no assets except for potential claims against its own directors. The purpose for which the order was sought
was to achieve a better result for the creditors than would be likely on a winding
up (during which such claims could also be pursued). The applicant had offered to
provide funding towards the claim. It was held that the administration order would
be granted. While liquidation was an alternative to administration, the provision of

---

[8] As to s.390 see p.639.
[9] Subject to certain qualifications: see below.
[10] para.8.
[11] Below.
[12] para.37. See below as to the definition of a qualifying floating charge holder.
[13] Para.38.
[14] Insolvency Act 1986 s.8(1).
[15] And see *AMCD (Property Holdings) Ltd, Re* [2004] All E.R. (D) 125.
[16] *Hammonds v Pro-Fit USA Ltd* [2007] EWHC 1998.

funding, which might not be available in liquidation, suggested that the specified purpose was reasonably likely to be achieved.[17]

The courts appear to agree that there must be a real prospect of the purpose of the administration being achieved for para.11(1)(b) to be satisfied, and this will usually fall to be decided according to the circumstance of the particular application. Thus, where the court is presented with evidence as to the expected outcome of the administration as compared to a liquidation, it may be persuaded to make an administration order notwithstanding the objection of the company's majority creditor.[18] It is not, however, necessary to produce detailed outcome statements in support of the application, as it has been stated that if it can be shown that the administration will, in all but the most unlikely of circumstances, produce a result no worse than a liquidation *and* that is reasonably likely that the result in an administration will be better, then an administration will be made.[19] An administration order has been made in order that a "pre-packaged" sale of the business of a firm of solicitors be executed, as this would achieve a better result for the company's creditors in that it would forestall the intervention of the Law Society and so preserve the value of the firm's work-in-progress.[20] However, where the applicant's debt was disputed and the administrator's proposals were somewhat vague, as he was not fully apprised of the company's financial situation, the court refused to grant an order.[21]

An administration order is acquired by an application to the court (an "administration application": para.12(1)). Such an application may be made by the company, its directors or any one or more of its creditors.[22] The applicant is under a duty to notify any person who has appointed or is entitled to appoint an administrative receiver or an administrator: para.12(2). An application made by directors may be made by a majority of the company's directors: para.105. A creditor, for these purposes, includes a contingent or prospective creditor: para.12(4).[23] The court's powers on hearing an administration application are listed in para.13, which is subject to para.39, whereby the court must dismiss the application if an administrative receiver is in office and the receiver's appointor does not consent to the making of the administration order unless the court "thinks" the security under which the receiver was appointed may be vulnerable.[24] Paragraph 39 applies whether the administrative receiver is appointed before or after the making of the administration application, so that the notification requirement in

---

[17] *Logitext UK Ltd, Re* [2004] EWHC 2899. See also *Redman Construction Ltd, Re* [2004] All E.R. (D) 146, *MCA Coffee Shops Ltd, Re* [2004] All E.R. (D) 320.

[18] *Professional Computer Group Ltd, Re* [2008] EWHC 1761.

[19] *Auto Management Services Ltd v Oracle Fleet UK Ltd* [2007] EWHC 392 (Ch.).

[20] *DKLL Solicitors v Revenue and Customs Commissioners* [2007] EWHC 2067 (Ch.), and see also *Kayley Vending Ltd, Re* [2009] EWHC 904 (Ch). See below, p.682 on pre-pack administrations.

[21] *Corbett v Nysir UK Ltd* [2008] EWHC 2670 (Ch.).

[22] para.12(1). An application may also be made by the designated officer in the exercise of the power conferred by Magistrates' Courts Act 1980 s.87A (para.12(1)(d)), or by the supervisor of a company voluntary arrangement (para.12(5)).

[23] And see *Thunderbird Industries LLC v Simico Digital UK Ltd* [2004] EWHC 209; *Hammonds v Pro-Fit USA Ltd* [2007] EWHC 1998

[24] i.e. open to challenge under ss.238, 239 or 245, as to which see pp.744 et seq. For an example of the court refusing to make an administration order by reason of para.39, see *Chesterton International Group Plc v Deka Immobilien Inv GmbH* [2005] EWHC 656 (Ch.).

para.12(2) allows a person entitled to appoint an administrative receiver to pre-empt the administration applicant by making such an appointment.

Appointment by qualifying floating charge holder

A qualifying floating charge holder may appoint an administrator of the company: **28–005** para.14(1). Prior to the Enterprise Act 2002, such a charge holder would be entitled to appoint an administrative receiver. Where the charge was granted on or after September 15, 2003, such an appointment is now prohibited by s.72A of the Insolvency Act,[25] and it is clearly envisaged that the appointment of an administrator will serve as a substitute method of enforcing the security.[26] However, such an appointment may also be made in order to achieve either of the other two statutory purposes in para.3(1), and as an alternative to the appointment of an administrative receiver in the case of a charge granted prior to September 15, 2003.

A qualifying floating charge is defined in para.14(2) as one which states that para.14 applies to a floating charge, or purports to empower its holder to appoint an administrator or a receiver who would be an administrative receiver within the meaning of s.29(2) of the Insolvency Act 1986. These are alternatives. A qualifying floating charge holder is defined in para.14(3). No appointment may be made under para.14 unless two business days' written notice has been given to the holder of a prior floating charge or that holder consents to the making of an appointment: para.15.[27] No appointment may be made if the floating charge is not enforceable (if, for example, no default has been made by the company or the charge has not been registered in accordance with s.860 of the Companies Act 2006[28]) or if a provisional liquidator or administrative receiver has been appointed: paras 16, 17.

By para.18, the appointor of an administrator under para.14 must file a notice of appointment with the court which must include a statutory declaration that he holds an enforceable qualifying floating charge in relation to the company's property. The notice must identify the administrator and be accompanied by his statement that he consents to the appointment and that in his opinion the purpose of administration is reasonably likely to be achieved. It is only when the requirements of this paragraph have been complied with that the appointment takes effect: para.19.

The appointment of administrators who were proposing to accept the surrender of leases granted by the company was challenged on the grounds of invalidity. The chargee made the appointment on November 20, at which time the company had not defaulted on its obligations under the charge. Notice of the appointment was filed on November 24, by which time default had taken place and the charge had become enforceable. It was held that the appointment was valid. According to para.19, it could not take effect until the requirements of para.18 had been satisfied and this had not occurred until November 24. Therefore the appointment had been made at a time when the charge was enforceable.[29]

---

[25] See above p.659.
[26] The enforcement of security is included in the hierarchy of objectives in administration: para.3(1)(c), above.
[27] Priority is determined, for these purposes, by the test in para.15(2), (3).
[28] See above, pp.630 et seq.
[29] *Fliptex v Hogg* [2004] EWHC 1280.

When the para.18 requirements have been satisfied, the appointor must notify the administrator as soon as reasonably practicable: para.20. If the appointment subsequently turns out to be invalid, the court may order the appointor to indemnify the appointee against any liability arising by reason of the invalidity: para.21. It is worth noting that where a qualifying floating charge holder makes an administration appointment there is no requirement that the company is or is likely to become unable to pay its debts. This may well allow a rescue attempt through administration to be commenced at a time when a company is experiencing financial difficulties but has not yet reached the point of insolvency (perhaps at the request of the company's directors). Such an attempt very likely stands a better chance of success.

Appointment by company/directors

28–006 Paragraph 22 empowers the company or its directors[30] to appoint an administrator, but not if such an appointment has been made before and less than 12 months have elapsed since the earlier appointment ceased to have effect: para.23. Nor may a para.22 appointment be made where a petition for winding up or an administration application under para.12 has been presented and remains undisposed of, or an administrative receiver is in office: para.25. Where it is proposed to appoint under para.22 the prospective appointor must give five business days' written notice to any person entitled to appoint an administrative receiver or an administrator under para.14, that notice specifying the proposed administrator: para.26.[31] This will allow such a person to appoint an administrative receiver or the administrator of his choice if he wishes. Such a notice must be filed with the court and be accompanied by a statement that the company is or is unlikely to become unable to pay its debts: para.27.[32] Once the notice of intention to appoint has been filed the company or its directors have 10 days within which to make the appointment: para.28.

Notice of a para.22 appointment must be filed with the court and accompanied by a statutory declaration that the person making the appointment is entitled to make it. The notice must identify the administrator and be accompanied by his statement that he consents to the appointment and that, in his opinion, the purpose of administration is reasonably likely to be achieved: para.29.[33] The appointment takes effect when the requirements of para.29 are complied with and the appointor must notify the administrator as soon as reasonably practicable thereafter: paras 31, 32. If an appointment by a qualifying floating charge holder is made under para.14 prior to the para.29 requirements being satisfied the para.22 appointment shall not take effect: para.33. If the para.22 appointment

---

[30] Or a majority of them: para.105.

[31] It appears that a notice by e-mail would be invalid: *Sporting Options Plc, Re* [2004] EWHC 3128 (Ch.).

[32] cf. on an appointment under para.14, where no such requirement is imposed.

[33] Where the wrong form was used in relation to this provision, it was held that the court could, under para.13 of Sch.B1, retrospectively validate the appointment of an administrator who had in fact acted as such for one year before the mistake was discovered: *G-Tech Construction Ltd, Re* [2007] B.P.I.R. 1275.

turns out to be invalid the court may order the appointor to indemnify the administrator against any liability arising by reason of the appointment's invalidity: para.34.

The effect of an administration order or appointment

If an administration order or appointment under any of the preceding provisions **28–007** is made certain consequences follow, all of which are intended to allow the administrator to assume control of the company's property and affairs and to provide him with a certain "breathing space" within which to attempt to achieve the objective of the administration. Paragraphs 40–43 are in similar or identical terms to provisions of Pt II Insolvency Act 1986, and therefore case law relating to the latter is likely to be highly persuasive as regards interpretation of the former. The consequences are as follows:

1. any winding up petition is dismissed, except for a petition under Insolvency Act 1986 s.124A (public interest) or s.367 of the Financial Services and Markets Act 2000: para.40;

2. any administrative receiver shall vacate office: para.41[34];

3. no resolution may be passed or order made for the company's winding up, except under s.124A of the Insolvency Act 1986 (public interest) or Financial Services and Markets Act 2000 s.367: para.42;

4. no steps may be taken to enforce security over the company's property, to repossess goods in the company's possession under a hire purchase-agreement,[35] or to forfeit a lease by peaceable re-entry[36] except with the consent of the administrator or permission of the court: para.43.

In *Bristol Airport v Powdrill*[37] it was held that the right of an airport under s.88 of the Civil Aviation Act 1982 to detain an aircraft for non-payment of airport charges is a security (the enforcement of which therefore requires consent or permission) within s.11 of the Insolvency Act 1986, and there would appear to be no change of substance in the wording of the provisions in Sch.B1. A contractual lien arising after the commencement of an administration is also a security requiring consent or permission to enforce: *London Flight Centre (Stansted) Ltd v Osprey Aviation* [2002] B.P.I.R. 1115.[38] Goods subject to a hire-purchase or leasing agreement are in the possession of the company even if it has sublet

---

[34] The receiver's remuneration (including his expenses and any indemnity to which he is entitled) become payable out of the company's property under his control immediately prior to vacation of office: para.41(3), (4).

[35] Which includes a conditional sale agreement, a chattel leasing agreement or a retention of title agreement: para.111.

[36] Overturning case law under the old administration regime which held that forfeiture by peaceable re-entry did not amount to an enforcement of security and therefore did not require the administrator's consent or the court's permission.

[37] [1990] 2.All E.R. 493.

[38] So too is a solicitor's lien: *Carter Commercial Developments Ltd, Re* [2002] B.C.C. 803.

them[39] or the agreement has been terminated prior to the commencement of the administration.[40]

The substantive rights of a security holder are not affected by this provision but rather rendered subject to a moratorium on enforcement.[41] On an application for leave to enforce the court has a wide discretion. The principles upon which the court will determine the issue were extensively considered by the Court of Appeal in *Atlantic Computer Systems Plc, Re*,[42] and are likely to remain relevant to applications under Sch.B1. The Court of Appeal considered that it is for the person seeking leave to make out a case, and that the court should have regard to the purpose of the moratorium, which is to enable the company, through its administrator, to achieve the objective of the administration, and to balance that purpose against the legitimate interests of the security holder in enforcing his security. In general, great importance is usually attached to the proprietary rights of the security holder, which should not be prejudiced purely in the interests of unsecured creditors. The court will, however, seek to achieve proportionality: if a substantially greater loss would be caused to others by a grant of leave than would be suffered by the security holder by a refusal to grant leave, the latter course may be appropriate.[43]

A company which had supplied goods on retention-of-title terms to a company in administration sought leave to repossess those goods under para.43(3). The administrators had negotiated a sale of the company's stock, including the applicant's goods, to a third party, on condition that the third party honour any valid retention of title claims. The third party resisted the applicant's claim to be able to repossess the goods on the bases that the clause was invalid. The applicant then waited eight months to commence proceedings under para.43. Permission to repossess the goods was refused. The applicant's delay was contrary to the scheme of the Insolvency Act and, in itself, sufficient to justify a refusal of permission.[44]

Leave may be granted, or refused, subject to conditions.[45] Where an administrator wrongfully refuses consent, as where he seeks to use the goods as a bargaining chip against the owner, he may be liable in conversion and, additionally, the court may require him to pay rental and compensation to the owner.[46]

28–008
    5.   no legal process (including legal proceedings, execution, distress or diligence) may be instituted or continued against the company or its property without the administrator's consent or the leave of the court: para.43(6).

The meaning of "legal process" has been considered in a number of contexts in relation to this provision's predecessor (s.11(3)(d) Insolvency Act 1986). In

[39] *Atlantic Computer Systems Plc, Re* [1992] 1 All E.R. 476 CA.
[40] *David Meek Access Ltd, Re* [1993] B.C.C. 175.
[41] *Barclays Mercantile Business Finance Ltd v Sibec Developments Ltd* [1992] 1 W.L.R. 1253.
[42] [1992] Ch. 505.
[43] [1992] Ch. 505 pp.542–544.
[44] *Fashoff (UK) Ltd (t/a Moschino) v Linton* [2008] EWHC 537 (Ch.).
[45] [1992] Ch. 505.
[46] *Barclays Mercantile Business Finance Ltd v Sibec Developments Ltd* [1992] 1 W.L.R. 1253

Olympia & York Canary Wharf Ltd, Re[47] Millett J. considered that the phrase suggested a process which required the assistance of the court, and so did not include the serving of a contractual notice making time of the essence or the acceptance of a repudiatory breach of contract which would terminate the contract itself. The bringing of criminal proceedings against the company has been held to require leave,[48] as does a claim for unfair dismissal,[49] and the reference of a contractual dispute to a statutory adjudication procedure.[50] An application to court seeking an extension of time for the registration of a floating charge is not a proceeding against the company or its property and therefore does not require leave: *Barrow Borough Transport Ltd, Re* [1989] B.C.C. 646.

As far as the court's discretion to give permission to commence proceedings is concerned, the approach in *Atlantic Computer Systems Plc, Re*[51] is followed.

The administrators of a company granted a licence to the purchaser of its business to occupy the company's leased premises, in contravention of a clause in the lease itself prohibiting such a course. The administrators offered to pay over to the applicant landlord all sums received from the purchaser under the licence (which were equivalent to the company's obligations under the lease, but payable in arrears). The applicant sought leave to commence proceedings seeking an immediate termination of the licence agreement. It was held that permission to commence proceedings would be refused. The applicant would suffer no great detriment, as the administrators had agreed to remit the licence payments to him, whereas, if leave were granted, the performance of the company's contracts by the purchaser would be prejudiced in turn jeopardising the collection of debts owed to the company, and this would be of disproportionate detriment to the company's other creditors.[52]

6. no appointment of an administrative receiver may be made: para.43(6A);

7. all business documents[53] issued by or on behalf of the company must state the name of the administrator and that the company's affairs, business and property are being managed by him, and this fact must also be stated on all of the company's websites: para.45;

8. suppliers of utilities cannot make it a precondition of further supplies that pre-administration debts be paid: Insolvency Act 1986 s.233.[54]

A similar, interim moratorium exists where an administration application has been made and not yet granted, or granted but has yet to take effect: para.44.

---

[47] [1993] B.C.C. 154.
[48] *Rhondda Waste Disposal Ltd, Re* [2001] Ch. 57.
[49] *Carr v British Intl Helicopters Ltd* [1993] B.C.C. 855, although leave should rarely be refused, given the emphasis of employment protection legislation.
[50] *Straume (UK) Ltd v Bradlor Developments Ltd* [2000] B.C.C. 333.
[51] Above, n.39.
[52] *Innovate Logistics Ltd v Sunberry Properties Ltd* [2008] EWCA Civ. 1321.
[53] Meaning invoices, orders for goods or services, order forms or business letters: para.45(3).
[54] See below, p.709.

POWERS OF AN ADMINISTRATOR

General powers

28–009 In general, an administrator will manage the company's business and property with a view to achieving one of the para.3 purposes of administration. He is given extensive powers in this regard. First, he may do anything necessary or expedient for the management of the affairs, business and property of the company, and any person dealing with the administrator in good faith and for value need not enquire whether he is acting within his powers: para.59. He may summon a meeting of shareholders[55] or of creditors,[56] and may apply to the court for directions.[57] An administrator may remove or appoint a director of the company[58] and the company, or any of its officers, may not exercise management powers (meaning any power the exercise of which could interfere with the exercise of the administrator's powers) without the administrator's consent: para.64.

The administrator is also given the specific powers in Sch.1 of the Insolvency Act 1986: para.60.[59] These are as follows:

1. power to take possession of, collect and get in the property of the company and, for that purpose, to take such proceedings as may seem to him expedient;

2. power to sell or otherwise dispose of the property of the company by public auction or private contract or, in Scotland, to sell, feu, hire out or otherwise dispose of the property of the company by public roup or private bargain;

3. power to raise or borrow money and grant security therefore over the property of the company;

4. power to appoint a solicitor or accountant or other professionally qualified person to assist him in the performance of his functions;

5. power to bring or defend any action or other legal proceedings in the name and on behalf of the company;

6. power to refer to arbitration any question affecting the company;

7. power to effect and maintain insurances in respect of the business and property of the company;

8. power to use the company's seal;

9. power to do all acts and to execute in the name and on behalf of the company any deed, receipt or other document;

---

[55] Insolvency Rules, r.2.49.
[56] para.62.
[57] para.63.
[58] para.61.
[59] As is an administrative receiver: see above, p.659.

10. power to draw, accept, make and endorse any bill of exchange or promissory note in the name and on behalf of the company;

11. power to appoint any agent to do any business that he is unable to do himself or which can more conveniently be done by an agent and power to employ and dismiss employees;[60]

12. power to do all such things (including the carrying out of works) as may be necessary for the realisation of the property of the company;

13. power to make any payment that is necessary or incidental to the **28–010** performance of his functions;

This power has been held to apply to the payment of a distribution to creditors who might otherwise insist on a liquidation[61] and to the payment of pre-administration debts where it is necessary to the survival of the company as a going concern.[62] However, a distribution to preferential creditors was not included in the purpose of the administration order and so was not "necessary or incidental" to the performance of the administrator's functions.[63] The position as to the payment of pre-administration debts and the making of distributions is now expressly covered in Sch.B1.[64]

14. power to carry on the business of the company;

15. power to establish subsidiaries of the company;

16. power to transfer to subsidiaries of the company the whole or any part of the business and property of the company;

17. power to grant or accept a surrender of a lease or tenancy of any of the property of the company, and to take a lease or tenancy of any property required or convenient for the business of the company;

18. power to make any arrangement or compromise on behalf of the company;

19. power to call up any uncalled capital of the company;

20. power to rank and claim in the bankruptcy, insolvency, sequestration or liquidation of any person indebted to the company and to receive dividends, and to accede to trust deeds for the creditors of any such person;

21. power to present of defend a petition for the winding up of the company;

22. power to change the situation of the company's registered office;

23. power to do all other things incidental to the exercise of the foregoing powers.

---

[60] Compliance with the consultation requirements of s.188 of the Trade Union and Labour Relations (Consolidation) Act 1992 is required: *Hartlebury Printers Ltd, Re* [1993] 1 All E.R. 470.

[61] *W.B.S.L Realisations 1992 Ltd, Re* [1995] B.C.C. 1118.

[62] *John Slack Ltd, Re* [1995] B.C.C. 1116.

[63] *The Designer Room Ltd, Re* [2004] EWHC 720.

[64] Below p.676.

28–011 Sch.B1 explicitly adds the power to make distributions to creditors of the company: para.65. However, where it is proposed to make a distribution to a creditor who is neither secured nor preferential the court must give permission. As will be seen below, an administration can be converted into a creditors' voluntary liquidation to allow for distributions to unsecured creditors to be made, so this paragraph will only be called upon where such a course is considered inappropriate. As far as the court's discretion is concerned, it was suggested in *GHE Realisations Ltd, Re*[65] that the primary consideration is whether the proposed distribution would be in the interests of the company's creditors as a whole. In *MG Rover Belux SA/NV, Re*[66] further considerations were enumerated, including whether the distribution would facilitate the achievement of the objectives of the administration, whether provision had been made to deal with the claims of secured and preferential creditors, whether there were realistic alternatives to making the distribution and whether the creditors had in fact approved the making of any such distribution. Paragraph 65 has been interpreted so as to allow a distribution to be made in respect of a compromised claim which was not pari passu with other unsecured claims.[67]

Preferential debts of the company are given priority over the claims of floating charge holders in much the same way as in liquidation and administrative receivership by para.65(2). Moreover, a payment may be made otherwise than in accordance with para.65 if the administrator thinks it likely to assist achievement of the purpose of the administration: para.66. Recourse to this power has so far been sought in relation to payments made in "cross-border" insolvencies, and the relationship between paras 65 and 66 was considered in some detail in *Collins & Aikman Europe SA, Re*.[68]

Any exercise of powers by the administrator is as agent of the company: para.69.

Powers to deal with charged property

28–012 In order that the achievement of the purpose of administration (especially where that purpose is to rescue the company or achieve a better result for its creditors than on liquidation) is facilitated, administrators are given powers to deal with charged property as though it were not subject to the charge. In the case of property subject to a floating charge, the administrator may dispose of it or take action in relation to it without leave of the court. The charge-holder retains his priority in respect of any acquired property which directly or indirectly represents the property disposed of: para.70.

In relation to property which is subject to a security other than a floating charge, the court may make an order enabling the administrator to dispose of such property. Such an order is subject to the condition that the court thinks that such disposal would be likely to promote the purpose of the administration and that the

[65] [2005] EWHC 2400 (Ch.).
[66] [2007] B.C.C. 446.
[67] *HPJ UK Ltd (In Administration)* [2007] B.C.C. 284.
[68] [2006] EWHC 1343 (Ch.). See also *MG Rover Espana SA, Re* [2006] B.C.C. 599; *MG Rover Belux SA/NV, Re* [2007] B.C.C. 446.

net proceeds of disposal (and any additional sum required to produce the amount which would be realised on a sale of the property at market value[69]) be applied towards discharging the sums secured by the security: para.71. A similar provision applies in relation to the disposal of goods in the company's possession under a hire-purchase agreement: para.72.[70] Where an administrator in fact deals with property subject to a security other than a floating charge or subject to a hire-purchase agreement without making an application under para.71 or 72, as the case may be, he may be liable in the tort of conversion.[71]

DUTIES OF AN ADMINISTRATOR

General duties

As an officer of the court,[72] an administrator is under a duty to act "honourably" **28–013** in accordance with the rule in *Ex p. James*.[73] Thus, where he is found liable to pay over an amount as an expense of the administration, and he has that amount invested pending the outcome of the dispute, he is liable to pay the amount together with the interest it has earned: *Powdrill v Watson, Paramount Airways Ltd, Re* (No.3).[74] An administrator need not, however, advise a creditor on what steps he should take to enforce his security.[75]

On appointment the administrator must take custody or control or all property to which he thinks the company is entitled: para.67. He owes a duty to take reasonable care to obtain a proper price for the company's property and in choosing the time to sell,[76] although it appears that he owes no general duty of care to the company's unsecured creditors absent an assumption of responsibility towards them.[77] This proposition must now be read subject to the provisions of Sch.B1, which impose upon the administrator a duty to perform his functions as quickly and efficiently as is reasonably practicable,[78] and in the interests of the creditors as a whole.[79]

An administrator will also be under a duty to meet preferential claims, to be calculated according to the date at which the company enters administration: para.65(2), s.387 of the Insolvency Act 1986. Furthermore, he is subject to the s.176A of the Insolvency Act 1986 duty to set aside a "prescribed part" of the

---

[69] See *Stanley J Holmes & Sons Ltd v Davenham Trust Plc* [2006] EWCA Civ. 1568.
[70] Which would include goods subject to a chattel lease, a conditional sale agreement or a retention of title clause: para.111.
[71] *Hachette UK Ltd v Borders (UK) Ltd* [2009] EWHC 3487 (Ch.).
[72] para.5.
[73] (1874) 9 Ch. App 609. See Dawson, *The Administrator, Morality and the Court* [1996] J.B.L 437.
[74] [1994] B.C.C. 172 at 182, CA.
[75] *Sabre International Products, Re* [1991] B.C.L.C. 470.
[76] *Charnley Davies (No.2) Ltd, Re* [1990] B.C.L.C. 760
[77] *Kyrris v Oldham* [2003] EWCA Civ. 1506; *Charalambous v B&C Associates* [2009] EWHC 2601 (Ch.).
[78] para.4
[79] para.3(2), subject to para.3(4) (administrator realising property in order to make a distribution to secured or preferential creditors). In this event the administrator must not unnecessarily harm the interests of the company's general creditors: para.3(4)(b). As to creditors' actions against the administrator, see below.

company's net property for distribution to unsecured creditors.[80] Moreover, as soon as is reasonably practicable after appointment, the administrator should require one or more "relevant persons"[81] to provide him with a statement of affairs of the company: para.47. The statement must show, inter alia, the company's assets and liabilities, the names and addresses of its creditors, details of security held by those making it and any other prescribed information: para.47(2). It must be provided within 11 days of the administrator's request and there are fines on default: para.48.

The administrator and creditors

28–014 Notwithstanding the breadth of an administrator's powers, he does not have carte blanche to do as he sees fit. One of the central planks of administration is that it is inclusive in nature, so that the company's creditors have a real stake in its outcome. In order to achieve this the administrator is required to formulate proposals for achieving the purpose of the administration, a copy of which must be sent to the Registrar of companies, every creditor of whom the administrator is aware and every member[82] of the company as soon as reasonably practicable after his appointment, and in any event within eight weeks of it: para.49.[83]

The statement of proposals must be accompanied by an invitation to an "initial" creditors' meeting, which must be scheduled as soon as reasonably practicable after the company enters administration and, in any event, within ten weeks of that time: para.51.[84] Notice of this meeting should normally be advertised in accordance with the Insolvency Rules 1986[85] and be sent to past or present directors of the company whose presence the administrator thinks is required.[86] The initial creditors meeting need not be called where the administrator thinks that the company has sufficient property to enable each creditor to be paid in full, that the company has insufficient property to enable a distribution to be made other than by virtue of s.176A(2),[87] or where he thinks that neither of the objectives in para.3(1)(a) or (b) can be achieved: para.52(1). Such a meeting must be summoned, however, if requested by creditors whose debts amount to at least 10 per cent of the total debts of the company; para.52(2).

The administrator must present a statement of his proposals at the initial creditors' meeting[88] and the meeting may approve them without modification or with any modification to which the administrator consents. The decision of the initial creditors' meeting must be reported to the court and the Registrar of companies, and there are penalties for non-compliance: para.53. Should the proposals be

---

[80] This duty applies mutatis mutandi to administrative receivers and liquidators. For details of the workings of s.176A see above, p.618.

[81] Defined in para.47(3).

[82] The duty to members is complied with if the administrator publishes a notice undertaking to provide a copy of his proposals to any member applying in writing to a specified address: para.49(6).

[83] Notices by email have been held not to be in compliance with the requirements of paras 46 and 49: *Sporting Options Plc, Re* [2004] All E.R. D 30.

[84] The periods specified in this paragraph may be varied in accordance with para.107.

[85] Rule 2.34(1).

[86] Insolvency Rules, r.2.34(2).

[87] See above, p.618.

[88] para.51(3).

approved (with or without modification), and should the administrator wish to revise them in a manner which he thinks is substantial, he should summon a further creditors' meeting and send a statement of the proposed revision to each creditor and member of the company.[89] A statement of the proposed revision must be presented to the creditors' meeting which may approve it without modification or with such modification as the administrator consents to: para.54. As with the initial creditors' meeting, its decision must be notified to the court and Registrar of companies and there are penalties for non-compliance.[90]

Should the initial creditors' meeting, or a creditors' meeting called to approve revised proposals, fail to approve the original or revised proposals (as the case may be) the administrator must report this to the court, which can then provide that his appointment shall cease to have effect from a specified time, adjourn the hearing, make an interim order, make an order on a petition for winding up suspended under para.49 or make any order it thinks appropriate: para.55. It was suggested in *Structures and Computer Ltds, Re*[91] that the court could, under its discretionary power in the predecessor provision to para.55, make an order implementing the rejected proposals, and, in *DKLL Solicitors v Revenue and Customs Commissioners*[92] Andrew Simmons QC agreed that that court had a discretionary power under para.55(2) to authorise the implementation of rejected proposals notwithstanding the opposition of the majority creditor. It is suggested, however, that such an order would only be made in exceptional circumstances, and perhaps only where a single creditor formed the majority and the proposals had otherwise been approved.

It seems likely that if a meeting has failed to approve revised proposals the **28–015** administrator is free to continue to act in accordance with the approved original proposals. Further creditors' meetings are to be called if requested in the prescribed manner[93] by creditors whose debts amount to not less than 10 per cent of the total debts of the company, or if the court so directs: para.56. The important issue of entitlement to vote at creditors' meetings is governed by the Insolvency Rules 1986.[94] Finally, creditors' meetings may now be conducted by "correspondence",[95] which includes correspondence by telephone or other electronic means.[96]

A creditors' meeting may establish a creditors' committee: para.57(1).[97] The committee may require the administrator to attend on it and provide it with information: para.57. The Insolvency Service is currently consulting on the possibility of holding "virtual" creditors meetings as a means of saving the costs associated with the present regime.

A question that has arisen in relation to the above provisions is whether an administrator may exercise his powers prior to the approval of any proposals by

---

[89] Members may be notified in the manner described in n.82, above.
[90] para.54(6), (7).
[91] [1998] B.C.C. 348.
[92] [2007] EWHC 2067 (Ch.).
[93] See Insolvency Rules r.2.37.
[94] See, in particular, rr.2.38–2.43.
[95] para.58, and see Insolvency Rules r.2.48.
[96] para.111.
[97] For the constitution and procedural aspects of the creditors' committee see Insolvency Rules rr.2.50–2.65.

the creditors meeting. There may be good reasons why an administrator might wish to do so: in particular, if he is seeking to dispose of assets, or even the entire undertaking of the company, in order to achieve a better result for creditors as a whole it may well be the case that speed is of the essence, and that a purchaser is unwilling to wait until the meeting has approved this course of action. It would, of course, be open to an administrator to apply to the court for directions in this respect under para.63, but, again, this may prove costly in terms of time.

Under the "old" Pt II of the Insolvency Act 1986, a note of caution was sounded in *Consumer & Industrial Press Ltd, Re* (No.2)[98] where it was considered that such a course of action would frustrate the statutory purposes of administration. Later authorities suggested that that an administrator need not seek the court's approval to dispose of the company's property or undertaking in advance of the creditors' meeting sanctioning such a course.[99] In *T & D Industries Plc, Re*,[100] Neuberger J. opined that, in cases of extreme urgency, the administrator should be free to proceed without the sanction of the court or creditors' committee, although he noted that it might be expedient to informally consult the company's major creditors (where there are only a few). An administrator was only required to act in accordance with the court's directions where such had been given. This approach has been adopted in relate to the "new" administration regime under Sch.B1.

Administrators applied to the court for directions as to whether they required a court order to sell the undertaking of the company prior to obtaining the approval of the creditors' meeting. It was held that no such order was required. The wording of para.68(2) appeared to mirror the authority of *Re T & D Industries*, reflecting a policy of non-interference by the courts in commercial decisions of administrators.[101]

28–016   Notwithstanding the above, creditors are given power to challenge the administrator's conduct of the company by application to court. By para.74, any creditor or member may apply to court claiming that the administrator has acted or is acting in such a way as to "unfairly harm the interests of the applicant" (whether alone or in common with some or all other creditors or members).[102] An application may also be made on the grounds that an administrator is proposing to act in such a way.[103] Creditors and members may also make an application based on an allegation that the administrator is not performing his functions as quickly or efficiently as is reasonably practicable: para.74(2). The court, on hearing such an application, may grant relief, dismiss it, adjourn the hearing, make an interim order or make any order it thinks appropriate,[104] and in particular may regulate the administrator's exercise of his functions, require him to do or not to do a specified thing, require creditors' meeting to be held or provide for the administrator's appointment to cease to have effect.[105] No order may be made where it would

[98] (1988) B.C.C. 72.
[99] *NS Distribution Ltd, Re* [1990] B.C.L.C. 169 (single asset); *Charnley Davies Ltd, Re* [1990] B.C.C. 605 (entire undertaking).
[100] [2000] 1 W.L.R. 646.
[101] *Transbus International, Re* [2004] EWCA 932.
[102] para.74(1)(a).
[103] para.74(1)(b).
[104] para.74(3).
[105] para.74(4).

impede or prevent the implementation of a voluntary arrangement, a scheme of arrangement or proposals (original or revised) approved more than 28 days before the application: para.74(6).

This provision is worded slightly differently to its predecessor, s.27 Insolvency Act 1986, in that it refers to conduct which would "unfairly harm" the interests of the applicant, rather than "unfairly prejudice" those interests. There was, perhaps surprisingly, little authority on s.27, save that holding that it did not apply where the allegation was that the administrator had been negligent.[106] In general, the courts have been reluctant to interfere with commercial decisions taken by administrators and have thus discouraged the use of s.27 to attempt to persuade them to second guess his judgment.[107] It appears that a similar approach will be taken in relation to para.74.

A group of investors has deposited certain securities with a company as collateral should the company make advances to them, these securities, along with those of many others in a similar position, constituting property held by the company on trust. The company entered administration and directions were given to the administrators to establish a "Trust Property Team" to deal with the question of ownership of the many securities. Administrators' proposals to this effect were approved by a creditors' meeting. The claimants argued that the agreement of terms for the transfer of their securities immediately prior to the company's insolvency meant that the administrators were in a position to provide further information requested and that failure to do so amounted to unfair prejudice for the purposes of para.74. It was held that no instance of *unfair* harm had occurred. While the administrators' refusal to provide the information requested might harm the applicants' interests it did not do so *unfairly*. The administrators were acting at all times in accordance with court directions and approved proposals, and it was therefore difficult to see how this could amount to unfairness. Compliance with the applicants' request would require the administrators to divert time and resources which may prove detrimental to the interests of other parties in their position.[108]

This important case acknowledges, absolutely correctly it is submitted, that **28–017** administration is a procedure requiring the exercise of professional commercial judgment, and that where such judgment has been exercised in favour of a particular course of action, and that course has been sanctioned by the creditors generally, it is not for the court to substitute its own opinion of the commercial exigencies of the circumstances at the behest of one or more creditors whose interests may be harmed by the execution of the proposals.

Paragraph 75 provides that the court may examine the conduct of an administrator on the grounds of misfeasance. An application may be made under this paragraph by the official receiver, an administrator[109], the liquidator of the company, a creditor of the company or a contributory of the company[110] and must allege that the administrator has misapplied or retained money or other property of the company, has become accountable for such money or property, has breached a

---

[106] *Charnley Davies, Re* [1990] B.C.C. 605, per Millett J. at 624.
[107] See, e.g. *MTI Trading Systems Ltd v Winter* [1998] B.C.C. 591.
[108] *Lehman Bros International (Europe), Re* [2008] EWHC 2869.
[109] Obviously, a subsequent administrator!
[110] para.75(2).

fiduciary or other duty owed to the company or has been guilty of misfeasance.[111] On an examination under para.75, the court may order the administrator to repay, restore or account for money or other property of the company, to pay interest, or to contribute a sum of money to the company's property by way of compensation for breach of duty or misfeasance.[112] Where the administrator in question has been discharged under para.98[113] an application may only be made with the permission of the court: para.75(6).

PRE-PACKAGED ADMINISTRATIONS[114]

28–018 The relationship between an administrator and creditors, particularly the company's unsecured creditors, has been brought sharply into focus in recent years by the emergence of the "pre-pack" strategy as a method of selling the business of an insolvent company. The defining characteristic of the pre-pack is that the going concern sale is negotiated *prior to the commencement of a formal insolvency procedure*. The purchaser is identified, as are the assets to be transferred and the consideration to be paid for those assets, in what might be termed the run-up to the formal insolvency. Once the insolvency procedure, usually administration, commences, the contract for sale is very quickly executed, and often on the opening day of the administration. This can be compared with the position where the procedure commences and the practitioner, believing the business to be saleable, takes steps to market it with a view to concluding an agreement for its sale as a going concern sale.

In a pre-pack, the negotiation stage will involve, inter alia, the obtaining of valuations, discussions on what assets are to be transferred, what price is to be paid for those assets, how and when payment is to be made, and to what extent creditors of the company should be consulted prior to the actual insolvency appointment. It may be crucial to consult certain contracting partners in order to determine whether they would be willing to novate executory agreements *after* the pre-pack has been completed, and, indeed, major suppliers, customers and employees whose business or co-operation is as vital to "Newco" as it was to "Oldco" may also be contacted. While it is important to acknowledge that there is no definitive template for a pre-pack sale, and that the process will vary enormously depending on the individual circumstances of the case, there will invariably be a negotiation stage of greater or lesser duration.

The pre-pack strategy has generated an unprecedented level of debate, and it is not proposed to consider in detail the propriety or otherwise of the pre-pack here. In brief, the main complaints concerning pre-packs are: (a) that they disenfranchise creditors

---

[111] para.75(3). This paragraph is now a substitute for Insolvency Act 1986 s.212, from which all references to an administrator have been removed. Case law on s.212 may still be of relevance, however, given the close similarity between the wording of the two provisions.

[112] para. 75(4).

[113] Below.

[114] There is a growing body of literature on pre-packs: for an "early" consideration of the issues see Finch, *Pre-packaged Administrations: Bargains in the Shadow of Insolvency or Shadowy Bargains?* [2006] JBL 568; Walton, *Pre-packaged administrations—trick or treat?* 2006 Insolv. Int. 19(8), 113–122. For an empirical view, see Frisby, *A preliminary analysis of pre-packaged administrations* (2007) available at: *https://www.r3.org.uk/uploads/documents/preliminary%20analysis%20of%20pre-packed%20administrations.pdf* [accessed June 5, 2010].

who, by definition, will be prevented from exercising their rights to approve an administrator's proposals where a pre-pack has occurred, as they are presented with a fait accompli; (b) that they may result in the business in question being sold at an undervalue, as it has not been exposed to the competitive forces of the market; and (c) that they encourage and facilitate "debt dumping" on the part of owner/managers of insolvent companies: such owner/managers are able, through the use of the administration procedure, to appoint an administrator who will sell the business of the insolvent company to them free of its unsecured debts. In favour of pre-packs, it is argued that they operate to prevent the depreciation of the value of the business which would inevitably occur on the announcement of its insolvency; that they are, in many cases, the *only* means of selling the business, especially where there is no funding available to trade the business whilst a purchaser is sought; and that they are exceptionally effective in preserving employment within the insolvent business, as the employees of the insolvent company are transferred to the new purchasing entity.

As far as the *legality* of pre-packs is concerned, the position now seems reason- **28–019** ably well settled. Whilst no court has ever explicitly addressed the question of whether a pre-pack effected through administration is lawful, plenty have had the opportunity to answer it in the negative and have studiously avoided doing so. Indeed, applications to court for the appointment of an administrator frequently result in administration orders being made where the court is well aware that a pre-pack is contemplated.[115] In *Johnson Machine and Tool Co Ltd, Re*[116] Judge Purle QC observed that ". . . [t]he legitimacy of pre-packs and the jurisdiction to make an order allowing pre-appointment costs are not in doubt" and the Court of Appeal, in *Innovate Logistics Ltd v Sunberry Properties Ltd*,[117] has inferentially sanctioned the practice of pre-packing. This position is probably correct, and it was noted above that there is no legal impediment to administrators acting without the approval of the creditors or the court.[118] However, certain elements of a pre-packaged administration may be open to challenge by other means.

The business of a firm of solicitors was sold by way of a pre-pack administration. The firm's major creditor was informed minutes before the agreement was executed and objected strongly to the value ascribed to the business. The creditor brought proceedings under para.88 of Sch.B1 of the Insolvency Act 1986 seeking the removal of the administrator who had assisted in the negotiations for the sale of the business, contending that the arrangement gave rise to suspicions and should be the subject of scrutiny by an independent liquidator. It was held that the administrator should be removed on the application of the creditor in question. There were sufficient elements of uncertainty regarding the sale agreement to warrant an investigation of it in a subsequent liquidation, and the incumbent administrator, having been involved in its negotiation and execution, was in a position of conflict as regards such investigation and so should be replaced: *Clydesdale Financial Services v Smailes* [2009] EWHC 1745 (Ch.).

---

[115] See, e.g. *DKLL Solicitors v Revenue and Customs Commissioners* [2007] EWHC 2067 (Ch.); *Kayley Vending Ltd, Re* [2009] EWHC 904 (Ch.).
[116] [2010] EWHC 582 (Ch.).
[117] [2008] EWCA Civ. 1321.
[118] See above, p.680, and see *Re T & D Industries Plc* [2000] 1 W.L.R. 646; *Transbus International, Re* [2004] EWCA 932.

ENDING ADMINISTRATION

28–020 An administration appointment automatically ceases to have effect one year after the date on which it took effect: para.76(1). However, the administrator may apply to court to have his term of office extended for a specified period or that term may be extended by consent for a specified period not exceeding six months: para.76(2).[119] In the latter case, consent means the consent of each secured creditor of the company and that of at least 50 per cent of the company's unsecured creditors: para.78(1). A court extension may be made where there has already been an extension by consent, but not after the expiry of the administrator's term of office: para.77.[120] The Registrar of companies must be notified of any order made under para.76: para.77(3).

An administrator's term of office may be extended by consent only once, and not after an extension by the court or after expiry: para.78(4). The court and the Registrar of companies must be notified of any extension by consent and there are penalties for non-compliance: para.78(5), (6).

An administration appointment may also come to an end where the administrator applies to the court if he thinks the purpose of the administration cannot be achieved, that the company should not have entered administration or where a creditors' meeting requires him to make an application: para.79. Further, where the appointment was made by court order, the administrator must make an application if he thinks the purpose of the administration has been sufficiently achieved: para.79(3). A similar provision applies where the administrator was appointed out of court[121] and the administrator thinks the purpose of the administration has been sufficiently achieved: para.80. In this latter case the administrator may file a notice in the prescribed form with the court and the Registrar of companies, at which point his appointment ceases to have effect: para.80(2), (3).

28–021 The court may end an administration on the application of a creditor of the company under para.81. Such an application must allege an improper motive on the part of the person making an administration application (in the case of a court-ordered administration) or the administrator's appointor (in the case of an appointment under paras 14 or 22): para.81. Where a winding up order is made in the public interest[122] or under s.367 of the Financial Services and Markets Act the court may order that the appointment of an administrator shall cease to have effect or that it shall continue to have effect: para.82.

It is now possible, under Sch.B1, to move the company from administration to creditors' voluntary liquidation or to dissolution. Where an administrator thinks that the total amount payable to secured creditors has been paid or set aside and that a distribution will be made to unsecured creditors he may send a notice to the Registrar of companies stating that para.83 applies: para.83(1), (2) (in Scotland), (3). Such notice should also be sent to the court and creditors: para.83(5). On the registration of the notice the appointment of the administrator ceases to have

---

[119] For an example of such an extension, see *Top Marques Car Rental, Re* [2006] EWHC 745 (Ch.).
[120] But see, exceptionally, *TT Industries Ltd, Re* [2006] B.C.C. 372.
[121] i.e., under paras 14 or 22.
[122] Under Insolvency Act 1986 s.124A.

effect and the company is wound up as though a resolution for voluntary winding up had been passed. The liquidator may be a person nominated by the creditors or, if no nomination is made, the administrator: para.83(6)(7).

If the administrator thinks that there will be no property to distribute to creditors he may send a notice to this effect to the Registrar and, on registration of the notice, his appointment ceases to have effect and the company proceeds to dissolution: para.84. It has been held that nothing in either paras 83 or 84 requires the administrator to obtain a court order for a move to a creditors' voluntary liquidation or dissolution. The appointment is brought to an end by the registration of the notice and it is a matter for the administrator whether to send the notice. These provisions are designed to produce administrative efficiency and costs savings: *Re Ballast Plc.*[123]

An administrator may resign in circumstances prescribed by the Insolvency Rules 1986, r.2.119[124] and only by giving written notice to the person who appointed him (i.e., the court, a qualifying floating charge holder, the company or its directors): para.87. He must vacate office if he ceases to be qualified to act as an insolvency practitioner: para.89. The court is also given power under para.88 to remove an administrator from office.[125] In any of the above cases, and in the case of the death of the administrator, paras 91–95 have effect to fill the vacancy left by the administrator. Depending upon the mode of appointment, the court, a qualifying floating charge holder, the company or its directors may replace the administrator. Where the company or its directors propose to replace the administrator they may only do so with the consent of any qualifying floating charge holder or permission of the court: para.94.

VACATION OF OFFICE: CHARGES AND LIABILITIES

Where a person ceases to be administrator of a company his remuneration and **28–022** expenses shall be charged on and payable property over which he had custody or control immediately before cessation and in priority to any security to which para.70 applies: para.99(3). This provision elevates the administrator's remuneration and expenses above the claims of floating charge holders. The expenses of the administration are payable in the order listed in the Insolvency Rules 1986 r.2.67, the ruling in *Toshoku Finance UK Plc, Re*[126] will apply in this regard. The charge referred to in para.99(3) is deferred to any liability arising under a contract of employment adopted by him or his predecessor to the extent that sum sums constitute "qualifying liabilities". An administrator adopts a contract of employment if he causes the company to continue the employment for mare than fourteen days after his appointment: para.99(5). No adoption will take place where no positive action is taken by the administrator.

Administrators were appointed and continued to use the services of employees they believed to be employed by the company's subsidiary. In fact these employees

---

[123] [2004] EWHC 2356.
[124] Intention to cease practice as an insolvency practitioner, conflict of interest, change in personal circumstances or, on other grounds, with the permission of the court.
[125] See, e.g. *Clydesdale Financial Services v Smailes* [2009] EWHC 1745.
[126] [2002] UKHL 6.

were employed by the company in administration. This fact was discovered 16 days after the administrators' appointment, at which point steps were taken to terminate the employment. It was held that the administrators had not adopted the contracts of employment. Adoption involved a choice on the part of the administrators to adopt the contracts in question: *Antal International Ltd, Re* [2003] B.C.L.C. 406.

Qualifying liabilities are defined in terms similar to those applicable to administrative receivers.[127]

Where a person ceases to be administrator of a company he is discharged from liability in respect of any action of his as administrator: para.98(1). This does not prevent a challenge to the conduct of the administrator on the grounds of misfeasance under para.75: para.98(4).[128]

ADJUSTMENT OF PRIOR TRANSACTIONS

28–023 In administration, certain charges and other transactions may be liable to be set aside under ss.238–246 of the Insolvency Act 1986. These sections also apply on a liquidation and are dealt with in Ch.29 below.

---

[127] See above, p.659.
[128] For misfeasance, see above, p.681.

Chapter 29

WINDING UP BY THE COURT

This chapter and the following two chapters deal with the winding up of a **29–001**
company, which is governed by the Insolvency Act 1986. That Act is a consolidation of parts of the Companies Act 1985 (itself a consolidation) and the
Insolvency Act 1985. A winding up may be:

1.   by the court; or

2.   voluntary (s.73).[1]

and there are two kinds of voluntary winding up, namely:

1.   a members' voluntary winding up (IA 1986 Ch.III); and

2.   a creditors' voluntary winding up (IA 1986 Ch.IV).

It will be recalled that winding up by the court on the "just and equitable ground"
was explained in Ch.18. Chapter 31 (Contributories and Creditors; Completion of
the Winding Up) is partly concerned with winding up by the court, as well as the
present chapter. Chapter 30 is concerned with voluntary winding up.

Section 1000 of the Companies Act 2006, which is explained in Ch.31,[2]
provides a method of dissolving a defunct company by striking it off the register
without a winding up, and under s.900(2)(d) of the Companies Act 1985, below,[3]
the court may order dissolution without winding up where there is a compromise
or an arrangement to facilitate a reconstruction or an amalgamation. In addition
to the statutory provisions, the Insolvency Rules[4] (hereinafter IR) make numerous
provisions as to the winding up of companies.

JURISDICTION TO WIND UP COMPANIES

To obtain a winding up by the court, a petition must be presented to the court **29–002**
having the necessary jurisdiction. Section 117 provides that the courts having
jurisdiction are:

---

[1] A third form, winding up subject to supervision of the court, was abolished by the Insolvency Act
  1985. In practice that form was not used.
[2] Below, p.756.
[3] p.780.
[4] SI 1986/1925.

1.   the High Court, i.e. the Companies Court,[5] in the case of all companies registered in England;

2.   where the paid-up share capital does not exceed £120,000,[6] the county court of the district in which the registered office is situated, provided that such county court has winding up jurisdiction.[7]

GROUNDS FOR WINDING UP BY THE COURT

29–003 Section 122 provides that a company[8] may be wound up by the court if:

1.   the company has by special resolution resolved to be wound up by the court[9];

2.   in the case of a public company first registered as such, no certificate of entitlement to commence business has been issued and the company has been registered for more than one year[10];

3.   it is an old public company, within the meaning of Sch.3 to the Companies Act 2006 (Consequential Amendments, Transitional Provisions and Savings) Order 2009;

4.   the company does not commence business within a year after its incorporation, or suspends business for a whole year[11];

5.   except in the case of a private company limited by shares or by guarantee, the number of members is reduced below two;

6.   the company is unable to pay its debts;

7.   the time for a moratorium under s.1A has come to an end without the approval of a voluntary arrangement; or

8.   the court is of opinion that it is just and equitable that the company should be wound up. This part of the section was explained in connection with statutory protection of the minority.[12] It should be added that the power to wind up a company under this part is not confined to cases in which there are grounds analogous to those mentioned earlier in the section[13].

---

[5] *Eastern Holdings v Singer & Friedlander Ltd* [1967] 1 W.L.R. 1017.

[6] This amount can be varied by order.

[7] See Civil Courts Order 1983 (SI 1983/713) as amended; s.117(4).

[8] i.e. one formed or registered under the Companies Act 2006 or a former Companies Act: CA 2006 ss.1(1), 1171: IA 1986 s.73.

[9] cf. s.84, below, p.726, which is more commonly resorted to, under which a company may pass a special resolution to be wound up voluntarily.

[10] See above, p.55.

[11] cf. CA 2006 s.1000, below, p.756, under which a defunct company may be struck off the register and so dissolved without being wound up.

[12] Above, p.526.

[13] *Loch v John Blackwood Ltd* [1924] A.C. 783, PC; *Symington v Symingtons' Quarries Ltd* (1905) 8 F. 121; *Baird v Lees*, 1924 S.C. 83; *Ebrahimi v Westbourne Galleries Ltd* [1973] A.C. 360.

Ground (4): Company not carrying on business

The period of a year is fixed by s.122, above, so as to give the company a reason-   **29–004**
able time in which to commence or resume business, as the case may be. A
winding up order will only be made on this ground if the company has no intention of carrying on business.[14]

A company was formed to build and use assembly rooms. Owing to a depression in trade in the neighbourhood, building was suspended for more than three
years although the company intended to continue its operations when trade
prospects improved. A shareholder presented a winding up petition which was
opposed by four-fifths of the shareholders. It was held that the petition should be
dismissed. Since the conduct of the majority was not unreasonable or something
of which the minority had a right to complain, the wishes of the majority were not
to be disregarded. It would have been different if business could not have been
carried on or there was an intention to abandon the undertaking.[15]

If a company is formed to carry on business in England and abroad and has
carried on business abroad, it will not be wound up merely on the ground that it
has not started its business in England within the year if it intends to do so as soon
as possible.[16] There is no need to wait a year if it is apparent within the year that
the company cannot carry out the objects for which it was formed.[17]

Ground (5): Company unable to pay its debts

This is the ground on which a petition for a compulsory winding up is usually   **29–005**
presented A company is deemed to be unable to pay its debts[18] under s.123 of the
IA 1986 if:

1.   a creditor, by assignment or otherwise, to whom the company is
     indebted in a sum exceeding £750[19] then due has served on the
     company, by leaving it at the registered office,[20] a demand in the
     prescribed form[21] requiring the company to pay the sum so due, and
     the company has for three weeks thereafter neglected to pay the sum
     due or to secure[22] or compound for it to the creditor's satisfaction;

---

[14] *Metropolitan Rlwy Warehousing Co, Re* (1867) 36 L.J. Ch. 827.
[15] *Middlesborough Assembly Rooms Co, Re* (1880) 14 Ch.D. 104, CA.
[16] *Capital Fire Insurance Association, Re* (1882) 21 Ch.D. 209.
[17] *German Date Coffee Co, Re* (1882) 20 Ch.D. 169, CA (petition on the "just and equitable" ground).
[18] The definition of "debts" for this purpose is found in IR 1986 r.13.12.
[19] This sum may be increased by order.
[20] The demand need not be served by an officer of the court (*Lord Advocate v Traprain*, 1989 S.L.T.
(Sh. Ct.) 99), but, if it is not, the court must have evidence that the person who served the statutory
demand was duly authorised by the creditor (*Lord Advocate v Blairwest Investment Ltd*, 1989 S.L.T.
(Sh. Ct.) 97). A statutory demand by a person bearing to act for and on behalf of the creditor is sufficient service: *Lord Advocate, Petitioner*, 1993 S.L.T. 1324, OH. It has been held that a demand sent
by telex did not comply with the statutory requirement: *A Company, Re* [1985] B.C.L.C. 37.
[21] See IR 1986 rr.4.4–4.6; Form 4.1.
[22] The security must be a marketable security covering the amount of the debt: *Commercial Bank of
Scotland Ltd v Lanark Oil Co Ltd* (1986) 14 R. 147.

2. in England and Wales, execution issued on a judgment in favour of a creditor is returned unsatisfied in whole or in part;

3. in Scotland, the induciae of a charge for payment on an extract decree have expired without payment being made;

4. it is proved to the satisfaction of the court that the company is unable to pay its debts as they fall due; or

5. if it is proved to the satisfaction of the court that, taking the company's contingent and prospective liabilities into account, the value of its assets is less than the amount of its liabilities: s.123(2).

A company has not neglected to pay a debt within 1 above, if it bona fide and upon substantial grounds disputes the debt.[23] Winding up proceedings are not appropriate for the adjudication of the question whether the petitioner is a creditor or not.[24] The creditor must prove that the demand was left at the company's registered office; if this can be proved, it does not matter whether it was left by the creditor personally or by an agent or employee. If it is put in the post, it is properly served if delivery is accepted or proved.[25]

The period of three weeks' neglect required in 1. above, has been held to be a period of three clear weeks, excluding the day of service of the demand for payment and the day of presentation of the petition.[26] A creditor will not rely upon a statutory demand where there is a risk of dissipation of the assets in the three-week interval. If available, he may use 2 3 or 5 above, although the evidence necessary under 5 may be difficult to obtain as far as the creditor is concerned. An alternative route is therefore to employ the more general ground in 4—that the company is unable to pay its debts as they fall due.

29–006   Thus in *Taylor's Industrial Flooring Ltd v M.H. Plant Hire Manchester Ltd*[27] it was held that if a debt was due and unpaid and could not be disputed on some substantial ground, the presentation of a petition under ground 4 above, was amply warranted even in the absence of a statutory demand. The Court of Appeal commented that the practice of prevaricating in the payment of due debts was to be discouraged, and this approach has been followed even where, in the past a creditor has consistently accepted late payments of due and undisputed debts[28] and where a company has failed to pay a due and undisputed debt but there is evidence of a substantial surplus of assets over liabilities.[29]

A company is also unable to pay its debts if its acceptances have been dishonoured[30] or it has informed a judgment creditor that it has no assets on which to

[23] *London and Paris Banking Corporation, Re* (1874) L.R. 19 Eq. 444; *Cunninghame v Walkinshaw Oil Co Ltd* (1866) 14 R. 87.
[24] *Stonegate Securities Ltd v Gregory* [1980] 1 All E.R. 241, per Buckley L.J. at 243; *Richbell Strategic Holdings Ltd, Re* [1997] 2 B.C.L.C. 429; *Customs and Excise v Broomco (1984) Ltd* [2000] B.T.C. 8035.
[25] *A Company, Re (No 008790 of 1990)* [1992] B.C.C. 11; cf. *A Company, Re* [1985] B.C.L.C. 37.
[26] See *Lympne Investments Ltd, Re* [1972] 1 W.L.R. 523.
[27] [1990] B.C.L.C. 216.
[28] *Easy Letting and Leasing, Re* [2008] EWHC 3175 (Ch.).
[29] *Cornhill Insurance Plc v Improvement Services Ltd* [1986] 1 W.L.R. 114.
[30] *Globe, etc. Steel Co, Re* (1875) L.R. 20 Eq. 337; *Gandy, Petitioner*, 1912 2 S.L.T. 276.

levy execution,[31] or the petitioner has demanded the sum due to him without success,[32] or the company disputes a comparatively small amount but fails to pay a much larger outstanding balance due to the same creditor.[33] A company is not unable to pay its debts just because it is carrying on a losing business, if its assets exceed its liabilities.[34] However, a company may be unable to pay its debts under 4 where its assets exceed its liabilities if its assets are not presently available to meet its current liabilities. Where a company persistently fails or neglects to pay its debts until forced to do so,[35] the court may find that it is unable to pay its debts under 4: *A Company, Re* [1986] B.C.L.C. 261. Where a petition is dismissed by consent on the company making late payment, costs may be awarded against the company.[36]

While grounds 2–4, above, do not require the petitioner's debt to be £750 or more, in practice, an order will not usually be made unless this condition is complied with, since there must be circumstances which justify an inference that the company is insolvent.[37] On the other hand, where a company refused to pay a debt of £35 on the ground that it was too small to be the foundation of a petition, an order was made.[38]

PERSONS WHO MAY PETITION FOR WINDING UP BY THE COURT

Subject as below, a winding up petition may be presented by any of the following **29–007** parties:

1. the company or its directors, under s.124(1) of the IA 1986. Where the petition is presented by the directors of the company they must act unanimously[39];

2. a creditor or creditors under s.124(1) of the IA 1986 (including contingent and prospective creditors);

3. a contributory under s.124(1), (2) of the IA 1986[40];

4. the Secretary of State (IA 1986 s.124(4))[41];

---

[31] *Flagstaff etc. Co of Utah, Re* (1875) L.R. 20 Eq. 268; *Douglas Griggs Engineering Ltd, Re* [1963] Ch. 19.

[32] *Stephen, Petitioner* (1884) 21 S.L.R. 764.

[33] *Blue Star Security Services (Scotland) Ltd, Petitioners*, 1992 S.L.T. (Sh. Ct.) 80.

[34] *Joint Stock Coal Company, Re* (1869) L.R. 8 Eq. 146.

[35] See, in this regard, the Late Payment of Commercial Debts (Interest) Act 1998 which implies a term into contracts for the supply of goods and services, where both parties are acting in the course of a business, entitling the supplier to statutory interest in the event of late payment.

[36] *Nowmost Co Ltd, Re* [1997] B.C.C. 105. See also *Yell.com v Internet Business Centres Ltd* 2003 S.L.T. (Sh Ct) 80.

[37] *Industrial Assurance Association, Re* [1910] W.N. 245.

[38] *World Industrial Bank, Re* [1909] W.N. 148.

[39] *Instrumentation Electrical Services, Re* (1988) 4 B.C.L.C. 550.

[40] Where a party has agreed to take shares in the company but the transfer has yet to be registered, that party is not a contributory for the purposes of IA 1986 s.124(1): *Quickdome Ltd, Re* (1988) 4 B.C.C. 296.

[41] If the case falls within s.122(1)(b) or (c), or 124A.

5. the Regulator of Community Interest Companies in cases falling under s.50 of the Companies (Audit, Investigations and Community Enterprise) Act 2004: s.124(4A)

6. in England and Wales, where the company is already being wound up voluntarily, the official receiver (s.124(5));

7. in the case of a charitable company, the Attorney General (Charities Act 1993 s.63(1)).

A creditor

29–008 A compulsory liquidation is usually initiated by a creditor's petition. A secured creditor may petition but will normally rely on his security so that the petitioner is almost always an unsecured creditor. Where a petitioning creditor's debt is disputed on a substantial ground the court will usually restrain the prosecution of the petition as an abuse of the process of the court, even if the company appears to be insolvent.[42] On the other hand, even if the company is solvent, a creditor whose debt is clearly established can present a petition if there is a persistent refusal to pay the debt,[43] and no bona fide defence.[44]

A creditor whose debt is presently due and who cannot obtain payment normally has a right as between himself and the company ex debito justitiae to a winding up order,[45] even if the company is being wound up voluntarily[46] or is in receivership.[47] This is not displaced merely by showing that the company has appealed against the judgment giving rise to the debt,[48] or has a disputed claim against the petitioning judgment creditor which is the subject of litigation in other proceedings.[49] Where there is a cross-claim the matter is one for the discretion of the judge.[50] If the company has a serious claim for an amount exceeding that of the petitioning creditors debt which it has been unable to litigate, the petition should be dismissed or stayed, unless there are special circumstances.[51] Such circumstances include the fact that the petitioner's undisputed claim significantly exceeds the amount of the cross-claim,[52] that the company had made no serious

---

[42] *Mann v Goldstein* [1968] 1 W.L.R. 1091. A creditor must show an interest in the winding up; a petitioner who has been paid in full after the presentation of petition no longer has such an interest: *Furmston, Petitioner*, 1987 S.L.T. (Sh. Ct.) 10.

[43] *Cornhill Insurance Plc v Improvement Services Ltd* [1986] 1 W.L.R. 114.

[44] *A Company, Re (No.0012209 of 1991)* [1992] 2 All E.R. 797; *A Compay, Re (No.0160 of 2004)* [2004] EWHC 380.

[45] See *Chapel House Colliery Co, Re* (1883) 24 Ch.D. 259, CA; *Gardner & Co v Link* (1894) 21 R. 967.

[46] *James Millward & Co Ltd, Re* [1940] Ch. 333, CA; *Smyth & Co v The Salem (Oregon) Capitol Flour Mills Co Ltd* (1887) 14 R. 441.

[47] *Foxhall & Gyle (Nurseries) Ltd, Petitioners*, 1978 S.L.T. (Notes) 29, OH.

[48] *Amalgamated Properties of Rhodesia, Re* (1913) Ltd [1917] 2 Ch. 115, CA.

[49] *Douglas Griggs Engineering Ltd, Re* [1963] Ch. 19; cf. *Fitness Centre (South East) Ltd, Re* [1986] B.C.L.C. 518.

[50] *L.H.F. Wools Ltd, Re* [1969] 3 All E.R. 882, CA; *A Company, Re (No.006273 of 1992)* [1992] B.C.C. 794.

[51] *Bayoil, S.A., Re* [1998] B.C.C. 988. CA.

[52] *Alexander Sheridan Ltd v Beaujersey Ltd* [2004] EWHC 2072.

attempt to litigate the cross-claim,[53] and that there is insufficient evidence to support the existence of the cross-claim.[54]

It is, however, an improper use of the court to present a petition on the basis of a debt which has never been demanded and for which no opportunity to repay has been given.[55] It is an abuse of the process of the court to maximise pressure on the company by simultaneously serving the petition on the company and faxing notice to its bankers precipitating the disruption of the company's bank account and depriving it of the opportunity to consider its position.[56] The re-presentation of a dishonoured cheque suspends the creditor's right to payment and the presentation of a petition to wind up is in these circumstances an abuse of the process of the court.[57] A petitioning creditor's solicitor may be ordered to pay the company's costs where the petition was filed improperly, unreasonably or negligently.[58]

The ex debito justitiae rule applies only between the petitioning creditor and the **29–009** company. As between the petitioning creditor and the other creditors he is invoking a class right and so it is improper for him to present a petition for some private purpose. On the other hand if the petition is genuinely for the benefit of the class of creditors, malice on his part will not make the petition improper.[59] As with all matters relating to winding up, the court may have regard to the wishes of the creditors or contributories of the company, as proved by sufficient evidence, and may, for the purpose of ascertaining those wishes, direct meetings to be called, and in the case of creditors regard must be had to the value of each creditor's debt: s.195.[60] This gives the judge a wide unfettered discretion to decide whether to make the order or not. Once an administrator has been appointed, however, no winding-up order can be made and any such petition must be dismissed.[61]

Where the company is insolvent the views of the creditors alone, as the only persons interested, are considered. In other cases the views of the contributories are considered.[62] Where there are different classes of creditors the wishes of those particularly interested will be given most weight and, in particular, where the company's assets are not entirely charged in favour of debenture holders the wishes of the unsecured creditors will be primarily considered. Where the assets are entirely charged in favour of debenture holders, if the petition of an unsecured creditor is opposed by the debenture holders the petitioner is entitled to a winding up order unless the opposing creditors can show that there is no reasonable possibility of the unsecured creditors obtaining a benefit from a winding up.[63] The court must

[53] *Bolsover DC v Dennis Rye Ltd* [2009] EWCA Civ 372.
[54] *Accessory People Ltd v Rouass* [2010] EWCA Civ 302.
[55] *A Company, Re* [1983] B.C.L.C. 492.
[56] *Bill Hennessey Associates Ltd, Re* [1992] B.C.C. 386.
[57] *Ex p. Medialite* [1991] B.C.L.C. 594.
[58] *Ridehalgh v Horsefield* [1994] 3 All E.R. 848, CA; *A Company, Re (No.006798 of 1995)* [1996] 2 All E.R. 417.
[59] ibid.
[60] If there is a real prospect of formulating a voluntary arrangement (above pp.640 et seq.) which will command majority support a petition may be dismissed or suspended: *Dollar Land (Feltham) Ltd, Re* [1995] B.C.C. 740.
[61] Above, p.671.
[62] If only a contributory opposes a petition it will usually be granted: *Camburn Petroleum Products Ltd, Re* [1979] 1 W.L.R. 86, but see *Allso v Secretary of State for Trade and Industry* [2004] EWHC 862.
[63] Crigglestone Coal Co Ltd, Re* [1906] 2 Ch. 327, CA; Gardner's case, above.

not refuse a winding up order just because the assets of the company have been mortgaged to an amount in excess of those assets or there are no assets: s.125(1).

If the petition of an unsecured creditor is opposed by the majority in value of the unsecured creditors, although the court has a complete discretion under s.125(1), above, to make or refuse an order and the fact of the majority opposition is not conclusive, if they oppose for good reason (e.g. because the assets exceed the liabilities and there are prospects of the company being able to continue business) their wishes will prevail in the absence of special circumstances making winding up desirable.[64] Similarly if the petition is opposed by a minority of creditors this will normally not prevent the order being made although the wishes of the minority may prevail in special cases.[65]

If a company is being wound up voluntarily a compulsory order will not usually be made if the majority of the creditors want the voluntary liquidation to continue.[66] Where there are special circumstances the court may give effect to the wishes of the minority.[67]

Any assignee of a debt or a definite part of a debt can petition,[68] even if a petition was presented in respect of the debt before the assignment.[69] An equitable assignment of a debt by way of security does not affect the rights of the legal owner of the debt and the equity of redemption to petition for a winding up order.[70] However, a failure by a reinsurer to replenish a trust account established by agreement with an insurer did not render the latter a creditor of the former, so that the insurer had no locus standi to present a winding up petition.[71] A secured creditor can petition, and his security will not be prejudiced; the holder of bearer debentures can also petition.[72] It has been held that the holder of debenture stock secured by a normal trust deed cannot present a petition as he is not a creditor of the company,[73] the trustees being the proper persons to present the petition in such case.[74]

It has been held in England that a garnishor of a debt due from the company cannot petition, because he is not a creditor, a garnishee order only giving him a lien on the debt and not operating as a transfer of the debt,[75] and that a petition

---

[64] *Vuma Ltd, Re* [1960] 1 W.L.R. 1283, CA; *P & J Macrae Ltd, Re* [1961] 1 W.L.R. 229, CA. See also *A.B.C. Coupler Co, Re* [1961] 1 W.L.R. 243, *Fitness Centre (South East) Ltd, Re* [1986] B.C.L.C. 518.

[65] *Southard & Co Ltd, Re* [1979] 1 W.L.R. 1198, CA.

[66] *Home Remedies Ltd, Re* [1943] Ch. 1; *B. Karsberg Ltd, Re* [1956] 1 W.L.R. 57, CA; *J.D. Swain Ltd, Re* [1965] 1 W.L.R. 909, CA; cf. *Pattisons Ltd v Kinnear* (1899) 1 F. 551, *Elsmie & Son v The Tomatin etc. Distillery Ltd* (1906) 8 F. 434 and *Fitness Centre (South East) Ltd, Re* [1986] B.C.L.C. 518.

[67] *Bell's Trustees v The Holmes Oil Co Ltd* (1900) 3 F. 23; *Bouboulis v Mann, Macneal & Co Ltd*, 1926 S.C. 637; *Southard & Co Ltd, Re* [1979] 1 W.L.R. 1198, CA; *H.J. Tomkins & Son, Re* [1990] B.C.L.C. 76.

[68] See *Re Steel Wing Co* [1921] 1 Ch. 349.

[69] *Perak Pioneer Ltd v Petroleum National Bhd* [1986] 3 W.L.R. 105, PC; cf. *Re Paris Skating Rink* (1877) 5 Ch.D. 959.

[70] *Parmalat Capital Finance Ltd v Food Holdings Ltd (In Liquidation)* [2008] UKPC 23.

[71] *New Hampshire Insurance Co v Magellan Reinsurance Co Ltd* [2009] UKPC 33

[72] *Re Olathe Silver Mining Co* (1884) 27 Ch.D. 278.

[73] *Re Dunderland Iron Ore Co Ltd* [1909] 1 Ch. 446.

[74] But see Palmer's Company Law, para.14.312.

[75] *Combined Weighing Machine Co, Re* (1889) 43 Ch.D. 99, CA.

cannot be presented by a person with a claim against the company for unliquidated damages.[76] However, it may be that such persons can petition as
"contingent or prospective creditors."[77]

A contributory

The term "contributory" means every person liable to contribute to the assets of **29–010**
the company in the event of its being wound up. As we shall see, it includes the
present members and certain past members of the company: IA 1986 s.79.[78] A
holder of fully paid-up shares in a limited company is a contributory.[79]

   By s.124(2), the right of a contributory to present a petition is limited to cases
where:

   (1)   the number of members is reduced below two[80]: s.124(2)(a); or

   (2)   his shares, or some of them, were originally allotted to him or have been
         held by him, and registered in his name, for at least six months[81] during
         the 18 months before the commencement of the winding up, or have
         devolved on him through the death of a former holder: s.124(2)(b). The
         object of the latter provision is to prevent a person acquiring shares to
         qualify himself to present a petition to wreck the company.[82]

A shareholder whose calls are in arrear can petition, but he must first pay the
amount of the call into court.[83] A person to whom shares have been allotted can
petition even though the shares have not been registered in his name, unless there
is a bona fide dispute as to the allotment.[84] A person who is not an original
allottee cannot petition unless he has been registered as a shareholder.[85] A registered shareholder has locus standi to petition notwithstanding that he is disputing
the beneficial ownership of other shares. However, the court may order that the

---

[76] *Pen-y-Van Colliery Co, Re* (1877) 6 Ch.D. 477.

[77] *A Company, Re* [1973] 1 W.L.R. 1566 it was pointed out by Megarry J. at 1571 that the *Pen-y-Van*
case was decided on s.82 of the 1862 Act which, unlike the present section, says nothing about
contingent or prospective creditors and it is very doubtful whether it is an authority for the proposition that a claim for unliquidated damages will not support a petition. See also *Dollar Land
Holdings Plc, Re* [1993] B.C.C. 823.

[78] Below, p.738.

[79] *National Savings Bank Association, Re* (1866) L.R. 1 Ch. App. 547; *Walker and Others, Petitioners*
(1894) 2 S.L.T. 230 and 397, OH.

[80] The section does not apply where the company has always only had one shareholder. *Pimlico
Capital Ltd, Re* [2002] EWHC 878.

[81] See *Gattopardo Ltd, Re* [1969] 1 W.L.R. 619, CA, where an order was made that a name be entered
on the register of members but the company was not a party to the proceedings and therefore was
not bound to register the individual as a shareholder, and so the six months' period did not
commence when the order was made.

[82] Where the locus standi of a petitioner is disputed the court will consider all the circumstances,
including the likelihood of damage to the company if the petition is not dismissed, in deciding
whether to require the petitioner to seek the determination of his status outside the petition: *Alipour
v Ary (a Company), Re (No.002180 of 1996)* [1997] 1 B.C.L.C. 557, CA.

[83] *Diamond Fuel Co, Re* (1879) 13 Ch.D. 499, CA.

[84] *J.N. 2, Re* [1978] 1 W.L.R. 183.

[85] *Quickdome, Re* (1988) B.C.L.C. 370 (mere agreement to acquire shares).

petition should not be advertised until the dispute has been settled.[86] In the case of the holder of a share warrant the shares are not "registered in his name", so that unless, e.g. he is an original allottee, he cannot petition.[87]

29–011   The trustee in bankruptcy of a bankrupt shareholder, where the trustee is not on the register of members, is not a contributory and cannot petition.[88] It seems that the personal representative of a deceased shareholder is a contributory.[89]

A person who may be required to repay an amount to an insolvent private company following a payment out of capital by that company for the purchase or redemption of its own shares under s.76,[90] may petition to wind up the company on either the just and equitable or insolvency grounds, but no others: s.124(3).

The court will not, as a rule, make an order on a contributory's petition unless the contributory alleges and proves a financial interest in the winding up. A member's liability to contribute to the assets of the company on a winding up will suffice for this purpose. A holder of fully paid shares however will have to show, at least to the extent of a prima facie case, that there will be assets for distribution among the shareholders,[91] or that the affairs of the company require investigation in respects which are likely to produce a surplus of assets available for such distribution.[92] However, where a contributory's petition is based on the just and equitable ground[93] and alleges a failure by the company to supply accounts and information about its affairs, so that he cannot tell whether there will be a surplus for contributories,[94] a surplus need not be shown. The jurisdiction of the court to order the winding up of a company on the just and equitable ground on a contributory's petition is very wide and depends upon a full investigation of the facts at the hearing. A contributory may rely on a report by Department of Trade and Industry inspectors to support his petition.[95] A petition by a contributory is uncommon. Such a petition which is opposed by the majority of the contributories will not be granted except where the conduct of the majority is something of which the minority have a right to complain.[96] The right of a contributory to petition cannot be excluded or limited by the articles.

---

[86] *Garage Door Associates Ltd, Re* [1984] 1 W.L.R. 35.

[87] Chitty J. in *Wala Wynaad India Gold Mining Co, Re* (1882) 21 Ch.D. 849 at 853.

[88] *H.L. Bolton Engineering Co Ltd, Re* [1956] Ch. 577 (s.82(2), by which the trustee represents the bankrupt shareholder, does not come into effect until a winding up order is made).

[89] See *Norwich Yarn Co, Re* (1850) 12 Beav. 366; *Cuthbert Cooper & Sons Ltd, Re* [1937] Ch. 392 at 399, where Simonds J. assumed, without deciding, that such a personal representative is a contributory, per Wynn-Parry J. in *H.L. Bolton Engineering Co Ltd, Re* [1956] Ch. 577 at 582; and *Meyer Douglas Pty Ltd, Re* [1965] V.R. 638, where Gowans J. pointed out at 655 that in *Norwich Yarn Co, Re* the statutory definition of "contributory" included not only every member, but also every other person liable to contribute, whether as an heir, devisee, executor or administrator of a deceased member. See also *Bayswater Trading Co Ltd, Re* [1970] 1 W.L.R. 343, and *Howling's Trustees v Smith* (1905) 7 F. 390.

[90] Above, Ch.10.

[91] *Rica Gold Washing Co, Re* (1879) 11 Ch.D. 36, CA; followed in *Expanded Plugs Ltd, Re* [1966] 1 W.L.R. 514; *Black v United Collieries Ltd* (1904) 7 F. 18, per Lord Trayner at 20. *O'Connor v Atlantis Fisheries Ltd*, 1998 G.W.D. 8–359 (Sh. Ct.).

[92] *Re Othery Construction Ltd* [1966] 1 W.L.R. 69, considering *Haycraft Gold etc., Co, Re* [1900] 2 Ch. 230 and *Newman and Howard, Re* [1962] Ch. 257.

[93] Above, p.526.

[94] *Newman and Howard Ltd, Re* [1962] Ch. 257.

[95] *St. Piran Ltd, Re* [1981] 3 All E.R. 270.

[96] *Middlesborough Assembly Rooms Co, Re* (1880) 14 Ch.D. 104, CA, above; *Galbraith v Merito Shpg Co Ltd*, 1947 S.C. 446; *Tivoli Freeholds Ltd, Re* [1972] V.R. 445; *St. Piran Ltd, Re* [1981] 3 All E.R. 270.

The articles provided that no winding-up petition could be presented without the consent of two directors, or unless a resolution to wind up was passed at a general meeting, or unless the petitioner held one-fifth of the share capital. None of these conditions was fulfilled. Held, the restrictions were invalid and a petition could be presented.[97]

The Official Receiver

The official receiver can petition for a winding up by the court when a company is **29–012** already in voluntary liquidation in England. An order will only be made if the court is satisfied on a balance of probabilities,[98] that the existing liquidation cannot be continued with due regard to the interests of the creditors or contributories: s.124(5). The fact that a liquidator must now be a qualified insolvency practitioner and, in a creditors' voluntary winding up, his powers are restricted prior to the creditors' meeting, may reduce the occasions upon which this can be shown. However, the court may be disposed to grant an order where there is suspicion of "sharp practice" that calls for independent and impartial investigation.[99]

The Secretary of State

Where a petition for compulsory winding up is presented by the Secretary of **29–013** State after he has reached the conclusion (which need not to be based on evidence of illegality[100]) that it is expedient in the public interest to wind up the company compulsorily,[101] it is for the court to decide on the material before it whether it is just and equitable to make the winding up order.[102] Where there are circumstances of suspicion or some evidence of commercially unacceptable conduct it is highly desirable that the winding up be by the court.[103] However, where a winding up order was sought on this ground and the company in question demonstrated that it had adopted a new business model and given undertakings as to the future conduct of its agents and representatives, the petition was dismissed.[104] the passing of a resolution for voluntary winding up shortly before the petition is presented ought not to be allowed to put the voluntary winding up in an entrenched position which can only be demolished if the Secretary of State can show that voluntary winding up would be markedly inferior to compulsory winding up.[105]

A report of inspectors appointed by him is prima facie evidence on which the court may act in deciding to make a winding up order on a petition by the

---

[97] *Peveril Gold Mines Ltd* [1898] 1 Ch. 122, CA.

[98] *J. Russell Electronics Ltd, Re* [1968] 1 W.L.R. 1252.

[99] *Gordon & Breach Science Publishers Ltd, Re* [1995] B.C.C. 261.

[100] *S.H.V. Senator Hanseatische Verwaltungs GmbH, Re* [1997] B.C.C. 112 (lottery).

[101] See IA 1986 s.124A and p.562 above.

[102] *Walter L Jacob & Co Ltd, Re* [1989] B.C.L.C. 345.

[103] See, e.g. *Equity & Provident Ltd, Re* [2002] EWHC 186.

[104] *Secretary of State for Business, Enterprise and Regulatory Reform v Amway (UK) Ltd* [2009] EWCA Civ. 32.

[105] *Lubin, Rosen and Associates, Re* [1975] 1 W.L.R. 122.

Secretary of State.[106] The Secretary of State's petition is in his own capacity and not that of a notional creditor.[107] Where the petition is subsequently withdrawn, the company is liable for the costs if the petition was properly presented.[108] In certain circumstances, on the presentation of a successful petition, the courts have ordered directors of the company to personally meet the applicant's and the company's costs.[109]

PETITION FOR WINDING UP BY THE COURT

29-014 The winding up petition must be in one of the forms specified in the Insolvency Rules 1986.[110]

Unless the court otherwise directs, the petition must be advertised in accordance with the rules. The rule in question is 4.11,[111] which requires notice of the petition to be given by the petitioner,[112] and the notice to be gazetted, unless this in not reasonably practicable, in which case notice shall be given in such other manner as the court thinks fit.[113] The rules require the notice to appear not less than seven clear days after the petition has been served on the company and not less than seven clear days before the day fixed for the hearing.[114] This gives the company the opportunity to discharge, or dispute, the debt or apply for validation of its transactions under s.127 before the advertisement appears.[115] The court will restrain the issue of the advertisement if the detriment to the petitioner from an injunction is outweighed by the potential harm caused to the company from the advertisement,[116] if the petition is an abuse of the process of the court,[117] or if the debt is bona fide disputed.[118] Premature advertisement is an abuse of the process of the court.

In *Doreen Boards Ltd, Re*[119] T and L formed a company but their relationship broke down and L began telephoning the company's creditors informing them that she intended to have the company wound up. Serious damage to the company resulted. It was held that L's petition should be struck out.

---

[106] *Armvent Ltd, Re* [1975] 3 All E.R. 441.

[107] *Highfield Commodities Ltd, Re* [1985] 1 W.L.R. 149.

[108] *XYLLYX, Re (No.2)* [1992] B.C.L.C. 378; cf. *Secure & Provide Plc, Re* [1992] B.C.C. 405.

[109] *Secretary of State for Trade and Industry v Aurum Marketing Ltd* [2002] B.C.C. 31. See also *Secretary of State for Trade and Industry v Liquid Acquisitions Ltd* [2002] EWHC 180 (Ch.) (costs order against majority shareholder).

[110] SI 1986/1925 r.12.7(1); Forms 4.2 and 4.3.

[111] As amended by the Insolvency (Amendment) Rules 2010 (SI 2010/686).

[112] Unless the court directs otherwise: r.4.11(1).

[113] IR 1986 r.4.11(2), (3).

[114] r.4.11(4). This rule is mandatory. It is designed to ensure that the class remedy of winding up is made available to all creditors and is not used merely as a means of putting pressure on the company to pay the petitioner's debt: *Practice Direction (No.1 of 1996)* Ch.D. (Companies Court) [1996] B.C.C. 677.

[115] *Bill Hennessey Associates Ltd, Re* [1992] B.C.C. 506.

[116] *A Company, Re (No.009080 of 1992)* [1993] B.C.L.C. 269. See also *A Company, Re (No.0079239 of 1994)* [1995] B.C.C. 634 (an advertisement liable to cause serious damage to the reputation and financial stability of the company was restrained).

[117] *A Company, Re (No.0012209 of 1991)* [1992] 2 All E.R. 797.

[118] *Ex p Avocet Aviation* [1992] B.C.L.C. 869 (costs awarded against petitioner on an indemnity basis).

[119] [1996] 1 B.C.L.C. 501.

It has been held (in a case where the Secretary of State presented the petition on the ground that winding up was expedient by reason of matters referred to in a report of inspectors appointed to investigate the affairs of the company) that when grave charges are levelled against individuals in a petition, the court will not be satisfied with merely prima facie evidence. The petitioner must, if practicable, prove facts by the evidence of witnesses who have first-hand knowledge of the matters on which they give evidence.[120] However, in a later case it was held that the report of inspectors stands in a wholly different position from the ordinary affidavit evidence and represents the conclusions of a statutory fact-finding body, after hearing oral evidence and examination of books. The court is entitled to look at the report and accept it not as hearsay evidence but as material of a different character. At least where the report is not challenged by the company, the court does not have to be satisfied anew by evidence of the ordinary nature as to the facts found in the report.[121] There is, however, no general rule that hearsay evidence is admissible in a winding up petition.[122]

After the presentation of a petition (which has not been struck out or **29–015** dismissed[123]) an application may be made to the court for the appointment of a provisional liquidator: IA 1986 s.135.[124] The application must be made to a Companies Court judge and will be held in public, unless otherwise ordered.[125] The applicant must provide a deposit or security for the appointee's remuneration.[126] In an ex parte application, the applicant owes a duty to the court to make full disclosure of all material facts, and failure to do so may result in any order made being set aside.[127] The appointment may be made at any time before the making of a winding up order, and the person usually appointed is the official receiver.

The provisional liquidator takes all the company's property into his custody or under his control (s.144), and after his appointment no legal proceedings can be commenced or continued against the company without leave of the court: s.130(2). An interpleader summons to which the company is made respondent is a proceeding against the company[128]; so also is distress levied on the company's property by the Commissioners of Customs and Excise for non-payment of VAT.[129] In general, when asked to give leave to commence proceedings under this provision, to court will consider what is fair in all the circumstances.[130] In one case

---

[120] *A.B.C. Coupler Co, Re (No.2)* [1962] 1 W.L.R. 1236; not followed in *Re Travel & Holiday Clubs Ltd*, below.

[121] *Re Travel & Holidays Clubs Ltd* [1967] 1 W.L.R. 711, where it was said (at 716c) that it is undesirable that inspectors who have conducted an enquiry should have to give evidence of their findings upon which they would be liable to be cross-examined. This case was followed in *S.B.A. Properties Ltd, Re* [1967] 1 W.L.R. 799. And see *Allied Produce, Re* [1967] 1 W.L.R. 1469.

[122] *Koscot Interplanetary (UK) Ltd, Re* [1972] 3 All E.R. 829.

[123] *A Company, Re* [1973] 1 W.L.R. 1566.

[124] Directors who improperly oppose the application may be ordered to pay the costs thrown away personally: *Gamelstaden Plc v Brackland Magazines Ltd* [1993] B.C.C. 194. The application may be heard in camera: Practice Direction (No.3 of 1996) [1997] 1 W.L.R. 3.

[125] See *Practice Direction; Insolvency Proceedings* [2007] B.C.C. 842.

[126] IR 1986 rr.4.27 and 4.28.

[127] *OJSC Ank Yugraneft, Re* [2008] EWHC 2614 (Ch.).

[128] *Eastern Holdings v Singer & Friedlander Ltd* [1967] 1 W.L.R. 1017.

[129] *Memco Engineering Ltd, Re* [1986] Ch 86.

[130] *New Cap Reinsurance Corp Ltd v HIH Casualty & General Insurance Ltd* [2002] EWCA Civ 300.

the court gave leave to proceed to a person who had an unimpugnable right to a claim for specific performance of an agreement to sell property belonging to the company.[131] Leave will be given to enable a person to enforce a debt against the company under an existing contract which the liquidator chose to continue for the benefit of the liquidation or a debt under a new contract with the liquidator entered into for the purposes of the liquidation.[132] The appointment of a provisional liquidator has the same result as the making of a winding up order in that the board of directors of the company becomes functus officio and its powers are assumed by the liquidator,[133] but notwithstanding the appointment the board has some residuary powers, e.g. it can instruct solicitors and counsel to oppose the petition and, if a winding up order is made, to appeal against it.[134] The board can also act in interlocutory proceedings, including a motion to discharge the provisional liquidator.

The court may also, after the presentation of a petition (which is still subsisting[135]) and before a winding up order has been made, on the application of the company or of any creditor or contributory, stay or restrain any pending legal proceedings against the company: s.126. Section 126 is an exception to the rule that proceedings pending in the Supreme Court cannot be restrained by injunction. The object of ss.126 and 130(2) is "to put all unsecured creditors upon an equality, and to pay them pari passu."[136]

Withdrawal of petition

29–016 A petitioner can apply to the court for leave to withdraw his petition so long as he does so at least five days prior to the hearing and satisfies the court that the petition has not been advertised, that no notices (whether in support or in opposition) have been received by him with reference to the petition, and that the company consents to an order being made.[137]

Hearing of petition

29–017 The company and any creditor or contributory may attend the hearing of the petition. For this purpose a person is a creditor if he is a creditor for a present debt, a prospective debt or a contingent debt. Whether a person is a contingent creditor depends on circumstances existing at the date of the hearing.[138]

On the hearing of a petition the court may dismiss it, or adjourn the hearing conditionally or unconditionally, or make any interim order, or any other order

---

[131] *Coregrange Ltd, Re* [1984] B.C.L.C. 453.

[132] *Atlantic Computer Systems Plc, Re* [1992] 1 All E.R. 476, CA.

[133] Below, p.721. The authority of agents appointed on behalf of a company by the directors is revoked: see *Pacific & General Insurance Co Ltd v Home & Overseas Insurance Co Ltd* [1997] B.C.C. 400.

[134] *Union Accident Insce. Co Ltd, Re* [1972] 1 W.L.R. 640.

[135] See n.13, above.

[136] Per Lindley L.J. in *Oak Pits Colliery Co, Re* (1882) Ch.D. 322, CA, at 329.

[137] IR 1986 r.4.15 and see *Practice Direction: Insolvency Proceedings* [2007] B.C.C. 842.

[138] *S.B.A. Properties Ltd, Re* [1967] 1 W.L.R. 799.

that it thinks it fit: s.125(1).[139] The court may have regard to the wishes of the creditors or contributories: s.195.[140] When exercising its discretion to adjourn the hearing of a petition for the winding up of an international bank, the court had to consider the interests of the creditors worldwide rather than the interests of one class of creditor within the jurisdiction; English law does not permit the court to erect a ring fence around assets or creditors in any one jurisdiction.[141]

When a judgment creditor is deprived of the right ex debito justitiae to a winding up order because his petition is opposed by the majority of the creditors, the fair practice is to make no order as to costs.[142] The same is true where the petitioning creditor is not a judgment creditor but his debt is undisputed.[143] *Aliter*, if the petitioning creditor acted unreasonably in presenting or prosecuting his petition,[144] or the company is being wound up voluntarily and no evidence is filed on behalf of the petitioner beyond an affidavit verifying the petition.[145] In special circumstances costs may be awarded against one party, e.g. where the company failed to defend an action so that the plaintiff petitioned to wind up the company, on the petition being dismissed and the action set aside, the company was held liable for the costs of the petition.[146] However, where a petitioner was paid in full by the company, apart from his costs, the petitioner was unable to recover his costs because he had not complied with the rules as to advertisement of the petition.[147]

When a winding up order is made, it is usual to order the costs of (1) the petitioner, (2) the company, and (3) one set of creditors and one set of contributories, to be paid out of the assets. Any other creditor who wishes to appear does so at his own expense. As a general rule no order for costs will be made in favour of one creditor against another.[148]

A copy of the order must be sent by the company to the Registrar of **29–018** Companies: s.130(1). Section 1078 of the Companies Act 2006 provides that the Registrar must cause notice of the receipt by him of the copy of the order to be published in the Gazette. The notice must state the company's name, a description of the document received and the date of receipt.

The court has power to stay a winding up order either altogether or for a limited time,[149] on such terms and conditions as it thinks fit, if an application is made to it by the liquidator or the official receiver or any creditor or contributory. The court may require the official receiver to furnish a report on matters relevant to

---

[139] Above.

[140] See also *Middlesborough Assembly Rooms Co, Re* (1880) 14 Ch.D. 104, CA, and *Galbraith v Merito Shpg Co Ltd*, 1947 S.C. 446.

[141] *Bank of Credit & Commerce International S.A., Re* [1992] B.C.C. 83.

[142] *R.W. Sharman Ltd, Re* [1957] 1 W.L.R. 774; *A.B.C. Coupler Co, Re* [1961] 1 W.L.R. 243.

[143] *Sklan Ltd, Re* [1961] 1 W.L.R. 1013.

[144] *A.E. Hayter & Sons, Re (Porchester) Ltd* [1961] 1 W.L.R. 1008.

[145] *Riviera Pearls Ltd, Re* [1962] 1 W.L.R. 722.

[146] *Lanaghan Bros Ltd, Re* [1977] 1 All E.R. 265. See also *M. McCarthy & Co (Builders) Ltd, Re (No.2)* [1976] 2 All E.R. 339; *Arrow Leeds Ltd, Re* [1986] B.C.L.C. 538; *Holmes v Mainstream Ventures Ltd* [2009] EWHC 3330 (Ch.).

[147] *The Shusella Ltd* (1982) 126 S.J. 577.

[148] *Esal (Commodities) Ltd, Re* [1985] B.C.L.C. 450. This case also provides guidance for costs where an alternative scheme of arrangement under Pt 26 of the Companies Act 2006 is under consideration.

[149] See *Boston Timber Fabrications Ltd, Re* [1984] B.C.L.C. 328.

the application. A copy of any order made by the court under this provision must be sent to the Registrar: s.147. Such an order is not usually made unless all the creditors are paid or satisfied, but the court will have regard to commercial morality and not just to the interests of the creditors.[150] As a matter of practice a stay is almost never granted, for good reasons,[151] but there may be circumstances when a court will do so.[152] An appeal from the making of a winding up order in England may be brought within four weeks: RSC Ord.59 r.4.[153]

Where an order winding up a solvent company was made on a contributory's petition opposed by the company and another contributory, and the company appealed against the order, the company had to provide security for the costs of the appeal otherwise than from the company's assets. It would have been wrong, if the appeal failed, for the petitioner to be liable to bear any proportion of the costs of the appeal or of a liquidation. An order was made that security be provided by the directors or shareholders promoting the appeal.[154]

CONSEQUENCES OF A WINDING UP ORDER

29–019 The consequences of the making of a winding up order date back to an earlier date than that on which the order was actually made. This date is called the commencement of the winding up and is, according to s.129 of the IA 1986:

1.   the time of the presentation of the petition (s.129(2)); or

2.   where, before the presentation of the petition, the company was in voluntary liquidation, the time of the passing of the resolution for voluntary winding up (s.129(1));

3.   the date on which the court makes an order for winding up on the hearing of an administration application under para.13(1)(e) of Sch.B1 (s.129(1A)).

The consequences of a winding up order are:

1.   Any disposition of the property of the company, and any transfer of shares or alteration in the status of the members, after the commencement of the winding up, is void unless the court otherwise orders: s.127.

The company is divested of beneficial ownership of its assets which fall subject to a "statutory trust".[155]

The object of s.127 is to prevent, during the period which must elapse before a petition can be heard, the improper alienation and dissipation of the property of a

---

[150] *Telescriptor Ltd, Re* [1903] 2 Ch. 174; see also for general principles *Lowston Ltd, Re* [1991] B.C.L.C. 570.
[151] See, per Plowman J. in *A & B.C. Chewing Gum Ltd, Re* [1975] 1 W.L.R. 579 at 592.
[152] As in *McGruther v James Scott Ltd* 2004 S.C. 514, ED.
[153] See IR 1986 r.7.47.
[154] *E. K. Wilson & Sons Ltd, Re* [1972] 1 W.L.R. 791, CA.
[155] *Ayerst v C & K (Construction) Ltd* [1976] A.C. 167.

company in extremis. However, where a company is trading, the court can sanction transactions in the ordinary course of business—otherwise the presentation of a petition, whether well- or ill-founded, would paralyse the company's trade.[156] Thus the court may sanction the continued operation of the company's bank account in the ordinary course of business, so long as there is no serious doubt as to the company's solvency.[157] Further in the case of a solvent company the court will normally sanction a disposition which the directors consider to be necessary or expedient in the interests of the company for reasons which an intelligent and honest man could reasonably hold.[158]

In *Park, Ward & Co, Re*,[159] between the date of the presentation of the petition and the making of a winding up order X advanced £1,200 to the company to enable it to pay wages due to the staff and took a debenture as security. X knew, at the time of the issue of the debenture, of the presentation of the petition. It was held that the debenture was valid.

The court may order that a debenture taken after the commencement of the **29–020** winding up is not void if the money is advanced, not for the payment of wages, but for the company's benefit to enable it to carry out its contracts and the lender has acted in good faith and with the honest intention of benefiting the company.[160] If however the disposition was made with a view to assisting the company's creditors, it will not be validated.[161]

Payments into or out of the company's bank account were held to fall within the section in *Gray's Inn Construction Co Ltd, Re*.[162] This proposition has since been held to be too broad. Payments into an account in credit were held not to be a disposition of the company's property in *Barn Crown Ltd, Re*,[163] and in *Bank of Ireland v Hollicourt (Contractors) Ltd*[164] the Court of Appeal held that a payment made by cheque out of an account, whether in credit or overdrawn, similarly would not be such a disposition by the bank.

After the presentation of a petition property may safely be transferred or payment made to the company,[165] but payments made by the company in respect of debts previously incurred must be refunded by the recipient,[166] and property transferred is held by the recipient on trust for the company, unless an order under s.127 is obtained.[167]

---

[156] Per Lord Cairns in *Wiltshire Iron Co, Re* (1868) L.R. 3 Ch. App. 443 at 447; see also *United Dominions Trust Ltd, Noters*, 1977 S.L.T. (Notes) 56, OH (warrant to sell security subjects valid).
[157] *A Company, Re (No.007532 of 1986)* [1987] B.C.L.C. 200.
[158] *Burton & Deakin Ltd, Re* [1977] 1 W.L.R. 390.
[159] [1926] Ch.828.
[160] *Steane's (Bournemouth) Ltd, Re* [1950] 1 All E.R. 21, applied in *Clifton Place Garage Ltd, Re* [1970] 1 All E.R. 352, CA.
[161] *Webb's Electrical, Re* [1988] B.C.L.C. 332.
[162] [1980] 1 W.L.R. 711, C.A.
[163] [1994] 1 W.L.R. 147.
[164] [2001] Ch. 555.
[165] *Mersey Steel Co v Naylor, Benzon & Co* (1882) 9 Q.B.D. 648, CA; (1884) 9 App. Cas. 434; *Millar v The National Bank of Scotland Ltd* (1891) 28 S.L.R. 884, OH.
[166] *Civil Service and General Store Ltd, Re* (1888) 57 L.J.Ch. 119; *McLintock v Lithauer*, 1924 S.L.T. 755, OH.
[167] *French's Wine Bar, Re* [1987] B.C.L.C. 499.

After the commencement of winding up, a company paid for petrol delivered prior to that date. The payments, which were made in good faith, in ignorance of the petition and were beneficial to the company and the unsecured creditors in that they were necessary to ensure further supplies, were validated by the court:[168]

29–021　　The word "disposition" in s.127 includes dispositions of a company's property whether made by the company or by a third party, or whether made directly or indirectly.[169] However where, prior to the petition, the company has entered into an unconditional contract capable of specific performance to sell its property the completion of the contract after the presentation of the petition is not a disposition of its property within s.127 because whatever interest the company has at that time gives it no control over the property. Leave is therefore not required.[170]

The court may, under the section, authorise a disposition of a company's property after presentation of the petition notwithstanding that a winding up order has not yet been made and will do so if the disposition will benefit creditors of the company if an order is made.[171]

Section 127 contains no express provision as to who can apply for the validation of dispositions. However, an applicant must have some discernible interest in the matter. The company can apply under the section. A shareholder has a sufficient locus standi to apply. A director may have a sufficient locus standi.[172] By s.127(2), the paragraph does not apply in respect of anything done by an administrator of a company while a winding up petition is suspended under para.40 of Sch.B1.

2.　　Any attachment, sequestration, distress or execution put in force against the estate or effects of the company after the commencement of the winding up is void: s.128.[173] In spite of its plain words, s.128 is subject to the provisions of s.126, above, and s.130(2), below, the combined effect of which is that a creditor who wishes validly to proceed to execution can apply to the court for leave.[174]

3.　　After a winding up order has been made or a provisional liquidator has been appointed, no action can be proceeded with or commenced against the company except by leave of the court: s.130(2).

---

[168] *Denny v John Hudson & Co Ltd* [1992] B.C.C. 110.

[169] *Leslie Engineers Co Ltd, Re* [1976] 1 W.L.R. 292. But see *Mal Bower's Macquarie Electrical Centre Pty. Ltd, Re* (in Liqdn) etc. [1974] 1 N.S.W.L.R. 254 (to the effect that the section does not affect agencies such as a bank interposing between a company, as disponor, and the recipient of the property, as disponee) and also *Barn Crown Ltd, Re* [1994] B.C.C. 381 and *Bank of Ireland v Hollicourt (Contractors) Ltd* [2001] Ch. 555.

[170] *French's Wine Bar, Re* [1987] B.C.L.C. 499. In *Site Preparations v Buchan Developments Co*, 1983 S.L.T. 317, OH, a floating charge created after the presentation of a petition was held to be a disposition.

[171] *A.I. Levy (Holdings) Ltd, Re* [1964] Ch.19; See also *Newport County Association Football Club, Re* (1987) 3 B.C.C. 635; *Royal Bank of Scotland Plc v Bhardwaj* [2002] B.C.C. 57.

[172] *Argentum Reductions (UK) Ltd, Re* [1975] 1 W.L.R. 186.

[173] A prior charging order nisi will not be confirmed after a liquidation: *Roberts Petroleum Ltd v Bernard Kenny Ltd* [1983] A.C. 192.

[174] *Lancashire Cotton Spinning Co, Re* (1887) 35 Ch.D. 656, CA; *The Constellation* [1966] 1 W.L.R. 272.

The purpose of s.130(2) is to ensure that when a company goes into liquidation **29–022** the assets are administered for the benefit of all the creditors.[175] It has been held that an action commenced without leave is a nullity and cannot be retrospectively authorised, although this contention must now be considered doubtful.[176]

Notwithstanding the section, if a company in liquidation brings an action the defendant may, without leave of the court, set up a cross-demand for liquidated or unliquidated damages, but only as a set-off to reduce or extinguish the plaintiff's claim.[177]

4. On a winding up order being made in England, the official receiver becomes the liquidator, and he continues to act until another person becomes liquidator. He also acts as liquidator during any vacancy: s.136(2), (3).

5. On a winding up order being made, the powers of the directors cease,[178] and are assumed by the liquidator. Some of the duties of the directors cease, too, e.g. as to the mode of keeping the company's accounting records under ss.386 to 389 of the Companies Act 2006.[179] One of the duties which remains after the making of a winding up order is the duty not to disclose confidential information.[180]

6. On a winding up order being made, the employees of the company are ipso facto, dismissed,[181] and may be able to sue for damages for breach of contract, but an employee who continues to discharge the same duties and receive the same wages as before may be held to have entered by tacit relocation into a contract of service with the liquidator.[182] Where a liquidator re-engaged employees in order to complete certain contracts and thereafter dismissed them on the ground of redundancy, the employees were held, for the purposes of the Redundancy Payments Act 1965, to have been continuously employed by one employer (i.e. the company) from the dates of their initial engagement by the company down to the dates of their dismissal by the liquidator.[183]

Every invoice, order for goods or business letter issued by or on behalf of the company or the liquidator, on which the company's name appears, must contain a statement that the company is being wound up and the same statement must appear on all of the company's websites. Non-compliance with this provision results in a fine: s.188(1), (2).

[175] Per Widgery L.J. in *Langley Constructions (Brixham) Ltd v Wells* [1969] 1 W.L.R. 503, CA, at 508; cf. the effects of an administration order, above, p.671.
[176] See *National Employers Mutual General Insurance Association, Re* [1995] B.C.C. 774. But cf. *Linkrealm Ltd, Re* [1998] B.C.C. 478 and *Palmer's Company Law*, Vol.3. See also, in a different but likely relevant context, *Seal v Chief Constable of South Wales* [2007] UKHL 31.
[177] *Langley Constructions (Brixham) Ltd v Wells*, above, n.175.
[178] *Fowler v Broad's Patent Night Light Co* [1893] 1 Ch. 724.
[179] Above, Ch.20.
[180] *Country Traders Distributors Ltd etc., Re* [1974] 2 N.S.W.L.R. 135.
[181] *Chapman's Case* (1866) L.R. 1 Eq. 346; *Laing v Gowans* (1902) 10 S.L.T. 461, OH.
[182] *Day v Tait* (1900) 8 S.L.T. 40, OH.
[183] *Smith v Lord Advocate*, 1978 S.C. 259.

Appointment of special manager

29–023 Where either a company has gone into liquidation or a provisional liquidator has been appointed, the liquidator or provisional liquidator, as appropriate, may apply to the court for the appointment of a special manager of the company's business or property if the nature of that business or property or the interests of the creditors, members or contributories require it.[184] The court may give the special manager such powers as it thinks fit. Such a person need not, however, be a qualified insolvency practitioner but must give such security as is prescribed[185]: s.177. This power applies to all kinds of liquidation.

PROCEEDINGS AFTER A WINDING UP

Statement of company's affairs and investigation by the official receiver

29–024 Where the court has made a winding up order or appointed a provisional liquidator the official receiver may require a statement of affairs to be produced. The persons who may be required to make such a statement, its contents and the procedural aspects are the same as those on the appointment of an administrative receiver[186] or administrator[187]: s.131.

In England, it is the duty of the official receiver after a winding up order has been made to carry out two investigations: (1) if the company has failed, into the causes of the failure, and (2), in any case, into the promotion, formation, business dealing and affairs of the company. Consequently, he may make a report to the court, which is prima facie evidence of the facts stated in it in any proceedings: s.132. The official receiver is therefore bound under (2) to investigate all compulsory liquidations and not just those concerned with insolvency, but he need only make a report to the court if he thinks fit.

If the company has insufficient assets to cover the expenses of the liquidation and the official receiver is satisfied that no further investigation is required he may apply for an early dissolution, in which case his responsibilities cease. This procedure is dealt with in Ch.31, below.[188]

Public examination of officers

29–025 Section 133(1) provides that the official receiver[189] may at any time before the dissolution of the company apply to the court for the public examination of (a) anyone who is or has been an officer of the company; (b) has acted as liquidator, administrator, receiver, or manager of its property; or (c) anyone else who has been concerned or has taken part in the promotion, formation or management of the

---

[184] The appointee may be an outgoing provisional liquidator so as to maintain continuity: *WF Fearman (No.2) Ltd, Re* (1988) 4 B.C.C. 141.
[185] IR 1986 rr.4.206–4.210, I(S)R 1986 rr.4.69–4.73.
[186] Above, Ch.27.
[187] Above, Ch.28.
[188] p.753.
[189] In Scotland, the liquidator.

company.[190] A public examination serves to expose serious misconduct and to promote a higher standard of commercial morality.[191]

The official receiver must apply for a public examination if he is requested to do so by either one half of the creditors or three quarters of the contributories: s.133(2). Failure to attend without a reasonable excuse is a contempt of court: s.134(1). Questions as to the company's formation, promotion, management or as to the person's conduct of its affairs or dealings with that company may be put by the official receiver, liquidator, special manager,[192] any creditor who has tendered a claim or any contributory: s.133(3), (4). The person examined is not entitled to refuse to reply on the ground of self-incrimination.[193]

Appointment of a liquidator

In England the official receiver becomes the first liquidator until another person **29–026** is appointed. There are two ways in which such a successor may be appointed:

1. Within 12 weeks of the winding up order the official receiver must decide whether or not to summon separate meetings of the company's creditors and contributories so that they might choose a liquidator in his place. If he decides not to do so he must notify the court, creditors and contributories to that effect but he must summon the meetings if requested by one quarter in value of the creditors, and any notice to the creditors of his refusal to summon the meetings must refer to that obligation: s.136.

If such meetings are held, each meeting may nominate a liquidator and, in the event of a disagreement, the creditors' nominee is to be the liquidator of the company subject to an application by any creditor or contributory to the court for the appointment of the contributories' nominee or some other person: s.139. This is similar to the appointment of a liquidator in a creditors' voluntary winding up except that the directors as such cannot apply to the court.[194] If no person is chosen as liquidator by the meetings, the official receiver must decide whether to refer the question of the appointment to the Secretary of State: s.137(2).

2. The official receiver always has the alternative of applying to the Secretary of State for the appointment of a liquidator rather than summoning the meetings of creditors and contributories. The Secretary of State has complete discretion whether to appoint a liquidator but if he does so, the liquidator must give notice of his appointment to the creditors or advertise his appointment as directed by the court: s.137(3), (4), (5).

---

[190] The jurisdiction is not confined to British subjects or to persons within the jurisdiction at the relevant time: *Seagull Manufacturing Co (In liquidation), Re* [1993] B.C.C. 241, CA; *Casterbridge Properties Ltd, Re* [2002] B.C.C. 453 cf., below, private examinations.
[191] Cork Report (1982), Cmnd.8558, para.656.
[192] Above, p.706.
[193] *Paget, Re* [1927] 2 Ch. 85; *Bishopsgate Investment Management Ltd v Maxwell* [1992] 2 All E.R. 856, 869–871, CA.
[194] Below, p.732.

Where a winding up order either follows the cessation of effect of the appointment of an administrator[195] or is made at the time of a voluntary arrangement,[196] the court may appoint the administrator or supervisor, as appropriate, as liquidator. In such cases the official receiver does not become the liquidator at all: s.140.

The liquidator is to be known by the style of "the liquidator" of the particular company unless he is also the official receiver, where he is to be known as "the official receiver and liquidator" of the company: s.163.

Liquidation committees

29–027 If meetings of creditors and contributories are summoned to choose a liquidator, they may also appoint a committee (of creditors and contributories) to be known as the liquidation committee. This committee then fulfils several functions in the liquidation procedure the main one being to sanction certain actions of the liquidator.[197] Its exact composition and functions are governed by the Rules.[198] Such a committee may alternatively be appointed by general meetings of creditors and contributories summoned by the liquidator (not the official receiver). The liquidator must summon such meetings if requested to do so by one tenth in value of the creditors. If there is no liquidation committee or the liquidator is the official receiver the functions of the committee are vested in the Secretary of State: s.141.

THE LIQUIDATOR AS OFFICE HOLDER

Office holders

29–028 The Insolvency Act applies certain basic rules and gives certain common powers to office holders. These are an administrator,[199] an administrative receiver,[200] a liquidator and a provisional liquidator (in any form of winding up). All such persons must be qualified insolvency practitioners[201]: s.230, Sch.B1, para.6. If any joint appointment is made the terms of the appointment must specify whether they are required to act together or may operate individually: s.231, Sch.B1, para.100(2). The acts of an office holder are valid despite any defect in his appointment, nomination or qualifications: s.232, Sch.B1, para.104.

Administrative receivers and administrators have been the subject of Chs 27 and 28 but it is convenient to deal with the provisions applicable to all office holders in one place. The following provisions apply therefore to both those earlier Chapters, this Chapter and Ch.30 on voluntary winding up.

---

[195] Above, p.684.
[196] Above, p.646.
[197] See, e.g. IA 1986 s.167.
[198] IR 1986 rr.4.151–4.172A., and where the winding up follows immediately on liquidation, rr.4.173–4.178. As to its constitution and rights, see *W & A Glaser Ltd, Re* [1994] B.C.C. 199.
[199] Above, Ch.28.
[200] Above, Ch.27.
[201] Above, p.638.

Supplies by public utilities

Although the utilities, such as gas, water and electricity are unsecured creditors, **29–029** they could exercise considerable power against an office holder by refusing to continue supplies unless their debts from the company were paid in full. If the company's business was continuing this would be a potent threat. The Cork Committee therefore recommended[202] that an office holder must be treated as a new customer with a statutory right to receive supplies independently of the company whose account is in arrears. This recommendation was accepted and is contained in s.233. The supplies affected are a supply of gas, a supply of electricity, a supply of water and a supply of telecommunications services by a public telecommunications operator.[203]

Although they may not require outstanding bills of the company to be paid[204] before supplying the office holder, they may require a personal guarantee from him for any subsequent supplies. This section also applies to the supervisor of a voluntary arrangement who is not an office holder for any other purpose.[205]

Getting in the company's property

The court may order any person who possesses any property, books, papers or **29–030** records apparently belonging to the company to transfer them to the office holder: s.234(2). "Property" is widely defined by s.436 as including

> "money, goods, things in action, land and every description of property wherever situated and also obligations and every description of interest, whether present or future or vested or contingent, arising out of, or incidental to, property".

If the office holder seizes or disposes of property which does not belong to the company but which he reasonably believes he is entitled to take or deal with, he is not liable for any loss or damage except that caused by his own negligence and is entitled to a lien on the property to recover any expenses: s.234(3), (4).[206]

Co-operation with the office holder—private examination

Any person referred to in s.235(3)[207] must on request give to the office holder **29–031** (including the official receiver: s.235(1)) such information concerning the company's affairs as the office holder may reasonably require and must attend on

---

[202] Paras 1451–1462.

[203] IA 1986 s.233(5)

[204] Directly or indirectly, e.g. by insisting on a coin-operated meter supply so calibrated as to recoup the previous unpaid amounts.

[205] Above, p.646.

[206] It has been held, however, that the protection afforded to office holders by s.234(3), (4) does not extend to wrongful dealings with choses in action: *Welsh Development Agency Ltd v Export Finance Co* [1992] B.C.C. 270.

[207] i.e. those who are, or have been officers of the company, have taken part in its formation, are or have been employed by the company or have acted as administrator, administrative receiver or liquidator of the company.

him when required to do so: s.235(2). These provisions are designed to assist the office holder to carry out his task quickly and effectively, and where a person fails, without reasonable excuse, to comply with any obligation imposed by them he is liable to a fine: s.235(5). Information or documents obtained or disclosed may be disclosed to the Secretary of State so that he may consider whether to bring disqualification proceedings[208] and the use of statements obtained under s.235 in subsequent disqualification proceedings does not of itself breach the provisions of the European Convention on Human Rights or, inferentially, the Human Rights Act 1998.[209]

Private examinations

29–032 The office holder[210] is given powers to apply to the court if there is insufficient co-operation under the provisions detailed above. The application[211] is lodged with a confidential report, parts of which may be made available to the proposed examinee.[212] On such an application the court may summon any officer of the company, any person known or suspected of possessing company property or supposed to be indebted to the company, or any person it thinks capable of giving information about the company's affairs,[213] to appear before it and to submit an affidavit detailing his dealings with the company, or to produce any relevant documents: s.236.[214]

The principles upon which the court exercises its discretion under s.236 were set out in *British & Commonwealth Holdings Plc v Spicer & Oppenheimer*.[215] A balance must be struck between the requirements of the office holder and oppression of the examinee.

> "An application is not necessarily unreasonable because it is inconvenient for the addressee or causes him a lot of work or may make him vulnerable to future claims or is addressed to a person who not an officer or employee of, or contractor with, the company . . . but all these factors will be relevant, together no doubt with many others."[216]

---

[208] On such proceedings, see Ch.17 above.

[209] *Westminster Property Management Ltd, Re* [2000] 1 W.L.R. 2230.

[210] Including at any time, the official receiver.

[211] Which may be made ex parte if there is good reason: see *Maxwell Communications Corporation Plc, Re, Homan v Vogel* [1994] B.C.C. 741 at 747.

[212] *British & Commonwealth Holdings Plc, Re* [1992] B.C.L.C. 641, CA; *Bishopsgate Investment Management Ltd, Re (No.2)* [1994] B.C.C. 732.

[213] In some cases, notwithstanding legal professional privilege: cf. *Barclays Bank Plc v Eustice* [1995] B.C.C. 978, CA; *Royscott Spa Leasing Ltd v Lovett* [1995] B.C.C. 502, CA.

[214] The jurisdiction is subject to territorial limitations: see s.237(3); *Seagull Manufacturing Co Ltd, Re* [1993] B.C.C. 241, CA. The section applies to the Crown: see *Soden v Burns* [1996] 3 All E.R. 967 (disclosure by the DTI of witness statements given to inspectors appointed under s.432 Companies Act 1985).

[215] [1992] 3 W.L.R. 853, HL, followed in *McIsaac and Wilson, Petitioners*, 1995 S.L.T. 498, OH (reference to "any person" in s.236 indicated that the provisions were not confined to persons resident in the jurisdiction of the court; in this case the order was limited to the production of documents by a firm of accountants). In relation to solvent companies, see *Galileo Ltd, Re* [1998] B.C.C. 228.

[216] Lord Slynn, ibid., 885. See also *Sasea Finance Ltd, Re* (in liquidation) [1998] 1 B.C.L.C. 559; *Cowlishaw v O&D Building Contractors Ltd* [2009] EWHC 2445 (Ch.).

While the court can exercise its power to enable the office-holder to reconstitute the state of knowledge which the company should possess, the discretion is broader and may be exercised to provide the office-holder with any information he reasonably requires to carry out his functions.[217]

In *British & Commonwealth Holdings Plc v Spicer & Oppenheimer*,[218] BC Plc had taken over A Ltd for £420 million and subsequently invested a further £117 million in it. Two years later A Ltd became insolvent with a deficiency of £279 million. BC Plc itself went into administration and its administrator sought an order under s.236 requiring the auditors of A Ltd to produce books and papers relating to certain audits and to the takeover. The House of Lords granted the order even though BC Plc would not have been entitled to such information when solvent.

The court[219] may examine a person on oath and he may be ordered to hand over **29–033** property, or to pay amounts due, to the company: IA 1986 s.237. A person being examined under these provisions, and under s.236, is not entitled to remain silent: the privilege against self-incrimination is impliedly abrogated by the statute in the interests of enabling the office holder more effectively to perform his investigative functions.[220] However, the use of statements obtained under compulsion in later criminal proceedings was held to be contrary to the European Convention on Human Rights in *Saunders v United Kingdom*.[221] The court is less inclined to make an order where proceedings have been commenced and pursued against the proposed examinee or where he is suspected of wrongdoing,[222] although the House of Lords has held that an order may be made where the purpose is to obtain information with a view to instituting disqualification proceedings against the director in question.[223]

It was recognised in *Barlow Clowes Gilt Managers Ltd, Re*[224] that the confidentiality of a private examination is important for the efficient functioning of the investigation, encouraging speedy, voluntary disclosure to the office holder. However, the ability of the office holder to ensure confidentiality is impaired by s.433 of the Insolvency Act 1986 which provides that a statement made, inter alia,

---

[217] Compare *Joint Administrators of Cloverbay v Bank of Credit & Commerce International SA* [1991] Ch.90. See also *First Tokyo Index Trust Ltd v Gould* [1993] G.W.D. 36–2298, OH.

[218] [1992] 3 W.L.R. 853, HL.

[219] Usually acting through the office holder: see *Kingscroft Insurance Co Ltd, Re* [1994] B.C.C. 343 (effect of the lapse of the office holder's appointment); *Maxwell Communications Corporation Plc, Re (No.3)* [1995] 1 B.C.L.C. 521 (non-office holders).

[220] *Bishopsgate Investment Management Ltd v Maxwell* [1992] B.C.C. 214, CA; an order made in favour of a company in the course of an action for an account of assets is outside the scope of the statutory exception and the director can claim the right to silence (ibid.); see also *Jeffrey S. Levett, Re* [1992] B.C.C. 137 (Vinelott J.); *Brook Martin & Co, Re* [1993] B.C.L.C. 328. The privilege against self-incrimination is not available to persons examined by the Director of the Serious Fraud Office exercising powers under s.2 of the Criminal Justice Act 1987; *Smith v Director of the Serious Fraud Office* [1992] 3 W.L.R. 66, HL.

[221] [1997] B.C.C. 872. The ruling was not applied in *R. v Secretary of State for Trade and Industry Ex p. McCormick* [1998] B.C.C. 379 (evidence obtained under compulsion by DTI inspectors admissible is subsequent disqualification proceedings, as these are not criminal proceedings); see, however, *Rottmann, Re* [2008] EWHC 1794 (Ch.) (examination of bankrupt to be held in private where criminal proceedings commenced abroad).

[222] *Bank of Credit & Commerce International SA, Morris v Bank of America, Re* [1997] B.C.C. 561, 572; *James McHale Automobiles Ltd, Re* [1997] B.C.C. 202.

[223] *Pantmaenog Timber Co Ltd, Re* [2003] UKHL 49.

[224] [1991] 4 All E.R. 385.

under s.236 can be used in evidence against the person making it and also by s.2(3) of the Criminal Justice Act 1987 which authorises the Director of the Serious Fraud Office to request transcripts from the office holder (notwithstanding any assurances of confidence which may have been given and notwithstanding a direction of the court under s.168(3)[225] that access should be denied as being prejudicial to the conduct of the investigation: *Arrows Ltd, Re (No.4)*).[226] However, the use against the examinee, in a criminal trial, of statements acquired in this way may violate the right under art.6 of the European Convention for the Protection of Human Rights and Fundamental Freedoms.[227]

THE PROPERTY OF THE COMPANY IN A WINDING UP BY THE COURT

Custody of company's property

29–034　When a winding up order has been made, or a provisional liquidator appointed, the liquidator must take into his custody or under his control all the property to which the company is or appears to be entitled: s.144. Winding up does not, as does bankruptcy, operate as a *cessio bonorum* or transfer of property; the company's property remains vested in it as before[228] unless, under s.145, the court makes an order vesting it in him in his official name.[229] Sections 234[230] and 160[231] also contain wide powers to enable the liquidator to get the company's property into his custody.

Restriction of rights of creditor as to execution or attachment

29–035　Section 183 provides that where a creditor has issued execution against the goods or lands of a company or has attached any debt due to it, and the company is subsequently wound up, he is not entitled to retain the benefit of the execution or attachment against the liquidator unless he completed the execution or attachment before the commencement of the winding up[232] or, if he had notice of a meeting at which a resolution for voluntary winding up was to be proposed, before such notice. A purchaser in good faith, under a sale by an enforcement officer[233] of goods on which execution has been levied acquires a good title to them against

---

[225] And IR 1986 r.9.5(4).

[226] [1993] B.C.C. 473, CA; [1995] 2 A.C. 75, HL. The liquidator does not, at the same time, have to disclose to the person charged: *Headington Investments Ltd, Re* [1993] B.C.C. 500 CA.

[227] See *Saunders v United Kingdom* (Case 43/1994/490/572). On civil proceedings, see *R. v Secretary of State for Trade & Industry, Ex p. McCormick* [1998] B.C.C. 379.

[228] Per Warrington L.J. in *H.J. Webb & Co (Smithfield, London), Re Ltd* [1922] 2 Ch. 369, CA, at 388; per Lord President Inglis in *Queensland Mercantile etc. Co Ltd v Australasian Investment Co Ltd* (1888) 15 R. 935 at 939; per Lord Hailsham in *Alexander Ward & Co Ltd v Samyang Navigation Co Ltd*, 1975 S.C. 26, HL at 47.

[229] See, for example, *Cambridge Gas Transport Corp v Official Committee of Unsecured Creditors of Navigator Holdings Plc* [2006] UKPC 26.

[230] Above.

[231] Applies to England only.

[232] Above, p.702.

[233] See s.183(4).

the liquidator: s.183(2)(b). The section does not apply to a distress for rent by a landlord.[234]

An execution against goods is taken to be completed either by seizure and sale or by the making of a charging order,[235] and an attachment of a debt by receipt of the debt, and an execution against land by seizure, the appointment of a receiver or by the making of a charging order: s.183(3).

Where a judgment creditor issued a writ of fi. fa. in respect of the judgment and the sheriff seized the company's goods and, after a petition for a compulsory winding up had been presented (although this was unknown to the sheriff), sold them, when an order for winding up was made the sheriff had to hand over the proceeds to the liquidator.[236]

The phrase "the benefit of the execution" does not refer to "the fruits of the execution" but to the charge conferred on the creditor by the issue of execution. Where a creditor has issued a writ of fi. fa. against a company, money paid to the sheriff or his officers in order to avoid a sale and which remains in their hands at the commencement of the winding up is outside "the benefit of the execution" so that the liquidator is not entitled to such money as against the creditor.[237] "The benefit of the attachment" means the right to take the necessary steps to complete it.

If a judgment creditor who has obtained a garnishee order obtains payment **29–036** after receipt by him of notice of a meeting called for the winding up of the company, he must, subject to the court's discretion under s.183(2)(c), below, account to the liquidator for the money.[238]

By s.183(2)(c), the rights conferred by s.183(1), above, on the liquidator may be set aside by the court in favour of the creditor. The basic scheme of the Insolvency Act is that in a winding up unsecured creditors rank pari passu and an execution creditor who has not completed his execution at the commencement of the winding up is for this purpose in the same position as any other unsecured creditor. Section 183(2)(c) gives the court a free hand to do what is right and fair according to the circumstances of the case,[239] but weighty reasons are necessary to justify the court in exercising its discretion.[240]

Where a judgment creditor of a company refrained from levying immediate execution because of a promise of payment by a director, there being no dishonesty by the director, and the execution was not completed before the commencement of the winding up, the court refused to set the liquidator's rights aside. To allow the creditor to retain the benefit of the execution would have been contrary to the basic scheme of the Acts and unfair to the other creditors. During the year before the winding up the company was keeping its general body of trade

---

[234] *Bellaglade Ltd, Re* [1977] 1 All E.R. 319. See also *Modern Jet Support Centre Ltd, Re* [2005] EWHC 1161 (Ch.) (distress levied by the Revenue).

[235] Under s.1 of the Charging Orders Act 1979.

[236] *Bluston & Bramley Ltd v Leigh* [1950] 2 K.B. 548. Giving the sheriff notice of a creditors' meeting is not sufficient to defeat the execution creditor's right: *Walton (TD), Re* [1966] 2 All E.R. 157.

[237] *Walkden Sheet Metal Co Ltd, Re* [1960] Ch. 170.

[238] *Caribbean Products (Yam Importers) Ltd, Re* [1966] Ch. 331, CA; overruling *Rainbow Tours Ltd, Re* [1964] Ch. 66.

[239] *Redman (Builders) Ltd, Re* [1964] 1 W.L.R. 541.

[240] *Caribbean Products (Yam Importers) Ltd, Re*, above, n.238.

creditors at bay and there was no reason why one execution creditor who had not completed execution should be preferred to the other creditors whether or not they had obtained judgment or commenced execution.[241] On the other hand, where before the action the company stalled the creditors' claims by promises and defended the action by disputing a debt already admitted, the liquidator's rights were set aside.[242]

Duties of enforcement officers as to goods taken in execution

29–037 Section 184 provides that where goods are taken in execution in England and Wales and, before their sale or the completion of the execution, notice of the appointment of a provisional liquidator, of a winding up order or resolution for voluntary winding up, is served upon the enforcement officer, he must, if required, deliver up the goods to the liquidator. The costs of execution are however a first charge upon them: s.184(2). Where goods are seized in respect of a judgment exceeding £500 the sheriff must deduct the costs of execution and retain the balance for 14 days and pay it to the liquidator if so required. The rights of the liquidator may be set aside in favour of the creditor as the court thinks fit.

Fraudulent trading

29–038 Section 213 provides that if in the winding up of a company it appears that business has been carried on with intent to defraud creditors or for any fraudulent purpose, the court, on the application of the liquidator, may declare that any persons who were knowingly parties to the fraudulent trading shall make such contributions to the company's assets as the court thinks proper.[243] Fraudulent trading (so defined) is also a criminal offence under s.993 of the Companies Act 2006.[244] The criminal offence, unlike the civil penalties in the Insolvency Act, however, is not linked to a winding up.

In general it may be properly inferred that there is an intent to defraud creditors if a company carries on business and incurs debts when, to the knowledge of the directors, there is no reasonable prospect of the company being able to pay them.[245] It is not necessary to show that there was no prospect of the creditors ever being paid. It is enough that there is no reason for thinking that they will be paid as the debts fall due or shortly thereafter.[246] In general, the courts have used the benchmark of "actual dishonesty" in determining whether the requirements of the section are made out.[247] However, the fact that one transaction carried out by the company could be described as fraudulent does not amount to the business

---

[241] *Grosvenor Metal Co Ltd, Re* [1950] Ch. 3.

[242] *Suidair International Airways Ltd, Re* [1951] Ch. 165.

[243] Any order is in favour of the liquidator not an individual shareholder: *Esal (Commodities) Ltd, Re* [1997] 1 B.C.L.C. 705, CA.

[244] There must be a finding of dishonesty for the criminal offence to be committed: *R. v Cox* [1983] B.C.L.C. 169. For the purposes of s.458 Companies Act 1985 the predecessor to s.993 "creditors" have been held to include future creditors: *R. v Smith* [1996] 2 B.C.L.C. 109, CA.

[245] *William C. Leitch Bros Ltd, Re* [1932] 2 Ch. 71.

[246] *R. v Grantham* [1984] Q.B. 675.

[247] *Patrick and Lyon Ltd, Re* [1933] Ch. 786; *Bernasconi v Nicholas Bennett & Co* [2000] B.C.C. 921.

of the company being carried on with the intention to defraud.[248] It is not fraudulent trading to intend to prefer one creditor to another even if all could not be paid in full,[249] nor to sell goods which prove to be defective knowing that liability for such defects might not be met.[250]

The expression "parties to" the fraudulent trading in s.213(2) indicates no more than "take part in" or "concur in" and involves some positive steps. Mere omission by the secretary to give certain advice (that the company is insolvent and should cease to trade) is not being a party to carrying on the business in a fraudulent manner.[251] However, a creditor who, knowing of the circumstances, accepts money fraudulently obtained by the company may be liable to repay it even if he took no part in the fraudulent trading itself.[252] The general rules as to the attribution of knowledge to a company[253] may result in a form of "vicarious" liability for fraudulent trading.

In *Morris v Bank of India*,[254] an international bank had engaged in a systematic fraud involving the manipulation of its accounts to conceal losses. The defendant bank had engaged in a series of transactions with the insolvent company whereby receipts from it had been used to credit heavily overdrawn accounts to give a false impression of solvency. It was found as a fact that employees of the defendant bank had "blind-eye knowledge" of the fraud. It was held that the defendant bank, by virtue of the knowledge of its employees, was a party to fraudulent trading.

It is not, however, fraudulent trading for a parent company to give promises of **29–039** support to a subsidiary which are not implemented. The fraud of the parent company cannot be linked to the subsidiary, since to establish liability the fraudulent trading must be committed by someone carrying on the business, i.e. the subsidiary. In any event such general statements would not be sufficient to prove fraud.[255]

The cause of action under s.213 arises on the date that the winding up order is made,[256] and although the court is given discretion, under s.213(2), to make any order as to contribution as it thinks proper it has been held that an appropriate contribution should be restricted to the amount equal to that by which the company's assets have been diminished; there should not be a penal element in this respect.[257] Where two or more parties are found liable under the provision, it may be appropriate to make separate orders regarding contribution against each.[258] The court may charge the liability of a person declared liable under s.213 on any debt due to him from the company, or on any charge on any assets of the company held by him, or any company or person on his behalf, or certain assignees from him or such a company or person: s.215.

---

[248] *Morphitis v Bernasconi* [2003] EWCA Civ. 289.
[249] *Sarflax Ltd, Re* [1979] Ch. 592.
[250] *Norcross Ltd v Amos* (1981) 131 N.L.J. 1213. See also *Rossleigh Ltd v Carlaw*, 1986 S.L.T. 204 in Scotland as to the knowledge required of the intent to defraud.
[251] *Maidstone Buildings Provisions Ltd, Re* [1971] 1 W.L.R. 1085, *R. v Miles* [1992] Crim.L.R. 657.
[252] *Gerald Cooper Chemicals Ltd, Re* [1978] Ch. 262.
[253] See above, Ch.23.
[254] [2005] EWCA Civ. 693.
[255] *Augustus Barnett & Son Ltd, Re* [1986] B.C.L.C. 170.
[256] *Overnight Ltd (In Liquidation), Re* [2009] EWHC 601 (Ch.).
[257] *Morphitis v Bernasconi* [2003] EWCA Civ. 289.
[258] *Overnight Ltd (In Liquidation), Re* [2010] EWHC 613 (Ch.).

Wrongful trading

29–040 The difficulties of establishing the "fraudulent" element of fraudulent trading led to many directors who had carried on the business recklessly being exempt. The Insolvency Act introduced another concept, that of wrongful trading which is designed to apply to such cases. Wrongful trading, which applies only to directors and to insolvent liquidations, has been dealt with in Ch.15, above.[259] As far as directors are concerned wrongful trading will largely replace fraudulent trading. Fraudulent trading, however, remains for other persons and as a criminal offence for serious cases (wrongful trading is not a criminal offence).

Summary remedy against delinquent directors, etc.

29–041 This was explained in the chapter on directors.[260]

Disclaimer

29–042 Where any part of the property of a company which is being wound up is onerous property, the liquidator may on giving notice disclaim that property. Onerous property for this purpose is (a) any unprofitable contract; or (b) any other property of the company which is unsaleable or not readily saleable or is such that may give rise to a liability to pay money or perform any other onerous act: s.178(1)–(3). A waste management licence has been held to be "property" or a right incidental to property for the purposes of the section: *Celtic Extraction Ltd & Bluestone Chemicals Ltd v Environment Agency* [2001] Ch. 475, CA.[261]

A disclaimer operates to determine the rights and liabilities of the company in respect of the property disclaimed but does not, except for the purpose of releasing the company from liability, affect the rights or liabilities of any other person: s.178(4).[262] Thus, where an insolvent company is the tenant under a lease, a disclaimer by the liquidator releases the future rent liability of the company but not that of its surety or of former tenants.[263] Furthermore, payment by a surety or former tenant gives rise to no right of indemnity against the company: see *Hindcastle Ltd v Barbara Attenborough Associates Ltd* [1996] 1 All E.R. 737, HL.[264] The liquidator cannot disclaim any property if notice in writing is served on him by a person interested in the property, requiring him to decide whether he will disclaim or not, and he does not, within 28 days, or any longer period allowed by the court, give notice of disclaimer: s.178(5).

---

[259] Above, p.587.
[260] Above, p.590.
[261] See also *Swift v Dairywise Farms Ltd (No.1)* [2000] 1 All E.R. 320 (milk quota).
[262] See *Capital Prime Properties Plc v Worthgate Ltd* [2000] B.C.C. 525.
[263] In relation to pre-1996 leases the liability of former tenants is contractual; in relation to leases granted on or after January 1, 1996 liability may arise under an authorised guarantee agreement: see Landlord & Tenant (Covenants) Act 1995, s.16.
[264] Overruling *Stacey v Hill* [1901] 1 Q.B. 660. See also *Shaw v Doleman* [2009] EWCA Civ. 279.

Any person injured by a disclaimer is deemed a creditor of the company to the extent of his loss or damage and may prove for that amount in the winding up: s.178(6).[265]

Where the property is a leasehold, no disclaimer can take effect unless the liquidator has served a notice on every person claiming under the company as underlessee or mortgagee and either no application for a vesting order (see below) has been made by such a person within 14 days or, if such application has been made, the court nevertheless directs that the disclaimer shall take effect: s.179.

The court may, on the application of any person interested in the property,[266] or **29–043** who is under an undischarged liability in respect of the disclaimed property,[267] make an order for the vesting or delivery of the property to that person or his trustee on such terms as it thinks fit.[268] However, the applicant must have a proprietary interest in the disclaimed property for such an order to be granted.[269] The effect of any such order must be taken into account in assessing any loss subsequently provable in the winding up: s.181. Where the property is a leasehold, such a vesting order cannot be made in favour of an underlessee or mortgagee, unless it is either (a) subject to the same liabilities and obligations as those to which the company was subject under the lease at the commencement of the winding up, or (b), if the court thinks fit, subject only to the same liabilities and obligations as if the lease had been assigned to that person at that date: s.182.

Any person who is, as against the liquidator, entitled to the benefit or subject to the burden of a contract with the company may apply to the court for an order rescinding the contract. The court may grant rescission on such terms as it thinks fit, including the payment of damages for breach of contract. Any damages payable to such a person under the order may be proved for in the liquidation: s.186.

The Insolvency Act widened the former disclaimer provisions in two major respects. First, the consent of the court is no longer required. The discretion previously vested in the court is now vested in the liquidator and its exercise can only be challenged[270] on the grounds of mala fides or perversity.[271] Second, the definition of onerous property has been widened to include unsaleable property.[272]

---

[265] In relation to the disclaimer of a lease, the landlord can claim the difference between the aggregate of the rent and other amounts which it was entitled to be paid by the tenant for the residue of the lease subject to a discount for accelerated receipt and the income which it could obtain from another tenant entering into the same lease (save as to rent) for a term equivalent to the residue of the term: *Park Air Services Plc, Re* [2000] 2 A.C. 172.

[266] This includes a statutory tenant: *Vedmay, Re* [1994] 10 E.G. 108.

[267] e.g. the tenant-company's surety, see *A.E. Realisations, Re* (1985) [1987] B.C.L.C. 486. Compare *Spirit Motorsport Ltd, Re* [1996] 1 B.C.L.C. 684.

[268] For example that on sale the surplus should be repaid to the liquidator for the benefit of the other creditors: cf. In *Lee, Re* (a Bankrupt), *The Times*, February 24, 1998.

[269] *Ballast Plc, Re* [2006] EWHC 3189 (Ch.) (insurer's subrogated right to assured company's claim was not a proprietary right).

[270] See IA 1986 s.168(5).

[271] *Hans Place Ltd, Re* [1992] B.C.C. 737; *Cavendish Offices & Houses Investments Ltd v Adams* [1992] E.G. 107.

[272] cf. Re *Potters Oils Ltd, Re* [1986] 1 W.L.R. 201 decided on the old law.

THE LIQUIDATOR IN A WINDING UP BY THE COURT

29–044 The liquidator in a winding up by the court is an officer of the court.[273]

Appointment

29–045 The liquidator is appointed in the manner already discussed.[274] He is an office holder[275] and as such must be a qualified insolvency practitioner.[276] The court has appointed as liquidator a person resident beyond the jurisdiction of the court but such an appointment was only made where there was an adequate reason.[277] Any person who gives, or agrees or offers to give, any member or creditor of the company any valuable consideration with a view to securing his own appointment or nomination, or to securing or preventing the appointment or nomination of someone else, as the liquidator, is liable to a fine: s.164.

Resignation and removal

29–046 A liquidator may resign by giving notice to the court before the completion of the liquidation: s.172(6). A liquidator must vacate his office on ceasing to be a qualified insolvency practitioner[278] and on the holding of the final meeting of creditors[279]: s.172(5), (8).

A liquidator may be removed either by the court or by a meeting of the creditors: s.172(2). Grounds on which a liquidator has been removed by the court include personal unfitness (due to, e.g. his character, his residence,[280] or his personal interest or involvement[281]), insanity,[282] prosecuting a claim against the wishes of a majority of the creditors where the company is insolvent,[283] or failing to carry out his duties with sufficient vigour and displaying a relaxed and complacent attitude towards wrongdoing by the directors.[284] On the other hand the court has refused to remove a liquidator merely because he is a shareholder and former

---

[273] Per Megarry J. in *Rolls Razor Ltd, Re (No.2)* [1970] Ch. 576 at 586. In *International Factors Ltd v Ves Voltech Electronic Services Ltd*, 1995 S.L.T. (Sh.Ct.) 40, it was observed that a provisional liquidator was an officer of the court and was required to comply with an order of the court and the statutory regulations governing his appointment; should advertisement of his appointment not be appropriate, he should immediately apply to the court for dispensation from the requirement to advertise; as the provisional liquidator had not done so in this case, the sheriff refused payment of his fees and expenses out of the property of the company.

[274] Above, p.707.

[275] Above, p.708.

[276] Above, p.638.

[277] *Brightwen & Co v City of Glasgow Bank* (1878) 6 R. 244 (appointment as joint liquidator of accountant resident in London refused); see *also Barberton Development etc. Ltd, Petitioners* (1898) 25 R. 654, and contrast *Liquidators of Bruce Peebles & Co Ltd v Shiells*, 1908 S.C. 692.

[278] Above, p.638.

[279] Below, p.793.

[280] *Skinner, Petitioner* (1899) 6 S.L.T. 388, OH (residence in England of sole liquidator).

[281] *Lysons v Liquidator of the Miraflores Gold Syndicate Ltd* (1895) 22 R. 605; *Corbenstoke, Re (No.2)* [1990] B.C.L.C. 60 (liquidator was the company's debtor).

[282] *The North Molton Mining Co Ltd, Re* (1886) 54 L.T. 602.

[283] *Tavistock Ironworks Co, Re* (1871) 24 L.T. 605.

[284] *Keypak Homecare, Re* [1987] B.C.L.C. 409.

director,[285] or because the majority of the creditors or of the contributories desire it[286] or because the liquidator has made a serious mistake.[287] The conduct of the liquidator must give rise to a reasonable loss of confidence on the part of the creditors.[288] In general, whether or not the removal of the liquidator should be ordered will depend upon the facts of each case, but it has been held that the court should be wary of acceding to creditors' applications based simply on a contention that the liquidator's conduct had fallen short of the ideal.[289]

The meeting of the creditors to replace a liquidator may be called by the liquidator himself, the court or one quarter in value of the creditors. If the liquidator was appointed by the Secretary of State only the Secretary of State may remove him. A vacancy in the office of the liquidator appointed by the court is filled in England by the official receiver: s.136(3).

Duties

The functions of a liquidator are to secure that the assets of the company are got   **29–047**
in, realised and distributed to the company's creditors and, if there is a surplus, to the persons entitled to it: s.143(1).

A liquidator must:

1. to give all information, assistance and documents to the official receiver as he may reasonably require: s.143(2);

2. take all the property of the company into his custody as soon as possible: s.144;

3. as soon as may be, settle a list of contributories,[290] collect the company's assets, apply them in discharge of its liabilities and distribute any surplus among the members according to their rights and interests in the company: ss.148, 154, 160.

The word "liabilities" excludes claims which are not legally enforceable. Thus it does not include arrears of tax claimed by a foreign state, even one which adheres to the Commonwealth.[291] If the liquidator distributes the assets without making provision for the liabilities he is liable to pay damages to the unpaid creditors.

In *James Smith & Sons (Norwood) Ltd v Goodman*,[292] the company had a lease of premises expiring in 1938 at a yearly rent of £1,217 10s. The lease was assigned to M, and in 1933 the company went into voluntary liquidation. M was insolvent and unable to pay the rent. The liquidator distributed the assets without making any

---

[285] *M'Knight & Co Ltd v Montgomerie* (1892) 19 R. 501; but see *Corbenstoke, Re* above n.281, where Harman J. considered it unlikely that a director would ever be a suitable person to act as liquidator.
[286] *Ker, Petitioner* (1897) 5 S.L.T. 126, OH.
[287] *Edennote Ltd, Re* [1996] B.C.C. 718.
[288] *Edennote Ltd* [1996] B.C.C. 718.
[289] *AMP Enterprises Ltd v Hoffman* [2002] EWHC 1899 (Ch.).
[290] But see below, p.739.
[291] *Government of India v Taylor* [1955] A.C. 491; cf. *Clyde Marine Insurance Co Ltd v Renwick & Co*, 1924 S.C. 113.
[292] [1936] Ch. 216, CA.

provision for the company's liabilities under the lease. It was held that the liquidator had committed a breach of his duty and was liable in damages to the lessor.

(4) summon meetings of the creditors or contributories when directed by resolution of the creditors or contributories or requested in writing by one-tenth in value of the creditors or contributories: s.168(2). He may summon meetings on his own initiative whenever he wants to ascertain the wishes of the creditors or contributories: s.168(2).

(5) Summon a final meeting in accordance with s.146.[293]

(6) In common with administrative receivers and administrators,[294] a liquidator must set aside a prescribed part of the company's property to be made available to the company's unsecured creditors: s.176A.

Powers of the liquidator

29–048 Section 167 of the IA 1986, and Sch.4 to that Act, provide that:

1. The liquidator (including a provisional liquidator[295]) in a winding up by the court has power, with the sanction of the court or of the liquidation committee:

    (a) to bring or defend actions and legal proceedings in the name and on behalf of the company.

It is a matter for his discretion whether he should litigate or not and so the court will not give guidance as to whether he should appeal to a higher court.[296] If the liquidator brings an unsuccessful action, only in exceptional circumstances (involving impropriety) will he be ordered to pay the costs personally.[297] Where the company has insufficient funds to meet the costs, the defendant should seek an order for security of costs.[298] An agreement between a liquidator and third parties that the latter would fund an action brought by the company in return for half of the amount recovered contravenes the law of maintenance and champerty and the action will be stayed.[299]

---

[293] Below, p.753.

[294] See Chs 27 and 28.

[295] *Wilsons (Glasgow and Trinidad) Ltd, Petitioners*, 1912 2 S.L.T. 330.

[296] *Note for Liquidator in Liquidation of S.S. "Camelot" Ltd* (1893) 1 S.L.T. 358, OH.

[297] See *Metalloy Supplies Ltd v M.A. (UK) Ltd* [1997] B.C.C. 165, CA; *Roods of Queensferry Ltd v Shand Construction Ltd (costs)* [2002] EWCA Civ. 918. Compare where he brings an action in his own name: *Wilson Lovatt & Sons Ltd, Re* [1977] 1 All E.R. 274.

[298] *Mettaloy*, above.

[299] See *Grovewood Holdings Plc v James Capel & Co Ltd* [1995] B.C.C. 760. A liquidator can sell a bare cause of action on terms providing for the division of recoveries (ibid.) and the validity of the assignment is not impaired by the fact that its purpose was to enable the litigation to be conducted with the benefit of Legal Aid: *Norglen Ltd v Reeds Rains Prudential Ltd* [1998] B.C.C. 44, HL. See also *Quest Trading Co Ltd (In Liquidation) v Revenue and Customs Commissioners* [2006] V. & D.R. 202.

(b) to carry on the business of the company so far as may be necessary for beneficial winding up.

In *Liquidator of Burntisland Oil Co Ltd v Dawson* (1892) 20 R. 180, the court refused the liquidator's application to carry on the business for an indefinite period on the ground that the company's property could not then be sold except on ruinous terms but granted power to carry on for six weeks while the property was advertised for sale. However, in *McIntyre, Petitioner* (1893) 30 S.L.R. 386, OH, power was granted to carry on business until the time of the year when the company's property, which consisted of a hall let for public entertainments, could be sold to best advantage.

When a liquidator carries on the business of the company he does so as the company's agent[300] and is not personally liable on contracts which he enters into as liquidator.[301]

(c) to pay any classes of creditors in full.
(d) to make any compromise or arrangement with creditors.[302]
(e) to compromise all calls and liabilities to calls and other debts and liabilities.

If a liquidator does any of the acts listed without the necessary sanction of the court or the liquidation committee he is personally liable although the court may retrospectively sanction such an act.[303] It appears, however, that no prospective sanction may be given by the Secretary of State.[304]

2. On his own responsibility and without obtaining any sanction, the liquidator can:

(a) Sell the property of the company.[305]
(b) Do all acts and execute, in the name and on behalf of the company, all deeds and documents, and use the company's seal therefore.
(c) Prove, rank and claim in the bankruptcy, insolvency or sequestration of any contributory.
(d) Draw, accept, make and indorse any bill of exchange or promissory note in the name and on behalf of the company.

---

[300] See *Smith v Lord Advocate*, 1978 S.C. 259.
[301] *Stead, Hazel & Co v Cooper* [1933] 1 K.B. 840; *Stewart v Engel* [2000] B.C.C. 741.
[302] This was held, in *Taylor, Noter*, 1993 S.L.T. 375, to extend to entering into a compromise with the trustee on the sequestrated estate of a director where the director's own assets and those of his two companies were so confused that it was impossible to identify the assets of each.
[303] *Associated Travel Leisure and Services Ltd (in Liquidation), Re* [1978] 1 W.L.R. 547.
[304] *Gresham International Ltd (In Liquidation) v Moonie* [2009] EWHC 1093 (Ch.).
[305] This includes a bare cause of action, *Norglen Ltd v Reeds Rains Prudential Ltd*, above, n.299, but not the fruits of wrongful or fraudulent trading litigation under ss.213 and 214: *Oasis Merchandising Services Ltd, Re* [1997] B.C.C. 282, CA.

    (e) Raise money on the security of the company's assets.

    (f) Take out letters of administration to any deceased contributory and do any other act necessary for obtaining payment of money due from a contributory or his estate.

    (g) Appoint an agent to do business which he cannot do himself.

    (h) Do all such other things as are necessary for winding up the affairs of the company and distributing its assets.

29–049 The exercise of these powers is subject to the control of the court and any creditor or contributory may apply to the court with respect to such exercise: s.167(3). If, in England, any person is aggrieved by any act or decision of the liquidator, that person may apply to the court, which may make such order as it thinks just: s.168(5).

    In *Edennote Ltd, Re*,[306] the liquidator assigned the company's cause of action to V for £7,000 plus 10 per cent of the proceeds of the action without considering whether others would have made a higher offer. It was held that the liquidator's act was utterly unreasonable and absurd and the assignment should be set aside.

    Aside from creditors and contributories, persons who may apply to the court under this section are restricted to those directly affected by the exercise of a specific power.[307]

    In England, the liquidator may apply to the court for directions in relation to any particular matter arising under the winding up: s.168(3). The right should be exercised in every case of serious doubt or difficulty in relation to the performance by the liquidator of his statutory duties. The omission to exercise it may lead the liquidator into serious liabilities.[308] Subject to the various statutory provisions the liquidator may use his own discretion as to the management and distribution of the company's assets: s.168(4).

Liability

29–050 A liquidator is not strictly speaking a trustee for the individual creditors or contributories, his position being that of agent of the company.

    During a liquidation a claim was made by a contributory for damages for delay in handing over to the contributory his proportion of the surplus assets of the company. It was held that in the absence of fraud, bad faith or personal misconduct, an action for damages would not lie against the liquidator at the suit of a creditor or contributory, the proper remedy being an application to the court to control the liquidator in the exercise of his powers.[309]

---

[306] [1996] B.C.C. 718, CA.

[307] *Mahomed v Morris (No.2)* [2001] B.C.C. 233. See also *Ultraframe (UK) Ltd v Rigby* [2005] EWCA Civ. 276.

[308] See *Windsor Steam Coal Co, Re* (1901) Ltd [1929] 1 Ch. 151; and *Home and Colonial Insurance Co Ltd, Re* [1930] 1 Ch. 102, below.

[309] *Knowles v Scott* [1891] 1 Ch. 717. See also *Leon v York-o-Matic Ltd* [1966] 3 All E.R. 277.

On the other hand, for breach of any of his statutory duties the liquidator will be liable in damages to a creditor or contributory for injury caused to them.

In *Pulsford v Devenish*,[310] a liquidator distributed the assets of the company without paying X, a creditor, who had no notice of the liquidation. The books of the company showed X to be a creditor but the liquidator made no attempt to communicate with X beyond issuing an insufficient advertisement for creditors. The company was dissolved. It was held that the liquidator was liable in damages to X. The duty of the liquidator was not merely to advertise for creditors but to write to those of whom he knew and who did not send in claims.

A liquidator should make provision for contingent claims of which he has notice, e.g. where the company, having assigned a lease, remains liable for the rent,[311] or where he knows of possible claims by workmen for injuries not covered by insurance.[312] If a liquidator applies the company's assets in paying a doubtful claim, which turns out to be unfounded, without taking proper legal advice or applying to the court for directions, he will be liable to refund the amount paid on a misfeasance summons taken out by a creditor or contributory.[313]

A liquidator, however, is not liable for admitting a proof of debt which is **29-051** ill-founded, provided he exercises all due care beforehand. But a

"high standard of care and diligence is required from a liquidator in a . . . winding up. He is of course paid for his services; he is able to obtain wherever it is expedient the assistance of solicitors and counsel; and, which is a most important consideration, he is entitled, in every serious case of doubt or difficulty . . . to submit the matter to the Court and to obtain its guidance".[314]

In *Home and Colonial Insurance Co, Re*,[315] H Co made a reinsurance agreement with L Co which was invalid. On H going into liquidation, L tendered a proof which the liquidator ultimately accepted for £89,100, on which £38,000 was paid to L in dividends. On learning that he should have disallowed the claim, the liquidator sued L but the claim was dismissed, as no mistake of fact on the part of the liquidator was made. A creditor took out a misfeasance summons. It was held that the liquidator was negligent in admitting so large a proof without taking legal advice or applying for directions, and was liable to pay compensation to the company.

Where a liquidator has paid money to shareholders under an error in law, caused, e.g. by an underestimation of tax liability, he is not entitled to recover it under the

---

[310] [1903] 2 Ch. 625. See also *Austin Securities Ltd v Northgate and English Stores Ltd* [1969] 2 All E.R. 753.

[311] *James Smith & Sons (Norwood) Ltd v Goodman* [1936] Ch. 216, CA; cf. *Lord Elphinstone v Monkland Iron etc. Co Ltd* (1886) 13 R. HL 98. See now Landlord and Tenant (Covenants) Act 1995.

[312] *Armstrong Whitworth Securities Co Ltd, Re* [1947] Ch. 673.

[313] *Windsor Steam Coal Co, Re* (1901) Ltd [1929] 1 Ch. 151, CA, where the court refused to grant him relief under s.61 of the Trustee Act 1925.

[314] per Maugham J. in *Home and Colonial Insurance Co Ltd, Re* [1930] 1 Ch. 102 at 125.

[315] [1930] 1 Ch. 102.

condictio indebiti, there being no special relationship between the liquidator and the shareholders such as to take the situation outside the general rule.[316]

Release

29–052 When a liquidator ceases to hold office, the question is whether and when he can be released from his obligations. If the liquidator is the official receiver he can be released either by notifying the Secretary of State that the winding up is for all practical purposes complete or, if he is replaced by another liquidator, on giving notice to the court that he has been so replaced. If he is replaced by a liquidator appointed by the court, it is for the court to determine his release: s.174(2)(3).

If the liquidator is someone other than the official receiver his release takes effect as follows:

1. if he was removed by the creditors' meeting which did not resolve against his release, or if he has died, at the time when notice of removal or death is given to the court;

2. if the creditors' meeting voted against his release but removed him from office, or he ceases to be a qualified insolvency practitioner he must apply to the Secretary of State for his release;

3. on resignation his release is governed by the rules[317];

4. if he has vacated office having called the final meeting of creditors he is released at that time unless the meeting votes to the contrary, in which case (b) applies: s.174(4).

The effect of a release is to discharge the liquidator from all liability in respect of his acts or omissions as such: s.174(6).

WINDING UP OF UNREGISTERED COMPANIES

29–053 Section 221(5) provides that an unregistered company may be wound up by the court[318] if:

1. it is dissolved, or has ceased business, or is carrying on business only for the purpose of winding up its affairs;

2. it is unable to pay its debts[319]; or

3. the court is of the opinion that it is just and equitable that the company should be wound up.

---

[316] *Taylor v Wilson's Trustees*, 1975 S.C. 146.

[317] IR 1986 r.4.121.

[318] Such a company cannot be wound up voluntarily other than in accordance with the EU Regulation: IA 1986 s.221(4).

[319] This will be deemed in the circumstances set out in ss.222–224.

The expression "unregistered company" includes any association or company[320] with the exception of a company registered in any part of the UK under the Joint Stock Companies Acts or under legislation (past or present) relating to companies in Great Britain (s.220(1)). Examples include companies incorporated by special Act or Royal Charter and certain foreign companies,[321] Investment Companies with Variable Capital[322] and a European Economic Interest Group may also be wound up under these provisions.[323]

Section 227 extends s.126[324] (stay of proceedings against company) to proceedings against a contributory where the application to stay is by a creditor, and s.228 provides that where an order has been made for winding up an unregistered company, no action or proceeding shall be proceeded with or commenced against any contributory of the company in respect of any debt of the company, except by leave of the court.

The provisions of Pt V of the Act (ss.220–229) with respect to unregistered companies are in addition to and not in restriction of the provisions with respect to the winding up of companies by the court, and the court or liquidator has the same powers in the case of unregistered companies as in the case of the winding up of companies formed and registered under the Act: s.229.

---

[320] While these words are very wide, they do not include an association which Parliament could not reasonably have intended should be subject to the winding up process: *International Tin Council, Re* [1988] 3 All E.R. 257 at 361 C.A. approving *St James Club, Re* (1852) 2 D & GM & G 383; see also *Witney Town Football & Social Club, Re* [1993] B.C.C. 874. The word "company" includes those incorporated elsewhere than in Great Britain: *Normandy Marketing Ltd, Re* [1993] B.C.C. 879 (Northern Ireland). A limited partnership was included in the definition of an unregistered company in s.665 of the 1985 Companies Act but was removed by the Insolvency Act 1985; as the 1986 Act was a consolidating Act which was not intended to alter the existing law, a limited partnership was not an unregistered company which could be wound up under s.220: *Smith v Smith*, 1998 G.W.D. 26–1341.

[321] See *Palmer's Company Law*, Vol.3, para.15–222.

[322] See Open-Ended Investment Companies (Investment Companies with Variable Capital) Regs 1996 (SI 1996/2827), regs 25–27.

[323] Council Regulation 2137/85, [1985] OJ L199/1, art.35.2.

[324] Above, p.700.

Chapter 30

VOLUNTARY WINDING UP

30–001 From the point of view of the company itself, a voluntary winding up has many advantages over a compulsory winding up, the chief being that there are not so many formalities to be complied with. In consequence the great majority of liquidations are voluntary liquidations. The Cork Committee, however, made several recommendations to prevent abuses in the system of voluntary liquidation and some of these were adopted by the Insolvency Act 1985, since consolidated into the Insolvency Act 1986.

INTRODUCTION

Initiation of voluntary winding up

30–002 Section 84 provides that a company may be wound up voluntarily:

1. When the period, if any, fixed for its duration by the articles expires, or the event, if any, occurs, on the occurrence of which the articles provide that it is to be dissolved, and the company in general meeting passes a resolution (i.e. an ordinary resolution) to be wound up voluntarily.

2. If it resolves by special resolution[1] to be wound up voluntarily.

A company can be wound up by special resolution without any reason being assigned, but the resolution cannot be passed conditionally to take effect on the happening of some other event.[2]

An extraordinary resolution is allowed here because time is of the essence since the company is insolvent and a special resolution would normally require a longer period of notice.[3]

Before any resolution is passed for voluntary winding up, the company must give notice of the resolution to the holder of a qualifying floating charge[4] to which s.72A applies: s.84(2A). This is to allow the holder of such a charge to

---

[1] Above, p.505. In the case of a company registered as a social landlord under the Housing Act 1996, such a resolution has no effect unless the Housing Corporation gives its prior consent: see Housing Act 1996 Sch.1 para.13(6)

[2] See *Norditrak (UK) Ltd, Re* [2000] B.C.C. 441.

[3] Above, p.505.

[4] For the meaning of qualifying floating charge, see IA 1986 Sch.B1 para.14.

appoint an administrator[5] under para.14 of Sch.B1 if he sees fit. Once notice has been given, no resolution for voluntary winding up may be passed unless the qualifying floating charge holder consents or until after five business days have elapsed without the appointment of an administrator having been made. A resolution for voluntary winding up must be advertised in the Gazette within 14 days after it is passed: s.85.[6] A voluntary winding up commences at the time of the passing of the resolution: s.86.

Kinds of voluntary winding up

A voluntary winding up may be either (1) a members' voluntary winding up; or (2) a creditors' voluntary winding up: s.90. **30–003**

MEMBERS' VOLUNTARY WINDING UP

A members' voluntary winding up takes place only when the company is solvent. It is entirely managed by the members, and the liquidator is appointed by them. No meeting of creditors is held and no liquidation committee is appointed. To obtain the benefit of this form of winding up, a declaration of solvency must be filed: s.89. **30–004**

Declaration of solvency

This is a statutory declaration made by the directors or, if there are more than two of them, by the majority, at a board meeting, that they have made a full inquiry into the company's affairs and, having done so, they have formed the opinion that the company will be able to pay its debts in full together with interest at the official rate[7] within a specified period not exceeding 12 months from the commencement of the winding up.[8] The declaration has no effect unless it is made within the five weeks immediately preceding the date of the passing of the winding up resolution. It may even be made on that date providing that it precedes the resolution. **30–005**

The declaration must be filed with the Registrar within 15 days of the passing of the resolution. Further, the declaration has no effect unless it embodies a statement of the company's assets and liabilities as at the latest practicable date before it is made: s.89. If there is something which can reasonably be described as "a statement of the company's assets and liabilities," then, even if it subsequently appears that there were errors and omissions, these will not prevent it from being a statement within s.89.[9] Nor will minor inaccuracies in the statement of assets and liabilities relied upon by directors in making the declaration of solvency invalidate it.[10]

---

[5] See, generally, Ch.28, above.
[6] A copy must be forwarded to the Registrar of Companies within 15 days.
[7] See IA 1986 s.251.
[8] See above.
[9] *De Courcy v Clement* [1971] Ch. 693.
[10] *New Millennium Experience Ltd, Re* [2003] EWHC 1823 (Ch.).

A director making a declaration of solvency without reasonable grounds is liable to imprisonment or a fine or both: s.89(6)[11] If the debts plus interest are not paid or provided for within the period stated, he is presumed not to have had reasonable grounds: s.89(5). If a declaration is made in accordance with the section the winding up is a members' voluntary winding up: s.90.

The liquidator

30–006 Unlike the liquidator in a winding up by the court, a liquidator in a voluntary winding up is not an officer of the court.[12] He is the agent of the company, but not of the individual members.[13] He is appointed, by the company in general meeting (s.91), and within 14 days he must give notice of his appointment to the Registrar of companies and publish it in the Gazette: s.109.[14] He may be appointed at the meeting at which the resolution for voluntary winding up is passed. If there is no liquidator acting, the court may appoint one. The court may also, on cause shown, remove a liquidator and appoint another: s.108[15] Thus, where a liquidator ceased to be qualified to act as an insolvency practitioner the court exercised its power under s.108(2).[16] Where, however, a person had been appointed liquidator without his knowledge and he declined to act, it was held that the appointment was invalid and there was therefore no need to remove him.[17] Anyone subject to a disqualification order under the Company Directors Disqualification Act 1986 cannot act as a liquidator.[18] The liquidator is also an office holder under the Insolvency Act.[19] He must be a qualified insolvency practitioner[20] and has the powers and duties of an office holder.

If a liquidator appointed by the company vacates office, whether by death, resignation or otherwise, the company at a general meeting, summoned by any contributory or by a continuing liquidator, may, subject to any arrangement with creditors, fill the vacancy: s.92.

In the period before the appointment of a liquidator the directors cannot exercise their powers without the sanction of the court, except to dispose of perishable goods or goods which are likely to fall in value if not disposed of immediately and to do anything necessary for the protection of the company's assets: s.114. This provision was introduced following a recommendation of the Cork Committee to prevent dissipation of the company's assets prior to the appointment

---

[11] See also IA 1986 s.430 and Sch.10.
[12] per Megarry J. in *Rolls Razor Ltd, Re (No.2)* [1970] Ch. 576 at 586.
[13] See *Taylor v Wilson's Trustees*, 1975 S.C. 146.
[14] This provision applies to all voluntary liquidations. In a members voluntary winding up the powers of the directors cease unless the general meeting or the liquidator sanction their continuance: see s.91(2).
[15] This provision applies to all voluntary liquidations.
[16] *Bridgend Goldsmiths Ltd, Re* [1995] B.C.C. 226.
[17] *Liquidator of Highland etc. Dairy Farms Ltd and Another, Petitioners*, 1964 S.C. 1.
[18] Above, p.639.
[19] Above, p.708.
[20] Above, p.638.

of a liquidator.[21] Failure to comply with s.114 is a criminal offence[22] on the part of the directors and transactions effected are invalid.[23]

A special manager may also be appointed under s.177.[24]

Vacation of office by or removal of a liquidator

Being an office holder, a liquidator must vacate office if he ceases to be a quali- **30–007** fied insolvency practitioner.[25] He may resign in accordance with the rules.[26] He vacates office on giving notice to the Registrar of the final meetings held under s.94.[27] He may be removed at any time by a general meeting of the company summoned for that purpose or by the court. If the liquidator has been appointed by the court (e.g. to fill a vacancy) he may be removed and replaced by a meeting of members holding not less than one half of the total voting rights,[28] or by a general meeting of the company summoned by the liquidator or the court:[29] s.171(2).

Release of a liquidator

The liquidator is released at the time of the final meeting. If he has been removed **30–008** from office by a general meeting of the company his release operates from the date at which notice was given to the Registrar in accordance with the rules. If he has been removed by the court he must apply to the Secretary of State for his release. If the liquidator has resigned he is released in accordance with the rules: s.173[30] Such a release absolves him from all liability in relation to the winding up except for proceedings against him under s.212.[31]

Conduct of liquidation

Subject to s.96,[32] within three months after the end of the first and every **30–009** succeeding year of the liquidation, the liquidator must summon a general meeting of the company and lay before it an account of his acts and dealings and of the conduct of the winding up during the preceding year: s.93. As soon as the affairs of the company are fully wound up the liquidator must call a general meeting of

---

[21] A practice know as "centrebinding"—see below.

[22] s.114(4).

[23] *A Company, Re (No.006341 of 1992), Ex p. B Ltd* [1994] B.C.L.C. 225. Where a third party deals in good faith with the directors, in circumstances where he does not, and could not be expected to, know of the limitation on the directors' authority (as where the resolution to wind up has been neither registered nor advertised) the transaction may be binding on the company by virtue of ostensible authority. Judge Paul Baker, QC, ibid.

[24] Above, p.706.

[25] Above, p.638.

[26] IR 1986 r.4.142.

[27] Below.

[28] In a members' voluntary winding up.

[29] In a creditors' voluntary winding up.

[30] IR 1986 r.4.144.

[31] IA 1986 s.173(4).

[32] Below.

the company. This is done by advertisement in the Gazette at least one month before the meeting. At the meeting the liquidator must present an account of the winding up, showing how the winding up has been conducted and how the company's property has been disposed of. A copy of this account, together with a return of the holding of meeting, must be sent to the Registrar within a week after the meeting: s.94. It is not necessary for the affairs of the company to be fully wound up before the liquidator can validly make his return, only that they should be fully wound up so far as the liquidator is aware.[33]

If a quorum is not present at the final meeting, the liquidator must make a return that the meeting was summoned but no quorum was present, and this has the same effect as a return of the holding of the meeting: s.94(5). The Registrar must publish in the Gazette notice of the receipt of the return (Companies Act 2006 ss.1077, 1078).

Effect of insolvency on a members' voluntary winding up

30–010 If the liquidator is of the opinion that the company will in fact be unable to pay its debts in full (including interest) within the time specified by the directors in their declaration of solvency he must call a creditors' meeting within 28 days, giving them at least seven days' notice by post and advertising it in the Gazette or an appropriate publication.[34] He must also supply the creditors with any information they might reasonably require in that period: s.95(1), (2).

The liquidator must lay before the meeting a statement of affairs set out in accordance with the rules,[35] showing, in particular, the company's assets, debts and liabilities, its creditors and their securities, together with the dates on which they were created: s.95(3), (4). The effect of holding such a meeting is that the winding up proceeds as if the declaration of solvency had never been made; i.e. as a creditors' voluntary winding up: s.96.

CREDITORS' VOLUNTARY WINDING UP

30–011 If no declaration of solvency is filed with the Registrar, a voluntary winding up is a creditors' voluntary winding up: s.90. In such a case the company must summon a meeting of creditors[36] for a date not later than 14 days after the passing of the resolution to wind up the company. Notices of the meeting must be sent to the creditors at least seven days before the meeting. Notice of the meeting must also be advertised in the Gazette. The notice must also state either the name and address of a person qualified to act as an insolvency practitioner in relation to the company who will provide such information as the creditors may reasonably request prior to the meeting or a place in the locality where on two business days prior to the meeting a list of the creditors' names and addresses will be available

---

[33] *Cornish Manures Ltd, Re* [1967] 1 W.L.R. 807.
[34] i.e. within the location of its principal place of business during the preceding six months.
[35] IR 1986 r.4.34–CVL.
[36] If the winding up has been converted to a creditors' winding up the creditors' meeting making such a decision under s.95, above, is the creditors' meeting for this purpose: s.102.

free of charge: s.98. Section 98, amended by the Legislative Reform (Insolvency) (Advertising Requirements) Order 2009, which, for England and Wales, removes the previous requirement for the notice of the creditors' meeting to be advertised in a newspaper besides the Gazette. Instead, by s.98(1A)(d), the directors are given a discretion to advertise the notice in such manner as they think fit.

Management of such a winding up is shared by the members and creditors but in all cases the creditors have the ultimate control by virtue of the following provisions.

Meeting of creditors

The meeting of creditors is presided over by one of the directors nominated for **30–012** that purpose by the directors: s.99(1)(c). The business of the meeting is:

1. to receive a full statement by the directors as to the company's affairs, together with a list of the creditors, and details of any securities and other information required by the rules[37]: s.99(1)(b), (2);

2. to appoint a liquidator: s.100, below;

3. to appoint a liquidation committee: s.101, below.

The liquidator

The creditors and the company at their respective meetings may nominate a **30–013** liquidator and, if different persons are nominated, the person nominated by the creditors is the liquidator, subject to any order made by the court. If the creditors make no nomination the company's nominee is the liquidator. If different persons are nominated, any director, member or creditor of the company may, within seven days after the creditors' nomination, apply to the court for an order that the company's nominee be liquidator instead of or jointly with the creditors' nominee, or that some other person be liquidator: s.100. A liquidator appointed under this section is not an officer of the court: *TH Knitwear (Wholesale) Ltd, Re* [1988] Ch. 275.

Under this system of appointing a liquidator it is still possible for the company to appoint a liquidator elect for the 14 days before a creditors' meeting is required to be held. Prior to the Insolvency Act it was possible to delay the creditors' meeting for several weeks because of the decision in *Centrebind Ltd, Re*[38] to the effect that while failure to call the meeting was a criminal offence, it did not invalidate the appointment of the nominated liquidator or his actions. This abuse, known as "centre-binding", whereby the company's assets were in fact unprotected and beyond the creditors' control, has been countered by many provisions, following recommendations of the Cork Committee.[39] These include the

---

[37] IR 1986 r.4.34–CVL.
[38] [1967] 1 W.L.R. 377.
[39] paras 667–673.

requirement that any liquidator be a qualified insolvency practitioner,[40] that until any liquidator is appointed the directors' powers are subject to the court's control[41] and the 14-day time limit within which the creditors' meeting must now be held.[42]

In addition where the company nominates a liquidator prior to the creditors' meeting his powers can only be exercised with the court's consent. He may, however, assume custody of the company's property, dispose of perishable goods and those likely to diminish in value unless disposed of, and protect the company's assets. He must attend the creditors' meeting and report to that meeting on the exercise of any of his powers in the meantime. He is also charged with the duty to apply to the court if the company or the directors fail to comply with the requirement vis-à-vis the creditors' meeting: s.166. This effectively prevents "centre-binding" since any liquidator acting in default can be fined and will be liable under s.212.[43]

Any vacancy, by reason of death, resignation or otherwise, in the office of a liquidator, other than a liquidator appointed by the court may be filled by the creditors: s.104. A liquidator may vacate office by removal and be released from liability in the same way as a liquidator in a members' voluntary winding up, except that the function of the members' meetings are carried out by a meeting of creditors: ss.171, 173, above.[44]

Liquidation committee

30–014 The creditors, at their first or any subsequent meeting, may appoint a liquidation committee of not more than five persons to act with the liquidator.[45] If they do so, the company in general meeting may appoint not more than five persons to act as members of the committee, but the creditors may resolve that these persons ought not to be members of the committee, and thereupon, unless the court otherwise directs, they cannot act on the committee: s.101.

Conduct of liquidation

30–015 Within three months after the end of the first and every succeeding year of the liquidation the liquidator must summon a general meeting of the company and a meeting of creditors, and lay before the meetings an account of his acts and dealings and of the conduct of the winding up during the preceding year: s.105.

When the liquidation is complete, the liquidator must, by at least one month's notice in the Gazette, call final meetings of the company and the creditors, and present his account. Within a week after these meetings, a copy of the account and a return of the holding of the meetings or a return that no quorum was present thereat must be filed with the Registrar, who must publish it in the Gazette (Companies Act 2006 ss.1077, 1078): s.106.

---

[40] Above, p.638.
[41] s.114.
[42] Below.
[43] Above, p.590.
[44] p.729.
[45] Below.

CONSEQUENCES OF ANY VOLUNTARY WINDING UP

The commencement of a voluntary winding up is the date of the passing of the **30–016** resolution for voluntary winding up: s.86. Even if the company is subsequently wound up by the court, the commencement of the winding up is the date of the passing of the resolution: s.129.

The consequences of a voluntary winding up are as follows—

1. As from the commencement of the winding up the company must cease to carry on business except so far as is required for its beneficial winding up, although the corporate state and powers continue until the company is dissolved: s.87. Notification that the company is in liquidation must be given on the company's documents on which its name appears and on all the company's websites: s.188.[46]

2. No transfer of shares can be made without the sanction of the liquidator and any alteration in the status of the members is void: s.88. A transfer of debentures can, however, be made.[47]

3. On the appointment of a liquidator the powers of the directors cease except so far as the company in general meeting or the liquidator (in a members' voluntary winding up), or the liquidation committee or, if there is no such committee, the creditors (in a creditors' voluntary winding up), sanction their continuance: ss.91(2) and 103.

A voluntary winding up does not automatically operate as a discharge of the company's employees.[48] However, the liquidator has power to terminate contracts of employment and may do so by his conduct.[49] The liquidator may equally continue the employment of the company's employees if required to ensure a more beneficial winding up of the company.[50]

In England there is no statutory provision for the stay of actions and other proceedings against the company in the case of a voluntary winding up (cf. ss.126, 128, 130, above[51]), but on an application under s.112, below,[52] the court has a discretion to stay proceedings.[53] Executions will usually be stayed when it is necessary to ensure the distribution of assets among the creditors pari passu,[54] but actions will not be stayed when there is a dispute as to liability, or when no advantage will be gained, e.g. no expense will be saved, by a stay.[55]

---

[46] Above, p.705.
[47] *Goy & Co Ltd, Re* [1900] 2 Ch. 149.
[48] Compare a winding up by the court; above, p.705.
[49] *Fowler v Commercial Timber Co Ltd* [1930] 2 K.B. 1, CA.
[50] cf. *Day v Tait* (1900) 8 S.L.T. 40, OH. See also *Commercial Finance Co Ltd v Ramsingh-Mahabir* [1994] 1 W.L.R. 1297, PC.
[51] Ch.29, pp.702 et seq.
[52] p.735.
[53] *Currie v Consolidated Kent Collieries Corp Ltd* [1906] 1 K.B. 134, CA.
[54] *Anglo-Baltic Bank v Barber & Co* [1924] 2 K.B. 410, CA.
[55] *Cook v "X" Chair Patents Co Ltd* [1960] 1 W.L.R. 60.

DISTRIBUTION OF THE PROPERTY OF THE COMPANY IN A VOLUNTARY WINDING UP

30–017 The costs, charges and expenses properly incurred in a voluntary winding up, including the remuneration of the liquidator, are payable in priority to all other claims: s.115. The pre-liquidation expenses of a person who expected to be liquidator but was not, in the event, appointed, can be paid but only in so far as they were incurred to enable the company to pass the winding up resolution. Expense incurred in collecting the assets was not recoverable: *Sandwell Copiers, Re*.[56] The liquidator must then apply the property[57] of the company first in paying the preferential debts[58] and then in discharging the liabilities of the company pari passu. The liquidator has a duty to inquire into all claims against the company.[59] Even where the company is solvent, statute-barred debts cannot be paid unless the contributories consent.[60] Any surplus must then be distributed amongst the members according to their rights and interests in the company: IA 1986 s.107. A distribution which fails to take a creditor's claim into account exposes the liquidator to liability for breach of statutory duty.[61]

Provision may be made for employees on the cessation of business if it is approved by the members or otherwise in accordance with the articles either before or during the liquidation. Such payment must be made out of the assets available to the members: Companies Act 1985 s.719. Any exercise of this power is not subject to s.107: s.187.

A contracting out of the provisions of s.107 is contrary to public policy.[62] Section 107 does not, however, affect contracts which bona fide deprive the company of ownership prior to the winding up, e.g. the creation of a trust fund.[63] Such contracts may, however, be invalid under alternative provisions.[64]

POWERS AND DUTIES OF THE LIQUIDATOR IN A VOLUNTARY WINDING UP

30–018 In every voluntary winding up it is the duty of the liquidator to pay the debts of the company and adjust the rights of the contributories among themselves. To enable him to do this, s.165[65] and Sch.4 provide that he may without sanction:

---

[56] [1988] B.C.L.C. 209.

[57] Below, Ch.31.

[58] See s.175, below, p.751.

[59] *Austin Securities Ltd v Northgate and English Stores Ltd* [1969] 1 W.L.R. 529, CA applying *Pulsford v Devenish* and *Armstrong Whitworth Securities Co Ltd, Re* (above, p.733). See also *Royton Industries Ltd v Lawrence* (1994) *The Independent*, February 28, 1994 (rent liability on a lease which the company has assigned).

[60] *Art Reproduction Co Ltd, Re* [1952] Ch. 89.

[61] *AMF International Ltd v Ellis* [1995] B.C.C. 439; [1996] B.C.C. 335.

[62] *British Eagle International Air Lines Ltd v Compagnie Nationale Air France* [1975] 1 W.L.R. 758, HL, where the rules of the general liquidation prevailed over the International Air Transport Association clearing house arrangements and, despite such arrangements, the plaintiff company was entitled to recover the sums payable to it by other airlines for services rendered by it and not cleared through the IATA system and vice versa. See also *Money Markets International Stockbrokers Ltd (In Liquidation) v London Stock Exchange Ltd* [2002] 1 W.L.R. 1150; *Fraser v Oystertec Plc* [2004] B.C.C. 233; *Perpetual Trustee Co Ltd v BNY Corporate Trustee Services Ltd* [2009] EWHC 1912 (Ch.).

[63] *Carreras Rothmans Ltd v Freeman Matthews Treasure Ltd* [1985] Ch. 207.

[64] Below, Ch.31.

[65] Subject to s.166.

1. commence or defend legal proceedings on behalf of the company;

2. carry on the company's business so far as it is beneficial for the winding up;

He may carry on the business of the company, if he reasonably thinks it is necessary for the beneficial winding up of the company. If he does so, those to whom he incurs obligations are entitled to be paid in priority to the creditors at the commencement of the winding up: *Great Eastern Electric Co Ltd, Re* [1941] Ch. 241.[66]

3. exercise all the general powers of a liquidator listed in Pt III of Sch.4 to the IA 1986.

In a members' voluntary winding up, with the sanction of an extraordinary resolution of the company, and in a creditors' voluntary winding up, with the sanction of the court or the liquidation committee or (if there is no such committee) a meeting of the creditors, the liquidator may:

1. pay any classes of creditors in full;

2. make any compromise or arrangement with creditors;

3. compromise all calls and liabilities to calls and other debts and liabilities: s.165, Sch.4.

Power to apply to court

In a voluntary winding up the liquidator, or any contributory or creditor, may **30–019** apply to the court to determine any question arising in the winding up or to exercise any of the powers which the court could exercise if the company were being wound up by the court: s.112.[67] This gives the liquidator in a voluntary winding up the same right to the guidance of the court as in a compulsory liquidation. For example, in England, if he is of opinion that fraud has been committed in the formation or promotion of the company or in relation to the company since its formation, he can obtain an order of the court for the public examination[68] of any promoter, director or other officer of the company concerned. Again, he can apply for an order for private examination.[69]

In *R-R Realisations Ltd, Re*,[70] a company went into voluntary liquidation in 1971. In 1976, it became apparent that it might be liable for claims in tort for

---

[66] cf. *Day v Tait* (1900) 8 S.L.T. 40, OH.

[67] For examples of applications under s.112 see *Madoff Securities International Ltd, Re* [2009] EWHC 442; *Cooper v PRG Powerhouse Ltd* [2008] EWHC 498 (Ch.) (declaration as to whether property held on trust); *Rusjon Ltd, Re* [2007] EWHC 2943 (Ch.).

[68] *Campbell Coverings Ltd, Re (No.2)* [1954] Ch. 225 and see above p.706 (Public Examination of Officers) and p.708 (Private Examination).

[69] As in *Rolls Razor Ltd, Re (No.2)* [1970] Ch. 576. See also *England v Smith* [2001] Ch. 419. Despite the wording of s.112(1), it seems that a creditor cannot apply: *James McHale Automobiles Ltd, Re* [1997] B.C.C. 202.

[70] [1980] 1 All E.R. 1019.

negligence during its operations. In 1979, after the liquidators had started preparing the final accounts, solicitors warned the liquidators of the possible claims. The liquidators applied for an order that they should distribute the final dividend to the members without regard to the claims on the basis of delay. Alternatively they sought an order that the claimants should bear the costs of the delay in distribution. Megarry V.C. held that the test was whether in all the circumstances it was just to make either of the orders sought. Default or lack of diligence by either party was relevant and the court was less likely to facilitate a distribution among the members than among the creditors. In the circumstances, both orders would be refused.

Duty to report criminal offences

30–020 If the liquidator thinks that any past or present officer, or any member, of the company has committed a criminal offence in relation to the company, he must report the matter, in an English winding up, to the Director of Public Prosecutions. The matter may then be referred to the Department of Business, Innovation and Skills[71], who have the same powers of investigating the company's affairs as in an investigation into the affairs of a company under ss.431 or 432 of the Companies Act 1985:[72] s.218.

Compulsory Liquidation after Commencement of Voluntary Liquidation

30–021 A voluntary liquidation does not bar the right of any creditor or contributory to have the company wound up by the court: s.116. A creditor of a company in voluntary liquidation is not entitled ex debito justitiae as between himself and the company to a compulsory winding up order and the views of the contributories must be taken into consideration,[73] unless the company is insolvent.[74] Even in such a case it had been said that the court will require reasons as to why the voluntary winding up is inappropriate: it is not inappropriate merely because the petitioner would prefer a different liquidator.[75] However, more recently it has been stated that a compulsory order should be made wherever the creditors would otherwise be left with a justifiable feeling of grievance that they had been prevented from having the company's affairs investigated by a liquidator who was not appointed by the directors.[76] There is no rule that the probity or competence of the liquidator must be attacked[77] but he must not only be independent but must be seen to be independent.[78] Further, the court is bound to have regard to the wishes of all the cred-

---

[71] Formerly the DTI and DBERR.
[72] These provisions of the Companies Act 1985 are not affected by the coming into force of the Companies Act 2006.
[73] *Surplus Properties (Huddersfield) Ltd, Re* [1984] B.C.L.C. 89.
[74] *James Millward & Co Ltd, Re* [1940] Ch. 333, CA.
[75] *Medisco Equipment Ltd, Re* [1983] B.C.L.C. 305, per Harman J.
[76] *M.C.H. Services, Re* [1987] B.C.L.C. 535, Vinelott J.; *Pinstripe Farming Co Ltd, Re* [1996] B.C.C. 913.
[77] *Palmer Marine Services Ltd, Re* [1986] 1 W.L.R. 573.
[78] *Lowestoft Traffic Services Ltd, Re* [1986] B.C.L.C. 81: and see *H.J. Tomkins & Son* [1990] B.C.L.C. 76.

itors,[79] and if the majority favour the continuance of the voluntary liquidation an order will not be made unless the petitioner can show special circumstances.[80] The court can, however, examine the motives of the creditors,[81] and, in particular, of those creditors who are also members.[82] Considerations of fairness and commercial morality should also be taken into account.[83] In the case of a financial company, the wish of the regulatory authority, based upon reasonable material, to have the sort of investigation which would follow on from a compulsory winding up may outweigh factors like inconvenience and expense.[84] A contributory must satisfy the court that the rights of the contributories will be prejudiced by a voluntary winding up: s.116. What the Secretary of State must show when he is the petitioner has been dealt with already.[85]

When a voluntary winding up is superseded by a compulsory winding up, all proceedings in the voluntary winding up are deemed to have been validly taken unless the court, on proof of fraud or mistake, thinks fit to direct otherwise: s.129, above.

[79] *Home Remedies Ltd, Re* [1943] Ch. 1; *Lowestoft Traffic Services Ltd, Re* [1986] B.C.L.C. 81; cf. *Pattisons Ltd v Kinnear* (1899) 1 F. 551 and *Elsmie & Son v The Tomatin etc. Distillery Ltd* (1906) 8 F. 434.
[80] *B. Karsberg Ltd, Re* [1956] 1 W.L.R. 57, CA; *J.D. Swain Ltd, Re* [1965] 1 W.L.R. 909, CA; for special circumstances, see *Bouboulis v Mann, Macneal & Co Ltd*, 1926 S.C. 637: and see *H.J. Tomkins, Re*, above n.77, where the court followed the wishes of creditors representing a majority in value, though not in number; *Magnus Consultants Ltd, Re* [1995] 1 B.C.L.C. 203.
[81] *Falcon (R.J.) Developments, Re* [1987] B.C.L.C. 437.
[82] *Palmer Marine Surveys Ltd, Re* [1986] 1 W.L.R. 573.
[83] ibid. See also *Gordon & Breach Science Publishers Ltd, Re* [1995] B.C.C. 261.
[84] *Securities & Investments Board v Lancashire and Yorkshire Portfolio Management Ltd* [1992] B.C.C. 381.
[85] Above, p.697; and see *Re Pinstripe Farming*, above n.76.

Chapter 31

CONTRIBUTORIES AND CREDITORS: COMPLETION OF THE WINDING UP

31–001 As soon as may be after a winding up order is made, it is the duty of the liquidator to:

(1) settle a list of contributories;

(2) collect the company's assets and apply them in discharge of its liabilities: ss.148, 160.

CONTRIBUTORIES

31–002 A contributory is a person liable to contribute to the assets of a company in the event of its being wound up: s.79. A fully paid-up shareholder in a company limited by shares falls within this definition.[1] Section 79(2), however, makes it clear that parties ordered to contribute to the company's assets under ss.213 or 214 Insolvency Act 1986[2] are not contributories within the meaning of the section. Section 74 provides that on a winding up every present and past member is liable to contribute to the assets of the company to an amount sufficient for payment of its debts and liabilities, and the expenses of the winding up, and for the adjustment of the rights of the contributories among themselves. This is subject to certain qualifications, below, e.g. a past member is not liable to contribute if he ceased to be a member one year or more before the commencement of the winding up[3]: s.74(2)(a).

Where a private company which has purchased or redeemed its own shares out of capital under ss.709 et seq. of the Companies Act 2005 goes into liquidation within one year of such payment, and is found to be insolvent, the directors and the recipient are liable to contribute up to the amount of the payment to cover any insufficiency: s.76.[4]

---

[1] *Anglesea Colliery Co, Re* (1866) L.R. 1 Ch. App. 555, followed, e.g. in *Paterson v M'Farlane* (1875) 2 R. 490.

[2] Fraudulent and wrongful trading (see above, Chs 23 and 29 respectively)

[3] Above, p.702, this qualification does not apply to the winding up of an unlimited company which has re-registered as limited, see s.77.

[4] Above, p.201. However, their liability falls outside ss.74 and 75 (s.76(5)) and they are not true contributories (s.79(3)).

The list of contributories

The list of contributories is in two parts, the A list and the B list. The A list consists **31–003** of the members of the company at the commencement of the winding up, i.e. present members. The B list consists of persons who were members within a year before the commencement of the winding up. The B list is often not settled at all, and is never settled unless it appears that the A contributories are unable to satisfy their contributions.[5] The list must distinguish between contributories who are liable in their own right and those liable as representatives of others[6]: s.148(3).

The court may dispense with the settlement of a list of contributories where it appears that it will not be necessary to make calls on or adjust the rights of contributories: s.148(2). The distribution of surplus assets among the contributories does not of itself involve an adjustment of the rights of the contributories among themselves and therefore no list need be settled.[7] The court should not exercise its discretion to dispense with a list of contributories if the company has a large number of shares held by a large number of shareholders.[8]

Liability of contributories

The liability of a contributory in a company limited by shares[9] is qualified as **31–004** follows:

1. The liability of a contributory, whether on the A list or the B list, is limited to the amount unpaid on his shares: s.74(2)(d). Where shares are partly paid, a past member only has to contribute if the existing member has not paid up in full. Where there are several past members in the year before the winding up, all will appear on the B list but the primary liability will be on the latest transferor.[10] The fact that all debts have been paid does not necessarily absolve the holder of partly paid shares from his liability: a contribution may still be required to adjust the rights of the contributories amongst themselves.[11]

2. B contributories are not liable to contribute in respect of any debt or liability of the company contracted after he ceased to be a member: s.74(2)(b).

The assets of the company, including the amount received from A contributories, are first applied pari passu in payment of the debts of the company, irrespective of the time when they were contracted.[12] The liability of the B contributories is

---

[5] See IA 1986 s.74(2)(c).
[6] See below.
[7] *Phoenix Oil, etc., Co, Re* [1958] Ch. 560.
[8] *Paragon Holdings Ltd, Re* [1961] Ch. 346.
[9] See s.74(3) for companies limited by guarantee.
[10] *Humby's Case* (1872) 26 L.T. 936.
[11] *Anglesea Colliery Co, Re* (1866) L.R. 1 Ch. 555.
[12] *Morris' Case* (1871) L.R. 7 Ch. App. 200. See also *Apex Film Distributors, Re* [1960] Ch. 378.

therefore further restricted, because they are liable only for such of the company's debts contracted before they ceased to be members as have not been satisfied by the distribution of the company's other assets among the creditors generally. The B contributories may therefore not be fully called upon although the creditors are not paid in full.

In *City of London Insurance Co Ltd, Re*,[13] the liquidator made calls on the B contributories of 5p a share in 1925, and 7½ p a share in 1927. The amount so realised exceeded by about £10,000 the debts of the company contracted while the B contributories were members but the total of all the calls did not suffice to pay the creditors in full. The liquidator asked to retain the full amount of the calls on the B contributories as assets available for the creditors. It was held that he could not retain the full amount, but must return the £10,000 to the B contributories.

B contributions are part of the general assets of the company, and are not to be applied, preferentially or exclusively, to the payment of debts incurred before the B shareholders ceased to be members.[14]

3.   B contributories are not liable to contribute unless it appears to the court that the existing members are unable to satisfy their contributions: s.74(2)(c).

Example: C and D are holders of £1 shares, 37½ p. paid. C transfers his shares to X and D transfers to Y. Within a year the company is wound up, and is insolvent. X pays up his shares in full, but Y pays nothing. No contribution will be required from C. A contribution will be required from D.

31–005   A member[15] cannot claim a sum due to him in his character of member (e.g. by way of dividend, profits or otherwise) in competition with any other creditor not a member of the company: s.74(2)(f). A sum is so due if it arises under the statutory contract between the members and the company constituted by s.33(1) of the Companies Act 2006.[16] Such debts are deferred as the price members pay for limited liability:

In *Soden v British & Commonwealth Holdings Plc*,[17] B & C Plc purchased all the shares in A Plc for £434 million. Both companies later went into administration. The administrators of B & C Plc brought an action against A Plc for damages for negligent misrepresentation inducing the purchase. The administrator of A Plc sought directions as to whether any damages recoverable by B & C Plc were due to them in their character of a member of A Plc. It was held that they were not so due and should not be deferred.

The section has been applied to dividends due to a holding company but retained by the subsidiary for use in its business. The judge decided that the onus of proving that such sums were not due as dividends to a member in his capacity as a member was on the holding company. This could be done by an express or

---

[13] [1932] 1 Ch. 226.
[14] *Webb v Whiffin* (1872) L.R. 5 H.L. 711.
[15] Includes past members, see *Consolidated Goldfields of New Zealand Ltd, Re* [1953] Ch. 689.
[16] Above, pp.92 et seq.
[17] [1997] 4 All E.R. 353, HL. The House of Lords left open the status of a damages claim arising from a contract to subscribe for shares.

implied agreement which created a loan by the holding company of the money involved or recognition of that fact with the passage of time, but there was no such evidence in that case.[18]

The liability of a contributory creates a debt (in England of the nature of an ordinary contract debt)[19] accruing at the time when his liability commenced, but payable when a call is made: s.80.

If a contributory dies either before or after he has been placed on the list of contributories, his personal representatives are liable. They are not personally liable; they are liable in their representative character. In England, if they make a default in payment, proceedings may be taken for administering the estate of the deceased: s.81.

If a contributory becomes bankrupt, his trustee in bankruptcy represents him for all the purposes of the winding up and is a contributory accordingly. Calls already made and the estimated value of the bankrupt's liability to future calls may be proved against the estate.[20]

There are special provisions as to the liability of B contributories where a company has re-registered under s.102 or s.105 of the Companies Act 2006[21]: ss.77, 78.

Calls on contributories

In England calls on contributories are made by the liquidator with the leave of the **31–006** court or the sanction of the liquidation committee: s.160(1)(d). Calls may be made either before or after the insufficiency of the assets has been ascertained. They are made for an amount necessary to satisfy the debts and liabilities of the company, and the costs of winding up, and for adjustment of the rights of the contributories among themselves. In fixing the amount regard is had to the probability that some contributories may fail to pay the call: s.150.

A debt due from the company to a contributory cannot be set off against calls, whether made before or after the winding up,[22] except:

1. where all the creditors have been paid in full (s.149(3));

2. in the case of an unlimited company, where the debt is due to him on an independent dealing with the company and not due to him as a member in respect of dividend or profit (s.149(2)); or

3. where the contributory is bankrupt.[23]

---

[18] *L.B. Holliday & Co Ltd, Re* [1986] 2 All E.R. 367.

[19] See Companies Act 2006 (Consequential Amendments, Transitional Provisions and Savings) Order 2009 art.2. The limitation period is therefore six years.

[20] s.82.

[21] Above, Ch.3.

[22] *Grissell's Case* (1866) L.R. 1 Ch. App. 528; *Cowan v Gowans* (1878) 5 R. 581; this has been held to be so where a shareholder deposited money with the company against calls: *Millar v Aikman* (1891) 28 S.L.R. 955, OH.

[23] *Duckworth, Re* (1867) L.R. 2 Ch. App. 578. On s.149, see *Penningtons Corporate Insolvency Law* 2nd edn (1997) pp.159 and 276.

A contributory on the list may be ordered by the court, at any time after the making of a winding up order, to pay any money due from him to the company: s.149.[24] The court can also order the arrest of, and seizure of the movable personal property of, a contributory believed to be about to abscond or to remove his property with the object of evading payment of calls: s.158.

CREDITORS

31–007 The rules apply with regard to (1) the respective rights of secured and unsecured creditors, (2) debts provable, and (3) the valuation of annuities and future and contingent liabilities.

Secured creditors

31–008 A secured creditor is one who holds some security for a debt due to him from the company, such as a mortgage, charge or lien.[25] He must give credit for the realised or estimated value of his security unless he surrenders it. Thus he may[26]:

1. realise his security and prove, as an unsecured creditor, for any balance due to him after deducting the amount realised;

2. value his security and prove, as an unsecured creditor, for any balance due after deducting the value of the security;

3. surrender his security and prove, as an unsecured creditor, for the whole debt; or

4. where he is fully secured, rely on his security and not prove at all.

A secured creditor who has realised his security for less than the total amount of his debt, part of which is preferential,[27] can appropriate the proceeds of sale to that part of his debt which is not preferential, so that he can prove for the preferential part.[28] If the creditor has made a mistake in the valuation of his security, he may amend it by application to the court. If he subsequently realises his security, the amount realised must be substituted for the amount in the proof.

Proof of debts

31–009 The debts which are provable on a winding up, and the manner of proof, are governed by the Insolvency Rules 1986.[29] The liability must exist at the commencement of the winding up[30] but, subject to that, it may be present or future, certain or

---

[24] The effect of s.149 dies with the company when it is dissolved: *Butler v Broadhead* [1975] Ch.D. 97.

[25] See, generally, Ch.25, above.

[26] Under Insolvency Rules 1986 r.4.88.

[27] Below, pp.750, et seq.

[28] *William Hall (Contractors) Ltd, Re* [1967] 1 W.L.R. 948.

[29] r.12.3 and rr.4.73–4.99.

[30] *Oriental Commercial Bank, Re* (1871) 7 Ch. App. 99 103–104.

contingent, ascertained or sounding only in damages. Where two creditors lodge proof in respect of what is, in substance, the same debt only one dividend can be paid (the rule against double proof)[31] notwithstanding the existence of two contracts.[32] The liquidator can estimate the value of any debt of uncertain amount[33] or, in difficult cases, he can apply to the court for directions: s.168(3).[34] It is no longer the case that in an insolvent winding up unliquidated claims in tort are excluded. Some claims can only be proved when those of all other creditors have been paid in full, with interest, e.g. those arising by virtue of restitution orders under s.382 of the Financial Services and Markets Act 2000. Statute-barred debts cannot be proved.[35]

If a debt is owed in foreign currency it must be paid at the rate of exchange prevailing at the commencement of the liquidation and not at the date of payment.[36]

Where there have been mutual credits, mutual debts or other mutual dealings between the company and one of its creditors, an account is taken of what is due from one to the other, and the balance of that account and no more can be claimed or paid.[37]

A Co borrowed money from B Co on the security of bills of sale charging some machinery and providing for its insurance against fire. The policies were in the name of B, and A paid the premiums. The machinery was destroyed by fire and the insurance amounting to £1,600 paid to B. A then went into liquidation. £744 was owing to B on the bills of sale at the date of the fire, so that B had £856 in hand, but A owed B £2,009 unsecured book debts. It was held that B could set off the £856 against the £2,009.[38]

The holder of a life policy in an assurance company mortgaged the policy to the issuing company. On the company's going into liquidation the policy holder claimed to set off the value of the policy against his mortgage debt. It was held that he was entitled to do so.[39]

This statutory set-off cannot be excluded by agreement between the parties.[40] **31–010** It applies automatically, irrespective of the wishes of the parties, wherever there are mutual debts (or provable claims) between the company and a creditor, so that

[31] *Oriental Commercial Bank, Re* (1871) 7 Ch. App. 99 103–104.

[32] For example, in a suretyship situation, between the creditor and the debtor and between the creditor and the surety. The rule is explained in *Polly Peck International Plc (in administration), Re* [1996] B.C.C. 486, per Robert Walker J. at 492.

[33] IR 1986 r.4.86; I(S)R 1986 rr.4.15, 4.16.

[34] Any person aggrieved can also apply: s.168(5).

[35] *Art Reproduction Co Ltd, Re* [1952] Ch. 89; *Overmark Smith Warden Ltd, Re, The Times*, March 22, 1982. In a compulsory winding up the limitation period is ascertained by reference to the date of the winding up order not the petition: *Case of Taffs Well, Re* [1991] 3 W.L.R. 731. If the debt is not time-barred at the commencement of the winding up, it does not become so by the passage of time thereafter: *Financial Services Compensation Scheme v Larnell Insurance* [2005] EWCA Civ 1408.

[36] *Lines Brothers Ltd, Re* [1983] Ch. 1, CA.

[37] IR 1986 r.4.90; on mutuality see Palmer's Company Law, Vol.3, paras 15.415–15.41, and see *Stein v Blake (No.1)* [1996] A.C. 243. Note also *Norman Holding Co Ltd, Re* [1990] 3 All E.R. 757 (a secured creditor who opts to rely upon his security rather than prove is not subject to r.4.90).

[38] *H.E. Thorne & Son Ltd, Re* [1914] 2 Ch. 438.

[39] *City Life Assurance Co Ltd, Re* [1926] Ch.191.

[40] *National Westminster Bank Ltd v Halesowen Presswork & Assemblies Ltd* [1972] A.C. 785.

the liquidator cannot deal with the subject of such mutual cross-claims free of the right of set-off.[41] Where the company is entitled to set-off a claim against a preferential creditor[42] who is also a non-preferential creditor, the company's claim must be set-off rateably in proportion to the amounts of the preferential and non-preferential claims.[43] It has been held that directors who had guaranteed a loan to their company, had constituted themselves principal debtors with their company,[44] and had lodged deposits with the lender as further security, could, when the lender went into liquidation, set-off the amount of the deposits against both their own and the company's debt.[45]

Interest is payable on all debts provable in the winding up, including interest which has accrued under the contract rate prior to the winding up. Post-winding up interest is only payable, however, if there is a surplus after paying all debts (including pre-winding-up interest), and is paid before any surplus is returned to the contributories. The rate of post-winding-up interest is that specified by order made under s.17 of the Judgments Act 1838 on the commencement of the winding up, unless the contract itself provided for a higher rate of interest:[46] s.189. If interest is payable on a foreign currency debt it should be calculated with respect to the exchange rate at the date of winding up and not when it is paid.[47]

Adjustment of prior transactions

31–011   The Insolvency Act contains provisions which enable the liquidator to apply to the court to set aside certain prior transactions which are unfairly disadvantageous to the general body of creditors. These provisions also apply where an administration order has been made.[48]

Transactions at an undervalue and preferences in England

31–012   A transaction at an undervalue entered into by a company is a transaction whereby a company makes a gift to another person or enters into a transaction on terms which provide that the company either receives no consideration or significantly less consideration than the value of the consideration it provides, measured in money or money's worth: s.238(4).[49] In valuing the consideration received by the company for the purposes of s.238(4), the court should have regard to the

---

[41] *Stein v Blake* [1996] A.C. 243, HL (bankruptcy).
[42] Below, p.750.
[43] *Unit 2 Windows Ltd, Re* [1986] B.C.L.C. 31.
[44] It may be otherwise where such a liability has not been assumed: see *Morris v Rayners Enterprises Inc* [1997] B.C.C. 965, HL.
[45] *High Street Services Ltd v Bank of Credit and Commerce International S.A.* [1993] B.C.C. 360, CA.
[46] Such a rate may be challenged by the liquidator under s.244, below, p.748.
[47] *Lines Brothers Ltd, Re (No.2)* [1984] Ch. 438.
[48] Above, Ch.28.
[49] The creation of a security over the company's assets has been held not to be a transaction at an undervalue: *M.C. Bacon Ltd, Re* [1990] B.C.C. 78, although see *Hill v Spread Trustee Co Ltd* [2006] B.C.C. 646. In determining whether there is an undervalue the court will look at the transaction as a whole not merely a discrete part of it: see *Agricultural Mortgage Corporation Plc v Woodward* [1994] B.C.C. 688, CA.

reality of the situation, and this may require viewing the impugned transaction with hindsight.

For example, in *Phillips (Liquidator of AJ Bekhor & Co) v Brewin Dolphin Bell Lawrie*,[50] the consideration for a sale of the company's business included an agreement that the purchaser would pay four annual instalments of £312,500 for sub-rental of the company's leased computer equipment. The head lease contained a prohibition against sub-leasing which, when breached, entitled the lessor to repossess the equipment. This occurred before any instalments had been paid and the purchaser terminated the agreement. It was held that the instalments should be ignored for the purpose of determining the value received by the company. The court should, when an agreement provided for a consideration that was speculative, have regard to circumstances after the agreement was entered into.

Where part of the consideration flowing to the company amounts to a preference under s.239 of the Insolvency Act 1986[51] it cannot be taken into account in determining the equivalence of the consideration for the purposes of s.238(4).[52]

However, this does not include transactions entered into by the company in good faith for the purpose of carrying on its business and at the time there were reasonable grounds for believing that the transaction would benefit the company: s.238(5). Further such a transaction must have taken place at a time when the company was unable to pay its debts[53] (or became unable to pay them as a result of the transaction (s.240(2)) and also within two years prior to the commencement of the winding up: s.240(1)(a).[54] If the transaction is with a person connected with the company the company is assumed to have been insolvent at the time unless the contrary is shown: s.240(2).

A company gives a preference to a creditor[55] under s.239 of the IA if it does **31–013** anything or suffers anything to be done which has the effect of putting the creditor into a position which, in the event of the company going into insolvent liquidation, would be better than the position he would have been in if that thing had not been done,[56] and the company in doing that was influenced by a desire to produce that effect. Such a motive is presumed if the creditor is connected with the company; s.239(6).[57] The preference must have been given at a time when the company was unable to pay its debts[58] (or became unable to do so as a result of the preference) and also within six months of the commencement of the winding up: s.240(1)(b). The time limit is extended to two years if the creditor is connected with the company: s.240(1)(a). The relevant time for considering the company's motive is not when it decides to pay the creditor but when it does so.[59]

---

[50] [2001] UKHL 2.
[51] See below.
[52] *Barber v CI Ltd* [2006] B.C.C. 927.
[53] As defined in s.123, above p.689.
[54] Or on the date an administration application is made or an administrator is appointed under paras 14 or 22 of Sch.B1.
[55] Including a surety or guarantor for any of its debts or liabilities.
[56] If a payment intended to be preferential does not, in the event, have that effect it cannot be impugned: cf. *Lewis v Hyde* [1997] B.C.C. 976, PC.
[57] See, e.g. *Exchange Travel (Holdings) Ltd, Re* [1996] B.C.C. 933; *Weisgard v Pilkington* [1995] B.C.C. 1108.
[58] See n.53.
[59] *Wills v Corfe Joinery Ltd* [1997] B.C.C. 511.

Both transactions at an undervalue and preferences may be challenged by the liquidator who can apply for a court order to return the position to what it would have been if the company had not entered into the transaction or given the preference: ss.238, 239. The court can make any order it thinks fit[60] and s.241 gives it wide powers relating to the transfer of property, return of benefits received and release of any security. A charge may therefore be set aside under these provisions.[61] An order under s.238 or 239 may affect the property of, or impose an obligation on, any person whether or not he is the person with whom the company entered the transaction or to whom the preference was given. However, the position of such third parties is protected by s.241 (as amended by s.1 of the Insolvency (No.2) Act 1994) which limits the orders which the court can make where a person has acted in good faith and for value. Lack of good faith is presumed if, at the time of the acquisition of the property or the receipt of the benefit, the person had notice of the relevant surrounding circumstances and the relevant proceedings[62] or was connected with, or an associate of, either the company, the person with whom the company entered the transaction or the person to whom the company gave the preference. The relevant surrounding circumstances are the fact that the transaction was at an undervalue or the circumstances which amounted to the giving of the preference.[63]

In relation to preferences, in the past, a liquidator had to prove that the giving of the preference was accompanied by a dominant intention to prefer on the part of the company. Section 239(5) requires merely that the company be influenced by a desire to prefer, even if there was no dominant intention to do so. If, however, the company has no positive desire to prefer at all and the preference was given solely as a result of commercial pressure (e.g. to avoid the appointment of a receiver by the bank) or for proper commercial considerations, it is not subject to avoidance.[64] Where several parties to a transaction are found to have been preferred, an order can only be made against those which the company desired to prefer.

In *Agriplant Services Ltd, Re*,[65] a company hired machinery from CAF. S, a director, gave a personal guarantee for the rental. When the company was on the brink of liquidation, CAF threatened to repossess unless rental arrears were cleared. S caused the company to pay CAF. It was held that CAF had to repay. The company (through S) was influenced by a desire to improve the position of CAF because only by such improvement could it achieve its desire to protect its director, S.

Transactions defrauding creditors

31–014 Transactions defrauding creditors are dealt with in ss.423–425 of the Insolvency Act 1986 and are transactions at an undervalue (defined as in s.238, above)

---

[60] Even against a person resident abroad: *Paramount Airways Ltd, Re* [1992] 3 All E.R. 7, CA.
[61] A floating charge may also be attacked under s.245, below, p.747.
[62] See s.241(3A)–(3C).
[63] For an unsuccessful attempt to rely on s.241(2), see *Sonatacus Ltd, Re* [2007] EWCA Civ. 31.
[64] *M. C. Bacon Ltd, Re* [1990] B.C.C. 78; *Fairway Magazines Ltd, Re* [1992] B.C.C. 924; *Beacon Leisure Ltd, Re* [1991] B.C.C. 213; cf. *D.K.G. Contractors Ltd, Re* [1990] B.C.C. 903.
[65] [1997] B.C.C. 842.

entered into for the purpose of putting assets beyond the reach of creditors or otherwise prejudicing their interests: s.423(1). It is sufficient that removing assets from the reach of creditors is a substantial purpose as regards the transaction, and it need not be the sole purpose.[66] To provide evidence of a defendant's purpose, the court may order discovery of documents passing between him and his legal advisor in connection with structuring a transaction.[67] A wide meaning has been given to "transaction".

In *Agricultural Mortgage Corp Plc v Woodward*,[68] D owned a farm which was mortgaged to P. D was unable to keep up the re-payments and P was likely to re-possess the farm and sell it. D leased the farm, at full market rent, to his wife, W, with the result that the proceeds of any sale by P would be insufficient to meet the mortgage debt. It was held that while D received a full market rent for the lease, the transaction as a whole was at an undervalue taking into account that it placed W in a position to secure payment from P for the surrender of the lease.

The relevant purpose can be established in relation to future and unknown creditors as where assets are transferred to protect them from the consequences of a possible failure of a new business venture.[69] An order can be made, on the application of the official receiver, a liquidator, and administrator or a "victim" of the transaction in question.[70] Any order made is aimed at restoring the position to what it would have been had the transaction not been entered into and protecting the interests of persons who are victims of the transaction.: s.423(2). The court does not have to set aside the transaction but should seek both to restore the position and protect the victims so far as practicable and s.425(1) lists a series of orders that may be made, without prejudice to the generality of s.423(2). Unlike s.238, s.423 operates independently of insolvency and is subject to no time limits.[71]

Avoidance of certain floating charges

As we have seen s.245 provides that certain floating charges created within **31–015** 12 months prior to the liquidation are voidable unless new consideration was supplied by the creditor.[72] This provision operates in addition to ss.238–244 detailed above.

---

[66] See *Chohan v Saggar* [1992] B.C.C. 306 at 321; *Inland Revenue Commissioners v Hashmir* [2002] EWCA Civ. 981. *Papanicola v Fagan* [2008] EWHC 3348 (bankruptcy).

[67] *Barclays Bank Plc v Eustice* [1995] B.C.C. 978, CA.

[68] [1994] B.C.C. 688, CA. See also *National Westminster Bank Plc v Jones* [2001] EWCA Civ. 1541. See, however, *Delaney v Chen* [2010] EWHC 6 (Ch.): sale and leaseback of property at consideration substantially below market value did not amount to an undervalue as the premium value of the tenancy made up the shortfall.

[69] *Midland Bank Plc v Wyatt* [1997] 1 B.C.L.C. 242.

[70] Defined in s.423(5) as a person who is, or is capable of being, prejudiced by the transaction. See *Pinewood Joinery v Starelm Properties Ltd* [1994] B.C.C. 569. The victim need not be a party whom the defendant had in mind at the time of the transaction: *Sands v Clitheroe* [2006] B.P.I.R. 1000.

[71] *Arbuthnot Leasing International Ltd v Havelet Leasing Ltd (No.2)* [1990] B.C.C. 636; *Chohan v Saggar* [1994] B.C.C. 134.

[72] Above, p.624.

Extortionate credit transactions

31–016 By virtue of s.244 of the Insolvency Act 1986, a transaction is an extortionate credit transaction if credit has been supplied to a company on terms which are extortionate (grossly exorbitant) having regard to the risk involved or it otherwise grossly contravenes the ordinary principles of fair dealing: s.244(3).[73] All credit transactions are presumed to be extortionate until the contrary is proved. The transaction must have been entered into within three years prior to the commencement of the winding up.

In such cases the liquidator may apply to the court for an order setting aside the transaction, varying its terms, for repayment of money or property held as security to the company or for the taking of accounts. This power may be used concurrently with the power to avoid a transaction at an undervalue: s.244(5).

Unenforceability of liens

31–017 Under s.246, a liquidator can override any lien or other right to retain possession of any books, papers or records of the company in order to gain possession of them. The only exception is a lien on documents which give a title to property and are held as such.[74]

Order of application of assets

31–018 The effect of ss.175, 176, 176A and the Insolvency Rules is that in a winding up the assets of the company are applicable in the following order:

1. costs, charges and expenses properly incurred in the winding up,[75] including the remuneration of the liquidator;

2. the preferential debts;

3. the prescribed part[76];

4. debts secured by a charge which as created was a floating charge[77];

5. the ordinary unsecured debts;

6. post insolvency interest on debts;

7. deferred debts;

8. the balance (if any) to be returned to the contributories.

---

[73] cf. Consumer Credit Act 1974, ss.137–139 (now repealed by Consumer Credit Act 2006 ss.19–22).

[74] See *SEIL Trade Finance Ltd, Re* [1992] B.C.C. 538.

[75] For example liabilities under contracts made or continued by the liquidator for the purposes of the winding up: *Atlantic Computer Systems Plc, Re* [1992] 1 All E.R. 476.

[76] See Ch.25, above, p.618.

[77] s.175(2)(b) and s.251; where necessary the property subject to the charge can be used to pay liabilities in categories 1., 2. and 3. For the position where a fixed charge is made subject to a floating charge see: *Portbase Clothing Ltd, Re* [1993] 3 All E.R. 829.

It should be noted that whilst preferential debts are payable out of the proceeds of floating charge realisations,[78] the House of Lords, in *Buchler v Talbot* held that the expenses of the liquidation were not to be paid out those proceeds.[79] The Companies Act 2006 s.1282 restored, to some extent, the previous position as stated in *Barleycorn Enterprises Ltd, Re*,[80] by inserting s.176ZA of the Insolvency Act. This provision provides that the expenses of the winding up, so far as the unencumbered assets of the company are insufficient to meet them, have priority over claims to property comprised in a floating charge. This general proposition is qualified by s.176ZA(3), which provides that rules may be made which restrict the priority of liquidation expenses unless they are approved by floating charge holders or by the court.

The Insolvency (Amendment) Rules 2008[81] make provision for the approval or authorisation of "litigation expenses" by secured or preferential creditors or by the court. Where a liquidator proposes to bring legal proceedings,[82] any "litigation expenses"[83] will not take priority to the floating charge holder unless they are approved or authorised in accordance with rr.4.218B to 4.218E.[84] In essence, where the liquidator considers that he will have to have recourse to property subject to a floating charge to meet such expenses[85] he must request approval or authorisation for such amount of litigation expenses as he thinks fit.[86] The manner in which approval or authorisation is taken to have been given is dealt with in r.4.218D. The liquidator may also seek approval or authorisation for litigation expenses from the court under r.4.218E where the floating charge creditor is to be the defendant in the legal proceedings or where that creditor declines to approve or authorise the incurring of litigation expenses.

As far as the hierarchy liabilities in of the assets is concerned, all liabilities belonging to a higher category must be paid for or provided for in full before any payment can be made in respect of liabilities of a lower category. None of this will affect creditors with a fixed charge (so long as it is valid and properly registered[87]): they may simply pay themselves out of their security. In relation to any balance remaining unpaid, they rank as ordinary or preferential unsecured creditors.[88]

In the event of the assets being insufficient to satisfy the costs, charges and **31–019** expenses incurred in the winding up, there is an internal order of priority: s.156 and Insolvency Rules 1986, r.4.218. Unless the court orders otherwise, the order of priority is[89]:

---

[78] Below, p.750
[79] [2004] UKHL 9, overruling *Barleycorn Enterprises Ltd, Re* [1970] Ch. 465. *cf* the position in administration, above, p.685
[80] Above, n.79.
[81] SI 2008/737, r.5.
[82] Defined in r.4.218A(1)(c).
[83] r.4.218A(1)(d): expenses incurred in the preparation and conduct of legal proceedings likely to exceed £5,000.
[84] r.4.218A(2).
[85] i.e. because there are insufficient unencumbered assets.
[86] r.4.218B(3), (4), (5), 4.218(c).
[87] See Ch.25, above, pp.626 et seq.
[88] See, e.g. *Mesco Properties, Re* [1980] 1 W.L.R. 96.
[89] For a detailed list, see IR 1986 r.4.218.

1. fees and expenses properly incurred in preserving, realising or getting in the assets. These can include costs relating to the bringing of legal proceedings under ss.214, 238, 239, etc.[90] The cost of employing a shorthand writer appointed by the court to conduct an examination is included here[91];

2. costs of the petition[92] including costs of those appearing on the petition whose costs are allowed by the court[93];

3. remuneration of the special manager (if any);

4. costs and expenses of any person who makes the company's statement of affairs;

5. charges of a shorthand writer appointed by the court;

6. disbursements of the liquidator including expenses of the liquidation committee;

7. costs of any person properly employed by the liquidator;

8. remuneration of the liquidator.[94]

Where the company is a lessee, rent accrued due after the winding up order is an expense of the liquidation if the liquidator retained the lease solely for the benefit of the liquidation, and not for the joint benefit of himself and the lessors.[95] Instalments of non-domestic rates, for which the company had been billed before liquidation but which were payable after liquidation, in respect of property of which the liquidator retained possession for the purposes of the company, should be paid as a liquidation expenses.[96]

Rule 4.218(1) is a definitive statement of what constitutes a liquidation expense and is not subject to any implied qualification: *Toshoku Finance UK Plc, Re* [2002] UKHL 6. The preferential debts rank equally among themselves and must be paid in full, after the expenses of winding up, unless the assets are insufficient to meet

---

[90] The provision was amended by SI 2002/2712 so as to bring such proceedings within the category of liquidation expenses and effectively overrules a line of cases deciding otherwise: see, e.g *M.C. Bacon Ltd, Re (No.2)* [1991] Ch. 127, *Floor Fourteen Ltd, Re* [2001] 3 All E.R. 499. Litigation expenses will, however, have to be approved or authorised if they are to take priority over the claims of a floating charge holder: see above.

[91] r.4.218(3)(a)(iii).

[92] See *Bostels, Re* [1968] Ch. 346.

[93] In *Bathampton Properties Ltd, Re* [1976] 1 W.L.R. 168 the company's costs were increased by its unsuccessful and unjustifiable opposition to the petition, and only its costs down to and including the first hearing, when it could have consented were paid out of the assets. See also *North West Holdings Plc, Re* [200] B.C.C. 731.

[94] As for priority between successive liquidators, see r.4.219 and *Salters Hall School Ltd (in liquidation), Re* [1998] B.C.C. 503.

[95] *A.B.C. Coupler & Engineering Co Ltd, Re (No.3)* [1970] 1 W.L.R. 702; and see *Downer Enterprises Ltd, Re* [1974] 1 W.L.R. 1460, where an intermediate lessee paid the arrears of rent and was held entitled to the lessor's rights by way of subrogation; such rent does not however fall within the para.(a) but para.(f), see *Linda Marie, Re* [1989] B.C.L.C. 46. For the position in administration, see *Goldacre (Office) Ltd v Nortel Networks UK Ltd* [2009] EWHC 3389.

[96] *Noltan Business Centre Ltd, Re* [1996] B.C.C. 500 (presumably, under para.(f).

them, in which case the preferential debts abate in equal proportions: s.175(2)(a). The Enterprise Act 2002 abolished the preferential status of debts due to Inland Revenue (generally, arrears of employees' PAYE contributions), debts due to Customs and Excise (arrears of Value Added Tax) and arrears of social security contributions due under the Social Security Contributions & Benefits Act 1992: Enterprise Act 2002 s.251. The remaining categories of preferential debts are found in Sch.6 of the Insolvency Act 1986: s.386(1). They include:

(a) Category 4: any sum owed by the debtor to which Sch.4 to the Pension Schemes Act 1993 applies;

(b) Category 5: remuneration owed to an employee in respect of services rendered to the company within four months next before the relevant date, not exceeding £800 per claimant.[97]

The expression "the relevant date" means, when the company is being wound up **31–020** compulsorily, the date of the appointment of a provisional liquidator or, if no such appointment was made, the date of the winding up-order; if the company is or was being wound up voluntarily, it means the date of the passing of the resolution for winding up. If the winding up follows a conversion from administration to winding up, the relevant date is that on which the company entered administration: s.387.

There are equivalent rules for voluntary arrangements, administrations and receiverships: s.387. In England a full-time company secretary is probably an employee.[98] A managing director[99] is not an employee nor is a director as such. However, a director may, under power in the articles, be employed in a salaried position with the company and so be an employee. Thus, where a director could be, and was, employed as editor of a periodical, he was a preferential creditor.[100] A chemist engaged two days a week at a salary to work on formulae for perfumiers is an employee.[101] A contributor, even a regular contributor, to a newspaper, although paid by a fixed salary, is not.[102]

(c) Category 6: debts in respect of levies on the production of coal and steel, or any surcharge for delay, as imposed under the European Coal and Steel Treaty.[103]

In England, if a landlord or other person has distrained on the company's goods within three months next before a winding up order, the preferential debts are a first charge on the goods or the proceeds of the distress. The landlord or other person, however, has the same priority as the persons paid out of the proceeds:

---

[97] This includes other sums payable to employees by virtue of Pts III and VII and ss.53 and 56 of the Employment Rights Act 1996 and ss.169 and 189 of the Trade Union and Labour Relations (Consolidation) Act 1992: see Sch.6, para.13.

[98] *Cairney v Back* [1906] 2 K.G. 746. The former wording was "clerk or servant".

[99] *Newspaper Proprietary Syndicate Ltd, Re* [1900] 2 Ch. 349.

[100] *Beeton & Co Ltd, Re* (1913) 2 Ch. 279.

[101] *G.H. Morison & Co Ltd, Re* (1912) 106 L.T. 731.

[102] See n.99, above.

[103] See SI 1987/2093.

s.176. This section applies to anyone who has seized goods and is holding them for the purpose of sale at the time of the winding up order.[104]

The ordinary debts rank and abate equally inter se.[105] There is, however, no objection to an agreement whereby a creditor agrees to subordinate his debt and such agreements are accordingly valid.[106] This is the case even where, under a group subordination agreement, the creditors of some members of the group are subordinated to a creditor of the parent by virtue of the agreement.[107]

It may be mentioned here that a sum of money paid into a company's bank account for behoof of the company's employees and which is at the date of the liquidation "clearly distinguishable and capable of being disentangled from the company's own funds" do not form part of the company's assets but must be paid to the employees.[108]

Where a company fails to implement an agreement to purchase its shares under s.690 of the Companies Act 2006[109] or to redeem its shares under s.684 of that Act,[110] and the company subsequently goes into liquidation the vendor/shareholder may enforce the agreement as a creditor. This will not apply if at any time between the date for purchase or redemption and the commencement of the winding up the company could not have fulfilled its obligation out of distributable profits: Companies Act 2006, s.735.[111]

COMPLETION OF WINDING UP BY THE COURT

31–021 When the liquidator has collected the assets and received the proofs of the creditors, he proceeds to divide the assets among the creditors.

If there is any surplus after the costs of the liquidation and the company's debts have been paid, the court must adjust the rights of the contributories among themselves and distribute any surplus among the persons entitled thereto: s.154. The section requires a court order before the liquidator can distribute surplus assets, whether or not an adjustment has to be made[112] among the contributories. It will be remembered that under normal articles preference shareholders are entitled to priority over ordinary shareholders in the return of capital.[113] Persons not registered as members but in possession of share certificates as collectors or scriptophilists are not beneficially entitled to the shares to which the certificates relate and have been excluded from a distribution of surplus assets.[114]

---

[104] *Memco Engineering Ltd, Re* [1986] Ch. 86. The position is different in a voluntary winding up: *Herbert Berry Associates Ltd, Re* [1977] 1 W.L.R. 1437, CA.

[105] Per Lord Selbourne in *Black & Co's Case* (1872) L.R. 8 Ch. 254 at 262. *Maxwell Communications Corp Plc, Re (No.2)* [1994] 1 All E.R. 737.

[106] *Maxwell Communications Corp Plc, Re (No.2)* [1994] 1 All E.R. 737.

[107] *Manning v AIG Europe UK Ltd* [2006] EWCA Civ 7.

[108] *Smith v Liquidator of James Birrell Ltd*, 1968 S.L.T. 174, OH.

[109] Above, Ch.10.

[110] Above, Ch.10.

[111] Above, Ch.10.

[112] As where shares are unequally paid up, see *Phoenix Oil, etc. Co Ltd, Re* [1958] Ch. 560.

[113] Above, Ch.16.

[114] *In Baku Consolidated Oilfields Ltd, Re* [1993] B.C.C. 653.

If the liquidation is not completed within a year after its commencement, the liquidator must send to the Registrar of Companies, at such intervals as may be prescribed, a statement in the prescribed form and giving prescribed particulars as to the position of the liquidation: s.192.[115]

Final meetings and release of the liquidator

The holding of final meetings of the company or its creditors as appropriate in the **31–022** case of a voluntary winding up has been dealt with already,[116] together with the release of the liquidator consequential upon such a meeting.[117]

In a compulsory winding up the liquidator, other than the official receiver, if he is satisfied that the liquidation is for practical purposes complete, must call a final general meeting of the creditors. The liquidator will then make his report to that meeting which must then decide whether to release him. He may also give notice of any final distribution of the company's property at the same time. If he cannot do so the meeting must be adjourned until he can do so. The costs of the final meeting must be covered by the company's assets and so the liquidator must retain sufficient for this purpose: s.146. The release of a liquidator consequential on this meeting has been dealt with above.[118]

Early dissolution of company in England

If the company is in compulsory liquidation and the official receiver, who is auto- **31–023** matically the first liquidator,[119] discovers that the realisable assets of the company will be insufficient to cover even the expenses of the winding up he may apply to the Registrar of Companies for an early dissolution of the company. Before he can do this, however, he must be satisfied that the company's affairs do not require any further investigation and he must give 28 days' notice of his intention to the creditors, contributories and any administrative receiver. Once such a notice is given the official receiver's duties are at an end, although any creditor, contributory, administrative receiver or even the official receiver himself, may apply to the Secretary of State for directions within three months on the grounds either that the assets are sufficient to cover the expenses, the company's affairs do merit further investigation or that an early dissolution would be inappropriate: ss.202, 203.

If no such application is made the company is automatically dissolved three months after the Registrar receives the application. If the Secretary of State does give directions, those would be that the winding up should proceed as if no notice of early dissolution had been given and he may defer the date of dissolution as he thinks fit. Notice of such directions must be given to the Registrar of Companies by the applicant within seven days. There is an appeal from the Secretary of State's decision to the court: ss.202, 203.

---

[115] See IR 1986 r.4.223.
[116] Above, Ch.30.
[117] ibid.
[118] ibid.
[119] Above p.697.

This procedure was adopted on the recommendation of the Cork Committee.[120] Up to one-third or even more of companies in compulsory liquidation are likely to be subject to these provisions.

Dissolution of company

31–024 In the case of a compulsory winding up where either the liquidator gives notice to the Registrar that the final meeting has been held and that he has vacated office,[121] or the official receiver gives notice that the winding up is complete, the registration of that notice begins a period of three months at the end of which the company will be automatically dissolved unless on the application of an interested party the Secretary of State defers that date. There is an appeal to the court from any such decision: s.205.

In a voluntary winding up the three months' period ending with the automatic dissolution of the company begins with the registration of the liquidator's final account and return under either s.94 or s.106.[122] Otherwise the procedure is the same as on a compulsory winding up: s.201.[123]

Subject to any order which may at any time be made by the court under s.1005 of the Companies Act 2006, any property vested in or held on trust for a company immediately before its dissolution (excluding property held by the company on trust for any other person) vests in the Crown as bona vacantia: s.1012 of the Companies Act 2006. The Crown may disclaim such property by a notice signed in the case of property in England by the Treasury Solicitor (and in the case of property in Scotland by the Queen's and Lord Treasurer's Remembrancer): s.1013 of the Companies Act 2006. The effect of such disclaimer is much the same as if the property had been disclaimed under the Insolvency Act 1986 s.178, above.[124] The notice of disclaimer must be executed within 12 months after the vesting of the property came to the notice of the Crown representative or, where any person interested in the property applies in writing to the Crown representative requiring him to decide whether he will disclaim, usually within three months after the application. The notice of disclaimer must be delivered to the Registrar of Companies and registered by him, and copies must be published in the *Gazette* and sent to persons who have given the Crown representative notice of their interest in the property: ss.1013, 1014 of the Companies Act 2006.

Restoration of dissolved company to the register

31–025 Where a company has been dissolved that dissolution may be reversed, and the company restored to the register by one of two methods under the Companies Act 2006. The second, dealt with briefly below, was introduced on the recommendation of the Company Law Review *Final Report*.[125] The 2006 Act also modified

---

[120] paras 649–651.
[121] Above, Ch.29.
[122] Above, Ch.30.
[123] The position where a company is dissolved after an administration was dealt with in Ch.28, above,
[124] Ch.29. See also *Allied Dunbar Assurance Plc v Fowle* (1994) B.C.C. 422.
[125] paras. 11-17–11-19.

ss.651 and 653 of the Companies Act 1985 which provided for restoration by the court. Section 1029 of the 2006 Act is based on s.653 of the 1985 Act and provides that an application may be made to the court to restore to the register a company that has been dissolved or struck off the register. A broad range of persons are entitled to make such an application, including former members, creditors directors and liquidators of the company, as well as persons having proprietary rights in property in which the company held some right or contractual rights against the company: s.1029(2). Finally, an application may be made by any person appearing to the court to have an interest in the matter (s.1029(2)), as was provided for in s.651 of the Companies Act 1985. Cases decided under that Act and its predecessors may, therefore, continue to be of authoritative value.

A solicitor acting on behalf of a client with a claim against the dissolved company, and having neither a financial nor a proprietary interest, was not a "person . . . interested" within s.651 of the Companies Act 1985.[126] A liquidator de son tort, i.e. a person who has never been a duly appointed liquidator of the company but who has, without lawful authority, been carrying on the liquidation of the company, was so interested.[127] So to was a contributory in the liquidation.[128] The Inland Revenue could apply where an assessment for taxes had been made but the assessments were under appeal when the company was struck off the register.[129]

Aside from cases within s.1030(1),[130] the application cannot be made more than six years after the date of the dissolution: s.1030(4).[131] This is subject to s.1030(5). The court may order restoration of a company to the register in any case where the company was struck off under ss.1000 or 1001 of the Companies Act 2006[132] or, where the company was struck off voluntarily, any of the requirements of ss.1004–1009 were not complied with, or if in any case it considers it just to do so: s.1031(1). Restoration takes effect on a copy of the court's order being delivered to the Registrar of Companies (s.1031(2)), who must publish a notice in the Gazette regarding the restoration (s.1031(3), (4)). The effect of the order is that the company is deemed to have continued in existence as if it had not been dissolved or struck off the register: s.1032

When a company is restored to the register, any property of the company which **31–026** vested in the Crown under s.1012 of the Companies Act 2006 remains the Crown's property: Companies Act 2006 s.1034. Instead the company will receive a cash payment equivalent to those assets. This payment will be either the sum the Crown received or the value of any property which has since been disposed of by the Crown. This provision allows the Crown to dispose of such property without fear of a revival of the company: Companies Act 2006 s.1034(2).

---

[126] *Roehampton Swimming Pool Ltd* [1968] 1 W.L.R. 1693.
[127] *Wood and Martin (Bricklaying Contractors) Ltd, Re* [1971] 1 W.L.R. 293.
[128] *Thompson and Riches Ltd, Re* [1981] 2 All E.R. 477. Presumably such a contributory would now be included by virtue of being a former member of the company under s.1029(2).
[129] *Belmont and Co Ltd, Re* [1952] Ch.10; followed in *Test Holdings (Clifton) Ltd, Re* [1970] Ch. 285.
[130] Where an application is made for the purposes of bringing proceedings against the company for damages for personal injury.
[131] The previous limit under s.s.651(4) of the Companies Act 1985 was two years.
[132] Defunct companies: see below.

The second method of restoration to the register, introduced for the first time by the Companies Act 2006, is "administrative restoration" under s.1024 of the 2006 Act, and applies only in relation to companies struck off the register as "defunct" under ss.1000 and 1001 of the 2006 Act. It is therefore intended to provide a cheap and quick method of restoration for companies which probably should not have been struck off as defunct in the first place.

Application is made under s.1024 to the Registrar, rather than to the court,[133] and an application may only be made by a former director or member of the company. The application must be made within six years of the striking off: s.1024(3), (4). The Registrar may only restore the company to the register if he is satisfied that the company was carrying on business at the time of the striking off, that, where property has vested in the Crown under s.1012 of the 2006 Act as a result of the striking off, the Crown Representative consents to the restoration, and that the applicant has delivered to him all documents necessary to bring his records up to date: s.1025. If the Registrar decides to restore the company to the register, restoration takes effect for the date that he sends notice of his decision to the applicant (s.1027(1), (2)) and the Registrar must publish a notice in the Gazette regarding the restoration (s.1027(3)). The effect of restoration is that the company is deemed to have continued in existence as if it had not been dissolved or struck off the register: s.1028.

Defunct Companies

31–027 By ss.1000 and 1001 of the Companies Act 1986, if the Registrar of Companies has reasonable cause to believe that a company is not carrying on business or is not in operation, he may, after carrying out a specified procedure, strike the company's name off the register, after which it is dissolved.

The procedure under these provisions is:

1. The Registrar sends to the company by post a letter asking whether the company is carrying on business.

2. If no answer is received within one month, he sends within the next 14 days a registered letter, stating that if no reply is received within one month a notice will be published in the Gazette with a view to striking the company's name off the register.

3. If no satisfactory reply is received he sends to the company by post and publishes in the Gazette a notice, stating that unless cause is shown to the contrary the company will be struck off after three months.

4. If cause is not shown to the contrary, he strikes the company off and publishes notice thereof in the Gazette, whereupon the company is dissolved.

Companies have, in the past, by inviting the Registrar to exercise his powers, used s.1000 as a form of voluntary dissolution. There is now a statutory procedure for

---

[133] Thus saving time and cost.

voluntary dissolution of private companies: Companies Act 2006, ss.1003–1011. It applies where the company has not traded, and otherwise complies with s.1004(1), in the three months prior to the application.

Striking the company's name off the register does not affect the liability of any director or member of the company, and the company may still be wound up by the court. If the company is to be wound up, it should first be restored to the register under s.1024 or s.1029 of the Companies Act 2006.[134]

---

[134] *Cambridge Coffee Room Association Ltd, Re* [1952] All E.R. 112.

CORPORATE REORGANISATION

Chapter 32

MERGERS, DIVISIONS AND OTHER CORPORATE REORGANISATIONS

THE NATURE OF CORPORATE REORGANISATIONS

The reasons for corporate reorganisations

Such is the pace of commerce in the modern world that companies frequently **32–001** change in form, or the human beings who have given birth to them change their views about the usefulness of organising their affairs in a particular manner, or the human beings who operate the companies change and are replaced by people with different views. Therefore, within groups of companies it is common for companies to be dissolved, new companies formed, or old companies merged into new companies. More importantly for the purposes of this chapter, it is common for different business undertakings to choose to consolidate themselves into one single entity or for existing companies to separate so that business can be conducted more effectively by different managers. Companies are, it should be remembered, merely the playthings of the human minds who actually conduct business.

In the late twentieth century the globalisation of markets brought with it a large amount of "mergers and acquisitions" activity by which large businesses bought up smaller businesses or businesses merged together so as to form larger businesses with "synergies" between them: that is, the merged entity was expected to build on the different talents of the various companies which existed before that merger. In essence, a commercial strategy is formed by which an enlarged or reorganised business undertaking is thought to be more likely to succeed, or more likely to generate larger profits through increased market share or economies of scale, or more likely to ward off attack from competing organisations. Alternatively, a reorganisation may have the effect of moving the undertaking's principal operations to another jurisdiction, or it may simply offer a better tax treatment or a lighter form of regulatory oversight. The reorganisation of the corporate entities through which that business is done is therefore a means to an end.

There are various forms of corporate reorganisation which are considered in this part of this book. They are principally: mergers, divisions, takeovers, reconstructions and cross-border mergers. We shall consider each type of reorganisation in outline terms here. Each is analysed in the various chapters of this part of this book.

Mergers

32–002   Mergers can take effect in different ways. If two corporate entities genuinely wish to combine their business activities for their mutual benefit then a merger may be a harmonious union of two companies with the result that a new company is formed which comprises both of their previous shareholders, employees and management ("merger by formation of a new company"[1]). The practice of mergers tends to be that they are anything but harmonious because the new company ("the resulting entity") usually finds itself with two people doing the same job which had been performed when the businesses were in separate companies. Therefore, there will be a period of adjustment in which one group in management tends to acquire the upper hand, the resulting company logo or name or business culture may resemble one of the previous companies more than the other, and so on. Another means by which a merger can take place is that one company is absorbed into another company so that there is a merger but the resultant entity is effectively an enlarged form of one of the companies ("merger by absorption"[2]). In any event, the resulting company will have to recognise the shareholding of shareholders in the previous companies, the contractual obligations of the previous companies, and so forth.

As is considered in Ch.34, this can be particularly difficult when a merger is effected across borders such that there are different systems of company law governing the companies' various obligations. When groups of companies merge (as opposed to two companies) then there may be a very large number of holding companies, trading companies and subsidiary companies which are combined. Those companies may be active or registered in a number of different jurisdictions, with the result that systems of law other than UK company law are at issue. In essence, in all mergers, the two companies must reach an agreement as to the way in which the resulting entity will operate and how the rights of the various stakeholders in a company (shareholders, employees, creditors, etc.) will be recognised. The twenty-first century has seen a period of consolidation of businesses into ever larger groups of companies, particularly in the banking sector where the massification of banks has caused great problems of competition law as well as problems of company law. When large companies merge, this may have the effect that there are fewer companies left offering competing services in that marketplace, with the result that consumers may receive a worse bargain, price or service than hitherto.

Divisions

32–003   A division takes place when a company transfers its assets to one or more new companies with substantially the same shareholders. This is also known as a "demerger" or a "reconstruction". Unlike the mergers considered immediately above, it may be that a large corporate entity wishes to divide itself into smaller units. It may be that a company carries on a number of different businesses and

---

[1] Companies Act 2006 s.904(1)(b).
[2] Companies Act 2006 s.904(1)(a).

wishes to reorganise its operations so that each business is conducted in a separate company. This may simplify the management of each business sector, or it may permit separate companies to acquire financing more readily if its business model is easier to understand once it is distinct from other businesses, or it may permit that separate part of the business to be sold off as a separate concern either to third parties or by way of a management buy-out by the people who control it. In the event of a private equity acquisition of a public company, for example, the private equity firm behind the purchase may wish to realise cash quickly by selling off distinct parts of the business. This process of selling off business assets (also known as "asset-stripping") works on the private equity firm's calculation that the business is worth more when broken up into its constituent parts than it is if kept as a single corporate unit. Division of operations may attract a beneficial tax treatment, or it may permit one business unit to expand its operations overseas and so set up in another jurisdictions. As with mergers, which in some senses divisions mirror, there is a commercial decision in the background as to the most beneficial means of organising the business.

Takeovers

Takeovers are discussed in Ch.33. Whereas mergers appear ostensibly to involve **32–004** the consensual union of two or more different companies, takeovers may not necessarily be harmonious. A takeover is a situation in which one company acquires all of the shares in another company and so takes over that other company's assets, business and so forth. The company conducting the takeover will make an offer to the "target company's" shareholders to buy their shares from them at a given price. In relation to takeovers of public companies, whose shares are traded on regulated markets, the purchaser will (usually) build up its shareholding in the target company slowly until it holds a majority of its shares sufficient to take control of its business. In relation to the takeover of public companies in the European Union, there are a number of principles identified by the Takeover Directive to govern takeovers of public companies, and in the United Kingdom there is the Takeover Code administered by the Takeover Panel which regulates takeover activity in this jurisdiction. As was suggested above in relation to mergers, there may be situations in which there may be little practical difference between a consensual takeover of a target company whose management is willing to be taken over and a merger in which one company effectively appears to gain more than it loses from a merger. The difference would appear to be that in a takeover one company consumes the other company by acquiring its shares, whereas in a merger there is an agreement between companies that they will come together to form a resulting company. Such a reorganisation may raise as many tax questions as it will raise regulatory questions considered in this part of this book. Mergers and takeovers are now regulated separately under the Companies Act 2006.

Reconstructions

Reconstructions of a corporate body may take place without there being any sale of **32–005** the business to any third person. As outlined above, a business undertaking will be organised in whichever way its managers and advisors consider to be the most profitable, efficient and prudent. A large public company will typically have a number of subsidiary companies within its group so as to organise its management, so as to separate business activities off from some mundane administrative activities, so as to minimise the group's liability to tax, and so forth. When this model appears to be unprofitable, inefficient, or otherwise less desirable than some other structure, then the group of companies and individual companies within that group will be subject to a reconstruction. A reconstruction will typically involve an alteration in the assets owned by various companies, an alteration in the share capital of the various companies and an alteration of each company's day-to-day activities. Self-evidently, the reconstruction of a company will be of concern to its creditors, its employees and other third parties who may consider that that company no longer represents materially the same entity with which they had dealt originally or by which they are employed, as appropriate. Therefore, corporate reconstructions require regulation to ensure that the position of such third parties is not harmed.

MERGERS UNDER THE COMPANIES ACT 2006

The fundamental principles of mergers

32–006 When a merger of public companies is proposed to be made, whether by absorption of one company into another or by the formation of a new company into which the pre-existing companies will merge, then a draft of the proposed terms of the scheme are to be drawn up and adopted by the directors of the emerging companies.[3] Among the information which must be included in this document is a statement of the share exchange ratio between the companies.[4] These draft terms must be published at least one month before the company meetings which will discuss and vote on them.[5] The merger must then be approved by a majority of 75 per cent of the shareholders in all of the merging companies.[6] The directors must prepare a report for the vote at that meeting which explains the effect of the merger on the company and setting out the legal and economic grounds for the proposal.[7] There must also be a report prepared on the proposal on behalf of both companies, including commentary on questions of valuation.[8] Similar provisions apply, mutatis mutandis, in relation to divisions of companies.[9] In relation to shareholders to whose shares special rights are attached, the proposal must explain the manner in which those shares will be dealt with.[10]

Different regulations deal with the concentration of ownership between companies[11] in the form of mergers of companies, or the acquisition of effective control

[3] Companies Act 2006 s.905.
[4] Companies Act 2006 s.905.
[5] Companies Act 2006 s.906.
[6] Companies Act 2006 s.907.
[7] Companies Act 2006 s.908.
[8] Companies Act 2006 s.909. This requires that experts and valuers are independent: Companies Act 2006 s.936.
[9] Companies Act 2006 s.920 et seq.
[10] Companies Act 2006 s.913.
[11] Subject to the Council Regulation 139/2004 on control of concentrations between under takings ("EC Merger Regulation [2004] OJ L24/1) and the Enterprise Act 2002.

of one entity by another, and some joint ventures. For these purposes, the holding of "decisive influence" by one company over another may constitute "control",[12] just as a 25 per cent shareholding by one company in another company may constitute "control".

The Companies Act 2006 provisions in relation to mergers and divisions

Part 27 of the Companies Act 2006 deals with mergers and divisions. The scope **32–007** of Pt 27 is set out in s.902 of the CA 2006 which provides as follows:

"(1) This Part applies where—

(a) a compromise or arrangement is proposed between a public company and—

(i) its creditors or any class of them, or
(ii) its members or any class of them,
for the purposes of, or in connection with, a scheme for the reconstruction of any company or companies or the amalgamation of any two or more companies,

(b) the scheme involves—

(i) a merger (as defined in section 904), or
(ii) a division (as defined in section 919), and

(c) the consideration for the transfer (or each of the transfers) envisaged is to be shares in the transferee company (or one or more of the transferee companies) receivable by members of the transferor company (or transferor companies), with or without any cash payment to members."

Therefore, these provisions apply either where a public company (as opposed to a private company) reaches an agreement with either its creditors or its shareholders (or members) to effect a merger or a division. Creditors may agree to a reorganisation of a company if that allocates assets to their use as a means of providing the creditors with security or if it is part of a business strategy which promises to improve the company's prospects. The reasons for the company's members agreeing to a reorganisation were considered at the beginning of the chapter. Part 27 does not apply, however, in relation to the winding up of a company.

The procedure for effecting a merger

The definition of "merger"

A "merger" is defined in s.904 of the CA 2006 in the following terms: **32–008**

---

[12] EC Merger Regulation, art.3. By contrast, the threshold was 30 per cent in relation to takeovers.

"(1) The scheme involves a merger where under the scheme—

    (a) the undertaking, property and liabilities of one or more public companies, including the company in respect of which the compromise or arrangement is proposed, are to be transferred to another existing public company (a 'merger by absorption'), or

    (b) the undertaking, property and liabilities of two or more public companies, including the company in respect of which the compromise or arrangement is proposed, are to be transferred to a new company, whether or not a public company, (a 'merger by formation of a new company')."

As considered at the beginning of this chapter, there are two circumstances in which a merger can take place: either by one company merging into another company, or by two companies forming a new company by means of their merger. The statute applies only to mergers between public companies. It does not apply to mergers involving private companies.

The need for draft merger terms

32–009 As identified above, a merger between public companies of either sort identified in s.904 must comply with the procedure set out in s.905. Section 905 of the CA 2006 provides that "a draft of the proposed terms of the scheme must be drawn up and adopted by the directors of the merging companies".[13] The draft proposed terms of the scheme must include the following information:

"The draft terms must give particulars of at least the following matters—

    (a) in respect of each transferor company and the transferee company—

        (i) its name,

        (ii) the address of its registered office, and

        (iii) whether it is a company limited by shares or a company limited by guarantee and having a share capital;

    (b) the number of shares in the transferee company to be allotted to members of a transferor company for a given number of their shares (the 'share exchange ratio') and the amount of any cash payment;

    (c) the terms relating to the allotment of shares in the transferee company;

    (d) the date from which the holding of shares in the transferee company will entitle the holders to participate in profits, and any special conditions affecting that entitlement;

    (e) the date from which the transactions of a transferor company are to be treated for accounting purposes as being those of the transferee company;

---

[13] Companies Act 2006 s.905(1).

(f) any rights or restrictions attaching to shares or other securities in the transferee company to be allotted under the scheme to the holders of shares or other securities in a transferor company to which any special rights or restrictions attach, or the measures proposed concerning them;

(g) any amount of benefit paid or given or intended to be paid or given—

(i) to any of the experts referred to in section 909 (expert's report), or

(ii) to any director of a merging company,

and the consideration for the payment of benefit."

The draft proposed terms must then be delivered to the Registrar and notification of receipt must then be published in the Gazette at least one month before any meeting of that company to discuss the proposed merger.[14] The scheme must then be approved by 75 per cent of the membership of each class of shares in relation to each company which is intended to be a party to the merger.[15] The directors of each of the merging companies must "draw up and adopt a report": the statute expresses one report in the singular, which suggests that the report must be one report representing their agreed position.[16] The report must be in a form which complies with s.908(2) of the CA 2006:

"The report must consist of—

(a) the statement required by section 897 (statement explaining effect of compromise or arrangement), and

(b) insofar as that statement does not deal with the following matters, a further statement—

(i) setting out the legal and economic grounds for the draft terms, and in particular for the share exchange ratio, and

(ii) specifying any special valuation difficulties."

Furthermore an "expert's report must be drawn up on behalf of each of the **32–010** merging companies".[17] That report is addressed to the members of each company which is proposed to take part in the merger.[18] The contents of the report must comply with s.909(5) of the CA 2006 which provides that:

"The expert's report must—

(a) indicate the method or methods used to arrive at the share exchange ratio;

(b) give an opinion as to whether the method or methods used are reasonable in all the circumstances of the case, indicate the values arrived at

---

[14] Companies Act 2006 s.906.
[15] Companies Act 2006 s.907.
[16] Companies Act 2006 s.908(1).
[17] Companies Act 2006 s.909(1).
[18] Companies Act 2006 s.909(2).

using each such method and (if there is more than one method) give an opinion on the relative importance attributed to such methods in arriving at the value decided on;

(c) describe any special valuation difficulties that have arisen;

(d) state whether in the expert's opinion the share exchange ratio is reasonable; and

(e) in the case of a valuation made by a person other than himself (see section 935), state that it appeared to him reasonable to arrange for it to be so made or to accept a valuation so made."

The expert has a right to access all documents and other information which he considers to be "necessary" to complete his report.[19] Therefore, the shareholders have a report from the directors of the various companies and also an independent[20] expert's report on which to base their decision whether or not to vote for or against the proposed merger. That the expert must be a person who is eligible to be appointed as a statutory auditor[21] means that the focus of the report will be on the financial aspects of the transaction, whereas other, strategic questions beyond the expertise of that person may also be of significance in many cases. The members of each company also have a statutory right to inspect documents relating to the companies subject to the proposed merger in a period one month before the meeting to vote on that merger proposal.[22] A supplementary accounting statement is required if the accounts for any of the companies were prepared more than seven months before the preparation of the report.[23] Furthermore, in the event of a merger, a draft of the articles of association of the transferee company must be approved by an ordinary resolution of the members of the transferor company.[24]

MERGERS OR DIVISIONS: SECTION 110 OF THE INSOLVENCY ACT 1986

The scope of section 110 of the IA 1986

32–011   There is a specific mechanism for the merger or division of companies provided for by means of IA 1986. Under s.110 of the IA 1986, a company which is in voluntary winding up may transfer or sell the whole or part of its business or property to another company. The company may, in the case of a members' voluntary winding up, pass a special resolution authorising the liquidator to receive a variety of types of property as consideration: cash, shares, policies, or other like interests in the transferee company for distribution among the

---

[19] Companies Act 2006 s.909(6).
[20] The expert must be independent of the company and have no connection with the company: Companies Act 2006 s.936.
[21] Companies Act 2006 s.909(4).
[22] Companies Act 2006 s.911.
[23] Companies Act 2006 s.910.
[24] Companies Act 2006 s.912.

members of the transferor company according to their rights and interests in that company. The sanction of the court is unnecessary in a members' voluntary winding up. In the case of a creditors' winding up the liquidator's authority for the passage of the special resolution must come either from the court or from the liquidation committee. At common law, the sale may be made to a foreign company.[25] However, it has been held that such a sale must be made to a company and not to a speculator who hopes to form a company to take over the assets.[26]

The procedure under section 110

The following procedure may well be the procedure which is adopted under s.110 **32–012** if a members' voluntary winding up is involved. Typically, in such circumstances, a meeting of the transferor company is summoned in order to pass resolutions for reconstruction or amalgamation. At the meeting, resolutions are passed for the voluntary winding up of the company, the appointment of a liquidator, and the grant of authority to the liquidator to enter into an agreement with the transferee company on the terms of a draft submitted to the meeting.

The agreement typically provides that the transferee company shall purchase the assets of the transferor company, except a sum retained by the liquidator to discharge its liabilities. Furthermore, the agreement usually provides that the consideration shall be met by the allotment of shares in the transferee company to the liquidator or his nominees, whether fully or partly paid up. Moreover, the liquidator will give notice to the shareholders of the transferor company of the number of shares to which they are entitled and the time within which they must apply for those shares, and the notice will stipulate that failure to apply for shares within that time will preclude their rights to any shares. So, in *Postlethwaite v Port Philip, etc. Gold Mining Co*[27] a reconstruction scheme provided that shareholders in the old company should apply for shares in the new company within ten days after being given notice requiring them to apply for those shares. It was further provided the liquidator would dispose of all shares not applied for. It was on June 12 that the liquidator sent out notices requiring application for shares in the new company to be made before June 25. P, a shareholder in the old company, applied on August 24. It was held that P was not entitled to an allotment of shares in the new company, nor to any other relief, because he had applied outside the specified period.

In the case of a creditors' winding up the necessary authority would come either from the court or from the liquidation committee. Instead of the liquidator being authorised to dispose of all shares which the members of the transferor company had not applied for, an underwriting agreement may be created in respect to such shares.[28] If the agreement is silent as to the disposal of the proceeds of sale of any shares which are not applied for, then the proceeds must

---

[25] *Irrigation Co of France, Re* (1871) L.R. 6 Ch. App. 176.
[26] *Bird v Bird's Patent, etc. Sewage Co* (1874) L.R. 9 Ch. App. 358.
[27] (1889) 43 Ch.D. 452.
[28] *Barrow v Paringo Mines (1909) Ltd* (1909) 2 Ch. 658.

be distributed among the members of the transferor company who have not applied for shares in the transferee company.[29] Alternatively, shares may be given directly to the members of the transferor company instead of being applied for in this manner.

Protection of dissentient members

32–013 A sale or arrangement under s.110 of the Insolvency Act 1986 is binding on all members of the transferor company, whether they agree to it or not.[30] However, in the case of a member who both did not vote in favour of the special resolution, and who also expressed his dissent from it in writing to the liquidator which was left at the registered office within seven days after the passing of the resolution, that member may require the liquidator either to abstain from carrying the resolution into effect or may purchase his interest at a price which is to be determined by agreement or arbitration.[31] Section 111(3) has the effect that the election is exercisable by the liquidator. If the liquidator elects to purchase the member's interest, then the purchase money must be paid before the transferor company is dissolved, and must be raised by the liquidator in the manner determined by special resolution. The agreement usually provides for the retention by the liquidator out of the assets of the transferor company of a sum to cover the interests of the dissentient shareholders.

A transferee of shares whose transfer was not registered when a special resolution is passed may be entitled to have the register of members rectified and to dissent from the resolution.[32] The articles cannot deprive a member of his statutory right to the value of his shareholding if he dissents.[33]

Protection of dissentient creditors

32–014 The liquidator must pay the creditors of the transferor company in the usual way in a winding up. If, however, the creditors form the view that they will be prejudiced by the transfer of all the company's assets to the transferee company, then they may petition for a compulsory winding-up order. Section 110(6) of the Insolvency Act 1986 provides that the special resolution for reconstruction shall not be valid if, within a year, an order is made for winding up the company by the court, unless the court sanctions the resolution.

Sale under a power in memorandum

32–015 If a company has a memorandum of association (as was required under the law before the Companies Act 2006) then that memorandum of association may give power to a company to sell its undertaking for shares in another company. If, however, the whole of the undertaking is to be sold and the proceeds are to be

[29] *Lake View Extended Gold Mine Co, Re* [1900] W.N. 44.
[30] Insolvency Act 1986 s.110(5).
[31] Insolvency Act 1986 s.111.
[32] *Sussex Brick Co, Re* [1904] 1 Ch. 598, CA.
[33] *Payne v The Cork Co Ltd* [1900] 1 Ch. 308.

distributed among the shareholders, the procedure laid down in s.110 of the Insolvency Act 1986, including the provisions for the protection of dissentient shareholders and creditors, cannot be excluded.[34]

ARRANGEMENTS AND RECONSTRUCTIONS

Scope of the section

Arrangements and reconstructions are governed by Pt 26 of the Companies Act **32–016** 2006. As considered above, the Insolvency Act contains provisions whereby the administrator or liquidator may make an arrangement with a company's creditors.[35] Such schemes are not suitable for mergers or divisions. However, the provisions of Pt 26 of the CA 2006 (sections 895 et seq.) provide that a company can also enter into a compromise or arrangement with its creditors, and its members (or any class thereof) without going into liquidation. Schemes of arrangement under s.895 of the CA 2006 have a wider potential than voluntary arrangements under the Insolvency Act and can be used for an agreed merger or division of two or more companies subject to the statutory requirements as to consent of the members and the court.

The proper way to distribute the assets of a company, otherwise than strictly in accordance with creditors' rights, has been held to require a scheme of arrangement under s.895 which binds all creditors, and not by an agreement or compromise under s.167 of the Insolvency Act 1986 which would deprive non-assenting creditors of the court's protection and prevent them from expressing their views.[36] Under s.895 the court may approve a scheme which differs from the statutory scheme on a liquidator.[37] Although this chapter is concerned primarily with mergers and divisions, since schemes of arrangement can be used for many other purposes, especially in relation to creditors, the following discussion involves all aspects of the procedure.

Statutory requirements

A compromise or arrangement will fall within Pt 26 of the CA 2006 if it is **32–017** proposed between a company and either its creditors, or any class of them, or its members, or any class of them.[38] This definition of what constitutes an arrangement is expanded on in the case law considered in this section of this chapter.[39] Section 895 of the CA 2006 provides that a compromise or arrangement will be binding on the company and the creditors or class of creditors or the members or class of members, as the case may be, if it complies with three requirements. First, under s.896(1) of the CA 2006—

---

[34] *Bisgood v Henderson's Transvaal Estates Ltd* [1908] 1 Ch. 743, CA; cf. *Waverley Hydropathic Co Ltd, Petitioners*, 1948 S.C. 59.
[35] ss.1–7A and 167.
[36] *Trix Ltd, Re* [1970] 1 W.L.R. 1421.
[37] *Anglo American Insurance Ltd, Re* [2001] 1 B.C.L.C. 755.
[38] Companies Act 2006 s.895(1).
[39] See *Savoy Hotel Ltd, Re* [1981] Ch. 351; *BTR Plc, Re* [2000] 1 B.C.L.C.740; *T &N Ltd, Re* [2006] 2 B.C.L.C. 374

"The court may, on an application under this section, order a meeting of the creditors or class of creditors, or of the members of the company or class of members (as the case may be), to be summoned in such manner as the court directs."

This is a change from the old law in that the court may now order a meeting on a separate application for that purpose without necessarily having to wait for the final application to sanction the merger in toto. In any event, the court is not obliged to summon such a meeting. It has been held that creditors who cannot possibly benefit, for example because the company's assets are too low, need not be involved in the scheme[40] and that members of the company who could not benefit from the scheme have no right to object.[41] Second, the compromise or arrangement must be agreed to by a majority in number representing three-quarters in value[42] of those present and voting either in person or by proxy at the meeting. Third, it must be sanctioned by the court. To effect a Pt 26 merger or division, the scheme, involving a transfer of one company's assets to another in return for shares in that company, must therefore be approved by at least 75 per cent of the members and creditors of the transferor company, and by the court. The benefit is that, if the scheme is approved, dissenting shareholders and creditors are bound by it.[43] This is not possible under s.110 of the Insolvency Act, considered above. If the scheme involves the merger or division of one of the more public companies, then additional requirements are imposed in the manner considered below.

The word "company" in this context means any company liable to be wound up under the Act. This definition encompasses a company formed and registered under the 2006 Act, an existing company (in effect, a company formed and registered under a previous Companies Act), or an unregistered company.[44]

The definition of "compromise or arrangement" at common law

32–018   The word "arrangement" has a very wide meaning, and is wider than the word "compromise".[45] An arrangement may involve debenture holders giving an extension of time for payment, accepting a cash payment less than the face value of their debentures,[46] giving up their security in whole or in part, exchanging their debentures for shares in the company[47] or in a new company,[48] or having the

---

[40] *British & Commonwealth Holdings Plc, Re (No.3)* [1992] B.C.C. 58; *Maxwell Communications Corp Plc, Re* [1994] 1 B.C.L.C. 1.

[41] *RAC Motoring Services Ltd, Re* [2000] 1 B.C.L.C. 307.

[42] Companies Act 2006 s.899. In the case of creditors the value of their debt is the relevant criterion; see, e.g. *Exchange Securities and Commodities Ltd, Re* (1987) 3 B.C.C. 48.

[43] Companies Act 2006 s.895(2). For examples of the effect of such approval see *Barclays Bank Plc v British & Commonwealth Holdings Plc* [1995] B.C.C. 19 and *Waste Recycling Group Plc, Re* [2004] B.C.C. 328.

[44] Which the court has power to wind up under s.221 of the IA 1986. This can include companies incorporated abroad: See, e.g. *Drax Holdings Ltd, Re* [2004] B.C.C. 334.

[45] *Guardian Assce Co, Re* [1917] 1 Ch. 431, CA.

[46] e.g. *The Philadelphia Securities Co v The Realisation etc. Corp of Scotland Ltd* (1903) 11 S.L.T. 217, OH.

[47] e.g. *Telewest Communications Plc, Re* [2005] B.C.C. 36.

[48] *Empire Mining Co, Re* (1890) 44 Ch.D. 402.

rights attached to their debentures varied in some other respect.[49] Creditors may take cash in part payment of their claims and the balance in shares or debentures in the company. Preference shareholders may give up their rights to arrears of dividends,[50] agree to accept a reduced rate of dividend in the future, or have their class rights otherwise varied.[51] The Pt 26 structure is also widely used for compromises with policy holders by insurance companies.[52] The members of a company in liquidation may agree with the company to seek or not to oppose a stay of the winding up, with the result that the members will give up their existing right to have all the proceeds of the company's assets distributed among them and instead have their rights remitted to their contractual rights under the articles.[53] It even includes a scheme whereby the shareholders transfer their shares to another company, since that affects the contractual arrangements between the shareholders and their company so that there is an arrangement between them.[54]

Section 895 provides that the expression "arrangement" includes a reorganisation of the share capital of the company by the consolidation of shares of different classes or by the division of shares into shares of different classes. The word "compromise" implies some element of accommodation on each side, although it is not defined in the statute. The word "compromise" is not apt to describe a total surrender. Similarly, the word "arrangement" implies some element of give and take.[55]

Where an arrangement under s.895 is essentially being used as a scheme for the purchase by an outsider of all the issued shares of a company, then the scheme will not be sanctioned unless that company consents. Such consent may be expressed by the members in general meeting or by the board of directors.[56] It cannot be used therefore for a contested takeover or merger. Even if the takeover or merger is an agreed one, one judge has held that the court will not allow the remaining provisions of Pt 28 (relating to takeovers) to be circumvented by the use of s.895 where the necessary resolution under s.895 can only be passed with the assistance of votes of the wholly-owned subsidiary of the offeror company.[57] However, there is no general principle that s.895 is subordinate to the rights of minority shareholders under Pt 28 (relating to takeovers). The lower majority required is balanced by the need for the court's approval.[58]

Summoning the class meetings

The first stage in effecting a scheme of arrangement is to ask the court to summon **32–019** the appropriate meetings of shareholders or creditors. Under s.896 of the CA

---

[49] e.g. *Wright & Greig Ltd, Petitioners* 1911 1 S.L.T. 353.

[50] e.g. *Balmenach-Glenlivet Distillery Ltd, Petitioners*, 1916 S.C. 639.

[51] *City, etc. Trust Corporation Ltd, Petitioners*, 1951 S.C. 570.

[52] See, e.g. *Equitable Life Assurance Society, Re* [2002] 2 B.C.L.C. 510.

[53] *Calgary and Edmonton Land Co Ltd, Re* [1975] 1 W.L.R. 355 at 363, per Megarry J.

[54] *N.F.U. Development Trust, Re* [1972] 1 W.L.R. 1548.

[55] *Savoy Hotel Ltd, Re* [1961] 3 All E.R. 646.

[56] ibid. But not all such cases will fail, see *National Bank Ltd, Re* [1966] 1 W.L.R. 819; *The Singer Manufacturing Co Ltd v Robinow*, 1971 S.C. 11 (scheme to enable parent company to acquire remaining 7.3 per cent shareholding in subsidiary held competent).

[57] *Hellenic & General Trust Ltd, Re* [1976] 1 W.L.R. 123.

[58] *BTR Plc, Re* [2000] 1 B.C.L.C. 740, CA.

2006, the court may order a meeting of the creditors or class of creditors, or of the members of the company or class of members (as the case may be), to be summoned in such manner as the court directs if an application is made under that section seeking such a meeting. This process therefore requires identification of the different classes (if any) of shareholders or creditors, since each class must meet and vote separately. Until recently, the court would simply act on the company's proposals and would not consider the issue as to whether the classes were properly constituted until it came to approve the scheme after the meetings had been held. The problem was that this sometimes meant that a scheme would be turned down at that late stage because of incorrect class identification even if there were no objections, when the issue could have been dealt with at the beginning, thus saving a great deal of expense. The courts finally began to appreciate this anomaly,[59] and the procedure was changed by a Practice Statement in 2002.[60] Thus, if there is a potential problem as to the identity of the classes, the matter is now considered at the initial stage.[61] The onus is on the company to draw the court's attention to any potential problems and to notify those affected so that they can raise objections. It is still possible for there to be objections on this point at the final stage but the court will want to know why those objections were not raised earlier.

Identifying the correct classes

32–020   The litigation concerning the correct classes which require separate meetings has involved both members and creditors. The central test is that set out by Bowen L.J. in *Sovereign Life Assurance Co v Dodd*[62]:

> "It must be confined to those whose rights are not so dissimilar as to make it impossible for them to consult together with a view to their common interest."

Thus it is a question of looking at the rights of those involved and not their personal interests. Members or creditors with the same legal rights may well have different or even conflicting interests, but that is an issue to be looked at in the context of fairness, at the final approval stage. Otherwise there would be a plethora of classes.[63] Further, even the existence of different rights does not always require separate class meetings. In *Hawk Insurance Co Ltd, Re*[64] Chadwick L.J. held that, having looked at the rights to be released and those to

---

[59] *Hawk Insurance Co Ltd, Re* [2001] 2 B.C.L.C. 480 at 513, per Chadwick L.J.; *Equitable Life Assurance Society, Re* [2002] B.C.L.C. 510.

[60] See [2002] 3 All E.R. 96.

[61] See, e.g. *Telewest Communications Plc, Re* [2004] B.C.C. 342, affirmed [2005] B.C.C. 29 CA.

[62] [1892] 2 Q.B. 573 at 583.

[63] *BTR Plc, Re* [1999] 2 B.C.L.C. 675, affirmed [2000] 1 B.C.L.C. 740, CA (where even the objectors could not identify all the classes on that basis); *Anglo American Insurance Ltd, Re* [2001] 1 B.C.L.C. 755; *Waste Recycling Group Plc, Re* [2004] B.C.C. 328; *Telewest Communications Plc, Re* [2004] B.C.C. 342, affirmed [2005] B.C.C. 29, CA; cf. *Hellenic and General Trust Ltd, Re* [1976] 1 W.L.R. 123, explained on other grounds in *BTR Plc, Re*.

[64] [2001] 2 B.C.L.C. 480 at 519. See also *Equitable Life Assurance Co, Re* [2002] 2 B.C.L.C. 510, per Lloyd J. where the concept of "consulting together" was said to be an outdated idea.

be gained, the court should ask whether those rights are really so dissimilar that they cannot consult together. Too zealous an application could give a minority an inappropriate veto. It has been the view of successive authors of this book that the rights of such minority shareholders should be considered at the sanction stage. So, in *Telewest Communications Plc, Re*,[65] bondholders who had different rights in insolvency proceedings (because some of them were denominated in sterling while others were denominated in US dollars) were nevertheless held to constitute a single class for the purpose of agreeing to the scheme. This was because there was a single scheme whereby they would all be credited with shares in a new holding company, pro rata to their claims, in place of their bonds. It was a single scheme with all the bondholders. The difference would come in the conversion rate to be applied, which it was argued would unfairly discriminate against the sterling bondholders and would be different from that applied on a liquidation. That issue could be considered as a matter of the overall fairness of the scheme at the approval stage.[66] Shareholders or creditors with no interest in the company need not be included, for example an insolvent company in relation to which such people would not be entitled to anything on a winding up.[67]

Other jurisdictional issues

At the preliminary hearing the court will also decide other jurisdictional issues. **32–021** Among those issues would be the question as to whether or not the court would have the power to approve the scheme if were approved by the class meetings. For example, in circumstances in which an order was sought which the court had no power to order, it was held that holding the meetings would have been pointless and so the court refused to summon the meetings.[68]

The need for an explanatory statement in relation to a meeting

Where a meeting of creditors or members is summoned, further to s.897 of the **32–022** CA 2006, a statement must be sent with every notice of the meeting explaining the effect of the compromise or arrangement and, in particular, stating any material interests of the directors in any capacity and the effect thereon of the compromise or arrangement in so far as it is different from the effect on the same interest of other persons. If the meeting is summoned by advertisement, a similar statement, or a notification of the place where such a statement may be obtained, must be included. Where the compromise or arrangement affects the rights of debenture holders the statement must give the same explanation as respects the trustees of a deed for securing the issue of debentures as it is required to give as respects the directors.

These formal requirements must be complied with faithfully. It has been held that the court "has no discretionary power to dispense with the procedural

---

[65] [2004] B.C.C. 342, affirmed [2005] B.C.C. 29, CA.
[66] See [2005] B.C.C. 36 where the scheme was held to be inherently fair.
[67] *Mytravel Plc, Re* [2004] EWHC 2741 (Ch.).
[68] ibid. The matter was not raised before the Court of Appeal in that case.

requirements of section [897]."[69] Thus a scheme will not be sanctioned even if an explanatory statement states that the company's assets have been revalued where that statement does not give the amount of the revaluation.[70] Similarly, if a copy of the petition[71] or a copy of the scheme[72] has been sent without any further explanation, then that scheme will not be sanctioned.[73]

Any material interests of directors must always be stated, even if those interests are in no way different from the interests of other persons in their treatment under the scheme.[74] In deciding whether the members of the class have been properly informed, the notice summoning the meeting and the circular can be read together.[75] Further to s.898 of the CA 2006, it is the duty of any director of the company, and any trustee for its debenture holders, "to give notice to the company of such matters relating to himself as may be necessary for the purposes of section 897".[76] Failure to do so constitutes an offence.[77]

Where there is a change in the material interests of the directors or of any other material circumstances between the issue of the statement and the meetings to consider the scheme the court will nevertheless sanction the scheme, even though the meetings are not informed of the change, if it is satisfied that no reasonable shareholder would have altered his decision as to the scheme had he known of the changes.[78] The test is whether all material changes of circumstances which have come to the attention of the board between the issuing of the circular and the meeting have been disclosed to those entitled to vote at the meeting. A material change for this purpose is one which would be likely to affect a reasonable shareholder's voting intentions.[79]

The requirement which is now contained in s.899 that "75% in value of the members or class of members" agree to the compromise of arrangement refers to the size of the stake which each member has in the company. It has been held that

> "the purpose is to prevent a numerical majority with a small stake outvoting a minority with a large stake, e.g. to prevent 51 members with one share each outvoting 49 members with 10 shares each."[80]

Any proper form of proxy may be used and it is not necessary as to its validity that it should be sent to the company's offices before the meeting.[81] Directors

---

[69] *The Scottish Eastern, etc. Trust Ltd, Petitioners*, 1966 S.L.T. 285 at 288, per Lord Guthrie.
[70] *Dorman, Long & Co Ltd, Re* [1934] Ch. 635.
[71] *Rankin & Blackmore Ltd, Petitioners*, 1950 S.C. 218.
[72] *Peter Scott & Co Ltd, Petitioners*, 1950 S.C. 507.
[73] The fact that some creditors have more background information than others is not fatal, however: *Heron International NV, Re* [1994] 1 B.C.L.C. 667.
[74] *Coltness Iron Co Ltd, Petitioners*, 1951 S.C. 476; contrast *Second Scottish Investment Trust, etc., Petitioners*, 1962 S.L.T. 392.
[75] *RAC Motoring Services Ltd, Re* [2000] 1 B.C.L.C. 307.
[76] Companies Act 2006 s.898(1).
[77] Companies Act 2006 s.898(2).
[78] *Jessel Trust Ltd, Re* [1985] B.C.L.C. 119; *Minster Assets Plc, Re* [1985] B.C.L.C. 200; *Allied Domecq Plc, Re* [2000] 1 B.C.L.C. 134.
[79] *MB Group Plc, Re* (1989) 5 B.C.C. 584.
[80] *N.F.U. Development Trust Ltd, Re* [1972] 1 W.L.R. 1548 at 1553, per Brightman J.
[81] *Dorman, Long & Co Ltd, Re* [1934] Ch. 635; *La Lainière de Roubaix v Glen Glove, etc. Co Ltd*, 1926 S.C. 91.

who, pursuant to the court's order, receive proxies must use them whether they are for or against the scheme.

The sanction of the court

The sanction of the court is given in accordance with s.899 of the CA 2006. **32–023** Section 899(1) provides that:

> "If a majority in number representing 75% in value of the creditors or class of creditors or members or class of members (as the case may be), present and voting either in person or by proxy at the meeting summoned under section 896, agree a compromise or arrangement, the court may, on an application under this section, sanction the compromise or arrangement."

Section 899(2) then provides that an application can be made under s.899 by the company; or by any creditor or member of the company; or, if the company is being wound up, by the liquidator; or, if the company is in administration, by the administrator. A compromise which is sanctioned by the court is then binding on any applicable creditors or members, the company itself, and any liquidator and any "contributories of the company" if the company is being wound up.[82] Such an order is effective once a copy has been delivered to the Registrar.[83]

It has been held that, before giving its sanction to a scheme of arrangement, the court will ensure that the following things have taken place:

> "First, that the provisions of the statute have been complied with. Secondly, that the class was fairly represented by those who attended the meeting and that the statutory majority are acting bona fide and are not coercing the minority in order to promote interests adverse to those of the class whom they purport to represent; and, thirdly, that the arrangement is such as a man of business would reasonably approve."[84]

That judgment is to be made assuming that the intelligent and honest person was acting as a member of the class concerned and in respect of his interests as such.

While the courts are concerned to state that approving a scheme is not merely a matter of checking that all the procedural requirements of the sections have been met with,[85] they are reluctant to interfere if the scheme has been approved by the correct majority, and typically the majority is usually far in excess of that required. Thus, for example, in *Waste Recycling Group, Re*,[86] the judge was impressed by the facts that the scheme (a merger) was approved by 99.7 per cent in value of the shares voted and that those votes came principally from the smaller shareholders.

---

[82] Companies Act 2006 s.899(3).

[83] Companies Act 2006 s.899(4).

[84] *Anglo-Continental Supply Co Ltd, Re* [1922] 2 Ch. 723 at 736, per Astbury J.; CA at 238. For adoption in Scotland, see per Lord President Dunedin in *Shandon Hydropathic Co Ltd, Petitioners*, 1911 S.C. 1153 at 1155. This statement is always applied.

[85] The important point as to establishing the correct identity of the classes is now mainly dealt with at the earlier stage: see above.

[86] [2004] B.C.C. 328. See also, e.g. *Equitable Life Assurance Society, Re* [2002] 2 B.C.L.C. 510.

That was so even though the number of shareholders who actually voted was small and only 74 per cent of the potential votes were actually exercised. In *Telewest Communications Plc, Re (No.2)*,[87] the scheme (to convert bonds into shares) was approved by 88 per cent of the bondholders. The dissenters were some of those who held only bonds denominated in sterling and who complained as to the unfairness of the proposed exchange rate vis-a-vis the US dollar bondholders. Again the judge was impressed by the strength of the majority[88] and by the fact that some of those who owned only sterling bonds had voted for the scheme. In any event, the scheme apart from the exchange rate was very much in the bondholders' interests and the exchange rate proposals were not inherently unfair.

In *Allied Domecq Plc, Re*,[89] the judge also relied on the fact that the scheme (for the disposal of a subsidiary) had been recommended by the board. In that case the intended and named buyer dropped out after the approval by the meeting but before the court's sanction was obtained. The court nevertheless approved the scheme since the mechanics of the sale were not dependent on any particular buyer.[90] However, the approval was made on terms that no actual sale could proceed without a special resolution as required by the original scheme. In another unusual case, *BAT Industries Plc, Re*,[91] the judge considered that contingent creditors (i.e. those with a potential tort action against the company) had the right to object at this stage, although on the facts he rejected their objections.

The court cannot alter the scheme and impose one that the relevant classes have not agreed to,[92] but it would be prepared to set aside a scheme where the court's consent has been obtained by fraud, even if that means unravelling the scheme. However, no such award would be made if the result would have been the same without the fraud[93] or if it would not assist the objectors.[94] The costs of the scheme may be borne by the company and there may be one set of costs for opposing creditors but not for any supporting creditors. In general, costs should be kept to a minimum and one set of creditors should not be ordered to pay the costs of another set of creditors.[95]

Human rights issues

32–024   The argument has been made that the procedure under s.895 by which, as we have seen, dissenting shareholders or creditors can be compelled to accept a scheme which changes their rights, is contrary to art.1 of the First Protocol to the European Convention on Human Rights, now part of UK law by virtue of the Human Rights Act 1998. That article provides that:

---

[87] [2005] B.C.C. 36.
[88] Although this was inevitable once it had been decided that all the bondholders could meet as a single class: *Telewest Communications Plc, Re* [2004] B.C.C. 342, affirmed [2005] B.C.C. 29, CA, above.
[89] [2000] 1 B.C.L.C. 134.
[90] Moreover, this would have been clear to those voting at the meeting, and even, if not, it would not have affected the way a reasonable shareholder would have cast his vote.
[91] Unreported, September 3, 1998.
[92] *Kempe v Ambassador Insurance Co* [1998] 1 B.C.L.C. 234, PC.
[93] There are other sanctions available to the court against the fraudsters.
[94] *Fletcher v Royal Automobile Club Ltd* [2000] 1 B.C.L.C. 331.
[95] *Esal (Commodities) Ltd, Re* [1985] B.C.L.C. 450.

"Every natural and legal person is entitled to the peaceful enjoyment of his possessions. No one shall be deprived of his possessions except in the public interest and subject to the conditions provided for by law and by the general principles of international law. The preceding provisions shall not, however, in any way impair the right of a State to enforce such laws as it deems necessary to control the use of property in accordance with the general interest . . ."

In *Equitable Life Assurance Society, Re*,[96] Lloyd J. rejected that argument on two grounds. First, he relied on a decision of the European Commission of Human Rights,[97] that provisions such as s.895 are only caught by art.1 of the First Protocol if the law creates such inequality that one person could be arbitrarily and unjustly deprived of property in favour of another. The terms of s.895 and the case law made it clear that that was not the case. Second, that it did not amount to a confiscation of property since all schemes require some exchange of rights. No scheme capable of being confirmed could amount to a confiscation in breach of art.1. The same judge heard the case of *Waste Recycling Group Plc, Re*,[98] where the objector argued that, since he had bought his shares on environmental grounds, being deprived of those shares under the scheme meant that he would no longer be able to influence the company's policies on that issue at meetings, and so forth. That interest, being non-financial, invoked art.1 since it could not be compensated for by a financial exchange. The judge said that s.895 took account of rights but not interests and that art.1, in its operation in relation to s.895, did not distinguish between shareholders as to why they purchased their shares, be it for financial or public benefit reasons.

A different issue arose in *Pan Atlantic Insurance Co Ltd, Re*,[99] where a scheme which involved claims being settled by an independent adjudicator was challenged as being contrary to art.6(1) of the Convention itself. That Article provides for a fair and public hearing of any dispute as to civil rights by an independent and impartial tribunal established by law. Lloyd J., again, heard the case and, after reviewing the case law on art.6(1),[100] decided that the right of access to the courts was not absolute and could be subject to limitations, provided they do not go to the very essence of the right but pursue a legitimate and proportional aim. On the facts the scheme did exactly that since the arbitrator's decision was final and binding only insofar as the law allowed and was proportional in the context of the scheme (an alternative to a winding up).

Facilitating a division or a merger

In order to facilitate schemes which can be classified as a reconstruction,[101] or **32–025** amalgamation, s.900 et seq. provides that when an application is made to the

---

[96] [2002] 2 B.C.L.C. 510 at 535–537.
[97] *Bamelid and Malström v Sweden* (1982) 29 D.R. 64.
[98] [2004] B.C.C. 328.
[99] [2003] B.C.C. 847.
[100] *Ashingdane v United Kingdom* (1985) E.H.R.R. 528.
[101] A reconstruction has been held to require that the members of the old and new company are the same: *Mytravel Plc, Re* [2004] E.W.H.C. 2741 (Ch.). The CA was not concerned with this point.

court under s.895 for the sanctioning of a compromise or arrangement, where the compromise or arrangement is for the purposes of a scheme for the division of a company[102] or the merger of two or more companies and the scheme involves the transfer of the whole or part of the undertaking or property of a company (called "a transferor company") to another company (called "the transferee company"), the court has the power to do the following things:[103]

"The court may, either by the order sanctioning the compromise or arrangement or by a subsequent order, make provision for all or any of the following matters—

(a) the transfer to the transferee company of the whole or any part of the undertaking and of the property or liabilities of any transferor company;

(b) the allotting or appropriation by the transferee company of any shares, debentures, policies or other like interests in that company which under the compromise or arrangement are to be allotted or appropriated by that company to or for any person;

(c) the continuation by or against the transferee company of any legal proceedings pending by or against any transferor company;

(d) the dissolution, without winding up, of any transferor company;

(e) the provision to be made for any persons who, within such time and in such manner as the court directs, dissent from the compromise or arrangement;

(f) such incidental, consequential and supplemental matters as are necessary to secure that the reconstruction or amalgamation is fully and effectively carried out."

The transfer to the transferee company of the whole or part of the undertaking and of the property or liabilities of a transferor company cannot apply to non-assignable rights,[104] nor can it transfer the office of executor from one bank to another; such an office of personal trust is incapable of assignment.[105] However, contracts of employment are transferred under the Transfer of Undertaking, (Protection of Employment) Regulations 1981.[106] An office copy of such an order made must be registered with the Registrar of Companies within seven days.

Mergers and divisions of public companies—additional requirements

32–026 Following the implementation of the third and sixth EC directives on company law[107] by the Companies (Mergers and Divisions) Regulations 1987,[108] additional

---

[102] The definition of company" here is different from its predecessor: *Re SEVIC Systems AG* [2006] 2 B.C.L.C. 510.

[103] Companies Act 2006 s.900(2).

[104] *L Hotel Co Ltd, Re* [1946] 1 All E.R. 319.

[105] *In the Estate of Skinner (Decd)* [1958] 1 W.L.R. 1043.

[106] SI 1981/794.

[107] Directive 78/885 [1978] OJ L295/36 and Directive 82/891, [1982] OJ L378/47.

[108] SI 1987/1991.

requirements to those already required by Pt 26 are imposed where the scheme of arrangement falls within one of the following three categories as defined in s.902 (a); in relation to mergers by acquisition, where a public company proposes to transfer all of its undertaking, property and liabilities to another public company (which has not been formed for that purpose) in return for shares in the transferee company to be held by the transferor shareholders (b); in relation to mergers by formation of a new company, where two or more public companies propose to transfer all their undertakings, etc. to any type of company formed for that purpose, members of the transferor company receiving shares in the new company by way of total or part consideration; in relation to divisions, where a public company proposes to divide all its undertakings and so forth between two or more companies which are either public companies or companies formed for the purpose of the division, then members of the transferor company may receive shares in the transferee companies by way of total or part consideration. In all these cases there is therefore an agreed arrangement involving a share exchange by the transferee company's shareholders. It is envisaged that the transferor company or companies will be dissolved after the scheme has gone through.[109] The legislation sets out additional requirements which must be complied with in different circumstances before the arrangement can be sanctioned, but those items of detail are outwith the scope of this book.

---

[109] These requirements do not apply if the transferor company is already in liquidation and so do not apply to reconstructions under s.110 of the Insolvency Act 1986, above.

Chapter 33

TAKEOVERS

INTRODUCTION

33–001 This chapter considers takeovers by one company of another company. The most significant takeover activity is governed by the Takeover Code which was implemented in the United Kingdom further to the Takeover Directive and Pt 28 of the Companies Act 2006, as considered below. Before turning to the detail of those provisions, however, it would be as well to consider the means by which takeovers are effected in general terms (and how they may be effected outwith the scope of the Takeover Directive otherwise than on a regulated market). Takeovers may take effect by means of the simple method of one company acquiring a majority or the whole of the shares of another company from its shareholders. In such a case it is usual for the acquiring company (the offeror company) to make an offer (called a takeover bid) to the shareholders in the other company (the target or offeree company) to purchase their shares at a stated price and to fix a time within which the offer is to be accepted, with a condition that if a named percentage of the shareholders do not accept the offer, the offer is to be void. The offer is usually at a higher price than the current market price of the shares as quoted on the Stock Exchange and it may be in cash (e.g. £2 per share) or in kind (e.g. two of the offeror company's shares for each of the target company's shares). There are many economic reasons why such an offer is made. Sometimes more than one takeover bid is made for the same company so that there are rival bidders. The Takeover Code provides a means of regulating takeover activity on regulated markets so as to prevent market abuse and other inappropriate conduct.

TAKEOVERS

Sources of the law on takeovers

33–002 The principal source of law on takeovers is the EU Takeovers Directive, further to which the control of takeovers of public companies is administered in the United Kingdom by the Takeover Panel, as discussed below. The Takeover Directive[1] came into force on May 20, 2004, and was implemented by means of

---

[1] Directive 2004/25/EC on takeover bids ("the Takeover Directive") [2004] OJ L142/12.

the Takeovers Directive (Interim Implementation) Regulations 2006[2] on May 20, 2006, and latterly superseded by Pt 28 of the Companies Act 2006. The directive relates to takeover offers for companies whose shares have been admitted to trading on a regulated market. Those offers must be public offers to take control of a company admitted to a regulated market.[3] This section will focus on the Takeover Code ("the Code") because it both effects the relevant provisions of the CA 2006 which in turn implement the directive and also because it stretches beyond the remit of that Directive.[4] The discussion of the larger will thus accommodate discussion of the smaller.

However, it is important to identify the purpose and extent of the Directive. Article 1 of the Directive provides that:

"This Directive lays down measures coordinating the laws, regulations, administrative provisions, codes of practice and other arrangements of the Member States, including arrangements established by organisations officially authorised to regulate the markets (hereinafter referred to as 'rules'), relating to takeover bids for the securities of companies governed by the laws of Member States, where all or some of those securities are admitted to trading on a regulated market within the meaning of Directive 93/22/EEC(11) in one or more Member States (hereinafter referred to as a 'regulated market')."

The focus of the directive is therefore on securities which are traded on regulated markets, such as the London Stock Exchange. The Financial Services Authority maintains a list of "regulated markets" in the United Kingdom, as do the competent authorities of all Member States in relation to their jurisdictions.[5]

The statutory powers of the Takeover Panel

The Takeover Panel ("the Panel") is the body which has been identified as the **33–003** authority responsible for the regulation of takeover activity in the United Kingdom,[6] further to the United Kingdom's obligations under the Takeover Directive. The Panel has proven itself to be a highly effective regulator even though it has hitherto been primarily an example of a self-regulatory body arising organically from the market. Its success has meant that implementation of the Takeover Directive has been conducted so as to retain the Panel in effectively the same form as before, albeit that the Panel has now been given statutory power to regulate takeovers by s.942 of the CA 2006. The power of the Panel to make rules is consequently now on a statutory footing.[7]

---

[2] SI 2006/1183.
[3] Takeover Directive, art.2.1(a).
[4] The Companies Act 2006 relates to broader matters than the offers for companies traded on a regulated market that are covered by the Takeover Directive. Part 27 of the CA 2006 is concerned with mergers and divisions of public companies; whereas Pt 28 of the CA 2006 is concerned with takeovers.
[5] This term is defined in Ch.13.
[6] Companies Act 2006 s.942.
[7] Companies Act 2006 s.943.

The rules referred to in the statute are the rules comprising the Code. The Panel's principal activity is the issue and the administration of the Code; although strictly speaking the Panel's remit stretches beyond the public offers in relation to takeovers described in the Takeover Directive. The Panel is permitted to act in relation to takeovers in implementation of the Directive as a result of para.7 of the Preamble to the Directive and art.4.1 of the Directive which specifically permit the supervisory body for takeover offers to be a private body. While it is a self-regulatory organisation, albeit one with statutory recognition, the Panel is required to take such steps as are necessary to co-operate with the FSA.

The Panel is empowered to give rulings on "the interpretation, application or effect of rules".[8] The Panel is also empowered to give directions to restrain actions in breach of the rules and to compel compliance with the rules.[9] The Panel also has the power to require the production of any documents or the provision of any information as it shall require, by written notice.[10] The Panel must keep confidential any matters relating to the private affairs of any individual or any information relating to a business.[11] The disclosure of any such information constitutes an offence.[12] If the Panel considers that there is a reasonable likelihood that a person will contravene one of the rules in the Code or that a rule has already been contravened, then it may apply to the court: the court may then make such order as it thinks fit to secure compliance with the requirements of those rules.[13] Contravention of the Code does not, however, constitute a breach of statutory duty in tort.[14] Before the enactment of the 2006 Act, the penalties for breach of the Code were limited to the censure of those who broke the Code and an expectation that corporate finance services would be withdrawn from the transgressor. The consensus view is that this regulation and penalisation through peer pressure was effective. The Panel itself may not be sued for damages for anything done in the performance of its duties.[15]

The functions of the Panel and the Executive

33–004 The City Code on Mergers and Takeovers which preceded the Takeover Code, created an Executive which considered takeover bids and which referred problems to the Panel. The same structure exists under the Takeover Code. In relation to the administration of the City Code on Mergers and Takeovers, in *R. v Panel on Takeovers and Mergers, Ex p. Guinness Plc* Watkins L.J. expressed the function of the executive as being as follows[16]:

"It is the executive which takes the lead in examining the circumstances of takeover bids and, if thought necessary, referring them to the Panel for consideration and adjudication according to the rules. Almost daily it is called upon to

---

[8] Companies Act 2006 s.945.
[9] Companies Act 2006 s.946.
[10] Companies Act 2006 s.947.
[11] Companies Act 2006 s.948.
[12] Companies Act 2006 s.949.
[13] Companies Act 2006 s.955.
[14] Companies Act 2006 s.956.
[15] Companies Act 2006 s.961.
[16] (1988) 4 B.C.C. 325, DC.

give advice and rulings, which mostly are accepted. . . . It acts as a sort of fire brigade to extinguish quickly the flames of unacceptable and unfair practice."[17]

If the Executive or either of the parties considers that the matter is serious enough it will be referred to the Panel for a full hearing. This is a quasi-judicial affair and at the end the Panel may give a definitive ruling imposing either disciplinary sanctions or a course of action which the parties must adhere to.

The Takeover Code provides that the role of the Executive is as follows:

"The day-to-day work of takeover supervision and regulation is carried out by the Executive. In carrying out these functions, the Executive operates independently of the Panel. This includes, either on its own initiative or at the instigation of third parties, the conduct of investigations, the monitoring of relevant dealings in connection with the Code and the giving of rulings on the interpretation, application or effect of the Code."

The Executive therefore has an important role to play in relation to the interpretation of the Code and in relation to communication with market participants. It is also the Executive which provides the first line of implementing the Code in individual cases. The Hearings Committee, comprised of five members, hears claimants who wish to contest any decision of the Executive.[18] Alternatively, the Executive may refer questions to the Hearings Committee, and it may institute disciplinary hearings in relation to any breach of the Code. A hearing need not be held if the Chairman of the Committee considers that any request for a hearing was frivolous or vexatious. Appeals from the Hearings Committee are then made to the Takeover Appeal Board.

Under the common law governing the predecessor to the Code, there was only an automatic right of appeal from a decision of the Panel if disciplinary action was taken[19] or the dispute related to the Panel's jurisdiction. In other cases there was only a right of appeal with the Panel's consent. Any appeal lay to the Appeals Committee with an independent chairman. That Committee would only interfere if it concluded that the Panel was wrong or, where the Panel's exercise of a discretion was being challenged, if either that power had been wrongly exercised or the Panel had misdirected itself.[20]

The Takeover Code

The purpose of the Takeover Code

The Takeover Code is the regulatory rulebook created and administered by the **33–005** Panel on Takeovers and Mergers.[21] The underlying purpose of the Code is expressed as being as follows:

---

[17] See, e.g. Panel statement on British Coal Pension Funds/Globe Investment Trust Plc [1991] J.B.L. 67.
[18] As provided for by Companies Act 2006 s.951.
[19] Including a ruling as to exempt principal trader or market maker status, below.
[20] Appeal statement on *BAT Industries Plc* [1990] J.B.L. 67.
[21] The version referred to here is that introduced on May 20, 2006. For an excellent discussion of this Code, see Macaulay, "The Regulation of Takeovers", in *Palmer's Company Law*, para.12.263 et seq.

"The Code is designed principally to ensure that shareholders are treated fairly and are not denied an opportunity to decide on the merits of a takeover and that shareholders of the same class are afforded equivalent treatment by an offeror. The Code also provides an orderly framework within which takeovers are conducted. In addition, it is designed to promote, in conjunction with other regulatory regimes, the integrity of the financial markets. The Code is not concerned with the financial or commercial advantages or disadvantages of a takeover. These are matters for the company and its shareholders. Nor is the Code concerned with those issues, such as competition policy, which are the responsibility of government and other bodies."

The Code has developed as a consensus position among those in the "market" as to the best means of treating takeovers.

The general principles underpinning the Code

33–006 The Code operates on the basis of six "general principles".[22] These six principles "are essentially statements of standards of commercial behaviour". Those principles are:

1. All holders of the securities of an offeree company of the same class must be afforded equivalent treatment; moreover, if a person acquires control of a company, the other holders of securities must be protected.

2. The holders of the securities of an offeree company must have sufficient time and information to enable them to reach a properly informed decision on the bid; where it advises the holders of securities, the board of the offeree company must give its views on the effects of implementation of the bid on employment, conditions of employment and the locations of the company's places of business.

3. The board of an offeree company must act in the interests of the company as a whole and must not deny the holders of securities the opportunity to decide on the merits of the bid.

4. False markets must not be created in the securities of the offeree company, of the offeror company or of any other company concerned by the bid in such a way that the rise or fall of the prices of the securities becomes artificial and the normal functioning of the markets is distorted.

5. An offeror must announce a bid only after ensuring that he can fulfil in full any cash consideration, if such is offered, and after taking all reasonable measures to secure the implementation of any other type of consideration.

6. An offeree company must not be hindered in the conduct of its affairs for longer than is reasonable by a bid for its securities.

---

[22] Set out in s.B1 of the Code.

These principles mirror those in art.3 of the Takeover Directive. Each of them is considered in turn.

Equal treatment of shareholders

The first general principle in the Code provides that: **33–007**

"1. All holders of the securities of an offeree company of the same class must be afforded equivalent treatment; moreover, if a person acquires control of a company, the other holders of securities must be protected."

Thus the requirement of shareholder equality is to be preserved, even though in takeover situations, different camps may develop among the shareholders some of whom are in favour and others against the mooted bid for the company. This principle has impacts in other contexts too. For example, a potential offeror who seeks to build a stake in the target company should not treat shareholders differently by paying different amounts for shares to different shareholders. Where stakebuilding takes effect over a long period of time it is likely that the market price of the shares will vary. The effect of the Code, however, is to require announcements to be made at appropriate junctures to make this process transparent and inter alia to ensure that all shareholders are put in the same position.

Sufficient time and information for shareholders to consider the bid

The second general principle underpinning the Code provides that: **33–008**

"2. The holders of the securities of an offeree company must have sufficient time and information to enable them to reach a properly informed decision on the bid . . ."

This principle is in tune with the general objective of securities regulation that investors must be provided with sufficient information to make an informed assessment of the securities, as in s.87A of the Financial Services and Markets Act 2000 in relation to the general duty of disclosure in prospectuses, as considered in Ch.13. The core of all securities regulation is the management of the flow of information to the investing public. The second general principle therefore requires that the securities holders (including the shareholders) of a company have sufficient time and information to make an informed decision on any offer that is made for the company.

Shareholder democracy

The third general principle provides as follows: **33–009**

"3. The board of an offeree company must act in the interests of the company as a whole and must not deny the holders of securities the opportunity to decide on the merits of the bid."

During a takeover bid, the board of the target company may have an opinion of its own as to the desirability of the bid. The board of directors may want the takeover to go ahead either because it considers that to be in the best interests of the company relating to the vision which the directors have for the company, or because the directors have some personal interest of their own in such a takeover (this is particularly true in relation to a management buy-out of a company where the directors are seeking to take the company over themselves). Alternatively, the directors may consider that the takeover would be undesirable because the prospective owners would harm the company's business prospects or because they would sell off the company by breaking up its business or because the directors consider that their personal positions within the company would be terminated or altered after the takeover. The third principle therefore requires that the directors must permit the holders of the securities in question (whether shares or other securities) to decide for themselves on the desirability or otherwise of the takeover bid.

The avoidance of false markets

33–010 The fourth general principle underpinning the Code provides that:

> "4. False markets must not be created in the securities of the offeree company, of the offeror company or of any other company concerned by the bid in such a way that the rise or fall of the prices of the securities becomes artificial and the normal functioning of the markets is distorted."

This principle clearly overlaps with the restrictions on market abuse (for example, insider dealing, as considered in Ch.11) which both restricts the abuse of inside information and seeks to prevent market manipulation by means of the publication or dissemination of false information with a view to generating a false market in those securities. In relation to takeover bids, there will clearly be an effect on the market value of securities as the possibility of a takeover waxes and wanes. There is some consideration of the regulation of market abuse and its overlap with takeover regulation below.

Ability to pay

33–011 The fifth principle provides as follows:

> "5. An offeror must announce a bid only after ensuring that he/she can fulfil in full any cash consideration, if such is offered, and after taking all reasonable measures to secure the implementation of any other type of consideration."

Therefore, a bid must only be made once the bidder is able to pay for the securities, in effect, depending on the terms of the offer. It would clearly be disruptive to the management and operation of a company if an offer were made to take it over without the bidder being able to make the acquisition. A bidder may otherwise make a speculative bid for a company and, if it is successful and accepted at a reasonable price, then seek the funding to make the acquisition. This would introduce unnecessary volatility to the stock market and be very disturbing to the management of public companies.

Avoiding disruption to a company's activities

The sixth principle provides as follows: **33–012**

> "6. An offeree company must not be hindered in the conduct of its affairs for longer than is reasonable by a bid for its securities."

One of the key commercial effects of being on the receiving end of a takeover bid is that the attention of senior management is diverted away from the detail of the business and devoted instead on the legal, accounting, public relations and other issues associated with beating back or negotiating (depending on its desirability) any takeover bid. Consequently, the longer that a bid or rumours of a bid continue, the longer the business will be under-developed. It is possible therefore that profits will be reduced during this period. Furthermore, the cost of employing professional advisors to deal with the takeover bid will also be a drain on the company's cash resources. A "hostile takeover" may therefore interfere with a company's profitability and morale for some considerable time. Consequently, the sixth principle creates a concept of "reasonableness" to govern the length of time for which a takeover bid may drag on. From the perspective of the Panel, the length of the bid and the effect it is having on the target company may lead the Panel to adjust its attitude to the bid and its decision to permit or deny its contin- uation within the terms of the Code.

Offences under the Companies Act 2006

It is an offence knowingly to publish an offer document in relation to a takeover   **33–013** bid which does not comply with the "offer document rules" created further to Pt 28 of the CA 2006 and without having taken reasonable steps to ensure compli- ance with those rules.[23] Similarly, knowing failure to comply with the "response document rules" created further to Pt 28 without taking reasonable steps to ensure compliance, is an offence.[24]

Civil procedure and the Code

Compensation under the Code

The Panel has the power to create rules by reference to which payment of   **33–014** compensation may be ordered. Compensation may be ordered where the Panel considers it to be "just and reasonable" to require such payment because there has been a breach of some rule in the Code.[25] The Code itself provides that:

---

[23] Companies Act 2006 s.953(2) and (3).
[24] Companies Act 2006 s.953(4).
[25] Companies Act 2006 s.954.

"Where a person has breached the requirements of any of Rules 6, 9, 11, 14, 15, 16 or 35.3 of the Code, the Panel may make a ruling requiring the person concerned to pay, within such period as is specified, to the holders, or former holders, of securities of the offeree company such amount as it thinks just and reasonable so as to ensure that such holders receive what they would have been entitled to receive if the relevant Rule had been complied with."

Those rules are considered below. In essence, whenever there is a breach of a duty in one of those rules relating to the procedure for takeovers, then compensation may be payable provided that the Panel considers it "just and reasonable" to order such a payment. The measure of compensation is such as to put the claimant in the position it would have been in if the defendant had complied with its obligations under the rules.

Enforcement orders and limitation on tactical litigation

33–015 The Panel may make an application to the court to seek an order if the Panel considers that some person is reasonably likely to contravene an obligation placed on it by a rule in the Code.[26] There is no right to seek an injunction beyond this right in the Panel to petition the court.[27] Moreover, there is no right to claim for breach of statutory duty in relation to the breach of a rule in the Code.[28]

These provisions are designed to continue the efficacy of the provisions and to prevent tactical litigation. The limits of an application for judicial review effectively prevented tactical litigation designed to hamper or frustrate a bid or a defence to a bid. This was seen as a great advantage of the previous regulatory system and the Government indicated that it wished to preserve that advantage.[29] It was indicated that the new takeovers legislation which was to implement the Directive would neither undermine nor be inconsistent with the *Datafin* principles, considered below.[30] With regard to other types of litigation, such as civil litigation between parties to a bid on the interpretation of the Code, which became possible when the Code became a legal document for the first time under Pt 28 of the CA 2006, the Government proposed to enact three specific measures. The first is that there is no action against any person for breach of statutory duty as a result of the Code's new status, as set out above. The second, to promote certainty, provides that transactions will not be set aside simply because of a breach of the Code or failure to comply with a Panel ruling. The third was that parties to Panel hearings will not be able to challenge their rulings apart from before the Panel's own Appeal Tribunal or under the limited current judicial review process, as set out above.

---

[26] Companies Act 2006 s.955.
[27] Companies Act 2006 s.955.
[28] Companies Act 2006, s.956.
[29] Consultative Document on Implementing the 13th Directive, January 20, 2005. The Directive itself expressly allows Member States to preserve these limitations in art.4.6.
[30] para.2.38 of the Consultative Document.

The mechanics of offers under the Code

The goals of the Code

The Code aims to provide the market, including shareholders in a company which **33–016** is the subject of a takeover bid (a "target company"), with information about the strategy of a person (a "bidder") who is considering making a bid to take over a target company. Because takeover or merger speculation can cause such volatility in the price of shares, particularly if the takeover were able to take place in secret, that insider dealing and other abuse would be easy to perpetrate, and the integrity of the markets would be called into question.

The way in which the initial offer is made and then publicised

The initial offer is to be made to the board of the offeree company or to its advi- **33–017** sors. The provisions relating to the making of an offer in the first place are contained in Rule 2. The board must satisfy itself whether or not the offeror can implement the offer in full. In tandem with the requirement that inside information be treated appropriately, there must be "absolute secrecy" before an announcement of an offer. Transmission of this information to other people can only be made if it is "necessary". The primary responsibility for making an announcement rests with the offeree once it has been notified of the offer. Under r.9 there is a mandatory obligation to make an announcement of the takeover offer. The offeree may impose a timetable on the offeror as to the firming up of its offer. Further to r.2.5, the offeror should only announce a firm intention to make an offer once it has given the matter the most careful and responsible consideration: then this either leads to a "firm announcement" trailing an offer, or a statement of an intention not to make an offer. Announcements are to be made in accordance with the procedures and formalities set out in r.2.5, detailing the terms of the offer, the securities in question, and so forth. This rule necessarily involves the commencement of a due diligence process by the offeror.

The board of the offeree company is required to obtain competent independent advice on any offer under r.3. The substance of such advice must be made known to the shareholders of the offeree company. The parties must be aware of conflicts of interest between advisors' duties to the company and its own position, particularly where there are cross-shareholdings involved or where the advisor stands to earn higher fees if the bid is a success.

Prevention of abuse of "price sensitive" information

In relation to the control of insider dealing relating to price sensitive inside infor- **33–018** mation, r.4.1 provides that "no dealings of any kind in securities of the offeree company by any person . . . who is privy to confidential price-sensitive information concerning an offer or contemplated offer may take place" between the time when an approach is contemplated and an announcement is eventually made.[31]

---

[31] The Code, r.4.1.

Clearly, this is because an announcement of a takeover bid will usually lead to a sharp increase in the value of shares and if someone could acquire shares once they knew that a takeover bid was in the offing then that would constitute insider dealing, as discussed in Ch.24. This provision links in with the general regulation of inside information across securities regulation in the FSA Listing Rules "Model Code" on market abuse and the FSA regulation of market abuse more generally. The prohibition on dealings encompasses making recommendations to anyone about dealings in relevant securities and dealing in the securities of the offeror. Rule 4.2 then prohibits dealings in securities by the offeror and "concert parties" in restricted periods. Rule 4.6 prohibits the unwinding of a borrowing or lending transaction in relation to relevant securities by the offeror, the offeree company, their associates, their connected advisors, their pension funds and so forth, without the consent of the Panel.

Acquiring control of the target company by crossing specified thresholds: Rule 5

33–019 A key part of the Code's regulation of takeovers is the identification of threshold levels of ownership which, when crossed, require the bidder for a company to act in particular ways. Rather than limiting itself to direct ownership of shares in a company, the Code refers to bidders having "control" of a given proportion of the voting rights derived from the company's shares either directly or indirectly. The Code's definitions provisions define "control" of a company as constituting a 30 per cent holding of voting rights in that company. Therefore, a holding of 30 per cent of the total voting rights in the target company is a significant threshold in the Code. So, r.5.1 prevents acquisitions of shares being made which would carry the purchaser across the 30 per cent threshold or across the 50 per cent threshold.

The threshold is crossed not on completion of a sale of shares but rather is crossed when the bidder acquires interests in shares which would cross that threshold. If this were not the case, the bidder could line up call options[32] which would be sufficient to call in 50 per cent of the shares in the target company but only actually own 2 per cent of the company's shares: thus avoiding the Code. Thus, derivatives such as options to acquire shares cannot be used as a means of eluding the restrictions in the Code by building *de facto* control of voting shares even if those options are not intended to be exercised until a later date. Exceptions to this restriction are set out in r.5.2, including the acquisition of shares from a single shareholder or where a firm intention to make an offer is to be announced immediately thereafter. This places a brake on "stakebuilding" as a takeover strategy without the making of an offer in accordance with the Code. "Stakebuilding" is a process by which a bidder acquires the right to buy incrementally larger parcels of shares in the target company slowly over time but without actually having to buy them in. The r.5 restrictions will also apply to irrevocable offers, as will the requirements of r.9, considered next.

---

[32] That means, rights to acquire shares in the target company which the holder of the option may or may not exercise as he chooses.

The requirement for a "mandatory offer": Rule 9

To prevent too much delay, market unrest, and concomitant pressure being put on **33–020** the target company, its shareholders and its business, the Code provides that an offer for the target company must be made in certain circumstances. That means that a coy rumour that an offer may or not be made cannot be maintained for too long without an offer actually being made eventually. A mandatory offer is required under r.9 once a person acquires, alone or in concert with others, 30 per cent of the voting rights in the offeree company.[33] That mandatory offer must be made to the holders of any class of equity share capital.[34] The offer must be made for a cash consideration or for an appropriate cash alternative. Where directors of the offeree or their close relatives or related trusts sell their shares to someone who will thus acquire 30 per cent of the voting rights, then those people must make compliance with r.9 a condition of the sale.[35] No one may be appointed to the board of the offeree company if that person is a nominee of the offeror, unless the Panel has consented to that action.[36] Rule 10 provides that the offer may be declared to be unconditional as to acceptances from the time when the offeror holds more than 50 per cent of the voting rights in the offeree company. Stakebuilding of this sort, by means of progressive acquisition of shares, does run the risk that the offeror will be left with unwanted shares if the bid is unsuccessful.

"Squeeze outs" for the unwilling sellers

The question then arises as to what happens in relation to shareholders who have **33–021** not agreed to sell their shares in response to a takeover offer. Once a person making a takeover offer has contracted, conditionally or unconditionally, to acquire not less than 90 per cent of the shares to which the offer relates, then that person may give notice to the holder of any of the other shares that she desires to acquire those shares.[37] This is referred to as a "squeeze-out". The same principle applies to offers made in relation to any particular class of shares in a company.[38] The notice must be prepared in the prescribed form.[39] The effect of the giving of a notice is that the offeror is entitled and bound to buy any of the shares to which the offer relates.[40] If a takeover offer has been made,[41] then the holder of any non-voting shares or of any shares of a particular class to which the offer relates (as is

---

[33] Under r.6.1 of the Code, when an offeror has acquired shares in an offeree company within three months of the beginning of an offer period, or after the commencement of the offer period but before a r.2.5 announcement, then offers to the existing shareholders must be on the same or better terms than those original acquisitions. When an offer is made during the offer period, then r.6.2 provides that the offeror must make its offer at the highest price which it has made for the acquisition of shares in the market before that time.

[34] The Code, r.9.1 [accessed June 14, 2010].

[35] The Code, r.9.6 [accessed June 14, 2010].

[36] The Code, r.9.7 [accessed June 14, 2010].

[37] Companies Act 2006 s.979(2).

[38] Companies Act 2006 s.979(4).

[39] Companies Act 2006 s.980.

[40] Companies Act 2006 s.981(2).

[41] As defined in Companies Act 2006 s.974.

relevant) may require the offeror to buy their shares, provided that (as before) the offeror had contracted to acquire 90 per cent of the relevant shares and that the holder of these shares is part of the outstanding minority holding.[42]

The common law governing the squeeze out provisions

33–022 Under the former statutory regime, the court decided that it would only make such an order if it was satisfied that the scheme was unfair to the general body of shareholders in the transferor company. There was normally a heavy burden of proof on the dissentients[43]—since the scheme has been approved by nine-tenths of the shareholders, prima facie it must be taken to be a fair one.[44] The test was one of fairness to the body of shareholders as a whole and not to individual shareholders, and it was not enough merely to prove that the scheme was open to criticism or capable of improvements.[45] It was not enough that the materials put before the shareholders were inadequate to enable them to form a just conclusion as to the acceptance or refusal of the offer.[46] Where there was a Stock Exchange quotation for the shares, prima facie that could be taken as the value of the shares.[47] The element of control of the transferor company, which would accrue to the transferee company from the acquisition of all the shares in the transferor company, was not taken into account in determining the value of the shares of a minority shareholder. It was also held, however, that dissentient shareholders, who were not satisfied with the price offered, could not obtain an order for discovery so as to enable them to carry out an investigation into the value of the shares, unless there were special circumstances[48] but a more recent decision has established that discovery will apply unless the court is satisfied that it is unnecessary.[49]

However, if the dissentient shareholders showed that in substance the transferee company was the same as the majority holding in the transferor company the onus was on the majority to satisfy the court that the scheme was one which the minority ought reasonably to be compelled to fall in with. In *Bugle Press Ltd, Re*[50] A and B were the two shareholders, each holding 50 shares, in the transferee company which offered to purchase the shares in the transferor company in which there were three shareholders, A and B, who each held 4,500 shares and who accepted the offer, and C, who held 1,000 shares and who dissented. It was held that C, by showing that the transferee company was for practical purposes equivalent to the holders of nine-tenths of the shares in the transferor company who accepted the offer, had prima facie shown that the case was one in which the

---

[42] Companies Act 2006 s.983.

[43] *Sussex Brick Co Ltd, Re* [1961] Ch. 289: *Nidditch v The Calico Printers' Association Ltd*, 1961 S.L.T. 282.

[44] The onus is the other way round per Templeman J. in *Hellenic & General Trust Ltd, Re* [1976] 1 W.L.R. 123, at 130, 131.

[45] *Grierson, Oldham & Adams Ltd, Re* [1968] Ch. 17.

[46] *Evertite Locknuts Ltd, Re* [1945] Ch. 220.

[47] See *Press Caps Ltd, Re* [1949] Ch. 434, CA.

[48] *Press Caps Ltd, Re* [1948] 2 All E.R. 638.

[49] *Lifecare International Plc, Re* [1990] B.C.L.C. 222.

[50] [1961] Ch. 270, CA.

circumstances were special and the court ought to "order otherwise", and the majority had not shown that there was some good reason in the interests of the company (for example, if the minority shareholder was acting in a manner highly damaging to the interests of the company) for allowing the section to be invoked for the purposes of enabling the majority to expropriate the minority. In *Britoil Plc, Re*[51] the Court of Appeal ruled that an application will not be vexatious (and so will not incur a penalty in costs) if there is evidence justifying the court's looking at the offer to make sure it is fair.

The general attitude of the courts on the former section has been followed in **33–023** two decisions. In *Lifecare International Plc, Re*,[52] the dissentients were said to have a heavy burden of proof to discharge, especially where their directors took independent advice and recommended acceptance of the bid. In *Chez Nico (Restaurants) Ltd, Re*,[53] on the other hand, where the offeror was an insider, as in the Bugle Press case, it was held that the burden of proof would be reversed, so that the offeror would need to show that the offer was fair. Since there had been breaches of the code in that case, that had not been discharged.

There were two decisions on the new right to apply for the terms of the acquisition to be varied under the old s.430C of the Companies Act 1985, the forerunner to s.986 of the CA 2006. In *Greythorn Plc, Re*,[54] the offeror was seeking to withdraw its compulsory offer altogether. The claimant, having originally sought an order to prevent the acquisition under s.430C(1)(a), now sought to hold the offeror to the acquisition but on different terms from the offer under s.430C(1)(b). The judge considered, but did not decide, that it was perfectly possible for the court to make such an order against the offeror even though the claimant had originally specified a different remedy and the offeror no longer wished to acquire the shares at all. If the offeror, however, still wishes to proceed with the acquisition, there is no doubt that the court may vary the terms of the acquisition. Such an order was made in *Fiske Nominees Ltd v Dwyka Diamonds Ltd*,[55] where the claimant successfully argued that not enough information had been given to them (as distinct minority shareholders) as to the valuation of the offer[56] so that they were unable to make an informed decision. Their shares would be valued by an independent expert and then acquired by the offeror.

FSA REGULATION OF MARKET ABUSE AS IT RELATES TO TAKEOVERS

The FSA regulates "market abuse" further to the EC Market Abuse Directive.[57] **33–024** Market abuse covers insider dealing and market manipulation, in the manner implemented into UK law by the Financial Services and Markets Act 2000 in ss.118 et seq. There are few market events which cause as rapid movements in the

---

[51] [1990] B.C.C. 70, CA.
[52] [1990] B.C.L.C. 222.
[53] [1992] B.C.L.C. 192.
[54] [2002] B.C.C. 559.
[55] [2002] B.C.C. 707.
[56] Although the City Code was not in issue, its Rules were cited as good practice as to what the acquisition documents should contain.
[57] Directive 2003/6/EC on market abuse [2003] OJ L96/16.

price of securities than rumours that a takeover will or will not take place. Consequently, it is in relation to takeover activity that market abuse regulation may be most significant. So, this section aims to connect FSA regulation of market abuse with the regulation of takeover activity because it is in this context that market abuse is particularly possible.

The EC Market Abuse Directive requires that Member States prohibit insiders from misusing inside information, whether directly or indirectly, to deal in financial instruments so as to earn personal profits or for other personal ends.[58] The policy underpinning this requirement is a perception that insider dealing and market abuse "prevent full and proper market transparency, which is a prerequisite for trading for all economic actors in integrated financial markets".[59] The categories of "insider" for this purpose are members of the issuing company's administrative, management or supervisory bodies; or shareholders or people otherwise holding capital in the issuer; or people having access to the information through the exercise of an employment, profession or other duties; or by virtue of criminal activities.[60] The reference in the Market Abuse Directive to "inside information" is a reference to

"information of a precise nature which has not been made public, relating, directly or indirectly, to one or more issuers of financial instruments or to one or more financial instruments and which, if it were made public, would be likely to have a significant effect on the prices of those financial instruments or on the price of related derivative financial instruments [such as options to buy or sell shares]".[61]

There are other matters which member states are required to prohibit: the disclosure of inside information to another person[62]; recommending that a person deal in securities on the basis of the inside information[63]; inducing a person to deal in securities on the basis of the inside information[64]; and making sure that all of the foregoing prohibitions apply to any person in possession of the inside information who should have been aware that it was inside information.[65]

33–025   The FSA market abuse code is known as the Code on Market Conduct ("MAR 1") and is located in ch.1 of the FSA Market Abuse Rulebook.[66] Section 118 FSMA 2000 sets out the general categories of behaviour which constitute market abuse, and then MAR 1 provides detail as to the FSA's attitude to those various categories. MAR 1 provides that "dealing on the basis of inside information

---

[58] The coverage of financial instruments in the Directive is to units in collective investment schemes, money-market instruments, forward rate agreements, futures, swaps, cash-settled and physically-settled options, and any other instruments admitted to trading on a regulated market: MAD, art.1(3).

[59] MAD recital (15).

[60] MAD art.2(1). These definitions include any human being who takes part in a decision taken by a corporate entity which constitutes that entity one of the categories of insider.

[61] MAD art.1(1).

[62] MAD art.3(1).

[63] MAD art.3(2).

[64] MAD art.3(2).

[65] MAD art.4.

[66] Published under the Financial Services Authority, *Market Conduct Sourcebook Instrument 2001* (MAR 1) further to Financial Services and Markets Act 2000, s.119.

which is not trading information" constitutes market abuse.[67] Under this head, three examples of market abuse are given in MAR 1 which relate to takeover activity. First, "front-running" whereby a person deals in securities in advance of the publication of the information by taking advantage of the "anticipated impact" of the order on the market price.[68] Secondly, in relation to takeovers, there is market abuse when an offeror or potential offeror takes a position which provides "a merely economic exposure to movements in the price of the target company's shares",[69] which occurs when an insider discloses information to another person. Disclosure will not constitute market abuse, however, if the disclosure is part of a body's proper functions or if it is made to a proper authority such as the Takeover Panel.[70]

The third form of market abuse is significant for present purposes. In relation to takeovers, if a person acting for the offeror or a potential offeror deals on her own account in relation to the target company's shares then that will constitute market abuse.[71] This encompasses any situation in which a person fails to observe proper market conduct when dealing with price sensitive information which is not in the public domain. An example would be a director of a target company in a takeover offer telling a friend at lunch that the company is subject to such an offer, and that friend then placing a bet at fixed odds with a bookmaker that the company will be subject to a bid.[72] Similarly, if the same process occurred, in relation to a bet placed by a friend after lunch, but in relation to the termination (the "non-contractual icing") of takeover negotiations in private then that would also constitute market abuse.[73]

The fourth category relates to market manipulation, and the fifth to transmitting misleading information through the media. Both of these forms of activity could be performed while leaking information or misinformation relating to possible takeover bids. Thus the fourth general principle under the Code precludes making false markets, for example, by market manipulation or misleading trails of information. The sixth category relates to disseminating information so as to give a false or misleading impression. In relation to Rule 5.1 of the Code, the requirement to give proper consideration to the making of an offer and the obligations to make announcements at the identified point may chime in with this requirement not to create a false impression as to whether or not a bid is to be made or not made. The seventh form of behaviour constituting market abuse relates to activities which are likely to create a false impression in the minds of others. The examples given in MAR 1 are typically related to movements of physical commodities so as to create the impression that the person moving them has greater stocks than is actually the case. Stakebuilding strategies, possibly involving acquisitions or disposals of shares or positioning of connected investors, so as to make it appear that stakebuilding has begun or is about to begin

[67] MAR 1.3.2(1)E.
[68] MAR 1.3.2(2)E.
[69] MAR 1.3.2(3)E.
[70] MAR 1.4.3C.
[71] MAR 1.3.2(4)E.
[72] MAR 1.5.10(1)E.
[73] MAR 1.5.10(2)E.

may also constitute such an activity which "is likely to give a regular user of the market a false or misleading impression" as to the value or market for the shares in question.[74]

THE LISTING RULES AND ACQUISITIONS

The Listing Rules and acquisitions in relation to listed companies

The applicability of the Listing Rules

33–026 The principal regulations dealing with transactions which may alter the effective size of a shareholder's holding in a listed company are contained in the Listing Rules, as discussed in Ch.15 of this book. Those regulations concern significant acquisitions or disposals by listed companies, and therefore relate closely to takeovers and to mergers and so forth. The general principles underpinning the Listing Rules still govern these transactions. Significantly, therefore, listed companies have an obligation under the Disclosure and Transparency Rules to disclose any major new developments if that information is not already in the public domain.[75] A takeover bid would be a clear example of that sort of information. The rules governing acquisitions and disposals therefore add to the ordinary provisions of the Listing Rules, and relate primarily to the level of disclosure which is required at which stage in a transaction depending on the significance of the acquisition or disposal transaction for a company and of the nature and size of the listed company in question.

The methodology for the classification of transactions: the class tests

33–027 Chapter 10 of the Listing Rules contains detailed provision for the classification of transactions according to their significance in the context of any given company. In effect the classification provisions are concerned to identify the significance of a transaction by measuring its impact variously on the gross assets, profits, and gross capital position of the company, and also the size of the consideration for the transaction relative to the company's market value. These four tests give an amount expressed as a percentage which is then used to identify the class of transaction involved, and hence the regulatory treatment which is appropriate to it. The rationale behind these percentage ratios is that they measure the significance of the transaction for a company of the size of the company in question: so, a transaction worth £x will be small transaction in relation to a company with assets of £200y, but may be significant in relation to a company with assets of only £y. Expressing these four tests as ratios then takes into account the nature of the individual company and the significance of the deal for that company by reference to four different measurement indicators in the four class tests.

---

[74] Financial Services and Markets Act 2000 s.118(8).
[75] Disclosure and Transparency Rules, 2.2.1R.

The class tests impose duties of disclosure of information to a recognised information service ("RIS") if the transaction involves an acquisition. The more important the transaction as a proportion of the total capital base of the target company, the more information that is required to be disclosed. With large "Class 1 transactions", for example, the company is required to notify the RIS once terms are agreed[76]; all of the stipulated information must be communicated to the RIS including a statement as to the anticipated effect of the transaction on the listed company[77]; the FSA must approve an explanatory circular which the company must then circulate to shareholders[78]; the company must obtain the agreement of the shareholders by ordinary resolution in general meeting[79]; and the agreement must be conditional on shareholder approval being obtained.[80]

It is only if a company is making a disposal because it is in severe financial difficulty that it may seek approval from the FSA to waive the requirement to prepare a circular and to obtain shareholder approval.[81] Such a company must convince the FSA that it could not have entered into negotiations earlier so that shareholder approval could have been sought[82] and the company's sponsor must be able to confirm that the company is in severe financial difficulties.[83]

Related party transactions

Transactions with "related parties" are subject to a different code. The aim of **33–028** these rules is to prevent a person with a close connection to a listed company from taking advantage of that relationship with the company. The categories of "related party" are: people who have been significant shareholders in the company in the previous 12 months; a director or shadow director of the company in the previous 12 months; a 50/50 partner in a joint venture; a person who exercises "significant influence"; or an associate of anyone in any of these categories.[84] A transaction is caught if it is one which is not part of the listed company's ordinary business, or if it conducted so as to provide financing to another undertaking in which that related party has an investment, or if it benefits a related party.[85] In such a situation, the listed company must notify a RIS as soon as possible after the terms of the transaction are agreed,[86] together with all of the information required in the regulations.[87]

---

[76] Listing Rules, 10.5.1(1)R and 10.4.1(1)R.
[77] Listing Rules, 10.4.1(2)R.
[78] Listing Rules, 10.5.1(2)R.
[79] Listing Rules, 10.5.1(2)R.
[80] Listing Rules, 10.5.1(3)R.
[81] Listing Rules, 10.8.1R.
[82] Listing Rules, 10.8.2R.
[83] Listing Rules, 10.8.3R.
[84] Listing Rules, 11.1.4R.
[85] Listing Rules, 11.1.5R.
[86] Listing Rules, 10.4.1(1)R.
[87] Listing Rules, 10.4.1(2)R.

THE GENERAL LAW AS IT APPLIES TO TAKEOVERS

Common law provisions relating to takeovers

33–029 The Takeover Code, as considered above, applies to securities traded on regulated markets. Therefore, it relates to public companies. Before the implementation of a code on takeover rules and outside the scope of the Code there have been various common law and equitable rules which also play a part in the legal regulation of takeovers. In relation to takeovers which fall within the scope of the Code, there is also an important contractual element to the offer and acceptance process by reference to which the bidding company and the target company will effect contractual relations with the target company and its shareholders. It should be recalled that the bidder will be acquiring shares from the shareholders and therefore there will be a contract of sale between those parties, as well as any further contractual agreement between other people involved in the transaction as to the rights of the target company and its directors and employees after the takeover. The directors of both the bidding company and target companies will continue to owe fiduciary duties to their companies.[88] The impact of these duties in a takeover situation has arisen where the target directors have entered into an agreement with a bidding company whereby they agree to recommend the bid to their shareholders but subsequently decide that a better offer has been made by another offeror and they recommend that bid instead. Therefore, the general law will be of great importance to all takeovers outwith the Code considered thus far. It is this law which is considered in this section.

The obligations of directors

33–030 The duties of directors in relation to a takeover may be complex. The directors owe their duties to the company further to s.170 of the Companies Act 2006.[89] The most significant question may be whether or not the directors were genuinely pursuing the company's best interests. It was held in *Fulham Football Club Ltd v Cabra Estates Plc*[90] by the Court of Appeal that the test should be whether at the time of the agreement the directors were acting bona fide for the benefit of the company. If they were, then any agreement would be binding on them, even if they latterly considered that to implement it would be contrary to the company's interests.

While the ordinary law of contract applies to takeovers, there have been numerous occasions where parties have resorted to the law of tort. Thus in *Lonrho Plc v Fayed*[91] claims were made involving the torts of conspiracy and wrongful interference with trade, alleging that false information was given by one potential offeror to the Secretary of State causing him not to refer that offer to the Monopolies and Mergers Commission which prejudiced the chances of a rival offeror. Similarly, in *Lonrho Plc v Tebbit*[92] the Secretary of State was held to owe a potential duty of care to that second offeror in deciding whether or not to release

---

[88] See Ch.15, above.
[89] cf. *Dawson International Plc v Coats Patons Plc*, 1988 S.L.T. 854, OH; (1989) 5 B.C.C. 405.
[90] [1992] B.C.L.C. 863.
[91] [1991] B.C.L.C. 779, HL.
[92] [1993] B.C.L.C. 96.

them from a monopolies' restriction. In *Partco Group Ltd v Wragg*,[93] it was held that the mere supply of information by the directors of a target company as required by the City Code (the forerunner to the Takeover Code) did not necessarily make them liable to an action for negligent misstatement. There had to be some assumption of personal responsibility further to the *Hedley Byrne* principle (discussed in Ch.14).

Challenging decisions of the Takeover Panel

In 1987 a Canadian-based company, Datafin, became the first party to challenge a **33–031** Panel decision in the courts by way of an application for judicial review. In the Court of Appeal it was established that the Panel was subject to the process of judicial review.[94] Lord Donaldson M.R., however, stressed that an application for judicial review should not be used as a ploy to hinder a bid and that in general the Panel's decisions would remain binding until otherwise directed. He considered that a challenge could be made against the Panel acting as legislator if it made a rule contrary to its own terms of reference; as interpreter of the Code; and as a disciplinary body, but in that case the internal appeals procedure should be used first.

The dispute in *Datafin* was as to the Panel's interpretation of a particular rule. The Court of Appeal rejected the application on the basis that a challenge would have to show that the Panel's view was so far removed from the natural and ordinary meaning of the words that no ordinary user of the market could reasonably be misled. In the case of an exercise of the Panel's discretion the Court would only interfere in a totally inequitable case.

A second challenge to the Panel by way of judicial review was mounted by Guinness Plc on the basis of a breach of natural justice in the Panel's proceedings. This too failed, the Court finding that although the Panel had been inconsiderate and harsh there was no procedural impropriety and no breach of the rules of natural justice.[95] The Court of Appeal accepted again, however, that judicial review could apply and Lord Donaldson M.R. suggested the test as being whether something had gone wrong of a nature and degree which required the intervention of the court.

The third challenge mounted against the Panel by way of judicial review **33–032** concerned a Panel executive's ruling that there had been a breach of the Code and a proposed hearing of the Panel to investigate this. This was challenged by the Fayed brothers on two grounds. First, that the ruling would be prejudicial to civil litigation then in progress relating to the same matter, and second that the hearing would rely on the report of DTI inspectors which was hearsay evidence. This challenge was rejected by the Court of Appeal.[96] There was no general risk of prejudice to the civil litigation and the judge in that trial would not be unduly influenced by any decision of the Panel. Further, the Panel would be aware that the evidence before them was hearsay and take that factor into account.

---

[93] [2004] BCC 782, CA. No such restriction would apply to an action for deceit.
[94] *R. v Panel on Takeovers and Mergers, Ex p. Datafin* [1987] Q.B. 815, CA.
[95] *R. v Panel on Takeovers and Mergers, Ex p. Guinness Plc* [1990] Q.B. 147, CA.
[96] *R. v Panel on Takeovers and Mergers, Ex p. Fayed* [1992] B.C.L.C. 938.

That decision also raises the issue as to how the Code is viewed in legal proceedings in which it is raised. In *Dunford & Elliott Ltd v Johnson & Firth Brown Ltd*[97] one party to a bid sought an injunction to prevent the abuse of alleged confidential information in a takeover situation. Both Lord Denning M.R. and Roskill L.J. quoted the Code and used it as a guide to good commercial practice in an area where the court had a discretion. Again in *St. Piran Ltd, Re*[98] the Court said that when considering whether to wind up a company on the just and equitable ground the fact that the directors of a public company chose to flout the City Code or to ignore, without good reason, the consequent directions of the City Panel so that the minority shareholders were hurt by a withdrawal of the company's Stock Exchange quotation,[99] would be strong evidence in favour of granting the petition. Conversely in *Astec (BSR) Plc, Re*,[100] it was held that the provisions of the Code could not give rise to any legitimate expectations for the shareholders for the purposes of a petition for unfairly prejudicial conduct. It did not form part of the company's constitution.

In *R. v Spens*[101] the question arose in a criminal trial as to whether the Code was a document which should be left to the jury to consider or a form of quasi-legislation which was a matter for the judge to interpret for the benefit of the jury. The Court of Appeal had no doubt:

"As to the present case, our view is that the code sufficiently resembles legis-lation as to be likewise regarded as demanding construction of its provisions by a judge. Moreover, the code is a form of consensual agreement between the affected parties with penal consequences."

The court has held that statements made during the course of a bid did not amount to a binding legal agreement because they were made in the context of the oper-ation of the Code to that bid.[102] On the other hand where a shareholder agreed to accept an offer unless a higher offer was announced by midnight on a certain date, the provisions of the Code were used to determine whether such an announce-ment had been so made,[103] and in considering the concepts of "control" and "acting in concert" in a contract.[104] In earlier times, however, the Court awarded injunctions preventing the Panel from issuing statements,[105] and the Panel had, on one occasion, a battle of words with the Department of Trade and Industry following an inspectors' report.[106]

[97] [1977] 1 Lloyd's Rep. 505, CA.
[98] [1981] 3 All E.R. 270.
[99] This effectively prevents the shares being sold.
[100] [1998] 2 B.C.L.C. 556.
[101] [1991] B.C.C. 140.
[102] *Dawson International Plc v Coats Patons Plc*, 1989 S.L.T. 655; [1991] B.C.C. 276.
[103] *Hasbro U.K. Ltd v Harris* [1994] B.C.C. 839.
[104] *Philip Morris Products Inc v Rothmans International Enterprises Ltd* [2002] B.C.C. 265.
[105] Panel statement on *Sandstar Ltd v Graff Diamonds Ltd* [1979] J.B.L. 274.
[106] Panel statement of May 14, 1979 [1979] J.B.L. 364.

Chapter 34

CROSS-BORDER MERGERS, MIGRATION AND THE EUROPEAN COMPANY

INTRODUCTION

This chapter considers some important aspects of the European dimension of **34–001** company law. As has been discussed already in this book in various places, both company law and securities law in the United Kingdom are informed by and frequently based on EU law. The drive towards a single market in the European Union requires that there is greater harmonisation between the laws of the EU so that, for example, offers of companies' securities can take place simultaneously across the European Union, and so that companies from different Member States can effect mergers and transact in ways which would be entirely normal within a single Member State. The first issue which is considered in this chapter is precisely that: the problem of effecting mergers across borders in the European Union. Secondly, we consider the problem of undertakings moving across borders. Finally we consider the latest development in the European company project whereby the European Union has sought to develop a form of company which can be used across the EU instead of undertakings having to rely on the company law of one Member State or another when incorporating. This could happen in two ways: either undertakings which are already in existence under the laws of various Member States could merge with one another to form European undertakings or a new form of undertaking entirely could be developed. In essence, the movement towards the single market requires that the obstacles of needing to comply with the very different company laws of the 27 Member States are removed either by creating a new form of entity which can have effect across the EU or by harmonising those national laws. The harmonisation project hits difficulties, however, every time it attempts to find a compromise between the cherished principles of the various jurisdictions' corporate codes because no agreement can be reached on a single model which should replace all states' existing laws. Similarly, in seeking to develop a new form of European company model there is disagreement as to which features of existing models from the Member States should be used in it and which features should be discarded. Much of the discussion to follow traces the development of EU policy in these areas in seeking to find compromise and outlines the EU legislation which has been created thus far.

CROSS-BORDER MERGERS

Problems with migration and cross-border mergers

34–002   The movement towards a single market requires that undertakings in different parts of the European Union should be able to merge together just as two companies in a single jurisdiction could merge together. Each jurisdiction in its company law will have a means of legislating for mergers and dealing with the complications of two companies becoming one, or of one company being assimilated into another: the approach in the United Kingdom was considered in Ch.32. At the EU level, however, the problems become more complicated because companies incorporated in two jurisdictions will have at least the laws of those two Member States to take into account when seeking to merge, as well as any other systems of law where the company may have operations, and those two systems of law may have contradictory principles as to the domicile of the companies, the procedure for merger, and so on. Let us begin with the problem of domicile as an illustration.

Companies, like individuals, must have a domicile. A domicile is a country whose laws govern a company's existence and internal affairs. The company law of the United Kingdom regards a company's domicile as being the country in which the company has its registered office, irrespective of where its head office or major activities are located. Thus, the registered office may be in one convenient location for regulatory or other purposes, while the company's real business is conducted elsewhere.[1] It follows, however, that nothing in our company law prevents a company from moving its operations and control to another country— it will still be a UK company so far as UK law is concerned. The complication in such a case is that many other countries, including most Member States of the European Community, apply a different test to determine a company's domicile. Those jurisdictions apply the *siège réel* (real seat) theory: that is, a company is deemed to be domiciled wherever its central management is located because that is considered to be, de facto, the place where the company's directing mind and will is located. Thus a company incorporated in London but whose head office is in Paris would be regarded as a UK company in the United Kingdom and as a French company in France, which since it would not be registered in France (in this example) presents problems as to whether it even has legal personality under French law. This clash of legal systems has been recognised by the EU from its earliest days, but a convention for the mutual recognition of each other's companies was never ratified, even by the original six Member States, and the position is still unresolved. The issue has, however, since come before the European Court of Justice on a few occasions in connection with the freedom of establishment.

The differences between UK company law jurisprudence and the jurisprudence of other jurisdictions in the EU has been illustrated by the case law. So, in *Centros*

---

[1] It is common, for example, for companies to have their corporate headquarters in expensive parts of London while their factories or call centres are located in much cheaper parts of the United Kingdom or in other countries entirely.

Ltd v Erhverus-og Selkabsstyrelsen,[2] the Court upheld the right of an English-registered company to operate as a branch in Denmark. The Danish authorities had refused to allow it to do so on the basis that this was, in reality, a Danish company which had simply registered in London to avoid the minimum capital rules applied to Danish private companies. In *Überseering BV v Nordic Construction Company Baumanagement GmbH,*[3] a Dutch company transferred its head office to Germany. Under Dutch law, which uses the place of registration or the incorporation theory, as we do, it still remained a Dutch company. Under German law (which uses the real-seat theory), it was held to be subject to German law and accordingly it was refused legal personality there. The European Court held that although there should be some controls on migration, denial of legal personality was a clear breach of the freedom of establishment. The basic problems on migration remain, however, although there is a draft proposal for a 14th Directive in an attempt to solve some these issues. This is discussed at the end of this chapter.

A different, but related issue concerns the lack of any mechanism for cross-border mergers between companies. Although the domestic merger procedures within the Community were harmonised by the Third Directive, none of them works well if companies from more than one jurisdiction are involved. Complex arrangements are needed to get round the problem. There are also tax and administrative problems, and difficulties arising from non-harmonised areas of company law, especially in the area of worker participation, which differ as between Member States. These issues are also in the minds of the Community, and there is a draft 10th Directive on this issue in circulation at the moment which is discussed at the end of this chapter. This is less of a problem for UK companies which generally use the takeover rather than the scheme of arrangement as a means of achieving cross-border mergers.

One solution: the European Company

All these problems of cross-border migration and mergers are clearly concerns **34–003** with which the Community is bound to be involved. As long ago as 1959, a very radical solution was put forward, to have a totally separate entity, which would not belong to any Member State but would be domiciled in the Community. This European Company would have its own complete code of company law and allow such companies to operate throughout the Community free of national restrictions. That ideal proved, however, to be illusory. Proposals made in 1970 and 1975 were in effect abandoned in 1982. But in 1988, the idea, on a less grand scale, was revived. After prolonged negotiation and consultation, drafting and redrafting, the EU Regulation establishing the European Company Statute was adopted in 2001 and automatically became law throughout the Community on October 8, 2004.[4] The contentious issue of employee participation was dealt

---

[2] [1999] E.C.R. 1–1458.
[3] [2002] E.C.R. 1–9919.
[4] Regulation 2001/2157 on the Statute for a European Company (SE) [2001] OJ L294/1 (the "EU Reg"). This has been passed under art.308 of the Treaty.

with in a separate directive which had to be implemented into national law on the same day.[5]

Although the Regulation is free-standing and needs no implementation in the United Kingdom, it did need some enabling changes to be made to UK company law and it did allow for some its articles to be optional so that choices had to be made. These changes and options have been made by the European Public Limited Liability Company Regulations 2004[6] (the enabling Regulations) which also implemented the employee participation directive. However, this model of the European Company is far removed from the original concept. It must be registered in one Member State and much of the law applicable to it will be the public company law of that state.[7] In addition, each Member State can decide whether to choose some or all of the options in the EU Regulation. Thus there will be as many variants of the European Company as there are Member States of the Community. We can therefore speak of a British or a French European Company, which ought to be a contradiction in terms. It does, however, retain one aspect of the original proposal, its name, which will end with the abbreviation SE rather than the domestic LLP. SE is the abbreviation for the Latin "Societas Europea" and will be used in the remainder of this chapter.

Whether the SE will ever be more than a political flagship exercise is far too early to tell. There has been little enthusiasm shown in Britain in the various consultation exercises. Given the incredible complexity of the employee participation provisions, the difficulty in divining the applicable laws (from the EU Regulation, the enabling regulations and parts of existing UK company law) and the still apparently intransigent tax issues, the future does not look too promising. On the other hand, it may prove to be rather more popular in some other Member States and so involve British employees of a non-British SE, and British companies wishing to participate in the formation of a non-British SE. It may well also be the forerunner of more realistic and genuine attempts to promote cross-border migration and mergers within the Community in the shape of the proposed 10th and 14th Directives. As such it is therefore worth noting the more important aspects of the SE, 2004-style. The key development in policy at the EU level came with the 2005 Cross-Border Merger Directive, which is considered next.

The Cross-Border Merger Directive 2005

The purpose and scope of the directive

34–004   The Cross-Border Merger Directive 2005[8] provides for the methods by which mergers can take place between limited liability companies in different Member States of the EU. At least two of the companies involved in the merger must have their registered office, their central administration, or their place of business in the

---

[5] Directive 2001/86/EU supplementing Statute for a European Company (SE) [2001] OJ L294/22.
[6] SI 2004/2326, effective from October 8, 2004.
[7] See EU Reg. art.10.
[8] Directive 2005/56/EU on cross-border mergers of limited liability companies ("CBMD" [2005] OJ L310/1).

European Union.[9] The Directive is concerned with the need for "co-ordination and consolidation" between limited liability companies "from different Member States" of the EU.[10] It "facilitates the cross-border merger of limited liability companies".[11] The central principles are that[12]:

> "each company taking part in a cross-border merger, and each third party concerned, remains subject to the provisions and formalities of the national law which would be applicable in the case of a national merger. None of the provisions and formalities of national law ... should introduce restrictions on freedom of establishment or on the free movement of capital save where these can be justified in accordance with the case-law of the Court of Justice and in particular by requirements of the general interest and are both necessary for, and proportionate to, the attainment of such overriding requirements."

In essence, therefore, there are two key principles underpinning the Directive. First, in the event of a cross-border merger it will still be a system of national law which will be applicable and that national law will be the law which would have applied before the Directive. Secondly, however, the applicable provisions of that national law may not impose unjustifiable restrictions on either freedom of establishment of the merged entity or freedom of movement of capital. The directive provides in effect for "common draft terms" to be applied in merger agreements between companies, along with the further terms that the parties may choose to use.[13] There are two types of merger envisaged here[14]: where a new company emerges from the dissolution of two existing companies with the transfer of their assets to a new company, or where one company is effectively assimilated into another company. In either case, there must not have been a liquidation of either of the companies. It is required that the appropriate national regulator assumes responsibility for overseeing the formalities in the operation of the resulting company and for ensuring the protection of the interests of shareholders and other third parties. This is therefore a consolidation of the existing legal position with the super-added obligation that the applicable law does not interfere with the achievement of EU legal goals of freedom of movement. Otherwise, the traditional provisions of national company laws will continue to apply, depending on which jurisdiction and which national system of rules are applicable to the merger. There is also a directive providing for tax neutrality on such mergers.[15]

Pre-conditions to a cross-border merger

There are pre-conditions to the operation of the Directive.[16] First, it must be **34–005** possible for a merger to take effect between these two types of company under

[9] CBMD, art.1.
[10] CBMD, recital 1.
[11] CBMD, recital 2.
[12] CBMD, recital 3.
[13] CBMD, recital 4.
[14] CBMD, art.2(2).
[15] Directive 90/434/EEC on a common system of taxation, [1990] OJ L2251.
[16] CBMD, art.4.

the applicable national laws. Second, the merging companies must comply with all of the relevant provisions of their respective national laws. Third, the authorities of any Member State to object to a merger on public interest grounds shall continue to apply to a cross-border merger in the European Union. Those public interest grounds may include rules concerning the approval process for the merger itself, the protection of creditors and debenture holders, the protection of shareholders, and the rights of employees. Furthermore, a company may decide to adopt measures to ensure the protection of minority shareholders who opposed the merger.

The procedure for effecting a cross-border merger

34–006 A cross-border merger will take effect in the following way. The companies must prepare "common draft terms" for their merger, containing certain prescribed information[17] (as considered below) and then those terms must be published.[18] The management of the various companies which are proposing to merge must then prepare a separate report which explains and justifies the legal and economic aspects of the merger: that report is then to be made available to "members, creditors and employees".[19] In time the members of the companies will be entitled to vote on the proposed merger. One month before that meeting, a report prepared by independent experts assessing the merger proposal must have been made available to those members.[20] Those experts shall be entitled to acquire all of the information which they require in the preparation of their report.[21] A general meeting of the companies will then vote on the proposed merger.[22] This may be conditional on ratification by any organ of the company including employees.[23] If approval is given by the company in general meeting, then each relevant Member State will designate a court or notary which is required to consider the legality of the merger under its national law.[24] Assuming that the merger is considered to be lawful, the national law of the Member State to which the resulting company[25] is subject will decide when the merger takes effect.[26] At that point, all of the assets of the former company or companies are transferred to the resulting company; the members of any company which has ceased to exist due to the merger shall become members of the resulting company; and a company being acquired or otherwise extinguished in the merger shall cease to exist.[27]

[17] CBMD, art.5.
[18] CBMD, art.6.
[19] CBMD, art.7.
[20] CBMD, art.8(1).
[21] CBMD, art.8(3).
[22] CBMD, art.9.
[23] CBMD, art.9(2).
[24] CBMD, art.10.
[25] That is, whether it is a new company acquiring the assets of both former companies, or a pre-existing company which has assimilated another company by means of the merger.
[26] CBMD, art.12.
[27] CBMD, art.14.

The common draft terms of cross-border mergers

The directive provides for "common draft terms" to be included in merger agree- **34–007** ments where they take effect cross-border in the EU. The common terms of the cross-border merger are set out in art.5 of the Directive. Article 5 provides that the following provisions must be included in the "common draft terms" of the merger, in the following terms:

"(a) the form, name and registered office of the merging companies and those proposed for the company resulting from the cross-border merger;
(b) the ratio applicable to the exchange of securities or shares representing the company capital and the amount of any cash payment;
(c) the terms for the allotment of securities or shares representing the capital of the company resulting from the cross-border merger;
(d) the likely repercussions of the cross-border merger on employment;
(e) the date from which the holding of such securities or shares representing the company capital will entitle the holders to share in profits and any special conditions affecting that entitlement;
(f) the date from which the transactions of the merging companies will be treated for accounting purposes as being those of the company resulting from the cross-border merger;
(g) the rights conferred by the company resulting from the cross-border merger on members enjoying special rights or on holders of securities other than shares representing the company capital, or the measures proposed concerning them;
(h) any special advantages granted to the experts who examine the draft terms of the cross-border merger or to members of the administrative, manage-ment, supervisory or controlling organs of the merging companies;
(i) the statutes of the company resulting from the cross-border merger;
(j) where appropriate, information on the procedures by which arrangements for the involvement of employees in the definition of their rights to participation in the company resulting from the cross-border merger are determined pursuant to Article 16;
(k) information on the evaluation of the assets and liabilities which are trans-ferred to the company resulting from the cross-border merger;
(l) dates of the merging companies' accounts used to establish the conditions of the cross-border merger."

The common draft terms of the merger must then be published.[28]

The rights of employees

Importantly, it may be that one company operated in a jurisdiction in which its **34–008** workers had rights to participate in the management of the company, for example

---

[28] CBMD, art.6.

through a supervisory board, whereas the national law of the merged company may not provide for such participation. In that instance, the EU Regulation[29] applies to regulate those workers' rights.[30] In essence, the resulting company will be subject to the company law of one Member State, and that resulting company will therefore be subject to the employee rights provided by that system of law.[31] The resulting company in a merger acquires all of the obligations of employees' contracts of employment.[32]

THE EUROPEAN COMPANY

Laws applicable to an "SE"

34–009 Article 9 of the EU Regulation[33] on the European company ("SE") provides that there is a distinct order of priority as to which law is applicable to an SE. This is: (i) the provisions of the Regulation; (ii) those areas specified by the Regulation as being a matter for the company's constitution; (iii) the harmonised domestic company law applicable to LLPs; (iv) other domestic LLP law; and (v) the SE's constitution. The SE is domiciled in the state in which it has its registered office and in which it must also have its head office.[34]

Forming an SE

34–010 Article 2 of the Regulation provides for four methods of formation. The common theme is that it involves companies from more than one Member State.[35] The four methods are as follows.

1. Merger of two or more EU public companies from at least two Member States.[36] In the UK, this would be achieved by a scheme of arrangement. The cross-border issues[37] are dealt with by requiring the law of each Member State to be applied, taking into account the cross-border protection of creditors, etc. The pre-merger procedure must be certified by the appropriate authority of each relevant Member State but the final scrutiny of the merger will be by the court of the intended state of registration. Other provisions are similar to those applicable to mergers of public companies subject to s.902 et seq. of the Companies Act 2006.

---

[29] EU Reg.
[30] CBMD, recital 13.
[31] CBMD, art.16.
[32] CBMD, art.14(4).
[33] As discussed above: EU Reg.
[34] EU Reg. art.7. This allows the real-seat theory to operate.
[35] A British SE can also include a company with a head office outside the EU to be involved provided it is registered in a Member State and has a real and continuous link with a Member State's economy: EPLLC reg.55 regs 2004.
[36] This will be in accordance with the existing mergers by acquisition and by the formation of a new company procedures in the third Directive and which are now part of ss.900–904 (see Ch.30 above).
[37] Of some interest in connection with cross-border mergers generally: see below.

The UK has taken up the option of being able to object to a merger on public interest grounds;[38]

2. Formation of an SE as a holding company with subsidiaries[39] in at least two Member States. The draft terms must be identical from each participating company, none of which can have a controlling interest in the SE. Otherwise the procedure is that laid down by the third directive;

3. Formation as a joint[40] subsidiary of two or more EU companies from at least two Member States under the law applicable to forming a subsidiary under the national law of each participating company.

4. Transformation of an existing EU public company provided it has had a subsidiary in another Member State for at least two years. There is no winding up of the old company and no new legal person is created. Terms of the conversion must be drawn up and approved by the general meeting. The company's net assets must also be equivalent to its capital and undistributable reserves.

Once formed, an SE has both legal personality and limited liability.[41] An SE organised in the United Kingdom can express its share capital in either Euros or sterling.[42] Otherwise UK law applies to its share and loan capital, accounts and insolvency.[43] Registration is the same as for a UK public company, but no SE can be registered unless it has in place arrangements for worker participation in accordance with the directive (as discussed below). The management of UK SEs will be able to change the constitution to comply with any new arrangements for worker participation in the directive without a general meeting.[44] An SE can also form an SE as a subsidiary of itself.

Migration of an SE

An SE may move from one Member State to another. Article 8 of the EU **34–011** Regulation provides the necessary safeguards for employees, creditors and shareholders but does not mention tax.[45] There must be a transfer proposal giving details of the proposed safeguards for those rights, and approval by a special resolution after a delay of at least two months. Further, the outgoing Member State must certify to the new Member State that the interests of creditors arising prior

---

[38] EPLLC Regs, reg.60.
[39] These may be public or private companies.
[40] But not necessarily equal.
[41] EU Reg. art.1. In Britain it is a body corporate—EPLLC Regs, reg.81.
[42] This is the combined effect of arts 4 and 67 of the EU Reg. and reg.67 of the EPLLC Regs 2004.
[43] Arts 5, 61 and 63, EU Reg. The existing domestic sanctions have been applied to SEs by the EPLLC Regs.
[44] EPLLC Regs, reg.59.
[45] These formed the basis for the CLR's proposals for migration generally (above) which were rejected by the British government.

to the transfer[46] have been adequately protected. In the case of a UK SE, it will have to produce a statement of solvency.[47] The proposal must be filed and officially notified. The UK Government has also taken advantage of options to strengthen the rights of creditors and shareholders to examine the proposal prior to the meeting[48] and for it to be able to oppose a transfer of an SE from the UK on public interest grounds.[49]

Structure of an SE

34–012 Article 38 of the EU Regulation provides that an SE shall comprise a general meeting of shareholders and either a one tier system with a single management/administrative organ or a two tier system with separate supervisory and management organs. This reflects the two management systems which are in place in the European Union.

With regard to meetings, there must be one each year.[50] In addition to the members of the management board(s), the holders of 10 per cent of the shares can request that a meeting be convened and 5 per cent can ask for additional items to be placed on the agenda.[51] The Secretary of State can convene a meeting in default. Ordinary and special resolutions are the same as for domestic companies. A quorum is to be one half of the members.[52]

At first sight the requirement that all SEs be allowed the choice of the two-tier management/supervisory board system would seem to be difficult for UK company law which has only a unitary system of the board of directors. But the Government has taken the view that the UK structure, allowing virtually complete freedom to companies to provide any form of management structure they like in their articles, is flexible enough to provide for the prescribed two-tier system as a practical proposition without the need for any specially enabling legislation.[53]

34–013 That prescribed two-tier system requires that no one can be a member of both the management and supervisory boards. The managers must be appointed by the supervisory board, the function of which is supervise the work of the management board. Its membership is in turn appointed by the general meeting and under any worker participation arrangements made under the directive. The management board must make quarterly reports to the supervisory board on progress and foreseeable developments and provide "any information on events likely to have

---

[46] Britain has exercised its option to extend this from liabilities prior to the publication of the transfer proposal; EPLLC Regs, reg.57.

[47] EPLLC Regs, reg.73.

[48] EPLLC Regs, reg.56.

[49] EPLLC Regs, reg.58.

[50] Although the first one may be within 18 months of the company's formation: EPLLC Regs reg.65.

[51] EPLLC Regs reg.66.

[52] EU Reg. art.50.

[53] It is arguable that many existing large companies with executive and non-executive directors have a de facto two-tier board system anyway. The existing rules in the Companies Act as to directors duties, disclosure, etc are to apply to all members of either the one tier or two tier boards (but separately in the latter case) and there is to be a register of members of the supervisory board kept by the SE and open for inspection: EPLLC Regs regs.77–79.

an appreciable effect on the SE". For a UK SE, the minimum number of members of the management and supervisory board is two in each case. In the case of a single-tier system there must be at least two directors of a UK SE.[54]

No manager or supervisor can be appointed for more than six years but can be re-appointed. The SE's constitution is to set out the categories of transactions which require authorisation by the board(s).[55] Persons disqualified as directors of UK companies cannot be a member of any of the boards of an SE and conduct as a director/manager/supervisor of an SE could lead to disqualification proceedings.[56]

Conversion of an SE into a Plc

Article 66 of the EU Regulation allows for an SE to convert back into a domestic **34-014** public company but not within the first two years of registration or before at least two sets of accounts have been approved. There is no winding up or creation of a new legal entity. Draft terms of the conversion must be drawn up and approved by a special resolution and an independent expert must confirm that the company has net assets equivalent to its capital. The draft constitution of the plc must also be approved. The enabling Regulations provide all the necessary formal registration and notification requirements for the conversion.[57]

Employee involvement in the SE

One of the most fundamental differences within the European Union is the extent **34-015** and form of employee involvement in the affairs and management of companies. The German system of co-determination (equality of employees and shareholders representatives on the supervisory board) is the most formalistic. The United Kingdom has, arguably, the most flexible system. Agreeing a formula for the SE was therefore a major stumbling block, which was only resolved when the matter was hived off to a Directive[58] which requires implementation by national law. In the United Kingdom this has been done by Pt 3 of the enabling regulations. We have already seen that no SE can be registered unless it has in place arrangements for employee participation as required by the directive. As a minimum, these will cover information and consultation but may also include employee involvement in the management structure itself.

Part 3 of the enabling regulations has transposed these requirements into UK law. They apply to all UK SEs and in some cases to UK employees of non-UK SEs. They set out the composition and appointment of the special negotiating body (SNB) which is to be set up to negotiate the arrangements with the participating companies of the proposed SE.[59] They also set out the consequences of the

---

[54] EPLLC Regs reg.62. This must be three if worker participation is involved: EU Reg art.43.
[55] EU Reg. art.48.
[56] EU Reg. art.47 and 9.1(c)(ii).
[57] Regs 85–89.
[58] Directive 2001/86/EU supplementing Statute for a European Company (SE) [2001] OJ L294/22.
[59] These apply to all British employees of an SE.

various possibilities arising from those negotiations, the default arrangements if there is no agreement and it is still proposed to set up an SE, and, finally, rules to ensure the compliance, enforcement, confidentiality and protection of the members of the SNB.[60]

The structure, as envisaged by the Directive, is in essence as follows:

1. the participating companies in the proposed SE provide employee representatives with information for the purpose of calculating the number and allocation of members of the SNB;

2. the SNB members are elected either by ballot of the employees or appointed by consultative committee and the six-month negotiating period begins;[61]

3. if an agreement is reached within that period the SE may be registered. This agreement may be (a) to rely on the national information and consultation rules,[62] (b) for some other employee involvement arrangement; or (c) to implement the default or standard rules as set out in the Annex to the Directive;

4. if no agreement is reached but the participating companies wish to continue to set up an SE then the standard rules will be automatically applied and the SE can be registered.

The default or standard rules for employee involvement are reproduced in Sch.3 to the enabling regulations. There must be a representative body of the employees of an SE and its subsidiaries and establishments elected or appointed by the members of the SNB. Such a body must after four years decide whether to open negotiations for a specific agreement or continue to rely on the standard rules. It may elect a select committee, be assisted by experts and is to be funded by the SE.[63]

34–016   With regard to information and consultation, the management of any SE is required to give the representative body regular reports on the progress and prospects for the SE's business, provide it with copies of the agenda for management meetings[64] and general meetings, and inform it of "any exceptional circumstances affecting the employees' interests to a considerable extent". If requested, there must be a meeting between the representative body and the management at least once a year to discuss those reports.[65] The representative body is entitled to

---

[60] These latter apply if any UK company or employee is involved in the special negotiating body.
[61] This can be extended by a further six months if the parties agree.
[62] This can be decided by a two-thirds majority of the SNB.
[63] But only for one expert.
[64] Including, where appropriate, of the supervisory board.
[65] In particular those meetings are to look at:

"the structure, economic and financial situation, the probable development of business and of production and sales, the situation and probable trends of employment, investments and substantial changes concerning organisation, introduction of new working methods or production processes, transfers of production, mergers, cut-backs or closures of undertakings, establishments or important parts thereof and collective redundancies."

a pre-meeting on its own. If there are "exceptional circumstances" (as above), then the select committee may meet with the top management; although any member of the representative body who represents workers directly affected may attend. If, after the meeting, the management has not acted in accordance with the opinion of the representative body, the latter may request another meeting. After the meetings and so forth the representative body must inform the employees or their representatives of the content and results of the process.

In the more divisive area of direct employee participation in the management structure of the SE, the directive draws a distinction between an SE formed by transformation from an existing national LLP and the other methods of formation. In the first case any existing rules as to employee participation in the management (or supervisory boards) will be continued into the SE. In the case of a UK company there are none. In other cases, where in at least one of the participating companies there were employee participation rights, the representative body will be able to appoint[66] members to the appropriate board. The number of such members is to be the highest proportion (of the board) in force in the participating companies at the time of registration. Thus employees in any participating company will be protected as to their existing rights on the formation of an SE. For example, if a German and a UK company decide to form a UK SE, the pre-existing co-determination rights of the German employees will be applicable to the SE.

Membership of the board(s) will in all cases be allocated as between employees in different Member States according to the ratio of employees in each state, but with at least one member from each Member State involved. Employee members of the board(s) are to be treated as full members of the relevant board and as having full voting rights.

---

[66] The wording is elect, appoint, recommend or oppose.

INDEX

LEGAL TAXONOMY
FROM SWEET & MAXWELL

This index has been prepared using Sweet & Maxwell's Legal Taxonomy. Main index entries conform to keywords provided by the Legal Taxonomy except where references to specific documents or non-standard terms (denoted by quotation marks) have been included. These keywords provide a means of identifying similar concepts in other Sweet & Maxwell publications and online services to which keywords from the Legal Taxonomy have been applied. Readers may find some minor differences between terms used in the text and those which appear in the index. Suggestions to *sweet&maxwell.taxonomy@thomson.com*.